DATABASE
SYSTEM CONCEPTS

SIXTH EDITION

Abraham Silberschatz
Yale University

Henry F. Korth
Lehigh University

S. Sudarshan
Indian Institute of Technology, Bombay

The McGraw·Hill Companies

Connect
Learn
Succeed™

DATABASE SYSTEM CONCEPTS, SIXTH EDITION

Published by McGraw-Hill, a business unit of The McGraw-Hill Companies, Inc., 1221 Avenue of the Americas, New York, NY 10020. Copyright © 2011 by The McGraw-Hill Companies, Inc. All rights reserved. Previous editions © 2006, 2002, and 1999. No part of this publication may be reproduced or distributed in any form or by any means, or stored in a database or retrieval system, without the prior written consent of The McGraw-Hill Companies, Inc., including, but not limited to, in any network or other electronic storage or transmission, or broadcast for distance learning.

Some ancillaries, including electronic and print components, may not be available to customers outside the United States.

This book is printed on acid-free paper.

1 2 3 4 5 6 7 8 9 0 DOC/DOC 1 0 9 8 7 6 5 4 3 2 1 0

ISBN 978-0-07-352332-3
MHID 0-07-352332-1

Global Publisher: *Raghothaman Srinivasan*
Director of Development: *Kristine Tibbetts*
Senior Marketing Manager: *Curt Reynolds*
Project Manager: *Melissa M. Leick*
Senior Production Supervisor: *Laura Fuller*
Design Coordinator: *Brenda A. Rolwes*
Cover Designer: *Studio Montage, St. Louis, Missouri*
(USE) Cover Image: *© Brand X Pictures/PunchStock*
Compositor: *Aptara®, Inc.*
Typeface: *10/12 Palatino*
Printer: *R. R. Donnelley*

All credits appearing on page or at the end of the book are considered to be an extension of the copyright page.

Library of Congress Cataloging-in-Publication Data

Silberschatz, Abraham.
  Database system concepts / Abraham Silberschatz. — 6th ed.
    p. cm.
  ISBN 978-0-07-352332-3 (alk. paper)
1. Database management. I. Title.
  QA76.9.D3S5637 2011
  005.74—dc22

                                    2009039039

The Internet addresses listed in the text were accurate at the time of publication. The inclusion of a Web site does not indicate an endorsement by the authors of McGraw-Hill, and McGraw-Hill does not guarantee the accuracy of the information presented at these sites.

www.mhhe.com

Contents

PART TWO   ■   DATABASE DESIGN

Chapter 8   Relational Database Design

Chapter 9   Application Design and Development

PART THREE   ■   DATA STORAGE AND QUERYING

Chapter 10   Storage and File Structure

Chapter 11   Indexing and Hashing

PART FOUR ■ TRANSACTION MANAGEMENT

Chapter 16   Recovery System

PART FIVE   ■   SYSTEM ARCHITECTURE

Chapter 17   Database-System Architectures

Chapter 18   Parallel Databases

Chapter 19   Distributed Databases

PART SIX ■ DATA WAREHOUSING, DATA MINING, AND INFORMATION RETRIEVAL

Chapter 20   Data Warehousing and Mining

Chapter 21   Information Retrieval

PART SEVEN ■ SPECIALTY DATABASES

Chapter 22   Object-Based Databases

Chapter 23   XML

PART EIGHT ■ ADVANCED TOPICS

Chapter 24   Advanced Application Development

Chapter 25   Spatial and Temporal Data and Mobility

Chapter 26   Advanced Transaction Processing

PART NINE ■ CASE STUDIES

Chapter 27   PostgreSQL

Chapter 28   Oracle

Chapter 29   IBM DB2 Universal Database

Chapter 30   Microsoft SQL Server

PART TEN   ■   APPENDICES

Appendix A   Detailed University Schema

Appendix B   Advanced Relational Design (contents online)

Appendix C   Other Relational Query Languages (contents online)

Appendix D   Network Model (contents online)

Appendix E   Hierarchical Model (contents online)

Bibliography   1283

Index   1315

Preface

Database management has evolved from a specialized computer application to a central component of a modern computing environment, and, as a result, knowledge about database systems has become an essential part of an education in computer science. In this text, we present the fundamental concepts of database management. These concepts include aspects of database design, database languages, and database-system implementation.

This text is intended for a first course in databases at the junior or senior undergraduate, or first-year graduate, level. In addition to basic material for a first course, the text contains advanced material that can be used for course supplements, or as introductory material for an advanced course.

We assume only a familiarity with basic data structures, computer organization, and a high-level programming language such as Java, C, or Pascal. We present concepts as intuitive descriptions, many of which are based on our running example of a university. Important theoretical results are covered, but formal proofs are omitted. In place of proofs, figures and examples are used to suggest why a result is true. Formal descriptions and proofs of theoretical results may be found in research papers and advanced texts that are referenced in the bibliographical notes.

The fundamental concepts and algorithms covered in the book are often based on those used in existing commercial or experimental database systems. Our aim is to present these concepts and algorithms in a general setting that is not tied to one particular database system. Details of particular database systems are discussed in Part 9, "Case Studies."

In this, the sixth edition of *Database System Concepts*, we have retained the overall style of the prior editions while evolving the content and organization to reflect the changes that are occurring in the way databases are designed, managed, and used. We have also taken into account trends in the teaching of database concepts and made adaptations to facilitate these trends where appropriate.

Organization

The text is organized in nine major parts, plus five appendices.

- **Overview** (Chapter 1). Chapter 1 provides a general overview of the nature and purpose of database systems. We explain how the concept of a database system has developed, what the common features of database systems are, what a database system does for the user, and how a database system interfaces with operating systems. We also introduce an example database application: a university organization consisting of multiple departments, instructors, students, and courses. This application is used as a running example throughout the book. This chapter is motivational, historical, and explanatory in nature.

- **Part 1: Relational Databases** (Chapters 2 through 6). Chapter 2 introduces the relational model of data, covering basic concepts such as the structure of relational databases, database schemas, keys, schema diagrams, relational query languages, and relational operations. Chapters 3, 4, and 5 focus on the most influential of the user-oriented relational languages: SQL. Chapter 6 covers the formal relational query languages: relational algebra, tuple relational calculus, and domain relational calculus.

  The chapters in this part describe data manipulation: queries, updates, insertions, and deletions, assuming a schema design has been provided. Schema design issues are deferred to Part 2.

- **Part 2: Database Design** (Chapters 7 through 9). Chapter 7 provides an overview of the database-design process, with major emphasis on database design using the entity-relationship data model. The entity-relationship data model provides a high-level view of the issues in database design, and of the problems that we encounter in capturing the semantics of realistic applications within the constraints of a data model. UML class-diagram notation is also covered in this chapter.

  Chapter 8 introduces the theory of relational database design. The theory of functional dependencies and normalization is covered, with emphasis on the motivation and intuitive understanding of each normal form. This chapter begins with an overview of relational design and relies on an intuitive understanding of logical implication of functional dependencies. This allows the concept of normalization to be introduced prior to full coverage of functional-dependency theory, which is presented later in the chapter. Instructors may choose to use only this initial coverage in Sections 8.1 through 8.3 without loss of continuity. Instructors covering the entire chapter will benefit from students having a good understanding of normalization concepts to motivate some of the challenging concepts of functional-dependency theory.

  Chapter 9 covers application design and development. This chapter emphasizes the construction of database applications with Web-based interfaces. In addition, the chapter covers application security.

- **Part 3: Data Storage and Querying** (Chapters 10 through 13). Chapter 10 deals with storage devices, files, and data-storage structures. A variety of data-access techniques are presented in Chapter 11, including B^+-tree indices and hashing. Chapters 12 and 13 address query-evaluation algorithms and query optimization. These chapters provide an understanding of the internals of the storage and retrieval components of a database.

- **Part 4: Transaction Management** (Chapters 14 through 16). Chapter 14 focuses on the fundamentals of a transaction-processing system: atomicity, consistency, isolation, and durability. It provides an overview of the methods used to ensure these properties, including locking and snapshot isolation.

  Chapter 15 focuses on concurrency control and presents several techniques for ensuring serializability, including locking, timestamping, and optimistic (validation) techniques. The chapter also covers deadlock issues. Alternatives to serializability are covered, most notably the widely-used snapshot isolation, which is discussed in detail.

  Chapter 16 covers the primary techniques for ensuring correct transaction execution despite system crashes and storage failures. These techniques include logs, checkpoints, and database dumps. The widely-used ARIES algorithm is presented.

- **Part 5: System Architecture** (Chapters 17 through 19). Chapter 17 covers computer-system architecture, and describes the influence of the underlying computer system on the database system. We discuss centralized systems, client–server systems, and parallel and distributed architectures in this chapter.

  Chapter 18, on parallel databases, explores a variety of parallelization techniques, including I/O parallelism, interquery and intraquery parallelism, and interoperation and intraoperation parallelism. The chapter also describes parallel-system design.

  Chapter 19 covers distributed database systems, revisiting the issues of database design, transaction management, and query evaluation and optimization, in the context of distributed databases. The chapter also covers issues of system availability during failures, heterogeneous distributed databases, cloud-based databases, and distributed directory systems.

- **Part 6: Data Warehousing, Data Mining, and Information Retrieval** (Chapters 20 and 21). Chapter 20 introduces the concepts of data warehousing and data mining. Chapter 21 describes information-retrieval techniques for querying textual data, including hyperlink-based techniques used in Web search engines.

  Part 6 uses the modeling and language concepts from Parts 1 and 2, but does not depend on Parts 3, 4, or 5. It can therefore be incorporated easily into a course that focuses on SQL and on database design.

- **Part 7: Specialty Databases** (Chapters 22 and 23). Chapter 22 covers object-based databases. The chapter describes the object-relational data model, which extends the relational data model to support complex data types, type inheritance, and object identity. The chapter also describes database access from object-oriented programming languages.

  Chapter 23 covers the XML standard for data representation, which is seeing increasing use in the exchange and storage of complex data. The chapter also describes query languages for XML.

- **Part 8: Advanced Topics** (Chapters 24 through 26). Chapter 24 covers advanced issues in application development, including performance tuning, performance benchmarks, database-application testing, and standardization.

  Chapter 25 covers spatial and geographic data, temporal data, multimedia data, and issues in the management of mobile and personal databases.

  Finally, Chapter 26 deals with advanced transaction processing. Topics covered in the chapter include transaction-processing monitors, transactional workflows, electronic commerce, high-performance transaction systems, real-time transaction systems, and long-duration transactions.

- **Part 9: Case Studies** (Chapters 27 through 30). In this part, we present case studies of four of the leading database systems, PostgreSQL, Oracle, IBM DB2, and Microsoft SQL Server. These chapters outline unique features of each of these systems, and describe their internal structure. They provide a wealth of interesting information about the respective products, and help you see how the various implementation techniques described in earlier parts are used in real systems. They also cover several interesting practical aspects in the design of real systems.

- **Appendices**. We provide five appendices that cover material that is of historical nature or is advanced; these appendices are available only online on the Web site of the book (http://www.db-book.com). An exception is Appendix A, which presents details of our university schema including the full schema, DDL, and all the tables. This appendix appears in the actual text.

  Appendix B describes other relational query languages, including QBE Microsoft Access, and Datalog.

  Appendix C describes advanced relational database design, including the theory of multivalued dependencies, join dependencies, and the project-join and domain-key normal forms. This appendix is for the benefit of individuals who wish to study the theory of relational database design in more detail, and instructors who wish to do so in their courses. This appendix, too, is available only online, on the Web site of the book.

  Although most new database applications use either the relational model or the object-relational model, the network and hierarchical data models are still in use in some legacy applications. For the benefit of readers who wish to learn about these data models, we provide appendices describing the network and hierarchical data models, in Appendices D and E respectively.

The Sixth Edition

The production of this sixth edition has been guided by the many comments and suggestions we received concerning the earlier editions, by our own observations while teaching at Yale University, Lehigh University, and IIT Bombay, and by our analysis of the directions in which database technology is evolving.

We have replaced the earlier running example of bank enterprise with a university example. This example has an immediate intuitive connection to students that assists not only in remembering the example, but, more importantly, in gaining deeper insight into the various design decisions that need to be made.

We have reorganized the book so as to collect all of our SQL coverage together and place it early in the book. Chapters 3, 4, and 5 present complete SQL coverage. Chapter 3 presents the basics of the language, with more advanced features in Chapter 4. In Chapter 5, we present JDBC along with other means of accessing SQL from a general-purpose programming language. We present triggers and recursion, and then conclude with coverage of online analytic processing (OLAP). Introductory courses may choose to cover only certain sections of Chapter 5 or defer sections until after the coverage of database design without loss of continuity.

Beyond these two major changes, we revised the material in each chapter, bringing the older material up-to-date, adding discussions on recent developments in database technology, and improving descriptions of topics that students found difficult to understand. We have also added new exercises and updated references. The list of specific changes includes the following:

- **Earlier coverage of SQL.** Many instructors use SQL as a key component of term projects (see our Web site, www.db-book.com, for sample projects). In order to give students ample time for the projects, particularly for universities and colleges on the quarter system, it is essential to teach SQL as early as possible. With this in mind, we have undertaken several changes in organization:

  ○ A new chapter on the relational model (Chapter 2) precedes SQL, laying the conceptual foundation, without getting lost in details of relational algebra.

  ○ Chapters 3, 4, and 5 provide detailed coverage of SQL. These chapters also discuss variants supported by different database systems, to minimize problems that students face when they execute queries on actual database systems. These chapters cover all aspects of SQL, including queries, data definition, constraint specification, OLAP, and the use of SQL from within a variety of languages, including Java/JDBC.

  ○ Formal languages (Chapter 6) have been postponed to after SQL, and can be omitted without affecting the sequencing of other chapters. Only our discussion of query optimization in Chapter 13 depends on the relational algebra coverage of Chapter 6.

- **New database schema.** We adopted a new schema, which is based on university data, as a running example throughout the book. This schema is more intuitive and motivating for students than the earlier bank schema, and illustrates more complex design trade-offs in the database-design chapters.

- **More support for a hands-on student experience.** To facilitate following our running example, we list the database schema and the sample relation instances for our university database together in Appendix A as well as where they are used in the various regular chapters. In addition, we provide, on our Web site http://www.db-book.com, SQL data-definition statements for the entire example, along with SQL statements to create our example relation instances. This encourages students to run example queries directly on a database system and to experiment with modifying those queries.

- **Revised coverage of E-R model.** The E-R diagram notation in Chapter 7 has been modified to make it more compatible with UML. The chapter also makes good use of the new university database schema to illustrate more complex design trade-offs.

- **Revised coverage of relational design.** Chapter 8 now has a more readable style, providing an intuitive understanding of functional dependencies and normalization, before covering functional dependency theory; the theory is motivated much better as a result.

- **Expanded material on application development and security.** Chapter 9 has new material on application development, mirroring rapid changes in the field. In particular, coverage of security has been expanded, considering its criticality in today's interconnected world, with an emphasis on practical issues over abstract concepts.

- **Revised and updated coverage of data storage, indexing and query optimization**. Chapter 10 has been updated with new technology, including expanded coverage of flash memory.

    Coverage of B^+-trees in Chapter 11 has been revised to reflect practical implementations, including coverage of bulk loading, and the presentation has been improved. The B^+-tree examples in Chapter 11 have now been revised with $n = 4$, to avoid the special case of empty nodes that arises with the (unrealistic) value of $n = 3$.

    Chapter 13 has new material on advanced query-optimization techniques.

- **Revised coverage of transaction management.** Chapter 14 provides full coverage of the basics for an introductory course, with advanced details following in Chapters 15 and 16. Chapter 14 has been expanded to cover the practical issues in transaction management faced by database users and database-application developers. The chapter also includes an expanded overview of topics covered in Chapters 15 and 16, ensuring that even if Chapters 15 and 16 are omitted, students have a basic knowledge of the concepts of concurrency control and recovery.

Chapters 14 and 15 now include detailed coverage of snapshot isolation, which is widely supported and used today, including coverage of potential hazards when using it.

Chapter 16 now has a simplified description of basic log-based recovery leading up to coverage of the ARIES algorithm.

- **Revised and expanded coverage of distributed databases.** We now cover cloud data storage, which is gaining significant interest for business applications. Cloud storage offers enterprises opportunities for improved cost-management and increased storage scalability, particularly for Web-based applications. We examine those advantages along with the potential drawbacks and risks.

  Multidatabases, which were earlier in the advanced transaction processing chapter, are now covered earlier as part of the distributed database chapter.

- **Postponed coverage of object databases and XML.** Although object-oriented languages and XML are widely used outside of databases, their use in databases is still limited, making them appropriate for more advanced courses, or as supplementary material for an introductory course. These topics have therefore been moved to later in the book, in Chapters 22 and 23.

- **QBE, Microsoft Access, and Datalog in an online appendix.** These topics, which were earlier part of a chapter on "other relational languages," are now covered in online Appendix C.

All topics not listed above are updated from the fifth edition, though their overall organization is relatively unchanged.

Review Material and Exercises

Each chapter has a list of review terms, in addition to a summary, which can help readers review key topics covered in the chapter.

The exercises are divided into two sets: **practice exercises** and **exercises**. The solutions for the practice exercises are publicly available on the Web site of the book. Students are encouraged to solve the practice exercises on their own, and later use the solutions on the Web site to check their own solutions. Solutions to the other exercises are available only to instructors (see "Instructor's Note," below, for information on how to get the solutions).

Many chapters have a tools section at the end of the chapter that provides information on software tools related to the topic of the chapter; some of these tools can be used for laboratory exercises. SQL DDL and sample data for the university database and other relations used in the exercises are available on the Web site of the book, and can be used for laboratory exercises.

Instructor's Note

The book contains both basic and advanced material, which might not be covered in a single semester. We have marked several sections as advanced, using the symbol "**". These sections may be omitted if so desired, without a loss of continuity. Exercises that are difficult (and can be omitted) are also marked using the symbol "**".

It is possible to design courses by using various subsets of the chapters. Some of the chapters can also be covered in an order different from their order in the book. We outline some of the possibilities here:

- Chapter 5 (Advanced SQL) can be skipped or deferred to later without loss of continuity. We expect most courses will cover at least Section 5.1.1 early, as JDBC is likely to be a useful tool in student projects.

- Chapter 6 (Formal Relational Query Languages) can be covered immediately after Chapter 2, ahead of SQL. Alternatively, this chapter may be omitted from an introductory course.

  We recommend covering Section 6.1 (relational algebra) if the course also covers query processing. However, Sections 6.2 and 6.3 can be omitted if students will not be using relational calculus as part of the course.

- Chapter 7 (E-R Model) can be covered ahead of Chapters 3, 4 and 5 if you so desire, since Chapter 7 does not have any dependency on SQL.

- Chapter 13 (Query Optimization) can be omitted from an introductory course without affecting coverage of any other chapter.

- Both our coverage of transaction processing (Chapters 14 through 16) and our coverage of system architecture (Chapters 17 through 19) consist of an overview chapter (Chapters 14 and 17, respectively), followed by chapters with details. You might choose to use Chapters 14 and 17, while omitting Chapters 15, 16, 18 and 19, if you defer these latter chapters to an advanced course.

- Chapters 20 and 21, covering data warehousing, data mining, and information retrieval, can be used as self-study material or omitted from an introductory course.

- Chapters 22 (Object-Based Databases), and 23 (XML) can be omitted from an introductory course.

- Chapters 24 through 26, covering advanced application development, spatial, temporal and mobile data, and advanced transaction processing, are suitable for an advanced course or for self-study by students.

- The case-study Chapters 27 through 30 are suitable for self-study by students. Alternatively, they can be used as an illustration of concepts when the earlier chapters are presented in class.

Model course syllabi, based on the text, can be found on the Web site of the book.

Web Site and Teaching Supplements

A Web site for the book is available at the URL: http://www.db-book.com. The Web site contains:

- Slides covering all the chapters of the book.
- Answers to the practice exercises.
- The five appendices.
- An up-to-date errata list.
- Laboratory material, including SQL DDL and sample data for the university schema and other relations used in exercises, and instructions for setting up and using various database systems and tools.

The following additional material is available only to faculty:

- An instructor manual containing solutions to all exercises in the book.
- A question bank containing extra exercises.

For more information about how to get a copy of the instructor manual and the question bank, please send electronic mail to customer.service@mcgraw-hill.com. In the United States, you may call 800-338-3987. The McGraw-Hill Web site for this book is http://www.mhhe.com/silberschatz.

Contacting Us

We have endeavored to eliminate typos, bugs, and the like from the text. But, as in new releases of software, bugs almost surely remain; an up-to-date errata list is accessible from the book's Web site. We would appreciate it if you would notify us of any errors or omissions in the book that are not on the current list of errata.

We would be glad to receive suggestions on improvements to the book. We also welcome any contributions to the book Web site that could be of use to other readers, such as programming exercises, project suggestions, online labs and tutorials, and teaching tips.

Email should be addressed to db-book-authors@cs.yale.edu. Any other correspondence should be sent to Avi Silberschatz, Department of Computer Science, Yale University, 51 Prospect Street, P.O. Box 208285, New Haven, CT 06520-8285 USA.

Acknowledgments

Many people have helped us with this sixth edition, as well as with the previous five editions from which it is derived.

Sixth Edition

- Anastassia Ailamaki, Sailesh Krishnamurthy, Spiros Papadimitriou, and Bianca Schroeder (Carnegie Mellon University) for writing Chapter 27 describing the PostgreSQL database system.

- Hakan Jakobsson (Oracle), for writing Chapter 28 on the Oracle database system.

- Sriram Padmanabhan (IBM), for writing Chapter 29 describing the IBM DB2 database system.

- Sameet Agarwal, José A. Blakeley, Thierry D'Hers, Gerald Hinson, Dirk Myers, Vaqar Pirzada, Bill Ramos, Balaji Rathakrishnan, Michael Rys, Florian Waas, and Michael Zwilling (all of Microsoft) for writing Chapter 30 describing the Microsoft SQL Server database system, and in particular José Blakeley for coordinating and editing the chapter; César Galindo-Legaria, Goetz Graefe, Kalen Delaney, and Thomas Casey (all of Microsoft) for their contributions to the previous edition of the Microsoft SQL Server chapter.

- Daniel Abadi for reviewing the table of contents of the fifth edition and helping with the new organization.

- Steve Dolins, University of Florida; Rolando Fernanez, George Washington University; Frantisek Franek, McMaster University; Latifur Khan, University of Texas - Dallas; Sanjay Madria, University of Missouri - Rolla; Aris Ouksel, University of Illinois; and Richard Snodgrass, University of Waterloo; who served as reviewers of the book and whose comments helped us greatly in formulating this sixth edition.

- Judi Paige for her help in generating figures and presentation slides.

- Mark Wogahn for making sure that the software to produce the book, including LaTeX macros and fonts, worked properly.

- N. L. Sarda for feedback that helped us improve several chapters, in particular Chapter 11; Vikram Pudi for motivating us to replace the earlier bank schema; and Shetal Shah for feedback on several chapters.

- Students at Yale, Lehigh, and IIT Bombay, for their comments on the fifth edition, as well as on preprints of the sixth edition.

Previous Editions

- Chen Li and Sharad Mehrotra for providing material on JDBC and security for the fifth edition.

- Marilyn Turnamian and Nandprasad Joshi provided secretarial assistance for the fifth edition, and Marilyn also prepared an early draft of the cover design for the fifth edition.

- Lyn Dupré copyedited the third edition and Sara Strandtman edited the text of the third edition.

- Nilesh Dalvi, Sumit Sanghai, Gaurav Bhalotia, Arvind Hulgeri K. V. Raghavan, Prateek Kapadia, Sara Strandtman, Greg Speegle, and Dawn Bezviner helped to prepare the instructor's manual for earlier editions.

- The idea of using ships as part of the cover concept was originally suggested to us by Bruce Stephan.

- The following people pointed out errors in the fifth edition: Alex Coman, Ravindra Guravannavar, Arvind Hulgeri, Rohit Kulshreshtha, Sang-Won Lee, Joe H. C. Lu, Alex N. Napitupulu, H. K. Park, Jian Pei, Fernando Saenz Perez, Donnie Pinkston, Yma Pinto, Rajarshi Rakshit, Sandeep Satpal, Amon Seagull, Barry Soroka, Praveen Ranjan Srivastava, Hans Svensson, Moritz Wiese, and Eyob Delele Yirdaw.

- The following people offered suggestions and comments for the fifth and earlier editions of the book. R. B. Abhyankar, Hani Abu-Salem, Jamel R. Alsabbagh, Raj Ashar, Don Batory, Phil Bernhard, Christian Breimann, Gavin M. Bierman, Janek Bogucki, Haran Boral, Paul Bourgeois, Phil Bohannon, Robert Brazile, Yuri Breitbart, Ramzi Bualuan, Michael Carey, Soumen Chakrabarti, Tom Chappell, Zhengxin Chen, Y. C. Chin, Jan Chomicki, Laurens Damen, Prasanna Dhandapani, Qin Ding, Valentin Dinu, J. Edwards, Christos Faloutsos, Homma Farian, Alan Fekete, Frantisek Franek, Shashi Gadia, Hector Garcia-Molina, Goetz Graefe, Jim Gray, Le Gruenwald, Eitan M. Gurari, William Hankley, Bruce Hillyer, Ron Hitchens, Chad Hogg, Arvind Hulgeri, Yannis Ioannidis, Zheng Jiaping, Randy M. Kaplan, Graham J. L. Kemp, Rami Khouri, Hyoung-Joo Kim, Won Kim, Henry Korth (father of Henry F.), Carol Kroll, Hae Choon Lee, Sang-Won Lee, Irwin Levinstein, Mark Llewellyn, Gary Lindstrom, Ling Liu, Dave Maier, Keith Marzullo, Marty Maskarinec, Fletcher Mattox, Sharad Mehrotra, Jim Melton, Alberto Mendelzon, Ami Motro, Bhagirath Narahari, Yiu-Kai Dennis Ng, Thanh-Duy Nguyen, Anil Nigam, Cyril Orji, Meral Ozsoyoglu, D. B. Phatak, Juan Altmayer Pizzorno, Bruce Porter, Sunil Prabhakar, Jim Peterson, K. V. Raghavan, Nahid Rahman, Rajarshi Rakshit, Krithi Ramamritham, Mike Reiter, Greg Riccardi, Odinaldo Rodriguez, Mark Roth, Marek Rusinkiewicz, Michael Rys, Sunita Sarawagi, N. L. Sarda, Patrick Schmid, Nikhil Sethi, S. Seshadri, Stewart Shen, Shashi Shekhar, Amit Sheth, Max Smolens, Nandit Soparkar, Greg Speegle, Jeff Storey, Dilys Thomas, Prem Thomas, Tim Wahls, Anita Whitehall, Christopher Wilson, Marianne Winslett, Weining Zhang, and Liu Zhenming.

Book Production

The publisher was Raghu Srinivasan. The developmental editor was Melinda D. Bilecki. The project manager was Melissa Leick. The marketing manager was

Curt Reynolds. The production supervisor was Laura Fuller. The book designer was Brenda Rolwes. The cover designer was Studio Montage, St. Louis, Missouri. The copyeditor was George Watson. The proofreader was Kevin Campbell. The freelance indexer was Tobiah Waldron. The Aptara team consisted of Raman Arora and Sudeshna Nandy

Personal Notes

Sudarshan would like to acknowledge his wife, Sita, for her love and support, and children Madhur and Advaith for their love and joie de vivre. Hank would like to acknowledge his wife, Joan, and his children, Abby and Joe, for their love and understanding. Avi would like to acknowledge Valerie for her love, patience, and support during the revision of this book.

A. S.
H. F. K.
S. S.

CHAPTER 1

Introduction

A **database-management system (DBMS)** is a collection of interrelated data and a set of programs to access those data. The collection of data, usually referred to as the **database**, contains information relevant to an enterprise. The primary goal of a DBMS is to provide a way to store and retrieve database information that is both *convenient* and *efficient*.

Database systems are designed to manage large bodies of information. Management of data involves both defining structures for storage of information and providing mechanisms for the manipulation of information. In addition, the database system must ensure the safety of the information stored, despite system crashes or attempts at unauthorized access. If data are to be shared among several users, the system must avoid possible anomalous results.

Because information is so important in most organizations, computer scientists have developed a large body of concepts and techniques for managing data. These concepts and techniques form the focus of this book. This chapter briefly introduces the principles of database systems.

1.1   Database-System Applications

Databases are widely used. Here are some representative applications:

- *Enterprise Information*

  - *Sales*: For customer, product, and purchase information.

  - *Accounting*: For payments, receipts, account balances, assets and other accounting information.

  - *Human resources*: For information about employees, salaries, payroll taxes, and benefits, and for generation of paychecks.

  - *Manufacturing*: For management of the supply chain and for tracking production of items in factories, inventories of items in warehouses and stores, and orders for items.

1

○ *Online retailers*: For sales data noted above plus online order tracking, generation of recommendation lists, and maintenance of online product evaluations.

- *Banking and Finance*

  ○ *Banking*: For customer information, accounts, loans, and banking transactions.

  ○ *Credit card transactions*: For purchases on credit cards and generation of monthly statements.

  ○ *Finance*: For storing information about holdings, sales, and purchases of financial instruments such as stocks and bonds; also for storing real-time market data to enable online trading by customers and automated trading by the firm.

- *Universities*: For student information, course registrations, and grades (in addition to standard enterprise information such as human resources and accounting).

- *Airlines*: For reservations and schedule information. Airlines were among the first to use databases in a geographically distributed manner.

- *Telecommunication*: For keeping records of calls made, generating monthly bills, maintaining balances on prepaid calling cards, and storing information about the communication networks.

As the list illustrates, databases form an essential part of every enterprise today, storing not only types of information that are common to most enterprises, but also information that is specific to the category of the enterprise.

Over the course of the last four decades of the twentieth century, use of databases grew in all enterprises. In the early days, very few people interacted directly with database systems, although without realizing it, they interacted with databases indirectly—through printed reports such as credit card statements, or through agents such as bank tellers and airline reservation agents. Then automated teller machines came along and let users interact directly with databases. Phone interfaces to computers (interactive voice-response systems) also allowed users to deal directly with databases—a caller could dial a number, and press phone keys to enter information or to select alternative options, to find flight arrival/departure times, for example, or to register for courses in a university.

The Internet revolution of the late 1990s sharply increased direct user access to databases. Organizations converted many of their phone interfaces to databases into Web interfaces, and made a variety of services and information available online. For instance, when you access an online bookstore and browse a book or music collection, you are accessing data stored in a database. When you enter an order online, your order is stored in a database. When you access a bank Web site and retrieve your bank balance and transaction information, the information is retrieved from the bank's database system. When you access a Web site, information about you may be retrieved from a database to select which advertisements you should see. Furthermore, data about your Web accesses may be stored in a database.

Thus, although user interfaces hide details of access to a database, and most people are not even aware they are dealing with a database, accessing databases forms an essential part of almost everyone's life today.

The importance of database systems can be judged in another way—today, database system vendors like Oracle are among the largest software companies in the world, and database systems form an important part of the product line of Microsoft and IBM.

1.2 Purpose of Database Systems

Database systems arose in response to early methods of computerized management of commercial data. As an example of such methods, typical of the 1960s, consider part of a university organization that, among other data, keeps information about all instructors, students, departments, and course offerings. One way to keep the information on a computer is to store it in operating system files. To allow users to manipulate the information, the system has a number of application programs that manipulate the files, including programs to:

- Add new students, instructors, and courses

- Register students for courses and generate class rosters

- Assign grades to students, compute grade point averages (GPA), and generate transcripts

System programmers wrote these application programs to meet the needs of the university.

New application programs are added to the system as the need arises. For example, suppose that a university decides to create a new major (say, computer science). As a result, the university creates a new department and creates new permanent files (or adds information to existing files) to record information about all the instructors in the department, students in that major, course offerings, degree requirements, etc. The university may have to write new application programs to deal with rules specific to the new major. New application programs may also have to be written to handle new rules in the university. Thus, as time goes by, the system acquires more files and more application programs.

This typical **file-processing system** is supported by a conventional operating system. The system stores permanent records in various files, and it needs different application programs to extract records from, and add records to, the appropriate files. Before database management systems (DBMSs) were introduced, organizations usually stored information in such systems.

Keeping organizational information in a file-processing system has a number of major disadvantages:

- **Data redundancy and inconsistency**. Since different programmers create the files and application programs over a long period, the various files are likely to have different structures and the programs may be written in several programming languages. Moreover, the same information may be duplicated in several places (files). For example, if a student has a double major (say, music and mathematics) the address and telephone number of that student may appear in a file that consists of student records of students in the Music department and in a file that consists of student records of students in the Mathematics department. This redundancy leads to higher storage and access cost. In addition, it may lead to **data inconsistency**; that is, the various copies of the same data may no longer agree. For example, a changed student address may be reflected in the Music department records but not elsewhere in the system.

- **Difficulty in accessing data**. Suppose that one of the university clerks needs to find out the names of all students who live within a particular postal-code area. The clerk asks the data-processing department to generate such a list. Because the designers of the original system did not anticipate this request, there is no application program on hand to meet it. There is, however, an application program to generate the list of *all* students. The university clerk has now two choices: either obtain the list of all students and extract the needed information manually or ask a programmer to write the necessary application program. Both alternatives are obviously unsatisfactory. Suppose that such a program is written, and that, several days later, the same clerk needs to trim that list to include only those students who have taken at least 60 credit hours. As expected, a program to generate such a list does not exist. Again, the clerk has the preceding two options, neither of which is satisfactory.

  The point here is that conventional file-processing environments do not allow needed data to be retrieved in a convenient and efficient manner. More responsive data-retrieval systems are required for general use.

- **Data isolation**. Because data are scattered in various files, and files may be in different formats, writing new application programs to retrieve the appropriate data is difficult.

- **Integrity problems**. The data values stored in the database must satisfy certain types of **consistency constraints**. Suppose the university maintains an account for each department, and records the balance amount in each account. Suppose also that the university requires that the account balance of a department may never fall below zero. Developers enforce these constraints in the system by adding appropriate code in the various application programs. However, when new constraints are added, it is difficult to change the programs to enforce them. The problem is compounded when constraints involve several data items from different files.

- **Atomicity problems**. A computer system, like any other device, is subject to failure. In many applications, it is crucial that, if a failure occurs, the data be restored to the consistent state that existed prior to the failure. Consider a program to transfer $500 from the account balance of department A to the account balance of department B. If a system failure occurs during the execution of the program, it is possible that the $500 was removed from the balance of department A but was not credited to the balance of department B, resulting in an inconsistent database state. Clearly, it is essential to database consistency that either both the credit and debit occur, or that neither occur. That is, the funds transfer must be *atomic*—it must happen in its entirety or not at all. It is difficult to ensure atomicity in a conventional file-processing system.

- **Concurrent-access anomalies**. For the sake of overall performance of the system and faster response, many systems allow multiple users to update the data simultaneously. Indeed, today, the largest Internet retailers may have millions of accesses per day to their data by shoppers. In such an environment, interaction of concurrent updates is possible and may result in inconsistent data. Consider department A, with an account balance of $10,000. If two department clerks debit the account balance (by say $500 and $100, respectively) of department A at almost exactly the same time, the result of the concurrent executions may leave the budget in an incorrect (or inconsistent) state. Suppose that the programs executing on behalf of each withdrawal read the old balance, reduce that value by the amount being withdrawn, and write the result back. If the two programs run concurrently, they may both read the value $10,000, and write back $9500 and $9900, respectively. Depending on which one writes the value last, the account balance of department A may contain either $9500 or $9900, rather than the correct value of $9400. To guard against this possibility, the system must maintain some form of supervision. But supervision is difficult to provide because data may be accessed by many different application programs that have not been coordinated previously.

  As another example, suppose a registration program maintains a count of students registered for a course, in order to enforce limits on the number of students registered. When a student registers, the program reads the current count for the courses, verifies that the count is not already at the limit, adds one to the count, and stores the count back in the database. Suppose two students register concurrently, with the count at (say) 39. The two program executions may both read the value 39, and both would then write back 40, leading to an incorrect increase of only 1, even though two students successfully registered for the course and the count should be 41. Furthermore, suppose the course registration limit was 40; in the above case both students would be able to register, leading to a violation of the limit of 40 students.

- **Security problems**. Not every user of the database system should be able to access all the data. For example, in a university, payroll personnel need to see only that part of the database that has financial information. They do not need access to information about academic records. But, since application programs are added to the file-processing system in an ad hoc manner, enforcing such security constraints is difficult.

These difficulties, among others, prompted the development of database systems. In what follows, we shall see the concepts and algorithms that enable database systems to solve the problems with file-processing systems. In most of this book, we use a university organization as a running example of a typical data-processing application.

1.3   View of Data

A database system is a collection of interrelated data and a set of programs that allow users to access and modify these data. A major purpose of a database system is to provide users with an *abstract* view of the data. That is, the system hides certain details of how the data are stored and maintained.

1.3.1   Data Abstraction

For the system to be usable, it must retrieve data efficiently. The need for efficiency has led designers to use complex data structures to represent data in the database. Since many database-system users are not computer trained, developers hide the complexity from users through several levels of abstraction, to simplify users' interactions with the system:

- **Physical level**. The lowest level of abstraction describes *how* the data are actually stored. The physical level describes complex low-level data structures in detail.

- **Logical level**. The next-higher level of abstraction describes *what* data are stored in the database, and what relationships exist among those data. The logical level thus describes the entire database in terms of a small number of relatively simple structures. Although implementation of the simple structures at the logical level may involve complex physical-level structures, the user of the logical level does not need to be aware of this complexity. This is referred to as **physical data independence**. Database administrators, who must decide what information to keep in the database, use the logical level of abstraction.

- **View level**. The highest level of abstraction describes only part of the entire database. Even though the logical level uses simpler structures, complexity remains because of the variety of information stored in a large database. Many users of the database system do not need all this information; instead, they need to access only a part of the database. The view level of abstraction exists to simplify their interaction with the system. The system may provide many views for the same database.

Figure 1.1 shows the relationship among the three levels of abstraction.

An analogy to the concept of data types in programming languages may clarify the distinction among levels of abstraction. Many high-level programming

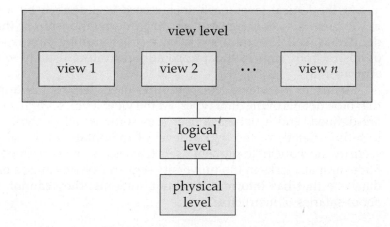

Figure 1.1 The three levels of data abstraction.

languages support the notion of a structured type. For example, we may describe a record as follows:[1]

type *instructor* = **record**
        ID : **char** (5);
        name : **char** (20);
        dept_name : **char** (20);
        salary : **numeric** (8,2);
    end;

This code defines a new record type called *instructor* with four fields. Each field has a name and a type associated with it. A university organization may have several such record types, including

- *department*, with fields *dept_name*, *building*, and *budget*
- *course*, with fields *course_id*, *title*, *dept_name*, and *credits*
- *student*, with fields *ID*, *name*, *dept_name*, and *tot_cred*

At the physical level, an *instructor*, *department*, or *student* record can be described as a block of consecutive storage locations. The compiler hides this level of detail from programmers. Similarly, the database system hides many of the lowest-level storage details from database programmers. Database administrators, on the other hand, may be aware of certain details of the physical organization of the data.

---

[1] The actual type declaration depends on the language being used. C and C++ use **struct** declarations. Java does not have such a declaration, but a simple class can be defined to the same effect.

At the logical level, each such record is described by a type definition, as in the previous code segment, and the interrelationship of these record types is defined as well. Programmers using a programming language work at this level of abstraction. Similarly, database administrators usually work at this level of abstraction.

Finally, at the view level, computer users see a set of application programs that hide details of the data types. At the view level, several views of the database are defined, and a database user sees some or all of these views. In addition to hiding details of the logical level of the database, the views also provide a security mechanism to prevent users from accessing certain parts of the database. For example, clerks in the university registrar office can see only that part of the database that has information about students; they cannot access information about salaries of instructors.

1.3.2   Instances and Schemas

Databases change over time as information is inserted and deleted. The collection of information stored in the database at a particular moment is called an **instance** of the database. The overall design of the database is called the database **schema**. Schemas are changed infrequently, if at all.

The concept of database schemas and instances can be understood by analogy to a program written in a programming language. A database schema corresponds to the variable declarations (along with associated type definitions) in a program. Each variable has a particular value at a given instant. The values of the variables in a program at a point in time correspond to an *instance* of a database schema.

Database systems have several schemas, partitioned according to the levels of abstraction. The **physical schema** describes the database design at the physical level, while the **logical schema** describes the database design at the logical level. A database may also have several schemas at the view level, sometimes called **subschemas**, that describe different views of the database.

Of these, the logical schema is by far the most important, in terms of its effect on application programs, since programmers construct applications by using the logical schema. The physical schema is hidden beneath the logical schema, and can usually be changed easily without affecting application programs. Application programs are said to exhibit **physical data independence** if they do not depend on the physical schema, and thus need not be rewritten if the physical schema changes.

We study languages for describing schemas after introducing the notion of data models in the next section.

1.3.3   Data Models

Underlying the structure of a database is the **data model**: a collection of conceptual tools for describing data, data relationships, data semantics, and consistency constraints. A data model provides a way to describe the design of a database at the physical, logical, and view levels.

There are a number of different data models that we shall cover in the text. The data models can be classified into four different categories:

- **Relational Model**. The relational model uses a collection of tables to represent both data and the relationships among those data. Each table has multiple columns, and each column has a unique name. Tables are also known as **relations**. The relational model is an example of a record-based model. Record-based models are so named because the database is structured in fixed-format records of several types. Each table contains records of a particular type. Each record type defines a fixed number of fields, or attributes. The columns of the table correspond to the attributes of the record type. The relational data model is the most widely used data model, and a vast majority of current database systems are based on the relational model. Chapters 2 through 8 cover the relational model in detail.

- **Entity-Relationship Model**. The entity-relationship (E-R) data model uses a collection of basic objects, called *entities*, and *relationships* among these objects. An entity is a "thing" or "object" in the real world that is distinguishable from other objects. The entity-relationship model is widely used in database design, and Chapter 7 explores it in detail.

- **Object-Based Data Model**. Object-oriented programming (especially in Java, C++, or C#) has become the dominant software-development methodology. This led to the development of an object-oriented data model that can be seen as extending the E-R model with notions of encapsulation, methods (functions), and object identity. The object-relational data model combines features of the object-oriented data model and relational data model. Chapter 22 examines the object-relational data model.

- **Semistructured Data Model**. The semistructured data model permits the specification of data where individual data items of the same type may have different sets of attributes. This is in contrast to the data models mentioned earlier, where every data item of a particular type must have the same set of attributes. The **Extensible Markup Language (XML)** is widely used to represent semistructured data. Chapter 23 covers it.

Historically, the **network data model** and the **hierarchical data model** preceded the relational data model. These models were tied closely to the underlying implementation, and complicated the task of modeling data. As a result they are used little now, except in old database code that is still in service in some places. They are outlined online in Appendices D and E for interested readers.

1.4 Database Languages

A database system provides a **data-definition language** to specify the database schema and a **data-manipulation language** to express database queries and updates. In practice, the data-definition and data-manipulation languages are not two separate languages; instead they simply form parts of a single database language, such as the widely used SQL language.

1.4.1   Data-Manipulation Language

A **data-manipulation language (DML)** is a language that enables users to access or manipulate data as organized by the appropriate data model. The types of access are:

- Retrieval of information stored in the database
- Insertion of new information into the database
- Deletion of information from the database
- Modification of information stored in the database

There are basically two types:

- **Procedural DMLs** require a user to specify *what* data are needed and *how* to get those data.
- **Declarative DMLs** (also referred to as **nonprocedural DMLs**) require a user to specify *what* data are needed *without* specifying how to get those data.

Declarative DMLs are usually easier to learn and use than are procedural DMLs. However, since a user does not have to specify how to get the data, the database system has to figure out an efficient means of accessing data.

A **query** is a statement requesting the retrieval of information. The portion of a DML that involves information retrieval is called a **query language**. Although technically incorrect, it is common practice to use the terms *query language* and *data-manipulation language* synonymously.

There are a number of database query languages in use, either commercially or experimentally. We study the most widely used query language, SQL, in Chapters 3, 4, and 5. We also study some other query languages in Chapter 6.

The levels of abstraction that we discussed in Section 1.3 apply not only to defining or structuring data, but also to manipulating data. At the physical level, we must define algorithms that allow efficient access to data. At higher levels of abstraction, we emphasize ease of use. The goal is to allow humans to interact efficiently with the system. The query processor component of the database system (which we study in Chapters 12 and 13) translates DML queries into sequences of actions at the physical level of the database system.

1.4.2   Data-Definition Language

We specify a database schema by a set of definitions expressed by a special language called a **data-definition language** (DDL). The DDL is also used to specify additional properties of the data.

We specify the storage structure and access methods used by the database system by a set of statements in a special type of DDL called a **data storage and definition** language. These statements define the implementation details of the database schemas, which are usually hidden from the users.

The data values stored in the database must satisfy certain **consistency constraints**. For example, suppose the university requires that the account balance of a department must never be negative. The DDL provides facilities to specify such constraints. The database system checks these constraints every time the database is updated. In general, a constraint can be an arbitrary predicate pertaining to the database. However, arbitrary predicates may be costly to test. Thus, database systems implement integrity constraints that can be tested with minimal overhead:

- **Domain Constraints**. A domain of possible values must be associated with every attribute (for example, integer types, character types, date/time types). Declaring an attribute to be of a particular domain acts as a constraint on the values that it can take. Domain constraints are the most elementary form of integrity constraint. They are tested easily by the system whenever a new data item is entered into the database.

- **Referential Integrity**. There are cases where we wish to ensure that a value that appears in one relation for a given set of attributes also appears in a certain set of attributes in another relation (referential integrity). For example, the department listed for each course must be one that actually exists. More precisely, the *dept_name* value in a *course* record must appear in the *dept_name* attribute of some record of the *department* relation. Database modifications can cause violations of referential integrity. When a referential-integrity constraint is violated, the normal procedure is to reject the action that caused the violation.

- **Assertions**. An assertion is any condition that the database must always satisfy. Domain constraints and referential-integrity constraints are special forms of assertions. However, there are many constraints that we cannot express by using only these special forms. For example, "Every department must have at least five courses offered every semester" must be expressed as an assertion. When an assertion is created, the system tests it for validity. If the assertion is valid, then any future modification to the database is allowed only if it does not cause that assertion to be violated.

- **Authorization**. We may want to differentiate among the users as far as the type of access they are permitted on various data values in the database. These differentiations are expressed in terms of **authorization**, the most common being: **read authorization**, which allows reading, but not modification, of data; **insert authorization**, which allows insertion of new data, but not modification of existing data; **update authorization**, which allows modification, but not deletion, of data; and **delete authorization**, which allows deletion of data. We may assign the user all, none, or a combination of these types of authorization.

The DDL, just like any other programming language, gets as input some instructions (statements) and generates some output. The output of the DDL is placed in the **data dictionary**, which contains **metadata**—that is, data about data. The data dictionary is considered to be a special type of table that can only be accessed and updated by the database system itself (not a regular user). The database system consults the data dictionary before reading or modifying actual data.

1.5   Relational Databases

A relational database is based on the relational model and uses a collection of tables to represent both data and the relationships among those data. It also includes a DML and DDL. In Chapter 2 we present a gentle introduction to the fundamentals of the relational model. Most commercial relational database systems employ the SQL language, which we cover in great detail in Chapters 3, 4, and 5. In Chapter 6 we discuss other influential languages.

1.5.1   Tables

Each table has multiple columns and each column has a unique name. Figure 1.2 presents a sample relational database comprising two tables: one shows details of university instructors and the other shows details of the various university departments.

The first table, the *instructor* table, shows, for example, that an instructor named Einstein with *ID* 22222 is a member of the Physics department and has an annual salary of $95,000. The second table, *department*, shows, for example, that the Biology department is located in the Watson building and has a budget of $90,000. Of course, a real-world university would have many more departments and instructors. We use small tables in the text to illustrate concepts. A larger example for the same schema is available online.

The relational model is an example of a record-based model. Record-based models are so named because the database is structured in fixed-format records of several types. Each table contains records of a particular type. Each record type defines a fixed number of fields, or attributes. The columns of the table correspond to the attributes of the record type.

It is not hard to see how tables may be stored in files. For instance, a special character (such as a comma) may be used to delimit the different attributes of a record, and another special character (such as a new-line character) may be used to delimit records. The relational model hides such low-level implementation details from database developers and users.

We also note that it is possible to create schemas in the relational model that have problems such as unnecessarily duplicated information. For example, suppose we store the department *budget* as an attribute of the *instructor* record. Then, whenever the value of a particular budget (say that one for the Physics department) changes, that change must to be reflected in the records of all instructors

ID	name	dept_name	salary
22222	Einstein	Physics	95000
12121	Wu	Finance	90000
32343	El Said	History	60000
45565	Katz	Comp. Sci.	75000
98345	Kim	Elec. Eng.	80000
76766	Crick	Biology	72000
10101	Srinivasan	Comp. Sci.	65000
58583	Califieri	History	62000
83821	Brandt	Comp. Sci.	92000
15151	Mozart	Music	40000
33456	Gold	Physics	87000
76543	Singh	Finance	80000

(a) The *instructor* table

dept_name	building	budget
Comp. Sci.	Taylor	100000
Biology	Watson	90000
Elec. Eng.	Taylor	85000
Music	Packard	80000
Finance	Painter	120000
History	Painter	50000
Physics	Watson	70000

(b) The *department* table

Figure 1.2 A sample relational database.

associated with the Physics department. In Chapter 8, we shall study how to distinguish good schema designs from bad schema designs.

1.5.2 Data-Manipulation Language

The SQL query language is nonprocedural. A query takes as input several tables (possibly only one) and always returns a single table. Here is an example of an SQL query that finds the names of all instructors in the History department:

> **select** *instructor.name*
> **from** *instructor*
> **where** *instructor.dept_name* = 'History';

The query specifies that those rows from the table *instructor* where the *dept_name* is History must be retrieved, and the *name* attribute of these rows must be displayed. More specifically, the result of executing this query is a table with a single column labeled *name,* and a set of rows, each of which contains the name of an instructor whose *dept_name,* is History. If the query is run on the table in Figure 1.2, the result will consist of two rows, one with the name El Said and the other with the name Califieri.

Queries may involve information from more than one table. For instance, the following query finds the instructor ID and department name of all instructors associated with a department with budget of greater than $95,000.

> **select** *instructor.ID, department.dept_name*
> **from** *instructor, department*
> **where** *instructor.dept_name= department.dept_name* **and**
>   *department.budget* > 95000;

If the above query were run on the tables in Figure 1.2, the system would find that there are two departments with budget of greater than $95,000—Computer Science and Finance; there are five instructors in these departments. Thus, the result will consist of a table with two columns (*ID, dept_name*) and five rows: (12121, Finance), (45565, Computer Science), (10101, Computer Science), (83821, Computer Science), and (76543, Finance).

1.5.3   Data-Definition Language

SQL provides a rich DDL that allows one to define tables, integrity constraints, assertions, etc.

For instance, the following SQL DDL statement defines the *department* table:

> **create table** *department*
>   (*dept_name*   **char** (20),
>   *building*   **char** (15),
>   *budget*   **numeric** (12,2));

Execution of the above DDL statement creates the *department* table with three columns: *dept_name, building,* and *budget,* each of which has a specific data type associated with it. We discuss data types in more detail in Chapter 3. In addition, the DDL statement updates the data dictionary, which contains metadata (see Section 1.4.2). The schema of a table is an example of metadata.

1.5.4   Database Access from Application Programs

SQL is not as powerful as a universal Turing machine; that is, there are some computations that are possible using a general-purpose programming language but are not possible using SQL. SQL also does not support actions such as input from users, output to displays, or communication over the network. Such computations and actions must be written in a *host* language, such as C, C++, or Java, with embedded SQL queries that access the data in the database. **Application programs** are programs that are used to interact with the database in this fashion.

Examples in a university system are programs that allow students to register for courses, generate class rosters, calculate student GPA, generate payroll checks, etc.

To access the database, DML statements need to be executed from the host language. There are two ways to do this:

- By providing an application program interface (set of procedures) that can be used to send DML and DDL statements to the database and retrieve the results.

  The Open Database Connectivity (ODBC) standard for use with the C language is a commonly used application program interface standard. The Java Database Connectivity (JDBC) standard provides corresponding features to the Java language.

- By extending the host language syntax to embed DML calls within the host language program. Usually, a special character prefaces DML calls, and a preprocessor, called the **DML precompiler**, converts the DML statements to normal procedure calls in the host language.

1.6   Database Design

Database systems are designed to manage large bodies of information. These large bodies of information do not exist in isolation. They are part of the operation of some enterprise whose end product may be information from the database or may be some device or service for which the database plays only a supporting role.

Database design mainly involves the design of the database schema. The design of a complete database application environment that meets the needs of the enterprise being modeled requires attention to a broader set of issues. In this text, we focus initially on the writing of database queries and the design of database schemas. Chapter 9 discusses the overall process of application design.

1.6.1   Design Process

A high-level data model provides the database designer with a conceptual framework in which to specify the data requirements of the database users, and how the database will be structured to fulfill these requirements. The initial phase of database design, then, is to characterize fully the data needs of the prospective database users. The database designer needs to interact extensively with domain experts and users to carry out this task. The outcome of this phase is a specification of user requirements.

Next, the designer chooses a data model, and by applying the concepts of the chosen data model, translates these requirements into a conceptual schema of the database. The schema developed at this **conceptual-design** phase provides a detailed overview of the enterprise. The designer reviews the schema to confirm that all data requirements are indeed satisfied and are not in conflict with one another. The designer can also examine the design to remove any redundant features. The focus at this point is on describing the data and their relationships, rather than on specifying physical storage details.

In terms of the relational model, the conceptual-design process involves decisions on *what* attributes we want to capture in the database and *how to group* these attributes to form the various tables. The "what" part is basically a business decision, and we shall not discuss it further in this text. The "how" part is mainly a computer-science problem. There are principally two ways to tackle the problem. The first one is to use the entity-relationship model (Section 1.6.3); the other is to employ a set of algorithms (collectively known as *normalization*) that takes as input the set of all attributes and generates a set of tables (Section 1.6.4).

A fully developed conceptual schema indicates the functional requirements of the enterprise. In a **specification of functional requirements**, users describe the kinds of operations (or transactions) that will be performed on the data. Example operations include modifying or updating data, searching for and retrieving specific data, and deleting data. At this stage of conceptual design, the designer can review the schema to ensure it meets functional requirements.

The process of moving from an abstract data model to the implementation of the database proceeds in two final design phases. In the **logical-design phase**, the designer maps the high-level conceptual schema onto the implementation data model of the database system that will be used. The designer uses the resulting system-specific database schema in the subsequent **physical-design phase**, in which the physical features of the database are specified. These features include the form of file organization and the internal storage structures; they are discussed in Chapter 10.

1.6.2 Database Design for a University Organization

To illustrate the design process, let us examine how a database for a university could be designed. The initial specification of user requirements may be based on interviews with the database users, and on the designer's own analysis of the organization. The description that arises from this design phase serves as the basis for specifying the conceptual structure of the database. Here are the major characteristics of the university.

- The university is organized into departments. Each department is identified by a unique name (*dept_name*), is located in a particular *building*, and has a *budget*.

- Each department has a list of courses it offers. Each course has associated with it a *course_id*, *title*, *dept_name*, and *credits*, and may also have have associated *prerequisites*.

- Instructors are identified by their unique *ID*. Each instructor has *name*, associated department (*dept_name*), and *salary*.

- Students are identified by their unique *ID*. Each student has a *name*, an associated major department (*dept_name*), and *tot_cred* (total credit hours the student earned thus far).

- The university maintains a list of classrooms, specifying the name of the *building*, *room_number*, and room *capacity*.

- The university maintains a list of all classes (sections) taught. Each section is identified by a *course_id*, *sec_id*, *year*, and *semester*, and has associated with it a *semester*, *year*, *building*, *room_number*, and *time_slot_id* (the time slot when the class meets).

- The department has a list of teaching assignments specifying, for each instructor, the sections the instructor is teaching.

- The university has a list of all student course registrations, specifying, for each student, the courses and the associated sections that the student has taken (registered for).

A real university database would be much more complex than the preceding design. However we use this simplified model to help you understand conceptual ideas without getting lost in details of a complex design.

1.6.3 The Entity-Relationship Model

The entity-relationship (E-R) data model uses a collection of basic objects, called *entities*, and *relationships* among these objects. An entity is a "thing" or "object" in the real world that is distinguishable from other objects. For example, each person is an entity, and bank accounts can be considered as entities.

Entities are described in a database by a set of **attributes**. For example, the attributes *dept_name*, *building*, and *budget* may describe one particular department in a university, and they form attributes of the *department* entity set. Similarly, attributes *ID*, *name*, and *salary* may describe an *instructor* entity.[2]

The extra attribute *ID* is used to identify an instructor uniquely (since it may be possible to have two instructors with the same name and the same salary). A unique instructor identifier must be assigned to each instructor. In the United States, many organizations use the social-security number of a person (a unique number the U.S. government assigns to every person in the United States) as a unique identifier.

A **relationship** is an association among several entities. For example, a *member* relationship associates an instructor with her department. The set of all entities of the same type and the set of all relationships of the same type are termed an **entity set** and **relationship set**, respectively.

The overall logical structure (schema) of a database can be expressed graphically by an *entity-relationship (E-R) diagram*. There are several ways in which to draw these diagrams. One of the most popular is to use the **Unified Modeling Language (UML)**. In the notation we use, which is based on UML, an E-R diagram is represented as follows:

---

[2]The astute reader will notice that we dropped the attribute *dept_name* from the set of attributes describing the *instructor* entity set; this is not an error. In Chapter 7 we shall provide a detailed explanation of why this is the case.

Figure 1.3 A sample E-R diagram.

- Entity sets are represented by a rectangular box with the entity set name in the header and the attributes listed below it.

- Relationship sets are represented by a diamond connecting a pair of related entity sets. The name of the relationship is placed inside the diamond.

As an illustration, consider part of a university database consisting of instructors and the departments with which they are associated. Figure 1.3 shows the corresponding E-R diagram. The E-R diagram indicates that there are two entity sets, *instructor* and *department*, with attributes as outlined earlier. The diagram also shows a relationship *member* between *instructor* and *department*.

In addition to entities and relationships, the E-R model represents certain constraints to which the contents of a database must conform. One important constraint is **mapping cardinalities**, which express the number of entities to which another entity can be associated via a relationship set. For example, if each instructor must be associated with only a single department, the E-R model can express that constraint.

The entity-relationship model is widely used in database design, and Chapter 7 explores it in detail.

1.6.4 Normalization

Another method for designing a relational database is to use a process commonly known as normalization. The goal is to generate a set of relation schemas that allows us to store information without unnecessary redundancy, yet also allows us to retrieve information easily. The approach is to design schemas that are in an appropriate *normal form*. To determine whether a relation schema is in one of the desirable normal forms, we need additional information about the real-world enterprise that we are modeling with the database. The most common approach is to use **functional dependencies**, which we cover in Section 8.4.

To understand the need for normalization, let us look at what can go wrong in a bad database design. Among the undesirable properties that a bad design may have are:

- Repetition of information

- Inability to represent certain information

ID	name	salary	dept_name	building	budget
22222	Einstein	95000	Physics	Watson	70000
12121	Wu	90000	Finance	Painter	120000
32343	El Said	60000	History	Painter	50000
45565	Katz	75000	Comp. Sci.	Taylor	100000
98345	Kim	80000	Elec. Eng.	Taylor	85000
76766	Crick	72000	Biology	Watson	90000
10101	Srinivasan	65000	Comp. Sci.	Taylor	100000
58583	Califieri	62000	History	Painter	50000
83821	Brandt	92000	Comp. Sci.	Taylor	100000
15151	Mozart	40000	Music	Packard	80000
33456	Gold	87000	Physics	Watson	70000
76543	Singh	80000	Finance	Painter	120000

Figure 1.4 The *faculty* table.

We shall discuss these problems with the help of a modified database design for our university example.

Suppose that instead of having the two separate tables *instructor* and *department*, we have a single table, *faculty*, that combines the information from the two tables (as shown in Figure 1.4). Notice that there are two rows in *faculty* that contain repeated information about the History department, specifically, that department's building and budget. The repetition of information in our alternative design is undesirable. Repeating information wastes space. Furthermore, it complicates updating the database. Suppose that we wish to change the budget amount of the History department from $50,000 to $46,800. This change must be reflected in the two rows; contrast this with the original design, where this requires an update to only a single row. Thus, updates are more costly under the alternative design than under the original design. When we perform the update in the alternative database, we must ensure that *every* tuple pertaining to the History department is updated, or else our database will show two different budget values for the History department.

Now, let us shift our attention to the issue of "inability to represent certain information." Suppose we are creating a new department in the university. In the alternative design above, we cannot represent directly the information concerning a department (*dept_name*, *building*, *budget*) unless that department has at least one instructor at the university. This is because rows in the faculty table require values for *ID*, *name*, and *salary*. This means that we cannot record information about the newly created department until the first instructor is hired for the new department.

One solution to this problem is to introduce **null** values. The *null* value indicates that the value does not exist (or is not known). An unknown value may be either *missing* (the value does exist, but we do not have that information) or *not known* (we do not know whether or not the value actually exists). As we shall see later, null values are difficult to handle, and it is preferable not to resort to them. If we are not willing to deal with null values, then we can create a particular item of department information only when the department has at least one instructor associated with the department. Furthermore, we would have to delete this information when the last instructor in the department departs. Clearly, this situation is undesirable, since, under our original database design, the department information would be available regardless of whether or not there is an instructor associated with the department, and without resorting to null values.

An extensive theory of normalization has been developed that helps formally define what database designs are undesirable, and how to obtain desirable designs. Chapter 8 covers relational-database design, including normalization.

1.7   Data Storage and Querying

A database system is partitioned into modules that deal with each of the responsibilities of the overall system. The functional components of a database system can be broadly divided into the storage manager and the query processor components.

The storage manager is important because databases typically require a large amount of storage space. Corporate databases range in size from hundreds of gigabytes to, for the largest databases, terabytes of data. A gigabyte is approximately 1000 megabytes (actually 1024) (1 billion bytes), and a terabyte is 1 million megabytes (1 trillion bytes). Since the main memory of computers cannot store this much information, the information is stored on disks. Data are moved between disk storage and main memory as needed. Since the movement of data to and from disk is slow relative to the speed of the central processing unit, it is imperative that the database system structure the data so as to minimize the need to move data between disk and main memory.

The query processor is important because it helps the database system to simplify and facilitate access to data. The query processor allows database users to obtain good performance while being able to work at the view level and not be burdened with understanding the physical-level details of the implementation of the system. It is the job of the database system to translate updates and queries written in a nonprocedural language, at the logical level, into an efficient sequence of operations at the physical level.

1.7.1   Storage Manager

The *storage manager* is the component of a database system that provides the interface between the low-level data stored in the database and the application programs and queries submitted to the system. The storage manager is responsible for the interaction with the file manager. The raw data are stored on the disk using the file system provided by the operating system. The storage manager translates the various DML statements into low-level file-system commands.

Thus, the storage manager is responsible for storing, retrieving, and updating data in the database.

The storage manager components include:

- **Authorization and integrity manager**, which tests for the satisfaction of integrity constraints and checks the authority of users to access data.

- **Transaction manager**, which ensures that the database remains in a consistent (correct) state despite system failures, and that concurrent transaction executions proceed without conflicting.

- **File manager**, which manages the allocation of space on disk storage and the data structures used to represent information stored on disk.

- **Buffer manager**, which is responsible for fetching data from disk storage into main memory, and deciding what data to cache in main memory. The buffer manager is a critical part of the database system, since it enables the database to handle data sizes that are much larger than the size of main memory.

The storage manager implements several data structures as part of the physical system implementation:

- **Data files**, which store the database itself.

- **Data dictionary**, which stores metadata about the structure of the database, in particular the schema of the database.

- **Indices**, which can provide fast access to data items. Like the index in this textbook, a database index provides pointers to those data items that hold a particular value. For example, we could use an index to find the *instructor* record with a particular *ID*, or all *instructor* records with a particular *name*. Hashing is an alternative to indexing that is faster in some but not all cases.

We discuss storage media, file structures, and buffer management in Chapter 10. Methods of accessing data efficiently via indexing or hashing are discussed in Chapter 11.

1.7.2   The Query Processor

The query processor components include:

- DDL **interpreter**, which interprets DDL statements and records the definitions in the data dictionary.

- DML **compiler**, which translates DML statements in a query language into an evaluation plan consisting of low-level instructions that the query evaluation engine understands.

A query can usually be translated into any of a number of alternative evaluation plans that all give the same result. The DML compiler also performs **query optimization**; that is, it picks the lowest cost evaluation plan from among the alternatives.

- **Query evaluation engine**, which executes low-level instructions generated by the DML compiler.

Query evaluation is covered in Chapter 12, while the methods by which the query optimizer chooses from among the possible evaluation strategies are discussed in Chapter 13.

1.8   Transaction Management

Often, several operations on the database form a single logical unit of work. An example is a funds transfer, as in Section 1.2, in which one department account (say A) is debited and another department account (say B) is credited. Clearly, it is essential that either both the credit and debit occur, or that neither occur. That is, the funds transfer must happen in its entirety or not at all. This all-or-none requirement is called **atomicity**. In addition, it is essential that the execution of the funds transfer preserve the consistency of the database. That is, the value of the sum of the balances of A and B must be preserved. This correctness requirement is called **consistency**. Finally, after the successful execution of a funds transfer, the new values of the balances of accounts A and B must persist, despite the possibility of system failure. This persistence requirement is called **durability**.

A **transaction** is a collection of operations that performs a single logical function in a database application. Each transaction is a unit of both atomicity and consistency. Thus, we require that transactions do not violate any database-consistency constraints. That is, if the database was consistent when a transaction started, the database must be consistent when the transaction successfully terminates. However, during the execution of a transaction, it may be necessary temporarily to allow inconsistency, since either the debit of A or the credit of B must be done before the other. This temporary inconsistency, although necessary, may lead to difficulty if a failure occurs.

It is the programmer's responsibility to define properly the various transactions, so that each preserves the consistency of the database. For example, the transaction to transfer funds from the account of department A to the account of department B could be defined to be composed of two separate programs: one that debits account A, and another that credits account B. The execution of these two programs one after the other will indeed preserve consistency. However, each program by itself does not transform the database from a consistent state to a new consistent state. Thus, those programs are not transactions.

Ensuring the atomicity and durability properties is the responsibility of the database system itself—specifically, of the **recovery manager**. In the absence of failures, all transactions complete successfully, and atomicity is achieved easily.

However, because of various types of failure, a transaction may not always complete its execution successfully. If we are to ensure the atomicity property, a failed transaction must have no effect on the state of the database. Thus, the database must be restored to the state in which it was before the transaction in question started executing. The database system must therefore perform **failure recovery**, that is, detect system failures and restore the database to the state that existed prior to the occurrence of the failure.

Finally, when several transactions update the database concurrently, the consistency of data may no longer be preserved, even though each individual transaction is correct. It is the responsibility of the **concurrency-control manager** to control the interaction among the concurrent transactions, to ensure the consistency of the database. The **transaction manager** consists of the concurrency-control manager and the recovery manager.

The basic concepts of transaction processing are covered in Chapter 14. The management of concurrent transactions is covered in Chapter 15. Chapter 16 covers failure recovery in detail.

The concept of a transaction has been applied broadly in database systems and applications. While the initial use of transactions was in financial applications, the concept is now used in real-time applications in telecommunication, as well as in the management of long-duration activities such as product design or administrative workflows. These broader applications of the transaction concept are discussed in Chapter 26.

1.9   Database Architecture

We are now in a position to provide a single picture (Figure 1.5) of the various components of a database system and the connections among them.

The architecture of a database system is greatly influenced by the underlying computer system on which the database system runs. Database systems can be centralized, or client-server, where one server machine executes work on behalf of multiple client machines. Database systems can also be designed to exploit parallel computer architectures. Distributed databases span multiple geographically separated machines.

In Chapter 17 we cover the general structure of modern computer systems. Chapter 18 describes how various actions of a database, in particular query processing, can be implemented to exploit parallel processing. Chapter 19 presents a number of issues that arise in a distributed database, and describes how to deal with each issue. The issues include how to store data, how to ensure atomicity of transactions that execute at multiple sites, how to perform concurrency control, and how to provide high availability in the presence of failures. Distributed query processing and directory systems are also described in this chapter.

Most users of a database system today are not present at the site of the database system, but connect to it through a network. We can therefore differentiate between **client** machines, on which remote database users work, and **server** machines, on which the database system runs.

Database applications are usually partitioned into two or three parts, as in Figure 1.6. In a **two-tier architecture**, the application resides at the client machine, where it invokes database system functionality at the server machine through

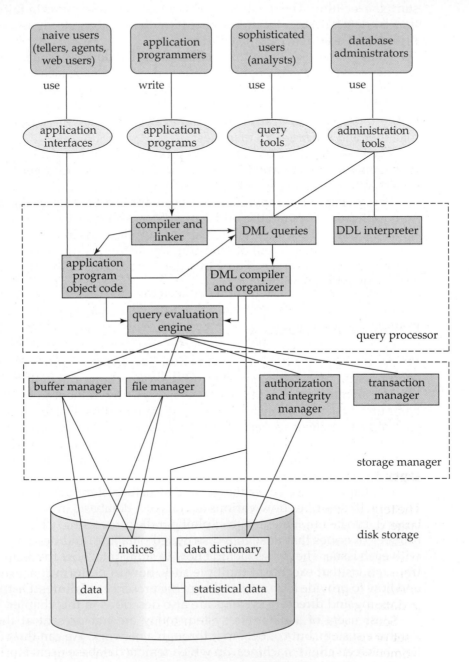

Figure 1.5 System structure.

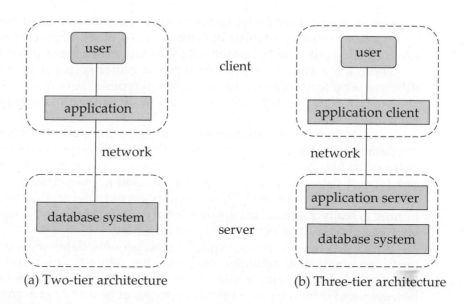

Figure 1.6 Two-tier and three-tier architectures.

query language statements. Application program interface standards like ODBC and JDBC are used for interaction between the client and the server.

In contrast, in a **three-tier architecture**, the client machine acts as merely a front end and does not contain any direct database calls. Instead, the client end communicates with an **application server**, usually through a forms interface. The application server in turn communicates with a database system to access data. The **business logic** of the application, which says what actions to carry out under what conditions, is embedded in the application server, instead of being distributed across multiple clients. Three-tier applications are more appropriate for large applications, and for applications that run on the World Wide Web.

1.10   Data Mining and Information Retrieval

The term **data mining** refers loosely to the process of semiautomatically analyzing large databases to find useful patterns. Like knowledge discovery in artificial intelligence (also called **machine learning**) or statistical analysis, data mining attempts to discover rules and patterns from data. However, data mining differs from machine learning and statistics in that it deals with large volumes of data, stored primarily on disk. That is, data mining deals with "knowledge discovery in databases."

Some types of knowledge discovered from a database can be represented by a set of **rules**. The following is an example of a rule, stated informally: "Young women with annual incomes greater than $50,000 are the most likely people to buy small sports cars." Of course such rules are not universally true, but rather have degrees of "support" and "confidence." Other types of knowledge are represented by equations relating different variables to each other, or by other mechanisms for predicting outcomes when the values of some variables are known.

There are a variety of possible types of patterns that may be useful, and different techniques are used to find different types of patterns. In Chapter 20 we study a few examples of patterns and see how they may be automatically derived from a database.

Usually there is a manual component to data mining, consisting of preprocessing data to a form acceptable to the algorithms, and postprocessing of discovered patterns to find novel ones that could be useful. There may also be more than one type of pattern that can be discovered from a given database, and manual interaction may be needed to pick useful types of patterns. For this reason, data mining is really a semiautomatic process in real life. However, in our description we concentrate on the automatic aspect of mining.

Businesses have begun to exploit the burgeoning data online to make better decisions about their activities, such as what items to stock and how best to target customers to increase sales. Many of their queries are rather complicated, however, and certain types of information cannot be extracted even by using SQL.

Several techniques and tools are available to help with decision support. Several tools for data analysis allow analysts to view data in different ways. Other analysis tools precompute summaries of very large amounts of data, in order to give fast responses to queries. The SQL standard contains additional constructs to support data analysis.

Large companies have diverse sources of data that they need to use for making business decisions. To execute queries efficiently on such diverse data, companies have built *data warehouses*. Data warehouses gather data from multiple sources under a unified schema, at a single site. Thus, they provide the user a single uniform interface to data.

Textual data, too, has grown explosively. Textual data is unstructured, unlike the rigidly structured data in relational databases. Querying of unstructured textual data is referred to as *information retrieval*. Information retrieval systems have much in common with database systems—in particular, the storage and retrieval of data on secondary storage. However, the emphasis in the field of information systems is different from that in database systems, concentrating on issues such as querying based on keywords; the relevance of documents to the query; and the analysis, classification, and indexing of documents. In Chapters 20 and 21, we cover decision support, including online analytical processing, data mining, data warehousing, and information retrieval.

1.11   Specialty Databases

Several application areas for database systems are limited by the restrictions of the relational data model. As a result, researchers have developed several data models to deal with these application domains, including object-based data models and semistructured data models.

1.11.1 Object-Based Data Models

Object-oriented programming has become the dominant software-development methodology. This led to the development of an **object-oriented data model** that can be seen as extending the E-R model with notions of encapsulation, methods (functions), and object identity. Inheritance, object identity, and encapsulation (information hiding), with methods to provide an interface to objects, are among the key concepts of object-oriented programming that have found applications in data modeling. The object-oriented data model also supports a rich type system, including structured and collection types. In the 1980s, several database systems based on the object-oriented data model were developed.

The major database vendors presently support the **object-relational data model**, a data model that combines features of the object-oriented data model and relational data model. It extends the traditional relational model with a variety of features such as structured and collection types, as well as object orientation. Chapter 22 examines the object-relational data model.

1.11.2 Semistructured Data Models

Semistructured data models permit the specification of data where individual data items of the same type may have different sets of attributes. This is in contrast with the data models mentioned earlier, where every data item of a particular type must have the same set of attributes.

The XML language was initially designed as a way of adding markup information to text documents, but has become important because of its applications in data exchange. XML provides a way to represent data that have nested structure, and furthermore allows a great deal of flexibility in structuring of data, which is important for certain kinds of nontraditional data. Chapter 23 describes the XML language, different ways of expressing queries on data represented in XML, and transforming XML data from one form to another.

1.12 Database Users and Administrators

A primary goal of a database system is to retrieve information from and store new information into the database. People who work with a database can be categorized as database users or database administrators.

1.12.1 Database Users and User Interfaces

There are four different types of database-system users, differentiated by the way they expect to interact with the system. Different types of user interfaces have been designed for the different types of users.

- **Naïve users** are unsophisticated users who interact with the system by invoking one of the application programs that have been written previously. For example, a clerk in the university who needs to add a new instructor to department *A* invokes a program called *new_hire*. This program asks the clerk for the name of the new instructor, her new *ID*, the name of the department (that is, *A*), and the salary.

The typical user interface for naïve users is a forms interface, where the user can fill in appropriate fields of the form. Naïve users may also simply read *reports* generated from the database.

As another example, consider a student, who during class registration period, wishes to register for a class by using a Web interface. Such a user connects to a Web application program that runs at a Web server. The application first verifies the identity of the user, and allows her to access a form where she enters the desired information. The form information is sent back to the Web application at the server, which then determines if there is room in the class (by retrieving information from the database) and if so adds the student information to the class roster in the database.

- **Application programmers** are computer professionals who write application programs. Application programmers can choose from many tools to develop user interfaces. **Rapid application development (RAD)** tools are tools that enable an application programmer to construct forms and reports with minimal programming effort.

- **Sophisticated users** interact with the system without writing programs. Instead, they form their requests either using a database query language or by using tools such as data analysis software. Analysts who submit queries to explore data in the database fall in this category.

- **Specialized users** are sophisticated users who write specialized database applications that do not fit into the traditional data-processing framework. Among these applications are computer-aided design systems, knowledge-base and expert systems, systems that store data with complex data types (for example, graphics data and audio data), and environment-modeling systems. Chapter 22 covers several of these applications.

1.12.2 Database Administrator

One of the main reasons for using DBMSs is to have central control of both the data and the programs that access those data. A person who has such central control over the system is called a **database administrator (DBA)**. The functions of a DBA include:

- **Schema definition**. The DBA creates the original database schema by executing a set of data definition statements in the DDL.

- **Storage structure and access-method definition**.

- **Schema and physical-organization modification**. The DBA carries out changes to the schema and physical organization to reflect the changing needs of the organization, or to alter the physical organization to improve performance.

- **Granting of authorization for data access**. By granting different types of authorization, the database administrator can regulate which parts of the database various users can access. The authorization information is kept in a special system structure that the database system consults whenever someone attempts to access the data in the system.

- **Routine maintenance**. Examples of the database administrator's routine maintenance activities are:

  - Periodically backing up the database, either onto tapes or onto remote servers, to prevent loss of data in case of disasters such as flooding.

  - Ensuring that enough free disk space is available for normal operations, and upgrading disk space as required.

  - Monitoring jobs running on the database and ensuring that performance is not degraded by very expensive tasks submitted by some users.

1.13   History of Database Systems

Information processing drives the growth of computers, as it has from the earliest days of commercial computers. In fact, automation of data processing tasks predates computers. Punched cards, invented by Herman Hollerith, were used at the very beginning of the twentieth century to record U.S. census data, and mechanical systems were used to process the cards and tabulate results. Punched cards were later widely used as a means of entering data into computers.

Techniques for data storage and processing have evolved over the years:

- **1950s and early 1960s**: Magnetic tapes were developed for data storage. Data processing tasks such as payroll were automated, with data stored on tapes. Processing of data consisted of reading data from one or more tapes and writing data to a new tape. Data could also be input from punched card decks, and output to printers. For example, salary raises were processed by entering the raises on punched cards and reading the punched card deck in synchronization with a tape containing the master salary details. The records had to be in the same sorted order. The salary raises would be added to the salary read from the master tape, and written to a new tape; the new tape would become the new master tape.

  Tapes (and card decks) could be read only sequentially, and data sizes were much larger than main memory; thus, data processing programs were forced to process data in a particular order, by reading and merging data from tapes and card decks.

- **Late 1960s and 1970s**: Widespread use of hard disks in the late 1960s changed the scenario for data processing greatly, since hard disks allowed direct access to data. The position of data on disk was immaterial, since any location on disk could be accessed in just tens of milliseconds. Data were thus freed from the tyranny of sequentiality. With disks, network and hierarchical databases could be created that allowed data structures such as lists and trees to be stored on disk. Programmers could construct and manipulate these data structures.

A landmark paper by Codd [1970] defined the relational model and nonprocedural ways of querying data in the relational model, and relational databases were born. The simplicity of the relational model and the possibility of hiding implementation details completely from the programmer were enticing indeed. Codd later won the prestigious Association of Computing Machinery Turing Award for his work.

- **1980s**: Although academically interesting, the relational model was not used in practice initially, because of its perceived performance disadvantages; relational databases could not match the performance of existing network and hierarchical databases. That changed with System R, a groundbreaking project at IBM Research that developed techniques for the construction of an efficient relational database system. Excellent overviews of System R are provided by Astrahan et al. [1976] and Chamberlin et al. [1981]. The fully functional System R prototype led to IBM's first relational database product, SQL/DS. At the same time, the Ingres system was being developed at the University of California at Berkeley. It led to a commercial product of the same name. Initial commercial relational database systems, such as IBM DB2, Oracle, Ingres, and DEC Rdb, played a major role in advancing techniques for efficient processing of declarative queries. By the early 1980s, relational databases had become competitive with network and hierarchical database systems even in the area of performance. Relational databases were so easy to use that they eventually replaced network and hierarchical databases; programmers using such databases were forced to deal with many low-level implementation details, and had to code their queries in a procedural fashion. Most importantly, they had to keep efficiency in mind when designing their programs, which involved a lot of effort. In contrast, in a relational database, almost all these low-level tasks are carried out automatically by the database, leaving the programmer free to work at a logical level. Since attaining dominance in the 1980s, the relational model has reigned supreme among data models.

  The 1980s also saw much research on parallel and distributed databases, as well as initial work on object-oriented databases.

- **Early 1990s**: The SQL language was designed primarily for decision support applications, which are query-intensive, yet the mainstay of databases in the 1980s was transaction-processing applications, which are update-intensive. Decision support and querying re-emerged as a major application area for databases. Tools for analyzing large amounts of data saw large growths in usage.

  Many database vendors introduced parallel database products in this period. Database vendors also began to add object-relational support to their databases.

- **1990s**: The major event of the 1990s was the explosive growth of the World Wide Web. Databases were deployed much more extensively than ever before. Database systems now had to support very high transaction-processing rates, as well as very high reliability and 24×7 availability (availability 24 hours a day, 7 days a week, meaning no downtime for scheduled maintenance activities). Database systems also had to support Web interfaces to data.

- **2000s**: The first half of the 2000s saw the emerging of XML and the associated query language XQuery as a new database technology. Although XML is widely used for data exchange, as well as for storing certain complex data types, relational databases still form the core of a vast majority of large-scale database applications. In this time period we have also witnessed the growth in "autonomic-computing/auto-admin" techniques for minimizing system administration effort. This period also saw a significant growth in use of open-source database systems, particularly PostgreSQL and MySQL.

  The latter part of the decade has seen growth in specialized databases for data analysis, in particular column-stores, which in effect store each column of a table as a separate array, and highly parallel database systems designed for analysis of very large data sets. Several novel distributed data-storage systems have been built to handle the data management requirements of very large Web sites such as Amazon, Facebook, Google, Microsoft and Yahoo!, and some of these are now offered as Web services that can be used by application developers. There has also been substantial work on management and analysis of streaming data, such as stock-market ticker data or computer network monitoring data. Data-mining techniques are now widely deployed; example applications include Web-based product-recommendation systems and automatic placement of relevant advertisements on Web pages.

1.14   Summary

- A **database-management system** (DBMS) consists of a collection of interrelated data and a collection of programs to access that data. The data describe one particular enterprise.

- The primary goal of a DBMS is to provide an environment that is both convenient and efficient for people to use in retrieving and storing information.

- Database systems are ubiquitous today, and most people interact, either directly or indirectly, with databases many times every day.

- Database systems are designed to store large bodies of information. The management of data involves both the definition of structures for the storage of information and the provision of mechanisms for the manipulation of information. In addition, the database system must provide for the safety of the information stored, in the face of system crashes or attempts at unauthorized access. If data are to be shared among several users, the system must avoid possible anomalous results.

- A major purpose of a database system is to provide users with an abstract view of the data. That is, the system hides certain details of how the data are stored and maintained.

- Underlying the structure of a database is the **data model**: a collection of conceptual tools for describing data, data relationships, data semantics, and data constraints.

- The relational data model is the most widely deployed model for storing data in databases. Other data models are the object-oriented model, the object-relational model, and semistructured data models.

- A **data-manipulation language (DML)** is a language that enables users to access or manipulate data. Nonprocedural DMLs, which require a user to specify only what data are needed, without specifying exactly how to get those data, are widely used today.

- A **data-definition language (DDL)** is a language for specifying the database schema and as well as other properties of the data.

- Database design mainly involves the design of the database schema. The entity-relationship (E-R) data model is a widely used data model for database design. It provides a convenient graphical representation to view data, relationships, and constraints.

- A database system has several subsystems.

  ○ The **storage manager** subsystem provides the interface between the low-level data stored in the database and the application programs and queries submitted to the system.

  ○ The **query processor** subsystem compiles and executes DDL and DML statements.

- **Transaction management** ensures that the database remains in a consistent (correct) state despite system failures. The transaction manager ensures that concurrent transaction executions proceed without conflicting.

- The architecture of a database system is greatly influenced by the underlying computer system on which the database system runs. Database systems can be centralized, or client-server, where one server machine executes work on behalf of multiple client machines. Database systems can also be designed to exploit parallel computer architectures. Distributed databases span multiple geographically separated machines.

- Database applications are typically broken up into a front-end part that runs at client machines and a part that runs at the back end. In two-tier architectures, the front end directly communicates with a database running at the back end. In three-tier architectures, the back end part is itself broken up into an application server and a database server.

- Knowledge-discovery techniques attempt to discover automatically statistical rules and patterns from data. The field of **data mining** combines knowledge-discovery techniques invented by artificial intelligence researchers and statistical analysts, with efficient implementation techniques that enable them to be used on extremely large databases.

- There are four different types of database-system users, differentiated by the way they expect to interact with the system. Different types of user interfaces have been designed for the different types of users.

Review Terms

- Database-management system (DBMS)
- Database-system applications
- File-processing systems
- Data inconsistency
- Consistency constraints
- Data abstraction
- Instance
- Schema
  - Physical schema
  - Logical schema
- Physical data independence
- Data models
  - Entity-relationship model
  - Relational data model
  - Object-based data model
  - Semistructured data model
- Database languages

- Data-definition language
- Data-manipulation language
- Query language
- Metadata
- Application program
- Normalization
- Data dictionary
- Storage manager
- Query processor
- Transactions
  - Atomicity
  - Failure recovery
  - Concurrency control
- Two- and three-tier database architectures
- Data mining
- Database administrator (DBA)

Practice Exercises

1.1 This chapter has described several major advantages of a database system. What are two disadvantages?

1.2 List five ways in which the type declaration system of a language such as Java or C++ differs from the data definition language used in a database.

1.3   List six major steps that you would take in setting up a database for a particular enterprise.

1.4   List at least 3 different types of information that a university would maintain, beyond those listed in Section 1.6.2.

1.5   Suppose you want to build a video site similar to YouTube. Consider each of the points listed in Section 1.2, as disadvantages of keeping data in a file-processing system. Discuss the relevance of each of these points to the storage of actual video data, and to metadata about the video, such as title, the user who uploaded it, tags, and which users viewed it.

1.6   Keyword queries used in Web search are quite different from database queries. List key differences between the two, in terms of the way the queries are specified, and in terms of what is the result of a query.

Exercises

1.7   List four applications you have used that most likely employed a database system to store persistent data.

1.8   List four significant differences between a file-processing system and a DBMS.

1.9   Explain the concept of physical data independence, and its importance in database systems.

1.10   List five responsibilities of a database-management system. For each responsibility, explain the problems that would arise if the responsibility were not discharged.

1.11   List at least two reasons why database systems support data manipulation using a declarative query language such as SQL, instead of just providing a a library of C or C++ functions to carry out data manipulation.

1.12   Explain what problems are caused by the design of the table in Figure 1.4.

1.13   What are five main functions of a database administrator?

1.14   Explain the difference between two-tier and three-tier architectures. Which is better suited for Web applications? Why?

1.15   Describe at least 3 tables that might be used to store information in a social-networking system such as Facebook.

Tools

There are a large number of commercial database systems in use today. The major ones include: IBM DB2 (www.ibm.com/software/data/db2), Oracle (www.oracle.com), Microsoft SQL Server (www.microsoft.com/sql), Sybase (www.sybase.com), and IBM Informix (www.ibm.com/software/data/informix). Some of these systems are available free for personal or noncommercial use, or for development, but are not free for actual deployment.

There are also a number of free/public domain database systems; widely used ones include MySQL (www.mysql.com) and PostgreSQL (www.postgresql.org).

A more complete list of links to vendor Web sites and other information is available from the home page of this book, at www.db-book.com.

Bibliographical Notes

We list below general-purpose books, research paper collections, and Web sites on databases. Subsequent chapters provide references to material on each topic outlined in this chapter.

Codd [1970] is the landmark paper that introduced the relational model.

Textbooks covering database systems include Abiteboul et al. [1995], O'Neil and O'Neil [2000], Ramakrishnan and Gehrke [2002], Date [2003], Kifer et al. [2005], Elmasri and Navathe [2006], and Garcia-Molina et al. [2008]. Textbook coverage of transaction processing is provided by Bernstein and Newcomer [1997] and Gray and Reuter [1993]. A book containing a collection of research papers on database management is offered by Hellerstein and Stonebraker [2005].

A review of accomplishments in database management and an assessment of future research challenges appears in Silberschatz et al. [1990], Silberschatz et al. [1996], Bernstein et al. [1998], Abiteboul et al. [2003], and Agrawal et al. [2009]. The home page of the ACM Special Interest Group on Management of Data (www.acm.org/sigmod) provides a wealth of information about database research. Database vendor Web sites (see the Tools section above) provide details about their respective products.

PART 1

RELATIONAL DATABASES

A data model is a collection of conceptual tools for describing data, data relationships, data semantics, and consistency constraints. In this part, we focus on the relational model.

The relational model, which is covered in Chapter 2, uses a collection of tables to represent both data and the relationships among those data. Its conceptual simplicity has led to its widespread adoption; today a vast majority of database products are based on the relational model. The relational model describes data at the logical and view levels, abstracting away low-level details of data storage. The entity-relationship model, discussed later in Chapter 7 (in Part 2), is a higher-level data model which is widely used for database design.

To make data from a relational database available to users, we have to address several issues. The most important issue is how users specify requests for retrieving and updating data; several query languages have been developed for this task. A second, but still important, issue is data integrity and protection; databases need to protect data from damage by user actions, whether unintentional or intentional.

Chapters 3, 4 and 5 cover the SQL language, which is the most widely used query language today. Chapters 3 and 4 provide introductory and intermediate level descriptions of SQL. Chapter 4 also covers integrity constraints which are enforced by the database, and authorization mechanisms, which control what access and update actions can be carried out by a user. Chapter 5 covers more advanced topics, including access to SQL from programming languages, and the use of SQL for data analysis.

Chapter 6 covers three formal query languages, the relational algebra, the tuple relational calculus and the domain relational calculus, which are declarative query languages based on mathematical logic. These formal languages form the basis for SQL, and for two other user-friendly languages, QBE and Datalog, which are described in Appendix B (available online at db-book.com).

CHAPTER 2

Introduction to the Relational Model

The relational model is today the primary data model for commercial data-processing applications. It attained its primary position because of its simplicity, which eases the job of the programmer, compared to earlier data models such as the network model or the hierarchical model.

In this chapter, we first study the fundamentals of the relational model. A substantial theory exists for relational databases. We study the part of this theory dealing with queries in Chapter 6. In Chapters 7 through 8, we shall examine aspects of database theory that help in the design of relational database schemas, while in Chapters 12 and 13 we discuss aspects of the theory dealing with efficient processing of queries.

2.1 Structure of Relational Databases

A relational database consists of a collection of **tables**, each of which is assigned a unique name. For example, consider the *instructor* table of Figure 2.1, which stores information about instructors. The table has four column headers: *ID*, *name*, *dept_name*, and *salary*. Each row of this table records information about an instructor, consisting of the instructor's *ID*, *name*, *dept_name*, and *salary*. Similarly, the *course* table of Figure 2.2 stores information about courses, consisting of a *course_id*, *title*, *dept_name*, and *credits*, for each course. Note that each instructor is identified by the value of the column *ID*, while each course is identified by the value of the column *course_id*.

Figure 2.3 shows a third table, *prereq*, which stores the prerequisite courses for each course. The table has two columns, *course_id* and *prereq_id*. Each row consists of a pair of course identifiers such that the second course is a prerequisite for the first course.

Thus, a row in the *prereq* table indicates that two courses are *related* in the sense that one course is a prerequisite for the other. As another example, we consider the table *instructor*, a row in the table can be thought of as representing

ID	name	dept_name	salary
10101	Srinivasan	Comp. Sci.	65000
12121	Wu	Finance	90000
15151	Mozart	Music	40000
22222	Einstein	Physics	95000
32343	El Said	History	60000
33456	Gold	Physics	87000
45565	Katz	Comp. Sci.	75000
58583	Califieri	History	62000
76543	Singh	Finance	80000
76766	Crick	Biology	72000
83821	Brandt	Comp. Sci.	92000
98345	Kim	Elec. Eng.	80000

Figure 2.1 The *instructor* relation.

the relationship between a specified *ID* and the corresponding values for *name*, *dept_name*, and *salary* values.

In general, a row in a table represents a *relationship* among a set of values. Since a table is a collection of such relationships, there is a close correspondence between the concept of *table* and the mathematical concept of *relation*, from which the relational data model takes its name. In mathematical terminology, a *tuple* is simply a sequence (or list) of values. A relationship between *n* values is represented mathematically by an *n-tuple* of values, i.e., a tuple with *n* values, which corresponds to a row in a table.

course_id	title	dept_name	credits
BIO-101	Intro. to Biology	Biology	4
BIO-301	Genetics	Biology	4
BIO-399	Computational Biology	Biology	3
CS-101	Intro. to Computer Science	Comp. Sci.	4
CS-190	Game Design	Comp. Sci.	4
CS-315	Robotics	Comp. Sci.	3
CS-319	Image Processing	Comp. Sci.	3
CS-347	Database System Concepts	Comp. Sci.	3
EE-181	Intro. to Digital Systems	Elec. Eng.	3
FIN-201	Investment Banking	Finance	3
HIS-351	World History	History	3
MU-199	Music Video Production	Music	3
PHY-101	Physical Principles	Physics	4

Figure 2.2 The *course* relation.

course_id	prereq_id
BIO-301	BIO-101
BIO-399	BIO-101
CS-190	CS-101
CS-315	CS-101
CS-319	CS-101
CS-347	CS-101
EE-181	PHY-101

Figure 2.3 The *prereq* relation.

Thus, in the relational model the term **relation** is used to refer to a table, while the term **tuple** is used to refer to a row. Similarly, the term **attribute** refers to a column of a table.

Examining Figure 2.1, we can see that the relation *instructor* has four attributes: *ID*, *name*, *dept_name*, and *salary*.

We use the term **relation instance** to refer to a specific instance of a relation, i.e., containing a specific set of rows. The instance of *instructor* shown in Figure 2.1 has 12 tuples, corresponding to 12 instructors.

In this chapter, we shall be using a number of different relations to illustrate the various concepts underlying the relational data model. These relations represent part of a university. They do not include all the data an actual university database would contain, in order to simplify our presentation. We shall discuss criteria for the appropriateness of relational structures in great detail in Chapters 7 and 8.

The order in which tuples appear in a relation is irrelevant, since a relation is a *set* of tuples. Thus, whether the tuples of a relation are listed in sorted order, as in Figure 2.1, or are unsorted, as in Figure 2.4, does not matter; the relations in

ID	name	dept_name	salary
22222	Einstein	Physics	95000
12121	Wu	Finance	90000
32343	El Said	History	60000
45565	Katz	Comp. Sci.	75000
98345	Kim	Elec. Eng.	80000
76766	Crick	Biology	72000
10101	Srinivasan	Comp. Sci.	65000
58583	Califieri	History	62000
83821	Brandt	Comp. Sci.	92000
15151	Mozart	Music	40000
33456	Gold	Physics	87000
76543	Singh	Finance	80000

Figure 2.4 Unsorted display of the *instructor* relation.

the two figures are the same, since both contain the same set of tuples. For ease of exposition, we will mostly show the relations sorted by their first attribute.

For each attribute of a relation, there is a set of permitted values, called the **domain** of that attribute. Thus, the domain of the *salary* attribute of the *instructor* relation is the set of all possible salary values, while the domain of the *name* attribute is the set of all possible instructor names.

We require that, for all relations r, the domains of all attributes of r be atomic. A domain is **atomic** if elements of the domain are considered to be indivisible units. For example, suppose the table *instructor* had an attribute *phone_number*, which can store a set of phone numbers corresponding to the instructor. Then the domain of *phone_number* would not be atomic, since an element of the domain is a set of phone numbers, and it has subparts, namely the individual phone numbers in the set.

The important issue is not what the domain itself is, but rather how we use domain elements in our database. Suppose now that the *phone_number* attribute stores a single phone number. Even then, if we split the value from the phone number attribute into a country code, an area code and a local number, we would be treating it as a nonatomic value. If we treat each phone number as a single indivisible unit, then the attribute *phone_number* would have an atomic domain.

In this chapter, as well as in Chapters 3 through 6, we assume that all attributes have atomic domains. In Chapter 22, we shall discuss extensions to the relational data model to permit nonatomic domains.

The **null** value is a special value that signifies that the value is unknown or does not exist. For example, suppose as before that we include the attribute *phone _number* in the *instructor* relation. It may be that an instructor does not have a phone number at all, or that the telephone number is unlisted. We would then have to use the null value to signify that the value is unknown or does not exist. We shall see later that null values cause a number of difficulties when we access or update the database, and thus should be eliminated if at all possible. We shall assume null values are absent initially, and in Section 3.6 we describe the effect of nulls on different operations.

2.2   Database Schema

When we talk about a database, we must differentiate between the **database schema**, which is the logical design of the database, and the **database instance**, which is a snapshot of the data in the database at a given instant in time.

The concept of a relation corresponds to the programming-language notion of a variable, while the concept of a **relation schema** corresponds to the programming-language notion of type definition.

In general, a relation schema consists of a list of attributes and their corresponding domains. We shall not be concerned about the precise definition of the domain of each attribute until we discuss the SQL language in Chapter 3.

The concept of a relation instance corresponds to the programming-language notion of a value of a variable. The value of a given variable may change with time;

dept_name	building	budget
Biology	Watson	90000
Comp. Sci.	Taylor	100000
Elec. Eng.	Taylor	85000
Finance	Painter	120000
History	Painter	50000
Music	Packard	80000
Physics	Watson	70000

Figure 2.5 The *department* relation.

similarly the contents of a relation instance may change with time as the relation is updated. In contrast, the schema of a relation does not generally change.

Although it is important to know the difference between a relation schema and a relation instance, we often use the same name, such as *instructor*, to refer to both the schema and the instance. Where required, we explicitly refer to the schema or to the instance, for example "the *instructor* schema," or "an instance of the *instructor* relation." However, where it is clear whether we mean the schema or the instance, we simply use the relation name.

Consider the *department* relation of Figure 2.5. The schema for that relation is

$$department \ (dept\_name, building, budget)$$

Note that the attribute *dept_name* appears in both the *instructor* schema and the *department* schema. This duplication is not a coincidence. Rather, using common attributes in relation schemas is one way of relating tuples of distinct relations. For example, suppose we wish to find the information about all the instructors who work in the Watson building. We look first at the *department* relation to find the *dept_name* of all the departments housed in Watson. Then, for each such department, we look in the *instructor* relation to find the information about the instructor associated with the corresponding *dept_name*.

Let us continue with our university database example.

Each course in a university may be offered multiple times, across different semesters, or even within a semester. We need a relation to describe each individual offering, or section, of the class. The schema is

$$section \ (course\_id, sec\_id, semester, year, building, room\_number, time\_slot\_id)$$

Figure 2.6 shows a sample instance of the *section* relation.

We need a relation to describe the association between instructors and the class sections that they teach. The relation schema to describe this association is

$$teaches \ (ID, course\_id, sec\_id, semester, year)$$

course_id	sec_id	semester	year	building	room_number	time_slot_id
BIO-101	1	Summer	2009	Painter	514	B
BIO-301	1	Summer	2010	Painter	514	A
CS-101	1	Fall	2009	Packard	101	H
CS-101	1	Spring	2010	Packard	101	F
CS-190	1	Spring	2009	Taylor	3128	E
CS-190	2	Spring	2009	Taylor	3128	A
CS-315	1	Spring	2010	Watson	120	D
CS-319	1	Spring	2010	Watson	100	B
CS-319	2	Spring	2010	Taylor	3128	C
CS-347	1	Fall	2009	Taylor	3128	A
EE-181	1	Spring	2009	Taylor	3128	C
FIN-201	1	Spring	2010	Packard	101	B
HIS-351	1	Spring	2010	Painter	514	C
MU-199	1	Spring	2010	Packard	101	D
PHY-101	1	Fall	2009	Watson	100	A

Figure 2.6   The *section* relation.

Figure 2.7 shows a sample instance of the *teaches* relation.

As you can imagine, there are many more relations maintained in a real university database. In addition to those relations we have listed already, *instructor*, *department*, *course*, *section*, *prereq*, and *teaches*, we use the following relations in this text:

ID	course_id	sec_id	semester	year
10101	CS-101	1	Fall	2009
10101	CS-315	1	Spring	2010
10101	CS-347	1	Fall	2009
12121	FIN-201	1	Spring	2010
15151	MU-199	1	Spring	2010
22222	PHY-101	1	Fall	2009
32343	HIS-351	1	Spring	2010
45565	CS-101	1	Spring	2010
45565	CS-319	1	Spring	2010
76766	BIO-101	1	Summer	2009
76766	BIO-301	1	Summer	2010
83821	CS-190	1	Spring	2009
83821	CS-190	2	Spring	2009
83821	CS-319	2	Spring	2010
98345	EE-181	1	Spring	2009

Figure 2.7   The *teaches* relation.

- *student* (*ID*, *name*, *dept_name*, *tot_cred*)

- *advisor* (*s_id*, *i_id*)

- *takes* (*ID*, *course_id*, *sec_id*, *semester*, *year*, *grade*)

- *classroom* (*building*, *room_number*, *capacity*)

- *time_slot* (*time_slot_id*, *day*, *start_time*, *end_time*)

2.3   Keys

We must have a way to specify how tuples within a given relation are distinguished. This is expressed in terms of their attributes. That is, the values of the attribute values of a tuple must be such that they can *uniquely identify* the tuple. In other words, no two tuples in a relation are allowed to have exactly the same value for all attributes.

A **superkey** is a set of one or more attributes that, taken collectively, allow us to identify uniquely a tuple in the relation. For example, the *ID* attribute of the relation *instructor* is sufficient to distinguish one instructor tuple from another. Thus, *ID* is a superkey. The *name* attribute of *instructor*, on the other hand, is not a superkey, because several instructors might have the same name.

Formally, let R denote the set of attributes in the schema of relation r. If we say that a subset K of R is a *superkey* for r, we are restricting consideration to instances of relations r in which no two distinct tuples have the same values on all attributes in K. That is, if t_1 and t_2 are in r and $t_1 \neq t_2$, then $t_1.K \neq t_2.K$.

A superkey may contain extraneous attributes. For example, the combination of *ID* and *name* is a superkey for the relation *instructor*. If K is a superkey, then so is any superset of K. We are often interested in superkeys for which no proper subset is a superkey. Such minimal superkeys are called **candidate keys**.

It is possible that several distinct sets of attributes could serve as a candidate key. Suppose that a combination of *name* and *dept_name* is sufficient to distinguish among members of the *instructor* relation. Then, both {*ID*} and {*name*, *dept_name*} are candidate keys. Although the attributes *ID* and *name* together can distinguish *instructor* tuples, their combination, {*ID*, *name*}, does not form a candidate key, since the attribute *ID* alone is a candidate key.

We shall use the term **primary key** to denote a candidate key that is chosen by the database designer as the principal means of identifying tuples within a relation. A key (whether primary, candidate, or super) is a property of the entire relation, rather than of the individual tuples. Any two individual tuples in the relation are prohibited from having the same value on the key attributes at the same time. The designation of a key represents a constraint in the real-world enterprise being modeled.

Primary keys must be chosen with care. As we noted, the name of a person is obviously not sufficient, because there may be many people with the same name. In the United States, the social-security number attribute of a person would be a candidate key. Since non-U.S. residents usually do not have social-security numbers, international enterprises must generate their own unique identifiers. An alternative is to use some unique combination of other attributes as a key.

The primary key should be chosen such that its attribute values are never, or very rarely, changed. For instance, the address field of a person should not be part of the primary key, since it is likely to change. Social-security numbers, on the other hand, are guaranteed never to change. Unique identifiers generated by enterprises generally do not change, except if two enterprises merge; in such a case the same identifier may have been issued by both enterprises, and a reallocation of identifiers may be required to make sure they are unique.

It is customary to list the primary key attributes of a relation schema before the other attributes; for example, the *dept_name* attribute of *department* is listed first, since it is the primary key. Primary key attributes are also underlined.

A relation, say r_1, may include among its attributes the primary key of another relation, say r_2. This attribute is called a **foreign key** from r_1, referencing r_2. The relation r_1 is also called the **referencing relation** of the foreign key dependency, and r_2 is called the **referenced relation** of the foreign key. For example, the attribute *dept_name* in *instructor* is a foreign key from *instructor*, referencing *department*, since *dept_name* is the primary key of *department*. In any database instance, given any tuple, say t_a, from the *instructor* relation, there must be some tuple, say t_b, in the *department* relation such that the value of the *dept_name* attribute of t_a is the same as the value of the primary key, *dept_name*, of t_b.

Now consider the *section* and *teaches* relations. It would be reasonable to require that if a section exists for a course, it must be taught by at least one instructor; however, it could possibly be taught by more than one instructor. To enforce this constraint, we would require that if a particular (*course_id*, *sec_id*, *semester*, *year*) combination appears in *section*, then the same combination must appear in *teaches*. However, this set of values does not form a primary key for *teaches*, since more than one instructor may teach one such section. As a result, we cannot declare a foreign key constraint from *section* to *teaches* (although we can define a foreign key constraint in the other direction, from *teaches* to *section*).

The constraint from *section* to *teaches* is an example of a **referential integrity constraint**; a referential integrity constraint requires that the values appearing in specified attributes of any tuple in the referencing relation also appear in specified attributes of at least one tuple in the referenced relation.

2.4   Schema Diagrams

A database schema, along with primary key and foreign key dependencies, can be depicted by **schema diagrams**. Figure 2.8 shows the schema diagram for our university organization. Each relation appears as a box, with the relation name at the top in blue, and the attributes listed inside the box. Primary key attributes are shown underlined. Foreign key dependencies appear as arrows from the foreign key attributes of the referencing relation to the primary key of the referenced relation.

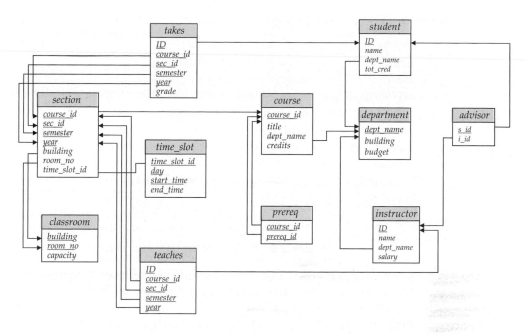

Figure 2.8 Schema diagram for the university database.

Referential integrity constraints other than foreign key constraints are not shown explicitly in schema diagrams. We will study a different diagrammatic representation called the entity-relationship diagram later, in Chapter 7. Entity-relationship diagrams let us represent several kinds of constraints, including general referential integrity constraints.

Many database systems provide design tools with a graphical user interface for creating schema diagrams. We shall discuss diagrammatic representation of schemas at length in Chapter 7.

The enterprise that we use in the examples in later chapters is a university. Figure 2.9 gives the relational schema that we use in our examples, with primary-key attributes underlined. As we shall see in Chapter 3, this corresponds to the approach to defining relations in the SQL data-definition language.

2.5 Relational Query Languages

A **query language** is a language in which a user requests information from the database. These languages are usually on a level higher than that of a standard programming language. Query languages can be categorized as either procedural or nonprocedural. In a **procedural language**, the user instructs the system to perform a sequence of operations on the database to compute the desired result. In a **nonprocedural language**, the user describes the desired information without giving a specific procedure for obtaining that information.

classroom(*building*, *room_number*, *capacity*)
department(*dept_name*, *building*, *budget*)
course(*course_id*, *title*, *dept_name*, *credits*)
instructor(*ID*, *name*, *dept_name*, *salary*)
section(*course_id*, *sec_id*, *semester*, *year*, *building*, *room_number*, *time_slot_id*)
teaches(*ID*, *course_id*, *sec_id*, *semester*, *year*)
student(*ID*, *name*, *dept_name*, *tot_cred*)
takes(*ID*, *course_id*, *sec_id*, *semester*, *year*, *grade*)
advisor(*s_ID*, *i_ID*)
time_slot(*time_slot_id*, *day*, *start_time*, *end_time*)
prereq(*course_id*, *prereq_id*)

Figure 2.9 Schema of the university database.

Query languages used in practice include elements of both the procedural and the nonprocedural approaches. We study the very widely used query language SQL in Chapters 3 through 5.

There are a number of "pure" query languages: The relational algebra is procedural, whereas the tuple relational calculus and domain relational calculus are nonprocedural. These query languages are terse and formal, lacking the "syntactic sugar" of commercial languages, but they illustrate the fundamental techniques for extracting data from the database. In Chapter 6, we examine in detail the relational algebra and the two versions of the relational calculus, the tuple relational calculus and domain relational calculus. The relational algebra consists of a set of operations that take one or two relations as input and produce a new relation as their result. The relational calculus uses predicate logic to define the result desired without giving any specific algebraic procedure for obtaining that result.

2.6   Relational Operations

All procedural relational query languages provide a set of operations that can be applied to either a single relation or a pair of relations. These operations have the nice and desired property that their result is always a single relation. This property allows one to combine several of these operations in a modular way. Specifically, since the result of a relational query is itself a relation, relational operations can be applied to the results of queries as well as to the given set of relations.

The specific relational operations are expressed differently depending on the language, but fit the general framework we describe in this section. In Chapter 3, we show the specific way the operations are expressed in SQL.

The most frequent operation is the selection of specific tuples from a single relation (say *instructor*) that satisfies some particular predicate (say *salary* > $85,000). The result is a new relation that is a subset of the original relation (*in-*

ID	name	dept_name	salary
12121	Wu	Finance	90000
22222	Einstein	Physics	95000
33456	Gold	Physics	87000
83821	Brandt	Comp. Sci.	92000

Figure 2.10 Result of query selecting *instructor* tuples with salary greater than $85000.

structor). For example, if we select tuples from the *instructor* relation of Figure 2.1, satisfying the predicate "*salary* is greater than $85000", we get the result shown in Figure 2.10.

Another frequent operation is to select certain attributes (columns) from a relation. The result is a new relation having only those selected attributes. For example, suppose we want a list of instructor *ID*s and salaries without listing the *name* and *dept_name* values from the *instructor* relation of Figure 2.1, then the result, shown in Figure 2.11, has the two attributes *ID* and *salary*. Each tuple in the result is derived from a tuple of the *instructor* relation but with only selected attributes shown.

The *join* operation allows the combining of two relations by merging pairs of tuples, one from each relation, into a single tuple. There are a number of different ways to join relations (as we shall see in Chapter 3). Figure 2.12 shows an example of joining the tuples from the *instructor* and *department* tables with the new tuples showing the information about each instructor and the department in which she is working. This result was formed by combining each tuple in the *instructor* relation with the tuple in the *department* relation for the instructor's department.

In the form of join shown in Figure 2.12, which is called a *natural join*, a tuple from the *instructor* relation matches a tuple in the *department* relation if the values

ID	salary
10101	65000
12121	90000
15151	40000
22222	95000
32343	60000
33456	87000
45565	75000
58583	62000
76543	80000
76766	72000
83821	92000
98345	80000

Figure 2.11 Result of query selecting attributes *ID* and *salary* from the *instructor* relation.

ID	name	salary	dept_name	building	budget
10101	Srinivasan	65000	Comp. Sci.	Taylor	100000
12121	Wu	90000	Finance	Painter	120000
15151	Mozart	40000	Music	Packard	80000
22222	Einstein	95000	Physics	Watson	70000
32343	El Said	60000	History	Painter	50000
33456	Gold	87000	Physics	Watson	70000
45565	Katz	75000	Comp. Sci.	Taylor	100000
58583	Califieri	62000	History	Painter	50000
76543	Singh	80000	Finance	Painter	120000
76766	Crick	72000	Biology	Watson	90000
83821	Brandt	92000	Comp. Sci.	Taylor	100000
98345	Kim	80000	Elec. Eng.	Taylor	85000

Figure 2.12 Result of natural join of the *instructor* and *department* relations.

of their *dept_name* attributes are the same. All such matching pairs of tuples are present in the join result. In general, the natural join operation on two relations matches tuples whose values are the same on all attribute names that are common to both relations.

The *Cartesian product* operation combines tuples from two relations, but unlike the join operation, its result contains *all* pairs of tuples from the two relations, regardless of whether their attribute values match.

Because relations are sets, we can perform normal set operations on relations. The *union* operation performs a set union of two "similarly structured" tables (say a table of all graduate students and a table of all undergraduate students). For example, one can obtain the set of all students in a department. Other set operations, such as *intersection* and *set difference* can be performed as well.

As we noted earlier, we can perform operations on the results of queries. For example, if we want to find the *ID* and *salary* for those instructors who have salary greater than $85,000, we would perform the first two operations in our example above. First we select those tuples from the *instructor* relation where the *salary* value is greater than $85,000 and then, from that result, select the two attributes *ID* and *salary*, resulting in the relation shown in Figure 2.13 consisting of the *ID*

ID	salary
12121	90000
22222	95000
33456	87000
83821	92000

Figure 2.13 Result of selecting attributes *ID* and *salary* of instructors with salary greater than $85,000.

RELATIONAL ALGEBRA

The relational algebra defines a set of operations on relations, paralleling the usual algebraic operations such as addition, subtraction or multiplication, which operate on numbers. Just as algebraic operations on numbers take one or more numbers as input and return a number as output, the relational algebra operations typically take one or two relations as input and return a relation as output.

Relational algebra is covered in detail in Chapter 6, but we outline a few of the operations below.

Symbol (Name)	Example of Use
σ (Selection)	$\sigma_{salary>=85000}(instructor)$
	Return rows of the input relation that satisfy the predicate.
Π (Projection)	$\Pi_{ID,salary}(instructor)$
	Output specified attributes from all rows of the input relation. Remove duplicate tuples from the output.
$\bowtie$ (Natural join)	$instructor \bowtie department$
	Output pairs of rows from the two input relations that have the same value on all attributes that have the same name.
$\times$ (Cartesian product)	$instructor \times department$
	Output all pairs of rows from the two input relations (regardless of whether or not they have the same values on common attributes)
$\cup$ (Union)	$\Pi_{name}(instructor) \cup \Pi_{name}(student)$
	Output the union of tuples from the two input relations.

---

and *salary*. In this example, we could have performed the operations in either order, but that is not the case for all situations, as we shall see.

Sometimes, the result of a query contains duplicate tuples. For example, if we select the *dept_name* attribute from the *instructor* relation, there are several cases of duplication, including "Comp. Sci.", which shows up three times. Certain relational languages adhere strictly to the mathematical definition of a set and remove duplicates. Others, in consideration of the relatively large amount of processing required to remove duplicates from large result relations, retain duplicates. In these latter cases, the relations are not truly relations in the pure mathematical sense of the term.

Of course, data in a database must be changed over time. A relation can be updated by inserting new tuples, deleting existing tuples, or modifying tuples by changing the values of certain attributes. Entire relations can be deleted and new ones created.

We shall discuss relational queries and updates using the SQL language in Chapters 3 through 5.

2.7   Summary

- The **relational data model** is based on a collection of tables. The user of the database system may query these tables, insert new tuples, delete tuples, and update (modify) tuples. There are several languages for expressing these operations.

- The **schema** of a relation refers to its logical design, while an **instance** of the relation refers to its contents at a point in time. The schema of a database and an instance of a database are similarly defined. The schema of a relation includes its attributes, and optionally the types of the attributes and constraints on the relation such as primary and foreign key constraints.

- A **superkey** of a relation is a set of one or more attributes whose values are guaranteed to identify tuples in the relation uniquely. A candidate key is a minimal superkey, that is, a set of attributes that forms a superkey, but none of whose subsets is a superkey. One of the candidate keys of a relation is chosen as its **primary key**.

- A **foreign key** is a set of attributes in a referencing relation, such that for each tuple in the referencing relation, the values of the foreign key attributes are guaranteed to occur as the primary key value of a tuple in the referenced relation.

- A **schema diagram** is a pictorial depiction of the schema of a database that shows the relations in the database, their attributes, and primary keys and foreign keys.

- The **relational query languages** define a set of operations that operate on tables, and output tables as their results. These operations can be combined to get expressions that express desired queries.

- The **relational algebra** provides a set of operations that take one or more relations as input and return a relation as an output. Practical query languages such as SQL are based on the relational algebra, but add a number of useful syntactic features.

Review Terms

- Table
- Relation
- Tuple
- Attribute
- Domain
- Atomic domain

- Null value
- Database schema
- Database instance
- Relation schema
- Relation instance
- Keys
  - Superkey
  - Candidate key
  - Primary key
- Foreign key
  - Referencing relation
  - Referenced relation

- Referential integrity constraint
- Schema diagram
- Query language
  - Procedural language
  - Nonprocedural language
- Operations on relations
  - Selection of tuples
  - Selection of attributes
  - Natural join
  - Cartesian product
  - Set operations
- Relational algebra

Practice Exercises

2.1   Consider the relational database of Figure 2.14. What are the appropriate primary keys?

2.2   Consider the foreign key constraint from the *dept_name* attribute of *instructor* to the *department* relation. Give examples of inserts and deletes to these relations, which can cause a violation of the foreign key constraint.

2.3   Consider the *time_slot* relation. Given that a particular time slot can meet more than once in a week, explain why *day* and *start_time* are part of the primary key of this relation, while *end_time* is not.

2.4   In the instance of *instructor* shown in Figure 2.1, no two instructors have the same name. From this, can we conclude that *name* can be used as a superkey (or primary key) of *instructor*?

2.5   What is the result of first performing the cross product of *student* and *advisor*, and then performing a selection operation on the result with the predicate *s_id* = ID? (Using the symbolic notation of relational algebra, this query can be written as $\sigma_{s\_id=ID}(student \times advisor)$.)

> *employee* (*person_name, street, city*)
> *works* (*person_name, company_name, salary*)
> *company* (*company_name, city*)

Figure 2.14   Relational database for Exercises 2.1, 2.7, and 2.12.

branch(*branch_name, branch_city, assets*)
customer (*customer_name, customer_street, customer_city*)
loan (*loan_number, branch_name, amount*)
borrower (*customer_name, loan_number*)
account (*account_number, branch_name, balance*)
depositor (*customer_name, account_number*)

Figure 2.15   Banking database for Exercises 2.8, 2.9, and 2.13.

2.6 Consider the following expressions, which use the result of a relational algebra operation as the input to another operation. For each expression, explain in words what the expression does.

   a. $\sigma_{year \geq 2009}(takes) \bowtie student$

   b. $\sigma_{year \geq 2009}(takes \bowtie student)$

   c. $\Pi_{ID, name, course\_id}(student \bowtie takes)$

2.7 Consider the relational database of Figure 2.14. Give an expression in the relational algebra to express each of the following queries:

   a.   Find the names of all employees who live in city "Miami".

   b.   Find the names of all employees whose salary is greater than $100,000.

   c.   Find the names of all employees who live in "Miami" and whose salary is greater than $100,000.

2.8 Consider the bank database of Figure 2.15. Give an expression in the relational algebra for each of the following queries.

   a.   Find the names of all branches located in "Chicago".

   b.   Find the names of all borrowers who have a loan in branch "Downtown".

Exercises

2.9 Consider the bank database of Figure 2.15.

   a.   What are the appropriate primary keys?

   b.   Given your choice of primary keys, identify appropriate foreign keys.

2.10 Consider the *advisor* relation shown in Figure 2.8, with *s_id* as the primary key of *advisor*. Suppose a student can have more than one advisor. Then, would *s_id* still be a primary key of the *advisor* relation? If not, what should the primary key of *advisor* be?

2.11 Describe the differences in meaning between the terms *relation* and *relation schema*.

2.12   Consider the relational database of Figure 2.14. Give an expression in the relational algebra to express each of the following queries:

   a.   Find the names of all employees who work for "First Bank Corporation".

   b.   Find the names and cities of residence of all employees who work for "First Bank Corporation".

   c.   Find the names, street address, and cities of residence of all employees who work for "First Bank Corporation" and earn more than $10,000.

2.13   Consider the bank database of Figure 2.15. Give an expression in the relational algebra for each of the following queries:

   a.   Find all loan numbers with a loan value greater than $10,000.

   b.   Find the names of all depositors who have an account with a value greater than $6,000.

   c.   Find the names of all depositors who have an account with a value greater than $6,000 at the "Uptown" branch.

2.14   List two reasons why null values might be introduced into the database.

2.15   Discuss the relative merits of procedural and nonprocedural languages.

Bibliographical Notes

E. F. Codd of the IBM San Jose Research Laboratory proposed the relational model in the late 1960s (Codd [1970]). This work led to the prestigious ACM Turing Award to Codd in 1981 (Codd [1982]).

After Codd published his original paper, several research projects were formed with the goal of constructing practical relational database systems, including System R at the IBM San Jose Research Laboratory, Ingres at the University of California at Berkeley, and Query-by-Example at the IBM T. J. Watson Research Center.

Many relational database products are now commercially available. These include IBM's DB2 and Informix, Oracle, Sybase, and Microsoft SQL Server. Open source relational database systems include MySQL and PostgreSQL. Microsoft Access is a single-user database product that is part of the Microsoft Office suite.

Atzeni and Antonellis [1993], Maier [1983], and Abiteboul et al. [1995] are texts devoted exclusively to the theory of the relational data model.

CHAPTER 3

Introduction to SQL

There are a number of database query languages in use, either commercially or experimentally. In this chapter, as well as in Chapters 4 and 5, we study the most widely used query language, SQL.

Although we refer to the SQL language as a "query language," it can do much more than just query a database. It can define the structure of the data, modify data in the database, and specify security constraints.

It is not our intention to provide a complete users' guide for SQL. Rather, we present SQL's fundamental constructs and concepts. Individual implementations of SQL may differ in details, or may support only a subset of the full language.

3.1 Overview of the SQL Query Language

IBM developed the original version of SQL, originally called Sequel, as part of the System R project in the early 1970s. The Sequel language has evolved since then, and its name has changed to SQL (Structured Query Language). Many products now support the SQL language. SQL has clearly established itself as *the* standard relational database language.

In 1986, the American National Standards Institute (ANSI) and the International Organization for Standardization (ISO) published an SQL standard, called SQL-86. ANSI published an extended standard for SQL, SQL-89, in 1989. The next version of the standard was SQL-92 standard, followed by SQL:1999, SQL:2003, SQL:2006, and most recently SQL:2008. The bibliographic notes provide references to these standards.

The SQL language has several parts:

- **Data-definition language** (DDL). The SQL DDL provides commands for defining relation schemas, deleting relations, and modifying relation schemas.

- **Data-manipulation language** (DML). The SQL DML provides the ability to query information from the database and to insert tuples into, delete tuples from, and modify tuples in the database.

- **Integrity**. The SQL DDL includes commands for specifying integrity constraints that the data stored in the database must satisfy. Updates that violate integrity constraints are disallowed.

- **View definition**. The SQL DDL includes commands for defining views.

- **Transaction control**. SQL includes commands for specifying the beginning and ending of transactions.

- **Embedded SQL** and **dynamic SQL**. Embedded and dynamic SQL define how SQL statements can be embedded within general-purpose programming languages, such as C, C++, and Java.

- **Authorization**. The SQL DDL includes commands for specifying access rights to relations and views.

In this chapter, we present a survey of basic DML and the DDL features of SQL. Features described here have been part of the SQL standard since SQL-92.

In Chapter 4, we provide a more detailed coverage of the SQL query language, including (a) various join expressions; (b) views; (c) transactions; (d) integrity constraints; (e) type system; and (f) authorization.

In Chapter 5, we cover more advanced features of the SQL language, including (a) mechanisms to allow accessing SQL from a programming language; (b) SQL functions and procedures; (c) triggers; (d) recursive queries; (e) advanced aggregation features; and (f) several features designed for data analysis, which were introduced in SQL:1999, and subsequent versions of SQL. Later, in Chapter 22, we outline object-oriented extensions to SQL, which were introduced in SQL:1999.

Although most SQL implementations support the standard features we describe here, you should be aware that there are differences between implementations. Most implementations support some nonstandard features, while omitting support for some of the more advanced features. In case you find that some language features described here do not work on the database system that you use, consult the user manuals for your database system to find exactly what features it supports.

3.2   SQL Data Definition

The set of relations in a database must be specified to the system by means of a data-definition language (DDL). The SQL DDL allows specification of not only a set of relations, but also information about each relation, including:

- The schema for each relation.

- The types of values associated with each attribute.

- The integrity constraints.

- The set of indices to be maintained for each relation.

- The security and authorization information for each relation.

- The physical storage structure of each relation on disk.

We discuss here basic schema definition and basic types; we defer discussion of the other SQL DDL features to Chapters 4 and 5.

3.2.1 Basic Types

The SQL standard supports a variety of built-in types, including:

- **char**(*n*): A fixed-length character string with user-specified length *n*. The full form, **character**, can be used instead.

- **varchar**(*n*): A variable-length character string with user-specified maximum length *n*. The full form, **character varying**, is equivalent.

- **int**: An integer (a finite subset of the integers that is machine dependent). The full form, **integer**, is equivalent.

- **smallint**: A small integer (a machine-dependent subset of the integer type).

- **numeric**(*p, d*): A fixed-point number with user-specified precision. The number consists of *p* digits (plus a sign), and *d* of the *p* digits are to the right of the decimal point. Thus, **numeric**(3,1) allows 44.5 to be stored exactly, but neither 444.5 or 0.32 can be stored exactly in a field of this type.

- **real, double precision**: Floating-point and double-precision floating-point numbers with machine-dependent precision.

- **float**(*n*): A floating-point number, with precision of at least *n* digits.

Additional types are covered in Section 4.5.

Each type may include a special value called the **null** value. A null value indicates an absent value that may exist but be unknown or that may not exist at all. In certain cases, we may wish to prohibit null values from being entered, as we shall see shortly.

The **char** data type stores fixed length strings. Consider, for example, an attribute *A* of type **char**(10). If we store a string "Avi" in this attribute, 7 spaces are appended to the string to make it 10 characters long. In contrast, if attribute *B* were of type **varchar**(10), and we store "Avi" in attribute *B*, no spaces would be added. When comparing two values of type **char**, if they are of different lengths extra spaces are automatically added to the shorter one to make them the same size, before comparison.

When comparing a **char** type with a **varchar** type, one may expect extra spaces to be added to the **varchar** type to make the lengths equal, before comparison; however, this may or may not be done, depending on the database system. As a result, even if the same value "Avi" is stored in the attributes *A* and *B* above, a comparison *A=B* may return false. We recommend you always use the **varchar** type instead of the **char** type to avoid these problems.

SQL also provides the **nvarchar** type to store multilingual data using the Unicode representation. However, many databases allow Unicode (in the UTF-8 representation) to be stored even in **varchar** types.

3.2.2   Basic Schema Definition

We define an SQL relation by using the **create table** command. The following command creates a relation *department* in the database.

> **create table** *department*
> (*dept_name* **varchar** (20),
>   *building*   **varchar** (15),
>   *budget*   **numeric** (12,2),
>   **primary key** (*dept_name*));

The relation created above has three attributes, *dept_name*, which is a character string of maximum length 20, *building*, which is a character string of maximum length 15, and *budget*, which is a number with 12 digits in total, 2 of which are after the decimal point. The **create table** command also specifies that the *dept_name* attribute is the primary key of the *department* relation.

The general form of the **create table** command is:

> **create table** r
> (A_1 D_1,
> A_2 D_2,
> $\ldots$,
> A_n D_n,
> $\langle$integrity-constraint$_1\rangle$,
> $\ldots$,
> $\langle$integrity-constraint$_k\rangle$);

where r is the name of the relation, each A_i is the name of an attribute in the schema of relation r, and D_i is the domain of attribute A_i; that is, D_i specifies the type of attribute A_i along with optional constraints that restrict the set of allowed values for A_i.

The semicolon shown at the end of the **create table** statements, as well as at the end of other SQL statements later in this chapter, is optional in many SQL implementations.

SQL supports a number of different integrity constraints. In this section, we discuss only a few of them:

- **primary key** ($A_{j_1}, A_{j_2}, \ldots, A_{j_m}$): The **primary-key** specification says that attributes $A_{j_1}, A_{j_2}, \ldots, A_{j_m}$ form the primary key for the relation. The primary-key attributes are required to be *nonnull* and *unique*; that is, no tuple can have a null value for a primary-key attribute, and no two tuples in the relation can be equal on all the primary-key attributes. Although the primary-key specification is optional, it is generally a good idea to specify a primary key for each relation.

- **foreign key** $(A_{k_1}, A_{k_2}, \dots, A_{k_n})$ **references** s: The **foreign key** specification says that the values of attributes $(A_{k_1}, A_{k_2}, \dots, A_{k_n})$ for any tuple in the relation must correspond to values of the primary key attributes of some tuple in relation s.

  Figure 3.1 presents a partial SQL DDL definition of the university database we use in the text. The definition of the *course* table has a declaration "**foreign key** (*dept_name*) **references** *department*". This foreign-key declaration specifies that for each course tuple, the department name specified in the tuple must exist in the primary key attribute (*dept_name*) of the *department* relation. Without this constraint, it is possible for a course to specify a nonexistent department name. Figure 3.1 also shows foreign key constraints on tables *section*, *instructor* and *teaches*.

- **not null**: The **not null** constraint on an attribute specifies that the null value is not allowed for that attribute; in other words, the constraint excludes the null value from the domain of that attribute. For example, in Figure 3.1, the **not null** constraint on the *name* attribute of the *instructor* relation ensures that the name of an instructor cannot be null.

More details on the foreign-key constraint, as well as on other integrity constraints that the **create table** command may include, are provided later, in Section 4.4.

SQL prevents any update to the database that violates an integrity constraint. For example, if a newly inserted or modified tuple in a relation has null values for any primary-key attribute, or if the tuple has the same value on the primary-key attributes as does another tuple in the relation, SQL flags an error and prevents the update. Similarly, an insertion of a *course* tuple with a *dept_name* value that does not appear in the *department* relation would violate the foreign-key constraint on *course*, and SQL prevents such an insertion from taking place.

A newly created relation is empty initially. We can use the **insert** command to load data into the relation. For example, if we wish to insert the fact that there is an instructor named Smith in the Biology department with *instructor_id* 10211 and a salary of $66,000, we write:

> **insert into** *instructor*
> **values** (10211, 'Smith', 'Biology', 66000);

The values are specified in the *order* in which the corresponding attributes are listed in the relation schema. The insert command has a number of useful features, and is covered in more detail later, in Section 3.9.2.

We can use the **delete** command to delete tuples from a relation. The command

> **delete from** *student*;

```
create table department
    (dept_name      varchar (20),
     building       varchar (15),
     budget         numeric (12,2),
     primary key (dept_name));

create table course
    (course_id      varchar (7),
     title          varchar (50),
     dept_name      varchar (20),
     credits        numeric (2,0),
     primary key (course_id),
     foreign key (dept_name) references department);

create table instructor
    (ID             varchar (5),
     name           varchar (20) not null,
     dept_name      varchar (20),
     salary         numeric (8,2),
     primary key (ID),
     foreign key (dept_name) references department);

create table section
    (course_id      varchar (8),
     sec_id         varchar (8),
     semester       varchar (6),
     year           numeric (4,0),
     building       varchar (15),
     room_number    varchar (7),
     time_slot_id   varchar (4),
     primary key (course_id, sec_id, semester, year),
     foreign key (course_id) references course);

create table teaches
    (ID             varchar (5),
     course_id      varchar (8),
     sec_id         varchar (8),
     semester       varchar (6),
     year           numeric (4,0),
     primary key (ID, course_id, sec_id, semester, year),
     foreign key (course_id, sec_id, semester, year) references section,
     foreign key (ID) references instructor);
```

Figure 3.1   SQL data definition for part of the university database.

would delete all tuples from the *student* relation. Other forms of the delete command allow specific tuples to be deleted; the delete command is covered in more detail later, in Section 3.9.1.

To remove a relation from an SQL database, we use the **drop table** command. The **drop table** command deletes all information about the dropped relation from the database. The command

$$\text{\textbf{drop table} } r;$$

is a more drastic action than

$$\text{\textbf{delete from} } r;$$

The latter retains relation r, but deletes all tuples in r. The former deletes not only all tuples of r, but also the schema for r. After r is dropped, no tuples can be inserted into r unless it is re-created with the **create table** command.

We use the **alter table** command to add attributes to an existing relation. All tuples in the relation are assigned *null* as the value for the new attribute. The form of the **alter table** command is

$$\text{\textbf{alter table} } r \text{ \textbf{add} } A \ D;$$

where r is the name of an existing relation, A is the name of the attribute to be added, and D is the type of the added attribute. We can drop attributes from a relation by the command

$$\text{\textbf{alter table} } r \text{ \textbf{drop} } A;$$

where r is the name of an existing relation, and A is the name of an attribute of the relation. Many database systems do not support dropping of attributes, although they will allow an entire table to be dropped.

3.3   Basic Structure of SQL Queries

The basic structure of an SQL query consists of three clauses: **select**, **from**, and **where**. The query takes as its input the relations listed in the **from** clause, operates on them as specified in the **where** and **select** clauses, and then produces a relation as the result. We introduce the SQL syntax through examples, and describe the general structure of SQL queries later.

3.3.1   Queries on a Single Relation

Let us consider a simple query using our university example, "Find the names of all instructors." Instructor names are found in the *instructor* relation, so we

name
Srinivasan
Wu
Mozart
Einstein
El Said
Gold
Katz
Califieri
Singh
Crick
Brandt
Kim

Figure 3.2 Result of "**select** *name* **from** *instructor*".

put that relation in the **from** clause. The instructor's name appears in the *name* attribute, so we put that in the **select** clause.

> **select** *name*
> **from** *instructor*;

The result is a relation consisting of a single attribute with the heading *name*. If the *instructor* relation is as shown in Figure 2.1, then the relation that results from the preceding query is shown in Figure 3.2.

Now consider another query, "Find the department names of all instructors," which can be written as:

> **select** *dept_name*
> **from** *instructor*;

Since more than one instructor can belong to a department, a department name could appear more than once in the *instructor* relation. The result of the above query is a relation containing the department names, shown in Figure 3.3.

In the formal, mathematical definition of the relational model, a relation is a set. Thus, duplicate tuples would never appear in relations. In practice, duplicate elimination is time-consuming. Therefore, SQL allows duplicates in relations as well as in the results of SQL expressions. Thus, the preceding SQL query lists each department name once for every tuple in which it appears in the *instructor* relation.

In those cases where we want to force the elimination of duplicates, we insert the keyword **distinct** after **select**. We can rewrite the preceding query as:

> **select distinct** *dept_name*
> **from** *instructor*;

dept_name
Comp. Sci.
Finance
Music
Physics
History
Physics
Comp. Sci.
History
Finance
Biology
Comp. Sci.
Elec. Eng.

Figure 3.3 Result of "**select** *dept_name* **from** *instructor*".

if we want duplicates removed. The result of the above query would contain each department name at most once.

SQL allows us to use the keyword **all** to specify explicitly that duplicates are not removed:

> **select all** *dept_name*
> **from** *instructor*;

Since duplicate retention is the default, we shall not use **all** in our examples. To ensure the elimination of duplicates in the results of our example queries, we shall use **distinct** whenever it is necessary.

The **select** clause may also contain arithmetic expressions involving the operators $+$, $-$, $*$, and $/$ operating on constants or attributes of tuples. For example, the query:

> **select** *ID, name, dept_name, salary* * 1.1
> **from** *instructor*;

returns a relation that is the same as the *instructor* relation, except that the attribute *salary* is multiplied by 1.1. This shows what would result if we gave a 10% raise to each instructor; note, however, that it does not result in any change to the *instructor* relation.

SQL also provides special data types, such as various forms of the *date* type, and allows several arithmetic functions to operate on these types. We discuss this further in Section 4.5.1.

The **where** clause allows us to select only those rows in the result relation of the **from** clause that satisfy a specified predicate. Consider the query "Find the names of all instructors in the Computer Science department who have salary greater than $70,000." This query can be written in SQL as:

Figure 3.4   Result of "Find the names of all instructors in the Computer Science department who have salary greater than $70,000."

> **select** *name*
> **from** *instructor*
> **where** *dept_name* = 'Comp. Sci.' **and** *salary* > 70000;

If the *instructor* relation is as shown in Figure 2.1, then the relation that results from the preceding query is shown in Figure 3.4.

SQL allows the use of the logical connectives **and**, **or**, and **not** in the **where** clause. The operands of the logical connectives can be expressions involving the comparison operators <, <=, >, >=, =, and <>. SQL allows us to use the comparison operators to compare strings and arithmetic expressions, as well as special types, such as date types.

We shall explore other features of **where** clause predicates later in this chapter.

3.3.2   Queries on Multiple Relations

So far our example queries were on a single relation. Queries often need to access information from multiple relations. We now study how to write such queries.

An an example, suppose we want to answer the query "Retrieve the names of all instructors, along with their department names and department building name."

Looking at the schema of the relation *instructor*, we realize that we can get the department name from the attribute *dept_name*, but the department building name is present in the attribute *building* of the relation *department*. To answer the query, each tuple in the *instructor* relation must be matched with the tuple in the *department* relation whose *dept_name* value matches the *dept_name* value of the *instructor* tuple.

In SQL, to answer the above query, we list the relations that need to be accessed in the **from** clause, and specify the matching condition in the **where** clause. The above query can be written in SQL as

> **select** *name, instructor.dept_name, building*
> **from** *instructor, department*
> **where** *instructor.dept_name= department.dept_name;*

If the *instructor* and *department* relations are as shown in Figures 2.1 and 2.5 respectively, then the result of this query is shown in Figure 3.5.

Note that the attribute *dept_name* occurs in both the relations *instructor* and *department*, and the relation name is used as a prefix (in *instructor.dept_name*, and

name	dept_name	building
Srinivasan	Comp. Sci.	Taylor
Wu	Finance	Painter
Mozart	Music	Packard
Einstein	Physics	Watson
El Said	History	Painter
Gold	Physics	Watson
Katz	Comp. Sci.	Taylor
Califieri	History	Painter
Singh	Finance	Painter
Crick	Biology	Watson
Brandt	Comp. Sci.	Taylor
Kim	Elec. Eng.	Taylor

Figure 3.5 The result of "Retrieve the names of all instructors, along with their department names and department building name."

department.dept_name) to make clear to which attribute we are referring. In contrast, the attributes *name* and *building* appear in only one of the relations, and therefore do not need to be prefixed by the relation name.

This naming convention *requires* that the relations that are present in the **from** clause have distinct names. This requirement causes problems in some cases, such as when information from two different tuples in the same relation needs to be combined. In Section 3.4.1, we see how to avoid these problems by using the rename operation.

We now consider the general case of SQL queries involving multiple relations. As we have seen earlier, an SQL query can contain three types of clauses, the **select** clause, the **from** clause, and the **where** clause. The role of each clause is as follows:

- The **select** clause is used to list the attributes desired in the result of a query.

- The **from** clause is a list of the relations to be accessed in the evaluation of the query.

- The **where** clause is a predicate involving attributes of the relation in the **from** clause.

A typical SQL query has the form

$$\textbf{select } A_1, \ A_2, \ldots, A_n$$
$$\textbf{from } r_1, \ r_2, \ldots, r_m$$
$$\textbf{where } P;$$

Each A_i represents an attribute, and each r_i a relation. P is a predicate. If the **where** clause is omitted, the predicate P is **true**.

Although the clauses must be written in the order **select**, **from**, **where**, the easiest way to understand the operations specified by the query is to consider the clauses in operational order: first **from**, then **where**, and then **select**.[1]

The **from** clause by itself defines a Cartesian product of the relations listed in the clause. It is defined formally in terms of set theory, but is perhaps best understood as an iterative process that generates tuples for the result relation of the **from** clause.

> **for each** tuple t_1 **in** relation r_1
> > **for each** tuple t_2 **in** relation r_2
> > > $\ldots$
> > > **for each** tuple t_m **in** relation r_m
> > > > Concatenate t_1, t_2, $\ldots$, t_m into a single tuple t
> > > > Add t into the result relation

The result relation has all attributes from all the relations in the **from** clause. Since the same attribute name may appear in both r_i and r_j, as we saw earlier, we prefix the the name of the relation from which the attribute originally came, before the attribute name.

For example, the relation schema for the Cartesian product of relations *instructor* and *teaches* is:

> (*instructor.ID, instructor.name, instructor.dept_name, instructor.salary*
> *teaches.ID, teaches.course_id, teaches.sec_id, teaches.semester, teaches.year*)

With this schema, we can distinguish *instructor.ID* from *teaches.ID*. For those attributes that appear in only one of the two schemas, we shall usually drop the relation-name prefix. This simplification does not lead to any ambiguity. We can then write the relation schema as:

> (*instructor.ID, name, dept_name, salary*
> *teaches.ID, course_id, sec_id, semester, year*)

To illustrate, consider the *instructor* relation in Figure 2.1 and the *teaches* relation in Figure 2.7. Their Cartesian product is shown in Figure 3.6, which includes only a portion of the tuples that make up the Cartesian product result.[2]

The Cartesian product by itself combines tuples from *instructor* and *teaches* that are unrelated to each other. Each tuple in *instructor* is combined with *every* tuple in *teaches*, even those that refer to a different instructor. The result can be an extremely large relation, and it rarely makes sense to create such a Cartesian product.

---

[1] In practice, SQL may convert the expression into an equivalent form that can be processed more efficiently. However, we shall defer concerns about efficiency to Chapters 12 and 13.
[2] Note that we renamed *instructor.ID* as *inst.ID* to reduce the width of the table in Figure 3.6.

inst.ID	name	dept_name	salary	teaches.ID	course_id	sec_id	semester	year
10101	Srinivasan	Physics	95000	10101	CS-101	1	Fall	2009
10101	Srinivasan	Physics	95000	10101	CS-315	1	Spring	2010
10101	Srinivasan	Physics	95000	10101	CS-347	1	Fall	2009
10101	Srinivasan	Physics	95000	10101	FIN-201	1	Spring	2010
10101	Srinivasan	Physics	95000	15151	MU-199	1	Spring	2010
10101	Srinivasan	Physics	95000	22222	PHY-101	1	Fall	2009
...	...	...	...	...	...	...	...	...
...	...	...	...	...	...	...	...	...
12121	Wu	Physics	95000	10101	CS-101	1	Fall	2009
12121	Wu	Physics	95000	10101	CS-315	1	Spring	2010
12121	Wu	Physics	95000	10101	CS-347	1	Fall	2009
12121	Wu	Physics	95000	10101	FIN-201	1	Spring	2010
12121	Wu	Physics	95000	15151	MU-199	1	Spring	2010
12121	Wu	Physics	95000	22222	PHY-101	1	Fall	2009
...	...	...	...	...	...	...	...	...
...	...	...	...	...	...	...	...	...
15151	Mozart	Physics	95000	10101	CS-101	1	Fall	2009
15151	Mozart	Physics	95000	10101	CS-315	1	Spring	2010
15151	Mozart	Physics	95000	10101	CS-347	1	Fall	2009
15151	Mozart	Physics	95000	10101	FIN-201	1	Spring	2010
15151	Mozart	Physics	95000	15151	MU-199	1	Spring	2010
15151	Mozart	Physics	95000	22222	PHY-101	1	Fall	2009
...	...	...	...	...	...	...	...	...
...	...	...	...	...	...	...	...	...
22222	Einstein	Physics	95000	10101	CS-101	1	Fall	2009
22222	Einstein	Physics	95000	10101	CS-315	1	Spring	2010
22222	Einstein	Physics	95000	10101	CS-347	1	Fall	2009
22222	Einstein	Physics	95000	10101	FIN-201	1	Spring	2010
22222	Einstein	Physics	95000	15151	MU-199	1	Spring	2010
22222	Einstein	Physics	95000	22222	PHY-101	1	Fall	2009
...	...	...	...	...	...	...	...	...
...	...	...	...	...	...	...	...	...

Figure 3.6 The Cartesian product of the *instructor* relation with the *teaches* relation.

Instead, the predicate in the **where** clause is used to restrict the combinations created by the Cartesian product to those that are meaningful for the desired answer. We would expect a query involving *instructor* and *teaches* to combine a particular tuple *t* in *instructor* with only those tuples in *teaches* that refer to the same instructor to which *t* refers. That is, we wish only to match *teaches* tuples with *instructor* tuples that have the same *ID* value. The following SQL query ensures this condition, and outputs the instructor name and course identifiers from such matching tuples.

select *name, course_id*
from *instructor, teaches*
where *instructor.ID= teaches.ID*;

Note that the above query outputs only instructors who have taught some course. Instructors who have not taught any course are not output; if we wish to output such tuples, we could use an operation called the *outer join*, which is described in Section 4.1.2.

If the *instructor* relation is as shown in Figure 2.1 and the *teaches* relation is as shown in Figure 2.7, then the relation that results from the preceding query is shown in Figure 3.7. Observe that instructors Gold, Califieri, and Singh, who have not taught any course, do not appear in the above result.

If we only wished to find instructor names and course identifiers for instructors in the Computer Science department, we could add an extra predicate to the **where** clause, as shown below.

select *name, course_id*
from *instructor, teaches*
where *instructor.ID= teaches.ID* **and** *instructor.dept_name* = 'Comp. Sci.';

Note that since the *dept_name* attribute occurs only in the *instructor* relation, we could have used just *dept_name*, instead of *instructor.dept_name* in the above query.

In general, the meaning of an SQL query can be understood as follows:

name	course_id
Srinivasan	CS-101
Srinivasan	CS-315
Srinivasan	CS-347
Wu	FIN-201
Mozart	MU-199
Einstein	PHY-101
El Said	HIS-351
Katz	CS-101
Katz	CS-319
Crick	BIO-101
Crick	BIO-301
Brandt	CS-190
Brandt	CS-190
Brandt	CS-319
Kim	EE-181

Figure 3.7   Result of "For all instructors in the university who have taught some course, find their names and the course ID of all courses they taught."

1. Generate a Cartesian product of the relations listed in the **from** clause

2. Apply the predicates specified in the **where** clause on the result of Step 1.

3. For each tuple in the result of Step 2, output the attributes (or results of expressions) specified in the **select** clause.

The above sequence of steps helps make clear what the result of an SQL query should be, *not* how it should be executed. A real implementation of SQL would not execute the query in this fashion; it would instead optimize evaluation by generating (as far as possible) only elements of the Cartesian product that satisfy the **where** clause predicates. We study such implementation techniques later, in Chapters 12 and 13.

When writing queries, you should be careful to include appropriate **where** clause conditions. If you omit the **where** clause condition in the preceding SQL query, it would output the Cartesian product, which could be a huge relation. For the example *instructor* relation in Figure 2.1 and the example *teaches* relation in Figure 2.7, their Cartesian product has $12 * 13 = 156$ tuples — more than we can show in the text! To make matters worse, suppose we have a more realistic number of instructors than we show in our sample relations in the figures, say 200 instructors. Let's assume each instructor teaches 3 courses, so we have 600 tuples in the *teaches* relation. Then the above iterative process generates $200 * 600 = 120,000$ tuples in the result.

3.3.3 The Natural Join

In our example query that combined information from the *instructor* and *teaches* table, the matching condition required *instructor.ID* to be equal to *teaches.ID*. These are the only attributes in the two relations that have the same name. In fact this is a common case; that is, the matching condition in the **from** clause most often requires all attributes with matching names to be equated.

To make the life of an SQL programmer easier for this common case, SQL supports an operation called the *natural join*, which we describe below. In fact SQL supports several other ways in which information from two or more relations can be **joined** together. We have already seen how a Cartesian product along with a **where** clause predicate can be used to join information from multiple relations. Other ways of joining information from multiple relations are discussed in Section 4.1.

The **natural join** operation operates on two relations and produces a relation as the result. Unlike the Cartesian product of two relations, which concatenates each tuple of the first relation with every tuple of the second, natural join considers only those pairs of tuples with the same value on those attributes that appear in the schemas of both relations. So, going back to the example of the relations *instructor* and *teaches*, computing *instructor* **natural join** *teaches* considers only those pairs of tuples where both the tuple from *instructor* and the tuple from *teaches* have the same value on the common attribute, *ID*.

ID	name	dept_name	salary	course_id	sec_id	semester	year
10101	Srinivasan	Comp. Sci.	65000	CS-101	1	Fall	2009
10101	Srinivasan	Comp. Sci.	65000	CS-315	1	Spring	2010
10101	Srinivasan	Comp. Sci.	65000	CS-347	1	Fall	2009
12121	Wu	Finance	90000	FIN-201	1	Spring	2010
15151	Mozart	Music	40000	MU-199	1	Spring	2010
22222	Einstein	Physics	95000	PHY-101	1	Fall	2009
32343	El Said	History	60000	HIS-351	1	Spring	2010
45565	Katz	Comp. Sci.	75000	CS-101	1	Spring	2010
45565	Katz	Comp. Sci.	75000	CS-319	1	Spring	2010
76766	Crick	Biology	72000	BIO-101	1	Summer	2009
76766	Crick	Biology	72000	BIO-301	1	Summer	2010
83821	Brandt	Comp. Sci.	92000	CS-190	1	Spring	2009
83821	Brandt	Comp. Sci.	92000	CS-190	2	Spring	2009
83821	Brandt	Comp. Sci.	92000	CS-319	2	Spring	2010
98345	Kim	Elec. Eng.	80000	EE-181	1	Spring	2009

Figure 3.8   The natural join of the *instructor* relation with the *teaches* relation.

The result relation, shown in Figure 3.8, has only 13 tuples, the ones that give information about an instructor and a course that that instructor actually teaches. Notice that we do not repeat those attributes that appear in the schemas of both relations; rather they appear only once. Notice also the order in which the attributes are listed: first the attributes common to the schemas of both relations, second those attributes unique to the schema of the first relation, and finally, those attributes unique to the schema of the second relation.

Consider the query "For all instructors in the university who have taught some course, find their names and the course ID of all courses they taught", which we wrote earlier as:

> **select** *name, course_id*
> **from** *instructor, teaches*
> **where** *instructor.ID= teaches.ID;*

This query can be written more concisely using the natural-join operation in SQL as:

> **select** *name, course_id*
> **from** *instructor* **natural join** *teaches;*

Both of the above queries generate the same result.

As we saw earlier, the result of the natural join operation is a relation. Conceptually, expression "*instructor* **natural join** *teaches*" in the **from** clause is replaced by the relation obtained by evaluating the natural join.[3] The **where** and **select** clauses are then evaluated on this relation, as we saw earlier in Section 3.3.2.

A **from** clause in an SQL query can have multiple relations combined using natural join, as shown here:

> **select** $A_1, A_2, \ldots, A_n$
> **from** r_1 **natural join** r_2 **natural join** ... **natural join** r_m
> **where** P;

More generally, a **from** clause can be of the form

$$\textbf{from } E_1, E_2, \ldots, E_n$$

where each E_i can be a single relation or an expression involving natural joins. For example, suppose we wish to answer the query "List the names of instructors along with the the titles of courses that they teach." The query can be written in SQL as follows:

> **select** *name, title*
> **from** *instructor* **natural join** *teaches, course*
> **where** *teaches.course_id= course.course_id*;

The natural join of *instructor* and *teaches* is first computed, as we saw earlier, and a Cartesian product of this result with *course* is computed, from which the **where** clause extracts only those tuples where the course identifier from the join result matches the course identifier from the *course* relation. Note that *teaches.course_id* in the **where** clause refers to the *course_id* field of the natural join result, since this field in turn came from the *teaches* relation.

In contrast the following SQL query does *not* compute the same result:

> **select** *name, title*
> **from** *instructor* **natural join** *teaches* **natural join** *course*;

To see why, note that the natural join of *instructor* and *teaches* contains the attributes (*ID, name, dept_name, salary, course_id, sec_id*), while the *course* relation contains the attributes (*course_id, title, dept_name, credits*). As a result, the natural join of these two would require that the *dept_name* attribute values from the two inputs be the same, in addition to requiring that the *course_id* values be the same. This query would then omit all (instructor name, course title) pairs where the instructor teaches a course in a department other than the instructor's own department. The previous query, on the other hand, correctly outputs such pairs.

---

[3] As a consequence, it is not possible to use attribute names containing the original relation names, for instance *instructor.name* or *teaches.course_id*, to refer to attributes in the natural join result; we can, however, use attribute names such as *name* and *course_id*, without the relation names.

To provide the benefit of natural join while avoiding the danger of equating attributes erroneously, SQL provides a form of the natural join construct that allows you to specify exactly which columns should be equated. This feature is illustrated by the following query:

> **select** *name, title*
> **from** (*instructor* **natural join** *teaches*) **join** *course* **using** (*course_id*);

The operation **join** . . . **using** requires a list of attribute names to be specified. Both inputs must have attributes with the specified names. Consider the operation r_1 **join** r_2 **using**(A_1, A_2). The operation is similar to r_1 **natural join** r_2, except that a pair of tuples t_1 from r_1 and t_2 from r_2 match if $t_1.A_1 = t_2.A_1$ and $t_1.A_2 = t_2.A_2$; even if r_1 and r_2 both have an attribute named A_3, it is *not* required that $t_1.A_3 = t_2.A_3$.

Thus, in the preceding SQL query, the **join** construct permits *teaches.dept_name* and *course.dept_name* to differ, and the SQL query gives the correct answer.

3.4   Additional Basic Operations

There are number of additional basic operations that are supported in SQL.

3.4.1   The Rename Operation

Consider again the query that we used earlier:

> **select** *name, course_id*
> **from** *instructor, teaches*
> **where** *instructor.ID= teaches.ID*;

The result of this query is a relation with the following attributes:

> *name, course_id*

The names of the attributes in the result are derived from the names of the attributes in the relations in the **from** clause.

We cannot, however, always derive names in this way, for several reasons: First, two relations in the **from** clause may have attributes with the same name, in which case an attribute name is duplicated in the result. Second, if we used an arithmetic expression in the **select** clause, the resultant attribute does not have a name. Third, even if an attribute name can be derived from the base relations as in the preceding example, we may want to change the attribute name in the result. Hence, SQL provides a way of renaming the attributes of a result relation. It uses the **as** clause, taking the form:

> *old-name* **as** *new-name*

The **as** clause can appear in both the **select** and **from** clauses.[4]

For example, if we want the attribute name *name* to be replaced with the name *instructor_name*, we can rewrite the preceding query as:

> **select** *name* **as** *instructor_name*, *course_id*
> **from** *instructor*, *teaches*
> **where** *instructor.ID= teaches.ID*;

The **as** clause is particularly useful in renaming relations. One reason to rename a relation is to replace a long relation name with a shortened version that is more convenient to use elsewhere in the query. To illustrate, we rewrite the query "For all instructors in the university who have taught some course, find their names and the course ID of all courses they taught."

> **select** *T.name*, *S.course_id*
> **from** *instructor* **as** *T*, *teaches* **as** *S*
> **where** *T.ID= S.ID*;

Another reason to rename a relation is a case where we wish to compare tuples in the same relation. We then need to take the Cartesian product of a relation with itself and, without renaming, it becomes impossible to distinguish one tuple from the other. Suppose that we want to write the query "Find the names of all instructors whose salary is greater than at least one instructor in the Biology department." We can write the SQL expression:

> **select distinct** *T.name*
> **from** *instructor* **as** *T*, *instructor* **as** *S*
> **where** *T.salary > S.salary* **and** *S.dept_name =* 'Biology';

Observe that we could not use the notation *instructor.salary*, since it would not be clear which reference to *instructor* is intended.

In the above query, *T* and *S* can be thought of as copies of the relation *instructor*, but more precisely, they are declared as aliases, that is as alternative names, for the relation *instructor*. An identifier, such as *T* and *S*, that is used to rename a relation is referred to as a **correlation name** in the SQL standard, but is also commonly referred to as a **table alias**, or a **correlation variable**, or a **tuple variable**.

Note that a better way to phrase the previous query in English would be "Find the names of all instructors who earn more than the lowest paid instructor in the Biology department." Our original wording fits more closely with the SQL that we wrote, but the latter wording is more intuitive, and can in fact be expressed directly in SQL as we shall see in Section 3.8.2.

---

[4]Early versions of SQL did not include the keyword **as**. As a result, some implementations of SQL, notably Oracle, do not permit the keyword **as** in the from clause. In Oracle, "*old-name* **as** *new-name*" is written instead as "*old-name new-name*" in the **from** clause. The keyword **as** is permitted for renaming attributes in the **select** clause, but it is optional and may be omitted in Oracle.

3.4.2 String Operations

SQL specifies strings by enclosing them in single quotes, for example, 'Computer'. A single quote character that is part of a string can be specified by using two single quote characters; for example, the string "It's right" can be specified by "It''s right".

The SQL standard specifies that the equality operation on strings is case sensitive; as a result the expression "'comp. sci.' = 'Comp. Sci.'" evaluates to false. However, some database systems, such as MySQL and SQL Server, do not distinguish uppercase from lowercase when matching strings; as a result "'comp. sci.' = 'Comp. Sci.'" would evaluate to true on these databases. This default behavior can, however, be changed, either at the database level or at the level of specific attributes.

SQL also permits a variety of functions on character strings, such as concatenating (using "||"), extracting substrings, finding the length of strings, converting strings to uppercase (using the function **upper**(*s*) where *s* is a string) and lowercase (using the function **lower**(*s*)), removing spaces at the end of the string (using **trim**(*s*)) and so on. There are variations on the exact set of string functions supported by different database systems. See your database system's manual for more details on exactly what string functions it supports.

Pattern matching can be performed on strings, using the operator **like**. We describe patterns by using two special characters:

- Percent (%): The % character matches any substring.

- Underscore (_): The _ character matches any character.

Patterns are case sensitive; that is, uppercase characters do not match lowercase characters, or vice versa. To illustrate pattern matching, we consider the following examples:

- 'Intro%' matches any string beginning with "Intro".

- '%Comp%' matches any string containing "Comp" as a substring, for example, 'Intro. to Computer Science', and 'Computational Biology'.

- '_ _ _' matches any string of exactly three characters.

- '_ _ _%' matches any string of at least three characters.

SQL expresses patterns by using the **like** comparison operator. Consider the query "Find the names of all departments whose building name includes the substring 'Watson'." This query can be written as:

> **select** *dept_name*
> **from** *department*
> **where** *building* **like** '%Watson%';

For patterns to include the special pattern characters (that is, % and _), SQL allows the specification of an escape character. The escape character is used immediately before a special pattern character to indicate that the special pattern character is to be treated like a normal character. We define the escape character for a **like** comparison using the **escape** keyword. To illustrate, consider the following patterns, which use a backslash (\) as the escape character:

- **like** 'ab\%cd%' **escape** '\' matches all strings beginning with "ab%cd".
- **like** 'ab\\cd%' **escape** '\' matches all strings beginning with "ab\cd".

SQL allows us to search for mismatches instead of matches by using the **not like** comparison operator. Some databases provide variants of the **like** operation which do not distinguish lower and upper case.

SQL:1999 also offers a **similar to** operation, which provides more powerful pattern matching than the **like** operation; the syntax for specifying patterns is similar to that used in Unix regular expressions.

3.4.3 Attribute Specification in Select Clause

The asterisk symbol " * " can be used in the **select** clause to denote "all attributes." Thus, the use of *instructor.* * in the **select** clause of the query:

$$
\begin{aligned}
&\textbf{select } \textit{instructor.*} \\
&\textbf{from } \textit{instructor, teaches} \\
&\textbf{where } \textit{instructor.ID= teaches.ID};
\end{aligned}
$$

indicates that all attributes of *instructor* are to be selected. A **select** clause of the form **select** * indicates that all attributes of the result relation of the **from** clause are selected.

3.4.4 Ordering the Display of Tuples

SQL offers the user some control over the order in which tuples in a relation are displayed. The **order by** clause causes the tuples in the result of a query to appear in sorted order. To list in alphabetic order all instructors in the Physics department, we write:

$$
\begin{aligned}
&\textbf{select } \textit{name} \\
&\textbf{from } \textit{instructor} \\
&\textbf{where } \textit{dept\_name} = \text{'Physics'} \\
&\textbf{order by } \textit{name};
\end{aligned}
$$

By default, the **order by** clause lists items in ascending order. To specify the sort order, we may specify **desc** for descending order or **asc** for ascending order. Furthermore, ordering can be performed on multiple attributes. Suppose that we wish to list the entire *instructor* relation in descending order of *salary*. If several instructors have the same salary, we order them in ascending order by name. We express this query in SQL as follows:

> **select** *
> **from** *instructor*
> **order by** *salary* **desc**, *name* **asc**;

3.4.5   Where Clause Predicates

SQL includes a **between** comparison operator to simplify **where** clauses that specify that a value be less than or equal to some value and greater than or equal to some other value. If we wish to find the names of instructors with salary amounts between $90,000 and $100,000, we can use the **between** comparison to write:

> **select** *name*
> **from** *instructor*
> **where** *salary* **between** 90000 **and** 100000;

instead of:

> **select** *name*
> **from** *instructor*
> **where** *salary* $<=$ 100000 **and** *salary* $>=$ 90000;

Similarly, we can use the **not between** comparison operator.

We can extend the preceding query that finds instructor names along with course identifiers, which we saw earlier, and consider a more complicated case in which we require also that the instructors be from the Biology department: "Find the instructor names and the courses they taught for all instructors in the Biology department who have taught some course." To write this query, we can modify either of the SQL queries we saw earlier, by adding an extra condition in the **where** clause. We show below the modified form of the SQL query that does not use natural join.

> **select** *name, course_id*
> **from** *instructor, teaches*
> **where** *instructor.ID*$=$ *teaches.ID* **and** *dept_name* $=$ 'Biology';

SQL permits us to use the notation $(v_1, v_2, \ldots, v_n)$ to denote a tuple of arity n containing values $v_1, v_2, \ldots, v_n$. The comparison operators can be used on tuples, and the ordering is defined lexicographically. For example, $(a_1, a_2) <= (b_1, b_2)$

course_id
CS-101
CS-347
PHY-101

Figure 3.9 The *c1* relation, listing courses taught in Fall 2009.

is true if $a_1 <= b_1$ **and** $a_2 <= b_2$; similarly, the two tuples are equal if all their attributes are equal. Thus, the preceding SQL query can be rewritten as follows:[5]

> **select** *name, course_id*
> **from** *instructor, teaches*
> **where** *(instructor.ID, dept_name) = (teaches.ID, 'Biology');*

3.5 Set Operations

The SQL operations **union**, **intersect**, and **except** operate on relations and correspond to the mathematical set-theory operations ∪, ∩, and −. We shall now construct queries involving the **union**, **intersect**, and **except** operations over two sets.

- The set of all courses taught in the Fall 2009 semester:

> **select** *course_id*
> **from** *section*
> **where** *semester =* 'Fall' **and** *year=* 2009;

- The set of all courses taught in the Spring 2010 semester:

> **select** *course_id*
> **from** *section*
> **where** *semester =* 'Spring' **and** *year=* 2010;

In our discussion that follows, we shall refer to the relations obtained as the result of the preceding queries as *c1* and *c2*, respectively, and show the results when these queries are run on the *section* relation of Figure 2.6 in Figures 3.9 and 3.10. Observe that *c2* contains two tuples corresponding to *course_id* CS-319, since two sections of the course have been offered in Spring 2010.

---

[5]Although it is part of the SQL-92 standard, some SQL implementations may not support this syntax.

course_id
CS-101
CS-315
CS-319
CS-319
FIN-201
HIS-351
MU-199

Figure 3.10 The *c2* relation, listing courses taught in Spring 2010.

3.5.1 The Union Operation

To find the set of all courses taught either in Fall 2009 or in Spring 2010, or both, we write:[6]

> (**select** *course_id*
> **from** *section*
> **where** *semester* = 'Fall' **and** *year*= 2009)
> **union**
> (**select** *course_id*
> **from** *section*
> **where** *semester* = 'Spring' **and** *year*= 2010);

The **union** operation automatically eliminates duplicates, unlike the **select** clause. Thus, using the *section* relation of Figure 2.6, where two sections of CS-319 are offered in Spring 2010, and a section of CS-101 is offered in the Fall 2009 as well as in the Fall 2010 semester, CS-101 and CS-319 appear only once in the result, shown in Figure 3.11.

If we want to retain all duplicates, we must write **union all** in place of **union**:

> (**select** *course_id*
> **from** *section*
> **where** *semester* = 'Fall' **and** *year*= 2009)
> **union all**
> (**select** *course_id*
> **from** *section*
> **where** *semester* = 'Spring' **and** *year*= 2010);

The number of duplicate tuples in the result is equal to the total number of duplicates that appear in both *c1* and *c2*. So, in the above query, each of CS-319 and CS-101 would be listed twice. As a further example, if it were the case that 4 sections of ECE-101 were taught in the Fall 2009 semester and 2 sections of ECE-101

---

[6]The parentheses we include around each **select-from-where** statement are optional, but useful for ease of reading.

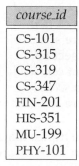

Figure 3.11 The result relation for *c1* union *c2*.

were taught in the Fall 2010 semester, then there would be 6 tuples with ECE-101 in the result.

3.5.2 The Intersect Operation

To find the set of all courses taught in the Fall 2009 as well as in Spring 2010 we write:

> (**select** *course_id*
> **from** *section*
> **where** *semester* = 'Fall' **and** *year*= 2009)
> **intersect**
> (**select** *course_id*
> **from** *section*
> **where** *semester* = 'Spring' **and** *year*= 2010);

The result relation, shown in Figure 3.12, contains only one tuple with CS-101. The **intersect** operation automatically eliminates duplicates. For example, if it were the case that 4 sections of ECE-101 were taught in the Fall 2009 semester and 2 sections of ECE-101 were taught in the Spring 2010 semester, then there would be only 1 tuple with ECE-101 in the result.

If we want to retain all duplicates, we must write **intersect all** in place of **intersect**:

Figure 3.12 The result relation for *c1* intersect *c2*.

> (**select** *course_id*
> **from** *section*
> **where** *semester* = 'Fall' **and** *year*= 2009)
> **intersect all**
> (**select** *course_id*
> **from** *section*
> **where** *semester* = 'Spring' **and** *year*= 2010);

The number of duplicate tuples that appear in the result is equal to the minimum number of duplicates in both *c1* and *c2*. For example, if 4 sections of ECE-101 were taught in the Fall 2009 semester and 2 sections of ECE-101 were taught in the Spring 2010 semester, then there would be 2 tuples with ECE-101 in the result.

3.5.3 The Except Operation

To find all courses taught in the Fall 2009 semester but not in the Spring 2010 semester, we write:

> (**select** *course_id*
> **from** *section*
> **where** *semester* = 'Fall' **and** *year*= 2009)
> **except**
> (**select** *course_id*
> **from** *section*
> **where** *semester* = 'Spring' **and** *year*= 2010);

The result of this query is shown in Figure 3.13. Note that this is exactly relation *c1* of Figure 3.9 except that the tuple for CS-101 does not appear. The **except** operation[7] outputs all tuples from its first input that do not occur in the second input; that is, it performs set difference. The operation automatically eliminates duplicates in the inputs before performing set difference. For example, if 4 sections of ECE-101 were taught in the Fall 2009 semester and 2 sections of ECE-101 were taught in the Spring 2010 semester, the result of the **except** operation would not have any copy of ECE-101.

If we want to retain duplicates, we must write **except all** in place of **except**:

> (**select** *course_id*
> **from** *section*
> **where** *semester* = 'Fall' **and** *year*= 2009)
> **except all**
> (**select** *course_id*
> **from** *section*
> **where** *semester* = 'Spring' **and** *year*= 2010);

---

[7]Some SQL implementations, notably Oracle, use the keyword **minus** in place of **except**.

$$\begin{array}{|c|}
\hline
\textit{course\_id} \\
\hline
\text{CS-347} \\
\text{PHY-101} \\
\hline
\end{array}$$

Figure 3.13 The result relation for *c1* except *c2*.

The number of duplicate copies of a tuple in the result is equal to the number of duplicate copies in *c1* minus the number of duplicate copies in *c2*, provided that the difference is positive. Thus, if 4 sections of ECE-101 were taught in the Fall 2009 semester and 2 sections of ECE-101 were taught in Spring 2010, then there are 2 tuples with ECE-101 in the result. If, however, there were two or fewer sections of ECE-101 in the the Fall 2009 semester, and two sections of ECE-101 in the Spring 2010 semester, there is no tuple with ECE-101 in the result.

3.6   Null Values

Null values present special problems in relational operations, including arithmetic operations, comparison operations, and set operations.

The result of an arithmetic expression (involving, for example $+$, $-$, $*$, or $/$) is null if any of the input values is null. For example, if a query has an expression $r.A + 5$, and $r.A$ is null for a particular tuple, then the expression result must also be null for that tuple.

Comparisons involving nulls are more of a problem. For example, consider the comparison "1 < **null**". It would be wrong to say this is true since we do not know what the null value represents. But it would likewise be wrong to claim this expression is false; if we did, "**not** (1 < **null**)" would evaluate to true, which does not make sense. SQL therefore treats as **unknown** the result of any comparison involving a *null* value (other than predicates **is null** and **is not null**, which are described later in this section). This creates a third logical value in addition to *true* and *false*.

Since the predicate in a **where** clause can involve Boolean operations such as **and**, **or**, and **not** on the results of comparisons, the definitions of the Boolean operations are extended to deal with the value **unknown**.

- **and**: The result of *true* **and** *unknown* is *unknown*, *false* **and** *unknown* is *false*, while *unknown* **and** *unknown* is *unknown*.

- **or**: The result of *true* **or** *unknown* is *true*, *false* **or** *unknown* is *unknown*, while *unknown* **or** *unknown* is *unknown*.

- **not**: The result of **not** *unknown* is *unknown*.

You can verify that if $r.A$ is null, then "1 < $r.A$" as well as "**not** (1 < $r.A$)" evaluate to unknown.

If the **where** clause predicate evaluates to either **false** or **unknown** for a tuple, that tuple is not added to the result.

SQL uses the special keyword **null** in a predicate to test for a null value. Thus, to find all instructors who appear in the *instructor* relation with null values for *salary*, we write:

$$
\begin{aligned}
&\textbf{select } name \\
&\textbf{from } instructor \\
&\textbf{where } salary \textbf{ is null};
\end{aligned}
$$

The predicate **is not null** succeeds if the value on which it is applied is not null.

Some implementations of SQL also allow us to test whether the result of a comparison is unknown, rather than true or false, by using the clauses **is unknown** and **is not unknown**.

When a query uses the **select distinct** clause, duplicate tuples must be eliminated. For this purpose, when comparing values of corresponding attributes from two tuples, the values are treated as identical if either both are non-null and equal in value, or both are null. Thus two copies of a tuple, such as {('A',null), ('A',null)}, are treated as being identical, even if some of the attributes have a null value. Using the **distinct** clause then retains only one copy of such identical tuples. Note that the treatment of null above is different from the way nulls are treated in predicates, where a comparison "null=null" would return unknown, rather than true.

The above approach of treating tuples as identical if they have the same values for all attributes, even if some of the values are null, is also used for the set operations union, intersection and except.

3.7   Aggregate Functions

Aggregate functions are functions that take a collection (a set or multiset) of values as input and return a single value. SQL offers five built-in aggregate functions:

- Average: **avg**
- Minimum: **min**
- Maximum: **max**
- Total: **sum**
- Count: **count**

The input to **sum** and **avg** must be a collection of numbers, but the other operators can operate on collections of nonnumeric data types, such as strings, as well.

3.7.1 Basic Aggregation

Consider the query "Find the average salary of instructors in the Computer Science department." We write this query as follows:

> **select avg** (*salary*)
> **from** *instructor*
> **where** *dept_name*= 'Comp. Sci.';

The result of this query is a relation with a single attribute, containing a single tuple with a numerical value corresponding to the average salary of instructors in the Computer Science department. The database system may give an arbitrary name to the result relation attribute that is generated by aggregation; however, we can give a meaningful name to the attribute by using the **as** clause as follows:

> **select avg** (*salary*) **as** *avg_salary*
> **from** *instructor*
> **where** *dept_name*= 'Comp. Sci.';

In the *instructor* relation of Figure 2.1, the salaries in the Computer Science department are $75,000, $65,000, and $92,000. The average balance is $232,000/3 = $77,333.33.

Retaining duplicates is important in computing an average. Suppose the Computer Science department adds a fourth instructor whose salary happens to be $75,000. If duplicates were eliminated, we would obtain the wrong answer ($232,000/4 = $58.000) rather than the correct answer of $76,750.

There are cases where we must eliminate duplicates before computing an aggregate function. If we do want to eliminate duplicates, we use the keyword **distinct** in the aggregate expression. An example arises in the query "Find the total number of instructors who teach a course in the Spring 2010 semester." In this case, an instructor counts only once, regardless of the number of course sections that the instructor teaches. The required information is contained in the relation *teaches*, and we write this query as follows:

> **select count** (**distinct** *ID*)
> **from** *teaches*
> **where** *semester* = 'Spring' **and** *year* = 2010;

Because of the keyword **distinct** preceding *ID*, even if an instructor teaches more than one course, she is counted only once in the result.

We use the aggregate function **count** frequently to count the number of tuples in a relation. The notation for this function in SQL is **count** (*). Thus, to find the number of tuples in the *course* relation, we write

> **select count** (*)
> **from** *course*;

ID	name	dept_name	salary
76766	Crick	Biology	72000
45565	Katz	Comp. Sci.	75000
10101	Srinivasan	Comp. Sci.	65000
83821	Brandt	Comp. Sci.	92000
98345	Kim	Elec. Eng.	80000
12121	Wu	Finance	90000
76543	Singh	Finance	80000
32343	El Said	History	60000
58583	Califieri	History	62000
15151	Mozart	Music	40000
33456	Gold	Physics	87000
22222	Einstein	Physics	95000

Figure 3.14 Tuples of the *instructor* relation, grouped by the *dept_name* attribute.

SQL does not allow the use of **distinct** with **count** (*). It is legal to use **distinct** with **max** and **min**, even though the result does not change. We can use the keyword **all** in place of **distinct** to specify duplicate retention, but, since **all** is the default, there is no need to do so.

3.7.2 Aggregation with Grouping

There are circumstances where we would like to apply the aggregate function not only to a single set of tuples, but also to a group of sets of tuples; we specify this wish in SQL using the **group by** clause. The attribute or attributes given in the **group by** clause are used to form groups. Tuples with the same value on all attributes in the **group by** clause are placed in one group.

As an illustration, consider the query "Find the average salary in each department." We write this query as follows:

> **select** *dept_name*, **avg** (*salary*) **as** *avg_salary*
> **from** *instructor*
> **group by** *dept_name*;

Figure 3.14 shows the tuples in the *instructor* relation grouped by the *dept _name* attribute, which is the first step in computing the query result. The specified aggregate is computed for each group, and the result of the query is shown in Figure 3.15.

In contrast, consider the query "Find the average salary of all instructors." We write this query as follows:

> **select avg** (*salary*)
> **from** *instructor*;

dept_name	avg_salary
Biology	72000
Comp. Sci.	77333
Elec. Eng.	80000
Finance	85000
History	61000
Music	40000
Physics	91000

Figure 3.15 The result relation for the query "Find the average salary in each department".

In this case the **group by** clause has been omitted, so the entire relation is treated as a single group.

As another example of aggregation on groups of tuples, consider the query "Find the number of instructors in each department who teach a course in the Spring 2010 semester." Information about which instructors teach which course sections in which semester is available in the *teaches* relation. However, this information has to be joined with information from the *instructor* relation to get the department name of each instructor. Thus, we write this query as follows:

select *dept_name*, **count** (**distinct** *ID*) **as** *instr_count*
from *instructor* **natural join** *teaches*
where *semester* = 'Spring' **and** *year* = 2010
group by *dept_name*;

The result is shown in Figure 3.16.

When an SQL query uses grouping, it is important to ensure that the only attributes that appear in the **select** statement without being aggregated are those that are present in the **group by** clause. In other words, any attribute that is not present in the **group by** clause must appear only inside an aggregate function if it appears in the **select** clause, otherwise the query is treated as erroneous. For example, the following query is erroneous since *ID* does not appear in the **group by** clause, and yet it appears in the **select** clause without being aggregated:

dept_name	instr_count
Comp. Sci.	3
Finance	1
History	1
Music	1

Figure 3.16 The result relation for the query "Find the number of instructors in each department who teach a course in the Spring 2010 semester."

```
/* erroneous query */
select dept_name, ID, avg (salary)
from instructor
group by dept_name;
```

Each instructor in a particular group (defined by *dept_name*) can have a different *ID*, and since only one tuple is output for each group, there is no unique way of choosing which *ID* value to output. As a result, such cases are disallowed by SQL.

3.7.3 The Having Clause

At times, it is useful to state a condition that applies to groups rather than to tuples. For example, we might be interested in only those departments where the average salary of the instructors is more than $42,000. This condition does not apply to a single tuple; rather, it applies to each group constructed by the **group by** clause. To express such a query, we use the **having** clause of SQL. SQL applies predicates in the **having** clause after groups have been formed, so aggregate functions may be used. We express this query in SQL as follows:

```
select dept_name, avg (salary) as avg_salary
from instructor
group by dept_name
having avg (salary) > 42000;
```

The result is shown in Figure 3.17.

As was the case for the **select** clause, any attribute that is present in the **having** clause without being aggregated must appear in the **group by** clause, otherwise the query is treated as erroneous.

The meaning of a query containing aggregation, **group by**, or **having** clauses is defined by the following sequence of operations:

1. As was the case for queries without aggregation, the **from** clause is first evaluated to get a relation.

dept_name	avg(avg_salary)
Physics	91000
Elec. Eng.	80000
Finance	85000
Comp. Sci.	77333
Biology	72000
History	61000

Figure 3.17 The result relation for the query "Find the average salary of instructors in those departments where the average salary is more than $42,000."

2. If a **where** clause is present, the predicate in the **where** clause is applied on the result relation of the **from** clause.

3. Tuples satisfying the **where** predicate are then placed into groups by the **group by** clause if it is present. If the **group by** clause is absent, the entire set of tuples satisfying the **where** predicate is treated as being in one group.

4. The **having** clause, if it is present, is applied to each group; the groups that do not satisfy the **having** clause predicate are removed.

5. The **select** clause uses the remaining groups to generate tuples of the result of the query, applying the aggregate functions to get a single result tuple for each group.

To illustrate the use of both a **having** clause and a **where** clause in the same query, we consider the query "For each course section offered in 2009, find the average total credits (*tot_cred*) of all students enrolled in the section, if the section had at least 2 students."

> **select** *course_id, semester, year, sec_id,* **avg** (*tot_cred*)
> **from** *takes* **natural join** *student*
> **where** *year* = 2009
> **group by** *course_id, semester, year, sec_id*
> **having count** (*ID*) >= 2;

Note that all the required information for the preceding query is available from the relations *takes* and *student*, and that although the query pertains to sections, a join with *section* is not needed.

3.7.4   Aggregation with Null and Boolean Values

Null values, when they exist, complicate the processing of aggregate operators. For example, assume that some tuples in the *instructor* relation have a null value for *salary*. Consider the following query to total all salary amounts:

> **select sum** (*salary*)
> **from** *instructor*;

The values to be summed in the preceding query include null values, since some tuples have a null value for *salary*. Rather than say that the overall sum is itself *null*, the SQL standard says that the **sum** operator should ignore *null* values in its input.

In general, aggregate functions treat nulls according to the following rule: All aggregate functions except **count (*)** ignore null values in their input collection. As a result of null values being ignored, the collection of values may be empty. The **count** of an empty collection is defined to be 0, and all other aggregate operations return a value of null when applied on an empty collection. The effect of null values on some of the more complicated SQL constructs can be subtle.

A **Boolean** data type that can take values **true**, **false**, and **unknown**, was introduced in SQL:1999. The aggregate functions **some** and **every**, which mean exactly what you would intuitively expect, can be applied on a collection of Boolean values.

3.8   Nested Subqueries

SQL provides a mechanism for nesting subqueries. A subquery is a **select-from-where** expression that is nested within another query. A common use of subqueries is to perform tests for set membership, make set comparisons, and determine set cardinality, by nesting subqueries in the **where** clause. We study such uses of nested subqueries in the **where** clause in Sections 3.8.1 through 3.8.4. In Section 3.8.5, we study nesting of subqueries in the **from** clause. In Section 3.8.7, we see how a class of subqueries called scalar subqueries can appear wherever an expression returning a value can occur.

3.8.1   Set Membership

SQL allows testing tuples for membership in a relation. The **in** connective tests for set membership, where the set is a collection of values produced by a **select** clause. The **not in** connective tests for the absence of set membership.

As an illustration, reconsider the query "Find all the courses taught in the both the Fall 2009 and Spring 2010 semesters." Earlier, we wrote such a query by intersecting two sets: the set of courses taught in Fall 2009 and the set of courses taught in Spring 2010. We can take the alternative approach of finding all courses that were taught in Fall 2009 and that are also members of the set of courses taught in Spring 2010. Clearly, this formulation generates the same results as the previous one did, but it leads us to write our query using the **in** connective of SQL. We begin by finding all courses taught in Spring 2010, and we write the subquery

> (**select** *course_id*
> **from** *section*
> **where** *semester* = 'Spring' **and** *year* = 2010)

We then need to find those courses that were taught in the Fall 2009 and that appear in the set of courses obtained in the subquery. We do so by nesting the subquery in the **where** clause of an outer query. The resulting query is

> **select distinct** *course_id*
> **from** *section*
> **where** *semester* = 'Fall' **and** *year* = 2009 **and**
>   *course_id* **in** (**select** *course_id*
>   **from** *section*
>   **where** *semester* = 'Spring' **and** *year* = 2010);

This example shows that it is possible to write the same query several ways in SQL. This flexibility is beneficial, since it allows a user to think about the query in the way that seems most natural. We shall see that there is a substantial amount of redundancy in SQL.

We use the **not in** construct in a way similar to the **in** construct. For example, to find all the courses taught in the Fall 2009 semester but not in the Spring 2010 semester, we can write:

> **select distinct** *course_id*
> **from** *section*
> **where** *semester* = 'Fall' **and** *year*= 2009 **and**
> *course_id* **not in** (**select** *course_id*
> **from** *section*
> **where** *semester* = 'Spring' **and** *year*= 2010);

The **in** and **not in** operators can also be used on enumerated sets. The following query selects the names of instructors whose names are neither "Mozart" nor "Einstein".

> **select distinct** *name*
> **from** *instructor*
> **where** *name* **not in** ('Mozart', 'Einstein');

In the preceding examples, we tested membership in a one-attribute relation. It is also possible to test for membership in an arbitrary relation in SQL. For example, we can write the query "find the total number of (distinct) students who have taken course sections taught by the instructor with *ID* 110011" as follows:

> **select count** (**distinct** *ID*)
> **from** *takes*
> **where** (*course_id*, *sec_id*, *semester*, *year*) **in** (**select** *course_id*, *sec_id*, *semester*, *year*
> **from** *teaches*
> **where** *teaches.ID*= 10101);

3.8.2 Set Comparison

As an example of the ability of a nested subquery to compare sets, consider the query "Find the names of all instructors whose salary is greater than at least one instructor in the Biology department." In Section 3.4.1, we wrote this query as follows:

> **select distinct** *T.name*
> **from** *instructor* **as** *T*, *instructor* **as** *S*
> **where** *T.salary* > *S.salary* **and** *S.dept_name* = 'Biology';

SQL does, however, offer an alternative style for writing the preceding query. The phrase "greater than at least one" is represented in SQL by > **some**. This construct allows us to rewrite the query in a form that resembles closely our formulation of the query in English.

> **select** *name*
> **from** *instructor*
> **where** *salary* > **some** (**select** *salary*
> **from** *instructor*
> **where** *dept_name* = 'Biology');

The subquery:

> (**select** *salary*
> **from** *instructor*
> **where** *dept_name* = 'Biology')

generates the set of all salary values of all instructors in the Biology department. The > **some** comparison in the **where** clause of the outer **select** is true if the *salary* value of the tuple is greater than at least one member of the set of all salary values for instructors in Biology.

SQL also allows < **some**, <= **some**, >= **some**, = **some**, and <> **some** comparisons. As an exercise, verify that = **some** is identical to **in**, whereas <> **some** is *not* the same as **not in**.[8]

Now we modify our query slightly. Let us find the names of all instructors that have a salary value greater than that of each instructor in the Biology department. The construct > **all** corresponds to the phrase "greater than all." Using this construct, we write the query as follows:

> **select** *name*
> **from** *instructor*
> **where** *salary* > **all** (**select** *salary*
> **from** *instructor*
> **where** *dept_name* = 'Biology');

As it does for **some**, SQL also allows < **all**, <= **all**, >= **all**, = **all**, and <> **all** comparisons. As an exercise, verify that <> **all** is identical to **not in**, whereas = **all** is *not* the same as **in**.

As another example of set comparisons, consider the query "Find the departments that have the highest average salary." We begin by writing a query to find all average salaries, and then nest it as a subquery of a larger query that finds

---

[8]The keyword **any** is synonymous to **some** in SQL. Early versions of SQL allowed only **any**. Later versions added the alternative **some** to avoid the linguistic ambiguity of the word *any* in English.

those departments for which the average salary is greater than or equal to all average salaries:

> **select** *dept_name*
> **from** *instructor*
> **group by** *dept_name*
> **having avg** (*salary*) $>=$ **all** (**select avg** (*salary*)
> **from** *instructor*
> **group by** *dept_name*);

3.8.3 Test for Empty Relations

SQL includes a feature for testing whether a subquery has any tuples in its result. The **exists** construct returns the value **true** if the argument subquery is nonempty. Using the **exists** construct, we can write the query "Find all courses taught in both the Fall 2009 semester and in the Spring 2010 semester" in still another way:

> **select** *course_id*
> **from** *section* **as** *S*
> **where** *semester* $=$ 'Fall' **and** *year*$=$ 2009 **and**
>   **exists** (**select** *
>   **from** *section* **as** *T*
>   **where** *semester* $=$ 'Spring' **and** *year*$=$ 2010 **and**
>   *S.course_id*$=$ *T.course_id*);

The above query also illustrates a feature of SQL where a correlation name from an outer query (*S* in the above query), can be used in a subquery in the **where** clause. A subquery that uses a correlation name from an outer query is called a **correlated subquery**.

In queries that contain subqueries, a scoping rule applies for correlation names. In a subquery, according to the rule, it is legal to use only correlation names defined in the subquery itself or in any query that contains the subquery. If a correlation name is defined both locally in a subquery and globally in a containing query, the local definition applies. This rule is analogous to the usual scoping rules used for variables in programming languages.

We can test for the nonexistence of tuples in a subquery by using the **not exists** construct. We can use the **not exists** construct to simulate the set containment (that is, superset) operation: We can write "relation *A* contains relation *B*" as "**not exists** (*B* **except** *A*)." (Although it is not part of the current SQL standards, the **contains** operator was present in some early relational systems.) To illustrate the **not exists** operator, consider the query "Find all students who have taken all courses offered in the Biology department." Using the **except** construct, we can write the query as follows:

> **select distinct** *S.ID*, *S.name*
> **from** *student* **as** *S*
> **where not exists** ((**select** *course_id*
>   **from** *course*
>   **where** *dept_name* = 'Biology')
>   **except**
>   (**select** *T.course_id*
>   **from** *takes* **as** *T*
>   **where** *S.ID* = *T.ID*));

Here, the subquery:

> (**select** *course_id*
> **from** *course*
> **where** *dept_name* = 'Biology')

finds the set of all courses offered in the Biology department. The subquery:

> (**select** *T.course_id*
> **from** *takes* **as** *T*
> **where** *S.ID* = *T.ID*)

finds all the courses that student *S.ID* has taken. Thus, the outer **select** takes each student and tests whether the set of all courses that the student has taken contains the set of all courses offered in the Biology department.

3.8.4   Test for the Absence of Duplicate Tuples

SQL includes a boolean function for testing whether a subquery has duplicate tuples in its result. The **unique** construct[9] returns the value **true** if the argument subquery contains no duplicate tuples. Using the **unique** construct, we can write the query "Find all courses that were offered at most once in 2009" as follows:

> **select** *T.course_id*
> **from** *course* **as** *T*
> **where unique** (**select** *R.course_id*
>   **from** *section* **as** *R*
>   **where** *T.course_id*= *R.course_id* **and**
>   *R.year* = 2009);

Note that if a course is not offered in 2009, the subquery would return an empty result, and the **unique** predicate would evaluate to true on the empty set.

An equivalent version of the above query not using the **unique** construct is:

---

[9]This construct is not yet widely implemented.

> **select** $T.course\_id$
> **from** $course$ **as** T
> **where** $1 <=$ (**select count**($R.course\_id$)
>   **from** $section$ **as** R
>   **where** $T.course\_id= R.course\_id$ **and**
> $R.year = 2009$);

We can test for the existence of duplicate tuples in a subquery by using the **not unique** construct. To illustrate this construct, consider the query "Find all courses that were offered at least twice in 2009" as follows:

> **select** $T.course\_id$
> **from** $course$ **as** T
> **where not unique** (**select** $R.course\_id$
>   **from** $section$ **as** R
>   **where** $T.course\_id= R.course\_id$ **and**
> $R.year = 2009$);

Formally, the **unique** test on a relation is defined to fail if and only if the relation contains two tuples t_1 and t_2 such that $t_1 = t_2$. Since the test $t_1 = t_2$ fails if any of the fields of t_1 or t_2 are null, it is possible for **unique** to be true even if there are multiple copies of a tuple, as long as at least one of the attributes of the tuple is null.

3.8.5 Subqueries in the From Clause

SQL allows a subquery expression to be used in the **from** clause. The key concept applied here is that any **select-from-where** expression returns a relation as a result and, therefore, can be inserted into another **select-from-where** anywhere that a relation can appear.

Consider the query "Find the average instructors' salaries of those departments where the average salary is greater than \$42,000." We wrote this query in Section 3.7 by using the **having** clause. We can now rewrite this query, without using the **having** clause, by using a subquery in the **from** clause, as follows:

> **select** $dept\_name, avg\_salary$
> **from** (**select** $dept\_name$, **avg** ($salary$) **as** avg_salary
>   **from** $instructor$
>   **group by** $dept\_name$)
> **where** $avg\_salary > 42000$;

The subquery generates a relation consisting of the names of all departments and their corresponding average instructors' salaries. The attributes of the subquery result can be used in the outer query, as can be seen in the above example.

Note that we do not need to use the **having** clause, since the subquery in the **from** clause computes the average salary, and the predicate that was in the **having** clause earlier is now in the **where** clause of the outer query.

We can give the subquery result relation a name, and rename the attributes, using the **as** clause, as illustrated below.

> **select** *dept_name, avg_salary*
> **from** (**select** *dept_name,* **avg** (*salary*)
>   **from** *instructor*
>   **group by** *dept_name*)
>   **as** *dept_avg* (*dept_name, avg_salary*)
> **where** *avg_salary* > 42000;

The subquery result relation is named *dept_avg*, with the attributes *dept_name* and *avg_salary*.

Nested subqueries in the **from** clause are supported by most but not all SQL implementations. However, some SQL implementations, notably Oracle, do not support renaming of the result relation in the **from** clause.

As another example, suppose we wish to find the maximum across all departments of the total salary at each department. The **having** clause does not help us in this task, but we can write this query easily by using a subquery in the **from** clause, as follows:

> **select max** (*tot_salary*)
> **from** (**select** *dept_name,* **sum**(*salary*)
>   **from** *instructor*
>   **group by** *dept_name*) **as** *dept_total* (*dept_name, tot_salary*);

We note that nested subqueries in the **from** clause cannot use correlation variables from other relations in the **from** clause. However, SQL:2003 allows a subquery in the **from** clause that is prefixed by the **lateral** keyword to access attributes of preceding tables or subqueries in the **from** clause. For example, if we wish to print the names of each instructor, along with their salary and the average salary in their department, we could write the query as follows:

> **select** *name, salary, avg_salary*
> **from** *instructor I1,* **lateral** (**select avg**(*salary*) as *avg_salary*
>   **from** *instructor I2*
>   **where** *I2.dept_name= I1.dept_name*);

Without the **lateral** clause, the subquery cannot access the correlation variable *I1* from the outer query. Currently, only a few SQL implementations, such as IBM DB2, support the **lateral** clause.

3.8.6   The with Clause

The **with** clause provides a way of defining a temporary relation whose definition is available only to the query in which the **with** clause occurs. Consider the following query, which finds those departments with the maximum budget.

> **with** *max_budget* (*value*) **as**
>   (**select max**(*budget*)
>   **from** *department*)
> **select** *budget*
> **from** *department*, *max_budget*
> **where** *department.budget* = *max_budget.value*;

The **with** clause defines the temporary relation *max_budget*, which is used in the immediately following query. The **with** clause, introduced in SQL:1999, is supported by many, but not all, database systems.

We could have written the above query by using a nested subquery in either the **from** clause or the **where** clause. However, using nested subqueries would have made the query harder to read and understand. The **with** clause makes the query logic clearer; it also permits a view definition to be used in multiple places within a query.

For example, suppose we want to find all departments where the total salary is greater than the average of the total salary at all departments. We can write the query using the **with** clause as follows.

> **with** *dept_total* (*dept_name, value*) **as**
>   (**select** *dept_name*, **sum**(*salary*)
>   **from** *instructor*
>   **group by** *dept_name*),
> *dept_total_avg*(*value*) **as**
>   (**select avg**(*value*)
>   **from** *dept_total*)
> **select** *dept_name*
> **from** *dept_total*, *dept_total_avg*
> **where** *dept_total.value* >= *dept_total_avg.value*;

We can, of course, create an equivalent query without the **with** clause, but it would be more complicated and harder to understand. You can write the equivalent query as an exercise.

3.8.7   Scalar Subqueries

SQL allows subqueries to occur wherever an expression returning a value is permitted, provided the subquery returns only one tuple containing a single attribute; such subqueries are called **scalar subqueries**. For example, a subquery can be used in the **select** clause as illustrated in the following example that lists all departments along with the number of instructors in each department:

$$\begin{aligned}
&\textbf{select } dept\_name, \\
&\qquad\quad (\textbf{select count}(*) \\
&\qquad\qquad \textbf{from } instructor \\
&\qquad\qquad \textbf{where } department.dept\_name = instructor.dept\_name) \\
&\qquad\quad \textbf{as } num\_instructors \\
&\qquad \textbf{from } department;
\end{aligned}$$

The subquery in the above example is guaranteed to return only a single value since it has a **count**(*) aggregate without a **group by**. The example also illustrates the usage of correlation variables, that is, attributes of relations in the **from** clause of the outer query, such as *department.dept_name* in the above example.

Scalar subqueries can occur in **select**, **where**, and **having** clauses. Scalar subqueries may also be defined without aggregates. It is not always possible to figure out at compile time if a subquery can return more than one tuple in its result; if the result has more than one tuple when the subquery is executed, a run-time error occurs.

Note that technically the type of a scalar subquery result is still a relation, even if it contains a single tuple. However, when a scalar subquery is used in an expression where a value is expected, SQL implicitly extracts the value from the single attribute of the single tuple in the relation, and returns that value.

3.9   Modification of the Database

We have restricted our attention until now to the extraction of information from the database. Now, we show how to add, remove, or change information with SQL.

3.9.1   Deletion

A delete request is expressed in much the same way as a query. We can delete only whole tuples; we cannot delete values on only particular attributes. SQL expresses a deletion by

$$\begin{aligned}
&\textbf{delete from } r \\
&\textbf{where } P;
\end{aligned}$$

where P represents a predicate and r represents a relation. The **delete** statement first finds all tuples t in r for which $P(t)$ is true, and then deletes them from r. The **where** clause can be omitted, in which case all tuples in r are deleted.

Note that a **delete** command operates on only one relation. If we want to delete tuples from several relations, we must use one **delete** command for each relation. The predicate in the **where** clause may be as complex as a **select** command's **where** clause. At the other extreme, the **where** clause may be empty. The request

delete from *instructor*;

deletes all tuples from the *instructor* relation. The *instructor* relation itself still exists, but it is empty.

Here are examples of SQL delete requests:

- Delete all tuples in the *instructor* relation pertaining to instructors in the Finance department.

$$\begin{array}{l} \textbf{delete from } instructor \\ \textbf{where } dept\_name = \text{'Finance'}; \end{array}$$

- Delete all instructors with a salary between $13,000 and $15,000.

$$\begin{array}{l} \textbf{delete from } instructor \\ \textbf{where } salary \textbf{ between } 13000 \textbf{ and } 15000; \end{array}$$

- Delete all tuples in the *instructor* relation for those instructors associated with a department located in the Watson building.

$$\begin{array}{l} \textbf{delete from } instructor \\ \textbf{where } dept\_name \textbf{ in } (\textbf{select } dept\_name \\ \qquad\qquad\qquad\quad \textbf{from } department \\ \qquad\qquad\qquad\quad \textbf{where } building = \text{'Watson'}); \end{array}$$

This **delete** request first finds all departments located in Watson, and then deletes all *instructor* tuples pertaining to those departments.

Note that, although we may delete tuples from only one relation at a time, we may reference any number of relations in a **select-from-where** nested in the **where** clause of a **delete**. The **delete** request can contain a nested **select** that references the relation from which tuples are to be deleted. For example, suppose that we want to delete the records of all instructors with salary below the average at the university. We could write:

$$\begin{array}{l} \textbf{delete from } instructor \\ \textbf{where } salary < (\textbf{select avg } (salary) \\ \qquad\qquad\qquad\quad \textbf{from } instructor); \end{array}$$

The **delete** statement first tests each tuple in the relation *instructor* to check whether the salary is less than the average salary of instructors in the university. Then, all tuples that fail the test—that is, represent an instructor with a lower-than-average salary—are deleted. Performing all the tests before performing any deletion is important—if some tuples are deleted before other tuples have been tested, the average salary may change, and the final result of the **delete** would depend on the order in which the tuples were processed!

3.9.2 Insertion

To insert data into a relation, we either specify a tuple to be inserted or write a query whose result is a set of tuples to be inserted. Obviously, the attribute values for inserted tuples must be members of the corresponding attribute's domain. Similarly, tuples inserted must have the correct number of attributes.

The simplest **insert** statement is a request to insert one tuple. Suppose that we wish to insert the fact that there is a course CS-437 in the Computer Science department with title "Database Systems", and 4 credit hours. We write:

> **insert into** *course*
>   **values** ('CS-437', 'Database Systems', 'Comp. Sci.', 4);

In this example, the values are specified in the order in which the corresponding attributes are listed in the relation schema. For the benefit of users who may not remember the order of the attributes, SQL allows the attributes to be specified as part of the **insert** statement. For example, the following SQL **insert** statements are identical in function to the preceding one:

> **insert into** *course* (*course_id*, *title*, *dept_name*, *credits*)
>   **values** ('CS-437', 'Database Systems', 'Comp. Sci.', 4);

> **insert into** *course* (*title*, *course_id*, *credits*, *dept_name*)
>   **values** ('Database Systems', 'CS-437', 4, 'Comp. Sci.');

More generally, we might want to insert tuples on the basis of the result of a query. Suppose that we want to make each student in the Music department who has earned more than 144 credit hours, an instructor in the Music department, with a salary of $18,000. We write:

> **insert into** *instructor*
>   **select** *ID*, *name*, *dept_name*, 18000
>   **from** *student*
>   **where** *dept_name* = 'Music' **and** *tot_cred* > 144;

Instead of specifying a tuple as we did earlier in this section, we use a **select** to specify a set of tuples. SQL evaluates the **select** statement first, giving a set of tuples that is then inserted into the *instructor* relation. Each tuple has an *ID*, a *name*, a *dept_name* (Music), and an salary of $18,000.

It is important that we evaluate the **select** statement fully before we carry out any insertions. If we carry out some insertions even as the **select** statement is being evaluated, a request such as:

> **insert into** *student*
> **select** *
> **from** *student*;

might insert an infinite number of tuples, if the primary key constraint on *student* were absent. Without the primary key constraint, the request would insert the first tuple in *student* again, creating a second copy of the tuple. Since this second copy is part of *student* now, the **select** statement may find it, and a third copy would be inserted into *student*. The **select** statement may then find this third copy and insert a fourth copy, and so on, forever. Evaluating the **select** statement completely before performing insertions avoids such problems. Thus, the above **insert** statement would simply duplicate every tuple in the *student* relation, if the relation did not have a primary key constraint.

Our discussion of the **insert** statement considered only examples in which a value is given for every attribute in inserted tuples. It is possible for inserted tuples to be given values on only some attributes of the schema. The remaining attributes are assigned a null value denoted by *null*. Consider the request:

> **insert into** *student*
> **values** ('3003', 'Green', 'Finance', *null*);

The tuple inserted by this request specified that a student with *ID* "3003" is in the Finance department, but the *tot_cred* value for this student is not known. Consider the query:

> **select** *student*
> **from** *student*
> **where** *tot_cred* > 45;

Since the *tot_cred* value of student "3003" is not known, we cannot determine whether it is greater than 45.

Most relational database products have special "bulk loader" utilities to insert a large set of tuples into a relation. These utilities allow data to be read from formatted text files, and can execute much faster than an equivalent sequence of insert statements.

3.9.3 Updates

In certain situations, we may wish to change a value in a tuple without changing *all* values in the tuple. For this purpose, the **update** statement can be used. As we could for **insert** and **delete**, we can choose the tuples to be updated by using a query.

Suppose that annual salary increases are being made, and salaries of all instructors are to be increased by 5 percent. We write:

> **update** *instructor*
> **set** *salary= salary* * 1.05;

The preceding update statement is applied once to each of the tuples in *instructor* relation.

If a salary increase is to be paid only to instructors with salary of less than $70,000, we can write:

> **update** *instructor*
> **set** *salary = salary* * 1.05
> **where** *salary* < 70000;

In general, the **where** clause of the **update** statement may contain any construct legal in the **where** clause of the **select** statement (including nested **select**s). As with **insert** and **delete**, a nested **select** within an **update** statement may reference the relation that is being updated. As before, SQL first tests all tuples in the relation to see whether they should be updated, and carries out the updates afterward. For example, we can write the request "Give a 5 percent salary raise to instructors whose salary is less than average" as follows:

> **update** *instructor*
> **set** *salary = salary* * 1.05
> **where** *salary* < (**select avg** (*salary*)
>   **from** *instructor*);

Let us now suppose that all instructors with salary over $100,000 receive a 3 percent raise, whereas all others receive a 5 percent raise. We could write two **update** statements:

> **update** *instructor*
> **set** *salary = salary* * 1.03
> **where** *salary* > 100000;

> **update** *instructor*
> **set** *salary = salary* * 1.05
> **where** *salary* <= 100000;

Note that the order of the two **update** statements is important. If we changed the order of the two statements, an instructor with a salary just under $100,000 would receive an over 8 percent raise.

SQL provides a **case** construct that we can use to perform both the updates with a single **update** statement, avoiding the problem with the order of updates.

```
update instructor
set salary = case
            when salary <= 100000 then salary * 1.05
            else salary * 1.03
    end
```

The general form of the case statement is as follows.

```
case
    when pred₁ then result₁
    when pred₂ then result₂
    ...
    when predₙ then resultₙ
    else result₀
end
```

The operation returns $result_i$, where i is the first of $pred_1, pred_2, \ldots, pred_n$ that is satisfied; if none of the predicates is satisfied, the operation returns $result_0$. Case statements can be used in any place where a value is expected.

Scalar subqueries are also useful in SQL update statements, where they can be used in the **set** clause. Consider an update where we set the *tot_cred* attribute of each *student* tuple to the sum of the credits of courses successfully completed by the student. We assume that a course is successfully completed if the student has a grade that is not 'F' or null. To specify this update, we need to use a subquery in the **set** clause, as shown below:

```
update student S
set tot_cred = (
    select sum(credits)
    from takes natural join course
    where S.ID= takes.ID and
          takes.grade <> 'F' and
          takes.grade is not null);
```

Observe that the subquery uses a correlation variable S from the **update** statement. In case a student has not successfully completed any course, the above update statement would set the *tot_cred* attribute value to null. To set the value to 0 instead, we could use another **update** statement to replace null values by 0; a better alternative is to replace the clause "**select sum**(*credits*)" in the preceding subquery by the following **select** clause using a **case** expression:

```
select case
       when sum(credits) is not null then sum(credits)
       else 0
       end
```

3.10   Summary

- SQL is the most influential commercially marketed relational query language. The SQL language has several parts:

  - **Data-definition language** (DDL), which provides commands for defining relation schemas, deleting relations, and modifying relation schemas.

  - **Data-manipulation language** (DML), which includes a query language and commands to insert tuples into, delete tuples from, and modify tuples in the database.

- The SQL data-definition language is used to create relations with specified schemas. In addition to specifying the names and types of relation attributes, SQL also allows the specification of integrity constraints such as primary-key constraints and foreign-key constraints.

- SQL includes a variety of language constructs for queries on the database. These include the **select**, **from**, and **where** clauses, and support for the natural join operation.

- SQL also provides mechanisms to rename both attributes and relations, and to order query results by sorting on specified attributes.

- SQL supports basic set operations on relations including **union**, **intersect**, and **except**, which correspond to the mathematical set-theory operations ∪, ∩, and −.

- SQL handles queries on relations containing null values by adding the truth value "unknown" to the usual truth values of true and false.

- SQL supports aggregation, including the ability to divide a relation into groups, applying aggregation separately on each group. SQL also supports set operations on groups.

- SQL supports nested subqueries in the **where**, and **from** clauses of an outer query. It also supports scalar subqueries, wherever an expression returning a value is permitted.

- SQL provides constructs for updating, inserting, and deleting information.

Review Terms

- Data-definition language
- Data-manipulation language
- Database schema
- Database instance
- Relation schema
- Relation instance
- Primary key
- Foreign key
  - Referencing relation
  - Referenced relation

- Null value
- Query language
- SQL query structure
  - **select** clause
  - **from** clause
  - **where** clause
- Natural join operation
- **as** clause
- **order** by clause
- Correlation name (correlation variable, tuple variable)
- Set operations
  - **union**
  - **intersect**
  - **except**
- Null values
  - Truth value "unknown"

- Aggregate functions
  - **avg, min, max, sum, count**
  - **group by**
  - **having**
- Nested subqueries
- Set comparisons
  - $\{<, <=, >, >=\}$ { **some, all** }
  - **exists**
  - **unique**
- **lateral** clause
- **with** clause
- Scalar subquery
- Database modification
  - Deletion
  - Insertion
  - Updating

Practice Exercises

3.1 Write the following queries in SQL, using the university schema. (We suggest you actually run these queries on a database, using the sample data that we provide on the Web site of the book, db-book.com. Instructions for setting up a database, and loading sample data, are provided on the above Web site.)

    a. Find the titles of courses in the Comp. Sci. department that have 3 credits.

    b. Find the IDs of all students who were taught by an instructor named Einstein; make sure there are no duplicates in the result.

    c. Find the highest salary of any instructor.

    d. Find all instructors earning the highest salary (there may be more than one with the same salary).

    e. Find the enrollment of each section that was offered in Autumn 2009.

    f. Find the maximum enrollment, across all sections, in Autumn 2009.

    g. Find the sections that had the maximum enrollment in Autumn 2009.

person (*driver_id*, name, address)
car (*license*, model, year)
accident (*report_number*, date, location)
owns (*driver_id*, *license*)
participated (*report_number*, *license*, driver_id, damage_amount)

Figure 3.18   Insurance database for Exercises 3.4 and 3.14.

3.2   Suppose you are given a relation *grade_points*(*grade*, points), which provides a conversion from letter grades in the *takes* relation to numeric scores; for example an "A" grade could be specified to correspond to 4 points, an "A−" to 3.7 points, a "B+" to 3.3 points, a "B" to 3 points, and so on. The grade points earned by a student for a course offering (section) is defined as the number of credits for the course multiplied by the numeric points for the grade that the student received.

Given the above relation, and our university schema, write each of the following queries in SQL. You can assume for simplicity that no *takes* tuple has the *null* value for *grade*.

a.   Find the total grade-points earned by the student with ID 12345, across all courses taken by the student.

b.   Find the grade-point average (*GPA*) for the above student, that is, the total grade-points divided by the total credits for the associated courses.

c.   Find the ID and the grade-point average of every student.

3.3   Write the following inserts, deletes or updates in SQL, using the university schema.

a.   Increase the salary of each instructor in the Comp. Sci. department by 10%.

b.   Delete all courses that have never been offered (that is, do not occur in the *section* relation).

c.   Insert every student whose *tot_cred* attribute is greater than 100 as an instructor in the same department, with a salary of $10,000.

3.4   Consider the insurance database of Figure 3.18, where the primary keys are underlined. Construct the following SQL queries for this relational database.

a.   Find the total number of people who owned cars that were involved in accidents in 2009.

b.   Add a new accident to the database; assume any values for required attributes.

c.   Delete the Mazda belonging to "John Smith".

branch(*branch_name*, branch_city, assets)
customer (*customer_name*, customer_street, customer_city)
loan (*loan_number*, branch_name, amount)
borrower (*customer_name*, *loan_number*)
account (*account_number*, branch_name, balance)
depositor (*customer_name*, *account_number*)

Figure 3.19   Banking database for Exercises 3.8 and 3.15.

3.5   Suppose that we have a relation *marks*(ID, *score*) and we wish to assign grades to students based on the score as follows: grade *F* if *score* < 40, grade *C* if 40 ≤ *score* < 60, grade *B* if 60 ≤ *score* < 80, and grade *A* if 80 ≤ *score*. Write SQL queries to do the following:

   a.   Display the grade for each student, based on the *marks* relation.

   b.   Find the number of students with each grade.

3.6   The SQL **like** operator is case sensitive, but the lower() function on strings can be used to perform case insensitive matching. To show how, write a query that finds departments whose names contain the string "sci" as a substring, regardless of the case.

3.7   Consider the SQL query

   select distinct *p.a*1
   from *p, r*1, *r*2
   where *p.a*1 = *r*1.*a*1 **or** *p.a*1 = *r*2.*a*1

   Under what conditions does the preceding query select values of *p.a*1 that are either in *r*1 or in *r*2? Examine carefully the cases where one of *r*1 or *r*2 may be empty.

3.8   Consider the bank database of Figure 3.19, where the primary keys are underlined. Construct the following SQL queries for this relational database.

   a.   Find all customers of the bank who have an account but not a loan.

   b.   Find the names of all customers who live on the same street and in the same city as "Smith".

   c.   Find the names of all branches with customers who have an account in the bank and who live in "Harrison".

3.9   Consider the employee database of Figure 3.20, where the primary keys are underlined. Give an expression in SQL for each of the following queries.

   a.   Find the names and cities of residence of all employees who work for "First Bank Corporation".

$$employee\ (\underline{employee\_name},\ street,\ city)$$
$$works\ (\underline{employee\_name},\ company\_name,\ salary)$$
$$company\ (\underline{company\_name},\ city)$$
$$manages\ (\underline{employee\_name},\ manager\_name)$$

Figure 3.20 Employee database for Exercises 3.9, 3.10, 3.16, 3.17, and 3.20.

b. Find the names, street addresses, and cities of residence of all employees who work for "First Bank Corporation" and earn more than $10,000.

c. Find all employees in the database who do not work for "First Bank Corporation".

d. Find all employees in the database who earn more than each employee of "Small Bank Corporation".

e. Assume that the companies may be located in several cities. Find all companies located in every city in which "Small Bank Corporation" is located.

f. Find the company that has the most employees.

g. Find those companies whose employees earn a higher salary, on average, than the average salary at "First Bank Corporation".

3.10 Consider the relational database of Figure 3.20. Give an expression in SQL for each of the following queries.

a. Modify the database so that "Jones" now lives in "Newtown".

b. Give all managers of "First Bank Corporation" a 10 percent raise unless the salary becomes greater than $100,000; in such cases, give only a 3 percent raise.

Exercises

3.11 Write the following queries in SQL, using the university schema.

a. Find the names of all students who have taken at least one Comp. Sci. course; make sure there are no duplicate names in the result.

b. Find the IDs and names of all students who have not taken any course offering before Spring 2009.

c. For each department, find the maximum salary of instructors in that department. You may assume that every department has at least one instructor.

d. Find the lowest, across all departments, of the per-department maximum salary computed by the preceding query.

3.12   Write the following queries in SQL, using the university schema.

   a.   Create a new course "CS-001", titled "Weekly Seminar", with 0 credits.

   b.   Create a section of this course in Autumn 2009, with *sec_id* of 1.

   c.   Enroll every student in the Comp. Sci. department in the above section.

   d.   Delete enrollments in the above section where the student's name is Chavez.

   e.   Delete the course CS-001. What will happen if you run this delete statement without first deleting offerings (sections) of this course.

   f.   Delete all *takes* tuples corresponding to any section of any course with the word "database" as a part of the title; ignore case when matching the word with the title.

3.13   Write SQL DDL corresponding to the schema in Figure 3.18. Make any reasonable assumptions about data types, and be sure to declare primary and foreign keys.

3.14   Consider the insurance database of Figure 3.18, where the primary keys are underlined. Construct the following SQL queries for this relational database.

   a.   Find the number of accidents in which the cars belonging to "John Smith" were involved.

   b.   Update the damage amount for the car with the license number "AABB2000" in the accident with report number "AR2197" to $3000.

3.15   Consider the bank database of Figure 3.19, where the primary keys are underlined. Construct the following SQL queries for this relational database.

   a.   Find all customers who have an account at *all* the branches located in "Brooklyn".

   b.   Find out the total sum of all loan amounts in the bank.

   c.   Find the names of all branches that have assets greater than those of at least one branch located in "Brooklyn".

3.16   Consider the employee database of Figure 3.20, where the primary keys are underlined. Give an expression in SQL for each of the following queries.

   a.   Find the names of all employees who work for "First Bank Corporation".

   b.   Find all employees in the database who live in the same cities as the companies for which they work.

   c.   Find all employees in the database who live in the same cities and on the same streets as do their managers.

     d.   Find all employees who earn more than the average salary of all employees of their company.

     e.   Find the company that has the smallest payroll.

3.17   Consider the relational database of Figure 3.20. Give an expression in SQL for each of the following queries.

     a.   Give all employees of "First Bank Corporation" a 10 percent raise.

     b.   Give all managers of "First Bank Corporation" a 10 percent raise.

     c.   Delete all tuples in the *works* relation for employees of "Small Bank Corporation".

3.18   List two reasons why null values might be introduced into the database.

3.19   Show that, in SQL, $<>$ **all** is identical to **not in**.

3.20   Give an SQL schema definition for the employee database of Figure 3.20. Choose an appropriate domain for each attribute and an appropriate primary key for each relation schema.

3.21   Consider the library database of Figure 3.21. Write the following queries in SQL.

     a.   Print the names of members who have borrowed any book published by "McGraw-Hill".

     b.   Print the names of members who have borrowed all books published by "McGraw-Hill".

     c.   For each publisher, print the names of members who have borrowed more than five books of that publisher.

     d.   Print the average number of books borrowed per member. Take into account that if an member does not borrow any books, then that member does not appear in the *borrowed* relation at all.

3.22   Rewrite the **where** clause

$$\textbf{where unique (select } \textit{title} \textbf{ from } \textit{course})$$

without using the **unique** construct.

member(<u>*memb no*</u>, *name, age*)
book(<u>*isbn*</u>, *title, authors, publisher*)
borrowed(<u>*memb no, isbn*</u>, *date*)

Figure 3.21 Library database for Exercise 3.21.

3.23   Consider the query:

> **select** *course_id, semester, year, sec_id,* **avg** (*tot_cred*)
> **from** *takes* **natural join** *student*
> **where** *year* = 2009
> **group by** *course_id, semester, year, sec_id*
> **having count** (*ID*) >= 2;

Explain why joining *section* as well in the **from** clause would not change the result.

3.24   Consider the query:

> **with** *dept_total* (*dept_name, value*) **as**
>   (**select** *dept_name,* **sum**(*salary*)
>   **from** *instructor*
>   **group by** *dept_name*),
> *dept_total_avg*(*value*) **as**
>   (**select avg**(*value*)
>   **from** *dept_total*)
> **select** *dept_name*
> **from** *dept_total, dept_total_avg*
> **where** *dept_total.value* >= *dept_total_avg.value*;

Rewrite this query without using the **with** construct.

Tools

A number of relational database systems are available commercially, including IBM DB2, IBM Informix, Oracle, Sybase, and Microsoft SQL Server. In addition several database systems can be downloaded and used free of charge, including PostgreSQL, MySQL (free except for certain kinds of commercial use), and Oracle Express edition.

Most database systems provide a command line interface for submitting SQL commands. In addition, most databases also provide graphical user interfaces (GUIs), which simplify the task of browsing the database, creating and submitting queries, and administering the database. Commercial IDEs for SQL that work across multiple database platforms, include Embarcadero's RAD Studio and Aqua Data Studio.

For PostgreSQL, the pgAdmin tool provides GUI functionality, while for MySQL, phpMyAdmin provides GUI functionality. The NetBeans IDE provides a GUI front end that works with a number of different databases, but with limited functionality, while the Eclipse IDE supports similar functionality through several different plugins such as the Data Tools Platform (DTP) and JBuilder.

SQL schema definitions and sample data for the university schema are provided on the Web site for this book, db-book.com. The Web site also contains instructions on how to set up and access some popular database systems. The SQL constructs discussed in this chapter are part of the SQL standard, but certain features are not supported by some databases. The Web site lists these incompatibilities, which you will need to take into account when executing queries on those databases.

Bibliographical Notes

The original version of SQL, called Sequel 2, is described by Chamberlin et al. [1976]. Sequel 2 was derived from the language Square (Boyce et al. [1975] and Chamberlin and Boyce [1974]). The American National Standard SQL-86 is described in ANSI [1986]. The IBM Systems Application Architecture definition of SQL is defined by IBM [1987]. The official standards for SQL-89 and SQL-92 are available as ANSI [1989] and ANSI [1992], respectively.

Textbook descriptions of the SQL-92 language include Date and Darwen [1997], Melton and Simon [1993], and Cannan and Otten [1993]. Date and Darwen [1997] and Date [1993a] include a critique of SQL-92 from a programming-languages perspective.

Textbooks on SQL:1999 include Melton and Simon [2001] and Melton [2002]. Eisenberg and Melton [1999] provide an overview of SQL:1999. Donahoo and Speegle [2005] covers SQL from a developers' perspective. Eisenberg et al. [2004] provides an overview of SQL:2003.

The SQL:1999, SQL:2003, SQL:2006 and SQL:2008 standards are published as a collection of ISO/IEC standards documents, which are described in more detail in Section 24.4. The standards documents are densely packed with information and hard to read, and of use primarily for database system implementers. The standards documents are available from the Web site http://webstore.ansi.org, but only for purchase.

Many database products support SQL features beyond those specified in the standard, and may not support some features of the standard. More information on these features may be found in the SQL user manuals of the respective products.

The processing of SQL queries, including algorithms and performance issues, is discussed in Chapters 12 and 13. Bibliographic references on these matters appear in those chapters.

CHAPTER 4

Intermediate SQL

In this chapter, we continue our study of SQL. We consider more complex forms of SQL queries, view definition, transactions, integrity constraints, more details regarding SQL data definition, and authorization.

4.1   Join Expressions

In Section 3.3.3, we introduced the **natural join** operation. SQL provides other forms of the join operation, including the ability to specify an explicit **join predicate**, and the ability to include in the result tuples that are excluded by **natural join**. We shall discuss these forms of join in this section.

The examples in this section involve the two relations *student* and *takes*, shown in Figures 4.1 and 4.2, respectively. Observe that the attribute *grade* has a value null for the student with *ID* 98988, for the course BIO-301, section 1, taken in Summer 2010. The null value indicates that the grade has not been awarded yet.

ID	name	dept_name	tot_cred
00128	Zhang	Comp. Sci.	102
12345	Shankar	Comp. Sci.	32
19991	Brandt	History	80
23121	Chavez	Finance	110
44553	Peltier	Physics	56
45678	Levy	Physics	46
54321	Williams	Comp. Sci.	54
55739	Sanchez	Music	38
70557	Snow	Physics	0
76543	Brown	Comp. Sci.	58
76653	Aoi	Elec. Eng.	60
98765	Bourikas	Elec. Eng.	98
98988	Tanaka	Biology	120

Figure 4.1 The *student* relation.

ID	course_id	sec_id	semester	year	grade
00128	CS-101	1	Fall	2009	A
00128	CS-347	1	Fall	2009	A-
12345	CS-101	1	Fall	2009	C
12345	CS-190	2	Spring	2009	A
12345	CS-315	1	Spring	2010	A
12345	CS-347	1	Fall	2009	A
19991	HIS-351	1	Spring	2010	B
23121	FIN-201	1	Spring	2010	C+
44553	PHY-101	1	Fall	2009	B-
45678	CS-101	1	Fall	2009	F
45678	CS-101	1	Spring	2010	B+
45678	CS-319	1	Spring	2010	B
54321	CS-101	1	Fall	2009	A-
54321	CS-190	2	Spring	2009	B+
55739	MU-199	1	Spring	2010	A-
76543	CS-101	1	Fall	2009	A
76543	CS-319	2	Spring	2010	A
76653	EE-181	1	Spring	2009	C
98765	CS-101	1	Fall	2009	C-
98765	CS-315	1	Spring	2010	B
98988	BIO-101	1	Summer	2009	A
98988	BIO-301	1	Summer	2010	*null*

Figure 4.2 The *takes* relation.

4.1.1 Join Conditions

In Section 3.3.3, we saw how to express natural joins, and we saw the **join** ...
using clause, which is a form of natural join that only requires values to match
on specified attributes. SQL supports another form of join, in which an arbitrary
join condition can be specified.

The **on** condition allows a general predicate over the relations being joined.
This predicate is written like a **where** clause predicate except for the use of the
keyword **on** rather than **where**. Like the **using** condition, the **on** condition appears
at the end of the join expression.

Consider the following query, which has a join expression containing the **on**
condition.

> **select** *
> **from** *student* **join** *takes* **on** *student.ID= takes.ID*;

The **on** condition above specifies that a tuple from *student* matches a tuple from
takes if their *ID* values are equal. The join expression in this case is almost the same
as the join expression *student* **natural join** *takes*, since the natural join operation

also requires that for a *student* tuple and a *takes* tuple to match. The one difference is that the result has the *ID* attribute listed twice, in the join result, once for *student* and once for *takes*, even though their *ID* values must be the same.

In fact, the above query is equivalent to the following query (in other words, they generate exactly the same results):

> **select** *
> **from** *student*, *takes*
> **where** *student.ID= takes.ID;*

As we have seen earlier, the relation name is used to disambiguate the attribute name *ID*, and thus the two occurrences can be referred to as *student.ID* and *takes.ID* respectively. A version of this query that displays the *ID* value only once is as follows:

> **select** *student.ID* **as** *ID*, *name*, *dept_name*, *tot_cred*,
>   *course_id*, *sec_id*, *semester*, *year*, *grade*
> **from** *student* **join** *takes* **on** *student.ID= takes.ID;*

The result of the above query is shown in Figure 4.3.

The **on** condition can express any SQL predicate, and thus a join expressions using the **on** condition can express a richer class of join conditions than **natural join**. However, as illustrated by our preceding example, a query using a join expression with an **on** condition can be replaced by an equivalent expression without the **on** condition, with the predicate in the **on** clause moved to the **where** clause. Thus, it may appear that the **on** condition is a redundant feature of SQL.

However, there are two good reasons for introducing the **on** condition. First, we shall see shortly that for a kind of join called an outer join, **on** conditions do behave in a manner different from **where** conditions. Second, an SQL query is often more readable by humans if the join condition is specified in the **on** clause and the rest of the conditions appear in the **where** clause.

4.1.2 Outer Joins

Suppose we wish to display a list of all students, displaying their *ID*, and *name*, *dept_name*, and *tot_cred*, along with the courses that they have taken. The following SQL query may appear to retrieve the required information:

> **select** *
> **from** *student* **natural join** *takes;*

Unfortunately, the above query does not work quite as intended. Suppose that there is some student who takes no courses. Then the tuple in the *student* relation for that particular student would not satisfy the condition of a natural join with any tuple in the *takes* relation, and that student's data would not appear in the result. We would thus not see any information about students who have not taken

ID	name	dept_name	tot_cred	course_id	sec_id	semester	year	grade
00128	Zhang	Comp. Sci.	102	CS-101	1	Fall	2009	A
00128	Zhang	Comp. Sci.	102	CS-347	1	Fall	2009	A-
12345	Shankar	Comp. Sci.	32	CS-101	1	Fall	2009	C
12345	Shankar	Comp. Sci.	32	CS-190	2	Spring	2009	A
12345	Shankar	Comp. Sci.	32	CS-315	1	Spring	2010	A
12345	Shankar	Comp. Sci.	32	CS-347	1	Fall	2009	A
19991	Brandt	History	80	HIS-351	1	Spring	2010	B
23121	Chavez	Finance	110	FIN-201	1	Spring	2010	C+
44553	Peltier	Physics	56	PHY-101	1	Fall	2009	B-
45678	Levy	Physics	46	CS-101	1	Fall	2009	F
45678	Levy	Physics	46	CS-101	1	Spring	2010	B+
45678	Levy	Physics	46	CS-319	1	Spring	2010	B
54321	Williams	Comp. Sci.	54	CS-101	1	Fall	2009	A-
54321	Williams	Comp. Sci.	54	CS-190	2	Spring	2009	B+
55739	Sanchez	Music	38	MU-199	1	Spring	2010	A-
76543	Brown	Comp. Sci.	58	CS-101	1	Fall	2009	A
76543	Brown	Comp. Sci.	58	CS-319	2	Spring	2010	A
76653	Aoi	Elec. Eng.	60	EE-181	1	Spring	2009	C
98765	Bourikas	Elec. Eng.	98	CS-101	1	Fall	2009	C-
98765	Bourikas	Elec. Eng.	98	CS-315	1	Spring	2010	B
98988	Tanaka	Biology	120	BIO-101	1	Summer	2009	A
98988	Tanaka	Biology	120	BIO-301	1	Summer	2010	null

Figure 4.3 The result of *student* **join** *takes* **on** *student.ID= takes.ID* with second occurrence of *ID* omitted.

any courses. For example, in the *student* and *takes* relations of Figures 4.1 and 4.2, note that student Snow, with ID 70557, has not taken any courses. Snow appears in *student*, but Snow's ID number does not appear in the *ID* column of *takes*. Thus, Snow does not appear in the result of the natural join.

More generally, some tuples in either or both of the relations being joined may be "lost" in this way. The **outer join** operation works in a manner similar to the join operations we have already studied, but preserve those tuples that would be lost in a join, by creating tuples in the result containing null values.

For example, to ensure that the student named Snow from our earlier example appears in the result, a tuple could be added to the join result with all attributes from the *student* relation set to the corresponding values for the student Snow, and all the remaining attributes which come from the *takes* relation, namely *course_id*, *sec_id*, *semester*, and *year*, set to *null*. Thus the tuple for the student Snow is preserved in the result of the outer join.

There are in fact three forms of outer join:

- The **left outer join** preserves tuples only in the relation named before (to the left of) the **left outer join** operation.

- The **right outer join** preserves tuples only in the relation named after (to the right of) the **right outer join** operation.

- The **full outer join** preserves tuples in both relations.

In contrast, the join operations we studied earlier that do not preserve nonmatched tuples are called **inner join** operations, to distinguish them from the outer-join operations.

We now explain exactly how each form of outer join operates. We can compute the left outer-join operation as follows. First, compute the result of the inner join as before. Then, for every tuple t in the left-hand-side relation that does not match any tuple in the right-hand-side relation in the inner join, add a tuple r to the result of the join constructed as follows:

- The attributes of tuple r that are derived from the left-hand-side relation are filled in with the values from tuple t.

- The remaining attributes of r are filled with null values.

Figure 4.4 shows the result of:

> **select** *
> **from** *student* **natural left outer join** *takes*;

That result includes student Snow (*ID* 70557), unlike the result of an inner join, but the tuple for Snow includes nulls for the attributes that appear only in the schema of the *takes* relation.

As another example of the use of the outer-join operation, we can write the query "Find all students who have not taken a course" as:

> **select** *ID*
> **from** *student* **natural left outer join** *takes*
> **where** *course_id* **is** *null*;

The **right outer join** is symmetric to the **left outer join**. Tuples from the right-hand-side relation that do not match any tuple in the left-hand-side relation are padded with nulls and are added to the result of the right outer join. Thus, if we rewrite our above query using a right outer join and swapping the order in which we list the relations as follows:

> **select** *
> **from** *takes* **natural right outer join** *student*;

we get the same result except for the order in which the attributes appear in the result (see Figure 4.5).

The **full outer join** is a combination of the left and right outer-join types. After the operation computes the result of the inner join, it extends with nulls those tuples from the left-hand-side relation that did not match with any from the

ID	name	dept_name	tot_cred	course_id	sec_id	semester	year	grade
00128	Zhang	Comp. Sci.	102	CS-101	1	Fall	2009	A
00128	Zhang	Comp. Sci.	102	CS-347	1	Fall	2009	A-
12345	Shankar	Comp. Sci.	32	CS-101	1	Fall	2009	C
12345	Shankar	Comp. Sci.	32	CS-190	2	Spring	2009	A
12345	Shankar	Comp. Sci.	32	CS-315	1	Spring	2010	A
12345	Shankar	Comp. Sci.	32	CS-347	1	Fall	2009	A
19991	Brandt	History	80	HIS-351	1	Spring	2010	B
23121	Chavez	Finance	110	FIN-201	1	Spring	2010	C+
44553	Peltier	Physics	56	PHY-101	1	Fall	2009	B-
45678	Levy	Physics	46	CS-101	1	Fall	2009	F
45678	Levy	Physics	46	CS-101	1	Spring	2010	B+
45678	Levy	Physics	46	CS-319	1	Spring	2010	B
54321	Williams	Comp. Sci.	54	CS-101	1	Fall	2009	A-
54321	Williams	Comp. Sci.	54	CS-190	2	Spring	2009	B+
55739	Sanchez	Music	38	MU-199	1	Spring	2010	A-
70557	Snow	Physics	0	*null*	*null*	*null*	*null*	*null*
76543	Brown	Comp. Sci.	58	CS-101	1	Fall	2009	A
76543	Brown	Comp. Sci.	58	CS-319	2	Spring	2010	A
76653	Aoi	Elec. Eng.	60	EE-181	1	Spring	2009	C
98765	Bourikas	Elec. Eng.	98	CS-101	1	Fall	2009	C-
98765	Bourikas	Elec. Eng.	98	CS-315	1	Spring	2010	B
98988	Tanaka	Biology	120	BIO-101	1	Summer	2009	A
98988	Tanaka	Biology	120	BIO-301	1	Summer	2010	*null*

Figure 4.4 Result of *student* **natural left outer join** *takes*.

right-hand side relation, and adds them to the result. Similarly, it extends with nulls those tuples from the right-hand-side relation that did not match with any tuples from the left-hand-side relation and adds them to the result.

As an example of the use of full outer join, consider the following query: "Display a list of all students in the Comp. Sci. department, along with the course sections, if any, that they have taken in Spring 2009; all course sections from Spring 2009 must be displayed, even if no student from the Comp. Sci. department has taken the course section." This query can be written as:

```
select *
from (select *
        from student
        where dept_name= 'Comp. Sci')
      natural full outer join
      (select *
       from takes
       where semester = 'Spring' and year = 2009);
```

ID	course_id	sec_id	semester	year	grade	name	dept_name	tot_cred
00128	CS-101	1	Fall	2009	A	Zhang	Comp. Sci.	102
00128	CS-347	1	Fall	2009	A-	Zhang	Comp. Sci.	102
12345	CS-101	1	Fall	2009	C	Shankar	Comp. Sci.	32
12345	CS-190	2	Spring	2009	A	Shankar	Comp. Sci.	32
12345	CS-315	1	Spring	2010	A	Shankar	Comp. Sci.	32
12345	CS-347	1	Fall	2009	A	Shankar	Comp. Sci.	32
19991	HIS-351	1	Spring	2010	B	Brandt	History	80
23121	FIN-201	1	Spring	2010	C+	Chavez	Finance	110
44553	PHY-101	1	Fall	2009	B-	Peltier	Physics	56
45678	CS-101	1	Fall	2009	F	Levy	Physics	46
45678	CS-101	1	Spring	2010	B+	Levy	Physics	46
45678	CS-319	1	Spring	2010	B	Levy	Physics	46
54321	CS-101	1	Fall	2009	A-	Williams	Comp. Sci.	54
54321	CS-190	2	Spring	2009	B+	Williams	Comp. Sci.	54
55739	MU-199	1	Spring	2010	A-	Sanchez	Music	38
70557	null	null	null	null	null	Snow	Physics	0
76543	CS-101	1	Fall	2009	A	Brown	Comp. Sci.	58
76543	CS-319	2	Spring	2010	A	Brown	Comp. Sci.	58
76653	EE-181	1	Spring	2009	C	Aoi	Elec. Eng.	60
98765	CS-101	1	Fall	2009	C-	Bourikas	Elec. Eng.	98
98765	CS-315	1	Spring	2010	B	Bourikas	Elec. Eng.	98
98988	BIO-101	1	Summer	2009	A	Tanaka	Biology	120
98988	BIO-301	1	Summer	2010	null	Tanaka	Biology	120

Figure 4.5 The result of *takes* **natural right outer join** *student*.

The **on** clause can be used with outer joins. The following query is identical to the first query we saw using "*student* **natural left outer join** *takes*," except that the attribute *ID* appears twice in the result.

> **select** *
> **from** *student* **left outer join** *takes* **on** *student.ID= takes.ID*;

As we noted earlier, **on** and **where** behave differently for outer join. The reason for this is that outer join adds null-padded tuples only for those tuples that do not contribute to the result of the corresponding inner join. The **on** condition is part of the outer join specification, but a **where** clause is not. In our example, the case of the *student* tuple for student "Snow" with ID 70557, illustrates this distinction. Suppose we modify the preceding query by moving the **on** clause predicate to the **where** clause, and instead using an **on** condition of *true*.

> **select** *
> **from** *student* **left outer join** *takes* **on** *true*
> **where** *student.ID= takes.ID*;

Join types	Join conditions
inner join **left outer join** **right outer join** **full outer join**	**natural** **on** <predicate> **using** ($A_1, A_2, ..., A_n$)

Figure 4.6   Join types and join conditions.

The earlier query, using the left outer join with the **on** condition, includes a tuple (70557, Snow, Physics, 0, *null, null, null, null, null, null*), because there is no tuple in *takes* with *ID* = 70557. In the latter query, however, every tuple satisfies the join condition *true*, so no null-padded tuples are generated by the outer join. The outer join actually generates the Cartesian product of the two relations. Since there is no tuple in *takes* with *ID* = 70557, every time a tuple appears in the outer join with *name* = "Snow", the values for *student.ID* and *takes.ID* must be different, and such tuples would be eliminated by the **where** clause predicate. Thus student Snow never appears in the result of the latter query.

4.1.3   Join Types and Conditions

To distinguish normal joins from outer joins, normal joins are called **inner joins** in SQL. A join clause can thus specify **inner join** instead of **outer join** to specify that a normal join is to be used. The keyword **inner** is, however, optional. The default join type, when the **join** clause is used without the **outer** prefix is the **inner join**. Thus,

> **select** *
> **from** *student* **join** *takes* **using** (ID);

is equivalent to:

> **select** *
> **from** *student* **inner join** *takes* **using** (ID);

Similarly, **natural join** is equivalent to **natural inner join**.

Figure 4.6 shows a full list of the various types of join that we have discussed. As can be seen from the figure, any form of join (inner, left outer, right outer, or full outer) can be combined with any join condition (natural, using, or on).

4.2   Views

In our examples up to this point, we have operated at the logical-model level. That is, we have assumed that the relations in the collection we are given are the actual relations stored in the database.

It is not desirable for all users to see the entire logical model. Security considerations may require that certain data be hidden from users. Consider a clerk who needs to know an instructor's ID, name and department name, but does not have authorization to see the instructor's salary amount. This person should see a relation described in SQL, by:

$$\textbf{select } ID, name, dept\_name$$
$$\textbf{from } instructor;$$

Aside from security concerns, we may wish to create a personalized collection of relations that is better matched to a certain user's intuition than is the logical model. We may want to have a list of all course sections offered by the Physics department in the Fall 2009 semester, with the building and room number of each section. The relation that we would create for obtaining such a list is:

$$\textbf{select } course.course\_id, sec\_id, building, room\_number$$
$$\textbf{from } course, section$$
$$\textbf{where } course.course\_id = section.course\_id$$
$$\textbf{and } course.dept\_name = \text{'Physics'}$$
$$\textbf{and } section.semester = \text{'Fall'}$$
$$\textbf{and } section.year = \text{'2009'};$$

It is possible to compute and store the results of the above queries and then make the stored relations available to users. However, if we did so, and the underlying data in the relations *instructor*, *course*, or *section* changes, the stored query results would then no longer match the result of reexecuting the query on the relations. In general, it is a bad idea to compute and store query results such as those in the above examples (although there are some exceptions, which we study later).

Instead, SQL allows a "virtual relation" to be defined by a query, and the relation conceptually contains the result of the query. The virtual relation is not precomputed and stored, but instead is computed by executing the query whenever the virtual relation is used.

Any such relation that is not part of the logical model, but is made visible to a user as a virtual relation, is called a **view**. It is possible to support a large number of views on top of any given set of actual relations.

4.2.1 View Definition

We define a view in SQL by using the **create view** command. To define a view, we must give the view a name and must state the query that computes the view. The form of the **create view** command is:

$$\textbf{create view } v \textbf{ as } <\text{query expression}>;$$

where <query expression> is any legal query expression. The view name is represented by *v*.

Consider again the clerk who needs to access all data in the *instructor* relation, except *salary*. The clerk should not be authorized to access the *instructor* relation (we see later, in Section 4.6, how authorizations can be specified). Instead, a view relation *faculty* can be made available to the clerk, with the view defined as follows:

> **create view** *faculty* **as**
> **select** *ID, name, dept_name*
> **from** *instructor*;

As explained earlier, the view relation conceptually contains the tuples in the query result, but is not precomputed and stored. Instead, the database system stores the query expression associated with the view relation. Whenever the view relation is accessed, its tuples are created by computing the query result. Thus, the view relation is created whenever needed, on demand.

To create a view that lists all course sections offered by the Physics department in the Fall 2009 semester with the building and room number of each section, we write:

> **create view** *physics_fall_2009* **as**
>   **select** *course.course_id, sec_id, building, room_number*
>   **from** *course, section*
>   **where** *course.course_id* = *section.course_id*
>   **and** *course.dept_name* = 'Physics'
>   **and** *section.semester* = 'Fall'
>   **and** *section.year* = '2009';

4.2.2   Using Views in SQL Queries

Once we have defined a view, we can use the view name to refer to the virtual relation that the view generates. Using the view *physics_fall_2009*, we can find all Physics courses offered in the Fall 2009 semester in the Watson building by writing:

> **select** *course_id*
> **from** *physics_fall_2009*
> **where** *building*= 'Watson';

View names may appear in a query any place where a relation name may appear, The attribute names of a view can be specified explicitly as follows:

> **create view** *departments_total_salary(dept_name, total_salary)* **as**
>   **select** *dept_name,* **sum** (*salary*)
>   **from** *instructor*
>   **group by** *dept_name*;

The preceding view gives for each department the sum of the salaries of all the instructors at that department. Since the expression **sum**(*salary*) does not have a name, the attribute name is specified explicitly in the view definition.

Intuitively, at any given time, the set of tuples in the view relation is the result of evaluation of the query expression that defines the view. Thus, if a view relation is computed and stored, it may become out of date if the relations used to define it are modified. To avoid this, views are usually implemented as follows. When we define a view, the database system stores the definition of the view itself, rather than the result of evaluation of the query expression that defines the view. Wherever a view relation appears in a query, it is replaced by the stored query expression. Thus, whenever we evaluate the query, the view relation is recomputed.

One view may be used in the expression defining another view. For example, we can define a view *physics_fall_2009_watson* that lists the course ID and room number of all Physics courses offered in the Fall 2009 semester in the Watson building as follows:

> **create view** *physics_fall_2009_watson* **as**
> **select** *course_id, room_number*
> **from** *physics_fall_2009*
> **where** *building*= 'Watson';

where *physics_fall_2009_watson* is itself a view relation. This is equivalent to:

> **create view** *physics_fall_2009_watson* **as**
> (**select** *course_id, room_number*
> **from** (**select** *course.course_id, building, room_number*
>   **from** *course, section*
>   **where** *course.course_id* = *section.course_id*
>   **and** *course.dept_name* = 'Physics'
>   **and** *section.semester* = 'Fall'
>   **and** *section.year* = '2009')
> **where** *building*= 'Watson';

4.2.3   Materialized Views

Certain database systems allow view relations to be stored, but they make sure that, if the actual relations used in the view definition change, the view is kept up-to-date. Such views are called **materialized views**.

For example, consider the view *departments_total_salary*. If the above view is materialized, its results would be stored in the database. However, if an *instructor* tuple is added to or deleted from the *instructor* relation, the result of the query defining the view would change, and as a result the materialized view's contents must be updated. Similarly, if an instructor's salary is updated, the tuple in *departments_total_salary* corresponding to that instructor's department must be updated.

The process of keeping the materialized view up-to-date is called **materialized view maintenance** (or often, just **view maintenance**) and is covered in Section 13.5. View maintenance can be done immediately when any of the relations on which the view is defined is updated. Some database systems, however, perform view maintenance lazily, when the view is accessed. Some systems update materialized views only periodically; in this case, the contents of the materialized view may be stale, that is, not up-to-date, when it is used, and should not be used if the application needs up-to-date data. And some database systems permit the database administrator to control which of the above methods is used for each materialized view.

Applications that use a view frequently may benefit if the view is materialized. Applications that demand fast response to certain queries that compute aggregates over large relations can also benefit greatly by creating materialized views corresponding to the queries. In this case, the aggregated result is likely to be much smaller than the large relations on which the view is defined; as a result the materialized view can be used to answer the query very quickly, avoiding reading the large underlying relations. Of course, the benefits to queries from the materialization of a view must be weighed against the storage costs and the added overhead for updates.

SQL does not define a standard way of specifying that a view is materialized, but many database systems provide their own SQL extensions for this task. Some database systems always keep materialized views up-to-date when the underlying relations change, while others permit them to become out of date, and periodically recompute them.

4.2.4   Update of a View

Although views are a useful tool for queries, they present serious problems if we express updates, insertions, or deletions with them. The difficulty is that a modification to the database expressed in terms of a view must be translated to a modification to the actual relations in the logical model of the database.

Suppose the view *faculty*, which we saw earlier, is made available to a clerk. Since we allow a view name to appear wherever a relation name is allowed, the clerk can write:

> **insert into** *faculty*
> **values** ('30765', 'Green', 'Music');

This insertion must be represented by an insertion into the relation *instructor*, since *instructor* is the actual relation from which the database system constructs the view *faculty*. However, to insert a tuple into *instructor*, we must have some value for *salary*. There are two reasonable approaches to dealing with this insertion:

- Reject the insertion, and return an error message to the user.

- Insert a tuple ('30765', 'Green', 'Music', *null*) into the *instructor* relation.

Another problem with modification of the database through views occurs with a view such as:

> **create view** *instructor_info* **as**
> **select** *ID, name, building*
> **from** *instructor, department*
> **where** *instructor.dept_name= department.dept_name;*

This view lists the *ID, name,* and building-name of each instructor in the university. Consider the following insertion through this view:

> **insert into** *instructor_info*
> **values** ('69987', 'White', 'Taylor');

Suppose there is no instructor with ID 69987, and no department in the Taylor building. Then the only possible method of inserting tuples into the *instructor* and *department* relations is to insert ('69987', 'White', *null, null*) into *instructor* and (*null*, 'Taylor', *null*) into *department*. Then, we obtain the relations shown in Figure 4.7. However, this update does not have the desired effect, since the view relation *instructor_info* still does *not* include the tuple ('69987', 'White', 'Taylor'). Thus, there is no way to update the relations *instructor* and *department* by using nulls to get the desired update on *instructor_info*.

Because of problems such as these, modifications are generally not permitted on view relations, except in limited cases. Different database systems specify different conditions under which they permit updates on view relations; see the database system manuals for details. The general problem of database modification through views has been the subject of substantial research, and the bibliographic notes provide pointers to some of this research.

In general, an SQL view is said to be **updatable** (that is, inserts, updates or deletes can be applied on the view) if the following conditions are all satisfied by the query defining the view:

- The **from** clause has only one database relation.

- The **select** clause contains only attribute names of the relation, and does not have any expressions, aggregates, or **distinct** specification.

- Any attribute not listed in the **select** clause can be set to *null*; that is, it does not have a **not null** constraint and is not part of a primary key.

- The query does not have a **group by** or **having** clause.

Under these constraints, the **update**, **insert**, and **delete** operations would be allowed on the following view:

> **create view** *history_instructors* **as**
> **select** *
> **from** *instructor*
> **where** *dept_name=* 'History';

ID	name	dept_name	salary
10101	Srinivasan	Comp. Sci.	65000
12121	Wu	Finance	90000
15151	Mozart	Music	40000
22222	Einstein	Physics	95000
32343	El Said	History	60000
33456	Gold	Physics	87000
45565	Katz	Comp. Sci.	75000
58583	Califieri	History	62000
76543	Singh	Finance	80000
76766	Crick	Biology	72000
83821	Brandt	Comp. Sci.	92000
98345	Kim	Elec. Eng.	80000
69987	White	null	null

instructor

dept_name	building	budget
Biology	Watson	90000
Comp. Sci.	Taylor	100000
Electrical Eng.	Taylor	85000
Finance	Painter	120000
History	Painter	50000
Music	Packard	80000
Physics	Watson	70000
null	Painter	null

department

Figure 4.7 Relations *instructor* and *department* after insertion of tuples.

Even with the conditions on updatability, the following problem still remains. Suppose that a user tries to insert the tuple ('25566', 'Brown', 'Biology', 100000) into the *history_instructors* view. This tuple can be inserted into the *instructor* relation, but it would not appear in the *history_instructors* view since it does not satisfy the selection imposed by the view.

By default, SQL would allow the above update to proceed. However, views can be defined with a **with check option** clause at the end of the view definition; then, if a tuple inserted into the view does not satisfy the view's **where** clause condition, the insertion is rejected by the database system. Updates are similarly rejected if the new value does not satisfy the **where** clause conditions.

SQL:1999 has a more complex set of rules about when inserts, updates, and deletes can be executed on a view, that allows updates through a larger class of views; however, the rules are too complex to be discussed here.

4.3   Transactions

A **transaction** consists of a sequence of query and/or update statements. The SQL standard specifies that a transaction begins implicitly when an SQL statement is executed. One of the following SQL statements must end the transaction:

- **Commit work** commits the current transaction; that is, it makes the updates performed by the transaction become permanent in the database. After the transaction is committed, a new transaction is automatically started.

- **Rollback work** causes the current transaction to be rolled back; that is, it undoes all the updates performed by the SQL statements in the transaction. Thus, the database state is restored to what it was before the first statement of the transaction was executed.

The keyword **work** is optional in both the statements.

Transaction rollback is useful if some error condition is detected during execution of a transaction. Commit is similar, in a sense, to saving changes to a document that is being edited, while rollback is similar to quitting the edit session without saving changes. Once a transaction has executed **commit work**, its effects can no longer be undone by **rollback work**. The database system guarantees that in the event of some failure, such as an error in one of the SQL statements, a power outage, or a system crash, a transaction's effects will be rolled back if it has not yet executed **commit work**. In the case of power outage or other system crash, the rollback occurs when the system restarts.

For instance, consider a banking application, where we need to transfer money from one bank account to another in the same bank. To do so, we need to update two account balances, subtracting the amount transferred from one, and adding it to the other. If the system crashes after subtracting the amount from the first account, but before adding it to the second account, the bank balances would be inconsistent. A similar problem would occur, if the second account is credited before subtracting the amount from the first account, and the system crashes just after crediting the amount.

As another example, consider our running example of a university application. We assume that the attribute *tot_cred* of each tuple in the *student* relation is kept up-to-date by modifying it whenever the student successfully completes a course. To do so, whenever the *takes* relation is updated to record successful completion of a course by a student (by assigning an appropriate grade) the corresponding *student* tuple must also be updated. If the application performing these two updates crashes after one update is performed, but before the second one is performed, the data in the database would be inconsistent.

By either committing the actions of a transaction after all its steps are completed, or rolling back all its actions in case the transaction could not complete all its actions successfully, the database provides an abstraction of a transaction as being **atomic**, that is, indivisible. Either all the effects of the transaction are reflected in the database, or none are (after rollback).

Applying the notion of transactions to the above applications, the update statements should be executed as a single transaction. An error while a transaction executes one of its statements would result in undoing of the effects of the earlier statements of the transaction, so that the database is not left in a partially updated state.

If a program terminates without executing either of these commands, the updates are either committed or rolled back. The standard does not specify which of the two happens, and the choice is implementation dependent.

In many SQL implementations, by default each SQL statement is taken to be a transaction on its own, and gets committed as soon as it is executed. Automatic commit of individual SQL statements must be turned off if a transaction consisting of multiple SQL statements needs to be executed. How to turn off automatic commit depends on the specific SQL implementation, although there is a standard way of doing this using application program interfaces such as JDBC or ODBC, which we study later, in Sections 5.1.1 and 5.1.2, respectively.

A better alternative, which is part of the SQL:1999 standard (but supported by only some SQL implementations currently), is to allow multiple SQL statements to be enclosed between the keywords **begin atomic** ... **end**. All the statements between the keywords then form a single transaction.

We study further properties of transactions in Chapter 14; issues in implementing transactions in a single database are addressed in Chapters 15 and 16, while Chapter 19 addresses issues in implementing transactions across multiple databases, to deal with problems such as transfer of money across accounts in different banks, which have different databases.

4.4   Integrity Constraints

Integrity constraints ensure that changes made to the database by authorized users do not result in a loss of data consistency. Thus, integrity constraints guard against accidental damage to the database.

Examples of integrity constraints are:

- An instructor name cannot be *null*.

- No two instructors can have the same instructor ID.

- Every department name in the *course* relation must have a matching department name in the *department* relation.

- The budget of a department must be greater than $0.00.

In general, an integrity constraint can be an arbitrary predicate pertaining to the database. However, arbitrary predicates may be costly to test. Thus, most database systems allow one to specify integrity constraints that can be tested with minimal overhead.

We have already seen some forms of integrity constraints in Section 3.2.2. We study some more forms of integrity constraints in this section. In Chapter 8, we study another form of integrity constraint, called **functional dependencies**, that is used primarily in the process of schema design.

Integrity constraints are usually identified as part of the database schema design process, and declared as part of the **create table** command used to create relations. However, integrity constraints can also be added to an existing relation by using the command **alter table** *table-name* **add** *constraint*, where *constraint* can be any constraint on the relation. When such a command is executed, the system first ensures that the relation satisfies the specified constraint. If it does, the constraint is added to the relation; if not, the command is rejected.

4.4.1 Constraints on a Single Relation

We described in Section 3.2 how to define tables using the **create table** command. The **create table** command may also include integrity-constraint statements. In addition to the primary-key constraint, there are a number of other ones that can be included in the **create table** command. The allowed integrity constraints include

- **not null**
- **unique**
- **check**(<predicate>)

We cover each of these types of constraints in the following sections.

4.4.2 Not Null Constraint

As we discussed in Chapter 3, the null value is a member of all domains, and as a result is a legal value for every attribute in SQL by default. For certain attributes, however, null values may be inappropriate. Consider a tuple in the *student* relation where *name* is *null*. Such a tuple gives student information for an unknown student; thus, it does not contain useful information. Similarly, we would not want the department budget to be *null*. In cases such as this, we wish to forbid null values, and we can do so by restricting the domain of the attributes *name* and *budget* to exclude null values, by declaring it as follows:

$$\textit{name} \quad \textbf{varchar}(20) \textbf{ not null}$$
$$\textit{budget} \ \textbf{numeric}(12,2) \textbf{ not null}$$

The **not null** specification prohibits the insertion of a null value for the attribute. Any database modification that would cause a null to be inserted in an attribute declared to be **not null** generates an error diagnostic.

There are many situations where we want to avoid null values. In particular, SQL prohibits null values in the primary key of a relation schema. Thus, in our university example, in the *department* relation, if the attribute *dept_name* is declared as the primary key for *department*, it cannot take a null value. As a result it would not need to be declared explicitly to be **not null**.

4.4.3 Unique Constraint

SQL also supports an integrity constraint:

$$\textbf{unique } (A_{j_1}, A_{j_2}, \ldots, A_{j_m})$$

The **unique** specification says that attributes $A_{j_1}, A_{j_2}, \ldots, A_{j_m}$ form a candidate key; that is, no two tuples in the relation can be equal on all the listed attributes. However, candidate key attributes are permitted to be *null* unless they have explicitly been declared to be **not null**. Recall that a null value does not equal any other value. (The treatment of nulls here is the same as that of the **unique** construct defined in Section 3.8.4.)

4.4.4 The check Clause

When applied to a relation declaration, the clause **check**(P) specifies a predicate P that must be satisfied by every tuple in a relation.

A common use of the **check** clause is to ensure that attribute values satisfy specified conditions, in effect creating a powerful type system. For instance, a clause **check** (*budget* > 0) in the **create table** command for relation *department* would ensure that the value of **budget** is nonnegative.

As another example, consider the following:

```
create table section
    (course_id      varchar (8),
     sec_id         varchar (8),
     semester       varchar (6),
     year           numeric (4,0),
     building       varchar (15),
     room_number    varchar (7),
     time_slot_id   varchar (4),
     primary key (course_id, sec_id, semester, year),
     check (semester in ('Fall', 'Winter', 'Spring', 'Summer')));
```

Here, we use the **check** clause to simulate an enumerated type, by specifying that *semester* must be one of 'Fall', 'Winter', 'Spring', or 'Summer'. Thus, the **check** clause permits attribute domains to be restricted in powerful ways that most programming-language type systems do not permit.

The predicate in the **check** clause can, according to the SQL standard, be an arbitrary predicate that can include a subquery. However, currently none of the widely used database products allows the predicate to contain a subquery.

4.4.5 Referential Integrity

Often, we wish to ensure that a value that appears in one relation for a given set of attributes also appears for a certain set of attributes in another relation. This condition is called **referential integrity**.

Foreign keys can be specified as part of the SQL **create table** statement by using the **foreign key** clause, as we saw earlier in Section 3.2.2. We illustrate foreign-key declarations by using the SQL DDL definition of part of our university database, shown in Figure 4.8. The definition of the *course* table has a declaration "**foreign key** (*dept_name*) **references** *department*". This foreign-key declaration specifies that for each course tuple, the department name specified in the tuple must exist in the *department* relation. Without this constraint, it is possible for a course to specify a nonexistent department name.

More generally, let r_1 and r_2 be relations whose set of attributes are R_1 and R_2, respectively, with primary keys K_1 and K_2. We say that a subset α of R_2 is a **foreign key** referencing K_1 in relation r_1 if it is required that, for every tuple t_2 in r_2, there must be a tuple t_1 in r_1 such that $t_1.K_1 = t_2.\alpha$.

Requirements of this form are called **referential-integrity constraints**, or **subset dependencies**. The latter term arises because the preceding referential-integrity constraint can be stated as a requirement that the set of values on α in r_2 must be a subset of the values on K_1 in r_1. Note that, for a referential-integrity constraint to make sense, α and K_1 must be compatible sets of attributes; that is, either α must be equal to K_1, or they must contain the same number of attributes, and the types of corresponding attributes must be compatible (we assume here that α and K_1 are ordered). Unlike foreign-key constraints, in general a referential integrity constraint does not require K_1 to be a primary key of r_1; as a result, more than one tuple in r_1 can have the same value for attributes K_1.

By default, in SQL a foreign key references the primary-key attributes of the referenced table. SQL also supports a version of the **references** clause where a list of attributes of the referenced relation can be specified explicitly. The specified list of attributes must, however, be declared as a candidate key of the referenced relation, using either a **primary key** constraint, or a **unique** constraint. A more general form of a referential-integrity constraint, where the referenced columns need not be a candidate key, cannot be directly specified in SQL. The SQL standard specifies other constructs that can be used to implement such constraints; they are described in Section 4.4.7.

We can use the following short form as part of an attribute definition to declare that the attribute forms a foreign key:

dept_name **varchar**(20) **references** *department*

When a referential-integrity constraint is violated, the normal procedure is to reject the action that caused the violation (that is, the transaction performing the update action is rolled back). However, a **foreign key** clause can specify that if a delete or update action on the referenced relation violates the constraint, then,

create table *classroom*
   (*building*   **varchar** (15),
   room_number **varchar** (7),
   capacity   **numeric** (4,0),
   primary key (*building, room_number*))

create table *department*
   (*dept_name*   **varchar** (20),
   building   **varchar** (15),
   budget   **numeric** (12,2) **check** (*budget* > 0),
   primary key (*dept_name*))

create table *course*
   (*course_id*   **varchar** (8),
   title   **varchar** (50),
   dept_name   **varchar** (20),
   credits   **numeric** (2,0) **check** (*credits* > 0),
   primary key (*course_id*),
   foreign key (*dept_name*) **references** *department*)

create table *instructor*
   (*ID*   **varchar** (5),
   name   **varchar** (20), **not null**
   dept_name   **varchar** (20),
   salary   **numeric** (8,2), **check** (*salary* > 29000),
   primary key (*ID*),
   foreign key (*dept_name*) **references** *department*)

create table *section*
   (*course_id*   **varchar** (8),
   sec_id   **varchar** (8),
   semester   **varchar** (6), **check** (*semester* **in**
                            ('Fall', 'Winter', 'Spring', 'Summer'),
   year   **numeric** (4,0), **check** (*year* > 1759 **and** *year* < 2100)
   building   **varchar** (15),
   room_number **varchar** (7),
   time_slot_id   **varchar** (4),
   primary key (*course_id, sec_id, semester, year*),
   foreign key (*course_id*) **references** *course*,
   foreign key (*building, room_number*) **references** *classroom*)

Figure 4.8 SQL data definition for part of the university database.

instead of rejecting the action, the system must take steps to change the tuple in the referencing relation to restore the constraint. Consider this definition of an integrity constraint on the relation *course*:

create table *course*
 (. . .
 foreign key (*dept_name*) **references** *department*
    on delete cascade
    on update cascade,
 . . .);

Because of the clause **on delete cascade** associated with the foreign-key declaration, if a delete of a tuple in *department* results in this referential-integrity constraint being violated, the system does not reject the delete. Instead, the delete "cascades" to the *course* relation, deleting the tuple that refers to the department that was deleted. Similarly, the system does not reject an update to a field referenced by the constraint if it violates the constraint; instead, the system updates the field *dept_name* in the referencing tuples in *course* to the new value as well. SQL also allows the **foreign key** clause to specify actions other than **cascade**, if the constraint is violated: The referencing field (here, *dept_name*) can be set to *null* (by using **set null** in place of **cascade**), or to the default value for the domain (by using **set default**).

If there is a chain of foreign-key dependencies across multiple relations, a deletion or update at one end of the chain can propagate across the entire chain. An interesting case where the **foreign key** constraint on a relation references the same relation appears in Practice Exercises 4.9. If a cascading update or delete causes a constraint violation that cannot be handled by a further cascading operation, the system aborts the transaction. As a result, all the changes caused by the transaction and its cascading actions are undone.

Null values complicate the semantics of referential-integrity constraints in SQL. Attributes of foreign keys are allowed to be *null*, provided that they have not otherwise been declared to be **not null**. If all the columns of a foreign key are nonnull in a given tuple, the usual definition of foreign-key constraints is used for that tuple. If any of the foreign-key columns is *null*, the tuple is defined automatically to satisfy the constraint.

This definition may not always be the right choice, so SQL also provides constructs that allow you to change the behavior with null values; we do not discuss the constructs here.

4.4.6   Integrity Constraint Violation During a Transaction

Transactions may consist of several steps, and integrity constraints may be violated temporarily after one step, but a later step may remove the violation. For instance, suppose we have a relation *person* with primary key *name*, and an attribute *spouse*, and suppose that *spouse* is a foreign key on *person*. That is, the constraint says that the *spouse* attribute must contain a name that is present in the *person* table. Suppose we wish to note the fact that John and Mary are married to each other by inserting two tuples, one for John and one for Mary, in the above relation, with the spouse attributes set to Mary and John, respectively. The insertion of the first tuple would violate the foreign-key constraint, regardless of which of the two tuples is inserted first. After the second tuple is inserted the foreign-key constraint would hold again.

To handle such situations, the SQL standard allows a clause **initially deferred** to be added to a constraint specification; the constraint would then be checked at the end of a transaction, and not at intermediate steps. A constraint can alternatively be specified as **deferrable**, which means it is checked immediately by default, but can be deferred when desired. For constraints declared as deferrable, executing a statement **set constraints** *constraint-list* **deferred** as part of a transaction causes the checking of the specified constraints to be deferred to the end of that transaction.

However, you should be aware that the default behavior is to check constraints immediately, and many database implementations do not support deferred constraint checking.

We can work around the problem in the above example in another way, if the *spouse* attribute can be set to *null*: We set the spouse attributes to *null* when inserting the tuples for John and Mary, and we update them later. However, this technique requires more programming effort, and does not work if the attributes cannot be set to *null*.

4.4.7   Complex Check Conditions and Assertions

The SQL standard supports additional constructs for specifying integrity constraints that are described in this section. However, you should be aware that these constructs are not currently supported by most database systems.

As defined by the SQL standard, the predicate in the **check** clause can be an arbitrary predicate, which can include a subquery. If a database implementation supports subqueries in the **check** clause, we could specify the following referential-integrity constraint on the relation *section*:

$$\textbf{check } (time\_slot\_id \textbf{ in } (\textbf{select } time\_slot\_id \textbf{ from } time\_slot))$$

The **check** condition verifies that the *time_slot_id* in each tuple in the *section* relation is actually the identifier of a time slot in the *time_slot* relation. Thus, the condition has to be checked not only when a tuple is inserted or modified in *section*, but also when the relation *time_slot* changes (in this case, when a tuple is deleted or modified in relation *time_slot*).

Another natural constraint on our university schema would be to require that every section has at least one instructor teaching the section. In an attempt to enforce this, we may try to declare that the attributes (*course_id*, *sec_id*, *semester*, *year*) of the *section* relation form a foreign key referencing the corresponding attributes of the *teaches* relation. Unfortunately, these attributes do not form a candidate key of the relation *teaches*. A check constraint similar to that for the *time_slot* attribute can be used to enforce this constraint, if check constraints with subqueries were supported by a database system.

Complex **check** conditions can be useful when we want to ensure integrity of data, but may be costly to test. For example, the predicate in the **check** clause

```
create assertion credits_earned_constraint check
(not exists (select ID
              from student
              where tot_cred <> (select sum(credits)
              from takes natural join course
              where student.ID= takes.ID
                      and grade is not null and grade<> 'F' )
```

Figure 4.9 An assertion example.

would not only have to be evaluated when a modification is made to the *section* relation, but may have to be checked if a modification is made to the *time_slot* relation because that relation is referenced in the subquery.

An **assertion** is a predicate expressing a condition that we wish the database always to satisfy. Domain constraints and referential-integrity constraints are special forms of assertions. We have paid substantial attention to these forms of assertions because they are easily tested and apply to a wide range of database applications. However, there are many constraints that we cannot express by using only these special forms. Two examples of such constraints are:

- For each tuple in the *student* relation, the value of the attribute *tot_cred* must equal the sum of credits of courses that the student has completed successfully.

- An instructor cannot teach in two different classrooms in a semester in the same time slot.[1]

An assertion in SQL takes the form:

create assertion <assertion-name> **check** <predicate>;

In Figure 4.9, we show how the first example of constraints can be written in SQL. Since SQL does not provide a "for all X, $P(X)$" construct (where P is a predicate), we are forced to implement the constraint by an equivalent construct, "not exists X such that not $P(X)$", that can be expressed in SQL.

We leave the specification of the second constraint as an exercise.

When an assertion is created, the system tests it for validity. If the assertion is valid, then any future modification to the database is allowed only if it does not cause that assertion to be violated. This testing may introduce a significant amount of overhead if complex assertions have been made. Hence, assertions should be used with great care. The high overhead of testing and maintaining assertions has led some system developers to omit support for general assertions, or to provide specialized forms of assertion that are easier to test.

---

[1]We assume that lectures are not displayed remotely in a second classroom! An alternative constraint that specifies that "an instructor cannot teach two courses in a given semester in the same time slot" may not hold since courses are sometimes cross-listed; that is, the same course is given two identifiers and titles.

Currently, none of the widely used database systems supports either subqueries in the **check** clause predicate, or the **create assertion** construct. However, equivalent functionality can be implemented using triggers, which are described in Section 5.3, if they are supported by the database system. Section 5.3 also describes how the referential integrity constraint on *time_slot_id* can be implemented using triggers.

4.5   SQL Data Types and Schemas

In Chapter 3, we covered a number of built-in data types supported in SQL, such as integer types, real types, and character types. There are additional built-in data types supported by SQL, which we describe below. We also describe how to create basic user-defined types in SQL.

4.5.1   Date and Time Types in SQL

In addition to the basic data types we introduced in Section 3.2, the SQL standard supports several data types relating to dates and times:

- **date**: A calendar date containing a (four-digit) year, month, and day of the month.

- **time**: The time of day, in hours, minutes, and seconds. A variant, **time**(p), can be used to specify the number of fractional digits for seconds (the default being 0). It is also possible to store time-zone information along with the time by specifying **time with timezone**.

- **timestamp**: A combination of **date** and **time**. A variant, **timestamp**(p), can be used to specify the number of fractional digits for seconds (the default here being 6). Time-zone information is also stored if **with timezone** is specified.

Date and time values can be specified like this:

> **date** '2001-04-25'
> **time** '09:30:00'
> **timestamp** '2001-04-25 10:29:01.45'

Dates must be specified in the format year followed by month followed by day, as shown. The seconds field of **time** or **timestamp** can have a fractional part, as in the timestamp above.

We can use an expression of the form **cast** e **as** t to convert a character string (or string valued expression) e to the type t, where t is one of **date, time**, or **timestamp**. The string must be in the appropriate format as illustrated at the beginning of this paragraph. When required, time-zone information is inferred from the system settings.

To extract individual fields of a **date** or **time** value d, we can use **extract** (*field* **from** d), where *field* can be one of **year, month, day, hour, minute**, or **second**. Time-zone information can be extracted using **timezone_hour** and **timezone_minute**.

SQL defines several functions to get the current date and time. For example, **current_date** returns the current date, **current_time** returns the current time (with time zone), and **localtime** returns the current local time (without time zone). Timestamps (date plus time) are returned by **current_timestamp** (with time zone) and **localtimestamp** (local date and time without time zone).

SQL allows comparison operations on all the types listed here, and it allows both arithmetic and comparison operations on the various numeric types. SQL also provides a data type called **interval**, and it allows computations based on dates and times and on intervals. For example, if x and y are of type **date**, then $x - y$ is an interval whose value is the number of days from date x to date y. Similarly, adding or subtracting an interval to a date or time gives back a date or time, respectively.

4.5.2 Default Values

SQL allows a default value to be specified for an attribute as illustrated by the following **create table** statement:

> **create table** *student*
>   (*ID*   **varchar** (5),
>   *name*   **varchar** (20) **not null**,
>   *dept_name*   **varchar** (20),
>   *tot_cred*   **numeric** (3,0) **default** 0,
>   **primary key** (*ID*));

The default value of the *tot_cred* attribute is declared to be 0. As a result, when a tuple is inserted into the *student* relation, if no value is provided for the *tot_cred* attribute, its value is set to 0. The following insert statement illustrates how an insertion can omit the value for the *tot_cred* attribute.

> **insert into** *student*(*ID*, *name*, *dept_name*)
>   **values** ('12789', 'Newman', 'Comp. Sci.');

4.5.3 Index Creation

Many queries reference only a small proportion of the records in a file. For example, a query like "Find all instructors in the Physics department" or "Find the *tot_cred* value of the student with *ID* 22201" references only a fraction of the student records. It is inefficient for the system to read every record and to check *ID* field for the *ID* "32556," or the *building* field for the value "Physics".

An **index** on an attribute of a relation is a data structure that allows the database system to find those tuples in the relation that have a specified value for that attribute efficiently, without scanning through all the tuples of the relation. For example, if we create in index on attribute *ID* of relation *student*, the database system can find the record with any specified *ID* value, such as 22201, or 44553, directly, without reading all the tuples of the *student* relation. An index can also be created on a list of attributes, for example on attributes *name*, and *dept_name* of *student*.

We study later, in Chapter 11, how indices are actually implemented, including a particularly widely used kind of index called a B^+-tree index.

Although the SQL language does not formally define any syntax for creating indices, many databases support index creation using the syntax illustrated below.

create index *studentID_index* **on** *student*(ID);

The above statement creates an index named *studentID_index* on the attribute *ID* of the relation *student*.

When a user submits an SQL query that can benefit from using an index, the SQL query processor automatically uses the index. For example, given an SQL query that selects the *student* tuple with *ID* 22201, the SQL query processor would use the index *studentID_index* defined above to find the required tuple without reading the whole relation.

4.5.4 Large-Object Types

Many current-generation database applications need to store attributes that can be large (of the order of many kilobytes), such as a photograph, or very large (of the order of many megabytes or even gigabytes), such as a high-resolution medical image or video clip. SQL therefore provides large-object data types for character data (**clob**) and binary data (**blob**). The letters "lob" in these data types stand for "Large OBject." For example, we may declare attributes

book_review **clob**(10KB)
image **blob**(10MB)
movie **blob**(2GB)

For result tuples containing large objects (multiple megabytes to gigabytes), it is inefficient or impractical to retrieve an entire large object into memory. Instead, an application would usually use an SQL query to retrieve a "locator" for a large object and then use the locator to manipulate the object from the host language in which the application itself is written. For instance, the JDBC application program interface (described in Section 5.1.1) permits a locator to be fetched instead of the entire large object; the locator can then be used to fetch the large object in small pieces, rather than all at once, much like reading data from an operating system file using a read function call.

4.5.5 User-Defined Types

SQL supports two forms of user-defined data types. The first form, which we cover here, is called **distinct types**. The other form, called **structured data types**, allows the creation of complex data types with nested record structures, arrays, and multisets. We do not cover structured data types in this chapter, but describe them later, in Chapter 22.

It is possible for several attributes to have the same data type. For example, the *name* attributes for student name and instructor name might have the same domain: the set of all person names. However, the domains of *budget* and *dept_name* certainly ought to be distinct. It is perhaps less clear whether *name* and *dept_name* should have the same domain. At the implementation level, both instructor names and department names are character strings. However, we would normally not consider the query "Find all instructors who have the same name as a department" to be a meaningful query. Thus, if we view the database at the conceptual, rather than the physical, level, *name* and *dept_name* should have distinct domains.

More importantly, at a practical level, assigning an instructor's name to a department name is probably a programming error; similarly, comparing a monetary value expressed in dollars directly with a monetary value expressed in pounds is also almost surely a programming error. A good type system should be able to detect such assignments or comparisons. To support such checks, SQL provides the notion of **distinct types**.

The **create type** clause can be used to define new types. For example, the statements:

$$\textbf{create type } Dollars \textbf{ as numeric}(12,2) \textbf{ final};$$
$$\textbf{create type } Pounds \textbf{ as numeric}(12,2) \textbf{ final};$$

define the user-defined types *Dollars* and *Pounds* to be decimal numbers with a total of 12 digits, two of which are placed after the decimal point. (The keyword **final** isn't really meaningful in this context but is required by the SQL:1999 standard for reasons we won't get into here; some implementations allow the **final** keyword to be omitted.) The newly created types can then be used, for example, as types of attributes of relations. For example, we can declare the *department* table as:

```
create table department
    (dept_name     varchar (20),
     building      varchar (15),
     budget        Dollars);
```

An attempt to assign a value of type *Dollars* to a variable of type *Pounds* results in a compile-time error, although both are of the same numeric type. Such an assignment is likely to be due to a programmer error, where the programmer forgot about the differences in currency. Declaring different types for different currencies helps catch such errors.

As a result of strong type checking, the expression (*department.budget*+20) would not be accepted since the attribute and the integer constant 20 have different types. Values of one type can be *cast* (that is, converted) to another domain, as illustrated below:

$$\textbf{cast } (department.budget \textbf{ to } numeric(12,2))$$

We could do addition on the numeric type, but to save the result back to an attribute of type *Dollars* we would have to use another cast expression to convert the type back to *Dollars*.

SQL provides **drop type** and **alter type** clauses to drop or modify types that have been created earlier.

Even before user-defined types were added to SQL (in SQL:1999), SQL had a similar but subtly different notion of **domain** (introduced in SQL-92), which can add integrity constraints to an underlying type. For example, we could define a domain *DDollars* as follows.

create domain *DDollars* **as numeric**(12,2) **not null;**

The domain *DDollars* can be used as an attribute type, just as we used the type *Dollars*. However, there are two significant differences between types and domains:

1. Domains can have constraints, such as **not null**, specified on them, and can have default values defined for variables of the domain type, whereas user-defined types cannot have constraints or default values specified on them. User-defined types are designed to be used not just for specifying attribute types, but also in procedural extensions to SQL where it may not be possible to enforce constraints.

2. Domains are not strongly typed. As a result, values of one domain type can be assigned to values of another domain type as long as the underlying types are compatible.

When applied to a domain, the **check** clause permits the schema designer to specify a predicate that must be satisfied by any attribute declared to be from this domain. For instance, a **check** clause can ensure that an instructor's salary domain allows only values greater than a specified value:

create domain *YearlySalary* **numeric**(8,2)
            constraint *salary_value_test* **check**(**value** $>=$ 29000.00);

The domain *YearlySalary* has a constraint that ensures that the YearlySalary is greater than or equal to $29,000.00. The clause **constraint** *salary_value_test* is optional, and is used to give the name *salary_value_test* to the constraint. The name is used by the system to indicate the constraint that an update violated.

As another example, a domain can be restricted to contain only a specified set of values by using the **in** clause:

create domain *degree_level* **varchar**(10)
        constraint *degree_level_test*
            check (**value in** ('Bachelors', 'Masters', or 'Doctorate'));

SUPPORT FOR TYPES AND DOMAINS IN DATABASE IMPLEMENTATIONS

Although the **create type** and **create domain** constructs described in this section are part of the SQL standard, the forms of these constructs described here are not fully supported by most database implementations. PostgreSQL supports the **create domain** construct, but its **create type** construct has a different syntax and interpretation.

IBM DB2 supports a version of the **create type** that uses the syntax **create distinct type**, but does not support **create domain**. Microsoft SQL Server implements a version of **create type** construct that supports domain constraints, similar to the SQL **create domain** construct.

Oracle does not support either construct as described here. However, SQL also defines a more complex object-oriented type system, which we study later in Chapter 22. Oracle, IBM DB2, PostgreSQL, and SQL Server all support object-oriented type systems using different forms of the **create type** construct.

4.5.6 Create Table Extensions

Applications often require creation of tables that have the same schema as an existing table. SQL provides a **create table like** extension to support this task:

create table *temp_instructor* **like** *instructor*;

The above statement creates a new table *temp_instructor* that has the same schema as *instructor*.

When writing a complex query, it is often useful to store the result of a query as a new table; the table is usually temporary. Two statements are required, one to create the table (with appropriate columns) and the second to insert the query result into the table. SQL:2003 provides a simpler technique to create a table containing the results of a query. For example the following statement creates a table *t1* containing the results of a query.

create table *t1* **as**
(**select** *
from *instructor*
where *dept_name*= 'Music')
with data;

By default, the names and data types of the columns are inferred from the query result. Names can be explicitly given to the columns by listing the column names after the relation name.

As defined by the SQL:2003 standard, if the **with data** clause is omitted, the table is created but not populated with data. However many implementations populate the table with data by default even if the **with data** clause is omitted.

Note that several implementations support the functionality of **create table** ...
like and **create table** ... **as** using different syntax; see the respective system
manuals for further details.

The above **create table** ... **as** statement closely resembles the **create view**
statement and both are defined by using queries. The main difference is that the
contents of the table are set when the table is created, whereas the contents of a
view always reflect the current query result.

4.5.7   Schemas, Catalogs, and Environments

To understand the motivation for schemas and catalogs, consider how files are
named in a file system. Early file systems were flat; that is, all files were stored
in a single directory. Current file systems, of course, have a directory (or, synonymously, folder) structure, with files stored within subdirectories. To name
a file uniquely, we must specify the full path name of the file, for example,
`/users/avi/db-book/chapter3.tex`.

Like early file systems, early database systems also had a single name space
for all relations. Users had to coordinate to make sure they did not try to use
the same name for different relations. Contemporary database systems provide a
three-level hierarchy for naming relations. The top level of the hierarchy consists
of **catalogs**, each of which can contain **schemas**. SQL objects such as relations and
views are contained within a **schema**. (Some database implementations use the
term "database" in place of the term catalog.)

In order to perform any actions on a database, a user (or a program) must
first *connect* to the database. The user must provide the user name and usually,
a password for verifying the identity of the user. Each user has a default catalog
and schema, and the combination is unique to the user. When a user connects to
a database system, the default catalog and schema are set up for the connection;
this corresponds to the current directory being set to the user's home directory
when the user logs into an operating system.

To identify a relation uniquely, a three-part name may be used, for example,

catalog5.univ_schema.course

We may omit the catalog component, in which case the catalog part of the name
is considered to be the default catalog for the connection. Thus if *catalog5* is
the default catalog, we can use *univ_schema.course* to identify the same relation
uniquely.

If a user wishes to access a relation that exists in a different schema than the
default schema for that user, the name of the schema must be specified. However,
if a relation is in the default schema for a particular user, then even the schema
name may be omitted. Thus we can use just *course* if the default catalog is *catalog5*
and the default schema is *univ_schema*.

With multiple catalogs and schemas available, different applications and
different users can work independently without worrying about name clashes.
Moreover, multiple versions of an application—one a production version, other
test versions—can run on the same database system.

The default catalog and schema are part of an **SQL environment** that is set up for each connection. The environment additionally contains the user identifier (also referred to as the *authorization identifier*). All the usual SQL statements, including the DDL and DML statements, operate in the context of a schema.

We can create and drop schemas by means of **create schema** and **drop schema** statements. In most database systems, schemas are also created automatically when user accounts are created, with the schema name set to the user account name. The schema is created in either a default catalog, or a catalog specified in creating the user account. The newly created schema becomes the default schema for the user account.

Creation and dropping of catalogs is implementation dependent and not part of the SQL standard.

4.6 Authorization

We may assign a user several forms of authorizations on parts of the database. Authorizations on data include:

- Authorization to read data.

- Authorization to insert new data.

- Authorization to update data.

- Authorization to delete data.

Each of these types of authorizations is called a **privilege**. We may authorize the user all, none, or a combination of these types of privileges on specified parts of a database, such as a relation or a view.

When a user submits a query or an update, the SQL implementation first checks if the query or update is authorized, based on the authorizations that the user has been granted. If the query or update is not authorized, it is rejected.

In addition to authorizations on data, users may also be granted authorizations on the database schema, allowing them, for example, to create, modify, or drop relations. A user who has some form of authorization may be allowed to pass on (grant) this authorization to other users, or to withdraw (revoke) an authorization that was granted earlier. In this section, we see how each of these authorizations can be specified in SQL.

The ultimate form of authority is that given to the database administrator. The database administrator may authorize new users, restructure the database, and so on. This form of authorization is analogous to that of a **superuser**, administrator, or operator for an operating system.

4.6.1 Granting and Revoking of Privileges

The SQL standard includes the privileges **select**, **insert**, **update**, and **delete**. The privilege **all privileges** can be used as a short form for all the allowable privileges. A user who creates a new relation is given all privileges on that relation automatically.

The SQL data-definition language includes commands to grant and revoke privileges. The **grant** statement is used to confer authorization. The basic form of this statement is:

grant <privilege list>
on <relation name or view name>
to <user/role list>;

The *privilege list* allows the granting of several privileges in one command. The notion of roles is covered later, in Section 4.6.2.

The **select** authorization on a relation is required to read tuples in the relation. The following **grant** statement grants database users Amit and Satoshi **select** authorization on the *department* relation:

grant select on *department* **to** *Amit, Satoshi;*

This allows those users to run queries on the *department* relation.

The **update** authorization on a relation allows a user to update any tuple in the relation. The **update** authorization may be given either on all attributes of the relation or on only some. If **update** authorization is included in a **grant** statement, the list of attributes on which update authorization is to be granted optionally appears in parentheses immediately after the **update** keyword. If the list of attributes is omitted, the update privilege will be granted on all attributes of the relation.

This **grant** statement gives users Amit and Satoshi update authorization on the *budget* attribute of the *department* relation:

grant update (*budget*) **on** *department* **to** *Amit, Satoshi;*

The **insert** authorization on a relation allows a user to insert tuples into the relation. The **insert** privilege may also specify a list of attributes; any inserts to the relation must specify only these attributes, and the system either gives each of the remaining attributes default values (if a default is defined for the attribute) or sets them to *null.*

The **delete** authorization on a relation allows a user to delete tuples from a relation.

The user name **public** refers to all current and future users of the system. Thus, privileges granted to **public** are implicitly granted to all current and future users.

By default, a user/role that is granted a privilege is not authorized to grant that privilege to another user/role. SQL allows a privilege grant to specify that the recipient may further grant the privilege to another user. We describe this feature in more detail in Section 4.6.5.

It is worth noting that the SQL authorization mechanism grants privileges on an entire relation, or on specified attributes of a relation. However, it does not permit authorizations on specific tuples of a relation.

To revoke an authorization, we use the **revoke** statement. It takes a form almost identical to that of **grant**:

> **revoke** <privilege list>
> **on** <relation name or view name>
> **from** <user/role list>;

Thus, to revoke the privileges that we granted previously, we write

> **revoke select on** *department* **from** *Amit, Satoshi*;
> **revoke update** (budget) **on** *department* **from** *Amit, Satoshi*;

Revocation of privileges is more complex if the user from whom the privilege is revoked has granted the privilege to another user. We return to this issue in Section 4.6.5.

4.6.2 Roles

Consider the real-world roles of various people in a university. Each instructor must have the same types of authorizations on the same set of relations. Whenever a new instructor is appointed, she will have to be given all these authorizations individually.

A better approach would be to specify the authorizations that every instructor is to be given, and to identify separately which database users are instructors. The system can use these two pieces of information to determine the authorizations of each instructor. When a new instructor is hired, a user identifier must be allocated to him, and he must be identified as an instructor. Individual permissions given to instructors need not be specified again.

The notion of **roles** captures this concept. A set of roles is created in the database. Authorizations can be granted to roles, in exactly the same fashion as they are granted to individual users. Each database user is granted a set of roles (which may be empty) that she is authorized to perform.

In our university database, examples of roles could include *instructor, teaching_assistant, student, dean*, and *department_chair*.

A less preferable alternative would be to create an *instructor* userid, and permit each instructor to connect to the database using the *instructor* userid. The problem with this approach is that it would not be possible to identify exactly which instructor carried out a database update, leading to security risks. The use of roles has the benefit of requiring users to connect to the database with their own userid.

Any authorization that can be granted to a user can be granted to a role. Roles are granted to users just as authorizations are.

Roles can be created in SQL as follows:

create role *instructor*;

Roles can then be granted privileges just as the users can, as illustrated in this statement:

grant select on *takes*
to *instructor*;

Roles can be granted to users, as well as to other roles, as these statements show:

grant *dean* **to** Amit;
create role *dean*;
grant *instructor* **to** *dean*;
grant *dean* **to** Satoshi;

Thus the privileges of a user or a role consist of:

- All privileges directly granted to the user/role.
- All privileges granted to roles that have been granted to the user/role.

Note that there can be a chain of roles; for example, the role *teaching_assistant* may be granted to all *instructors*. In turn the role *instructor* is granted to all *deans*. Thus, the *dean* role inherits all privileges granted to the roles *instructor* and to *teaching_assistant* in addition to privileges granted directly to *dean*.

When a user logs in to the database system, the actions executed by the user during that session have all the privileges granted directly to the user, as well as all privileges granted to roles that are granted (directly or indirectly via other roles) to that user. Thus, if a user Amit has been granted the role *dean*, user Amit holds all privileges granted directly to Amit, as well as privileges granted to *dean*, plus privileges granted to *instructor*, and *teaching_assistant* if, as above, those roles were granted (directly or indirectly) to the role *dean*.

It is worth noting that the concept of role-based authorization is not specific to SQL, and role-based authorization is used for access control in a wide variety of shared applications.

4.6.3 Authorization on Views

In our university example, consider a staff member who needs to know the salaries of all faculty in a particular department, say the Geology department. This staff member is not authorized to see information regarding faculty in other departments. Thus, the staff member must be denied direct access to the *instructor* relation. But, if he is to have access to the information for the Geology department, he might be granted access to a view that we shall call *geo_instructor*, consisting of only those *instructor* tuples pertaining to the Geology department. This view can be defined in SQL as follows:

create view *geo_instructor* **as**
(**select** *
from *instructor*
where *dept_name* = 'Geology');

Suppose that the staff member issues the following SQL query:

select *
from *geo_instructor*;

Clearly, the staff member is authorized to see the result of this query. However, when the query processor translates it into a query on the actual relations in the database, it produces a query on *instructor*. Thus, the system must check authorization on the clerk's query before it begins query processing.

A user who creates a view does not necessarily receive all privileges on that view. She receives only those privileges that provide no additional authorization beyond those that she already had. For example, a user who creates a view cannot be given **update** authorization on a view without having **update** authorization on the relations used to define the view. If a user creates a view on which no authorization can be granted, the system will deny the view creation request. In our *geo_instructor* view example, the creator of the view must have **select** authorization on the *instructor* relation.

As we will see later, in Section 5.2, SQL supports the creation of functions and procedures, which may in turn contain queries and updates. The **execute** privilege can be granted on a function or procedure, enabling a user to execute the function/procedure. By default, just like views, functions and procedures have all the privileges that the creator of the function or procedure had. In effect, the function or procedure runs as if it were invoked by the user who created the function.

Although this behavior is appropriate in many situations, it is not always appropriate. Starting with SQL:2003, if the function definition has an extra clause **sql security invoker**, then it is executed under the privileges of the user who invokes the function, rather than the privileges of the **definer** of the function. This allows the creation of libraries of functions that can run under the same authorization as the invoker.

4.6.4 Authorizations on Schema

The SQL standard specifies a primitive authorization mechanism for the database schema: Only the owner of the schema can carry out any modification to the schema, such as creating or deleting relations, adding or dropping attributes of relations, and adding or dropping indices.

However, SQL includes a **references** privilege that permits a user to declare foreign keys when creating relations. The SQL **references** privilege is granted on specific attributes in a manner like that for the **update** privilege. The following **grant** statement allows user Mariano to create relations that reference the key *branch_name* of the *branch* relation as a foreign key:

grant references (*dept_name*) **on** *department* **to** Mariano;

Initially, it may appear that there is no reason ever to prevent users from creating foreign keys referencing another relation. However, recall that foreign-key constraints restrict deletion and update operations on the referenced relation. Suppose Mariano creates a foreign key in a relation *r* referencing the *dept_name* attribute of the *department* relation and then inserts a tuple into *r* pertaining to the Geology department. It is no longer possible to delete the Geology department from the *department* relation without also modifying relation *r*. Thus, the definition of a foreign key by Mariano restricts future activity by other users; therefore, there is a need for the **references** privilege.

Continuing to use the example of the *department* relation, the references privilege on *department* is also required to create a **check** constraint on a relation *r* if the constraint has a subquery referencing *department*. This is reasonable for the same reason as the one we gave for foreign-key constraints; a check constraint that references a relation limits potential updates to that relation.

4.6.5 Transfer of Privileges

A user who has been granted some form of authorization may be allowed to pass on this authorization to other users. By default, a user/role that is granted a privilege is not authorized to grant that privilege to another user/role. If we wish to grant a privilege and to allow the recipient to pass the privilege on to other users, we append the **with grant option** clause to the appropriate **grant** command. For example, if we wish to allow Amit the **select** privilege on *department* and allow Amit to grant this privilege to others, we write:

grant select on *department* **to** Amit **with grant option**;

The creator of an object (relation/view/role) holds all privileges on the object, including the privilege to grant privileges to others.

Consider, as an example, the granting of update authorization on the *teaches* relation of the university database. Assume that, initially, the database administrator grants update authorization on *teaches* to users U_1, U_2, and U_3, who may in turn pass on this authorization to other users. The passing of a specific authorization from one user to another can be represented by an **authorization graph**. The nodes of this graph are the users.

Consider the graph for update authorization on *teaches*. The graph includes an edge $U_i \rightarrow U_j$ if user U_i grants update authorization on *teaches* to U_j. The root of the graph is the database administrator. In the sample graph in Figure 4.10,

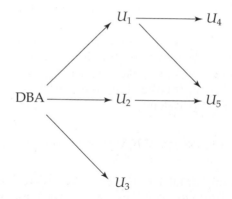

Figure 4.10 Authorization-grant graph ($U_1, U_2, \ldots, U_5$ are users and DBA refers to the database administrator).

observe that user U_5 is granted authorization by both U_1 and U_2; U_4 is granted authorization by only U_1.

A user has an authorization *if and only if* there is a path from the root of the authorization graph (the node representing the database administrator) down to the node representing the user.

4.6.6 Revoking of Privileges

Suppose that the database administrator decides to revoke the authorization of user U_1. Since U_4 has authorization from U_1, that authorization should be revoked as well. However, U_5 was granted authorization by both U_1 and U_2. Since the database administrator did not revoke update authorization on *teaches* from U_2, U_5 retains update authorization on *teaches*. If U_2 eventually revokes authorization from U_5, then U_5 loses the authorization.

A pair of devious users might attempt to defeat the rules for revocation of authorization by granting authorization to each other. For example, if U_2 is initially granted an authorization by the database administrator, and U_2 further grants it to U_3. Suppose U_3 now grants the privilege back to U_2. If the database administrator revokes authorization from U_2, it might appear that U_2 retains authorization through U_3. However, note that once the administrator revokes authorization from U_2, there is no path in the authorization graph from the root to either U_2 or to U_3. Thus, SQL ensures that the authorization is revoked from both the users.

As we just saw, revocation of a privilege from a user/role may cause other users/roles also to lose that privilege. This behavior is called *cascading revocation*. In most database systems, cascading is the default behavior. However, the **revoke** statement may specify **restrict** in order to prevent cascading revocation:

revoke select on *department* **from** Amit, Satoshi **restrict;**

In this case, the system returns an error if there are any cascading revocations, and does not carry out the revoke action.

The keyword **cascade** can be used instead of **restrict** to indicate that revocation should cascade; however, it can be omitted, as we have done in the preceding examples, since it is the default behavior.

The following **revoke** statement revokes only the grant option, rather than the actual **select** privilege:

revoke grant option for select on *department* **from** Amit;

Note that some database implementations do not support the above syntax; instead, the privilege itself can be revoked, and then granted again without the grant option.

Cascading revocation is inappropriate in many situations. Suppose Satoshi has the role of *dean*, grants *instructor* to Amit, and later the role *dean* is revoked from Satoshi (perhaps because Satoshi leaves the university); Amit continues to be employed on the faculty, and should retain the *instructor* role.

To deal with the above situation, SQL permits a privilege to be granted by a role rather than by a user. SQL has a notion of the current role associated with a session. By default, the current role associated with a session is null (except in some special cases). The current role associated with a session can be set by executing **set role** *role_name*. The specified role must have been granted to the user, else the **set role** statement fails.

To grant a privilege with the grantor set to the current role associated with a session, we can add the clause:

granted by current_role

to the grant statement, provided the current role is not null.

Suppose the granting of the role *instructor* (or other privileges) to Amit is done using the **granted by current_role** clause, with the current role set to *dean*), instead of the grantor being the user Satoshi. Then, revoking of roles/privileges (including the role *dean*) from Satoshi will not result in revoking of privileges that had the grantor set to the role *dean*, even if Satoshi was the user who executed the grant; thus, Amit would retain the *instructor* role even after Satoshi's privileges are revoked.

4.7   Summary

- SQL supports several types of joins including inner and outer joins and several types of join conditions.

- View relations can be defined as relations containing the result of queries. Views are useful for hiding unneeded information, and for collecting together information from more than one relation into a single view.

- Transactions are a sequence of queries and updates that together carry out a task. Transactions can be committed, or rolled back; when a transaction is rolled back, the effects of all updates performed by the transaction are undone.

- Integrity constraints ensure that changes made to the database by authorized users do not result in a loss of data consistency.

- Referential-integrity constraints ensure that a value that appears in one relation for a given set of attributes also appears for a certain set of attributes in another relation.

- Domain constraints specify the set of possible values that may be associated with an attribute. Such constraints may also prohibit the use of null values for particular attributes.

- Assertions are declarative expressions that state predicates that we require always to be true.

- The SQL data-definition language provides support for defining built-in domain types such as **date** and **time**, as well as user-defined domain types.

- SQL authorization mechanisms allow one to differentiate among the users of the database as far as the type of access they are permitted on various data values in the database.

- A user who has been granted some form of authority may be allowed to pass on this authority to other users. However, we must be careful about how authorization can be passed among users if we are to ensure that such authorization can be revoked at some future time.

- Roles help to assign a set of privileges to a user according to the role that the user plays in the organization.

Review Terms

- Join types
  - Inner and outer join
  - Left, right and full outer join
  - Natural, using, and on
- View definition
- Materialized views
- View update
- Transactions
  - Commit work
  - Rollback work
  - Atomic transaction
- Integrity constraints
- Domain constraints
- Unique constraint
- Check clause
- Referential integrity
  - Cascading deletes
  - Cascading updates

- Assertions
- Date and time types
- Default values
- Indices
- Large objects
- User-defined types
- Domains
- Catalogs
- Schemas
- Authorization
- Privileges
    - **select**
    - **insert**

  - **update**
  - **all privileges**
  - Granting of privileges
  - Revoking of privileges
  - Privilege to grant privileges
  - Grant option
- Roles
- Authorization on views
- Execute authorization
- Invoker privileges
- Row-level authorization

Practice Exercises

4.1 Write the following queries in SQL:

a. Display a list of all instructors, showing their ID, name, and the number of sections that they have taught. Make sure to show the number of sections as 0 for instructors who have not taught any section. Your query should use an outerjoin, and should not use scalar subqueries.

b. Write the same query as above, but using a scalar subquery, without outerjoin.

c. Display the list of all course sections offered in Spring 2010, along with the names of the instructors teaching the section. If a section has more than one instructor, it should appear as many times in the result as it has instructors. If it does not have any instructor, it should still appear in the result with the instructor name set to "—".

d. Display the list of all departments, with the total number of instructors in each department, without using scalar subqueries. Make sure to correctly handle departments with no instructors.

4.2 Outer join expressions can be computed in SQL without using the SQL **outer join** operation. To illustrate this fact, show how to rewrite each of the following SQL queries without using the **outer join** expression.

a. **select** * **from** *student* **natural left outer join** *takes*

b. **select** * **from** *student* **natural full outer join** *takes*

4.3 Suppose we have three relations $r(A, B)$, $s(B, C)$, and $t(B, D)$, with all attributes declared as **not null**. Consider the expressions

- r **natural left outer join** (s **natural left outer join** t), and

- (r **natural left outer join** s) **natural left outer join** t

a. Give instances of relations r, s and t such that in the result of the second expression, attribute C has a null value but attribute D has a non-null value.

b. Is the above pattern, with C null and D not null possible in the result of the first expression? Explain why or why not.

4.4 **Testing SQL queries**: To test if a query specified in English has been correctly written in SQL, the SQL query is typically executed on multiple test databases, and a human checks if the SQL query result on each test database matches the intention of the specification in English.

a. In Section 3.3.3 we saw an example of an erroneous SQL query which was intended to find which courses had been taught by each instructor; the query computed the natural join of *instructor*, *teaches*, and *course*, and as a result unintentionally equated the *dept_name* attribute of *instructor* and *course*. Give an example of a dataset that would help catch this particular error.

b. When creating test databases, it is important to create tuples in referenced relations that do not have any matching tuple in the referencing relation, for each foreign key. Explain why, using an example query on the university database.

c. When creating test databases, it is important to create tuples with null values for foreign key attributes, provided the attribute is nullable (SQL allows foreign key attributes to take on null values, as long as they are not part of the primary key, and have not been declared as **not null**). Explain why, using an example query on the university database.

Hint: use the queries from Exercise 4.1.

4.5 Show how to define the view *student_grades* (ID, GPA) giving the grade-point average of each student, based on the query in Exercise 3.2; recall that we used a relation *grade_points*(grade, points) to get the numeric points associated with a letter grade. Make sure your view definition correctly handles the case of *null* values for the *grade* attribute of the *takes* relation.

4.6 Complete the SQL DDL definition of the university database of Figure 4.8 to include the relations *student*, *takes*, *advisor*, and *prereq*.

$$employee\ (\underline{employee\_name},\ street,\ city)$$
$$works\ (\underline{employee\_name},\ company\_name,\ salary)$$
$$company\ (\underline{company\_name},\ city)$$
$$manages\ (\underline{employee\_name},\ manager\_name)$$

Figure 4.11   Employee database for Figure 4.7 and 4.12.

4.7   Consider the relational database of Figure 4.11. Give an SQL DDL definition of this database. Identify referential-integrity constraints that should hold, and include them in the DDL definition.

4.8   As discussed in Section 4.4.7, we expect the constraint "an instructor cannot teach sections in two different classrooms in a semester in the same time slot" to hold.

   a.   Write an SQL query that returns all (*instructor*, *section*) combinations that violate this constraint.

   b.   Write an SQL assertion to enforce this constraint (as discussed in Section 4.4.7, current generation database systems do not support such assertions, although they are part of the SQL standard).

4.9   SQL allows a foreign-key dependency to refer to the same relation, as in the following example:

> **create table** *manager*
>   (*employee_name*   **varchar**(20) **not null**
>   *manager_name*   **varchar**(20) **not null**,
>   **primary key** *employee_name*,
>   **foreign key** (*manager_name*) **references** *manager*
>   **on delete cascade**)

Here, *employee_name* is a key to the table *manager*, meaning that each employee has at most one manager. The foreign-key clause requires that every manager also be an employee. Explain exactly what happens when a tuple in the relation *manager* is deleted.

4.10   SQL provides an *n*-ary operation called **coalesce**, which is defined as follows: **coalesce**$(A_1, A_2, \ldots, A_n)$ returns the first nonnull A_i in the list $A_1, A_2, \ldots, A_n$, and returns *null* if all of $A_1, A_2, \ldots, A_n$ are *null*.

Let *a* and *b* be relations with the schemas A(*name, address, title*), and B(*name, address, salary*), respectively. Show how to express *a* **natural full outer join** *b* using the **full outer-join** operation with an **on** condition and the **coalesce** operation. Make sure that the result relation does not contain two copies of the attributes *name* and *address*, and that the solution is correct even if some tuples in *a* and *b* have null values for attributes *name* or *address*.

salaried_worker (*name, office, phone, salary*)
hourly_worker (*name, hourly_wage*)
address (*name, street, city*)

Figure 4.12   Employee database for Exercise 4.16.

4.11   Some researchers have proposed the concept of *marked* nulls. A marked null $\perp_i$ is equal to itself, but if $i \neq j$, then $\perp_i \neq \perp_j$. One application of marked nulls is to allow certain updates through views. Consider the view *instructor_info* (Section 4.2). Show how you can use marked nulls to allow the insertion of the tuple (99999, "Johnson", "Music") through *instructor _info*.

Exercises

4.12   For the database of Figure 4.11, write a query to find those employees with no manager. Note that an employee may simply have no manager listed or may have a *null* manager. Write your query using an outer join and then write it again using no outer join at all.

4.13   Under what circumstances would the query

   select *
   from *student* **natural full outer join** *takes* **natural full outer join** *course*

   include tuples with null values for the *title* attribute?

4.14   Show how to define a view *tot_credits* (*year, num_credits*), giving the total number of credits taken by students in each year.

4.15   Show how to express the **coalesce** operation from Exercise 4.10 using the **case** operation.

4.16   Referential-integrity constraints as defined in this chapter involve exactly two relations. Consider a database that includes the relations shown in Figure 4.12. Suppose that we wish to require that every name that appears in *address* appears in either *salaried_worker* or *hourly_worker*, but not necessarily in both.

   a.   Propose a syntax for expressing such constraints.

   b.   Discuss the actions that the system must take to enforce a constraint of this form.

4.17   Explain why, when a manager, say Satoshi, grants an authorization, the grant should be done by the manager role, rather than by the user Satoshi.

4.18   Suppose user A, who has all authorizations on a relation r, grants select on relation r to **public** with grant option. Suppose user B then grants select on r to A. Does this cause a cycle in the authorization graph? Explain why.

4.19   Database systems that store each relation in a separate operating-system file may use the operating system's authorization scheme, instead of defining a special scheme themselves. Discuss an advantage and a disadvantage of such an approach.

Bibliographical Notes

See the bibliographic notes of Chapter 3 for SQL reference material.

The rules used by SQL to determine the updatability of a view, and how updates are reflected on the underlying database relations, are defined by the SQL:1999 standard, and are summarized in Melton and Simon [2001].

CHAPTER 5

Advanced SQL

In Chapters 3 and 4, we provided detailed coverage of the basic structure of SQL. In this chapter, we cover some of the more advanced features of SQL.[1] We address the issue of how to access SQL from a general-purpose programming language, which is very important for building applications that use a database to store and retrieve data. We describe how procedural code can be executed within the database, either by extending the SQL language to support procedural actions, or by allowing functions defined in procedural languages to be executed within the database. We describe triggers, which can be used to specify actions that are to be carried out automatically on certain events such as insertion, deletion, or update of tuples in a specified relation. We discuss recursive queries and advanced aggregation features supported by SQL. Finally, we describe online analytic processing (OLAP) systems, which support interactive analysis of very large datasets.

5.1   Accessing SQL From a Programming Language

SQL provides a powerful declarative query language. Writing queries in SQL is usually much easier than coding the same queries in a general-purpose programming language. However, a database programmer must have access to a general-purpose programming language for at least two reasons:

1. Not all queries can be expressed in SQL, since SQL does not provide the full expressive power of a general-purpose language. That is, there exist queries that can be expressed in a language such as C, Java, or Cobol that cannot be expressed in SQL. To write such queries, we can embed SQL within a more powerful language.

---

[1]**Note regarding chapter and section sequencing:** Database design—Chapters 7 and 8—can be studied independently of the material in this chapter. It is quite possible to study database design first, and study this chapter later. However, for courses with a programming emphasis, a richer variety of laboratory exercises is possible after studying Section 5.1, and we recommend that it be covered before database design for such courses.

2. Nondeclarative actions—such as printing a report, interacting with a user, or sending the results of a query to a graphical user interface—cannot be done from within SQL. Applications usually have several components, and querying or updating data is only one component; other components are written in general-purpose programming languages. For an integrated application, there must be a means to combine SQL with a general-purpose programming language.

There are two approaches to accessing SQL from a general-purpose programming language:

- **Dynamic SQL**: A general-purpose program can connect to and communicate with a database server using a collection of functions (for procedural languages) or methods (for object-oriented languages). Dynamic SQL allows the program to construct an SQL query as a character string at runtime, submit the query, and then retrieve the result into program variables a tuple at a time. The *dynamic SQL* component of SQL allows programs to construct and submit SQL queries at runtime.

  In this chapter, we look at two standards for connecting to an SQL database and performing queries and updates. One, JDBC (Section 5.1.1), is an application program interface for the Java language. The other, ODBC (Section 5.1.2), is an application program interface originally developed for the C language, and subsequently extended to other languages such as C++, C#, and Visual Basic.

- **Embedded SQL**: Like dynamic SQL, embedded SQL provides a means by which a program can interact with a database server. However, under embedded SQL, the SQL statements are identified at compile time using a preprocessor. The preprocessor submits the SQL statements to the database system for precompilation and optimization; then it replaces the SQL statements in the application program with appropriate code and function calls before invoking the programming-language compiler. Section 5.1.3 covers embedded SQL.

A major challenge in mixing SQL with a general-purpose language is the mismatch in the ways these languages manipulate data. In SQL, the primary type of data is the relation. SQL statements operate on relations and return relations as a result. Programming languages normally operate on a variable at a time, and those variables correspond roughly to the value of an attribute in a tuple in a relation. Thus, integrating these two types of languages into a single application requires providing a mechanism to return the result of a query in a manner that the program can handle.

5.1.1   JDBC

The **JDBC** standard defines an **application program interface (API)** that Java programs can use to connect to database servers. (The word JDBC was originally

```
public static void JDBCexample(String userid, String passwd)
{
    try
    {
        Class.forName ("oracle.jdbc.driver.OracleDriver");
        Connection conn = DriverManager.getConnection(
                "jdbc:oracle:thin:@db.yale.edu:1521:univdb",
                userid, passwd);
        Statement stmt = conn.createStatement();
        try {
            stmt.executeUpdate(
                "insert into instructor values('77987', 'Kim', 'Physics', 98000)");
        } catch (SQLException sqle)
        {
            System.out.println("Could not insert tuple. " + sqle);
        }
        ResultSet rset = stmt.executeQuery(
                "select dept_name, avg (salary) "+
                " from instructor "+
                " group by dept_name");
        while (rset.next()) {
            System.out.println(rset.getString("dept_name") + " " +
                    rset.getFloat(2));
        }
        stmt.close();
        conn.close();
    }
    catch (Exception sqle)
    {
        System.out.println("Exception : " + sqle);
    }
}
```

Figure 5.1   An example of JDBC code.

an abbreviation for **Java Database Connectivity**, but the full form is no longer used.)

Figure 5.1 shows an example Java program that uses the JDBC interface. It illustrates how connections are opened, how statements are executed and results processed, and how connections are closed. We discuss this example in detail in this section. The Java program must import java.sql.*, which contains the interface definitions for the functionality provided by JDBC.

5.1.1.1   Connecting to the Database

The first step in accessing a database from a Java program is to open a connection to the database. This step is required to select which database to use, for example, an instance of Oracle running on your machine, or a PostgreSQL database running on another machine. Only after opening a connection can a Java program execute SQL statements.

A connection is opened using the getConnection method of the Driver-Manager class (within java.sql). This method takes three parameters.[2]

- The first parameter to the getConnection call is a string that specifies the URL, or machine name, where the server runs (in our example, db.yale.edu), along with possibly some other information such as the protocol to be used to communicate with the database (in our example, jdbc:oracle:thin:; we shall shortly see why this is required), the port number the database system uses for communication (in our example, 2000), and the specific database on the server to be used (in our example, univdb). Note that JDBC specifies only the API, not the communication protocol. A JDBC driver may support multiple protocols, and we must specify one supported by both the database and the driver. The protocol details are vendor specific.

- The second parameter to getConnection is a database user identifier, which is a string.

- The third parameter is a password, which is also a string. (Note that the need to specify a password within the JDBC code presents a security risk if an unauthorized person accesses your Java code.)

In our example in the figure, we have created a Connection object whose handle is conn.

Each database product that supports JDBC (all the major database vendors do) provides a JDBC driver that must be dynamically loaded in order to access the database from Java. In fact, loading the driver must be done first, before connecting to the database.

This is done by invoking Class.forName with one argument specifying a concrete class implementing the java.sql.Driver interface, in the first line of the program in Figure 5.1. This interface provides for the translation of product-independent JDBC calls into the product-specific calls needed by the specific database management system being used. The example in the figure shows the Oracle driver, oracle.jdbc.driver.OracleDriver.[3] The driver is available in a .jar file at vendor Web sites and should be placed within the classpath so that the Java compiler can access it.

The actual protocol used to exchange information with the database depends on the driver that is used, and is not defined by the JDBC standard. Some

---

[2]There are multiple versions of the getConnection method, which differ in the parameters that they accept. We present the most commonly used version.
[3]The equivalent driver names for other products are as follows: IBM DB2: com.ibm.db2.jdbc.app.DB2Driver; Microsoft SQL Server: com.microsoft.sqlserver.jdbc.SQLServerDriver; PostgreSQL: org.postgresql.Driver; and MySQL: com.mysql.jdbc.Driver. Sun also offers a "bridge driver" that converts JDBC calls to ODBC. This should be used only for vendors that support ODBC but not JDBC.

drivers support more than one protocol, and a suitable protocol must be chosen depending on what protocol the database that you are connecting to supports. In our example, when opening a connection with the database, the string `jdbc:oracle:thin:` specifies a particular protocol supported by Oracle.

5.1.1.2 Shipping SQL Statements to the Database System

Once a database connection is open, the program can use it to send SQL statements to the database system for execution. This is done via an instance of the class `Statement`. A `Statement` object is not the SQL statement itself, but rather an object that allows the Java program to invoke methods that ship an SQL statement given as an argument for execution by the database system. Our example creates a `Statement` handle (`stmt`) on the connection `conn`.

To execute a statement, we invoke either the `executeQuery` method or the `executeUpdate` method, depending on whether the SQL statement is a query (and, thus, returns a result set) or nonquery statement such as **update**, **insert**, **delete**, **create table**, etc. In our example, `stmt.executeUpdate` executes an update statement that inserts into the *instructor* relation. It returns an integer giving the number of tuples inserted, updated, or deleted. For DDL statements, the return value is zero. The `try { ... } catch { ... }` construct permits us to catch any exceptions (error conditions) that arise when JDBC calls are made, and print an appropriate message to the user.

5.1.1.3 Retrieving the Result of a Query

The example program executes a query by using `stmt.executeQuery`. It retrieves the set of tuples in the result into a `ResultSet` object `rset` and fetches them one tuple at a time. The `next` method on the result set tests whether or not there remains at least one unfetched tuple in the result set and if so, fetches it. The return value of the `next` method is a Boolean indicating whether it fetched a tuple. Attributes from the fetched tuple are retrieved using various methods whose names begin with `get`. The method `getString` can retrieve any of the basic SQL data types (converting the value to a Java String object), but more restrictive methods such as `getFloat` can be used as well. The argument to the various get methods can either be an attribute name specified as a string, or an integer indicating the position of the desired attribute within the tuple. Figure 5.1 shows two ways of retrieving the values of attributes in a tuple: using the name of the attribute (*dept_name*) and using the position of the attribute (2, to denote the second attribute).

The statement and connection are both closed at the end of the Java program. Note that it is important to close the connection because there is a limit imposed on the number of connections to the database; unclosed connections may cause that limit to be exceeded. If this happens, the application cannot open any more connections to the database.

```
PreparedStatement pStmt = conn.prepareStatement(
            "insert into instructor values(?,?,?,?)");
pStmt.setString(1, "88877");
pStmt.setString(2, "Perry");
pStmt.setString(3, "Finance");
pStmt.setInt(4, 125000);
pStmt.executeUpdate();
pStmt.setString(1, "88878");
pStmt.executeUpdate();
```

Figure 5.2 Prepared statements in JDBC code.

5.1.1.4   Prepared Statements

We can create a prepared statement in which some values are replaced by "?", thereby specifying that actual values will be provided later. The database system compiles the query when it is prepared. Each time the query is executed (with new values to replace the "?"s), the database system can reuse the previously compiled form of the query and apply the new values. The code fragment in Figure 5.2 shows how prepared statements can be used.

The prepareStatement method of the Connection class submits an SQL statement for compilation. It returns an object of class PreparedStatement. At this point, no SQL statement has been executed. The executeQuery and executeUpdate methods of PreparedStatement class do that. But before they can be invoked, we must use methods of class PreparedStatement that assign values for the "?" parameters. The setString method and other similar methods such as setInt for other basic SQL types allow us to specify the values for the parameters. The first argument specifies the "?" parameter for which we are assigning a value (the first parameter is 1, unlike most other Java constructs, which start with 0). The second argument specifies the value to be assigned.

In the example in the figure, we prepare an **insert** statement, set the "?" parameters, and then invoke executeUpdate. The final two lines of our example show that parameter assignments remain unchanged until we specifically reassign them. Thus, the final statement, which invokes executeUpdate, inserts the tuple ("88878", "Perry", "Finance", 125000).

Prepared statements allow for more efficient execution in cases where the same query can be compiled once and then run multiple times with different parameter values. However, there is an even more significant advantage to prepared statements that makes them the preferred method of executing SQL queries whenever a user-entered value is used, even if the query is to be run only once. Suppose that we read in a user-entered value and then use Java string manipulation to construct the SQL statement. If the user enters certain special characters, such as a single quote, the resulting SQL statement may be syntactically incorrect unless we take extraordinary care in checking the input. The setString method does this for us automatically and inserts the needed escape characters to ensure syntactic correctness.

In our example, suppose that the values for the variables *ID*, *name*, *dept_name*, and *salary* have been entered by a user, and a corresponding row is to be inserted into the *instructor* relation. Suppose that, instead of using a prepared statement, a query is constructed by concatenating the strings using the following Java expression:

"insert into instructor values(' " + ID + " ',' " + name + " ', " +
" ' + dept_name + " ', " ' balance + ")"

and the query is executed directly using the executeQuery method of a Statement object. Now, if the user typed a single quote in the ID or name fields, the query string would have a syntax error. It is quite possible that an instructor name may have a quotation mark in its name (for example, "O'Henry").

While the above example might be considered an annoyance, the situation can be much worse. A technique called **SQL injection** can be used by malicious hackers to steal data or damage the database.

Suppose a Java program inputs a string *name* and constructs the query:

"select * from instructor where name = '" + name + "'"

If the user, instead of entering a name, enters:

X' or 'Y' = 'Y

then the resulting statement becomes:

"select * from instructor where name = '" + "X' or 'Y' = 'Y" + "'"

which is:

select * from instructor where name = 'X' or 'Y' = 'Y'

In the resulting query, the **where** clause is always true and the entire instructor relation is returned. More clever malicious users could arrange to output even more data. Use of a prepared statement would prevent this problem because the input string would have escape characters inserted, so the resulting query becomes:

"select * from instructor where name = 'X\' or \'Y\' = \'Y'

which is harmless and returns the empty relation.

Older systems allow multiple statements to be executed in a single call, with statements separated by a semicolon. This feature is being eliminated because the SQL injection technique was used by malicious hackers to insert whole SQL statements. Because these statements run with the privileges of the owner of the

Java program, devastating SQL statements such as **drop table** could be executed. Developers of SQL applications need to be wary of such potential security holes.

5.1.1.5   Callable Statements

JDBC also provides a `CallableStatement` interface that allows invocation of SQL stored procedures and functions (described later, in Section 5.2). These play the same role for functions and procedures as `prepareStatement` does for queries.

```
CallableStatement cStmt1 = conn.prepareCall("{? = call some_function(?)}");
CallableStatement cStmt2 = conn.prepareCall("{call some_procedure(?,?)}");
```

The data types of function return values and out parameters of procedures must be registered using the method `registerOutParameter()`, and can be retrieved using get methods similar to those for result sets. See a JDBC manual for more details.

5.1.1.6   Metadata Features

As we noted earlier, a Java application program does not include declarations for data stored in the database. Those declarations are part of the SQL DDL statements. Therefore, a Java program that uses JDBC must either have assumptions about the database schema hard-coded into the program or determine that information directly from the database system at runtime. The latter approach is usually preferable, since it makes the application program more robust to changes in the database schema.

Recall that when we submit a query using the `executeQuery` method, the result of the query is contained in a `ResultSet` object. The interface `ResultSet` has a method, `getMetaData()`, that returns a `ResultSetMetaData` object that contains metadata about the result set. `ResultSetMetaData`, in turn, has methods to find metadata information, such as the number of columns in the result, the name of a specified column, or the type of a specified column. In this way, we can execute a query even if we have no idea of the schema of the result.

The Java code segment below uses JDBC to print out the names and types of all columns of a result set. The variable `rs` in the code below is assumed to refer to a `ResultSet` instance obtained by executing a query.

```
ResultSetMetaData rsmd = rs.getMetaData();
for(int i = 1; i <= rsmd.getColumnCount(); i++) {
        System.out.println(rsmd.getColumnName(i));
        System.out.println(rsmd.getColumnTypeName(i));
}
```

The `getColumnCount` method returns the arity (number of attributes) of the result relation. That allows us to iterate through each attribute (note that we start

```
DatabaseMetaData dbmd = conn.getMetaData();
ResultSet rs = dbmd.getColumns(null, "univdb", "department", "%");
    // Arguments to getColumns: Catalog, Schema-pattern, Table-pattern,
    //              and Column-Pattern
    // Returns: One row for each column; row has a number of attributes
    //              such as COLUMN_NAME, TYPE_NAME
while( rs.next()) {
    System.out.println(rs.getString("COLUMN_NAME"),
              rs.getString("TYPE_NAME");
}
```

Figure 5.3   Finding column information in JDBC using `DatabaseMetaData`.

at 1, as is conventional in JDBC). For each attribute, we retrieve its name and data type using the methods `getColumnName` and `getColumnTypeName`, respectively.

The `DatabaseMetaData` interface provides a way to find metadata about the database. The interface `Connection` has a method `getMetaData` that returns a `DatabaseMetaData` object. The `DatabaseMetaData` interface in turn has a very large number of methods to get metadata about the database and the database system to which the application is connected.

For example, there are methods that return the product name and version number of the database system. Other methods allow the application to query the database system about its supported features.

Still other methods return information about the database itself. The code in Figure 5.3 illustrates how to find information about columns (attributes) of relations in a database. The variable `conn` is assumed to be a handle for an already opened database connection. The method `getColumns` takes four arguments: a catalog name (null signifies that the catalog name is to be ignored), a schema name pattern, a table name pattern, and a column name pattern. The schema name, table name, and column name patterns can be used to specify a name or a pattern. Patterns can use the SQL string matching special characters "%" and "_"; for instance, the pattern "%" matches all names. Only columns of tables of schemas satisfying the specified name or pattern are retrieved. Each row in the result set contains information about one column. The rows have a number of columns such as the name of the catalog, schema, table and column, the type of the column, and so on.

Examples of other methods provided by `DatabaseMetaData` that provide information about the database include those for retrieval of metadata about relations (`getTables()`), foreign-key references (`getCrossReference()`), authorizations, database limits such as maximum number of connections, and so on.

The metadata interfaces can be used for a variety of tasks. For example, they can be used to write a database browser that allows a user to find the tables in a database, examine their schema, examine rows in a table, apply selections to see desired rows, and so on. The metadata information can be used to make code used for these tasks generic; for example, code to display the rows in a relation can be written in such a way that it would work on all possible relations regardless of their schema. Similarly, it is possible to write code that takes a query string, executes the query, and prints out the results as a formatted table; the code can work regardless of the actual query submitted.

5.1.1.7   Other Features

JDBC provides a number of other features, such as **updatable result sets**. It can create an updatable result set from a query that performs a selection and/or a projection on a database relation. An update to a tuple in the result set then results in an update to the corresponding tuple of the database relation.

Recall from Section 4.3 that a transaction allows multiple actions to be treated as a single atomic unit which can be committed or rolled back.

By default, each SQL statement is treated as a separate transaction that is committed automatically. The method `setAutoCommit()` in the JDBC `Connection` interface allows this behavior to be turned on or off. Thus, if conn is an open connection, `conn.setAutoCommit(false)` turns off automatic commit. Transactions must then be committed or rolled back explicitly using either `conn.commit()` or `conn.rollback()`. `conn.setAutoCommit(true)` turns on automatic commit.

JDBC provides interfaces to deal with large objects without requiring an entire large object to be created in memory. To fetch large objects, the `ResultSet` interface provides methods `getBlob()` and `getClob()` that are similar to the `getString()` method, but return objects of type `Blob` and `Clob`, respectively. These objects do not store the entire large object, but instead store "locators" for the large objects, that is, logical pointers to the actual large object in the database. Fetching data from these objects is very much like fetching data from a file or an input stream, and can be performed using methods such as `getBytes` and `getSubString`.

Conversely, to store large objects in the database, the `PreparedStatement` class permits a database column whose type is **blob** to be linked to an input stream (such as a file that has been opened) using the method `setBlob(int parameterIndex, InputStream inputStream)`. When the prepared statement is executed, data are read from the input stream, and written to the **blob** in the database. Similarly, a **clob** column can be set using the `setClob` method, which takes as arguments a parameter index and a character stream.

JDBC includes a *row set* feature that allows result sets to be collected and shipped to other applications. Row sets can be scanned both backward and forward and can be modified. Because row sets are not part of the database itself once they are downloaded, we do not cover details of their use here.

5.1.2   ODBC

The **Open Database Connectivity** (ODBC) standard defines an API that applications can use to open a connection with a database, send queries and updates, and get back results. Applications such as graphical user interfaces, statistics pack-

```
void ODBCexample()
{
      RETCODE error;
      HENV env; /* environment */
      HDBC conn; /* database connection */

      SQLAllocEnv(&env);
      SQLAllocConnect(env, &conn);
      SQLConnect(conn, "db.yale.edu", SQL_NTS, "avi", SQL_NTS,
                        "avipasswd", SQL_NTS);
      {
            char deptname[80];
            float salary;
            int lenOut1, lenOut2;
            HSTMT stmt;

            char * sqlquery = "select dept_name, sum (salary)
                                  from instructor
                                  group by dept_name";
            SQLAllocStmt(conn, &stmt);
            error = SQLExecDirect(stmt, sqlquery, SQL_NTS);
            if (error == SQL_SUCCESS) {
                  SQLBindCol(stmt, 1, SQL_C_CHAR, deptname , 80, &lenOut1);
                  SQLBindCol(stmt, 2, SQL_C_FLOAT, &salary, 0 , &lenOut2);
                  while (SQLFetch(stmt) == SQL_SUCCESS) {
                        printf (" %s %g\n", depthname, salary);
                  }
            }
            SQLFreeStmt(stmt, SQL_DROP);
      }
      SQLDisconnect(conn);
      SQLFreeConnect(conn);
      SQLFreeEnv(env);
}
```

Figure 5.4   ODBC code example.

ages, and spreadsheets can make use of the same ODBC API to connect to any database server that supports ODBC.

Each database system supporting ODBC provides a library that must be linked with the client program. When the client program makes an ODBC API call, the code in the library communicates with the server to carry out the requested action, and fetch results.

Figure 5.4 shows an example of C code using the ODBC API. The first step in using ODBC to communicate with a server is to set up a connection with the server. To do so, the program first allocates an SQL environment, then a database connection handle. ODBC defines the types HENV, HDBC, and RETCODE. The program then opens the database connection by using SQLConnect. This call takes several parameters, including the connection handle, the server to which to connect, the user identifier, and the password for the database. The constant SQL_NTS denotes that the previous argument is a null-terminated string.

Once the connection is set up, the program can send SQL commands to the database by using SQLExecDirect. C language variables can be bound to attributes of the query result, so that when a result tuple is fetched using SQLFetch, its attribute values are stored in corresponding C variables. The SQLBindCol function does this task; the second argument identifies the position of the attribute in the query result, and the third argument indicates the type conversion required from SQL to C. The next argument gives the address of the variable. For variable-length types like character arrays, the last two arguments give the maximum length of the variable and a location where the actual length is to be stored when a tuple is fetched. A negative value returned for the length field indicates that the value is **null**. For fixed-length types such as integer or float, the maximum length field is ignored, while a negative value returned for the length field indicates a null value.

The SQLFetch statement is in a **while** loop that is executed until SQLFetch returns a value other than SQL_SUCCESS. On each fetch, the program stores the values in C variables as specified by the calls on SQLBindCol and prints out these values.

At the end of the session, the program frees the statement handle, disconnects from the database, and frees up the connection and SQL environment handles. Good programming style requires that the result of every function call must be checked to make sure there are no errors; we have omitted most of these checks for brevity.

It is possible to create an SQL statement with parameters; for example, consider the statement insert into department values(?,?,?). The question marks are placeholders for values which will be supplied later. The above statement can be "prepared," that is, compiled at the database, and repeatedly executed by providing actual values for the placeholders—in this case, by providing an department name, building, and budget for the relation *department*.

ODBC defines functions for a variety of tasks, such as finding all the relations in the database and finding the names and types of columns of a query result or a relation in the database.

By default, each SQL statement is treated as a separate transaction that is committed automatically. The SQLSetConnectOption(conn, SQL_AUTOCOMMIT, 0) turns off automatic commit on connection conn, and transactions must then be committed explicitly by SQLTransact(conn, SQL_COMMIT) or rolled back by SQLTransact(conn, SQL_ROLLBACK).

The ODBC standard defines *conformance levels*, which specify subsets of the functionality defined by the standard. An ODBC implementation may provide only core level features, or it may provide more advanced (level 1 or level 2) features. Level 1 requires support for fetching information about the catalog, such as information about what relations are present and the types of their attributes.

> **ADO.NET**
>
> The ADO.NET API, designed for the Visual Basic .NET and C# languages, provides functions to access data, which at a high level are not dissimilar to the JDBC functions, although details differ. Like JDBC and ODBC, the ADO.NET API allows access to results of SQL queries, as well as to metadata, but is considerably simpler to use than ODBC. A database that supports ODBC can be accessed using the ADO.NET API, and the ADO.NET calls are translated into ODBC calls. The ADO.NET API can also be used with some kinds of nonrelational data sources such as Microsoft's OLE-DB, XML (covered in Chapter 23), and more recently, the Entity Framework developed by Microsoft. See the bibliographic notes for more information on ADO.NET.

Level 2 requires further features, such as the ability to send and retrieve arrays of parameter values and to retrieve more detailed catalog information.

The SQL standard defines a **call level interface (CLI)** that is similar to the ODBC interface.

5.1.3 Embedded SQL

The SQL standard defines embeddings of SQL in a variety of programming languages, such as C, C++, Cobol, Pascal, Java, PL/I, and Fortran. A language in which SQL queries are embedded is referred to as a *host* language, and the SQL structures permitted in the host language constitute *embedded* SQL.

Programs written in the host language can use the embedded SQL syntax to access and update data stored in a database. An embedded SQL program must be processed by a special preprocessor prior to compilation. The preprocessor replaces embedded SQL requests with host-language declarations and procedure calls that allow runtime execution of the database accesses. Then, the resulting program is compiled by the host-language compiler. This is the main distinction between embedded SQL and JDBC or ODBC.

In JDBC, SQL statements are interpreted at runtime (even if they are prepared first using the prepared statement feature). When embedded SQL is used, some SQL-related errors (including data-type errors) may be caught at compile time.

To identify embedded SQL requests to the preprocessor, we use the EXEC SQL statement; it has the form:

$$\text{EXEC SQL } <\text{embedded SQL statement }>;$$

The exact syntax for embedded SQL requests depends on the language in which SQL is embedded. In some languages, such as Cobol, the semicolon is replaced with END-EXEC.

We place the statement SQL INCLUDE SQLCA in the program to identify the place where the preprocessor should insert the special variables used for communication between the program and the database system.

Before executing any SQL statements, the program must first connect to the database. This is done using:

> EXEC SQL **connect to** *server* **user** *user-name* **using** *password*;

Here, *server* identifies the server to which a connection is to be established.

Variables of the host language can be used within embedded SQL statements, but they must be preceded by a colon (:) to distinguish them from SQL variables. Variables used as above must be declared within a DECLARE section, as illustrated below. The syntax for declaring the variables, however, follows the usual host language syntax.

> EXEC SQL BEGIN DECLARE SECTION;
>   int *credit_amount*;
> EXEC SQL END DECLARE SECTION;

Embedded SQL statements are similar in form to regular SQL statements. There are, however, several important differences, as we note here.

To write a relational query, we use the **declare cursor** statement. The result of the query is not yet computed. Rather, the program must use the **open** and **fetch** commands (discussed later in this section) to obtain the result tuples. As we shall see, use of a cursor is analogous to iterating through a result set in JDBC.

Consider the university schema. Assume that we have a host-language variable *credit_amount* in our program, declared as we saw earlier, and that we wish to find the names of all students who have taken more than *credit_amount* credit hours. We can write this query as follows:

> EXEC SQL
>   **declare** *c* **cursor for**
>   **select** *ID*, *name*
>   **from** *student*
>   **where** *tot_cred* > :*credit_amount*;

The variable *c* in the preceding expression is called a *cursor* for the query. We use this variable to identify the query. We then use the **open** statement, which causes the query to be evaluated.

The **open** statement for our sample query is as follows:

> EXEC SQL **open** *c*;

This statement causes the database system to execute the query and to save the results within a temporary relation. The query uses the value of the host-language variable (*credit_amount*) at the time the **open** statement is executed.

If the SQL query results in an error, the database system stores an error diagnostic in the SQL communication-area (SQLCA) variables.

We then use a series of **fetch** statements, each of which causes the values of one tuple to be placed in host-language variables. The **fetch** statement requires one host-language variable for each attribute of the result relation. For our example query, we need one variable to hold the *ID* value and another to hold the *name* value. Suppose that those variables are *si* and *sn*, respectively, and have been declared within a DECLARE section. Then the statement:

EXEC SQL **fetch** *c* **into** :*si*, :*sn*;

produces a tuple of the result relation. The program can then manipulate the variables *si* and *sn* by using the features of the host programming language.

A single **fetch** request returns only one tuple. To obtain all tuples of the result, the program must contain a loop to iterate over all tuples. Embedded SQL assists the programmer in managing this iteration. Although a relation is conceptually a set, the tuples of the result of a query are in some fixed physical order. When the program executes an **open** statement on a cursor, the cursor is set to point to the first tuple of the result. Each time it executes a **fetch** statement, the cursor is updated to point to the next tuple of the result. When no further tuples remain to be processed, the character array variable SQLSTATE in the SQLCA is set to '02000' (meaning "no more data"); the exact syntax for accessing this variable depends on the specific database system you use. Thus, we can use a **while** loop (or equivalent loop) to process each tuple of the result.

We must use the **close** statement to tell the database system to delete the temporary relation that held the result of the query. For our example, this statement takes the form

EXEC SQL **close** *c*;

Embedded SQL expressions for database modification (**update**, **insert**, and **delete**) do not return a result. Thus, they are somewhat simpler to express. A database-modification request takes the form

EXEC SQL < any valid **update, insert,** or **delete**>;

Host-language variables, preceded by a colon, may appear in the SQL database-modification expression. If an error condition arises in the execution of the statement, a diagnostic is set in the SQLCA.

Database relations can also be updated through cursors. For example, if we want to add 100 to the *salary* attribute of every instructor in the Music department, we could declare a cursor as follows.

SQLJ

The Java embedding of SQL, called SQLJ, provides the same features as other embedded SQL implementations, but using a different syntax that more closely matches features already present in Java, such as iterators. For example, SQLJ uses the syntax #sql instead of EXEC SQL, and instead of cursors, uses the Java iterator interface to fetch query results. Thus the result of executing a query is a Java iterator, and the next() method of the Java iterator interface can be used to step through the result tuples, just as the preceding examples use **fetch** on the cursor. The iterator must have attributes declared, whose types match the types of the attributes in the SQL query result. The code snippet below illustrates the use of iterators.

```
#sql iterator deptInfoIter ( String dept_name, int avgSal);
deptInfoIter iter = null;

#sql iter = { select dept_name, avg(salary)
              from instructor
              group by dept_name };
while (iter.next()) {
    String deptName = iter.dept_name();
    int avgSal = iter.avgSal();
    System.out.println(deptName + " " + avgSal);
}
iter.close();
```

SQLJ is supported by IBM DB2 and Oracle; both provide translators that convert SQLJ code into JDBC code. The translator can connect to the database in order to check the syntactic correctness of queries at compile time, and to ensure that the SQL types of query results are compatible with the Java types of variables they are assigned to. As of early 2009, SQLJ is not supported by other database systems.

We do not describe SQLJ in detail here; see the bibliographic notes for more information.

```
EXEC SQL
        declare c cursor for
        select *
        from instructor
        where dept_name= 'Music'
        for update;
```

We then iterate through the tuples by performing **fetch** operations on the cursor (as illustrated earlier), and after fetching each tuple we execute the following code:

EXEC SQL
    update *instructor*
    set *salary = salary* + 100
    where current of *c;*

Transactions can be committed using EXEC SQL COMMIT, or rolled back using EXEC SQL ROLLBACK.

Queries in embedded SQL are normally defined when the program is written. There are rare situations where a query needs to be defined at runtime. For example, an application interface may allow a user to specify selection conditions on one or more attributes of a relation, and may construct the **where** clause of an SQL query at runtime, with conditions on only those attributes for which the user specifies selections. In such cases, a query string can be constructed and prepared at runtime, using a statement of the form EXEC SQL PREPARE <query-name> FROM :<variable>, and a cursor can be opened on the query name.

5.2   Functions and Procedures

We have already seen several functions that are built into the SQL language. In this section, we show how developers can write their own functions and procedures, store them in the database, and then invoke them from SQL statements. Functions are particularly useful with specialized data types such as images and geometric objects. For instance, a line-segment data type used in a map database may have an associated function that checks whether two line segments overlap, and an image data type may have associated functions to compare two images for similarity.

Procedures and functions allow "business logic" to be stored in the database, and executed from SQL statements. For example, universities usually have many rules about how many courses a student can take in a given semester, the minimum number of courses a full-time instructor must teach in a year, the maximum number of majors a student can be enrolled in, and so on. While such business logic can be encoded as programming-language procedures stored entirely outside the database, defining them as stored procedures in the database has several advantages. For example, it allows multiple applications to access the procedures, and it allows a single point of change in case the business rules change, without changing other parts of the application. Application code can then call the stored procedures, instead of directly updating database relations.

SQL allows the definition of functions, procedures, and methods. These can be defined either by the procedural component of SQL, or by an external programming language such as Java, C, or C++. We look at definitions in SQL first, and then see how to use definitions in external languages in Section 5.2.3.

Although the syntax we present here is defined by the SQL standard, most databases implement nonstandard versions of this syntax. For example, the procedural languages supported by Oracle (PL/SQL), Microsoft SQL Server (TransactSQL), and PostgreSQL (PL/pgSQL) all differ from the standard syntax we present

```
create function dept_count(dept_name varchar(20))
    returns integer
    begin
    declare d_count integer;
        select count(*) into d_count
        from instructor
        where instructor.dept_name= dept_name
    return d_count;
    end
```

Figure 5.5   Function defined in SQL.

here. We illustrate some of the differences, for the case of Oracle, later (page 178). See the respective system manuals for further details. Although parts of the syntax we present here may not be supported on such systems, the concepts we describe are applicable across implementations, although with a different syntax.

5.2.1   Declaring and Invoking SQL Functions and Procedures

Suppose that we want a function that, given the name of a department, returns the count of the number of instructors in that department. We can define the function as shown in Figure 5.5.[4] This function can be used in a query that returns names and budgets of all departments with more than 12 instructors:

```
select dept_name, budget
from instructor
where dept_count(dept_name) > 12;
```

The SQL standard supports functions that can return tables as results; such functions are called **table functions**.[5] Consider the function defined in Figure 5.6. The function returns a table containing all the instructors of a particular department. Note that the function's parameter is referenced by prefixing it with the name of the function (*instructor_of.dept_name*).

The function can be used in a query as follows:

```
select *
from table(instructor_of('Finance'));
```

This query returns all instructors of the 'Finance' department. In the above simple case it is straightforward to write this query without using table-valued functions. In general, however, table-valued functions can be thought of as **parameterized views** that generalize the regular notion of views by allowing parameters.

---

[4]If you are entering your own functions or procedures, you should write "**create or replace**" rather than **create** so that it is easy to modify your code (by replacing the function) during debugging.
[5]This feature first appeared in SQL:2003.

create function *instructors_of* (*dept_name* **varchar**(20))
    returns table (
        ID **varchar** (5),
        name **varchar** (20),
        dept_name **varchar** (20),
        salary **numeric** (8,2))
    return table
        (**select** *ID, name, dept_name, salary*
        from *instructor*
        where *instructor.dept_name* = *instructor_of.dept_name*);

Figure 5.6 Table function in SQL.

SQL also supports procedures. The *dept_count* function could instead be written as a procedure:

create procedure *dept_count_proc*(**in** *dept_name* **varchar(20)**,
                              out *d_count* **integer**)
    begin
        select count(*) **into** *d_count*
        from *instructor*
        where *instructor.dept_name*= *dept_count_proc.dept_name*
    end

The keywords **in** and **out** indicate, respectively, parameters that are expected to have values assigned to them and parameters whose values are set in the procedure in order to return results.

Procedures can be invoked either from an SQL procedure or from embedded SQL by the **call** statement:

declare *d_count* **integer**;
call *dept_count_proc*('Physics', *d_count*);

Procedures and functions can be invoked from dynamic SQL, as illustrated by the JDBC syntax in Section 5.1.1.4.

SQL permits more than one procedure of the same name, so long as the number of arguments of the procedures with the same name is different. The name, along with the number of arguments, is used to identify the procedure. SQL also permits more than one function with the same name, so long as the different functions with the same name either have different numbers of arguments, or for functions with the same number of arguments, they differ in the type of at least one argument.

5.2.2 Language Constructs for Procedures and Functions

SQL supports constructs that give it almost all the power of a general-purpose programming language. The part of the SQL standard that deals with these constructs is called the **Persistent Storage Module (PSM)**.

Variables are declared using a **declare** statement and can have any valid SQL data type. Assignments are performed using a **set** statement.

A compound statement is of the form **begin** ... **end**, and it may contain multiple SQL statements between the **begin** and the **end**. Local variables can be declared within a compound statement, as we have seen in Section 5.2.1. A compound statement of the form **begin atomic** ... **end** ensures that all the statements contained within it are executed as a single transaction.

SQL:1999 supports the **while** statements and the **repeat** statements by the following syntax:

> **while** *boolean expression* **do**
> *sequence of statements;*
> **end while**
>
> **repeat**
> *sequence of statements;*
> **until** *boolean expression*
> **end repeat**

There is also a **for** loop that permits iteration over all results of a query:

> **declare** *n* **integer default** 0;
> **for** *r* **as**
> **select** *budget* **from** *department*
> **where** *dept_name* = 'Music'
> **do**
> **set** *n* = *n*− *r.budget*
> **end for**

The program fetches the query results one row at a time into the **for** loop variable (*r*, in the above example). The statement **leave** can be used to exit the loop, while **iterate** starts on the next tuple, from the beginning of the loop, skipping the remaining statements.

The conditional statements supported by SQL include if-then-else statements by using this syntax:

> **if** *boolean expression*
> **then** *statement or compound statement*
> **elseif** *boolean expression*
> **then** *statement or compound statement*
> **else** *statement or compound statement*
> **end if**

-- Registers a student after ensuring classroom capacity is not exceeded
-- Returns 0 on success, and -1 if capacity is exceeded.
create function *registerStudent(*
        in *s_id* **varchar**(5),
        in *s_courseid* **varchar** (8),
        in *s_secid* **varchar** (8),
        in *s_semester* **varchar** (6),
        in *s_year* **numeric** (4,0),
        out *errorMsg* **varchar**(100)
returns integer
begin
    declare *currEnrol* **int**;
    select **count**(*) **into** *currEnrol*
        from *takes*
        where *course_id* = *s_courseid* **and** *sec_id* = *s_secid*
            and *semester* = *s_semester* **and** *year* = *s_year*;
    declare *limit* **int**;
    select *capacity* **into** *limit*
        from *classroom* **natural join** *section*
        where *course_id* = *s_courseid* **and** *sec_id* = *s_secid*
            and *semester* = *s_semester* **and** *year* = *s_year*;
    if (*currEnrol* < *limit*)
        begin
            insert into *takes* **values**
                (*s_id*, *s_courseid*, *s_secid*, *s_semester*, *s_year*, null);
            return(0);
        end
    -- Otherwise, section capacity limit already reached
    set *errorMsg* = 'Enrollment limit reached for course ' || *s_courseid*
        || ' section ' || *s_secid*;
    return(-1);
end;

Figure 5.7   Procedure to register a student for a course section.

SQL also supports a case statement similar to the C/C++ language case statement (in addition to case expressions, which we saw in Chapter 3).

Figure 5.7 provides a larger example of the use of procedural constructs in SQL. The function *registerStudent* defined in the figure, registers a student in a course section, after verifying that the number of students in the section does not exceed the capacity of the room allocated to the section. The function returns an error code, with a value greater than or equal to 0 signifying success, and a negative value signifying an error condition, and a message indicating the reason for the failure is returned as an **out** parameter.

NONSTANDARD SYNTAX FOR PROCEDURES AND FUNCTIONS

Although the SQL standard defines the syntax for procedures and functions, most databases do not follow the standard strictly, and there is considerable variation in the syntax supported. One of the reasons for this situation is that these databases typically introduced support for procedures and functions before the syntax was standardized, and they continue to support their original syntax. It is not possible to list the syntax supported by each database here, but we illustrate a few of the differences in the case of Oracle's PL/SQL, by showing below a version of the function from Figure 5.5, as it would be defined in PL/SQL.

```
create or replace function dept_count(dept_name in instructor.dept_name%type)
return integer
as
    d_count integer;
    begin
        select count(*) into d_count
        from instructor
        where instructor.dept_name = dept_name;
        return d_count;
    end;
```

While the two versions are similar in concept, there are a number of minor syntactic differences, some of which are evident when comparing the two versions of the function. Although not shown here, the syntax for control flow in PL/SQL also has several differences from the syntax presented here.

Observe that PL/SQL allows a type to be specified as the type of an attribute of a relation, by adding the suffix %type. On the other hand, PL/SQL does not directly support the ability to return a table, although there is an indirect way of implementing this functionality by creating a table type. The procedural languages supported by other databases also have a number of syntactic and semantic differences. See the respective language references for more information.

The SQL procedural language also supports the signaling of **exception conditions**, and declaring of **handlers** that can handle the exception, as in this code:

```
declare out_of_classroom_seats condition
declare exit handler for out_of_classroom_seats
begin
sequence of statements
end
```

The statements between the **begin** and the **end** can raise an exception by executing **signal** *out_of_classroom_seats*. The handler says that if the condition arises, the action to be taken is to exit the enclosing **begin end** statement. Alternative actions would be **continue**, which continues execution from the next statement following the one that raised the exception. In addition to explicitly defined conditions, there are also predefined conditions such as **sqlexception, sqlwarning**, and **not found**.

5.2.3 External Language Routines

Although the procedural extensions to SQL can be very useful, they are unfortunately not supported in a standard way across databases. Even the most basic features have different syntax or semantics in different database products. As a result, programmers have to essentially learn a new language for each database product. An alternative that is gaining in support is to define procedures in an imperative programming language, but allow them to be invoked from SQL queries and trigger definitions.

SQL allows us to define functions in a programming language such as Java, C#, C or C++. Functions defined in this fashion can be more efficient than functions defined in SQL, and computations that cannot be carried out in SQL can be executed by these functions.

External procedures and functions can be specified in this way (note that the exact syntax depends on the specific database system you use):

> **create procedure** dept_count_proc(**in** *dept_name* **varchar**(20),
> > **out** count **integer**)
>
> **language** C
> **external name** '/usr/avi/bin/dept_count_proc'
>
> **create function** dept_count (*dept_name* **varchar**(20))
> **returns** integer
> **language** C
> **external name** '/usr/avi/bin/dept_count'

In general, the external language procedures need to deal with null values in parameters (both **in** and **out**) and return values. They also need to communicate failure/success status, to deal with exceptions. This information can be communicated by extra parameters: an **sqlstate** value to indicate failure/success status, a parameter to store the return value of the function, and indicator variables for each parameter/function result to indicate if the value is null. Other mechanisms are possible to handle null values, for example by passing pointers instead of values. The exact mechanisms depend on the database. However, if a function does not deal with these situations, an extra line **parameter style general** can be added to the declaration to indicate that the external procedures/functions take only the arguments shown and do not handle null values or exceptions.

Functions defined in a programming language and compiled outside the database system may be loaded and executed with the database-system code.

However, doing so carries the risk that a bug in the program can corrupt the database internal structures, and can bypass the access-control functionality of the database system. Database systems that are concerned more about efficient performance than about security may execute procedures in such a fashion. Database systems that are concerned about security may execute such code as part of a separate process, communicate the parameter values to it, and fetch results back, via interprocess communication. However, the time overhead of interprocess communication is quite high; on typical CPU architectures, tens to hundreds of thousands of instructions can execute in the time taken for one interprocess communication.

If the code is written in a "safe" language such as Java or C#, there is another possibility: executing the code in a **sandbox** within the database query execution process itself. The sandbox allows the Java or C# code to access its own memory area, but prevents the code from reading or updating the memory of the query execution process, or accessing files in the file system. (Creating a sandbox is not possible for a language such as C, which allows unrestricted access to memory through pointers.) Avoiding interprocess communication reduces function call overhead greatly.

Several database systems today support external language routines running in a sandbox within the query execution process. For example, Oracle and IBM DB2 allow Java functions to run as part of the database process. Microsoft SQL Server allows procedures compiled into the Common Language Runtime (CLR) to execute within the database process; such procedures could have been written, for example, in C# or Visual Basic. PostgreSQL allows functions defined in several languages, such as Perl, Python, and Tcl.

5.3   Triggers

A **trigger** is a statement that the system executes automatically as a side effect of a modification to the database. To design a trigger mechanism, we must meet two requirements:

1. Specify when a trigger is to be executed. This is broken up into an *event* that causes the trigger to be checked and a *condition* that must be satisfied for trigger execution to proceed.

2. Specify the *actions* to be taken when the trigger executes.

Once we enter a trigger into the database, the database system takes on the responsibility of executing it whenever the specified event occurs and the corresponding condition is satisfied.

5.3.1   Need for Triggers

Triggers can be used to implement certain integrity constraints that cannot be specified using the constraint mechanism of SQL. Triggers are also useful mechanisms for alerting humans or for starting certain tasks automatically when certain conditions are met. As an illustration, we could design a trigger that, whenever a tuple is inserted into the *takes* relation, updates the tuple in the *student* relation for the student taking the course by adding the number of credits for the course to the student's total credits. As another example, suppose a warehouse wishes to maintain a minimum inventory of each item; when the inventory level of an item falls below the minimum level, an order can be placed automatically. On an update of the inventory level of an item, the trigger compares the current inventory level with the minimum inventory level for the item, and if the level is at or below the minimum, a new order is created.

Note that trigger systems cannot usually perform updates outside the database, and hence, in the inventory replenishment example, we cannot use a trigger to place an order in the external world. Instead, we add an order to a relation holding reorders. We must create a separate permanently running system process that periodically scans that relation and places orders. Some database systems provide built-in support for sending email from SQL queries and triggers, using the above approach.

5.3.2 Triggers in SQL

We now consider how to implement triggers in SQL. The syntax we present here is defined by the SQL standard, but most databases implement nonstandard versions of this syntax. Although the syntax we present here may not be supported on such systems, the concepts we describe are applicable across implementations. We discuss nonstandard trigger implementations later in this section (page 184).

Figure 5.8 shows how triggers can be used to ensure referential integrity on the *time_slot_id* attribute of the *section* relation. The first trigger definition in the figure specifies that the trigger is initiated *after* any insert on the relation *section* and it ensures that the *time_slot_id* value being inserted is valid. An SQL insert statement could insert multiple tuples of the relation, and the **for each row** clause in the trigger code would then explicitly iterate over each inserted row. The **referencing new row as** clause creates a variable *nrow* (called a **transition variable**) that stores the value of an inserted row after the insertion.

The **when** statement specifies a condition. The system executes the rest of the trigger body only for tuples that satisfy the condition. The **begin atomic** ... **end** clause can serve to collect multiple SQL statements into a single compound statement. In our example, though, there is only one statement, which rolls back the transaction that caused the trigger to get executed. Thus any transaction that violates the referential integrity constraint gets rolled back, ensuring the data in the database satisfies the constraint.

It is not sufficient to check referential integrity on inserts alone, we also need to consider updates of *section*, as well as deletes and updates to the referenced table *time_slot*. The second trigger definition in Figure 5.8 considers the case of deletes to *time_slot*. This trigger checks that the *time_slot_id* of the tuple being deleted is either still present in *time_slot*, or that no tuple in *section* contains that particular *time_slot_id* value; otherwise, referential integrity would be violated.

```
create trigger timeslot_check1 after insert on section
referencing new row as nrow
for each row
when (nrow.time_slot_id not in (
            select time_slot_id
            from time_slot)) /* time_slot_id not present in time_slot */
begin
    rollback
end;

create trigger timeslot_check2 after delete on timeslot
referencing old row as orow
for each row
when (orow.time_slot_id not in (
            select time_slot_id
            from time_slot) /* last tuple for time_slot_id deleted from time_slot */
    and orow.time_slot_id in (
            select time_slot_id
            from section)) /* and time_slot_id still referenced from section*/
begin
    rollback
end;
```

Figure 5.8   Using triggers to maintain referential integrity.

To ensure referential integrity, we would also have to create triggers to handle updates to *section* and *time_slot*; we describe next how triggers can be executed on updates, but leave the definition of these triggers as an exercise to the reader.

For updates, the trigger can specify attributes whose update causes the trigger to execute; updates to other attributes would not cause it to be executed. For example, to specify that a trigger executes after an update to the *grade* attribute of the *takes* relation, we write:

after update of *takes* **on** *grade*

The **referencing old row as** clause can be used to create a variable storing the old value of an updated or deleted row. The **referencing new row as** clause can be used with updates in addition to inserts.

Figure 5.9 shows how a trigger can be used to keep the *tot_cred* attribute value of *student* tuples up-to-date when the *grade* attribute is updated for a tuple in the *takes* relation. The trigger is executed only when the *grade* attribute is updated from a value that is either null or 'F', to a grade that indicates the course is successfully completed. The **update** statement is normal SQL syntax except for the use of the variable *nrow*.

```
create trigger credits_earned after update of takes on (grade)
referencing new row as nrow
referencing old row as orow
for each row
when nrow.grade <> 'F' and nrow.grade is not null
    and (orow.grade = 'F' or orow.grade is null)
begin atomic
    update student
    set tot_cred= tot_cred+
            (select credits
             from course
             where course.course_id= nrow.course_id)
    where student.id = nrow.id;
end;
```

Figure 5.9   Using a trigger to maintain *credits_earned* values.

A more realistic implementation of this example trigger would also handle grade corrections that change a successful completion grade to a fail grade, and handle insertions into the *takes* relation where the *grade* indicates successful completion. We leave these as an exercise for the reader.

As another example of the use of a trigger, the action on **delete** of a *student* tuple could be to check if the student has any entries in the *takes* relation, and if so, to delete them.

Many database systems support a variety of other triggering events, such as when a user (application) logs on to the database (that is, opens a connection), the system shuts down, or changes are made to system settings.

Triggers can be activated **before** the event (insert, delete, or update) instead of **after** the event. Triggers that execute before an event can serve as extra constraints that can prevent invalid updates, inserts, or deletes. Instead of letting the invalid action proceed and cause an error, the trigger might take action to correct the problem so that the update, insert, or delete becomes valid. For example, if we attempt to insert an instructor into a department whose name does not appear in the *department* relation, the trigger could insert a tuple into the *department* relation for that department name before the insertion generates a foreign-key violation. As another example, suppose the value of an inserted grade is blank, presumably to indicate the absence of a grade. We can define a trigger that replaces the value by the **null** value. The **set** statement can be used to carry out such modifications. An example of such a trigger appears in Figure 5.10.

Instead of carrying out an action for each affected row, we can carry out a single action for the entire SQL statement that caused the insert, delete, or update. To do so, we use the **for each statement** clause instead of the **for each row** clause. The clauses **referencing old table as** or **referencing new table as** can then be used to refer to temporary tables (called *transition tables*) containing all the affected rows. Transition tables cannot be used with **before** triggers, but can be

```
create trigger setnull before update on takes
referencing new row as nrow
for each row
when (nrow.grade = ' ')
begin atomic
    set nrow.grade = null;
end;
```

Figure 5.10   Example of using **set** to change an inserted value.

used with **after** triggers, regardless of whether they are statement triggers or row triggers. A single SQL statement can then be used to carry out multiple actions on the basis of the transition tables.

NONSTANDARD TRIGGER SYNTAX

Although the trigger syntax we describe here is part of the SQL standard, and is supported by IBM DB2, most other database systems have nonstandard syntax for specifying triggers, and may not implement all features in the SQL standard. We outline a few of the differences below; see the respective system manuals for further details.

For example, in the Oracle syntax, unlike the SQL standard syntax, the keyword **row** does not appear in the **referencing** statement. The keyword **atomic** does not appear after **begin**. The reference to *nrow* in the **select** statement nested in the **update** statement must begin with a colon (:) to inform the system that the variable *nrow* is defined externally from the SQL statement. Further, subqueries are not allowed in the **when** and **if** clauses. It is possible to work around this problem by moving complex predicates from the **when** clause into a separate query that saves the result into a local variable, and then reference that variable in an **if** clause, and the body of the trigger then moves into the corresponding **then** clause. Further, in Oracle, triggers are not allowed to execute a transaction rollback directly; however, they can instead use a function called raise_application_error to not only roll back the transaction, but also return an error message to the user/application that performed the update.

As another example, in Microsoft SQL Server the keyword **on** is used instead of **after**. The **referencing** clause is omitted, and old and new rows are referenced by the tuple variables **deleted** and **inserted**. Further, the **for each row** clause is omitted, and **when** is replaced by **if**. The **before** specification is not supported, but an **instead of** specification is supported.

In PostgreSQL, triggers do not have a body, but instead invoke a procedure for each row, which can access variables **new** and **old** containing the old and new values of the row. Instead of performing a rollback, the trigger can raise an exception, with an associated error message.

create trigger *reorder* **after update of** *amount* **on** *inventory*
referencing old row as *orow,* **new row as** *nrow*
for each row
when *nrow.level* <= (**select** *level*
                from *minlevel*
                where *minlevel.item = orow.item*)
and *orow.level* > (**select** *level*
              from *minlevel*
              where *minlevel.item = orow.item*)
begin atomic
    insert into *orders*
        (**select** *item, amount*
        from *reorder*
        where *reorder.item = orow.item*);
end;

Figure 5.11 Example of trigger for reordering an item.

Triggers can be disabled or enabled; by default they are enabled when they are created, but can be disabled by using **alter trigger** *trigger_name* **disable** (some databases use alternative syntax such as **disable trigger** *trigger_name*). A trigger that has been disabled can be enabled again. A trigger can instead be dropped, which removes it permanently, by using the command **drop trigger** *trigger_name*.

Returning to our warehouse inventory example, suppose we have the following relations:

- *inventory* (*item, level*), which notes the current amount of the item in the warehouse.

- *minlevel* (*item, level*), which notes the minimum amount of the item to be maintained.

- *reorder* (*item, amount*), which notes the amount of the item to be ordered when its level falls below the minimum.

- *orders* (*item, amount*), which notes the amount of the item to be ordered.

Note that we have been careful to place an order only when the amount falls from above the minimum level to below the minimum level. If we check only that the new value after an update is below the minimum level, we may place an order erroneously when the item has already been reordered. We can then use the trigger shown in Figure 5.11 for reordering the item.

SQL-based database systems use triggers widely, although before SQL:1999 they were not part of the SQL standard. Unfortunately, each database system implemented its own syntax for triggers, leading to incompatibilities. The SQL:1999 syntax for triggers that we use here is similar, but not identical, to the syntax in the IBM DB2 and Oracle database systems.

5.3.3   When Not to Use Triggers

There are many good uses for triggers, such as those we have just seen in Section 5.3.2, but some uses are best handled by alternative techniques. For example, we could implement the **on delete cascade** feature of a foreign-key constraint by using a trigger, instead of using the cascade feature. Not only would this be more work to implement, but also, it would be much harder for a database user to understand the set of constraints implemented in the database.

As another example, triggers can be used to maintain materialized views. For instance, if we wished to support very fast access to the total number of students registered for each course section, we could do this by creating a relation

section_registration(*course_id*, *sec_id*, *semester*, *year*, *total_students*)

defined by the query

> **select** *course_id*, *sec_id*, *semester*, *year*, **count**(*ID*) **as** *total_students*
> **from** *takes*
> **group by** *course_id*, *sec_id*, *semester*, *year*;

The value of *total_students* for each course must be maintained up-to-date by triggers on insert, delete, or update of the *takes* relation. Such maintenance may require insertion, update or deletion of tuples from *section_registration*, and triggers must be written accordingly.

However, many database systems now support materialized views, which are automatically maintained by the database system (see Section 4.2.3). As a result, there is no need to write trigger code for maintaining such materialized views.

Triggers have been used for maintaining copies, or replicas, of databases. A collection of triggers on insert, delete, or update can be created on each relation to record the changes in relations called **change** or **delta** relations. A separate process copies over the changes to the replica of the database. Modern database systems, however, provide built-in facilities for database replication, making triggers unnecessary for replication in most cases. Replicated databases are discussed in detail in Chapter 19.

Another problem with triggers lies in unintended execution of the triggered action when data are loaded from a backup copy,[6] or when database updates at a site are replicated on a backup site. In such cases, the triggered action has already been executed, and typically should not be executed again. When loading data, triggers can be disabled explicitly. For backup replica systems that may have to take over from the primary system, triggers would have to be disabled initially, and enabled when the backup site takes over processing from the primary system. As an alternative, some database systems allow triggers to be specified as **not**

---

[6]We discuss database backup and recovery from failures in detail in Chapter 16.

course_id	prereq_id
BIO-301	BIO-101
BIO-399	BIO-101
CS-190	CS-101
CS-315	CS-101
CS-319	CS-101
CS-347	CS-101
EE-181	PHY-101

Figure 5.12 The *prereq* relation.

for replication, which ensures that they are not executed on the backup site during database replication. Other database systems provide a system variable that denotes that the database is a replica on which database actions are being replayed; the trigger body should check this variable and exit if it is true. Both solutions remove the need for explicit disabling and enabling of triggers.

Triggers should be written with great care, since a trigger error detected at runtime causes the failure of the action statement that set off the trigger. Furthermore, the action of one trigger can set off another trigger. In the worst case, this could even lead to an infinite chain of triggering. For example, suppose an insert trigger on a relation has an action that causes another (new) insert on the same relation. The insert action then triggers yet another insert action, and so on ad infinitum. Some database systems limit the length of such chains of triggers (for example, to 16 or 32) and consider longer chains of triggering an error. Other systems flag as an error any trigger that attempts to reference the relation whose modification caused the trigger to execute in the first place.

Triggers can serve a very useful purpose, but they are best avoided when alternatives exist. Many trigger applications can be substituted by appropriate use of stored procedures, which we discussed in Section 5.2.

5.4   Recursive Queries **

Consider the instance of the relation *prereq* shown in Figure 5.12 containing information about the various courses offered at the university and the prerequisite for each course.[7]

Suppose now that we want to find out which courses are a prerequisite whether directly or indirectly, for a specific course—say, CS-347. That is, we wish to find a course that is a direct prerequisite for CS-347, or is a prerequisite for a course that is a prerequisite for CS-347, and so on.

---

[7]This instance of *prereq* differs from that used earlier for reasons that will become apparent as we use it to explain recursive queries.

Thus, if CS-301 is a prerequisite for CS-347, and CS-201 is a prerequisite for CS-301, and CS-101 is a prerequisite for CS-201, then CS-301, CS-201, and CS-101 are all prerequisites for CS-347.

The **transitive closure** of the relation *prereq* is a relation that contains all pairs (*cid*, *pre*) such that *pre* is a direct or indirect prerequisite of *cid*. There are numerous applications that require computation of similar transitive closures on **hierarchies**. For instance, organizations typically consist of several levels of organizational units. Machines consist of parts that in turn have subparts, and so on; for example, a bicycle may have subparts such as wheels and pedals, which in turn have subparts such as tires, rims, and spokes. Transitive closure can be used on such hierarchies to find, for example, all parts in a bicycle.

5.4.1 Transitive Closure Using Iteration

One way to write the above query is to use iteration: First find those courses that are a direct prerequisite of CS-347, then those courses that are a prerequisite of all the courses under the first set, and so on. This iterative process continues until we reach an iteration where no courses are added. Figure 5.13 shows a function *findAllPrereqs(cid)* to carry out this task; the function takes the *course _id* of the course as a parameter (*cid*), computes the set of all direct and indirect prerequisites of that course, and returns the set.

The procedure uses three temporary tables:

- *c_prereq*: stores the set of tuples to be returned.
- *new_c_prereq*: stores the courses found in the previous iteration.
- *temp*: used as temporary storage while sets of courses are manipulated.

Note that SQL allows the creation of temporary tables using the command **create temporary table**; such tables are available only within the transaction executing the query, and are dropped when the transaction finishes. Moreover, if two instances of *findAllPrereqs* run concurrently, each gets its own copy of the temporary tables; if they shared a copy, their result could be incorrect.

The procedure inserts all direct prerequisites of course *cid* into *new_c_prereq* before the **repeat** loop. The **repeat** loop first adds all courses in *new_c_prereq* to *c_prereq*. Next, it computes prerequisites of all those courses in *new_c_prereq*, except those that have already been found to be prerequisites of *cid*, and stores them in the temporary table *temp*. Finally, it replaces the contents of *new_c_prereq* by the contents of *temp*. The **repeat** loop terminates when it finds no new (indirect) prerequisites.

Figure 5.14 shows the prerequisites that would be found in each iteration, if the procedure were called for the course named CS-347.

We note that the use of the **except** clause in the function ensures that the function works even in the (abnormal) case where there is a cycle of prerequisites. For example, if *a* is a prerequisite for *b*, *b* is a prerequisite for *c*, and *c* is a prerequisite for *a*, there is a cycle.

```
create function findAllPrereqs(cid varchar(8))
    -- Finds all courses that are prerequisite (directly or indirectly) for cid
returns table (course_id varchar(8))
    -- The relation prereq(course_id, prereq_id) specifies which course is
    -- directly a prerequisite for another course.
begin
    create temporary table c_prereq (course_id varchar(8));
        -- table c_prereq stores the set of courses to be returned
    create temporary table new_c_prereq (course_id varchar(8));
        -- table new_c_prereq contains courses found in the previous iteration
    create temporary table temp (course_id varchar(8));
        -- table temp is used to store intermediate results
    insert into new_c_prereq
        select prereq_id
        from prereq
        where course_id = cid;
    repeat
        insert into c_prereq
            select course_id
            from new_c_prereq;

        insert into temp
            (select prereq.course_id
                from new_c_prereq, prereq
                where new_c_prereq.course_id = prereq.prereq_id
            )
            except (
                select course_id
                from c_prereq
            );
        delete from new_c_prereq;
        insert into new_c_prereq
            select *
            from temp;
        delete from temp;

    until not exists (select * from new_c_prereq)
    end repeat;
    return table c_prereq;
end
```

Figure 5.13 Finding all prerequisites of a course.

While cycles may be unrealistic in course prerequisites, cycles are possible in other applications. For instance, suppose we have a relation *flights(to, from)* that says which cities can be reached from which other cities by a direct flight. We can

Iteration Number	Tuples in c1
0	
1	(CS-301)
2	(CS-301), (CS-201)
3	(CS-301), (CS-201)
4	(CS-301), (CS-201), (CS-101)
5	(CS-301), (CS-201), (CS-101)

Figure 5.14 Prerequisites of CS-347 in iterations of function *findAllPrereqs*.

write code similar to that in the *findAllPrereqs* function, to find all cities that are reachable by a sequence of one or more flights from a given city. All we have to do is to replace *prereq* by *flight* and replace attribute names correspondingly. In this situation, there can be cycles of reachability, but the function would work correctly since it would eliminate cities that have already been seen.

5.4.2 Recursion in SQL

It is rather inconvenient to specify transitive closure using iteration. There is an alternative approach, using recursive view definitions, that is easier to use.

We can use recursion to define the set of courses that are prerequisites of a particular course, say CS-347, as follows. The courses that are prerequisites (directly or indirectly) of CS-347 are:

1. Courses that are prerequisites for CS-347.

2. Courses that are prerequisites for those courses that are prerequisites (directly or indirectly) for CS-347.

Note that case 2 is recursive, since it defines the set of courses that are prerequisites of CS-347 in terms of the set of courses that are prerequisites of CS-347. Other examples of transitive closure, such as finding all subparts (direct or indirect) of a given part can also be defined in a similar manner, recursively.

Since the SQL:1999 version, the SQL standard supports a limited form of recursion, using the **with recursive** clause, where a view (or temporary view) is expressed in terms of itself. Recursive queries can be used, for example, to express transitive closure concisely. Recall that the **with** clause is used to define a temporary view whose definition is available only to the query in which it is defined. The additional keyword **recursive** specifies that the view is recursive.

For example, we can find every pair (*cid,pre*) such that *pre* is directly or indirectly a prerequisite for course *cid*, using the recursive SQL view shown in Figure 5.15.

Any recursive view must be defined as the union of two subqueries: a **base query** that is nonrecursive and a **recursive query** that uses the recursive view. In the example in Figure 5.15, the base query is the select on *prereq* while the recursive query computes the join of *prereq* and *rec_prereq*.

> **with recursive** *c_prereq*(*course_id*, *prereq_id*) **as** (
> > **select** *course_id*, *prereq_id*
> > **from** *prereq*
> **union**
> > **select** *prereq.prereq_id*, *c_prereq.course_id*
> > **from** *prereq*, *c_prereq*
> > **where** *prereq.course_id* = *c_prereq.prereq_id*
>)
> **select** ∗
> **from** *c_prereq*;

Figure 5.15 Recursive query in SQL.

The meaning of a recursive view is best understood as follows. First compute the base query and add all the resultant tuples to the recursively defined view relation *rec_prereq* (which is initially empty). Next compute the recursive query using the current contents of the view relation, and add all the resulting tuples back to the view relation. Keep repeating the above step until no new tuples are added to the view relation. The resultant view relation instance is called a **fixed point** of the recursive view definition. (The term "fixed" refers to the fact that there is no further change.) The view relation is thus defined to contain exactly the tuples in the fixed-point instance.

Applying the above logic to our example, we first find all direct prerequisites of each course by executing the base query. The recursive query adds one more level of courses in each iteration, until the maximum depth of the course-prereq relationship is reached. At this point no new tuples are added to the view, and a fixed point is reached.

To find the prerequisites of a specific course, such as CS-347, we can modify the outer level query by adding a where clause "**where** *rec_prereq.course_id* = 'CS-347'". One way to evaluate the query with the selection is to compute the full contents of *rec_prereq* using the iterative technique, and then select from this result only those tuples whose *course_id* is CS-347. However, this would result in computing (course, prerequisite) pairs for all courses, all of which are irrelevant except for those for the course CS-347. In fact the database system is not required to use the above iterative technique to compute the full result of the recursive query and then perform the selection. It may get the same result using other techniques that may be more efficient, such as that used in the function *findAllPrereqs* which we saw earlier. See the bibliographic notes for references to more information on this topic.

There are some restrictions on the recursive query in a recursive view; specifically, the query should be **monotonic**, that is, its result on a view relation instance V_1 should be a superset of its result on a view relation instance V_2 if V_1 is a superset of V_2. Intuitively, if more tuples are added to the view relation, the recursive query should return at least the same set of tuples as before, and possibly return additional tuples.

In particular, recursive queries should not use any of the following constructs, since they would make the query nonmonotonic:

- Aggregation on the recursive view.

- **not exists** on a subquery that uses the recursive view.

- Set difference (**except**) whose right-hand side uses the recursive view.

For instance, if the recursive query was of the form $r - v$ where v is the recursive view, if we add a tuple to v the result of the query can become smaller; the query is therefore not monotonic.

The meaning of recursive views can be defined by the iterative procedure as long as the recursive query is monotonic; if the recursive query is nonmonotonic, the meaning of the view is hard to define. SQL therefore requires the queries to be monotonic. Recursive queries are discussed in more detail in the context of the Datalog query language, in Section B.3.6.

SQL also allows creation of recursively defined permanent views by using **create recursive view** in place of **with recursive**. Some implementations support recursive queries using a different syntax; see the respective system manuals for further details.

5.5   Advanced Aggregation Features**

The aggregation support in SQL, which we have seen earlier, is quite powerful, and handles most common tasks with ease. However, there are some tasks that are hard to implement efficiently with the basic aggregation features. In this section, we study features that were added to SQL to handle some such tasks.

5.5.1   Ranking

Finding the position of a value in a larger set is a common operation. For instance, we may wish to assign students a rank in class based on their grade-point average (GPA), with the rank 1 going to the student with the highest GPA, the rank 2 to the student with the next highest GPA, and so on. A related type of query is to find the percentile in which a value in a (multi)set belongs, for example, the bottom third, middle third, or top third. While such queries can be expressed using the SQL constructs we have seen so far, they are difficult to express and inefficient to evaluate. Programmers may resort to writing the query partly in SQL and partly in a programming language. We study SQL support for direct expression of these types of queries here.

In our university example, the *takes* relation shows the grade each student earned in each course taken. To illustrate ranking, let us assume we have a view *student_grades* (*ID, GPA*) giving the grade-point average of each student.[8]

---

[8]The SQL statement to create the view *student_grades* is somewhat complex since we must convert the letter grades in the *takes* relation to numbers and weight the grades for each course by the number of credits for that course. The definition of this view is the goal of Exercise 4.5.

Ranking is done with an **order by** specification. The following query gives the rank of each student:

> **select** *ID*, **rank() over (order by** (*GPA*) **desc) as** *s_rank*
> **from** *student_grades*;

Note that the order of tuples in the output is not defined, so they may not be sorted by rank. An extra **order by** clause is needed to get them in sorted order, as shown below.

> **select** *ID*, **rank () over (order by** (*GPA*) **desc) as** *s_rank*
> **from** *student_grades*
> **order by** *s_rank*;

A basic issue with ranking is how to deal with the case of multiple tuples that are the same on the ordering attribute(s). In our example, this means deciding what to do if there are two students with the same GPA. The **rank** function gives the same rank to all tuples that are equal on the **order by** attributes. For instance, if the highest GPA is shared by two students, both would get rank 1. The next rank given would be 3, not 2, so if three students get the next highest GPA, they would all get rank 3, and the next student(s) would get rank 6, and so on. There is also a **dense_rank** function that does not create gaps in the ordering. In the above example, the tuples with the second highest value all get rank 2, and tuples with the third highest value get rank 3, and so on.

It is possible to express the above query with the basic SQL aggregation functions, using the following query:

> **select** *ID*, (1 + (**select count**(*)
> **from** *student_grades B*
> **where** *B.GPA* > *A.GPA*)) **as** *s_rank*
> **from** *student_grades A*
> **order by** *s_rank*;

It should be clear that the rank of a student is merely 1 plus the number of students with a higher *GPA*, which is exactly what the above query specifies. However, this computation of each student's rank takes time linear in the size of the relation, leading to an overall time quadratic in the size of the relation. On large relations, the above query could take a very long time to execute. In contrast, the system's implementation of the **rank** clause can sort the relation and compute the rank in much less time.

Ranking can be done within partitions of the data. For instance, suppose we wish to rank students by department rather than across the entire university. Assume that a view is defined like *student_grades* but including the department name: *dept_grades(ID, dept_name, GPA)*. The following query then gives the rank of students within each section:

```
select ID, dept_name,
       rank () over (partition by dept_name order by GPA desc) as dept_rank
from dept_grades
order by dept_name, dept_rank;
```

The outer **order by** clause orders the result tuples by department name, and within each department by the rank.

Multiple **rank** expressions can be used within a single **select** statement; thus we can obtain the overall rank and the rank within the department by using two **rank** expressions in the same **select** clause. When ranking (possibly with partitioning) occurs along with a **group by** clause, the **group by** clause is applied first, and partitioning and ranking are done on the results of the group by. Thus aggregate values can then be used for ranking. We could have written our ranking over the *student_grades* view without using the view, using a single **select** clause. We leave details as an exercise for you.

The ranking functions can be used to find the top n tuples by embedding a ranking query within an outer-level query; we leave details as an exercise. Note that the bottom n is simply the same as the top n with a reverse sorting order. Several database systems provide nonstandard SQL extensions to specify directly that only the top n results are required; such extensions do not require the rank function and simplify the job of the optimizer. For example, some databases allow a clause **limit** n to be added at the end of an SQL query to specify that only the first n tuples should be output; this clause is used in conjunction with an **order by** clause to fetch the top n tuples, as illustrated by the following query, which retrieves the IDs and GPAs of the top 10 students in order of GPA:

```
select ID, GPA)
from student_grades
order by GPA
limit 10;
```

However, the **limit** clause does not support partitioning, so we cannot get the top n within each partition without performing ranking; further, if more than one student gets the same GPA, it is possible that one is included in the top 10, while another is excluded.

Several other functions can be used in place of **rank**. For instance, **percent_rank** of a tuple gives the rank of the tuple as a fraction. If there are n tuples in the partition[9] and the rank of the tuple is r, then its percent rank is defined as $(r-1)/(n-1)$ (and as *null* if there is only one tuple in the partition). The function **cume_dist**, short for cumulative distribution, for a tuple is defined as p/n where p is the number of tuples in the partition with ordering values preceding or equal to the ordering value of the tuple and n is the number of tuples in the partition. The function **row_number** sorts the rows and gives each row a unique number corre-

---

[9]The entire set is treated as a single partition if no explicit partition is used.

sponding to its position in the sort order; different rows with the same ordering value would get different row numbers, in a nondeterministic fashion.

Finally, for a given constant n, the ranking function **ntile**(n) takes the tuples in each partition in the specified order and divides them into n buckets with equal numbers of tuples.[10] For each tuple, **ntile**(n) then gives the number of the bucket in which it is placed, with bucket numbers starting with 1. This function is particularly useful for constructing histograms based on percentiles. We can show the quartile into which each student falls based on GPA by the following query:

> **select** *ID*, **ntile**(4) **over** (**order by** (*GPA* **desc**)) **as** *quartile*
> **from** *student_grades*;

The presence of null values can complicate the definition of rank, since it is not clear where they should occur first in the sort order. SQL permits the user to specify where they should occur by using **nulls first** or **nulls last**, for instance:

> **select** *ID*, **rank** () **over** (**order by** *GPA* **desc nulls last**) **as** *s_rank*
> **from** *student_grades*;

5.5.2 Windowing

Window queries compute an aggregate function over ranges of tuples. This is useful, for example, to compute an aggregate of a fixed range of time; the time range is called a *window*. Windows may overlap, in which case a tuple may contribute to more than one window. This is unlike the partitions we saw earlier, where a tuple could contribute to only one partition.

An example of the use of windowing is trend analysis. Consider our earlier sales example. Sales may fluctuate widely from day to day based on factors like weather (for example a snowstorm, flood, hurricane, or earthquake might reduce sales for a period of time). However, over a sufficiently long period of time, fluctuations might be less (continuing the example, sales may "make up" for weather-related downturns). Stock market trend analysis is another example of the use of the windowing concept. Various "moving averages" are found on business and investment Web sites.

It is relatively easy to write an SQL query using those features we have already studied to compute an aggregate over one window, for example, sales over a fixed 3-day period. However, if we want to do this for *every* 3-day period, the query becomes cumbersome.

SQL provides a windowing feature to support such queries. Suppose we are given a view *tot_credits* (*year*, *num_credits*) giving the total number of credits taken

---

[10]If the total number of tuples in a partition is not divisible by n, then the number of tuples in each bucket can differ by at most 1. Tuples with the same value for the ordering attribute may be assigned to different buckets, nondeterministically, in order to make the number of tuples in each bucket equal.

by students in each year.[11] Note that this relation can contain at most one tuple for each year. Consider the following query:

> **select** *year*, **avg**(*num_credits*)
> > **over** (**order by** *year* **rows** 3 **preceding**)
> > **as** *avg_total_credits*
> **from** *tot_credits*;

This query computes averages over the 3 *preceding* tuples in the specified sort order. Thus, for 2009, if tuples for years 2008 and 2007 are present in the relation *tot_credits*, with each year represented by only one tuple, the result of the window definition is the average of the values for years 2007, 2008, and 2009. The averages each year would be computed in a similar manner. For the earliest year in the relation *tot_credits*, the average would be over only that year itself, while for the next year, the average would be over two years. Note that if the relation *tot _credits* has more than one tuple for a specific year, there may be multiple possible orderings of tuples, that are sorted by year. In this case, the definition of preceding tuples is based on the implementation dependent sort order, and is not uniquely defined.

Suppose that instead of going back a fixed number of tuples, we want the window to consist of all prior years. That means the number of prior years considered is not fixed. To get the average total credits over all prior years we write:

> **select** *year*, **avg**(*num_credits*)
> > **over** (**order by** *year* **rows unbounded preceding**)
> > **as** *avg_total_credits*
> **from** *tot_credits*;

It is possible to use the keyword **following** in place of **preceding**. If we did this in our example the *year* value specifies the beginning of the window instead of the end. Similarly, we can specify a window beginning before the current tuple and ending after it:

> **select** *year*, **avg**(*num_credits*)
> > **over** (**order by** *year* **rows between** 3 **preceding and** 2 **following**)
> > **as** *avg_total_credits*
> **from** *tot_credits*;

Instead of a specific count of tuples, we can specify a range based on the value of the **order by** attribute. To specify a range going back 4 years and including the current year, we write:

---

[11]We leave the definition of this view in terms of our university example as an exercise.

```
    select year, avg(num_credits)
                        over (order by year range between year - 4 and year)
                        as avg_total_credits
    from tot_credits;
```

Be sure to note the use of the keyword **range** in the above example. For the year 2010, data for years 2006 to 2010 inclusive would be included regardless of how many tuples actually exist for that range.

In our example, all tuples pertain to the entire university. Suppose instead, we have credit data for each department in a view *tot_credits_dept* (*dept_name, year, num_credits*) giving the total number of credits students took with the particular department in the specified year. (Again, we leave writing this view definition as an exercise.) We can write windowing queries that treat each department separately by partitioning by *dept_name*:

```
  select dept_name, year, avg(num_credits)
                over (partition by dept_name
                      order by year rows between 3 preceding and current row)
                as avg_total_credits
  from tot_credits_dept;
```

5.6 OLAP**

An online analytical processing (OLAP) system is an interactive system that permits an analyst to view different summaries of multidimensional data. The word *online* indicates that an analyst must be able to request new summaries and get responses online, within a few seconds, and should not be forced to wait for a long time to see the result of a query.

There are many OLAP products available, including some that ship with database products such as Microsoft SQL Server, and Oracle, and other standalone tools. The initial versions of many OLAP tools assumed that data is memory resident. Data analysis on small amounts of data can in fact be performed using spreadsheet applications, such as Excel. However, OLAP on very large amounts of data requires that data be resident in a database, and requires support from the database for efficient preprocessing of data as well as for online query processing. In this section, we study extensions of SQL to support such tasks.

5.6.1 Online Analytical Processing

Consider an application where a shop wants to find out what kinds of clothes are popular. Let us suppose that clothes are characterized by their item_name, color, and size, and that we have a relation *sales* with the schema.

sales (*item_name, color, clothes_size, quantity*)

item_name	color	clothes_size	quantity
skirt	dark	small	2
skirt	dark	medium	5
skirt	dark	large	1
skirt	pastel	small	11
skirt	pastel	medium	9
skirt	pastel	large	15
skirt	white	small	2
skirt	white	medium	5
skirt	white	large	3
dress	dark	small	2
dress	dark	medium	6
dress	dark	large	12
dress	pastel	small	4
dress	pastel	medium	3
dress	pastel	large	3
dress	white	small	2
dress	white	medium	3
dress	white	large	0
shirt	dark	small	2
shirt	dark	medium	6
shirt	dark	large	6
shirt	pastel	small	4
shirt	pastel	medium	1
shirt	pastel	large	2
shirt	white	small	17
shirt	white	medium	1
shirt	white	large	10
pants	dark	small	14
pants	dark	medium	6
pants	dark	large	0
pants	pastel	small	1
pants	pastel	medium	0
pants	pastel	large	1
pants	white	small	3
pants	white	medium	0
pants	white	large	2

Figure 5.16 An example of *sales* relation.

Suppose that *item_name* can take on the values (skirt, dress, shirt, pants), *color* can take on the values (dark, pastel, white), *clothes_size* can take on values (small, medium, large), and *quantity* is an integer value representing the total number of items of a given {*item_name*, *color*, *clothes_size* }. An instance of the *sales* relation is shown in Figure 5.16.

Statistical analysis often requires grouping on multiple attributes. Given a relation used for data analysis, we can identify some of its attributes as **measure** attributes, since they measure some value, and can be aggregated upon. For instance, the attribute *quantity* of the *sales* relation is a measure attribute, since it measures the number of units sold. Some (or all) of the other attributes of the relation are identified as **dimension attributes**, since they define the dimensions on which measure attributes, and summaries of measure attributes, are viewed. In the *sales* relation, *item_name*, *color*, and *clothes_size* are dimension attributes. (A more realistic version of the *sales* relation would have additional dimensions, such as time and sales location, and additional measures such as monetary value of the sale.)

Data that can be modeled as dimension attributes and measure attributes are called **multidimensional data**.

To analyze the multidimensional data, a manager may want to see data laid out as shown in the table in Figure 5.17. The table shows total quantities for different combinations of *item_name* and *color*. The value of *clothes_size* is specified to be **all**, indicating that the displayed values are a summary across all values of *clothes_size* (that is, we want to group the "small", "medium", and "large" items into one single group.

The table in Figure 5.17 is an example of a **cross-tabulation** (or **cross-tab**, for short), also referred to as a **pivot-table**. In general, a cross-tab is a table derived from a relation (say R), where values for one attribute of relation R (say A) form the row headers and values for another attribute of relation R (say B) form the column header. For example, in Figure 5.17, the attribute *item_name* corresponds to A (with values "dark", "pastel", and "white"), and the attribute *color* corresponds to to B (with attributes "skirt", "dress", "shirt", and "pants").

Each cell in the pivot-table can be identified by (a_i, b_j), where a_i is a value for A and b_j a value for B. The values of the various cells in the pivot-table are derived from the relation R as follows: If there is at most one tuple in R with any (a_i, b_j) value, the value in the cell is derived from that single tuple (if any); for instance, it could be the value of one or more other attributes of the tuple. If there can be multiple tuples with an (a_i, b_j) value, the value in the cell must be derived

clothes_size **all**

color

	dark	pastel	white	total
skirt	8	35	10	53
dress	20	10	5	35
shirt	14	7	28	49
pants	20	2	5	27
total	62	54	48	164

item_name

Figure 5.17 Cross tabulation of *sales* by *item_name* and *color*.

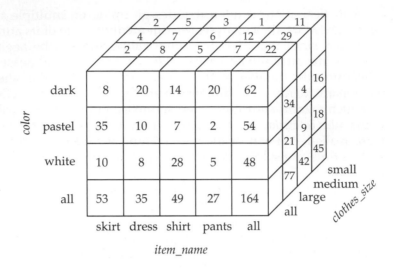

Figure 5.18 Three-dimensional data cube.

by aggregation on the tuples with that value. In our example, the aggregation used is the sum of the values for attribute *quantity*, across all values for *clothes _size*, as indicated by "*clothes_size*: **all**" above the cross-tab in Figure 5.17. Thus, the value for cell (skirt, pastel) is 35, since there are 3 tuples in the *sales* table that meet that criteria, with values 11, 9, and 15.

In our example, the cross-tab also has an extra column and an extra row storing the totals of the cells in the row/column. Most cross-tabs have such summary rows and columns.

The generalization of a cross-tab, which is two-dimensional, to n dimensions can be visualized as an n-dimensional cube, called the **data cube**. Figure 5.18 shows a data cube on the *sales* relation. The data cube has three dimensions, *item_name*, *color*, and *clothes_size*, and the measure attribute is *quantity*. Each cell is identified by values for these three dimensions. Each cell in the data cube contains a value, just as in a cross-tab. In Figure 5.18, the value contained in a cell is shown on one of the faces of the cell; other faces of the cell are shown blank if they are visible. All cells contain values, even if they are not visible. The value for a dimension may be **all**, in which case the cell contains a summary over all values of that dimension, as in the case of cross-tabs.

The number of different ways in which the tuples can be grouped for aggregation can be large. In the example of Figure 5.18, there are 3 colors, 4 items, and 3 sizes resulting in a cube size of $3 \times 4 \times 3 = 36$. Including the summary values, we obtain a $4 \times 5 \times 4$ cube, whose size is 80. In fact, for a table with n dimensions, aggregation can be performed with grouping on each of the 2^n subsets of the n dimensions.[12]

---

[12]Grouping on the set of all n dimensions is useful only if the table may have duplicates.

With an OLAP system, a data analyst can look at different cross-tabs on the same data by interactively selecting the attributes in the cross-tab. Each cross-tab is a two-dimensional view on a multidimensional data cube. For instance, the analyst may select a cross-tab on *item_name* and *clothes_size* or a cross-tab on *color* and *clothes_size*. The operation of changing the dimensions used in a cross-tab is called **pivoting**.

OLAP systems allow an analyst to see a cross-tab on *item_name* and *color* for a fixed value of *clothes_size*, for example, large, instead of the sum across all sizes. Such an operation is referred to as **slicing**, since it can be thought of as viewing a slice of the data cube. The operation is sometimes called **dicing**, particularly when values for multiple dimensions are fixed.

When a cross-tab is used to view a multidimensional cube, the values of dimension attributes that are not part of the cross-tab are shown above the cross-tab. The value of such an attribute can be **all**, as shown in Figure 5.17, indicating that data in the cross-tab are a summary over all values for the attribute. Slicing/dicing simply consists of selecting specific values for these attributes, which are then displayed on top of the cross-tab.

OLAP systems permit users to view data at any desired level of granularity. The operation of moving from finer-granularity data to a coarser granularity (by means of aggregation) is called a **rollup**. In our example, starting from the data cube on the *sales* table, we got our example cross-tab by rolling up on the attribute *clothes_size*. The opposite operation—that of moving from coarser-granularity data to finer-granularity data—is called a **drill down**. Clearly, finer-granularity data cannot be generated from coarse-granularity data; they must be generated either from the original data, or from even finer-granularity summary data.

Analysts may wish to view a dimension at different levels of detail. For instance, an attribute of type **datetime** contains a date and a time of day. Using time precise to a second (or less) may not be meaningful: An analyst who is interested in rough time of day may look at only the hour value. An analyst who is interested in sales by day of the week may map the date to a day of the week and look only at that. Another analyst may be interested in aggregates over a month, or a quarter, or for an entire year.

The different levels of detail for an attribute can be organized into a **hierarchy**. Figure 5.19a shows a hierarchy on the **datetime** attribute. As another example, Figure 5.19b shows a hierarchy on location, with the city being at the bottom of the hierarchy, state above it, country at the next level, and region being the top level. In our earlier example, clothes can be grouped by category (for instance, menswear or womenswear); *category* would then lie above *item_name* in our hierarchy on clothes. At the level of actual values, skirts and dresses would fall under the womenswear category and pants and shirts under the menswear category.

An analyst may be interested in viewing sales of clothes divided as menswear and womenswear, and not interested in individual values. After viewing the aggregates at the level of womenswear and menswear, an analyst may *drill down the hierarchy* to look at individual values. An analyst looking at the detailed level may *drill up the hierarchy* and look at coarser-level aggregates. Both levels can be displayed on the same cross-tab, as in Figure 5.20.

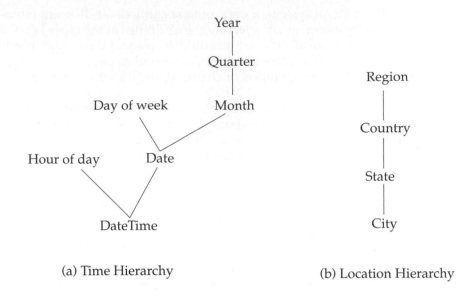

(a) Time Hierarchy   (b) Location Hierarchy

Figure 5.19   Hierarchies on dimensions.

5.6.2   Cross-Tab and Relational Tables

A cross-tab is different from relational tables usually stored in databases, since the number of columns in the cross-tab depends on the actual data. A change in the data values may result in adding more columns, which is not desirable for data storage. However, a cross-tab view is desirable for display to users. It is straightforward to represent a cross-tab without summary values in a relational form with a fixed number of columns. A cross-tab with summary rows/columns can be represented by introducing a special value **all** to represent subtotals, as in Figure 5.21. The SQL standard actually uses the **null** value in place of **all**, but to avoid confusion with regular null values, we shall continue to use **all**.

clothes_size: **all**

category	item_name	color				
		dark	pastel	white	total	
womenswear	skirt	8	8	10	53	
	dress	20	20	5	35	
	subtotal	28	28	15		88
menswear	pants	14	14	28	49	
	shirt	20	20	5	27	
	subtotal	34	34	33		76
total		62	62	48		164

Figure 5.20   Cross tabulation of *sales* with hierarchy on *item_name*.

item_name	color	clothes_size	quantity
skirt	dark	**all**	8
skirt	pastel	**all**	35
skirt	white	**all**	10
skirt	**all**	**all**	53
dress	dark	**all**	20
dress	pastel	**all**	10
dress	white	**all**	5
dress	**all**	**all**	35
shirt	dark	**all**	14
shirt	pastel	**all**	7
shirt	white	**all**	28
shirt	**all**	**all**	49
pants	dark	**all**	20
pants	pastel	**all**	2
pants	white	**all**	5
pants	**all**	**all**	27
all	dark	**all**	62
all	pastel	**all**	54
all	white	**all**	48
all	**all**	**all**	164

Figure 5.21 Relational representation of the data in Figure 5.17.

Consider the tuples (skirt, **all**, **all**, 53) and (dress, **all**, **all**, 35). We have obtained these tuples by eliminating individual tuples with different values for *color* and *clothes_size*, and by replacing the value of *quantity* by an aggregate—namely, the sum of the quantities. The value **all** can be thought of as representing the set of all values for an attribute. Tuples with the value **all** for the *color* and *clothes_size* dimensions can be obtained by an aggregation on the *sales* relation with a **group by** on the column *item_name*. Similarly, a **group by** on *color*, *clothes_size* can be used to get the tuples with the value **all** for *item_name*, and a **group by** with no attributes (which can simply be omitted in SQL) can be used to get the tuple with value **all** for *item_name*, *color*, and *clothes_size*.

Hierarchies can also be represented by relations. For example, the fact that skirts and dresses fall under the womenswear category, and the pants and shirts under the menswear category can be represented by a relation *itemcategory*(*item_name*, category). This relation can be joined with the *sales* relation, to get a relation that includes the category for each item. Aggregation on this joined relation allows us to get a cross-tab with hierarchy. As another example, a hierarchy on city can be represented by a single relation *city_hierarchy* (ID, *city*, *state*, *country*, *region*), or by multiple relations, each mapping values in one level of the hierarchy to values at the next level. We assume here that cities have unique identifiers, stored in the attribute ID, to avoid confusing between two cities with the same name, e.g., the Springfield in Missouri and the Springfield in Illinois.

OLAP IMPLEMENTATION

The earliest OLAP systems used multidimensional arrays in memory to store data cubes, and are referred to as **multidimensional OLAP (MOLAP)** systems. Later, OLAP facilities were integrated into relational systems, with data stored in a relational database. Such systems are referred to as **relational OLAP (ROLAP)** systems. Hybrid systems, which store some summaries in memory and store the base data and other summaries in a relational database, are called **hybrid OLAP (HOLAP)** systems.

Many OLAP systems are implemented as client-server systems. The server contains the relational database as well as any MOLAP data cubes. Client systems obtain views of the data by communicating with the server.

A naïve way of computing the entire data cube (all groupings) on a relation is to use any standard algorithm for computing aggregate operations, one grouping at a time. The naïve algorithm would require a large number of scans of the relation. A simple optimization is to compute an aggregation on, say, (*item _name*, *color*) from an aggregation (*item_name*, *color*, *clothes_size*), instead of from the original relation.

For the standard SQL aggregate functions, we can compute an aggregate with grouping on a set of attributes A from an aggregate with grouping on a set of attributes B if $A \subseteq B$; you can do so as an exercise (see Exercise 5.24), but note that to compute **avg**, we additionally need the **count** value. (For some nonstandard aggregate functions, such as median, aggregates cannot be computed as above; the optimization described here does not apply to such *non-decomposable* aggregate functions.) The amount of data read drops significantly by computing an aggregate from another aggregate, instead of from the original relation. Further improvements are possible; for instance, multiple groupings can be computed on a single scan of the data.

Early OLAP implementations precomputed and stored entire data cubes, that is, groupings on all subsets of the dimension attributes. Precomputation allows OLAP queries to be answered within a few seconds, even on datasets that may contain millions of tuples adding up to gigabytes of data. However, there are 2^n groupings with n dimension attributes; hierarchies on attributes increase the number further. As a result, the entire data cube is often larger than the original relation that formed the data cube and in many cases it is not feasible to store the entire data cube.

Instead of precomputing and storing all possible groupings, it makes sense to precompute and store some of the groupings, and to compute others on demand. Instead of computing queries from the original relation, which may take a very long time, we can compute them from other precomputed queries. For instance, suppose that a query requires grouping by (*item_name*, *color*), and this has not been precomputed. The query result can be computed from summaries by (*item _name*, *color*, *clothes_size*), if that has been precomputed. See the bibliographical notes for references on how to select a good set of groupings for precomputation, given limits on the storage available for precomputed results.

5.6.3 OLAP in SQL

Several SQL implementations, such as Microsoft SQL Server, and Oracle, support a **pivot** clause in SQL, which allows creation of cross-tabs. Given the *sales* relation from Figure 5.16, the query:

> **select** *
> **from** *sales*
> **pivot** (
>   **sum**(*quantity*)
>   **for** *color* **in** ('dark','pastel','white')
>)
> **order by** *item_name*;

returns the cross-tab shown in Figure 5.22. Note that the **for** clause within the **pivot** clause specifies what values from the attribute *color* should appears as attribute names in the pivot result. The attribute *color* itself is eliminated from the result, although all other attributes are retained, except that the values for the newly created attributes are specified to come from the attribute *quantity*. In case more than one tuple contributes values to a given cell, the aggregate operation within the **pivot** clause specifies how the values should be combined. In the above example, the *quantity* values are summed up.

Note that the pivot clause by itself does not compute the subtotals we saw in the pivot table from Figure 5.17. However, we can first generate the relational representation shown in Figure 5.21, as outlined shortly, and then apply the pivot clause on that representation to get an equivalent result. In this case, the value **all** must also be listed in the **for** clause, and the **order by** clause needs to be modified to order **all** at the end.

item_name	clothes_size	dark	pastel	white
skirt	small	2	11	2
skirt	medium	5	9	5
skirt	large	1	15	3
dress	small	2	4	2
dress	medium	6	3	3
dress	large	12	3	0
shirt	small	2	4	17
shirt	medium	6	1	1
shirt	large	6	2	10
pants	small	14	1	3
pants	medium	6	0	0
pants	large	0	1	2

Figure 5.22 Result of SQL pivot operation on the *sales* relation of Figure 5.16.

item_name	quantity
skirt	53
dress	35
shirt	49
pants	27

Figure 5.23   Query result.

The data in a data cube cannot be generated by a single SQL query, using the basic **group by** constructs, since aggregates are computed for several different groupings of the dimension attributes. For this reason, SQL includes functions to form the grouping needed for OLAP. We discuss these below.

SQL supports generalizations of the **group by** construct to perform the **cube** and **rollup** operations. The **cube** and **rollup** constructs in the **group by** clause allow multiple **group by** queries to be run in a single query with the result returned as a single relation in a style similar to that of the relation of Figure 5.21.

Consider again our retail shop example and the relation:

$$sales\ (item\_name,\ color,\ clothes\_size,\ quantity)$$

We can find the number of items sold in each item name by writing a simple **group by** query:

> **select** item_name, **sum**(quantity)
> **from** sales
> **group by** item_name;

The result of this query is shown in Figure 5.23. Note that this represents the same data as the last column of Figure 5.17 (or equivalently, the first row in the cube of Figure 5.18).

Similarly, we can find the number of items sold in each color, etc. By using multiple attributes in the **group by** clause, we can find how many items were sold with a certain set of properties. For example, we can find a breakdown of sales by item-name and color by writing:

> **select** item_name, color, **sum**(quantity)
> **from** sales
> **group by** item_name, color;

The result of this query is shown in Figure 5.24. Note that this represents the same data as is shown in the the first 4 rows and first 4 columns of Figure 5.17 (or equivalently, the first 4 rows and columns in the cube of Figure 5.18).

If, however, we want to generate the entire data cube using this approach, we would have to write a separate query for each of the following sets of attributes:

item_name	color	quantity
skirt	dark	8
skirt	pastel	35
skirt	white	10
dress	dark	20
dress	pastel	10
dress	white	5
shirt	dark	14
shirt	pastel	7
shirt	white	28
pants	dark	20
pants	pastel	2
pants	white	5

Figure 5.24 Query result.

{ (*item_name, color, clothes_size*), (*item_name, color*), (*item_name, clothes_size*),
(*color, clothes_size*), (*item_name*), (*color*), (*clothes_size*), () }

where () denotes an empty **group by** list.

The **cube** construct allows us to accomplish this in one query:

> **select** *item_name*, color, *clothes_size*, **sum**(*quantity*)
> **from** *sales*
> **group by cube**(*item_name, color, clothes_size*);

The above query produces a relation whose schema is:

> (*item_name, color, clothes_size*, **sum**(*quantity*))

So that the result of this query is indeed a relation, tuples in the result contain *null* as the value of those attributes not present in a particular grouping. For example, tuples produced by grouping on *clothes_size* have a schema (*clothes _size*, **sum**(*quantity*)). They are converted to tuples on (*item_name, color, clothes_size*, **sum**(*quantity*)) by inserting *null* for *item_name* and *color*.

Data cube relations are often very large. The cube query above, with 3 possible colors, 4 possible item names, and 3 sizes, has 80 tuples. The relation of Figure 5.21 is generated using grouping by *item_name* and *color*. It also uses **all** in place of *null* so as to be more readable to the average user. To generate that relation in SQL, we arrange to substitute **all** for *null*. The query:

> **select** *item_name, color*, **sum**(*quantity*)
> **from** *sales*
> **group by cube**(*item_name, color*);

THE DECODE FUNCTION

The **decode** function allows substitution of values in an attribute of a tuple. The general form of **decode** is:

> **decode** (*value, match-1, replacement-1, match-2, replacement-2, . . .,*
> *match-N, replacement-N, default-replacement*);

It compares *value* against the *match* values and if a match is found, it replaces the attribute value with the corresponding replacement value. If no match succeeds, then the attribute value is replaced with the default replacement value.

The **decode** function does not work as we might like for null values because, as we saw in Section 3.6, predicates on nulls evaluate to **unknown**, which ultimately becomes **false**. To deal with this, we apply the **grouping** function, which returns 1 if its argument is a null value generated by a **cube** or **rollup** and 0 otherwise. Then the relation in Figure 5.21, with occurrences of **all** replaced by *null*, can be computed by the query:

> **select decode(grouping**(*item_name*), 1, 'all', *item_name*) **as** *item_name*
> **decode(grouping**(*color*), 1, 'all', *color*) **as** *color*
> **sum**(*quantity*) **as** *quantity*
> **from** *sales*
> **group by cube**(*item_name, color*);

generates the relation of Figure 5.21 with nulls. The substitution of **all** is achieved using the SQL **decode** and **grouping** functions. The **decode** function is conceptually simple but its syntax is somewhat hard to read. See blue box for details.

The **rollup** construct is the same as the **cube** construct except that **rollup** generates fewer **group by** queries. We saw that **group by cube** (*item_name, color, clothes_size*) generated all 8 ways of forming a **group by** query using some (or all or none) of the attributes. In:

> **select** *item_name, color, clothes_size,* **sum**(*quantity*)
> **from** *sales*
> **group by rollup**(*item_name, color, clothes_size*);

group by rollup(*item_name, color, clothes_size*) generates only 4 groupings:

> { (*item_name, color, clothes_size*), (*item_name, color*), (*item_name*), () }

Notice that the order of the attributes in the **rollup** makes a difference; the final attribute (*clothes_size*, in our example) appears in only one grouping, the penultimate (second last) attribute in 2 groupings, and so on, with the first attribute appearing in all groups but one (the empty grouping).

Why might we want the specific groupings that are used in **rollup**? These groups are of frequent practical interest for hierarchies (as in Figure 5.19, for example). For the location hierarchy (*Region, Country, State, City*), we may want to group by *Region* to get sales by region. Then we may want to "drill down" to the level of countries within each region, which means we would group by *Region, Country*. Drilling down further, we may wish to group by *Region, Country, State* and then by *Region, Country, State, City*. The **rollup** construct allows us to specify this sequence of drilling down for further detail.

Multiple **rollup**s and **cube**s can be used in a single **group by** clause. For instance, the following query:

> **select** *item_name, color, clothes_size*, **sum**(*quantity*)
> **from** *sales*
> **group by rollup**(*item_name*), **rollup**(*color, clothes_size*);

generates the groupings:

> { (*item_name, color, clothes_size*), (*item_name, color*), (*item_name*),
> (*color, clothes_size*), (*color*), () }

To understand why, observe that **rollup**(*item_name*) generates two groupings, {(*item_name*), ()}, and **rollup**(*color, clothes_size*) generates three groupings, {(*color, clothes_size*), (*color*), () }. The Cartesian product of the two gives us the six groupings shown.

Neither the **rollup** nor the **cube** clause gives complete control on the groupings that are generated. For instance, we cannot use them to specify that we want only groupings {(*color, clothes_size*), (*clothes_size, item_name*)}. Such restricted groupings can be generated by using the **grouping** construct in the **having** clause; we leave the details as an exercise for you.

5.7 Summary

- SQL queries can be invoked from host languages, via embedded and dynamic SQL. The ODBC and JDBC standards define application program interfaces to access SQL databases from C and Java language programs. Increasingly, programmers use these APIs to access databases.

- Functions and procedures can be defined using SQLprocedural extensions that allow iteration and conditional (if-then-else) statements.

- Triggers define actions to be executed automatically when certain events occur and corresponding conditions are satisfied. Triggers have many uses, such as implementing business rules, audit logging, and even carrying out actions outside the database system. Although triggers were not added to the

SQL standard until SQL:1999, most database systems have long implemented triggers.

- Some queries, such as transitive closure, can be expressed either by using iteration or by using recursive SQL queries. Recursion can be expressed using either recursive views or recursive **with** clause definitions.

- SQL supports several advanced aggregation features, including ranking and windowing queries that simplify the expression of some aggregates and allow more efficient evaluation.

- Online analytical processing (OLAP) tools help analysts view data summarized in different ways, so that they can gain insight into the functioning of an organization.

  - OLAP tools work on multidimensional data, characterized by dimension attributes and measure attributes.

  - The data cube consists of multidimensional data summarized in different ways. Precomputing the data cube helps speed up queries on summaries of data.

  - Cross-tab displays permit users to view two dimensions of multidimensional data at a time, along with summaries of the data.

  - Drill down, rollup, slicing, and dicing are among the operations that users perform with OLAP tools.

- SQL, starting with the SQL:1999 standard, provides a variety of operators for data analysis, including **cube** and **rollup** operations. Some systems support a **pivot** clause, which allows easy creation of cross-tabs.

Review Terms

- JDBC
- ODBC
- Prepared statements
- Accessing metadata
- SQL injection
- Embedded SQL
- Cursors
- Updatable cursors
- Dynamic SQL
- SQL functions
- Stored procedures
- Procedural constructs
- External language routines
- Trigger
- Before and after triggers
- Transition variables and tables
- Recursive queries
- Monotonic queries
- Ranking functions
  - Rank
  - Dense rank
  - Partition by
- Windowing

- Online analytical processing (OLAP)
- Multidimensional data

  ○ Measure attributes

  ○ Dimension attributes

○ Pivoting

○ Data cube

○ Slicing and dicing

○ Rollup and drill down

- Cross-tabulation

Practice Exercises

5.1 Describe the circumstances in which you would choose to use embedded SQL rather than SQL alone or only a general-purpose programming language.

5.2 Write a Java function using JDBC metadata features that takes a `ResultSet` as an input parameter, and prints out the result in tabular form, with appropriate names as column headings.

5.3 Write a Java function using JDBC metadata features that prints a list of all relations in the database, displaying for each relation the names and types of its attributes.

5.4 Show how to enforce the constraint "an instructor cannot teach in two different classrooms in a semester in the same time slot." using a trigger (remember that the constraint can be violated by changes to the *teaches* relation as well as to the *section* relation).

5.5 Write triggers to enforce the referential integrity constraint from *section* to *time_slot*, on updates to *section*, and *time_slot*. Note that the ones we wrote in Figure 5.8 do not cover the **update** operation.

5.6 To maintain the *tot_cred* attribute of the *student* relation, carry out the following:

   a. Modify the trigger on updates of *takes*, to handle all updates that can affect the value of *tot_cred*.

   b. Write a trigger to handle inserts to the *takes* relation.

   c. Under what assumptions is it reasonable not to create triggers on the *course* relation?

5.7 Consider the bank database of Figure 5.25. Let us define a view *branch_cust* as follows:

        create view *branch_cust* **as**
            select *branch_name, customer_name*
            from *depositor, account*
            where *depositor.account_number = account.account_number*

branch(*branch_name*, *branch_city*, *assets*)
customer (*customer_name*, *customer_street*, *cust omer_city*)
loan (*loan_number*, *branch_name*, *amount*)
borrower (*customer_name*, *loan_number*)
account (*account_number*, *branch_name*, *balance*)
depositor (*customer_name*, *account_number*)

Figure 5.25   Banking database for Exercises 5.7, 5.8, and 5.28 .

Suppose that the view is *materialized*; that is, the view is computed and stored. Write triggers to *maintain* the view, that is, to keep it up-to-date on insertions to and deletions from *depositor* or *account*. Do not bother about updates.

5.8   Consider the bank database of Figure 5.25. Write an SQL trigger to carry out the following action: On **delete** of an account, for each owner of the account, check if the owner has any remaining accounts, and if she does not, delete her from the *depositor* relation.

5.9   Show how to express **group by cube**(a, b, c, d) using **rollup**; your answer should have only one **group by** clause.

5.10   Given a relation S(*student*, *subject*, *marks*), write a query to find the top n students by total marks, by using ranking.

5.11   Consider the *sales* relation from Section 5.6. Write an SQL query to compute the cube operation on the relation, giving the relation in Figure 5.21. Do not use the **cube** construct.

Exercises

5.12   Consider the following relations for a company database:

- *emp* (*ename*, *dname*, *salary*)
- *mgr* (*ename*, *mname*)

and the Java code in Figure 5.26, which uses the JDBC API. Assume that the userid, password, machine name, etc. are all okay. Describe in concise English what the Java program does. (That is, produce an English sentence like "It finds the manager of the toy department," not a line-by-line description of what each Java statement does.)

5.13   Suppose you were asked to define a class MetaDisplay in Java, containing a method static void printTable(String r); the method takes a relation name r as input, executes the query "**select * from** r", and prints the result out in nice tabular format, with the attribute names displayed in the header of the table.

```
import java.sql.*;
public class Mystery {
    public static void main(String[] args) {
        try {
            Connection con=null;
            Class.forName("oracle.jdbc.driver.OracleDriver");
            con=DriverManager.getConnection(
                "jdbc:oracle:thin:star/X@//edgar.cse.lehigh.edu:1521/XE");
            Statement s=con.createStatement();
            String q;
            String empName = "dog";
            boolean more;
            ResultSet result;
            do {
                q = "select mname from mgr where ename = '" + empName + "'";
                result = s.executeQuery(q);
                more = result.next();
                if (more) {
                    empName = result.getString("mname");
                    System.out.println (empName);
                }
            } while (more);
            s.close();
            con.close();
        } catch(Exception e){e.printStackTrace();} }}
```

Figure 5.26   Java code for Exercise 5.12.

    a.   What do you need to know about relation r to be able to print the result in the specified tabular format.

    b.   What JDBC methods(s) can get you the required information?

    c.   Write the method printTable(String r) using the JDBC API.

5.14   Repeat Exercise 5.13 using ODBC, defining void printTable(char *r) as a function instead of a method.

5.15   Consider an employee database with two relations

$$employee \ (\underline{employee\_name}, \ street, \ city)$$
$$works \ (\underline{employee\_name}, \ company\_name, \ salary)$$

where the primary keys are underlined. Write a query to find companies whose employees earn a higher salary, on average, than the average salary at "First Bank Corporation".

      a.   Using SQL functions as appropriate.

      b.   Without using SQL functions.

5.16   Rewrite the query in Section 5.2.1 that returns the name and budget of all departments with more than 12 instructors, using the **with** clause instead of using a function call.

5.17   Compare the use of embedded SQL with the use in SQL of functions defined in a general-purpose programming language. Under what circumstances would you use each of these features?

5.18   Modify the recursive query in Figure 5.15 to define a relation

$$prereq\_depth(course\_id, prereq\_id, depth)$$

where the attribute *depth* indicates how many levels of intermediate prerequisites are there between the course and the prerequisite. Direct prerequisites have a depth of 0.

5.19   Consider the relational schema

$$part(\underline{part\_id}, name, cost)$$
$$subpart(\underline{part\_id, subpart\_id}, count)$$

A tuple $(p_1, p_2, 3)$ in the *subpart* relation denotes that the part with part-id p_2 is a direct subpart of the part with part-id p_1, and p_1 has 3 copies of p_2. Note that p_2 may itself have further subparts. Write a recursive SQL query that outputs the names of all subparts of the part with part-id "P-100".

5.20   Consider again the relational schema from Exercise 5.19. Write a JDBC function using non-recursive SQL to find the total cost of part "P-100", including the costs of all its subparts. Be sure to take into account the fact that a part may have multiple occurrences of a subpart. You may use recursion in Java if you wish.

5.21   Suppose there are two relations r and s, such that the foreign key B of r references the primary key A of s. Describe how the trigger mechanism can be used to implement the **on delete cascade** option, when a tuple is deleted from s.

5.22   The execution of a trigger can cause another action to be triggered. Most database systems place a limit on how deep the nesting can be. Explain why they might place such a limit.

5.23   Consider the relation, r, shown in Figure 5.27. Give the result of the following query:

building	room_number	time_slot_id	course_id	sec_id
Garfield	359	A	BIO-101	1
Garfield	359	B	BIO-101	2
Saucon	651	A	CS-101	2
Saucon	550	C	CS-319	1
Painter	705	D	MU-199	1
Painter	403	D	FIN-201	1

Figure 5.27 The relation *r* for Exercise 5.23.

> **select** *building, room_number, time_slot_id,* **count**(*)
> **from** r
> **group by rollup** (*building, room_number, time_slot_id*)

5.24 For each of the SQL aggregate functions **sum, count, min**, and **max**, show how to compute the aggregate value on a multiset $S_1 \cup S_2$, given the aggregate values on multisets S_1 and S_2.

On the basis of the above, give expressions to compute aggregate values with grouping on a subset S of the attributes of a relation $r(A, B, C, D, E)$, given aggregate values for grouping on attributes $T \supseteq S$, for the following aggregate functions:

   a. **sum, count, min**, and **max**

   b. **avg**

   c. Standard deviation

5.25 In Section 5.5.1, we used the *student_grades* view of Exercise 4.5 to write a query to find the rank of each student based on grade-point average. Modify that query to show only the top 10 students (that is, those students whose rank is 1 through 10).

5.26 Give an example of a pair of groupings that cannot be expressed by using a single **group by** clause with **cube** and **rollup**.

5.27 Given relation $s(a, b, c)$, show how to use the extended SQL features to generate a histogram of c versus a, dividing a into 20 equal-sized partitions (that is, where each partition contains 5 percent of the tuples in s, sorted by a).

5.28 Consider the bank database of Figure 5.25 and the *balance* attribute of the *account* relation. Write an SQL query to compute a histogram of *balance* values, dividing the range 0 to the maximum account balance present, into three equal ranges.

Tools

Most database vendors provide OLAP tools as part of their database systems, or as add-on applications. These include OLAP tools from Microsoft Corp., Oracle Express, and Informix Metacube. Tools may be integrated with a larger "business intelligence" product such as IBM Cognos. Many companies also provide analysis tools for specific applications, such as customer relationship management (for example, Oracle Siebel CRM).

Bibliographical Notes

See the bibliographic notes of Chapter 3 for references to SQL standards and books on SQL.

An excellent source for more (and up-to-date) information on JDBC, and on Java in general, is java.sun.com/docs/books/tutorial. References to books on Java (including JDBC) are also available at this URL. The ODBC API is described in Microsoft [1997] and Sanders [1998]. Melton and Eisenberg [2000] provides a guide to SQLJ, JDBC, and related technologies. More information on ODBC, ADO, and ADO.NET can be found on msdn.microsoft.com/data.

In the context of functions and procedures in SQL, many database products support features beyond those specified in the standards, and do not support many of the features of the standard. More information on these features may be found in the SQL user manuals of the respective products.

The original SQL proposals for assertions and triggers are discussed in Astrahan et al. [1976], Chamberlin et al. [1976], and Chamberlin et al. [1981]. Melton and Simon [2001], Melton [2002], and Eisenberg and Melton [1999] provide textbook coverage of SQL:1999, the version of the SQL standard that first included triggers.

Recursive query processing was first studied in detail in the context of a query language called Datalog, which was based on mathematical logic and followed the syntax of the logic programming language Prolog. Ramakrishnan and Ullman [1995] provides a survey of results in this area, including techniques to optimize queries that select a subset of tuples from a recursively defined view.

Gray et al. [1995] and Gray et al. [1997] describe the data-cube operator. Efficient algorithms for computing data cubes are described by Agarwal et al. [1996], Harinarayan et al. [1996], and Ross and Srivastava [1997]. Descriptions of extended aggregation support in SQL:1999 can be found in the product manuals of database systems such as Oracle and IBM DB2.

There has been a substantial amount of research on the efficient processing of "top-k" queries that return only the top-k-ranked results. A survey of that work appears in Ilyas et al. [2008].

CHAPTER 6

Formal Relational Query Languages

In Chapters 2 through 5 we introduced the relational model and covered SQL in great detail. In this chapter we present the formal model upon which SQL as well as other relational query languages are based.

We cover three formal languages. We start by presenting the relational algebra, which forms the basis of the widely used SQL query language. We then cover the tuple relational calculus and the domain relational calculus, which are declarative query languages based on mathematical logic.

6.1 The Relational Algebra

The relational algebra is a *procedural* query language. It consists of a set of operations that take one or two relations as input and produce a new relation as their result. The fundamental operations in the relational algebra are *select, project, union, set difference, Cartesian product,* and *rename.* In addition to the fundamental operations, there are several other operations—namely, *set intersection, natural join,* and *assignment.* We shall define these operations in terms of the fundamental operations.

6.1.1 Fundamental Operations

The select, project, and rename operations are called *unary* operations, because they operate on one relation. The other three operations operate on pairs of relations and are, therefore, called *binary* operations.

6.1.1.1 The Select Operation

The **select** operation selects tuples that satisfy a given predicate. We use the lowercase Greek letter sigma (σ) to denote selection. The predicate appears as a subscript to σ. The argument relation is in parentheses after the σ. Thus, to select

217

ID	name	dept_name	salary
10101	Srinivasan	Comp. Sci.	65000
12121	Wu	Finance	90000
15151	Mozart	Music	40000
22222	Einstein	Physics	95000
32343	El Said	History	60000
33456	Gold	Physics	87000
45565	Katz	Comp. Sci.	75000
58583	Califieri	History	62000
76543	Singh	Finance	80000
76766	Crick	Biology	72000
83821	Brandt	Comp. Sci.	92000
98345	Kim	Elec. Eng.	80000

Figure 6.1   The *instructor* relation.

those tuples of the *instructor* relation where the instructor is in the "Physics" department, we write:

$$\sigma_{dept\_name = \text{"Physics"}} (instructor)$$

If the *instructor* relation is as shown in Figure 6.1, then the relation that results from the preceding query is as shown in Figure 6.2.

We can find all instructors with salary greater than \$90,000 by writing:

$$\sigma_{salary > 90000} (instructor)$$

In general, we allow comparisons using $=, \neq, <, \leq, >$, and $\geq$ in the selection predicate. Furthermore, we can combine several predicates into a larger predicate by using the connectives *and* ($\wedge$), *or* ($\vee$), and *not* ($\neg$). Thus, to find the instructors in Physics with a salary greater than \$90,000, we write:

$$\sigma_{dept\_name = \text{"Physics"} \wedge salary > 90000} (instructor)$$

The selection predicate may include comparisons between two attributes. To illustrate, consider the relation *department*. To find all departments whose name is the same as their building name, we can write:

$$\sigma_{dept\_name = building}(department)$$

ID	name	dept_name	salary
22222	Einstein	Physics	95000
33456	Gold	Physics	87000

Figure 6.2   Result of $\sigma_{dept\_name = \text{"Physics"}} (instructor)$.

SQL VERSUS RELATIONAL ALGEBRA

The term *select* in relational algebra has a different meaning than the one used in SQL, which is an unfortunate historical fact. In relational algebra, the term *select* corresponds to what we refer to in SQL as *where*. We emphasize the different interpretations here to minimize potential confusion.

6.1.1.2 The Project Operation

Suppose we want to list all instructors' *ID*, *name*, and *salary*, but do not care about the *dept_name*. The **project** operation allows us to produce this relation. The project operation is a unary operation that returns its argument relation, with certain attributes left out. Since a relation is a set, any duplicate rows are eliminated. Projection is denoted by the uppercase Greek letter pi (Π). We list those attributes that we wish to appear in the result as a subscript to Π. The argument relation follows in parentheses. We write the query to produce such a list as:

$$\Pi_{ID,\ name,\ salary}(instructor)$$

Figure 6.3 shows the relation that results from this query.

6.1.1.3 Composition of Relational Operations

The fact that the result of a relational operation is itself a relation is important. Consider the more complicated query "Find the name of all instructors in the Physics department." We write:

ID	name	salary
10101	Srinivasan	65000
12121	Wu	90000
15151	Mozart	40000
22222	Einstein	95000
32343	El Said	60000
33456	Gold	87000
45565	Katz	75000
58583	Califieri	62000
76543	Singh	80000
76766	Crick	72000
83821	Brandt	92000
98345	Kim	80000

Figure 6.3 Result of $\Pi_{ID,\ name,\ salary}(instructor)$.

$$\Pi_{name} \left(\sigma_{dept\_name = \text{"Physics"}} (instructor) \right)$$

Notice that, instead of giving the name of a relation as the argument of the projection operation, we give an expression that evaluates to a relation.

In general, since the result of a relational-algebra operation is of the same type (relation) as its inputs, relational-algebra operations can be composed together into a **relational-algebra expression**. Composing relational-algebra operations into relational-algebra expressions is just like composing arithmetic operations (such as $+$, $-$, $*$, and $\div$) into arithmetic expressions. We study the formal definition of relational-algebra expressions in Section 6.1.2.

6.1.1.4   The Union Operation

Consider a query to find the set of all courses taught in the Fall 2009 semester, the Spring 2010 semester, or both. The information is contained in the *section* relation (Figure 6.4). To find the set of all courses taught in the Fall 2009 semester, we write:

$$\Pi_{course\_id} \left(\sigma_{semester = \text{"Fall"} \land year = 2009} (section) \right)$$

To find the set of all courses taught in the Spring 2010 semester, we write:

$$\Pi_{course\_id} \left(\sigma_{semester = \text{"Spring"} \land year = 2010} (section) \right)$$

To answer the query, we need the **union** of these two sets; that is, we need all section IDs that appear in either or both of the two relations. We find these data

course_id	sec_id	semester	year	building	room_number	time_slot_id
BIO-101	1	Summer	2009	Painter	514	B
BIO-301	1	Summer	2010	Painter	514	A
CS-101	1	Fall	2009	Packard	101	H
CS-101	1	Spring	2010	Packard	101	F
CS-190	1	Spring	2009	Taylor	3128	E
CS-190	2	Spring	2009	Taylor	3128	A
CS-315	1	Spring	2010	Watson	120	D
CS-319	1	Spring	2010	Watson	100	B
CS-319	2	Spring	2010	Taylor	3128	C
CS-347	1	Fall	2009	Taylor	3128	A
EE-181	1	Spring	2009	Taylor	3128	C
FIN-201	1	Spring	2010	Packard	101	B
HIS-351	1	Spring	2010	Painter	514	C
MU-199	1	Spring	2010	Packard	101	D
PHY-101	1	Fall	2009	Watson	100	A

Figure 6.4   The *section* relation.

course_id
CS-101
CS-315
CS-319
CS-347
FIN-201
HIS-351
MU-199
PHY-101

Figure 6.5 Courses offered in either Fall 2009, Spring 2010 or both semesters.

by the binary operation union, denoted, as in set theory, by $\cup$. So the expression needed is:

$$\Pi_{course\_id} \left(\sigma_{semester = \text{"Fall"} \wedge year=2009} (section) \right) \cup$$
$$\Pi_{course\_id} \left(\sigma_{semester = \text{"Spring"} \wedge year=2010} (section) \right)$$

The result relation for this query appears in Figure 6.5. Notice that there are 8 tuples in the result, even though there are 3 distinct courses offered in the Fall 2009 semester and 6 distinct courses offered in the Spring 2010 semester. Since relations are sets, duplicate values such as CS-101, which is offered in both semesters, are replaced by a single occurrence.

Observe that, in our example, we took the union of two sets, both of which consisted of *course_id* values. In general, we must ensure that unions are taken between *compatible* relations. For example, it would not make sense to take the union of the *instructor* relation and the *student* relation. Although both relations have four attributes, they differ on the *salary* and *tot_cred* domains. The union of these two attributes would not make sense in most situations. Therefore, for a union operation $r \cup s$ to be valid, we require that two conditions hold:

1. The relations r and s must be of the same arity. That is, they must have the same number of attributes.

2. The domains of the ith attribute of r and the ith attribute of s must be the same, for all i.

Note that r and s can be either database relations or temporary relations that are the result of relational-algebra expressions.

6.1.1.5 The Set-Difference Operation

The **set-difference** operation, denoted by $-$, allows us to find tuples that are in one relation but are not in another. The expression $r - s$ produces a relation containing those tuples in r but not in s.

course_id
CS-347
PHY-101

Figure 6.6 Courses offered in the Fall 2009 semester but not in Spring 2010 semester.

We can find all the courses taught in the Fall 2009 semester but not in Spring 2010 semester by writing:

$$\Pi_{course\_id} \left(\sigma_{semester = \text{"Fall"} \wedge year=2009} \left(section \right) \right) \; - $$
$$\Pi_{course\_id} \left(\sigma_{semester = \text{"Spring"} \wedge year=2010} \left(section \right) \right)$$

The result relation for this query appears in Figure 6.6.

As with the union operation, we must ensure that set differences are taken between *compatible* relations. Therefore, for a set-difference operation $r - s$ to be valid, we require that the relations r and s be of the same arity, and that the domains of the ith attribute of r and the ith attribute of s be the same, for all i.

6.1.1.6   The Cartesian-Product Operation

The **Cartesian-product** operation, denoted by a cross ($\times$), allows us to combine information from any two relations. We write the Cartesian product of relations r_1 and r_2 as $r_1 \times r_2$.

Recall that a relation is by definition a subset of a Cartesian product of a set of domains. From that definition, we should already have an intuition about the definition of the Cartesian-product operation. However, since the same attribute name may appear in both r_1 and r_2, we need to devise a naming schema to distinguish between these attributes. We do so here by attaching to an attribute the name of the relation from which the attribute originally came. For example, the relation schema for $r = instructor \times teaches$ is:

$(instructor.ID, instructor.name, instructor.dept\_name, instructor.salary$
$teaches.ID, teaches.course\_id, teaches.sec\_id, teaches.semester, teaches.year)$

With this schema, we can distinguish *instructor.ID* from *teaches.ID*. For those attributes that appear in only one of the two schemas, we shall usually drop the relation-name prefix. This simplification does not lead to any ambiguity. We can then write the relation schema for r as:

$(instructor.ID, name, dept\_name, salary$
$teaches.ID, course\_id, sec\_id, semester, year)$

This naming convention *requires* that the relations that are the arguments of the Cartesian-product operation have distinct names. This requirement causes problems in some cases, such as when the Cartesian product of a relation with itself is desired. A similar problem arises if we use the result of a relational-algebra expression in a Cartesian product, since we shall need a name for the relation so

ID	course_id	sec_id	semester	year
10101	CS-101	1	Fall	2009
10101	CS-315	1	Spring	2010
10101	CS-347	1	Fall	2009
12121	FIN-201	1	Spring	2010
15151	MU-199	1	Spring	2010
22222	PHY-101	1	Fall	2009
32343	HIS-351	1	Spring	2010
45565	CS-101	1	Spring	2010
45565	CS-319	1	Spring	2010
76766	BIO-101	1	Summer	2009
76766	BIO-301	1	Summer	2010
83821	CS-190	1	Spring	2009
83821	CS-190	2	Spring	2009
83821	CS-319	2	Spring	2010
98345	EE-181	1	Spring	2009

Figure 6.7 The *teaches* relation.

that we can refer to the relation's attributes. In Section 6.1.1.7, we see how to avoid these problems by using the rename operation.

Now that we know the relation schema for $r = instructor \times teaches$, what tuples appear in r? As you may suspect, we construct a tuple of r out of each possible pair of tuples: one from the *instructor* relation (Figure 6.1) and one from the *teaches* relation (Figure 6.7). Thus, r is a large relation, as you can see from Figure 6.8, which includes only a portion of the tuples that make up r.[1]

Assume that we have n_1 tuples in *instructor* and n_2 tuples in *teaches*. Then, there are $n_1 * n_2$ ways of choosing a pair of tuples—one tuple from each relation; so there are $n_1 * n_2$ tuples in r. In particular, note that for some tuples t in r, it may be that $t[instructor.ID] \neq t[teaches.ID]$.

In general, if we have relations $r_1(R_1)$ and $r_2(R_2)$, then $r_1 \times r_2$ is a relation whose schema is the concatenation of R_1 and R_2. Relation R contains all tuples t for which there is a tuple t_1 in r_1 and a tuple t_2 in r_2 for which $t[R_1] = t_1[R_1]$ and $t[R_2] = t_2[R_2]$.

Suppose that we want to find the names of all instructors in the Physics department together with the *course_id* of all courses they taught. We need the information in both the *instructor* relation and the *teaches* relation to do so. If we write:

$$\sigma_{dept\_name = \text{"Physics"}}(instructor \times teaches)$$

then the result is the relation in Figure 6.9.

---

[1]Note that we renamed *instructor.ID* as *inst.ID* to reduce the width of the tables in Figures 6.8 and 6.9.

inst.ID	name	dept_name	salary	teaches.ID	course_id	sec_id	semester	year
10101	Srinivasan	Physics	95000	10101	CS-101	1	Fall	2009
10101	Srinivasan	Physics	95000	10101	CS-315	1	Spring	2010
10101	Srinivasan	Physics	95000	10101	CS-347	1	Fall	2009
10101	Srinivasan	Physics	95000	10101	FIN-201	1	Spring	2010
10101	Srinivasan	Physics	95000	15151	MU-199	1	Spring	2010
10101	Srinivasan	Physics	95000	22222	PHY-101	1	Fall	2009
...	...	...	...	...	...	...	...	...
...	...	...	...	...	...	...	...	...
12121	Wu	Physics	95000	10101	CS-101	1	Fall	2009
12121	Wu	Physics	95000	10101	CS-315	1	Spring	2010
12121	Wu	Physics	95000	10101	CS-347	1	Fall	2009
12121	Wu	Physics	95000	10101	FIN-201	1	Spring	2010
12121	Wu	Physics	95000	15151	MU-199	1	Spring	2010
12121	Wu	Physics	95000	22222	PHY-101	1	Fall	2009
...	...	...	...	...	...	...	...	...
...	...	...	...	...	...	...	...	...
15151	Mozart	Physics	95000	10101	CS-101	1	Fall	2009
15151	Mozart	Physics	95000	10101	CS-315	1	Spring	2010
15151	Mozart	Physics	95000	10101	CS-347	1	Fall	2009
15151	Mozart	Physics	95000	10101	FIN-201	1	Spring	2010
15151	Mozart	Physics	95000	15151	MU-199	1	Spring	2010
15151	Mozart	Physics	95000	22222	PHY-101	1	Fall	2009
...	...	...	...	...	...	...	...	...
...	...	...	...	...	...	...	...	...
22222	Einstein	Physics	95000	10101	CS-101	1	Fall	2009
22222	Einstein	Physics	95000	10101	CS-315	1	Spring	2010
22222	Einstein	Physics	95000	10101	CS-347	1	Fall	2009
22222	Einstein	Physics	95000	10101	FIN-201	1	Spring	2010
22222	Einstein	Physics	95000	15151	MU-199	1	Spring	2010
22222	Einstein	Physics	95000	22222	PHY-101	1	Fall	2009
...	...	...	...	...	...	...	...	...
...	...	...	...	...	...	...	...	...

Figure 6.8 Result of *instructor* × *teaches*.

We have a relation that pertains only to instructors in the Physics department. However, the *course_id* column may contain information about courses that were not taught by the corresponding instructor. (If you do not see why that is true, recall that the Cartesian product takes all possible pairings of one tuple from *instructor* with one tuple of *teaches*.)

Since the Cartesian-product operation associates *every* tuple of *instructor* with every tuple of *teaches*, we know that if a an instructor is in the Physics department, and has taught a course (as recorded in the *teaches* relation), then there is some

inst.ID	name	dept_name	salary	teaches.ID	course_id	sec_id	semester	year
22222	Einstein	Physics	95000	10101	CS-437	1	Fall	2009
22222	Einstein	Physics	95000	10101	CS-315	1	Spring	2010
22222	Einstein	Physics	95000	12121	FIN-201	1	Spring	2010
22222	Einstein	Physics	95000	15151	MU-199	1	Spring	2010
22222	Einstein	Physics	95000	22222	PHY-101	1	Fall	2009
22222	Einstein	Physics	95000	32343	HIS-351	1	Spring	2010
...	...	...	...	...	...	...	...	...
...	...	...	...	...	...	...	...	...
33456	Gold	Physics	87000	10101	CS-437	1	Fall	2009
33456	Gold	Physics	87000	10101	CS-315	1	Spring	2010
33456	Gold	Physics	87000	12121	FIN-201	1	Spring	2010
33456	Gold	Physics	87000	15151	MU-199	1	Spring	2010
33456	Gold	Physics	87000	22222	PHY-101	1	Fall	2009
33456	Gold	Physics	87000	32343	HIS-351	1	Spring	2010
...	...	...	...	...	...	...	...	...
...	...	...	...	...	...	...	...	...

Figure 6.9 Result of $\sigma_{dept\_name = \text{"Physics"}}(instructor \times teaches)$.

tuple in $\sigma_{dept\_name = \text{"Physics"}}(instructor \times teaches)$ that contains his name, and which satisfies $instructor.ID = teaches.ID$. So, if we write:

$$\sigma_{instructor.ID = teaches.ID}(\sigma_{dept\_name = \text{"Physics"}}(instructor \times teaches))$$

we get only those tuples of $instructor \times teaches$ that pertain to instructors in Physics and the courses that they taught.

Finally, since we only want the names of all instructors in the Physics department together with the $course\_id$ of all courses they taught, we do a projection:

$$\Pi_{name,\ course\_id} (\sigma_{instructor.ID = teaches.ID}(\sigma_{dept\_name = \text{"Physics"}}(instructor \times teaches)))$$

The result of this expression, shown in Figure 6.10, is the correct answer to our query. Observe that although instructor Gold is in the Physics department, he does not teach any course (as recorded in the *teaches* relation), and therefore does not appear in the result.

name	course_id
Einstein	PHY-101

Figure 6.10 Result of
$\Pi_{name,\ course\_id} (\sigma_{instructor.ID = teaches.ID}(\sigma_{dept\_name = \text{"Physics"}}(instructor \times teaches)))$.

Note that there is often more than one way to write a query in relational algebra. Consider the following query:

$$\Pi_{name,\ course\_id}\ (\sigma_{instructor.ID\ =\ teaches.ID}((\sigma_{dept\_name\ =\ \text{``Physics''}}(instructor))\ \times\ teaches))$$

Note the subtle difference between the two queries: in the query above, the selection that restricts *dept_name* to Physics is applied to *instructor*, and the Cartesian product is applied subsequently; in contrast, the Cartesian product was applied before the selection in the earlier query. However, the two queries are **equivalent**; that is, they give the same result on any database.

6.1.1.7   The Rename Operation

Unlike relations in the database, the results of relational-algebra expressions do not have a name that we can use to refer to them. It is useful to be able to give them names; the **rename** operator, denoted by the lowercase Greek letter rho (ρ), lets us do this. Given a relational-algebra expression E, the expression

$$\rho_x\ (E)$$

returns the result of expression E under the name x.

A relation r by itself is considered a (trivial) relational-algebra expression. Thus, we can also apply the rename operation to a relation r to get the same relation under a new name.

A second form of the rename operation is as follows: Assume that a relational-algebra expression E has arity n. Then, the expression

$$\rho_{x(A_1, A_2, ..., A_n)}\ (E)$$

returns the result of expression E under the name x, and with the attributes renamed to $A_1, A_2, \ldots, A_n$.

To illustrate renaming a relation, we consider the query "Find the highest salary in the university." Our strategy is to (1) compute first a temporary relation consisting of those salaries that are *not* the largest and (2) take the set difference between the relation $\Pi_{salary}\ (instructor)$ and the temporary relation just computed, to obtain the result.

1. Step 1: To compute the temporary relation, we need to compare the values of all salaries. We do this comparison by computing the Cartesian product *instructor* $\times$ *instructor* and forming a selection to compare the value of any two salaries appearing in one tuple. First, we need to devise a mechanism to distinguish between the two *salary* attributes. We shall use the rename operation to rename one reference to the instructor relation; thus we can reference the relation twice without ambiguity.

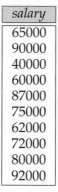

Figure 6.11 Result of the subexpression
$\Pi_{instructor.salary}\,(\sigma_{instructor.salary\,<\,d.salary}\,(instructor\,\times\,\rho_d\,(instructor)))$.

We can now write the temporary relation that consists of the salaries that are not the largest:

$$\Pi_{instructor.salary}\,(\sigma_{instructor.salary\,<\,d.salary}\,(instructor\,\times\,\rho_d\,(instructor)))$$

This expression gives those salaries in the *instructor* relation for which a larger salary appears somewhere in the *instructor* relation (renamed as *d*). The result contains all salaries *except* the largest one. Figure 6.11 shows this relation.

2. Step 2: The query to find the largest salary in the university can be written as:

$$\Pi_{salary}\,(instructor)\,-$$
$$\Pi_{instructor.salary}\,(\sigma_{instructor.salary\,<\,d.salary}\,(instructor\,\times\,\rho_d\,(instructor)))$$

Figure 6.12 shows the result of this query.

The rename operation is not strictly required, since it is possible to use a positional notation for attributes. We can name attributes of a relation implicitly by using a positional notation, where $1, $2, ... refer to the first attribute, the second attribute, and so on. The positional notation also applies to results of relational-algebra operations. The following relational-algebra expression illustrates the

Figure 6.12 Highest salary in the university.

use of positional notation to write the expression we saw earlier, which computes salaries that are not the largest:

$$\Pi_{\$4} \left(\sigma_{\$4 \, < \, \$8} \left(instructor \, \times \, instructor \right) \right)$$

Note that the Cartesian product concatenates the attributes of the two relations. Thus, for the result of the Cartesian product (*instructor* × *instructor*), $4 refers to the *salary* attribute from the first occurrence of *instructor*, while $8 refers to the *salary* attribute from the second occurrence of *instructor*. A positional notation can also be used to refer to relation names, if a binary operation needs to distinguish between its two operand relations. For example, $R1 could refer to the first operand relation, and $R2 could refer to the second operand relation of a Cartesian product. However, the positional notation is inconvenient for humans, since the position of the attribute is a number, rather than an easy-to-remember attribute name. Hence, we do not use the positional notation in this textbook.

6.1.2   Formal Definition of the Relational Algebra

The operations in Section 6.1.1 allow us to give a complete definition of an expression in the relational algebra. A basic expression in the relational algebra consists of either one of the following:

- A relation in the database

- A constant relation

A constant relation is written by listing its tuples within { }, for example { (22222, Einstein, Physics, 95000), (76543, Singh, Finance, 80000) }.

A general expression in the relational algebra is constructed out of smaller subexpressions. Let E_1 and E_2 be relational-algebra expressions. Then, the following are all relational-algebra expressions:

- $E_1 \cup E_2$

- $E_1 - E_2$

- $E_1 \times E_2$

- $\sigma_P(E_1)$, where P is a predicate on attributes in E_1

- $\Pi_S(E_1)$, where S is a list consisting of some of the attributes in E_1

- $\rho_x(E_1)$, where x is the new name for the result of E_1

6.1.3   Additional Relational-Algebra Operations

The fundamental operations of the relational algebra are sufficient to express any relational-algebra query. However, if we restrict ourselves to just the fundamental operations, certain common queries are lengthy to express. Therefore, we define additional operations that do not add any power to the algebra, but simplify

course_id
CS-101

Figure 6.13 Courses offered in both the Fall 2009 and Spring 2010 semesters.

common queries. For each new operation, we give an equivalent expression that uses only the fundamental operations.

6.1.3.1   The Set-Intersection Operation

The first additional relational-algebra operation that we shall define is **set intersection** ($\cap$). Suppose that we wish to find the set of all courses taught in both the Fall 2009 and the Spring 2010 semesters. Using set intersection, we can write

$$\Pi_{course\_id} \left(\sigma_{semester = \text{"Fall"} \wedge year=2009} \left(section \right) \right) \cap$$
$$\Pi_{course\_id} \left(\sigma_{semester = \text{"Spring"} \wedge year=2010} \left(section \right) \right)$$

The result relation for this query appears in Figure 6.13.

Note that we can rewrite any relational-algebra expression that uses set intersection by replacing the intersection operation with a pair of set-difference operations as:

$$r \cap s = r - (r - s)$$

Thus, set intersection is not a fundamental operation and does not add any power to the relational algebra. It is simply more convenient to write $r \cap s$ than to write $r - (r - s)$.

6.1.3.2   The Natural-Join Operation

It is often desirable to simplify certain queries that require a Cartesian product. Usually, a query that involves a Cartesian product includes a selection operation on the result of the Cartesian product. The selection operation most often requires that all attributes that are common to the relations that are involved in the Cartesian product be equated.

In our example query from Section 6.1.1.6 that combined information from the *instructor* and *teaches* tables, the matching condition required *instructor.ID* to be equal to *teaches.ID*. These are the only attributes in the two relations that have the same name.

The *natural join* is a binary operation that allows us to combine certain selections and a Cartesian product into one operation. It is denoted by the **join** symbol $\bowtie$. The natural-join operation forms a Cartesian product of its two arguments, performs a selection forcing equality on those attributes that appear in both relation schemas, and finally removes duplicate attributes. Returning to the example of the relations *instructor* and *teaches*, computing *instructor* **natural join** *teaches* considers only those pairs of tuples where both the tuple from *instructor* and the

ID	name	dept_name	salary	course_id	sec_id	semester	year
10101	Srinivasan	Comp. Sci.	65000	CS-101	1	Fall	2009
10101	Srinivasan	Comp. Sci.	65000	CS-315	1	Spring	2010
10101	Srinivasan	Comp. Sci.	65000	CS-347	1	Fall	2009
12121	Wu	Finance	90000	FIN-201	1	Spring	2010
15151	Mozart	Music	40000	MU-199	1	Spring	2010
22222	Einstein	Physics	95000	PHY-101	1	Fall	2009
32343	El Said	History	60000	HIS-351	1	Spring	2010
45565	Katz	Comp. Sci.	75000	CS-101	1	Spring	2010
45565	Katz	Comp. Sci.	75000	CS-319	1	Spring	2010
76766	Crick	Biology	72000	BIO-101	1	Summer	2009
76766	Crick	Biology	72000	BIO-301	1	Summer	2010
83821	Brandt	Comp. Sci.	92000	CS-190	1	Spring	2009
83821	Brandt	Comp. Sci.	92000	CS-190	2	Spring	2009
83821	Brandt	Comp. Sci.	92000	CS-319	2	Spring	2010
98345	Kim	Elec. Eng.	80000	EE-181	1	Spring	2009

Figure 6.14 The natural join of the *instructor* relation with the *teaches* relation.

tuple from *teaches* have the same value on the common attribute ID. The result relation, shown in Figure 6.14, has only 13 tuples, the ones that give information about an instructor and a course that that instructor actually teaches. Notice that we do not repeat those attributes that appear in the schemas of both relations; rather they appear only once. Notice also the order in which the attributes are listed: first the attributes common to the schemas of both relations, second those attributes unique to the schema of the first relation, and finally, those attributes unique to the schema of the second relation.

Although the definition of natural join is complicated, the operation is easy to apply. As an illustration, consider again the example "Find the names of all instructors together with the *course_id* of all courses they taught." We express this query by using the natural join as follows:

$$\Pi_{name,\ course\_id}\ (instructor \bowtie teaches)$$

Since the schemas for *instructor* and *teaches* have the attribute ID in common, the natural-join operation considers only pairs of tuples that have the same value on ID. It combines each such pair of tuples into a single tuple on the union of the two schemas; that is, (ID, name, dept_name, salary, course_id). After performing the projection, we obtain the relation in Figure 6.15.

Consider two relation schemas R and S—which are, of course, lists of attribute names. If we consider the schemas to be *sets*, rather than lists, we can denote those attribute names that appear in both R and S by $R \cap S$, and denote those attribute names that appear in R, in S, or in both by $R \cup S$. Similarly, those attribute names that appear in R but not S are denoted by $R - S$, whereas $S - R$ denotes those

name	course_id
Srinivasan	CS-101
Srinivasan	CS-315
Srinivasan	CS-347
Wu	FIN-201
Mozart	MU-199
Einstein	PHY-101
El Said	HIS-351
Katz	CS-101
Katz	CS-319
Crick	BIO-101
Crick	BIO-301
Brandt	CS-190
Brandt	CS-319
Kim	EE-181

Figure 6.15 Result of $\Pi_{name,\ course\_id}$ (*instructor* ⋈ *teaches*).

attribute names that appear in S but not in R. Note that the union, intersection, and difference operations here are on sets of attributes, rather than on relations.

We are now ready for a formal definition of the natural join. Consider two relations $r(R)$ and $s(S)$. The **natural join** of r and s, denoted by $r ⋈ s$, is a relation on schema $R \cup S$ formally defined as follows:

$$r ⋈ s = \Pi_{R \cup S} (\sigma_{r.A_1 = s.A_1 \wedge r.A_2 = s.A_2 \wedge \ldots \wedge r.A_n = s.A_n} (r \times s))$$

where $R \cap S = \{A_1, A_2, \ldots, A_n\}$.

Please note that if $r(R)$ and $s(S)$ are relations without any attributes in common, that is, $R \cap S = \emptyset$, then $r ⋈ s = r \times s$.

Let us consider one more example of the use of natural join, to write the query "Find the names of all instructors in the Comp. Sci. department together with the course titles of all the courses that the instructors teach."

$$\Pi_{name, title} (\sigma_{dept\_name = \text{"Comp. Sci."}} (\textit{instructor} ⋈ \textit{teaches} ⋈ \textit{course}))$$

The result relation for this query appears in Figure 6.16.

Notice that we wrote *instructor* ⋈ *teaches* ⋈ *course* without inserting parentheses to specify the order in which the natural-join operations on the three relations should be executed. In the preceding case, there are two possibilities:

$$(\textit{instructor} ⋈ \textit{teaches}) ⋈ \textit{course}$$
$$\textit{instructor} ⋈ (\textit{teaches} ⋈ \textit{course})$$

We did not specify which expression we intended, because the two are equivalent. That is, the natural join is **associative**.

name	title
Brandt	Game Design
Brandt	Image Processing
Katz	Image Processing
Katz	Intro. to Computer Science
Srinivasan	Intro. to Computer Science
Srinivasan	Robotics
Srinivasan	Database System Concepts

Figure 6.16 Result of
$\Pi_{name, title} \left(\sigma_{dept\_name =} \text{"Comp. Sci."} \left(instructor \bowtie teaches \bowtie course \right) \right)$.

The *theta join* operation is a variant of the natural-join operation that allows us to combine a selection and a Cartesian product into a single operation. Consider relations $r(R)$ and $s(S)$, and let θ be a predicate on attributes in the schema $R \cup S$. The **theta join** operation $r \bowtie_\theta s$ is defined as follows:

$$r \bowtie_\theta s = \sigma_\theta (r \times s)$$

6.1.3.3   The Assignment Operation

It is convenient at times to write a relational-algebra expression by assigning parts of it to temporary relation variables. The **assignment** operation, denoted by ←, works like assignment in a programming language. To illustrate this operation, consider the definition of the natural-join operation. We could write $r \bowtie s$ as:

$$temp1 \leftarrow R \times S$$
$$temp2 \leftarrow \sigma_{r.A_1 = s.A_1 \wedge r.A_2 = s.A_2 \wedge ... \wedge r.A_n = s.A_n} (temp1)$$
$$result = \Pi_{R \cup S} (temp2)$$

The evaluation of an assignment does not result in any relation being displayed to the user. Rather, the result of the expression to the right of the ← is assigned to the relation variable on the left of the ←. This relation variable may be used in subsequent expressions.

With the assignment operation, a query can be written as a sequential program consisting of a series of assignments followed by an expression whose value is displayed as the result of the query. For relational-algebra queries, assignment must always be made to a temporary relation variable. Assignments to permanent relations constitute a database modification. Note that the assignment operation does not provide any additional power to the algebra. It is, however, a convenient way to express complex queries.

6.1.3.4   Outer join Operations

The **outer-join** operation is an extension of the join operation to deal with missing information. Suppose that there is some instructor who teaches no courses. Then

ID	name	dept_name	salary	course_id	sec_id	semester	year
10101	Srinivasan	Comp. Sci.	65000	CS-101	1	Fall	2009
10101	Srinivasan	Comp. Sci.	65000	CS-315	1	Spring	2010
10101	Srinivasan	Comp. Sci.	65000	CS-347	1	Fall	2009
12121	Wu	Finance	90000	FIN-201	1	Spring	2010
15151	Mozart	Music	40000	MU-199	1	Spring	2010
22222	Einstein	Physics	95000	PHY-101	1	Fall	2009
32343	El Said	History	60000	HIS-351	1	Spring	2010
33456	Gold	Physics	87000	*null*	*null*	*null*	*null*
45565	Katz	Comp. Sci.	75000	CS-101	1	Spring	2010
45565	Katz	Comp. Sci.	75000	CS-319	1	Spring	2010
58583	Califieri	History	62000	*null*	*null*	*null*	*null*
76543	Singh	Finance	80000	*null*	*null*	*null*	*null*
76766	Crick	Biology	72000	BIO-101	1	Summer	2009
76766	Crick	Biology	72000	BIO-301	1	Summer	2010
83821	Brandt	Comp. Sci.	92000	CS-190	1	Spring	2009
83821	Brandt	Comp. Sci.	92000	CS-190	2	Spring	2009
83821	Brandt	Comp. Sci.	92000	CS-319	2	Spring	2010
98345	Kim	Elec. Eng.	80000	EE-181	1	Spring	2009

Figure 6.17 Result of *instructor* ⟗ *teaches*.

the tuple in the *instructor* relation (Figure 6.1) for that particular instructor would not satisfy the condition of a natural join with the *teaches* relation (Figure 6.7) and that instructor's data would not appear in the result of the natural join, shown in Figure 6.14. For example, instructors Califieri, Gold, and Singh do not appear in the result of the natural join, since they do not teach any course.

More generally, some tuples in either or both of the relations being joined may be "lost" in this way. The **outer join** operation works in a manner similar to the natural join operation we have already studied, but preserves those tuples that would be lost in an join by creating tuples in the result containing null values.

We can use the *outer-join* operation to avoid this loss of information. There are actually three forms of the operation: *left outer join*, denoted ⟕; *right outer join*, denoted ⟖; and *full outer join*, denoted ⟗. All three forms of outer join compute the join, and add extra tuples to the result of the join. For example, the results of the expression *instructor* ⟕ *teaches* and *teaches* ⟖ *instructor* appear in Figures 6.17 and 6.18, respectively.

The **left outer join** (⟕) takes all tuples in the left relation that did not match with any tuple in the right relation, pads the tuples with null values for all other attributes from the right relation, and adds them to the result of the natural join. In Figure 6.17, tuple (58583, Califieri, History, 62000, *null, null, null, null*), is such a tuple. All information from the left relation is present in the result of the left outer join.

ID	course_id	sec_id	semester	year	name	dept_name	salary
10101	CS-101	1	Fall	2009	Srinivasan	Comp. Sci.	65000
10101	CS-315	1	Spring	2010	Srinivasan	Comp. Sci.	65000
10101	CS-347	1	Fall	2009	Srinivasan	Comp. Sci.	65000
12121	FIN-201	1	Spring	2010	Wu	Finance	90000
15151	MU-199	1	Spring	2010	Mozart	Music	40000
22222	PHY-101	1	Fall	2009	Einstein	Physics	95000
32343	HIS-351	1	Spring	2010	El Said	History	60000
33456	null	null	null	null	Gold	Physics	87000
45565	CS-101	1	Spring	2010	Katz	Comp. Sci.	75000
45565	CS-319	1	Spring	2010	Katz	Comp. Sci.	75000
58583	null	null	null	null	Califieri	History	62000
76543	null	null	null	null	Singh	Finance	80000
76766	BIO-101	1	Summer	2009	Crick	Biology	72000
76766	BIO-301	1	Summer	2010	Crick	Biology	72000
83821	CS-190	1	Spring	2009	Brandt	Comp. Sci.	92000
83821	CS-190	2	Spring	2009	Brandt	Comp. Sci.	92000
83821	CS-319	2	Spring	2010	Brandt	Comp. Sci.	92000
98345	EE-181	1	Spring	2009	Kim	Elec. Eng.	80000

Figure 6.18 Result of *teaches* ⟗ *instructor*.

The **right outer join** (⟖) is symmetric with the left outer join: It pads tuples from the right relation that did not match any from the left relation with nulls and adds them to the result of the natural join. In Figure 6.18, tuple (58583, *null*, *null*, *null*, *null*, Califieri, History, 62000), is such a tuple. Thus, all information from the right relation is present in the result of the right outer join.

The **full outer join** (⟗) does both the left and right outer join operations, padding tuples from the left relation that did not match any from the right relation, as well as tuples from the right relation that did not match any from the left relation, and adding them to the result of the join.

Note that in going from our left-outer-join example to our right-outer-join example, we chose to swap the order of the operands. Thus both examples preserve tuples from the *instructor* relation, and thus contain the same information. In our example relations, *teaches* tuples always have matching *instructor* tuples, and thus *teaches* ⟗ *instructor* would give the same result as *teaches* ⟕ *instructor*. If there were tuples in *teaches* without matching tuples in *instructor*, such tuples would appear padded with nulls in *teaches* ⟗ *instructor* as well as in *teaches* ⟖ *instructor*. Further examples of outer joins (expressed in SQL syntax) may be found in Section 4.1.2.

Since outer-join operations may generate results containing null values, we need to specify how the different relational-algebra operations deal with null values. Section 3.6 dealt with this issue in the context of SQL. The same concepts apply for the case of relational algebra, and we omit details.

It is interesting to note that the outer-join operations can be expressed by the basic relational-algebra operations. For instance, the left outer join operation, $r ⟕ s$, can be written as:

$$(r ⋈ s) \cup (r - \Pi_R(r ⋈ s)) \times \{(null, \ldots, null)\}$$

where the constant relation $\{(null, \ldots, null)\}$ is on the schema $S - R$.

6.1.4 Extended Relational-Algebra Operations

We now describe relational-algebra operations that provide the ability to write queries that cannot be expressed using the basic relational-algebra operations. These operations are called **extended relational-algebra** operations.

6.1.4.1 Generalized Projection

The first operation is the **generalized-projection** operation, which extends the projection operation by allowing operations such as arithmetic and string functions to be used in the projection list. The generalized-projection operation has the form:

$$\Pi_{F_1, F_2, \ldots, F_n}(E)$$

where E is any relational-algebra expression, and each of $F_1, F_2, \ldots, F_n$ is an arithmetic expression involving constants and attributes in the schema of E. As a base case, the expression may be simply an attribute or a constant. In general, an expression can use arithmetic operations such as $+$, $-$, $*$, and $\div$ on numeric valued attributes, numeric constants, and on expressions that generate a numeric result. Generalized projection also permits operations on other data types, such as concatenation of strings.

For example, the expression:

$$\Pi_{ID, name, dept\_name, salary \div 12}(instructor)$$

gives the ID, $name$, $dept\_name$, and the monthly salary of each instructor.

6.1.4.2 Aggregation

The second extended relational-algebra operation is the aggregate operation $\mathcal{G}$, which permits the use of aggregate functions such as min or average, on sets of values.

Aggregate functions take a collection of values and return a single value as a result. For example, the aggregate function **sum** takes a collection of values and returns the sum of the values. Thus, the function **sum** applied on the collection:

$$\{1, 1, 3, 4, 4, 11\}$$

returns the value 24. The aggregate function **avg** returns the average of the values. When applied to the preceding collection, it returns the value 4. The aggregate function **count** returns the number of the elements in the collection, and returns 6 on the preceding collection. Other common aggregate functions include **min** and **max**, which return the minimum and maximum values in a collection; they return 1 and 11, respectively, on the preceding collection.

The collections on which aggregate functions operate can have multiple occurrences of a value; the order in which the values appear is not relevant. Such collections are called **multisets**. Sets are a special case of multisets where there is only one copy of each element.

To illustrate the concept of aggregation, we shall use the *instructor* relation. Suppose that we want to find out the sum of salaries of all instructors; the relational-algebra expression for this query is:

$$\mathcal{G}_{\textbf{sum}(salary)}(instructor)$$

The symbol $\mathcal{G}$ is the letter G in calligraphic font; read it as "calligraphic G." The relational-algebra operation $\mathcal{G}$ signifies that aggregation is to be applied, and its subscript specifies the aggregate operation to be applied. The result of the expression above is a relation with a single attribute, containing a single row with a numerical value corresponding to the sum of the salaries of all instructors.

There are cases where we must eliminate multiple occurrences of a value before computing an aggregate function. If we do want to eliminate duplicates, we use the same function names as before, with the addition of the hyphenated string "**distinct**" appended to the end of the function name (for example, **count-distinct**). An example arises in the query "Find the total number of instructors who teach a course in the Spring 2010 semester." In this case, an instructor counts only once, regardless of the number of course sections that the instructor teaches. The required information is contained in the relation *teaches*, and we write this query as follows:

$$\mathcal{G}_{\textbf{count-distinct}(ID)}(\sigma_{semester=\text{"Spring"} \land year=2010}(teaches))$$

The aggregate function **count-distinct** ensures that even if an instructor teaches more than one course, she is counted only once in the result.

There are circumstances where we would like to apply the aggregate function not to a single set of tuples, but instead to a group of sets of tuples. As an illustration, consider the query "Find the average salary in each department." We write this query as follows:

$$_{dept\_name}\mathcal{G}_{\textbf{average}(salary)}(instructor)$$

Figure 6.19 shows the tuples in the *instructor* relation grouped by the *dept _name* attribute. This is the first step in computing the query result. The specified aggregate is computed for each group, and the result of the query is shown in Figure 6.20.

ID	name	dept_name	salary
76766	Crick	Biology	72000
45565	Katz	Comp. Sci.	75000
10101	Srinivasan	Comp. Sci.	65000
83821	Brandt	Comp. Sci.	92000
98345	Kim	Elec. Eng.	80000
12121	Wu	Finance	90000
76543	Singh	Finance	80000
32343	El Said	History	60000
58583	Califieri	History	62000
15151	Mozart	Music	40000
33456	Gold	Physics	87000
22222	Einstein	Physics	95000

Figure 6.19 Tuples of the *instructor* relation, grouped by the *dept_name* attribute

In contrast, consider the query "Find the average salary of all instructors." We write this query as follows:

$$\mathcal{G}_{\textbf{average}(salary)}(instructor)$$

In this case the attribute *dept_name* has been omitted from the left side of the $\mathcal{G}$ operator, so the entire relation is treated as a single group.

The general form of the **aggregation operation** $\mathcal{G}$ is as follows:

$$_{G_1, G_2, ..., G_n}\mathcal{G}_{F_1(A_1),\ F_2(A_2), ...,\ F_m(A_m)}(E)$$

where E is any relational-algebra expression; $G_1, G_2, \ldots, G_n$ constitute a list of attributes on which to group; each F_i is an aggregate function; and each A_i is an attribute name. The meaning of the operation is as follows: The tuples in the result of expression E are partitioned into groups in such a way that:

dept_name	salary
Biology	72000
Comp. Sci.	77333
Elec. Eng.	80000
Finance	85000
History	61000
Music	40000
Physics	91000

Figure 6.20 The result relation for the query "Find the average salary in each department".

MULTISET RELATIONAL ALGEBRA

Unlike the relational algebra, SQL allows multiple copies of a tuple in an input relation as well as in a query result. The SQL standard defines how many copies of each tuple are there in the output of a query, which depends in turn on how many copies of tuples are present in the input relations.

To model this behavior of SQL, a version of relational algebra, called the **multiset relational algebra** is defined to work on multisets, that is, sets that may contain duplicates. The basic operations in the multiset relational algebra are defined as follows:

1. If there are c_1 copies of tuple t_1 in r_1, and t_1 satisfies selection σ_θ, then there are c_1 copies of t_1 in $\sigma_\theta(r_1)$.

2. For each copy of tuple t_1 in r_1, there is a copy of tuple $\Pi_A(t_1)$ in $\Pi_A(r_1)$, where $\Pi_A(t_1)$ denotes the projection of the single tuple t_1.

3. If there are c_1 copies of tuple t_1 in r_1 and c_2 copies of tuple t_2 in r_2, there are $c_1 * c_2$ copies of the tuple $t_1.t_2$ in $r_1 \times r_2$.

For example, suppose that relations r_1 with schema (A, B) and r_2 with schema (C) are the following multisets:

$$r_1 = \{(1, a), (2, a)\} \quad r_2 = \{(2), (3), (3)\}$$

Then $\Pi_B(r_1)$ would be $\{(a), (a)\}$, whereas $\Pi_B(r_1) \times r_2$ would be:

$$\{(a, 2), (a, 2), (a, 3), (a, 3), (a, 3), (a, 3)\}$$

Multiset union, intersection and set difference can also be defined in a similar way, following the corresponding definitions in SQL, which we saw in Section 3.5. There is no change in the definition of the aggregation operation.

1. All tuples in a group have the same values for $G_1, G_2, \ldots, G_n$.

2. Tuples in different groups have different values for $G_1, G_2, \ldots, G_n$.

Thus, the groups can be identified by the values of attributes $G_1, G_2, \ldots, G_n$. For each group $(g_1, g_2, \ldots, g_n)$, the result has a tuple $(g_1, g_2, \ldots, g_n, a_1, a_2, \ldots, a_m)$ where, for each i, a_i is the result of applying the aggregate function F_i on the multiset of values for attribute A_i in the group.

As a special case of the aggregate operation, the list of attributes $G_1, G_2, \ldots, G_n$ can be empty, in which case there is a single group containing all tuples in the relation. This corresponds to aggregation without grouping.

SQL AND RELATIONAL ALGEBRA

From a comparison of the relational algebra operations and the SQL operations, it should be clear that there is a close connection between the two. A typical SQL query has the form:

$$\textbf{select } A_1, \ A_2, \ldots, A_n$$
$$\textbf{from } r_1, \ r_2, \ldots, r_m$$
$$\textbf{where } P$$

Each A_i represents an attribute, and each r_i a relation. P is a predicate. The query is equivalent to the multiset relational-algebra expression:

$$\Pi_{A_1, \ A_2, \ldots, A_n}(\sigma_P (r_1 \times r_2 \times \cdots \times r_m))$$

If the **where** clause is omitted, the predicate P is **true**.

More complex SQL queries can also be rewritten in relational algebra. For example, the query:

$$\textbf{select } A_1, \ A_2, \textbf{sum}(A_3)$$
$$\textbf{from } r_1, \ r_2, \ldots, r_m$$
$$\textbf{where } P$$
$$\textbf{group by } A_1, \ A_2$$

is equivalent to:

$$_{A_1, \ A_2}\mathcal{G}_{\text{sum}(A_3)}(\Pi_{A_1, \ A_2, \ldots, \ A_n}(\sigma_P (r_1 \times r_2 \times \cdots \times r_m)))$$

Join expressions in the **from** clause can be written using equivalent join expressions in relational algebra; we leave the details as an exercise for the reader. However, subqueries in the **where** or **select** clause cannot be rewritten into relational algebra in such a straightforward manner, since there is no relational-algebra operation equivalent to the subquery construct. Extensions of relational algebra have been proposed for this task, but are beyond the scope of this book.

6.2 The Tuple Relational Calculus

When we write a relational-algebra expression, we provide a sequence of procedures that generates the answer to our query. The tuple relational calculus, by contrast, is a **nonprocedural** query language. It describes the desired information without giving a specific procedure for obtaining that information.

A query in the tuple relational calculus is expressed as:

$$\{t \mid P(t)\}$$

That is, it is the set of all tuples t such that predicate P is true for t. Following our earlier notation, we use $t[A]$ to denote the value of tuple t on attribute A, and we use $t \in r$ to denote that tuple t is in relation r.

Before we give a formal definition of the tuple relational calculus, we return to some of the queries for which we wrote relational-algebra expressions in Section 6.1.1.

6.2.1 Example Queries

Find the *ID*, *name*, *dept_name*, *salary* for instructors whose salary is greater than $80,000:

$$\{t \mid t \in instructor \land t[salary] > 80000\}$$

Suppose that we want only the *ID* attribute, rather than all attributes of the *instructor* relation. To write this query in the tuple relational calculus, we need to write an expression for a relation on the schema (*ID*). We need those tuples on (*ID*) such that there is a tuple in *instructor* with the *salary* attribute > 80000. To express this request, we need the construct "there exists" from mathematical logic. The notation:

$$\exists\, t \in r\, (Q(t))$$

means "there exists a tuple t in relation r such that predicate $Q(t)$ is true."

Using this notation, we can write the query "Find the instructor *ID* for each instructor with a salary greater than $80,000" as:

$$\{t \mid \exists\, s \in instructor\, (t[ID] = s[ID] \\ \land\, s[salary] > 80000)\}$$

In English, we read the preceding expression as "The set of all tuples t such that there exists a tuple s in relation *instructor* for which the values of t and s for the *ID* attribute are equal, and the value of s for the *salary* attribute is greater than $80,000."

Tuple variable t is defined on only the *ID* attribute, since that is the only attribute having a condition specified for t. Thus, the result is a relation on (*ID*).

Consider the query "Find the names of all instructors whose department is in the Watson building." This query is slightly more complex than the previous queries, since it involves two relations: *instructor* and *department*. As we shall see, however, all it requires is that we have two "there exists" clauses in our tuple-relational-calculus expression, connected by *and* ($\land$). We write the query as follows:

$$\{t \mid \exists\, s \in instructor\, (t[name] = s[name] \\ \land\, \exists\, u \in department\, (u[dept\_name] = s[dept\_name] \\ \land\, u[building] = \text{"Watson"}))\}$$

name
Einstein
Crick
Gold

Figure 6.21 Names of all instructors whose department is in the Watson building.

Tuple variable u is restricted to departments that are located in the Watson building, while tuple variable s is restricted to instructors whose *dept_name* matches that of tuple variable u. Figure 6.21 shows the result of this query.

To find the set of all courses taught in the Fall 2009 semester, the Spring 2010 semester, or both, we used the union operation in the relational algebra. In the tuple relational calculus, we shall need two "there exists" clauses, connected by *or* ($\vee$):

$$\{t \mid \exists s \in section \ (t[course\_id] = s[course\_id])$$
$$\wedge s[semester] = \text{"Fall"} \wedge s[year] = 2009)\}$$
$$\vee \exists u \in section \ (u[course\_id] = t[course\_id])\}$$
$$\wedge u[semester] = \text{"Spring"} \wedge u[year] = 2010)\}$$

This expression gives us the set of all *course_id* tuples for which at least one of the following holds:

- The *course_id* appears in some tuple of the *section* relation with *semester* = Fall and *year* = 2009.

- The *course_id* appears in some tuple of the *section* relation with *semester* = Spring and *year* = 2010.

If the same course is offered in both the Fall 2009 and Spring 2010 semesters, its *course_id* appears only once in the result, because the mathematical definition of a set does not allow duplicate members. The result of this query appeared earlier in Figure 6.5.

If we now want *only* those *course_id* values for courses that are offered in *both* the Fall 2009 and Spring 2010 semesters, all we need to do is to change the *or* ($\vee$) to *and* ($\wedge$) in the preceding expression.

$$\{t \mid \exists s \in section \ (t[course\_id] = s[course\_id])$$
$$\wedge s[semester] = \text{"Fall"} \wedge s[year] = 2009)\}$$
$$\wedge \exists u \in section \ (u[course\_id] = t[course\_id])\}$$
$$\wedge u[semester] = \text{"Spring"} \wedge u[year] = 2010)\}$$

The result of this query appeared in Figure 6.13.

Now consider the query "Find all the courses taught in the Fall 2009 semester but not in Spring 2010 semester." The tuple-relational-calculus expression for this query is similar to the expressions that we have just seen, except for the use of the *not* ($\neg$) symbol:

$$\{t \mid \exists \, s \in section \; (t[course\_id] = s[course\_id])$$
$$\wedge \; s[semester] = \text{``Fall''} \wedge \; s[year] = 2009)\}$$
$$\wedge \neg \, \exists \, u \in section \; (u[course\_id] = t[course\_id])\}$$
$$\wedge \; u[semester] = \text{``Spring''} \wedge \; u[year] = 2010)\}$$

This tuple-relational-calculus expression uses the $\exists s \in section \; (\ldots)$ clause to require that a particular *course_id* is taught in the Fall 2009 semester, and it uses the $\neg \exists u \in section \; (\ldots)$ clause to eliminate those *course_id* values that appear in some tuple of the *section* relation as having been taught in the Spring 2010 semester.

The query that we shall consider next uses implication, denoted by $\Rightarrow$. The formula $P \Rightarrow Q$ means "P implies Q"; that is, "if P is true, then Q must be true." Note that $P \Rightarrow Q$ is logically equivalent to $\neg P \vee Q$. The use of implication rather than *not* and *or* often suggests a more intuitive interpretation of a query in English.

Consider the query that "Find all students who have taken all courses offered in the Biology department." To write this query in the tuple relational calculus, we introduce the "for all" construct, denoted by $\forall$. The notation:

$$\forall \, t \in r \; (Q(t))$$

means "Q is true for all tuples t in relation r."

We write the expression for our query as follows:

$$\{t \mid \exists \, r \in student \; (r[ID] = t[ID]) \wedge$$
$$(\forall \, u \in course \; (u[dept\_name] = \text{`` Biology''} \Rightarrow$$
$$\exists \, s \in takes \; (t[ID] = s[ID]$$
$$\wedge \; s[course\_id] = u[course\_id])))\}$$

In English, we interpret this expression as "The set of all students (that is, (*ID*) tuples *t*) such that, for *all* tuples *u* in the *course* relation, if the value of *u* on attribute *dept_name* is 'Biology', then there exists a tuple in the *takes* relation that includes the student *ID* and the *course_id*."

Note that there is a subtlety in the above query: If there is no course offered in the Biology department, all student *ID*s satisfy the condition. The first line of the query expression is critical in this case—without the condition

$$\exists \, r \in student \; (r[ID] = t[ID])$$

if there is no course offered in the Biology department, any value of *t* (including values that are not student *ID*s in the *student* relation) would qualify.

6.2.2 Formal Definition

We are now ready for a formal definition. A tuple-relational-calculus expression is of the form:

$$\{t \mid P(t)\}$$

where P is a *formula*. Several tuple variables may appear in a formula. A tuple variable is said to be a *free variable* unless it is quantified by a $\exists$ or $\forall$. Thus, in:

$$t \in instructor \; \land \; \exists s \in department(t[dept\_name] = s[dept\_name])$$

t is a free variable. Tuple variable s is said to be a *bound* variable.

A tuple-relational-calculus formula is built up out of *atoms*. An atom has one of the following forms:

- $s \in r$, where s is a tuple variable and r is a relation (we do not allow use of the $\notin$ operator).

- $s[x] \; \Theta \; u[y]$, where s and u are tuple variables, x is an attribute on which s is defined, y is an attribute on which u is defined, and Θ is a comparison operator ($<, \leq, =, \neq, >, \geq$); we require that attributes x and y have domains whose members can be compared by Θ.

- $s[x] \; \Theta \; c$, where s is a tuple variable, x is an attribute on which s is defined, Θ is a comparison operator, and c is a constant in the domain of attribute x.

We build up formulae from atoms by using the following rules:

- An atom is a formula.
- If P_1 is a formula, then so are $\neg P_1$ and (P_1).
- If P_1 and P_2 are formulae, then so are $P_1 \lor P_2$, $P_1 \land P_2$, and $P_1 \Rightarrow P_2$.
- If $P_1(s)$ is a formula containing a free tuple variable s, and r is a relation, then

$$\exists s \in r \, (P_1(s)) \text{ and } \forall s \in r \, (P_1(s))$$

are also formulae.

As we could for the relational algebra, we can write equivalent expressions that are not identical in appearance. In the tuple relational calculus, these equivalences include the following three rules:

1. $P_1 \land P_2$ is equivalent to $\neg \, (\neg(P_1) \lor \neg(P_2))$.
2. $\forall t \in r \, (P_1(t))$ is equivalent to $\neg \exists t \in r \, (\neg P_1(t))$.
3. $P_1 \Rightarrow P_2$ is equivalent to $\neg(P_1) \lor P_2$.

6.2.3   Safety of Expressions

There is one final issue to be addressed. A tuple-relational-calculus expression may generate an infinite relation. Suppose that we write the expression:

$$\{t \mid \neg \, (t \, \in \, instructor)\}$$

There are infinitely many tuples that are not in *instructor*. Most of these tuples contain values that do not even appear in the database! Clearly, we do not wish to allow such expressions.

To help us define a restriction of the tuple relational calculus, we introduce the concept of the **domain** of a tuple relational formula, P. Intuitively, the domain of P, denoted $dom(P)$, is the set of all values referenced by P. They include values mentioned in P itself, as well as values that appear in a tuple of a relation mentioned in P. Thus, the domain of P is the set of all values that appear explicitly in P or that appear in one or more relations whose names appear in P. For example, $dom(t \in instructor \wedge t[salary] > 80000)$ is the set containing 80000 as well as the set of all values appearing in any attribute of any tuple in the *instructor* relation. Similarly, $dom(\neg \, (t \, \in \, instructor))$ is also the set of all values appearing in *instructor*, since the relation *instructor* is mentioned in the expression.

We say that an expression $\{t \mid P(t)\}$ is *safe* if all values that appear in the result are values from $dom(P)$. The expression $\{t \mid \neg \, (t \, \in \, instructor)\}$ is not safe. Note that $dom(\neg \, (t \, \in \, instructor))$ is the set of all values appearing in *instructor*. However, it is possible to have a tuple t not in *instructor* that contains values that do not appear in *instructor*. The other examples of tuple-relational-calculus expressions that we have written in this section are safe.

The number of tuples that satisfy an unsafe expression, such as $\{t \mid \neg \, (t \, \in \, instructor)\}$, could be infinite, whereas safe expressions are guaranteed to have finite results. The class of tuple-relational-calculus expressions that are allowed is therefore restricted to those that are safe.

6.2.4   Expressive Power of Languages

The tuple relational calculus restricted to safe expressions is equivalent in expressive power to the basic relational algebra (with the operators $\cup$, $-$, $\times$, σ, and ρ, but without the extended relational operations such as generalized projection and aggregation ($\mathcal{G}$)). Thus, for every relational-algebra expression using only the basic operations, there is an equivalent expression in the tuple relational calculus, and for every tuple-relational-calculus expression, there is an equivalent relational-algebra expression. We shall not prove this assertion here; the bibliographic notes contain references to the proof. Some parts of the proof are included in the exercises. We note that the tuple relational calculus does not have any equivalent of the aggregate operation, but it can be extended to support aggregation. Extending the tuple relational calculus to handle arithmetic expressions is straightforward.

6.3   The Domain Relational Calculus

A second form of relational calculus, called **domain relational calculus**, uses *domain* variables that take on values from an attributes domain, rather than values for an entire tuple. The domain relational calculus, however, is closely related to the tuple relational calculus.

Domain relational calculus serves as the theoretical basis of the widely used QBE language (see Appendix B.1), just as relational algebra serves as the basis for the SQL language.

6.3.1   Formal Definition

An expression in the domain relational calculus is of the form

$$\{< x_1, \ x_2, \ldots, x_n > \ | \ P(x_1, \ x_2, \ldots, x_n)\}$$

where $x_1, \ x_2, \ldots, x_n$ represent domain variables. P represents a formula composed of atoms, as was the case in the tuple relational calculus. An atom in the domain relational calculus has one of the following forms:

- $< x_1, \ x_2, \ldots, x_n > \ \in \ r$, where r is a relation on n attributes and $x_1, \ x_2, \ldots, x_n$ are domain variables or domain constants.

- $x \ \Theta \ y$, where x and y are domain variables and Θ is a comparison operator $(<, \leq, =, \neq, >, \geq)$. We require that attributes x and y have domains that can be compared by Θ.

- $x \ \Theta \ c$, where x is a domain variable, Θ is a comparison operator, and c is a constant in the domain of the attribute for which x is a domain variable.

We build up formulae from atoms by using the following rules:

- An atom is a formula.
- If P_1 is a formula, then so are $\neg P_1$ and (P_1).
- If P_1 and P_2 are formulae, then so are $P_1 \ \vee \ P_2$, $P_1 \ \wedge \ P_2$, and $P_1 \ \Rightarrow \ P_2$.
- If $P_1(x)$ is a formula in x, where x is a free domain variable, then

$$\exists \ x \ (P_1(x)) \text{ and } \forall \ x \ (P_1(x))$$

  are also formulae.

As a notational shorthand, we write $\exists a, b, c \ (P(a, b, c))$ for $\exists a \ (\exists b \ (\exists c \ (P(a, b, c))))$.

6.3.2 Example Queries

We now give domain-relational-calculus queries for the examples that we considered earlier. Note the similarity of these expressions and the corresponding tuple-relational-calculus expressions.

- Find the instructor *ID*, *name*, *dept_name*, and *salary* for instructors whose salary is greater than $80,000:

$$\{< i, n, d, s > \ | \ < i, n, d, s > \in instructor \land s > 80000\}$$

- Find all instructor *ID* for instructors whose salary is greater than $80,000:

$$\{< n > \ | \exists \, i, d, s \, (< i, n, d, s > \in instructor \land s > 80000)\}$$

Although the second query appears similar to the one that we wrote for the tuple relational calculus, there is an important difference. In the tuple calculus, when we write $\exists s$ for some tuple variable s, we bind it immediately to a relation by writing $\exists s \in r$. However, when we write $\exists n$ in the domain calculus, n refers not to a tuple, but rather to a domain value. Thus, the domain of variable n is unconstrained until the subformula $< i, n, d, s > \in instructor$ constrains n to instructor names that appear in the *instructor* relation.

We now give several examples of queries in the domain relational calculus.

- Find the names of all instructors in the Physics department together with the *course_id* of all courses they teach:

$$\{< n, c > \ | \exists \, i, a \, (< i, c, a, s, y > \in teaches \\ \land \exists d, s \, (< i, n, d, s > \in instructor \land d = \text{``Physics''}))\}$$

- Find the set of all courses taught in the Fall 2009 semester, the Spring 2010 semester, or both:

$$\{< c > \ | \exists s \, (< c, a, s, y, b, r, t > \in section \\ \land s = \text{``Fall''} \land y = \text{``2009''} \\ \lor \exists u \, (< c, a, s, y, b, r, t > \in section \\ \land s = \text{``Spring''} \land y = \text{``2010''}$$

- Find all students who have taken all courses offered in the Biology department:

$$\{< i > \ | \exists n, \, d, t \, (< i, n, d, t > \in student) \land \\ \forall x, y, z, w \, (< x, y, z, w > \in course \land z = \text{``Biology''} \Rightarrow \\ \exists a, b \, (< a, x, b, r, p, q > \in takes \land \ < c, a > \in depositor))\}$$

Note that as was the case for tuple-relational-calculus, if no courses are offered in the Biology department, all students would be in the result.

6.3.3 Safety of Expressions

We noted that, in the tuple relational calculus (Section 6.2), it is possible to write expressions that may generate an infinite relation. That led us to define *safety* for tuple-relational-calculus expressions. A similar situation arises for the domain relational calculus. An expression such as

$$\{< i, n, d, s > \mid \neg(< i, n, d, s > \in \ instructor)\}$$

is unsafe, because it allows values in the result that are not in the domain of the expression.

For the domain relational calculus, we must be concerned also about the form of formulae within "there exists" and "for all" clauses. Consider the expression

$$\{< x > \mid \exists \, y \, (< x, \, y > \in \ r) \ \wedge \ \exists z \, (\neg(< x, \, z > \in \ r) \ \wedge \ P(x, z))\}$$

where P is some formula involving x and z. We can test the first part of the formula, $\exists \, y \, (< x, \, y > \in \ r)$, by considering only the values in r. However, to test the second part of the formula, $\exists z \, (\neg \, (< x, \, z > \in \ r) \wedge P(x, z))$, we must consider values for z that do not appear in r. Since all relations are finite, an infinite number of values do not appear in r. Thus, it is not possible, in general, to test the second part of the formula without considering an infinite number of potential values for z. Instead, we add restrictions to prohibit expressions such as the preceding one.

In the tuple relational calculus, we restricted any existentially quantified variable to range over a specific relation. Since we did not do so in the domain calculus, we add rules to the definition of safety to deal with cases like our example. We say that an expression

$$\{< x_1, \ x_2, \ldots, x_n > \mid P \, (x_1, \ x_2, \ldots, x_n)\}$$

is safe if all of the following hold:

1. All values that appear in tuples of the expression are values from $dom(P)$.

2. For every "there exists" subformula of the form $\exists \, x \, (P_1(x))$, the subformula is true if and only if there is a value x in $dom(P_1)$ such that $P_1(x)$ is true.

3. For every "for all" subformula of the form $\forall x \, (P_1(x))$, the subformula is true if and only if $P_1(x)$ is true for all values x from $dom(P_1)$.

The purpose of the additional rules is to ensure that we can test "for all" and "there exists" subformulae without having to test infinitely many possibilities. Consider the second rule in the definition of safety. For $\exists \, x \, (P_1(x))$ to be true, we need to find only one x for which $P_1(x)$ is true. In general, there would be infinitely many values to test. However, if the expression is safe, we know that we can restrict our attention to values from $dom(P_1)$. This restriction reduces to a finite number the tuples we must consider.

The situation for subformulae of the form $\forall x\ (P_1(x))$ is similar. To assert that $\forall x\ (P_1(x))$ is true, we must, in general, test all possible values, so we must examine infinitely many values. As before, if we know that the expression is safe, it is sufficient for us to test $P_1(x)$ for those values taken from $dom(P_1)$.

All the domain-relational-calculus expressions that we have written in the example queries of this section are safe, except for the example unsafe query we saw earlier.

6.3.4 Expressive Power of Languages

When the domain relational calculus is restricted to safe expressions, it is equivalent in expressive power to the tuple relational calculus restricted to safe expressions. Since we noted earlier that the restricted tuple relational calculus is equivalent to the relational algebra, all three of the following are equivalent:

- The basic relational algebra (without the extended relational-algebra operations)

- The tuple relational calculus restricted to safe expressions

- The domain relational calculus restricted to safe expressions

We note that the domain relational calculus also does not have any equivalent of the aggregate operation, but it can be extended to support aggregation, and extending it to handle arithmetic expressions is straightforward.

6.4   Summary

- The **relational algebra** defines a set of algebraic operations that operate on tables, and output tables as their results. These operations can be combined to get expressions that express desired queries. The algebra defines the basic operations used within relational query languages.

- The operations in relational algebra can be divided into:

  - Basic operations

  - Additional operations that can be expressed in terms of the basic operations

  - Extended operations, some of which add further expressive power to relational algebra

- The relational algebra is a terse, formal language that is inappropriate for casual users of a database system. Commercial database systems, therefore, use languages with more "syntactic sugar." In Chapters 3 through 5, we cover the most influential language—SQL, which is based on relational algebra.

- The **tuple relational calculus** and the **domain relational calculus** are non-procedural languages that represent the basic power required in a relational query language. The basic relational algebra is a procedural language that is equivalent in power to both forms of the relational calculus when they are restricted to safe expressions.

- The relational calculi are terse, formal languages that are inappropriate for casual users of a database system. These two formal languages form the basis for two more user-friendly languages, QBE and Datalog, that we cover in Appendix B.

Review Terms

- Relational algebra
- Relational-algebra operations
  - Select σ
  - Project Π
  - Union ∪
  - Set difference −
  - Cartesian product ×
  - Rename ρ
- Additional operations
  - Set intersection ∩
  - Natural join ⋈

- Assignment operation
- Outer join
  - Left outer join ⟕
  - Right outer join ⟖
  - Full outer join ⟗
- Multisets
- Grouping
- Null value
- Tuple relational calculus
- Domain relational calculus
- Safety of expressions
- Expressive power of languages

Practice Exercises

6.1 Write the following queries in relational algebra, using the university schema.

a. Find the titles of courses in the Comp. Sci. department that have 3 credits.

b. Find the IDs of all students who were taught by an instructor named Einstein; make sure there are no duplicates in the result.

c. Find the highest salary of any instructor.

d. Find all instructors earning the highest salary (there may be more than one with the same salary).

employee (*person_name*, *street*, *city*)
works (*person_name*, *company_name*, *salary*)
company (*company_name*, *city*)
manages (*person_name*, *manager_name*)

Figure 6.22   Relational database for Exercises 6.2, 6.8, 6.11, 6.13, and 6.15

e. Find the enrollment of each section that was offered in Autumn 2009.

f. Find the maximum enrollment, across all sections, in Autumn 2009.

g. Find the sections that had the maximum enrollment in Autumn 2009.

6.2 Consider the relational database of Figure 6.22, where the primary keys are underlined. Give an expression in the relational algebra to express each of the following queries:

a. Find the names of all employees who live in the same city and on the same street as do their managers.

b. Find the names of all employees in this database who do not work for "First Bank Corporation".

c. Find the names of all employees who earn more than every employee of "Small Bank Corporation".

6.3 The natural outer-join operations extend the natural-join operation so that tuples from the participating relations are not lost in the result of the join. Describe how the theta-join operation can be extended so that tuples from the left, right, or both relations are not lost from the result of a theta join.

6.4 (**Division operation**): The division operator of relational algebra, "÷", is defined as follows. Let $r(R)$ and $s(S)$ be relations, and let $S \subseteq R$; that is, every attribute of schema S is also in schema R. Then $r \div s$ is a relation on schema $R - S$ (that is, on the schema containing all attributes of schema R that are not in schema S). A tuple t is in $r \div s$ if and only if both of two conditions hold:

- t is in $\Pi_{R-S}(r)$

- For every tuple t_s in s, there is a tuple t_r in r satisfying both of the following:
  a. $t_r[S] = t_s[S]$
  b. $t_r[R - S] = t$

Given the above definition:

a. Write a relational algebra expression using the division operator to find the IDs of all students who have taken all Comp. Sci. courses. (Hint: project *takes* to just ID and *course_id*, and generate the set of all Comp. Sci. *course_id*s using a select expression, before doing the division.)

b. Show how to write the above query in relational algebra, without using division. (By doing so, you would have shown how to define the division operation using the other relational algebra operations.)

6.5 Let the following relation schemas be given:

$$R = (A, B, C)$$
$$S = (D, E, F)$$

Let relations $r(R)$ and $s(S)$ be given. Give an expression in the tuple relational calculus that is equivalent to each of the following:

a. $\Pi_A(r)$

b. $\sigma_{B=17}(r)$

c. $r \times s$

d. $\Pi_{A,F}(\sigma_{C=D}(r \times s))$

6.6 Let $R = (A, B, C)$, and let r_1 and r_2 both be relations on schema R. Give an expression in the domain relational calculus that is equivalent to each of the following:

a. $\Pi_A(r_1)$

b. $\sigma_{B=17}(r_1)$

c. $r_1 \cup r_2$

d. $r_1 \cap r_2$

e. $r_1 - r_2$

f. $\Pi_{A,B}(r_1) \bowtie \Pi_{B,C}(r_2)$

6.7 Let $R = (A, B)$ and $S = (A, C)$, and let $r(R)$ and $s(S)$ be relations. Write expressions in relational algebra for each of the following queries:

a. $\{< a > \ | \ \exists b \ (< a, b > \in r \wedge b = 7)\}$

b. $\{< a, b, c > \ | \ < a, b > \in r \wedge < a, c > \in s\}$

c. $\{< a > \ | \ \exists c \ (< a, c > \in s \wedge \exists b_1, b_2 \ (< a, b_1 > \in r \wedge < c, b_2 > \in r \wedge b_1 > b_2))\}$

6.8 Consider the relational database of Figure 6.22 where the primary keys are underlined. Give an expression in tuple relational calculus for each of the following queries:

a. Find all employees who work directly for "Jones."

b. Find all cities of residence of all employees who work directly for "Jones."

c. Find the name of the manager of the manager of "Jones."

d. Find those employees who earn more than all employees living in the city "Mumbai."

6.9 Describe how to translate join expressions in SQL to relational algebra.

Exercises

6.10 Write the following queries in relational algebra, using the university schema.

a. Find the names of all students who have taken at least one Comp. Sci. course.

b. Find the IDs and names of all students who have not taken any course offering before Spring 2009.

c. For each department, find the maximum salary of instructors in that department. You may assume that every department has at least one instructor.

d. Find the lowest, across all departments, of the per-department maximum salary computed by the preceding query.

6.11 Consider the relational database of Figure 6.22, where the primary keys are underlined. Give an expression in the relational algebra to express each of the following queries:

a. Find the names of all employees who work for "First Bank Corporation".

b. Find the names and cities of residence of all employees who work for "First Bank Corporation".

c. Find the names, street addresses, and cities of residence of all employees who work for "First Bank Corporation" and earn more than $10,000.

d. Find the names of all employees in this database who live in the same city as the company for which they work.

e. Assume the companies may be located in several cities. Find all companies located in every city in which "Small Bank Corporation" is located.

6.12 Using the university example, write relational-algebra queries to find the course sections taught by more than one instructor in the following ways:

    a. Using an aggregate function.

    b. Without using any aggregate functions.

6.13 Consider the relational database of Figure 6.22. Give a relational-algebra expression for each of the following queries:

    a. Find the company with the most employees.

    b. Find the company with the smallest payroll.

    c. Find those companies whose employees earn a higher salary, on average, than the average salary at First Bank Corporation.

6.14 Consider the following relational schema for a library:

$$member(\underline{memb\_no}, name, dob)$$
$$books(\underline{isbn}, title, authors, publisher)$$
$$borrowed(\underline{memb\_no}, \underline{isbn}, date)$$

Write the following queries in relational algebra.

    a. Find the names of members who have borrowed any book published by "McGraw-Hill".

    b. Find the name of members who have borrowed all books published by "McGraw-Hill".

    c. Find the name and membership number of members who have borrowed more than five different books published by "McGraw-Hill".

    d. For each publisher, find the name and membership number of members who have borrowed more than five books of that publisher.

    e. Find the average number of books borrowed per member. Take into account that if an member does not borrow any books, then that member does not appear in the *borrowed* relation at all.

6.15 Consider the employee database of Figure 6.22. Give expressions in tuple relational calculus and domain relational calculus for each of the following queries:

    a. Find the names of all employees who work for "First Bank Corporation".

    b. Find the names and cities of residence of all employees who work for "First Bank Corporation".

    c. Find the names, street addresses, and cities of residence of all employees who work for "First Bank Corporation" and earn more than $10,000.

    d.   Find all employees who live in the same city as that in which the company for which they work is located.

    e.   Find all employees who live in the same city and on the same street as their managers.

    f.   Find all employees in the database who do not work for "First Bank Corporation".

    g.   Find all employees who earn more than every employee of "Small Bank Corporation".

    h.   Assume that the companies may be located in several cities. Find all companies located in every city in which "Small Bank Corporation" is located.

6.16 Let $R = (A, B)$ and $S = (A, C)$, and let $r(R)$ and $s(S)$ be relations. Write relational-algebra expressions equivalent to the following domain-relational-calculus expressions:

    a. $\{<a> \mid \exists b (<a, b> \in r \land b = 17)\}$

    b. $\{<a, b, c> \mid <a, b> \in r \land <a, c> \in s\}$

    c. $\{<a> \mid \exists b (<a, b> \in r) \lor \forall c (\exists d (<d, c> \in s) \Rightarrow <a, c> \in s)\}$

    d. $\{<a> \mid \exists c (<a, c> \in s \land \exists b_1, b_2 (<a, b_1> \in r \land <c, b_2> \in r \land b_1 > b_2))\}$

6.17 Repeat Exercise 6.16, writing SQL queries instead of relational-algebra expressions.

6.18 Let $R = (A, B)$ and $S = (A, C)$, and let $r(R)$ and $s(S)$ be relations. Using the special constant *null*, write tuple-relational-calculus expressions equivalent to each of the following:

    a. $r \bowtie\!\!\!\!\!\rule[-0.2ex]{0.1ex}{1.6ex}\;\; s$

    b. $r \;\rule[-0.2ex]{0.1ex}{1.6ex}\!\!\!\!\!\bowtie s$

    c. $r \;\rule[-0.2ex]{0.1ex}{1.6ex}\!\!\!\!\!\bowtie\!\!\!\!\!\rule[-0.2ex]{0.1ex}{1.6ex}\;\; s$

6.19 Give a tuple-relational-calculus expression to find the maximum value in relation $r(A)$.

Bibliographical Notes

The original definition of relational algebra is in Codd [1970]. Extensions to the relational model and discussions of incorporation of null values in the relational algebra (the RM/T model), as well as outer joins, are in Codd [1979]. Codd [1990] is a compendium of E. F. Codd's papers on the relational model. Outer joins are also discussed in Date [1993b].

The original definition of tuple relational calculus is in Codd [1972]. A formal proof of the equivalence of tuple relational calculus and relational algebra is in Codd [1972]. Several extensions to the relational calculus have been proposed. Klug [1982] and Escobar-Molano et al. [1993] describe extensions to scalar aggregate functions.

PART 2

DATABASE DESIGN

Database systems are designed to manage large bodies of information. These large bodies of information do not exist in isolation. They are part of the operation of some enterprise whose end product may be information from the database or may be some device or service for which the database plays only a supporting role.

The first two chapters of this part focus on the design of database schemas. The entity-relationship (E-R) model described in Chapter 7 is a high-level data model. Instead of representing all data in tables, it distinguishes between basic objects, called *entities*, and *relationships* among these objects. It is often used as a first step in database-schema design.

Relational database design—the design of the relational schema— was covered informally in earlier chapters. There are, however, principles that can be used to distinguish good database designs from bad ones. These are formalized by means of several "normal forms" that offer different trade-offs between the possibility of inconsistencies and the efficiency of certain queries. Chapter 8 describes the formal design of relational schemas.

The design of a complete database application environment that meets the needs of the enterprise being modeled requires attention to a broader set of issues, many of which are covered in Chapter 9. This chapter first covers the design of Web-based interfaces to applications. The chapter then describes how large applications are architected using multiple layers of abstraction. Finally, the chapter provides a detailed discussion of security at the application and database levels.

CHAPTER 7

Database Design and the E-R Model

Up to this point in the text, we have assumed a given database schema and studied how queries and updates are expressed. We now consider how to design a database schema in the first place. In this chapter, we focus on the entity-relationship data model (E-R), which provides a means of identifying entities to be represented in the database and how those entities are related. Ultimately, the database design will be expressed in terms of a relational database design and an associated set of constraints. We show in this chapter how an E-R design can be transformed into a set of relation schemas and how some of the constraints can be captured in that design. Then, in Chapter 8, we consider in detail whether a set of relation schemas is a good or bad database design and study the process of creating good designs using a broader set of constraints. These two chapters cover the fundamental concepts of database design.

7.1 Overview of the Design Process

The task of creating a database application is a complex one, involving design of the database schema, design of the programs that access and update the data, and design of a security scheme to control access to data. The needs of the users play a central role in the design process. In this chapter, we focus on the design of the database schema, although we briefly outline some of the other design tasks later in the chapter.

The design of a complete database application environment that meets the needs of the enterprise being modeled requires attention to a broad set of issues. These additional aspects of the expected use of the database influence a variety of design choices at the physical, logical, and view levels.

7.1.1 Design Phases

For small applications, it may be feasible for a database designer who understands the application requirements to decide directly on the relations to be created, their attributes, and constraints on the relations. However, such a direct design process is difficult for real-world applications, since they are often highly complex. Often no one person understands the complete data needs of an application. The database designer must interact with users of the application to understand the needs of the application, represent them in a high-level fashion that can be understood by the users, and then translate the requirements into lower levels of the design. A high-level data model serves the database designer by providing a conceptual framework in which to specify, in a systematic fashion, the data requirements of the database users, and a database structure that fulfills these requirements.

- The initial phase of database design is to characterize fully the data needs of the prospective database users. The database designer needs to interact extensively with domain experts and users to carry out this task. The outcome of this phase is a specification of user requirements. While there are techniques for diagrammatically representing user requirements, in this chapter we restrict ourselves to textual descriptions of user requirements.

- Next, the designer chooses a data model and, by applying the concepts of the chosen data model, translates these requirements into a conceptual schema of the database. The schema developed at this **conceptual-design** phase provides a detailed overview of the enterprise. The entity-relationship model, which we study in the rest of this chapter, is typically used to represent the conceptual design. Stated in terms of the entity-relationship model, the conceptual schema specifies the entities that are represented in the database, the attributes of the entities, the relationships among the entities, and constraints on the entities and relationships. Typically, the conceptual-design phase results in the creation of an entity-relationship diagram that provides a graphic representation of the schema.

  The designer reviews the schema to confirm that all data requirements are indeed satisfied and are not in conflict with one another. She can also examine the design to remove any redundant features. Her focus at this point is on describing the data and their relationships, rather than on specifying physical storage details.

- A fully developed conceptual schema also indicates the functional requirements of the enterprise. In a **specification of functional requirements**, users describe the kinds of operations (or transactions) that will be performed on the data. Example operations include modifying or updating data, searching for and retrieving specific data, and deleting data. At this stage of conceptual design, the designer can review the schema to ensure it meets functional requirements.

- The process of moving from an abstract data model to the implementation of the database proceeds in two final design phases.

  ○ In the **logical-design phase**, the designer maps the high-level conceptual schema onto the implementation data model of the database system that will be used. The implementation data model is typically the relational data model, and this step typically consists of mapping the conceptual schema defined using the entity-relationship model into a relation schema.

- ○ Finally, the designer uses the resulting system-specific database schema in the subsequent **physical-design phase**, in which the physical features of the database are specified. These features include the form of file organization and choice of index structures, discussed in Chapters 10 and 11.

The physical schema of a database can be changed relatively easily after an application has been built. However, changes to the logical schema are usually harder to carry out, since they may affect a number of queries and updates scattered across application code. It is therefore important to carry out the database design phase with care, before building the rest of the database application.

7.1.2 Design Alternatives

A major part of the database design process is deciding how to represent in the design the various types of "things" such as people, places, products, and the like. We use the term *entity* to refer to any such distinctly identifiable item. In a university database, examples of entities would include instructors, students, departments, courses, and course offerings.[1] The various entities are related to each other in a variety of ways, all of which need to be captured in the database design. For example, a student takes a course offering, while an instructor teaches a course offering; teaches and takes are examples of relationships between entities.

In designing a database schema, we must ensure that we avoid two major pitfalls:

1. **Redundancy:** A bad design may repeat information. For example, if we store the course identifier and title of a course with each course offering, the title would be stored redundantly (that is, multiple times, unnecessarily) with each course offering. It would suffice to store only the course identifier with each course offering, and to associate the title with the course identifier only once, in a course entity.

   Redundancy can also occur in a relational schema. In the university example we have used so far, we have a relation with section information and a separate relation with course information. Suppose that instead we have a single relation where we repeat all of the course information (course _id, title, dept_name, credits) once for each section (offering) of the course. Clearly, information about courses would then be stored redundantly.

   The biggest problem with such redundant representation of information is that the copies of a piece of information can become inconsistent if the

---

[1] A course may have run in multiple semesters, as well as multiple times in a semester. We refer to each such offering of a course as a section.

information is updated without taking precautions to update all copies of the information. For example, different offerings of a course may have the same course identifier, but may have different titles. It would then become unclear what the correct title of the course is. Ideally, information should appear in exactly one place.

2. **Incompleteness:** A bad design may make certain aspects of the enterprise difficult or impossible to model. For example, suppose that, as in case (1) above, we only had entities corresponding to course offering, without having an entity corresponding to courses. Equivalently, in terms of relations, suppose we have a single relation where we repeat all of the course information once for each section that the course is offered. It would then be impossible to represent information about a new course, unless that course is offered. We might try to make do with the problematic design by storing null values for the section information. Such a work-around is not only unattractive, but may be prevented by primary-key constraints.

Avoiding bad designs is not enough. There may be a large number of good designs from which we must choose. As a simple example, consider a customer who buys a product. Is the sale of this product a relationship between the customer and the product? Alternatively, is the sale itself an entity that is related both to the customer and to the product? This choice, though simple, may make an important difference in what aspects of the enterprise can be modeled well. Considering the need to make choices such as this for the large number of entities and relationships in a real-world enterprise, it is not hard to see that database design can be a challenging problem. Indeed we shall see that it requires a combination of both science and "good taste."

7.2   The Entity-Relationship Model

The **entity-relationship** (E-R) data model was developed to facilitate database design by allowing specification of an *enterprise schema* that represents the overall logical structure of a database.

The E-R model is very useful in mapping the meanings and interactions of real-world enterprises onto a conceptual schema. Because of this usefulness, many database-design tools draw on concepts from the E-R model. The E-R data model employs three basic concepts: entity sets, relationship sets, and attributes, which we study first. The E-R model also has an associated diagrammatic representation, the E-R diagram, which we study later in this chapter.

7.2.1   Entity Sets

An **entity** is a "thing" or "object" in the real world that is distinguishable from all other objects. For example, each person in a university is an entity. An entity has a set of properties, and the values for some set of properties may uniquely identify an entity. For instance, a person may have a *person_id* property whose value uniquely identifies that person. Thus, the value 677-89-9011 for *person_id* would uniquely identify one particular person in the university. Similarly, courses can be thought of as entities, and *course_id* uniquely identifies a course entity in the university. An entity may be concrete, such as a person or a book, or it may be abstract, such as a course, a course offering, or a flight reservation.

An **entity set** is a set of entities of the same type that share the same properties, or attributes. The set of all people who are instructors at a given university, for example, can be defined as the entity set *instructor*. Similarly, the entity set *student* might represent the set of all students in the university.

In the process of modeling, we often use the term *entity set* in the abstract, without referring to a particular set of individual entities. We use the term **extension** of the entity set to refer to the actual collection of entities belonging to the entity set. Thus, the set of actual instructors in the university forms the extension of the entity set *instructor*. The above distinction is similar to the difference between a relation and a relation instance, which we saw in Chapter 2.

Entity sets do not need to be disjoint. For example, it is possible to define the entity set of all people in a university (*person*). A *person* entity may be an *instructor* entity, a *student* entity, both, or neither.

An entity is represented by a set of **attributes**. Attributes are descriptive properties possessed by each member of an entity set. The designation of an attribute for an entity set expresses that the database stores similar information concerning each entity in the entity set; however, each entity may have its own value for each attribute. Possible attributes of the *instructor* entity set are *ID*, *name*, *dept_name*, and *salary*. In real life, there would be further attributes, such as street number, apartment number, state, postal code, and country, but we omit them to keep our examples simple. Possible attributes of the *course* entity set are *course_id*, *title*, *dept_name*, and *credits*.

Each entity has a **value** for each of its attributes. For instance, a particular *instructor* entity may have the value 12121 for *ID*, the value Wu for *name*, the value Finance for *dept_name*, and the value 90000 for *salary*.

The *ID* attribute is used to identify instructors uniquely, since there may be more than one instructor with the same name. In the United States, many enterprises find it convenient to use the *social-security* number of a person[2] as an attribute whose value uniquely identifies the person. In general the enterprise would have to create and assign a unique identifier for each instructor.

A database thus includes a collection of entity sets, each of which contains any number of entities of the same type. Figure 7.1 shows part of a university database that consists of two entity sets: *instructor* and *student*. To keep the figure simple, only some of the attributes of the two entity sets are shown.

A database for a university may include a number of other entity sets. For example, in addition to keeping track of instructors and students, the university also has information about courses, which are represented by the entity set *course*

---

[2]In the United States, the government assigns to each person in the country a unique number, called a social-security number, to identify that person uniquely. Each person is supposed to have only one social-security number, and no two people are supposed to have the same social-security number.

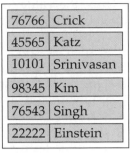

76766	Crick
45565	Katz
10101	Srinivasan
98345	Kim
76543	Singh
22222	Einstein

instructor

98988	Tanaka
12345	Shankar
00128	Zhang
76543	Brown
76653	Aoi
23121	Chavez
44553	Peltier

student

Figure 7.1 Entity sets *instructor* and *student*.

with attributes *course_id*, *title*, *dept_name* and *credits*. In a real setting, a university database may keep dozens of entity sets.

7.2.2 Relationship Sets

A **relationship** is an association among several entities. For example, we can define a relationship *advisor* that associates instructor Katz with student Shankar. This relationship specifies that Katz is an advisor to student Shankar.

A **relationship set** is a set of relationships of the same type. Formally, it is a mathematical relation on $n \geq 2$ (possibly nondistinct) entity sets. If $E_1, E_2, \ldots, E_n$ are entity sets, then a relationship set R is a subset of

$$\{(e_1, e_2, \ldots, e_n) \mid e_1 \in E_1, e_2 \in E_2, \ldots, e_n \in E_n\}$$

where $(e_1, e_2, \ldots, e_n)$ is a relationship.

Consider the two entity sets *instructor* and *student* in Figure 7.1. We define the relationship set *advisor* to denote the association between instructors and students. Figure 7.2 depicts this association.

As another example, consider the two entity sets *student* and *section*. We can define the relationship set *takes* to denote the association between a student and the course sections in which that student is enrolled.

The association between entity sets is referred to as participation; that is, the entity sets $E_1, E_2, \ldots, E_n$ **participate** in relationship set R. A **relationship instance** in an E-R schema represents an association between the named entities in the real-world enterprise that is being modeled. As an illustration, the individual *instructor* entity Katz, who has instructor ID 45565, and the *student* entity Shankar, who has student ID 12345, participate in a relationship instance of *advisor*. This relationship instance represents that in the university, the instructor Katz is advising student Shankar.

The function that an entity plays in a relationship is called that entity's **role**. Since entity sets participating in a relationship set are generally distinct, roles

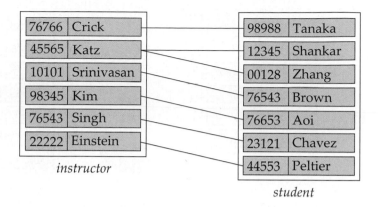

76766	Crick
45565	Katz
10101	Srinivasan
98345	Kim
76543	Singh
22222	Einstein

instructor

98988	Tanaka
12345	Shankar
00128	Zhang
76543	Brown
76653	Aoi
23121	Chavez
44553	Peltier

student

Figure 7.2 Relationship set *advisor*.

are implicit and are not usually specified. However, they are useful when the meaning of a relationship needs clarification. Such is the case when the entity sets of a relationship set are not distinct; that is, the same entity set participates in a relationship set more than once, in different roles. In this type of relationship set, sometimes called a **recursive** relationship set, explicit role names are necessary to specify how an entity participates in a relationship instance. For example, consider the entity set *course* that records information about all the courses offered in the university. To depict the situation where one course (C2) is a prerequisite for another course (C1) we have relationship set *prereq* that is modeled by ordered pairs of *course* entities. The first course of a pair takes the role of course C1, whereas the second takes the role of prerequisite course C2. In this way, all relationships of *prereq* are characterized by (C1, C2) pairs; (C2, C1) pairs are excluded.

A relationship may also have attributes called **descriptive attributes**. Consider a relationship set *advisor* with entity sets *instructor* and *student*. We could associate the attribute *date* with that relationship to specify the date when an instructor became the advisor of a student. The *advisor* relationship among the entities corresponding to instructor Katz and student Shankar has the value "10 June 2007" for attribute *date*, which means that Katz became Shankar's advisor on 10 June 2007.

Figure 7.3 shows the relationship set *advisor* with a descriptive attribute *date*. Please note that Katz advises two students with two different advising dates.

As a more realistic example of descriptive attributes for relationships, consider the entity sets *student* and *section*, which participate in a relationship set *takes*. We may wish to store a descriptive attribute *grade* with the relationship to record the grade that a student got in the class. We may also store a descriptive attribute *for _credit* to record whether a student has taken the course for credit, or is auditing (or sitting in on) the course.

A relationship instance in a given relationship set must be uniquely identifiable from its participating entities, without using the descriptive attributes. To understand this point, suppose we want to model all the dates when an instructor

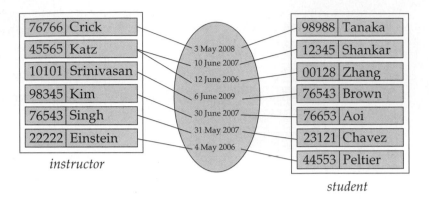

Figure 7.3 *date* as attribute of the *advisor* relationship set.

became an advisor of a particular student. The single-valued attribute *date* can store a single *date* only. We cannot represent multiple dates by multiple relationship instances between the same instructor and a student, since the relationship instances would not be uniquely identifiable using only the participating entities. The right way to handle this case is to create a multivalued attribute *date*, which can store all the dates.

It is possible to have more than one relationship set involving the same entity sets. In our example, the *instructor* and *student* entity sets participate in the relationship set *advisor*. Additionally, suppose each student must have another instructor who serves as a department advisor (undergraduate or graduate). Then the *instructor* and *student* entity sets may participate in another relationship set, *dept_advisor*.

The relationship sets *advisor* and *dept_advisor* provide examples of a **binary** relationship set—that is, one that involves two entity sets. Most of the relationship sets in a database system are binary. Occasionally, however, relationship sets involve more than two entity sets.

As an example, suppose that we have an entity set *project* that represents all the research projects carried out in the university. Consider the entity sets *instructor*, *student*, and *project*. Each project can have multiple associated students and multiple associated instructors. Furthermore, each student working on a project must have an associated instructor who guides the student on the project. For now, we ignore the first two relationships, between project and instructor, and between project and student. Instead, we focus on the information about which instructor is guiding which student on a particular project. To represent this information, we relate the three entity sets through the relationship set *proj_guide*, which indicates that a particular student is guided by a particular instructor on a particular project.

Note that a student could have different instructors as guides for different projects, which cannot be captured by a binary relationship between students and instructors.

The number of entity sets that participate in a relationship set is the **degree** of the relationship set. A binary relationship set is of degree 2; a ternary relationship set is of degree 3.

7.2.3   Attributes

For each attribute, there is a set of permitted values, called the **domain**, or **value set**, of that attribute. The domain of attribute *course_id* might be the set of all text strings of a certain length. Similarly, the domain of attribute *semester* might be strings from the set {Fall, Winter, Spring, Summer}.

Formally, an attribute of an entity set is a function that maps from the entity set into a domain. Since an entity set may have several attributes, each entity can be described by a set of (attribute, data value) pairs, one pair for each attribute of the entity set. For example, a particular *instructor* entity may be described by the set {(*ID*, 76766), (*name*, Crick), (*dept_name*, Biology), (*salary*, 72000)}, meaning that the entity describes a person named Crick whose instructor *ID* is 76766, who is a member of the Biology department with salary of $72,000. We can see, at this point, an integration of the abstract schema with the actual enterprise being modeled. The attribute values describing an entity constitute a significant portion of the data stored in the database.

An attribute, as used in the E-R model, can be characterized by the following attribute types.

- **Simple** and **composite** attributes. In our examples thus far, the attributes have been simple; that is, they have not been divided into subparts. **Composite** attributes, on the other hand, can be divided into subparts (that is, other attributes). For example, an attribute *name* could be structured as a composite attribute consisting of *first_name*, *middle_initial*, and *last_name*. Using composite attributes in a design schema is a good choice if a user will wish to refer to an entire attribute on some occasions, and to only a component of the attribute on other occasions. Suppose we were to to add an address to the *student* entity-set. The address can be defined as the composite attribute *address* with the attributes *street*, *city*, *state*, and *zip_code*.[3] Composite attributes help us to group together related attributes, making the modeling cleaner.

  Note also that a composite attribute may appear as a hierarchy. In the composite attribute *address*, its component attribute *street* can be further divided into *street_number*, *street_name*, and *apartment_number*. Figure 7.4 depicts these examples of composite attributes for the *instructor* entity set.

- **Single-valued** and **multivalued** attributes. The attributes in our examples all have a single value for a particular entity. For instance, the *student_ID* attribute for a specific student entity refers to only one student *ID*. Such attributes are said to be **single valued**. There may be instances where an attribute has a set of values for a specific entity. Suppose we add to the *instructor* entity set

---

[3]We assume the address format used in the United States, which includes a numeric postal code called a zip code.

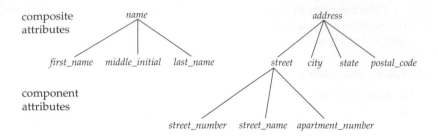

Figure 7.4 Composite attributes instructor *name* and *address*.

a *phone_number* attribute. An *instructor* may have zero, one, or several phone numbers, and different instructors may have different numbers of phones. This type of attribute is said to be **multivalued**. As another example, we could add to the *instructor* entity set an attribute *dependent_name* listing all the dependents. This attribute would be multivalued, since any particular instructor may have zero, one, or more dependents.

To denote that an attribute is multivalued, we enclose it in braces, for example {*phone_number*} or {*dependent_name*}.

Where appropriate, upper and lower bounds may be placed on the number of values in a multivalued attribute. For example, a university may limit the number of phone numbers recorded for a single instructor to two. Placing bounds in this case expresses that the *phone_number* attribute of the *instructor* entity set may have between zero and two values.

- **Derived** attribute. The value for this type of attribute can be derived from the values of other related attributes or entities. For instance, let us say that the *instructor* entity set has an attribute *students_advised*, which represents how many students an instructor advises. We can derive the value for this attribute by counting the number of *student* entities associated with that instructor.

  As another example, suppose that the *instructor* entity set has an attribute *age* that indicates the instructor's age. If the *instructor* entity set also has an attribute *date_of_birth*, we can calculate *age* from *date_of_birth* and the current date. Thus, *age* is a derived attribute. In this case, *date_of_birth* may be referred to as a *base* attribute, or a *stored* attribute. The value of a derived attribute is not stored but is computed when required.

An attribute takes a **null** value when an entity does not have a value for it. The *null* value may indicate "not applicable"—that is, that the value does not exist for the entity. For example, one may have no middle name. *Null* can also designate that an attribute value is unknown. An unknown value may be either *missing* (the value does exist, but we do not have that information) or *not known* (we do not know whether or not the value actually exists).

For instance, if the *name* value for a particular instructor is *null*, we assume that the value is missing, since every instructor must have a name. A null value for the *apartment_number* attribute could mean that the address does not include an apartment number (not applicable), that an apartment number exists but we do not know what it is (missing), or that we do not know whether or not an apartment number is part of the instructor's address (unknown).

7.3 Constraints

An E-R enterprise schema may define certain constraints to which the contents of a database must conform. In this section, we examine mapping cardinalities and participation constraints.

7.3.1 Mapping Cardinalities

Mapping cardinalities, or cardinality ratios, express the number of entities to which another entity can be associated via a relationship set.

Mapping cardinalities are most useful in describing binary relationship sets, although they can contribute to the description of relationship sets that involve more than two entity sets. In this section, we shall concentrate on only binary relationship sets.

For a binary relationship set R between entity sets A and B, the mapping cardinality must be one of the following:

- **One-to-one**. An entity in A is associated with *at most* one entity in B, and an entity in B is associated with *at most* one entity in A. (See Figure 7.5a.)

- **One-to-many**. An entity in A is associated with any number (zero or more) of entities in B. An entity in B, however, can be associated with *at most* one entity in A. (See Figure 7.5b.)

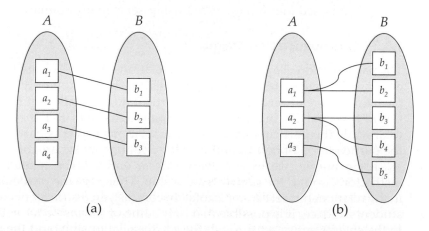

Figure 7.5 Mapping cardinalities. (a) One-to-one. (b) One-to-many.

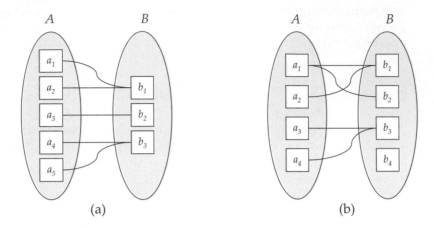

Figure 7.6 Mapping cardinalities. (a) Many-to-one. (b) Many-to-many.

- **Many-to-one.** An entity in A is associated with *at most* one entity in B. An entity in B, however, can be associated with any number (zero or more) of entities in A. (See Figure 7.6a.)

- **Many-to-many.** An entity in A is associated with any number (zero or more) of entities in B, and an entity in B is associated with any number (zero or more) of entities in A. (See Figure 7.6b.)

The appropriate mapping cardinality for a particular relationship set obviously depends on the real-world situation that the relationship set is modeling.

As an illustration, consider the *advisor* relationship set. If, in a particular university, a student can be advised by only one instructor, and an instructor can advise several students, then the relationship set from *instructor* to *student* is one-to-many. If a student can be advised by several instructors (as in the case of students advised jointly), the relationship set is many-to-many.

7.3.2   Participation Constraints

The participation of an entity set E in a relationship set R is said to be **total** if every entity in E participates in at least one relationship in R. If only some entities in E participate in relationships in R, the participation of entity set E in relationship R is said to be **partial**. In Figure 7.5a, the participation of B in the relationship set is total while the participation of A in the relationship set is partial. In Figure 7.5b, the participation of both A and B in the relationship set are total.

For example, we expect every *student* entity to be related to at least one instructor through the *advisor* relationship. Therefore the participation of *student* in the relationship set *advisor* is total. In contrast, an *instructor* need not advise any students. Hence, it is possible that only some of the *instructor* entities are related to the *student* entity set through the *advisor* relationship, and the participation of *instructor* in the *advisor* relationship set is therefore partial.

7.3.3 Keys

We must have a way to specify how entities within a given entity set are distinguished. Conceptually, individual entities are distinct; from a database perspective, however, the differences among them must be expressed in terms of their attributes.

Therefore, the values of the attribute values of an entity must be such that they can *uniquely identify* the entity. In other words, no two entities in an entity set are allowed to have exactly the same value for all attributes.

The notion of a *key* for a relation schema, as defined in Section 2.3, applies directly to entity sets. That is, a key for an entity is a set of attributes that suffice to distinguish entities from each other. The concepts of superkey, candidate key, and primary key are applicable to entity sets just as they are applicable to relation schemas.

Keys also help to identify relationships uniquely, and thus distinguish relationships from each other. Below, we define the corresponding notions of keys for relationships.

The primary key of an entity set allows us to distinguish among the various entities of the set. We need a similar mechanism to distinguish among the various relationships of a relationship set.

Let R be a relationship set involving entity sets $E_1, E_2, \ldots, E_n$. Let *primary-key*(E_i) denote the set of attributes that forms the primary key for entity set E_i. Assume for now that the attribute names of all primary keys are unique. The composition of the primary key for a relationship set depends on the set of attributes associated with the relationship set R.

If the relationship set R has no attributes associated with it, then the set of attributes

$$primary\text{-}key(E_1) \cup primary\text{-}key(E_2) \cup \cdots \cup primary\text{-}key(E_n)$$

describes an individual relationship in set R.

If the relationship set R has attributes $a_1, a_2, \ldots, a_m$ associated with it, then the set of attributes

$$primary\text{-}key(E_1) \cup primary\text{-}key(E_2) \cup \cdots \cup primary\text{-}key(E_n) \cup \{a_1, a_2, \ldots, a_m\}$$

describes an individual relationship in set R.

In both of the above cases, the set of attributes

$$primary\text{-}key(E_1) \cup primary\text{-}key(E_2) \cup \cdots \cup primary\text{-}key(E_n)$$

forms a superkey for the relationship set.

If the attribute names of primary keys are not unique across entity sets, the attributes are renamed to distinguish them; the name of the entity set combined with the name of the attribute would form a unique name. If an entity set participates more than once in a relationship set (as in the *prereq* relationship in

Section 7.2.2), the role name is used instead of the name of the entity set, to form a unique attribute name.

The structure of the primary key for the relationship set depends on the mapping cardinality of the relationship set. As an illustration, consider the entity sets *instructor* and *student*, and the relationship set *advisor*, with attribute *date*, in Section 7.2.2. Suppose that the relationship set is many-to-many. Then the primary key of *advisor* consists of the union of the primary keys of *instructor* and *student*. If the relationship is many-to-one from *student* to *instructor*—that is, each student can have have at most one advisor—then the primary key of *advisor* is simply the primary key of *student*. However, if an instructor can advise only one student— that is, if the *advisor* relationship is many-to-one from *instructor* to *student*—then the primary key of *advisor* is simply the primary key of *instructor*. For one-to-one relationships either candidate key can be used as the primary key.

For nonbinary relationships, if no cardinality constraints are present then the superkey formed as described earlier in this section is the only candidate key, and it is chosen as the primary key. The choice of the primary key is more complicated if cardinality constraints are present. Since we have not discussed how to specify cardinality constraints on nonbinary relations, we do not discuss this issue further in this chapter. We consider the issue in more detail later, in Sections 7.5.5 and 8.4.

7.4   Removing Redundant Attributes in Entity Sets

When we design a database using the E-R model, we usually start by identifying those entity sets that should be included. For example, in the university organization we have discussed thus far, we decided to include such entity sets as *student*, *instructor*, etc. Once the entity sets are decided upon, we must choose the appropriate attributes. These attributes are supposed to represent the various values we want to capture in the database. In the university organization, we decided that for the *instructor* entity set, we will include the attributes *ID*, *name*, *dept_name*, and *salary*. We could have added the attributes: *phone_number*, *office_number*, *home_page*, etc. The choice of what attributes to include is up to the designer, who has a good understanding of the structure of the enterprise.

Once the entities and their corresponding attributes are chosen, the relationship sets among the various entities are formed. These relationship sets may result in a situation where attributes in the various entity sets are redundant and need to be removed from the original entity sets. To illustrate, consider the entity sets *instructor* and *department*:

- The entity set *instructor* includes the attributes *ID*, *name*, *dept_name*, and *salary*, with *ID* forming the primary key.

- The entity set *department* includes the attributes *dept_name*, *building*, and *budget*, with *dept_name* forming the primary key.

We model the fact that each instructor has an associated department using a relationship set *inst_dept* relating *instructor* and *department*.

The attribute *dept_name* appears in both entity sets. Since it is the primary key for the entity set *department*, it is redundant in the entity set *instructor* and needs to be removed.

Removing the attribute *dept_name* from the *instructor* entity set may appear rather unintuitive, since the relation *instructor* that we used in the earlier chapters had an attribute *dept_name*. As we shall see later, when we create a relational schema from the E-R diagram, the attribute *dept_name* in fact gets added to the relation *instructor*, but only if each instructor has at most one associated department. If an instructor has more than one associated department, the relationship between instructors and departments is recorded in a separate relation *inst_dept*.

Treating the connection between instructors and departments uniformly as a relationship, rather than as an attribute of *instructor*, makes the logical relationship explicit, and helps avoid a premature assumption that each instructor is associated with only one department.

Similarly, the *student* entity set is related to the *department* entity set through the relationship set *student_dept* and thus there is no need for a *dept_name* attribute in *student*.

As another example, consider course offerings (sections) along with the time slots of the offerings. Each time slot is identified by a *time_slot_id*, and has associated with it a set of weekly meetings, each identified by a day of the week, start time, and end time. We decide to model the set of weekly meeting times as a multivalued composite attribute. Suppose we model entity sets *section* and *time_slot* as follows:

- The entity set *section* includes the attributes *course_id*, *sec_id*, *semester*, *year*, *building*, *room_number*, and *time_slot_id*, with (*course_id*, *sec_id*, *year*, *semester*) forming the primary key.

- The entity set *time_slot* includes the attributes *time_slot_id*, which is the primary key,[4] and a multivalued composite attribute $\{(day, start\_time, end\_time)\}$.[5]

These entities are related through the relationship set *sec_time_slot*.

The attribute *time_slot_id* appears in both entity sets. Since it is the primary key for the entity set *time_slot*, it is redundant in the entity set *section* and needs to be removed.

As a final example, suppose we have an entity set *classroom*, with attributes *building*, *room_number*, and *capacity*, with *building* and *room_number* forming the primary key. Suppose also that we have a relationship set *sec_class* that relates *section* to *classroom*. Then the attributes {*building*, *room_number*} are redundant in the entity set *section*.

A good entity-relationship design does not contain redundant attributes. For our university example, we list the entity sets and their attributes below, with primary keys underlined:

---

[4]We shall see later on that the primary key for the relation created from the entity set *time_slot* includes *day* and *start_time*; however, *day* and *start_time* do not form part of the primary key of the entity set *time_slot*.

[5]We could optionally give a name, such as *meeting*, for the composite attribute containing *day*, *start_time*, and *end_time*.

- **classroom**: with attributes (*building*, *room_number*, *capacity*).
- **department**: with attributes (*dept_name*, *building*, *budget*).
- **course**: with attributes (*course_id*, *title*, *credits*).
- **instructor**: with attributes (*ID*, *name*, *salary*).
- **section:** with attributes (*course_id*, *sec_id*, *semester*, *year*).
- **student**: with attributes (*ID*, *name*, *tot_cred*).
- **time_slot**: with attributes (*time_slot_id*, {(*day*, *start_time*, *end_time*) }).

The relationship sets in our design are listed below:

- **inst_dept**: relating instructors with departments.
- **stud_dept**: relating students with departments.
- **teaches**: relating instructors with sections.
- **takes**: relating students with sections, with a descriptive attribute *grade*.
- **course_dept**: relating courses with departments.
- **sec_course**: relating sections with courses.
- **sec_class**: relating sections with classrooms.
- **sec_time_slot**: relating sections with time slots.
- **advisor**: relating students with instructors.
- **prereq**: relating courses with prerequisite courses.

You can verify that none of the entity sets has any attribute that is made redundant by one of the relationship sets. Further, you can verify that all the information (other than constraints) in the relational schema for our university database, which we saw earlier in Figure 2.8 in Chapter 2, has been captured by the above design, but with several attributes in the relational design replaced by relationships in the E-R design.

7.5   Entity-Relationship Diagrams

As we saw briefly in Section 1.3.3, an **E-R diagram** can express the overall logical structure of a database graphically. E-R diagrams are simple and clear—qualities that may well account in large part for the widespread use of the E-R model.

7.5.1   Basic Structure

An E-R diagram consists of the following major components:

Figure 7.7 E-R diagram corresponding to instructors and students.

- **Rectangles divided into two parts** represent entity sets. The first part, which in this textbook is shaded blue, contains the name of the entity set. The second part contains the names of all the attributes of the entity set.

- **Diamonds** represent relationship sets.

- **Undivided rectangles** represent the attributes of a relationship set. Attributes that are part of the primary key are underlined.

- **Lines** link entity sets to relationship sets.

- **Dashed lines** link attributes of a relationship set to the relationship set.

- **Double lines** indicate total participation of an entity in a relationship set.

- **Double diamonds** represent identifying relationship sets linked to weak entity sets (we discuss identifying relationship sets and weak entity sets later, in Section 7.5.6).

Consider the E-R diagram in Figure 7.7, which consists of two entity sets, *instructor* and *student* related through a binary relationship set *advisor*. The attributes associated with *instructor* are *ID*, *name*, and *salary*. The attributes associated with *student* are *ID*, *name*, and *tot_cred*. In Figure 7.7, attributes of an entity set that are members of the primary key are underlined.

If a relationship set has some attributes associated with it, then we enclose the attributes in a rectangle and link the rectangle with a dashed line to the diamond representing that relationship set. For example, in Figure 7.8, we have the *date* descriptive attribute attached to the relationship set *advisor* to specify the date on which an instructor became the advisor.

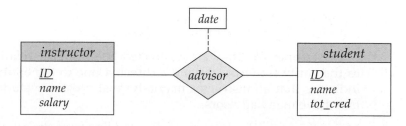

Figure 7.8 E-R diagram with an attribute attached to a relationship set.

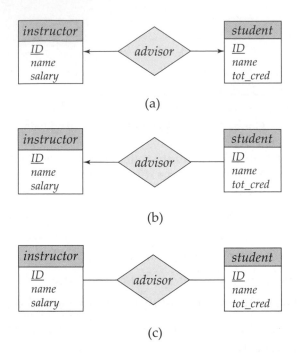

Figure 7.9   Relationships. (a) One-to-one. (b) One-to-many. (c) Many-to-many.

7.5.2   Mapping Cardinality

The relationship set *advisor*, between the *instructor* and *student* entity sets may be one-to-one, one-to-many, many-to-one, or many-to-many. To distinguish among these types, we draw either a directed line ($\rightarrow$) or an undirected line (—) between the relationship set and the entity set in question, as follows:

- **One-to-one:** We draw a directed line from the relationship set *advisor* to both entity sets *instructor* and *student* (see Figure 7.9a). This indicates that an instructor may advise at most one student, and a student may have at most one advisor.

- **One-to-many:** We draw a directed line from the relationship set *advisor* to the entity set *instructor* and an undirected line to the entity set *student* (see Figure 7.9b). This indicates that an instructor may advise many students, but a student may have at most one advisor.

- **Many-to-one:** We draw an undirected line from the relationship set *advisor* to the entity set *instructor* and a directed line to the entity set *student*. This indicates that an instructor may advise at most one student, but a student may have many advisors.

- **Many-to-many:** We draw an undirected line from the relationship set *advisor* to both entity sets *instructor* and *student* (see Figure 7.9c). This indicates that an instructor may advise many students, and a student may have many advisors.

E-R diagrams also provide a way to indicate more complex constraints on the number of times each entity participates in relationships in a relationship set. A line may have an associated minimum and maximum cardinality, shown in the form *l..h*, where *l* is the minimum and *h* the maximum cardinality. A minimum value of 1 indicates total participation of the entity set in the relationship set; that is, each entity in the entity set occurs in at least one relationship in that relationship set. A maximum value of 1 indicates that the entity participates in at most one relationship, while a maximum value ∗ indicates no limit.

For example, consider Figure 7.10. The line between *advisor* and *student* has a cardinality constraint of 1..1, meaning the minimum and the maximum cardinality are both 1. That is, each student must have exactly one advisor. The limit 0..∗ on the line between *advisor* and *instructor* indicates that an instructor can have zero or more students. Thus, the relationship *advisor* is one-to-many from *instructor* to *student*, and further the participation of *student* in *advisor* is total, implying that a student must have an advisor.

It is easy to misinterpret the 0..∗ on the left edge and think that the relationship *advisor* is many-to-one from *instructor* to *student*—this is exactly the reverse of the correct interpretation.

If both edges have a maximum value of 1, the relationship is one-to-one. If we had specified a cardinality limit of 1..∗ on the left edge, we would be saying that each instructor must advise at least one student.

The E-R diagram in Figure 7.10 could alternatively have been drawn with a double line from *student* to *advisor*, and an arrow on the line from *advisor* to *instructor*, in place of the cardinality constraints shown. This alternative diagram would enforce exactly the same constraints as the constraints shown in the figure.

7.5.3   Complex Attributes

Figure 7.11 shows how composite attributes can be represented in the E-R notation. Here, a composite attribute *name*, with component attributes *first_name, middle _initial*, and *last_name* replaces the simple attribute *name* of *instructor*. As another example, suppose we were to add an address to the *instructor* entity-set. The address can be defined as the composite attribute *address* with the attributes

Figure 7.10   Cardinality limits on relationship sets.

instructor
<u>*ID*</u>
name
first_name
middle_initial
last_name
address
street
street_number
street_name
apt_number
city
state
zip
{ phone_number }
date_of_birth
age ( )

Figure 7.11 E-R diagram with composite, multivalued, and derived attributes.

street, *city*, *state*, and *zip_code*. The attribute *street* is itself a composite attribute whose component attributes are *street_number*, *street_name*, and *apartment_number*.

Figure 7.11 also illustrates a multivalued attribute *phone_number*, denoted by "*{phone_number}*", and a derived attribute *age*, depicted by a "*age ( )*".

7.5.4 Roles

We indicate roles in E-R diagrams by labeling the lines that connect diamonds to rectangles. Figure 7.12 shows the role indicators *course_id* and *prereq_id* between the *course* entity set and the *prereq* relationship set.

7.5.5 Nonbinary Relationship Sets

Nonbinary relationship sets can be specified easily in an E-R diagram. Figure 7.13 consists of the three entity sets *instructor*, *student*, and *project*, related through the relationship set *proj_guide*.

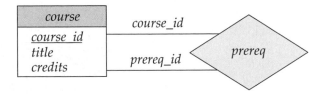

Figure 7.12 E-R diagram with role indicators.

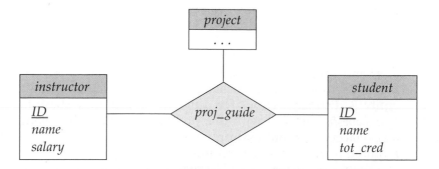

Figure 7.13   E-R diagram with a ternary relationship.

We can specify some types of many-to-one relationships in the case of non-binary relationship sets. Suppose a *student* can have at most one instructor as a guide on a project. This constraint can be specified by an arrow pointing to *instructor* on the edge from *proj_guide*.

We permit at most one arrow out of a relationship set, since an E-R diagram with two or more arrows out of a nonbinary relationship set can be interpreted in two ways. Suppose there is a relationship set R between entity sets $A_1, A_2, \ldots, A_n$, and the only arrows are on the edges to entity sets $A_{i+1}, A_{i+2}, \ldots, A_n$. Then, the two possible interpretations are:

1. A particular combination of entities from $A_1, A_2, \ldots, A_i$ can be associated with at most one combination of entities from $A_{i+1}, A_{i+2}, \ldots, A_n$. Thus, the primary key for the relationship R can be constructed by the union of the primary keys of $A_1, A_2, \ldots, A_i$.

2. For each entity set A_k, $i < k \leq n$, each combination of the entities from the other entity sets can be associated with at most one entity from A_k. Each set $\{A_1, A_2, \ldots, A_{k-1}, A_{k+1}, \ldots, A_n\}$, for $i < k \leq n$, then forms a candidate key.

Each of these interpretations has been used in different books and systems. To avoid confusion, we permit only one arrow out of a relationship set, in which case the two interpretations are equivalent. In Chapter 8 (Section 8.4), we study *functional dependencies*, which allow either of these interpretations to be specified in an unambiguous manner.

7.5.6   Weak Entity Sets

Consider a *section* entity, which is uniquely identified by a course identifier, semester, year, and section identifier. Clearly, section entities are related to course entities. Suppose we create a relationship set *sec_course* between entity sets *section* and *course*.

Now, observe that the information in *sec_course* is redundant, since *section* already has an attribute *course_id*, which identifies the course with which the section is related. One option to deal with this redundancy is to get rid of the relationship *sec_course*; however, by doing so the relationship between *section* and *course* becomes implicit in an attribute, which is not desirable.

An alternative way to deal with this redundancy is to not store the attribute *course_id* in the *section* entity and to only store the remaining attributes *sec_id*, *year*, and *semester*.[6] However, the entity set *section* then does not have enough attributes to identify a particular *section* entity uniquely; although each *section* entity is distinct, sections for different courses may share the same *sec_id*, *year*, and *semester*. To deal with this problem, we treat the relationship *sec_course* as a special relationship that provides extra information, in this case the *course_id*, required to identify *section* entities uniquely.

The notion of *weak entity set* formalizes the above intuition. An entity set that does not have sufficient attributes to form a primary key is termed a **weak entity set**. An entity set that has a primary key is termed a **strong entity set**.

For a weak entity set to be meaningful, it must be associated with another entity set, called the **identifying** or **owner entity set**. Every weak entity must be associated with an identifying entity; that is, the weak entity set is said to be **existence dependent** on the identifying entity set. The identifying entity set is said to **own** the weak entity set that it identifies. The relationship associating the weak entity set with the identifying entity set is called the **identifying relationship**.

The identifying relationship is many-to-one from the weak entity set to the identifying entity set, and the participation of the weak entity set in the relationship is total. The identifying relationship set should not have any descriptive attributes, since any such attributes can instead be associated with the weak entity set.

In our example, the identifying entity set for *section* is *course*, and the relationship *sec_course*, which associates *section* entities with their corresponding *course* entities, is the identifying relationship.

Although a weak entity set does not have a primary key, we nevertheless need a means of distinguishing among all those entities in the weak entity set that depend on one particular strong entity. The **discriminator** of a weak entity set is a set of attributes that allows this distinction to be made. For example, the discriminator of the weak entity set *section* consists of the attributes *sec_id*, *year*, and *semester*, since, for each course, this set of attributes uniquely identifies one single section for that course. The discriminator of a weak entity set is also called the *partial key* of the entity set.

The primary key of a weak entity set is formed by the primary key of the identifying entity set, plus the weak entity set's discriminator. In the case of the entity set *section*, its primary key is {*course_id*, *sec_id*, *year*, *semester*}, where *course_id* is the primary key of the identifying entity set, namely *course*, and {*sec_id*, *year*, *semester*} distinguishes *section* entities for the same course.

Note that we could have chosen to make *sec_id* globally unique across all courses offered in the university, in which case the *section* entity set would have

---

[6]Note that the relational schema we eventually create from the entity set *section* does have the attribute *course_id*, for reasons that will become clear later, even though we have dropped the attribute *course_id* from the entity set *section*.

Figure 7.14 E-R diagram with a weak entity set.

had a primary key. However, conceptually, a *section* is still dependent on a *course* for its existence, which is made explicit by making it a weak entity set.

In E-R diagrams, a weak entity set is depicted via a rectangle, like a strong entity set, but there are two main differences:

- The discriminator of a weak entity is underlined with a dashed, rather than a solid, line.

- The relationship set connecting the weak entity set to the identifying strong entity set is depicted by a double diamond.

In Figure 7.14, the weak entity set *section* depends on the strong entity set *course* via the relationship set *sec_course*.

The figure also illustrates the use of double lines to indicate *total participation*; the participation of the (weak) entity set *section* in the relationship *sec_course* is total, meaning that every section must be related via *sec_course* to some course. Finally, the arrow from *sec_course* to *course* indicates that each section is related to a single course.

A weak entity set can participate in relationships other than the identifying relationship. For instance, the *section* entity could participate in a relationship with the *time_slot* entity set, identifying the time when a particular class section meets. A weak entity set may participate as owner in an identifying relationship with another weak entity set. It is also possible to have a weak entity set with more than one identifying entity set. A particular weak entity would then be identified by a combination of entities, one from each identifying entity set. The primary key of the weak entity set would consist of the union of the primary keys of the identifying entity sets, plus the discriminator of the weak entity set.

In some cases, the database designer may choose to express a weak entity set as a multivalued composite attribute of the owner entity set. In our example, this alternative would require that the entity set *course* have a multivalued, composite attribute *section*. A weak entity set may be more appropriately modeled as an attribute if it participates in only the identifying relationship, and if it has few attributes. Conversely, a weak entity set representation more aptly models a situation where the set participates in relationships other than the identifying relationship, and where the weak entity set has several attributes. It is clear that *section* violates the requirements for being modeled as a multivalued composite attribute, and is modeled more aptly as a weak entity set.

7.5.7 E-R diagram for the University Enterprise

In Figure 7.15, we show an E-R diagram that corresponds to the university enterprise that we have been using thus far in the text. This E-R diagram is equivalent to the textual description of the university E-R model that we saw in Section 7.4, but with several additional constraints, and *section* now being a weak entity.

In our university database, we have a constraint that each instructor must have exactly one associated department. As a result, there is a double line in Figure 7.15 between *instructor* and *inst_dept*, indicating total participation of *instructor* in *inst_dept*; that is, each instructor must be associated with a department. Further, there is an arrow from *inst_dept* to *department*, indicating that each instructor can have at most one associated department.

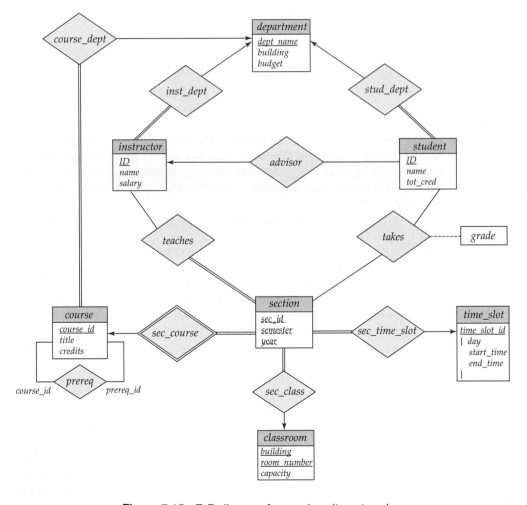

Figure 7.15   E-R diagram for a university enterprise.

Similarly, entity sets *course* and *student* have double lines to relationship sets *course_dept* and *stud_dept* respectively, as also entity set *section* to relationship set *sec_time_slot*. The first two relationships, in turn, have an arrow pointing to the other relationship, *department*, while the third relationship has an arrow pointing to *time_slot*.

Further, Figure 7.15 shows that the relationship set *takes* has a descriptive attribute *grade*, and that each student has at most one advisor. The figure also shows that *section* is now a weak entity set, with attributes *sec_id*, *semester*, and *year* forming the discriminator; *sec_course* is the identifying relationship set relating weak entity set *section* to the strong entity set *course*.

In Section 7.6, we shall show how this E-R diagram can be used to derive the various relation schemas we use.

7.6   Reduction to Relational Schemas

We can represent a database that conforms to an E-R database schema by a collection of relation schemas. For each entity set and for each relationship set in the database design, there is a unique relation schema to which we assign the name of the corresponding entity set or relationship set.

Both the E-R model and the relational database model are abstract, logical representations of real-world enterprises. Because the two models employ similar design principles, we can convert an E-R design into a relational design.

In this section, we describe how an E-R schema can be represented by relation schemas and how constraints arising from the E-R design can be mapped to constraints on relation schemas.

7.6.1   Representation of Strong Entity Sets with Simple Attributes

Let E be a strong entity set with only simple descriptive attributes a_1, a_2, . . . , a_n. We represent this entity by a schema called E with n distinct attributes. Each tuple in a relation on this schema corresponds to one entity of the entity set E.

For schemas derived from strong entity sets, the primary key of the entity set serves as the primary key of the resulting schema. This follows directly from the fact that each tuple corresponds to a specific entity in the entity set.

As an illustration, consider the entity set *student* of the E-R diagram in Figure 7.15. This entity set has three attributes: *ID*, *name*, *tot_cred*. We represent this entity set by a schema called *student* with three attributes:

$$student \; (\underline{ID}, \; name, \; tot\_cred)$$

Note that since student *ID* is the primary key of the entity set, it is also the primary key of the relation schema.

Continuing with our example, for the E-R diagram in Figure 7.15, all the strong entity sets, except *time_slot*, have only simple attributes. The schemas derived from these strong entity sets are:

> *classroom* (*building*, *room_number*, *capacity*)
> *department* (*dept_name*, *building*, *budget*)
> *course* (*course_id*, *title*, *credits*)
> *instructor* (*ID*, *name*, *salary*)
> *student* (*ID*, *name*, *tot_cred*)

As you can see, both the *instructor* and *student* schemas are different from the schemas we have used in the previous chapters (they do not contain the attribute *dept_name*). We shall revisit this issue shortly.

7.6.2 Representation of Strong Entity Sets with Complex Attributes

When a strong entity set has nonsimple attributes, things are a bit more complex. We handle composite attributes by creating a separate attribute for each of the component attributes; we do not create a separate attribute for the composite attribute itself. To illustrate, consider the version of the *instructor* entity set depicted in Figure 7.11. For the composite attribute *name*, the schema generated for *instructor* contains the attributes *first_name*, *middle_name*, and *last_name*; there is no separate attribute or schema for *name*. Similarly, for the composite attribute *address*, the schema generated contains the attributes *street*, *city*, *state*, and *zip_code*. Since *street* is a composite attribute it is replaced by *street_number*, *street_name*, and *apt_number*. We revisit this matter in Section 8.2.

Multivalued attributes are treated differently from other attributes. We have seen that attributes in an E-R diagram generally map directly into attributes for the appropriate relation schemas. Multivalued attributes, however, are an exception; new relation schemas are created for these attributes, as we shall see shortly.

Derived attributes are not explicitly represented in the relational data model. However, they can be represented as "methods" in other data models such as the object-relational data model, which is described later in Chapter 22.

The relational schema derived from the version of entity set *instructor* with complex attributes, without including the multivalued attribute, is thus:

> *instructor* (*ID*, *first_name*, *middle_name*, *last_name*,
> *street_number*, *street_name*, *apt_number*,
> *city*, *state*, *zip_code*, *date_of_birth*)

For a multivalued attribute M, we create a relation schema R with an attribute A that corresponds to M and attributes corresponding to the primary key of the entity set or relationship set of which M is an attribute.

As an illustration, consider the E-R diagram in Figure 7.11 that depicts the entity set *instructor*, which includes the multivalued attribute *phone_number*. The primary key of *instructor* is *ID*. For this multivalued attribute, we create a relation schema

> *instructor_phone* (*ID*, *phone_number*)

Each phone number of an instructor is represented as a unique tuple in the relation on this schema. Thus, if we had an instructor with *ID* 22222, and phone numbers 555-1234 and 555-4321, the relation *instructor_phone* would have two tuples (22222, 555-1234) and (22222, 555-4321).

We create a primary key of the relation schema consisting of all attributes of the schema. In the above example, the primary key consists of both attributes of the relation *instructor_phone*.

In addition, we create a foreign-key constraint on the relation schema created from the multivalued attribute, with the attribute generated from the primary key of the entity set referencing the relation generated from the entity set. In the above example, the foreign-key constraint on the *instructor_phone* relation would be that attribute *ID* references the *instructor* relation.

In the case that an entity set consists of only two attributes — a single primary-key attribute B and a single multivalued attribute M — the relation schema for the entity set would contain only one attribute, namely the primary-key attribute B. We can drop this relation, while retaining the relation schema with the attribute B and attribute A that corresponds to M.

To illustrate, consider the entity set *time_slot* depicted in Figure 7.15. Here, *time_slot_id* is the primary key of the *time_slot* entity set and there is a single multivalued attribute that happens also to be composite. The entity set can be represented by just the following schema created from the multivalued composite attribute:

$$time\_slot\ (\underline{time\_slot\_id},\ \underline{day},\ \underline{start\_time},\ end\_time)$$

Although not represented as a constraint on the E-R diagram, we know that there cannot be two meetings of a class that start at the same time of the same day-of-the-week but end at different times; based on this constraint, *end_time* has been omitted from the primary key of the *time_slot* schema.

The relation created from the entity set would have only a single attribute *time_slot_id*; the optimization of dropping this relation has the benefit of simplifying the resultant database schema, although it has a drawback related to foreign keys, which we briefly discuss in Section 7.6.4.

7.6.3 Representation of Weak Entity Sets

Let A be a weak entity set with attributes $a_1, a_2, \ldots, a_m$. Let B be the strong entity set on which A depends. Let the primary key of B consist of attributes $b_1, b_2, \ldots, b_n$. We represent the entity set A by a relation schema called A with one attribute for each member of the set:

$$\{a_1, a_2, \ldots, a_m\} \cup \{b_1, b_2, \ldots, b_n\}$$

For schemas derived from a weak entity set, the combination of the primary key of the strong entity set and the discriminator of the weak entity set serves as the primary key of the schema. In addition to creating a primary key, we also create a foreign-key constraint on the relation A, specifying that the attributes $b_1, b_2, \ldots, b_n$ reference the primary key of the relation B. The foreign-key constraint ensures that for each tuple representing a weak entity, there is a corresponding tuple representing the corresponding strong entity.

As an illustration, consider the weak entity set *section* in the E-R diagram of Figure 7.15. This entity set has the attributes: *sec_id*, *semester*, and *year*. The primary key of the *course* entity set, on which *section* depends, is *course_id*. Thus, we represent *section* by a schema with the following attributes:

$$section\ (\underline{course\_id},\ \underline{sec\_id},\ \underline{semester},\ \underline{year})$$

The primary key consists of the primary key of the entity set *course*, along with the discriminator of *section*, which is *sec_id*, *semester*, and *year*. We also create a foreign-key constraint on the *section* schema, with the attribute *course_id* referencing the primary key of the *course* schema, and the integrity constraint "on delete cascade".[7] Because of the "on delete cascade" specification on the foreign key constraint, if a *course* entity is deleted, then so are all the associated *section* entities.

7.6.4   Representation of Relationship Sets

Let R be a relationship set, let $a_1, a_2, \ldots, a_m$ be the set of attributes formed by the union of the primary keys of each of the entity sets participating in R, and let the descriptive attributes (if any) of R be $b_1, b_2, \ldots, b_n$. We represent this relationship set by a relation schema called R with one attribute for each member of the set:

$$\{a_1, a_2, \ldots, a_m\} \cup \{b_1, b_2, \ldots, b_n\}$$

We described earlier, in Section 7.3.3, how to choose a primary key for a binary relationship set. As we saw in that section, taking all the primary-key attributes from all the related entity sets serves to identify a particular tuple, but for one-to-one, many-to-one, and one-to-many relationship sets, this turns out to be a larger set of attributes than we need in the primary key. The primary key is instead chosen as follows:

- For a binary many-to-many relationship, the union of the primary-key attributes from the participating entity sets becomes the primary key.

- For a binary one-to-one relationship set, the primary key of either entity set can be chosen as the primary key. The choice can be made arbitrarily.

- For a binary many-to-one or one-to-many relationship set, the primary key of the entity set on the "many" side of the relationship set serves as the primary key.

---

[7]The "on delete cascade" feature of foreign key constraints in SQL is described in Section 4.4.5.

- For an *n*-ary relationship set without any arrows on its edges, the union of the primary key-attributes from the participating entity sets becomes the primary key.

- For an *n*-ary relationship set with an arrow on one of its edges, the primary keys of the entity sets not on the "arrow" side of the relationship set serve as the primary key for the schema. Recall that we allowed only one arrow out of a relationship set.

We also create foreign-key constraints on the relation schema R as follows: For each entity set E_i related to relationship set R, we create a foreign-key constraint from relation schema R, with the attributes of R that were derived from primary-key attributes of E_i referencing the primary key of the relation schema representing E_i.

As an illustration, consider the relationship set *advisor* in the E-R diagram of Figure 7.15. This relationship set involves the following two entity sets:

- *instructor* with the primary key *ID*.

- *student* with the primary key *ID*.

Since the relationship set has no attributes, the *advisor* schema has two attributes, the primary keys of *instructor* and *student*. Since both attributes have the same name, we rename them *i_ID* and *s_ID*. Since the *advisor* relationship set is many-to-one from *student* to *instructor* the primary key for the *advisor* relation schema is *s_ID*.

We also create two foreign-key constraints on the *advisor* relation, with attribute *i_ID* referencing the primary key of *instructor* and attribute *s_ID* referencing the primary key of *student*.

Continuing with our example, for the E-R diagram in Figure 7.15, the schemas derived from a relationship set are depicted in Figure 7.16.

Observe that for the case of the relationship set *prereq*, the role indicators associated with the relationship are used as attribute names, since both roles refer to the same relation *course*.

Similar to the case of *advisor*, the primary key for each of the relations *sec_course*, *sec_time_slot*, *sec_class*, *inst_dept*, *stud_dept* and *course_dept* consists of the primary key of only one of the two related entity sets, since each of the corresponding relationships is many-to-one.

Foreign keys are not shown in Figure 7.16, but for each of the relations in the figure there are two foreign-key constraints, referencing the two relations created from the two related entity sets. Thus, for example, *sec_course* has foreign keys referencing *section* and *classroom*, *teaches* has foreign keys referencing *instructor* and *section*, and *takes* has foreign keys referencing *student* and *section*.

The optimization that allowed us to create only a single relation schema from the entity set *time_slot*, which had a multivalued attribute, prevents the creation of a foreign key from the relation schema *sec_time_slot* to the relation created from entity set *time_slot*, since we dropped the relation created from the entity set *time teaches* (<u>ID</u>, <u>course_id</u>, <u>sec_id</u>, <u>semester</u>, <u>year</u>)

takes (<u>ID</u>, <u>course_id</u>, <u>sec_id</u>, <u>semester</u>, <u>year</u>, grade)

prereq (<u>course_id</u>, <u>prereq_id</u>)

advisor (<u>s_ID</u>, i_ID)

sec_course (<u>course_id</u>, <u>sec_id</u>, <u>semester</u>, <u>year</u>)

sec_time_slot (<u>course_id</u>, <u>sec_id</u>, <u>semester</u>, <u>year</u>, time_slot_id)

sec_class (<u>course_id</u>, <u>sec_id</u>, <u>semester</u>, <u>year</u>, building, room_number)

inst_dept (<u>ID</u>, dept_name)

stud_dept (<u>ID</u>, dept_name)

course_dept (<u>course_id</u>, dept_name)

Figure 7.16   Schemas derived from relationship sets in the E-R diagram in Figure 7.15.

_slot. We retained the relation created from the multivalued attribute, and named it *time_slot*, but this relation may potentially have no tuples corresponding to a *time_slot_id*, or may have multiple tuples corresponding to a *time_slot_id*; thus, *time _slot_id* in *sec_time_slot* cannot reference this relation.

The astute reader may wonder why we have not seen the schemas *sec_course*, *sec_time_slot*, *sec_class*, *inst_dept*, *stud_dept*, and *course_dept* in the previous chapters. The reason is that the algorithm we have presented thus far results in some schemas that can be either eliminated or combined with other schemas. We explore this issue next.

7.6.4.1   Redundancy of Schemas

A relationship set linking a weak entity set to the corresponding strong entity set is treated specially. As we noted in Section 7.5.6, these relationships are many-to-one and have no descriptive attributes. Furthermore, the primary key of a weak entity set includes the primary key of the strong entity set. In the E-R diagram of Figure 7.14, the weak entity set *section* is dependent on the strong entity set *course* via the relationship set *sec_course*. The primary key of *section* is {*course_id*, *sec_id*, *semester*, *year*} and the primary key of *course* is *course_id*. Since *sec_course* has no descriptive attributes, the *sec_course* schema has attributes *course_id*, *sec_id*, *semester*, and *year*. The schema for the entity set *section* includes the attributes *course_id*, *sec_id*, *semester*, and *year* (among others). Every (*course_id*, *sec_id*, *semester*, *year*) combination in a *sec_course* relation would also be present in the relation on schema *section*, and vice versa. Thus, the *sec_course* schema is redundant.

In general, the schema for the relationship set linking a weak entity set to its corresponding strong entity set is redundant and does not need to be present in a relational database design based upon an E-R diagram.

7.6.4.2   Combination of Schemas

Consider a many-to-one relationship set *AB* from entity set *A* to entity set *B*. Using our relational-schema construction algorithm outlined previously, we get three schemas: *A*, *B*, and *AB*. Suppose further that the participation of *A* in the relationship is total; that is, every entity *a* in the entity set *B* must participate in the relationship *AB*. Then we can combine the schemas *A* and *AB* to form a single schema consisting of the union of attributes of both schemas. The primary key of the combined schema is the primary key of the entity set into whose schema the relationship set schema was merged.

To illustrate, let's examine the various relations in the E-R diagram of Figure 7.15 that satisfy the above criteria:

- *inst_dept*. The schemas *instructor* and *department* correspond to the entity sets *A* and *B*, respectively. Thus, the schema *inst_dept* can be combined with the *instructor* schema. The resulting *instructor* schema consists of the attributes {*ID*, *name*, *dept_name*, *salary*}.

- *stud_dept*. The schemas *student* and *department* correspond to the entity sets *A* and *B*, respectively. Thus, the schema *stud_dept* can be combined with the *student* schema. The resulting *student* schema consists of the attributes {*ID*, *name*, *dept_name*, *tot_cred*}.

- *course_dept*. The schemas *course* and *department* correspond to the entity sets *A* and *B*, respectively. Thus, the schema *course_dept* can be combined with the *course* schema. The resulting *course* schema consists of the attributes {*course_id*, *title*, *dept_name*, *credits*}.

- *sec_class*. The schemas *section* and *classroom* correspond to the entity sets *A* and *B*, respectively. Thus, the schema *sec_class* can be combined with the *section* schema. The resulting *section* schema consists of the attributes {*course_id*, *sec_id*, *semester*, *year*, *building*, *room_number*}.

- *sec_time_slot*. The schemas *section* and *time_slot* correspond to the entity sets *A* and *B* respectively, Thus, the schema *sec_time_slot* can be combined with the *section* schema obtained in the previous step. The resulting *section* schema consists of the attributes {*course_id*, *sec_id*, *semester*, *year*, *building*, *room_number*, *time_slot_id*}.

In the case of one-to-one relationships, the relation schema for the relationship set can be combined with the schemas for either of the entity sets.

We can combine schemas even if the participation is partial by using null values. In the above example, if *inst_dept* were partial, then we would store null values for the *dept_name* attribute for those instructors who have no associated department.

Finally, we consider the foreign-key constraints that would have appeared in the schema representing the relationship set. There would have been foreign-key constraints referencing each of the entity sets participating in the relationship set. We drop the constraint referencing the entity set into whose schema the relationship set schema is merged, and add the other foreign-key constraints to the combined schema. For example, *inst_dept* has a foreign key constraint of the attribute *dept_name* referencing the *department* relation. This foreign constraint is added to the *instructor* relation when the schema for *inst_dept* is merged into *instructor*.

7.7   Entity-Relationship Design Issues

The notions of an entity set and a relationship set are not precise, and it is possible to define a set of entities and the relationships among them in a number of different ways. In this section, we examine basic issues in the design of an E-R database schema. Section 7.10 covers the design process in further detail.

7.7.1   Use of Entity Sets versus Attributes

Consider the entity set *instructor* with the additional attribute *phone_number* (Figure 7.17a.) It can easily be argued that a phone is an entity in its own right with attributes *phone_number* and *location*; the location may be the office or home where the phone is located, with mobile (cell) phones perhaps represented by the value "mobile." If we take this point of view, we do not add the attribute *phone_number* to the *instructor*. Rather, we create:

- A *phone* entity set with attributes *phone_number* and *location*.

- A relationship set *inst_phone*, denoting the association between instructors and the phones that they have.

This alternative is shown in Figure 7.17b.

What, then, is the main difference between these two definitions of an instructor? Treating a phone as an attribute *phone_number* implies that instructors have precisely one phone number each. Treating a phone as an entity *phone* permits instructors to have several phone numbers (including zero) associated with them. However, we could instead easily define *phone_number* as a multivalued attribute to allow multiple phones per instructor.

The main difference then is that treating a phone as an entity better models a situation where one may want to keep extra information about a phone, such as its location, or its type (mobile, IP phone, or plain old phone), or all who share

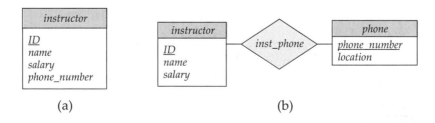

Figure 7.17 Alternatives for adding *phone* to the *instructor* entity set.

the phone. Thus, treating phone as an entity is more general than treating it as an attribute and is appropriate when the generality may be useful.

In contrast, it would not be appropriate to treat the attribute *name* (of an instructor) as an entity; it is difficult to argue that *name* is an entity in its own right (in contrast to the phone). Thus, it is appropriate to have *name* as an attribute of the *instructor* entity set.

Two natural questions thus arise: What constitutes an attribute, and what constitutes an entity set? Unfortunately, there are no simple answers. The distinctions mainly depend on the structure of the real-world enterprise being modeled, and on the semantics associated with the attribute in question.

A common mistake is to use the primary key of an entity set as an attribute of another entity set, instead of using a relationship. For example, it is incorrect to model the *ID* of a *student* as an attribute of an *instructor* even if each instructor advises only one student. The relationship *advisor* is the correct way to represent the connection between students and instructors, since it makes their connection explicit, rather than implicit via an attribute.

Another related mistake that people sometimes make is to designate the primary-key attributes of the related entity sets as attributes of the relationship set. For example, *ID* (the primary-key attributes of *student*) and *ID* (the primary key of *instructor*) should not appear as attributes of the relationship *advisor*. This should not be done since the primary-key attributes are already implicit in the relationship set.[8]

7.7.2 Use of Entity Sets versus Relationship Sets

It is not always clear whether an object is best expressed by an entity set or a relationship set. In Figure 7.15, we used the *takes* relationship set to model the situation where a student takes a (section of a) course. An alternative is to imagine that there is a course-registration record for each course that each student takes. Then, we have an entity set to represent the course-registration record. Let us call that entity set *registration*. Each *registration* entity is related to exactly one student and to exactly one section, so we have two relationship sets, one to relate course-registration records to students and one to relate course-registration records to sections. In Figure 7.18, we show the entity sets *section* and *student* from Figure 7.15 with the *takes* relationship set replaced by one entity set and two relationship sets:

- *registration*, the entity set representing course-registration records.
- *section_reg*, the relationship set relating *registration* and *course*.
- *student_reg*, the relationship set relating *registration* and *student*.

Note that we use double lines to indicate total participation by *registration* entities.

---

[8]When we create a relation schema from the E-R schema, the attributes may appear in a schema created from the *advisor* relationship set, as we shall see later; however, they should not appear in the *advisor* relationship set.

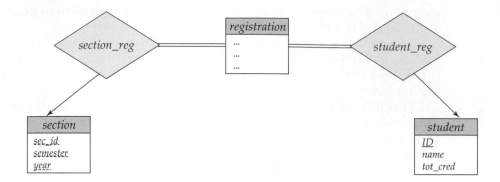

Figure 7.18 Replacement of *takes* by *registration* and two relationship sets

Both the approach of Figure 7.15 and that of Figure 7.18 accurately represent the university's information, but the use of *takes* is more compact and probably preferable. However, if the registrar's office associates other information with a course-registration record, it might be best to make it an entity in its own right.

One possible guideline in determining whether to use an entity set or a relationship set is to designate a relationship set to describe an action that occurs between entities. This approach can also be useful in deciding whether certain attributes may be more appropriately expressed as relationships.

7.7.3   Binary versus *n*-ary Relationship Sets

Relationships in databases are often binary. Some relationships that appear to be nonbinary could actually be better represented by several binary relationships. For instance, one could create a ternary relationship *parent*, relating a child to his/her mother and father. However, such a relationship could also be represented by two binary relationships, *mother* and *father*, relating a child to his/her mother and father separately. Using the two relationships *mother* and *father* provides us a record of a child's mother, even if we are not aware of the father's identity; a null value would be required if the ternary relationship *parent* is used. Using binary relationship sets is preferable in this case.

In fact, it is always possible to replace a nonbinary (*n*-ary, for $n > 2$) relationship set by a number of distinct binary relationship sets. For simplicity, consider the abstract ternary ($n = 3$) relationship set R, relating entity sets A, B, and C. We replace the relationship set R by an entity set E, and create three relationship sets as shown in Figure 7.19:

- R_A, relating E and A.
- R_B, relating E and B.
- R_C, relating E and C.

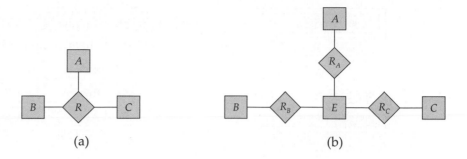

Figure 7.19   Ternary relationship versus three binary relationships.

If the relationship set R had any attributes, these are assigned to entity set E; further, a special identifying attribute is created for E (since it must be possible to distinguish different entities in an entity set on the basis of their attribute values). For each relationship (a_i, b_i, c_i) in the relationship set R, we create a new entity e_i in the entity set E. Then, in each of the three new relationship sets, we insert a relationship as follows:

- (e_i, a_i) in R_A.

- (e_i, b_i) in R_B.

- (e_i, c_i) in R_C.

We can generalize this process in a straightforward manner to n-ary relationship sets. Thus, conceptually, we can restrict the E-R model to include only binary relationship sets. However, this restriction is not always desirable.

- An identifying attribute may have to be created for the entity set created to represent the relationship set. This attribute, along with the extra relationship sets required, increases the complexity of the design and (as we shall see in Section 7.6) overall storage requirements.

- An n-ary relationship set shows more clearly that several entities participate in a single relationship.

- There may not be a way to translate constraints on the ternary relationship into constraints on the binary relationships. For example, consider a constraint that says that R is many-to-one from A, B to C; that is, each pair of entities from A and B is associated with at most one C entity. This constraint cannot be expressed by using cardinality constraints on the relationship sets R_A, R_B, and R_C.

Consider the relationship set *proj_guide* in Section 7.2.2, relating *instructor*, *student*, and *project*. We cannot directly split *proj_guide* into binary relationships between *instructor* and *project* and between *instructor* and *student*. If we did so,

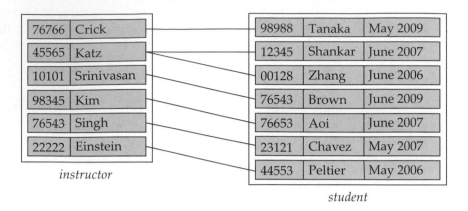

Figure 7.20 *date* as an attribute of the *student* entity set.

we would be able to record that instructor Katz works on projects *A* and *B* with students Shankar and Zhang; however, we would not be able to record that Katz works on project *A* with student Shankar and works on project *B* with student Zhang, but does not work on project *A* with Zhang or on project *B* with Shankar.

The relationship set *proj_guide* can be split into binary relationships by creating a new entity set as described above. However, doing so would not be very natural.

7.7.4 Placement of Relationship Attributes

The cardinality ratio of a relationship can affect the placement of relationship attributes. Thus, attributes of one-to-one or one-to-many relationship sets can be associated with one of the participating entity sets, rather than with the relationship set. For instance, let us specify that *advisor* is a one-to-many relationship set such that one instructor may advise several students, but each student can be advised by only a single instructor. In this case, the attribute *date*, which specifies when the instructor became the advisor of a student, could be associated with the *student* entity set, as Figure 7.20 depicts. (To keep the figure simple, only some of the attributes of the two entity sets are shown.) Since each *student* entity participates in a relationship with at most one instance of *instructor*, making this attribute designation has the same meaning as would placing *date* with the *advisor* relationship set. Attributes of a one-to-many relationship set can be repositioned to only the entity set on the "many" side of the relationship. For one-to-one relationship sets, on the other hand, the relationship attribute can be associated with either one of the participating entities.

The design decision of where to place descriptive attributes in such cases —as a relationship or entity attribute—should reflect the characteristics of the enterprise being modeled. The designer may choose to retain *date* as an attribute of *advisor* to express explicitly that the date refers to the advising relationship and not some other aspect of the student's university status (for example, date of acceptance to the university).

The choice of attribute placement is more clear-cut for many-to-many relationship sets. Returning to our example, let us specify the perhaps more realistic case that *advisor* is a many-to-many relationship set expressing that an instructor may advise one or more students, and that a student may be advised by one or more instructors. If we are to express the date on which a specific instructor became the advisor of a specific student, *date* must be an attribute of the *advisor* relationship set, rather than either one of the participating entities. If *date* were an attribute of *student*, for instance, we could not determine which instructor became the advisor on that particular date. When an attribute is determined by the combination of participating entity sets, rather than by either entity separately, that attribute must be associated with the many-to-many relationship set. Figure 7.3 depicts the placement of *date* as a relationship attribute; again, to keep the figure simple, only some of the attributes of the two entity sets are shown.

7.8 Extended E-R Features

Although the basic E-R concepts can model most database features, some aspects of a database may be more aptly expressed by certain extensions to the basic E-R model. In this section, we discuss the extended E-R features of specialization, generalization, higher- and lower-level entity sets, attribute inheritance, and aggregation.

To help with the discussions, we shall use a slightly more elaborate database schema for the university. In particular, we shall model the various people within a university by defining an entity set *person*, with attributes *ID*, *name*, and *address*.

7.8.1 Specialization

An entity set may include subgroupings of entities that are distinct in some way from other entities in the set. For instance, a subset of entities within an entity set may have attributes that are not shared by all the entities in the entity set. The E-R model provides a means for representing these distinctive entity groupings.

As an example, the entity set *person* may be further classified as one of the following:

- *employee*.
- *student*.

Each of these person types is described by a set of attributes that includes all the attributes of entity set *person* plus possibly additional attributes. For example, *employee* entities may be described further by the attribute *salary*, whereas *student* entities may be described further by the attribute *tot_cred*. The process of designating subgroupings within an entity set is called **specialization**. The specialization of *person* allows us to distinguish among person entities according to whether they correspond to employees or students: in general, a person could be an employee, a student, both, or neither.

As another example, suppose the university divides students into two categories: graduate and undergraduate. Graduate students have an office assigned to them. Undergraduate students are assigned to a residential college. Each of these student types is described by a set of attributes that includes all the attributes of the entity set *student* plus additional attributes.

The university could create two specializations of *student*, namely *graduate* and *undergraduate*. As we saw earlier, student entities are described by the attributes *ID*, *name*, *address*, and *tot_cred*. The entity set *graduate* would have all the attributes of *student* and an additional attribute *office_number*. The entity set *undergraduate* would have all the attributes of *student*, and an additional attribute *residential _college*.

We can apply specialization repeatedly to refine a design. For instance, university employees may be further classified as one of the following:

- *instructor*.

- *secretary*.

Each of these employee types is described by a set of attributes that includes all the attributes of entity set *employee* plus additional attributes. For example, *instructor* entities may be described further by the attribute *rank* while *secretary* entities are described by the attribute *hours_per_week*. Further, *secretary* entities may participate in a relationship *secretary_for* between the *secretary* and *employee* entity sets, which identifies the employees who are assisted by a secretary.

An entity set may be specialized by more than one distinguishing feature. In our example, the distinguishing feature among employee entities is the job the employee performs. Another, coexistent, specialization could be based on whether the person is a temporary (limited_term) employee or a permanent employee, resulting in the entity sets *temporary_employee* and *permanent_employee*. When more than one specialization is formed on an entity set, a particular entity may belong to multiple specializations. For instance, a given employee may be a temporary employee who is a secretary.

In terms of an E-R diagram, specialization is depicted by a hollow arrow-head pointing from the specialized entity to the other entity (see Figure 7.21). We refer to this relationship as the ISA relationship, which stands for "is a" and represents, for example, that an instructor "is a" employee.

The way we depict specialization in an E-R diagram depends on whether an entity may belong to multiple specialized entity sets or if it must belong to at most one specialized entity set. The former case (multiple sets permitted) is called **overlapping specialization**, while the latter case (at most one permitted) is called **disjoint specialization**. For an overlapping specialization (as is the case for *student* and *employee* as specializations of *person*), two separate arrows are used. For a disjoint specialization (as is the case for *instructor* and *secretary* as specializations of *employee*), a single arrow is used. The specialization relationship may also be referred to as a **superclass-subclass** relationship. Higher- and lower-level entity

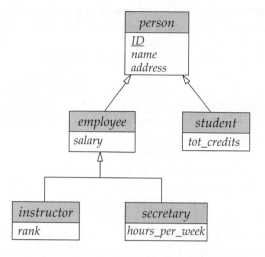

Figure 7.21 Specialization and generalization.

sets are depicted as regular entity sets—that is, as rectangles containing the name of the entity set.

7.8.2 Generalization

The refinement from an initial entity set into successive levels of entity subgroupings represents a **top-down** design process in which distinctions are made explicit. The design process may also proceed in a **bottom-up** manner, in which multiple entity sets are synthesized into a higher-level entity set on the basis of common features. The database designer may have first identified:

- *instructor* entity set with attributes *instructor_id*, *instructor_name*, *instructor _salary*, and *rank*.

- *secretary* entity set with attributes *secretary_id*, *secretary_name*, *secretary_salary*, and *hours_per_week*.

There are similarities between the *instructor* entity set and the *secretary* entity set in the sense that they have several attributes that are conceptually the same across the two entity sets: namely, the identifier, name, and salary attributes. This commonality can be expressed by **generalization**, which is a containment relationship that exists between a *higher-level* entity set and one or more *lower-level* entity sets. In our example, *employee* is the higher-level entity set and *instructor* and *secretary* are lower-level entity sets. In this case, attributes that are conceptually the same had different names in the two lower-level entity sets. To create a generalization, the attributes must be given a common name and represented with the higher-level entity *person*. We can use the attribute names *ID*, *name*, *address*, as we saw in the example in Section 7.8.1.

Higher- and lower-level entity sets also may be designated by the terms **superclass** and **subclass**, respectively. The *person* entity set is the superclass of the *employee* and *student* subclasses.

For all practical purposes, generalization is a simple inversion of specialization. We apply both processes, in combination, in the course of designing the E-R schema for an enterprise. In terms of the E-R diagram itself, we do not distinguish between specialization and generalization. New levels of entity representation are distinguished (specialization) or synthesized (generalization) as the design schema comes to express fully the database application and the user requirements of the database. Differences in the two approaches may be characterized by their starting point and overall goal.

Specialization stems from a single entity set; it emphasizes differences among entities within the set by creating distinct lower-level entity sets. These lower-level entity sets may have attributes, or may participate in relationships, that do not apply to all the entities in the higher-level entity set. Indeed, the reason a designer applies specialization is to represent such distinctive features. If *student* and *employee* have exactly the same attributes as *person* entities, and participate in exactly the same relationships as *person* entities, there would be no need to specialize the *person* entity set.

Generalization proceeds from the recognition that a number of entity sets share some common features (namely, they are described by the same attributes and participate in the same relationship sets). On the basis of their commonalities, generalization synthesizes these entity sets into a single, higher-level entity set. Generalization is used to emphasize the similarities among lower-level entity sets and to hide the differences; it also permits an economy of representation in that shared attributes are not repeated.

7.8.3   Attribute Inheritance

A crucial property of the higher- and lower-level entities created by specialization and generalization is **attribute inheritance**. The attributes of the higher-level entity sets are said to be **inherited** by the lower-level entity sets. For example, *student* and *employee* inherit the attributes of *person*. Thus, *student* is described by its *ID*, *name*, and *address* attributes, and additionally a *tot_cred* attribute; *employee* is described by its *ID*, *name*, and *address* attributes, and additionally a *salary* attribute. Attribute inheritance applies through all tiers of lower-level entity sets; thus, *instructor* and *secretary*, which are subclasses of *employee*, inherit the attributes *ID*, *name*, and *address* from *person*, in addition to inheriting *salary* from *employee*.

A lower-level entity set (or subclass) also inherits participation in the relationship sets in which its higher-level entity (or superclass) participates. Like attribute inheritance, participation inheritance applies through all tiers of lower-level entity sets. For example, suppose the *person* entity set participates in a relationship *person_dept* with *department*. Then, the *student*, *employee*, *instructor* and *secretary* entity sets, which are subclasses of the *person* entity set, also implicitly participate in the *person_dept* relationship with *department*. The above entity sets can participate in any relationships in which the *person* entity set participates.

Whether a given portion of an E-R model was arrived at by specialization or generalization, the outcome is basically the same:

- A higher-level entity set with attributes and relationships that apply to all of its lower-level entity sets.

- Lower-level entity sets with distinctive features that apply only within a particular lower-level entity set.

In what follows, although we often refer to only generalization, the properties that we discuss belong fully to both processes.

Figure 7.21 depicts a **hierarchy** of entity sets. In the figure, *employee* is a lower-level entity set of *person* and a higher-level entity set of the *instructor* and *secretary* entity sets. In a hierarchy, a given entity set may be involved as a lower-level entity set in only one ISA relationship; that is, entity sets in this diagram have only **single inheritance**. If an entity set is a lower-level entity set in more than one ISA relationship, then the entity set has **multiple inheritance**, and the resulting structure is said to be a *lattice*.

7.8.4 Constraints on Generalizations

To model an enterprise more accurately, the database designer may choose to place certain constraints on a particular generalization. One type of constraint involves determining which entities can be members of a given lower-level entity set. Such membership may be one of the following:

- **Condition-defined**. In condition-defined lower-level entity sets, membership is evaluated on the basis of whether or not an entity satisfies an explicit condition or predicate. For example, assume that the higher-level entity set *student* has the attribute *student_type*. All *student* entities are evaluated on the defining *student_type* attribute. Only those entities that satisfy the condition *student_type* = "graduate" are allowed to belong to the lower-level entity set *graduate_student*. All entities that satisfy the condition *student_type* = "undergraduate" are included in *undergraduate_student*. Since all the lower-level entities are evaluated on the basis of the same attribute (in this case, on *student_type*), this type of generalization is said to be **attribute-defined**.

- **User-defined**. User-defined lower-level entity sets are not constrained by a membership condition; rather, the database user assigns entities to a given entity set. For instance, let us assume that, after 3 months of employment, university employees are assigned to one of four work teams. We therefore represent the teams as four lower-level entity sets of the higher-level *employee* entity set. A given employee is not assigned to a specific team entity automatically on the basis of an explicit defining condition. Instead, the user in charge of this decision makes the team assignment on an individual basis. The assignment is implemented by an operation that adds an entity to an entity set.

A second type of constraint relates to whether or not entities may belong to more than one lower-level entity set within a single generalization. The lower-level entity sets may be one of the following:

- **Disjoint**. A *disjointness constraint* requires that an entity belong to no more than one lower-level entity set. In our example, *student* entity can satisfy only one condition for the *student_type* attribute; an entity can be either a graduate student or an undergraduate student, but cannot be both.

- **Overlapping**. In *overlapping generalizations*, the same entity may belong to more than one lower-level entity set within a single generalization. For an illustration, consider the employee work-team example, and assume that certain employees participate in more than one work team. A given employee may therefore appear in more than one of the team entity sets that are lower-level entity sets of *employee*. Thus, the generalization is overlapping.

In Figure 7.21, we assume a person may be both an employee and a student. We show this overlapping generalization via separate arrows: one from employee to person and another from student to person. However, the generalization of instructor and secretaries is disjoint. We show this using a single arrow.

A final constraint, the **completeness constraint** on a generalization or specialization, specifies whether or not an entity in the higher-level entity set must belong to at least one of the lower-level entity sets within the generalization/specialization. This constraint may be one of the following:

- **Total generalization** or **specialization**. Each higher-level entity must belong to a lower-level entity set.

- **Partial generalization** or **specialization**. Some higher-level entities may not belong to any lower-level entity set.

Partial generalization is the default. We can specify total generalization in an E-R diagram by adding the keyword "total" in the diagram and drawing a dashed line from the keyword to the corresponding hollow arrow-head to which it applies (for a total generalization), or to the set of hollow arrow-heads to which it applies (for an overlapping generalization).

The *student* generalization is total: All student entities must be either graduate or undergraduate. Because the higher-level entity set arrived at through generalization is generally composed of only those entities in the lower-level entity sets, the completeness constraint for a generalized higher-level entity set is usually total. When the generalization is partial, a higher-level entity is not constrained to appear in a lower-level entity set. The work team entity sets illustrate a partial specialization. Since employees are assigned to a team only after 3 months on the job, some *employee* entities may not be members of any of the lower-level team entity sets.

We may characterize the team entity sets more fully as a partial, overlapping specialization of *employee*. The generalization of *graduate_student* and *undergrad-*

uate_student into *student* is a total, disjoint generalization. The completeness and disjointness constraints, however, do not depend on each other. Constraint patterns may also be partial-disjoint and total-overlapping.

We can see that certain insertion and deletion requirements follow from the constraints that apply to a given generalization or specialization. For instance, when a total completeness constraint is in place, an entity inserted into a higher-level entity set must also be inserted into at least one of the lower-level entity sets. With a condition-defined constraint, all higher-level entities that satisfy the condition must be inserted into that lower-level entity set. Finally, an entity that is deleted from a higher-level entity set also is deleted from all the associated lower-level entity sets to which it belongs.

7.8.5 Aggregation

One limitation of the E-R model is that it cannot express relationships among relationships. To illustrate the need for such a construct, consider the ternary relationship *proj_guide*, which we saw earlier, between an *instructor*, *student* and *project* (see Figure 7.13).

Now suppose that each instructor guiding a student on a project is required to file a monthly evaluation report. We model the evaluation report as an entity *evaluation*, with a primary key *evaluation_id*. One alternative for recording the (*student*, *project*, *instructor*) combination to which an *evaluation* corresponds is to create a quaternary (4-way) relationship set *eval_for* between *instructor*, *student*, *project*, and *evaluation*. (A quaternary relationship is required—a binary relationship between *student* and *evaluation*, for example, would not permit us to represent the (*project*, *instructor*) combination to which an *evaluation* corresponds.) Using the basic E-R modeling constructs, we obtain the E-R diagram of Figure 7.22. (We have omitted the attributes of the entity sets, for simplicity.)

It appears that the relationship sets *proj_guide* and *eval_for* can be combined into one single relationship set. Nevertheless, we should not combine them into a single relationship, since some *instructor*, *student*, *project* combinations may not have an associated *evaluation*.

There is redundant information in the resultant figure, however, since every *instructor*, *student*, *project* combination in *eval_for* must also be in *proj_guide*. If the *evaluation* were a value rather than a entity, we could instead make *evaluation* a multivalued composite attribute of the relationship set *proj_guide*. However, this alternative may not be be an option if an *evaluation* may also be related to other entities; for example, each evaluation report may be associated with a *secretary* who is responsible for further processing of the evaluation report to make scholarship payments.

The best way to model a situation such as the one just described is to use aggregation. **Aggregation** is an abstraction through which relationships are treated as higher-level entities. Thus, for our example, we regard the relationship set *proj_guide* (relating the entity sets *instructor*, *student*, and *project*) as a higher-level entity set called *proj_guide*. Such an entity set is treated in the same manner as is any other entity set. We can then create a binary relationship *eval_for* between *proj*

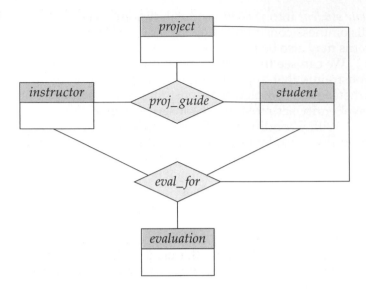

Figure 7.22   E-R diagram with redundant relationships.

_guide and *evaluation* to represent which (*student, project, instructor*) combination an *evaluation* is for. Figure 7.23 shows a notation for aggregation commonly used to represent this situation.

7.8.6   Reduction to Relation Schemas

We are in a position now to describe how the extended E-R features can be translated into relation schemas.

7.8.6.1   Representation of Generalization

There are two different methods of designing relation schemas for an E-R diagram that includes generalization. Although we refer to the generalization in Figure 7.21 in this discussion, we simplify it by including only the first tier of lower-level entity sets—that is, *employee* and *student*. We assume that *ID* is the primary key of *person*.

1. Create a schema for the higher-level entity set. For each lower-level entity set, create a schema that includes an attribute for each of the attributes of that entity set plus one for each attribute of the primary key of the higher-level entity set. Thus, for the E-R diagram of Figure 7.21 (ignoring the *instructor* and *secretary* entity sets) we have three schemas:

    > *person* (*ID*, *name, street, city*)
    > *employee* (*ID*, *salary*)
    > *student* (*ID*, *tot_cred*)

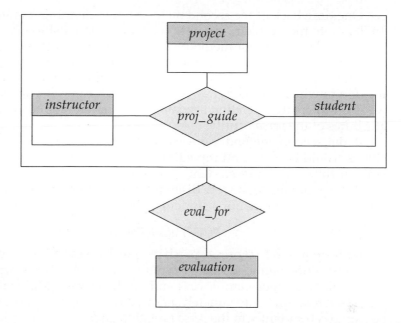

Figure 7.23   E-R diagram with aggregation.

The primary-key attributes of the higher-level entity set become primary-key attributes of the higher-level entity set as well as all lower-level entity sets. These can be seen underlined in the above example.

In addition, we create foreign-key constraints on the lower-level entity sets, with their primary-key attributes referencing the primary key of the relation created from the higher-level entity set. In the above example, the *ID* attribute of *employee* would reference the primary key of *person*, and similarly for *student*.

2. An alternative representation is possible, if the generalization is disjoint and complete—that is, if no entity is a member of two lower-level entity sets directly below a higher-level entity set, and if every entity in the higher-level entity set is also a member of one of the lower-level entity sets. Here, we do not create a schema for the higher-level entity set. Instead, for each lower-level entity set, we create a schema that includes an attribute for each of the attributes of that entity set plus one for *each* attribute of the higher-level entity set. Then, for the E-R diagram of Figure 7.21, we have two schemas:

employee (<u>ID</u>, *name, street, city, salary*)
student (<u>ID</u>, *name, street, city, tot_cred*)

Both these schemas have *ID*, which is the primary-key attribute of the higher-level entity set *person*, as their primary key.

One drawback of the second method lies in defining foreign-key constraints. To illustrate the problem, suppose we had a relationship set R involving entity set *person*. With the first method, when we create a relation schema R from the relationship set, we would also define a foreign-key constraint on R, referencing the schema *person*. Unfortunately, with the second method, we do not have a single relation to which a foreign-key constraint on R can refer. To avoid this problem, we need to create a relation schema *person* containing at least the primary-key attributes of the *person* entity.

If the second method were used for an overlapping generalization, some values would be stored multiple times, unnecessarily. For instance, if a person is both an employee and a student, values for *street* and *city* would be stored twice.

If the generalization were disjoint but not complete—that is, if some person is neither an employee nor a student—then an extra schema

$$person \ (\underline{ID}, \ name, \ street, \ city)$$

would be required to represent such people. However, the problem with foreign-key constraints mentioned above would remain. As an attempt to work around the problem, suppose employees and students are additionally represented in the *person* relation. Unfortunately, name, street, and city information would then be stored redundantly in the *person* relation and the *student* relation for students, and similarly in the *person* relation and the *employee* relation for employees. That suggests storing name, street, and city information only in the *person* relation and removing that information from *student* and *employee*. If we do that, the result is exactly the first method we presented.

7.8.6.2   Representation of Aggregation

Designing schemas for an E-R diagram containing aggregation is straightforward. Consider the diagram of Figure 7.23. The schema for the relationship set *eval_for* between the aggregation of *proj_guide* and the entity set *evaluation* includes an attribute for each attribute in the primary keys of the entity set *evaluation*, and the relationship set *proj_guide*. It also includes an attribute for any descriptive attributes, if they exist, of the relationship set *eval_for*. We then transform the relationship sets and entity sets within the aggregated entity set following the rules we have already defined.

The rules we saw earlier for creating primary-key and foreign-key constraints on relationship sets can be applied to relationship sets involving aggregations as well, with the aggregation treated like any other entity set. The primary key of the aggregation is the primary key of its defining relationship set. No separate relation is required to represent the aggregation; the relation created from the defining relationship is used instead.

7.9   Alternative Notations for Modeling Data

A diagrammatic representation of the data model of an application is a very important part of designing a database schema. Creation of a database schema requires not only data modeling experts, but also domain experts who know the requirements of the application but may not be familiar with data modeling. An intuitive diagrammatic representation is particularly important since it eases communication of information between these groups of experts.

A number of alternative notations for modeling data have been proposed, of which E-R diagrams and UML class diagrams are the most widely used. There is no universal standard for E-R diagram notation, and different books and E-R diagram software use different notations. We have chosen a particular notation

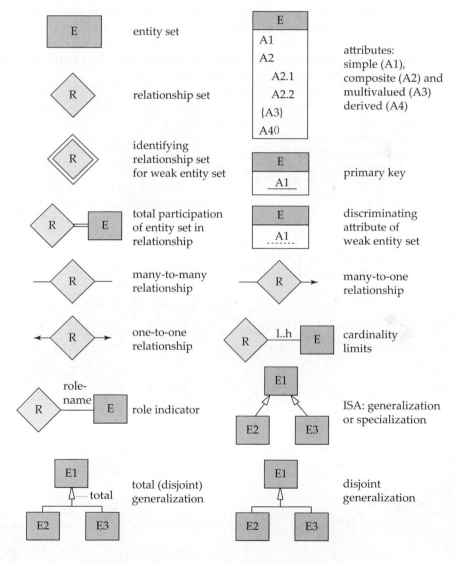

Figure 7.24 Symbols used in the E-R notation.

in this sixth edition of this book which actually differs from the notation we used in earlier editions, for reasons that we explain later in this section.

In the rest of this section, we study some of the alternative E-R diagram notations, as well as the UML class diagram notation. To aid in comparison of our notation with these alternatives, Figure 7.24 summarizes the set of symbols we have used in our E-R diagram notation.

7.9.1 Alternative E-R Notations

Figure 7.25 indicates some of the alternative E-R notations that are widely used. One alternative representation of attributes of entities is to show them in ovals connected to the box representing the entity; primary key attributes are indicated by underlining them. The above notation is shown at the top of the figure. Relationship attributes can be similarly represented, by connecting the ovals to the diamond representing the relationship.

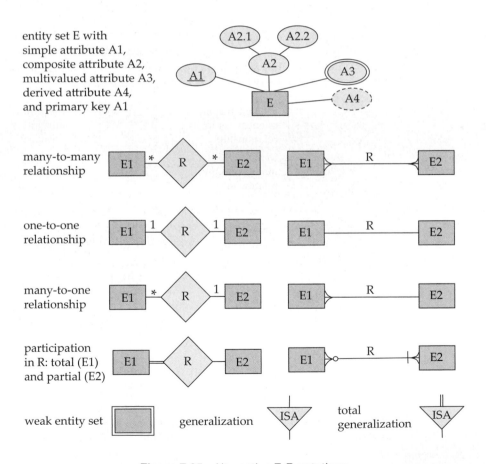

Figure 7.25   Alternative E-R notations.

Cardinality constraints on relationships can be indicated in several different ways, as shown in Figure 7.25. In one alternative, shown on the left side of the figure, labels ∗ and 1 on the edges out of the relationship are used for depicting many-to-many, one-to-one, and many-to-one relationships. The case of one-to-many is symmetric to many-to-one, and is not shown.

In another alternative notation shown on the right side of the figure, relationship sets are represented by lines between entity sets, without diamonds; only binary relationships can be modeled thus. Cardinality constraints in such a notation are shown by "crow's-foot" notation, as in the figure. In a relationship R between $E1$ and $E2$, crow's feet on both sides indicates a many-to-many relationship, while crow's feet on just the $E1$ side indicates a many-to-one relationship from $E1$ to $E2$. Total participation is specified in this notation by a vertical bar. Note however, that in a relationship R between entities $E1$ and $E2$, if the participation of $E1$ in R is total, the vertical bar is placed on the opposite side, adjacent to entity $E2$. Similarly, partial participation is indicated by using a circle, again on the opposite side.

The bottom part of Figure 7.25 shows an alternative representation of generalization, using triangles instead of hollow arrow-heads.

In prior editions of this text up to the fifth edition, we used ovals to represent attributes, with triangles representing generalization, as shown in Figure 7.25. The notation using ovals for attributes and diamonds for relationships is close to the original form of E-R diagrams used by Chen in his paper that introduced the notion of E-R modeling. That notation is now referred to as Chen's notation.

The U.S. National Institute for Standards and Technology defined a standard called IDEF1X in 1993. IDEF1X uses the crow's-foot notation, with vertical bars on the relationship edge to denote total participation and hollow circles to denote partial participation, and includes other notations that we have not shown.

With the growth in the use of Unified Markup Language (UML), described later in Section 7.9.2, we have chosen to update our E-R notation to make it closer to the form of UML class diagrams; the connections will become clear in Section 7.9.2. In comparison with our previous notation, our new notation provides a more compact representation of attributes, and is also closer to the notation supported by many E-R modeling tools, in addition to being closer to the UML class diagram notation.

There are a variety of tools for constructing E-R diagrams, each of which has its own notational variants. Some of the tools even provide a choice between several E-R notation variants. See the references in the bibliographic notes for more information.

One key difference between entity sets in an E-R diagram and the relation schemas created from such entities is that attributes in the relational schema corresponding to E-R relationships, such as the *dept_name* attribute of *instructor*, are not shown in the entity set in the E-R diagram. Some data modeling tools allow users to choose between two views of the same entity, one an entity view without such attributes, and other a relational view with such attributes.

7.9.2   The Unified Modeling Language UML

Entity-relationship diagrams help model the data representation component of a software system. Data representation, however, forms only one part of an overall system design. Other components include models of user interactions with the system, specification of functional modules of the system and their interaction, etc. The **Unified Modeling Language** (UML) is a standard developed under the auspices of the Object Management Group (OMG) for creating specifications of various components of a software system. Some of the parts of UML are:

- **Class diagram**. A class diagram is similar to an E-R diagram. Later in this section we illustrate a few features of class diagrams and how they relate to E-R diagrams.

- **Use case diagram**. Use case diagrams show the interaction between users and the system, in particular the steps of tasks that users perform (such as withdrawing money or registering for a course).

- **Activity diagram**. Activity diagrams depict the flow of tasks between various components of a system.

- **Implementation diagram**. Implementation diagrams show the system components and their interconnections, both at the software component level and the hardware component level.

We do not attempt to provide detailed coverage of the different parts of UML here. See the bibliographic notes for references on UML. Instead we illustrate some features of that part of UML that relates to data modeling through examples.

Figure 7.26 shows several E-R diagram constructs and their equivalent UML class diagram constructs. We describe these constructs below. UML actually models objects, whereas E-R models entities. Objects are like entities, and have attributes, but additionally provide a set of functions (called methods) that can be invoked to compute values on the basis of attributes of the objects, or to update the object itself. Class diagrams can depict methods in addition to attributes. We cover objects in Chapter 22. UML does not support composite or multivalued attributes, and derived attributes are equivalent to methods that take no parameters. Since classes support encapsulation, UML allows attributes and methods to be prefixed with a "+", "-", or "#", which denote respectively public, private and protected access. Private attributes can only be used in methods of the class, while protected attributes can be used only in methods of the class and its subclasses; these should be familiar to anyone who knows Java, C++ or C#.

In UML terminology, relationship sets are referred to as **associations**; we shall refer to them as relationship sets for consistency with E-R terminology. We represent binary relationship sets in UML by just drawing a line connecting the entity sets. We write the relationship set name adjacent to the line. We may also specify the role played by an entity set in a relationship set by writing the role name on the line, adjacent to the entity set. Alternatively, we may write the relationship set name in a box, along with attributes of the relationship set, and connect the

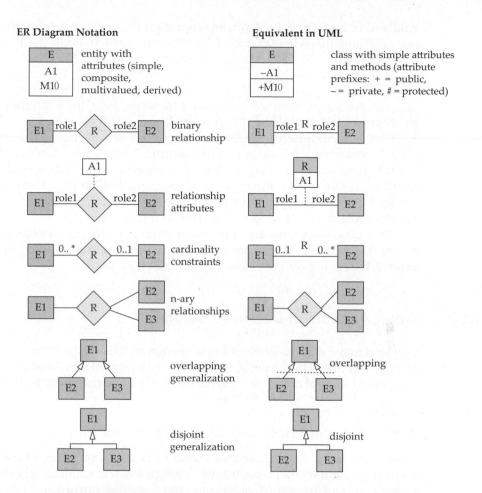

Figure 7.26 Symbols used in the UML class diagram notation.

box by a dotted line to the line depicting the relationship set. This box can then be treated as an entity set, in the same way as an aggregation in E-R diagrams, and can participate in relationships with other entity sets.

Since UML version 1.3, UML supports nonbinary relationships, using the same diamond notation used in E-R diagrams. Nonbinary relationships could not be directly represented in earlier versions of UML—they had to be converted to binary relationships by the technique we have seen earlier in Section 7.7.3. UML allows the diamond notation to be used even for binary relationships, but most designers use the line notation.

Cardinality constraints are specified in UML in the same way as in E-R diagrams, in the form $l..h$, where l denotes the minimum and h the maximum number of relationships an entity can participate in. However, you should be aware that the positioning of the constraints is exactly the reverse of the positioning of constraints in E-R diagrams, as shown in Figure 7.26. The constraint $0..*$ on the $E2$

side and 0..1 on the $E1$ side means that each $E2$ entity can participate in at most one relationship, whereas each $E1$ entity can participate in many relationships; in other words, the relationship is many-to-one from $E2$ to $E1$.

Single values such as 1 or $*$ may be written on edges; the single value 1 on an edge is treated as equivalent to 1..1, while $*$ is equivalent to 0..$*$. UML supports generalization; the notation is basically the same as in our E-R notation, including the representation of disjoint and overlapping generalizations.

UML class diagrams include several other notations that do not correspond to the E-R notations we have seen. For example, a line between two entity sets with a small diamond at one end specifies that the entity on the diamond side contains the other entity (containment is called "aggregation" in UML terminology; do not confuse this use of aggregation with the sense in which it is used in the E-R model). For example, a vehicle entity may contain an engine entity.

UML class diagrams also provide notations to represent object-oriented language features such as interfaces. See the references in the bibliographic notes for more information on UML class diagrams.

7.10   Other Aspects of Database Design

Our extensive discussion of schema design in this chapter may create the false impression that schema design is the only component of a database design. There are indeed several other considerations that we address more fully in subsequent chapters, and survey briefly here.

7.10.1   Data Constraints and Relational Database Design

We have seen a variety of data constraints that can be expressed using SQL, including primary-key constraints, foreign-key constraints, **check** constraints, assertions, and triggers. Constraints serve several purposes. The most obvious one is the automation of consistency preservation. By expressing constraints in the SQL data-definition language, the designer is able to ensure that the database system itself enforces the constraints. This is more reliable than relying on each application program individually to enforce constraints. It also provides a central location for the update of constraints and the addition of new ones.

A further advantage of stating constraints explicitly is that certain constraints are particularly useful in designing relational database schemas. If we know, for example, that a social-security number uniquely identifies a person, then we can use a person's social-security number to link data related to that person even if these data appear in multiple relations. Contrast that with, for example, eye color, which is not a unique identifier. Eye color could not be used to link data pertaining to a specific person across relations because that person's data could not be distinguished from data pertaining to other people with the same eye color.

In Section 7.6, we generated a set of relation schemas for a given E-R design using the constraints specified in the design. In Chapter 8, we formalize this idea and related ones, and show how they can assist in the design of relational database schemas. The formal approach to relational database design allows us to state in a precise manner when a given design is a good one and to transform poor designs into better ones. We shall see that the process of starting with an entity-relationship design and generating relation schemas algorithmically from that design provides a good start to the design process.

Data constraints are useful as well in determining the physical structure of data. It may be useful to store data that are closely related to each other in physical proximity on disk so as to gain efficiencies in disk access. Certain index structures work better when the index is on a primary key.

Constraint enforcement comes at a potentially high price in performance each time the database is updated. For each update, the system must check all of the constraints and either reject updates that fail the constraints or execute appropriate triggers. The significance of the performance penalty depends not only on the frequency of update but also on how the database is designed. Indeed efficiency of the testing of certain types of constraints is an important aspect of the discussion of relational database schema design in Chapter 8.

7.10.2 Usage Requirements: Queries, Performance

Database system performance is a critical aspect of most enterprise information systems. Performance pertains not only to the efficient use of the computing and storage hardware being used, but also to the efficiency of people who interact with the system and of processes that depend upon database data.

There are two main metrics for performance:

- **Throughput**—the number of queries or updates (often referred to as *transactions*) that can be processed on average per unit of time.

- **Response time**—the amount of time a *single* transaction takes from start to finish in either the average case or the worst case.

Systems that process large numbers of transactions in a batch style focus on having high throughput. Systems that interact with people or time-critical systems often focus on response time. These two metrics are not equivalent. High throughput arises from obtaining high utilization of system components. Doing so may result in certain transactions being delayed until such time that they can be run more efficiently. Those delayed transactions suffer poor response time.

Most commercial database systems historically have focused on throughput; however, a variety of applications including Web-based applications and telecommunication information systems require good response time on average and a reasonable bound on worst-case response time.

An understanding of types of queries that are expected to be the most frequent helps in the design process. Queries that involve joins require more resources to evaluate than those that do not. In cases where a join is required, the database administrator may choose to create an index that facilitates evaluation of that join. For queries—whether a join is involved or not—indices can be created to speed evaluation of selection predicates (SQL **where** clause) that are likely to appear.

Another aspect of queries that affects the choice of indices is the relative mix of update and read operations. While an index may speed queries, it also slows updates, which are forced to do extra work to maintain the accuracy of the index.

7.10.3 Authorization Requirements

Authorization constraints affect design of the database as well because SQL allows access to be granted to users on the basis of components of the logical design of the database. A relation schema may need to be decomposed into two or more schemas to facilitate the granting of access rights in SQL. For example, an employee record may include data relating to payroll, job functions, and medical benefits. Because different administrative units of the enterprise may manage each of these types of data, some users will need access to payroll data while being denied access to the job data, medical data, etc. If these data are all in one relation, the desired division of access, though still feasible through the use of views, is more cumbersome. Division of data in this manner becomes even more critical when the data are distributed across systems in a computer network, an issue we consider in Chapter 19.

7.10.4 Data Flow, Workflow

Database applications are often part of a larger enterprise application that interacts not only with the database system but also with various specialized applications. For example, in a manufacturing company, a computer-aided design (CAD) system may assist in the design of new products. The CAD system may extract data from the database via an SQL statement, process the data internally, perhaps interacting with a product designer, and then update the database. During this process, control of the data may pass among several product designers as well as other people. As another example, consider a travel-expense report. It is created by an employee returning from a business trip (possibly by means of a special software package) and is subsequently routed to the employee's manager, perhaps other higher-level managers, and eventually to the accounting department for payment (at which point it interacts with the enterprise's accounting information systems).

The term *workflow* refers to the combination of data and tasks involved in processes like those of the preceding examples. Workflows interact with the database system as they move among users and users perform their tasks on the workflow. In addition to the data on which workflows operate, the database may store data about the workflow itself, including the tasks making up a workflow and how they are to be routed among users. Workflows thus specify a series of queries and updates to the database that may be taken into account as part of the database-design process. Put in other terms, modeling the enterprise requires us not only to understand the semantics of the data but also the business processes that use those data.

7.10.5 Other Issues in Database Design

Database design is usually not a one-time activity. The needs of an organization evolve continually, and the data that it needs to store also evolve corresponding-ly. During the initial database-design phases, or during the development of an application, the database designer may realize that changes are required at the conceptual, logical, or physical schema levels. Changes in the schema can affect all aspects of the database application. A good database design anticipates future needs of an organization, and ensures that the schema requires minimal changes as the needs evolve.

It is important to distinguish between fundamental constraints that are ex-pected to be permanent and constraints that are anticipated to change. For exam-ple, the constraint that an instructor-id identify a unique instructor is fundamen-tal. On the other hand, a university may have a policy that an instructor can have only one department, which may change at a later date if joint appointments are allowed. A database design that only allows one department per instructor might require major changes if joint appointments are allowed. Such joint appointments can be represented by adding an extra relationship, without modifying the *in-structor* relation, as long as each instructor has only one primary department affiliation; a policy change that allows more than one primary affiliation may require a larger change in the database design. A good design should account not only for current policies, but should also avoid or minimize changes due to changes that are anticipated, or have a reasonable chance of happening.

Furthermore, the enterprise that the database is serving likely interacts with other enterprises and, therefore, multiple databases may need to interact. Con-version of data between different schemas is an important problem in real-world applications. Various solutions have been proposed for this problem. The XML data model, which we study in Chapter 23, is widely used for representing data when it is exchanged between different applications.

Finally, it is worth noting that database design is a human-oriented activity in two senses: the end users of the system are people (even if an application sits between the database and the end users); and the database designer needs to interact extensively with experts in the application domain to understand the data requirements of the application. All of the people involved with the data have needs and preferences that should be taken into account in order for a database design and deployment to succeed within the enterprise.

7.11 Summary

- Database design mainly involves the design of the database schema. The **entity-relationship (E-R)** data model is a widely used data model for database design. It provides a convenient graphical representation to view data, rela-tionships, and constraints.

- The E-R model is intended primarily for the database-design process. It was developed to facilitate database design by allowing the specification of an

enterprise schema. Such a schema represents the overall logical structure of the database. This overall structure can be expressed graphically by an **E-R diagram**.

- An **entity** is an object that exists in the real world and is distinguishable from other objects. We express the distinction by associating with each entity a set of attributes that describes the object.

- A **relationship** is an association among several entities. A **relationship set** is a collection of relationships of the same type, and an **entity set** is a collection of entities of the same type.

- The terms **superkey**, **candidate key**, and **primary key** apply to entity and relationship sets as they do for relation schemas. Identifying the primary key of a relationship set requires some care, since it is composed of attributes from one or more of the related entity sets.

- **Mapping cardinalities** express the number of entities to which another entity can be associated via a relationship set.

- An entity set that does not have sufficient attributes to form a primary key is termed a **weak entity set**. An entity set that has a primary key is termed a **strong entity set**.

- The various features of the E-R model offer the database designer numerous choices in how to best represent the enterprise being modeled. Concepts and objects may, in certain cases, be represented by entities, relationships, or attributes. Aspects of the overall structure of the enterprise may be best described by using weak entity sets, generalization, specialization, or aggregation. Often, the designer must weigh the merits of a simple, compact model versus those of a more precise, but more complex, one.

- A database design specified by an E-R diagram can be represented by a collection of relation schemas. For each entity set and for each relationship set in the database, there is a unique relation schema that is assigned the name of the corresponding entity set or relationship set. This forms the basis for deriving a relational database design from an E-R diagram.

- **Specialization** and **generalization** define a containment relationship between a higher-level entity set and one or more lower-level entity sets. Specialization is the result of taking a subset of a higher-level entity set to form a lower-level entity set. Generalization is the result of taking the union of two or more disjoint (lower-level) entity sets to produce a higher-level entity set. The attributes of higher-level entity sets are inherited by lower-level entity sets.

- **Aggregation** is an abstraction in which relationship sets (along with their associated entity sets) are treated as higher-level entity sets, and can participate in relationships.

- UML is a popular modeling language. UML class diagrams are widely used for modeling classes, as well as for general purpose data modeling.

Review Terms

- Entity-relationship data model
- Entity and entity set
  - Attributes
  - Domain
  - Simple and composite attributes
  - Single-valued and multivalued attributes
  - Null value
  - Derived attribute
  - Superkey, candidate key, and primary key
- Relationship and relationship set
  - Binary relationship set
  - Degree of relationship set
  - Descriptive attributes
  - Superkey, candidate key, and primary key
  - Role
  - Recursive relationship set
- E-R diagram
- Mapping cardinality:
  - One-to-one relationship
- One-to-many relationship
- Many-to-one relationship
- Many-to-many relationship
- Participation
  - Total participation
  - Partial participation
- Weak entity sets and strong entity sets
  - Discriminator attributes
  - Identifying relationship
- Specialization and generalization
  - Superclass and subclass
  - Attribute inheritance
  - Single and multiple inheritance
  - Condition-defined and user-defined membership
  - Disjoint and overlapping generalization
  - Total and partial generalization
- Aggregation
- UML
- UML class diagram

Practice Exercises

7.1 Construct an E-R diagram for a car insurance company whose customers own one or more cars each. Each car has associated with it zero to any number of recorded accidents. Each insurance policy covers one or more cars, and has one or more premium payments associated with it. Each payment is for a particular period of time, and has an associated due date, and the date when the payment was received.

7.2 Consider a database used to record the marks that students get in different exams of different course offerings (sections).

a. Construct an E-R diagram that models exams as entities, and uses a ternary relationship, for the database.

b. Construct an alternative E-R diagram that uses only a binary relationship between *student* and *section*. Make sure that only one relationship exists between a particular *student* and *section* pair, yet you can represent the marks that a student gets in different exams.

7.3 Design an E-R diagram for keeping track of the exploits of your favorite sports team. You should store the matches played, the scores in each match, the players in each match, and individual player statistics for each match. Summary statistics should be modeled as derived attributes.

7.4 Consider an E-R diagram in which the same entity set appears several times, with its attributes repeated in more than one occurrence. Why is allowing this redundancy a bad practice that one should avoid?

7.5 An E-R diagram can be viewed as a graph. What do the following mean in terms of the structure of an enterprise schema?

a. The graph is disconnected.

b. The graph has a cycle.

7.6 Consider the representation of a ternary relationship using binary relationships as described in Section 7.7.3 and illustrated in Figure 7.27b (attributes not shown).

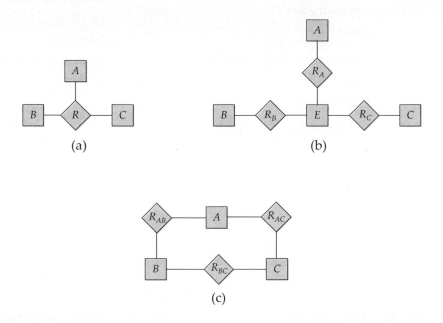

Figure 7.27 E-R diagram for Practice Exercise 7.6 and Exercise 7.24.

a. Show a simple instance of E, A, B, C, R_A, R_B, and R_C that cannot correspond to any instance of A, B, C, and R.

b. Modify the E-R diagram of Figure 7.27b to introduce constraints that will guarantee that any instance of E, A, B, C, R_A, R_B, and R_C that satisfies the constraints will correspond to an instance of A, B, C, and R.

c. Modify the translation above to handle total participation constraints on the ternary relationship.

d. The above representation requires that we create a primary-key attribute for E. Show how to treat E as a weak entity set so that a primary-key attribute is not required.

7.7 A weak entity set can always be made into a strong entity set by adding to its attributes the primary-key attributes of its identifying entity set. Outline what sort of redundancy will result if we do so.

7.8 Consider a relation such as *sec_course*, generated from a many-to-one relationship *sec_course*. Do the primary and foreign key constraints created on the relation enforce the many-to-one cardinality constraint? Explain why.

7.9 Suppose the *advisor* relationship were one-to-one. What extra constraints are required on the relation *advisor* to ensure that the one-to-one cardinality constraint is enforced?

7.10 Consider a many-to-one relationship R between entity sets A and B. Suppose the relation created from R is combined with the relation created from A. In SQL, attributes participating in a foreign key constraint can be null. Explain how a constraint on total participation of A in R can be enforced using **not null** constraints in SQL.

7.11 In SQL, foreign key constraints can only reference the primary key attributes of the referenced relation, or other attributes declared to be a super key using the **unique** constraint. As a result, total participation constraints on a many-to-many relationship (or on the "one" side of a one-to-many relationship) cannot be enforced on the relations created from the relationship, using primary key, foreign key and not null constraints on the relations.

a. Explain why.

b. Explain how to enforce total participation constraints using complex check constraints or assertions (see Section 4.4.7). (Unfortunately, these features are not supported on any widely used database currently.)

7.12 Figure 7.28 shows a lattice structure of generalization and specialization (attributes not shown). For entity sets A, B, and C, explain how attributes

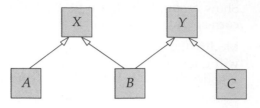

Figure 7.28   E-R diagram for Practice Exercise 7.12.

are inherited from the higher-level entity sets X and Y. Discuss how to handle a case where an attribute of X has the same name as some attribute of Y.

7.13 **Temporal changes**: An E-R diagram usually models the state of an enterprise at a point in time. Suppose we wish to track *temporal changes*, that is, changes to data over time. For example, Zhang may have been a student between 1 September 2005 31 May 2009, while Shankar may have had instructor Einstein as advisor from 31 May 2008 to 5 December 2008, and again from 1 June 2009 to 5 January 2010. Similarly, attribute values of an entity or relationship, such as *title* and *credits* of *course*, *salary*, or even *name* of *instructor*, and *tot_cred* of *student*, can change over time.

One way to model temporal changes is as follows. We define a new data type called **valid_time**, which is a time-interval, or a set of time-intervals. We then associate a *valid_time* attribute with each entity and relationship, recording the time periods during which the entity or relationship is valid. The end-time of an interval can be infinity; for example, if Shankar became a student on 2 September 2008, and is still a student, we can represent the end-time of the *valid_time* interval as infinity for the Shankar entity. Similarly, we model attributes that can change over time as a set of values, each with its own *valid_time*.

a. Draw an E-R diagram with the *student* and *instructor* entities, and the *advisor* relationship, with the above extensions to track temporal changes.

b. Convert the above E-R diagram into a set of relations.

It should be clear that the set of relations generated above is rather complex, leading to difficulties in tasks such as writing queries in SQL. An alternative approach, which is used more widely is to ignore temporal changes when designing the E-R model (in particular, temporal changes to attribute values), and to modify the relations generated from the E-R model to track temporal changes, as discussed later in Section 8.9.

Exercises

7.14 Explain the distinctions among the terms primary key, candidate key, and superkey.

7.15 Construct an E-R diagram for a hospital with a set of patients and a set of medical doctors. Associate with each patient a log of the various tests and examinations conducted.

7.16 Construct appropriate relation schemas for each of the E-R diagrams in Practice Exercises 7.1 to 7.3.

7.17 Extend the E-R diagram of Practice Exercise 7.3 to track the same information for all teams in a league.

7.18 Explain the difference between a weak and a strong entity set.

7.19 We can convert any weak entity set to a strong entity set by simply adding appropriate attributes. Why, then, do we have weak entity sets?

7.20 Consider the E-R diagram in Figure 7.29, which models an online bookstore.

    a. List the entity sets and their primary keys.

    b. Suppose the bookstore adds Blu-ray discs and downloadable video to its collection. The same item may be present in one or both formats, with differing prices. Extend the E-R diagram to model this addition, ignoring the effect on shopping baskets.

    c. Now extend the E-R diagram, using generalization, to model the case where a shopping basket may contain any combination of books, Blu-ray discs, or downloadable video.

7.21 Design a database for an automobile company to provide to its dealers to assist them in maintaining customer records and dealer inventory and to assist sales staff in ordering cars.

Each vehicle is identified by a vehicle identification number (VIN). Each individual vehicle is a particular model of a particular brand offered by the company (e.g., the XF is a model of the car brand Jaguar of Tata Motors). Each model can be offered with a variety of options, but an individual car may have only some (or none) of the available options. The database needs to store information about models, brands, and options, as well as information about individual dealers, customers, and cars.

Your design should include an E-R diagram, a set of relational schemas, and a list of constraints, including primary-key and foreign-key constraints.

7.22 Design a database for a world-wide package delivery company (e.g., DHL or FedEX). The database must be able to keep track of customers (who ship items) and customers (who receive items); some customers may do both.

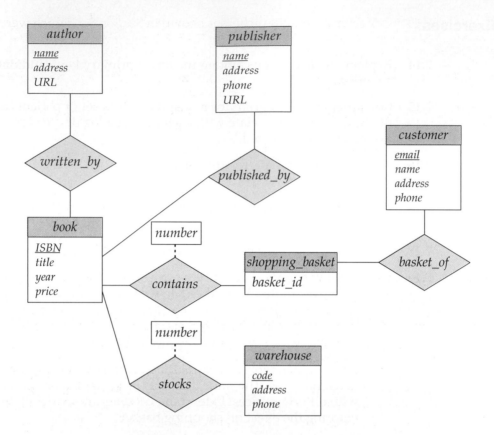

Figure 7.29 E-R diagram for Exercise 7.20.

Each package must be identifiable and trackable, so the database must be able to store the location of the package and its history of locations. Locations include trucks, planes, airports, and warehouses.

Your design should include an E-R diagram, a set of relational schemas, and a list of constraints, including primary-key and foreign-key constraints.

7.23 Design a database for an airline. The database must keep track of customers and their reservations, flights and their status, seat assignments on individual flights, and the schedule and routing of future flights.

Your design should include an E-R diagram, a set of relational schemas, and a list of constraints, including primary-key and foreign-key constraints.

7.24 In Section 7.7.3, we represented a ternary relationship (repeated in Figure 7.27a) using binary relationships, as shown in Figure 7.27b. Consider the alternative shown in Figure 7.27c. Discuss the relative merits of these two alternative representations of a ternary relationship by binary relationships.

7.25 Consider the relation schemas shown in Section 7.6, which were generated from the E-R diagram in Figure 7.15. For each schema, specify what foreign-key constraints, if any, should be created.

7.26 Design a generalization–specialization hierarchy for a motor vehicle sales company. The company sells motorcycles, passenger cars, vans, and buses. Justify your placement of attributes at each level of the hierarchy. Explain why they should not be placed at a higher or lower level.

7.27 Explain the distinction between condition-defined and user-defined constraints. Which of these constraints can the system check automatically? Explain your answer.

7.28 Explain the distinction between disjoint and overlapping constraints.

7.29 Explain the distinction between total and partial constraints.

Tools

Many database systems provide tools for database design that support E-R diagrams. These tools help a designer create E-R diagrams, and they can automatically create corresponding tables in a database. See bibliographic notes of Chapter 1 for references to database-system vendors' Web sites.

There are also several database-independent data modeling tools that support E-R diagrams and UML class diagrams. The drawing tool Dia, which is available as freeware, supports E-R diagrams and UML class diagrams. Commercial tools include IBM Rational Rose (www.ibm.com/software/rational), Microsoft Visio (see www.microsoft.com/office/visio), CA's ERwin (www.ca.com/us/data-modeling.aspx), Poseidon for UML (www.gentleware.com), and SmartDraw (www.smartdraw.com).

Bibliographical Notes

The E-R data model was introduced by Chen [1976]. A logical design methodology for relational databases using the extended E-R model is presented by Teorey et al. [1986]. The Integration Definition for Information Modeling (IDEF1X) standard NIST [1993] released by the United States National Institute of Standards and Technology (NIST) defined standards for E-R diagrams. However, a variety of E-R notations are in use today.

Thalheim [2000] provides a detailed textbook coverage of research in E-R modeling. Basic textbook discussions are offered by Batini et al. [1992] and Elmasri and Navathe [2006]. Davis et al. [1983] provides a collection of papers on the E-R model.

As of 2009, the current UML version was 2.2, with UML version 2.3 near final adoption. See www.uml.org for more information on UML standards and tools.

CHAPTER 8

Relational Database Design

In this chapter, we consider the problem of designing a schema for a relational database. Many of the issues in doing so are similar to design issues we considered in Chapter 7 using the E-R model.

In general, the goal of relational database design is to generate a set of relation schemas that allows us to store information without unnecessary redundancy, yet also allows us to retrieve information easily. This is accomplished by designing schemas that are in an appropriate *normal form*. To determine whether a relation schema is in one of the desirable normal forms, we need information about the real-world enterprise that we are modeling with the database. Some of this information exists in a well-designed E-R diagram, but additional information about the enterprise may be needed as well.

In this chapter, we introduce a formal approach to relational database design based on the notion of functional dependencies. We then define normal forms in terms of functional dependencies and other types of data dependencies. First, however, we view the problem of relational design from the standpoint of the schemas derived from a given entity-relationship design.

8.1 Features of Good Relational Designs

Our study of entity-relationship design in Chapter 7 provides an excellent starting point for creating a relational database design. We saw in Section 7.6 that it is possible to generate a set of relation schemas directly from the E-R design. Obviously, the goodness (or badness) of the resulting set of schemas depends on how good the E-R design was in the first place. Later in this chapter, we shall study precise ways of assessing the desirability of a collection of relation schemas. However, we can go a long way toward a good design using concepts we have already studied.

For ease of reference, we repeat the schemas for the university database in Figure 8.1.

classroom(*building*, *room_number*, *capacity*)
department(*dept_name*, *building*, *budget*)
course(*course_id*, *title*, *dept_name*, *credits*)
instructor(*ID*, *name*, *dept_name*, *salary*)
section(*course_id*, *sec_id*, *semester*, *year*, *building*, *room_number*, *time_slot_id*)
teaches(*ID*, *course_id*, *sec_id*, *semester*, *year*)
student(*ID*, *name*, *dept_name*, *tot_cred*)
takes(*ID*, *course_id*, *sec_id*, *semester*, *year*, *grade*)
advisor(*s_ID*, *i_ID*)
time_slot(*time_slot_id*, *day*, *start_time*, *end_time*)
prereq(*course_id*, *prereq_id*)

Figure 8.1   Schema for the university database.

8.1.1   Design Alternative: Larger Schemas

Now, let us explore features of this relational database design as well as some alternatives. Suppose that instead of having the schemas *instructor* and *department*, we have the schema:

$$inst\_dept\ (ID,\ name,\ salary,\ dept\_name,\ building,\ budget)$$

This represents the result of a natural join on the relations corresponding to *instructor* and *department*. This seems like a good idea because some queries can be expressed using fewer joins, until we think carefully about the facts about the university that led to our E-R design.

Let us consider the instance of the *inst_dept* relation shown in Figure 8.2. Notice that we have to repeat the department information ("building" and "budget") once for each instructor in the department. For example, the information about the Comp. Sci. department (Taylor, 100000) is included in the tuples of instructors Katz, Srinivasan, and Brandt.

It is important that all these tuples agree as to the budget amount since otherwise our database would be inconsistent. In our original design using *instructor* and *department*, we stored the amount of each budget exactly once. This suggests that using *inst_dept* is a bad idea since it stores the budget amounts redundantly and runs the risk that some user might update the budget amount in one tuple but not all, and thus create inconsistency.

Even if we decided to live with the redundancy problem, there is still another problem with the *inst_dept* schema. Suppose we are creating a new department in the university. In the alternative design above, we cannot represent directly the information concerning a department (*dept_name*, *building*, *budget*) unless that department has at least one instructor at the university. This is because tuples in the *inst_dept* table require values for *ID*, *name*, and *salary*. This means that we cannot record information about the newly created department until the first instructor

ID	name	salary	dept_name	building	budget
22222	Einstein	95000	Physics	Watson	70000
12121	Wu	90000	Finance	Painter	120000
32343	El Said	60000	History	Painter	50000
45565	Katz	75000	Comp. Sci.	Taylor	100000
98345	Kim	80000	Elec. Eng.	Taylor	85000
76766	Crick	72000	Biology	Watson	90000
10101	Srinivasan	65000	Comp. Sci.	Taylor	100000
58583	Califieri	62000	History	Painter	50000
83821	Brandt	92000	Comp. Sci.	Taylor	100000
15151	Mozart	40000	Music	Packard	80000
33456	Gold	87000	Physics	Watson	70000
76543	Singh	80000	Finance	Painter	120000

Figure 8.2 The *inst_dept* table.

is hired for the new department. In the old design, the schema *department* can handle this, but under the revised design, we would have to create a tuple with a null value for *building* and *budget*. In some cases null values are troublesome, as we saw in our study of SQL. However, if we decide that this is not a problem to us in this case, then we can proceed to use the revised design.

8.1.2 Design Alternative: Smaller Schemas

Suppose again that, somehow, we had started out with the schema *inst_dept*. How would we recognize that it requires repetition of information and should be split into the two schemas *instructor* and *department*?

By observing the contents of actual relations on schema *inst_dept*, we could note the repetition of information resulting from having to list the building and budget once for each instructor associated with a department. However, this is an unreliable process. A real-world database has a large number of schemas and an even larger number of attributes. The number of tuples can be in the millions or higher. Discovering repetition would be costly. There is an even more fundamental problem with this approach. It does not allow us to determine whether the lack of repetition is just a "lucky" special case or whether it is a manifestation of a general rule. In our example, how would we *know* that in our university organization, each department (identified by its department name) *must* reside in a single building and must have a single budget amount? Is the fact that the budget amount for the Comp. Sci. department appears three times with the same budget amount just a coincidence? We cannot answer these questions without going back to the enterprise itself and understanding its rules. In particular, we would need to discover that the university requires that every department (identified by its department name) *must* have only one building and one budget value.

In the case of *inst_dept*, our process of creating an E-R design successfully avoided the creation of this schema. However, this fortuitous situation does not always occur. Therefore, we need to allow the database designer to specify rules such as "each specific value for *dept_name* corresponds to at most one *budget*" even in cases where *dept_name* is not the primary key for the schema in question. In other words, we need to write a rule that says "if there were a schema (*dept_name*, *budget*), then *dept_name* is able to serve as the primary key." This rule is specified as a **functional dependency**

$$dept\_name \rightarrow budget$$

Given such a rule, we now have sufficient information to recognize the problem of the *inst_dept* schema. Because *dept_name* cannot be the primary key for *inst_dept* (because a department may need several tuples in the relation on schema *inst_dept*), the amount of a budget may have to be repeated.

Observations such as these and the rules (functional dependencies in particular) that result from them allow the database designer to recognize situations where a schema ought to be split, or *decomposed*, into two or more schemas. It is not hard to see that the right way to decompose *inst_dept* is into schemas *instructor* and *department* as in the original design. Finding the right decomposition is much harder for schemas with a large number of attributes and several functional dependencies. To deal with this, we shall rely on a formal methodology that we develop later in this chapter.

Not all decompositions of schemas are helpful. Consider an extreme case where all we had were schemas consisting of one attribute. No interesting relationships of any kind could be expressed. Now consider a less extreme case where we choose to decompose the *employee* schema (Section 7.8):

$$employee \ (ID, name, street, city, salary)$$

into the following two schemas:

$$employee1 \ (ID, name)$$
$$employee2 \ (name, street, city, salary)$$

The flaw in this decomposition arises from the possibility that the enterprise has two employees with the same name. This is not unlikely in practice, as many cultures have certain highly popular names. Of course each person would have a unique employee-id, which is why *ID* can serve as the primary key. As an example, let us assume two employees, both named Kim, work at the university and have the following tuples in the relation on schema *employee* in the original design:

$$(57766, Kim, Main, Perryridge, 75000)$$
$$(98776, Kim, North, Hampton, 67000)$$

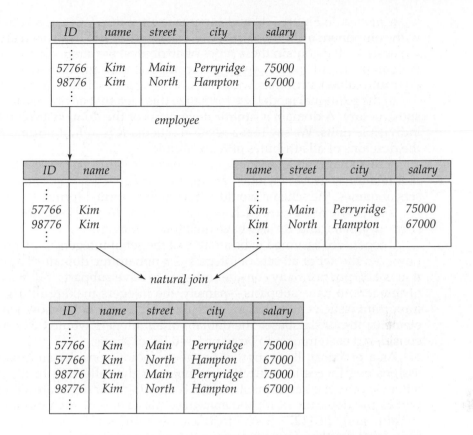

Figure 8.3   Loss of information via a bad decomposition.

Figure 8.3 shows these tuples, the resulting tuples using the schemas resulting from the decomposition, and the result if we attempted to regenerate the original tuples using a natural join. As we see in the figure, the two original tuples appear in the result along with two new tuples that incorrectly mix data values pertaining to the two employees named Kim. Although we have more tuples, we actually have less information in the following sense. We can indicate that a certain street, city, and salary pertain to someone named Kim, but we are unable to distinguish which of the Kims. Thus, our decomposition is unable to represent certain important facts about the university employees. Clearly, we would like to avoid such decompositions. We shall refer to such decompositions as being **lossy decompositions**, and, conversely, to those that are not as **lossless decompositions**.

8.2   Atomic Domains and First Normal Form

The E-R model allows entity sets and relationship sets to have attributes that have some degree of substructure. Specifically, it allows multivalued attributes such as *phone_number* in Figure 7.11 and composite attributes (such as an attribute *address* with component attributes *street*, *city*, *state*, and *zip*). When we create tables from E-R designs that contain these types of attributes, we eliminate this substructure. For composite attributes, we let each component be an attribute in its own right. For multivalued attributes, we create one tuple for each item in a multivalued set.

In the relational model, we formalize this idea that attributes do not have any substructure. A domain is **atomic** if elements of the domain are considered to be indivisible units. We say that a relation schema R is in **first normal form** (1NF) if the domains of all attributes of R are atomic.

A set of names is an example of a nonatomic value. For example, if the schema of a relation *employee* included an attribute *children* whose domain elements are sets of names, the schema would not be in first normal form.

Composite attributes, such as an attribute *address* with component attributes *street*, *city*, *state*, and *zip* also have nonatomic domains.

Integers are assumed to be atomic, so the set of integers is an atomic domain; however, the set of all sets of integers is a nonatomic domain. The distinction is that we do not normally consider integers to have subparts, but we consider sets of integers to have subparts—namely, the integers making up the set. But the important issue is not what the domain itself is, but rather how we use domain elements in our database. The domain of all integers would be nonatomic if we considered each integer to be an ordered list of digits.

As a practical illustration of the above point, consider an organization that assigns employees identification numbers of the following form: The first two letters specify the department and the remaining four digits are a unique number within the department for the employee. Examples of such numbers would be "CS001" and "EE1127". Such identification numbers can be divided into smaller units, and are therefore nonatomic. If a relation schema had an attribute whose domain consists of identification numbers encoded as above, the schema would not be in first normal form.

When such identification numbers are used, the department of an employee can be found by writing code that breaks up the structure of an identification number. Doing so requires extra programming, and information gets encoded in the application program rather than in the database. Further problems arise if such identification numbers are used as primary keys: When an employee changes departments, the employee's identification number must be changed everywhere it occurs, which can be a difficult task, or the code that interprets the number would give a wrong result.

From the above discussion, it may appear that our use of course identifiers such as "CS-101", where "CS" indicates the Computer Science department, means that the domain of course identifiers is not atomic. Such a domain is not atomic as far as humans using the system are concerned. However, the database application still treats the domain as atomic, as long as it does not attempt to split the identifier and interpret parts of the identifier as a department abbreviation. The *course* schema stores the department name as a separate attribute, and the database application can use this attribute value to find the department of a course, instead of interpreting particular characters of the course identifier. Thus, our university schema can be considered to be in first normal form.

The use of set-valued attributes can lead to designs with redundant storage of data, which in turn can result in inconsistencies. For instance, instead of having the relationship between instructors and sections being represented as a separate relation *teaches*, a database designer may be tempted to store a set of course section identifiers with each instructor and a set of instructor identifiers with each section. (The primary keys of *section* and *instructor* are used as identifiers.) Whenever data pertaining to which instructor teaches which section is changed, the update has to be performed at two places: in the set of instructors for the section, and the set of sections for the instructor. Failure to perform both updates can leave the database in an inconsistent state. Keeping only one of these sets, that either the set of instructors of a section, or the set of sections of an instructor, would avoid repeated information; however keeping only one of these would complicate some queries, and it is unclear which of the two to retain.

Some types of nonatomic values can be useful, although they should be used with care. For example, composite-valued attributes are often useful, and set-valued attributes are also useful in many cases, which is why both are supported in the E-R model. In many domains where entities have a complex structure, forcing a first normal form representation represents an unnecessary burden on the application programmer, who has to write code to convert data into atomic form. There is also the runtime overhead of converting data back and forth from the atomic form. Support for nonatomic values can thus be very useful in such domains. In fact, modern database systems do support many types of nonatomic values, as we shall see in Chapter 22. However, in this chapter we restrict ourselves to relations in first normal form and, thus, all domains are atomic.

8.3   Decomposition Using Functional Dependencies

In Section 8.1, we noted that there is a formal methodology for evaluating whether a relational schema should be decomposed. This methodology is based upon the concepts of keys and functional dependencies.

In discussing algorithms for relational database design, we shall need to talk about arbitrary relations and their schema, rather than talking only about examples. Recalling our introduction to the relational model in Chapter 2, we summarize our notation here.

- In general, we use Greek letters for sets of attributes (for example, α). We use a lowercase Roman letter followed by an uppercase Roman letter in parentheses to refer to a relation schema (for example, $r(R)$). We use the notation $r(R)$ to show that the schema is for relation r, with R denoting the set of attributes, but at times simplify our notation to use just R when the relation name does not matter to us.

  Of course, a relation schema is a set of attributes, but not all sets of attributes are schemas. When we use a lowercase Greek letter, we are referring to a set of attributes that may or may not be a schema. A Roman letter is used when we wish to indicate that the set of attributes is definitely a schema.

- When a set of attributes is a superkey, we denote it by K. A superkey pertains to a specific relation schema, so we use the terminology "K is a superkey of $r(R)$."

- We use a lowercase name for relations. In our examples, these names are intended to be realistic (for example, *instructor*), while in our definitions and algorithms, we use single letters, like r.

- A relation, of course, has a particular value at any given time; we refer to that as an instance and use the term "instance of r". When it is clear that we are talking about an instance, we may use simply the relation name (for example, r).

8.3.1   Keys and Functional Dependencies

A database models a set of entities and relationships in the real world. There are usually a variety of constraints (rules) on the data in the real world. For example, some of the constraints that are expected to hold in a university database are:

1. Students and instructors are uniquely identified by their ID.

2. Each student and instructor has only one name.

3. Each instructor and student is (primarily) associated with only one department.[1]

4. Each department has only one value for its budget, and only one associated building.

An instance of a relation that satisfies all such real-world constraints is called a **legal instance** of the relation; a legal instance of a database is one where all the relation instances are legal instances.

Some of the most commonly used types of real-world constraints can be represented formally as keys (superkeys, candidate keys and primary keys), or as functional dependencies, which we define below.

In Section 2.3, we defined the notion of a *superkey* as a set of one or more attributes that, taken collectively, allows us to identify uniquely a tuple in the relation. We restate that definition here as follows: Let $r(R)$ be a relation schema. A subset K of R is a **superkey** of $r(R)$ if, in any legal instance of $r(R)$, for all pairs t_1 and t_2 of tuples in the instance of r if $t_1 \neq t_2$, then $t_1[K] \neq t_2[K]$. That is, no two tuples in any legal instance of relation $r(R)$ may have the same value on

---

[1] An instructor or a student can be associated with more than one department, for example as an adjunct faculty, or as a minor department. Our simplified university schema models only the primary department associated with each instructor or student. A real university schema would capture secondary associations in other relations.

attribute set K. Clearly, if no two tuples in r have the same value on K, then a K-value uniquely identifies a tuple in r.

Whereas a superkey is a set of attributes that uniquely identifies an entire tuple, a functional dependency allows us to express constraints that uniquely identify the values of certain attributes. Consider a relation schema $r(R)$, and let $\alpha \subseteq R$ and $\beta \subseteq R$.

- Given an instance of $r(R)$, we say that the instance **satisfies** the **functional dependency** $\alpha \rightarrow \beta$ if for all pairs of tuples t_1 and t_2 in the instance such that $t_1[\alpha] = t_2[\alpha]$, it is also the case that $t_1[\beta] = t_2[\beta]$.

- We say that the functional dependency $\alpha \rightarrow \beta$ **holds** on schema $r(R)$ if, in every legal instance of $r(R)$ it satisfies the functional dependency.

Using the functional-dependency notation, we say that K *is a superkey of* $r(R)$ if the functional dependency $K \rightarrow R$ holds on $r(R)$. In other words, K is a superkey if, for every legal instance of $r(R)$, for every pair of tuples t_1 and t_2 from the instance, whenever $t_1[K] = t_2[K]$, it is also the case that $t_1[R] = t_2[R]$ (that is, $t_1 = t_2$).[2]

Functional dependencies allow us to express constraints that we cannot express with superkeys. In Section 8.1.2, we considered the schema:

$$inst\_dept \ (ID, name, salary, dept\_name, building, budget)$$

in which the functional dependency $dept\_name \rightarrow budget$ holds because for each department (identified by $dept\_name$) there is a unique budget amount.

We denote the fact that the pair of attributes $(ID, dept\_name)$ forms a superkey for $inst\_dept$ by writing:

$$ID, dept\_name \rightarrow name, salary, building, budget$$

We shall use functional dependencies in two ways:

1. To test instances of relations to see whether they satisfy a given set F of functional dependencies.

2. To specify constraints on the set of legal relations. We shall thus concern ourselves with *only* those relation instances that satisfy a given set of functional dependencies. If we wish to constrain ourselves to relations on schema $r(R)$ that satisfy a set F of functional dependencies, we say that F **holds** on $r(R)$.

Let us consider the instance of relation r of Figure 8.4, to see which functional dependencies are satisfied. Observe that $A \rightarrow C$ is satisfied. There are two tuples

---

[2]Note that we assume here that relations are sets. SQL deals with multisets, and a **primary key** declaration in SQL for a set of attributes K requires not only that $t_1 = t_2$ if $t_1[K] = t_2[K]$, but also that there be no duplicate tuples. SQL also requires that attributes in the set K cannot be assigned a *null* value.

A	B	C	D
a_1	b_1	c_1	d_1
a_1	b_2	c_1	d_2
a_2	b_2	c_2	d_2
a_2	b_3	c_2	d_3
a_3	b_3	c_2	d_4

Figure 8.4 Sample instance of relation r.

that have an A value of a_1. These tuples have the same C value—namely, c_1. Similarly, the two tuples with an A value of a_2 have the same C value, c_2. There are no other pairs of distinct tuples that have the same A value. The functional dependency $C \rightarrow A$ is not satisfied, however. To see that it is not, consider the tuples $t_1 = (a_2, b_3, c_2, d_3)$ and $t_2 = (a_3, b_3, c_2, d_4)$. These two tuples have the same C values, c_2, but they have different A values, a_2 and a_3, respectively. Thus, we have found a pair of tuples t_1 and t_2 such that $t_1[C] = t_2[C]$, but $t_1[A] \neq t_2[A]$.

Some functional dependencies are said to be **trivial** because they are satisfied by all relations. For example, $A \rightarrow A$ is satisfied by all relations involving attribute A. Reading the definition of functional dependency literally, we see that, for all tuples t_1 and t_2 such that $t_1[A] = t_2[A]$, it is the case that $t_1[A] = t_2[A]$. Similarly, $AB \rightarrow A$ is satisfied by all relations involving attribute A. In general, a functional dependency of the form $\alpha \rightarrow \beta$ is **trivial** if $\beta \subseteq \alpha$.

It is important to realize that an instance of a relation may satisfy some functional dependencies that are not required to hold on the relation's schema. In the instance of the *classroom* relation of Figure 8.5, we see that *room_number* $\rightarrow$ *capacity* is satisfied. However, we believe that, in the real world, two classrooms in different buildings can have the same room number but with different room capacity. Thus, it is possible, at some time, to have an instance of the *classroom* relation in which *room_number* $\rightarrow$ *capacity* is not satisfied. So, we would not include *room_number* $\rightarrow$ *capacity* in the set of functional dependencies that hold on the schema for the *classroom* relation. However, we would expect the functional dependency *building, room_number* $\rightarrow$ *capacity* to hold on the *classroom* schema.

Given that a set of functional dependencies F holds on a relation $r(R)$, it may be possible to infer that certain other functional dependencies must also hold on

building	*room_number*	*capacity*
Packard	101	500
Painter	514	10
Taylor	3128	70
Watson	100	30
Watson	120	50

Figure 8.5 An instance of the *classroom* relation.

the relation. For example, given a schema $r(A, B, C)$, if functional dependencies $A \to B$ and $B \to C$, hold on r, we can infer the functional dependency $A \to C$ must also hold on r. This is because, given any value of A there can be only one corresponding value for B, and for that value of B, there can only be one corresponding value for C. We study later, in Section 8.4.1, how to make such inferences.

We will use the notation F^+ to denote the **closure** of the set F, that is, the set of all functional dependencies that can be inferred given the set F. Clearly F^+ contains all of the functional dependencies in F.

8.3.2 Boyce–Codd Normal Form

One of the more desirable normal forms that we can obtain is **Boyce–Codd normal form** (**BCNF**). It eliminates all redundancy that can be discovered based on functional dependencies, though, as we shall see in Section 8.6, there may be other types of redundancy remaining. A relation schema R is in BCNF with respect to a set F of functional dependencies if, for all functional dependencies in F^+ of the form $\alpha \to \beta$, where $\alpha \subseteq R$ and $\beta \subseteq R$, at least one of the following holds:

- $\alpha \to \beta$ is a trivial functional dependency (that is, $\beta \subseteq \alpha$).

- α is a superkey for schema R.

A database design is in BCNF if each member of the set of relation schemas that constitutes the design is in BCNF.

We have already seen in Section 8.1 an example of a relational schema that is not in BCNF:

$$inst\_dept \ (ID, name, salary, dept\_name, building, budget)$$

The functional dependency $dept\_name \to budget$ holds on $inst\_dept$, but $dept\_name$ is not a superkey (because, a department may have a number of different instructors). In Section 8.1.2, we saw that the decomposition of $inst\_dept$ into $instructor$ and $department$ is a better design. The $instructor$ schema is in BCNF. All of the nontrivial functional dependencies that hold, such as:

$$ID \to name, dept\_name, salary$$

include ID on the left side of the arrow, and ID is a superkey (actually, in this case, the primary key) for $instructor$. (In other words, there is no nontrivial functional dependency with any combination of $name$, $dept\_name$, and $salary$, without ID, on the side.) Thus, $instructor$ is in BCNF.

Similarly, the $department$ schema is in BCNF because all of the nontrivial functional dependencies that hold, such as:

$$dept\_name \to building, budget$$

include *dept_name* on the left side of the arrow, and *dept_name* is a superkey (and the primary key) for *department*. Thus, *department* is in BCNF.

We now state a general rule for decomposing that are not in BCNF. Let R be a schema that is not in BCNF. Then there is at least one nontrivial functional dependency $\alpha \rightarrow \beta$ such that α is not a superkey for R. We replace R in our design with two schemas:

- $(\alpha \cup \beta)$
- $(R - (\beta - \alpha))$

In the case of *inst_dept* above, $\alpha = dept\_name$, $\beta = \{building, budget\}$, and *inst_dept* is replaced by

- $(\alpha \cup \beta) = (dept\_name, building, budget)$
- $(R - (\beta - \alpha)) = (ID, name, dept\_name, salary)$

In this example, it turns out that $\beta - \alpha = \beta$. We need to state the rule as we did so as to deal correctly with functional dependencies that have attributes that appear on both sides of the arrow. The technical reasons for this are covered later in Section 8.5.1.

When we decompose a schema that is not in BCNF, it may be that one or more of the resulting schemas are not in BCNF. In such cases, further decomposition is required, the eventual result of which is a set of BCNF schemas.

8.3.3   BCNF and Dependency Preservation

We have seen several ways in which to express database consistency constraints: primary-key constraints, functional dependencies, **check** constraints, assertions, and triggers. Testing these constraints each time the database is updated can be costly and, therefore, it is useful to design the database in a way that constraints can be tested efficiently. In particular, if testing a functional dependency can be done by considering just one relation, then the cost of testing this constraint is low. We shall see that, in some cases, decomposition into BCNF can prevent efficient testing of certain functional dependencies.

To illustrate this, suppose that we make a small change to our university organization. In the design of Figure 7.15, a student may have only one advisor. This follows from the relationship set *advisor* being many-to-one from *student* to *advisor*. The "small" change we shall make is that an instructor can be associated with only a single department and a student may have more than one advisor, but at most one from a given department.[3]

One way to implement this change using the E-R design is by replacing the *advisor* relationship set with a ternary relationship set, *dept_advisor*, involving entity sets *instructor*, *student*, and *department* that is many-to-one from the pair

---

[3]Such an arrangement makes sense for students with a double major.

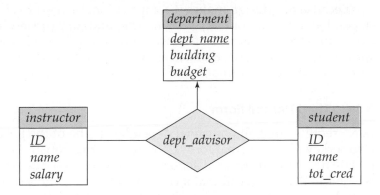

Figure 8.6 The *dept_advisor* relationship set.

{*student*, *instructor*} to *department* as shown in Figure 8.6. The E-R diagram specifies the constraint that "a student may have more than one advisor, but at most one corresponding to a given department".

With this new E-R diagram, the schemas for the *instructor*, *department*, and *student* are unchanged. However, the schema derived from *dept_advisor* is now:

$$dept\_advisor\ (s\_ID,\ i\_ID,\ dept\_name)$$

Although not specified in the E-R diagram, suppose we have the additional constraint that "an instructor can act as advisor for only a single department."

Then, the following functional dependencies hold on *dept_advisor*:

$$i\_ID \rightarrow dept\_name$$
$$s\_ID, dept\_name \rightarrow i\_ID$$

The first functional dependency follows from our requirement that "an instructor can act as an advisor for only one department." The second functional dependency follows from our requirement that "a student may have at most one advisor for a given department."

Notice that with this design, we are forced to repeat the department name once for each time an instructor participates in a *dept_advisor* relationship. We see that *dept_advisor* is not in BCNF because *i_ID* is not a superkey. Following our rule for BCNF decomposition, we get:

$$(s\_ID, i\_ID)$$
$$(i\_ID, dept\_name)$$

Both the above schemas are BCNF. (In fact, you can verify that any schema with only two attributes is in BCNF by definition.) Note however, that in our BCNF design, there is no schema that includes all the attributes appearing in the functional dependency *s_ID*, *dept_name* → *i_ID*.

Because our design makes it computationally hard to enforce this functional dependency, we say our design is not **dependency preserving**.[4] Because dependency preservation is usually considered desirable, we consider another normal form, weaker than BCNF, that will allow us to preserve dependencies. That normal form is called third normal form.[5]

8.3.4   Third Normal Form

BCNF requires that all nontrivial dependencies be of the form $\alpha \rightarrow \beta$, where α is a superkey. Third normal form (3NF) relaxes this constraint slightly by allowing certain nontrivial functional dependencies whose left side is not a superkey. Before we define 3NF, we recall that a candidate key is a minimal superkey—that is, a superkey no proper subset of which is also a superkey.

A relation schema R is in **third normal form** with respect to a set F of functional dependencies if, for all functional dependencies in F^+ of the form $\alpha \rightarrow \beta$, where $\alpha \subseteq R$ and $\beta \subseteq R$, at least one of the following holds:

- $\alpha \rightarrow \beta$ is a trivial functional dependency.

- α is a superkey for R.

- Each attribute A in $\beta - \alpha$ is contained in a candidate key for R.

Note that the third condition above does not say that a single candidate key must contain all the attributes in $\beta - \alpha$; each attribute A in $\beta - \alpha$ may be contained in a *different* candidate key.

The first two alternatives are the same as the two alternatives in the definition of BCNF. The third alternative of the 3NF definition seems rather unintuitive, and it is not obvious why it is useful. It represents, in some sense, a minimal relaxation of the BCNF conditions that helps ensure that every schema has a dependency-preserving decomposition into 3NF. Its purpose will become more clear later, when we study decomposition into 3NF.

Observe that any schema that satisfies BCNF also satisfies 3NF, since each of its functional dependencies would satisfy one of the first two alternatives. BCNF is therefore a more restrictive normal form than is 3NF.

The definition of 3NF allows certain functional dependencies that are not allowed in BCNF. A dependency $\alpha \rightarrow \beta$ that satisfies only the third alternative of the 3NF definition is not allowed in BCNF, but is allowed in 3NF.[6]

Now, let us again consider the *dept_advisor* relationship set, which has the following functional dependencies:

---

[4]Technically, it is possible that a dependency whose attributes do not all appear in any one schema is still implicitly enforced, because of the presence of other dependencies that imply it logically. We address that case later, in Section 8.4.5.
[5]You may have noted that we skipped second normal form. It is of historical significance only and is not used in practice.
[6]These dependencies are examples of **transitive dependencies** (see Practice Exercise 8.16). The original definition of 3NF was in terms of transitive dependencies. The definition we use is equivalent but easier to understand.

$$i\_ID \rightarrow dept\_name$$
$$s\_ID, dept\_name \rightarrow i\_ID$$

In Section 8.3.3 we argued that the functional dependency "$i\_ID \rightarrow dept\_name$" caused the *dept_advisor* schema not to be in BCNF. Note that here $\alpha = i\_ID$, $\beta = dept\_name$, and $\beta - \alpha = dept\_name$. Since the functional dependency $s\_ID, dept\_name \rightarrow i\_ID$ holds on *dept_advisor*, the attribute *dept_name* is contained in a candidate key and, therefore, *dept_advisor* is in 3NF.

We have seen the trade-off that must be made between BCNF and 3NF when there is no dependency-preserving BCNF design. These trade-offs are described in more detail in Section 8.5.4.

8.3.5   Higher Normal Forms

Using functional dependencies to decompose schemas may not be sufficient to avoid unnecessary repetition of information in certain cases. Consider a slight variation in the *instructor* entity-set definition in which we record with each instructor a set of children's names and a set of phone numbers. The phone numbers may be shared by multiple people. Thus, *phone_number* and *child_name* would be multivalued attributes and, following our rules for generating schemas from an E-R design, we would have two schemas, one for each of the multivalued attributes, *phone_number* and *child_name*:

(*ID*, *child_name*)
(*ID*, *phone_number*)

If we were to combine these schemas to get

(*ID*, *child_name*, *phone_number*)

we would find the result to be in BCNF because only nontrivial functional dependencies hold. As a result we might think that such a combination is a good idea. However, such a combination is a bad idea, as we can see by considering the example of an instructor with two children and two phone numbers. For example, let the instructor with *ID* 99999 have two children named "David" and "William" and two phone numbers, 512-555-1234 and 512-555-4321. In the combined schema, we must repeat the phone numbers once for each dependent:

(99999, David, 512-555-1234)
(99999, David, 512-555-4321)
(99999, William, 512-555-1234)
(99999, William, 512-555-4321)

If we did not repeat the phone numbers, and stored only the first and last tuple, we would have recorded the dependent names and the phone numbers, but the resultant tuples would imply that David corresponded to 512-555-1234, while William corresponded to 512-555-4321. As we know, this would be incorrect.

Because normal forms based on functional dependencies are not sufficient to deal with situations like this, other dependencies and normal forms have been defined. We cover these in Sections 8.6 and 8.7.

8.4   Functional-Dependency Theory

We have seen in our examples that it is useful to be able to reason systematically about functional dependencies as part of a process of testing schemas for BCNF or 3NF.

8.4.1   Closure of a Set of Functional Dependencies

We shall see that, given a set F of functional dependencies on a schema, we can prove that certain other functional dependencies also hold on the schema. We say that such functional dependencies are "logically implied" by F. When testing for normal forms, it is not sufficient to consider the given set of functional dependencies; rather, we need to consider *all* functional dependencies that hold on the schema.

More formally, given a relational schema $r(R)$, a functional dependency f on R is **logically implied** by a set of functional dependencies F on r if every instance of $r(R)$ that satisfies F also satisfies f.

Suppose we are given a relation schema $r(A, B, C, G, H, I)$ and the set of functional dependencies:

$$A \rightarrow B$$
$$A \rightarrow C$$
$$CG \rightarrow H$$
$$CG \rightarrow I$$
$$B \rightarrow H$$

The functional dependency:

$$A \rightarrow H$$

is logically implied. That is, we can show that, whenever a relation satisfies our given set of functional dependencies, $A \rightarrow H$ must also be satisfied by that relation. Suppose that t_1 and t_2 are tuples such that:

$$t_1[A] = t_2[A]$$

Since we are given that $A \rightarrow B$, it follows from the definition of functional dependency that:

$$t_1[B] = t_2[B]$$

Then, since we are given that $B \to H$, it follows from the definition of functional dependency that:

$$t_1[H] = t_2[H]$$

Therefore, we have shown that, whenever t_1 and t_2 are tuples such that $t_1[A] = t_2[A]$, it must be that $t_1[H] = t_2[H]$. But that is exactly the definition of $A \to H$.

Let F be a set of functional dependencies. The **closure** of F, denoted by F^+, is the set of all functional dependencies logically implied by F. Given F, we can compute F^+ directly from the formal definition of functional dependency. If F were large, this process would be lengthy and difficult. Such a computation of F^+ requires arguments of the type just used to show that $A \to H$ is in the closure of our example set of dependencies.

Axioms, or rules of inference, provide a simpler technique for reasoning about functional dependencies. In the rules that follow, we use Greek letters (α, β, γ, ...) for sets of attributes, and uppercase Roman letters from the beginning of the alphabet for individual attributes. We use $\alpha\beta$ to denote $\alpha \cup \beta$.

We can use the following three rules to find logically implied functional dependencies. By applying these rules *repeatedly*, we can find all of F^+, given F. This collection of rules is called **Armstrong's axioms** in honor of the person who first proposed it.

- **Reflexivity rule**. If α is a set of attributes and $\beta \subseteq \alpha$, then $\alpha \to \beta$ holds.

- **Augmentation rule**. If $\alpha \to \beta$ holds and γ is a set of attributes, then $\gamma\alpha \to \gamma\beta$ holds.

- **Transitivity rule**. If $\alpha \to \beta$ holds and $\beta \to \gamma$ holds, then $\alpha \to \gamma$ holds.

Armstrong's axioms are **sound**, because they do not generate any incorrect functional dependencies. They are **complete**, because, for a given set F of functional dependencies, they allow us to generate all F^+. The bibliographical notes provide references for proofs of soundness and completeness.

Although Armstrong's axioms are complete, it is tiresome to use them directly for the computation of F^+. To simplify matters further, we list additional rules. It is possible to use Armstrong's axioms to prove that these rules are sound (see Practice Exercises 8.4 and 8.5 and Exercise 8.26).

- **Union rule**. If $\alpha \to \beta$ holds and $\alpha \to \gamma$ holds, then $\alpha \to \beta\gamma$ holds.

- **Decomposition rule**. If $\alpha \to \beta\gamma$ holds, then $\alpha \to \beta$ holds and $\alpha \to \gamma$ holds.

- **Pseudotransitivity rule**. If $\alpha \to \beta$ holds and $\gamma\beta \to \delta$ holds, then $\alpha\gamma \to \delta$ holds.

Let us apply our rules to the example of schema $R = (A, B, C, G, H, I)$ and the set F of functional dependencies $\{A \to B, A \to C, CG \to H, CG \to I, B \to H\}$. We list several members of F^+ here:

- $A \rightarrow H$. Since $A \rightarrow B$ and $B \rightarrow H$ hold, we apply the transitivity rule. Observe that it was much easier to use Armstrong's axioms to show that $A \rightarrow H$ holds than it was to argue directly from the definitions, as we did earlier in this section.

- $CG \rightarrow HI$. Since $CG \rightarrow H$ and $CG \rightarrow I$, the union rule implies that $CG \rightarrow HI$.

- $AG \rightarrow I$. Since $A \rightarrow C$ and $CG \rightarrow I$, the pseudotransitivity rule implies that $AG \rightarrow I$ holds.

  Another way of finding that $AG \rightarrow I$ holds is as follows: We use the augmentation rule on $A \rightarrow C$ to infer $AG \rightarrow CG$. Applying the transitivity rule to this dependency and $CG \rightarrow I$, we infer $AG \rightarrow I$.

Figure 8.7 shows a procedure that demonstrates formally how to use Armstrong's axioms to compute F^+. In this procedure, when a functional dependency is added to F^+, it may be already present, and in that case there is no change to F^+. We shall see an alternative way of computing F^+ in Section 8.4.2.

The left-hand and right-hand sides of a functional dependency are both subsets of R. Since a set of size n has 2^n subsets, there are a total of $2^n \times 2^n = 2^{2n}$ possible functional dependencies, where n is the number of attributes in R. Each iteration of the repeat loop of the procedure, except the last iteration, adds at least one functional dependency to F^+. Thus, the procedure is guaranteed to terminate.

8.4.2   Closure of Attribute Sets

We say that an attribute B is **functionally determined** by α if $\alpha \rightarrow B$. To test whether a set α is a superkey, we must devise an algorithm for computing the set of attributes functionally determined by α. One way of doing this is to compute F^+, take all functional dependencies with α as the left-hand side, and take the union of the right-hand sides of all such dependencies. However, doing so can be expensive, since F^+ can be large.

An efficient algorithm for computing the set of attributes functionally determined by α is useful not only for testing whether α is a superkey, but also for several other tasks, as we shall see later in this section.

$F^+ = F$
repeat
     for each functional dependency f in F^+
          apply reflexivity and augmentation rules on f
          add the resulting functional dependencies to F^+
     for each pair of functional dependencies f_1 and f_2 in F^+
          if f_1 and f_2 can be combined using transitivity
               add the resulting functional dependency to F^+
until F^+ does not change any further

Figure 8.7   A procedure to compute F^+.

```
result := α;
repeat
        for each functional dependency β → γ in F do
            begin
                if β ⊆ result then result := result ∪ γ;
            end
until (result does not change)
```

Figure 8.8 An algorithm to compute α^+, the closure of α under F.

Let α be a set of attributes. We call the set of all attributes functionally determined by α under a set F of functional dependencies the **closure** of α under F; we denote it by α^+. Figure 8.8 shows an algorithm, written in pseudocode, to compute α^+. The input is a set F of functional dependencies and the set α of attributes. The output is stored in the variable *result*.

To illustrate how the algorithm works, we shall use it to compute $(AG)^+$ with the functional dependencies defined in Section 8.4.1. We start with $result = AG$. The first time that we execute the **repeat** loop to test each functional dependency, we find that:

- $A \rightarrow B$ causes us to include B in *result*. To see this fact, we observe that $A \rightarrow B$ is in F, $A \subseteq result$ (which is AG), so $result := result \cup B$.

- $A \rightarrow C$ causes *result* to become $ABCG$.

- $CG \rightarrow H$ causes *result* to become $ABCGH$.

- $CG \rightarrow I$ causes *result* to become $ABCGHI$.

The second time that we execute the **repeat** loop, no new attributes are added to *result*, and the algorithm terminates.

Let us see why the algorithm of Figure 8.8 is correct. The first step is correct, since $\alpha \rightarrow \alpha$ always holds (by the reflexivity rule). We claim that, for any subset β of *result*, $\alpha \rightarrow \beta$. Since we start the **repeat** loop with $\alpha \rightarrow result$ being true, we can add γ to *result* only if $\beta \subseteq result$ and $\beta \rightarrow \gamma$. But then $result \rightarrow \beta$ by the reflexivity rule, so $\alpha \rightarrow \beta$ by transitivity. Another application of transitivity shows that $\alpha \rightarrow \gamma$ (using $\alpha \rightarrow \beta$ and $\beta \rightarrow \gamma$). The union rule implies that $\alpha \rightarrow result \cup \gamma$, so α functionally determines any new result generated in the **repeat** loop. Thus, any attribute returned by the algorithm is in α^+.

It is easy to see that the algorithm finds all of α^+. If there is an attribute in α^+ that is not yet in *result* at any point during the execution, then there must be a functional dependency $\beta \rightarrow \gamma$ for which $\beta \subseteq result$, and at least one attribute in γ is not in *result*. When the algorithm terminates, all such functional dependencies have been processed, and the attributes in γ added to *result*; we can thus be sure that all attributes in α^+ are in *result*.

It turns out that, in the worst case, this algorithm may take an amount of time quadratic in the size of F. There is a faster (although slightly more complex) algorithm that runs in time linear in the size of F; that algorithm is presented as part of Practice Exercise 8.8.

There are several uses of the attribute closure algorithm:

- To test if α is a superkey, we compute α^+, and check if α^+ contains all attributes in R.

- We can check if a functional dependency $\alpha \rightarrow \beta$ holds (or, in other words, is in F^+), by checking if $\beta \subseteq \alpha^+$. That is, we compute α^+ by using attribute closure, and then check if it contains β. This test is particularly useful, as we shall see later in this chapter.

- It gives us an alternative way to compute F^+: For each $\gamma \subseteq R$, we find the closure γ^+, and for each $S \subseteq \gamma^+$, we output a functional dependency $\gamma \rightarrow S$.

8.4.3 Canonical Cover

Suppose that we have a set of functional dependencies F on a relation schema. Whenever a user performs an update on the relation, the database system must ensure that the update does not violate any functional dependencies, that is, all the functional dependencies in F are satisfied in the new database state.

The system must roll back the update if it violates any functional dependencies in the set F.

We can reduce the effort spent in checking for violations by testing a simplified set of functional dependencies that has the same closure as the given set. Any database that satisfies the simplified set of functional dependencies also satisfies the original set, and vice versa, since the two sets have the same closure. However, the simplified set is easier to test. We shall see how the simplified set can be constructed in a moment. First, we need some definitions.

An attribute of a functional dependency is said to be **extraneous** if we can remove it without changing the closure of the set of functional dependencies. The formal definition of **extraneous attributes** is as follows: Consider a set F of functional dependencies and the functional dependency $\alpha \rightarrow \beta$ in F.

- Attribute A is extraneous in α if $A \in \alpha$, and F logically implies $(F - \{\alpha \rightarrow \beta\}) \cup \{(\alpha - A) \rightarrow \beta\}$.

- Attribute A is extraneous in β if $A \in \beta$, and the set of functional dependencies $(F - \{\alpha \rightarrow \beta\}) \cup \{\alpha \rightarrow (\beta - A)\}$ logically implies F.

For example, suppose we have the functional dependencies $AB \rightarrow C$ and $A \rightarrow C$ in F. Then, B is extraneous in $AB \rightarrow C$. As another example, suppose we have the functional dependencies $AB \rightarrow CD$ and $A \rightarrow C$ in F. Then C would be extraneous in the right-hand side of $AB \rightarrow CD$.

Beware of the direction of the implications when using the definition of extraneous attributes: If you exchange the left-hand side with the right-hand side,

$F_c = F$
repeat
    Use the union rule to replace any dependencies in F_c of the form
        $\alpha_1 \rightarrow \beta_1$ and $\alpha_1 \rightarrow \beta_2$ with $\alpha_1 \rightarrow \beta_1 \beta_2$.
    Find a functional dependency $\alpha \rightarrow \beta$ in F_c with an extraneous
        attribute either in α or in β.
        /* Note: the test for extraneous attributes is done using F_c, not F */
    If an extraneous attribute is found, delete it from $\alpha \rightarrow \beta$ in F_c.
until (F_c does not change)

Figure 8.9 Computing canonical cover.

the implication will *always* hold. That is, $(F - \{\alpha \rightarrow \beta\}) \cup \{(\alpha - A) \rightarrow \beta\}$ always logically implies F, and also F always logically implies $(F - \{\alpha \rightarrow \beta\}) \cup \{\alpha \rightarrow (\beta - A)\}$.

Here is how we can test efficiently if an attribute is extraneous. Let R be the relation schema, and let F be the given set of functional dependencies that hold on R. Consider an attribute A in a dependency $\alpha \rightarrow \beta$.

- If $A \in \beta$, to check if A is extraneous, consider the set

$$F' = (F - \{\alpha \rightarrow \beta\}) \cup \{\alpha \rightarrow (\beta - A)\}$$

  and check if $\alpha \rightarrow A$ can be inferred from F'. To do so, compute α^+ (the closure of α) under F'; if α^+ includes A, then A is extraneous in β.

- If $A \in \alpha$, to check if A is extraneous, let $\gamma = \alpha - \{A\}$, and check if $\gamma \rightarrow \beta$ can be inferred from F. To do so, compute γ^+ (the closure of γ) under F; if γ^+ includes all attributes in β, then A is extraneous in α.

For example, suppose F contains $AB \rightarrow CD$, $A \rightarrow E$, and $E \rightarrow C$. To check if C is extraneous in $AB \rightarrow CD$, we compute the attribute closure of AB under $F' = \{AB \rightarrow D, A \rightarrow E,$ and $E \rightarrow C\}$. The closure is $ABCDE$, which includes CD, so we infer that C is extraneous.

A **canonical cover** F_c for F is a set of dependencies such that F logically implies all dependencies in F_c, and F_c logically implies all dependencies in F. Furthermore, F_c must have the following properties:

- No functional dependency in F_c contains an extraneous attribute.

- Each left side of a functional dependency in F_c is unique. That is, there are no two dependencies $\alpha_1 \rightarrow \beta_1$ and $\alpha_2 \rightarrow \beta_2$ in F_c such that $\alpha_1 = \alpha_2$.

A canonical cover for a set of functional dependencies F can be computed as depicted in Figure 8.9. It is important to note that when checking if an attribute is extraneous, the check uses the dependencies in the current value of F_c, and **not** the dependencies in F. If a functional dependency contains only one attribute in its right-hand side, for example $A \to C$, and that attribute is found to be extraneous, we would get a functional dependency with an empty right-hand side. Such functional dependencies should be deleted.

The canonical cover of F, F_c, can be shown to have the same closure as F; hence, testing whether F_c is satisfied is equivalent to testing whether F is satisfied. However, F_c is minimal in a certain sense—it does not contain extraneous attributes, and it combines functional dependencies with the same left side. It is cheaper to test F_c than it is to test F itself.

Consider the following set F of functional dependencies on schema (A, B, C):

$$A \to BC$$
$$B \to C$$
$$A \to B$$
$$AB \to C$$

Let us compute the canonical cover for F.

- There are two functional dependencies with the same set of attributes on the left side of the arrow:

$$A \to BC$$
$$A \to B$$

We combine these functional dependencies into $A \to BC$.

- A is extraneous in $AB \to C$ because F logically implies $(F - \{AB \to C\}) \cup \{B \to C\}$. This assertion is true because $B \to C$ is already in our set of functional dependencies.

- C is extraneous in $A \to BC$, since $A \to BC$ is logically implied by $A \to B$ and $B \to C$.

Thus, our canonical cover is:

$$A \to B$$
$$B \to C$$

Given a set F of functional dependencies, it may be that an entire functional dependency in the set is extraneous, in the sense that dropping it does not change the closure of F. We can show that a canonical cover F_c of F contains no such extraneous functional dependency. Suppose that, to the contrary, there were such an extraneous functional dependency in F_c. The right-side attributes of the dependency would then be extraneous, which is not possible by the definition of canonical covers.

A canonical cover might not be unique. For instance, consider the set of functional dependencies $F = \{A \to BC, B \to AC, \text{ and } C \to AB\}$. If we apply the extraneity test to $A \to BC$, we find that both B and C are extraneous under F. However, it is incorrect to delete both! The algorithm for finding the canonical cover picks one of the two, and deletes it. Then,

1. If C is deleted, we get the set $F' = \{A \to B, B \to AC, \text{and } C \to AB\}$. Now, B is not extraneous in the side of $A \to B$ under F'. Continuing the algorithm, we find A and B are extraneous in the right-hand side of $C \to AB$, leading to two canonical covers

$$F_c = \{A \to B, B \to C, C \to A\}$$
$$F_c = \{A \to B, B \to AC, C \to B\}.$$

2. If B is deleted, we get the set $\{A \to C, B \to AC, \text{and } C \to AB\}$. This case is symmetrical to the previous case, leading to the canonical covers

$$F_c = \{A \to C, C \to B, \text{and } B \to A\}$$
$$F_c = \{A \to C, B \to C, \text{and } C \to AB\}.$$

As an exercise, can you find one more canonical cover for F?

8.4.4   Lossless Decomposition

Let $r(R)$ be a relation schema, and let F be a set of functional dependencies on $r(R)$. Let R_1 and R_2 form a decomposition of R. We say that the decomposition is a **lossless decomposition** if there is no loss of information by replacing $r(R)$ with two relation schemas $r_1(R_1)$ and $r_2(R_2)$. More precisely, we say the decomposition is lossless if, for all legal database instances (that is, database instances that satisfy the specified functional dependencies and other constraints), relation r contains the same set of tuples as the result of the following SQL query:

> **select** *
> **from** (**select** R_1 **from** r)
> **natural join**
> (**select** R_2 **from** r)

This is stated more succinctly in the relational algebra as:

$$\Pi_{R_1}(r) \bowtie \Pi_{R_2}(r) = r$$

In other words, if we project r onto R_1 and R_2, and compute the natural join of the projection results, we get back exactly r. A decomposition that is not a lossless decomposition is called a **lossy decomposition**. The terms **lossless-join decomposition** and **lossy-join decomposition** are sometimes used in place of lossless decomposition and lossy decomposition.

As an example of a lossy decomposition, recall the decomposition of the *employee* schema into:

employee1 (ID, *name*)
employee2 (*name, street, city, salary*)

that we saw earlier in Section 8.1.2. As we saw in Figure 8.3, the result of *employee1* ⋈ *employee2* is a superset of the original relation *employee*, but the decomposition is lossy since the join result has lost information about which employee identifiers correspond to which addresses and salaries, in the case where two or more employees have the same name.

We can use functional dependencies to show when certain decompositions are lossless. Let R, R_1, R_2, and F be as above. R_1 and R_2 form a lossless decomposition of R if at least one of the following functional dependencies is in F^+:

- $R_1 \cap R_2 \rightarrow R_1$
- $R_1 \cap R_2 \rightarrow R_2$

In other words, if $R_1 \cap R_2$ forms a superkey of either R_1 or R_2, the decomposition of R is a lossless decomposition. We can use attribute closure to test efficiently for superkeys, as we have seen earlier.

To illustrate this, consider the schema

inst_dept (ID, *name, salary, dept_name, building, budget*)

that we decomposed in Section 8.1.2 into the *instructor* and *department* schemas:

instructor (ID, *name, dept_name, salary*)
department (*dept_name, building, budget*)

Consider the intersection of these two schemas, which is *dept_name*. We see that because *dept_name* → *dept_name, building, budget*, the lossless-decomposition rule is satisfied.

For the general case of decomposition of a schema into multiple schemas at once, the test for lossless decomposition is more complicated. See the bibliographical notes for references on the topic.

While the test for binary decomposition is clearly a sufficient condition for lossless decomposition, it is a necessary condition only if all constraints are functional dependencies. We shall see other types of constraints later (in particular, a type of constraint called multivalued dependencies discussed in Section 8.6.1), that can ensure that a decomposition is lossless even if no functional dependencies are present.

8.4.5   Dependency Preservation

Using the theory of functional dependencies, it is easier to characterize dependency preservation than using the ad-hoc approach we took in Section 8.3.3.

Let F be a set of functional dependencies on a schema R, and let $R_1, R_2, \ldots, R_n$ be a decomposition of R. The **restriction** of F to R_i is the set F_i of all functional dependencies in F^+ that include *only* attributes of R_i. Since all functional dependencies in a restriction involve attributes of only one relation schema, it is possible to test such a dependency for satisfaction by checking only one relation.

Note that the definition of restriction uses all dependencies in F^+, not just those in F. For instance, suppose $F = \{A \to B, B \to C\}$, and we have a decomposition into AC and AB. The restriction of F to AC includes $A \to C$, since $A \to C$ is in F^+, even though it is not in F.

The set of restrictions $F_1, F_2, \ldots, F_n$ is the set of dependencies that can be checked efficiently. We now must ask whether testing only the restrictions is sufficient. Let $F' = F_1 \cup F_2 \cup \cdots \cup F_n$. F' is a set of functional dependencies on schema R, but, in general, $F' \neq F$. However, even if $F' \neq F$, it may be that $F'^+ = F^+$. If the latter is true, then every dependency in F is logically implied by F', and, if we verify that F' is satisfied, we have verified that F is satisfied. We say that a decomposition having the property $F'^+ = F^+$ is a **dependency-preserving decomposition**.

Figure 8.10 shows an algorithm for testing dependency preservation. The input is a set $D = \{R_1, R_2, \ldots, R_n\}$ of decomposed relation schemas, and a set F of functional dependencies. This algorithm is expensive since it requires computation of F^+. Instead of applying the algorithm of Figure 8.10, we consider two alternatives.

First, note that if each member of F can be tested on one of the relations of the decomposition, then the decomposition is dependency preserving. This is an easy way to show dependency preservation; however, it does not always work. There are cases where, even though the decomposition is dependency preserving, there is a dependency in F that cannot be tested in any one relation in the decomposition. Thus, this alternative test can be used only as a sufficient condition that is easy

```
compute F⁺;
for each schema Rᵢ in D do
    begin
        Fᵢ : = the restriction of F⁺ to Rᵢ;
    end
F' := ∅
for each restriction Fᵢ do
    begin
        F' = F' ∪ Fᵢ
    end
compute F'⁺;
if (F'⁺ = F⁺) then return (true)
                else return (false);
```

Figure 8.10   Testing for dependency preservation.

to check; if it fails we cannot conclude that the decomposition is not dependency preserving; instead we will have to apply the general test.

We now give a second alternative test for dependency preservation that avoids computing F^+. We explain the intuition behind the test after presenting the test. The test applies the following procedure to each $\alpha \to \beta$ in F.

$$result = \alpha$$
repeat
  for each R_i in the decomposition
    $t = (result \cap R_i)^+ \cap R_i$
    $result = result \cup t$
until (*result* does not change)

The attribute closure here is under the set of functional dependencies F. If *result* contains all attributes in β, then the functional dependency $\alpha \to \beta$ is preserved. The decomposition is dependency preserving if and only if the procedure shows that all the dependencies in F are preserved.

The two key ideas behind the above test are as follows:

- The first idea is to test each functional dependency $\alpha \to \beta$ in F to see if it is preserved in F' (where F' is as defined in Figure 8.10). To do so, we compute the closure of α under F'; the dependency is preserved exactly when the closure includes β. The decomposition is dependency preserving if (and only if) all the dependencies in F are found to be preserved.

- The second idea is to use a modified form of the attribute-closure algorithm to compute closure under F', without actually first computing F'. We wish to avoid computing F' since computing it is quite expensive. Note that F' is the union of F_i, where F_i is the restriction of F on R_i. The algorithm computes the attribute closure of (*result* $\cap R_i$) with respect to F, intersects the closure with R_i, and adds the resultant set of attributes to *result*; this sequence of steps is equivalent to computing the closure of *result* under F_i. Repeating this step for each i inside the while loop gives the closure of *result* under F'.

  To understand why this modified attribute-closure approach works correctly, we note that for any $\gamma \subseteq R_i$, $\gamma \to \gamma^+$ is a functional dependency in F^+, and $\gamma \to \gamma^+ \cap R_i$ is a functional dependency that is in F_i, the restriction of F^+ to R_i. Conversely, if $\gamma \to \delta$ were in F_i, then δ would be a subset of $\gamma^+ \cap R_i$.

This test takes polynomial time, instead of the exponential time required to compute F^+.

8.5   Algorithms for Decomposition

Real-world database schemas are much larger than the examples that fit in the pages of a book. For this reason, we need algorithms for the generation of designs that are in appropriate normal form. In this section, we present algorithms for BCNF and 3NF.

8.5.1 BCNF Decomposition

The definition of BCNF can be used directly to test if a relation is in BCNF. However, computation of F^+ can be a tedious task. We first describe below simplified tests for verifying if a relation is in BCNF. If a relation is not in BCNF, it can be decomposed to create relations that are in BCNF. Later in this section, we describe an algorithm to create a lossless decomposition of a relation, such that the decomposition is in BCNF.

8.5.1.1 Testing for BCNF

Testing of a relation schema R to see if it satisfies BCNF can be simplified in some cases:

- To check if a nontrivial dependency $\alpha \rightarrow \beta$ causes a violation of BCNF, compute α^+ (the attribute closure of α), and verify that it includes all attributes of R; that is, it is a superkey of R.

- To check if a relation schema R is in BCNF, it suffices to check only the dependencies in the given set F for violation of BCNF, rather than check all dependencies in F^+.

  We can show that if none of the dependencies in F causes a violation of BCNF, then none of the dependencies in F^+ will cause a violation of BCNF, either.

Unfortunately, the latter procedure does not work when a relation is decomposed. That is, it *does not* suffice to use F when we test a relation R_i, in a decomposition of R, for violation of BCNF. For example, consider relation schema $R(A, B, C, D, E)$, with functional dependencies F containing $A \rightarrow B$ and $BC \rightarrow D$. Suppose this were decomposed into $R_1(A, B)$ and $R_2(A, C, D, E)$. Now, neither of the dependencies in F contains only attributes from (A, C, D, E) so we might be misled into thinking R_2 satisfies BCNF. In fact, there is a dependency $AC \rightarrow D$ in F^+ (which can be inferred using the pseudotransitivity rule from the two dependencies in F) that shows that R_2 is not in BCNF. Thus, we may need a dependency that is in F^+, but is not in F, to show that a decomposed relation is not in BCNF.

An alternative BCNF test is sometimes easier than computing every dependency in F^+. To check if a relation R_i in a decomposition of R is in BCNF, we apply this test:

- For every subset α of attributes in R_i, check that α^+ (the attribute closure of α under F) either includes no attribute of $R_i - \alpha$, or includes all attributes of R_i.

```
result := {R};
done := false;
compute F⁺;
while (not done) do
    if (there is a schema Rᵢ in result that is not in BCNF)
        then begin
                let α → β be a nontrivial functional dependency that holds
                    on Rᵢ such that α → Rᵢ is not in F⁺, and α ∩ β = ∅;
                result := (result − Rᵢ) ∪ (Rᵢ − β) ∪ (α, β);
            end
        else done := true;
```

Figure 8.11   BCNF decomposition algorithm.

If the condition is violated by some set of attributes α in R_i, consider the following functional dependency, which can be shown to be present in F^+:

$$\alpha \rightarrow (\alpha^+ - \alpha) \cap R_i.$$

The above dependency shows that R_i violates BCNF.

8.5.1.2   BCNF Decomposition Algorithm

We are now able to state a general method to decompose a relation schema so as to satisfy BCNF. Figure 8.11 shows an algorithm for this task. If R is not in BCNF, we can decompose R into a collection of BCNF schemas $R_1, R_2, \ldots, R_n$ by the algorithm. The algorithm uses dependencies that demonstrate violation of BCNF to perform the decomposition.

The decomposition that the algorithm generates is not only in BCNF, but is also a lossless decomposition. To see why our algorithm generates only lossless decompositions, we note that, when we replace a schema R_i with $(R_i - \beta)$ and (α, β), the dependency $\alpha \rightarrow \beta$ holds, and $(R_i - \beta) \cap (\alpha, \beta) = \alpha$.

If we did not require $\alpha \cap \beta = \emptyset$, then those attributes in $\alpha \cap \beta$ would not appear in the schema $(R_i - \beta)$ and the dependency $\alpha \rightarrow \beta$ would no longer hold.

It is easy to see that our decomposition of *inst_dept* in Section 8.3.2 would result from applying the algorithm. The functional dependency *dept_name* → *building, budget* satisfies the $\alpha \cap \beta = \emptyset$ condition and would therefore be chosen to decompose the schema.

The BCNF decomposition algorithm takes time exponential in the size of the initial schema, since the algorithm for checking if a relation in the decomposition satisfies BCNF can take exponential time. The bibliographical notes provide references to an algorithm that can compute a BCNF decomposition in polynomial time. However, the algorithm may "overnormalize," that is, decompose a relation unnecessarily.

As a longer example of the use of the BCNF decomposition algorithm, suppose we have a database design using the *class* schema below:

class (*course_id, title, dept_name, credits, sec_id, semester, year, building, room_number, capacity, time_slot_id*)

The set of functional dependencies that we require to hold on *class* are:

course_id → *title, dept_name, credits*
building, room_number → *capacity*
course_id, sec_id, semester, year → *building, room_number, time_slot_id*

A candidate key for this schema is {*course_id, sec_id, semester, year*}.
We can apply the algorithm of Figure 8.11 to the *class* example as follows:

- The functional dependency:

  course_id → *title, dept_name, credits*

  holds, but *course_id* is not a superkey. Thus, *class* is not in BCNF. We replace *class* by:

  course(*course_id, title, dept_name, credits*)
  class-1 (*course_id, sec_id, semester, year, building, room_number
          capacity, time_slot_id*)

  The only nontrivial functional dependencies that hold on *course* include *course_id* on the left side of the arrow. Since *course_id* is a key for *course*, the relation *course* is in BCNF.

- A candidate key for *class-1* is {*course_id, sec_id, semester, year*}. The functional dependency:

  building, room_number → *capacity*

  holds on *class-1*, but {*building, room_number*} is not a superkey for *class-1*. We replace *class-1* by:

  classroom (*building, room_number, capacity*)
  section (*course_id, sec_id, semester, year,
          building, room_number, time_slot_id*)

  classroom and *section* are in BCNF.

Thus, the decomposition of *class* results in the three relation schemas *course, classroom*, and *section*, each of which is in BCNF. These correspond to the schemas that we have used in this, and previous, chapters. You can verify that the decomposition is lossless and dependency preserving.

let F_c be a canonical cover for F;
$i := 0$;
for each functional dependency $\alpha \to \beta$ in F_c
    $i := i + 1$;
    $R_i := \alpha \beta$;
if none of the schemas R_j, $j = 1, 2, \ldots, i$ contains a candidate key for R
    then
        $i := i + 1$;
        $R_i :=$ any candidate key for R;
/* Optionally, remove redundant relations */
repeat
    if any schema R_j is contained in another schema R_k
        then
            /* Delete R_j */
            $R_j := R_i$;
            $i := i - 1$;
until no more R_js can be deleted
return $(R_1, R_2, \ldots, R_i)$

Figure 8.12   Dependency-preserving, lossless decomposition into 3NF.

8.5.2   3NF Decomposition

Figure 8.12 shows an algorithm for finding a dependency-preserving, lossless decomposition into 3NF. The set of dependencies F_c used in the algorithm is a canonical cover for F. Note that the algorithm considers the set of schemas R_j, $j = 1, 2, \ldots, i$; initially $i = 0$, and in this case the set is empty.

Let us apply this algorithm to our example of Section 8.3.4, where we showed that:

$$dept\_advisor\ (s\_ID, i\_ID, dept\_name)$$

is in 3NF even though it is not in BCNF. The algorithm uses the following functional dependencies in F:

$$f_1: i\_ID \to dept\_name$$
$$f_2: s\_ID, dept\_name \to i\_ID$$

There are no extraneous attributes in any of the functional dependencies in F, so F_c contains f_1 and f_2. The algorithm then generates as R_1 the schema, $(i\_ID\ dept\_name)$, and as R_2 the schema $(s\_ID, dept\_name, i\_ID)$. The algorithm then finds that R_2 contains a candidate key, so no further relation schema is created.

The resultant set of schemas can contain redundant schemas, with one schema R_k containing all the attributes of another schema R_j. For example, R_2 above contains all the attributes from R_1. The algorithm deletes all such schemas that are contained in another schema. Any dependencies that could be tested on an

R_j that is deleted can also be tested on the corresponding relation R_k, and the decomposition is lossless even if R_j is deleted.

Now let us consider again the *class* schema of Section 8.5.1.2 and apply the 3NF decomposition algorithm. The set of functional dependencies we listed there happen to be a canonical cover. As a result, the algorithm gives us the same three schemas *course*, *classroom*, and *section*.

The above example illustrates an interesting property of the 3NF algorithm. Sometimes, the result is not only in 3NF, but also in BCNF. This suggests an alternative method of generating a BCNF design. First use the 3NF algorithm. Then, for any schema in the 3NF design that is not in BCNF, decompose using the BCNF algorithm. If the result is not dependency-preserving, revert to the 3NF design.

8.5.3 Correctness of the 3NF Algorithm

The 3NF algorithm ensures the preservation of dependencies by explicitly building a schema for each dependency in a canonical cover. It ensures that the decomposition is a lossless decomposition by guaranteeing that at least one schema contains a candidate key for the schema being decomposed. Practice Exercise 8.14 provides some insight into the proof that this suffices to guarantee a lossless decomposition.

This algorithm is also called the **3NF synthesis algorithm**, since it takes a set of dependencies and adds one schema at a time, instead of decomposing the initial schema repeatedly. The result is not uniquely defined, since a set of functional dependencies can have more than one canonical cover, and, further, in some cases, the result of the algorithm depends on the order in which it considers the dependencies in F_c. The algorithm may decompose a relation even if it is already in 3NF; however, the decomposition is still guaranteed to be in 3NF.

If a relation R_i is in the decomposition generated by the synthesis algorithm, then R_i is in 3NF. Recall that when we test for 3NF it suffices to consider functional dependencies whose right-hand side is a single attribute. Therefore, to see that R_i is in 3NF you must convince yourself that any functional dependency $\gamma \to B$ that holds on R_i satisfies the definition of 3NF. Assume that the dependency that generated R_i in the synthesis algorithm is $\alpha \to \beta$. Now, B must be in α or β, since B is in R_i and $\alpha \to \beta$ generated R_i. Let us consider the three possible cases:

- B is in both α and β. In this case, the dependency $\alpha \to \beta$ would not have been in F_c since B would be extraneous in β. Thus, this case cannot hold.

- B is in β but not α. Consider two cases:

  - γ is a superkey. The second condition of 3NF is satisfied.

  - γ is not a superkey. Then α must contain some attribute not in γ. Now, since $\gamma \to B$ is in F^+, it must be derivable from F_c by using the attribute closure algorithm on γ. The derivation could not have used $\alpha \to \beta$— if it had been used, α must be contained in the attribute closure of γ, which is not possible, since we assumed γ is not a superkey. Now, using $\alpha \to (\beta - \{B\})$ and $\gamma \to B$, we can derive $\alpha \to B$ (since $\gamma \subseteq \alpha\beta$, and γ

cannot contain B because $\gamma \rightarrow B$ is nontrivial). This would imply that B is extraneous in the right-hand side of $\alpha \rightarrow \beta$, which is not possible since $\alpha \rightarrow \beta$ is in the canonical cover F_c. Thus, if B is in β, then γ must be a superkey, and the second condition of 3NF must be satisfied.

- B is in α but not β.
  Since α is a candidate key, the third alternative in the definition of 3NF is satisfied.

Interestingly, the algorithm we described for decomposition into 3NF can be implemented in polynomial time, even though testing a given relation to see if it satisfies 3NF is NP-hard (which means that it is very unlikely that a polynomial-time algorithm will ever be invented for this task).

8.5.4 Comparison of BCNF and 3NF

Of the two normal forms for relational database schemas, 3NF and BCNF there are advantages to 3NF in that we know that it is always possible to obtain a 3NF design without sacrificing losslessness or dependency preservation. Nevertheless, there are disadvantages to 3NF: We may have to use null values to represent some of the possible meaningful relationships among data items, and there is the problem of repetition of information.

Our goals of database design with functional dependencies are:

1. BCNF.

2. Losslessness.

3. Dependency preservation.

Since it is not always possible to satisfy all three, we may be forced to choose between BCNF and dependency preservation with 3NF.

It is worth noting that SQL does not provide a way of specifying functional dependencies, except for the special case of declaring superkeys by using the **primary key** or **unique** constraints. It is possible, although a little complicated, to write assertions that enforce a functional dependency (see Practice Exercise 8.9); unfortunately, currently no database system supports the complex assertions that are required to enforce a functional dependency, and the assertions would be expensive to test. Thus even if we had a dependency-preserving decomposition, if we use standard SQL we can test efficiently only those functional dependencies whose left-hand side is a key.

Although testing functional dependencies may involve a join if the decomposition is not dependency preserving, we could in principle reduce the cost by using materialized views, which many database systems support, provided the database system supports primary key constraints on materialized views. Given a BCNF decomposition that is not dependency preserving, we consider each dependency in a canonical cover F_c that is not preserved in the decomposition. For each such dependency $\alpha \rightarrow \beta$, we define a materialized view that computes a join of all relations in the decomposition, and projects the result on $\alpha\beta$. The functional dependency can be tested easily on the materialized view, using one of the constraints **unique** (α) or **primary key** (α).

On the negative side, there is a space and time overhead due to the materialized view, but on the positive side, the application programmer need not worry about writing code to keep redundant data consistent on updates; it is the job of the database system to maintain the materialized view, that is, keep it up to date when the database is updated. (Later in the book, in Section 13.5, we outline how a database system can perform materialized view maintenance efficiently.)

Unfortunately, most current database systems do not support constraints on materialized views. Although the Oracle database does support constraints on materialized views, by default it performs view maintenance when the view is accessed, not when the underlying relation is updated;[7] as a result a constraint violation may get detected well after the update has been performed, which makes the detection useless.

Thus, in case we are not able to get a dependency-preserving BCNF decomposition, it is generally preferable to opt for BCNF, since checking functional dependencies other than primary key constraints is difficult in SQL.

8.6 Decomposition Using Multivalued Dependencies

Some relation schemas, even though they are in BCNF, do not seem to be sufficiently normalized, in the sense that they still suffer from the problem of repetition of information. Consider a variation of the university organization where an instructor may be associated with multiple departments.

$$inst \ (ID, \ dept\_name, \ name, \ street, \ city)$$

The astute reader will recognize this schema as a non-BCNF schema because of the functional dependency

$$ID \rightarrow \ name, street, city$$

and because *ID* is not a key for *inst*.

Further assume that an instructor may have several addresses (say, a winter home and a summer home). Then, we no longer wish to enforce the functional dependency "*ID* → *street, city*", though, of course, we still want to enforce "*ID* → name*" (that is, the university is not dealing with instructors who operate under multiple aliases!). Following the BCNF decomposition algorithm, we obtain two schemas:

---

[7]At least as of Oracle version 10g.

$$r_1 \ (ID, name)$$
$$r_2 \ (ID, dept\_name, street, city)$$

Both of these are in BCNF (recall that an instructor can be associated with multiple departments and a department may have several instructors, and therefore, neither "$ID \rightarrow dept\_name$" nor "$dept\_name \rightarrow ID$" hold).

Despite r_2 being in BCNF, there is redundancy. We repeat the address information of each residence of an instructor once for each department with which the instructor is associated. We could solve this problem by decomposing r_2 further into:

$$r_{21}(dept\_name, ID)$$
$$r_{22}(ID, street, city)$$

but there is no constraint that leads us to do this.

To deal with this problem, we must define a new form of constraint, called a *multivalued dependency*. As we did for functional dependencies, we shall use multivalued dependencies to define a normal form for relation schemas. This normal form, called **fourth normal form** (4NF), is more restrictive than BCNF. We shall see that every 4NF schema is also in BCNF but there are BCNF schemas that are not in 4NF.

8.6.1   Multivalued Dependencies

Functional dependencies rule out certain tuples from being in a relation. If $A \rightarrow B$, then we cannot have two tuples with the same A value but different B values. Multivalued dependencies, on the other hand, do not rule out the existence of certain tuples. Instead, they *require* that other tuples of a certain form be present in the relation. For this reason, functional dependencies sometimes are referred to as **equality-generating dependencies**, and multivalued dependencies are referred to as **tuple-generating dependencies**.

Let $r(R)$ be a relation schema and let $\alpha \subseteq R$ and $\beta \subseteq R$. The **multivalued dependency**

$$\alpha \twoheadrightarrow \beta$$

holds on R if, in any legal instance of relation $r(R)$, for all pairs of tuples t_1 and t_2 in r such that $t_1[\alpha] = t_2[\alpha]$, there exist tuples t_3 and t_4 in r such that

$$t_1[\alpha] = t_2[\alpha] = t_3[\alpha] = t_4[\alpha]$$
$$t_3[\beta] = t_1[\beta]$$
$$t_3[R - \beta] = t_2[R - \beta]$$
$$t_4[\beta] = t_2[\beta]$$
$$t_4[R - \beta] = t_1[R - \beta]$$

	α	β	$R - \alpha - \beta$
t_1	$a_1 \ldots a_i$	$a_{i+1} \ldots a_j$	$a_{j+1} \ldots a_n$
t_2	$a_1 \ldots a_i$	$b_{i+1} \ldots b_j$	$b_{j+1} \ldots b_n$
t_3	$a_1 \ldots a_i$	$a_{i+1} \ldots a_j$	$b_{j+1} \ldots b_n$
t_4	$a_1 \ldots a_i$	$b_{i+1} \ldots b_j$	$a_{j+1} \ldots a_n$

Figure 8.13 Tabular representation of $\alpha \rightarrow\!\!\!\rightarrow \beta$.

This definition is less complicated than it appears to be. Figure 8.13 gives a tabular picture of t_1, t_2, t_3, and t_4. Intuitively, the multivalued dependency $\alpha \rightarrow\!\!\!\rightarrow \beta$ says that the relationship between α and β is independent of the relationship between α and $R - \beta$. If the multivalued dependency $\alpha \rightarrow\!\!\!\rightarrow \beta$ is satisfied by all relations on schema R, then $\alpha \rightarrow\!\!\!\rightarrow \beta$ is a *trivial* multivalued dependency on schema R. Thus, $\alpha \rightarrow\!\!\!\rightarrow \beta$ is trivial if $\beta \subseteq \alpha$ or $\beta \cup \alpha = R$.

To illustrate the difference between functional and multivalued dependencies, we consider the schema r_2 again, and an example relation on that schema shown in Figure 8.14. We must repeat the department name once for each address that an instructor has, and we must repeat the address for each department with which an instructor is associated. This repetition is unnecessary, since the relationship between an instructor and his address is independent of the relationship between that instructor and a department. If an instructor with *ID* 22222 is associated with the Physics department, we want that department to be associated with all of that instructor's addresses. Thus, the relation of Figure 8.15 is illegal. To make this relation legal, we need to add the tuples (Physics, 22222, Main, Manchester) and (Math, 22222, North, Rye) to the relation of Figure 8.15.

Comparing the preceding example with our definition of multivalued dependency, we see that we want the multivalued dependency:

$$ID \rightarrow\!\!\!\rightarrow street, city$$

to hold. (The multivalued dependency *ID* $\rightarrow\!\!\!\rightarrow$ *dept_name* will do as well. We shall soon see that they are equivalent.)

As with functional dependencies, we shall use multivalued dependencies in two ways:

1. To test relations to determine whether they are legal under a given set of functional and multivalued dependencies

ID	dept_name	street	city
22222	Physics	North	Rye
22222	Physics	Main	Manchester
12121	Finance	Lake	Horseneck

Figure 8.14 An example of redundancy in a relation on a BCNF schema.

ID	dept_name	street	city
22222	Physics	North	Rye
22222	Math	Main	Manchester

Figure 8.15 An illegal r_2 relation.

2. To specify constraints on the set of legal relations; we shall thus concern ourselves with *only* those relations that satisfy a given set of functional and multivalued dependencies

Note that, if a relation r fails to satisfy a given multivalued dependency, we can construct a relation r' that *does* satisfy the multivalued dependency by adding tuples to r.

Let D denote a set of functional and multivalued dependencies. The **closure** D^+ of D is the set of all functional and multivalued dependencies logically implied by D. As we did for functional dependencies, we can compute D^+ from D, using the formal definitions of functional dependencies and multivalued dependencies. We can manage with such reasoning for very simple multivalued dependencies. Luckily, multivalued dependencies that occur in practice appear to be quite simple. For complex dependencies, it is better to reason about sets of dependencies by using a system of inference rules.

From the definition of multivalued dependency, we can derive the following rules for $\alpha, \beta \subseteq R$:

- If $\alpha \to \beta$, then $\alpha \twoheadrightarrow \beta$. In other words, every functional dependency is also a multivalued dependency.

- If $\alpha \twoheadrightarrow \beta$, then $\alpha \twoheadrightarrow R - \alpha - \beta$

Appendix C.1.1 outlines a system of inference rules for multivalued dependencies.

8.6.2 Fourth Normal Form

Consider again our example of the BCNF schema:

$$r_2 \, (ID, dept\_name, street, city)$$

in which the multivalued dependency "$ID \twoheadrightarrow street, city$" holds. We saw in the opening paragraphs of Section 8.6 that, although this schema is in BCNF, the design is not ideal, since we must repeat an instructor's address information for each department. We shall see that we can use the given multivalued dependency to improve the database design, by decomposing this schema into a **fourth normal form** decomposition.

A relation schema $r(R)$ is in **fourth normal form** (4NF) with respect to a set D of functional and multivalued dependencies if, for all multivalued dependencies in D^+ of the form $\alpha \twoheadrightarrow \beta$, where $\alpha \subseteq R$ and $\beta \subseteq R$, at least one of the following holds:

- $\alpha \twoheadrightarrow \beta$ is a trivial multivalued dependency.
- α is a superkey for R.

A database design is in 4NF if each member of the set of relation schemas that constitutes the design is in 4NF.

Note that the definition of 4NF differs from the definition of BCNF in only the use of multivalued dependencies. Every 4NF schema is in BCNF. To see this fact, we note that, if a schema $r(R)$ is not in BCNF, then there is a nontrivial functional dependency $\alpha \rightarrow \beta$ holding on R, where α is not a superkey. Since $\alpha \rightarrow \beta$ implies $\alpha \twoheadrightarrow \beta$, $r(R)$ cannot be in 4NF.

Let $r(R)$ be a relation schema, and let $r_1(R_1), r_2(R_2), \ldots, r_n(R_n)$ be a decomposition of $r(R)$. To check if each relation schema r_i in the decomposition is in 4NF, we need to find what multivalued dependencies hold on each r_i. Recall that, for a set F of functional dependencies, the restriction F_i of F to R_i is all functional dependencies in F^+ that include *only* attributes of R_i. Now consider a set D of both functional and multivalued dependencies. The **restriction** of D to R_i is the set D_i consisting of:

1.   All functional dependencies in D^+ that include only attributes of R_i.

2.   All multivalued dependencies of the form:

$$\alpha \twoheadrightarrow \beta \cap R_i$$

where $\alpha \subseteq R_i$ and $\alpha \twoheadrightarrow \beta$ is in D^+.

8.6.3   4NF Decomposition

The analogy between 4NF and BCNF applies to the algorithm for decomposing a schema into 4NF. Figure 8.16 shows the 4NF decomposition algorithm. It is identical to the BCNF decomposition algorithm of Figure 8.11, except that it uses multivalued dependencies and uses the restriction of D^+ to R_i.

If we apply the algorithm of Figure 8.16 to (*ID, dept_name, street, city*), we find that *ID* $\twoheadrightarrow$ *dept_name* is a nontrivial multivalued dependency, and *ID* is not a superkey for the schema. Following the algorithm, we replace it by two schemas:

$$r_{21} \ (ID, dept\_name)$$
$$r_{22} \ (ID, street, city)$$

This pair of schemas, which is in 4NF, eliminates the redundancy we encountered earlier.

As was the case when we were dealing solely with functional dependencies, we are interested in decompositions that are lossless and that preserve dependen-

$result := \{R\}$;
$done :=$ false;
compute D^+; Given schema R_i, let D_i denote the restriction of D^+ to R_i
while (**not** *done*) **do**
    if (there is a schema R_i in *result* that is not in 4NF w.r.t. D_i)
        then begin
                let $\alpha \twoheadrightarrow \beta$ be a nontrivial multivalued dependency that holds
                on R_i such that $\alpha \rightarrow R_i$ is not in D_i, and $\alpha \cap \beta = \emptyset$;
                $result := (result - R_i) \cup (R_i - \beta) \cup (\alpha, \beta)$;
        end
    else *done* := true;

Figure 8.16 4NF decomposition algorithm.

cies. The following fact about multivalued dependencies and losslessness shows that the algorithm of Figure 8.16 generates only lossless decompositions:

- Let $r(R)$ be a relation schema, and let D be a set of functional and multivalued dependencies on R. Let $r_1(R_1)$ and $r_2(R_2)$ form a decomposition of R. This decomposition is lossless of R if and only if at least one of the following multivalued dependencies is in D^+:

$$R_1 \cap R_2 \twoheadrightarrow R_1$$
$$R_1 \cap R_2 \twoheadrightarrow R_2$$

Recall that we stated in Section 8.4.4 that, if $R_1 \cap R_2 \rightarrow R_1$ or $R_1 \cap R_2 \rightarrow R_2$, then $r_1(R_1)$ and $r_2(R_2)$ are a lossless decomposition $r(R)$. The preceding fact about multivalued dependencies is a more general statement about losslessness. It says that, for *every* lossless decomposition of $r(R)$ into two schemas $r_1(R_1)$ and $r_2(R_2)$, one of the two dependencies $R_1 \cap R_2 \twoheadrightarrow R_1$ or $R_1 \cap R_2 \twoheadrightarrow R_2$ must hold.

The issue of dependency preservation when we decompose a relation schema becomes more complicated in the presence of multivalued dependencies. Appendix C.1.2 pursues this topic.

8.7   More Normal Forms

The fourth normal form is by no means the "ultimate" normal form. As we saw earlier, multivalued dependencies help us understand and eliminate some forms of repetition of information that cannot be understood in terms of functional dependencies. There are types of constraints called **join dependencies** that generalize multivalued dependencies, and lead to another normal form called **project-join normal form (PJNF)** (PJNF is called **fifth normal form** in some books). There is a class of even more general constraints that leads to a normal form called **domain-key normal form (DKNF)**.

A practical problem with the use of these generalized constraints is that they are not only hard to reason with, but there is also no set of sound and complete inference rules for reasoning about the constraints. Hence PJNF and DKNF are used quite rarely. Appendix C provides more details about these normal forms.

Conspicuous by its absence from our discussion of normal forms is **second normal form** (2NF). We have not discussed it, because it is of historical interest only. We simply define it, and let you experiment with it in Practice Exercise 8.17.

8.8   Database-Design Process

So far we have looked at detailed issues about normal forms and normalization. In this section, we study how normalization fits into the overall database-design process.

Earlier in the chapter, starting in Section 8.3, we assumed that a relation schema $r(R)$ is given, and proceeded to normalize it. There are several ways in which we could have come up with the schema $r(R)$:

1. $r(R)$ could have been generated in converting an E-R diagram to a set of relation schemas.

2. $r(R)$ could have been a single relation schema containing *all* attributes that are of interest. The normalization process then breaks up $r(R)$ into smaller schemas.

3. $r(R)$ could have been the result of an ad-hoc design of relations that we then test to verify that it satisfies a desired normal form.

In the rest of this section, we examine the implications of these approaches. We also examine some practical issues in database design, including denormalization for performance and examples of bad design that are not detected by normalization.

8.8.1   E-R Model and Normalization

When we define an E-R diagram carefully, identifying all entities correctly, the relation schemas generated from the E-R diagram should not need much further normalization. However, there can be functional dependencies between attributes of an entity. For instance, suppose an *instructor* entity set had attributes *dept_name* and *dept_address*, and there is a functional dependency *dept_name* → *dept_address*. We would then need to normalize the relation generated from *instructor*.

Most examples of such dependencies arise out of poor E-R diagram design. In the above example, if we had designed the E-R diagram correctly, we would have created a *department* entity set with attribute *dept_address* and a relationship set between *instructor* and *department*. Similarly, a relationship set involving more than two entity sets may result in a schema that may not be in a desirable normal form. Since most relationship sets are binary, such cases are relatively rare. (In fact, some E-R-diagram variants actually make it difficult or impossible to specify nonbinary relationship sets.)

Functional dependencies can help us detect poor E-R design. If the generated relation schemas are not in desired normal form, the problem can be fixed in the E-R diagram. That is, normalization can be done formally as part of data modeling. Alternatively, normalization can be left to the designer's intuition during E-R modeling, and can be done formally on the relation schemas generated from the E-R model.

A careful reader will have noted that in order for us to illustrate a need for multivalued dependencies and fourth normal form, we had to begin with schemas that were not derived from our E-R design. Indeed, the process of creating an E-R design tends to generate 4NF designs. If a multivalued dependency holds and is not implied by the corresponding functional dependency, it usually arises from one of the following sources:

- A many-to-many relationship set.
- A multivalued attribute of an entity set.

For a many-to-many relationship set each related entity set has its own schema and there is an additional schema for the relationship set. For a multivalued attribute, a separate schema is created consisting of that attribute and the primary key of the entity set (as in the case of the *phone_number* attribute of the entity set *instructor*).

The universal-relation approach to relational database design starts with an assumption that there is one single relation schema containing all attributes of interest. This single schema defines how users and applications interact with the database.

8.8.2 Naming of Attributes and Relationships

A desirable feature of a database design is the **unique-role assumption**, which means that each attribute name has a unique meaning in the database. This prevents us from using the same attribute to mean different things in different schemas. For example, we might otherwise consider using the attribute *number* for phone number in the *instructor* schema and for room number in the *classroom* schema. The join of a relation on schema *instructor* with one on *classroom* is meaningless. While users and application developers can work carefully to ensure use of the right *number* in each circumstance, having a different attribute name for phone number and for room number serves to reduce user errors.

While it is a good idea to keep names for incompatible attributes distinct, if attributes of different relations have the same meaning, it may be a good idea to use the same attribute name. For this reason we used the same attribute name "*name*" for both the *instructor* and the *student* entity sets. If this was not the case (that is, we used different naming conventions for the instructor and student names), then if we wished to generalize these entity sets by creating a *person* entity set, we would have to rename the attribute. Thus, even if we did not currently have a generalization of *student* and *instructor*, if we foresee such a possibility it is best to use the same name in both entity sets (and relations).

Although technically, the order of attribute names in a schema does not matter, it is convention to list primary-key attributes first. This makes reading default output (as from **select** *) easier.

In large database schemas, relationship sets (and schemas derived therefrom) are often named via a concatenation of the names of related entity sets, perhaps with an intervening hyphen or underscore. We have used a few such names, for example *inst_sec* and *student_sec*. We used the names *teaches* and *takes* instead of using the longer concatenated names. This was acceptable since it is not hard for you to remember the associated entity sets for a few relationship sets. We cannot always create relationship-set names by simple concatenation; for example, a manager or works-for relationship between employees would not make much sense if it were called *employee_employee*! Similarly, if there are multiple relationship sets possible between a pair of entity sets, the relationship-set names must include extra parts to identify the relationship set.

Different organizations have different conventions for naming entity sets. For example, we may call an entity set of students *student* or *students*. We have chosen to use the singular form in our database designs. Using either singular or plural is acceptable, as long as the convention is used consistently across all entity sets.

As schemas grow larger, with increasing numbers of relationship sets, using consistent naming of attributes, relationships, and entities makes life much easier for the database designer and application programmers.

8.8.3 Denormalization for Performance

Occasionally database designers choose a schema that has redundant information; that is, it is not normalized. They use the redundancy to improve performance for specific applications. The penalty paid for not using a normalized schema is the extra work (in terms of coding time and execution time) to keep redundant data consistent.

For instance, suppose all course prerequisites have to be displayed along with a course information, every time a course is accessed. In our normalized schema, this requires a join of *course* with *prereq*.

One alternative to computing the join on the fly is to store a relation containing all the attributes of *course* and *prereq*. This makes displaying the "full" course information faster. However, the information for a course is repeated for every course prerequisite, and all copies must be updated by the application, whenever a course prerequisite is added or dropped. The process of taking a normalized schema and making it nonnormalized is called **denormalization**, and designers use it to tune performance of systems to support time-critical operations.

A better alternative, supported by many database systems today, is to use the normalized schema, and additionally store the join of *course* and *prereq* as a materialized view. (Recall that a materialized view is a view whose result is stored in the database and brought up to date when the relations used in the view are updated.) Like denormalization, using materialized views does have space and time overhead; however, it has the advantage that keeping the view up to date is the job of the database system, not the application programmer.

8.8.4   Other Design Issues

There are some aspects of database design that are not addressed by normalization, and can thus lead to bad database design. Data pertaining to time or to ranges of time have several such issues. We give examples here; obviously, such designs should be avoided.

Consider a university database, where we want to store the total number of instructors in each department in different years. A relation *total_inst*(*dept_name*, *year*, *size*) could be used to store the desired information. The only functional dependency on this relation is *dept_name*, *year*→ *size*, and the relation is in BCNF.

An alternative design is to use multiple relations, each storing the size information for a different year. Let us say the years of interest are 2007, 2008, and 2009; we would then have relations of the form *total_inst_2007*, *total_inst_2008*, *total_inst_2009*, all of which are on the schema (*dept_name*, *size*). The only functional dependency here on each relation would be *dept_name* → *size*, so these relations are also in BCNF.

However, this alternative design is clearly a bad idea—we would have to create a new relation every year, and we would also have to write new queries every year, to take each new relation into account. Queries would also be more complicated since they may have to refer to many relations.

Yet another way of representing the same data is to have a single relation *dept_year*(*dept_name*, *total_inst_2007*, *total_inst_2008*, *total_inst_2009*). Here the only functional dependencies are from *dept_name* to the other attributes, and again the relation is in BCNF. This design is also a bad idea since it has problems similar to the previous design—namely we would have to modify the relation schema and write new queries every year. Queries would also be more complicated, since they may have to refer to many attributes.

Representations such as those in the *dept_year* relation, with one column for each value of an attribute, are called **crosstabs**; they are widely used in spreadsheets and reports and in data analysis tools. While such representations are useful for display to users, for the reasons just given, they are not desirable in a database design. SQL includes features to convert data from a normal relational representation to a crosstab, for display, as we discussed in Section 5.6.1.

8.9   Modeling Temporal Data

Suppose we retain data in our university organization showing not only the address of each instructor, but also all former addresses of which the university is aware. We may then ask queries such as "Find all instructors who lived in Princeton in 1981." In this case, we may have multiple addresses for instructors. Each address has an associated start and end date, indicating when the instructor was resident at that address. A special value for the end date, e.g., null, or a value well into the future such as 9999-12-31, can be used to indicate that the instructor is still resident at that address.

In general, **temporal data** are data that have an associated time interval during which they are **valid**.[8] We use the term **snapshot** of data to mean the value of the data at a particular point in time. Thus a snapshot of *course* data gives the values of all attributes, such as title and department, of all courses at a particular point in time.

Modeling temporal data is a challenging problem for several reasons. For example, suppose we have an *instructor* entity set with which we wish to associate a time-varying address. To add temporal information to an address, we would then have to create a multivalued attribute, each of whose values is a composite value containing an address and a time interval. In addition to time-varying attribute values, entities may themselves have an associated valid time. For example, a student entity may have a valid time from the date the student entered the university to the date the student graduated (or left the university). Relationships too may have associated valid times. For example, the *prereq* relationship may record when a course became a prerequisite for another course. We would thus have to add valid time intervals to attribute values, entity sets, and relationship sets. Adding such detail to an E-R diagram makes it very difficult to create and to comprehend. There have been several proposals to extend the E-R notation to specify in a simple manner that an attribute value or relationship is time varying, but there are no accepted standards.

When we track data values across time, functional dependencies that we assumed to hold, such as:

$$ID \rightarrow street, city$$

may no longer hold. The following constraint (expressed in English) would hold instead: "An instructor *ID* has only one *street* and *city* value for any given time *t*."

Functional dependencies that hold at a particular point in time are called temporal functional dependencies. Formally, a **temporal functional dependency** $X \overset{\tau}{\rightarrow} Y$ holds on a relation schema $r(R)$ if, for all legal instances of $r(R)$, all snapshots of r satisfy the functional dependency $X \rightarrow Y$.

We could extend the theory of relational database design to take temporal functional dependencies into account. However, reasoning with regular functional dependencies is difficult enough already, and few designers are prepared to deal with temporal functional dependencies.

In practice, database designers fall back to simpler approaches to designing temporal databases. One commonly used approach is to design the entire database (including E-R design and relational design) ignoring temporal changes (equivalently, taking only a snapshot into consideration). After this, the designer

---

[8]There are other models of temporal data that distinguish between **valid time** and **transaction time**, the latter recording when a fact was recorded in the database. We ignore such details for simplicity.

studies the various relations and decides which relations require temporal variation to be tracked.

The next step is to add valid time information to each such relation, by adding
start and end time as attributes. For example, consider the *course* relation. The
title of the course may change over time, which can be handled by adding a valid
time range; the resultant schema would be

$$course \ (\underline{course\_id}, \ title, \ dept\_name, \ start, \ end)$$

An instance of this relation might have two records (CS-101, "Introduction to Programming", 1985-01-01, 2000-12-31) and (CS-101, "Introduction to C", 2001-01-01,
9999-12-31). If the relation is updated by changing the course title to "Introduction
to Java," the time "9999-12-31" would be updated to the time until which the old
value ("Introduction to C") is valid, and a new tuple would be added containing
the new title ("Introduction to Java"), with an appropriate start time.

If another relation had a foreign key referencing a temporal relation, the
database designer has to decide if the reference is to the current version of the
data or to the data as of a particular point in time. For example, we may extend
the *department* relation to track changes in the building or budget of a department
across time, but a reference from the *instructor* or *student* relation may not care
about the history of the building or budget, but may instead implicitly refer to the
temporally current record for the corresponding *dept_name*. On the other hand, a
record in a student's transcript should refer to the course title at the time when
the student took the course. In this latter case, the referencing relation must also
record time information, to identify a particular record from the *course* relation. In
our example, the *year* and *semester* when the course was taken can be mapped to a
representative time/date value such as midnight of the start date of the semester;
the resulting time/date value is used to identify a particular record from the
temporal version of the *course* relation, from which the *title* is retrieved.

The original primary key for a temporal relation would no longer uniquely
identify a tuple. To resolve this problem, we could add the start and end time
attributes to the primary key. However, some problems remain:

- It is possible to store data with overlapping intervals, which the primary-key
  constraint would not catch. If the system supports a native *valid time* type, it
  can detect and prevent such overlapping time intervals.

- To specify a foreign key referencing such a relation, the referencing tuples
  would have to include the start- and end-time attributes as part of their
  foreign key, and the values must match that in the referenced tuple. Further,
  if the referenced tuple is updated (and the end time which was in the future
  is updated), the update must propagate to all the referencing tuples.

  If the system supports temporal data in a better fashion, we can allow
  the referencing tuple to specify a point in time, rather than a range, and rely
  on the system to ensure that there is a tuple in the referenced relation whose
  valid time interval contains the point in time. For example, a transcript record

may specify a *course_id* and a time (say the start date of a semester), which is enough to identify the correct record in the *course* relation.

As a common special case, if all references to temporal data refer to only the current data, a simpler solution is to not add time information to the relation, but instead create a corresponding *history* relation that has temporal information, for past values. For example, in our bank database, we could use the design we have created, ignoring temporal changes, to store only the current information. All historical information is moved to historical relations. Thus, the *instructor* relation may store only the current address, while a relation *instructor_history* may contain all the attributes of *instructor*, with additional *start_time* and *end_time* attributes.

Although we have not provided any formal way to deal with temporal data, the issues we have discussed and the examples we have provided should help you in designing a database that records temporal data. Further issues in handling temporal data, including temporal queries, are covered later, in Section 25.2.

8.10   Summary

- We showed pitfalls in database design, and how to systematically design a database schema that avoids the pitfalls. The pitfalls included repeated information and inability to represent some information.

- We showed the development of a relational database design from an E-R design, when schemas may be combined safely, and when a schema should be decomposed. All valid decompositions must be lossless.

- We described the assumptions of atomic domains and first normal form.

- We introduced the concept of functional dependencies, and used it to present two normal forms, Boyce–Codd normal form (BCNF) and third normal form (3NF).

- If the decomposition is dependency preserving, given a database update, all functional dependencies can be verifiable from individual relations, without computing a join of relations in the decomposition.

- We showed how to reason with functional dependencies. We placed special emphasis on what dependencies are logically implied by a set of dependencies. We also defined the notion of a canonical cover, which is a minimal set of functional dependencies equivalent to a given set of functional dependencies.

- We outlined an algorithm for decomposing relations into BCNF. There are relations for which there is no dependency-preserving BCNF decomposition.

- We used the canonical covers to decompose a relation into 3NF, which is a small relaxation of the BCNF condition. Relations in 3NF may have some redundancy, but there is always a dependency-preserving decomposition into 3NF.

- We presented the notion of multivalued dependencies, which specify constraints that cannot be specified with functional dependencies alone. We defined fourth normal form (4NF) with multivalued dependencies. Appendix C.1.1 gives details on reasoning about multivalued dependencies.

- Other normal forms, such as PJNF and DKNF, eliminate more subtle forms of redundancy. However, these are hard to work with and are rarely used. Appendix C gives details on these normal forms.

- In reviewing the issues in this chapter, note that the reason we could define rigorous approaches to relational database design is that the relational data model rests on a firm mathematical foundation. That is one of the primary advantages of the relational model compared with the other data models that we have studied.

Review Terms

- E-R model and normalization
- Decomposition
- Functional dependencies
- Lossless decomposition
- Atomic domains
- First normal form (1NF)
- Legal relations
- Superkey
- R satisfies F
- F holds on R
- Boyce–Codd normal form (BCNF)
- Dependency preservation
- Third normal form (3NF)
- Trivial functional dependencies
- Closure of a set of functional dependencies

- Armstrong's axioms
- Closure of attribute sets
- Restriction of F to R_i
- Canonical cover
- Extraneous attributes
- BCNF decomposition algorithm
- 3NF decomposition algorithm
- Multivalued dependencies
- Fourth normal form (4NF)
- Restriction of a multivalued dependency
- Project-join normal form (PJNF)
- Domain-key normal form (DKNF)
- Universal relation
- Unique-role assumption
- Denormalization

Practice Exercises

8.1 Suppose that we decompose the schema $r(A, B, C, D, E)$ into

$$r_1(A, B, C)$$
$$r_2(A, D, E)$$

Show that this decomposition is a lossless decomposition if the following set F of functional dependencies holds:

$$A \rightarrow BC$$
$$CD \rightarrow E$$
$$B \rightarrow D$$
$$E \rightarrow A$$

8.2 List all functional dependencies satisfied by the relation of Figure 8.17.

8.3 Explain how functional dependencies can be used to indicate the following:

- A one-to-one relationship set exists between entity sets *student* and *instructor*.

- A many-to-one relationship set exists between entity sets *student* and *instructor*.

8.4 Use Armstrong's axioms to prove the soundness of the union rule. (*Hint*: Use the augmentation rule to show that, if $\alpha \rightarrow \beta$, then $\alpha \rightarrow \alpha\beta$. Apply the augmentation rule again, using $\alpha \rightarrow \gamma$, and then apply the transitivity rule.)

8.5 Use Armstrong's axioms to prove the soundness of the pseudotransitivity rule.

8.6 Compute the closure of the following set F of functional dependencies for relation schema $r\ (A,\ B,\ C,\ D,\ E)$.

$$A \rightarrow BC$$
$$CD \rightarrow E$$
$$B \rightarrow D$$
$$E \rightarrow A$$

List the candidate keys for R.

8.7 Using the functional dependencies of Practice Exercise 8.6, compute the canonical cover F_c.

A	B	C
a_1	b_1	c_1
a_1	b_1	c_2
a_2	b_1	c_1
a_2	b_1	c_3

Figure 8.17   Relation of Practice Exercise 8.2.

8.8   Consider the algorithm in Figure 8.18 to compute α^+. Show that this algorithm is more efficient than the one presented in Figure 8.8 (Section 8.4.2) and that it computes α^+ correctly.

8.9   Given the database schema $R(a, b, c)$, and a relation r on the schema R, write an SQL query to test whether the functional dependency $b \rightarrow c$ holds on relation r. Also write an SQL assertion that enforces the functional dependency; assume that no null values are present. (Although part of the SQL standard, such assertions are not supported by any database implementation currently.)

8.10   Our discussion of lossless-join decomposition implicitly assumed that attributes on the left-hand side of a functional dependency cannot take on null values. What could go wrong on decomposition, if this property is violated?

8.11   In the BCNF decomposition algorithm, suppose you use a functional dependency $\alpha \rightarrow \beta$ to decompose a relation schema $r(\alpha, \beta, \gamma)$ into $r_1(\alpha, \beta)$ and $r_2(\alpha, \gamma)$.

    a.   What primary and foreign-key constraint do you expect to hold on the decomposed relations?

    b.   Give an example of an inconsistency that can arise due to an erroneous update, if the foreign-key constraint were not enforced on the decomposed relations above.

    c.   When a relation is decomposed into 3NF using the algorithm in Section 8.5.2, what primary and foreign key dependencies would you expect will hold on the decomposed schema?

8.12   Let R_1, $R_2, \ldots, R_n$ be a decomposition of schema U. Let $u(U)$ be a relation, and let $r_i = \Pi_{R_i}(u)$. Show that

$$u \subseteq r_1 \bowtie r_2 \bowtie \cdots \bowtie r_n$$

8.13   Show that the decomposition in Practice Exercise 8.1 is not a dependency-preserving decomposition.

8.14   Show that it is possible to ensure that a dependency-preserving decomposition into 3NF is a lossless decomposition by guaranteeing that at least one schema contains a candidate key for the schema being decomposed. (*Hint*: Show that the join of all the projections onto the schemas of the decomposition cannot have more tuples than the original relation.)

8.15   Give an example of a relation schema R' and set F' of functional dependencies such that there are at least three distinct lossless decompositions of R' into BCNF.

$result := \emptyset;$
/* *fdcount* is an array whose *i*th element contains the number
of attributes on the left side of the *i*th *FD* that are
not yet known to be in α^+ */
for $i := 1$ **to** $|F|$ **do**
    begin
        let $\beta \rightarrow \gamma$ denote the *i*th *FD*;
        fdcount $[i] := |\beta|;$
    end
/* *appears* is an array with one entry for each attribute. The
entry for attribute A is a list of integers. Each integer
i on the list indicates that A appears on the left side
of the *i*th *FD* */
for each attribute A **do**
    begin
        appears $[A] := NIL;$
        for $i := 1$ **to** $|F|$ **do**
            begin
                let $\beta \rightarrow \gamma$ denote the *i*th *FD*;
                if $A \in \beta$ **then** add i to *appears* $[A];$
            end
    end
addin $(\alpha);$
return $(result);$

procedure addin $(\alpha);$
for each attribute A in α **do**
    begin
        if $A \notin result$ **then**
            begin
                $result := result \cup \{A\};$
                for each element i of *appears*$[A]$ **do**
                    begin
                        fdcount $[i] := fdcount [i] - 1;$
                        if *fdcount* $[i] := 0$ **then**
                            begin
                                let $\beta \rightarrow \gamma$ denote the *i*th *FD*;
                                addin $(\gamma);$
                          end
                    end
            end
    end

Figure 8.18 An algorithm to compute α^+.

8.16   Let a **prime** attribute be one that appears in at least one candidate key. Let α and β be sets of attributes such that $\alpha \rightarrow \beta$ holds, but $\beta \rightarrow \alpha$ does not hold. Let A be an attribute that is not in α, is not in β, and for which $\beta \rightarrow A$ holds. We say that A is **transitively dependent** on α. We can restate our definition of 3NF as follows: *A relation schema R is in 3NF with respect to a set F of functional dependencies if there are no nonprime attributes A in R for which A is transitively dependent on a key for R.* Show that this new definition is equivalent to the original one.

8.17   A functional dependency $\alpha \rightarrow \beta$ is called a **partial dependency** if there is a proper subset γ of α such that $\gamma \rightarrow \beta$. We say that β is *partially dependent* on α. A relation schema R is in **second normal form** (2NF) if each attribute A in R meets one of the following criteria:

- It appears in a candidate key.
- It is not partially dependent on a candidate key.

Show that every 3NF schema is in 2NF. (*Hint*: Show that every partial dependency is a transitive dependency.)

8.18   Give an example of a relation schema R and a set of dependencies such that R is in BCNF but is not in 4NF.

Exercises

8.19   Give a lossless-join decomposition into BCNF of schema R of Practice Exercise 8.1.

8.20   Give a lossless-join, dependency-preserving decomposition into 3NF of schema R of Practice Exercise 8.1.

8.21   Normalize the following schema, with given constraints, to 4NF.

$$books(accessionno, isbn, title, author, publisher)$$
$$users(userid, name, deptid, deptname)$$
$$accessionno \rightarrow isbn$$
$$isbn \rightarrow title$$
$$isbn \rightarrow publisher$$
$$isbn \rightarrow\!\!\!\rightarrow author$$
$$userid \rightarrow name$$
$$userid \rightarrow deptid$$
$$deptid \rightarrow deptname$$

8.22   Explain what is meant by *repetition of information* and *inability to represent information*. Explain why each of these properties may indicate a bad relational database design.

8.23 Why are certain functional dependencies called *trivial* functional dependencies?

8.24 Use the definition of functional dependency to argue that each of Armstrong's axioms (reflexivity, augmentation, and transitivity) is sound.

8.25 Consider the following proposed rule for functional dependencies: If $\alpha \to \beta$ and $\gamma \to \beta$, then $\alpha \to \gamma$. Prove that this rule is *not* sound by showing a relation r that satisfies $\alpha \to \beta$ and $\gamma \to \beta$, but does not satisfy $\alpha \to \gamma$.

8.26 Use Armstrong's axioms to prove the soundness of the decomposition rule.

8.27 Using the functional dependencies of Practice Exercise 8.6, compute B^+.

8.28 Show that the following decomposition of the schema R of Practice Exercise 8.1 is not a lossless decomposition:

$$(A, B, C)$$
$$(C, D, E)$$

Hint: Give an example of a relation r on schema R such that

$$\Pi_{A,B,C}(r) \bowtie \Pi_{C,D,E}(r) \neq r$$

8.29 Consider the following set F of functional dependencies on the relation schema $r(A, B, C, D, E, F)$:

$$A \to BCD$$
$$BC \to DE$$
$$B \to D$$
$$D \to A$$

a. Compute B^+.

b. Prove (using Armstrong's axioms) that AF is a superkey.

c. Compute a canonical cover for the above set of functional dependencies F; give each step of your derivation with an explanation.

d. Give a 3NF decomposition of r based on the canonical cover.

e. Give a BCNF decomposition of r using the original set of functional dependencies.

f. Can you get the same BCNF decomposition of r as above, using the canonical cover?

8.30 List the three design goals for relational databases, and explain why each is desirable.

8.31   In designing a relational database, why might we choose a non-BCNF design?

8.32   Given the three goals of relational database design, is there any reason to design a database schema that is in 2NF, but is in no higher-order normal form? (See Practice Exercise 8.17 for the definition of 2NF.)

8.33   Given a relational schema $r(A, B, C, D)$, does $A \twoheadrightarrow BC$ logically imply $A \twoheadrightarrow B$ and $A \twoheadrightarrow C$? If yes prove it, else give a counter example.

8.34   Explain why 4NF is a normal form more desirable than BCNF.

Bibliographical Notes

The first discussion of relational database design theory appeared in an early paper by Codd [1970]. In that paper, Codd also introduced functional dependencies and first, second, and third normal forms.

Armstrong's axioms were introduced in Armstrong [1974]. Significant development of relational database theory occurred in the late 1970s. These results are collected in several texts on database theory including Maier [1983], Atzeni and Antonellis [1993], and Abiteboul et al. [1995].

BCNF was introduced in Codd [1972]. Biskup et al. [1979] give the algorithm we used to find a lossless dependency-preserving decomposition into 3NF. Fundamental results on the lossless decomposition property appear in Aho et al. [1979a].

Beeri et al. [1977] gives a set of axioms for multivalued dependencies, and proves that the authors' axioms are sound and complete. The notions of 4NF, PJNF, and DKNF are from Fagin [1977], Fagin [1979], and Fagin [1981], respectively. See the bibliographical notes of Appendix C for further references to literature on normalization.

Jensen et al. [1994] presents a glossary of temporal-database concepts. A survey of extensions to E-R modeling to handle temporal data is presented by Gregersen and Jensen [1999]. Tansel et al. [1993] covers temporal database theory, design, and implementation. Jensen et al. [1996] describes extensions of dependency theory to temporal data.

CHAPTER 9

Application Design and Development

Practically all use of databases occurs from within application programs. Correspondingly, almost all user interaction with databases is indirect, via application programs. Not surprisingly, therefore, database systems have long supported tools such as form and GUI builders, which help in rapid development of applications that interface with users. In recent years, the Web has become the most widely used user interface to databases.

In this chapter, we study tools and technologies that are used to build applications, focussing on interactive applications that use databases to store data.

After an introduction to application programs and user interfaces in Section 9.1, we focus on developing applications with Web-based interfaces. We start with an overview of Web technologies in Section 9.2, and discuss the Java Servlets technology, which is widely used for building Web applications, in Section 9.3. A short overview of Web application architectures in presented Section 9.4. In Section 9.5, we discuss tools for rapid application development, while in Section 9.6 we cover performance issues in building large Web applications. In Section 9.7, we discuss issues in application security. We conclude the chapter with Section 9.8, which covers encryption and its use in applications.

9.1 Application Programs and User Interfaces

Although many people interact with databases, very few people use a query language to interact with a database system directly. The most common way in which users interact with databases is through an application program that provides a user interface at the front end, and interfaces with a database at the back end. Such applications take input from users, typically through a forms-based interface, and either enter data into a database or extract information from a database based on the user input, and generate output, which is displayed to the user.

As an example of an application, consider a university registration system. Like other such applications, the registration system first requires you to identify

---

375

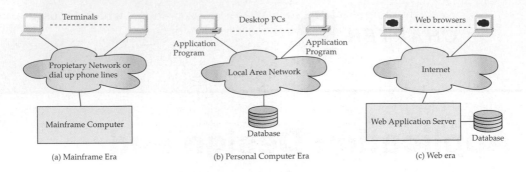

Figure 9.1 Application architectures in different eras

and authenticate yourself, typically by a user name and password. The application then uses your identity to extract information, such as your name and the courses for which you have registered, from the database and displays the information. The application provides a number of interfaces that let you register for courses and query a variety of other information such as course and instructor information. Organizations use such applications to automate a variety of tasks, such as sales, purchases, accounting and payroll, human-resources management, and inventory management, among many others.

Application programs may be used even when it is not apparent that they are being used. For example, a news site may provide a page that is transparently customized to individual users, even if the user does not explicitly fill any forms when interacting with the site. To do so, it actually runs an application program that generates a customized page for each user; customization can, for example, be based on the history of articles browsed by the user.

A typical application program includes a front-end component, which deals with the user interface, a back-end component, which communicates with a database, and a middle layer, which contains "business logic," that is, code that executes specific requests for information or updates, enforcing rules of business such as what actions should be carried out to execute a given task, or who can carry out what task.

Application architectures have evolved over time, as illustrated in Figure 9.1. Applications such as airline reservations have been around since the 1960s. In the early days of computer applications, applications ran on a large "mainframe" computer, and users interacted with the application through terminals, some of which even supported forms.

With the widespread use of personal computers, many organizations used a different architecture for internal applications, with applications running on the user's computer, and accessing a central database. This architecture, often called a "client–server" architecture, allowed the creation of powerful graphical user interfaces, which earlier terminal-based applications did not support. However, software had to be installed on each user's machine to run an application, making tasks such as upgrades harder. Even in the personal computer era, when client–server architectures became popular, mainframe architecture continued to be the choice for applications such as airline reservations, which are used from a large number of geographically distributed locations.

In the past 15 years, Web browsers have become the *universal front end* to database applications, connecting to the back end through the Internet. Browsers use a standardized syntax, the **HyperText Markup Language (HTML)** standard, which supports both formatted display of information, and creation of forms-based interfaces. The HTML standard is independent of the operating system or browser, and pretty much every computer today has a Web browser installed. Thus a Web-based application can be accessed from any computer that is connected to the Internet.

Unlike client–server architectures, there is no need to install any application-specific software on client machines in order to use Web-based applications. However, sophisticated user interfaces, supporting features well beyond what is possible using plain HTML, are now widely used, and are built with the scripting language JavaScript, which is supported by most Web browsers. JavaScript programs, unlike programs written in C, can be run in a safe mode, guaranteeing they cannot cause security problems. JavaScript programs are downloaded transparently to the browser and do not need any explicit software installation on the user's computer.

While the Web browser provides the front end for user interaction, application programs constitute the back end. Typically, requests from a browser are sent to a Web server, which in turn executes an application program to process the request. A variety of technologies are available for creating application programs that run at the back end, including Java servlets, Java Server Pages (JSP), Active Server Page (ASP), or scripting languages such as PHP, Perl, or Python.

In the rest of this chapter, we describe how to build such applications, starting with Web technologies and tools for building Web interfaces, and technologies for building application programs, and then covering application architectures, and performance and security issues in building applications.

9.2   Web Fundamentals

In this section, we review some of the fundamental technology behind the World Wide Web, for readers who are not familiar with the technology underlying the Web.

9.2.1   Uniform Resource Locators

A **uniform resource locator (URL)** is a globally unique name for each document that can be accessed on the Web. An example of a URL is:

http://www.acm.org/sigmod

The first part of the URL indicates how the document is to be accessed: "http" indicates that the document is to be accessed by the **HyperText Transfer Protocol**

```
<html>
<body>
<table border>
<tr> <th>ID</th>        <th>Name</th>      <th>Department</th> </tr>
<tr> <td>00128</td> <td>Zhang</td>    <td>Comp. Sci.</td> </tr>
<tr> <td>12345</td> <td>Shankar</td> <td>Comp. Sci.</td> </tr>
<tr> <td>19991</td> <td>Brandt</td>    <td>History</td> </tr>
</table>
</body>
</html>
```

Figure 9.2   Tabular data in HTML format.

(HTTP), which is a protocol for transferring HTML documents. The second part gives the name of a machine that has a Web server. The rest of the URL is the path name of the file on the machine, or other unique identifier of a document within the machine.

A URL can contain the identifier of a program located on the Web server machine, as well as arguments to be given to the program. An example of such a URL is

http://www.google.com/search?q=silberschatz

which says that the program search on the server www.google.com should be executed with the argument q=silberschatz. On receiving a request for such a URL, the Web server executes the program, using the given arguments. The program returns an HTML document to the Web server, which sends it back to the front end.

9.2.2   HyperText Markup Language

Figure 9.2 is an example of a table represented in the HTML format, while Figure 9.3 shows the displayed image generated by a browser from the HTML representation of the table. The HTML source shows a few of the HTML tags. Every HTML page should be enclosed in an html tag, while the body of the page is enclosed in a body tag. A table is specified by a table tag, which contains rows specified by a tr tag. The header row of the table has table cells specified by a th tag, while regular

ID	Name	Department
00128	Zhang	Comp. Sci.
12345	Shankar	Comp. Sci.
19991	Brandt	History

Figure 9.3   Display of HTML source from Figure 9.2.

```
<html>
<body>
<form action="PersonQuery" method=get>
Search for:
<select name="persontype">
        <option value="student" selected>Student </option>
        <option value="instructor"> Instructor </option>
</select> <br>
Name: <input type=text size=20 name="name">
<input type=submit value="submit">
</form>
</body>
</html>
```

Figure 9.4 An HTML form.

rows have table cells specified by a td tag. We do not go into more details about the tags here; see the bibliographic notes for references containing more detailed descriptions of HTML.

Figure 9.4 shows how to specify an HTML form that allows users to select the person type (student or instructor) from a menu and to input a number in a text box. Figure 9.5 shows how the above form is displayed in a Web browser. Two methods of accepting input are illustrated in the form, but HTML also supports several other input methods. The action attribute of the form tag specifies that when the form is submitted (by clicking on the submit button), the form data should be sent to the URL PersonQuery (the URL is relative to that of the page). The Web server is configured such that when this URL is accessed, a corresponding application program is invoked, with the user-provided values for the arguments persontype and name (specified in the select and input fields). The application program generates an HTML document, which is then sent back and displayed to the user; we shall see how to construct such programs later in this chapter.

HTTP defines two ways in which values entered by a user at the browser can be sent to the Web server. The get method encodes the values as part of the URL. For example, if the Google search page used a form with an input parameter named q with the get method, and the user typed in the string "silberschatz" and submitted the form, the browser would request the following URL from the Web server:

http://www.google.com/search?q=silberschatz

Search for: Student :
Name:
submit

Figure 9.5 Display of HTML source from Figure 9.4.

The post method would instead send a request for the URL http://www.google.com, and send the parameter values as part of the HTTP protocol exchange between the Web server and the browser. The form in Figure 9.4 specifies that the form uses the get method.

Although HTML code can be created using a plain text editor, there are a number of editors that permit direct creation of HTML text by using a graphical interface. Such editors allow constructs such as forms, menus, and tables to be inserted into the HTML document from a menu of choices, instead of manually typing in the code to generate the constructs.

HTML supports *stylesheets*, which can alter the default definitions of how an HTML formatting construct is displayed, as well as other display attributes such as background color of the page. The *cascading stylesheet* (CSS) standard allows the same stylesheet to be used for multiple HTML documents, giving a distinctive but uniform look to all the pages on a Web site.

9.2.3 Web Servers and Sessions

A **Web server** is a program running on the server machine, which accepts requests from a Web browser and sends back results in the form of HTML documents. The browser and Web server communicate via HTTP. Web servers provide powerful features, beyond the simple transfer of documents. The most important feature is the ability to execute programs, with arguments supplied by the user, and to deliver the results back as an HTML document.

As a result, a Web server can act as an intermediary to provide access to a variety of information services. A new service can be created by creating and installing an application program that provides the service. The **common gateway interface (CGI)** standard defines how the Web server communicates with application programs. The application program typically communicates with a database server, through ODBC, JDBC, or other protocols, in order to get or store data.

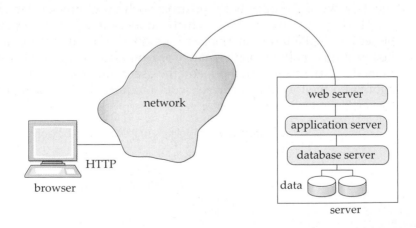

Figure 9.6 Three-layer Web application architecture.

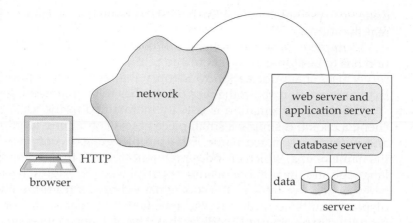

Figure 9.7 Two-layer Web application architecture.

Figure 9.6 shows a Web application built using a three-layer architecture, with a Web server, an application server, and a database server. Using multiple levels of servers increases system overhead; the CGI interface starts a new process to service each request, which results in even greater overhead.

Most Web applications today therefore use a two-layer Web application architecture, where the application program runs within the Web server, as in Figure 9.7. We study systems based on the two-layer architecture in more detail in subsequent sections.

There is no continuous connection between the client and the Web server; when a Web server receives a request, a connection is temporarily created to send the request and receive the response from the Web server. But the connection may then be closed, and the next request could come over a new connection. In contrast, when a user logs on to a computer, or connects to a database using ODBC or JDBC, a session is created, and session information is retained at the server and the client until the session is terminated—information such as the user-identifier of the user and session options that the user has set. One important reason that HTTP is **connectionless** is that most computers have limits on the number of simultaneous connections they can accommodate, and if a large number of sites on the Web open connections to a single server, this limit would be exceeded, denying service to further users. With a connectionless protocol, the connection can be broken as soon as a request is satisfied, leaving connections available for other requests.[1]

Most Web applications, however, need session information to allow meaningful user interaction. For instance, applications typically restrict access to information, and therefore need to authenticate users. Authentication should be

---

[1]For performance reasons, connections may be kept open for a short while, to allow subsequent requests to reuse the connection. However, there is no guarantee that the connection will be kept open, and applications must be designed assuming the connection may be closed as soon as a request is serviced.

done once per session, and further interactions in the session should not require reauthentication.

To implement sessions in spite of connections getting closed, extra information has to be stored at the client and returned with each request in a session; the server uses this information to identify that a request is part of a user session. Extra information about the session also has to be maintained at the server.

This extra information is usually maintained in the form of a **cookie** at the client; a cookie is simply a small piece of text containing identifying information and with an associated name. For example, google.com may set a cookie with the name prefs, which encodes preferences set by the user such as the preferred language and the number of answers displayed per page. On each search request, google.com can retrieve the cookie named prefs from the user's browser, and display results according to the specified preferences. A domain (Web site) is permitted to retrieve only cookies that it has set, not cookies set by other domains, and cookie names can be reused across domains.

For the purpose of tracking a user session, an application may generate a session identifier (usually a random number not currently in use as a session identifier), and send a cookie named (for instance) sessionid containing the session identifier. The session identifier is also stored locally at the server. When a request comes in, the application server requests the cookie named sessionid from the client. If the client does not have the cookie stored, or returns a value that is not currently recorded as a valid session identifier at the server, the application concludes that the request is not part of a current session. If the cookie value matches a stored session identifier, the request is identified as part of an ongoing session.

If an application needs to identify users securely, it can set the cookie only after authenticating the user; for example a user may be authenticated only when a valid user name and password are submitted.[2]

For applications that do not require high security, such as publicly available news sites, cookies can be stored permanently at the browser and at the server; they identify the user on subsequent visits to the same site, without any identification information being typed in. For applications that require higher security, the server may invalidate (drop) the session after a time-out period, or when the user logs out. (Typically a user logs out by clicking on a logout button, which submits a logout form, whose action is to invalidate the current session.) Invalidating a session merely consists of dropping the session identifier from the list of active sessions at the application server.

---

[2]The user identifier could be stored at the client end, in a cookie named, for example, userid. Such cookies can be used for low-security applications, such as free Web sites identifying their users. However, for applications that require a higher level of security, such a mechanism creates a security risk: The value of a cookie can be changed at the browser by a malicious user, who can then masquerade as a different user. Setting a cookie (named sessionid, for example) to a randomly generated session identifier (from a large space of numbers) makes it highly improbable that a user can masquerade as (that is, pretend to be) another user. A sequentially generated session identifier, on the other hand, would be susceptible to masquerading.

9.3   Servlets and JSP

In a two-layer Web architecture, an application runs as part of the Web server itself. One way of implementing such an architecture is to load Java programs into the Web server. The Java **servlet** specification defines an application programming interface for communication between the Web server and the application program. The HttpServlet class in Java implements the servlet API specification; servlet classes used to implement specific functions are defined as subclasses of this class.[3] Often the word *servlet* is used to refer to a Java program (and class) that implements the servlet interface. Figure 9.8 shows a servlet example; we explain it in detail shortly.

The code for a servlet is loaded into the Web server when the server is started, or when the server receives a remote HTTP request to execute a particular servlet. The task of a servlet is to process such a request, which may involve accessing a database to retrieve necessary information, and dynamically generate an HTML page to be returned to the client browser.

9.3.1   A Servlet Example

Servlets are commonly used to generate dynamic responses to HTTP requests. They can access inputs provided through HTML forms, apply "business logic" to decide what response to provide, and then generate HTML output to be sent back to the browser.

Figure 9.8 shows an example of servlet code to implement the form in Figure 9.4. The servlet is called PersonQueryServlet, while the form specifies that "action="PersonQuery"." The Web server must be told that this servlet is to be used to handle requests for PersonQuery. The form specifies that the HTTP get mechanism is used for transmitting parameters. So the doGet() method of the servlet, as defined in the code, is invoked.

Each request results in a new thread within which the call is executed, so multiple requests can be handled in parallel. Any values from the form menus and input fields on the Web page, as well as cookies, pass through an object of the HttpServletRequest class that is created for the request, and the reply to the request passes through an object of the class HttpServletResponse.

The doGet() method in the example extracts values of the parameter's type and number by using request.getParameter(), and uses these values to run a query against a database. The code used to access the database and to get attribute values from the query result is not shown; refer to Section 5.1.1.4 for details of how to use JDBC to access a database. The servlet code returns the results of the query to the requester by outputting them to the HttpServletResponse object response. Outputting the results is to response is implemented by first getting a PrintWriter object out from response, and then printing the result in HTML format to out.

---

[3]The servlet interface can also support non-HTTP requests, although our example uses only HTTP.

```
import java.io.*;
import javax.servlet.*;
import javax.servlet.http.*;

public class PersonQueryServlet extends HttpServlet {
    public void doGet(HttpServletRequest request,
                      HttpServletResponse response)
        throws ServletException, IOException
    {
        response.setContentType("text/html");
        PrintWriter out = response.getWriter();
        out.println("<HEAD><TITLE> Query Result</TITLE></HEAD>");
        out.println("<BODY>");

        String persontype = request.getParameter("persontype");
        String number = request.getParameter("name");
        if(persontype.equals("student")) {
            ... code to find students with the specified name ...
            ... using JDBC to communicate with the database ..
            out.println("<table BORDER COLS=3>");
            out.println(" <tr> <td>ID</td> <td>Name: </td>" +
                " <td>Department</td> </tr>");
            for(... each result ...){
                ... retrieve ID, name and dept_name
                ... into variables ID, name and deptname
                out.println("<tr> <td>" + ID + "</td>" +
                    "<td>" + name + "</td>" +
                    "<td>" + deptname + "</td></tr>");
            };
            out.println("</table>");
        }
        else {
            ... as above, but for instructors ...
        }
        out.println("</BODY>");
        out.close();
    }
}
```

Figure 9.8 Example of servlet code.

9.3.2 Servlet Sessions

Recall that the interaction between a browser and a Web server is stateless. That is, each time the browser makes a request to the server, the browser needs to connect to the server, request some information, then disconnect from the server. Cookies can be used to recognize that a request is from the same browser session as an earlier request. However, cookies form a low-level mechanism, and programmers require a better abstraction to deal with sessions.

The servlet API provides a method of tracking a session and storing information pertaining to it. Invocation of the method getSession(false) of the class HttpServletRequest retrieves the HttpSession object corresponding to the browser that sent the request. An argument value of true would have specified that a new session object must be created if the request is a new request.

When the getSession() method is invoked, the server first asks the client to return a cookie with a specified name. If the client does not have a cookie of that name, or returns a value that does not match any ongoing session, then the request is not part of an ongoing session. In this case, getSession() would return a null value, and the servlet could direct the user to a login page.

The login page could allow the user to provide a user name and password. The servlet corresponding to the login page could verify that the password matches the user (for example, by looking up authentication information in the database). If the user is properly authenticated, the login servlet would execute getSession(true), which would return a new session object. To create a new session the Web server would internally carry out the following tasks: set a cookie (called, for example, sessionId) with a session identifier as its associated value at the client browser, create a new session object, and associate the session identifier value with the session object.

The servlet code can also store and look up (attribute-name, value) pairs in the HttpSession object, to maintain state across multiple requests within a session. For example, after the user is authenticated and the session object has been created, the login servlet could store the user-id of the user as a session parameter by executing the method

```
session.setAttribute("userid", userid)
```

on the session object returned by getSession(); the Java variable userid is assumed to contain the user identifier.

If the request was part of an ongoing session, the browser would have returned the cookie value, and the corresponding session object is returned by getSession(). The servlet can then retrieve session parameters such as user-id from the session object by executing the method

```
session.getAttribute("userid")
```

on the session object returned above. If the attribute userid is not set, the function would return a null value, which would indicate that the client user has not been authenticated.

9.3.3 Servlet Life Cycle

The life cycle of a servlet is controlled by the Web server in which the servlet has been deployed. When there is a client request for a specific servlet, the server first checks if an instance of the servlet exists or not. If not, the Web server loads the servlet class into the Java virtual machine (JVM), and creates an instance of the servlet class. In addition, the server calls the init() method to initialize the servlet instance. Notice that each servlet instance is initialized only once when it is loaded.

After making sure the servlet instance does exist, the server invokes the service method of the servlet, with a request object and a response object as parameters. By default, the server creates a new thread to execute the service method; thus, multiple requests on a servlet can execute in parallel, without having to wait for earlier requests to complete execution. The service method calls doGet or doPost as appropriate.

When no longer required, a servlet can be shut down by calling the destroy() method. The server can be set up to automatically shut down a servlet if no requests have been made on a servlet within a time-out period; the time-out period is a server parameter that can be set as appropriate for the application.

9.3.4 Servlet Support

Many application servers provide built-in support for servlets. One of the most popular is the Tomcat Server from the Apache Jakarta Project. Other application servers that support servlets include Glassfish, JBoss, BEA Weblogic Application Server, Oracle Application Server, and IBM's WebSphere Application Server.

The best way to develop servlet applications is by using an IDE such as Eclipse or NetBeans, which come with Tomcat or Glassfish servers built in.

Application servers usually provide a variety of useful services, in addition to basic servlet support. They allow applications to be deployed or stopped, and provide functionality to monitor the status of the application server, including performance statistics. If a servlet file is modified, some application servers can detect this and recompile and reload the servlet transparently. Many application servers also allow the server to run on multiple machines in parallel to improve performance, and route requests to an appropriate copy. Many application servers also support the Java 2 Enterprise Edition (J2EE) platform, which provides support and APIs for a variety of tasks, such as for handling objects, parallel processing across multiple application servers, and for handling XML data (XML is described later in Chapter 23).

9.3.5 Server-Side Scripting

Writing even a simple Web application in a programming language such as Java or C is a time-consuming task that requires many lines of code and programmers who are familiar with the intricacies of the language. An alternative approach, that of **server-side scripting**, provides a much easier method for creating many applications. Scripting languages provide constructs that can be embedded within HTML documents. In server-side scripting, before delivering a Web page, the server executes the scripts embedded within the HTML contents of the page. Each piece of script, when executed, can generate text that is added to the page (or may even delete content from the page). The source code of the scripts is removed

```
<html>
<head> <title> Hello </title> </head>
<body>
  < % if (request.getParameter("name") == null)
    { out.println("Hello World"); }
    else { out.println("Hello, " + request.getParameter("name")); }
  %>
</body>
</html>
```

Figure 9.9 A JSP page with embedded Java code.

from the page, so the client may not even be aware that the page originally had any code in it. The executed script may contain SQL code that is executed against a database.

Some of the widely used scripting languages include Java Server Pages (JSP) from Sun, Active Server Pages (ASP) and its successor ASP.NET from Microsoft, the PHP scripting language, the ColdFusion Markup Language (CFML), and Ruby on Rails. Many scripting languages also allow code written in languages such as Java, C#, VBScript, Perl, and Python to be embedded into or invoked from HTML pages. For instance, JSP allows Java code to be embedded in HTML pages, while Microsoft's ASP.NET and ASP support embedded C# and VBScript. Many of these languages come with libraries and tools, that together constitute a framework for Web application development.

We briefly describe below **Java Server Pages** (JSP), a scripting language that allows HTML programmers to mix static HTML with dynamically generated HTML. The motivation is that, for many dynamic Web pages, most of their content is still static (that is, the same content is present whenever the page is generated). The dynamic content of the Web pages (which are generated, for example, on the basis of form parameters) is often a small part of the page. Creating such pages by writing servlet code results in a large amount of HTML being coded as Java strings. JSP instead allows Java code to be embedded in static HTML; the embedded Java code generates the dynamic part of the page. JSP scripts are actually translated into servlet code that is then compiled, but the application programmer is saved the trouble of writing much of the Java code to create the servlet.

Figure 9.9 shows the source text of an JSP page that includes embedded Java code. The Java code in the script is distinguished from the surrounding HTML code by being enclosed in <% ... %>. The code uses request.getParameter() to get the value of the attribute name.

When a JSP page is requested by a browser, the application server generates HTML output from the page, which is sent back to the browser. The HTML part of the JSP page is output as is.[4] Wherever Java code is embedded within <% ...%>,

---

[4]JSP allows a more complex embedding, where HTML code is within a Java if-else statement, and gets output conditionally depending on whether the if condition evaluates to true or not. We omit details here.

PHP

PHP is a scripting language that is widely used for server-side scripting. PHP code can be intermixed with HTML in a manner similar to JSP. The characters "<?php" indicate the start of PHP code, while the characters "?>" indicate the end of PHP code. The following code performs the same actions as the JSP code in Figure 9.9.

```
<html>
<head> <title> Hello </title> </head>
<body>
  <?php if (!isset($_REQUEST['name']))
  { echo 'Hello World'; }
  else { echo 'Hello, ' . $_REQUEST['name']; }
  ?>
</body>
</html>
```

The array $_REQUEST contains the request parameters. Note that the array is indexed by the parameter name; in PHP arrays can be indexed by arbitrary strings, not just numbers. The function `isset` checks if the element of the array has been initialized. The `echo` function prints its argument to the output HTML. The operator "." between two strings concatenates the strings.

A suitably configured Web server would interpret any file whose name ends in ".php" to be a PHP file. If the file is requested, the Web server process it in a manner similar to how JSP files are processed, and returns the generated HTML to the browser.

A number of libraries are available for the PHP language, including libraries for database access using ODBC (similar to JDBC in Java).

the code is replaced in the HTML output by the text it prints to the object out. In the JSP code in the above figure, if no value was entered for the form parameter name, the script prints "Hello World"; if a value was entered, the script prints "Hello" followed by the name.

A more realistic example may perform more complex actions, such as looking up values from a database using JDBC.

JSP also supports the concept of a *tag library*, which allows the use of tags that look much like HTML tags, but are interpreted at the server, and are replaced by appropriately generated HTML code. JSP provides a standard set of tags that define variables and control flow (iterators, if-then-else), along with an expression language based on JavaScript (but interpreted at the server). The set of tags is extensible, and a number of tag libraries have been implemented. For example, there is a tag library that supports paginated display of large data sets, and a library that simplifies display and parsing of dates and times. See the bibliographic notes for references to more information on JSP tag libraries.

9.3.6 Client-Side Scripting

Embedding of program code in documents allows Web pages to be **active**, carrying out activities such as animation by executing programs at the local site, instead of just presenting passive text and graphics. The primary use of such programs is flexible interaction with the user, beyond the limited interaction power provided by HTML and HTML forms. Further, executing programs at the client site speeds up interaction greatly, compared to every interaction being sent to a server site for processing.

A danger in supporting such programs is that, if the design of the system is done carelessly, program code embedded in a Web page (or equivalently, in an email message) can perform malicious actions on the user's computer. The malicious actions could range from reading private information, to deleting or modifying information on the computer, up to taking control of the computer and propagating the code to other computers (through email, for example). A number of email viruses have spread widely in recent years in this way.

One of the reasons that the Java language became very popular is that it provides a safe mode for executing programs on users' computers. Java code can be compiled into platform-independent "byte-code" that can be executed on any browser that supports Java. Unlike local programs, Java programs (applets) downloaded as part of a Web page have no authority to perform any actions that could be destructive. They are permitted to display data on the screen, or to make a network connection to the server from which the Web page was downloaded, in order to fetch more information. However, they are not permitted to access local files, to execute any system programs, or to make network connections to any other computers.

While Java is a full-fledged programming language, there are simpler languages, called **scripting languages**, that can enrich user interaction, while providing the same protection as Java. These languages provide constructs that can be embedded with an HTML document. **Client-side scripting languages** are languages designed to be executed on the client's Web browser.

Of these, the *JavaScript* language is by far the most widely used. The current generation of Web interfaces uses the JavaScript scripting language extensively to construct sophisticated user interfaces. JavaScript is used for a variety of tasks. For example, functions written in JavaScript can be used to perform error checks (validation) on user input, such as a date string being properly formatted, or a value entered (such as age) being in an appropriate range. These checks are carried out on the browser as data is entered, even before the data are sent to the Web server.

Figure 9.10 shows an example of a JavaScript function used to validate a form input. The function is declared in the head section of the HTML document. The function checks that the credits entered for a course is a number greater than 0, and less than 16. The form tag specifies that the validation function is to be invoked when the form is submitted. If the validation fails, an alert box is shown to the user, and if it succeeds, the form is submitted to the server.

JavaScript can be used to modify dynamically the HTML code being displayed. The browser parses HTML code into an in-memory tree structure defined by

```
<html>
<head>
<script type="text/javascript">
  function validate() {
    var credits=document.getElementById("credits").value;
    if (isNaN(credits)|| credits<=0 || credits>=16) {
      alert("Credits must be a number greater than 0 and less than 16");
      return false
    }
  }
</script>
</head>

<body>
<form action="createCourse" onsubmit="return validate()">
  Title: <input type="text" id="title" size="20"><br />
  Credits: <input type="text" id="credits" size="2"><br />
  <input type="submit" value="Submit">
</form>
</body>
</html>
```

Figure 9.10   Example of JavaScript used to validate form input

a standard called the **Document Object Model (DOM)**. JavaScript code can modify the tree structure to carry out certain operations. For example, suppose a user needs to enter a number of rows of data, for example multiple items in a single bill. A table containing text boxes and other form input methods can be used to gather user input. The table may have a default size, but if more rows are needed, the user may click on a button labeled (for example) "Add Item." This button can be set up to invoke a JavaScript function that modifies the DOM tree by adding an extra row in the table.

Although the JavaScript language has been standardized, there are differences between browsers, particularly in the details of the DOM model. As a result, JavaScript code that works on one browser may not work on another. To avoid such problems, it is best to use a JavaScript library, such as Yahoo's YUI library, which allows code to be written in a browser independent way. Internally, the functions in the library can find out which browser is in use, and send appropriately generated JavaScript to the browser. See the Tools section at the end of the chapter for more information on YUI and other libraries.

Today, JavaScript is widely used to create dynamic Web pages, using several technologies that are collectively called **Ajax**. Programs written in JavaScript communicate with the Web server asynchronously (that is, in the background, without blocking user interaction with the Web browser), and can fetch data and display it.

As an example of the use of Ajax, consider a Web site with a form that allows you to select a country, and once a country has been selected, you are allowed to select a state from a list of states in that country. Until the country is selected, the drop-down list of states is empty. The Ajax framework allows the list of states to be downloaded from the Web site in the background when the country is selected, and as soon as the list has been fetched, it is added to the drop-down list, which allows you to select the state.

There are also special-purpose scripting languages for specialized tasks such as animation (for example, Flash and Shockwave) and three-dimensional modeling (Virtual Reality Markup Language (VRML)). Flash is very widely used today not only for animation, but also for handling streaming video content.

9.4   Application Architectures

To handle their complexity, large applications are often broken into several layers:

- The *presentation* or *user interface* layer, which deals with user interaction. A single application may have several different versions of this layer, corresponding to distinct kinds of interfaces such as Web browsers, and user interfaces of mobile phones, which have much smaller screens.

    In many implementations, the presentation/user-interface layer is itself conceptually broken up into layers, based on the **model-view-controller** (MVC) architecture. The **model** corresponds to the business-logic layer, described below. The **view** defines the presentation of data; a single underlying model can have different views depending on the specific software/device used to access the application. The **controller** receives events (user actions), executes actions on the model, and returns a view to the user. The MVC architecture is used in a number of Web application frameworks, which are discussed later in Section 9.5.2.

- The **business-logic** layer, which provides a high-level view of data and actions on data. We discuss the business-logic layer in more detail in Section 9.4.1.

- The **data access** layer, which provides the interface between the business-logic layer and the underlying database. Many applications use an object-oriented language to code the business-logic layer, and use an object-oriented model of data, while the underlying database is a relational database. In such cases, the data-access layer also provides the mapping from the object-oriented data model used by the business logic to the relational model supported by the database. We discuss such mappings in more detail in Section 9.4.2.

Figure 9.11 shows the above layers, along with a sequence of steps taken to process a request from the Web browser. The labels on the arrows in the figure indicate the order of the steps. When the request is received by the application server, the controller sends a request to the model. The model processes the

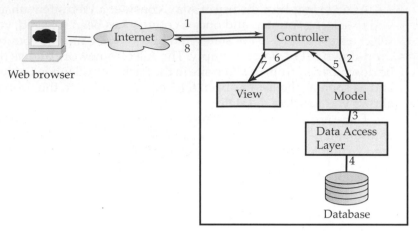

Figure 9.11   Web application architecture.

request, using business logic, which may involve updating objects that are part of the model, followed by creating a result object. The model in turn uses the data-access layer to update or retrieve information from a database. The result object created by the model is sent to the view module, which creates an HTML view of the result, to be displayed on the Web browser. The view may be tailored based on the characteristics of the device used to view the result, for example whether it is a computer monitor with a large screen, or a small screen on a phone.

9.4.1   The Business-Logic Layer

The business-logic layer of an application for managing a university may provide abstractions of entities such as students, instructors, courses, sections, etc., and actions such as admitting a student to the university, enrolling a student in a course, and so on. The code implementing these actions ensures that **business rules** are satisfied; for example the code would ensure that a student can enroll for a course only if she has already completed course prerequisites, and has paid her tuition fees.

In addition, the business logic includes **workflows**, which describe how a particular task that involves multiple participants is handled. For example, if a candidate applies to the university, there is a workflow that defines who should see and approve the application first, and if approved in the first step, who should see the application next, and so on until either an offer is made to the student, or a rejection note is sent out. Workflow management also needs to deal with error situations; for example, if a deadline for approval/rejection is not met, a supervisor may need to be informed so she can intervene and ensure the application is processed. Workflows are discussed in more detail in Section 26.2.

9.4.2 The Data-Access Layer and Object-Relational Mapping

In the simplest scenario, where the business-logic layer uses the same data model as the database, the data-access layer simply hides the details of interfacing with the database. However, when the business-logic layer is written using an object-oriented programming language, it is natural to model data as objects, with methods invoked on objects.

In early implementations, programmers had to write code for creating objects by fetching data from the database, and for storing updated objects back in the database. However, such manual conversions between data models is cumbersome and error prone. One approach to handling this problem was to develop a database system that natively stores objects, and relationships between objects. Such databases, called **object-oriented databases**, are discussed in more detail in Chapter 22. However, object-oriented databases did not achieve commercial success for a variety of technical and commercial reasons.

An alternative approach is to use traditional relational databases to store data, but to automate the mapping of data in relations to in-memory objects, which are created on demand (since memory is usually not sufficient to store all data in the database), as well as the reverse mapping to store updated objects back as relations in the database.

Several systems have been developed to implement such **object-relational mappings**. The **Hibernate** system is widely used for mapping from Java objects to relations. In Hibernate, the mapping from each Java class to one or more relations is specified in a mapping file. The mapping file can specify, for example, that a Java class called *Student* is mapped to the relation *student*, with the Java attribute ID mapped to the attribute *student*.ID, and so on. Information about the database, such as the host on which it is running, and user name and password for connecting to the database, etc., are specified in a *properties* file. The program has to open a *session*, which sets up the connection to the database. Once the session is set up, a *Student* object *stud* created in Java can be stored in the database by invoking **session.save**(*stud*). The Hibernate code generates the SQL commands required to store corresponding data in the *student* relation.

A list of objects can be retrieved from the database by executing a query written in the Hibernate query language; this is similar to executing a query using JDBC, which returns a **ResultSet** containing a set of tuples. Alternatively, a single object can be retrieved by providing its primary key. The retrieved objects can be updated in memory; when the transaction on the ongoing Hibernate session is committed, Hibernate automatically saves the updated objects by making corresponding updates on relations in the database.

While entities in an E-R model naturally correspond to objects in an object-oriented language such as Java, relationships often do not. Hibernate supports the ability to map such relationships as sets associated with objects. For example, the *takes* relationship between *student* and *section* can be modeled by associating a set of *section*s with each *student*, and a set of *student*s with each *section*. Once the appropriate mapping is specified, Hibernate populates these sets automatically from the database relation *takes*, and updates to the sets are reflected back to the database relation on commit.

HIBERNATE EXAMPLE

As an example of the use of Hibernate, we create a Java class corresponding to the *student* relation as follows.

```
public class Student {
        String ID;
        String name;
        String department;
        int tot_cred;
        Student(String id, String name, String dept, int totcreds); // constructor
}
```

To be precise, the class attributes should be declared as private, and getter/setter methods should be provided to access the attributes, but we omit these details.

The mapping of the class attributes of Student to attributes of the relation *student* is specified in a mapping file, in an XML format. Again, we omit details.

The following code snippet then creates a Student object and saves it to the database.

```
Session session = getSessionFactory().openSession();
Transaction txn = session.beginTransaction();
Student stud = new Student("12328", "John Smith", "Comp. Sci.", 0);
session.save(stud);
txn.commit();
session.close();
```

Hibernate automatically generates the required SQL **insert** statement to create a *student* tuple in the database.

To retrieve students, we can use the following code snippet

```
Session session = getSessionFactory().openSession();
Transaction txn = session.beginTransaction();
List students =
        session.find("from Student as s order by s.ID asc");
for ( Iterator iter = students.iterator(); iter.hasNext(); ) {
        Student stud = (Student) iter.next();
        .. print out the Student information ..
}
txn.commit();
session.close();
```

The above code snippet uses a query in Hibernate's HQL query language. The HQL query is automatically translated to SQL by Hibernate and executed, and the results are converted into a list of Student objects. The for loop iterates over the objects in this list and prints them out.

The above features help to provide the programmer a high-level model of data without bothering about the details of the relational storage. However, Hibernate, like other object-relational mapping systems, also allows programmers direct SQL access to the underlying relations. Such direct access is particularly important for writing complex queries used for report generation.

Microsoft has developed a data model called the **Entity Data Model**, which can be viewed as a variant of the entity-relationship model, and an associated framework called the ADO.NET Entity Framework, which can map data between the Entity Data Model and a relational database. The framework also provides an SQL-like query language called **Entity SQL**, which operates directly on the Entity Data Model.

9.4.3   Web Services

In the past, most Web applications used only data available at the application server and its associated database. In recent years, a wide variety of data is available on the Web that is intended to be processed by a program, rather than displayed directly to the user; the program may be running as part of a back-end application, or may be a script running in the browser. Such data are typically accessed using what is in effect a Web application programming interface; that is, a function call request is sent using the HTTP protocol, executed at an application server, and the results sent back to the calling program. A system that supports such an interface is called a **Web service**.

Two approaches are widely used to implement Web services. In the simpler approach, called **Representation State Transfer** (or **REST**), Web service function calls are executed by a standard HTTP request to a URL at an application server, with parameters sent as standard HTTP request parameters. The application server executes the request (which may involve updating the database at the server), generates and encodes the result, and returns the result as the result of the HTTP request. The server can use any encoding for a particular requested URL; XML, and an encoding of JavaScript objects called **JavaScript Object Notation**(JSON), are widely used. The requestor parses the returned page to access the returned data.

In many applications of such RESTful Web services (that is, Web services using REST), the requestor is JavaScript code running in a Web browser; the code updates the browser screen using the result of the function call. For example, when you scroll the display on a map interface on the Web, the part of the map that needs to be newly displayed may be fetched by JavaScript code using a RESTful interface, and then displayed on the screen.

A more complex approach, sometimes referred to as "Big Web Services," uses XML encoding of parameters as well as results, has a formal definition of the Web API using a special language, and uses a protocol layer built on top of the HTTP protocol. This approach is described in more detail in Section 23.7.3.

9.4.4   Disconnected Operation

Many applications wish to support some operations even when a client is disconnected from the application server. For example, a student may wish to fill an application form even if her laptop is disconnected from the network, but have it saved back when the laptop is reconnected. As another example, if an email client is built as a Web application, a user may wish to compose an email even if her laptop is disconnected from the network, and have it sent when it is reconnected. Building such applications requires local storage, preferably in the form of a database, in the client machine. The **Gears** software (originally developed by Google) is a browser plug-in that provides a database, a local Web server, and support for parallel execution of JavaScript at the client. The software works identically on multiple operating system/browser platforms, allowing applications to support rich functionality without installation of any software (other than Gears itself). Adobe's AIR software also provides similar functionality for building Internet applications that can run outside the Web browser.

9.5   Rapid Application Development

If Web applications are built without using tools or libraries for constructing the user interface, the programming effort required to construct the user interface can be significantly more than that required for business logic and database access. Several approaches have been developed to reduce the effort required to build applications:

- Provide a library of functions to generate user-interface elements with minimal programming.

- Provide drag-and-drop features in an integrated development environment that allows user-interface elements to be dragged from a menu into a design view of a page. The integrated development environment generates code that creates the user-interface element by invoking library functions.

- Automatically generate code for the user interface from a declarative specification.

All these approaches have been used for creating user interfaces, well before the Web was created, as part of **Rapid Application Development** (RAD) tools, and are now used extensively for creating Web applications as well.

Examples of tools designed for rapid development of interfaces for database applications include Oracle Forms, Sybase PowerBuilder, and Oracle Application Express (APEX). In addition, tools designed for Web application development, such as Visual Studio and Netbeans VisualWeb, support several features designed for rapid development of Web interfaces for database backed applications.

We study tools for construction of user interfaces in Section 9.5.1, and study frameworks that support automatic code generation from a system model, in Section 9.5.2.

9.5.1   Tools for Building User Interfaces

Many HTML constructs are best generated by using appropriately defined functions, instead of being written as part of the code of each Web page. For example, address forms typically require a menu containing country or state names. Instead of writing lengthy HTML code to create the required menu each time it is used, it is preferable to define a function that outputs the menu, and to call the function wherever required.

Menus are often best generated from data in the database, such as a table containing country names or state names. The function generating the menu executes a database query and populates the menu, using the query result. Adding a country or state then requires only a change to the database, not to the application code. This approach has the potential drawback of requiring increased database interaction, but such overhead can be minimized by caching query results at the application server.

Forms to input dates and times, or inputs that require validation, are similarly best generated by calling appropriately defined functions. Such functions can output JavaScript code to perform validation at the browser.

Displaying a set of results from a query is a common task for many database applications. It is possible to build a generic function that takes an SQL query (or ResultSet) as argument, and display the tuples in the query result (or ResultSet) in a tabular form. JDBC metadata calls can be used to find information such as the number of columns and the names and types of the columns in the query result; this information is then used to display the query result.

To handle situations where the query result is very large, such a query result display function can provide for *pagination* of results. The function can display a fixed number of records in a page and provide controls to step to the next or previous page or jump to a particular page of the results.

There is unfortunately no (widely used) standard Java API for functions to carry out the user-interface tasks described above. Building such a library can be an interesting programming project.

However, there are other tools, such as the JavaServer Faces (JSF) framework, that support the features listed above. The JSF framework includes a JSP tag library that implements these features. The Netbeans IDE has a component called VisualWeb that builds on JSF, providing a visual development environment where user interface components can be dragged and dropped into a page, and their properties customized. For example, JSF provides components to create drop-down menus, or display a table, which can be configured to get their data from a database query. JSF also supports validation specification on components, for example to make a selection or input mandatory, or to constrain a number or a date to be in a specified range.

Microsoft's Active Server Pages (ASP), and its more recent version, Active Server Pages.NET(ASP.NET), is a widely used alternative to JSP/Java. ASP.NET is similar to JSP, in that code in a language such as Visual Basic or C# can be embedded within HTML code. In addition, ASP.NET provides a variety of controls (scripting commands) that are interpreted at the server, and generate HTML that is then sent to the client. These controls can significantly simplify the construction of Web interfaces. We provide a brief overview of the benefits that these controls offer.

For example, controls such as drop-down menus and list boxes can be associated with a `DataSet` object. The `DataSet` object is similar to a JDBC `ResultSet` object, and is typically created by executing a query on the database. The HTML menu contents are then generated from the `DataSet` object's contents; for example, a query may retrieve the names of all departments in an organization into the `DataSet`, and the associated menu would contain these names. Thus, menus that depend on database contents can be created in a convenient manner with very little programming.

Validator controls can be added to form input fields; these declaratively specify validity constraints such as value ranges, or whether the input is a required input for which a value must be provided by the user. The server creates appropriate HTML code combined with JavaScript to perform the validation at the user's browser. Error messages to be displayed on invalid input can be associated with each validator control.

User actions can be specified to have an associated action at the server. For example, a menu control can specify that selecting a value from a menu has an associated server-side action (JavaScript code is generated to detect the selection event and initiate the server-side action). Visual Basic/C# code that displays data pertaining to the selected value can be associated with the action at the server. Thus, selecting a value from a menu can result in associated data on the page getting updated, without requiring the user to click on a submit button.

The `DataGrid` control provides a very convenient way of displaying query results. A `DataGrid` is associated with a `DataSet` object, which is typically the result of a query. The server generates HTML code that displays the query result as a table. Column headings are generated automatically from query result metadata. In addition, `DataGrids` provide several features, such as pagination, and allow the user to sort the result on chosen columns. All the HTML code as well as server-side functionality to implement these features is generated automatically by the server. The `DataGrid` even allows users to edit the data and submit changes back to the server. The application developer can specify a function, to be executed when a row is edited, that can perform the update on the database.

Microsoft Visual Studio provides a graphical user interface for creating ASP pages using these features, further reducing the programming effort.

See the bibliographic notes for references to more information on ASP.NET.

9.5.2   Web Application Frameworks

There are a variety of Web application development frameworks that provide several commonly used features such as:

- An object-oriented model with an object-relational mapping to store data in a relational database (as we saw in Section 9.4.2).

- A (relatively) declarative way of specifying a form with validation constraints on user inputs, from which the system generates HTML and Javascript/Ajax code to implement the form.

- A template scripting system (similar to JSP).

- A controller that maps user interaction events such as form submits to appropriate functions that handle the event. The controller also manages authentication and sessions. Some frameworks also provide tools for managing authorizations.

Thus, these frameworks provide a variety of features that are required to build Web applications, in an integrated manner. By generating forms from declarative specifications, and managing data access transparently, the frameworks minimize the amount of coding that a Web application programmer has to carry out.

There are a large number of such frameworks, based on different languages. Some of the more widely used frameworks include Ruby on Rails, which is based on the Ruby programming language, JBoss Seam, Apache Struts, Swing, Tapestry, and WebObjects, all based on Java/JSP. Some of these, such as Ruby on Rails and JBoss Seam provide a tool that can automatically create simple **CRUD** Web interfaces; that is, interfaces that support create, read, update and delete of objects/tuples, by generating code from an object model or a database. Such tools are particularly useful to get simple applications running quickly, and the generated code can be edited to build more sophisticated Web interfaces.

9.5.3 Report Generators

Report generators are tools to generate human-readable summary reports from a database. They integrate querying the database with the creation of formatted text and summary charts (such as bar or pie charts). For example, a report may show the total sales in each of the past 2 months for each sales region.

The application developer can specify report formats by using the formatting facilities of the report generator. Variables can be used to store parameters such as the month and the year and to define fields in the report. Tables, graphs, bar charts, or other graphics can be defined via queries on the database. The query definitions can make use of the parameter values stored in the variables.

Once we have defined a report structure on a report-generator facility, we can store it and can execute it at any time to generate a report. Report-generator systems provide a variety of facilities for structuring tabular output, such as defining table and column headers, displaying subtotals for each group in a table, automatically splitting long tables into multiple pages, and displaying subtotals at the end of each page.

Figure 9.12 is an example of a formatted report. The data in the report are generated by aggregation on information about orders.

Report-generation tools are available from a variety of vendors, such as Crystal Reports and Microsoft (SQL Server Reporting Services). Several application suites, such as Microsoft Office, provide a way of embedding formatted query results from a database directly into a document. Chart-generation facilities provided by Crystal Reports, or by spreadsheets such as Excel can be used to access data from databases, and generate tabular depictions of data or graphical depictions using charts or graphs. Such charts can be embedded within text documents.

Acme Supply Company, Inc.
Quarterly Sales Report

Period: Jan. 1 to March 31, 2009

Region	Category	Sales	Subtotal
North	Computer Hardware	1,000,000	
	Computer Software	500,000	
	All categories		1,500,000
South	Computer Hardware	200,000	
	Computer Software	400,000	
	All categories		600,000

Total Sales   2,100,000

Figure 9.12   A formatted report.

The charts are created initially from data generated by executing queries against the database; the queries can be re-executed and the charts regenerated when required, to generate a current version of the overall report.

In addition to generating static reports, report-generation tools support the creation of interactive reports. For example, a user can "drill down" into areas of interest, for example move from an aggregate view showing the total sales across an entire year to the monthly sales figures for a particular year. Such operations were discussed earlier, in Section 5.6.

9.6   Application Performance

Web sites may be accessed by millions of people from across the globe, at rates of thousands of requests per second, or even more, for the most popular sites. Ensuring that requests are served with low response times is a major challenge for Web site developers. To do so, application developers try to speed up the processing of individual requests by using techniques such as caching, and exploit parallel processing by using multiple application servers. We describe these techniques briefly below. Tuning of database applications is described in more detail later, in Chapter 24 (Section 24.1).

9.6.1   Reducing Overhead by Caching

Caching techniques of various types are used to exploit commonalities between transactions. For instance, suppose the application code for servicing each user request needs to contact a database through JDBC. Creating a new JDBC connection may take several milliseconds, so opening a new connection for each user request is not a good idea if very high transaction rates are to be supported.

The **Connection pooling** method is used to reduce this overhead; it works as follows. The connection pool manager (a part of the application server) creates a pool (that is, a set) of open ODBC/JDBC connections. Instead of opening a new connection to the database, the code servicing a user request (typically a servlet) asks for (requests) a connection from the connection pool and returns the connection to the pool when the code (servlet) completes its processing. If the pool has no unused connections when a connection is requested, a new connection is opened to the database (taking care not to exceed the maximum number of connections that the database system can support concurrently). If there are many open connections that have not been used for a while, the connection pool manager may close some of the open database connections. Many application servers, and newer ODBC/JDBC drivers provide a built-in connection pool manager.

A common error that many programmers make when creating Web applications is to forget to close an opened JDBC connection (or equivalently, when connection pooling is used, to forget to return the connection to the connection pool). Each request then opens a new connection to the database, and the database soon reaches the limit of how many open connections it can have at a time. Such problems often do not show up on small-scale testing, since databases often allow hundreds of open connections, but show up only on intensive usage. Some programmers assume that connections, like memory allocated by Java programs, are garbage collected automatically. Unfortunately, this does not happen, and programmers are responsible for closing connections that they have opened.

Certain requests may result in exactly the same query being resubmitted to the database. The cost of communication with the database can be greatly reduced by caching the results of earlier queries and reusing them, so long as the query result has not changed at the database. Some Web servers support such query-result caching; caching can otherwise be done explicitly in application code.

Costs can be further reduced by caching the final Web page that is sent in response to a request. If a new request comes with exactly the same parameters as a previous request, the request does not perform any updates, and the resultant Web page is in the cache, then it can be reused to avoid the cost of recomputing the page. Caching can be done at the level of fragments of Web pages, which are then assembled to create complete Web pages.

Cached query results and cached Web pages are forms of materialized views. If the underlying database data change, the cached results must be discarded, or recomputed, or even incrementally updated, as in materialized-view maintenance (described later, in Section 13.5). Some database systems (such as Microsoft SQL Server) provide a way for the application server to register a query with the database, and get a **notification** from the database when the result of the query changes. Such a notification mechanism can be used to ensure that query results cached at the application server are up-to-date.

9.6.2 Parallel Processing

A commonly used approach to handling such very heavy loads is to use a large number of application servers running in parallel, each handling a fraction of the requests. A Web server or a network router can be used to route each client request to one of the application servers. All requests from a particular client session must go to the same application server, since the server maintains state for a client session. This property can be ensured, for example, by routing all requests from a particular IP address to the same application server. The underlying database is, however, shared by all the application servers, so that users see a consistent view of the database.

With the above architecture, the database could easily become the bottleneck, since it is shared. Application designers pay particular attention to minimizing the number of requests to the database, by caching query results at the application server, as discussed earlier. In addition, parallel database systems, described in Chapter 18, are used when required.

9.7   Application Security

Application security has to deal with several security threats and issues beyond those handled by SQL authorization.

The first point where security has to be enforced is in the application. To do so, applications must authenticate users, and ensure that users are only allowed to carry out authorized tasks.

There are many ways in which an application's security can be compromised, even if the database system is itself secure, due to badly written application code. In this section, we first describe several security loopholes that can permit hackers to carry out actions that bypass the authentication and authorization checks carried out by the application, and explain how to prevent such loopholes. Later in the section, we describe techniques for secure authentication, and for fine-grained authorization. We then describe audit trails that can help in recovering from unauthorized access and from erroneous updates. We conclude the section by describing issues in data privacy.

9.7.1   SQL Injection

In **SQL injection** attacks, the attacker manages to get an application to execute an SQL query created by the attacker. In Section 5.1.1.4, we saw an example of an SQL injection vulnerability if user inputs are concatenated directly with an SQL query and submitted to the database. As another example of SQL injection vulnerability, consider the form source text shown in Figure 9.4. Suppose the corresponding servlet shown in Figure 9.8 creates an SQL query string using the following Java expression:

```
String query = "select * from student where name like '%"
                 + name + "%'"
```

where name is a variable containing the string input by the user, and then executes the query on the database. A malicious attacker using the Web form can then type a string such as "';<some SQL statement>; −− ", where <some SQL statement> denotes any SQL statement that the attacker desires, in place of a valid student name. The servlet would then execute the following string.

select * **from** *student* **where** *name* **like** ' '; <some SQL statement>; −− '

The quote inserted by the attacker closes the string, the following semicolon terminates the query, and the following text inserted by the attacker gets interpreted as a second SQL query, while the closing quote has been commented out. Thus, the malicious user has managed to insert an arbitrary SQL statement that is executed by the application. The statement can cause significant damage, since it can perform any action on the database, bypassing all security measures implemented in the application code.

As discussed in Section 5.1.1.4, to avoid such attacks, it is best to use prepared statements to execute SQL queries. When setting a parameter of a prepared query, JDBC automatically adds escape characters so that the user-supplied quote would no longer be able to terminate the string. Equivalently, a function that adds such escape characters could be applied on input strings before they are concatenated with the SQL query, instead of using prepared statements.

Another source of SQL-injection risk comes from applications that create queries dynamically, based on selection conditions and ordering attributes specified in a form. For example, an application may allow a user to specify what attribute should be used for sorting the results of a query. An appropriate SQL query is constructed, based on the attribute specified. Suppose the application takes the attribute name from a form, in the variable orderAttribute, and creates a query string such as the following:

```
String query = "select * from takes order by " + orderAttribute;
```

A malicious user can send an arbitrary string in place of a meaningful orderAttribute value, even if the HTML form used to get the input tried to restrict the allowed values by providing a menu. To avoid this kind of SQL injection, the application should ensure that the orderAttribute variable value is one of the allowed values (in our example, attribute names), before appending it.

9.7.2 Cross Site Scripting and Request Forgery

A Web site that allows users to enter text, such as a comment or a name, and then stores it and later displays it to other users, is potentially vulnerable to a kind of attack called a **cross-site scripting** (XSS) attack. In such an attack, a malicious user enters code written in a client-side scripting language such as JavaScript or Flash instead of entering a valid name or comment. When a different user views the entered text, the browser would execute the script, which can carry out actions such as sending private cookie information back to the malicious user, or even executing an action on a different Web server that the user may be logged into.

For example, suppose the user happens to be logged into her bank account at the time the script executes. The script could send cookie information related to the bank account login back to the malicious user, who could use the information to connect to the bank's Web server, fooling it into believing that the connection is from the original user. Or, the script could access appropriate pages on the bank's Web site, with appropriately set parameters, to execute a money transfer. In fact this particular problem can occur even without scripting by simply using a line of code such as

```
<img src=
    "http://mybank.com/transfermoney?amount=1000&toaccount=14523">
```

assuming that the URL mybank.com/transfermoney accepts the specified parameters, and carries out a money transfer. This latter kind of vulnerability is also called **cross-site request forgery** or **XSRF** (sometimes also called **CSRF**).

XSS can be done in other ways, such as luring a user into visiting a Web site that has malicious scripts embedded in its pages. There are other more complex kinds of XSS and XSRF attacks, which we shall not get into here. To protect against such attacks, two things need to be done:

- **Prevent your Web site from being used to launch XSS or XSRF attacks.**
  The simplest technique is to disallow any HTML tags whatsoever in text input by users. There are functions that detect, or strip all such tags. These functions can be used to prevent HTML tags, and as a result, any scripts, from being displayed to other users. In some cases HTML formatting is useful, and in that case functions that parse the text and allow limited HTML constructs, but disallow other dangerous constructs can be used instead; these must be designed carefully, since something as innocuous as an image include could potentially be dangerous in case there is a bug in the image display software that can be exploited.

- **Protect your Web site from XSS or XSRF attacks launched from other sites.**
  If the user has logged into your Web site, and visits a different Web site vulnerable to XSS, the malicious code executing on the user's browser could execute actions on your Web site, or pass session information related to your Web site back to the malicious user who could try to exploit it. This cannot be prevented altogether, but you can take a few steps to minimize the risk.

  ○ The HTTP protocol allows a server to check the **referer** of a page access, that is, the URL of the page that had the link that the user clicked on to initiate the page access. By checking that the referer is valid, for example, that the referer URL is a page on the same Web site, XSS attacks that originated on a different Web page accessed by the user can be prevented.

  ○ Instead of using only the cookie to identify a session, the session could also be restricted to the IP address from which it was originally authenticated.

As a result, even if a malicious user gets a cookie, he may not be able to log in from a different computer.

○ Never use a GET method to perform any updates. This prevents attacks using <img src ..> such as the one we saw earlier. In fact, the HTTP standard recommends that GET methods should never perform any updates, for other reasons such as a page refresh repeating an action that should have happened only once.

9.7.3 Password Leakage

Another problem that application developers must deal with is storing passwords in clear text in the application code. For example, programs such as JSP scripts often contain passwords in clear text. If such scripts are stored in a directory accessible by a Web server, an external user may be able to access the source code of the script, and get access to the password for the database account used by the application. To avoid such problems, many application servers provide mechanisms to store passwords in encrypted form, which the server decrypts before passing it on to the database. Such a feature removes the need for storing passwords as clear text in application programs. However, if the decryption key is also vulnerable to being exposed, this approach is not fully effective.

As another measure against compromised database passwords, many database systems allow access to the database to be restricted to a given set of Internet addresses, typically, the machines running the application servers. Attempts to connect to the database from other Internet addresses are rejected. Thus, unless the malicious user is able to log into the application server, she cannot do any damage even if she gains access to the database password.

9.7.4 Application Authentication

Authentication refers to the task of verifying the identity of a person/software connecting to an application. The simplest form of authentication consists of a secret password that must be presented when a user connects to the application. Unfortunately, passwords are easily compromised, for example, by guessing, or by sniffing of packets on the network if the passwords are not sent encrypted. More robust schemes are needed for critical applications, such as online bank accounts. Encryption is the basis for more robust authentication schemes. Authentication through encryption is addressed in Section 9.8.3.

Many applications use **two-factor authentication**, where two independent *factors* (that is, pieces of information or processes) are used to identify a user. The two factors should not share a common vulnerability; for example, if a system merely required two passwords, both could be vulnerable to leakage in the same manner (by network sniffing, or by a virus on the computer used by the user, for example). While biometrics such as fingerprints or iris scanners can be used in situations where a user is physically present at the point of authentication, they are not very meaningful across a network.

Passwords are used as the first factor in most such two-factor authentication schemes. Smart cards or other encryption devices connected through the USB interface, which can be used for authentication based on encryption techniques (see Section 9.8.3), are widely used as second factors.

One-time password devices, which generate a new pseudo-random number (say) every minute are also widely used as a second factor. Each user is given one of these devices, and must enter the number displayed by the device at the time of authentication, along with the password, to authenticate himself. Each device generates a different sequence of pseudo-random numbers. The application server can generate the same sequence of pseudo-random numbers as the device given to the user, stopping at the number that would be displayed at the time of authentication, and verify that the numbers match. This scheme requires that the clock in the device and at the server are synchronized reasonably closely.

Yet another second-factor approach is to send an SMS with a (randomly generated) one-time password to the user's phone (whose number is registered earlier) whenever the user wishes to log in to the application. The user must possess a phone with that number to receive the SMS, and then enter the one-time password, along with her regular password, to be authenticated.

It is worth noting that even with two-factor authentication, users may still be vulnerable to **man-in-the-middle** attacks. In such attacks, a user attempting to connect to the application is diverted to a fake Web site, which accepts the password (including second factor passwords) from the user, and uses it immediately to authenticate to the original application. The HTTPS protocol, described later in Section 9.8.3.2, is used to authenticate the Web site to the user (so the user does not connect to a fake site believing it to be the intended site). The HTTPS protocol also encrypts data, and prevents man-in-the-middle attacks.

When users access multiple Web sites, it is often annoying for a user to have to authenticate herself to each site separately, often with different passwords on each site. There are systems that allow the user to authenticate herself to one central authentication service, and other Web sites and applications can authenticate the user through the central authentication service; the same password can then be used to access multiple sites. The LDAP protocol is widely used to implement such a central point of authentication; organizations implement an LDAP server containing user names and password information, and applications use the LDAP server to authenticate users.

In addition to authenticating users, a central authentication service can provide other services, for example, providing information about the user such as name, email, and address information, to the application. This obviates the need to enter this information separately in each application. LDAP can be used for this task, as described later in Section 19.10.2. Other directory systems such Microsoft's Active Directories, also provide mechanisms for authenticating users as well as for providing user information.

A **single sign-on** system further allows the user to be authenticated once, and multiple applications can then verify the user's identity through an authentication service without requiring reauthentication. In other words, once a user is logged in at one site, he does not have to enter his user name and password at other sites that use the same single sign-on service. Such single sign-on mechanisms have long been used in network authentication protocols such as Kerberos, and implementations are now available for Web applications.

The **Security Assertion Markup Language (SAML)** is a standard for exchanging authentication and authorization information between different security domains, to provide cross-organization single sign-on. For example, suppose an application needs to provide access to all students from a particular university, say Yale. The university can set up a Web-based service that carries out authentication. Suppose a user connects to the application with a username such as "joe@yale.edu". The application, instead of directly authenticating a user, diverts the user to Yale University's authentication service, which authenticates the user, and then tells the application who the user is and may provide some additional information such as the category of the user (student or instructor) or other relevant information. The user's password and other authentication factors are never revealed to the application, and the user need not register explicitly with the application. However, the application must trust the university's authentication service when authenticating a user.

The **OpenID** standard is an alternative for single sign-on across organizations, and has seen increasing acceptance in recent years. A large number of popular Web sites, such as Google, Microsoft, Yahoo!, among many others, act as OpenID authentication providers. Any application that acts as an OpenID client can then use any of these providers to authenticate a user; for example, a user who has a Yahoo! account can choose Yahoo! as the authentication provider. The user is redirected to Yahoo! for authentication, and on successful authentication is transparently redirected back to the application, and can then continue using the application.

9.7.5 Application-Level Authorization

Although the SQL standard supports a fairly flexible system of authorization based on roles (described in Section 4.6), the SQL authorization model plays a very limited role in managing user authorizations in a typical application. For instance, suppose you want all students to be able to see their own grades, but not the grades of anyone else. Such authorization cannot be specified in SQL for at least two reasons:

1. **Lack of end-user information**. With the growth in the Web, database accesses come primarily from Web application servers. The end users typically do not have individual user identifiers on the database itself, and indeed there may only be a single user identifier in the database corresponding to all users of an application server. Thus, authorization specification in SQL cannot be used in the above scenario.

   It is possible for an application server to authenticate end users, and then pass the authentication information on to the database. In this section we will assume that the function *syscontext.user_id*() returns the identifier of the application user on whose behalf a query is being executed.[5]

2. **Lack of fine-grained authorization**. Authorization must be at the level of individual tuples, if we are to authorize students to see only their own grades. Such authorization is not possible in the current SQL standard, which permits authorization only on an entire relation or view, or on specified attributes of relations or views.

 We could try to get around this limitation by creating for each student a view on the *takes* relation that shows only that student's grades. While this would work in principle, it would be extremely cumbersome since we would have to create one such view for every single student enrolled in the university, which is completely impractical.[6]

 An alternative is to create a view of the form

> **create view** *studentTakes* **as**
> **select** *
> **from** *takes*
> **where** *takes.ID= syscontext.user_id*()

Users are then given authorization to this view, rather than to the underlying *takes* relation. However, queries executed on behalf of students must now be written on the view *studentTakes*, rather than on the original *takes* relation, whereas queries executed on behalf of instructors may need to use a different view. The task of developing applications becomes more complex as a result.

 The task of authorization is today typically carried out entirely in the application, bypassing the authorization facilities of SQL. At the application level, users are authorized to access specific interfaces, and may further be restricted to view or update certain data items only.

 While carrying out authorization in the application gives a great deal of flexibility to application developers, there are problems, too.

- The code for checking authorization becomes intermixed with the rest of the application code.

- Implementing authorization through application code, rather than specifying it declaratively in SQL, makes it hard to ensure the absence of loopholes. Because of an oversight, one of the application programs may not check for authorization, allowing unauthorized users access to confidential data.

---

[5]In Oracle, a JDBC connection using Oracle's JDBC drivers can set the end user identifier using the method OracleConnection.setClientIdentifier(userId), and an SQL query can use the function sys_context('USERENV', 'CLIENT_IDENTIFIER') to retrieve the user identifier.

[6]Database systems are designed to manage large relations, but manage schema information such as views in a way that assumes smaller data volumes so as to enhance overall performance.

Verifying that all application programs make all required authorization checks involves reading through all the application-server code, a formidable task in a large system. In other words, applications have a very large "surface area," making the task of protecting the application significantly harder. And in fact, security loopholes have been found in a variety of real-life applications.

In contrast, if a database directly supported fine-grained authorization, authorization policies could be specified and enforced at the SQL-level, which has a much smaller surface area. Even if some of the application interfaces inadvertently omit required authorization checks, the SQL-level authorization could prevent unauthorized actions from being executed.

Some database systems provide mechanisms for fine-grained authorization. For example, the Oracle **Virtual Private Database** (**VPD**) allows a system administrator to associate a function with a relation; the function returns a predicate that must be added to any query that uses the relation (different functions can be defined for relations that are being updated). For example, using our syntax for retrieving application user identifiers, the function for the *takes* relation can return a predicate such as:

$$ID = sys\_context.user\_id()$$

This predicate is added to the **where** clause of every query that uses the *takes* relation. As a result (assuming that the application program sets the *user_id* value to the student's *ID*), each student can see only the tuples corresponding to courses that she took.

Thus, VPD provides authorization at the level of specific tuples, or rows, of a relation, and is therefore said to be a *row-level authorization* mechanism. A potential pitfall with adding a predicate as described above is that it may change the meaning of a query significantly. For example, if a user wrote a query to find the average grade over all courses, she would end up getting the average of *her* grades, not all grades. Although the system would give the "right" answer for the rewritten query, that answer would not correspond to the query the user may have thought she was submitting.

See the bibliographic notes for pointers to more information on Oracle VPD.

9.7.6 Audit Trails

An **audit trail** is a log of all changes (inserts, deletes, and updates) to the application data, along with information such as which user performed the change and when the change was performed. If application security is breached, or even if security was not breached, but some update was carried out erroneously, an audit trail can (a) help find out what happened, and who may have carried out the actions, and (b) aid in fixing the damage caused by the security breach or erroneous update.

For example, if a student's grade is found to be incorrect, the audit log can be examined to locate when and how the grade was updated, as well as to find which user carried out the updates. The university could then also use the audit trail to trace all the updates performed by this user, in order to find other incorrect or fraudulent updates, and then correct them.

Audit trails can also be used to detect security breaches where a user's account is compromised and accessed by an intruder. For example, each time a user logs in, she may be informed about all updates in the audit trail that were done from that login in the recent past; if the user sees a update that she did not carry out, it is likely the account has been compromised.

It is possible to create a database-level audit trail by defining appropriate triggers on relation updates (using system-defined variables that identify the user name and time). However, many database systems provide built-in mechanisms to create audit trails that are much more convenient to use. Details of how to create audit trails vary across database systems, and you should refer to the database-system manuals for details.

Database-level audit trails are usually insufficient for applications, since they are usually unable to track who was the end user of the application. Further, updates are recorded at a low level, in terms of updates to tuples of a relation, rather than at a higher level, in terms of the business logic. Applications therefore usually create a higher-level audit trail, recording, for example, what action was carried out, by whom, when, and from which IP address the request originated.

A related issue is that of protecting the audit trail itself from being modified or deleted by users who breach application security. One possible solution is to copy the audit trail to a different machine, to which the intruder would not have access, with each record in the trail copied as soon as it is generated.

9.7.7   Privacy

In a world where an increasing amount of personal data are available online, people are increasingly worried about the privacy of their data. For example, most people would want their personal medical data to be kept private and not revealed publicly. However, the medical data must be made available to doctors and emergency medical technicians who treat the patient. Many countries have laws on privacy of such data that define when and to whom the data may be revealed. Violation of privacy law can result in criminal penalties in some countries. Applications that access such private data must be built carefully, keeping the privacy laws in mind.

On the other hand, aggregated private data can play an important role in many tasks such as detecting drug side effects, or in detecting the spread of epidemics. How to make such data available to researchers carrying out such tasks, without compromising the privacy of individuals, is an important real-world problem. As an example, suppose a hospital hides the name of the patient, but provides a researcher with the date of birth and the zip code (postal code) of the patient (both of which may be useful to the researcher). Just these two pieces of information can be used to uniquely identify the patient in many cases (using information from an external database), compromising his privacy. In this particular situation, one solution would be to give the year of birth but not the date of birth, along with the zip code, which may suffice for the researcher. This would not provide enough information to uniquely identify most individuals.[7]

As another example, Web sites often collect personal data such as address, telephone, email, and credit-card information. Such information may be required to carry out a transaction such as purchasing an item from a store. However, the customer may not want the information to be made available to other organizations, or may want part of the information (such as credit-card numbers) to be erased after some period of time as a way to prevent it from falling into unauthorized hands in the event of a security breach. Many Web sites allow customers to specify their privacy preferences, and must then ensure that these preferences are respected.

9.8 Encryption and Its Applications

Encryption refers to the process of transforming data into a form that is unreadable, unless the reverse process of decryption is applied. Encryption algorithms use an encryption key to perform encryption, and require a decryption key (which could be the same as the encryption key depending on the encryption algorithm used) to perform decryption.

The oldest uses of encryption were for transmitting messages, encrypted using a secret key known only to the sender and the intended receiver. Even if the message is intercepted by an enemy, the enemy, not knowing the key, will not be able to decrypt and understand the message. Encryption is widely used today for protecting data in transit in a variety of applications such as data transfer on the Internet, and on cellular phone networks. Encryption is also used to carry out other tasks, such as authentication, as we will see in Section 9.8.3.

In the context of databases, encryption is used to store data in a secure way, so that even if the data is acquired by an unauthorized user (for example, a laptop computer containing the data is stolen), the data will not be accessible without a decryption key.

Many databases today store sensitive customer information, such as credit-card numbers, names, fingerprints, signatures, and identification numbers such as, in the United States, social-security numbers. A criminal who gets access to such data can use it for a variety of illegal activities such as purchasing goods using a credit-card number, or even acquiring a credit card in someone else's name. Organizations such as credit-card companies use knowledge of personal information as a way of identifying who is requesting a service or goods. Leakage of such personal information allows a criminal to impersonate someone else and get access to service or goods; such impersonation is referred to as **identity theft**. Thus, applications that store such sensitive data must take great care to protect them from theft.

---

[7]For extremely old people, who are relatively rare, even the year of birth plus postal code may be enough to uniquely identify the individual, so a range of values, such as 80 years or older, may be provided instead of the actual age for people older than 80 years.

To reduce the chance of sensitive information being acquired by criminals, many countries and states today require by law that any database storing such sensitive information must store the information in an encrypted form. A business that does not protect its data thus could be held criminally liable in case of data theft. Thus, encryption is a critical component of any application that stores such sensitive information.

9.8.1 Encryption Techniques

There are a vast number of techniques for the encryption of data. Simple encryption techniques may not provide adequate security, since it may be easy for an unauthorized user to break the code. As an example of a weak encryption technique, consider the substitution of each character with the next character in the alphabet. Thus,

Perryridge

becomes

Qfsszsjehf

If an unauthorized user sees only "Qfsszsjehf," she probably has insufficient information to break the code. However, if the intruder sees a large number of encrypted branch names, she could use statistical data regarding the relative frequency of characters to guess what substitution is being made (for example, E is the most common letter in English text, followed by T, A, O, N, I, and so on).

A good encryption technique has the following properties:

- It is relatively simple for authorized users to encrypt and decrypt data.

- It depends not on the secrecy of the algorithm, but rather on a parameter of the algorithm called the *encryption key*, which is used to encrypt data. In a **symmetric-key** encryption technique, the encryption key is also used to decrypt data. In contrast, in **public-key** (also known as **asymmetric-key**) encryption techniques, there are two different keys, the public key and the private key, used to encrypt and decrypt the data.

- Its decryption key is extremely difficult for an intruder to determine, even if the intruder has access to encrypted data. In the case of asymmetric-key encryption, it is extremely difficult to infer the private key even if the public key is available.

The **Advanced Encryption Standard** (AES) is a symmetric-key encryption algorithm that was adopted as an encryption standard by the U.S. government in 2000, and is now widely used. The standard is based on the **Rijndael algorithm** (named for the inventors V. Rijmen and J. Daemen). The algorithm operates on a 128-bit block of data at a time, while the key can be 128, 192, or 256 bits in length.

The algorithm runs a series of steps to jumble up the bits in a data block in a way that can be reversed during decryption, and performs an XOR operation with a 128-bit "round key" that is derived from the encryption key. A new round key is generated from the encryption key for each block of data that is encrypted. During decryption, the round keys are generated again from the encryption key and the encryption process is reversed to recover the original data. An earlier standard called the *Data Encryption Standard* (DES), adopted in 1977, was very widely used earlier.

For any symmetric-key encryption scheme to work, authorized users must be provided with the encryption key via a secure mechanism. This requirement is a major weakness, since the scheme is no more secure than the security of the mechanism by which the encryption key is transmitted.

Public-key encryption is an alternative scheme that avoids some of the problems faced by symmetric-key encryption techniques. It is based on two keys: a *public key* and a *private key*. Each user U_i has a public key E_i and a private key D_i. All public keys are published: They can be seen by anyone. Each private key is known to only the one user to whom the key belongs. If user U_1 wants to store encrypted data, U_1 encrypts them using public key E_1. Decryption requires the private key D_1.

Because the encryption key for each user is public, it is possible to exchange information securely by this scheme. If user U_1 wants to share data with U_2, U_1 encrypts the data using E_2, the public key of U_2. Since only user U_2 knows how to decrypt the data, information can be transferred securely.

For public-key encryption to work, there must be a scheme for encryption such that it is infeasible (that is, extremely hard) to deduce the private key, given the public key. Such a scheme does exist and is based on these conditions:

- There is an efficient algorithm for testing whether or not a number is prime.

- No efficient algorithm is known for finding the prime factors of a number.

For purposes of this scheme, data are treated as a collection of integers. We create a public key by computing the product of two large prime numbers: P_1 and P_2. The private key consists of the pair (P_1, P_2). The decryption algorithm cannot be used successfully if only the product $P_1 P_2$ is known; it needs the individual values P_1 and P_2. Since all that is published is the product $P_1 P_2$, an unauthorized user would need to be able to factor $P_1 P_2$ to steal data. By choosing P_1 and P_2 to be sufficiently large (over 100 digits), we can make the cost of factoring $P_1 P_2$ prohibitively high (on the order of years of computation time, on even the fastest computers).

The details of public-key encryption and the mathematical justification of this technique's properties are referenced in the bibliographic notes.

Although public-key encryption by this scheme is secure, it is also computationally very expensive. A hybrid scheme widely used for secure communication is as follows: a symmetric encryption key (based, for example, on AES) is randomly generated and exchanged in a secure manner using a public-key encryption scheme, and symmetric-key encryption using that key is used on the data transmitted subsequently.

Encryption of small values, such as identifiers or names, is made complicated by the possibility of **dictionary attacks**, particularly if the encryption key is publicly available. For example, if date-of-birth fields are encrypted, an attacker trying to decrypt a particular encrypted value e could try encrypting every possible date of birth until he finds one whose encrypted value matches e. Even if the encryption key is not publicly available, statistical information about data distributions can be used to figure out what an encrypted value represents in some cases, such as age or zip code. For example, if the age 18 is the most common age in a database, the encrypted age value that occurs most often can be inferred to represent 18.

Dictionary attacks can be deterred by adding extra random bits to the end of the value before encryption (and removing them after decryption). Such extra bits, referred to as an **initialization vector** in AES, or as *salt* bits in other contexts, provide good protection against dictionary attack.

9.8.2   Encryption Support in Databases

Many file systems and database systems today support encryption of data. Such encryption protects the data from someone who is able to access the data, but is not able to access the decryption key. In the case of file-system encryption, the data to be encrypted are usually large files and directories containing information about files.

In the context of databases, encryption can be done at several different levels. At the lowest level, the disk blocks containing database data can be encrypted, using a key available to the database-system software. When a block is retrieved from disk, it is first decrypted and then used in the usual fashion. Such disk-block-level encryption protects against attackers who can access the disk contents but do not have access to the encryption key.

At the next higher level, specified (or all) attributes of a relation can be stored in encrypted form. In this case, each attribute of a relation could have a different encryption key. Many databases today support encryption at the level of specified attributes as well as at the level of an entire relation, or all relations in a database. Encryption of specified attributes minimizes the overhead of decryption, by allowing applications to encrypt only attributes that contain sensitive values such as credit-card numbers. However, when individual attributes or relations are encrypted, databases typically do not allow primary and foreign key attributes to be encrypted, and do not support indexing on encrypted attributes. Encryption also then needs to use extra random bits to prevent dictionary attacks, as described earlier.

A decryption key is obviously required to get access to encrypted data. A single master encryption key may be used for all the encrypted data; with attribute level encryption, different encryption keys could be used for different attributes.

In this case, the decryption keys for different attributes can be stored in a file or relation (often referred to as "wallet"), which is itself encrypted using a master key.

A connection to the database that needs to access encrypted attributes must then provide the master key; unless this is provided, the connection will not be able to access encrypted data. The master key would be stored in the application program (typically on a different computer), or memorized by the database user, and provided when the user connects to the database.

Encryption at the database level has the advantage of requiring relatively low time and space overhead, and does not require modification of applications. For example, if data in a laptop computer database need to be protected from theft of the computer itself, such encryption can be used. Similarly, someone who gets access to backup tapes of a database would not be able to access the data contained in the backups without knowing the decryption key.

An alternative to performing encryption in the database is to perform it *before* the data are sent to the database. The application must then encrypt the data before sending it to the database, and decrypt the data when it is retrieved. This approach to data encryption requires significant modifications to be done to the application, unlike encryption performed in a database system.

9.8.3 Encryption and Authentication

Password-based authentication is used widely by operating systems as well as databases. However, the use of passwords has some drawbacks, especially over a network. If an eavesdropper is able to "sniff" the data being sent over the network, she may be able to find the password as it is being sent across the network. Once the eavesdropper has a user name and password, she can connect to the database, pretending to be the legitimate user.

A more secure scheme involves a **challenge–response** system. The database system sends a challenge string to the user. The user encrypts the challenge string using a secret password as encryption key and then returns the result. The database system can verify the authenticity of the user by decrypting the string with the same secret password and checking the result with the original challenge string. This scheme ensures that no passwords travel across the network.

Public-key systems can be used for encryption in challenge–response systems. The database system encrypts a challenge string using the user's public key and sends it to the user. The user decrypts the string using her private key, and returns the result to the database system. The database system then checks the response. This scheme has the added benefit of not storing the secret password in the database, where it could potentially be seen by system administrators.

Storing the private key of a user on a computer (even a personal computer) has the risk that if the computer is compromised, the key may be revealed to an attacker who can then masquerade as the user. **Smart cards** provide a solution to this problem. In a smart card, the key can be stored on an embedded chip; the operating system of the smart card guarantees that the key can never be read, but allows data to be sent to the card for encryption or decryption, using the private key.[8]

9.8.3.1 Digital Signatures

Another interesting application of public-key encryption is in **digital signatures** to verify authenticity of data; digital signatures play the electronic role of physical signatures on documents. The private key is used to "sign," that is, encrypt, data, and the signed data can be made public. Anyone can verify the signature by decrypting the data using the public key, but no one could have generated the signed data without having the private key. (Note the reversal of the roles of the public and private keys in this scheme.) Thus, we can **authenticate** the data; that is, we can verify that the data were indeed created by the person who is supposed to have created them.

Furthermore, digital signatures also serve to ensure **nonrepudiation**. That is, in case the person who created the data later claims she did not create it (the electronic equivalent of claiming not to have signed the check), we can prove that that person must have created the data (unless her private key was leaked to others).

9.8.3.2 Digital Certificates

Authentication is, in general, a two-way process, where each of a pair of interacting entities authenticates itself to the other. Such pairwise authentication is needed even when a client contacts a Web site, to prevent a malicious site from masquerading as a legal Web site. Such masquerading could be done, for example, if the network routers were compromised, and data rerouted to the malicious site.

For a user to ensure that she is interacting with an authentic Web site, she must have the site's public key. This raises the problem of how the user can get the public key–if it is stored on the Web site, the malicious site could supply a different key, and the user would have no way of verifying if the supplied public key is itself authentic. Authentication can be handled by a system of **digital certificates**, whereby public keys are signed by a certification agency, whose public key is well known. For example, the public keys of the root certification authorities are stored in standard Web browsers. A certificate issued by them can be verified by using the stored public keys.

A two-level system would place an excessive burden of creating certificates on the root certification authorities, so a multilevel system is used instead, with one or more root certification authorities and a tree of certification authorities below each root. Each authority (other than the root authorities) has a digital certificate issued by its parent.

A digital certificate issued by a certification authority A consists of a public key K_A and an encrypted text E that can be decoded by using the public key

---

[8]Smart cards provide other functionality too, such as the ability to store cash digitally and make payments, which is not relevant in our context.

K_A. The encrypted text contains the name of the party to whom the certificate was issued and her public key K_c. In case the certification authority A is not a root certification authority, the encrypted text also contains the digital certificate issued to A by its parent certification authority; this certificate authenticates the key K_A itself. (That certificate may in turn contain a certificate from a further parent authority, and so on.)

To verify a certificate, the encrypted text E is decrypted by using the public key K_A to retrieve the name of the party (that is, the name of the organization owning the Web site); additionally, if A is not a root authority whose public key is known to the verifier, the public key K_A is verified recursively by using the digital certificate contained within E; recursion terminates when a certificate issued by the root authority is reached. Verifying the certificate establishes the chain through which a particular site was authenticated, and provides the name and authenticated public key for the site.

Digital certificates are widely used to authenticate Web sites to users, to prevent malicious sites from masquerading as other Web sites. In the HTTPS protocol (the secure version of the HTTP protocol), the site provides its digital certificate to the browser, which then displays it to the user. If the user accepts the certificate, the browser then uses the provided public key to encrypt data. A malicious site will have access to the certificate, but not the private key, and will thus not be able to decrypt the data sent by the browser. Only the authentic site, which has the corresponding private key, can decrypt the data sent by the browser. We note that public-/private-key encryption and decryption costs are much higher than encryption/decryption costs using symmetric private keys. To reduce encryption costs, HTTPS actually creates a one-time symmetric key after authentication, and uses it to encrypt data for the rest of the session.

Digital certificates can also be used for authenticating users. The user must submit a digital certificate containing her public key to a site, which verifies that the certificate has been signed by a trusted authority. The user's public key can then be used in a challenge–response system to ensure that the user possesses the corresponding private key, thereby authenticating the user.

9.9   Summary

- Application programs that use databases as back ends and interact with users have been around since the 1960s. Application architectures have evolved over this period. Today most applications use Web browsers as their front end, and a database as their back end, with an application server in between.

- HTML provides the ability to define interfaces that combine hyperlinks with forms facilities. Web browsers communicate with Web servers by the HTTP protocol. Web servers can pass on requests to application programs, and return the results to the browser.

- Web servers execute application programs to implement desired functionality. Servlets are a widely used mechanism to write application programs that run as part of the Web server process, in order to reduce overhead. There are also many server-side scripting languages that are interpreted by the Web server and provide application-program functionality as part of the Web server.

- There are several client-side scripting languages—JavaScript is the most widely used—that provide richer user interaction at the browser end.

- Complex applications usually have a multilayer architecture, including a model implementing business logic, a controller, and a view mechanism to display results. They may also include a data access layer that implements an object-relational mapping. Many applications implement and use Web services, allowing functions to be invoked over HTTP.

- A number of tools have been developed for rapid application development, and in particular to reduce the effort required to build user interfaces.

- Techniques such as caching of various forms, including query result caching and connection pooling, and parallel processing are used to improve application performance.

- Application developers must pay careful attention to security, to prevent attacks such as SQL injection attacks and cross-site scripting attacks.

- SQL authorization mechanisms are coarse grained and of limited value to applications that deal with large numbers of users. Today application programs implement fine-grained, tuple-level authorization, dealing with a large number of application users, completely outside the database system. Database extensions to provide tuple-level access control and to deal with large numbers of application users have been developed, but are not standard as yet.

- Protecting the privacy of data is an important task for database applications. Many countries have legal requirements on protection of certain kinds of data, such as credit-card information or medical data.

- Encryption plays a key role in protecting information and in authentication of users and Web sites. Symmetric-key encryption and public-key encryption are two contrasting but widely used approaches to encryption. Encryption of certain sensitive data stored in databases is a legal requirement in many countries and states.

- Encryption also plays a key role in authentication of users to applications, of Web sites to users, and for digital signatures.

Review Terms

- Application programs
- Web interfaces to databases
- HyperText Markup Language (HTML)

- Hyperlinks
- Uniform resource locator (URL)
- Forms
- HyperText Transfer Protocol (HTTP)
- Common Gateway Interface (CGI)
- Connectionless protocols
- Cookie
- Session
- Servlets and Servlet sessions
- Server-side scripting
- JSP
- PHP
- ASP.NET
- Client-side scripting
- JavaScript
- Document Object Model (DOM)
- Applets
- Application architecture
- Presentation layer
- Model-view-controller (MVC) architecture
- Business-logic layer
- Data-access layer
- Object-relational mapping
- Hibernate
- Web services
- RESTful services
- Rapid application development
- Web application frameworks
- Report generators
- Connection pooling
- Query result caching
- Application security
- SQL injection
- Cross-site scripting (XSS)
- Cross-site request forgery (XSRF)
- Authentication
- Two-factor authentication
- Man-in-the-middle attack
- Central authentication
- Single sign-on
- OpenID
- Virtual Private Database (VPD)
- Audit trail
- Encryption
- Symmetric-key encryption
- Public-key encryption
- Dictionary attack
- Challenge–response
- Digital signatures
- Digital certificates

Practice Exercises

9.1 What is the main reason why servlets give better performance than programs that use the common gateway interface (CGI), even though Java programs generally run slower than C or C++ programs?

9.2 List some benefits and drawbacks of connectionless protocols over protocols that maintain connections.

9.3 Consider a carelessly written Web application for an online-shopping site, which stores the price of each item as a hidden form variable in the Web page sent to the customer; when the customer submits the form, the information from the hidden form variable is used to compute the bill for the customer. What is the loophole in this scheme? (There was a real instance where the loophole was exploited by some customers of an online-shopping site, before the problem was detected and fixed.)

9.4   Consider another carelessly written Web application, which uses a servlet that checks if there was an active session, but does not check if the user is authorized to access that page, instead depending on the fact that a link to the page is shown only to authorized users. What is the risk with this scheme? (There was a real instance where applicants to a college admissions site could, after logging into the Web site, exploit this loophole and view information they were not authorized to see; the unauthorized access was however detected, and those who accessed the information were punished by being denied admission.)

9.5   List three ways in which caching can be used to speed up Web server performance.

9.6   The netstat command (available on Linux and on Windows) shows the active network connections on a computer. Explain how this command can be used to find out if a particular Web page is not closing connections that it opened, or if connection pooling is used, not returning connections to the connection pool. You should account for the fact that with connection pooling, the connection may not get closed immediately.

9.7   Testing for SQL-injection vulnerability:

   a.   Suggest an approach for testing an application to find if it is vulnerable to SQL injection attacks on text input.

   b.   Can SQL injection occur with other forms of input? If so, how would you test for vulnerability?

9.8   A database relation may have the values of certain attributes encrypted for security. Why do database systems not support indexing on encrypted attributes? Using your answer to this question, explain why database systems do not allow encryption of primary-key attributes.

9.9   Exercise 9.8 addresses the problem of encryption of certain attributes. However, some database systems support encryption of entire databases. Explain how the problems raised in Exercise 9.8 are avoided when the entire database is encrypted.

9.10   Suppose someone impersonates a company and gets a certificate from a certificate-issuing authority. What is the effect on things (such as purchase orders or programs) certified by the impersonated company, and on things certified by other companies?

9.11   Perhaps the most important data items in any database system are the passwords that control access to the database. Suggest a scheme for the secure storage of passwords. Be sure that your scheme allows the system to test passwords supplied by users who are attempting to log into the system.

Exercises

9.12 Write a servlet and associated HTML code for the following very simple application: A user is allowed to submit a form containing a value, say n, and should get a response containing n "*" symbols.

9.13 Write a servlet and associated HTML code for the following simple application: A user is allowed to submit a form containing a number, say n, and should get a response saying how many times the value n has been submitted previously. The number of times each value has been submitted previously should be stored in a database.

9.14 Write a servlet that authenticates a user (based on user names and passwords stored in a database relation), and sets a session variable called *userid* after authentication.

9.15 What is an SQL injection attack? Explain how it works, and what precautions must be taken to prevent SQL injection attacks.

9.16 Write pseudocode to manage a connection pool. Your pseudocode must include a function to create a pool (providing a database connection string, database user name, and password as parameters), a function to request a connection from the pool, a connection to release a connection to the pool, and a function to close the connection pool.

9.17 Explain the terms CRUD and REST.

9.18 Many Web sites today provide rich user-interfaces using Ajax. List two features each of which reveals if a site uses Ajax, without having to look at the source code. Using the above features, find three sites which use Ajax; you can view the HTML source of the page to check if the site is actually using Ajax.

9.19 XSS attacks:

    a.   What is an XSS attack?

    b.   How can the referer field be used to detect some XSS attacks?

9.20 What is multi-factor authentication? How does it help safeguard against stolen passwords?

9.21 Consider the Oracle **Virtual Private Database** (VPD) feature described in Section 9.7.5, and an application based on our university schema.

    a.   What predicate (using a subquery) should be generated to allow each faculty member to see only *takes* tuples corresponding to course sections that they have taught?

b.   Give an SQL query such that the query with the predicate added gives a result that is a subset of the original query result without the added predicate.

c.   Give an SQL query such that the query with the predicate added gives a result containing a tuple that is not in the result of the original query without the added predicate.

9.22   What are two advantages of encrypting data stored in the database?

9.23   Suppose you wish to create an audit trail of changes to the *takes* relation.

a.   Define triggers to create an audit trail, logging the information into a relation called, for example, *takes_trail*. The logged information should include the user-id (assume a function *user_id()* provides this information) and a timestamp, in addition to old and new values. You must also provide the schema of the *takes_trail* relation.

b.   Can the above implementation guarantee that updates made by a malicious database administrator (or someone who manages to get the administrator's password) will be in the audit trail? Explain your answer.

9.24   Hackers may be able to fool you into believing that their Web site is actually a Web site (such as a bank or credit card Web site) that you trust. This may be done by misleading email, or even by breaking into the network infrastructure and rerouting network traffic destined for, say mybank.com, to the hacker's site. If you enter your user name and password on the hacker's site, the site can record it, and use it later to break into your account at the real site. When you use a URL such as https://mybank.com, the HTTPS protocol is used to prevent such attacks. Explain how the protocol might use digital certificates to verify authenticity of the site.

9.25   Explain what is a challenge–response system for authentication. Why is it more secure than a traditional password-based system?

Project Suggestions

Each of the following is a large project, which can be a semester-long project done by a group of students. The difficulty of the project can be adjusted easily by adding or deleting features.

Project 9.1   Pick your favorite interactive Web site, such as Bebo, Blogger, Facebook, Flickr, Last.FM, Twitter, Wikipedia; these are just a few examples, there are many more. Most of these sites manage a large amount of data, and use databases to store and process the data. Implement a subset of the functionality of the Web site you picked. Clearly, implementing even a significant subset of the features of such a site is well beyond a course project, but it is possible to find a set of features that is interesting to implement, yet small enough for a course project.

Most of today's popular Web sites make extensive use of Javascript to create rich interfaces. You may wish to go easy on this for your project, at least initially, since it takes time to build such intefaces, and then add more features to your interfaces, as time permits. Make use of Web application development frameworks, or Javascript libraries available on the Web, such as the Yahoo User Interface library, to speed up your development.

Project 9.2 Create a "mashup" which uses Web services such as Google or Yahoo maps APIs to create an interactive Web sites. For example, the map APIs provide a way to display a map on the Web page, with other information overlayed on the maps. You could implement a restaurant recommendation system, with users contributing information about restaurants such as location, cuisine, price range, and ratings. Results of user searches could be displayed on the map. You could allow Wikipedia-like features, such as allowing users to add information and edit information added by other users, along with moderators who can weed out malicious updates. You could also implement social features, such as giving more importance to ratings provided by your friends.

Project 9.3 Your university probably uses a course-management systems such as Moodle, Blackboard, or WebCT. Implement a subset of the functionality of such a course-management system. For example, you can provide assignment submission and grading functionality, including mechanisms for students and teachers/teaching-assistants to discuss grading of a particular assignment. You could also provide polls and other mechanisms for getting feedback.

Project 9.4 Consider the E-R schema of Practice Exercise 7.3 (Chapter 7), which represents information about teams in a league. Design and implement a Web-based system to enter, update, and view the data.

Project 9.5 Design and implement a shopping cart system that lets shoppers collect items into a shopping cart (you can decide what information is to be supplied for each item) and purchased together. You can extend and use the E-R schema of Exercise 7.20 of Chapter 7. You should check for availability of the item and deal with nonavailable items as you feel appropriate.

Project 9.6 Design and implement a Web-based system to record student registration and grade information for courses at a university.

Project 9.7 Design and implement a system that permits recording of course performance information—specifically, the marks given to each student in each assignment or exam of a course, and computation of a (weighted) sum of marks to get the total course marks. The number of assignments/exams should not be predefined; that is, more assignments/exams can be added at any time. The system should also support grading, permitting cutoffs to be specified for various grades.

You may also wish to integrate it with the student registration system of Project 9.6 (perhaps being implemented by another project team).

Project 9.8   Design and implement a Web-based system for booking classrooms at your university. Periodic booking (fixed days/times each week for a whole semester) must be supported. Cancellation of specific lectures in a periodic booking should also be supported.

You may also wish to integrate it with the student registration system of Project 9.6 (perhaps being implemented by another project team) so that classrooms can be booked for courses, and cancellations of a lecture or addition of extra lectures can be noted at a single interface, and will be reflected in the classroom booking and communicated to students via email.

Project 9.9   Design and implement a system for managing online multiple-choice tests. You should support distributed contribution of questions (by teaching assistants, for example), editing of questions by whoever is in charge of the course, and creation of tests from the available set of questions. You should also be able to administer tests online, either at a fixed time for all students, or at any time but with a time limit from start to finish (support one or both), and give students feedback on their scores at the end of the allotted time.

Project 9.10   Design and implement a system for managing email customer service. Incoming mail goes to a common pool. There is a set of customer service agents who reply to email. If the email is part of an ongoing series of replies (tracked using the in-reply-to field of email) the mail should preferably be replied to by the same agent who replied earlier. The system should track all incoming mail and replies, so an agent can see the history of questions from a customer before replying to an email.

Project 9.11   Design and implement a simple electronic marketplace where items can be listed for sale or for purchase under various categories (which should form a hierarchy). You may also wish to support alerting services, whereby a user can register interest in items in a particular category, perhaps with other constraints as well, without publicly advertising her interest, and is notified when such an item is listed for sale.

Project 9.12   Design and implement a Web-based newsgroup system. Users should be able to subscribe to newsgroups, and browse articles in newsgroups. The system tracks which articles were read by a user, so they are not displayed again. Also provide search for old articles. You may also wish to provide a rating service for articles, so that articles with high rating are highlighted, permitting the busy reader to skip low-rated articles.

Project 9.13   Design and implement a Web-based system for managing a sports "ladder." Many people register, and may be given some initial rankings (perhaps based on past performance). Anyone can challenge anyone else to a match, and the rankings are adjusted according to the result. One simple system for adjusting rankings just moves the winner ahead of the loser in the rank order, in case the winner was behind earlier. You can try to invent more complicated rank-adjustment systems.

Project 9.14 Design and implement a publication-listing service. The service should permit entering of information about publications, such as title, authors, year, where the publication appeared, and pages. Authors should be a separate entity with attributes such as name, institution, department, email, address, and home page.

Your application should support multiple views on the same data. For instance, you should provide all publications by a given author (sorted by year, for example), or all publications by authors from a given institution or department. You should also support search by keywords, on the overall database as well as within each of the views.

Project 9.15 A common task in any organization is to collect structured information from a group of people. For example, a manager may need to ask employees to enter their vacation plans, a professor may wish to collect feedback on a particular topic from students, or a student organizing an event may wish to allow other students to register for the event, or someone may wish to conduct an online vote on some topic.

Create a system that will allow users to easily create information collection events. When creating an event, the event creator must define who is eligible to participate; to do so, your system must maintain user information, and allow predicates defining a subset of users. The event creator should be able to specify a set of inputs (with types, default values, and validation checks) that the users will have to provide. The event should have an associated deadline, and the system should have the ability to send reminders to users who have not yet submitted their information. The event creator may be given the option of automatic enforcement of the deadline based on a specified date/time, or choosing to login and declare the deadline is over. Statistics about the submissions should be generated—to do so, the event creator may be allowed to create simple summaries on the entered information. The event creator may choose to make some of the summaries public, viewable by all users, either continually (e.g., how many people have responded) or after the deadline (e.g., what was the average feedback score).

Project 9.16 Create a library of functions to simplify creation of Web interfaces. You must implement at least the following functions: a function to display a JDBC result set (with tabular formatting), functions to create different types of text and numeric inputs (with validation criteria such as input type and optional range, enforced at the client by appropriate JavaScript code), functions to input date and time values (with default values), and functions to create menu items based on a result set. For extra credit, allow the user to set style parameters such as colors and fonts, and provide pagination support in the tables (hidden form parameters can be used to specify which page is to be displayed). Build a sample database application to illustrate the use of these functions.

Project 9.17 Design and implement a Web-based multiuser calendar system. The system must track appointments for each person, including multioccurrence events, such as weekly meetings, and shared events (where an update made by the event creator gets reflected to all those who share the event). Provide interfaces to schedule multiuser events, where an event creator can add a number of users who are invited to the event. Provide email notification of events. For extra credits implement a Web service that can be used by a reminder program running on the client machine.

Tools

Development of a Web application requires several software tools such as an application server, a compiler, and an editor for a programming language such as Java or C#, and other optional tools such as a Web server. There are several integrated development environments that provide support for Web application development. The two most popular open-source IDEs are Eclipse, developed by IBM, and Netbeans, developed by Sun Microsystems. Microsoft's Visual Studio is the most widely used IDE in the Windows world.

The Apache Tomcat (jakarta.apache.org), Glassfish (glassfish.dev.java.net), JBoss (jboss.org), and Caucho's Resin (www.caucho.com), are application servers that support servlets and JSP. The Apache Web server (apache.org) is the most widely used Web server today. Microsoft's IIS (Internet Information Services) is a Web and application server that is widely used on Microsoft Windows platforms, supporting Microsoft's ASP.NET (msdn.microsoft.com/asp.net/).

IBM's WebSphere (www.software.ibm.com) software provides a variety of software tools for Web application development and deployment, including an application server, an IDE, application integration middleware, business process management software and system management tools.

Some of the above tools are open-source software that can be used free of cost, some are free for noncommercial use or for personal use, while others need to be paid for. See the respective Web sites for more information.

The Yahoo! User Interface (YUI) JavaScript library (developer.yahoo.com/yui) is widely used for creating JavaScript programs that work across multiple browsers.

Bibliographical Notes

Information about servlets, including tutorials, standard specifications, and software, is available on java.sun.com/products/servlet. Information about JSP is available at java.sun.com/products/jsp. Information on JSP tag libraries can also be found at this URL. Information about the .NET framework and about Web application development using ASP.NET can be found at msdn.microsoft.com.

Atreya et al. [2002] provide textbook coverage of digital signatures, including X.509 digital certificates and public-key infrastructure.

PART 3

DATA STORAGE AND QUERYING

Although a database system provides a high-level view of data, ultimately data have to be stored as bits on one or more storage devices. A vast majority of databases today store data on magnetic disk (and, increasingly, on flash storage) and fetch data into main memory for processing, or copy data onto tapes and other backup devices for archival storage. The physical characteristics of storage devices play a major role in the way data are stored, in particular because access to a random piece of data on disk is much slower than memory access: Disk access takes tens of milliseconds, whereas memory access takes a tenth of a microsecond.

Chapter 10 begins with an overview of physical storage media, including mechanisms to minimize the chance of data loss due to device failures. The chapter then describes how records are mapped to files, which in turn are mapped to bits on the disk.

Many queries reference only a small proportion of the records in a file. An index is a structure that helps locate desired records of a relation quickly, without examining all records. The index in this textbook is an example, although, unlike database indices, it is meant for human use. Chapter 11 describes several types of indices used in database systems.

User queries have to be executed on the database contents, which reside on storage devices. It is usually convenient to break up queries into smaller operations, roughly corresponding to the relational-algebra operations. Chapter 12 describes how queries are processed, presenting algorithms for implementing individual operations, and then outlining how the operations are executed in synchrony, to process a query.

There are many alternative ways of processing a query, which can have widely varying costs. Query optimization refers to the process of finding the lowest-cost method of evaluating a given query. Chapter 13 describes the process of query optimization.

CHAPTER **10**

Storage and File Structure

In preceding chapters, we have emphasized the higher-level models of a database. For example, at the *conceptual* or *logical* level, we viewed the database, in the relational model, as a collection of tables. Indeed, the logical model of the database is the correct level for database *users* to focus on. This is because the goal of a database system is to simplify and facilitate access to data; users of the system should not be burdened unnecessarily with the physical details of the implementation of the system.

In this chapter, however, as well as in Chapters 11, 12, and 13, we probe below the higher levels as we describe various methods for implementing the data models and languages presented in preceding chapters. We start with characteristics of the underlying storage media, such as disk and tape systems. We then define various data structures that allow fast access to data. We consider several alternative structures, each best suited to a different kind of access to data. The final choice of data structure needs to be made on the basis of the expected use of the system and of the physical characteristics of the specific machine.

10.1 Overview of Physical Storage Media

Several types of data storage exist in most computer systems. These storage media are classified by the speed with which data can be accessed, by the cost per unit of data to buy the medium, and by the medium's reliability. Among the media typically available are these:

- **Cache**. The cache is the fastest and most costly form of storage. Cache memory is relatively small; its use is managed by the computer system hardware. We shall not be concerned about managing cache storage in the database system. It is, however, worth noting that database implementors do pay attention to cache effects when designing query processing data structures and algorithms.

- **Main memory**. The storage medium used for data that are available to be operated on is main memory. The general-purpose machine instructions operate on main memory. Although main memory may contain several gigabytes of data on a personal computer, or even hundreds of gigabytes of data in large server systems, it is generally too small (or too expensive) for storing the entire database. The contents of main memory are usually lost if a power failure or system crash occurs.

- **Flash memory**. Flash memory differs from main memory in that stored data are retained even if power is turned off (or fails). There are two types of flash memory, called *NAND* and *NOR* flash. Of these, NAND flash has a much higher storage capacity for a given cost, and is widely used for data storage in devices such as cameras, music players, and cell phones, and increasingly, in laptop computers as well. Flash memory has a lower cost per byte than main memory, in addition to being nonvolatile; that is, it retains stored data even if power is switched off.

  Flash memory is also widely used for storing data in "USB keys," which can be plugged into the **Universal Serial Bus** (USB) slots of computing devices. Such USB keys have become a popular means of transporting data between computer systems ("floppy disks" played the same role in earlier days, but their limited capacity has made them obsolete now).

  Flash memory is also increasingly used as a replacement for magnetic disks for storing moderate amounts of data. Such disk-drive replacements are called *solid-state drives*. As of 2009, a 64 GB solid-state hard drive costs less than $200, and capacities range up to 160 GB. Further, flash memory is increasingly being used in server systems to improve performance by caching frequently used data, since it provides faster access than disk, with larger storage capacity than main memory (for a given cost).

- **Magnetic-disk storage**. The primary medium for the long-term online storage of data is the magnetic disk. Usually, the entire database is stored on magnetic disk. The system must move the data from disk to main memory so that they can be accessed. After the system has performed the designated operations, the data that have been modified must be written to disk.

  As of 2009, the size of magnetic disks ranges from 80 gigabytes to 1.5 terabytes, and a 1 terabyte disk costs about $100. Disk capacities have been growing at about 50 percent per year, and we can expect disks of much larger capacity every year. Disk storage survives power failures and system crashes. Disk-storage devices themselves may sometimes fail and thus destroy data, but such failures usually occur much less frequently than do system crashes.

- **Optical storage**. The most popular forms of optical storage are the *compact disk* (CD), which can hold about 700 megabytes of data and has a playtime of about 80 minutes, and the *digital video disk* (DVD), which can hold 4.7 or 8.5 gigabytes of data per side of the disk (or up to 17 gigabytes on a two-sided disk). The expression **digital versatile disk** is also used in place of **digital video disk**, since DVDs can hold any digital data, not just video data. Data are stored optically on a disk, and are read by a laser. A higher capacity format called *Blu-ray DVD* can store 27 gigabytes per layer, or 54 gigabytes in a double-layer disk.

The optical disks used in read-only compact disks (CD-ROM) or read-only digital video disks (DVD-ROM) cannot be written, but are supplied with data prerecorded. There are also "record-once" versions of compact disk (called CD-R) and digital video disk (called DVD-R and DVD+R), which can be written only once; such disks are also called **write-once, read-many** (WORM) disks. There are also "multiple-write" versions of compact disk (called CD-RW) and digital video disk (DVD-RW, DVD+RW, and DVD-RAM), which can be written multiple times.

Optical disk **jukebox** systems contain a few drives and numerous disks that can be loaded into one of the drives automatically (by a robot arm) on demand.

- **Tape storage**. Tape storage is used primarily for backup and archival data. Although magnetic tape is cheaper than disks, access to data is much slower, because the tape must be accessed sequentially from the beginning. For this reason, tape storage is referred to as **sequential-access** storage. In contrast, disk storage is referred to as **direct-access** storage because it is possible to read data from any location on disk.

  Tapes have a high capacity (40- to 300-gigabyte tapes are currently available), and can be removed from the tape drive, so they are well suited to cheap archival storage. Tape libraries (jukeboxes) are used to hold exceptionally large collections of data such as data from satellites, which could include as much as hundreds of terabytes (1 terabyte = 10^{12} bytes), or even multiple petabytes (1 petabyte = 10^{15} bytes) of data in a few cases.

The various storage media can be organized in a hierarchy (Figure 10.1) according to their speed and their cost. The higher levels are expensive, but are fast. As we move down the hierarchy, the cost per bit decreases, whereas the access time increases. This trade-off is reasonable; if a given storage system were both faster and less expensive than another—other properties being the same —then there would be no reason to use the slower, more expensive memory. In fact, many early storage devices, including paper tape and core memories, are relegated to museums now that magnetic tape and semiconductor memory have become faster and cheaper. Magnetic tapes themselves were used to store active data back when disks were expensive and had low storage capacity. Today, almost all active data are stored on disks, except in very rare cases where they are stored on tape or in optical jukeboxes.

The fastest storage media—for example, cache and main memory—are referred to as **primary storage**. The media in the next level in the hierarchy—for example, magnetic disks—are referred to as **secondary storage**, or **online storage**. The media in the lowest level in the hierarchy—for example, magnetic tape and optical-disk jukeboxes—are referred to as **tertiary storage**, or **offline storage**.

In addition to the speed and cost of the various storage systems, there is also the issue of storage volatility. **Volatile storage** loses its contents when the power to the device is removed. In the hierarchy shown in Figure 10.1, the storage systems from main memory up are volatile, whereas the storage systems below

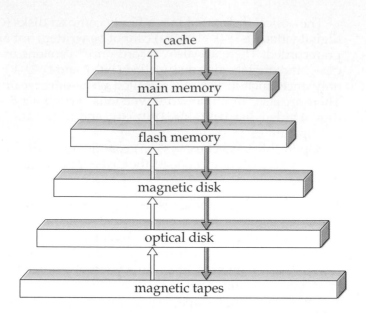

Figure 10.1 Storage device hierarchy.

main memory are nonvolatile. Data must be written to **nonvolatile storage** for safekeeping. We shall return to this subject in Chapter 16.

10.2   Magnetic Disk and Flash Storage

Magnetic disks provide the bulk of secondary storage for modern computer systems. Although disk capacities have been growing year after year, the storage requirements of large applications have also been growing very fast, in some cases even faster than the growth rate of disk capacities. A very large database may require hundreds of disks. In recent years, flash-memory storage sizes have grown rapidly, and flash storage is increasingly becoming a competitor to magnetic disk storage for several applications.

10.2.1   Physical Characteristics of Disks

Physically, disks are relatively simple (Figure 10.2). Each disk **platter** has a flat, circular shape. Its two surfaces are covered with a magnetic material, and information is recorded on the surfaces. Platters are made from rigid metal or glass.

When the disk is in use, a drive motor spins it at a constant high speed (usually 60, 90, or 120 revolutions per second, but disks running at 250 revolutions per second are available). There is a read–write head positioned just above the surface of the platter. The disk surface is logically divided into **tracks**, which are subdivided into **sectors**. A **sector** is the smallest unit of information that can be read from or written to the disk. In currently available disks, sector sizes are

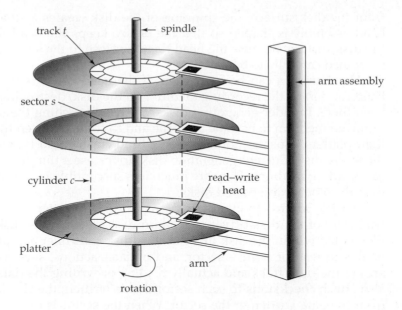

Figure 10.2   Moving head disk mechanism.

typically 512 bytes; there are about 50,000 to 100,000 tracks per platter, and 1 to 5 platters per disk. The inner tracks (closer to the spindle) are of smaller length, and in current-generation disks, the outer tracks contain more sectors than the inner tracks; typical numbers are around 500 to 1000 sectors per track in the inner tracks, and around 1000 to 2000 sectors per track in the outer tracks. The numbers vary among different models; higher-capacity models usually have more sectors per track and more tracks on each platter.

The **read–write head** stores information on a sector magnetically as reversals of the direction of magnetization of the magnetic material.

Each side of a platter of a disk has a read–write head that moves across the platter to access different tracks. A disk typically contains many platters, and the read–write heads of all the tracks are mounted on a single assembly called a **disk arm**, and move together. The disk platters mounted on a spindle and the heads mounted on a disk arm are together known as **head–disk assemblies**. Since the heads on all the platters move together, when the head on one platter is on the ith track, the heads on all other platters are also on the ith track of their respective platters. Hence, the ith tracks of all the platters together are called the ith **cylinder**.

Today, disks with a platter diameter of $3\frac{1}{2}$ inches dominate the market. They have a lower cost and faster seek times (due to smaller seek distances) than do the larger-diameter disks (up to 14 inches) that were common earlier, yet they provide high storage capacity. Disks with even smaller diameters are used in portable devices such as laptop computers, and some handheld computers and portable music players.

The read–write heads are kept as close as possible to the disk surface to increase the recording density. The head typically floats or flies only microns from the disk surface; the spinning of the disk creates a small breeze, and the head assembly is shaped so that the breeze keeps the head floating just above the disk surface. Because the head floats so close to the surface, platters must be machined carefully to be flat.

Head crashes can be a problem. If the head contacts the disk surface, the head can scrape the recording medium off the disk, destroying the data that had been there. In older-generation disks, the head touching the surface caused the removed medium to become airborne and to come between the other heads and their platters, causing more crashes; a head crash could thus result in failure of the entire disk. Current-generation disk drives use a thin film of magnetic metal as recording medium. They are much less susceptible to failure by head crashes than the older oxide-coated disks.

A **disk controller** interfaces between the computer system and the actual hardware of the disk drive; in modern disk systems, the disk controller is implemented within the disk drive unit. A disk controller accepts high-level commands to read or write a sector, and initiates actions, such as moving the disk arm to the right track and actually reading or writing the data. Disk controllers also attach **checksums** to each sector that is written; the checksum is computed from the data written to the sector. When the sector is read back, the controller computes the checksum again from the retrieved data and compares it with the stored checksum; if the data are corrupted, with a high probability the newly computed checksum will not match the stored checksum. If such an error occurs, the controller will retry the read several times; if the error continues to occur, the controller will signal a read failure.

Another interesting task that disk controllers perform is **remapping of bad sectors**. If the controller detects that a sector is damaged when the disk is initially formatted, or when an attempt is made to write the sector, it can logically map the sector to a different physical location (allocated from a pool of extra sectors set aside for this purpose). The remapping is noted on disk or in nonvolatile memory, and the write is carried out on the new location.

Disks are connected to a computer system through a high-speed interconnection. There are a number of common interfaces for connecting disks to computers of which the most commonly used today are (1) SATA (which stands for **serial ATA**,[1] and a newer version of SATA called SATA II or SATA3 Gb (older versions of the ATA standard called **PATA**, or Parallel ATA, and IDE, were widely used earlier, and are still available), (2) **small-computer-system interconnect** (SCSI; pronounced "scuzzy") , (3) SAS (which stands for **serial attached SCSI**), and (4) the Fibre Channel interface. Portable external disk systems often use the USB interface or the IEEE 1394 FireWire interface.

While disks are usually connected directly by cables to the disk interface of the computer system, they can be situated remotely and connected by a high-speed network to the disk controller. In the **storage area network** (SAN) architecture, large numbers of disks are connected by a high-speed network to a number

---

[1] ATA is a storage-device connection standard from the 1980s.

of server computers. The disks are usually organized locally using a storage organization technique called **redundant arrays of independent disks** (RAID) (described later, in Section 10.3), to give the servers a logical view of a very large and very reliable disk. The computer and the disk subsystem continue to use the SCSI, SAS, or Fiber Channel interface protocols to talk with each other, although they may be separated by a network. Remote access to disks across a storage area network means that disks can be shared by multiple computers that could run different parts of an application in parallel. Remote access also means that disks containing important data can be kept in a central server room where they can be monitored and maintained by system administrators, instead of being scattered in different parts of an organization.

Network attached storage (NAS) is an alternative to SAN. NAS is much like SAN, except that instead of the networked storage appearing to be a large disk, it provides a file system interface using networked file system protocols such as NFS or CIFS.

10.2.2 Performance Measures of Disks

The main measures of the qualities of a disk are capacity, access time, data-transfer rate, and reliability.

Access time is the time from when a read or write request is issued to when data transfer begins. To access (that is, to read or write) data on a given sector of a disk, the arm first must move so that it is positioned over the correct track, and then must wait for the sector to appear under it as the disk rotates. The time for repositioning the arm is called the **seek time**, and it increases with the distance that the arm must move. Typical seek times range from 2 to 30 milliseconds, depending on how far the track is from the initial arm position. Smaller disks tend to have lower seek times since the head has to travel a smaller distance.

The **average seek time** is the average of the seek times, measured over a sequence of (uniformly distributed) random requests. If all tracks have the same number of sectors, and we disregard the time required for the head to start moving and to stop moving, we can show that the average seek time is one-third the worst-case seek time. Taking these factors into account, the average seek time is around one-half of the maximum seek time. Average seek times currently range between 4 and 10 milliseconds, depending on the disk model.

Once the head has reached the desired track, the time spent waiting for the sector to be accessed to appear under the head is called the **rotational latency time**. Rotational speeds of disks today range from 5400 rotations per minute (90 rotations per second) up to 15,000 rotations per minute (250 rotations per second), or, equivalently, 4 milliseconds to 11.1 milliseconds per rotation. On an average, one-half of a rotation of the disk is required for the beginning of the desired sector to appear under the head. Thus, the **average latency time** of the disk is one-half the time for a full rotation of the disk.

The access time is then the sum of the seek time and the latency, and ranges from 8 to 20 milliseconds. Once the first sector of the data to be accessed has come under the head, data transfer begins. The **data-transfer rate** is the rate at which data can be retrieved from or stored to the disk. Current disk systems support maximum transfer rates of 25 to 100 megabytes per second; transfer rates are significantly lower than the maximum transfer rates for inner tracks of the disk, since they have fewer sectors. For example, a disk with a maximum transfer rate of 100 megabytes per second may have a sustained transfer rate of around 30 megabytes per second on its inner tracks.

The final commonly used measure of a disk is the **mean time to failure** (MTTF), which is a measure of the reliability of the disk. The mean time to failure of a disk (or of any other system) is the amount of time that, on average, we can expect the system to run continuously without any failure. According to vendors' claims, the mean time to failure of disks today ranges from 500,000 to 1,200,000 hours— about 57 to 136 years. In practice the claimed mean time to failure is computed on the probability of failure when the disk is new—the figure means that given 1000 relatively new disks, if the MTTF is 1,200,000 hours, on an average one of them will fail in 1200 hours. A mean time to failure of 1,200,000 hours does not imply that the disk can be expected to function for 136 years! Most disks have an expected life span of about 5 years, and have significantly higher rates of failure once they become more than a few years old.

Disk drives for desktop machines typically support the Serial ATA(SATA) interface, which supports 150 megabytes per second, or the SATA-II 3Gb interface, which supports 300 megabytes per second. The PATA 5 interface supported transfer rates of 133 megabytes per second. Disk drives designed for server systems typically support the Ultra320 SCSI interface, which provides transfer rates of up to 320 megabytes per second, or the Serial Attached SCSI (SAS) interface, versions of which provide transfer rates of 3 or 6 gigabits per second. Storage area network (SAN) devices, which are connected to servers by a network, typically use Fiber Channel FC 2-Gb or 4-Gb interface, which provides transfer rates of up to 256 or 512 megabytes per second. The transfer rate of an interface is shared between all disks attached to the interface, except for the serial interfaces which allow only one disk to be connected to each interface.

10.2.3   Optimization of Disk-Block Access

Requests for disk I/O are generated both by the file system and by the virtual memory manager found in most operating systems. Each request specifies the address on the disk to be referenced; that address is in the form of a *block number*. A **block** is a logical unit consisting of a fixed number of contiguous sectors. Block sizes range from 512 bytes to several kilobytes. Data are transferred between disk and main memory in units of blocks. The term **page** is often used to refer to blocks, although in a few contexts (such as flash memory) they refer to different things.

A sequence of requests for blocks from disk may be classified as a sequential access pattern or a random access pattern. In a **sequential access** pattern, successive requests are for successive block numbers, which are on the same track, or on adjacent tracks. To read blocks in sequential access, a disk seek may be required for the first block, but successive requests would either not require a seek, or require a seek to an adjacent track, which is faster than a seek to a track that is farther away.

In contrast, in a **random access** pattern, successive requests are for blocks that are randomly located on disk. Each such request would require a seek. The number of random block accesses that can be satisfied by a single disk in a second depends on the seek time, and is typically about 100 to 200 accesses per second. Since only a small amount (one block) of data is read per seek, the transfer rate is significantly lower with a random access pattern than with a sequential access pattern.

A number of techniques have been developed for improving the speed of access to blocks.

- **Buffering**. Blocks that are read from disk are stored temporarily in an in-memory buffer, to satisfy future requests. Buffering is done by both the operating system and the database system. Database buffering is discussed in more detail in Section 10.8.

- **Read-ahead**. When a disk block is accessed, consecutive blocks from the same track are read into an in-memory buffer even if there is no pending request for the blocks. In the case of sequential access, such read-ahead ensures that many blocks are already in memory when they are requested, and minimizes the time wasted in disk seeks and rotational latency per block read. Operating systems also routinely perform read-ahead for consecutive blocks of an operating system file. Read-ahead is, however, not very useful for random block accesses.

- **Scheduling**. If several blocks from a cylinder need to be transferred from disk to main memory, we may be able to save access time by requesting the blocks in the order in which they will pass under the heads. If the desired blocks are on different cylinders, it is advantageous to request the blocks in an order that minimizes disk-arm movement. **Disk-arm–scheduling** algorithms attempt to order accesses to tracks in a fashion that increases the number of accesses that can be processed. A commonly used algorithm is the **elevator algorithm**, which works in the same way many elevators do. Suppose that, initially, the arm is moving from the innermost track toward the outside of the disk. Under the elevator algorithm's control, for each track for which there is an access request, the arm stops at that track, services requests for the track, and then continues moving outward until there are no waiting requests for tracks farther out. At this point, the arm changes direction, and moves toward the inside, again stopping at each track for which there is a request, until it reaches a track where there is no request for tracks farther toward the center. Then, it reverses direction and starts a new cycle. Disk controllers usually perform the task of reordering read requests to improve performance, since they are intimately aware of the organization of blocks on disk, of the rotational position of the disk platters, and of the position of the disk arm.

- **File organization**. To reduce block-access time, we can organize blocks on disk in a way that corresponds closely to the way we expect data to be accessed. For example, if we expect a file to be accessed sequentially, then we should ideally keep all the blocks of the file sequentially on adjacent cylinders. Older operating systems, such as the IBM mainframe operating systems, provided programmers fine control on placement of files, allowing a programmer to reserve a set of cylinders for storing a file. However, this control places a burden on the programmer or system administrator to decide, for example, how many cylinders to allocate for a file, and may require costly reorganization if data are inserted to or deleted from the file.

    Subsequent operating systems, such as Unix and Microsoft Windows, hide the disk organization from users, and manage the allocation internally. Although they do not guarantee that all blocks of a file are laid out sequentially, they allocate multiple consecutive blocks (an **extent**) at a time to a file. Sequential access to the file then only needs one seek per extent, instead of one seek per block. Over time, a sequential file that has multiple small appends may become **fragmented**; that is, its blocks become scattered all over the disk. To reduce fragmentation, the system can make a backup copy of the data on disk and restore the entire disk. The restore operation writes back the blocks of each file contiguously (or nearly so). Some systems (such as different versions of the Windows operating system) have utilities that scan the disk and then move blocks to decrease the fragmentation. The performance increases realized from these techniques can be large.

- **Nonvolatile write buffers**. Since the contents of main memory are lost in a power failure, information about database updates has to be recorded on disk to survive possible system crashes. For this reason, the performance of update-intensive database applications, such as transaction-processing systems, is heavily dependent on the speed of disk writes.

    We can use **nonvolatile random-access memory** (NVRAM) to speed up disk writes drastically. The contents of NVRAM are not lost in power failure. A common way to implement NVRAM is to use battery–backed-up RAM, although flash memory is also increasingly being used for nonvolatile write buffering. The idea is that, when the database system (or the operating system) requests that a block be written to disk, the disk controller writes the block to an NVRAM buffer, and immediately notifies the operating system that the write completed successfully. The controller writes the data to their destination on disk whenever the disk does not have any other requests, or when the NVRAM buffer becomes full. When the database system requests a block write, it notices a delay only if the NVRAM buffer is full. On recovery from a system crash, any pending buffered writes in the NVRAM are written back to the disk. NVRAM buffers are found in certain high end disks, but are more frequently found in "RAID controllers"; we study RAID in Section 10.3.

- **Log disk**. Another approach to reducing write latencies is to use a log disk — that is, a disk devoted to writing a sequential log — in much the same way as a nonvolatile RAM buffer. All access to the log disk is sequential, essentially eliminating seek time, and several consecutive blocks can be written at once, making writes to the log disk several times faster than random writes. As before, the data have to be written to their actual location on disk as well, but the log disk can do the write later, without the database system having to wait for the write to complete. Furthermore, the log disk can reorder the writes to minimize disk-arm movement. If the system crashes before some writes to the actual disk location have completed, when the system comes back up it reads the log disk to find those writes that had not been completed, and carries them out then.

File systems that support log disks as above are called **journaling file systems**. Journaling file systems can be implemented even without a separate log disk, keeping data and the log on the same disk. Doing so reduces the monetary cost, at the expense of lower performance.

Most modern file systems implement journaling, and use the log disk when writing internal file system information such as file allocation information. Earlier-generation file systems allowed write reordering without using a log disk, and ran the risk that the file system data structures on disk would be corrupted if the system crashed. Suppose, for example, that a file system used a linked list, and inserted a new node at the end by first writing the data for the new node, then updating the pointer from the previous node. Suppose also that the writes were reordered, so the pointer was updated first, and the system crashes before the new node is written. The contents of the node would then be whatever junk was on disk earlier, resulting in a corrupted data structure.

To deal with the possibility of such data structure corruption, earlier-generation file systems had to perform a file system consistency check on system restart, to ensure that the data structures were consistent. And if they were not, extra steps had to be taken to restore them to consistency. These checks resulted in long delays in system restart after a crash, and the delays became worse as disk systems grew to higher capacities. Journaling file systems allow quick restart without the need for such file system consistency checks.

However, writes performed by applications are usually not written to the log disk. Database systems implement their own forms of logging, which we study later in Chapter 16.

10.2.4 Flash Storage

As mentioned in Section 10.1, there are two types of flash memory, NOR flash and NAND flash. NOR flash allows random access to individual words of memory, and has read time comparable to main memory. However, unlike NOR flash, reading from NAND flash requires an entire *page* of data, typically consisting of between 512 and 4096 bytes, to be fetched from NAND flash into main memory. Pages in a NAND flash are thus similar to sectors in a magnetic disk. But NAND flash is significantly cheaper than NOR flash, and has much higher storage capacity, and is by far the more widely used.

Storage systems built using NAND flash provide the same block-oriented interface as disk storage. Compared to magnetic disks, flash memory can provide much faster random access: a page of data can be retrieved in around 1 or 2 microseconds from flash, whereas a random access on disk would take 5 to 10 milliseconds. Flash memory has a lower transfer rate than magnetic disks, with 20 megabytes per second being common. Some more recent flash memories have increased transfer rates of 100 to 200 megabytes per second. However, solid state drives use multiple flash memory chips in parallel, to increase transfer rates to over 200 megabytes per second, which is faster than transfer rates of most disks.

Writes to flash memory are a little more complicated. A write to a page of flash memory typically takes a few microseconds. However, once written, a page of flash memory cannot be directly overwritten. Instead, it has to be erased and rewritten subsequently. The erase operation can be performed on a number of pages, called an **erase block**, at once, and takes about 1 to 2 milliseconds. The size of an erase block (often referred to as just "block" in flash literature) is usually significantly larger than the block size of the storage system. Further, there is a limit to how many times a flash page can be erased, typically around 100,000 to 1,000,000 times. Once this limit is reached, errors in storing bits are likely to occur.

Flash memory systems limit the impact of both the slow erase speed and the update limits by mapping logical page numbers to physical page numbers. When a logical page is updated, it can be remapped to any already erased physical page, and the original location can be erased later. Each physical page has a small area of memory where its logical address is stored; if the logical address is remapped to a different physical page, the original physical page is marked as deleted. Thus by scanning the physical pages, we can find where each logical page resides. The logical-to-physical page mapping is replicated in an in-memory **translation table** for quick access.

Blocks containing multiple deleted pages are periodically erased, taking care to first copy nondeleted pages in those blocks to a different block (the translation table is updated for these nondeleted pages). Since each physical page can be updated only a fixed number of times, physical pages that have been erased many times are assigned "cold data," that is, data that are rarely updated, while pages that have not been erased many times are used to store "hot data," that is, data that are updated frequently. This principle of evenly distributing erase operations across physical blocks is called **wear leveling**, and is usually performed transparently by flash-memory controllers. If a physical page is damaged due to an excessive number of updates, it can be removed from usage, without affecting the flash memory as a whole.

All the above actions are carried out by a layer of software called the **flash translation layer**; above this layer, flash storage looks identical to magnetic disk storage, providing the same page/sector-oriented interface, except that flash storage is much faster. File systems and database storage structures can thus see an identical logical view of the underlying storage structure, regardless of whether it is flash or magnetic storage.

Hybrid disk drives are hard-disk systems that combine magnetic storage with a smaller amount of flash memory, which is used as a cache for frequently accessed data. Frequently accessed data that are rarely updated are ideal for caching in flash memory.

10.3 RAID

The data-storage requirements of some applications (in particular Web, database, and multimedia applications) have been growing so fast that a large number of disks are needed to store their data, even though disk-drive capacities have been growing very fast.

Having a large number of disks in a system presents opportunities for improving the rate at which data can be read or written, if the disks are operated in parallel. Several independent reads or writes can also be performed in parallel. Furthermore, this setup offers the potential for improving the reliability of data storage, because redundant information can be stored on multiple disks. Thus, failure of one disk does not lead to loss of data.

A variety of disk-organization techniques, collectively called **redundant arrays of independent disks** (**RAID**), have been proposed to achieve improved performance and reliability.

In the past, system designers viewed storage systems composed of several small, cheap disks as a cost-effective alternative to using large, expensive disks; the cost per megabyte of the smaller disks was less than that of larger disks. In fact, the I in RAID, which now stands for *independent*, originally stood for *inexpensive*. Today, however, all disks are physically small, and larger-capacity disks actually have a lower cost per megabyte. RAID systems are used for their higher reliability and higher performance rate, rather than for economic reasons. Another key justification for RAID use is easier management and operations.

10.3.1 Improvement of Reliability via Redundancy

Let us first consider reliability. The chance that at least one disk out of a set of N disks will fail is much higher than the chance that a specific single disk will fail. Suppose that the mean time to failure of a disk is 100,000 hours, or slightly over 11 years. Then, the mean time to failure of some disk in an array of 100 disks will be 100,000/100 = 1000 hours, or around 42 days, which is not long at all! If we store only one copy of the data, then each disk failure will result in loss of a significant amount of data (as discussed in Section 10.2.1). Such a high frequency of data loss is unacceptable.

The solution to the problem of reliability is to introduce **redundancy**; that is, we store extra information that is not needed normally, but that can be used in the event of failure of a disk to rebuild the lost information. Thus, even if a disk fails, data are not lost, so the effective mean time to failure is increased, provided that we count only failures that lead to loss of data or to nonavailability of data.

The simplest (but most expensive) approach to introducing redundancy is to duplicate every disk. This technique is called **mirroring** (or, sometimes, *shadowing*). A logical disk then consists of two physical disks, and every write is carried out on both disks. If one of the disks fails, the data can be read from the other. Data will be lost only if the second disk fails before the first failed disk is repaired.

The mean time to failure (where failure is the loss of data) of a mirrored disk depends on the mean time to failure of the individual disks, as well as on the **mean time to repair**, which is the time it takes (on an average) to replace a failed disk and to restore the data on it. Suppose that the failures of the two disks are *independent*; that is, there is no connection between the failure of one disk and the failure of the other. Then, if the mean time to failure of a single disk is 100,000 hours, and the mean time to repair is 10 hours, the **mean time to data loss** of a mirrored disk system is $100,000^2/(2 * 10) = 500 * 10^6$ hours, or 57,000 years! (We do not go into the derivations here; references in the bibliographical notes provide the details.)

You should be aware that the assumption of independence of disk failures is not valid. Power failures, and natural disasters such as earthquakes, fires, and floods, may result in damage to both disks at the same time. As disks age, the probability of failure increases, increasing the chance that a second disk will fail while the first is being repaired. In spite of all these considerations, however, mirrored-disk systems offer much higher reliability than do single-disk systems. Mirrored-disk systems with mean time to data loss of about 500,000 to 1,000,000 hours, or 55 to 110 years, are available today.

Power failures are a particular source of concern, since they occur far more frequently than do natural disasters. Power failures are not a concern if there is no data transfer to disk in progress when they occur. However, even with mirroring of disks, if writes are in progress to the same block in both disks, and power fails before both blocks are fully written, the two blocks can be in an inconsistent state. The solution to this problem is to write one copy first, then the next, so that one of the two copies is always consistent. Some extra actions are required when we restart after a power failure, to recover from incomplete writes. This matter is examined in Practice Exercise 10.3.

10.3.2   Improvement in Performance via Parallelism

Now let us consider the benefit of parallel access to multiple disks. With disk mirroring, the rate at which read requests can be handled is doubled, since read requests can be sent to either disk (as long as both disks in a pair are functional, as is almost always the case). The transfer rate of each read is the same as in a single-disk system, but the number of reads per unit time has doubled.

With multiple disks, we can improve the transfer rate as well (or instead) by **striping data** across multiple disks. In its simplest form, data striping consists of splitting the bits of each byte across multiple disks; such striping is called **bit-level striping**. For example, if we have an array of eight disks, we write bit i of each byte to disk i. The array of eight disks can be treated as a single disk with sectors that are eight times the normal size, and, more important, that has eight times the transfer rate. In such an organization, every disk participates in every access (read or write), so the number of accesses that can be processed per second is about the same as on a single disk, but each access can read eight times as many data in the same time as on a single disk. Bit-level striping can be generalized to a number of disks that either is a multiple of 8 or a factor of 8. For example, if we use an array of four disks, bits i and $4 + i$ of each byte go to disk i.

Block-level striping stripes blocks across multiple disks. It treats the array of disks as a single large disk, and it gives blocks logical numbers; we assume the block numbers start from 0. With an array of n disks, block-level striping assigns logical block i of the disk array to disk $(i \bmod n) + 1$; it uses the $\lfloor i/n \rfloor$th physical

(a) RAID 0: nonredundant striping

(b) RAID 1: mirrored disks

(c) RAID 2: memory-style error-correcting codes

(d) RAID 3: bit-interleaved parity

(e) RAID 4: block-interleaved parity

(f) RAID 5: block-interleaved distributed parity

(g) RAID 6: P + Q redundancy

Figure 10.3 RAID levels.

block of the disk to store logical block i. For example, with 8 disks, logical block 0 is stored in physical block 0 of disk 1, while logical block 11 is stored in physical block 1 of disk 4. When reading a large file, block-level striping fetches n blocks at a time in parallel from the n disks, giving a high data-transfer rate for large reads. When a single block is read, the data-transfer rate is the same as on one disk, but the remaining $n - 1$ disks are free to perform other actions.

Block-level striping is the most commonly used form of data striping. Other levels of striping, such as bytes of a sector or sectors of a block, also are possible.

In summary, there are two main goals of parallelism in a disk system:

1. Load-balance multiple small accesses (block accesses), so that the throughput of such accesses increases.

2. Parallelize large accesses so that the response time of large accesses is reduced.

10.3.3   RAID Levels

Mirroring provides high reliability, but it is expensive. Striping provides high data-transfer rates, but does not improve reliability. Various alternative schemes aim to provide redundancy at lower cost by combining disk striping with "parity" bits (which we describe next). These schemes have different cost–performance trade-offs. The schemes are classified into **RAID levels**, as in Figure 10.3. (In the figure, P indicates error-correcting bits, and C indicates a second copy of the data.) For all levels, the figure depicts four disks' worth of data, and the extra disks depicted are used to store redundant information for failure recovery.

*   **RAID level 0** refers to disk arrays with striping at the level of blocks, but without any redundancy (such as mirroring or parity bits). Figure 10.3a shows an array of size 4.

*   **RAID level 1** refers to disk mirroring with block striping. Figure 10.3b shows a mirrored organization that holds four disks' worth of data.
    Note that some vendors use the term **RAID level 1+0** or **RAID level 10** to refer to mirroring with striping, and use the term RAID level 1 to refer to mirroring without striping. Mirroring without striping can also be used with arrays of disks, to give the appearance of a single large, reliable disk: if each disk has M blocks, logical blocks 0 to $M - 1$ are stored on disk 0, M to $2M - 1$ on disk 1(the second disk), and so on, and each disk is mirrored.[2]

*   **RAID level 2**, known as memory-style error-correcting-code (ECC) organization, employs parity bits. Memory systems have long used parity bits for

---

[2]Note that some vendors use the term RAID 0+1 to refer to a version of RAID that uses striping to create a RAID 0 array, and mirrors the array onto another array, with the difference from RAID 1 being that if a disk fails, the RAID 0 array containing the disk becomes unusable. The mirrored array can still be used, so there is no loss of data. This arrangement is inferior to RAID 1 when a disk has failed, since the other disks in the RAID 0 array can continue to be used in RAID 1, but remain idle in RAID 0+1.

error detection and correction. Each byte in a memory system may have a parity bit associated with it that records whether the numbers of bits in the byte that are set to 1 is even (parity = 0) or odd (parity = 1). If one of the bits in the byte gets damaged (either a 1 becomes a 0, or a 0 becomes a 1), the parity of the byte changes and thus will not match the stored parity. Similarly, if the stored parity bit gets damaged, it will not match the computed parity. Thus, all 1-bit errors will be detected by the memory system. Error-correcting schemes store 2 or more extra bits, and can reconstruct the data if a single bit gets damaged.

The idea of error-correcting codes can be used directly in disk arrays by striping bytes across disks. For example, the first bit of each byte could be stored in disk 0, the second bit in disk 1, and so on until the eighth bit is stored in disk 7, and the error-correction bits are stored in further disks.

Figure 10.3c shows the level 2 scheme. The disks labeled P store the error-correction bits. If one of the disks fails, the remaining bits of the byte and the associated error-correction bits can be read from other disks, and can be used to reconstruct the damaged data. Figure 10.3c shows an array of size 4; note RAID level 2 requires only three disks' overhead for four disks of data, unlike RAID level 1, which required four disks' overhead.

- **RAID level 3**, bit-interleaved parity organization, improves on level 2 by exploiting the fact that disk controllers, unlike memory systems, can detect whether a sector has been read correctly, so a single parity bit can be used for error correction, as well as for detection. The idea is as follows: If one of the sectors gets damaged, the system knows exactly which sector it is, and, for each bit in the sector, the system can figure out whether it is a 1 or a 0 by computing the parity of the corresponding bits from sectors in the other disks. If the parity of the remaining bits is equal to the stored parity, the missing bit is 0; otherwise, it is 1.

  RAID level 3 is as good as level 2, but is less expensive in the number of extra disks (it has only a one-disk overhead), so level 2 is not used in practice. Figure 10.3d shows the level 3 scheme.

  RAID level 3 has two benefits over level 1. It needs only one parity disk for several regular disks, whereas level 1 needs one mirror disk for every disk, and thus level 3 reduces the storage overhead. Since reads and writes of a byte are spread out over multiple disks, with N-way striping of data, the transfer rate for reading or writing a single block is N times faster than a RAID level 1 organization using N-way striping. On the other hand, RAID level 3 supports a lower number of I/O operations per second, since every disk has to participate in every I/O request.

- **RAID level 4**, block-interleaved parity organization, uses block-level striping, like RAID 0, and in addition keeps a parity block on a separate disk for corresponding blocks from N other disks. This scheme is shown pictorially in Figure 10.3e. If one of the disks fails, the parity block can be used with the corresponding blocks from the other disks to restore the blocks of the failed disk.

A block read accesses only one disk, allowing other requests to be processed by the other disks. Thus, the data-transfer rate for each access is slower, but multiple read accesses can proceed in parallel, leading to a higher overall I/O rate. The transfer rates for large reads is high, since all the disks can be read in parallel; large writes also have high transfer rates, since the data and parity can be written in parallel.

Small independent writes, on the other hand, cannot be performed in parallel. A write of a block has to access the disk on which the block is stored, as well as the parity disk, since the parity block has to be updated. Moreover, both the old value of the parity block and the old value of the block being written have to be read for the new parity to be computed. Thus, a single write requires four disk accesses: two to read the two old blocks, and two to write the two blocks.

- **RAID level 5**, block-interleaved distributed parity, improves on level 4 by partitioning data and parity among all $N + 1$ disks, instead of storing data in N disks and parity in one disk. In level 5, all disks can participate in satisfying read requests, unlike RAID level 4, where the parity disk cannot participate, so level 5 increases the total number of requests that can be met in a given amount of time. For each set of N logical blocks, one of the disks stores the parity, and the other N disks store the blocks.

  Figure 10.3f shows the setup. The P's are distributed across all the disks. For example, with an array of 5 disks, the parity block, labeled Pk, for logical blocks $4k$, $4k + 1$, $4k + 2$, $4k + 3$ is stored in disk k mod 5; the corresponding blocks of the other four disks store the 4 data blocks $4k$ to $4k + 3$. The following table indicates how the first 20 blocks, numbered 0 to 19, and their parity blocks are laid out. The pattern shown gets repeated on further blocks.

P0	0	1	2	3
4	P1	5	6	7
8	9	P2	10	11
12	13	14	P3	15
16	17	18	19	P4

  Note that a parity block cannot store parity for blocks in the same disk, since then a disk failure would result in loss of data as well as of parity, and hence would not be recoverable. Level 5 subsumes level 4, since it offers better read −write performance at the same cost, so level 4 is not used in practice.

- **RAID level 6**, the P + Q redundancy scheme, is much like RAID level 5, but stores extra redundant information to guard against multiple disk failures. Instead of using parity, level 6 uses error-correcting codes such as the Reed−Solomon codes (see the bibliographical notes). In the scheme in Figure 10.3g, 2 bits of redundant data are stored for every 4 bits of data—unlike 1 parity bit in level 5—and the system can tolerate two disk failures.

Finally, we note that several variations have been proposed to the basic RAID schemes described here, and different vendors use different terminologies for the variants.

10.3.4 Choice of RAID Level

The factors to be taken into account in choosing a RAID level are:

- Monetary cost of extra disk-storage requirements.

- Performance requirements in terms of number of I/O operations.

- Performance when a disk has failed.

- Performance during rebuild (that is, while the data in a failed disk are being rebuilt on a new disk).

The time to rebuild the data of a failed disk can be significant, and it varies with the RAID level that is used. Rebuilding is easiest for RAID level 1, since data can be copied from another disk; for the other levels, we need to access all the other disks in the array to rebuild data of a failed disk. The **rebuild performance** of a RAID system may be an important factor if continuous availability of data is required, as it is in high-performance database systems. Furthermore, since rebuild time can form a significant part of the repair time, rebuild performance also influences the mean time to data loss.

RAID level 0 is used in high-performance applications where data safety is not critical. Since RAID levels 2 and 4 are subsumed by RAID levels 3 and 5, the choice of RAID levels is restricted to the remaining levels. Bit striping (level 3) is inferior to block striping (level 5), since block striping gives as good data-transfer rates for large transfers, while using fewer disks for small transfers. For small transfers, the disk access time dominates anyway, so the benefit of parallel reads diminishes. In fact, level 3 may perform worse than level 5 for a small transfer, since the transfer completes only when corresponding sectors on all disks have been fetched; the average latency for the disk array thus becomes very close to the worst-case latency for a single disk, negating the benefits of higher transfer rates. Level 6 is not supported currently by many RAID implementations, but it offers better reliability than level 5 and can be used in applications where data safety is very important.

The choice between RAID level 1 and level 5 is harder to make. RAID level 1 is popular for applications such as storage of log files in a database system, since it offers the best write performance. RAID level 5 has a lower storage overhead than level 1, but has a higher time overhead for writes. For applications where data are read frequently, and written rarely, level 5 is the preferred choice.

Disk-storage capacities have been growing at a rate of over 50 percent per year for many years, and the cost per byte has been falling at the same rate. As a result, for many existing database applications with moderate storage requirements, the monetary cost of the extra disk storage needed for mirroring has become relatively small (the extra monetary cost, however, remains a significant issue for storage-intensive applications such as video data storage). Access speeds have improved at a much slower rate (around a factor of 3 over 10 years), while the number of I/O operations required per second has increased tremendously, particularly for Web application servers.

RAID level 5, which increases the number of I/O operations needed to write a single logical block, pays a significant time penalty in terms of write performance. RAID level 1 is therefore the RAID level of choice for many applications with moderate storage requirements and high I/O requirements.

RAID system designers have to make several other decisions as well. For example, how many disks should there be in an array? How many bits should be protected by each parity bit? If there are more disks in an array, data-transfer rates are higher, but the system will be more expensive. If there are more bits protected by a parity bit, the space overhead due to parity bits is lower, but there is an increased chance that a second disk will fail before the first failed disk is repaired, and that will result in data loss.

10.3.5 Hardware Issues

Another issue in the choice of RAID implementations is at the level of hardware. RAID can be implemented with no change at the hardware level, using only software modification. Such RAID implementations are called **software RAID**. However, there are significant benefits to be had by building special-purpose hardware to support RAID, which we outline below; systems with special hardware support are called **hardware RAID** systems.

Hardware RAID implementations can use nonvolatile RAM to record writes before they are performed. In case of power failure, when the system comes back up, it retrieves information about any incomplete writes from nonvolatile RAM and then completes the writes. Without such hardware support, extra work needs to be done to detect blocks that may have been partially written before power failure (see Practice Exercise 10.3).

Even if all writes are completed properly, there is a small chance of a sector in a disk becoming unreadable at some point, even though it was successfully written earlier. Reasons for loss of data on individual sectors could range from manufacturing defects, to data corruption on a track when an adjacent track is written repeatedly. Such loss of data that were successfully written earlier is sometimes referred to as a *latent failure*, or as *bit rot*. When such a failure happens, if it is detected early the data can be recovered from the remaining disks in the RAID organization. However, if such a failure remains undetected, a single disk failure could lead to data loss if a sector in one of the other disks has a latent failure.

To minimize the chance of such data loss, good RAID controllers perform **scrubbing**; that is, during periods when disks are idle, every sector of every disk is read, and if any sector is found to be unreadable, the data are recovered from the remaining disks in the RAID organization, and the sector is written back. (If the physical sector is damaged, the disk controller would remap the logical sector address to a different physical sector on disk.)

Some hardware RAID implementations permit **hot swapping**; that is, faulty disks can be removed and replaced by new ones without turning power off. Hot swapping reduces the mean time to repair, since replacement of a disk does not have to wait until a time when the system can be shut down. In fact many critical systems today run on a 24 × 7 schedule; that is, they run 24 hours a day, 7 days a week, providing no time for shutting down and replacing a failed disk. Further, many RAID implementations assign a spare disk for each array (or for a set of disk arrays). If a disk fails, the spare disk is immediately used as a replacement. As a result, the mean time to repair is reduced greatly, minimizing the chance of any data loss. The failed disk can be replaced at leisure.

The power supply, or the disk controller, or even the system interconnection in a RAID system could become a single point of failure that could stop functioning of the RAID system. To avoid this possibility, good RAID implementations have multiple redundant power supplies (with battery backups so they continue to function even if power fails). Such RAID systems have multiple disk interfaces, and multiple interconnections to connect the RAID system to the computer system (or to a network of computer systems). Thus, failure of any single component will not stop the functioning of the RAID system.

10.3.6 Other RAID Applications

The concepts of RAID have been generalized to other storage devices, including arrays of tapes, and even to the broadcast of data over wireless systems. When applied to arrays of tapes, the RAID structures are able to recover data even if one of the tapes in an array of tapes is damaged. When applied to broadcast of data, a block of data is split into short units and is broadcast along with a parity unit; if one of the units is not received for any reason, it can be reconstructed from the other units.

10.4   Tertiary Storage

In a large database system, some of the data may have to reside on tertiary storage. The two most common tertiary storage media are optical disks and magnetic tapes.

10.4.1   Optical Disks

Compact disks have been a popular medium for distributing software, multimedia data such as audio and images, and other electronically published information. They have a storage capacity of 640 to 700 megabytes, and they are cheap to mass-produce. Digital video disks (DVDs) have now replaced compact disks in applications that require larger amounts of data. Disks in the DVD-5 format can store 4.7 gigabytes of data (in one recording layer), while disks in the DVD-9 format can store 8.5 gigabytes of data (in two recording layers). Recording on both sides of a disk yields even larger capacities; DVD-10 and DVD-18 formats, which are the two-sided versions of DVD-5 and DVD-9, can store 9.4 gigabytes and 17 gigabytes, respectively. The *Blu-ray DVD* format has a significantly higher capacity of 27 to 54 gigabytes per disk.

CD and DVD drives have much longer seek times (100 milliseconds is common) than do magnetic-disk drives, since the head assembly is heavier. Rotational speeds are typically lower than those of magnetic disks, although the faster CD and DVD drives have rotation speeds of about 3000 rotations per minute, which is comparable to speeds of lower-end magnetic-disk drives. Rotational speeds of CD drives originally corresponded to the audio CD standards, and the speeds of DVD drives originally corresponded to the DVD video standards, but current-generation drives rotate at many times the standard rate.

Data-transfer rates are somewhat less than for magnetic disks. Current CD drives read at around 3 to 6 megabytes per second, and current DVD drives read at 8 to 20 megabytes per second. Like magnetic-disk drives, optical disks store more data in outside tracks and less data in inner tracks. The transfer rate of optical drives is characterized as $n\times$, which means the drive supports transfers at n times the standard rate; rates of around $50\times$ for CD and $16\times$ for DVD are now common.

The record-once versions of optical disks (CD-R, DVD-R, and DVD+R) are popular for distribution of data and particularly for archival storage of data because they have a high capacity, have a longer lifetime than magnetic disks, and can be removed and stored at a remote location. Since they cannot be overwritten, they can be used to store information that should not be modified, such as audit trails. The multiple-write versions (CD-RW, DVD-RW, DVD+RW, and DVD-RAM) are also used for archival purposes.

Jukeboxes are devices that store a large number of optical disks (up to several hundred) and load them automatically on demand to one of a small number of drives (usually 1 to 10). The aggregate storage capacity of such a system can be many terabytes. When a disk is accessed, it is loaded by a mechanical arm from a rack onto a drive (any disk that was already in the drive must first be placed back on the rack). The disk load/unload time is usually of the order of a few seconds —very much longer than disk access times.

10.4.2   Magnetic Tapes

Although magnetic tapes are relatively permanent, and can hold large volumes of data, they are slow in comparison to magnetic and optical disks. Even more important, magnetic tapes are limited to sequential access. Thus, they cannot provide random access for secondary-storage requirements, although historically, prior to the use of magnetic disks, tapes were used as a secondary-storage medium.

Tapes are used mainly for backup, for storage of infrequently used information, and as an off-line medium for transferring information from one system to another. Tapes are also used for storing large volumes of data, such as video or image data, that either do not need to be accessible quickly or are so voluminous that magnetic-disk storage would be too expensive.

A tape is kept in a spool, and is wound or rewound past a read–write head. Moving to the correct spot on a tape can take seconds or even minutes, rather than milliseconds; once positioned, however, tape drives can write data at densities and speeds approaching those of disk drives. Capacities vary, depending on the length and width of the tape and on the density at which the head can read and write. The market is currently fragmented among a wide variety of tape formats. Currently available tape capacities range from a few gigabytes with the **Digital Audio Tape** (DAT) format, 10 to 40 gigabytes with the **Digital Linear Tape** (DLT) format, 100 gigabytes and higher with the **Ultrium** format, to 330 gigabytes with **Ampex helical scan** tape formats. Data-transfer rates are of the order of a few to tens of megabytes per second.

Tape devices are quite reliable, and good tape drive systems perform a read of the just-written data to ensure that it has been recorded correctly. Tapes, however, have limits on the number of times that they can be read or written reliably.

Tape jukeboxes, like optical disk jukeboxes, hold large numbers of tapes, with a few drives onto which the tapes can be mounted; they are used for storing large volumes of data, ranging up to many petabytes (10^{15} bytes), with access times on the order of seconds to a few minutes. Applications that need such enormous data storage include imaging systems that gather data from remote-sensing satellites, and large video libraries for television broadcasters.

Some tape formats (such as the Accelis format) support faster seek times (of the order of tens of seconds), and are intended for applications that retrieve information from jukeboxes. Most other tape formats provide larger capacities, at the cost of slower access; such formats are ideal for data backup, where fast seeks are not important.

Tape drives have been unable to keep up with the enormous improvements in disk drive capacity and corresponding reduction in storage cost. While the cost of tapes is low, the cost of tape drives and tape libraries is significantly higher than the cost of a disk drive: a tape library capable of storing a few terabytes can costs tens of thousands of dollars. Backing up data to disk drives has become a cost-effective alternative to tape backup for a number of applications.

10.5 File Organization

A database is mapped into a number of different files that are maintained by the underlying operating system. These files reside permanently on disks. A **file** is organized logically as a sequence of records. These records are mapped onto disk blocks. Files are provided as a basic construct in operating systems, so we shall assume the existence of an underlying *file system*. We need to consider ways of representing logical data models in terms of files.

Each file is also logically partitioned into fixed-length storage units called **blocks**, which are the units of both storage allocation and data transfer. Most databases use block sizes of 4 to 8 kilobytes by default, but many databases allow the block size to be specified when a database instance is created. Larger block sizes can be useful in some database applications.

A block may contain several records; the exact set of records that a block contains is determined by the form of physical data organization being used. We shall assume that *no record is larger than a block*. This assumption is realistic for most data-processing applications, such as our university example. There are certainly several kinds of large data items, such as images, that can be significantly larger than a block. We briefly discuss how to handle such large data items later, in Section 10.5.2, by storing large data items separately, and storing a pointer to the data item in the record.

In addition, we shall require that *each record is entirely contained in a single block*; that is, no record is contained partly in one block, and partly in another. This restriction simplifies and speeds up access to data items.

In a relational database, tuples of distinct relations are generally of different sizes. One approach to mapping the database to files is to use several files, and to store records of only one fixed length in any given file. An alternative is to structure our files so that we can accommodate multiple lengths for records; however, files of fixed-length records are easier to implement than are files of variable-length records. Many of the techniques used for the former can be applied to the variable-length case. Thus, we begin by considering a file of fixed-length records, and consider storage of variable-length records later.

10.5.1 Fixed-Length Records

As an example, let us consider a file of *instructor* records for our university database. Each record of this file is defined (in pseudocode) as:

> **type** *instructor* = **record**
> > *ID* **varchar** (5);
> > *name* **varchar**(20);
> > *dept_name* **varchar** (20);
> > *salary* **numeric** (8,2);
> **end**

Assume that each character occupies 1 byte and that numeric (8,2) occupies 8 bytes. Suppose that instead of allocating a variable amount of bytes for the attributes *ID*, *name*, and *dept_name*, we allocate the maximum number of bytes that each attribute can hold. Then, the *instructor* record is 53 bytes long. A simple approach is to use the first 53 bytes for the first record, the next 53 bytes for the second record, and so on (Figure 10.4). However, there are two problems with this simple approach:

1. Unless the block size happens to be a multiple of 53 (which is unlikely), some records will cross block boundaries. That is, part of the record will be stored in one block and part in another. It would thus require two block accesses to read or write such a record.

2. It is difficult to delete a record from this structure. The space occupied by the record to be deleted must be filled with some other record of the file, or we must have a way of marking deleted records so that they can be ignored.

record 0	10101	Srinivasan	Comp. Sci.	65000
record 1	12121	Wu	Finance	90000
record 2	15151	Mozart	Music	40000
record 3	22222	Einstein	Physics	95000
record 4	32343	El Said	History	60000
record 5	33456	Gold	Physics	87000
record 6	45565	Katz	Comp. Sci.	75000
record 7	58583	Califieri	History	62000
record 8	76543	Singh	Finance	80000
record 9	76766	Crick	Biology	72000
record 10	83821	Brandt	Comp. Sci.	92000
record 11	98345	Kim	Elec. Eng.	80000

Figure 10.4 File containing *instructor* records.

To avoid the first problem, we allocate only as many records to a block as would fit entirely in the block (this number can be computed easily by dividing the block size by the record size, and discarding the fractional part). Any remaining bytes of each block are left unused.

When a record is deleted, we could move the record that came after it into the space formerly occupied by the deleted record, and so on, until every record following the deleted record has been moved ahead (Figure 10.5). Such an approach requires moving a large number of records. It might be easier simply to move the final record of the file into the space occupied by the deleted record (Figure 10.6).

It is undesirable to move records to occupy the space freed by a deleted record, since doing so requires additional block accesses. Since insertions tend to be more frequent than deletions, it is acceptable to leave open the space occupied by the

record 0	10101	Srinivasan	Comp. Sci.	65000
record 1	12121	Wu	Finance	90000
record 2	15151	Mozart	Music	40000
record 4	32343	El Said	History	60000
record 5	33456	Gold	Physics	87000
record 6	45565	Katz	Comp. Sci.	75000
record 7	58583	Califieri	History	62000
record 8	76543	Singh	Finance	80000
record 9	76766	Crick	Biology	72000
record 10	83821	Brandt	Comp. Sci.	92000
record 11	98345	Kim	Elec. Eng.	80000

Figure 10.5 File of Figure 10.4, with record 3 deleted and all records moved.

record 0	10101	Srinivasan	Comp. Sci.	65000
record 1	12121	Wu	Finance	90000
record 2	15151	Mozart	Music	40000
record 11	98345	Kim	Elec. Eng.	80000
record 4	32343	El Said	History	60000
record 5	33456	Gold	Physics	87000
record 6	45565	Katz	Comp. Sci.	75000
record 7	58583	Califieri	History	62000
record 8	76543	Singh	Finance	80000
record 9	76766	Crick	Biology	72000
record 10	83821	Brandt	Comp. Sci.	92000

Figure 10.6 File of Figure 10.4, with record 3 deleted and final record moved.

deleted record, and to wait for a subsequent insertion before reusing the space. A simple marker on a deleted record is not sufficient, since it is hard to find this available space when an insertion is being done. Thus, we need to introduce an additional structure.

At the beginning of the file, we allocate a certain number of bytes as a **file header**. The header will contain a variety of information about the file. For now, all we need to store there is the address of the first record whose contents are deleted. We use this first record to store the address of the second available record, and so on. Intuitively, we can think of these stored addresses as *pointers*, since they point to the location of a record. The deleted records thus form a linked list, which is often referred to as a **free list**. Figure 10.7 shows the file of Figure 10.4, with the free list, after records 1, 4, and 6 have been deleted.

On insertion of a new record, we use the record pointed to by the header. We change the header pointer to point to the next available record. If no space is available, we add the new record to the end of the file.

Insertion and deletion for files of fixed-length records are simple to implement, because the space made available by a deleted record is exactly the space needed to insert a record. If we allow records of variable length in a file, this match no longer holds. An inserted record may not fit in the space left free by a deleted record, or it may fill only part of that space.

10.5.2 Variable-Length Records

Variable-length records arise in database systems in several ways:

- Storage of multiple record types in a file.
- Record types that allow variable lengths for one or more fields.
- Record types that allow repeating fields, such as arrays or multisets.

header				
record 0	10101	Srinivasan	Comp. Sci.	65000
record 1				
record 2	15151	Mozart	Music	40000
record 3	22222	Einstein	Physics	95000
record 4				
record 5	33456	Gold	Physics	87000
record 6				
record 7	58583	Califieri	History	62000
record 8	76543	Singh	Finance	80000
record 9	76766	Crick	Biology	72000
record 10	83821	Brandt	Comp. Sci.	92000
record 11	98345	Kim	Elec. Eng.	80000

Figure 10.7 File of Figure 10.4, with free list after deletion of records 1, 4, and 6.

Different techniques for implementing variable-length records exist. Two different problems must be solved by any such technique:

- How to represent a single record in such a way that individual attributes can be extracted easily.

- How to store variable-length records within a block, such that records in a block can be extracted easily.

The representation of a record with variable-length attributes typically has two parts: an initial part with fixed length attributes, followed by data for variable-length attributes. Fixed-length attributes, such as numeric values, dates, or fixed-length character strings are allocated as many bytes as required to store their value. Variable-length attributes, such as varchar types, are represented in the initial part of the record by a pair (*offset*, *length*), where *offset* denotes where the data for that attribute begins within the record, and *length* is the length in bytes of the variable-sized attribute. The values for these attributes are stored consecutively, after the initial fixed-length part of the record. Thus, the initial part of the record stores a fixed size of information about each attribute, whether it is fixed-length or variable-length.

An example of such a record representation is shown in Figure 10.8. The figure shows an *instructor* record, whose first three attributes *ID*, *name*, and *dept_name* are variable-length strings, and whose fourth attribute *salary* is a fixed-sized number. We assume that the offset and length values are stored in two bytes each, for a total of 4 bytes per attribute. The *salary* attribute is assumed to be stored in 8 bytes, and each string takes as many bytes as it has characters.

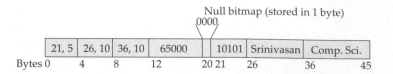

Figure 10.8   Representation of variable-length record.

The figure also illustrates the use of a **null bitmap**, which indicates which attributes of the record have a null value. In this particular record, if the salary were null, the fourth bit of the bitmap would be set to 1, and the *salary* value stored in bytes 12 through 19 would be ignored. Since the record has four attributes, the null bitmap for this record fits in 1 byte, although more bytes may be required with more attributes. In some representations, the null bitmap is stored at the beginning of the record, and for attributes that are null, no data (value, or offset/length) are stored at all. Such a representation would save some storage space, at the cost of extra work to extract attributes of the record. This representation is particularly useful for certain applications where records have a large number of fields, most of which are null.

We next address the problem of storing variable-length records in a block. The **slotted-page structure** is commonly used for organizing records within a block, and is shown in Figure 10.9.[3] There is a header at the beginning of each block, containing the following information:

1.   The number of record entries in the header.

2.   The end of free space in the block.

3.   An array whose entries contain the location and size of each record.

The actual records are allocated *contiguously* in the block, starting from the end of the block. The free space in the block is contiguous, between the final entry in the header array, and the first record. If a record is inserted, space is allocated for it at the end of free space, and an entry containing its size and location is added to the header.

If a record is deleted, the space that it occupies is freed, and its entry is set to *deleted* (its size is set to −1, for example). Further, the records in the block before the deleted record are moved, so that the free space created by the deletion gets occupied, and all free space is again between the final entry in the header array and the first record. The end-of-free-space pointer in the header is appropriately updated as well. Records can be grown or shrunk by similar techniques, as long as there is space in the block. The cost of moving the records is not too high, since the size of a block is limited: typical values are around 4 to 8 kilobytes.

The slotted-page structure requires that there be no pointers that point directly to records. Instead, pointers must point to the entry in the header that contains the

---

[3]Here, "page" is synonymous with "block."

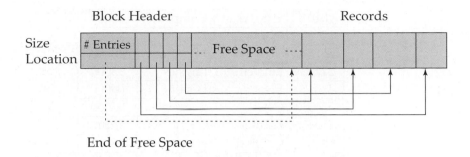

Figure 10.9 Slotted-page structure.

actual location of the record. This level of indirection allows records to be moved to prevent fragmentation of space inside a block, while supporting indirect pointers to the record.

Databases often store data that can be much larger than a disk block. For instance, an image or an audio recording may be multiple megabytes in size, while a video object may be multiple gigabytes in size. Recall that SQL supports the types **blob** and **clob**, which store binary and character large objects.

Most relational databases restrict the size of a record to be no larger than the size of a block, to simplify buffer management and free-space management. Large objects are often stored in a special file (or collection of files) instead of being stored with the other (short) attributes of records in which they occur. A (logical) pointer to the object is then stored in the record containing the large object. Large objects are often represented using B^+-tree file organizations, which we study in Section 11.4.1. B^+-tree file organizations permit us to read an entire object, or specified byte ranges in the object, as well as to insert and delete parts of the object.

10.6 Organization of Records in Files

So far, we have studied how records are represented in a file structure. A relation is a set of records. Given a set of records, the next question is how to organize them in a file. Several of the possible ways of organizing records in files are:

- **Heap file organization**. Any record can be placed anywhere in the file where there is space for the record. There is no ordering of records. Typically, there is a single file for each relation.

- **Sequential file organization**. Records are stored in sequential order, according to the value of a "search key" of each record. Section 10.6.1 describes this organization.

- **Hashing file organization**. A hash function is computed on some attribute of each record. The result of the hash function specifies in which block of the

10101	Srinivasan	Comp. Sci.	65000
12121	Wu	Finance	90000
15151	Mozart	Music	40000
22222	Einstein	Physics	95000
32343	El Said	History	60000
33456	Gold	Physics	87000
45565	Katz	Comp. Sci.	75000
58583	Califieri	History	62000
76543	Singh	Finance	80000
76766	Crick	Biology	72000
83821	Brandt	Comp. Sci.	92000
98345	Kim	Elec. Eng.	80000

Figure 10.10 Sequential file for *instructor* records.

file the record should be placed. Chapter 11 describes this organization; it is closely related to the indexing structures described in that chapter.

Generally, a separate file is used to store the records of each relation. However, in a **multitable clustering file organization**, records of several different relations are stored in the same file; further, related records of the different relations are stored on the same block, so that one I/O operation fetches related records from all the relations. For example, records of the two relations can be considered to be related if they would match in a join of the two relations. Section 10.6.2 describes this organization.

10.6.1   Sequential File Organization

A **sequential file** is designed for efficient processing of records in sorted order based on some search key. A **search key** is any attribute or set of attributes; it need not be the primary key, or even a superkey. To permit fast retrieval of records in search-key order, we chain together records by pointers. The pointer in each record points to the next record in search-key order. Furthermore, to minimize the number of block accesses in sequential file processing, we store records physically in search-key order, or as close to search-key order as possible.

Figure 10.10 shows a sequential file of *instructor* records taken from our university example. In that example, the records are stored in search-key order, using *ID* as the search key.

The sequential file organization allows records to be read in sorted order; that can be useful for display purposes, as well as for certain query-processing algorithms that we shall study in Chapter 12.

It is difficult, however, to maintain physical sequential order as records are inserted and deleted, since it is costly to move many records as a result of a single

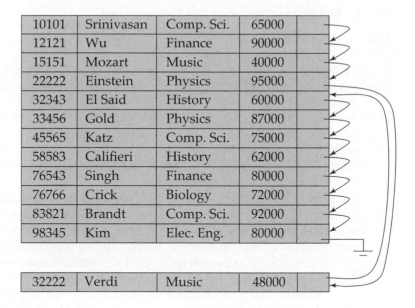

10101	Srinivasan	Comp. Sci.	65000	
12121	Wu	Finance	90000	
15151	Mozart	Music	40000	
22222	Einstein	Physics	95000	
32343	El Said	History	60000	
33456	Gold	Physics	87000	
45565	Katz	Comp. Sci.	75000	
58583	Califieri	History	62000	
76543	Singh	Finance	80000	
76766	Crick	Biology	72000	
83821	Brandt	Comp. Sci.	92000	
98345	Kim	Elec. Eng.	80000	

| 32222 | Verdi | Music | 48000 | |

Figure 10.11 Sequential file after an insertion.

insertion or deletion. We can manage deletion by using pointer chains, as we saw previously. For insertion, we apply the following rules:

1. Locate the record in the file that comes before the record to be inserted in search-key order.

2. If there is a free record (that is, space left after a deletion) within the same block as this record, insert the new record there. Otherwise, insert the new record in an *overflow block*. In either case, adjust the pointers so as to chain together the records in search-key order.

Figure 10.11 shows the file of Figure 10.10 after the insertion of the record (32222, Verdi, Music, 48000). The structure in Figure 10.11 allows fast insertion of new records, but forces sequential file-processing applications to process records in an order that does not match the physical order of the records.

If relatively few records need to be stored in overflow blocks, this approach works well. Eventually, however, the correspondence between search-key order and physical order may be totally lost over a period of time, in which case sequential processing will become much less efficient. At this point, the file should be **reorganized** so that it is once again physically in sequential order. Such reorganizations are costly, and must be done during times when the system load is low. The frequency with which reorganizations are needed depends on the frequency of insertion of new records. In the extreme case in which insertions rarely occur, it is possible always to keep the file in physically sorted order. In such a case, the pointer field in Figure 10.10 is not needed.

10.6.2 Multitable Clustering File Organization

Many relational database systems store each relation in a separate file, so that they can take full advantage of the file system that the operating system provides. Usually, tuples of a relation can be represented as fixed-length records. Thus, relations can be mapped to a simple file structure. This simple implementation of a relational database system is well suited to low-cost database implementations as in, for example, embedded systems or portable devices. In such systems, the size of the database is small, so little is gained from a sophisticated file structure. Furthermore, in such environments, it is essential that the overall size of the object code for the database system be small. A simple file structure reduces the amount of code needed to implement the system.

This simple approach to relational database implementation becomes less satisfactory as the size of the database increases. We have seen that there are performance advantages to be gained from careful assignment of records to blocks, and from careful organization of the blocks themselves. Clearly, a more complicated file structure may be beneficial, even if we retain the strategy of storing each relation in a separate file.

However, many large-scale database systems do not rely directly on the underlying operating system for file management. Instead, one large operating-system file is allocated to the database system. The database system stores all relations in this one file, and manages the file itself.

Even if multiple relations are stored in a single file, by default most databases store records of only one relation in a given block. This simplifies data management. However, in some cases it can be useful to store records of more than one relation in a single block. To see the advantage of storing records of multiple relations in one block, consider the following SQL query for the university database:

> **select** *dept_name, building, budget*, ID, *name, salary*
> **from** *department* **natural join** *instructor*;

This query computes a join of the *department* and *instructor* relations. Thus, for each tuple of *department*, the system must locate the *instructor* tuples with the same value for *dept_name*. Ideally, these records will be located with the help of *indices*, which we shall discuss in Chapter 11. Regardless of how these records are located, however, they need to be transferred from disk into main memory. In the worst case, each record will reside on a different block, forcing us to do one block read for each record required by the query.

dept_name	building	budget
Comp. Sci.	Taylor	100000
Physics	Watson	70000

Figure 10.12 The *department* relation.

ID	name	dept_name	salary
10101	Srinivasan	Comp. Sci.	65000
33456	Gold	Physics	87000
45565	Katz	Comp. Sci.	75000
83821	Brandt	Comp. Sci.	92000

Figure 10.13   The *instructor* relation.

As a concrete example, consider the *department* and *instructor* relations of Figures 10.12 and 10.13, respectively (for brevity, we include only a subset of the tuples of the relations we have used thus far). In Figure 10.14, we show a file structure designed for efficient execution of queries involving the natural join of *department* and *instructor*. The *instructor* tuples for each *ID* are stored near the *department* tuple for the corresponding *dept_name*. This structure mixes together tuples of two relations, but allows for efficient processing of the join. When a tuple of the *department* relation is read, the entire block containing that tuple is copied from disk into main memory. Since the corresponding *instructor* tuples are stored on the disk near the *department* tuple, the block containing the *department* tuple contains tuples of the *instructor* relation needed to process the query. If a department has so many instructors that the *instructor* records do not fit in one block, the remaining records appear on nearby blocks.

A **multitable clustering file organization** is a file organization, such as that illustrated in Figure 10.14, that stores related records of two or more relations in each block. Such a file organization allows us to read records that would satisfy the join condition by using one block read. Thus, we are able to process this particular query more efficiently.

In the representation shown in Figure 10.14, the *dept_name* attribute is omitted from *instructor* records since it can be inferred from the associated *department* record; the attribute may be retained in some implementations, to simplify access to the attributes. We assume that each record contains the identifier of the relation to which it belongs, although this is not shown in Figure 10.14.

Our use of clustering of multiple tables into a single file has enhanced processing of a particular join (that of *department* and *instructor*), but it results in slowing processing of other types of queries. For example,

Comp. Sci.	Taylor	100000
45564	Katz	75000
10101	Srinivasan	65000
83821	Brandt	92000
Physics	Watson	70000
33456	Gold	87000

Figure 10.14   Multitable clustering file structure.

Comp. Sci.	Taylor	100000	
45564	Katz	75000	
10101	Srinivasan	65000	
83821	Brandt	92000	
Physics	Watson	70000	
33456	Gold	87000	

Figure 10.15 Multitable clustering file structure with pointer chains.

select *
from *department*;

requires more block accesses than it did in the scheme under which we stored each relation in a separate file, since each block now contains significantly fewer *department* records. To locate efficiently all tuples of the *department* relation in the structure of Figure 10.14, we can chain together all the records of that relation using pointers, as in Figure 10.15.

When multitable clustering is to be used depends on the types of queries that the database designer believes to be most frequent. Careful use of multitable clustering can produce significant performance gains in query processing.

10.7   Data-Dictionary Storage

So far, we have considered only the representation of the relations themselves. A relational database system needs to maintain data *about* the relations, such as the schema of the relations. In general, such "data about data" is referred to as **metadata**.

Relational schemas and other metadata about relations are stored in a structure called the **data dictionary** or **system catalog**. Among the types of information that the system must store are these:

- Names of the relations.

- Names of the attributes of each relation.

- Domains and lengths of attributes.

- Names of views defined on the database, and definitions of those views.

- Integrity constraints (for example, key constraints).

In addition, many systems keep the following data on users of the system:

- Names of authorized users.

- Authorization and accounting information about users.

- Passwords or other information used to authenticate users.

Further, the database may store statistical and descriptive data about the relations, such as:

- Number of tuples in each relation.
- Method of storage for each relation (for example, clustered or nonclustered).

The data dictionary may also note the storage organization (sequential, hash, or heap) of relations, and the location where each relation is stored:

- If relations are stored in operating system files, the dictionary would note the names of the file (or files) containing each relation.
- If the database stores all relations in a single file, the dictionary may note the blocks containing records of each relation in a data structure such as a linked list.

In Chapter 11, in which we study indices, we shall see a need to store information about each index on each of the relations:

- Name of the index.
- Name of the relation being indexed.
- Attributes on which the index is defined.
- Type of index formed.

All this metadata information constitutes, in effect, a miniature database. Some database systems store such metadata by using special-purpose data structures and code. It is generally preferable to store the data about the database as relations in the database itself. By using database relations to store system metadata, we simplify the overall structure of the system and harness the full power of the database for fast access to system data.

The exact choice of how to represent system metadata by relations must be made by the system designers. One possible representation, with primary keys underlined, is shown in Figure 10.16. In this representation, the attribute *index_attributes* of the relation *Index_metadata* is assumed to contain a list of one or more attributes, which can be represented by a character string such as "*dept_name, building*". The *Index_metadata* relation is thus not in first normal form; it can be normalized, but the above representation is likely to be more efficient to access. The data dictionary is often stored in a nonnormalized form to achieve fast access.

Whenever the database system needs to retrieve records from a relation, it must first consult the *Relation_metadata* relation to find the location and storage organization of the relation, and then fetch records using this information. How-ever, the storage organization and location of the *Relation_metadata* relation itself

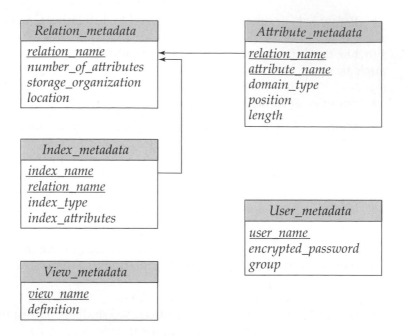

Figure 10.16   Relational schema representing system metadata.

must be recorded elsewhere (for example, in the database code itself, or in a fixed location in the database), since we need this information to find the contents of *Relation_metadata*.

10.8   Database Buffer

A major goal of the database system is to minimize the number of block transfers between the disk and memory. One way to reduce the number of disk accesses is to keep as many blocks as possible in main memory. The goal is to maximize the chance that, when a block is accessed, it is already in main memory, and, thus, no disk access is required.

Since it is not possible to keep all blocks in main memory, we need to manage the allocation of the space available in main memory for the storage of blocks. The **buffer** is that part of main memory available for storage of copies of disk blocks. There is always a copy kept on disk of every block, but the copy on disk may be a version of the block older than the version in the buffer. The subsystem responsible for the allocation of buffer space is called the **buffer manager**.

10.8.1   Buffer Manager

Programs in a database system make requests (that is, calls) on the buffer manager when they need a block from disk. If the block is already in the buffer, the buffer manager passes the address of the block in main memory to the requester. If the block is not in the buffer, the buffer manager first allocates space in the buffer for the block, throwing out some other block, if necessary, to make space for the new block. The thrown-out block is written back to disk only if it has been modified since the most recent time that it was written to the disk. Then, the buffer manager reads in the requested block from the disk to the buffer, and passes the address of the block in main memory to the requester. The internal actions of the buffer manager are transparent to the programs that issue disk-block requests.

If you are familiar with operating-system concepts, you will note that the buffer manager appears to be nothing more than a virtual-memory manager, like those found in most operating systems. One difference is that the size of the database might be larger than the hardware address space of a machine, so memory addresses are not sufficient to address all disk blocks. Further, to serve the database system well, the buffer manager must use techniques more sophisticated than typical virtual-memory management schemes:

- **Buffer replacement strategy**. When there is no room left in the buffer, a block must be removed from the buffer before a new one can be read in. Most operating systems use a **least recently used** (LRU) scheme, in which the block that was referenced least recently is written back to disk and is removed from the buffer. This simple approach can be improved on for database applications.

- **Pinned blocks**. For the database system to be able to recover from crashes (Chapter 16), it is necessary to restrict those times when a block may be written back to disk. For instance, most recovery systems require that a block should not be written to disk while an update on the block is in progress. A block that is not allowed to be written back to disk is said to be **pinned**. Although many operating systems do not support pinned blocks, such a feature is essential for a database system that is resilient to crashes.

- **Forced output of blocks**. There are situations in which it is necessary to write back the block to disk, even though the buffer space that it occupies is not needed. This write is called the **forced output** of a block. We shall see the reason for forced output in Chapter 16; briefly, main-memory contents and thus buffer contents are lost in a crash, whereas data on disk usually survive a crash.

10.8.2   Buffer-Replacement Policies

The goal of a replacement strategy for blocks in the buffer is to minimize accesses to the disk. For general-purpose programs, it is not possible to predict accurately which blocks will be referenced. Therefore, operating systems use the past pattern of block references as a predictor of future references. The assumption generally made is that blocks that have been referenced recently are likely to be referenced again. Therefore, if a block must be replaced, the least recently referenced block is replaced. This approach is called the **least recently used** (LRU) block-replacement scheme.

```
for each tuple i of instructor do
    for each tuple d of department do
        if i[dept_name] = d[dept_name]
        then begin
                let x be a tuple defined as follows:
                x[ID] := i[ID]
                x[dept_name] := i[dept_name]
                x[name] := i[name]
                x[salary] := i[salary]
                x[building] := d[building]
                x[budget] := d[budget]
                include tuple x as part of result of instructor ⋈ department
        end
    end
end
```

Figure 10.17   Procedure for computing join.

LRU is an acceptable replacement scheme in operating systems. However, a database system is able to predict the pattern of future references more accurately than an operating system. A user request to the database system involves several steps. The database system is often able to determine in advance which blocks will be needed by looking at each of the steps required to perform the user-requested operation. Thus, unlike operating systems, which must rely on the past to predict the future, database systems may have information regarding at least the short-term future.

To illustrate how information about future block access allows us to improve the LRU strategy, consider the processing of the SQL query:

> **select** *
> **from** *instructor* **natural join** *department*;

Assume that the strategy chosen to process this request is given by the pseudocode program shown in Figure 10.17. (We shall study other, more efficient, strategies in Chapter 12.)

Assume that the two relations of this example are stored in separate files. In this example, we can see that, once a tuple of *instructor* has been processed, that tuple is not needed again. Therefore, once processing of an entire block of *instructor* tuples is completed, that block is no longer needed in main memory, even though it has been used recently. The buffer manager should be instructed to free the space occupied by an *instructor* block as soon as the final tuple has been processed. This buffer-management strategy is called the **toss-immediate** strategy.

Now consider blocks containing *department* tuples. We need to examine every block of *department* tuples once for each tuple of the *instructor* relation. When processing of a *department* block is completed, we know that that block will not be accessed again until all other *department* blocks have been processed. Thus, the most recently used *department* block will be the final block to be re-referenced, and the least recently used *department* block is the block that will be referenced next. This assumption set is the exact opposite of the one that forms the basis for the LRU strategy. Indeed, the optimal strategy for block replacement for the above procedure is the **most recently used** (MRU) strategy. If a *department* block must be removed from the buffer, the MRU strategy chooses the most recently used block (blocks are not eligible for replacement while they are being used).

For the MRU strategy to work correctly for our example, the system must pin the *department* block currently being processed. After the final *department* tuple has been processed, the block is unpinned, and it becomes the most recently used block.

In addition to using knowledge that the system may have about the request being processed, the buffer manager can use statistical information about the probability that a request will reference a particular relation. For example, the data dictionary that (as we will see in detail in Section 10.7) keeps track of the logical schema of the relations as well as their physical storage information is one of the most frequently accessed parts of the database. Thus, the buffer manager should try not to remove data-dictionary blocks from main memory, unless other factors dictate that it do so. In Chapter 11, we discuss indices for files. Since an index for a file may be accessed more frequently than the file itself, the buffer manager should, in general, not remove index blocks from main memory if alternatives are available.

The ideal database block-replacement strategy needs knowledge of the database operations—both those being performed and those that will be performed in the future. No single strategy is known that handles all the possible scenarios well. Indeed, a surprisingly large number of database systems use LRU, despite that strategy's faults. The practice questions and exercises explore alternative strategies.

The strategy that the buffer manager uses for block replacement is influenced by factors other than the time at which the block will be referenced again. If the system is processing requests by several users concurrently, the concurrency-control subsystem (Chapter 15) may need to delay certain requests, to ensure preservation of database consistency. If the buffer manager is given information from the concurrency-control subsystem indicating which requests are being delayed, it can use this information to alter its block-replacement strategy. Specifically, blocks needed by active (nondelayed) requests can be retained in the buffer at the expense of blocks needed by the delayed requests.

The crash-recovery subsystem (Chapter 16) imposes stringent constraints on block replacement. If a block has been modified, the buffer manager is not allowed to write back the new version of the block in the buffer to disk, since that would destroy the old version. Instead, the block manager must seek permission from the crash-recovery subsystem before writing out a block. The crash-recovery subsystem may demand that certain other blocks be force-output before it grants permission to the buffer manager to output the block requested. In Chapter 16, we define precisely the interaction between the buffer manager and the crash-recovery subsystem.

10.9 Summary

- Several types of data storage exist in most computer systems. They are classified by the speed with which they can access data, by their cost per unit of data to buy the memory, and by their reliability. Among the media available are cache, main memory, flash memory, magnetic disks, optical disks, and magnetic tapes.

- Two factors determine the reliability of storage media: whether a power failure or system crash causes data to be lost, and what the likelihood is of physical failure of the storage device.

- We can reduce the likelihood of physical failure by retaining multiple copies of data. For disks, we can use mirroring. Or we can use more sophisticated methods based on redundant arrays of independent disks (RAID). By striping data across disks, these methods offer high throughput rates on large accesses; by introducing redundancy across disks, they improve reliability greatly. Several different RAID organizations are possible, each with different cost, performance, and reliability characteristics. RAID level 1 (mirroring) and RAID level 5 are the most commonly used.

- We can organize a file logically as a sequence of records mapped onto disk blocks. One approach to mapping the database to files is to use several files, and to store records of only one fixed length in any given file. An alternative is to structure files so that they can accommodate multiple lengths for records. The slotted-page method is widely used to handle varying length records within a disk block.

- Since data are transferred between disk storage and main memory in units of a block, it is worthwhile to assign file records to blocks in such a way that a single block contains related records. If we can access several of the records we want with only one block access, we save disk accesses. Since disk accesses are usually the bottleneck in the performance of a database system, careful assignment of records to blocks can pay significant performance dividends.

- The data dictionary, also referred to as the system catalog, keeps track of metadata, that is data about data, such as relation names, attribute names and types, storage information, integrity constraints, and user information.

- One way to reduce the number of disk accesses is to keep as many blocks as possible in main memory. Since it is not possible to keep all blocks in main memory, we need to manage the allocation of the space available in main memory for the storage of blocks. The *buffer* is that part of main memory available for storage of copies of disk blocks. The subsystem responsible for the allocation of buffer space is called the *buffer manager*.

Review Terms

- Physical storage media
  - Cache
  - Main memory
  - Flash memory
  - Magnetic disk
  - Optical storage
- Magnetic disk
  - Platter
  - Hard disks
  - Floppy disks
  - Tracks
  - Sectors
  - Read–write head
  - Disk arm
  - Cylinder
  - Disk controller
  - Checksums
  - Remapping of bad sectors
- Performance measures of disks
  - Access time
  - Seek time
  - Rotational latency
  - Data-transfer rate
  - Mean time to failure (MTTF)
- Disk block
- Optimization of disk-block access
  - Disk-arm scheduling
  - Elevator algorithm
  - File organization

- Defragmenting
- Nonvolatile write buffers
- Nonvolatile random-access memory (NVRAM)
- Log disk
- Redundant arrays of independent disks (RAID)
  - Mirroring
  - Data striping
  - Bit-level striping
  - Block-level striping
- RAID levels
  - Level 0 (block striping, no redundancy)
  - Level 1 (block striping, mirroring)
  - Level 3 (bit striping, parity)
  - Level 5 (block striping, distributed parity)
  - Level 6 (block striping, P + Q redundancy)
- Rebuild performance
- Software RAID
- Hardware RAID
- Hot swapping
- Tertiary storage
  - Optical disks
  - Magnetic tapes
  - Jukeboxes
- File
- File organization
  - File header

- ○ Free list
- Variable-length records
  - ○ Slotted-page structure
- Large objects
- Heap file organization
- Sequential file organization
- Hashing file organization
- Multitable clustering file organization
- Search key
- Data dictionary

- System catalog
- Buffer
  - ○ Buffer manager
  - ○ Pinned blocks
  - ○ Forced output of blocks
- Buffer-replacement policies
  - ○ Least recently used (LRU)
  - ○ Toss-immediate
  - ○ Most recently used (MRU)

Practice Exercises

10.1   Consider the data and parity-block arrangement on four disks depicted in Figure 10.18. The B_is represent data blocks; the P_is represent parity blocks. Parity block P_i is the parity block for data blocks B_{4i-3} to B_{4i}. What, if any, problem might this arrangement present?

10.2   Flash storage:

   a.   How is the flash translation table, which is used to map logical page numbers to physical page numbers, created in memory?

   b.   Suppose you have a 64 gigabyte flash storage system, with a 4096 byte page size. How big would the flash translation table be, assuming each page has a 32 bit address, and the table is stored as an array.

   c.   Suggest how to reduce the size of the translation table if very often long ranges of consecutive logical page numbers are mapped to consecutive physical page numbers.

Disk 1	Disk 2	Disk 3	Disk 4
B_1	B_2	B_3	B_4
P_1	B_5	B_6	B_7
B_8	P_2	B_9	B_{10}
⋮	⋮	⋮	⋮

Figure 10.18   Data and parity block arrangement.

10.3 A power failure that occurs while a disk block is being written could result in the block being only partially written. Assume that partially written blocks can be detected. An atomic block write is one where either the disk block is fully written or nothing is written (i.e., there are no partial writes). Suggest schemes for getting the effect of atomic block writes with the following RAID schemes. Your schemes should involve work on recovery from failure.

    a. RAID level 1 (mirroring)

    b. RAID level 5 (block interleaved, distributed parity)

10.4 Consider the deletion of record 5 from the file of Figure 10.6. Compare the relative merits of the following techniques for implementing the deletion:

    a. Move record 6 to the space occupied by record 5, and move record 7 to the space occupied by record 6.

    b. Move record 7 to the space occupied by record 5.

    c. Mark record 5 as deleted, and move no records.

10.5 Show the structure of the file of Figure 10.7 after each of the following steps:

    a. Insert (24556, Turnamian, Finance, 98000).

    b. Delete record 2.

    c. Insert (34556, Thompson, Music, 67000).

10.6 Consider the relations *section* and *takes*. Give an example instance of these two relations, with three sections, each of which has five students. Give a file structure of these relations that uses multitable clustering.

10.7 Consider the following bitmap technique for tracking free space in a file. For each block in the file, two bits are maintained in the bitmap. If the block is between 0 and 30 percent full the bits are 00, between 30 and 60 percent the bits are 01, between 60 and 90 percent the bits are 10, and above 90 percent the bits are 11. Such bitmaps can be kept in memory even for quite large files.

    a. Describe how to keep the bitmap up to date on record insertions and deletions.

    b. Outline the benefit of the bitmap technique over free lists in searching for free space and in updating free space information.

10.8 It is important to be able to quickly find out if a block is present in the buffer, and if so where in the buffer it resides. Given that database buffer sizes are very large, what (in-memory) data structure would you use for the above task?

10.9   Give an example of a relational-algebra expression and a query-processing strategy in each of the following situations:

    a.   MRU is preferable to LRU.

    b.   LRU is preferable to MRU.

Exercises

10.10   List the physical storage media available on the computers you use routinely. Give the speed with which data can be accessed on each medium.

10.11   How does the remapping of bad sectors by disk controllers affect data-retrieval rates?

10.12   RAID systems typically allow you to replace failed disks without stopping access to the system. Thus, the data in the failed disk must be rebuilt and written to the replacement disk while the system is in operation. Which of the RAID levels yields the least amount of interference between the rebuild and ongoing disk accesses? Explain your answer.

10.13   What is scrubbing, in the context of RAID systems, and why is scrubbing important?

10.14   In the variable-length record representation, a null bitmap is used to indicate if an attribute has the null value.

    a.   For variable length fields, if the value is null, what would be stored in the offset and length fields?

    b.   In some applications, tuples have a very large number of attributes, most of which are null. Can you modify the record representation such that the only overhead for a null attribute is the single bit in the null bitmap.

10.15   Explain why the allocation of records to blocks affects database-system performance significantly.

10.16   If possible, determine the buffer-management strategy used by the operating system running on your local computer system and what mechanisms it provides to control replacement of pages. Discuss how the control on replacement that it provides would be useful for the implementation of database systems.

10.17   List two advantages and two disadvantages of each of the following strategies for storing a relational database:

    a.   Store each relation in one file.

    b.   Store multiple relations (perhaps even the entire database) in one file.

10.18 In the sequential file organization, why is an overflow *block* used even if there is, at the moment, only one overflow record?

10.19 Give a normalized version of the *Index_metadata* relation, and explain why using the normalized version would result in worse performance.

10.20 If you have data that should not be lost on disk failure, and the data are write intensive, how would you store the data?

10.21 In earlier generation disks the number of sectors per track was the same across all tracks. Current generation disks have more sectors per track on outer tracks, and fewer sectors per track on inner tracks (since they are shorter in length). What is the effect of such a change on each of the three main indicators of disk speed?

10.22 Standard buffer managers assume each block is of the same size and costs the same to read. Consider a buffer manager that, instead of LRU, uses the rate of reference to objects, that is, how often an object has been accessed in the last n seconds. Suppose we want to store in the buffer objects of varying sizes, and varying read costs (such as Web pages, whose read cost depends on the site from which they are fetched). Suggest how a buffer manager may choose which block to evict from the buffer.

Bibliographical Notes

Hennessy et al. [2006] is a popular textbook on computer architecture, which includes coverage of hardware aspects of translation look-aside buffers, caches, and memory-management units. Rosch [2003] presents an excellent overview of computer hardware, including extensive coverage of all types of storage technology such as magnetic disks, optical disks, tapes, and storage interfaces. Patterson [2004] provides a good discussion on how latency improvements have lagged behind bandwidth (transfer rate) improvements.

With the rapid increase in CPU speeds, cache memory located along with the CPU has become much faster than main memory. Although database systems do not control what data is kept in cache, there is an increasing motivation to organize data in memory and write programs in such a way that cache utilization is maximized. Work in this area includes Rao and Ross [2000], Ailamaki et al. [2001], Zhou and Ross [2004], Garcia and Korth [2005], and Cieslewicz et al. [2009].

The specifications of current-generation disk drives can be obtained from the Web sites of their manufacturers, such as Hitachi, LaCie, Iomega, Seagate, Maxtor, and Western Digital.

Discussions of redundant arrays of inexpensive disks (RAID) are presented by Patterson et al. [1988]. Chen et al. [1994] presents an excellent survey of RAID principles and implementation. Reed–Solomon codes are covered in Pless [1998].

Buffering data in mobile systems is discussed in Imielinski and Badrinath [1994], Imielinski and Korth [1996], and Chandrasekaran et al. [2003].

The storage structure of specific database systems, such as IBM DB2, Oracle, Microsoft SQL Server, and PostgreSQL are documented in their respective system manuals.

Buffer management is discussed in most operating-system texts, including in Silberschatz et al. [2008]. Chou and Dewitt [1985] presents algorithms for buffer management in database systems, and describes a performance evaluation.

CHAPTER 11

Indexing and Hashing

Many queries reference only a small proportion of the records in a file. For example, a query like "Find all instructors in the Physics department" or "Find the total number of credits earned by the student with *ID* 22201" references only a fraction of the student records. It is inefficient for the system to read every tuple in the *instructor* relation to check if the *dept_name* value is "Physics". Likewise, it is inefficient to read the entire *student* relation just to find the one tuple for the *ID* "32556,". Ideally, the system should be able to locate these records directly. To allow these forms of access, we design additional structures that we associate with files.

11.1 Basic Concepts

An index for a file in a database system works in much the same way as the index in this textbook. If we want to learn about a particular topic (specified by a word or a phrase) in this textbook, we can search for the topic in the index at the back of the book, find the pages where it occurs, and then read the pages to find the information for which we are looking. The words in the index are in sorted order, making it easy to find the word we want. Moreover, the index is much smaller than the book, further reducing the effort needed.

Database-system indices play the same role as book indices in libraries. For example, to retrieve a *student* record given an *ID*, the database system would look up an index to find on which disk block the corresponding record resides, and then fetch the disk block, to get the appropriate *student* record.

Keeping a sorted list of students' *ID* would not work well on very large databases with thousands of students, since the index would itself be very big; further, even though keeping the index sorted reduces the search time, finding a student can still be rather time-consuming. Instead, more sophisticated indexing techniques may be used. We shall discuss several of these techniques in this chapter.

There are two basic kinds of indices:

- **Ordered indices**. Based on a sorted ordering of the values.

- **Hash indices**. Based on a uniform distribution of values across a range of buckets. The bucket to which a value is assigned is determined by a function, called a *hash function*.

We shall consider several techniques for both ordered indexing and hashing. No one technique is the best. Rather, each technique is best suited to particular database applications. Each technique must be evaluated on the basis of these factors:

- **Access types**: The types of access that are supported efficiently. Access types can include finding records with a specified attribute value and finding records whose attribute values fall in a specified range.

- **Access time**: The time it takes to find a particular data item, or set of items, using the technique in question.

- **Insertion time**: The time it takes to insert a new data item. This value includes the time it takes to find the correct place to insert the new data item, as well as the time it takes to update the index structure.

- **Deletion time**: The time it takes to delete a data item. This value includes the time it takes to find the item to be deleted, as well as the time it takes to update the index structure.

- **Space overhead**: The additional space occupied by an index structure. Provided that the amount of additional space is moderate, it is usually worthwhile to sacrifice the space to achieve improved performance.

We often want to have more than one index for a file. For example, we may wish to search for a book by author, by subject, or by title.

An attribute or set of attributes used to look up records in a file is called a **search key**. Note that this definition of *key* differs from that used in *primary key*, *candidate key*, and *superkey*. This duplicate meaning for *key* is (unfortunately) well established in practice. Using our notion of a search key, we see that if there are several indices on a file, there are several search keys.

11.2   Ordered Indices

To gain fast random access to records in a file, we can use an index structure. Each index structure is associated with a particular search key. Just like the index of a book or a library catalog, an ordered index stores the values of the search keys in sorted order, and associates with each search key the records that contain it.

The records in the indexed file may themselves be stored in some sorted order, just as books in a library are stored according to some attribute such as the Dewey decimal number. A file may have several indices, on different search keys. If the file containing the records is sequentially ordered, a **clustering index** is an index whose search key also defines the sequential order of the file. Clustering indices

10101	Srinivasan	Comp. Sci.	65000	
12121	Wu	Finance	90000	
15151	Mozart	Music	40000	
22222	Einstein	Physics	95000	
32343	El Said	History	60000	
33456	Gold	Physics	87000	
45565	Katz	Comp. Sci.	75000	
58583	Califieri	History	62000	
76543	Singh	Finance	80000	
76766	Crick	Biology	72000	
83821	Brandt	Comp. Sci.	92000	
98345	Kim	Elec. Eng.	80000	

Figure 11.1   Sequential file for *instructor* records.

are also called **primary indices**; the term primary index may appear to denote an index on a primary key, but such indices can in fact be built on any search key. The search key of a clustering index is often the primary key, although that is not necessarily so. Indices whose search key specifies an order different from the sequential order of the file are called **nonclustering indices**, or **secondary** indices. The terms "clustered" and "nonclustered" are often used in place of "clustering" and "nonclustering."

In Sections 11.2.1 through 11.2.3, we assume that all files are ordered sequentially on some search key. Such files, with a clustering index on the search key, are called **index-sequential files**. They represent one of the oldest index schemes used in database systems. They are designed for applications that require both sequential processing of the entire file and random access to individual records. In Section 11.2.4 we cover secondary indices.

Figure 11.1 shows a sequential file of *instructor* records taken from our university example. In the example of Figure 11.1, the records are stored in sorted order of instructor *ID*, which is used as the search key.

11.2.1   Dense and Sparse Indices

An **index entry**, or **index record**, consists of a search-key value and pointers to one or more records with that value as their search-key value. The pointer to a record consists of the identifier of a disk block and an offset within the disk block to identify the record within the block.

There are two types of ordered indices that we can use:

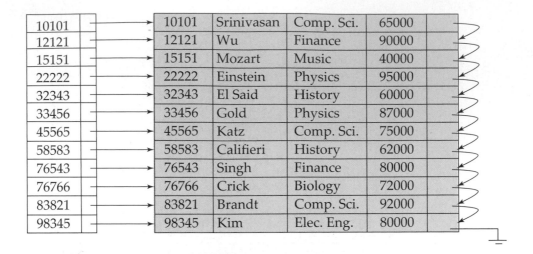

Figure 11.2 Dense index.

- **Dense index**: In a dense index, an index entry appears for every search-key value in the file. In a dense clustering index, the index record contains the search-key value and a pointer to the first data record with that search-key value. The rest of the records with the same search-key value would be stored sequentially after the first record, since, because the index is a clustering one, records are sorted on the same search key.

  In a dense nonclustering index, the index must store a list of pointers to all records with the same search-key value.

- **Sparse index**: In a sparse index, an index entry appears for only some of the search-key values. Sparse indices can be used only if the relation is stored in sorted order of the search key, that is, if the index is a clustering index. As is true in dense indices, each index entry contains a search-key value and a pointer to the first data record with that search-key value. To locate a record, we find the index entry with the largest search-key value that is less than or equal to the search-key value for which we are looking. We start at the record pointed to by that index entry, and follow the pointers in the file until we find the desired record.

Figures 11.2 and 11.3 show dense and sparse indices, respectively, for the *instructor* file. Suppose that we are looking up the record of instructor with *ID* "22222". Using the dense index of Figure 11.2, we follow the pointer directly to the desired record. Since *ID* is a primary key, there exists only one such record and the search is complete. If we are using the sparse index (Figure 11.3), we do not find an index entry for "22222". Since the last entry (in numerical order) before "22222" is "10101", we follow that pointer. We then read the *instructor* file in sequential order until we find the desired record.

Consider a (printed) dictionary. The header of each page lists the first word alphabetically on that page. The words at the top of each page of the book index together form a sparse index on the contents of the dictionary pages.

As another example, suppose that the search-key value is not not a primary key. Figure 11.4 shows a dense clustering index for the *instructor* file with the search key being *dept_name*. Observe that in this case the *instructor* file is sorted on the search key *dept_name*, instead of ID, otherwise the index on *dept_name* would be a nonclustering index. Suppose that we are looking up records for the History department. Using the dense index of Figure 11.4, we follow the pointer directly to the first History record. We process this record, and follow the pointer in that record to locate the next record in search-key (*dept_name*) order. We continue processing records until we encounter a record for a department other than History.

As we have seen, it is generally faster to locate a record if we have a dense index rather than a sparse index. However, sparse indices have advantages over dense indices in that they require less space and they impose less maintenance overhead for insertions and deletions.

There is a trade-off that the system designer must make between access time and space overhead. Although the decision regarding this trade-off depends on the specific application, a good compromise is to have a sparse index with one index entry per block. The reason this design is a good trade-off is that the dominant cost in processing a database request is the time that it takes to bring a block from disk into main memory. Once we have brought in the block, the time to scan the entire block is negligible. Using this sparse index, we locate the block containing the record that we are seeking. Thus, unless the record is on an overflow block (see Section 10.6.1), we minimize block accesses while keeping the size of the index (and thus our space overhead) as small as possible.

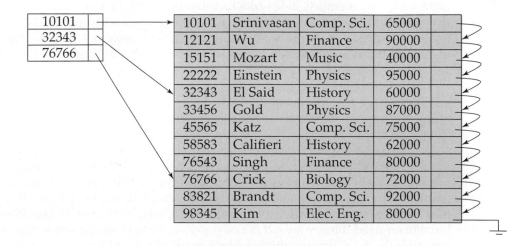

Figure 11.3   Sparse index.

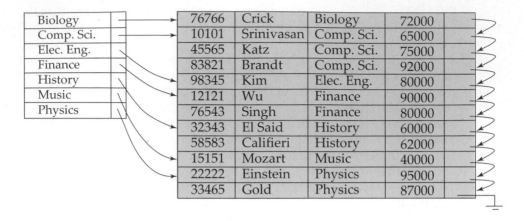

Figure 11.4 Dense index with search key *dept_name*.

For the preceding technique to be fully general, we must consider the case where records for one search-key value occupy several blocks. It is easy to modify our scheme to handle this situation.

11.2.2 Multilevel Indices

Suppose we build a dense index on a relation with 1,000,000 tuples. Index entries are smaller than data records, so let us assume that 100 index entries fit on a 4 kilobyte block. Thus, our index occupies 10,000 blocks. If the relation instead had 100,000,000 tuples, the index would instead occupy 1,000,000 blocks, or 4 gigabytes of space. Such large indices are stored as sequential files on disk.

If an index is small enough to be kept entirely in main memory, the search time to find an entry is low. However, if the index is so large that not all of it can be kept in memory, index blocks must be fetched from disk when required. (Even if an index is smaller than the main memory of a computer, main memory is also required for a number of other tasks, so it may not be possible to keep the entire index in memory.) The search for an entry in the index then requires several disk-block reads.

Binary search can be used on the index file to locate an entry, but the search still has a large cost. If the index would occupy b blocks, binary search requires as many as $\lceil \log_2(b) \rceil$ blocks to be read. ($\lceil x \rceil$ denotes the least integer that is greater than or equal to x; that is, we round upward.) For a 10,000-block index, binary search requires 14 block reads. On a disk system where a block read takes on average 10 milliseconds, the index search will take 140 milliseconds. This may not seem much, but we would be able to carry out only seven index searches a second, whereas a more efficient search mechanism would let us carry out far more searches per second, as we shall see shortly. Note that, if overflow blocks have been used, binary search is not possible. In that case, a sequential search is typically used, and that requires b block reads, which will take even longer. Thus, the process of searching a large index may be costly.

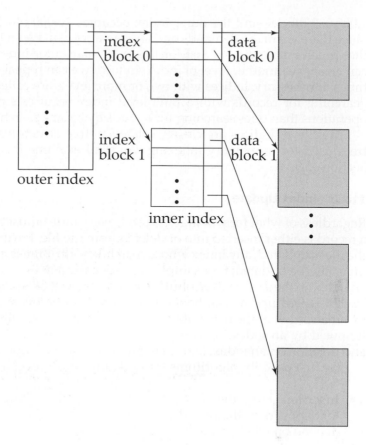

Figure 11.5 Two-level sparse index.

To deal with this problem, we treat the index just as we would treat any other sequential file, and construct a sparse outer index on the original index, which we now call the inner index, as shown in Figure 11.5. Note that the index entries are always in sorted order, allowing the outer index to be sparse. To locate a record, we first use binary search on the outer index to find the record for the largest search-key value less than or equal to the one that we desire. The pointer points to a block of the inner index. We scan this block until we find the record that has the largest search-key value less than or equal to the one that we desire. The pointer in this record points to the block of the file that contains the record for which we are looking.

In our example, an inner index with 10,000 blocks would require 10,000 entries in the outer index, which would occupy just 100 blocks. If we assume that the outer index is already in main memory, we would read only one index block for a search using a multilevel index, rather than the 14 blocks we read with binary search. As a result, we can perform 14 times as many index searches per second.

If our file is extremely large, even the outer index may grow too large to fit in main memory. With a 100,000,000 tuple relation, the inner index would occupy

1,000,000 blocks, and the outer index occupies 10,000 blocks, or 40 megabytes. Since there are many demands on main memory, it may not be possible to reserve that much main memory just for this particular outer index. In such a case, we can create yet another level of index. Indeed, we can repeat this process as many times as necessary. Indices with two or more levels are called **multilevel** indices. Searching for records with a multilevel index requires significantly fewer I/O operations than does searching for records by binary search.[1]

Multilevel indices are closely related to tree structures, such as the binary trees used for in-memory indexing. We shall examine the relationship later, in Section 11.3.

11.2.3   Index Update

Regardless of what form of index is used, every index must be updated whenever a record is either inserted into or deleted from the file. Further, in case a record in the file is updated, any index whose search-key attribute is affected by the update must also be updated; for example, if the department of an instructor is changed, an index on the *dept_name* attribute of *instructor* must be updated correspondingly. Such a record update can be modeled as a deletion of the old record, followed by an insertion of the new value of the record, which results in an index deletion followed by an index insertion. As a result we only need to consider insertion and deletion on an index, and do not need to consider updates explicitly.

We first describe algorithms for updating single-level indices.

- **Insertion**. First, the system performs a lookup using the search-key value that appears in the record to be inserted. The actions the system takes next depend on whether the index is dense or sparse:

  ○ Dense indices:
    1. If the search-key value does not appear in the index, the system inserts an index entry with the search-key value in the index at the appropriate position.
    2. Otherwise the following actions are taken:
      a. If the index entry stores pointers to all records with the same search-key value, the system adds a pointer to the new record in the index entry.
      b. Otherwise, the index entry stores a pointer to only the first record with the search-key value. The system then places the record being inserted after the other records with the same search-key values.

  ○ Sparse indices: We assume that the index stores an entry for each block. If the system creates a new block, it inserts the first search-key value (in

---

[1]In the early days of disk-based indices, each level of the index corresponded to a unit of physical storage. Thus, we may have indices at the track, cylinder, and disk levels. Such a hierarchy does not make sense today since disk subsystems hide the physical details of disk storage, and the number of disks and platters per disk is very small compared to the number of cylinders or bytes per track.

search-key order) appearing in the new block into the index. On the other hand, if the new record has the least search-key value in its block, the system updates the index entry pointing to the block; if not, the system makes no change to the index.

- **Deletion**. To delete a record, the system first looks up the record to be deleted. The actions the system takes next depend on whether the index is dense or sparse:

  ○ Dense indices:

    1. If the deleted record was the only record with its particular search-key value, then the system deletes the corresponding index entry from the index.

    2. Otherwise the following actions are taken:

      a. If the index entry stores pointers to all records with the same search-key value, the system deletes the pointer to the deleted record from the index entry.

      b. Otherwise, the index entry stores a pointer to only the first record with the search-key value. In this case, if the deleted record was the first record with the search-key value, the system updates the index entry to point to the next record.

  ○ Sparse indices:

    1. If the index does not contain an index entry with the search-key value of the deleted record, nothing needs to be done to the index.

    2. Otherwise the system takes the following actions:

      a. If the deleted record was the only record with its search key, the system replaces the corresponding index record with an index record for the next search-key value (in search-key order). If the next search-key value already has an index entry, the entry is deleted instead of being replaced.

      b. Otherwise, if the index entry for the search-key value points to the record being deleted, the system updates the index entry to point to the next record with the same search-key value.

Insertion and deletion algorithms for multilevel indices are a simple extension of the scheme just described. On deletion or insertion, the system updates the lowest-level index as described. As far as the second level is concerned, the lowest-level index is merely a file containing records—thus, if there is any change in the lowest-level index, the system updates the second-level index as described. The same technique applies to further levels of the index, if there are any.

11.2.4 Secondary Indices

Secondary indices must be dense, with an index entry for every search-key value, and a pointer to every record in the file. A clustering index may be sparse, storing only some of the search-key values, since it is always possible to find records with intermediate search-key values by a sequential access to a part of the file, as described earlier. If a secondary index stores only some of the search-key values, records with intermediate search-key values may be anywhere in the file and, in general, we cannot find them without searching the entire file.

A secondary index on a candidate key looks just like a dense clustering index, except that the records pointed to by successive values in the index are not stored sequentially. In general, however, secondary indices may have a different structure from clustering indices. If the search key of a clustering index is not a candidate key, it suffices if the index points to the first record with a particular value for the search key, since the other records can be fetched by a sequential scan of the file.

In contrast, if the search key of a secondary index is not a candidate key, it is not enough to point to just the first record with each search-key value. The remaining records with the same search-key value could be anywhere in the file, since the records are ordered by the search key of the clustering index, rather than by the search key of the secondary index. Therefore, a secondary index must contain pointers to all the records.

We can use an extra level of indirection to implement secondary indices on search keys that are not candidate keys. The pointers in such a secondary index do not point directly to the file. Instead, each points to a bucket that contains pointers to the file. Figure 11.6 shows the structure of a secondary index that uses an extra level of indirection on the *instructor* file, on the search key *salary*.

A sequential scan in clustering index order is efficient because records in the file are stored physically in the same order as the index order. However, we cannot (except in rare special cases) store a file physically ordered by both the search key of the clustering index and the search key of a secondary index.

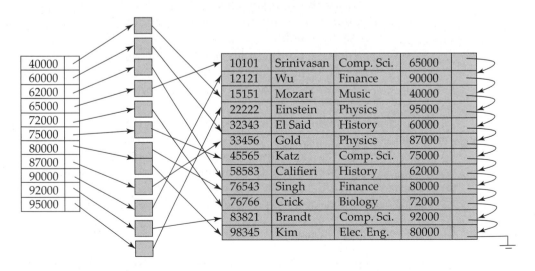

Figure 11.6 Secondary index on *instructor* file, on noncandidate key *salary*.

> **AUTOMATIC CREATION OF INDICES**
>
> If a relation is declared to have a primary key, most database implementations automatically create an index on the primary key. Whenever a tuple is inserted into the relation, the index can be used to check that the primary key constraint is not violated (that is, there are no duplicates on the primary key value). Without the index on the primary key, whenever a tuple is inserted, the entire relation would have to be read to ensure that the primary-key constraint is satisfied.

Because secondary-key order and physical-key order differ, if we attempt to scan the file sequentially in secondary-key order, the reading of each record is likely to require the reading of a new block from disk, which is very slow.

The procedure described earlier for deletion and insertion can also be applied to secondary indices; the actions taken are those described for dense indices storing a pointer to every record in the file. If a file has multiple indices, whenever the file is modified, *every* index must be updated.

Secondary indices improve the performance of queries that use keys other than the search key of the clustering index. However, they impose a significant overhead on modification of the database. The designer of a database decides which secondary indices are desirable on the basis of an estimate of the relative frequency of queries and modifications.

11.2.5 Indices on Multiple Keys

Although the examples we have seen so far have had a single attribute in a search key, in general a search key can have more than one attribute. A search key containing more than one attribute is referred to as a **composite search key**. The structure of the index is the same as that of any other index, the only difference being that the search key is not a single attribute, but rather is a list of attributes. The search key can be represented as a tuple of values, of the form $(a_1, \ldots, a_n)$, where the indexed attributes are $A_1, \ldots, A_n$. The ordering of search-key values is the *lexicographic ordering*. For example, for the case of two attribute search keys, $(a_1, a_2) < (b_1, b_2)$ if either $a_1 < b_1$ or $a_1 = b_1$ and $a_2 < b_2$. Lexicographic ordering is basically the same as alphabetic ordering of words.

As an example, consider an index on the *takes* relation, on the composite search key (*course_id*, *semester*, *year*). Such an index would be useful to find all students who have registered for a particular course in a particular semester/year. An ordered index on a composite key can also be used to answer several other kinds of queries efficiently, as we shall see later in Section 11.5.2.

11.3   B$^+$-Tree Index Files

The main disadvantage of the index-sequential file organization is that performance degrades as the file grows, both for index lookups and for sequential scans through the data. Although this degradation can be remedied by reorganization of the file, frequent reorganizations are undesirable.

The **B$^+$-tree** index structure is the most widely used of several index structures that maintain their efficiency despite insertion and deletion of data. A B$^+$-tree index takes the form of a **balanced tree** in which every path from the root of the tree to a leaf of the tree is of the same length. Each nonleaf node in the tree has between $\lceil n/2 \rceil$ and n children, where n is fixed for a particular tree.

We shall see that the B$^+$-tree structure imposes performance overhead on insertion and deletion, and adds space overhead. The overhead is acceptable even for frequently modified files, since the cost of file reorganization is avoided. Furthermore, since nodes may be as much as half empty (if they have the minimum number of children), there is some wasted space. This space overhead, too, is acceptable given the performance benefits of the B$^+$-tree structure.

11.3.1 Structure of a B$^+$-Tree

A B$^+$-tree index is a multilevel index, but it has a structure that differs from that of the multilevel index-sequential file. Figure 11.7 shows a typical node of a B$^+$-tree. It contains up to $n - 1$ search-key values $K_1, K_2, \ldots, K_{n-1}$, and n pointers $P_1, P_2, \ldots, P_n$. The search-key values within a node are kept in sorted order; thus, if $i < j$, then $K_i < K_j$.

We consider first the structure of the **leaf nodes**. For $i = 1, 2, \ldots, n-1$, pointer P_i points to a file record with search-key value K_i. Pointer P_n has a special purpose that we shall discuss shortly.

Figure 11.8 shows one leaf node of a B$^+$-tree for the *instructor* file, in which we have chosen n to be 4, and the search key is *name*.

Now that we have seen the structure of a leaf node, let us consider how search-key values are assigned to particular nodes. Each leaf can hold up to $n - 1$ values. We allow leaf nodes to contain as few as $\lceil (n - 1)/2 \rceil$ values. With $n = 4$ in our example B$^+$-tree, each leaf must contain at least 2 values, and at most 3 values.

The ranges of values in each leaf do not overlap, except if there are duplicate search-key values, in which case a value may be present in more than one leaf. Specifically, if L_i and L_j are leaf nodes and $i < j$, then every search-key value in L_i is less than or equal to every search-key value in L_j. If the B$^+$-tree index is used as a dense index (as is usually the case) every search-key value must appear in some leaf node.

Now we can explain the use of the pointer P_n. Since there is a linear order on the leaves based on the search-key values that they contain, we use P_n to chain

Figure 11.7 Typical node of a B$^+$-tree.

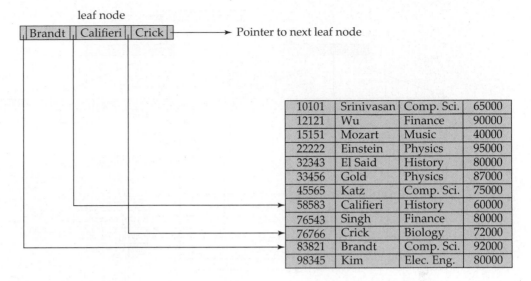

Figure 11.8 A leaf node for *instructor* B+-tree index ($n = 4$).

together the leaf nodes in search-key order. This ordering allows for efficient sequential processing of the file.

The **nonleaf nodes** of the B+-tree form a multilevel (sparse) index on the leaf nodes. The structure of nonleaf nodes is the same as that for leaf nodes, except that all pointers are pointers to tree nodes. A nonleaf node may hold up to n pointers, and *must* hold at least $\lceil n/2 \rceil$ pointers. The number of pointers in a node is called the *fanout* of the node. Nonleaf nodes are also referred to as **internal nodes**.

Let us consider a node containing m pointers ($m \le n$). For $i = 2, 3, \ldots, m - 1$, pointer P_i points to the subtree that contains search-key values less than K_i and greater than or equal to K_{i-1}. Pointer P_m points to the part of the subtree that contains those key values greater than or equal to K_{m-1}, and pointer P_1 points to the part of the subtree that contains those search-key values less than K_1.

Unlike other nonleaf nodes, the root node can hold fewer than $\lceil n/2 \rceil$ pointers; however, it must hold at least two pointers, unless the tree consists of only one node. It is always possible to construct a B+-tree, for any n, that satisfies the preceding requirements.

Figure 11.9 shows a complete B+-tree for the *instructor* file (with $n = 4$). We have shown instructor names abbreviated to 3 characters in order to depict the tree clearly; in reality, the tree nodes would contain the full names. We have also omitted null pointers for simplicity; any pointer field in the figure that does not have an arrow is understood to have a null value.

Figure 11.10 shows another B+-tree for the *instructor* file, this time with $n = 6$. As before, we have abbreviated instructor names only for clarity of presentation.

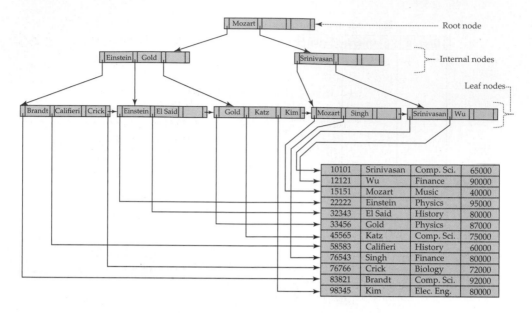

Figure 11.9 B$^+$-tree for *instructor* file ($n = 4$).

Observe that the height of this tree is less than that of the previous tree, which had $n = 4$.

These examples of B$^+$-trees are all balanced. That is, the length of every path from the root to a leaf node is the same. This property is a requirement for a B$^+$-tree. Indeed, the "B" in B$^+$-tree stands for "balanced." It is the balance property of B$^+$-trees that ensures good performance for lookup, insertion, and deletion.

11.3.2   Queries on B$^+$-Trees

Let us consider how we process queries on a B$^+$-tree. Suppose that we wish to find records with a search-key value of V. Figure 11.11 presents pseudocode for a function find() to carry out this task.

Intuitively, the function starts at the root of the tree, and traverses the tree down until it reaches a leaf node that would contain the specified value if it exists in the tree. Specifically, starting with the root as the current node, the function repeats the following steps until a leaf node is reached. First, the current node is examined, looking for the smallest i such that search-key value K_i is greater

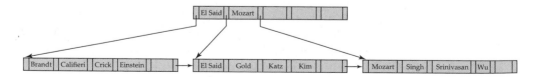

Figure 11.10 B$^+$-tree for *instructor* file with $n = 6$.

function find(*value V*)

/* Returns leaf node C and index i such that $C.P_i$ points to first record
* with search key value V */

  Set C = root node

  while (C is not a leaf node) **begin**

    Let i = smallest number such that $V \leq C.K_i$

    if there is no such number i **then begin**

      Let P_m = last non-null pointer in the node

      Set $C = C.P_m$

    end

    else if ($V = C.K_i$)

      then Set $C = C.P_{i+1}$

    else $C = C.P_i$ /* $V < C.K_i$ */

  end

  /* C is a leaf node */

  Let i be the least value such that $K_i = V$

  if there is such a value i

    then return (C, i)

    else return null ; /* No record with key value V exists*/

procedure printAll(*value V*)

/* prints all records with search key value V */

  Set done = false;

  Set (L, i) = find(V);

  if ((L, i) is null) **return**

  repeat

    repeat

      Print record pointed to by $L.P_i$

      Set $i = i + 1$

    until ($i >$ number of keys in L **or** $L.K_i > V$)

    if ($i >$ number of keys in L)

      then $L = L.P_n$

      else Set done = true;

  until (done **or** L is null)

Figure 11.11 Querying a B⁺-tree.

than or equal to V. Suppose such a value is found; then, if K_i is equal to V, the current node is set to the node pointed to by P_{i+1}, otherwise $K_i > V$, and the current node is set to the node pointed to by P_i. If no such value K_i is found, then clearly $V > K_{m-1}$, where P_m is the last nonnull pointer in the node. In this case the current node is set to that pointed to by P_m. The above procedure is repeated, traversing down the tree until a leaf node is reached.

At the leaf node, if there is a search-key value equal to V, let K_i be the first such value; pointer P_i directs us to a record with search-key value K_i. The function then returns the leaf node L and the index i. If no search-key with value V is found in the leaf node, no record with key value V exists in the relation, and function find returns null, to indicate failure.

If there is at most one record with a search key value V (for example, if the index is on a primary key) the procedure that calls the find function simply uses the pointer $L.P_i$ to retrieve the record and is done. However, in case there may be more than one matching record, the remaining records also need to be fetched.

Procedure printAll shown in Figure 11.11 shows how to fetch all records with a specified search key V. The procedure first steps through the remaining keys in the node L, to find other records with search-key value V. If node L contains at least one search-key value greater than V, then there are no more records matching V. Otherwise, the next leaf, pointed to by P_n may contain further entries for V. The node pointed to by P_n must then be searched to find further records with search-key value V. If the highest search-key value in the node pointed to by P_n is also V, further leaves may have to be traversed, in order to find all matching records. The **repeat** loop in printAll carries out the task of traversing leaf nodes until all matching records have been found.

A real implementation would provide a version of find supporting an iterator interface similar to that provided by the JDBC ResultSet, which we saw in Section 5.1.1. Such an iterator interface would provide a method next(), which can be called repeatedly to fetch successive records with the specified search-key. The next() method would step through the entries at the leaf level, in a manner similar to printAll, but each call takes only one step, and records where it left off, so that successive calls next step through successive records. We omit details for simplicity, and leave the pseudocode for the iterator interface as an exercise for the interested reader.

B$^+$-trees can also be used to find all records with search key values in a specified range (L, U). For example, with a B$^+$-tree on attribute *salary* of *instructor*, we can find all *instructor* records with salary in a specified range such as $(50000, 100000)$ (in other words, all salaries between 50000 and 100000). Such queries are called **range queries**. To execute such queries, we can create a procedure printRange(L, U), whose body is the same as printAll except for these differences: printRange calls find(L), instead of find(V), and then steps through records as in procedure printAll, but with the stopping condition being that $L.K_i > U$, instead of $L.K_i > V$.

In processing a query, we traverse a path in the tree from the root to some leaf node. If there are N records in the file, the path is no longer than $\lceil \log_{\lceil n/2 \rceil}(N) \rceil$.

In practice, only a few nodes need to be accessed. Typically, a node is made to be the same size as a disk block, which is typically 4 kilobytes. With a search-key size of 12 bytes, and a disk-pointer size of 8 bytes, n is around 200. Even with a more conservative estimate of 32 bytes for the search-key size, n is around 100. With $n = 100$, if we have 1 million search-key values in the file, a lookup requires only $\lceil \log_{50}(1,000,000) \rceil = 4$ nodes to be accessed. Thus, at most four blocks need to be read from disk for the lookup. The root node of the tree is usually heavily accessed and is likely to be in the buffer, so typically only three or fewer blocks need to be read from disk.

An important difference between B$^+$-tree structures and in-memory tree structures, such as binary trees, is the size of a node, and as a result, the height of the tree. In a binary tree, each node is small, and has at most two pointers. In a B$^+$-tree, each node is large—typically a disk block—and a node can have a large number of pointers. Thus, B$^+$-trees tend to be fat and short, unlike thin and tall binary trees. In a balanced binary tree, the path for a lookup can be of length $\lceil \log_2(N) \rceil$, where N is the number of records in the file being indexed. With $N = 1,000,000$ as in the previous example, a balanced binary tree requires around 20 node accesses. If each node were on a different disk block, 20 block reads would be required to process a lookup, in contrast to the four block reads for the B$^+$-tree. The difference is significant, since each block read could require a disk arm seek, and a block read together with the disk arm seek takes about 10 milliseconds on a typical disk.

11.3.3 Updates on B⁺-Trees

When a record is inserted into, or deleted from a relation, indices on the relation must be updated correspondingly. Recall that updates to a record can be modeled as a deletion of the old record followed by insertion of the updated record. Hence we only consider the case of insertion and deletion.

Insertion and deletion are more complicated than lookup, since it may be necessary to **split** a node that becomes too large as the result of an insertion, or to **coalesce** nodes (that is, combine nodes) if a node becomes too small (fewer than $\lceil n/2 \rceil$ pointers). Furthermore, when a node is split or a pair of nodes is combined, we must ensure that balance is preserved. To introduce the idea behind insertion and deletion in a B$^+$-tree, we shall assume temporarily that nodes never become too large or too small. Under this assumption, insertion and deletion are performed as defined next.

- **Insertion**. Using the same technique as for lookup from the find() function (Figure 11.11), we first find the leaf node in which the search-key value would appear. We then insert an entry (that is, a search-key value and record pointer pair) in the leaf node, positioning it such that the search keys are still in order.

- **Deletion**. Using the same technique as for lookup, we find the leaf node containing the entry to be deleted, by performing a lookup on the search-key value of the deleted record; if there are multiple entries with the same search-key value, we search across all entries with the same search-key value until we find the entry that points to the record being deleted. We then remove the entry from the leaf node. All entries in the leaf node that are to the right of the deleted entry are shifted left by one position, so that there are no gaps in the entries after the entry is deleted.

We now consider the general case of insertion and deletion, dealing with node splitting and node coalescing.

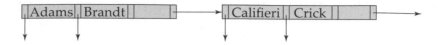

Figure 11.12 Split of leaf node on insertion of "Adams"

11.3.3.1   Insertion

We now consider an example of insertion in which a node must be split. Assume that a record is inserted on the *instructor* relation, with the *name* value being Adams. We then need to insert an entry for "Adams" into the B$^+$-tree of Figure 11.9. Using the algorithm for lookup, we find that "Adams" should appear in the leaf node containing "Brandt", "Califieri", and "Crick." There is no room in this leaf to insert the search-key value "Adams." Therefore, the node is *split* into two nodes. Figure 11.12 shows the two leaf nodes that result from the split of the leaf node on inserting "Adams". The search-key values "Adams" and "Brandt" are in one leaf, and "Califieri" and "Crick" are in the other. In general, we take the n search-key values (the $n - 1$ values in the leaf node plus the value being inserted), and put the first $\lceil n/2 \rceil$ in the existing node and the remaining values in a newly created node.

Having split a leaf node, we must insert the new leaf node into the B$^+$-tree structure. In our example, the new node has "Califieri" as its smallest search-key value. We need to insert an entry with this search-key value, and a pointer to the new node, into the parent of the leaf node that was split. The B$^+$-tree of Figure 11.13 shows the result of the insertion. It was possible to perform this insertion with no further node split, because there was room in the parent node for the new entry. If there were no room, the parent would have had to be split, requiring an entry to be added to its parent. In the worst case, all nodes along the path to the root must be split. If the root itself is split, the entire tree becomes deeper.

Splitting of a nonleaf node is a little different from splitting of a leaf node. Figure 11.14 shows the result of inserting a record with search key "Lamport" into the tree shown in Figure 11.13. The leaf node in which "Lamport" is to be inserted already has entries "Gold", "Katz", and "Kim", and as a result the leaf node has to be split. The new right-hand-side node resulting from the split contains the search-key values "Kim" and "Lamport". An entry (Kim, $n1$) must then be added

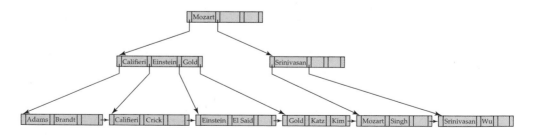

Figure 11.13 Insertion of "Adams" into the B$^+$-tree of Figure 11.9.

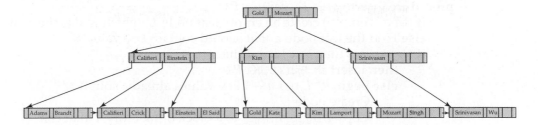

Figure 11.14 Insertion of "Lamport" into the B⁺-tree of Figure 11.13.

to the parent node, where $n1$ is a pointer to the new node, However, there is no space in the parent node to add a new entry, and the parent node has to be split. To do so, the parent node is conceptually expanded temporarily, the entry added, and the overfull node is then immediately split.

When an overfull nonleaf node is split, the child pointers are divided among the original and the newly created nodes; in our example, the original node is left with the first three pointers, and the newly created node to the right gets the remaining two pointers. The search key values are, however, handled a little differently. The search key values that lie between the pointers moved to the right node (in our example, the value "Kim") are moved along with the pointers, while those that lie between the pointers that stay on the left (in our example, "Califieri" and "Einstein") remain undisturbed.

However, the search key value that lies between the pointers that stay on the left, and the pointers that move to the right node is treated differently. In our example, the search key value "Gold" lies between the three pointers that went to the left node, and the two pointers that went to the right node. The value "Gold" is not added to either of the split nodes. Instead, an entry (Gold, $n2$) is added to the parent node, where $n2$ is a pointer to the newly created node that resulted from the split. In this case, the parent node is the root, and it has enough space for the new entry.

The general technique for insertion into a B⁺-tree is to determine the leaf node l into which insertion must occur. If a split results, insert the new node into the parent of node l. If this insertion causes a split, proceed recursively up the tree until either an insertion does not cause a split or a new root is created.

Figure 11.15 outlines the insertion algorithm in pseudocode. The procedure insert inserts a key-value pointer pair into the index, using two subsidiary procedures insert_in_leaf and insert_in_parent. In the pseudocode, L, N, P and T denote pointers to nodes, with L being used to denote a leaf node. $L.K_i$ and $L.P_i$ denote the ith value and the ith pointer in node L, respectively; $T.K_i$ and $T.P_i$ are used similarly. The pseudocode also makes use of the function parent(N) to find the parent of a node N. We can compute a list of nodes in the path from the root to the leaf while initially finding the leaf node, and can use it later to find the parent of any node in the path efficiently.

The procedure insert_in_parent takes as parameters N, K', N', where node N was split into N and N', with K' being the least value in N'. The procedure

procedure insert(*value K, pointer P*)
    if (tree is empty) create an empty leaf node L, which is also the root
    else Find the leaf node L that should contain key value K
    if (L has less than $n - 1$ key values)
        then insert_in_leaf (L, K, P)
        else begin /* L has $n - 1$ key values already, split it */
            Create node L'
            Copy $L.P_1 \ldots L.K_{n-1}$ to a block of memory T that can
                hold n (pointer, key-value) pairs
            insert_in_leaf (T, K, P)
            Set $L'.P_n = L.P_n$; Set $L.P_n = L'$
            Erase $L.P_1$ through $L.K_{n-1}$ from L
            Copy $T.P_1$ through $T.K_{\lceil n/2 \rceil}$ from T into L starting at $L.P_1$
            Copy $T.P_{\lceil n/2 \rceil+1}$ through $T.K_n$ from T into L' starting at $L'.P_1$
            Let K' be the smallest key-value in L'
            insert_in_parent(L, K', L')
        end

procedure insert_in_leaf (*node L, value K, pointer P*)
    if ($K < L.K_1$)
        then insert P, K into L just before $L.P_1$
        else begin
            Let K_i be the highest value in L that is less than K
            Insert P, K into L just after $T.K_i$
        end

procedure insert_in_parent(*node N, value K', node N'*)
    if (N is the root of the tree)
        then begin
            Create a new node R containing N, K', N' /* N and N' are pointers */
            Make R the root of the tree
            return
        end
    Let $P = parent (N)$
    if (P has less than n pointers)
        then insert (K', N') in P just after N
        else begin /* Split P */
            Copy P to a block of memory T that can hold P and (K', N')
            Insert (K', N') into T just after N
            Erase all entries from P; Create node P'
            Copy $T.P_1 \ldots T.P_{\lceil n/2 \rceil}$ into P
            Let $K'' = T.K_{\lceil n/2 \rceil}$
            Copy $T.P_{\lceil n/2 \rceil+1} \ldots T.P_{n+1}$ into P'
            insert_in_parent(P, K'', P')
    end

Figure 11.15 Insertion of entry in a B$^+$-tree.

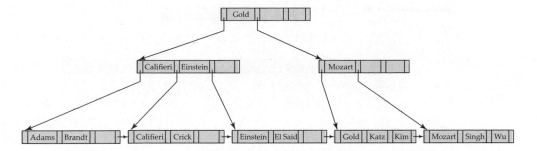

Figure 11.16 Deletion of "Srinivasan" from the B+-tree of Figure 11.13.

modifies the parent of N to record the split. The procedures `insert_into_index` and `insert_in_parent` use a temporary area of memory T to store the contents of a node being split. The procedures can be modified to copy data from the node being split directly to the newly created node, reducing the time required for copying data. However, the use of the temporary space T simplifies the procedures.

11.3.3.2 Deletion

We now consider deletions that cause tree nodes to contain too few pointers. First, let us delete "Srinivasan" from the B+-tree of Figure 11.13. The resulting B+-tree appears in Figure 11.16. We now consider how the deletion is performed. We first locate the entry for "Srinivasan" by using our lookup algorithm. When we delete the entry for "Srinivasan" from its leaf node, the node is left with only one entry, "Wu". Since, in our example, $n = 4$ and $1 < \lceil(n-1)/2\rceil$, we must either merge the node with a sibling node, or redistribute the entries between the nodes, to ensure that each node is at least half-full. In our example, the underfull node with the entry for "Wu" can be merged with its left sibling node. We merge the nodes by moving the entries from both the nodes into the left sibling, and deleting the now empty right sibling. Once the node is deleted, we must also delete the entry in the parent node that pointed to the just deleted node.

In our example, the entry to be deleted is (Srinivasan, $n3$), where $n3$ is a pointer to the leaf containing "Srinivasan". (In this case the entry to be deleted in the nonleaf node happens to be the same value as that deleted from the leaf; that would not be the case for most deletions.) After deleting the above entry, the parent node, which had a search key value "Srinivasan" and two pointers, now has one pointer (the leftmost pointer in the node) and no search-key values. Since $1 < \lceil n/2\rceil$ for $n = 4$, the parent node is underfull. (For larger n, a node that becomes underfull would still have some values as well as pointers.)

In this case, we look at a sibling node; in our example, the only sibling is the nonleaf node containing the search keys "Califieri", "Einstein", and "Gold". If possible, we try to coalesce the node with its sibling. In this case, coalescing is not possible, since the node and its sibling together have five pointers, against a maximum of four. The solution in this case is to **redistribute** the pointers between

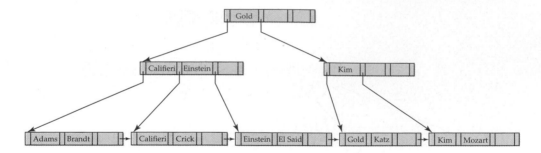

Figure 11.17   Deletion of "Singh" and "Wu" from the B$^+$-tree of Figure 11.16.

the node and its sibling, such that each has at least $\lceil n/2 \rceil = 2$ child pointers. To do so, we move the rightmost pointer from the left sibling (the one pointing to the leaf node containing "Mozart") to the underfull right sibling. However, the underfull right sibling would now have two pointers, namely its leftmost pointer, and the newly moved pointer, with no value separating them. In fact, the value separating them is not present in either of the nodes, but is present in the parent node, between the pointers from the parent to the node and its sibling. In our example, the value "Mozart" separates the two pointers, and is present in the right sibling after the redistribution. Redistribution of the pointers also means that the value "Mozart" in the parent no longer correctly separates search-key values in the two siblings. In fact, the value that now correctly separates search-key values in the two sibling nodes is the value "Gold", which was in the left sibling before redistribution.

As a result, as can be seen in the B$^+$-tree in Figure 11.16, after redistribution of pointers between siblings, the value "Gold" has moved up into the parent, while the value that was there earlier, "Mozart", has moved down into the right sibling.

We next delete the search-key values "Singh" and "Wu" from the B$^+$-tree of Figure 11.16. The result is shown in Figure 11.17. The deletion of the first of these values does not make the leaf node underfull, but the deletion of the second value does. It is not possible to merge the underfull node with its sibling, so a redistribution of values is carried out, moving the search-key value "Kim" into the node containing "Mozart", resulting in the tree shown in Figure 11.17. The value separating the two siblings has been updated in the parent, from "Mozart" to "Kim".

Now we delete "Gold" from the above tree; the result is shown in Figure 11.18. This results in an underfull leaf, which can now be merged with its sibling. The resultant deletion of an entry from the parent node (the nonleaf node containing "Kim") makes the parent underfull (it is left with just one pointer). This time around, the parent node can be merged with its sibling. This merge results in the search-key value "Gold" moving down from the parent into the merged node. As a result of this merge, an entry is deleted from its parent, which happens to be the root of the tree. And as a result of that deletion, the root is left with only one child pointer and no search-key value, violating the condition that the root

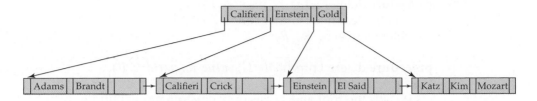

Figure 11.18 Deletion of "Gold" from the B+-tree of Figure 11.17.

have at least two children. As a result, the root node is deleted and its sole child becomes the root, and the depth of the B+-tree has been decreased by 1.

It is worth noting that, as a result of deletion, a key value that is present in a nonleaf node of the B+-tree may not be present at any leaf of the tree. For example, in Figure 11.18, the value "Gold" has been deleted from the leaf level, but is still present in a nonleaf node.

In general, to delete a value in a B+-tree, we perform a lookup on the value and delete it. If the node is too small, we delete it from its parent. This deletion results in recursive application of the deletion algorithm until the root is reached, a parent remains adequately full after deletion, or redistribution is applied.

Figure 11.19 outlines the pseudocode for deletion from a B+-tree. The procedure swap_variables(N, N') merely swaps the values of the (pointer) variables N and N'; this swap has no effect on the tree itself. The pseudocode uses the condition "too few pointers/values." For nonleaf nodes, this criterion means less than $\lceil n/2 \rceil$ pointers; for leaf nodes, it means less than $\lceil (n-1)/2 \rceil$ values. The pseudocode redistributes entries by borrowing a single entry from an adjacent node. We can also redistribute entries by repartitioning entries equally between the two nodes. The pseudocode refers to deleting an entry (K, P) from a node. In the case of leaf nodes, the pointer to an entry actually precedes the key value, so the pointer P precedes the key value K. For nonleaf nodes, P follows the key value K.

11.3.4   Nonunique Search Keys

If a relation can have more than one record containing the same search key value (that is, two or more records can have the same values for the indexed attributes), the search key is said to be a **nonunique search key**.

One problem with nonunique search keys is in the efficiency of record deletion. Suppose a particular search-key value occurs a large number of times, and one of the records with that search key is to be deleted. The deletion may have to search through a number of entries, potentially across multiple leaf nodes, to find the entry corresponding to the particular record being deleted.

A simple solution to this problem, used by most database systems, is to make search keys unique by creating a composite search key containing the original search key and another attribute, which together are unique across all records. The extra attribute can be a record-id, which is a pointer to the record, or any other attribute whose value is unique among all records with the same search-

procedure delete(*value K, pointer P*)
    find the leaf node L that contains (K, P)
    delete_entry(L, K, P)

procedure delete_entry(*node N, value K, pointer P*)
    delete (K, P) from N
    if (N is the root **and** N has only one remaining child)
    then make the child of N the new root of the tree and delete N
    else if (N has too few values/pointers) **then begin**
        Let N' be the previous or next child of *parent*(N)
        Let K' be the value between pointers N and N' in *parent*(N)
        if (entries in N and N' can fit in a single node)
            then begin /* Coalesce nodes */
                if (N is a predecessor of N') **then** swap_variables(N, N')
                if (N is not a leaf)
                    then append K' and all pointers and values in N to N'
                    else append all (K_i, P_i) pairs in N to N'; set $N'.P_n = N.P_n$
                delete_entry(*parent*(N), K', N); delete node N
            end
            else begin /* Redistribution: borrow an entry from N' */
                if (N' is a predecessor of N) **then begin**
                    if (N is a nonleaf node) **then begin**
                        let m be such that $N'.P_m$ is the last pointer in N'
                        remove $(N'.K_{m-1}, N'.P_m)$ from N'
                        insert $(N'.P_m, K')$ as the first pointer and value in N,
                            by shifting other pointers and values right
                        replace K' in *parent*(N) by $N'.K_{m-1}$
                    end
                    else begin
                        let m be such that $(N'.P_m, N'.K_m)$ is the last pointer/value
                            pair in N'
                        remove $(N'.P_m, N'.K_m)$ from N'
                        insert $(N'.P_m, N'.K_m)$ as the first pointer and value in N,
                            by shifting other pointers and values right
                        replace K' in *parent*(N) by $N'.K_m$
                    end
                end
                else ... symmetric to the **then** case ...
        end
    end

Figure 11.19 Deletion of entry from a B$^+$-tree.

key value. The extra attribute is called a **uniquifier** attribute. When a record is to be deleted, the composite search-key value is computed from the record, and then used to look up the index. Since the value is unique, the corresponding leaf-level entry can be found with a single traversal from root to leaf, with no further accesses at the leaf level. As a result, record deletion can be done efficiently.

A search with the original search-key attribute simply ignores the value of the uniquifier attribute when comparing search-key values.

With nonunique search keys, our B$^+$-tree structure stores each key value as many times as there are records containing that value. An alternative is to store each key value only once in the tree, and to keep a bucket (or list) of record pointers with a search-key value, to handle nonunique search keys. This approach is more space efficient since it stores the key value only once; however, it creates several complications when B$^+$-trees are implemented. If the buckets are kept in the leaf node, extra code is needed to deal with variable-size buckets, and to deal with buckets that grow larger than the size of the leaf node. If the buckets are stored in separate blocks, an extra I/O operation may be required to fetch records. In addition to these problems, the bucket approach also has the problem of inefficiency for record deletion if a search-key value occurs a large number of times.

11.3.5   Complexity of B$^+$-Tree Updates

Although insertion and deletion operations on B$^+$-trees are complicated, they require relatively few I/O operations, which is an important benefit since I/O operations are expensive. It can be shown that the number of I/O operations needed in the worst case for an insertion is proportional to $\log_{\lceil n/2 \rceil}(N)$, where n is the maximum number of pointers in a node, and N is the number of records in the file being indexed.

The worst-case complexity of the deletion procedure is also proportional to $\log_{\lceil n/2 \rceil}(N)$, provided there are no duplicate values for the search key. If there are duplicate values, deletion may have to search across multiple records with the same search-key value to find the correct entry to be deleted, which can be inefficient. However, making the search key unique by adding a uniquifier attribute, as described in Section 11.3.4, ensures the worst-case complexity of deletion is the same even if the original search key is nonunique.

In other words, the cost of insertion and deletion operations in terms of I/O operations is proportional to the height of the B$^+$-tree, and is therefore low. It is the speed of operation on B$^+$-trees that makes them a frequently used index structure in database implementations.

In practice, operations on B$^+$-trees result in fewer I/O operations than the worst-case bounds. With fanout of 100, and assuming accesses to leaf nodes are uniformly distributed, the parent of a leaf node is 100 times more likely to get accessed than the leaf node. Conversely, with the same fanout, the total number of nonleaf nodes in a B$^+$-tree would be just a little more than 1/100th of the number of leaf nodes. As a result, with memory sizes of several gigabytes being common today, for B$^+$-trees that are used frequently, even if the relation is very large it is quite likely that most of the nonleaf nodes are already in the database buffer when they are accessed. Thus, typically only one or two I/O operations are required to perform a lookup. For updates, the probability of a node split occurring is correspondingly very small. Depending on the ordering of inserts, with a fanout of 100, only between 1 in 100 to 1 in 50 insertions will result in a node split, requiring more than one block to be written. As a result, on an average an insert will require just a little more than one I/O operation to write updated blocks.

Although B$^+$-trees only guarantee that nodes will be at least half full, if entries are inserted in random order, nodes can be expected to be more than two-thirds full on average. If entries are inserted in sorted order, on the other hand, nodes will be only half full. (We leave it as an exercise to the reader to figure out why nodes would be only half full in the latter case.)

11.4   B$^+$-Tree Extensions

In this section, we discuss several extensions and variations of the B$^+$-tree index structure.

11.4.1   B$^+$-Tree File Organization

As mentioned in Section 11.3, the main drawback of index-sequential file organization is the degradation of performance as the file grows: With growth, an increasing percentage of index entries and actual records become out of order, and are stored in overflow blocks. We solve the degradation of index lookups by using B$^+$-tree indices on the file. We solve the degradation problem for storing the actual records by using the leaf level of the B$^+$-tree to organize the blocks containing the actual records. We use the B$^+$-tree structure not only as an index, but also as an organizer for records in a file. In a **B$^+$-tree file organization**, the leaf nodes of the tree store records, instead of storing pointers to records. Figure 11.20 shows an example of a B$^+$-tree file organization. Since records are usually larger than pointers, the maximum number of records that can be stored in a leaf node is less than the number of pointers in a nonleaf node. However, the leaf nodes are still required to be at least half full.

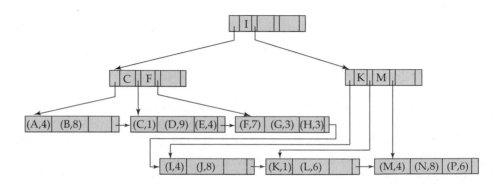

Figure 11.20   B$^+$-tree file organization.

Insertion and deletion of records from a B$^+$-tree file organization are handled in the same way as insertion and deletion of entries in a B$^+$-tree index. When a record with a given key value v is inserted, the system locates the block that should contain the record by searching the B$^+$-tree for the largest key in the tree that is $\leq v$. If the block located has enough free space for the record, the system stores the record in the block. Otherwise, as in B$^+$-tree insertion, the system splits the block in two, and redistributes the records in it (in the B$^+$-tree–key order) to create space for the new record. The split propagates up the B$^+$-tree in the normal fashion. When we delete a record, the system first removes it from the block containing it. If a block B becomes less than half full as a result, the records in B are redistributed with the records in an adjacent block B'. Assuming fixed-sized records, each block will hold at least one-half as many records as the maximum that it can hold. The system updates the nonleaf nodes of the B$^+$-tree in the usual fashion.

When we use a B$^+$-tree for file organization, space utilization is particularly important, since the space occupied by the records is likely to be much more than the space occupied by keys and pointers. We can improve the utilization of space in a B$^+$-tree by involving more sibling nodes in redistribution during splits and merges. The technique is applicable to both leaf nodes and nonleaf nodes, and works as follows:

During insertion, if a node is full the system attempts to redistribute some of its entries to one of the adjacent nodes, to make space for a new entry. If this attempt fails because the adjacent nodes are themselves full, the system splits the node, and splits the entries evenly among one of the adjacent nodes and the two nodes that it obtained by splitting the original node. Since the three nodes together contain one more record than can fit in two nodes, each node will be about two-thirds full. More precisely, each node will have at least $\lfloor 2n/3 \rfloor$ entries, where n is the maximum number of entries that the node can hold. ($\lfloor x \rfloor$ denotes the greatest integer that is less than or equal to x; that is, we drop the fractional part, if any.)

During deletion of a record, if the occupancy of a node falls below $\lfloor 2n/3 \rfloor$, the system attempts to borrow an entry from one of the sibling nodes. If both sibling nodes have $\lfloor 2n/3 \rfloor$ records, instead of borrowing an entry, the system redistributes the entries in the node and in the two siblings evenly between two of the nodes, and deletes the third node. We can use this approach because the total number of entries is $3\lfloor 2n/3 \rfloor - 1$, which is less than $2n$. With three adjacent nodes used for redistribution, each node can be guaranteed to have $\lfloor 3n/4 \rfloor$ entries. In general, if m nodes ($m - 1$ siblings) are involved in redistribution, each node can be guaranteed to contain at least $\lfloor (m - 1)n/m \rfloor$ entries. However, the cost of update becomes higher as more sibling nodes are involved in the redistribution.

Note that in a B$^+$-tree index or file organization, leaf nodes that are adjacent to each other in the tree may be located at different places on disk. When a file organization is newly created on a set of records, it is possible to allocate blocks that are mostly contiguous on disk to leaf nodes that are contiguous in the tree. Thus a sequential scan of leaf nodes would correspond to a mostly sequential scan on disk. As insertions and deletions occur on the tree, sequentiality is increasingly lost, and sequential access has to wait for disk seeks increasingly often. An index rebuild may be required to restore sequentiality.

B$^+$-tree file organizations can also be used to store large objects, such as SQL clobs and blobs, which may be larger than a disk block, and as large as multiple gigabytes. Such large objects can be stored by splitting them into sequences of smaller records that are organized in a B$^+$-tree file organization. The records can be sequentially numbered, or numbered by the byte offset of the record within the large object, and the record number can be used as the search key.

11.4.2 Secondary Indices and Record Relocation

Some file organizations, such as the B$^+$-tree file organization, may change the location of records even when the records have not been updated. As an example, when a leaf node is split in a B$^+$-tree file organization, a number of records are moved to a new node. In such cases, all secondary indices that store pointers to the relocated records would have to be updated, even though the values in the records may not have changed. Each leaf node may contain a fairly large number of records, and each of them may be in different locations on each secondary index. Thus a leaf-node split may require tens or even hundreds of I/O operations to update all affected secondary indices, making it a very expensive operation.

A widely used solution for this problem is as follows: In secondary indices, in place of pointers to the indexed records, we store the values of the primary-index search-key attributes. For example, suppose we have a primary index on the attribute *ID* of relation *instructor*; then a secondary index on *dept_name* would store with each department name a list of instructor's *ID* values of the corresponding records, instead of storing pointers to the records.

Relocation of records because of leaf-node splits then does not require any update on any such secondary index. However, locating a record using the secondary index now requires two steps: First we use the secondary index to find the primary-index search-key values, and then we use the primary index to find the corresponding records.

The above approach thus greatly reduces the cost of index update due to file reorganization, although it increases the cost of accessing data using a secondary index.

11.4.3 Indexing Strings

Creating B$^+$-tree indices on string-valued attributes raises two problems. The first problem is that strings can be of variable length. The second problem is that strings can be long, leading to a low fanout and a correspondingly increased tree height.

With variable-length search keys, different nodes can have different fanouts even if they are full. A node must then be split if it is full, that is, there is no space to add a new entry, regardless of how many search entries it has. Similarly, nodes can be merged or entries redistributed depending on what fraction of the space in the nodes is used, instead of being based on the maximum number of entries that the node can hold.

The fanout of nodes can be increased by using a technique called **prefix compression**. With prefix compression, we do not store the entire search key value at nonleaf nodes. We only store a prefix of each search key value that is sufficient to distinguish between the key values in the subtrees that it separates. For example, if we had an index on names, the key value at a nonleaf node could be a prefix of a name; it may suffice to store "Silb" at a nonleaf node, instead of the full "Silberschatz" if the closest values in the two subtrees that it separates are, say, "Silas" and "Silver" respectively.

11.4.4 Bulk Loading of B$^+$-Tree Indices

As we saw earlier, insertion of a record in a B$^+$-tree requires a number of I/O operations that in the worst case is proportional to the height of the tree, which is usually fairly small (typically five or less, even for large relations).

Now consider the case where a B$^+$-tree is being built on a large relation. Suppose the relation is significantly larger than main memory, and we are constructing a nonclustering index on the relation such that the index is also larger than main memory. In this case, as we scan the relation and add entries to the B$^+$-tree, it is quite likely that each leaf node accessed is not in the database buffer when it is accessed, since there is no particular ordering of the entries. With such randomly ordered accesses to blocks, each time an entry is added to the leaf, a disk seek will be required to fetch the block containing the leaf node. The block will probably be evicted from the disk buffer before another entry is added to the block, leading to another disk seek to write the block back to disk. Thus a random read and a random write operation may be required for each entry inserted.

For example, if the relation has 100 million records, and each I/O operation takes about 10 milliseconds, it would take at least 1 million seconds to build the index, counting only the cost of reading leaf nodes, not even counting the cost of writing the updated nodes back to disk. This is clearly a very large amount of time; in contrast, if each record occupies 100 bytes, and the disk subsystem can transfer data at 50 megabytes per second, it would take just 200 seconds to read the entire relation.

Insertion of a large number of entries at a time into an index is referred to as **bulk loading** of the index. An efficient way to perform bulk loading of an index is as follows. First, create a temporary file containing index entries for the relation, then sort the file on the search key of the index being constructed, and finally scan the sorted file and insert the entries into the index. There are efficient algorithms for sorting large relations, which are described later in Section 12.4, which can sort even a large file with an I/O cost comparable to that of reading the file a few times, assuming a reasonable amount of main memory is available.

There is a significant benefit to sorting the entries before inserting them into the B$^+$-tree. When the entries are inserted in sorted order, all entries that go to a particular leaf node will appear consecutively, and the leaf needs to be written out only once; nodes will never have to be read from disk during bulk load, if the B$^+$-tree was empty to start with. Each leaf node will thus incur only one I/O operation even though many entries may be inserted into the node. If each leaf contains 100 entries, the leaf level will contain 1 million nodes, resulting in only 1 million I/O operations for creating the leaf level. Even these I/O operations can be expected to be sequential, if successive leaf nodes are allocated on successive disk blocks, and few disk seeks would be required. With current disks, 1 millisecond per block is a reasonable estimate for mostly sequential I/O operations, in contrast to 10 milliseconds per block for random I/O operations.

We shall study the cost of sorting a large relation later, in Section 12.4, but as a rough estimate, the index which would have taken a million seconds to build otherwise, can be constructed in well under 1000 seconds by sorting the entries before inserting them into the B^+-tree, in contrast to more than 1,000,000 seconds for inserting in random order.

If the B^+-tree is initially empty, it can be constructed faster by building it bottom-up, from the leaf level, instead of using the usual insert procedure. In **bottom-up B^+-tree construction**, after sorting the entries as we just described, we break up the sorted entries into blocks, keeping as many entries in a block as can fit in the block; the resulting blocks form the leaf level of the B^+-tree. The minimum value in each block, along with the pointer to the block, is used to create entries in the next level of the B^+-tree, pointing to the leaf blocks. Each further level of the tree is similarly constructed using the minimum values associated with each node one level below, until the root is created. We leave details as an exercise for the reader.

Most database systems implement efficient techniques based on sorting of entries, and bottom-up construction, when creating an index on a relation, although they use the normal insertion procedure when tuples are added one at a time to a relation with an existing index. Some database systems recommend that if a very large number of tuples are added at once to an already existing relation, indices on the relation (other than any index on the primary key) should be dropped, and then re-created after the tuples are inserted, to take advantage of efficient bulk-loading techniques.

11.4.5   B-Tree Index Files

B-tree indices are similar to B^+-tree indices. The primary distinction between the two approaches is that a B-tree eliminates the redundant storage of search-key values. In the B^+-tree of Figure 11.13, the search keys "Califieri", "Einstein", "Gold", "Mozart", and "Srinivasan" appear in nonleaf nodes, in addition to appearing in the leaf nodes. Every search-key value appears in some leaf node; several are repeated in nonleaf nodes.

A B-tree allows search-key values to appear only once (if they are unique), unlike a B^+-tree, where a value may appear in a nonleaf node, in addition to appearing in a leaf node. Figure 11.21 shows a B-tree that represents the same search keys as the B^+-tree of Figure 11.13. Since search keys are not repeated in the B-tree, we may be able to store the index in fewer tree nodes than in the corresponding B^+-tree index. However, since search keys that appear in nonleaf nodes appear nowhere else in the B-tree, we are forced to include an additional

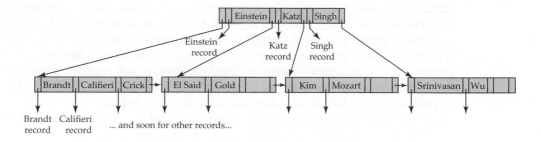

Figure 11.21   B-tree equivalent of B+-tree in Figure 11.13.

pointer field for each search key in a nonleaf node. These additional pointers point to either file records or buckets for the associated search key.

It is worth noting that many database system manuals, articles in industry literature, and industry professionals use the term B-tree to refer to the data structure that we call the B+-tree. In fact, it would be fair to say that in current usage, the term B-tree is assumed to be synonymous with B+-tree. However, in this book we use the terms B-tree and B+-tree as they were originally defined, to avoid confusion between the two data structures.

A generalized B-tree leaf node appears in Figure 11.22a; a nonleaf node appears in Figure 11.22b. Leaf nodes are the same as in B+-trees. In nonleaf nodes, the pointers P_i are the tree pointers that we used also for B+-trees, while the pointers B_i are bucket or file-record pointers. In the generalized B-tree in the figure, there are $n-1$ keys in the leaf node, but there are $m-1$ keys in the nonleaf node. This discrepancy occurs because nonleaf nodes must include pointers B_i, thus reducing the number of search keys that can be held in these nodes. Clearly, $m < n$, but the exact relationship between m and n depends on the relative size of search keys and pointers.

The number of nodes accessed in a lookup in a B-tree depends on where the search key is located. A lookup on a B+-tree requires traversal of a path from the root of the tree to some leaf node. In contrast, it is sometimes possible to find the desired value in a B-tree before reaching a leaf node. However, roughly n times as many keys are stored in the leaf level of a B-tree as in the nonleaf levels, and, since n is typically large, the benefit of finding certain values early is relatively

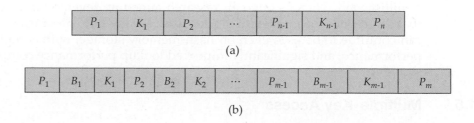

Figure 11.22   Typical nodes of a B-tree. (a) Leaf node. (b) Nonleaf node.

small. Moreover, the fact that fewer search keys appear in a nonleaf B-tree node, compared to B^+-trees, implies that a B-tree has a smaller fanout and therefore may have depth greater than that of the corresponding B^+-tree. Thus, lookup in a B-tree is faster for some search keys but slower for others, although, in general, lookup time is still proportional to the logarithm of the number of search keys.

Deletion in a B-tree is more complicated. In a B^+-tree, the deleted entry always appears in a leaf. In a B-tree, the deleted entry may appear in a nonleaf node. The proper value must be selected as a replacement from the subtree of the node containing the deleted entry. Specifically, if search key K_i is deleted, the smallest search key appearing in the subtree of pointer P_{i+1} must be moved to the field formerly occupied by K_i. Further actions need to be taken if the leaf node now has too few entries. In contrast, insertion in a B-tree is only slightly more complicated than is insertion in a B^+-tree.

The space advantages of B-trees are marginal for large indices, and usually do not outweigh the disadvantages that we have noted. Thus, pretty much all database-system implementations use the B^+-tree data structure, even if (as we discussed earlier) they refer to the data structure as a B-tree.

11.4.6   Flash Memory

In our description of indexing so far, we have assumed that data are resident on magnetic disks. Although this assumption continues to be true for the most part, flash memory capacities have grown significantly, and the cost of flash memory per gigabyte has dropped equally significantly, making flash memory storage a serious contender for replacing magnetic-disk storage for many applications. A natural question is, how would this change affect the index structure.

Flash-memory storage is structured as blocks, and the B^+-tree index structure can be used for flash-memory storage. The benefit of the much faster access speeds is clear for index lookups. Instead of requiring an average of 10 milliseconds to seek to and read a block, a random block can be read in about a microsecond from flash-memory. Thus lookups run significantly faster than with disk-based data. The optimum B^+-tree node size for flash-memory is typically smaller than that with disk.

The only real drawback with flash memory is that it does not permit in-place updates to data at the physical level, although it appears to do so logically. Every update turns into a copy+write of an entire flash-memory block, requiring the old copy of the block to be erased subsequently; a block erase takes about 1 millisecond. There is ongoing research aimed at developing index structures that can reduce the number of block erases. Meanwhile, standard B^+-tree indices can continue to be used even on flash-memory storage, with acceptable update performance, and significantly improved lookup performance compared to disk storage.

11.5   Multiple-Key Access

Until now, we have assumed implicitly that only one index on one attribute is used to process a query on a relation. However, for certain types of queries, it is advantageous to use multiple indices if they exist, or to use an index built on a multiattribute search key.

11.5.1   Using Multiple Single-Key Indices

Assume that the *instructor* file has two indices: one for *dept_name* and one for *salary*. Consider the following query: "Find all instructors in the Finance department with salary equal to $80,000." We write

> **select** *ID*
> **from** *instructor*
> **where** *dept_name* ='Finance' **and** *salary*= 80000;

There are three strategies possible for processing this query:

1. Use the index on *dept_name* to find all records pertaining to the Finance department. Examine each such record to see whether *salary*= 80000.

2. Use the index on *salary* to find all records pertaining to instructors with salary of $80,000. Examine each such record to see whether the department name is "Finance".

3. Use the index on *dept_name* to find *pointers* to all records pertaining to the Finance department. Also, use the index on *salary* to find pointers to all records pertaining to instructors with a salary of $80,000. Take the intersection of these two sets of pointers. Those pointers that are in the intersection point to records pertaining to instructors of the Finance department and with salary of $80,000.

The third strategy is the only one of the three that takes advantage of the existence of multiple indices. However, even this strategy may be a poor choice if all of the following hold:

*   There are many records pertaining to the Finance department.

*   There are many records pertaining to instructors with a salary of $80,000.

*   There are only a few records pertaining to *both* the Finance department and instructors with a salary of $80,000.

If these conditions hold, we must scan a large number of pointers to produce a small result. An index structure called a "bitmap index" can in some cases greatly speed up the intersection operation used in the third strategy. Bitmap indices are outlined in Section 11.9.

11.5.2 Indices on Multiple Keys

An alternative strategy for this case is to create and use an index on a composite search key (*dept_name*, *salary*)—that is, the search key consisting of the department name concatenated with the instructor salary.

We can use an ordered (B$^+$-tree) index on the above composite search key to answer efficiently queries of the form

> **select** *ID*
> **from** *instructor*
> **where** *dept_name* = 'Finance' **and** *salary*= 80000;

Queries such as the following query, which specifies an equality condition on the first attribute of the search key (*dept_name*) and a range on the second attribute of the search key (*salary*), can also be handled efficiently since they correspond to a range query on the search attribute.

> **select** *ID*
> **from** *instructor*
> **where** *dept_name* = 'Finance' **and** *salary*< 80000;

We can even use an ordered index on the search key (*dept_name*, *salary*) to answer the following query on only one attribute efficiently:

> **select** *ID*
> **from** *instructor*
> **where** *dept_name* = 'Finance';

An equality condition *dept_name* = "Finance" is equivalent to a range query on the range with lower end (Finance, $-\infty$) and upper end (Finance, $+\infty$). Range queries on just the *dept_name* attribute can be handled in a similar manner.

The use of an ordered-index structure on a composite search key, however, has a few shortcomings. As an illustration, consider the query

> **select** *ID*
> **from** *instructor*
> **where** *dept_name* < 'Finance' **and** *salary*< 80000;

We can answer this query by using an ordered index on the search key (*dept_name*, *salary*): For each value of *dept_name* that is less than "Finance" in alphabetic order, the system locates records with a *salary* value of 80000. However, each record is likely to be in a different disk block, because of the ordering of records in the file, leading to many I/O operations.

The difference between this query and the previous two queries is that the condition on the first attribute (*dept_name*) is a comparison condition, rather than an equality condition. The condition does not correspond to a range query on the search key.

To speed the processing of general composite search-key queries (which can involve one or more comparison operations), we can use several special structures. We shall consider *bitmap indices* in Section 11.9. There is another structure, called the *R-tree*, that can be used for this purpose. The R-tree is an extension of the B^+-tree to handle indexing on multiple dimensions. Since the R-tree is used primarily with geographical data types, we describe the structure in Chapter 25.

11.5.3 Covering Indices

Covering indices are indices that store the values of some attributes (other than the search-key attributes) along with the pointers to the record. Storing extra attribute values is useful with secondary indices, since they allow us to answer some queries using just the index, without even looking up the actual records.

For example, suppose that we have a nonclustering index on the *ID* attribute of the *instructor* relation. If we store the value of the *salary* attribute along with the record pointer, we can answer queries that require the salary (but not the other attribute, *dept_name*) without accessing the *instructor* record.

The same effect could be obtained by creating an index on the search key (*ID, salary*), but a covering index reduces the size of the search key, allowing a larger fanout in the nonleaf nodes, and potentially reducing the height of the index.

11.6   Static Hashing

One disadvantage of sequential file organization is that we must access an index structure to locate data, or must use binary search, and that results in more I/O operations. File organizations based on the technique of **hashing** allow us to avoid accessing an index structure. Hashing also provides a way of constructing indices. We study file organizations and indices based on hashing in the following sections.

In our description of hashing, we shall use the term **bucket** to denote a unit of storage that can store one or more records. A bucket is typically a disk block, but could be chosen to be smaller or larger than a disk block.

Formally, let K denote the set of all search-key values, and let B denote the set of all bucket addresses. A **hash function** h is a function from K to B. Let h denote a hash function.

To insert a record with search key K_i, we compute $h(K_i)$, which gives the address of the bucket for that record. Assume for now that there is space in the bucket to store the record. Then, the record is stored in that bucket.

To perform a lookup on a search-key value K_i, we simply compute $h(K_i)$, then search the bucket with that address. Suppose that two search keys, K_5 and K_7, have the same hash value; that is, $h(K_5) = h(K_7)$. If we perform a lookup on K_5, the bucket $h(K_5)$ contains records with search-key values K_5 and records with search-key values K_7. Thus, we have to check the search-key value of every record in the bucket to verify that the record is one that we want.

Deletion is equally straightforward. If the search-key value of the record to be deleted is K_i, we compute $h(K_i)$, then search the corresponding bucket for that record, and delete the record from the bucket.

Hashing can be used for two different purposes. In a **hash file organization**, we obtain the address of the disk block containing a desired record directly by computing a function on the search-key value of the record. In a **hash index organization** we organize the search keys, with their associated pointers, into a hash file structure.

11.6.1   Hash Functions

The worst possible hash function maps all search-key values to the same bucket. Such a function is undesirable because all the records have to be kept in the same bucket. A lookup has to examine every such record to find the one desired. An ideal hash function distributes the stored keys uniformly across all the buckets, so that every bucket has the same number of records.

Since we do not know at design time precisely which search-key values will be stored in the file, we want to choose a hash function that assigns search-key values to buckets in such a way that the distribution has these qualities:

- The distribution is *uniform*. That is, the hash function assigns each bucket the same number of search-key values from the set of *all* possible search-key values.

- The distribution is *random*. That is, in the average case, each bucket will have nearly the same number of values assigned to it, regardless of the actual distribution of search-key values. More precisely, the hash value will not be correlated to any externally visible ordering on the search-key values, such as alphabetic ordering or ordering by the length of the search keys; the hash function will appear to be random.

As an illustration of these principles, let us choose a hash function for the *instructor* file using the search key *dept_name*. The hash function that we choose must have the desirable properties not only on the example *instructor* file that we have been using, but also on an *instructor* file of realistic size for a large university with many departments.

Assume that we decide to have 26 buckets, and we define a hash function that maps names beginning with the ith letter of the alphabet to the ith bucket. This hash function has the virtue of simplicity, but it fails to provide a uniform distribution, since we expect more names to begin with such letters as B and R than Q and X, for example.

Now suppose that we want a hash function on the search key *salary*. Suppose that the minimum salary is $30,000 and the maximum salary is $130,000, and we use a hash function that divides the values into 10 ranges, $30,000–$40,000, $40,001–$50,000 and so on. The distribution of search-key values is uniform (since

bucket 0

bucket 1

15151	Mozart	Music	40000

bucket 2

32343	El Said	History	80000
58583	Califieri	History	60000

bucket 3

22222	Einstein	Physics	95000
33456	Gold	Physics	87000
98345	Kim	Elec. Eng.	80000

bucket 4

12121	Wu	Finance	90000
76543	Singh	Finance	80000

bucket 5

76766	Crick	Biology	72000

bucket 6

10101	Srinivasan	Comp. Sci.	65000
45565	Katz	Comp. Sci.	75000
83821	Brandt	Comp. Sci.	92000

bucket 7

Figure 11.23 Hash organization of *instructor* file, with *dept_name* as the key.

each bucket has the same number of different *salary* values), but is not random. Records with salaries between \$60,001 and \$70,000 are far more common than are records with salaries between \$30,001 and \$40,000. As a result, the distribution of records is not uniform—some buckets receive more records than others do. If the function has a random distribution, even if there are such correlations in the search keys, the randomness of the distribution will make it very likely that all buckets will have roughly the same number of records, as long as each search key occurs in only a small fraction of the records. (If a single search key occurs in a large fraction of the records, the bucket containing it is likely to have more records than other buckets, regardless of the hash function used.)

Typical hash functions perform computation on the internal binary machine representation of characters in the search key. A simple hash function of this type first computes the sum of the binary representations of the characters of a key, then returns the sum modulo the number of buckets.

Figure 11.23 shows the application of such a scheme, with eight buckets, to the *instructor* file, under the assumption that the ith letter in the alphabet is represented by the integer i.

The following hash function is a better alternative for hashing strings. Let s be a string of length n, and let $s[i]$ denote the ith byte of the string. The hash function is defined as:

$$s[0] * 31^{(n-1)} + s[1] * 31^{(n-2)} + \cdots + s[n-1]$$

The function can be implemented efficiently by setting the hash result initially to 0, and iterating from the first to the last character of the string, at each step multiplying the hash value by 31 and then adding the next character (treated as an integer). The above expression would appear to result in a very large number, but it is actually computed with fixed-size positive integers; the result of each multiplication and addition is thus automatically computed modulo the largest possible integer value plus 1. The result of the above function modulo the number of buckets can then be used for indexing.

Hash functions require careful design. A bad hash function may result in lookup taking time proportional to the number of search keys in the file. A well-designed function gives an average-case lookup time that is a (small) constant, independent of the number of search keys in the file.

11.6.2   Handling of Bucket Overflows

So far, we have assumed that, when a record is inserted, the bucket to which it is mapped has space to store the record. If the bucket does not have enough space, a **bucket overflow** is said to occur. Bucket overflow can occur for several reasons:

- **Insufficient buckets**. The number of buckets, which we denote n_B, must be chosen such that $n_B > n_r/f_r$, where n_r denotes the total number of records that will be stored and f_r denotes the number of records that will fit in a bucket. This designation, of course, assumes that the total number of records is known when the hash function is chosen.

- **Skew**. Some buckets are assigned more records than are others, so a bucket may overflow even when other buckets still have space. This situation is called bucket **skew**. Skew can occur for two reasons:

    1. Multiple records may have the same search key.

    2. The chosen hash function may result in nonuniform distribution of search keys.

So that the probability of bucket overflow is reduced, the number of buckets is chosen to be $(n_r/f_r) * (1 + d)$, where d is a fudge factor, typically around 0.2. Some space is wasted: About 20 percent of the space in the buckets will be empty. But the benefit is that the probability of overflow is reduced.

Despite allocation of a few more buckets than required, bucket overflow can still occur. We handle bucket overflow by using **overflow buckets**. If a record must be inserted into a bucket b, and b is already full, the system provides an overflow bucket for b, and inserts the record into the overflow bucket. If the overflow bucket is also full, the system provides another overflow bucket, and so on. All the overflow buckets of a given bucket are chained together in a linked list, as in Figure 11.24. Overflow handling using such a linked list is called **overflow chaining**.

We must change the lookup algorithm slightly to handle overflow chaining. As before, the system uses the hash function on the search key to identify a bucket

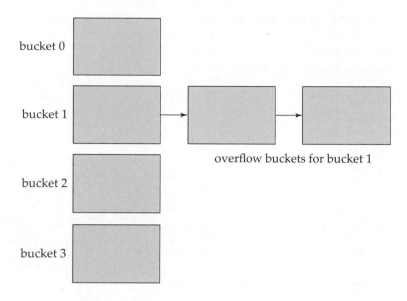

Figure 11.24 Overflow chaining in a hash structure.

b. The system must examine all the records in bucket b to see whether they match the search key, as before. In addition, if bucket b has overflow buckets, the system must examine the records in all the overflow buckets also.

The form of hash structure that we have just described is sometimes referred to as **closed hashing**. Under an alternative approach, called **open hashing**, the set of buckets is fixed, and there are no overflow chains. Instead, if a bucket is full, the system inserts records in some other bucket in the initial set of buckets B. One policy is to use the next bucket (in cyclic order) that has space; this policy is called *linear probing*. Other policies, such as computing further hash functions, are also used. Open hashing has been used to construct symbol tables for compilers and assemblers, but closed hashing is preferable for database systems. The reason is that deletion under open hashing is troublesome. Usually, compilers and assemblers perform only lookup and insertion operations on their symbol tables. However, in a database system, it is important to be able to handle deletion as well as insertion. Thus, open hashing is of only minor importance in database implementation.

An important drawback to the form of hashing that we have described is that we must choose the hash function when we implement the system, and it cannot be changed easily thereafter if the file being indexed grows or shrinks. Since the function h maps search-key values to a fixed set B of bucket addresses, we waste space if B is made large to handle future growth of the file. If B is too small, the buckets contain records of many different search-key values, and bucket overflows can occur. As the file grows, performance suffers. We study later, in Section 11.7, how the number of buckets and the hash function can be changed dynamically.

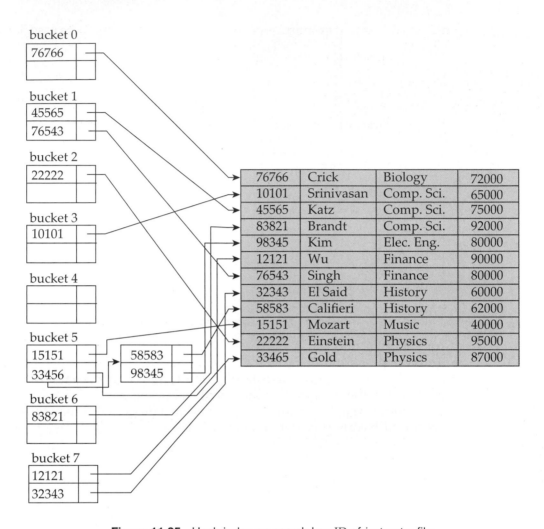

Figure 11.25   Hash index on search key *ID* of *instructor* file.

11.6.3   Hash Indices

Hashing can be used not only for file organization, but also for index-structure creation. A **hash index** organizes the search keys, with their associated pointers, into a hash file structure. We construct a hash index as follows. We apply a hash function on a search key to identify a bucket, and store the key and its associated pointers in the bucket (or in overflow buckets). Figure 11.25 shows a secondary hash index on the *instructor* file, for the search key *ID*. The hash function in the figure computes the sum of the digits of the *ID* modulo 8. The hash index has eight buckets, each of size 2 (realistic indices would, of course, have much larger bucket sizes). One of the buckets has three keys mapped to it, so it has an overflow bucket. In this example, *ID* is a primary key for *instructor*, so each search key has only one associated pointer. In general, multiple pointers can be associated with each key.

We use the term *hash index* to denote hash file structures as well as secondary hash indices. Strictly speaking, hash indices are only secondary index structures. A hash index is never needed as a clustering index structure, since, if a file itself is organized by hashing, there is no need for a separate hash index structure on it. However, since hash file organization provides the same direct access to records that indexing provides, we pretend that a file organized by hashing also has a clustering hash index on it.

11.7   Dynamic Hashing

As we have seen, the need to fix the set B of bucket addresses presents a serious problem with the static hashing technique of the previous section. Most databases grow larger over time. If we are to use static hashing for such a database, we have three classes of options:

1. Choose a hash function based on the current file size. This option will result in performance degradation as the database grows.

2. Choose a hash function based on the anticipated size of the file at some point in the future. Although performance degradation is avoided, a significant amount of space may be wasted initially.

3. Periodically reorganize the hash structure in response to file growth. Such a reorganization involves choosing a new hash function, recomputing the hash function on every record in the file, and generating new bucket assignments. This reorganization is a massive, time-consuming operation. Furthermore, it is necessary to forbid access to the file during reorganization.

Several **dynamic hashing** techniques allow the hash function to be modified dynamically to accommodate the growth or shrinkage of the database. In this section we describe one form of dynamic hashing, called **extendable hashing**. The bibliographical notes provide references to other forms of dynamic hashing.

11.7.1   Data Structure

Extendable hashing copes with changes in database size by splitting and coalescing buckets as the database grows and shrinks. As a result, space efficiency is retained. Moreover, since the reorganization is performed on only one bucket at a time, the resulting performance overhead is acceptably low.

With extendable hashing, we choose a hash function h with the desirable properties of uniformity and randomness. However, this hash function generates values over a relatively large range—namely, b-bit binary integers. A typical value for b is 32.

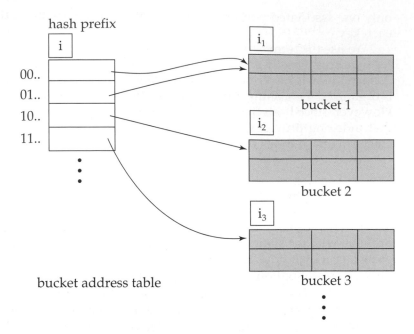

Figure 11.26 General extendable hash structure.

We do not create a bucket for each hash value. Indeed, 2^{32} is over 4 billion, and that many buckets is unreasonable for all but the largest databases. Instead, we create buckets on demand, as records are inserted into the file. We do not use the entire b bits of the hash value initially. At any point, we use i bits, where $0 \leq i \leq b$. These i bits are used as an offset into an additional table of bucket addresses. The value of i grows and shrinks with the size of the database.

Figure 11.26 shows a general extendable hash structure. The i appearing above the bucket address table in the figure indicates that i bits of the hash value $h(K)$ are required to determine the correct bucket for K. This number will, of course, change as the file grows. Although i bits are required to find the correct entry in the bucket address table, several consecutive table entries may point to the same bucket. All such entries will have a common hash prefix, but the length of this prefix may be less than i. Therefore, we associate with each bucket an integer giving the length of the common hash prefix. In Figure 11.26 the integer associated with bucket j is shown as i_j. The number of bucket-address-table entries that point to bucket j is

$$2^{(i - i_j)}$$

11.7.2 Queries and Updates

We now see how to perform lookup, insertion, and deletion on an extendable hash structure.

To locate the bucket containing search-key value K_l, the system takes the first i high-order bits of $h(K_l)$, looks at the corresponding table entry for this bit string, and follows the bucket pointer in the table entry.

To insert a record with search-key value K_l, the system follows the same procedure for lookup as before, ending up in some bucket—say, j. If there is room in the bucket, the system inserts the record in the bucket. If, on the other hand, the bucket is full, it must split the bucket and redistribute the current records, plus the new one. To split the bucket, the system must first determine from the hash value whether it needs to increase the number of bits that it uses.

- If $i = i_j$, only one entry in the bucket address table points to bucket j. Therefore, the system needs to increase the size of the bucket address table so that it can include pointers to the two buckets that result from splitting bucket j. It does so by considering an additional bit of the hash value. It increments the value of i by 1, thus doubling the size of the bucket address table. It replaces each entry by two entries, both of which contain the same pointer as the original entry. Now two entries in the bucket address table point to bucket j. The system allocates a new bucket (bucket z), and sets the second entry to point to the new bucket. It sets i_j and i_z to i. Next, it rehashes each record in bucket j and, depending on the first i bits (remember the system has added 1 to i), either keeps it in bucket j or allocates it to the newly created bucket.

  The system now reattempts the insertion of the new record. Usually, the attempt will succeed. However, if all the records in bucket j, as well as the new record, have the same hash-value prefix, it will be necessary to split a bucket again, since all the records in bucket j and the new record are assigned to the same bucket. If the hash function has been chosen carefully, it is unlikely that a single insertion will require that a bucket be split more than once, unless there are a large number of records with the same search key. If all the records in bucket j have the same search-key value, no amount of splitting will help. In such cases, overflow buckets are used to store the records, as in static hashing.

- If $i > i_j$, then more than one entry in the bucket address table points to bucket j. Thus, the system can split bucket j without increasing the size of the bucket address table. Observe that all the entries that point to bucket j correspond to hash prefixes that have the same value on the leftmost i_j bits. The system allocates a new bucket (bucket z), and sets i_j and i_z to the value that results from adding 1 to the original i_j value. Next, the system needs to adjust the entries in the bucket address table that previously pointed to bucket j. (Note that with the new value for i_j, not all the entries correspond to hash prefixes that have the same value on the leftmost i_j bits.) The system leaves the first half of the entries as they were (pointing to bucket j), and sets all the remaining entries to point to the newly created bucket (bucket z). Next, as in the previous case, the system rehashes each record in bucket j, and allocates it either to bucket j or to the newly created bucket z.

dept_name	h(dept_name)
Biology	0010 1101 1111 1011 0010 1100 0011 0000
Comp. Sci.	1111 0001 0010 0100 1001 0011 0110 1101
Elec. Eng.	0100 0011 1010 1100 1100 0110 1101 1111
Finance	1010 0011 1010 0000 1100 0110 1001 1111
History	1100 0111 1110 1101 1011 1111 0011 1010
Music	0011 0101 1010 0110 1100 1001 1110 1011
Physics	1001 1000 0011 1111 1001 1100 0000 0001

Figure 11.27   Hash function for *dept_name*.

The system then reattempts the insert. In the unlikely case that it again fails, it applies one of the two cases, $i = i_j$ or $i > i_j$, as appropriate.

Note that, in both cases, the system needs to recompute the hash function on only the records in bucket j.

To delete a record with search-key value K_l, the system follows the same procedure for lookup as before, ending up in some bucket—say, j. It removes both the search key from the bucket and the record from the file. The bucket, too, is removed if it becomes empty. Note that, at this point, several buckets can be coalesced, and the size of the bucket address table can be cut in half. The procedure for deciding on which buckets can be coalesced and how to coalesce buckets is left to you to do as an exercise. The conditions under which the bucket address table can be reduced in size are also left to you as an exercise. Unlike coalescing of buckets, changing the size of the bucket address table is a rather expensive operation if the table is large. Therefore it may be worthwhile to reduce the bucket-address-table size only if the number of buckets reduces greatly.

To illustrate the operation of insertion, we use the *instructor* file in Figure 11.1 and assume that the search key is *dept_name* with the 32-bit hash values as appear in Figure 11.27. Assume that, initially, the file is empty, as in Figure 11.28. We insert the records one by one. To illustrate all the features of extendable hashing in a small structure, we shall make the unrealistic assumption that a bucket can hold only two records.

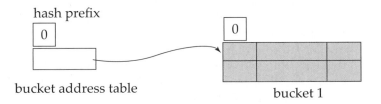

Figure 11.28   Initial extendable hash structure.

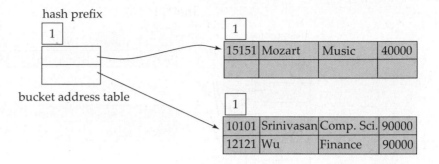

Figure 11.29 Hash structure after three insertions.

We insert the record (10101, Srinivasan, Comp. Sci., 65000). The bucket address table contains a pointer to the one bucket, and the system inserts the record. Next, we insert the record (12121, Wu, Finance, 90000). The system also places this record in the one bucket of our structure.

When we attempt to insert the next record (15151, Mozart, Music, 40000), we find that the bucket is full. Since $i = i_0$, we need to increase the number of bits that we use from the hash value. We now use 1 bit, allowing us $2^1 = 2$ buckets. This increase in the number of bits necessitates doubling the size of the bucket address table to two entries. The system splits the bucket, placing in the new bucket those records whose search key has a hash value beginning with 1, and leaving in the original bucket the other records. Figure 11.29 shows the state of our structure after the split.

Next, we insert (22222, Einstein, Physics, 95000). Since the first bit of h(Physics) is 1, we must insert this record into the bucket pointed to by the "1" entry in the

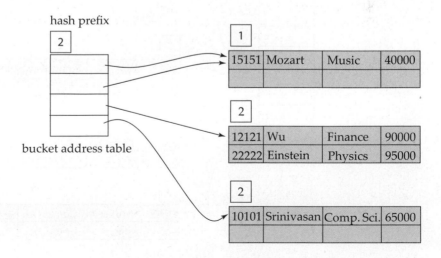

Figure 11.30 Hash structure after four insertions.

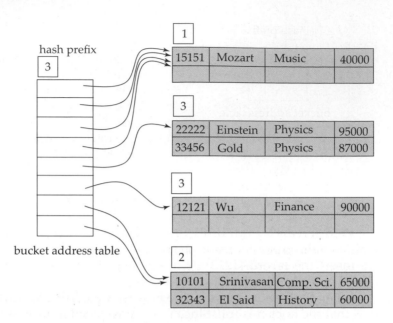

Figure 11.31 Hash structure after six insertions.

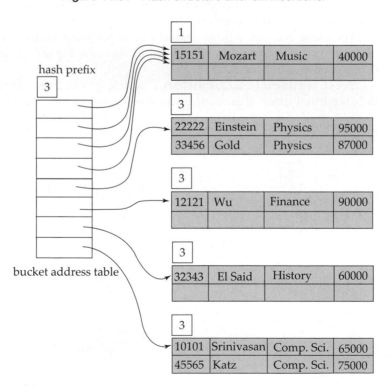

Figure 11.32 Hash structure after seven insertions.

bucket address table. Once again, we find the bucket full and $i = i_1$. We increase the number of bits that we use from the hash to 2. This increase in the number of bits necessitates doubling the size of the bucket address table to four entries, as in Figure 11.30. Since the bucket of Figure 11.29 for hash prefix 0 was not split, the two entries of the bucket address table of 00 and 01 both point to this bucket.

For each record in the bucket of Figure 11.29 for hash prefix 1 (the bucket being split), the system examines the first 2 bits of the hash value to determine which bucket of the new structure should hold it.

Next, we insert (32343, El Said, History, 60000), which goes in the same bucket as Comp. Sci. The following insertion of (33456, Gold, Physics, 87000) results in a bucket overflow, leading to an increase in the number of bits, and a doubling of the size of the bucket address table (see Figure 11.31).

The insertion of (45565, Katz, Comp. Sci., 75000) leads to another bucket overflow; this overflow, however, can be handled without increasing the number of bits, since the bucket in question has two pointers pointing to it (see Figure 11.32).

Next, we insert the records of "Califieri", "Singh", and "Crick" without any bucket overflow. The insertion of the third Comp. Sci. record (83821, Brandt, Comp. Sci., 92000), however, leads to another overflow. This overflow cannot be handled by increasing the number of bits, since there are three records with exactly the same hash value. Hence the system uses an overflow bucket, as in

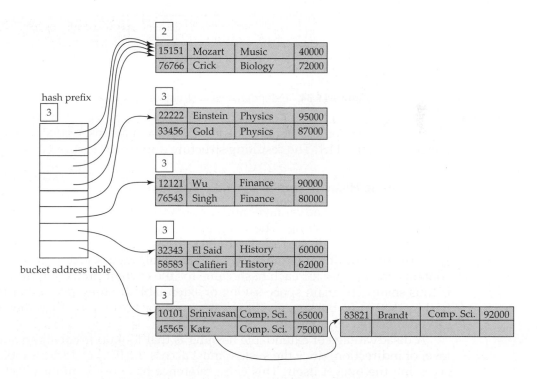

Figure 11.33 Hash structure after eleven insertions.

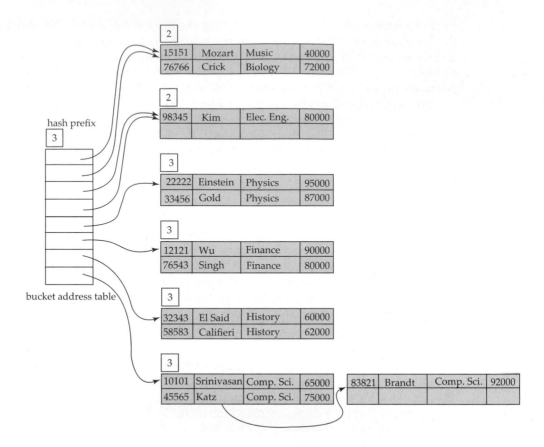

Figure 11.34   Extendable hash structure for the *instructor* file.

Figure 11.33. We continue in this manner until we have inserted all the *instructor* records of Figure 11.1. The resulting structure appears in Figure 11.34.

11.7.3   Static Hashing versus Dynamic Hashing

We now examine the advantages and disadvantages of extendable hashing, compared with static hashing. The main advantage of extendable hashing is that performance does not degrade as the file grows. Furthermore, there is minimal space overhead. Although the bucket address table incurs additional overhead, it contains one pointer for each hash value for the current prefix length. This table is thus small. The main space saving of extendable hashing over other forms of hashing is that no buckets need to be reserved for future growth; rather, buckets can be allocated dynamically.

A disadvantage of extendable hashing is that lookup involves an additional level of indirection, since the system must access the bucket address table before accessing the bucket itself. This extra reference has only a minor effect on performance. Although the hash structures that we discussed in Section 11.6 do not have this extra level of indirection, they lose their minor performance advantage as they become full.

Thus, extendable hashing appears to be a highly attractive technique, provided that we are willing to accept the added complexity involved in its implementation. The bibliographical notes reference more detailed descriptions of extendable hashing implementation.

The bibliographical notes also provide references to another form of dynamic hashing called **linear hashing**, which avoids the extra level of indirection associated with extendable hashing, at the possible cost of more overflow buckets.

11.8   Comparison of Ordered Indexing and Hashing

We have seen several ordered-indexing schemes and several hashing schemes. We can organize files of records as ordered files by using index-sequential organization or B^+-tree organizations. Alternatively, we can organize the files by using hashing. Finally, we can organize them as heap files, where the records are not ordered in any particular way.

Each scheme has advantages in certain situations. A database-system implementor could provide many schemes, leaving the final decision of which schemes to use to the database designer. However, such an approach requires the implementor to write more code, adding both to the cost of the system and to the space that the system occupies. Most database systems support B^+-trees and may additionally support some form of hash file organization or hash indices.

To make a choice of file organization and indexing techniques for a relation, the implementor or the database designer must consider the following issues:

- Is the cost of periodic reorganization of the index or hash organization acceptable?

- What is the relative frequency of insertion and deletion?

- Is it desirable to optimize average access time at the expense of increasing the worst-case access time?

- What types of queries are users likely to pose?

We have already examined the first three of these issues, first in our review of the relative merits of specific indexing techniques, and again in our discussion of hashing techniques. The fourth issue, the expected type of query, is critical to the choice of ordered indexing or hashing.

If most queries are of the form:

$$\textbf{select } A_1, A_2, \ldots, A_n$$
$$\textbf{from } r$$
$$\textbf{where } A_i = c;$$

then, to process this query, the system will perform a lookup on an ordered index or a hash structure for attribute A_i, for value c. For queries of this form, a hashing scheme is preferable. An ordered-index lookup requires time proportional to the log of the number of values in r for A_i. In a hash structure, however, the average lookup time is a constant independent of the size of the database. The only advantage to an index over a hash structure for this form of query is that the worst-case lookup time is proportional to the log of the number of values in r for A_i. By contrast, for hashing, the worst-case lookup time is proportional to the number of values in r for A_i. However, the worst-case lookup time is unlikely to occur with hashing, and hashing is preferable in this case.

Ordered-index techniques are preferable to hashing in cases where the query specifies a range of values. Such a query takes the following form:

> **select** A_1, A_2, ..., A_n
> **from** r
> **where** $A_i \leq c_2$ **and** $A_i \geq c_1$;

In other words, the preceding query finds all the records with A_i values between c_1 and c_2.

Let us consider how we process this query using an ordered index. First, we perform a lookup on value c_1. Once we have found the bucket for value c_1, we follow the pointer chain in the index to read the next bucket in order, and we continue in this manner until we reach c_2.

If, instead of an ordered index, we have a hash structure, we can perform a lookup on c_1 and can locate the corresponding bucket—but it is not easy, in general, to determine the next bucket that must be examined. The difficulty arises because a good hash function assigns values randomly to buckets. Thus, there is no simple notion of "next bucket in sorted order." The reason we cannot chain buckets together in sorted order on A_i is that each bucket is assigned many search-key values. Since values are scattered randomly by the hash function, the values in the specified range are likely to be scattered across many or all of the buckets. Therefore, we have to read all the buckets to find the required search keys.

Usually the designer will choose ordered indexing unless it is known in advance that range queries will be infrequent, in which case hashing would be chosen. Hash organizations are particularly useful for temporary files created during query processing, if lookups based on a key value are required, but no range queries will be performed.

11.9   Bitmap Indices

Bitmap indices are a specialized type of index designed for easy querying on multiple keys, although each bitmap index is built on a single key.

For bitmap indices to be used, records in a relation must be numbered sequentially, starting from, say, 0. Given a number n, it must be easy to retrieve the record numbered n. This is particularly easy to achieve if records are fixed in size, and allocated on consecutive blocks of a file. The record number can then be translated easily into a block number and a number that identifies the record within the block.

Consider a relation r, with an attribute A that can take on only one of a small number (for example, 2 to 20) values. For instance, a relation *instructor_info* may have an attribute *gender*, which can take only values m (male) or f (female). Another example would be an attribute *income_level*, where income has been broken up into 5 levels: $L1$: \$0−9999, $L2$: \$10,000−19,999, $L3$: 20,000−39,999, $L4$: 40,000−74,999, and $L5$: 75,000−∞. Here, the raw data can take on many values, but a data analyst has split the values into a small number of ranges to simplify analysis of the data.

11.9.1 Bitmap Index Structure

A **bitmap** is simply an array of bits. In its simplest form, a **bitmap index** on the attribute A of relation r consists of one bitmap for each value that A can take. Each bitmap has as many bits as the number of records in the relation. The ith bit of the bitmap for value v_j is set to 1 if the record numbered i has the value v_j for attribute A. All other bits of the bitmap are set to 0.

In our example, there is one bitmap for the value m and one for f. The ith bit of the bitmap for m is set to 1 if the *gender* value of the record numbered i is m. All other bits of the bitmap for m set to 0. Similarly, the bitmap for f has the value 1 for bits corresponding to records with the value f for the *gender* attribute; all other bits have the value 0. Figure 11.35 shows an example of bitmap indices on a relation *instructor_info*.

We now consider when bitmaps are useful. The simplest way of retrieving all records with value m (or value f) would be to simply read all records of the relation and select those records with value m (or f, respectively). The bitmap index doesn't really help to speed up such a selection. While it would allow us to

record number	ID	gender	income_level		Bitmaps for *gender*		Bitmaps for *income_level*
0	76766	m	L1	m	10010	L1	10100
1	22222	f	L2	f	01101	L2	01000
2	12121	f	L1			L3	00001
3	15151	m	L4			L4	00010
4	58583	f	L3			L5	00000

Figure 11.35 Bitmap indices on relation *instructor_info*.

read only those records for a specific gender, it is likely that every disk block for the file would have to be read anyway.

In fact, bitmap indices are useful for selections mainly when there are selections on multiple keys. Suppose we create a bitmap index on attribute *income _level*, which we described earlier, in addition to the bitmap index on *gender*.

Consider now a query that selects women with income in the range $10,000 *to* $19, 999. This query can be expressed as

> **select** *
> **from** *r*
> **where** *gender* = 'f' **and** *income_level* = 'L2';

To evaluate this selection, we fetch the bitmaps for *gender* value f and the bitmap for *income_level* value L2, and perform an **intersection** (logical-and) of the two bitmaps. In other words, we compute a new bitmap where bit *i* has value 1 if the *i*th bit of the two bitmaps are both 1, and has a value 0 otherwise. In the example in Figure 11.35, the intersection of the bitmap for *gender* = f (01101) and the bitmap for *income_level* = L2 (01000) gives the bitmap 01000.

Since the first attribute can take two values, and the second can take five values, we would expect only about 1 in 10 records, on an average, to satisfy a combined condition on the two attributes. If there are further conditions, the fraction of records satisfying all the conditions is likely to be quite small. The system can then compute the query result by finding all bits with value 1 in the intersection bitmap and retrieving the corresponding records. If the fraction is large, scanning the entire relation would remain the cheaper alternative.

Another important use of bitmaps is to count the number of tuples satisfying a given selection. Such queries are important for data analysis. For instance, if we wish to find out how many women have an income level L2, we compute the intersection of the two bitmaps and then count the number of bits that are 1 in the intersection bitmap. We can thus get the desired result from the bitmap index, without even accessing the relation.

Bitmap indices are generally quite small compared to the actual relation size. Records are typically at least tens of bytes to hundreds of bytes long, whereas a single bit represents the record in a bitmap. Thus the space occupied by a single bitmap is usually less than 1 percent of the space occupied by the relation. For instance, if the record size for a given relation is 100 bytes, then the space occupied by a single bitmap would be $\frac{1}{8}$ of 1 percent of the space occupied by the relation. If an attribute *A* of the relation can take on only one of eight values, a bitmap index on attribute *A* would consist of eight bitmaps, which together occupy only 1 percent of the size of the relation.

Deletion of records creates gaps in the sequence of records, since shifting records (or record numbers) to fill gaps would be extremely expensive. To recognize deleted records, we can store an **existence bitmap**, in which bit *i* is 0 if record *i* does not exist and 1 otherwise. We shall see the need for existence bitmaps in Section 11.9.2. Insertion of records should not affect the sequence numbering of other records. Therefore, we can do insertion either by appending records to the end of the file or by replacing deleted records.

11.9.2 Efficient Implementation of Bitmap Operations

We can compute the intersection of two bitmaps easily by using a **for** loop: the ith iteration of the loop computes the **and** of the ith bits of the two bitmaps. We can speed up computation of the intersection greatly by using bit-wise **and** instructions supported by most computer instruction sets. A *word* usually consists of 32 or 64 bits, depending on the architecture of the computer. A bit-wise **and** instruction takes two words as input and outputs a word where each bit is the logical **and** of the bits in corresponding positions of the input words. What is important to note is that a single bit-wise **and** instruction can compute the intersection of 32 or 64 bits *at once*.

If a relation had 1 million records, each bitmap would contain 1 million bits, or equivalently 128 kilobytes. Only 31,250 instructions are needed to compute the intersection of two bitmaps for our relation, assuming a 32-bit word length. Thus, computing bitmap intersections is an extremely fast operation.

Just as bitmap intersection is useful for computing the **and** of two conditions, bitmap union is useful for computing the **or** of two conditions. The procedure for bitmap union is exactly the same as for intersection, except we use bit-wise **or** instructions instead of bit-wise **and** instructions.

The complement operation can be used to compute a predicate involving the negation of a condition, such as **not** (*income-level* = L1). The complement of a bitmap is generated by complementing every bit of the bitmap (the complement of 1 is 0 and the complement of 0 is 1). It may appear that **not** (*income_level* = L1) can be implemented by just computing the complement of the bitmap for income level L1. If some records have been deleted, however, just computing the complement of a bitmap is not sufficient. Bits corresponding to such records would be 0 in the original bitmap, but would become 1 in the complement, although the records don't exist. A similar problem also arises when the value of an attribute is *null*. For instance, if the value of *income_level* is null, the bit would be 0 in the original bitmap for value L1, and 1 in the complement bitmap.

To make sure that the bits corresponding to deleted records are set to 0 in the result, the complement bitmap must be intersected with the existence bitmap to turn off the bits for deleted records. Similarly, to handle null values, the complement bitmap must also be intersected with the complement of the bitmap for the value *null*.[2]

Counting the number of bits that are 1 in a bitmap can be done quickly by a clever technique. We can maintain an array with 256 entries, where the ith entry stores the number of bits that are 1 in the binary representation of i. Set the total count initially to 0. We take each byte of the bitmap, use it to index into this array, and add the stored count to the total count. The number of addition operations is

---

[2]Handling predicates such as **is unknown** would cause further complications, which would in general require use of an extra bitmap to track which operation results are unknown.

$\frac{1}{8}$ of the number of tuples, and thus the counting process is very efficient. A large array (using $2^{16} = 65,536$ entries), indexed by pairs of bytes, would give even higher speedup, but at a higher storage cost.

11.9.3   Bitmaps and B⁺-Trees

Bitmaps can be combined with regular B⁺-tree indices for relations where a few attribute values are extremely common, and other values also occur, but much less frequently. In a B⁺-tree index leaf, for each value we would normally maintain a list of all records with that value for the indexed attribute. Each element of the list would be a record identifier, consisting of at least 32 bits, and usually more. For a value that occurs in many records, we store a bitmap instead of a list of records.

Suppose a particular value v_i occurs in $\frac{1}{16}$ of the records of a relation. Let N be the number of records in the relation, and assume that a record has a 64-bit number identifying it. The bitmap needs only 1 bit per record, or N bits in total. In contrast, the list representation requires 64 bits per record where the value occurs, or $64 * N/16 = 4N$ bits. Thus, a bitmap is preferable for representing the list of records for value v_i. In our example (with a 64-bit record identifier), if fewer than 1 in 64 records have a particular value, the list representation is preferable for identifying records with that value, since it uses fewer bits than the bitmap representation. If more than 1 in 64 records have that value, the bitmap representation is preferable.

Thus, bitmaps can be used as a compressed storage mechanism at the leaf nodes of B⁺-trees for those values that occur very frequently.

11.10   Index Definition in SQL

The SQL standard does not provide any way for the database user or administrator to control what indices are created and maintained in the database system. Indices are not required for correctness, since they are redundant data structures. However, indices are important for efficient processing of transactions, including both update transactions and queries. Indices are also important for efficient enforcement of integrity constraints.

In principle, a database system can decide automatically what indices to create. However, because of the space cost of indices, as well as the effect of indices on update processing, it is not easy to automatically make the right choices about what indices to maintain. Therefore, most SQL implementations provide the programmer control over creation and removal of indices via data-definition-language commands.

We illustrate the syntax of these commands next. Although the syntax that we show is widely used and supported by many database systems, it is not part of the SQL standard. The SQL standard does not support control of the physical database schema; it restricts itself to the logical database schema.

We create an index with the **create index** command, which takes the form:

create index <index-name> **on** <relation-name> (<attribute-list>);

The *attribute-list* is the list of attributes of the relations that form the search key for the index.

To define an index named *dept_index* on the *instructor* relation with *dept_name* as the search key, we write:

create index *dept_index* **on** *instructor* (*dept_name*);

If we wish to declare that the search key is a candidate key, we add the attribute **unique** to the index definition. Thus, the command:

create unique index *dept_index* **on** *instructor* (*dept_name*);

declares *dept_name* to be a candidate key for *instructor* (which is probably not what we actually would want for our university database). If, at the time we enter the **create unique index** command, *dept_name* is not a candidate key, the system will display an error message, and the attempt to create the index will fail. If the index-creation attempt succeeds, any subsequent attempt to insert a tuple that violates the key declaration will fail. Note that the **unique** feature is redundant if the database system supports the **unique** declaration of the SQL standard.

Many database systems also provide a way to specify the type of index to be used (such as B^+-tree or hashing). Some database systems also permit one of the indices on a relation to be declared to be clustered; the system then stores the relation sorted by the search-key of the clustered index.

The index name we specified for an index is required to drop an index. The **drop index** command takes the form:

drop index <index-name>;

11.11 Summary

- Many queries reference only a small proportion of the records in a file. To reduce the overhead in searching for these records, we can construct *indices* for the files that store the database.

- Index-sequential files are one of the oldest index schemes used in database systems. To permit fast retrieval of records in search-key order, records are stored sequentially, and out-of-order records are chained together. To allow fast random access, we use an index structure.

- There are two types of indices that we can use: dense indices and sparse indices. Dense indices contain entries for every search-key value, whereas sparse indices contain entries only for some search-key values.

- If the sort order of a search key matches the sort order of a relation, an index on the search key is called a *clustering index*. The other indices are called *nonclustering* or *secondary indices*. Secondary indices improve the performance of queries that use search keys other than the search key of the clustering index. However, they impose an overhead on modification of the database.

- The primary disadvantage of the index-sequential file organization is that performance degrades as the file grows. To overcome this deficiency, we can use a B^+-*tree index*.

- A B^+-tree index takes the form of a *balanced* tree, in which every path from the root of the tree to a leaf of the tree is of the same length. The height of a B^+-tree is proportional to the logarithm to the base N of the number of records in the relation, where each nonleaf node stores N pointers; the value of N is often around 50 or 100. B^+-trees are much shorter than other balanced binary-tree structures such as AVL trees, and therefore require fewer disk accesses to locate records.

- Lookup on B^+-trees is straightforward and efficient. Insertion and deletion, however, are somewhat more complicated, but still efficient. The number of operations required for lookup, insertion, and deletion on B^+-trees is proportional to the logarithm to the base N of the number of records in the relation, where each nonleaf node stores N pointers.

- We can use B^+-trees for indexing a file containing records, as well as to organize records into a file.

- B-tree indices are similar to B^+-tree indices. The primary advantage of a B-tree is that the B-tree eliminates the redundant storage of search-key values. The major disadvantages are overall complexity and reduced fanout for a given node size. System designers almost universally prefer B^+-tree indices over B-tree indices in practice.

- Sequential file organizations require an index structure to locate data. File organizations based on hashing, by contrast, allow us to find the address of a data item directly by computing a function on the search-key value of the desired record. Since we do not know at design time precisely which search-key values will be stored in the file, a good hash function to choose is one that assigns search-key values to buckets such that the distribution is both uniform and random.

- *Static hashing* uses hash functions in which the set of bucket addresses is fixed. Such hash functions cannot easily accommodate databases that grow significantly larger over time. There are several *dynamic hashing techniques* that allow the hash function to be modified. One example is *extendable hashing,* which copes with changes in database size by splitting and coalescing buckets as the database grows and shrinks.

- We can also use hashing to create secondary indices; such indices are called *hash indices*. For notational convenience, we assume hash file organizations have an implicit hash index on the search key used for hashing.

- Ordered indices such as B$^+$-trees and hash indices can be used for selections based on equality conditions involving single attributes. When multiple attributes are involved in a selection condition, we can intersect record identifiers retrieved from multiple indices.

- Bitmap indices provide a very compact representation for indexing attributes with very few distinct values. Intersection operations are extremely fast on bitmaps, making them ideal for supporting queries on multiple attributes.

Review Terms

- Access types
- Access time
- Insertion time
- Deletion time
- Space overhead
- Ordered index
- Clustering index
- Primary index
- Nonclustering index
- Secondary index
- Index-sequential file
- Index entry/record
- Dense index
- Sparse index
- Multilevel index
- Composite key
- Sequential scan
- B$^+$-tree index
- Leaf node
- Nonleaf node
- Balanced tree
- Range query
- Node split
- Node coalesce

- Nonunique search key
- B$^+$-tree file organization
- Bulk load
- Bottom-up B$^+$-tree construction
- B-tree index
- Static hashing
- Hash file organization
- Hash index
- Bucket
- Hash function
- Bucket overflow
- Skew
- Closed hashing
- Dynamic hashing
- Extendable hashing
- Multiple-key access
- Indices on multiple keys
- Bitmap index
- Bitmap operations
  - Intersection
  - Union
  - Complement
  - Existence bitmap

Practice Exercises

11.1 Indices speed query processing, but it is usually a bad idea to create indices on every attribute, and every combinations of attributes, that is a potential search keys. Explain why.

11.2 Is it possible in general to have two clustering indices on the same relation for different search keys? Explain your answer.

11.3 Construct a B^+-tree for the following set of key values:

$$(2, 3, 5, 7, 11, 17, 19, 23, 29, 31)$$

Assume that the tree is initially empty and values are added in ascending order. Construct B^+-trees for the cases where the number of pointers that will fit in one node is as follows:

  a. Four

  b. Six

  c. Eight

11.4 For each B^+-tree of Practice Exercise 11.3, show the form of the tree after each of the following series of operations:

  a. Insert 9.

  b. Insert 10.

  c. Insert 8.

  d. Delete 23.

  e. Delete 19.

11.5 Consider the modified redistribution scheme for B^+-trees described on page 501. What is the expected height of the tree as a function of n?

11.6 Suppose that we are using extendable hashing on a file that contains records with the following search-key values:

$$2, 3, 5, 7, 11, 17, 19, 23, 29, 31$$

Show the extendable hash structure for this file if the hash function is $h(x) = x \bmod 8$ and buckets can hold three records.

11.7 Show how the extendable hash structure of Practice Exercise 11.6 changes as the result of each of the following steps:

  a. Delete 11.

  b. Delete 31.

c. Insert 1.

d. Insert 15.

11.8 Give pseudocode for a B$^+$-tree function `findIterator()`, which is like the function `find()`, except that it returns an iterator object, as described in Section 11.3.2. Also give pseudocode for the iterator class, including the variables in the iterator object, and the `next()` method.

11.9 Give pseudocode for deletion of entries from an extendable hash structure, including details of when and how to coalesce buckets. Do not bother about reducing the size of the bucket address table.

11.10 Suggest an efficient way to test if the bucket address table in extendable hashing can be reduced in size, by storing an extra count with the bucket address table. Give details of how the count should be maintained when buckets are split, coalesced, or deleted. (*Note*: Reducing the size of the bucket address table is an expensive operation, and subsequent inserts may cause the table to grow again. Therefore, it is best not to reduce the size as soon as it is possible to do so, but instead do it only if the number of index entries becomes small compared to the bucket-address-table size.)

11.11 Consider the *instructor* relation shown in Figure 11.1.

a. Construct a bitmap index on the attribute *salary*, dividing *salary* values into 4 ranges: below 50000, 50000 to below 60000, 60000 to below 70000, and 70000 and above.

b. Consider a query that requests all instructors in the Finance department with salary of 80000 or more. Outline the steps in answering the query, and show the final and intermediate bitmaps constructed to answer the query.

11.12 What would the occupancy of each leaf node of a B$^+$-tree be, if index entries are inserted in sorted order? Explain why.

11.13 Suppose you have a relation r with n_r tuples on which a secondary B$^+$-tree is to be constructed.

a. Give a formula for the cost of building the B$^+$-tree index by inserting one record at a time. Assume each block will hold an average of f entries, and that all levels of the tree above the leaf are in memory.

b. Assuming a random disk access takes 10 milliseconds, what is the cost of index construction on a relation with 10 million records?

c. Write pseudocode for bottom-up construction of a B$^+$-tree, which was outlined in Section 11.4.4. You can assume that a function to efficiently sort a large file is available.

11.14 Why might the leaf nodes of a B$^+$-tree file organization lose sequentiality?

a.   Suggest how the file organization may be reorganized to restore sequentiality.

b.   An alternative to reorganization is to allocate leaf pages in units of n blocks, for some reasonably large n. When the first leaf of a B^+-tree is allocated, only one block of an n-block unit is used, and the remaining pages are free. If a page splits, and its n-block unit has a free page, that space is used for the new page. If the n-block unit is full, another n-block unit is allocated, and the first $n/2$ leaf pages are placed in one n-block unit, and the remaining in the second n-block unit. For simplicity, assume that there are no delete operations.

   i.   What is the worst case occupancy of allocated space, assuming no delete operations, after the first n-block unit is full.

   ii.   Is it possible that leaf nodes allocated to an n-node block unit are not consecutive, that is, is it possible that two leaf nodes are allocated to one n-node block, but another leaf node in between the two is allocated to a different n-node block?

   iii.   Under the reasonable assumption that buffer space is sufficient to store a n-page block, how many seeks would be required for a leaf-level scan of the B^+-tree, in the worst case? Compare this number with the worst case if leaf pages are allocated a block at a time.

   iv.   The technique of redistributing values to siblings to improve space utilization is likely to be more efficient when used with the above allocation scheme for leaf blocks. Explain why.

Exercises

11.15   When is it preferable to use a dense index rather than a sparse index? Explain your answer.

11.16   What is the difference between a clustering index and a secondary index?

11.17   For each B^+-tree of Practice Exercise 11.3, show the steps involved in the following queries:

a.   Find records with a search-key value of 11.

b.   Find records with a search-key value between 7 and 17, inclusive.

11.18   The solution presented in Section 11.3.4 to deal with nonunique search keys added an extra attribute to the search key. What effect could this change have on the height of the B^+-tree?

11.19   Explain the distinction between closed and open hashing. Discuss the relative merits of each technique in database applications.

11.20   What are the causes of bucket overflow in a hash file organization? What can be done to reduce the occurrence of bucket overflows?

11.21   Why is a hash structure not the best choice for a search key on which range queries are likely?

11.22   Suppose there is a relation $r(A, B, C)$, with a B^+-tree index with search key (A, B).

    a.   What is the worst-case cost of finding records satisfying $10 < A < 50$ using this index, in terms of the number of records retrieved n_1 and the height h of the tree?

    b.   What is the worst-case cost of finding records satisfying $10 < A < 50 \wedge 5 < B < 10$ using this index, in terms of the number of records n_2 that satisfy this selection, as well as n_1 and h defined above?

    c.   Under what conditions on n_1 and n_2 would the index be an efficient way of finding records satisfying $10 < A < 50 \wedge 5 < B < 10$?

11.23   Suppose you have to create a B^+-tree index on a large number of names, where the maximum size of a name may be quite large (say 40 characters) and the average name is itself large (say 10 characters). Explain how prefix compression can be used to maximize the average fanout of nonleaf nodes.

11.24   Suppose a relation is stored in a B^+-tree file organization. Suppose secondary indices stored record identifiers that are pointers to records on disk.

    a.   What would be the effect on the secondary indices if a node split happens in the file organization?

    b.   What would be the cost of updating all affected records in a secondary index?

    c.   How does using the search key of the file organization as a logical record identifier solve this problem?

    d.   What is the extra cost due to the use of such logical record identifiers?

11.25   Show how to compute existence bitmaps from other bitmaps. Make sure that your technique works even in the presence of null values, by using a bitmap for the value *null*.

11.26   How does data encryption affect index schemes? In particular, how might it affect schemes that attempt to store data in sorted order?

11.27   Our description of static hashing assumes that a large contiguous stretch of disk blocks can be allocated to a static hash table. Suppose you can allocate only C contiguous blocks. Suggest how to implement the hash table, if it can be much larger than C blocks. Access to a block should still be efficient.

Bibliographical Notes

Discussions of the basic data structures in indexing and hashing can be found in Cormen et al. [1990]. B-tree indices were first introduced in Bayer [1972] and Bayer and McCreight [1972]. B$^+$-trees are discussed in Comer [1979], Bayer and Unterauer [1977], and Knuth [1973]. The bibliographical notes in Chapter 15 provide references to research on allowing concurrent accesses and updates on B$^+$-trees. Gray and Reuter [1993] provide a good description of issues in the implementation of B$^+$-trees.

Several alternative tree and treelike search structures have been proposed. **Tries** are trees whose structure is based on the "digits" of keys (for example, a dictionary thumb index, which has one entry for each letter). Such trees may not be balanced in the sense that B$^+$-trees are. Tries are discussed by Ramesh et al. [1989], Orenstein [1982], Litwin [1981], and Fredkin [1960]. Related work includes the digital B-trees of Lomet [1981].

Knuth [1973] analyzes a large number of different hashing techniques. Several dynamic hashing schemes exist. Extendable hashing was introduced by Fagin et al. [1979]. Linear hashing was introduced by Litwin [1978] and Litwin [1980]. A performance comparison with extendable hashing is given by Rathi et al. [1990]. An alternative given by Ramakrishna and Larson [1989] allows retrieval in a single disk access at the price of a high overhead for a small fraction of database modifications. Partitioned hashing is an extension of hashing to multiple attributes, and is covered in Rivest [1976], Burkhard [1976], and Burkhard [1979].

Vitter [2001] provides an extensive survey of external-memory data structures and algorithms.

Bitmap indices, and variants called **bit-sliced indices** and **projection indices**, are described in O'Neil and Quass [1997]. They were first introduced in the IBM Model 204 file manager on the AS 400 platform. They provide very large speedups on certain types of queries, and are today implemented on most database systems. Research on bitmap indices includes Wu and Buchmann [1998], Chan and Ioannidis [1998], Chan and Ioannidis [1999], and Johnson [1999].

CHAPTER **12**

Query Processing

Query processing refers to the range of activities involved in extracting data from a database. The activities include translation of queries in high-level database languages into expressions that can be used at the physical level of the file system, a variety of query-optimizing transformations, and actual evaluation of queries.

12.1 Overview

The steps involved in processing a query appear in Figure 12.1. The basic steps are:

1. Parsing and translation.

2. Optimization.

3. Evaluation.

Before query processing can begin, the system must translate the query into a usable form. A language such as SQL is suitable for human use, but is ill suited to be the system's internal representation of a query. A more useful internal representation is one based on the extended relational algebra.

Thus, the first action the system must take in query processing is to translate a given query into its internal form. This translation process is similar to the work performed by the parser of a compiler. In generating the internal form of the query, the parser checks the syntax of the user's query, verifies that the relation names appearing in the query are names of the relations in the database, and so on. The system constructs a parse-tree representation of the query, which it then translates into a relational-algebra expression. If the query was expressed in terms of a view, the translation phase also replaces all uses of the view by the relational-algebra expression that defines the view.[1] Most compiler texts cover parsing in detail.

---

[1] For materialized views, the expression defining the view has already been evaluated and stored. Therefore, the stored relation can be used, instead of uses of the view being replaced by the expression defining the view. Recursive views are handled differently, via a fixed-point procedure, as discussed in Section 5.4 and Appendix B.3.6.

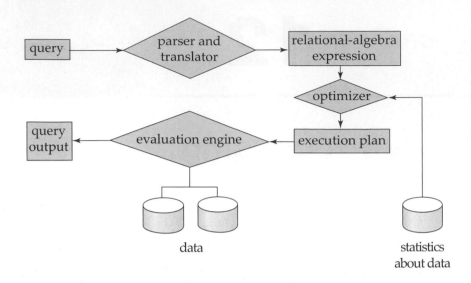

Figure 12.1 Steps in query processing.

Given a query, there are generally a variety of methods for computing the answer. For example, we have seen that, in SQL, a query could be expressed in several different ways. Each SQL query can itself be translated into a relational-algebra expression in one of several ways. Furthermore, the relational-algebra representation of a query specifies only partially how to evaluate a query; there are usually several ways to evaluate relational-algebra expressions. As an illustration, consider the query:

> **select** *salary*
> **from** *instructor*
> **where** *salary* < 75000;

This query can be translated into either of the following relational-algebra expressions:

- $\sigma_{salary\ <75000} \left(\Pi_{salary} \left(instructor \right) \right)$

- $\Pi_{salary} \left(\sigma_{salary<75000} \left(instructor \right) \right)$

Further, we can execute each relational-algebra operation by one of several different algorithms. For example, to implement the preceding selection, we can search every tuple in *instructor* to find tuples with salary less than 75000. If a B^+-tree index is available on the attribute *salary*, we can use the index instead to locate the tuples.

To specify fully how to evaluate a query, we need not only to provide the relational-algebra expression, but also to annotate it with instructions specifying how to evaluate each operation. Annotations may state the algorithm to be used

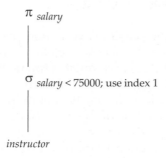

Figure 12.2 A query-evaluation plan.

for a specific operation, or the particular index or indices to use. A relational-algebra operation annotated with instructions on how to evaluate it is called an **evaluation primitive**. A sequence of primitive operations that can be used to evaluate a query is a **query-execution plan** or **query-evaluation plan**. Figure 12.2 illustrates an evaluation plan for our example query, in which a particular index (denoted in the figure as "index 1") is specified for the selection operation. The **query-execution engine** takes a query-evaluation plan, executes that plan, and returns the answers to the query.

The different evaluation plans for a given query can have different costs. We do not expect users to write their queries in a way that suggests the most efficient evaluation plan. Rather, it is the responsibility of the system to construct a query-evaluation plan that minimizes the cost of query evaluation; this task is called *query optimization*. Chapter 13 describes query optimization in detail.

Once the query plan is chosen, the query is evaluated with that plan, and the result of the query is output.

The sequence of steps already described for processing a query is representative; not all databases exactly follow those steps. For instance, instead of using the relational-algebra representation, several databases use an annotated parse-tree representation based on the structure of the given SQL query. However, the concepts that we describe here form the basis of query processing in databases.

In order to optimize a query, a query optimizer must know the cost of each operation. Although the exact cost is hard to compute, since it depends on many parameters such as actual memory available to the operation, it is possible to get a rough estimate of execution cost for each operation.

In this chapter we study how to evaluate individual operations in a query plan, and how to estimate their cost; we return to query optimization in Chapter 13. Section 12.2 outlines how we measure the cost of a query. Sections 12.3 through 12.6 cover the evaluation of individual relational-algebra operations. Several operations may be grouped together into a **pipeline**, in which each of the operations starts working on its input tuples even as they are being generated by another operation. In Section 12.7, we examine how to coordinate the execution of multiple operations in a query evaluation plan, in particular, how to use pipelined operations to avoid writing intermediate results to disk.

12.2   Measures of Query Cost

There are multiple possible evaluation plans for a query, and it is important to be able to compare the alternatives in terms of their (estimated) cost, and choose the best plan. To do so, we must estimate the cost of individual operations, and combine them to get the cost of a query evaluation plan. Thus, as we study evaluation algorithms for each operation later in this chapter, we also outline how to estimate the cost of the operation.

The cost of query evaluation can be measured in terms of a number of different resources, including disk accesses, CPU time to execute a query, and, in a distributed or parallel database system, the cost of communication (which we discuss later, in Chapters 18 and 19).

In large database systems, the cost to access data from disk is usually the most important cost, since disk accesses are slow compared to in-memory operations. Moreover, CPU speeds have been improving much faster than have disk speeds. Thus, it is likely that the time spent in disk activity will continue to dominate the total time to execute a query. The CPU time taken for a task is harder to estimate since it depends on low-level details of the execution code. Although real-life query optimizers do take CPU costs into account, for simplicity in this book we ignore CPU costs and use only disk-access costs to measure the cost of a query-evaluation plan.

We use the *number of block transfers* from disk and the *number of disk seeks* to estimate the cost of a query-evaluation plan. If the disk subsystem takes an average of t_T seconds to transfer a block of data, and has an average block-access time (disk seek time plus rotational latency) of t_S seconds, then an operation that transfers b blocks and performs S seeks would take $b * t_T + S * t_S$ seconds. The values of t_T and t_S must be calibrated for the disk system used, but typical values for high-end disks today would be $t_S = 4$ milliseconds and $t_T = 0.1$ milliseconds, assuming a 4-kilobyte block size and a transfer rate of 40 megabytes per second.[2]

We can refine our cost estimates further by distinguishing block reads from block writes, since block writes are typically about twice as expensive as reads (this is because disk systems read sectors back after they are written to verify that the write was successful). For simplicity, we ignore this detail, and leave it to you to work out more precise cost estimates for various operations.

The cost estimates we give do not include the cost of writing the final result of an operation back to disk. These are taken into account separately where required. The costs of all the algorithms that we consider depend on the size of the buffer in main memory. In the best case, all data can be read into the buffers, and the disk does not need to be accessed again. In the worst case, we assume that the buffer can hold only a few blocks of data—approximately one block per relation. When presenting cost estimates, we generally assume the worst case.

---

[2]Some database systems perform test seeks and block transfers to estimate average seek and block transfer costs, as part of the software installation process.

In addition, although we assume that data must be read from disk initially, it is possible that a block that is accessed is already present in the in-memory buffer. Again, for simplicity, we ignore this effect; as a result, the actual disk-access cost during the execution of a plan may be less than the estimated cost.

The **response time** for a query-evaluation plan (that is, the wall-clock time required to execute the plan), assuming no other activity is going on in the computer, would account for all these costs, and could be used as a measure of the cost of the plan. Unfortunately, the response time of a plan is very hard to estimate without actually executing the plan, for the following reasons:

1. The response time depends on the contents of the buffer when the query begins execution; this information is not available when the query is optimized, and is hard to account for even if it were available.

2. In a system with multiple disks, the response time depends on how accesses are distributed among disks, which is hard to estimate without detailed knowledge of data layout on disk.

Interestingly, a plan may get a better response time at the cost of extra resource consumption. For example, if a system has multiple disks, a plan A that requires extra disk reads, but performs the reads in parallel across multiple disks may finish faster than another plan B that has fewer disk reads, but from only one disk. However, if many instances of a query using plan A run concurrently, the overall response time may actually be more than if the same instances are executed using plan B, since plan A generates more load on the disks.

As a result, instead of trying to minimize the response time, optimizers generally try to minimize the total **resource consumption** of a query plan. Our model of estimating the total disk access time (including seek and data transfer) is an example of such a resource consumption–based model of query cost.

12.3 Selection Operation

In query processing, the **file scan** is the lowest-level operator to access data. File scans are search algorithms that locate and retrieve records that fulfill a selection condition. In relational systems, a file scan allows an entire relation to be read in those cases where the relation is stored in a single, dedicated file.

12.3.1 Selections Using File Scans and Indices

Consider a selection operation on a relation whose tuples are stored together in one file. The most straightforward way of performing a selection is as follows:

- **A1 (linear search)**. In a linear search, the system scans each file block and tests all records to see whether they satisfy the selection condition. An initial seek is required to access the first block of the file. In case blocks of the file are not stored contiguously, extra seeks may be required, but we ignore this effect for simplicity.

Although it may be slower than other algorithms for implementing selection, the linear-search algorithm can be applied to any file, regardless of the ordering of the file, or the availability of indices, or the nature of the selection operation. The other algorithms that we shall study are not applicable in all cases, but when applicable they are generally faster than linear search.

Cost estimates for linear scan, as well as for other selection algorithms, are shown in Figure 12.3. In the figure, we use h_i to represent the height of the B^+-tree. Real-life optimizers usually assume that the root of the tree is present in the in-memory buffer since it is frequently accessed. Some optimizers even assume that all but the leaf level of the tree is present in memory, since they are accessed relatively frequently, and usually less than 1 percent of the nodes of a B^+-tree are nonleaf nodes. The cost formulae can be modified appropriately.

Index structures are referred to as **access paths**, since they provide a path through which data can be located and accessed. In Chapter 11, we pointed out that it is efficient to read the records of a file in an order corresponding closely to physical order. Recall that a *primary index* (also referred to as a *clustering index*) is an index that allows the records of a file to be read in an order that corresponds to the physical order in the file. An index that is not a primary index is called a *secondary index*.

Search algorithms that use an index are referred to as **index scans**. We use the selection predicate to guide us in the choice of the index to use in processing the query. Search algorithms that use an index are:

- **A2 (primary index, equality on key).** For an equality comparison on a key attribute with a primary index, we can use the index to retrieve a single record that satisfies the corresponding equality condition. Cost estimates are shown in Figure 12.3.

- **A3 (primary index, equality on nonkey).** We can retrieve multiple records by using a primary index when the selection condition specifies an equality comparison on a nonkey attribute, A. The only difference from the previous case is that multiple records may need to be fetched. However, the records must be stored consecutively in the file since the file is sorted on the search key. Cost estimates are shown in Figure 12.3.

- **A4 (secondary index, equality).** Selections specifying an equality condition can use a secondary index. This strategy can retrieve a single record if the equality condition is on a key; multiple records may be retrieved if the indexing field is not a key.

  In the first case, only one record is retrieved. The time cost in this case is the same as that for a primary index (case A2).

  In the second case, each record may be resident on a different block, which may result in one I/O operation per retrieved record, with each I/O operation requiring a seek and a block transfer. The worst-case time cost in this case is

	Algorithm	Cost	Reason
A1	Linear Search	$t_S + b_r * t_T$	One initial seek plus b_r block transfers, where b_r denotes the number of blocks in the file.
A1	Linear Search, Equality on Key	Average case $t_S + (b_r/2) * t_T$	Since at most one record satisfies condition, scan can be terminated as soon as the required record is found. In the worst case, b_r blocks transfers are still required.
A2	Primary B^+-tree Index, Equality on Key	$(h_i + 1) * (t_T + t_S)$	(Where h_i denotes the height of the index.) Index lookup traverses the height of the tree plus one I/O to fetch the record; each of these I/O operations requires a seek and a block transfer.
A3	Primary B^+-tree Index, Equality on Nonkey	$h_i * (t_T + t_S) + b * t_T$	One seek for each level of the tree, one seek for the first block. Here b is the number of blocks containing records with the specified search key, all of which are read. These blocks are leaf blocks assumed to be stored sequentially (since it is a primary index) and don't require additional seeks.
A4	Secondary B^+-tree Index, Equality on Key	$(h_i + 1) * (t_T + t_S)$	This case is similar to primary index.
A4	Secondary B^+-tree Index, Equality on Nonkey	$(h_i + n) * (t_T + t_S)$	(Where n is the number of records fetched.) Here, cost of index traversal is the same as for A3, but each record may be on a different block, requiring a seek per record. Cost is potentially very high if n is large.
A5	Primary B^+-tree Index, Comparison	$h_i * (t_T + t_S) + b * t_T$	Identical to the case of A3, equality on nonkey.
A6	Secondary B^+-tree Index, Comparison	$(h_i + n) * (t_T + t_S)$	Identical to the case of A4, equality on nonkey.

Figure 12.3 Cost estimates for selection algorithms.

$(h_i + n) * (t_S + t_T)$, where n is the number of records fetched, if each record is in a different disk block, and the block fetches are randomly ordered. The worst-case cost could become even worse than that of linear search if a large number of records are retrieved.

If the in-memory buffer is large, the block containing the record may already be in the buffer. It is possible to construct an estimate of the *average* or *expected* cost of the selection by taking into account the probability of the block containing the record already being in the buffer. For large buffers, that estimate will be much less than the worst-case estimate.

In certain algorithms, including A2, the use of a B^+-tree file organization can save one access since records are stored at the leaf-level of the tree.

As described in Section 11.4.2, when records are stored in a B^+-tree file organization or other file organizations that may require relocation of records, secondary indices usually do not store pointers to the records.[3] Instead, secondary indices store the values of the attributes used as the search key in a B^+-tree file organization. Accessing a record through such a secondary index is then more expensive: First the secondary index is searched to find the primary index search-key values, then the primary index is looked up to find the records. The cost formulae described for secondary indices have to be modified appropriately if such indices are used.

12.3.2 Selections Involving Comparisons

Consider a selection of the form $\sigma_{A \leq v}(r)$. We can implement the selection either by using linear search or by using indices in one of the following ways:

- **A5 (primary index, comparison).** A primary ordered index (for example, a primary B^+-tree index) can be used when the selection condition is a comparison. For comparison conditions of the form $A > v$ or $A \geq v$, a primary index on A can be used to direct the retrieval of tuples, as follows: For $A \geq v$, we look up the value v in the index to find the first tuple in the file that has a value of $A = v$. A file scan starting from that tuple up to the end of the file returns all tuples that satisfy the condition. For $A > v$, the file scan starts with the first tuple such that $A > v$. The cost estimate for this case is identical to that for case A3.

  For comparisons of the form $A < v$ or $A \leq v$, an index lookup is not required. For $A < v$, we use a simple file scan starting from the beginning of the file, and continuing up to (but not including) the first tuple with attribute $A = v$. The case of $A \leq v$ is similar, except that the scan continues up to (but not including) the first tuple with attribute $A > v$. In either case, the index is not useful.

- **A6 (secondary index, comparison).** We can use a secondary ordered index to guide retrieval for comparison conditions involving $<, \leq, \geq$, or $>$. The lowest-level index blocks are scanned, either from the smallest value up to v (for $<$ and $\leq$), or from v up to the maximum value (for $>$ and $\geq$).

---

[3]Recall that if B^+-tree file organizations are used to store relations, records may be moved between blocks when leaf nodes are split or merged, and when records are redistributed.

The secondary index provides pointers to the records, but to get the actual records we have to fetch the records by using the pointers. This step may require an I/O operation for each record fetched, since consecutive records may be on different disk blocks; as before, each I/O operation requires a disk seek and a block transfer. If the number of retrieved records is large, using the secondary index may be even more expensive than using linear search. Therefore the secondary index should be used only if very few records are selected.

12.3.3 Implementation of Complex Selections

So far, we have considered only simple selection conditions of the form $A \; op \; B$, where op is an equality or comparison operation. We now consider more complex selection predicates.

- **Conjunction:** A *conjunctive selection* is a selection of the form:

$$\sigma_{\theta_1 \wedge \theta_2 \wedge \cdots \wedge \theta_n}(r)$$

- **Disjunction:** A *disjunctive selection* is a selection of the form:

$$\sigma_{\theta_1 \vee \theta_2 \vee \cdots \vee \theta_n}(r)$$

  A disjunctive condition is satisfied by the union of all records satisfying the individual, simple conditions θ_i.

- **Negation:** The result of a selection $\sigma_{\neg\theta}(r)$ is the set of tuples of r for which the condition θ evaluates to false. In the absence of nulls, this set is simply the set of tuples in r that are not in $\sigma_{\theta}(r)$.

We can implement a selection operation involving either a conjunction or a disjunction of simple conditions by using one of the following algorithms:

- **A7 (conjunctive selection using one index).** We first determine whether an access path is available for an attribute in one of the simple conditions. If one is, one of the selection algorithms A2 through A6 can retrieve records satisfying that condition. We complete the operation by testing, in the memory buffer, whether or not each retrieved record satisfies the remaining simple conditions.

  To reduce the cost, we choose a θ_i and one of algorithms A1 through A6 for which the combination results in the least cost for $\sigma_{\theta_i}(r)$. The cost of algorithm A7 is given by the cost of the chosen algorithm.

- **A8 (conjunctive selection using composite index).** An appropriate *composite index* (that is, an index on multiple attributes) may be available for some conjunctive selections. If the selection specifies an equality condition on two or more attributes, and a composite index exists on these combined attribute fields, then the index can be searched directly. The type of index determines which of algorithms A2, A3, or A4 will be used.

- **A9 (conjunctive selection by intersection of identifiers).** Another alternative for implementing conjunctive selection operations involves the use of record pointers or record identifiers. This algorithm requires indices with record pointers, on the fields involved in the individual conditions. The algorithm scans each index for pointers to tuples that satisfy an individual condition. The intersection of all the retrieved pointers is the set of pointers to tuples that satisfy the conjunctive condition. The algorithm then uses the pointers to retrieve the actual records. If indices are not available on all the individual conditions, then the algorithm tests the retrieved records against the remaining conditions.

  The cost of algorithm **A9** is the sum of the costs of the individual index scans, plus the cost of retrieving the records in the intersection of the retrieved lists of pointers. This cost can be reduced by sorting the list of pointers and retrieving records in the sorted order. Thereby, (1) all pointers to records in a block come together, hence all selected records in the block can be retrieved using a single I/O operation, and (2) blocks are read in sorted order, minimizing disk-arm movement. Section 12.4 describes sorting algorithms.

- **A10 (disjunctive selection by union of identifiers).** If access paths are available on all the conditions of a disjunctive selection, each index is scanned for pointers to tuples that satisfy the individual condition. The union of all the retrieved pointers yields the set of pointers to all tuples that satisfy the disjunctive condition. We then use the pointers to retrieve the actual records.

  However, if even one of the conditions does not have an access path, we have to perform a linear scan of the relation to find tuples that satisfy the condition. Therefore, if there is even one such condition in the disjunct, the most efficient access method is a linear scan, with the disjunctive condition tested on each tuple during the scan.

The implementation of selections with negation conditions is left to you as an exercise (Practice Exercise 12.6).

12.4   Sorting

Sorting of data plays an important role in database systems for two reasons. First, SQL queries can specify that the output be sorted. Second, and equally important for query processing, several of the relational operations, such as joins, can be implemented efficiently if the input relations are first sorted. Thus, we discuss sorting here before discussing the join operation in Section 12.5.

We can sort a relation by building an index on the sort key, and then using that index to read the relation in sorted order. However, such a process orders the relation only *logically*, through an index, rather than *physically*. Hence, the reading of tuples in the sorted order may lead to a disk access (disk seek plus block transfer) for each record, which can be very expensive, since the number of records can be much larger than the number of blocks. For this reason, it may be desirable to order the records physically.

The problem of sorting has been studied extensively, both for relations that fit entirely in main memory and for relations that are bigger than memory. In the first case, standard sorting techniques such as quick-sort can be used. Here, we discuss how to handle the second case.

12.4.1 External Sort-Merge Algorithm

Sorting of relations that do not fit in memory is called **external sorting**. The most commonly used technique for external sorting is the **external sort–merge** algorithm. We describe the external sort–merge algorithm next. Let M denote the number of blocks in the main-memory buffer available for sorting, that is, the number of disk blocks whose contents can be buffered in available main memory.

1. In the first stage, a number of sorted **runs** are created; each run is sorted, but contains only some of the records of the relation.

    > $i = 0$;
    > **repeat**
    >   read M blocks of the relation, or the rest of the relation,
    >   whichever is smaller;
    >   sort the in-memory part of the relation;
    >   write the sorted data to run file R_i;
    > $i = i + 1$;
    > **until** the end of the relation

2. In the second stage, the runs are *merged*. Suppose, for now, that the total number of runs, N, is less than M, so that we can allocate one block to each run and have space left to hold one block of output. The merge stage operates as follows:

    > read one block of each of the N files R_i into a buffer block in memory;
    > **repeat**
    >   choose the first tuple (in sort order) among all buffer blocks;
    >   write the tuple to the output, and delete it from the buffer block;
    >   **if** the buffer block of any run R_i is empty **and not** end-of-file(R_i)
    >   **then** read the next block of R_i into the buffer block;
    > **until** all input buffer blocks are empty

The output of the merge stage is the sorted relation. The output file is buffered to reduce the number of disk write operations. The preceding merge operation is a generalization of the two-way merge used by the standard in-memory sort–merge algorithm; it merges N runs, so it is called an N-**way merge**.

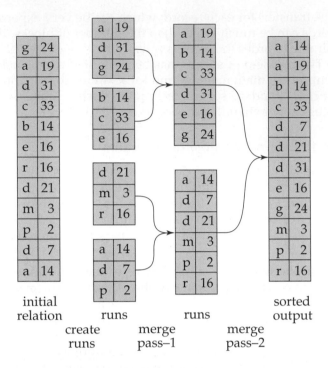

Figure 12.4 External sorting using sort–merge.

In general, if the relation is much larger than memory, there may be M or more runs generated in the first stage, and it is not possible to allocate a block for each run during the merge stage. In this case, the merge operation proceeds in multiple passes. Since there is enough memory for $M - 1$ input buffer blocks, each merge can take $M - 1$ runs as input.

The initial *pass* functions in this way: It merges the first $M - 1$ runs (as described in item 2 above) to get a single run for the next pass. Then, it merges the next $M - 1$ runs similarly, and so on, until it has processed all the initial runs. At this point, the number of runs has been reduced by a factor of $M - 1$. If this reduced number of runs is still greater than or equal to M, another pass is made, with the runs created by the first pass as input. Each pass reduces the number of runs by a factor of $M - 1$. The passes repeat as many times as required, until the number of runs is less than M; a final pass then generates the sorted output.

Figure 12.4 illustrates the steps of the external sort–merge for an example relation. For illustration purposes, we assume that only one tuple fits in a block ($f_r = 1$), and we assume that memory holds at most three blocks. During the merge stage, two blocks are used for input and one for output.

12.4.2 Cost Analysis of External Sort-Merge

We compute the disk-access cost for the external sort–merge in this way: Let b_r denote the number of blocks containing records of relation r. The first stage reads every block of the relation and writes them out again, giving a total of $2b_r$ block transfers. The initial number of runs is $\lceil b_r/M \rceil$. Since the number of runs decreases by a factor of $M-1$ in each merge pass, the total number of merge passes required is $\lceil \log_{M-1}(b_r/M) \rceil$. Each of these passes reads every block of the relation once and writes it out once, with two exceptions. First, the final pass can produce the sorted output without writing its result to disk. Second, there may be runs that are not read in or written out during a pass—for example, if there are M runs to be merged in a pass, $M-1$ are read in and merged, and one run is not accessed during the pass. Ignoring the (relatively small) savings due to the latter effect, the total number of block transfers for external sorting of the relation is:

$$b_r(2\lceil \log_{M-1}(b_r/M) \rceil + 1)$$

Applying this equation to the example in Figure 12.4, we get a total of $12 * (4+1)$ $= 60$ block transfers, as you can verify from the figure. Note that the above numbers do not include the cost of writing out the final result.

We also need to add the disk-seek costs. Run generation requires seeks for reading data for each of the runs as well as for writing the runs. During the merge phase, if data are read b_b blocks at a time from each run (that is, b_b buffer blocks are allocated to each run), then each merge pass would require around $\lceil b_r/b_b \rceil$ seeks for reading data.[4] Although the output is written sequentially, if it is on the same disk as the input runs the head may have moved away between writes of consecutive blocks. Thus we would have to add a total of $2\lceil b_r/b_b \rceil$ seeks for each merge pass, except the final pass (since we assume the final result is not written back to disk). The total number of seeks is then:

$$2\lceil b_r/M \rceil + \lceil b_r/b_b \rceil(2\lceil \log_{M-1}(b_r/M) \rceil - 1)$$

Applying this equation to the example in Figure 12.4, we get a total of $8 + 12 *$ $(2 * 2 - 1) = 44$ disk seeks if we set the number of buffer blocks per run, b_b to 1.

12.5 Join Operation

In this section, we study several algorithms for computing the join of relations, and we analyze their respective costs.

We use the term **equi-join** to refer to a join of the form $r \bowtie_{r.A=s.B} s$, where A and B are attributes or sets of attributes of relations r and s, respectively.

We use as a running example the expression:

$$student \bowtie takes$$

---

[4]To be more precise, since we read each run separately and may get fewer than b_b blocks when reading the end of a run, we may require an extra seek for each run. We ignore this detail for simplicity.

using the same relation schemas that we used in Chapter 2. We assume the following information about the two relations:

- Number of records of *student*: $n_{student} = 5,000$.

- Number of blocks of *student*: $b_{student} = 100$.

- Number of records of *takes*: $n_{takes} = 10,000$.

- Number of blocks of *takes*: $b_{takes} = 400$.

12.5.1   Nested-Loop Join

Figure 12.5 shows a simple algorithm to compute the theta join, $r \bowtie_\theta s$, of two relations r and s. This algorithm is called the **nested-loop join** algorithm, since it basically consists of a pair of nested **for** loops. Relation r is called the **outer relation** and relation s the **inner relation** of the join, since the loop for r encloses the loop for s. The algorithm uses the notation $t_r \cdot t_s$, where t_r and t_s are tuples; $t_r \cdot t_s$ denotes the tuple constructed by concatenating the attribute values of tuples t_r and t_s.

Like the linear file-scan algorithm for selection, the nested-loop join algorithm requires no indices, and it can be used regardless of what the join condition is. Extending the algorithm to compute the natural join is straightforward, since the natural join can be expressed as a theta join followed by elimination of repeated attributes by a projection. The only change required is an extra step of deleting repeated attributes from the tuple $t_r \cdot t_s$, before adding it to the result.

The nested-loop join algorithm is expensive, since it examines every pair of tuples in the two relations. Consider the cost of the nested-loop join algorithm. The number of pairs of tuples to be considered is $n_r * n_s$, where n_r denotes the number of tuples in r, and n_s denotes the number of tuples in s. For each record in r, we have to perform a complete scan on s. In the worst case, the buffer can hold only one block of each relation, and a total of $n_r * b_s + b_r$ block transfers would be required, where b_r and b_s denote the number of blocks containing tuples of r and s, respectively. We need only one seek for each scan on the inner relation s since it is read sequentially, and a total of b_r seeks to read r, leading to a total of $n_r + b_r$ seeks. In the best case, there is enough space for both relations to fit simultaneously in memory, so each block would have to be read only once; hence, only $b_r + b_s$ block transfers would be required, along with 2 seeks.

```
for each tuple t_r in r do begin
    for each tuple t_s in s do begin
        test pair (t_r, t_s) to see if they satisfy the join condition θ
        if they do, add t_r · t_s to the result;
    end
end
```

Figure 12.5   Nested-loop join.

```
for each block B_r of r do begin
    for each block B_s of s do begin
        for each tuple t_r in B_r do begin
            for each tuple t_s in B_s do begin
                test pair (t_r, t_s) to see if they satisfy the join condition
                if they do, add t_r · t_s to the result;
            end
        end
    end
end
```

Figure 12.6 Block nested-loop join.

If one of the relations fits entirely in main memory, it is beneficial to use that relation as the inner relation, since the inner relation would then be read only once. Therefore, if s is small enough to fit in main memory, our strategy requires only a total $b_r + b_s$ block transfers and 2 seeks—the same cost as that for the case where both relations fit in memory.

Now consider the natural join of *student* and *takes*. Assume for now that we have no indices whatsoever on either relation, and that we are not willing to create any index. We can use the nested loops to compute the join; assume that *student* is the outer relation and *takes* is the inner relation in the join. We will have to examine $5000 * 10,000 = 50 * 10^6$ pairs of tuples. In the worst case, the number of block transfers is $5000 * 400 + 100 = 2{,}000{,}100$, plus $5000 + 100 = 5100$ seeks. In the best-case scenario, however, we can read both relations only once, and perform the computation. This computation requires at most $100 + 400 = 500$ block transfers, plus 2 seeks—a significant improvement over the worst-case scenario. If we had used *takes* as the relation for the outer loop and *student* for the inner loop, the worst-case cost of our final strategy would have been $10{,}000 * 100 + 400 = 1{,}000{,}400$ block transfers, plus 10,400 disk seeks. The number of block transfers is significantly less, and although the number of seeks is higher, the overall cost is reduced, assuming $t_S = 4$ milliseconds and $t_T = 0.1$ milliseconds.

12.5.2 Block Nested-Loop Join

If the buffer is too small to hold either relation entirely in memory, we can still obtain a major saving in block accesses if we process the relations on a per-block basis, rather than on a per-tuple basis. Figure 12.6 shows **block nested-loop join**, which is a variant of the nested-loop join where every block of the inner relation is paired with every block of the outer relation. Within each pair of blocks, every tuple in one block is paired with every tuple in the other block, to generate all pairs of tuples. As before, all pairs of tuples that satisfy the join condition are added to the result.

The primary difference in cost between the block nested-loop join and the basic nested-loop join is that, in the worst case, each block in the inner relation s is read only once for each *block* in the outer relation, instead of once for each *tuple* in the outer relation. Thus, in the worst case, there will be a total of $b_r * b_s + b_r$ block transfers, where b_r and b_s denote the number of blocks containing records of r and s, respectively. Each scan of the inner relation requires one seek, and the scan of the outer relation requires one seek per block, leading to a total of $2 * b_r$ seeks. Clearly, it is more efficient to use the smaller relation as the outer relation, in case neither of the relations fits in memory. In the best case, where the inner relation fits in memory, there will be $b_r + b_s$ block transfers and just 2 seeks (we would choose the smaller relation as the inner relation in this case).

Now return to our example of computing *student* ⋈ *takes*, using the block nested-loop join algorithm. In the worst case, we have to read each block of *takes* once for each block of *student*. Thus, in the worst case, a total of $100 * 400 + 100 = 40{,}100$ block transfers plus $2*100 = 200$ seeks are required. This cost is a significant improvement over the $5000*400+100 = 2{,}000{,}100$ block transfers plus 5100 seeks needed in the worst case for the basic nested-loop join. The best-case cost remains the same—namely, $100 + 400 = 500$ block transfers and 2 seeks.

The performance of the nested-loop and block nested-loop procedures can be further improved:

- If the join attributes in a natural join or an equi-join form a key on the inner relation, then for each outer relation tuple the inner loop can terminate as soon as the first match is found.

- In the block nested-loop algorithm, instead of using disk blocks as the blocking unit for the outer relation, we can use the biggest size that can fit in memory, while leaving enough space for the buffers of the inner relation and the output. In other words, if memory has M blocks, we read in $M - 2$ blocks of the outer relation at a time, and when we read each block of the inner relation we join it with all the $M - 2$ blocks of the outer relation. This change reduces the number of scans of the inner relation from b_r to $\lceil b_r/(M - 2) \rceil$, where b_r is the number of blocks of the outer relation. The total cost is then $\lceil b_r/(M - 2) \rceil * b_s + b_r$ block transfers and $2\lceil b_r/(M - 2) \rceil$ seeks.

- We can scan the inner loop alternately forward and backward. This scanning method orders the requests for disk blocks so that the data remaining in the buffer from the previous scan can be reused, thus reducing the number of disk accesses needed.

- If an index is available on the inner loop's join attribute, we can replace file scans with more efficient index lookups. Section 12.5.3 describes this optimization.

12.5.3   Indexed Nested-Loop Join

In a nested-loop join (Figure 12.5), if an index is available on the inner loop's join attribute, index lookups can replace file scans. For each tuple t_r in the outer relation r, the index is used to look up tuples in s that will satisfy the join condition with tuple t_r.

This join method is called an **indexed nested-loop join**; it can be used with existing indices, as well as with temporary indices created for the sole purpose of evaluating the join.

Looking up tuples in s that will satisfy the join conditions with a given tuple t_r is essentially a selection on s. For example, consider $student \bowtie takes$. Suppose that we have a $student$ tuple with ID "00128". Then, the relevant tuples in $takes$ are those that satisfy the selection "$ID = 00128$".

The cost of an indexed nested-loop join can be computed as follows: For each tuple in the outer relation r, a lookup is performed on the index for s, and the relevant tuples are retrieved. In the worst case, there is space in the buffer for only one block of r and one block of the index. Then, b_r I/O operations are needed to read relation r, where b_r denotes the number of blocks containing records of r; each I/O requires a seek and a block transfer, since the disk head may have moved in between each I/O. For each tuple in r, we perform an index lookup on s. Then, the time cost of the join can be computed as $b_r(t_T + t_S) + n_r * c$, where n_r is the number of records in relation r, and c is the cost of a single selection on s using the join condition. We have seen in Section 12.3 how to estimate the cost of a single selection algorithm (possibly using indices); that estimate gives us the value of c.

The cost formula indicates that, if indices are available on both relations r and s, it is generally most efficient to use the one with fewer tuples as the outer relation.

For example, consider an indexed nested-loop join of $student \bowtie takes$, with $student$ as the outer relation. Suppose also that $takes$ has a primary B$^+$-tree index on the join attribute ID, which contains 20 entries on average in each index node. Since $takes$ has 10,000 tuples, the height of the tree is 4, and one more access is needed to find the actual data. Since $n_{student}$ is 5000, the total cost is $100 + 5000 * 5 = 25,100$ disk accesses, each of which requires a seek and a block transfer. In contrast, as we saw before, 40,100 block transfers plus 200 seeks were needed for a block nested-loop join. Although the number of block transfers has been reduced, the seek cost has actually increased, increasing the total cost since a seek is considerably more expensive than a block transfer. However, if we had a selection on the $student$ relation that reduces the number of rows significantly, indexed nested-loop join could be significantly faster than block nested-loop join.

12.5.4 Merge Join

The **merge-join** algorithm (also called the **sort-merge-join** algorithm) can be used to compute natural joins and equi-joins. Let $r(R)$ and $s(S)$ be the relations whose natural join is to be computed, and let $R \cap S$ denote their common attributes. Suppose that both relations are sorted on the attributes $R \cap S$. Then, their join can be computed by a process much like the merge stage in the merge–sort algorithm.

12.5.4.1 Merge-Join Algorithm

Figure 12.7 shows the merge-join algorithm. In the algorithm, *JoinAttrs* refers to the attributes in $R \cap S$, and $t_r \bowtie t_s$, where t_r and t_s are tuples that have the same

```
pr := address of first tuple of r;
ps := address of first tuple of s;
while (ps ≠ null and pr ≠ null) do
    begin
        tₛ := tuple to which ps points;
        Sₛ := {tₛ};
        set ps to point to next tuple of s;
        done := false;
        while (not done and ps ≠ null) do
            begin
                tₛ' := tuple to which ps points;
                if (tₛ'[JoinAttrs] = tₛ[JoinAttrs])
                    then begin
                                Sₛ := Sₛ ∪ {tₛ'};
                                set ps to point to next tuple of s;
                         end
                    else done := true;
            end
        tᵣ := tuple to which pr points;
        while (pr ≠ null and tᵣ[JoinAttrs] < tₛ[JoinAttrs]) do
            begin
                set pr to point to next tuple of r;
                tᵣ := tuple to which pr points;
            end
        while (pr ≠ null and tᵣ[JoinAttrs] = tₛ[JoinAttrs]) do
            begin
                for each tₛ in Sₛ do
                    begin
                        add tₛ ⋈ tᵣ to result;
                    end
                set pr to point to next tuple of r;
                tᵣ := tuple to which pr points;
            end
    end
end.
```

Figure 12.7   Merge join.

values for *JoinAttrs*, denotes the concatenation of the attributes of the tuples, followed by projecting out repeated attributes. The merge-join algorithm associates one pointer with each relation. These pointers point initially to the first tuple of the respective relations. As the algorithm proceeds, the pointers move through the relation. A group of tuples of one relation with the same value on the join attributes is read into S_s. The algorithm in Figure 12.7 *requires* that every set of tuples S_s fit in main memory; we discuss extensions of the algorithm to avoid this requirement shortly. Then, the corresponding tuples (if any) of the other relation are read in, and are processed as they are read.

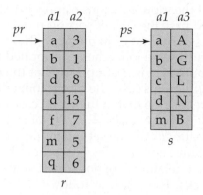

Figure 12.8 Sorted relations for merge join.

Figure 12.8 shows two relations that are sorted on their join attribute $a1$. It is instructive to go through the steps of the merge-join algorithm on the relations shown in the figure.

The merge-join algorithm of Figure 12.7 requires that each set S_s of all tuples with the same value for the join attributes must fit in main memory. This requirement can usually be met, even if the relation s is large. If there are some join attribute values for which S_s is larger than available memory, a block nested-loop join can be performed for such sets S_s, matching them with corresponding blocks of tuples in r with the same values for the join attributes.

If either of the input relations r and s is not sorted on the join attributes, they can be sorted first, and then the merge-join algorithm can be used. The merge-join algorithm can also be easily extended from natural joins to the more general case of equi-joins.

12.5.4.2 Cost Analysis

Once the relations are in sorted order, tuples with the same value on the join attributes are in consecutive order. Thereby, each tuple in the sorted order needs to be read only once, and, as a result, each block is also read only once. Since it makes only a single pass through both files (assuming all sets S_s fit in memory) the merge-join method is efficient; the number of block transfers is equal to the sum of the number of blocks in both files, $b_r + b_s$.

Assuming that b_b buffer blocks are allocated to each relation, the number of disk seeks required would be $\lceil b_r/b_b \rceil + \lceil b_s/b_b \rceil$ disk seeks. Since seeks are much more expensive than data transfer, it makes sense to allocate multiple buffer blocks to each relation, provided extra memory is available. For example, with $t_T = 0.1$ milliseconds per 4-kilobyte block, and $t_S = 4$ milliseconds, the buffer size is 400 blocks (or 1.6 megabytes), so the seek time would be 4 milliseconds for every 40 milliseconds of transfer time, in other words, seek time would be just 10 percent of the transfer time.

If either of the input relations r and s is not sorted on the join attributes, they must be sorted first; the cost of sorting must then be added to the above costs. If some some sets S_s do not fit in memory, the cost would increase slightly.

Suppose the merge-join scheme is applied to our example of *student* ⋈ *takes*. The join attribute here is *ID*. Suppose that the relations are already sorted on the join attribute *ID*. In this case, the merge join takes a total of $400 + 100 = 500$ block transfers. If we assume that in the worst case only one buffer block is allocated to each input relation (that is, $b_b = 1$), a total of $400 + 100 = 500$ seeks would also be required; in reality b_b can be set much higher since we need to buffer blocks for only two relations, and the seek cost would be significantly less.

Suppose the relations are not sorted, and the memory size is the worst case, only three blocks. The cost is as follows:

1. Using the formulae that we developed in Section 12.4, we can see that sorting relation *takes* requires $\lceil \log_{3-1}(400/3) \rceil = 8$ merge passes. Sorting of relation *takes* then takes $400 * (2\lceil \log_{3-1}(400/3) \rceil + 1)$, or 6800, block transfers, with 400 more transfers to write out the result. The number of seeks required is $2 * \lceil 400/3 \rceil + 400 * (2 * 8 - 1)$ or 6268 seeks for sorting, and 400 seeks for writing the output, for a total of 6668 seeks, since only one buffer block is available for each run.

2. Similarly, sorting relation *student* takes $\lceil \log_{3-1}(100/3) \rceil = 6$ merge passes and $100 * (2\lceil \log_{3-1}(100/3) \rceil + 1)$, or 1300, block transfers, with 100 more transfers to write it out. The number of seeks required for sorting *student* is $2 * \lceil 100/3 \rceil + 100 * (2 * 6 - 1) = 1164$, and 100 seeks are required for writing the output, for a total of 1264 seeks.

3. Finally, merging the two relations takes $400 + 100 = 500$ block transfers and 500 seeks.

Thus, the total cost is 9100 block transfers plus 8932 seeks if the relations are not sorted, and the memory size is just 3 blocks.

With a memory size of 25 blocks, and the relations not sorted, the cost of sorting followed by merge join would be as follows:

1. Sorting the relation *takes* can be done with just one merge step, and takes a total of just $400 * (2\lceil \log_{24}(400/25) \rceil + 1) = 1200$ block transfers. Similarly, sorting *student* takes 300 block transfers. Writing the sorted output to disk requires $400 + 100 = 500$ block transfers, and the merge step requires 500 block transfers to read the data back. Adding up these costs gives a total cost of 2500 block transfers.

2. If we assume that only one buffer block is allocated for each run, the number of seeks required in this case is $2 * \lceil 400/25 \rceil + 400 + 400 = 832$ seeks for sorting *takes* and writing the sorted output to disk, and similarly $2 * \lceil 100/25 \rceil + 100 + 100 = 208$ for *student*, plus $400 + 100$ seeks for reading the sorted data in the merge-join step. Adding up these costs gives a total cost of 1640 seeks.

The number of seeks can be significantly reduced by setting aside more buffer blocks for each run. For example, if 5 buffer blocks are allocated for each run and for the output from merging the 4 runs of *student*, the cost is reduced to $2 * \lceil 100/25 \rceil + \lceil 100/5 \rceil + \lceil 100/5 \rceil = 48$ seeks, from 208 seeks. If the merge-join step sets aside 12 blocks each for buffering *takes* and *student*, the number of seeks for the merge-join step goes down to $\lceil 400/12 \rceil + \lceil 100/12 \rceil = 43$, from 500. The total number of seeks is then 251.

Thus, the total cost is 2500 block transfers plus 251 seeks if the relations are not sorted, and the memory size is 25 blocks.

12.5.4.3 Hybrid Merge Join

It is possible to perform a variation of the merge-join operation on unsorted tuples, if secondary indices exist on both join attributes. The algorithm scans the records through the indices, resulting in their being retrieved in sorted order. This variation presents a significant drawback, however, since records may be scattered throughout the file blocks. Hence, each tuple access could involve accessing a disk block, and that is costly.

To avoid this cost, we can use a hybrid merge-join technique that combines indices with merge join. Suppose that one of the relations is sorted; the other is unsorted, but has a secondary B^+-tree index on the join attributes. The **hybrid merge-join algorithm** merges the sorted relation with the leaf entries of the secondary B^+-tree index. The result file contains tuples from the sorted relation and addresses for tuples of the unsorted relation. The result file is then sorted on the addresses of tuples of the unsorted relation, allowing efficient retrieval of the corresponding tuples, in physical storage order, to complete the join. Extensions of the technique to handle two unsorted relations are left as an exercise for you.

12.5.5 Hash Join

Like the merge-join algorithm, the hash-join algorithm can be used to implement natural joins and equi-joins. In the hash-join algorithm, a hash function h is used to partition tuples of both relations. The basic idea is to partition the tuples of each of the relations into sets that have the same hash value on the join attributes.

We assume that:

- h is a hash function mapping *JoinAttrs* values to $\{0, 1, \ldots, n_h\}$, where *JoinAttrs* denotes the common attributes of r and s used in the natural join.

- $r_0, r_1, \ldots, r_{n_h}$ denote partitions of r tuples, each initially empty. Each tuple $t_r \in r$ is put in partition r_i, where $i = h(t_r[\text{JoinAttrs}])$.

- $s_0, s_1, \ldots, s_{n_h}$ denote partitions of s tuples, each initially empty. Each tuple $t_s \in s$ is put in partition s_i, where $i = h(t_s[\text{JoinAttrs}])$.

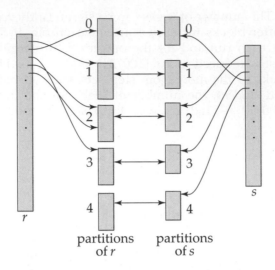

partitions   partitions
of r of s

Figure 12.9   Hash partitioning of relations.

The hash function h should have the "goodness" properties of randomness and uniformity that we discussed in Chapter 11. Figure 12.9 depicts the partitioning of the relations.

12.5.5.1   Basics

The idea behind the hash-join algorithm is this: Suppose that an r tuple and an s tuple satisfy the join condition; then, they have the same value for the join attributes. If that value is hashed to some value i, the r tuple has to be in r_i and the s tuple in s_i. Therefore, r tuples in r_i need only to be compared with s tuples in s_i; they do not need to be compared with s tuples in any other partition.

For example, if d is a tuple in *student*, c a tuple in *takes*, and h a hash function on the ID attributes of the tuples, then d and c must be tested only if $h(c) = h(d)$. If $h(c) \neq h(d)$, then c and d must have different values for ID. However, if $h(c) = h(d)$, we must test c and d to see whether the values in their join attributes are the same, since it is possible that c and d have different *iid*s that have the same hash value.

Figure 12.10 shows the details of the **hash-join** algorithm to compute the natural join of relations r and s. As in the merge-join algorithm, $t_r \bowtie t_s$ denotes the concatenation of the attributes of tuples t_r and t_s, followed by projecting out repeated attributes. After the partitioning of the relations, the rest of the hash-join code performs a separate indexed nested-loop join on each of the partition pairs i, for $i = 0, \ldots, n_h$. To do so, it first **builds** a hash index on each s_i, and then **probes** (that is, looks up s_i) with tuples from r_i. The relation s is the **build input**, and r is the **probe input**.

The hash index on s_i is built in memory, so there is no need to access the disk to retrieve the tuples. The hash function used to build this hash index must be different from the hash function h used earlier, but is still applied to only the join

```
/* Partition s */
for each tuple t_s in s do begin
    i := h(t_s[JoinAttrs]);
    H_{s_i} := H_{s_i} ∪ {t_s};
end
/* Partition r */
for each tuple t_r in r do begin
    i := h(t_r[JoinAttrs]);
    H_{r_i} := H_{r_i} ∪ {t_r};
end
/* Perform join on each partition */
for i := 0 to n_h do begin
    read H_{s_i} and build an in-memory hash index on it;
    for each tuple t_r in H_{r_i} do begin
        probe the hash index on H_{s_i} to locate all tuples t_s
            such that t_s[JoinAttrs] = t_r[JoinAttrs];
        for each matching tuple t_s in H_{s_i} do begin
            add t_r ⋈ t_s to the result;
        end
    end
end
```

Figure 12.10 Hash join.

attributes. In the course of the indexed nested-loop join, the system uses this hash index to retrieve records that match records in the probe input.

The build and probe phases require only a single pass through both the build and probe inputs. It is straightforward to extend the hash-join algorithm to compute general equi-joins.

The value n_h must be chosen to be large enough such that, for each i, the tuples in the partition s_i of the build relation, along with the hash index on the partition, fit in memory. It is not necessary for the partitions of the probe relation to fit in memory. Clearly, it is best to use the smaller input relation as the build relation. If the size of the build relation is b_s blocks, then, for each of the n_h partitions to be of size less than or equal to M, n_h must be at least $\lceil b_s/M \rceil$. More precisely stated, we have to account for the extra space occupied by the hash index on the partition as well, so n_h should be correspondingly larger. For simplicity, we sometimes ignore the space requirement of the hash index in our analysis.

12.5.5.2 Recursive Partitioning

If the value of n_h is greater than or equal to the number of blocks of memory, the relations cannot be partitioned in one pass, since there will not be enough buffer blocks. Instead, partitioning has to be done in repeated passes. In one pass, the input can be split into at most as many partitions as there are blocks available for use as output buffers. Each bucket generated by one pass is separately read in and partitioned again in the next pass, to create smaller partitions. The hash function used in a pass is, of course, different from the one used in the previous pass. The system repeats this splitting of the input until each partition of the build input fits in memory. Such partitioning is called **recursive partitioning**.

A relation does not need recursive partitioning if $M > n_h + 1$, or equivalently $M > (b_s/M) + 1$, which simplifies (approximately) to $M > \sqrt{b_s}$. For example, consider a memory size of 12 megabytes, divided into 4-kilobyte blocks; it would contain a total of 3K (3072) blocks. We can use a memory of this size to partition relations of size up to 3K $*$ 3K blocks, which is 36 gigabytes. Similarly, a relation of size 1 gigabyte requires just over $\sqrt{256K}$ blocks, or 2 megabytes, to avoid recursive partitioning.

12.5.5.3   Handling of Overflows

Hash-table overflow occurs in partition i of the build relation s if the hash index on s_i is larger than main memory. Hash-table overflow can occur if there are many tuples in the build relation with the same values for the join attributes, or if the hash function does not have the properties of randomness and uniformity. In either case, some of the partitions will have more tuples than the average, whereas others will have fewer; partitioning is then said to be **skewed**.

We can handle a small amount of skew by increasing the number of partitions so that the expected size of each partition (including the hash index on the partition) is somewhat less than the size of memory. The number of partitions is therefore increased by a small value, called the **fudge factor**, that is usually about 20 percent of the number of hash partitions computed as described in Section 12.5.5.

Even if, by using a fudge factor, we are conservative on the sizes of the partitions, overflows can still occur. Hash-table overflows can be handled by either *overflow resolution* or *overflow avoidance*. **Overflow resolution** is performed during the build phase, if a hash-index overflow is detected. Overflow resolution proceeds in this way: If s_i, for any i, is found to be too large, it is further partitioned into smaller partitions by using a different hash function. Similarly, r_i is also partitioned using the new hash function, and only tuples in the matching partitions need to be joined.

In contrast, **overflow avoidance** performs the partitioning carefully, so that overflows never occur during the build phase. In overflow avoidance, the build relation s is initially partitioned into many small partitions, and then some partitions are combined in such a way that each combined partition fits in memory. The probe relation r is partitioned in the same way as the combined partitions on s, but the sizes of r_i do not matter.

If a large number of tuples in s have the same value for the join attributes, the resolution and avoidance techniques may fail on some partitions. In that case, instead of creating an in-memory hash index and using a nested-loop join to join the partitions, we can use other join techniques, such as block nested-loop join, on those partitions.

12.5.5.4 Cost of Hash Join

We now consider the cost of a hash join. Our analysis assumes that there is no hash-table overflow. First, consider the case where recursive partitioning is not required.

- The partitioning of the two relations r and s calls for a complete reading of both relations, and a subsequent writing back of them. This operation requires $2(b_r + b_s)$ block transfers, where b_r and b_s denote the number of blocks containing records of relations r and s, respectively. The build and probe phases read each of the partitions once, calling for further $b_r + b_s$ block transfers. The number of blocks occupied by partitions could be slightly more than $b_r + b_s$, as a result of partially filled blocks. Accessing such partially filled blocks can add an overhead of at most $2n_h$ for each of the relations, since each of the n_h partitions could have a partially filled block that has to be written and read back. Thus, a hash join is estimated to require:

$$3(b_r + b_s) + 4n_h$$

block transfers. The overhead $4n_h$ is usually quite small compared to $b_r + b_s$, and can be ignored.

- Assuming b_b blocks are allocated for the input buffer and each output buffer, partitioning requires a total of $2(\lceil b_r/b_b \rceil + \lceil b_s/b_b \rceil)$ seeks. The build and probe phases require only one seek for each of the n_h partitions of each relation, since each partition can be read sequentially. The hash join thus requires $2(\lceil b_r/b_b \rceil + \lceil b_s/b_b \rceil) + 2n_h$ seeks.

Now consider the case where recursive partitioning is required. Each pass reduces the size of each of the partitions by an expected factor of $M - 1$; and passes are repeated until each partition is of size at most M blocks. The expected number of passes required for partitioning s is therefore $\lceil \log_{M-1}(b_s) - 1 \rceil$.

- Since, in each pass, every block of s is read in and written out, the total block transfers for partitioning of s is $2b_s \lceil \log_{M-1}(b_s) - 1 \rceil$. The number of passes for partitioning of r is the same as the number of passes for partitioning of s, therefore the join is estimated to require:

$$2(b_r + b_s)\lceil \log_{M-1}(b_s) - 1 \rceil + b_r + b_s$$

block transfers.

- Again assuming b_b blocks are allocated for buffering each partition, and ignoring the relatively small number of seeks during the build and probe phase, hash join with recursive partitioning requires:

$$2(\lceil b_r/b_b \rceil + \lceil b_s/b_b \rceil)\lceil \log_{M-1}(b_s) - 1 \rceil$$

disk seeks.

Consider, for example, the natural join *takes* ⋈ *student*. With a memory size of 20 blocks, the *student* relation can be partitioned into five partitions, each of size 20 blocks, which size will fit into memory. Only one pass is required for the partitioning. The relation *takes* is similarly partitioned into five partitions, each of size 80. Ignoring the cost of writing partially filled blocks, the cost is $3(100 + 400) = 1500$ block transfers. There is enough memory to allocate 3 buffers for the input and each of the 5 outputs during partitioning, leading to $2(\lceil 100/3 \rceil + \lceil 400/3 \rceil) = 336$ seeks.

The hash join can be improved if the main-memory size is large. When the entire build input can be kept in main memory, n_h can be set to 0; then, the hash-join algorithm executes quickly, without partitioning the relations into temporary files, regardless of the probe input's size. The cost estimate goes down to $b_r + b_s$ block transfers and two seeks.

12.5.5.5   Hybrid Hash Join

The **hybrid hash-join** algorithm performs another optimization; it is useful when memory sizes are relatively large, but not all of the build relation fits in memory. The partitioning phase of the hash-join algorithm needs a minimum of one block of memory as a buffer for each partition that is created, and one block of memory as an input buffer. To reduce the impact of seeks, a larger number of blocks would be used as a buffer; let b_b denote the number of blocks used as a buffer for the input and for each partition. Hence, a total of $(n_h + 1) * b_b$ blocks of memory are needed for partitioning the two relations. If memory is larger than $(n_h + 1) * b_b$, we can use the rest of memory ($M - (n_h + 1) * b_b$ blocks) to buffer the first partition of the build input (that is, s_0), so that it will not need to be written out and read back in. Further, the hash function is designed in such a way that the hash index on s_0 fits in $M - (n_h + 1) * b_b$ blocks, in order that, at the end of partitioning of s, s_0 is completely in memory and a hash index can be built on s_0.

When the system partitions r it again does not write tuples in r_0 to disk; instead, as it generates them, the system uses them to probe the memory-resident hash index on s_0, and to generate output tuples of the join. After they are used for probing, the tuples can be discarded, so the partition r_0 does not occupy any memory space. Thus, a write and a read access have been saved for each block of both r_0 and s_0. The system writes out tuples in the other partitions as usual, and joins them later. The savings of hybrid hash join can be significant if the build input is only slightly bigger than memory.

If the size of the build relation is b_s, n_h is approximately equal to b_s / M. Thus, hybrid hash join is most useful if $M >> (b_s / M) * b_b$, or $M >> \sqrt{b_s * b_b}$, where the notation $>>$ denotes *much larger than*. For example, suppose the block size is 4 kilobytes, the build relation size is 5 gigabytes, and b_b is 20. Then, the hybrid hash-join algorithm is useful if the size of memory is significantly more than 20 megabytes; memory sizes of gigabytes or more are common on computers today. If we devote 1 gigabyte for the join algorithm, s_0 would be nearly 1 gigabyte, and hybrid hash join would be nearly 20 percent cheaper than hash join.

12.5.6 Complex Joins

Nested-loop and block nested-loop joins can be used regardless of the join conditions. The other join techniques are more efficient than the nested-loop join and its variants, but can handle only simple join conditions, such as natural joins or equi-joins. We can implement joins with complex join conditions, such as conjunctions and disjunctions, by using the efficient join techniques, if we apply the techniques developed in Section 12.3.3 for handling complex selections.

Consider the following join with a conjunctive condition:

$$r \bowtie_{\theta_1 \wedge \theta_2 \wedge \cdots \wedge \theta_n} s$$

One or more of the join techniques described earlier may be applicable for joins on the individual conditions $r \bowtie_{\theta_1} s$, $r \bowtie_{\theta_2} s$, $r \bowtie_{\theta_3} s$, and so on. We can compute the overall join by first computing the result of one of these simpler joins $r \bowtie_{\theta_i} s$; each pair of tuples in the intermediate result consists of one tuple from r and one from s. The result of the complete join consists of those tuples in the intermediate result that satisfy the remaining conditions:

$$\theta_1 \wedge \cdots \wedge \theta_{i-1} \wedge \theta_{i+1} \wedge \cdots \wedge \theta_n$$

These conditions can be tested as tuples in $r \bowtie_{\theta_i} s$ are being generated.

A join whose condition is disjunctive can be computed in this way. Consider:

$$r \bowtie_{\theta_1 \vee \theta_2 \vee \cdots \vee \theta_n} s$$

The join can be computed as the union of the records in individual joins $r \bowtie_{\theta_i} s$:

$$(r \bowtie_{\theta_1} s) \cup (r \bowtie_{\theta_2} s) \cup \cdots \cup (r \bowtie_{\theta_n} s)$$

Section 12.6 describes algorithms for computing the union of relations.

12.6 Other Operations

Other relational operations and extended relational operations—such as duplicate elimination, projection, set operations, outer join, and aggregation—can be implemented as outlined in Sections 12.6.1 through 12.6.5.

12.6.1 Duplicate Elimination

We can implement duplicate elimination easily by sorting. Identical tuples will appear adjacent to each other as a result of sorting, and all but one copy can be removed. With external sort–merge, duplicates found while a run is being created can be removed before the run is written to disk, thereby reducing the number of block transfers. The remaining duplicates can be eliminated during merging, and the final sorted run has no duplicates. The worst-case cost estimate for duplicate elimination is the same as the worst-case cost estimate for sorting of the relation.

We can also implement duplicate elimination by hashing, as in the hash-join algorithm. First, the relation is partitioned on the basis of a hash function on the whole tuple. Then, each partition is read in, and an in-memory hash index is constructed. While constructing the hash index, a tuple is inserted only if it is not already present. Otherwise, the tuple is discarded. After all tuples in the partition have been processed, the tuples in the hash index are written to the result. The cost estimate is the same as that for the cost of processing (partitioning and reading each partition) of the build relation in a hash join.

Because of the relatively high cost of duplicate elimination, SQL requires an explicit request by the user to remove duplicates; otherwise, the duplicates are retained.

12.6.2 Projection

We can implement projection easily by performing projection on each tuple, which gives a relation that could have duplicate records, and then removing duplicate records. Duplicates can be eliminated by the methods described in Section 12.6.1. If the attributes in the projection list include a key of the relation, no duplicates will exist; hence, duplicate elimination is not required. Generalized projection can be implemented in the same way as projection.

12.6.3 Set Operations

We can implement the *union*, *intersection*, and *set-difference* operations by first sorting both relations, and then scanning once through each of the sorted relations to produce the result. In $r \cup s$, when a concurrent scan of both relations reveals the same tuple in both files, only one of the tuples is retained. The result of $r \cap s$ will contain only those tuples that appear in both relations. We implement *set difference*, $r - s$, similarly, by retaining tuples in r only if they are absent in s.

For all these operations, only one scan of the two sorted input relations is required, so the cost is $b_r + b_s$ block transfers if the relations are sorted in the same order. Assuming a worst case of one block buffer for each relation, a total of $b_r + b_s$ disk seeks would be required in addition to $b_r + b_s$ block transfers. The number of seeks can be reduced by allocating extra buffer blocks.

If the relations are not sorted initially, the cost of sorting has to be included. Any sort order can be used in evaluation of set operations, provided that both inputs have that same sort order.

Hashing provides another way to implement these set operations. The first step in each case is to partition the two relations by the same hash function, and thereby create the partitions $r_0, r_1, \ldots, r_{n_h}$ and $s_0, s_1, \ldots, s_{n_h}$. Depending on the operation, the system then takes these steps on each partition $i = 0, 1, \ldots, n_h$:

- $r \cup s$

    1. Build an in-memory hash index on r_i.

2. Add the tuples in s_i to the hash index only if they are not already present.

3. Add the tuples in the hash index to the result.

- $r \cap s$

    1. Build an in-memory hash index on r_i.

    2. For each tuple in s_i, probe the hash index and output the tuple to the result only if it is already present in the hash index.

- $r - s$

    1. Build an in-memory hash index on r_i.

    2. For each tuple in s_i, probe the hash index, and, if the tuple is present in the hash index, delete it from the hash index.

    3. Add the tuples remaining in the hash index to the result.

12.6.4   Outer Join

Recall the *outer-join operations* described in Section 4.1.2. For example, the natural left outer join *takes* ⟕ *student* contains the join of *takes* and *student*, and, in addition, for each *takes* tuple t that has no matching tuple in *student* (that is, where *ID* is not in *student*), the following tuple t_1 is added to the result. For all attributes in the schema of *takes*, tuple t_1 has the same values as tuple t. The remaining attributes (from the schema of *student*) of tuple t_1 contain the value null.

We can implement the outer-join operations by using one of two strategies:

1. Compute the corresponding join, and then add further tuples to the join result to get the outer-join result. Consider the left outer-join operation and two relations: $r(R)$ and $s(S)$. To evaluate $r ⟕_\theta s$, we first compute $r ⋈_\theta s$, and save that result as temporary relation q_1. Next, we compute $r - \Pi_R(q_1)$ to obtain those tuples in r that do not participate in the theta join. We can use any of the algorithms for computing the joins, projection, and set difference described earlier to compute the outer joins. We pad each of these tuples with null values for attributes from s, and add it to q_1 to get the result of the outer join.

    The right outer-join operation $r ⟖_\theta s$ is equivalent to $s ⟕_\theta r$, and can therefore be implemented in a symmetric fashion to the left outer join. We can implement the full outer-join operation $r ⟗_\theta s$ by computing the join $r ⋈ s$, and then adding the extra tuples of both the left and right outer-join operations, as before.

2. Modify the join algorithms. It is easy to extend the nested-loop join algorithms to compute the left outer join: Tuples in the outer relation that do not match any tuple in the inner relation are written to the output after being padded with null values. However, it is hard to extend the nested-loop join to compute the full outer join.

Natural outer joins and outer joins with an equi-join condition can be computed by extensions of the merge-join and hash-join algorithms. Merge join can be extended to compute the full outer join as follows: When the merge of the two relations is being done, tuples in either relation that do not match any tuple in the other relation can be padded with nulls and written to the output. Similarly, we can extend merge join to compute the left and right outer joins by writing out nonmatching tuples (padded with nulls) from only one of the relations. Since the relations are sorted, it is easy to detect whether or not a tuple matches any tuples from the other relation. For example, when a merge join of *takes* and *student* is done, the tuples are read in sorted order of *ID*, and it is easy to check, for each tuple, whether there is a matching tuple in the other.

The cost estimates for implementing outer joins using the merge-join algorithm are the same as are those for the corresponding join. The only difference lies in size of the result, and therefore in the block transfers for writing it out, which we did not count in our earlier cost estimates.

The extension of the hash-join algorithm to compute outer joins is left for you to do as an exercise (Exercise 12.15).

12.6.5   Aggregation

Recall the aggregation function (operator), discussed in Section 3.7. For example, the function

> **select** *dept_name*, **avg** (*salary*)
> **from** *instructor*
> **group by** *dept_name*;

computes the average salary in each university department.

The aggregation operation can be implemented in the same way as duplicate elimination. We use either sorting or hashing, just as we did for duplicate elimination, but based on the grouping attributes (*branch_name* in the preceding example). However, instead of eliminating tuples with the same value for the grouping attribute, we gather them into groups, and apply the aggregation operations on each group to get the result.

The cost estimate for implementing the aggregation operation is the same as the cost of duplicate elimination, for aggregate functions such as **min**, **max**, **sum**, **count**, and **avg**.

Instead of gathering all the tuples in a group and then applying the aggregation operations, we can implement the aggregation operations **sum**, **min**, **max**, **count**, and **avg** on the fly as the groups are being constructed. For the case of **sum**, **min**, and **max**, when two tuples in the same group are found, the system replaces them by a single tuple containing the **sum**, **min**, or **max**, respectively, of the columns being aggregated. For the **count** operation, it maintains a running count for each group for which a tuple has been found. Finally, we implement the

avg operation by computing the sum and the count values on the fly, and finally dividing the sum by the count to get the average.

If all tuples of the result fit in memory, both the sort-based and the hash-based implementations do not need to write any tuples to disk. As the tuples are read in, they can be inserted in a sorted tree structure or in a hash index. When we use on-the-fly aggregation techniques, only one tuple needs to be stored for each of the groups. Hence, the sorted tree structure or hash index fits in memory, and the aggregation can be processed with just b_r block transfers (and 1 seek) instead of the $3b_r$ transfers (and a worst case of up to $2b_r$ seeks) that would be required otherwise.

12.7   Evaluation of Expressions

So far, we have studied how individual relational operations are carried out. Now we consider how to evaluate an expression containing multiple operations. The obvious way to evaluate an expression is simply to evaluate one operation at a time, in an appropriate order. The result of each evaluation is **materialized** in a temporary relation for subsequent use. A disadvantage to this approach is the need to construct the temporary relations, which (unless they are small) must be written to disk. An alternative approach is to evaluate several operations simultaneously in a **pipeline**, with the results of one operation passed on to the next, without the need to store a temporary relation.

In Sections 12.7.1 and 12.7.2, we consider both the *materialization* approach and the *pipelining* approach. We shall see that the costs of these approaches can differ substantially, but also that there are cases where only the materialization approach is feasible.

12.7.1   Materialization

It is easiest to understand intuitively how to evaluate an expression by looking at a pictorial representation of the expression in an **operator tree**. Consider the expression:

$$\Pi_{name}(\sigma_{building\,=\,\text{"Watson"}}(department) \bowtie instructor)$$

in Figure 12.11.

If we apply the materialization approach, we start from the lowest-level operations in the expression (at the bottom of the tree). In our example, there is only one such operation: the selection operation on *department*. The inputs to the lowest-level operations are relations in the database. We execute these operations by the algorithms that we studied earlier, and we store the results in temporary relations. We can use these temporary relations to execute the operations at the next level up in the tree, where the inputs now are either temporary relations or relations stored in the database. In our example, the inputs to the join are the *instructor* relation and the temporary relation created by the selection on *department*. The join can now be evaluated, creating another temporary relation.

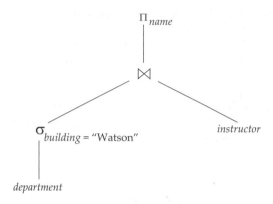

Figure 12.11   Pictorial representation of an expression.

By repeating the process, we will eventually evaluate the operation at the root of the tree, giving the final result of the expression. In our example, we get the final result by executing the projection operation at the root of the tree, using as input the temporary relation created by the join.

Evaluation as just described is called **materialized evaluation**, since the results of each intermediate operation are created (materialized) and then are used for evaluation of the next-level operations.

The cost of a materialized evaluation is not simply the sum of the costs of the operations involved. When we computed the cost estimates of algorithms, we ignored the cost of writing the result of the operation to disk. To compute the cost of evaluating an expression as done here, we have to add the costs of all the operations, as well as the cost of writing the intermediate results to disk. We assume that the records of the result accumulate in a buffer, and, when the buffer is full, they are written to disk. The number of blocks written out, b_r, can be estimated as n_r/f_r, where n_r is the estimated number of tuples in the result relation r, and f_r is the *blocking factor* of the result relation, that is, the number of records of r that will fit in a block. In addition to the transfer time, some disk seeks may be required, since the disk head may have moved between successive writes. The number of seeks can be estimated as $\lceil b_r/b_b \rceil$ where b_b is the size of the output buffer (measured in blocks).

Double buffering (using two buffers, with one continuing execution of the algorithm while the other is being written out) allows the algorithm to execute more quickly by performing CPU activity in parallel with I/O activity. The number of seeks can be reduced by allocating extra blocks to the output buffer, and writing out multiple blocks at once.

12.7.2   Pipelining

We can improve query-evaluation efficiency by reducing the number of temporary files that are produced. We achieve this reduction by combining several relational operations into a *pipeline* of operations, in which the results of one operation are passed along to the next operation in the pipeline. Evaluation as just described is called **pipelined evaluation**.

For example, consider the expression $(\Pi_{a1,a2}(r \bowtie s))$. If materialization were applied, evaluation would involve creating a temporary relation to hold the result of the join, and then reading back in the result to perform the projection. These operations can be combined: When the join operation generates a tuple of its result, it passes that tuple immediately to the project operation for processing. By combining the join and the projection, we avoid creating the intermediate result, and instead create the final result directly.

Creating a pipeline of operations can provide two benefits:

1. It eliminates the cost of reading and writing temporary relations, reducing the cost of query evaluation.

2. It can start generating query results quickly, if the root operator of a query-evaluation plan is combined in a pipeline with its inputs. This can be quite useful if the results are displayed to a user as they are generated, since otherwise there may be a long delay before the user sees any query results.

12.7.2.1 Implementation of Pipelining

We can implement a pipeline by constructing a single, complex operation that combines the operations that constitute the pipeline. Although this approach may be feasible for some frequently occurring situations, it is desirable in general to reuse the code for individual operations in the construction of a pipeline.

In the example of Figure 12.11, all three operations can be placed in a pipeline, which passes the results of the selection to the join as they are generated. In turn, it passes the results of the join to the projection as they are generated. The memory requirements are low, since results of an operation are not stored for long. However, as a result of pipelining, the inputs to the operations are not available all at once for processing.

Pipelines can be executed in either of two ways:

1. In a **demand-driven pipeline**, the system makes repeated requests for tuples from the operation at the top of the pipeline. Each time that an operation receives a request for tuples, it computes the next tuple (or tuples) to be returned, and then returns that tuple. If the inputs of the operation are not pipelined, the next tuple(s) to be returned can be computed from the input relations, while the system keeps track of what has been returned so far. If it has some pipelined inputs, the operation also makes requests for tuples from its pipelined inputs. Using the tuples received from its pipelined inputs, the operation computes tuples for its output, and passes them up to its parent.

2. In a **producer-driven pipeline**, operations do not wait for requests to produce tuples, but instead generate the tuples **eagerly**. Each operation in a producer-driven pipeline is modeled as a separate process or thread within

the system that takes a stream of tuples from its pipelined inputs and generates a stream of tuples for its output.

We describe below how demand-driven and producer-driven pipelines can be implemented.

Each operation in a demand-driven pipeline can be implemented as an **iterator** that provides the following functions: *open()*, *next()*, and *close()*. After a call to *open()*, each call to *next()* returns the next output tuple of the operation. The implementation of the operation in turn calls *open()* and *next()* on its inputs, to get its input tuples when required. The function *close()* tells an iterator that no more tuples are required. The iterator maintains the **state** of its execution in between calls, so that successive *next()* requests receive successive result tuples.

For example, for an iterator implementing the select operation using linear search, the *open()* operation starts a file scan, and the iterator's state records the point to which the file has been scanned. When the *next()* function is called, the file scan continues from after the previous point; when the next tuple satisfying the selection is found by scanning the file, the tuple is returned after storing the point where it was found in the iterator state. A merge-join iterator's *open()* operation would open its inputs, and if they are not already sorted, it would also sort the inputs. On calls to *next()*, it would return the next pair of matching tuples. The state information would consist of up to where each input had been scanned. Details of the implementation of iterators are left for you to complete in Practice Exercise 12.7.

Producer-driven pipelines, on the other hand, are implemented in a different manner. For each pair of adjacent operations in a producer-driven pipeline, the system creates a buffer to hold tuples being passed from one operation to the next. The processes or threads corresponding to different operations execute concurrently. Each operation at the bottom of a pipeline continually generates output tuples, and puts them in its output buffer, until the buffer is full. An operation at any other level of a pipeline generates output tuples when it gets input tuples from lower down in the pipeline, until its output buffer is full. Once the operation uses a tuple from a pipelined input, it removes the tuple from its input buffer. In either case, once the output buffer is full, the operation waits until its parent operation removes tuples from the buffer, so that the buffer has space for more tuples. At this point, the operation generates more tuples, until the buffer is full again. The operation repeats this process until all the output tuples have been generated.

It is necessary for the system to switch between operations only when an output buffer is full, or an input buffer is empty and more input tuples are needed to generate any more output tuples. In a parallel-processing system, operations in a pipeline may be run concurrently on distinct processors (see Chapter 18).

Using producer-driven pipelining can be thought of as **pushing** data up an operation tree from below, whereas using demand-driven pipelining can be thought of as **pulling** data up an operation tree from the top. Whereas tuples are generated *eagerly* in producer-driven pipelining, they are generated **lazily**, on demand, in demand-driven pipelining. Demand-driven pipelining is used more commonly than producer-driven pipelining, because it is easier to implement. However, producer-driven pipelining is very useful in parallel processing systems.

12.7.2.2 Evaluation Algorithms for Pipelining

Some operations, such as sorting, are inherently **blocking operations**, that is, they may not be able to output any results until all tuples from their inputs have been examined.[5]

Other operations, such as join, are not inherently blocking, but specific evaluation algorithms may be blocking. For example, the hash-join algorithm is a blocking operation, since it requires both its inputs to be fully retrieved and partitioned, before it outputs any tuples. On the other hand, the indexed nested loops join algorithm can output result tuples as it gets tuples for the outer relation. It is therefore said to be **pipelined** on its outer (left-hand side) relation, although it is blocking on its indexed (right-hand side) input, since the index must be fully constructed before the indexed nested-loop join algorithm can execute.

Hybrid hash join can be viewed as partially pipelined on the probe relation, since it can output tuples from the first partition as tuples are received for the probe relation. However, tuples that are not in the first partition will be output only after the entire pipelined input relation is received. Hybrid hash join thus provides pipelined evaluation on its probe input if the build input fits entirely in memory, or nearly pipelined evaluation if most of the build input fits in memory.

If both inputs are sorted on the join attribute, and the join condition is an equi-join, merge join can be used, with both its inputs pipelined.

However, in the more common case that the two inputs that we desire to pipeline into the join are not already sorted, another alternative is the **double-pipelined join** technique, shown in Figure 12.12. The algorithm assumes that the input tuples for both input relations, r and s, are pipelined. Tuples made available for both relations are queued for processing in a single queue. Special queue entries, called End_r and End_s, which serve as end-of-file markers, are inserted in the queue after all tuples from r and s (respectively) have been generated. For efficient evaluation, appropriate indices should be built on the relations r and s. As tuples are added to r and s, the indices must be kept up to date. When hash indices are used on r and s, the resultant algorithm is called the **double-pipelined hash-join** technique.

The double-pipelined join algorithm in Figure 12.12 assumes that both inputs fit in memory. In case the two inputs are larger than memory, it is still possible to use the double-pipelined join technique as usual until available memory is full. When available memory becomes full, r and s tuples that have arrived up to that point can be treated as being in partition r_0 and s_0, respectively. Tuples for r and s that arrive subsequently are assigned to partitions r_1 and s_1, respectively, which

---

[5]Blocking operations such as sorting may be able to output tuples early if the input is known to satisfy some special properties such as being sorted, or partially sorted, already. However, in the absence of such information, blocking operations cannot output tuples early.

$done_r := false;$
$done_s := false;$
$r := \emptyset;$
$s := \emptyset;$
$result := \emptyset;$
while not $done_r$ **or not** $done_s$ **do**
   begin
      if queue is empty, **then** wait until queue is not empty;
      $t :=$ top entry in queue;
      if $t = End_r$ **then** $done_r := true$
        else if $t = End_s$ **then** $done_s := true$
          else if t is from input r
           then
             begin
               $r := r \cup \{t\};$
               $result := result \cup (\{t\} \bowtie s);$
             end
           else /* t is from input s */
             begin
               $s := s \cup \{t\};$
               $result := result \cup (r \bowtie \{t\});$
             end
 end

Figure 12.12   Double-pipelined join algorithm.

are written to disk, and are not added to the in-memory index. However, tuples assigned to r_1 and s_1 are used to probe s_0 and r_0, respectively, before they are written to disk. Thus, the join of r_1 with s_0, and s_0 with r_1, is also carried out in a pipelined fashion. After r and s have been fully processed, the join of r_1 tuples with s_1 tuples must be carried out, to complete the join; any of the join techniques we have seen earlier can be used to join r_1 with s_1.

12.8   Summary

- The first action that the system must perform on a query is to translate the query into its internal form, which (for relational database systems) is usually based on the relational algebra. In the process of generating the internal form of the query, the parser checks the syntax of the user's query, verifies that the relation names appearing in the query are names of relations in the database, and so on. If the query was expressed in terms of a view, the parser replaces all references to the view name with the relational-algebra expression to compute the view.

- Given a query, there are generally a variety of methods for computing the answer. It is the responsibility of the query optimizer to transform the query as entered by the user into an equivalent query that can be computed more efficiently. Chapter 13 covers query optimization.

- We can process simple selection operations by performing a linear scan, or by making use of indices. We can handle complex selections by computing unions and intersections of the results of simple selections.

- We can sort relations larger than memory by the external sort–merge algorithm.

- Queries involving a natural join may be processed in several ways, depending on the availability of indices and the form of physical storage for the relations.

  ○ If the join result is almost as large as the Cartesian product of the two relations, a *block nested-loop* join strategy may be advantageous.

  ○ If indices are available, the *indexed nested-loop* join can be used.

  ○ If the relations are sorted, a *merge join* may be desirable. It may be advantageous to sort a relation prior to join computation (so as to allow use of the merge-join strategy).

  ○ The *hash-join* algorithm partitions the relations into several pieces, such that each piece of one of the relations fits in memory. The partitioning is carried out with a hash function on the join attributes, so that corresponding pairs of partitions can be joined independently.

- Duplicate elimination, projection, set operations (union, intersection, and difference), and aggregation can be done by sorting or by hashing.

- Outer-join operations can be implemented by simple extensions of join algorithms.

- Hashing and sorting are dual, in the sense that any operation such as duplicate elimination, projection, aggregation, join, and outer join that can be implemented by hashing can also be implemented by sorting, and vice versa; that is, any operation that can be implemented by sorting can also be implemented by hashing.

- An expression can be evaluated by means of materialization, where the system computes the result of each subexpression and stores it on disk, and then uses it to compute the result of the parent expression.

- Pipelining helps to avoid writing the results of many subexpressions to disk, by using the results in the parent expression even as they are being generated.

Review Terms

- Query processing
- Evaluation primitive
- Query-execution plan
- Query-evaluation plan
- Query-execution engine
- Measures of query cost

- Sequential I/O
- Random I/O
- File scan
- Linear search
- Selections using indices
- Access paths
- Index scans
- Conjunctive selection
- Disjunctive selection
- Composite index
- Intersection of identifiers
- External sorting
- External sort–merge
- Runs
- *N*-way merge
- Equi-join
- Nested-loop join
- Block nested-loop join
- Indexed nested-loop join
- Merge join
- Sort-merge join
- Hybrid merge join
- Hash join
  - Build
  - Probe
  - Build input
  - Probe input
  - Recursive partitioning
  - Hash-table overflow
  - Skew
  - Fudge factor
  - Overflow resolution
  - Overflow avoidance
- Hybrid hash join
- Operator tree
- Materialized evaluation
- Double buffering
- Pipelined evaluation
  - Demand-driven pipeline (lazy, pulling)
  - Producer-driven pipeline (eager, pushing)
  - Iterator
- Double-pipelined join

Practice Exercises

12.1 Assume (for simplicity in this exercise) that only one tuple fits in a block and memory holds at most 3 blocks. Show the runs created on each pass of the sort-merge algorithm, when applied to sort the following tuples on the first attribute: (kangaroo, 17), (wallaby, 21), (emu, 1), (wombat, 13), (platypus, 3), (lion, 8), (warthog, 4), (zebra, 11), (meerkat, 6), (hyena, 9), (hornbill, 2), (baboon, 12).

12.2 Consider the bank database of Figure 12.13, where the primary keys are underlined, and the following SQL query:

> **select** *T.branch_name*
> **from** *branch T, branch S*
> **where** *T.assets* > *S.assets* **and** *S.branch_city* = "Brooklyn"

Write an efficient relational-algebra expression that is equivalent to this query. Justify your choice.

12.3   Let relations $r_1(A, B, C)$ and $r_2(C, D, E)$ have the following properties: r_1 has 20,000 tuples, r_2 has 45,000 tuples, 25 tuples of r_1 fit on one block, and 30 tuples of r_2 fit on one block. Estimate the number of block transfers and seeks required, using each of the following join strategies for $r_1 \bowtie r_2$:

    a.   Nested-loop join.

    b.   Block nested-loop join.

    c.   Merge join.

    d.   Hash join.

12.4   The indexed nested-loop join algorithm described in Section 12.5.3 can be inefficient if the index is a secondary index, and there are multiple tuples with the same value for the join attributes. Why is it inefficient? Describe a way, using sorting, to reduce the cost of retrieving tuples of the inner relation. Under what conditions would this algorithm be more efficient than hybrid merge join?

12.5   Let r and s be relations with no indices, and assume that the relations are not sorted. Assuming infinite memory, what is the lowest-cost way (in terms of I/O operations) to compute $r \bowtie s$? What is the amount of memory required for this algorithm?

12.6   Consider the bank database of Figure 12.13, where the primary keys are underlined. Suppose that a B$^+$-tree index on *branch_city* is available on relation *branch*, and that no other index is available. List different ways to handle the following selections that involve negation:

    a. $\sigma_{\neg(branch\_city < \text{“Brooklyn”})}(branch)$

    b. $\sigma_{\neg(branch\_city = \text{“Brooklyn”})}(branch)$

    c. $\sigma_{\neg(branch\_city < \text{“Brooklyn”} \lor assets < 5000)}(branch)$

12.7   Write pseudocode for an iterator that implements indexed nested-loop join, where the outer relation is pipelined. Your pseudocode must define

        branch(*branch_name*, *branch_city*, *assets*)
        customer (*customer_name*, *customer_street*, *customer_city*)
        loan (*loan_number*, *branch_name*, *amount*)
        borrower (*customer_name*, *loan_number*)
        account (*account_number*, *branch_name*, *balance*)
        depositor (*customer_name*, *account_number*)

Figure 12.13   Banking database.

the standard iterator functions *open()*, *next()*, and *close()*. Show what state information the iterator must maintain between calls.

12.8 Design sort-based and hash-based algorithms for computing the relational division operation (see Practise Exercises of Chapter 6 for a definition of the division operation).

12.9 What is the effect on the cost of merging runs if the number of buffer blocks per run is increased, while keeping overall memory available for buffering runs fixed?

Exercises

12.10 Suppose you need to sort a relation of 40 gigabytes, with 4 kilobyte blocks, using a memory size of 40 megabytes. Suppose the cost of a seek is 5 milliseconds, while the disk transfer rate is 40 megabytes per second.

a. Find the cost of sorting the relation, in seconds, with $b_b = 1$ and with $b_b = 100$.

b. In each case, how many merge passes are required?

c. Suppose a flash storage device is used instead of a disk, and it has a seek time of 1 microsecond, and a transfer rate of 40 megabytes per second. Recompute the cost of sorting the relation, in seconds, with $b_b = 1$ and with $b_b = 100$, in this setting.

12.11 Consider the following extended relational-algebra operators. Describe how to implement each operation using sorting, and using hashing.

a. **Semijoin** ($\ltimes_\theta$): $r \ltimes_\theta s$ is defined as $\Pi_R(r \bowtie_\theta s)$, where R is the set of attributes in the schema of r; that it it selects those tuples r_i in r for which there is a tuple s_j in s such that r_i and s_j satisfy predicate θ.

b. **Anti-semijoin** ($\bar{\ltimes}_\theta$): $r \bar{\ltimes}_\theta s$ is defined as $r - \Pi_R(r \bowtie_\theta s)$; that it it selects those tuples r_i in r for which there is no tuple s_j in s such that r_i and s_j satisfy predicate θ.

12.12 Why is it not desirable to force users to make an explicit choice of a query-processing strategy? Are there cases in which it *is* desirable for users to be aware of the costs of competing query-processing strategies? Explain your answer.

12.13 Design a variant of the hybrid merge-join algorithm for the case where both relations are not physically sorted, but both have a sorted secondary index on the join attributes.

12.14 Estimate the number of block transfers and seeks required by your solution to Exercise 12.13 for $r_1 \bowtie r_2$, where r_1 and r_2 are as defined in Practice Exercise 12.3.

12.15   The hash-join algorithm as described in Section 12.5.5 computes the natural join of two relations. Describe how to extend the hash-join algorithm to compute the natural left outer join, the natural right outer join and the natural full outer join. (Hint: Keep extra information with each tuple in the hash index, to detect whether any tuple in the probe relation matches the tuple in the hash index.) Try out your algorithm on the *takes* and *student* relations.

12.16   Pipelining is used to avoid writing intermediate results to disk. Suppose you need to sort relation *r* using sort–merge and merge-join the result with an already sorted relation *s*.

   a.   Describe how the output of the sort of *r* can be pipelined to the merge join without being written back to disk.

   b.   The same idea is applicable even if both inputs to the merge join are the outputs of sort–merge operations. However, the available memory has to be shared between the two merge operations (the merge-join algorithm itself needs very little memory). What is the effect of having to share memory on the cost of each sort–merge operation?

12.17   Write pseudocode for an iterator that implements a version of the sort–merge algorithm where the result of the final merge is pipelined to its consumers. Your pseudocode must define the standard iterator functions *open()*, *next()*, and *close()*. Show what state information the iterator must maintain between calls.

12.18   Suppose you have to compute $_A\mathcal{G}_{sum(C)}(r)$ as well as $_{A,B}\mathcal{G}_{sum(C)}(r)$. Describe how to compute these together using a single sorting of *r*.

Bibliographical Notes

A query processor must parse statements in the query language, and must translate them into an internal form. Parsing of query languages differs little from parsing of traditional programming languages. Most compiler texts cover the main parsing techniques, and present optimization from a programming-language point of view.

Graefe and McKenna [1993b] presents an excellent survey of query-evaluation techniques.

Knuth [1973] presents an excellent description of external sorting algorithms, including an optimization called *replacement selection*, which can create initial runs that are (on the average) twice the size of memory. Nyberg et al. [1995] shows that due to poor processor-cache behavior, replacement selection performs worse than in-memory quicksort for run generation, negating the benefits of generating longer runs. Nyberg et al. [1995] presents an efficient external sorting algorithm that takes processor cache effects into account. Query evaluation algorithms that take cache effects into account have been extensively studied; see, for example, Harizopoulos and Ailamaki [2004].

According to performance studies conducted in the mid-1970s, database systems of that period used only nested-loop join and merge join. These studies, including Blasgen and Eswaran [1976], which was related to the development of System R, determined that either the nested-loop join or merge join nearly always provided the optimal join method. Hence, these two were the only join algorithms implemented in System R. However, Blasgen and Eswaran [1976] did not include an analysis of hash-join algorithms. Today, hash joins are considered to be highly efficient and widely used.

Hash-join algorithms were initially developed for parallel database systems. Hybrid hash join is described in Shapiro [1986]. Zeller and Gray [1990] and Davison and Graefe [1994] describe hash-join techniques that can adapt to the available memory, which is important in systems where multiple queries may be running at the same time. Graefe et al. [1998] describes the use of hash joins and *hash teams*, which allow pipelining of hash joins by using the same partitioning for all hash joins in a pipeline sequence, in the Microsoft SQL Server.

CHAPTER 13

Query Optimization

Query optimization is the process of selecting the most efficient query-evaluation plan from among the many strategies usually possible for processing a given query, especially if the query is complex. We do not expect users to write their queries so that they can be processed efficiently. Rather, we expect the system to construct a query-evaluation plan that minimizes the cost of query evaluation. This is where query optimization comes into play.

One aspect of optimization occurs at the relational-algebra level, where the system attempts to find an expression that is equivalent to the given expression, but more efficient to execute. Another aspect is selecting a detailed strategy for processing the query, such as choosing the algorithm to use for executing an operation, choosing the specific indices to use, and so on.

The difference in cost (in terms of evaluation time) between a good strategy and a bad strategy is often substantial, and may be several orders of magnitude. Hence, it is worthwhile for the system to spend a substantial amount of time on the selection of a good strategy for processing a query, even if the query is executed only once.

13.1 Overview

Consider the following relational-algebra expression, for the query "Find the names of all instructors in the Music department together with the course title of all the courses that the instructors teach."

$$\Pi_{name, title} \left(\sigma_{dept\_name = \text{``Music''}} \left(instructor \bowtie \left(teaches \bowtie \Pi_{course\_id, title}(course) \right) \right) \right)$$

Note that the projection of *course* on (*course_id,title*) is required since *course* shares an attribute *dept_name* with *instructor*; if we did not remove this attribute using the projection, the above expression using natural joins would return only courses from the Music department, even if some Music department instructors taught courses in other departments.

The above expression constructs a large intermediate relation, *instructor* $\bowtie$ *teaches* $\bowtie$ $\Pi_{course\_id, title}(course)$. However, we are interested in only a few tuples

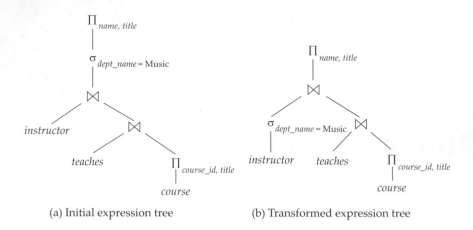

(a) Initial expression tree   (b) Transformed expression tree

Figure 13.1 Equivalent expressions.

of this relation (those pertaining to instructors in the Music department), and in only two of the ten attributes of this relation. Since we are concerned with only those tuples in the *instructor* relation that pertain to the Music department, we do not need to consider those tuples that do not have *dept_name* = "Music". By reducing the number of tuples of the *instructor* relation that we need to access, we reduce the size of the intermediate result. Our query is now represented by the relational-algebra expression:

$$\Pi_{name, title} \left((\sigma_{dept\_name = \text{"Music"}} (instructor)) \bowtie (teaches \bowtie \Pi_{course\_id, title} (course)) \right)$$

which is equivalent to our original algebra expression, but which generates smaller intermediate relations. Figure 13.1 depicts the initial and transformed expressions.

An evaluation plan defines exactly what algorithm should be used for each operation, and how the execution of the operations should be coordinated. Figure 13.2 illustrates one possible evaluation plan for the expression from Figure 13.1(b). As we have seen, several different algorithms can be used for each relational operation, giving rise to alternative evaluation plans. In the figure, hash join has been chosen for one of the join operations, while the other uses merge join, after sorting the relations on the join attribute, which is ID. Where edges are marked as pipelined, the output of the producer is pipelined directly to the consumer, without being written out to disk.

Given a relational-algebra expression, it is the job of the query optimizer to come up with a query-evaluation plan that computes the same result as the given expression, and is the least-costly way of generating the result (or, at least, is not much costlier than the least-costly way).

To find the least-costly query-evaluation plan, the optimizer needs to generate alternative plans that produce the same result as the given expression, and to choose the least-costly one. Generation of query-evaluation plans involves three steps: (1) generating expressions that are logically equivalent to the given ex-

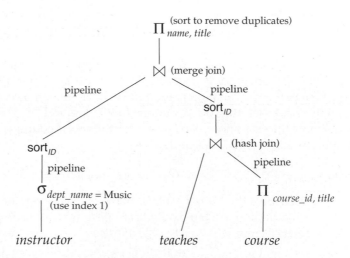

Figure 13.2 An evaluation plan.

pression, (2) annotating the resultant expressions in alternative ways to generate alternative query-evaluation plans, and (3) estimating the cost of each evaluation plan, and choosing the one whose estimated cost is the least.

Steps (1), (2), and (3) are interleaved in the query optimizer—some expressions are generated, and annotated to generate evaluation plans, then further expressions are generated and annotated, and so on. As evaluation plans are generated, their costs are estimated by using statistical information about the relations, such as relation sizes and index depths.

To implement the first step, the query optimizer must generate expressions equivalent to a given expression. It does so by means of *equivalence rules* that specify how to transform an expression into a logically equivalent one. We describe these rules in Section 13.2.

In Section 13.3 we describe how to estimate statistics of the results of each operation in a query plan. Using these statistics with the cost formulae in Chapter 12 allows us to estimate the costs of individual operations. The individual costs are combined to determine the estimated cost of evaluating a given relational-algebra expression, as outlined earlier in Section 12.7.

In Section 13.4, we describe how to choose a query-evaluation plan. We can choose one based on the estimated cost of the plans. Since the cost is an estimate, the selected plan is not necessarily the least-costly plan; however, as long as the estimates are good, the plan is likely to be the least-costly one, or not much more costly than it.

Finally, materialized views help to speed up processing of certain queries. In Section 13.5, we study how to "maintain" materialized views—that is, to keep them up-to-date—and how to perform query optimization with materialized views.

VIEWING QUERY EVALUATION PLANS

Most database systems provide a way to view the evaluation plan chosen to execute a given query. It is usually best to use the GUI provided with the database system to view evaluation plans. However, if you use a command line interface, many databases support variations of a command "**explain** <query>", which displays the execution plan chosen for the specified query <query>. The exact syntax varies with different databases:

- PostgreSQL uses the syntax shown above.

- Oracle uses the syntax **explain plan for**. However, the command stores the resultant plan in a table called *plan_table*, instead of displaying it. The query "**select * from table**(*dbms_xplan.display*);" displays the stored plan.

- DB2 follows a similar approach to Oracle, but requires the program db2exfmt to be executed to display the stored plan.

- SQL Server requires the command **set showplan_text on** to be executed before submitting the query; then, when a query is submitted, instead of executing the query, the evaluation plan is displayed.

The estimated costs for the plan are also displayed along with the plan. It is worth noting that the costs are usually not in any externally meaningful unit, such as seconds or I/O operations, but rather in units of whatever cost model the optimizer uses. Some optimizers such as PostgreSQL display two cost-estimate numbers; the first indicates the estimated cost for outputting the first result, and the second indicates the estimated cost for outputting all results.

13.2   Transformation of Relational Expressions

A query can be expressed in several different ways, with different costs of evaluation. In this section, rather than take the relational expression as given, we consider alternative, equivalent expressions.

Two relational-algebra expressions are said to be **equivalent** if, on every legal database instance, the two expressions generate the same set of tuples. (Recall that a legal database instance is one that satisfies all the integrity constraints specified in the database schema.) Note that the order of the tuples is irrelevant; the two expressions may generate the tuples in different orders, but would be considered equivalent as long as the set of tuples is the same.

In SQL, the inputs and outputs are multisets of tuples, and the multiset version of the relational algebra (described in the box in page 238) is used for evaluating SQL queries. Two expressions in the *multiset* version of the relational algebra are said to be equivalent if on every legal database the two expressions generate the same multiset of tuples. The discussion in this chapter is based on the relational

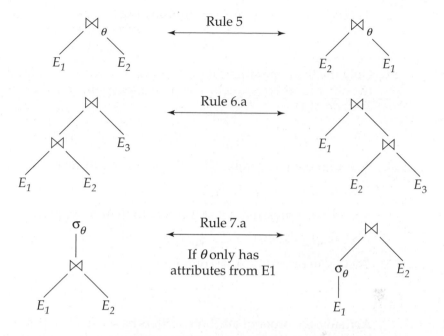

Figure 13.3 Pictorial representation of equivalences.

algebra. We leave extensions to the multiset version of the relational algebra to you as exercises.

13.2.1   Equivalence Rules

An **equivalence rule** says that expressions of two forms are equivalent. We can replace an expression of the first form by an expression of the second form, or vice versa—that is, we can replace an expression of the second form by an expression of the first form—since the two expressions generate the same result on any valid database. The optimizer uses equivalence rules to transform expressions into other logically equivalent expressions.

We now list a number of general equivalence rules on relational-algebra expressions. Some of the equivalences listed appear in Figure 13.3. We use θ, θ_1, θ_2, and so on to denote predicates, L_1, L_2, L_3, and so on to denote lists of attributes, and E, E_1, E_2, and so on to denote relational-algebra expressions. A relation name r is simply a special case of a relational-algebra expression, and can be used wherever E appears.

1. Conjunctive selection operations can be deconstructed into a sequence of individual selections. This transformation is referred to as a cascade of σ.

$$\sigma_{\theta_1 \wedge \theta_2}(E) = \sigma_{\theta_1}(\sigma_{\theta_2}(E))$$

2. Selection operations are **commutative**.

$$\sigma_{\theta_1}(\sigma_{\theta_2}(E)) = \sigma_{\theta_2}(\sigma_{\theta_1}(E))$$

3. Only the final operations in a sequence of projection operations are needed; the others can be omitted. This transformation can also be referred to as a cascade of Π.

$$\Pi_{L_1}(\Pi_{L_2}(\ldots(\Pi_{L_n}(E))\ldots)) = \Pi_{L_1}(E)$$

4. Selections can be combined with Cartesian products and theta joins.

   a. $\sigma_\theta(E_1 \times E_2) = E_1 \bowtie_\theta E_2$

       This expression is just the definition of the theta join.

   b. $\sigma_{\theta_1}(E_1 \bowtie_{\theta_2} E_2) = E_1 \bowtie_{\theta_1 \wedge \theta_2} E_2$

5. Theta-join operations are commutative.

$$E_1 \bowtie_\theta E_2 = E_2 \bowtie_\theta E_1$$

Actually, the order of attributes differs between the left-hand side and right-hand side, so the equivalence does not hold if the order of attributes is taken into account. A projection operation can be added to one of the sides of the equivalence to appropriately reorder attributes, but for simplicity we omit the projection and ignore the attribute order in most of our examples.

Recall that the natural-join operator is simply a special case of the theta-join operator; hence, natural joins are also commutative.

6.   a. Natural-join operations are **associative**.

$$(E_1 \bowtie E_2) \bowtie E_3 = E_1 \bowtie (E_2 \bowtie E_3)$$

   b. Theta joins are associative in the following manner:

$$(E_1 \bowtie_{\theta_1} E_2) \bowtie_{\theta_2 \wedge \theta_3} E_3 = E_1 \bowtie_{\theta_1 \wedge \theta_3} (E_2 \bowtie_{\theta_2} E_3)$$

       where θ_2 involves attributes from only E_2 and E_3. Any of these conditions may be empty; hence, it follows that the Cartesian product $(\times)$ operation is also associative. The commutativity and associativity of join operations are important for join reordering in query optimization.

7. The selection operation distributes over the theta-join operation under the following two conditions:

   a. It distributes when all the attributes in selection condition θ_0 involve only the attributes of one of the expressions (say, E_1) being joined.

$$\sigma_{\theta_0}(E_1 \bowtie_\theta E_2) = (\sigma_{\theta_0}(E_1)) \bowtie_\theta E_2$$

b. It distributes when selection condition θ_1 involves only the attributes of E_1 and θ_2 involves only the attributes of E_2.

$$\sigma_{\theta_1 \wedge \theta_2}(E_1 \bowtie_\theta E_2) = (\sigma_{\theta_1}(E_1)) \bowtie_\theta (\sigma_{\theta_2}(E_2))$$

8. The projection operation distributes over the theta-join operation under the following conditions.

   a. Let L_1 and L_2 be attributes of E_1 and E_2, respectively. Suppose that the join condition θ involves only attributes in $L_1 \cup L_2$. Then,

   $$\Pi_{L_1 \cup L_2}(E_1 \bowtie_\theta E_2) = (\Pi_{L_1}(E_1)) \bowtie_\theta (\Pi_{L_2}(E_2))$$

   b. Consider a join $E_1 \bowtie_\theta E_2$. Let L_1 and L_2 be sets of attributes from E_1 and E_2, respectively. Let L_3 be attributes of E_1 that are involved in join condition θ, but are not in $L_1 \cup L_2$, and let L_4 be attributes of E_2 that are involved in join condition θ, but are not in $L_1 \cup L_2$. Then,

   $$\Pi_{L_1 \cup L_2}(E_1 \bowtie_\theta E_2) = \Pi_{L_1 \cup L_2}((\Pi_{L_1 \cup L_3}(E_1)) \bowtie_\theta (\Pi_{L_2 \cup L_4}(E_2)))$$

9. The set operations union and intersection are commutative.

   $$E_1 \cup E_2 = E_2 \cup E_1$$

   $$E_1 \cap E_2 = E_2 \cap E_1$$

   Set difference is not commutative.

10. Set union and intersection are associative.

    $$(E_1 \cup E_2) \cup E_3 = E_1 \cup (E_2 \cup E_3)$$

    $$(E_1 \cap E_2) \cap E_3 = E_1 \cap (E_2 \cap E_3)$$

11. The selection operation distributes over the union, intersection, and set-difference operations.

    $$\sigma_P(E_1 - E_2) = \sigma_P(E_1) - \sigma_P(E_2)$$

    Similarly, the preceding equivalence, with $-$ replaced with either $\cup$ or $\cap$, also holds. Further:

    $$\sigma_P(E_1 - E_2) = \sigma_P(E_1) - E_2$$

    The preceding equivalence, with $-$ replaced by $\cap$, also holds, but does not hold if $-$ is replaced by $\cup$.

12. The projection operation distributes over the union operation.

    $$\Pi_L(E_1 \cup E_2) = (\Pi_L(E_1)) \cup (\Pi_L(E_2))$$

This is only a partial list of equivalences. More equivalences involving extended relational operators, such as the outer join and aggregation, are discussed in the exercises.

13.2.2 Examples of Transformations

We now illustrate the use of the equivalence rules. We use our university example with the relation schemas:

$$instructor(ID, name, dept\_name, salary)$$
$$teaches(ID, course\_id, sec\_id, semester, year)$$
$$course(course\_id, title, dept\_name, credits)$$

In our example in Section 13.1, the expression:

$$\Pi_{name, title} \left(\sigma_{dept\_name = \text{``Music''}} \left(instructor \bowtie \left(teaches \bowtie \Pi_{course\_id, title}(course) \right) \right) \right)$$

was transformed into the following expression:

$$\Pi_{name, title} \left(\left(\sigma_{dept\_name = \text{``Music''}} \left(instructor \right) \right) \bowtie \left(teaches \bowtie \Pi_{course\_id, title}(course) \right) \right)$$

which is equivalent to our original algebra expression, but generates smaller intermediate relations. We can carry out this transformation by using rule 7.a. Remember that the rule merely says that the two expressions are equivalent; it does not say that one is better than the other.

Multiple equivalence rules can be used, one after the other, on a query or on parts of the query. As an illustration, suppose that we modify our original query to restrict attention to instructors who have taught a course in 2009. The new relational-algebra query is:

$$\Pi_{name, title} \left(\sigma_{dept\_name = \text{``Music''} \wedge year = 2009} \right.$$
$$\left. \left(instructor \bowtie \left(teaches \bowtie \Pi_{course\_id, title}(course) \right) \right) \right)$$

We cannot apply the selection predicate directly to the *instructor* relation, since the predicate involves attributes of both the *instructor* and *teaches* relations. However, we can first apply rule 6.a (associativity of natural join) to transform the join $instructor \bowtie (teaches \bowtie \Pi_{course\_id, title}(course))$ into $(instructor \bowtie teaches) \bowtie \Pi_{course\_id, title}(course)$:

$$\Pi_{name, title} \left(\sigma_{dept\_name = \text{``Music''} \wedge year = 2009} \right.$$
$$\left. \left((instructor \bowtie teaches) \bowtie \Pi_{course\_id, title}(course) \right) \right)$$

Then, using rule 7.a, we can rewrite our query as:

$$\Pi_{name,\,title}\ \big((\sigma_{dept\_name\,=\,\text{“Music”}\,\wedge\,year\,=\,2009}$$
$$(instructor \bowtie teaches)) \bowtie \Pi_{course\_id,\,title}(course))$$

Let us examine the selection subexpression within this expression. Using rule 1, we can break the selection into two selections, to get the following subexpression:

$$\sigma_{dept\_name\,=\,\text{“Music”}}\ (\sigma_{year\,=\,2009}\ (instructor \bowtie teaches))$$

Both of the preceding expressions select tuples with $dept\_name =$ “Music” and $course\_id = 2009$. However, the latter form of the expression provides a new opportunity to apply Rule 7.a ("perform selections early"), resulting in the subexpression:

$$\sigma_{dept\_name\,=\,\text{“Music”}}\ (instructor) \bowtie \sigma_{year\,=\,2009}\ (teaches)$$

Figure 13.4 depicts the initial expression and the final expression after all these transformations. We could equally well have used rule 7.b to get the final expression directly, without using rule 1 to break the selection into two selections. In fact, rule 7.b can itself be derived from rules 1 and 7.a.

A set of equivalence rules is said to be **minimal** if no rule can be derived from any combination of the others. The preceding example illustrates that the set of equivalence rules in Section 13.2.1 is not minimal. An expression equivalent to the original expression may be generated in different ways; the number of different ways of generating an expression increases when we use a nonminimal set of equivalence rules. Query optimizers therefore use minimal sets of equivalence rules.

Now consider the following form of our example query:

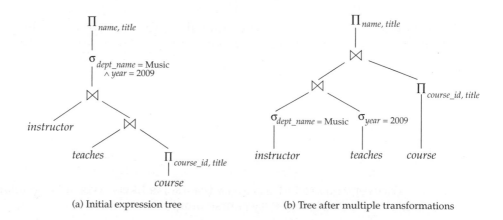

(a) Initial expression tree   (b) Tree after multiple transformations

Figure 13.4   Multiple transformations.

$$\Pi_{name,title} ((\sigma_{dept\_name = \text{``Music''}} (instructor) \bowtie teaches) \bowtie \Pi_{course\_id,title}(course))$$

When we compute the subexpression:

$$(\sigma_{dept\_name = \text{``Music''}} (instructor) \bowtie teaches)$$

we obtain a relation whose schema is:

$$(ID, name, dept\_name, salary, course\_id, sec\_id, semester, year)$$

We can eliminate several attributes from the schema by pushing projections based on equivalence rules 8.a and 8.b. The only attributes that we must retain are those that either appear in the result of the query or are needed to process subsequent operations. By eliminating unneeded attributes, we reduce the number of columns of the intermediate result. Thus, we reduce the size of the intermediate result. In our example, the only attributes we need from the join of *instructor* and *teaches* are *name* and *course_id*. Therefore, we can modify the expression to:

$$\Pi_{name,title} ((\Pi_{name,course\_id} ((\sigma_{dept\_name = \text{``Music''}} (instructor)) \bowtie teaches) \\ \bowtie \Pi_{course\_id,title}(course))$$

The projection $\Pi_{name,course\_id}$ reduces the size of the intermediate join results.

13.2.3 Join Ordering

A good ordering of join operations is important for reducing the size of temporary results; hence, most query optimizers pay a lot of attention to the join order. As mentioned in Chapter 6 and in equivalence rule 6.a, the natural-join operation is associative. Thus, for all relations r_1, r_2, and r_3:

$$(r_1 \bowtie r_2) \bowtie r_3 = r_1 \bowtie (r_2 \bowtie r_3)$$

Although these expressions are equivalent, the costs of computing them may differ. Consider again the expression:

$$\Pi_{name,title} ((\sigma_{dept\_name = \text{``Music''}} (instructor)) \bowtie teaches \bowtie \Pi_{course\_id,title}(course))$$

We could choose to compute $teaches \bowtie \Pi_{course\_id,title}(course)$ first, and then to join the result with:

$$\sigma_{dept\_name = \text{``Music''}} (instructor)$$

However, $teaches \bowtie \Pi_{course\_id,title}(course)$ is likely to be a large relation, since it contains one tuple for every course taught. In contrast:

$$\sigma_{dept\_name = \text{``Music''}} (instructor) \bowtie teaches$$

is probably a small relation. To see that it is, we note that, since a university has a large number of departments, it is likely that only a small fraction of the university instructors are associated with the Music department. Thus, the preceding expression results in one tuple for each course taught by an instructor in the Music department. Therefore, the temporary relation that we must store is smaller than it would have been had we computed $teaches \bowtie \Pi_{course\_id, title}(course)$ first.

There are other options to consider for evaluating our query. We do not care about the order in which attributes appear in a join, since it is easy to change the order before displaying the result. Thus, for all relations r_1 and r_2:

$$r_1 \bowtie r_2 = r_2 \bowtie r_1$$

That is, natural join is commutative (equivalence rule 5).

Using the associativity and commutativity of the natural join (rules 5 and 6), consider the following relational-algebra expression:

$$(instructor \bowtie \Pi_{course\_id, title}(course)) \bowtie teaches$$

Note that there are no attributes in common between $\Pi_{course\_id, title}(course)$ and *instructor*, so the join is just a Cartesian product. If there are a tuples in *instructor* and b tuples in $\Pi_{course\_id, title}(course)$, this Cartesian product generates $a * b$ tuples, one for every possible pair of instructor tuple and course (without regard for whether the instructor taught the course). This Cartesian product would produce a very large temporary relation. However, if the user had entered the preceding expression, we could use the associativity and commutativity of the natural join to transform this expression to the more efficient expression:

$$(instructor \bowtie teaches) \bowtie \Pi_{course\_id, title}(course)$$

13.2.4 Enumeration of Equivalent Expressions

Query optimizers use equivalence rules to systematically generate expressions equivalent to the given query expression. Conceptually, this can be done as outlined in Figure 13.5. The process proceeds as follows. Given a query expression E, the set of equivalent expressions EQ initially contains only E. Now, each expression in EQ is matched with each equivalence rule. If an expression, say E_i, of any subexpression e_i of E_i (which could, as a special case, be E_i itself) matches one side of an equivalence rule, the optimizer generates a new expression where e_i is transformed to match the other side of the rule. The resultant expression is added to EQ. This process continues until no more new expressions can be generated.

The preceding process is extremely costly both in space and in time, but optimizers can greatly reduce both the space and time cost, using two key ideas.

1. If we generate an expression E' from an expression E_1 by using an equivalence rule on subexpression e_i, then E' and E_1 have identical subexpressions

procedure genAllEquivalent(E)
$EQ = \{E\}$
repeat
    Match each expression E_i in EQ with each equivalence rule R_j
    if any subexpression e_i of E_i matches one side of R_j
        Create a new expression E' which is identical to E_i, except that
            e_i is transformed to match the other side of R_j
        Add E' to EQ if it is not already present in EQ
until no new expression can be added to EQ

Figure 13.5 Procedure to generate all equivalent expressions.

except for e_i and its transformation. Even e_i and its transformed version usually share many identical subexpressions. Expression-representation techniques that allow both expressions to point to shared subexpressions can reduce the space requirement significantly.

2. It is not always necessary to generate every expression that can be generated with the equivalence rules. If an optimizer takes cost estimates of evaluation into account, it may be able to avoid examining some of the expressions, as we shall see in Section 13.4. We can reduce the time required for optimization by using techniques such as these.

We revisit these issues in Section 13.4.2.

13.3   Estimating Statistics of Expression Results

The cost of an operation depends on the size and other statistics of its inputs. Given an expression such as $a \bowtie (b \bowtie c)$ to estimate the cost of joining a with $(b \bowtie c)$, we need to have estimates of statistics such as the size of $b \bowtie c$.

In this section, we first list some statistics about database relations that are stored in database-system catalogs, and then show how to use the statistics to estimate statistics on the results of various relational operations.

One thing that will become clear later in this section is that the estimates are not very accurate, since they are based on assumptions that may not hold exactly. A query-evaluation plan that has the lowest estimated execution cost may therefore not actually have the lowest actual execution cost. However, real-world experience has shown that even if estimates are not precise, the plans with the lowest estimated costs usually have actual execution costs that are either the lowest actual execution costs, or are close to the lowest actual execution costs.

13.3.1   Catalog Information

The database-system catalog stores the following statistical information about database relations:

- n_r, the number of tuples in the relation r.

- b_r, the number of blocks containing tuples of relation r.

- l_r, the size of a tuple of relation r in bytes.

- f_r, the blocking factor of relation r —that is, the number of tuples of relation r that fit into one block.

- $V(A, r)$, the number of distinct values that appear in the relation r for attribute A. This value is the same as the size of $\Pi_A(r)$. If A is a key for relation r, $V(A, r)$ is n_r.

The last statistic, $V(A, r)$, can also be maintained for sets of attributes, if desired, instead of just for individual attributes. Thus, given a set of attributes, A, $V(A, r)$ is the size of $\Pi_A(r)$.

If we assume that the tuples of relation r are stored together physically in a file, the following equation holds:

$$b_r = \left\lceil \frac{n_r}{f_r} \right\rceil$$

Statistics about indices, such as the heights of B^+-tree indices and number of leaf pages in the indices, are also maintained in the catalog.

If we wish to maintain accurate statistics, then, every time a relation is modified, we must also update the statistics. This update incurs a substantial amount of overhead. Therefore, most systems do not update the statistics on every modification. Instead, they update the statistics during periods of light system load. As a result, the statistics used for choosing a query-processing strategy may not be completely accurate. However, if not too many updates occur in the intervals between the updates of the statistics, the statistics will be sufficiently accurate to provide a good estimation of the relative costs of the different plans.

The statistical information noted here is simplified. Real-world optimizers often maintain further statistical information to improve the accuracy of their cost estimates of evaluation plans. For instance, most databases store the distribution of values for each attribute as a **histogram**: in a histogram the values for the attribute are divided into a number of ranges, and with each range the histogram associates the number of tuples whose attribute value lies in that range. Figure 13.6 shows an example of a histogram for an integer-valued attribute that takes values in the range 1 to 25.

Histograms used in database systems usually record the number of distinct values in each range, in addition to the number of tuples with attribute values in that range.

As an example of a histogram, the range of values for an attribute *age* of a relation *person* could be divided into 0–9, 10–19, ..., 90–99 (assuming a maximum age of 99). With each range we store a count of the number of *person* tuples whose *age* values lie in that range, and the number of distinct age values that lie in that

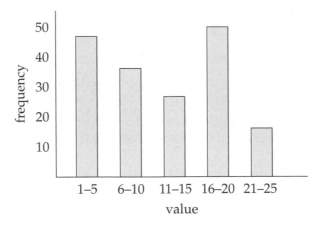

Figure 13.6 Example of histogram.

range. Without such histogram information, an optimizer would have to assume that the distribution of values is uniform; that is, each range has the same count.

A histogram takes up only a little space, so histograms on several different attributes can be stored in the system catalog. There are several types of histograms used in database systems. For example, an **equi-width histogram** divides the range of values into equal-sized ranges, whereas an **equi-depth** histogram adjusts the boundaries of the ranges such that each range has the same number of values.

13.3.2 Selection Size Estimation

The size estimate of the result of a selection operation depends on the selection predicate. We first consider a single equality predicate, then a single comparison predicate, and finally combinations of predicates.

- $\sigma_{A=a}(r)$: If we assume uniform distribution of values (that is, each value appears with equal probability), the selection result can be estimated to have $n_r/V(A, r)$ tuples, assuming that the value a appears in attribute A of some record of r. The assumption that the value a in the selection appears in some record is generally true, and cost estimates often make it implicitly. However, it is often not realistic to assume that each value appears with equal probability. The *course_id* attribute in the *takes* relation is an example where the assumption is not valid. It is reasonable to expect that a popular undergraduate course will have many more students than a smaller specialized graduate course. Therefore, certain *course_id* values appear with greater probability than do others. Despite the fact that the uniform-distribution assumption is often not correct, it is a reasonable approximation of reality in many cases, and it helps us to keep our presentation relatively simple.

  If a histogram is available on attribute A, we can locate the range that contains the value a, and modify the above-mentioned estimate $n_r/V(A, r)$

COMPUTING AND MAINTAINING STATISTICS

Conceptually, statistics on relations can be thought of as materialized views, which should be automatically maintained when relations are modified. Unfortunately, keeping statistics up-to-date on every insert, delete or update to the database can be very expensive. On the other hand, optimizers generally do not need exact statistics: an error of a few percent may result in a plan that is not quite optimal being chosen, but the alternative plan chosen is likely to have a cost which is within a few percent of the optimal cost. Thus, it is acceptable to have statistics that are approximate.

Database systems reduce the cost of generating and maintaining statistics, as outlined below, by exploiting the fact that statistics can be approximate.

- Statistics are often computed from a sample of the underlying data, instead of examining the entire collection of data. For example, a fairly accurate histogram can be computed from a sample of a few thousand tuples, even on a relation that has millions, or hundreds of millions of records. However, the sample used must be a **random sample**; a sample that is not random may have an excessive representation of one part of the relation, and can give misleading results. For example, if we used a sample of instructors to compute a histogram on salaries, if the sample has an overrepresentation of lower-paid instructors the histogram would result in wrong estimates. Database systems today routinely use random sampling to create statistics. See the bibliographic notes for references on sampling.

- Statistics are not maintained on every update to the database. In fact, some database systems never update statistics automatically. They rely on database administrators periodically running a command to update statistics. Oracle and PostgreSQL provide an SQL command called **analyze** that generates statistics on specified relations, or on all relations. IBM DB2 supports an equivalent command called **runstats**. See the system manuals for details. You should be aware that optimizers sometimes choose very bad plans due to incorrect statistics. Many database systems, such as IBM DB2, Oracle, and SQL Server, update statistics automatically at certain points of time. For example, the system can keep approximate track of how many tuples there are in a relation and recompute statistics if this number changes significantly. Another approach is to compare estimated cardinalities of a relation scan with actual cardinalities when a query is executed, and if they differ significantly, initiate an update of statistics for that relation.

by using the frequency count for that range instead of n_r, and the number of distinct values that occurs in that range instead of $V(A, r)$.

- $\sigma_{A \leq v}(r)$: Consider a selection of the form $\sigma_{A \leq v}(r)$. If the actual value used in the comparison (v) is available at the time of cost estimation, a more accurate estimate can be made. The lowest and highest values ($\min(A, r)$ and $\max(A, r)$) for the attribute can be stored in the catalog. Assuming that values are uniformly distributed, we can estimate the number of records that will satisfy the condition $A \leq v$ as 0 if $v < \min(A, r)$, as n_r if $v \geq \max(A, r)$, and:

$$n_r \cdot \frac{v - \min(A, r)}{\max(A, r) - \min(A, r)}$$

otherwise.

If a histogram is available on attribute A, we can get a more accurate estimate; we leave the details as an exercise for you. In some cases, such as when the query is part of a stored procedure, the value v may not be available when the query is optimized. In such cases, we assume that approximately one-half the records will satisfy the comparison condition. That is, we assume the result has $n_r / 2$ tuples; the estimate may be very inaccurate, but is the best we can do without any further information.

- Complex selections:

  ○ **Conjunction:** A *conjunctive selection* is a selection of the form:

  $$\sigma_{\theta_1 \wedge \theta_2 \wedge \cdots \wedge \theta_n}(r)$$

  We can estimate the result size of such a selection: For each θ_i, we estimate the size of the selection $\sigma_{\theta_i}(r)$, denoted by s_i, as described previously. Thus, the probability that a tuple in the relation satisfies selection condition θ_i is s_i / n_r.

  The preceding probability is called the **selectivity** of the selection $\sigma_{\theta_i}(r)$. Assuming that the conditions are *independent* of each other, the probability that a tuple satisfies all the conditions is simply the product of all these probabilities. Thus, we estimate the number of tuples in the full selection as:

  $$n_r * \frac{s_1 * s_2 * \cdots * s_n}{n_r^n}$$

  ○ **Disjunction:** A *disjunctive selection* is a selection of the form:

  $$\sigma_{\theta_1 \vee \theta_2 \vee \cdots \vee \theta_n}(r)$$

  A disjunctive condition is satisfied by the union of all records satisfying the individual, simple conditions θ_i.

  As before, let s_i / n_r denote the probability that a tuple satisfies condition θ_i. The probability that the tuple will satisfy the disjunction is then 1 minus the probability that it will satisfy *none* of the conditions:

  $$1 - (1 - \frac{s_1}{n_r}) * (1 - \frac{s_2}{n_r}) * \cdots * (1 - \frac{s_n}{n_r})$$

  Multiplying this value by n_r gives us the estimated number of tuples that satisfy the selection.

○ **Negation:** In the absence of nulls, the result of a selection $\sigma_{\neg\theta}(r)$ is simply the tuples of r that are not in $\sigma_\theta(r)$. We already know how to estimate the number of tuples in $\sigma_\theta(r)$. The number of tuples in $\sigma_{\neg\theta}(r)$ is therefore estimated to be $n(r)$ minus the estimated number of tuples in $\sigma_\theta(r)$.

We can account for nulls by estimating the number of tuples for which the condition θ would evaluate to *unknown*, and subtracting that number from the above estimate, ignoring nulls. Estimating that number would require extra statistics to be maintained in the catalog.

13.3.3 Join Size Estimation

In this section, we see how to estimate the size of the result of a join.

The Cartesian product $r \times s$ contains $n_r * n_s$ tuples. Each tuple of $r \times s$ occupies $l_r + l_s$ bytes, from which we can calculate the size of the Cartesian product.

Estimating the size of a natural join is somewhat more complicated than estimating the size of a selection or of a Cartesian product. Let $r(R)$ and $s(S)$ be relations.

- If $R \cap S = \emptyset$—that is, the relations have no attribute in common—then $r \bowtie s$ is the same as $r \times s$, and we can use our estimation technique for Cartesian products.

- If $R \cap S$ is a key for R, then we know that a tuple of s will join with at most one tuple from r. Therefore, the number of tuples in $r \bowtie s$ is no greater than the number of tuples in s. The case where $R \cap S$ is a key for S is symmetric to the case just described. If $R \cap S$ forms a foreign key of S, referencing R, the number of tuples in $r \bowtie s$ is exactly the same as the number of tuples in s.

- The most difficult case is when $R \cap S$ is a key for neither R nor S. In this case, we assume, as we did for selections, that each value appears with equal probability. Consider a tuple t of r, and assume $R \cap S = \{A\}$. We estimate that tuple t produces:

$$\frac{n_s}{V(A, s)}$$

tuples in $r \bowtie s$, since this number is the average number of tuples in s with a given value for the attributes A. Considering all the tuples in r, we estimate that there are:

$$\frac{n_r * n_s}{V(A, s)}$$

tuples in $r \bowtie s$. Observe that, if we reverse the roles of r and s in the preceding estimate, we obtain an estimate of:

$$\frac{n_r * n_s}{V(A, r)}$$

tuples in $r \bowtie s$. These two estimates differ if $V(A, r) \neq V(A, s)$. If this situation occurs, there are likely to be dangling tuples that do not participate in the join. Thus, the lower of the two estimates is probably the more accurate one.

The preceding estimate of join size may be too high if the $V(A, r)$ values for attribute A in r have few values in common with the $V(A, s)$ values for attribute A in s. However, this situation is unlikely to happen in the real world, since dangling tuples either do not exist or constitute only a small fraction of the tuples, in most real-world relations.

More important, the preceding estimate depends on the assumption that each value appears with equal probability. More sophisticated techniques for size estimation have to be used if this assumption does not hold. For example, if we have histograms on the join attributes of both relations, and both histograms have the same ranges, then we can use the above estimation technique within each range, using the number of rows with values in the range instead of n_r or n_s, and the number of distinct values in that range, instead of $V(A, r)$ or $V(A, s)$. We then add up the size estimates obtained for each range to get the overall size estimate. We leave the case where both relations have histograms on the join attribute, but the histograms have different ranges, as an exercise for you.

We can estimate the size of a theta join $r \bowtie_\theta s$ by rewriting the join as $\sigma_\theta(r \times s)$, and using the size estimates for Cartesian products along with the size estimates for selections, which we saw in Section 13.3.2.

To illustrate all these ways of estimating join sizes, consider the expression:

$$student \bowtie takes$$

Assume the following catalog information about the two relations:

- $n_{student} = 5000$.

- $f_{student} = 50$, which implies that $b_{student} = 5000/50 = 100$.

- $n_{takes} = 10000$.

- $f_{takes} = 25$, which implies that $b_{takes} = 10000/25 = 400$.

- $V(ID, takes) = 2500$, which implies that only half the students have taken any course (this is unrealistic, but we use it to show that our size estimates are correct even in this case), and on average, each student who has taken a course has taken four courses.

The attribute ID in *takes* is a foreign key on *student*, and null values do not occur in *takes.ID*, since *ID* is part of the primary key of *takes*; thus, the size of $student \bowtie takes$ is exactly n_{takes}, which is 10000.

We now compute the size estimates for $student \bowtie takes$ without using information about foreign keys. Since $V(ID, takes) = 2500$ and $V(ID, student) = 5000$, the two estimates we get are $5000 * 10000/2500 = 20000$ and $5000 * 10000/5000 = 10000$, and we choose the lower one. In this case, the lower of these estimates is the same as that which we computed earlier from information about foreign keys.

13.3.4 Size Estimation for Other Operations

We outline below how to estimate the sizes of the results of other relational-algebra operations.

- **Projection:** The estimated size (number of records or number of tuples) of a projection of the form $\Pi_A(r)$ is $V(A, r)$, since projection eliminates duplicates.

- **Aggregation:** The size of ${}_A\mathcal{G}_F(r)$ is simply $V(A, r)$, since there is one tuple in ${}_A\mathcal{G}_F(r)$ for each distinct value of A.

- **Set operations:** If the two inputs to a set operation are selections on the same relation, we can rewrite the set operation as disjunctions, conjunctions, or negations. For example, $\sigma_{\theta_1}(r) \cup \sigma_{\theta_2}(r)$ can be rewritten as $\sigma_{\theta_1 \vee \theta_2}(r)$. Similarly, we can rewrite intersections as conjunctions, and we can rewrite set difference by using negation, so long as the two relations participating in the set operations are selections on the same relation. We can then use the estimates for selections involving conjunctions, disjunctions, and negation in Section 13.3.2.

  If the inputs are not selections on the same relation, we estimate the sizes this way: The estimated size of $r \cup s$ is the sum of the sizes of r and s. The estimated size of $r \cap s$ is the minimum of the sizes of r and s. The estimated size of $r - s$ is the same size as r. All three estimates may be inaccurate, but provide upper bounds on the sizes.

- **Outer join:** The estimated size of $r ⟕ s$ is the size of $r ⋈ s$ plus the size of r; that of $r ⟖ s$ is symmetric, while that of $r ⟗ s$ is the size of $r ⋈ s$ plus the sizes of r and s. All three estimates may be inaccurate, but provide upper bounds on the sizes.

13.3.5 Estimation of Number of Distinct Values

For selections, the number of distinct values of an attribute (or set of attributes) A in the result of a selection, $V(A, \sigma_\theta(r))$, can be estimated in these ways:

- If the selection condition θ forces A to take on a specified value (e.g., $A = 3$), $V(A, \sigma_\theta(r)) = 1$.

- If θ forces A to take on one of a specified set of values (e.g., $(A = 1 \vee A = 3 \vee A = 4)$), then $V(A, \sigma_\theta(r))$ is set to the number of specified values.

- If the selection condition θ is of the form $A\ op\ v$, where op is a comparison operator, $V(A, \sigma_\theta(r))$ is estimated to be $V(A, r) * s$, where s is the selectivity of the selection.

- In all other cases of selections, we assume that the distribution of A values is independent of the distribution of the values on which selection conditions are specified, and we use an approximate estimate of $\min(V(A, r), n_{\sigma_\theta(r)})$. A more accurate estimate can be derived for this case using probability theory, but the above approximation works fairly well.

For joins, the number of distinct values of an attribute (or set of attributes) A in the result of a join, $V(A, r \bowtie s)$, can be estimated in these ways:

- If all attributes in A are from r, $V(A, r \bowtie s)$ is estimated as $\min(V(A, r), n_{r \bowtie s})$, and similarly if all attributes in A are from s, $V(A, r \bowtie s)$ is estimated to be $\min(V(A, s), n_{r \bowtie s})$.

- If A contains attributes $A1$ from r and $A2$ from s, then $V(A, r \bowtie s)$ is estimated as:

$$\min(V(A1, r) * V(A2 - A1, s), V(A1 - A2, r) * V(A2, s), n_{r \bowtie s})$$

Note that some attributes may be in $A1$ as well as in $A2$, and $A1 - A2$ and $A2 - A1$ denote, respectively, attributes in A that are only from r and attributes in A that are only from s. Again, more accurate estimates can be derived by using probability theory, but the above approximations work fairly well.

The estimates of distinct values are straightforward for projections: They are the same in $\Pi_A(r)$ as in r. The same holds for grouping attributes of aggregation. For results of **sum**, **count**, and **average**, we can assume, for simplicity, that all aggregate values are distinct. For **min**(A) and **max**(A), the number of distinct values can be estimated as $\min(V(A, r), V(G, r))$, where G denotes the grouping attributes. We omit details of estimating distinct values for other operations.

13.4   Choice of Evaluation Plans

Generation of expressions is only part of the query-optimization process, since each operation in the expression can be implemented with different algorithms. An evaluation plan defines exactly what algorithm should be used for each operation, and how the execution of the operations should be coordinated.

Given an evaluation plan, we can estimate its cost using statistics estimated by the techniques in Section 13.3 coupled with cost estimates for various algorithms and evaluation methods described in Chapter 12.

A **cost-based optimizer** explores the space of all query-evaluation plans that are equivalent to the given query, and chooses the one with the least estimated cost. We have seen how equivalence rules can be used to generate equivalent plans. However, cost-based optimization with arbitrary equivalence rules is fairly complicated. We first cover a simpler version of cost-based optimization, which involves only join-order and join algorithm selection, in Section 13.4.1. Later in Section 13.4.2 we briefly sketch how a general-purpose optimizer based on equivalence rules can be built, without going into details.

Exploring the space of all possible plans may be too expensive for complex queries. Most optimizers include heuristics to reduce the cost of query optimization, at the potential risk of not finding the optimal plan. We study some such heuristics in Section 13.4.3.

13.4.1   Cost-Based Join Order Selection

The most common type of query in SQL consists of a join of a few relations, with join predicates and selections specified in the **where** clause. In this section we consider the problem of choosing the optimal join order for such a query.

For a complex join query, the number of different query plans that are equivalent to the query can be large. As an illustration, consider the expression:

$$r_1 \bowtie r_2 \bowtie \cdots \bowtie r_n$$

where the joins are expressed without any ordering. With $n = 3$, there are 12 different join orderings:

$r_1 \bowtie (r_2 \bowtie r_3)$	$r_1 \bowtie (r_3 \bowtie r_2)$	$(r_2 \bowtie r_3) \bowtie r_1$	$(r_3 \bowtie r_2) \bowtie r_1$
$r_2 \bowtie (r_1 \bowtie r_3)$	$r_2 \bowtie (r_3 \bowtie r_1)$	$(r_1 \bowtie r_3) \bowtie r_2$	$(r_3 \bowtie r_1) \bowtie r_2$
$r_3 \bowtie (r_1 \bowtie r_2)$	$r_3 \bowtie (r_2 \bowtie r_1)$	$(r_1 \bowtie r_2) \bowtie r_3$	$(r_2 \bowtie r_1) \bowtie r_3$

In general, with n relations, there are $(2(n-1))!/(n-1)!$ different join orders. (We leave the computation of this expression for you to do in Exercise 13.10.) For joins involving small numbers of relations, this number is acceptable; for example, with $n = 5$, the number is 1680. However, as n increases, this number rises quickly. With $n = 7$, the number is 665,280; with $n = 10$, the number is greater than 17.6 billion!

Luckily, it is not necessary to generate all the expressions equivalent to a given expression. For example, suppose we want to find the best join order of the form:

$$(r_1 \bowtie r_2 \bowtie r_3) \bowtie r_4 \bowtie r_5$$

which represents all join orders where r_1, r_2, and r_3 are joined first (in some order), and the result is joined (in some order) with r_4 and r_5. There are 12 different join orders for computing $r_1 \bowtie r_2 \bowtie r_3$, and 12 orders for computing the join of this result with r_4 and r_5. Thus, there appear to be 144 join orders to examine. However, once we have found the best join order for the subset of relations $\{r_1, r_2, r_3\}$, we can use that order for further joins with r_4 and r_5, and can ignore all costlier join orders of $r_1 \bowtie r_2 \bowtie r_3$. Thus, instead of 144 choices to examine, we need to examine only $12 + 12$ choices.

Using this idea, we can develop a *dynamic-programming* algorithm for finding optimal join orders. Dynamic-programming algorithms store results of computations and reuse them, a procedure that can reduce execution time greatly.

A recursive procedure implementing the dynamic-programming algorithm appears in Figure 13.7. The procedure applies selections on individual relations at the earliest possible point, that is, when the relations are accessed. It is easiest to understand the procedure assuming that all joins are natural joins, although the procedure works unchanged with any join condition. With arbitrary join conditions, the join of two subexpressions is understood to include all join conditions that relate attributes from the two subexpressions.

procedure FindBestPlan(S)
    if (*bestplan*[S].*cost* $\neq \infty$) /* *bestplan*[S] already computed */
        return *bestplan*[S]
    if (S contains only 1 relation)
        set *bestplan*[S].*plan* and *bestplan*[S].*cost* based on best way of accessing S
    else for each non-empty subset S1 of S such that S1 $\neq$ S
        P1 = FindBestPlan(S1)
        P2 = FindBestPlan(S − S1)
        A = best algorithm for joining results of P1 and P2
        cost = P1.*cost* + P2.*cost* + cost of A
        if cost < *bestplan*[S].*cost*
            bestplan[S].*cost* = cost
            bestplan[S].*plan* = "execute P1.*plan*; execute P2.*plan*;
                          join results of P1 and P2 using A"
    return *bestplan*[S]

Figure 13.7 Dynamic-programming algorithm for join order optimization.

The procedure stores the evaluation plans it computes in an associative array *bestplan*, which is indexed by sets of relations. Each element of the associative array contains two components: the cost of the best plan of S, and the plan itself. The value of *bestplan*[S].*cost* is assumed to be initialized to ∞ if *bestplan*[S] has not yet been computed.

The procedure first checks if the best plan for computing the join of the given set of relations S has been computed already (and stored in the associative array *bestplan*); if so, it returns the already computed plan.

If S contains only one relation, the best way of accessing S (taking selections on S, if any, into account) is recorded in *bestplan*. This may involve using an index to identify tuples, and then fetching the tuples (often referred to as an *index scan*), or scanning the entire relation (often referred to as a *relation scan*).[1] If there is any selection condition on S, other than those ensured by an index scan, a selection operation is added to the plan, to ensure all selections on S are satisfied.

Otherwise, if S contains more than one relation, the procedure tries every way of dividing S into two disjoint subsets. For each division, the procedure recursively finds the best plans for each of the two subsets, and then computes the cost of the overall plan by using that division.[2] The procedure picks the cheapest plan from among all the alternatives for dividing S into two sets. The cheapest plan and its cost are stored in the array *bestplan*, and returned by the

---

[1] If an index contains all the attributes of a relation that are used in a query, it is possible to perform an *index-only scan*, which retrieves the required attribute values from the index, without fetching actual tuples.
[2] Note that an indexed nested loops join is considered for joining P1 and P2, with P2 as the inner relation, if P2 has only a single relation, say r, and an index is available on the join attributes of r. Plan P2 may contain an indexed access to r, based on selection conditions on r. To allow indexed nested loops join to be used, the index lookup using the selection condition on r would be dropped from P2; instead, the selection condition would be checked on tuples returned from the index on the join attributes of r.

procedure. The time complexity of the procedure can be shown to be $O(3^n)$ (see Practice Exercise 13.11).

Actually, the order in which tuples are generated by the join of a set of relations is also important for finding the best overall join order, since it can affect the cost of further joins (for instance, if merge join is used). A particular sort order of the tuples is said to be an **interesting sort order** if it could be useful for a later operation. For instance, generating the result of $r_1 \Join r_2 \Join r_3$ sorted on the attributes common with r_4 or r_5 may be useful, but generating it sorted on the attributes common to only r_1 and r_2 is not useful. Using merge join for computing $r_1 \Join r_2 \Join r_3$ may be costlier than using some other join technique, but it may provide an output sorted in an interesting sort order.

Hence, it is not sufficient to find the best join order for each subset of the set of n given relations. Instead, we have to find the best join order for each subset, for each interesting sort order of the join result for that subset. The number of subsets of n relations is 2^n. The number of interesting sort orders is generally not large. Thus, about 2^n join expressions need to be stored. The dynamic-programming algorithm for finding the best join order can be easily extended to handle sort orders. The cost of the extended algorithm depends on the number of interesting orders for each subset of relations; since this number has been found to be small in practice, the cost remains at $O(3^n)$. With $n = 10$, this number is around 59,000, which is much better than the 17.6 billion different join orders. More important, the storage required is much less than before, since we need to store only one join order for each interesting sort order of each of 1024 subsets of $r_1, \ldots, r_{10}$. Although both numbers still increase rapidly with n, commonly occurring joins usually have less than 10 relations, and can be handled easily.

13.4.2 Cost-Based Optimization with Equivalence Rules

The join order optimization technique we just saw handles the most common class of queries, which perform an inner join of a set of relations. However, clearly many queries use other features, such as aggregation, outer join, and nested queries, which are not addressed by join order selection.

Many optimizers follow an approach based on using heuristic transformations to handle constructs other than joins, and applying the cost-based join order selection algorithm to subexpressions involving only joins and selections. Details of such heuristics are for the most part specific to individual optimizers, and we do not cover them. However, heuristic transformations to handle nested queries are widely used, and are considered in more detail in Section 13.4.4.

In this section, however, we outline how to create a general-purpose cost-based optimizer based on equivalence rules, which can handle a wide variety of query constructs.

The benefit of using equivalence rules is that it is easy to extend the optimizer with new rules to handle different query constructs. For example, nested queries can be represented using extended relational-algebra constructs, and transformations of nested queries can be expressed as equivalence rules. We have already seen equivalence rules with aggregation operations, and equivalence rules can also be created for outer joins.

In Section 13.2.4, we saw how an optimizer could systematically generate all expressions equivalent to the given query. The procedure for generating equivalent expressions can be modified to generate all possible evaluation plans as follows: A new class of equivalence rules, called **physical equivalence rules**, is added that allows a logical operation, such as a join, to be transformed to a physical operation, such as a hash join, or a nested-loops join. By adding such rules to the original set of equivalence rules, the procedure can generate all possible evaluation plans. The cost estimation techniques we have seen earlier can then be used to choose the optimal (that is, the least-cost) plan.

However, the procedure shown in Section 13.2.4 is very expensive, even if we do not consider generation of evaluation plans. To make the approach work efficiently requires the following:

1. A space-efficient representation of expressions that avoids making multiple copies of the same subexpressions when equivalence rules are applied.

2. Efficient techniques for detecting duplicate derivations of the same expression.

3. A form of dynamic programming based on **memoization**, which stores the optimal query evaluation plan for a subexpression when it is optimized for the first time; subsequent requests to optimize the same subexpression are handled by returning the already memoized plan.

4. Techniques that avoid generating all possible equivalent plans, by keeping track of the cheapest plan generated for any subexpression up to any point of time, and pruning away any plan that is more expensive than the cheapest plan found so far for that subexpression.

The details are more complex than we wish to deal with here. This approach was pioneered by the Volcano research project, and the query optimizer of SQL Server is based on this approach. See the bibliographical notes for references containing further information.

13.4.3   Heuristics in Optimization

A drawback of cost-based optimization is the cost of optimization itself. Although the cost of query optimization can be reduced by clever algorithms, the number of different evaluation plans for a query can be very large, and finding the optimal plan from this set requires a lot of computational effort. Hence, optimizers use **heuristics** to reduce the cost of optimization.

An example of a heuristic rule is the following rule for transforming relational-algebra queries:

- Perform selection operations as early as possible.

A heuristic optimizer would use this rule without finding out whether the cost is reduced by this transformation. In the first transformation example in Section 13.2, the selection operation was pushed into a join.

We say that the preceding rule is a heuristic because it usually, but not always, helps to reduce the cost. For an example of where it can result in an increase in cost, consider an expression $\sigma_\theta(r \bowtie s)$, where the condition θ refers to only attributes in s. The selection can certainly be performed before the join. However, if r is extremely small compared to s, and if there is an index on the join attributes of s, but no index on the attributes used by θ, then it is probably a bad idea to perform the selection early. Performing the selection early—that is, directly on s—would require doing a scan of all tuples in s. It is probably cheaper, in this case, to compute the join by using the index, and then to reject tuples that fail the selection.

The projection operation, like the selection operation, reduces the size of relations. Thus, whenever we need to generate a temporary relation, it is advantageous to apply immediately any projections that are possible. This advantage suggests a companion to the "perform selections early" heuristic:

- Perform projections early.

It is usually better to perform selections earlier than projections, since selections have the potential to reduce the sizes of relations greatly, and selections enable the use of indices to access tuples. An example similar to the one used for the selection heuristic should convince you that this heuristic does not always reduce the cost.

Most practical query optimizers have further heuristics to reduce the cost of optimization. For example, many query optimizers, such as the System R optimizer,[3] do not consider all join orders, but rather restrict the search to particular kinds of join orders. The System R optimizer considers only those join orders where the right operand of each join is one of the initial relations $r_1, \ldots, r_n$. Such join orders are called **left-deep join orders**. Left-deep join orders are particularly convenient for pipelined evaluation, since the right operand is a stored relation, and thus only one input to each join is pipelined.

Figure 13.8 illustrates the difference between left-deep join trees and non-left-deep join trees. The time it takes to consider all left-deep join orders is $O(n!)$, which is much less than the time to consider all join orders. With the use of dynamic-programming optimizations, the System R optimizer can find the best join order in time $O(n2^n)$. Contrast this cost with the $O(3^n)$ time required to find the best overall join order. The System R optimizer uses heuristics to push selections and projections down the query tree.

A heuristic approach to reduce the cost of join-order selection, which was originally used in some versions of Oracle, works roughly this way: For an n-way join, it considers n evaluation plans. Each plan uses a left-deep join order, starting

---

[3]System R was one of the first implementations of SQL, and its optimizer pioneered the idea of cost-based join-order optimization.

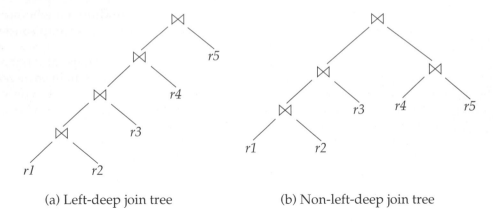

(a) Left-deep join tree   (b) Non-left-deep join tree

Figure 13.8   Left-deep join trees.

with a different one of the n relations. The heuristic constructs the join order for each of the n evaluation plans by repeatedly selecting the "best" relation to join next, on the basis of a ranking of the available access paths. Either nested-loop or sort-merge join is chosen for each of the joins, depending on the available access paths. Finally, the heuristic chooses one of the n evaluation plans in a heuristic manner, on the basis of minimizing the number of nested-loop joins that do not have an index available on the inner relation and on the number of sort-merge joins.

Query-optimization approaches that apply heuristic plan choices for some parts of the query, with cost-based choice based on generation of alternative access plans on other parts of the query, have been adopted in several systems. The approach used in System R and in its successor, the Starburst project, is a hierarchical procedure based on the nested-block concept of SQL. The cost-based optimization techniques described here are used for each block of the query separately. The optimizers in several database products, such as IBM DB2 and Oracle, are based on the above approach, with extensions to handle other operations such as aggregation. For compound SQL queries (using the ∪, ∩, or − operation), the optimizer processes each component separately, and combines the evaluation plans to form the overall evaluation plan.

Most optimizers allow a cost budget to be specified for query optimization. The search for the optimal plan is terminated when the **optimization cost budget** is exceeded, and the best plan found up to that point is returned. The budget itself may be set dynamically; for example, if a cheap plan is found for a query, the budget may be reduced, on the premise that there is no point spending a lot of time optimizing the query if the best plan found so far is already quite cheap. On the other hand, if the best plan found so far is expensive, it makes sense to invest more time in optimization, which could result in a significant reduction in execution time. To best exploit this idea, optimizers usually first apply cheap heuristics to find a plan, and then start full cost-based optimization with a budget based on the heuristically chosen plan.

Many applications execute the same query repeatedly, but with different values for the constants. For example, a university application may repeatedly execute a query to find the courses for which a student has registered, but each time for a different student with a different value for the student ID. As a heuristic, many optimizers optimize a query once, with whatever values were provided for the constants when the query was first submitted, and cache the query plan. Whenever the query is executed again, perhaps with new values for constants, the cached query plan is reused (using new values for the constants, of course). The optimal plan for the new constants may differ from the optimal plan for the initial values, but as a heuristic the cached plan is reused.[4] Caching and reuse of query plans is referred to as **plan caching**.

Even with the use of heuristics, cost-based query optimization imposes a substantial overhead on query processing. However, the added cost of cost-based query optimization is usually more than offset by the saving at query-execution time, which is dominated by slow disk accesses. The difference in execution time between a good plan and a bad one may be huge, making query optimization essential. The achieved saving is magnified in those applications that run on a regular basis, where a query can be optimized once, and the selected query plan can be used each time the query is executed. Therefore, most commercial systems include relatively sophisticated optimizers. The bibliographical notes give references to descriptions of the query optimizers of actual database systems.

13.4.4 Optimizing Nested Subqueries**

SQL conceptually treats nested subqueries in the **where** clause as functions that take parameters and return either a single value or a set of values (possibly an empty set). The parameters are the variables from an outer level query that are used in the nested subquery (these variables are called **correlation variables**). For instance, suppose we have the following query, to find the names of all instructors who taught a course in 2007:

> **select** *name*
> **from** *instructor*
> **where exists** (**select** *
>   **from** *teaches*
>   **where** *instructor.ID* = *teaches.ID*
>   **and** *teaches.year* = 2007);

Conceptually, the subquery can be viewed as a function that takes a parameter (here, *instructor.ID*) and returns the set of all courses taught in 2007 by instructors (with the same *ID*).

---

[4]For the student registration query, the plan would almost certainly be the same for any student ID. But a query that took a range of student IDs, and returned registration information for all student IDs in that range, would probably have a different optimal plan if the range is very small than if the range is large.

SQL evaluates the overall query (conceptually) by computing the Cartesian product of the relations in the outer **from** clause and then testing the predicates in the **where** clause for each tuple in the product. In the preceding example, the predicate tests if the result of the subquery evaluation is empty.

This technique for evaluating a query with a nested subquery is called **correlated evaluation**. Correlated evaluation is not very efficient, since the subquery is separately evaluated for each tuple in the outer level query. A large number of random disk I/O operations may result.

SQL optimizers therefore attempt to transform nested subqueries into joins, where possible. Efficient join algorithms help avoid expensive random I/O. Where the transformation is not possible, the optimizer keeps the subqueries as separate expressions, optimizes them separately, and then evaluates them by correlated evaluation.

As an example of transforming a nested subquery into a join, the query in the preceding example can be rewritten as:

> **select** *name*
> **from** *instructor, teaches*
> **where** *instructor.ID = teaches.ID* **and** *teaches.year = 2007;*

(To properly reflect SQL semantics, the number of duplicate derivations should not change because of the rewriting; the rewritten query can be modified to ensure this property, as we shall see shortly.)

In the example, the nested subquery was very simple. In general, it may not be possible to directly move the nested subquery relations into the **from** clause of the outer query. Instead, we create a temporary relation that contains the results of the nested query *without* the selections using correlation variables from the outer query, and join the temporary table with the outer level query. For instance, a query of the form:

> **select** ...
> **from** L_1
> **where** P_1 **and exists (select** *
>   **from** L_2
>   **where** P_2);

where P_2 is a conjunction of simpler predicates, can be rewritten as:

> **create table** t_1 **as**
>   **select distinct** V
>   **from** L_2
>   **where** P_2^1;
> **select** ...
> **from** L_1, t_1
> **where** P_1 **and** P_2^2;

where P_2^1 contains predicates in P_2 without selections involving correlation variables, and P_2^2 reintroduces the selections involving correlation variables (with relations referenced in the predicate appropriately renamed). Here, V contains all attributes that are used in selections with correlation variables in the nested subquery.

In our example, the original query would have been transformed to:

create table t_1 **as**
    select distinct *ID*
    from *teaches*
    where *year* = 2007;
select *name*
from *instructor*, t_1
where $t_1.ID = instructor.ID$;

The query we rewrote to illustrate creation of a temporary relation can be obtained by simplifying the above transformed query, assuming the number of duplicates of each tuple does not matter.

The process of replacing a nested query by a query with a join (possibly with a temporary relation) is called **decorrelation**.

Decorrelation is more complicated when the nested subquery uses aggregation, or when the result of the nested subquery is used to test for equality, or when the condition linking the nested subquery to the outer query is **not exists**, and so on. We do not attempt to give algorithms for the general case, and instead refer you to relevant items in the bibliographical notes.

Optimization of complex nested subqueries is a difficult task, as you can infer from the above discussion, and many optimizers do only a limited amount of decorrelation. It is best to avoid using complex nested subqueries, where possible, since we cannot be sure that the query optimizer will succeed in converting them to a form that can be evaluated efficiently.

13.5 Materialized Views**

When a view is defined, normally the database stores only the query defining the view. In contrast, a **materialized view** is a view whose contents are computed and stored. Materialized views constitute redundant data, in that their contents can be inferred from the view definition and the rest of the database contents. However, it is much cheaper in many cases to read the contents of a materialized view than to compute the contents of the view by executing the query defining the view.

Materialized views are important for improving performance in some applications. Consider this view, which gives the total salary in each department:

create view *department_total_salary*(*dept_name*, *total_salary*) **as**
select *dept_name*, **sum** (*salary*)
from *instructor*
group by *dept_name*;

Suppose the total salary amount at a department is required frequently. Computing the view requires reading every *instructor* tuple pertaining to a department, and summing up the salary amounts, which can be time-consuming. In contrast, if the view definition of the total salary amount were materialized, the total salary amount could be found by looking up a single tuple in the materialized view.[5]

13.5.1   View Maintenance

A problem with materialized views is that they must be kept up-to-date when the data used in the view definition changes. For instance, if the *salary* value of an instructor is updated, the materialized view will become inconsistent with the underlying data, and it must be updated. The task of keeping a materialized view up-to-date with the underlying data is known as **view maintenance**.

Views can be maintained by manually written code: That is, every piece of code that updates the *salary* value can be modified to also update the total salary amount for the corresponding department. However, this approach is error prone, since it is easy to miss some places where the *salary* is updated, and the materialized view will then no longer match the underlying data.

Another option for maintaining materialized views is to define triggers on insert, delete, and update of each relation in the view definition. The triggers must modify the contents of the materialized view, to take into account the change that caused the trigger to fire. A simplistic way of doing so is to completely recompute the materialized view on every update.

A better option is to modify only the affected parts of the materialized view, which is known as **incremental view maintenance**. We describe how to perform incremental view maintenance in Section 13.5.2.

Modern database systems provide more direct support for incremental view maintenance. Database-system programmers no longer need to define triggers for view maintenance. Instead, once a view is declared to be materialized, the database system computes the contents of the view and incrementally updates the contents when the underlying data change.

Most database systems perform **immediate view maintenance**; that is, incremental view maintenance is performed as soon as an update occurs, as part of the updating transaction. Some database systems also support **deferred view maintenance**, where view maintenance is deferred to a later time; for example, updates may be collected throughout a day, and materialized views may be updated at night. This approach reduces the overhead on update transactions. However, materialized views with deferred view maintenance may not be consistent with the underlying relations on which they are defined.

---

[5]The difference may not be all that large for a medium-sized university, but in other settings the difference can be very large. For example, if the materialized view computed total sales of each product, from a sales relation with tens of millions of tuples, the difference between computing the aggregate from the underlying data, and looking up the materialized view can be many orders of magnitude.

13.5.2 Incremental View Maintenance

To understand how to maintain materialized views incrementally, we start off by considering individual operations, and then we see how to handle a complete expression.

The changes to a relation that can cause a materialized view to become out-of-date are inserts, deletes, and updates. To simplify our description, we replace updates to a tuple by deletion of the tuple followed by insertion of the updated tuple. Thus, we need to consider only inserts and deletes. The changes (inserts and deletes) to a relation or expression are referred to as its **differential**.

13.5.2.1 Join Operation

Consider the materialized view $v = r \bowtie s$. Suppose we modify r by inserting a set of tuples denoted by i_r. If the old value of r is denoted by r^{old}, and the new value of r by r^{new}, $r^{new} = r^{old} \cup i_r$. Now, the old value of the view, v^{old}, is given by $r^{old} \bowtie s$, and the new value v^{new} is given by $r^{new} \bowtie s$. We can rewrite $r^{new} \bowtie s$ as $(r^{old} \cup i_r) \bowtie s$, which we can again rewrite as $(r^{old} \bowtie s) \cup (i_r \bowtie s)$. In other words:

$$v^{new} = v^{old} \cup (i_r \bowtie s)$$

Thus, to update the materialized view v, we simply need to add the tuples $i_r \bowtie s$ to the old contents of the materialized view. Inserts to s are handled in an exactly symmetric fashion.

Now suppose r is modified by deleting a set of tuples denoted by d_r. Using the same reasoning as above, we get:

$$v^{new} = v^{old} - (d_r \bowtie s)$$

Deletes on s are handled in an exactly symmetric fashion.

13.5.2.2 Selection and Projection Operations

Consider a view $v = \sigma_\theta(r)$. If we modify r by inserting a set of tuples i_r, the new value of v can be computed as:

$$v^{new} = v^{old} \cup \sigma_\theta(i_r)$$

Similarly, if r is modified by deleting a set of tuples d_r, the new value of v can be computed as:

$$v^{new} = v^{old} - \sigma_\theta(d_r)$$

Projection is a more difficult operation with which to deal. Consider a materialized view $v = \Pi_A(r)$. Suppose the relation r is on the schema $R = (A, B)$, and r contains two tuples $(a, 2)$ and $(a, 3)$. Then, $\Pi_A(r)$ has a single tuple (a). If we delete the tuple $(a, 2)$ from r, we cannot delete the tuple (a) from $\Pi_A(r)$: If we did so, the result would be an empty relation, whereas in reality $\Pi_A(r)$ still has a single tuple (a). The reason is that the same tuple (a) is derived in two ways, and deleting one tuple from r removes only one of the ways of deriving (a); the other is still present.

This reason also gives us the intuition for solution: For each tuple in a projection such as $\Pi_A(r)$, we will keep a count of how many times it was derived.

When a set of tuples d_r is deleted from r, for each tuple t in d_r we do the following: Let $t.A$ denote the projection of t on the attribute A. We find $(t.A)$ in the materialized view, and decrease the count stored with it by 1. If the count becomes 0, $(t.A)$ is deleted from the materialized view.

Handling insertions is relatively straightforward. When a set of tuples i_r is inserted into r, for each tuple t in i_r we do the following: If $(t.A)$ is already present in the materialized view, we increase the count stored with it by 1. If not, we add $(t.A)$ to the materialized view, with the count set to 1.

13.5.2.3 Aggregation Operations

Aggregation operations proceed somewhat like projections. The aggregate operations in SQL are **count, sum, avg, min,** and **max:**

- **count**: Consider a materialized view $v = {}_A\mathcal{G}_{count(B)}(r)$, which computes the count of the attribute B, after grouping r by attribute A.

    When a set of tuples i_r is inserted into r, for each tuple t in i_r we do the following: We look for the group $t.A$ in the materialized view. If it is not present, we add $(t.A, 1)$ to the materialized view. If the group $t.A$ is present, we add 1 to the count of the group.

    When a set of tuples d_r is deleted from r, for each tuple t in d_r we do the following: We look for the group $t.A$ in the materialized view, and subtract 1 from the count for the group. If the count becomes 0, we delete the tuple for the group $t.A$ from the materialized view.

- **sum**: Consider a materialized view $v = {}_A\mathcal{G}_{sum(B)}(r)$.

    When a set of tuples i_r is inserted into r, for each tuple t in i_r we do the following: We look for the group $t.A$ in the materialized view. If it is not present, we add $(t.A, t.B)$ to the materialized view; in addition, we store a count of 1 associated with $(t.A, t.B)$, just as we did for projection. If the group $t.A$ is present, we add the value of $t.B$ to the aggregate value for the group, and add 1 to the count of the group.

    When a set of tuples d_r is deleted from r, for each tuple t in d_r we do the following: We look for the group $t.A$ in the materialized view, and subtract $t.B$ from the aggregate value for the group. We also subtract 1 from the count for the group, and if the count becomes 0, we delete the tuple for the group $t.A$ from the materialized view.

    Without keeping the extra count value, we would not be able to distinguish a case where the sum for a group is 0 from the case where the last tuple in a group is deleted.

- **avg**: Consider a materialized view $v = {}_A\mathcal{G}_{avg(B)}(r)$.

  Directly updating the average on an insert or delete is not possible, since it depends not only on the old average and the tuple being inserted/deleted, but also on the number of tuples in the group.

  Instead, to handle the case of **avg**, we maintain the **sum** and **count** aggregate values as described earlier, and compute the average as the sum divided by the count.

- **min, max**: Consider a materialized view $v = {}_A\mathcal{G}_{min(B)}(r)$. (The case of **max** is exactly equivalent.)

  Handling insertions on r is straightforward. Maintaining the aggregate values **min** and **max** on deletions may be more expensive. For example, if the tuple corresponding to the minimum value for a group is deleted from r, we have to look at the other tuples of r that are in the same group to find the new minimum value.

13.5.2.4 Other Operations

The set operation *intersection* is maintained as follows: Given materialized view $v = r \cap s$, when a tuple is inserted in r we check if it is present in s, and if so we add it to v. If a tuple is deleted from r, we delete it from the intersection if it is present. The other set operations, *union* and *set difference*, are handled in a similar fashion; we leave details to you.

Outer joins are handled in much the same way as joins, but with some extra work. In the case of deletion from r we have to handle tuples in s that no longer match any tuple in r. In the case of insertion to r, we have to handle tuples in s that did not match any tuple in r. Again we leave details to you.

13.5.2.5 Handling Expressions

So far we have seen how to update incrementally the result of a single operation. To handle an entire expression, we can derive expressions for computing the incremental change to the result of each subexpression, starting from the smallest subexpressions.

For example, suppose we wish to incrementally update a materialized view $E_1 \bowtie E_2$ when a set of tuples i_r is inserted into relation r. Let us assume r is used in E_1 alone. Suppose the set of tuples to be inserted into E_1 is given by expression D_1. Then the expression $D_1 \bowtie E_2$ gives the set of tuples to be inserted into $E_1 \bowtie E_2$.

See the bibliographical notes for further details on incremental view maintenance with expressions.

13.5.3 Query Optimization and Materialized Views

Query optimization can be performed by treating materialized views just like regular relations. However, materialized views offer further opportunities for optimization:

- Rewriting queries to use materialized views:

Suppose a materialized view $v = r \bowtie s$ is available, and a user submits a query $r \bowtie s \bowtie t$. Rewriting the query as $v \bowtie t$ may provide a more efficient query plan than optimizing the query as submitted. Thus, it is the job of the query optimizer to recognize when a materialized view can be used to speed up a query.

- Replacing a use of a materialized view with the view definition:

  Suppose a materialized view $v = r \bowtie s$ is available, but without any index on it, and a user submits a query $\sigma_{A=10}(v)$. Suppose also that s has an index on the common attribute B, and r has an index on attribute A. The best plan for this query may be to replace v with $r \bowtie s$, which can lead to the query plan $\sigma_{A=10}(r) \bowtie s$; the selection and join can be performed efficiently by using the indices on $r.A$ and $s.B$, respectively. In contrast, evaluating the selection directly on v may require a full scan of v, which may be more expensive.

The bibliographical notes give pointers to research showing how to efficiently perform query optimization with materialized views.

13.5.4   Materialized View and Index Selection

Another related optimization problem is that of **materialized view selection**, namely, "What is the best set of views to materialize?" This decision must be made on the basis of the system **workload**, which is a sequence of queries and updates that reflects the typical load on the system. One simple criterion would be to select a set of materialized views that minimizes the overall execution time of the workload of queries and updates, including the time taken to maintain the materialized views. Database administrators usually modify this criterion to take into account the importance of different queries and updates: Fast response may be required for some queries and updates, but a slow response may be acceptable for others.

Indices are just like materialized views, in that they too are derived data, can speed up queries, and may slow down updates. Thus, the problem of **index selection** is closely related to that of materialized view selection, although it is simpler. We examine index and materialized view selection in more detail in Sections 24.1.6 and 24.1.7.

Most database systems provide tools to help the database administrator with index and materialized view selection. These tools examine the history of queries and updates, and suggest indices and views to be materialized. The Microsoft SQL Server Database Tuning Assistant, the IBM DB2 Design Advisor, and the Oracle SQL Tuning Wizard are examples of such tools.

13.6   Advanced Topics in Query Optimization**

There are a number of opportunities for optimizing queries, beyond those we have seen so far. We examine a few of these in this section.

13.6.1   Top-K Optimization

Many queries fetch results sorted on some attributes, and require only the top K results for some K. Sometimes the bound K is specified explicitly. For example, some databases support a **limit** K clause which results in only the top K results being returned by the query. Other databases support alternative ways of specifying similar limits. In other cases, the query may not specify such a limit, but the optimizer may allow a hint to be specified, indicating that only the top K results of the query are likely to be retrieved, even if the query generates more results.

When K is small, a query optimization plan that generates the entire set of results, then sorts and generates the top K, is very inefficient since it discards most of the intermediate results that it computes. Several techniques have been proposed to optimize such *top-K queries*. One approach is to use pipelined plans that can generate the results in sorted order. Another approach is to estimate what is the highest value on the sorted attributes that will appear in the top-K output, and introduce selection predicates that eliminate larger values. If extra tuples beyond the top-K are generated they are discarded, and if too few tuples are generated then the selection condition is changed and the query is re-executed. See the bibliographical notes for references to work on top-K optimization.

13.6.2   Join Minimization

When queries are generated through views, sometimes more relations are joined than are needed for computation of the query. For example, a view v may include the join of *instructor* and *department*, but a use of the view v may use only attributes from *instructor*. The join attribute *dept_name* of *instructor* is a foreign key referencing *department*. Assuming that *instructor.dept_name* has been declared **not null**, the join with *department* can be dropped, with no impact on the query. For, under the above assumption, the join with *department* does not eliminate any tuples from *instructor*, nor does it result in extra copies of any *instructor* tuple.

Dropping a relation from a join as above is an example of join minimization. In fact, join minimization can be performed in other situations as well. See the bibliographical notes for references on join minimization.

13.6.3   Optimization of Updates

Update queries often involve subqueries in the **set** and **where** clauses, which must also be taken into account in optimizing the update. Updates that involve a selection on the updated column (e.g., give a 10 percent salary raise to all employees whose salary is $\geq \$100,000$) must be handled carefully. If the update is done while the selection is being evaluated by an index scan, an updated tuple may be reinserted in the index ahead of the scan and seen again by the scan; the same employee tuple may then get incorrectly updated multiple times (an infinite number of times, in this case). A similar problem also arises with updates involving subqueries whose result is affected by the update.

The problem of an update affecting the execution of a query associated with the update is known as the **Halloween problem** (named so because it was first recognized on a Halloween day, at IBM). The problem can be avoided by executing the queries defining the update first, creating a list of affected tuples, and updating the tuples and indices as the last step. However, breaking up the execution plan in such a fashion increases the execution cost. Update plans can be optimized by checking if the Halloween problem can occur, and if it cannot occur, updates can be performed while the query is being processed, reducing the update overheads. For example, the Halloween problem cannot occur if the update does not affect index attributes. Even if it does, if the updates decrease the value, while the index is scanned in increasing order, updated tuples will not be encountered again during the scan. In such cases, the index can be updated even while the query is being executed, reducing the overall cost.

Update queries that result in a large number of updates can also be optimized by collecting the updates as a batch, and then applying the batch of updates separately to each affected index. When applying the batch of updates to an index, the batch is first sorted in the index order for that index; such sorting can greatly reduce the amount of random I/O required for updating indices.

Such optimizations of updates are implemented in most database systems. See the bibliographical notes for references to such optimization.

13.6.4 Multiquery Optimization and Shared Scans

When a batch of queries are submitted together, a query optimizer can potentially exploit common subexpressions between the different queries, evaluating them once and reusing them where required. Complex queries may in fact have subexpressions repeated in different parts of the query, which can be similarly exploited, to reduce query evaluation cost. Such optimization is known as **multiquery optimization**.

Common subexpression elimination optimizes subexpressions shared by different expressions in a program, by computing and storing the result, and reusing it wherever the subexpression occurs. Common subexpression elimination is a standard optimization applied on arithmetic expressions by programming-language compilers. Exploiting common subexpressions among evaluation plans chosen for each of a batch of queries is just as useful in database query evaluation, and is implemented by some databases. However, multiquery optimization can do even better in some cases: A query typically has more than one evaluation plan, and a judiciously chosen set of query evaluation plans for the queries may provide for a greater sharing and lesser cost than that afforded by choosing the lowest cost evaluation plan for each query. More details on multiquery optimization may be found in references cited in the bibliographical notes.

Sharing of relation scans between queries is another limited form of multiquery optimization that is implemented in some databases. The **shared-scan** optimization works as follows: Instead of reading the relation repeatedly from disk, once for each query that needs to scan a relation, data are read once from disk, and pipelined to each of the queries. The shared-scan optimization is particularly useful when multiple queries perform a scan on a single large relation (typically a "fact table").

13.6.5 Parametric Query Optimization

Plan caching, which we saw earlier in Section 13.4.3, is used as a heuristic in many databases. Recall that with plan caching, if a query is invoked with some constants, the plan chosen by the optimizer is cached, and reused if the query is submitted again, even if the constants in the query are different. For example, suppose a query takes a department name as a parameter, and retrieves all courses of the department. With plan caching, a plan chosen when the query is executed for the first time, say for the Music department, is reused if the query is executed for any other department.

Such reuse of plans by plan caching is reasonable if the optimal query plan is not significantly affected by the exact value of the constants in the query. However, if the plan is affected by the value of the constants, parametric query optimization is an alternative.

In **parametric query optimization**, a query is optimized without being provided specific values for its parameters, for example, *dept_name* in the preceding example. The optimizer then outputs several plans, each optimal for a different parameter value. A plan would be output by the optimizer only if it is optimal for some possible value of the parameters. The set of alternative plans output by the optimizer are stored. When a query is submitted with specific values for its parameters, instead of performing a full optimization, the cheapest plan from the set of alternative plans computed earlier is used. Finding the cheapest such plan usually takes much less time than reoptimization. See the bibliographical notes for references on parametric query optimization.

13.7 Summary

- Given a query, there are generally a variety of methods for computing the answer. It is the responsibility of the system to transform the query as entered by the user into an equivalent query that can be computed more efficiently. The process of finding a good strategy for processing a query is called *query optimization*.

- The evaluation of complex queries involves many accesses to disk. Since the transfer of data from disk is slow relative to the speed of main memory and the CPU of the computer system, it is worthwhile to allocate a considerable amount of processing to choose a method that minimizes disk accesses.

- There are a number of equivalence rules that we can use to transform an expression into an equivalent one. We use these rules to generate systematically all expressions equivalent to the given query.

- Each relational-algebra expression represents a particular sequence of operations. The first step in selecting a query-processing strategy is to find a relational-algebra expression that is equivalent to the given expression and is estimated to cost less to execute.

- The strategy that the database system chooses for evaluating an operation depends on the size of each relation and on the distribution of values within columns. So that they can base the strategy choice on reliable information, database systems may store statistics for each relation r. These statistics include:

  ○ The number of tuples in the relation r.

  ○ The size of a record (tuple) of relation r in bytes.

  ○ The number of distinct values that appear in the relation r for a particular attribute.

- Most database systems use histograms to store the number of values for an attribute within each of several ranges of values. Histograms are often computed using sampling.

- These statistics allow us to estimate the sizes of the results of various operations, as well as the cost of executing the operations. Statistical information about relations is particularly useful when several indices are available to assist in the processing of a query. The presence of these structures has a significant influence on the choice of a query-processing strategy.

- Alternative evaluation plans for each expression can be generated by equivalence rules, and the cheapest plan across all expressions can be chosen. Several optimization techniques are available to reduce the number of alternative expressions and plans that need to be generated.

- We use heuristics to reduce the number of plans considered, and thereby to reduce the cost of optimization. Heuristic rules for transforming relational-algebra queries include "Perform selection operations as early as possible," "Perform projections early," and "Avoid Cartesian products."

- Materialized views can be used to speed up query processing. Incremental view maintenance is needed to efficiently update materialized views when the underlying relations are modified. The differential of an operation can be computed by means of algebraic expressions involving differentials of the inputs of the operation. Other issues related to materialized views include how to optimize queries by making use of available materialized views, and how to select views to be materialized.

- A number of advanced optimization techniques have been proposed such as top-K optimization, join minimization, optimization of updates, multiquery optimization, and parametric query optimization.

Review Terms

- Query optimization
- Transformation of expressions
- Equivalence of expressions

- Equivalence rules
    - Join commutativity
    - Join associativity
- Minimal set of equivalence rules
- Enumeration of equivalent expressions
- Statistics estimation
- Catalog information
- Size estimation
    - Selection
    - Selectivity
    - Join
- Histograms
- Distinct value estimation
- Random sample
- Choice of evaluation plans
- Interaction of evaluation techniques
- Cost-based optimization
- Join-order optimization
    - Dynamic-programming algorithm

- Left-deep join order
- Interesting sort order
- Heuristic optimization
- Plan caching
- Access-plan selection
- Correlated evaluation
- Decorrelation
- Materialized views
- Materialized view maintenance
    - Recomputation
    - Incremental maintenance
    - Insertion
    - Deletion
    - Updates
- Query optimization with materialized views
- Index selection
- Materialized view selection
- Top-K optimization
- Join minimization
- Halloween problem
- Multiquery optimization

Practice Exercises

13.1 Show that the following equivalences hold. Explain how you can apply them to improve the efficiency of certain queries:

  a. $E_1 \bowtie_\theta (E_2 - E_3) = (E_1 \bowtie_\theta E_2 - E_1 \bowtie_\theta E_3)$.

  b. $\sigma_\theta(\,_A\mathcal{G}_F(E)) = \,_A\mathcal{G}_F(\sigma_\theta(E))$, where θ uses only attributes from A.

  c. $\sigma_\theta(E_1 \bowtie E_2) = \sigma_\theta(E_1) \bowtie E_2$, where θ uses only attributes from E_1.

13.2 For each of the following pairs of expressions, give instances of relations that show the expressions are not equivalent.

  a. $\Pi_A(R - S)$ and $\Pi_A(R) - \Pi_A(S)$.

  b. $\sigma_{B<4}(\,_A\mathcal{G}_{max(B) \text{ as } B}(R))$ and $\,_A\mathcal{G}_{max(B) \text{ as } B}(\sigma_{B<4}(R))$.

    c.   In the preceding expressions, if both occurrences of max were replaced by min would the expressions be equivalent?

    d. $(R ⟕ S) ⟕ T$ and $R ⟕ (S ⟕ T)$
In other words, the natural left outer join is not associative. (Hint: Assume that the schemas of the three relations are $R(a, b1)$, $S(a, b2)$, and $T(a, b3)$, respectively.)

    e. $\sigma_\theta(E_1 ⟕ E_2)$ and $E_1 ⟕ \sigma_\theta(E_2)$, where θ uses only attributes from E_2.

13.3   SQL allows relations with duplicates (Chapter 3).

    a.   Define versions of the basic relational-algebra operations σ, Π, $\times$, $⋈$, $-$, $\cup$, and $\cap$ that work on relations with duplicates, in a way consistent with SQL.

    b.   Check which of the equivalence rules 1 through 7.b hold for the multiset version of the relational-algebra defined in part a.

13.4   Consider the relations $r_1(A, B, C)$, $r_2(C, D, E)$, and $r_3(E, F)$, with primary keys A, C, and E, respectively. Assume that r_1 has 1000 tuples, r_2 has 1500 tuples, and r_3 has 750 tuples. Estimate the size of $r_1 ⋈ r_2 ⋈ r_3$, and give an efficient strategy for computing the join.

13.5   Consider the relations $r_1(A, B, C)$, $r_2(C, D, E)$, and $r_3(E, F)$ of Practice Exercise 13.4. Assume that there are no primary keys, except the entire schema. Let $V(C, r_1)$ be 900, $V(C, r_2)$ be 1100, $V(E, r_2)$ be 50, and $V(E, r_3)$ be 100. Assume that r_1 has 1000 tuples, r_2 has 1500 tuples, and r_3 has 750 tuples. Estimate the size of $r_1 ⋈ r_2 ⋈ r_3$ and give an efficient strategy for computing the join.

13.6   Suppose that a B^+-tree index on *building* is available on relation *department*, and that no other index is available. What would be the best way to handle the following selections that involve negation?

    a. $\sigma_{\neg(building <\text{"Watson"})}(department)$

    b. $\sigma_{\neg(building =\text{"Watson"})}(department)$

    c. $\sigma_{\neg(building <\text{"Watson"} \vee budget <50000)}(department)$

13.7   Consider the query:

> **select** *
> **from** r, s
> **where** upper($r.A$) = upper($s.A$);

where "upper" is a function that returns its input argument with all lowercase letters replaced by the corresponding uppercase letters.

    a.   Find out what plan is generated for this query on the database system you use.

b. Some database systems would use a (block) nested-loop join for this query, which can be very inefficient. Briefly explain how hash-join or merge-join can be used for this query.

13.8 Give conditions under which the following expressions are equivalent

$$_{A,B}\mathcal{G}_{agg(C)}(E_1 \bowtie E_2) \quad \text{and} \quad (_{A}\mathcal{G}_{agg(C)}(E_1)) \bowtie E_2$$

where *agg* denotes any aggregation operation. How can the above conditions be relaxed if *agg* is one of **min** or **max**?

13.9 Consider the issue of interesting orders in optimization. Suppose you are given a query that computes the natural join of a set of relations S. Given a subset $S1$ of S, what are the interesting orders of $S1$?

13.10 Show that, with n relations, there are $(2(n-1))!/(n-1)!$ different join orders. *Hint:* A **complete binary tree** is one where every internal node has exactly two children. Use the fact that the number of different complete binary trees with n leaf nodes is:

$$\frac{1}{n}\binom{2(n-1)}{(n-1)}$$

If you wish, you can derive the formula for the number of complete binary trees with n nodes from the formula for the number of binary trees with n nodes. The number of binary trees with n nodes is:

$$\frac{1}{n+1}\binom{2n}{n}$$

This number is known as the **Catalan number**, and its derivation can be found in any standard textbook on data structures or algorithms.

13.11 Show that the lowest-cost join order can be computed in time $O(3^n)$. Assume that you can store and look up information about a set of relations (such as the optimal join order for the set, and the cost of that join order) in constant time. (If you find this exercise difficult, at least show the looser time bound of $O(2^{2n})$.)

13.12 Show that, if only left-deep join trees are considered, as in the System R optimizer, the time taken to find the most efficient join order is around $n2^n$. Assume that there is only one interesting sort order.

13.13 Consider the bank database of Figure 13.9, where the primary keys are underlined. Construct the following SQL queries for this relational database.

a. Write a nested query on the relation *account* to find, for each branch with name starting with B, all accounts with the maximum balance at the branch.

> branch(*branch_name*, *branch_city*, *assets*)
> customer (*customer_name*, *customer_street*, *customer_city*)
> loan (*loan_number*, *branch_name*, *amount*)
> borrower (*customer_name*, *loan_number*)
> account (*account_number*, *branch_name*, *balance*)
> depositor (*customer_name*, *account_number*)

Figure 13.9   Banking database for Exercise 13.13.

    b.   Rewrite the preceding query, without using a nested subquery; in other words, decorrelate the query.

    c.   Give a procedure (similar to that described in Section 13.4.4) for decorrelating such queries.

13.14   The set version of the semijoin operator $\ltimes$ is defined as follows:

$$r \ltimes_\theta s = \Pi_R(r \Join_\theta s)$$

where R is the set of attributes in the schema of r. The multiset version of the semijoin operation returns the same set of tuples, but each tuple has exactly as many copies as it had in r.

Consider the nested query we saw in Section 13.4.4 which finds the names of all instructors who taught a course in 2007. Write the query in relational algebra using the multiset semjoin operation, ensuring that the number of duplicates of each name is the same as in the SQL query. (The semijoin operation is widely used for decorrelation of nested queries.)

Exercises

13.15   Suppose that a B^+-tree index on (*dept_name*, *building*) is available on relation *department*. What would be the best way to handle the following selection?

$$\sigma_{(building\ <\ \text{“Watson”})\ \wedge\ (budget\ <\ 55000)\ \wedge\ (dept\_name\ =\ \text{“Music”})}(department)$$

13.16   Show how to derive the following equivalences by a sequence of transformations using the equivalence rules in Section 13.2.1.

    a. $\sigma_{\theta_1 \wedge \theta_2 \wedge \theta_3}(E) = \sigma_{\theta_1}(\sigma_{\theta_2}(\sigma_{\theta_3}(E)))$

    b. $\sigma_{\theta_1 \wedge \theta_2}(E_1 \Join_{\theta_3} E_2) = \sigma_{\theta_1}(E_1 \Join_{\theta_3} (\sigma_{\theta_2}(E_2)))$, where θ_2 involves only attributes from E_2

13.17 Consider the two expressions $\sigma_\theta(E_1 \bowtie E_2)$ and $\sigma_\theta(E_1 \bowtie E_2)$.

    a. Show using an example that the two expressions are not equivalent in general.

    b. Give a simple condition on the predicate θ, which if satisfied will ensure that the two expressions are equivalent.

13.18 A set of equivalence rules is said to be *complete* if, whenever two expressions are equivalent, one can be derived from the other by a sequence of uses of the equivalence rules. Is the set of equivalence rules that we considered in Section 13.2.1 complete? Hint: Consider the equivalence $\sigma_{3=5}(r) = \{\ \}$.

13.19 Explain how to use a histogram to estimate the size of a selection of the form $\sigma_{A \leq v}(r)$.

13.20 Suppose two relations r and s have histograms on attributes $r.A$ and $s.A$, respectively, but with different ranges. Suggest how to use the histograms to estimate the size of $r \bowtie s$. Hint: Split the ranges of each histogram further.

13.21 Consider the query

> **select** A, B
> **from** r
> **where** $r.B <$ **some** (**select** B
>   **from** s
>   **where** $s.A = r.A$)

Show how to decorrelate the above query using the multiset version of the semijoin operation, defined in Exercise 13.14.

13.22 Describe how to incrementally maintain the results of the following operations, on both insertions and deletions:

    a. Union and set difference.

    b. Left outer join.

13.23 Give an example of an expression defining a materialized view and two situations (sets of statistics for the input relations and the differentials) such that incremental view maintenance is better than recomputation in one situation, and recomputation is better in the other situation.

13.24 Suppose you want to get answers to $r \bowtie s$ sorted on an attribute of r, and want only the top K answers for some relatively small K. Give a good way of evaluating the query:

    a. When the join is on a foreign key of r referencing s, where the foreign key attribute is declared to be not null.

    b. When the join is not on a foreign key.

13.25 Consider a relation $r(A, B, C)$, with an index on attribute A. Give an example of a query that can be answered by using the index only, without looking at the tuples in the relation. (Query plans that use only the index, without accessing the actual relation, are called *index-only* plans.)

13.26 Suppose you have an update query U. Give a simple sufficient condition on U that will ensure that the Halloween problem cannot occur, regardless of the execution plan chosen, or the indices that exist.

Bibliographical Notes

The seminal work of Selinger et al. [1979] describes access-path selection in the System R optimizer, which was one of the earliest relational-query optimizers. Query processing in Starburst, described in Haas et al. [1989], forms the basis for query optimization in IBM DB2.

Graefe and McKenna [1993a] describe Volcano, an equivalence-rule–based query optimizer that, along with its successor Cascades (Graefe [1995]), forms the basis of query optimization in Microsoft SQL Server.

Estimation of statistics of query results, such as result size, is addressed by Ioannidis and Poosala [1995], Poosala et al. [1996], and Ganguly et al. [1996], among others. Nonuniform distributions of values cause problems for estimation of query size and cost. Cost-estimation techniques that use histograms of value distributions have been proposed to tackle the problem. Ioannidis and Christodoulakis [1993], Ioannidis and Poosala [1995], and Poosala et al. [1996] present results in this area. The use of random sampling for constructing histograms is well known in statistics, but issues in histogram construction in the context of databases is discussed in Chaudhuri et al. [1998].

Klug [1982] was an early work on optimization of relational-algebra expressions with aggregate functions. Optimization of queries with aggregation is addressed by Yan and Larson [1995] and Chaudhuri and Shim [1994]. Optimization of queries containing outer joins is described in Rosenthal and Reiner [1984], Galindo-Legaria and Rosenthal [1992], and Galindo-Legaria [1994]. Optimization of top-K queries is addressed in Carey and Kossmann [1998] and Bruno et al. [2002].

Optimization of nested subqueries is discussed in Kim [1982], Ganski and Wong [1987], Dayal [1987], Seshadri et al. [1996] and Galindo-Legaria and Joshi [2001].

Blakeley et al. [1986] describe techniques for maintenance of materialized views. Optimization of materialized view maintenance plans is described by Vista [1998] and Mistry et al. [2001]. Query optimization in the presence of materialized views is addressed by Chaudhuri et al. [1995]. Index selection and materialized view selection are addressed by Ross et al. [1996], and Chaudhuri and Narasayya [1997].

Optimization of top-K queries is addressed in Carey and Kossmann [1998] and Bruno et al. [2002]. A collection of techniques for join minimization has been grouped under the name *tableau optimization*. The notion of a tableau was introduced by Aho et al. [1979b] and Aho et al. [1979a], and was further extended by Sagiv and Yannakakis [1981].

Parametric query-optimization algorithms have been proposed by Ioannidis et al. [1992], Ganguly [1998] and Hulgeri and Sudarshan [2003]. Sellis [1988] was an early work on multiquery optimization, while Roy et al. [2000] showed how to integrate multi-query optimization into a Volcano-based query optimizer.

Galindo-Legaria et al. [2004] describes query processing and optimization for database updates, including optimization of index maintenance, materialized view maintenance plans and integrity constraint checking, along with techniques to handle the Halloween problem.

PART 4

TRANSACTION MANAGEMENT

The term *transaction* refers to a collection of operations that form a single logical unit of work. For instance, transfer of money from one account to another is a transaction consisting of two updates, one to each account.

It is important that either all actions of a transaction be executed completely, or, in case of some failure, partial effects of each incomplete transaction be undone. This property is called *atomicity*. Further, once a transaction is successfully executed, its effects must persist in the database—a system failure should not result in the database forgetting about a transaction that successfully completed. This property is called *durability*.

In a database system where multiple transactions are executing concurrently, if updates to shared data are not controlled there is potential for transactions to see inconsistent intermediate states created by updates of other transactions. Such a situation can result in erroneous updates to data stored in the database. Thus, database systems must provide mechanisms to isolate transactions from the effects of other concurrently executing transactions. This property is called *isolation*.

Chapter 14 describes the concept of a transaction in detail, including the properties of atomicity, durability, isolation, and other properties provided by the transaction abstraction. In particular, the chapter makes precise the notion of isolation by means of a concept called serializability.

Chapter 15 describes several concurrency-control techniques that help implement the isolation property. Chapter 16 describes the recovery management component of a database, which implements the atomicity and durability properties.

Taken as a whole, the transaction-management component of a database system allows application developers to focus on the implementation of individual transactions, ignoring the issues of concurrency and fault tolerance.

CHAPTER 14

Transactions

Often, a collection of several operations on the database appears to be a single unit from the point of view of the database user. For example, a transfer of funds from a checking account to a savings account is a single operation from the customer's standpoint; within the database system, however, it consists of several operations. Clearly, it is essential that all these operations occur, or that, in case of a failure, none occur. It would be unacceptable if the checking account were debited but the savings account not credited.

Collections of operations that form a single logical unit of work are called **transactions**. A database system must ensure proper execution of transactions despite failures—either the entire transaction executes, or none of it does. Furthermore, it must manage concurrent execution of transactions in a way that avoids the introduction of inconsistency. In our funds-transfer example, a transaction computing the customer's total balance might see the checking-account balance before it is debited by the funds-transfer transaction, but see the savings balance after it is credited. As a result, it would obtain an incorrect result.

This chapter introduces the basic concepts of transaction processing. Details on concurrent transaction processing and recovery from failures are in Chapters 15 and 16, respectively. Further topics in transaction processing are discussed in Chapter 26.

14.1 Transaction Concept

A **transaction** is a **unit** of program execution that accesses and possibly updates various data items. Usually, a transaction is initiated by a user program written in a high-level data-manipulation language (typically SQL), or programming language (for example, C++, or Java), with embedded database accesses in JDBC or ODBC. A transaction is delimited by statements (or function calls) of the form **begin transaction** and **end transaction**. The transaction consists of all operations executed between the **begin transaction** and **end transaction**.

This collection of steps must appear to the user as a single, indivisible unit. Since a transaction is indivisible, it either executes in its entirety or not at all. Thus, if a transaction begins to execute but fails for whatever reason, any changes to the database that the transaction may have made must be undone. This requirement holds regardless of whether the transaction itself failed (for example, if it divided by zero), the operating system crashed, or the computer itself stopped operating. As we shall see, ensuring that this requirement is met is difficult since some changes to the database may still be stored only in the main-memory variables of the transaction, while others may have been written to the database and stored on disk. This "all-or-none" property is referred to as **atomicity**.

Furthermore, since a transaction is a single unit, its actions cannot appear to be separated by other database operations not part of the transaction. While we wish to present this user-level impression of transactions, we know that reality is quite different. Even a single SQL statement involves many separate accesses to the database, and a transaction may consist of several SQL statements. Therefore, the database system must take special actions to ensure that transactions operate properly without interference from concurrently executing database statements. This property is referred to as **isolation**.

Even if the system ensures correct execution of a transaction, this serves little purpose if the system subsequently crashes and, as a result, the system "forgets" about the transaction. Thus, a transaction's actions must persist across crashes. This property is referred to as **durability**.

Because of the above three properties, transactions are an ideal way of structuring interaction with a database. This leads us to impose a requirement on transactions themselves. A transaction must preserve database consistency—if a transaction is run atomically in isolation starting from a consistent database, the database must again be consistent at the end of the transaction. This consistency requirement goes beyond the data integrity constraints we have seen earlier (such as primary-key constraints, referential integrity, **check** constraints, and the like). Rather, transactions are expected to go beyond that to ensure preservation of those application-dependent consistency constraints that are too complex to state using the SQL constructs for data integrity. How this is done is the responsibility of the programmer who codes a transaction. This property is referred to as **consistency**.

To restate the above more concisely, we require that the database system maintain the following properties of the transactions:

- **Atomicity**. Either all operations of the transaction are reflected properly in the database, or none are.

- **Consistency**. Execution of a transaction in isolation (that is, with no other transaction executing concurrently) preserves the consistency of the database.

- **Isolation**. Even though multiple transactions may execute concurrently, the system guarantees that, for every pair of transactions T_i and T_j, it appears to T_i that either T_j finished execution before T_i started or T_j started execution after T_i finished. Thus, each transaction is unaware of other transactions executing concurrently in the system.

- **Durability**. After a transaction completes successfully, the changes it has made to the database persist, even if there are system failures.

These properties are often called the **ACID properties**; the acronym is derived from the first letter of each of the four properties.

As we shall see later, ensuring the isolation property may have a significant adverse effect on system performance. For this reason, some applications compromise on the isolation property. We shall study these compromises after first studying the strict enforcement of the ACID properties.

14.2   A Simple Transaction Model

Because SQL is a powerful and complex language, we begin our study of transactions with a simple database language that focuses on when data are moved from disk to main memory and from main memory to disk. In doing this, we ignore SQL **insert** and **delete** operations, and defer considering them until Section 15.8. The only actual operations on the data are restricted in our simple language to arithmetic operations. Later we shall discuss transactions in a realistic, SQL-based context with a richer set of operations. The data items in our simplified model contain a single data value (a number in our examples). Each data item is identified by a name (typically a single letter in our examples, that is, A, B, C, etc.).

We shall illustrate the transaction concept using a simple bank application consisting of several accounts and a set of transactions that access and update those accounts. Transactions access data using two operations:

- read(X), which transfers the data item X from the database to a variable, also called X, in a buffer in main memory belonging to the transaction that executed the read operation.

- write(X), which transfers the value in the variable X in the main-memory buffer of the transaction that executed the write to the data item X in the database.

It is important to know if a change to a data item appears only in main memory or if it has been written to the database on disk. In a real database system, the write operation does not necessarily result in the immediate update of the data on the disk; the write operation may be temporarily stored elsewhere and executed on the disk later. For now, however, we shall assume that the write operation updates the database immediately. We shall return to this subject in Chapter 16.

Let T_i be a transaction that transfers \$50 from account A to account B. This transaction can be defined as:

$$T_i: \text{read}(A);$$
$$A := A - 50;$$
$$\text{write}(A);$$
$$\text{read}(B);$$
$$B := B + 50;$$
$$\text{write}(B).$$

Let us now consider each of the ACID properties. (For ease of presentation, we consider them in an order different from the order A-C-I-D.)

- **Consistency**: The consistency requirement here is that the sum of A and B be unchanged by the execution of the transaction. Without the consistency requirement, money could be created or destroyed by the transaction! It can be verified easily that, if the database is consistent before an execution of the transaction, the database remains consistent after the execution of the transaction.

  Ensuring consistency for an individual transaction is the responsibility of the application programmer who codes the transaction. This task may be facilitated by automatic testing of integrity constraints, as we discussed in Section 4.4.

- **Atomicity**: Suppose that, just before the execution of transaction T_i, the values of accounts A and B are $1000 and $2000, respectively. Now suppose that, during the execution of transaction T_i, a failure occurs that prevents T_i from completing its execution successfully. Further, suppose that the failure happened after the write(A) operation but before the write(B) operation. In this case, the values of accounts A and B reflected in the database are $950 and $2000. The system destroyed $50 as a result of this failure. In particular, we note that the sum $A + B$ is no longer preserved.

  Thus, because of the failure, the state of the system no longer reflects a real state of the world that the database is supposed to capture. We term such a state an **inconsistent state**. We must ensure that such inconsistencies are not visible in a database system. Note, however, that the system must at some point be in an inconsistent state. Even if transaction T_i is executed to completion, there exists a point at which the value of account A is $950 and the value of account B is $2000, which is clearly an inconsistent state. This state, however, is eventually replaced by the consistent state where the value of account A is $950, and the value of account B is $2050. Thus, if the transaction never started or was guaranteed to complete, such an inconsistent state would not be visible except during the execution of the transaction. That is the reason for the atomicity requirement: If the atomicity property is present, all actions of the transaction are reflected in the database, or none are.

  The basic idea behind ensuring atomicity is this: The database system keeps track (on disk) of the old values of any data on which a transaction performs a write. This information is written to a file called the *log*. If the transaction does not complete its execution, the database system restores the old values from the log to make it appear as though the transaction never executed. We discuss these ideas further in Section 14.4. Ensuring atomicity is the responsibility of the database system; specifically, it is handled by a component of the database called the **recovery system**, which we describe in detail in Chapter 16.

- **Durability:** Once the execution of the transaction completes successfully, and the user who initiated the transaction has been notified that the transfer of funds has taken place, it must be the case that no system failure can result in a loss of data corresponding to this transfer of funds. The durability property guarantees that, once a transaction completes successfully, all the updates that it carried out on the database persist, even if there is a system failure after the transaction completes execution.

We assume for now that a failure of the computer system may result in loss of data in main memory, but data written to disk are never lost. Protection against loss of data on disk is discussed in Chapter 16. We can guarantee durability by ensuring that either:

1. The updates carried out by the transaction have been written to disk before the transaction completes.

2. Information about the updates carried out by the transaction and written to disk is sufficient to enable the database to reconstruct the updates when the database system is restarted after the failure.

The **recovery system** of the database, described in Chapter 16, is responsible for ensuring durability, in addition to ensuring atomicity.

- **Isolation:** Even if the consistency and atomicity properties are ensured for each transaction, if several transactions are executed concurrently, their operations may interleave in some undesirable way, resulting in an inconsistent state.

  For example, as we saw earlier, the database is temporarily inconsistent while the transaction to transfer funds from A to B is executing, with the deducted total written to A and the increased total yet to be written to B. If a second concurrently running transaction reads A and B at this intermediate point and computes $A+B$, it will observe an inconsistent value. Furthermore, if this second transaction then performs updates on A and B based on the inconsistent values that it read, the database may be left in an inconsistent state even after both transactions have completed.

  A way to avoid the problem of concurrently executing transactions is to execute transactions serially—that is, one after the other. However, concurrent execution of transactions provides significant performance benefits, as we shall see in Section 14.5. Other solutions have therefore been developed; they allow multiple transactions to execute concurrently.

  We discuss the problems caused by concurrently executing transactions in Section 14.5. The isolation property of a transaction ensures that the concurrent execution of transactions results in a system state that is equivalent to a state that could have been obtained had these transactions executed one at a time in some order. We shall discuss the principles of isolation further in Section 14.6. Ensuring the isolation property is the responsibility of a component of the database system called the **concurrency-control system**, which we discuss later, in Chapter 15.

14.3   Storage Structure

To understand how to ensure the atomicity and durability properties of a transaction, we must gain a better understanding of how the various data items in the database may be stored and accessed.

In Chapter 10 we saw that storage media can be distinguished by their relative speed, capacity, and resilience to failure, and classified as volatile storage or nonvolatile storage. We review these terms, and introduce another class of storage, called **stable storage**.

- **Volatile storage**. Information residing in volatile storage does not usually survive system crashes. Examples of such storage are main memory and cache memory. Access to volatile storage is extremely fast, both because of the speed of the memory access itself, and because it is possible to access any data item in volatile storage directly.

- **Nonvolatile storage**. Information residing in nonvolatile storage survives system crashes. Examples of nonvolatile storage include secondary storage devices such as magnetic disk and flash storage, used for online storage, and tertiary storage devices such as optical media, and magnetic tapes, used for archival storage. At the current state of technology, nonvolatile storage is slower than volatile storage, particularly for random access. Both secondary and tertiary storage devices, however, are susceptible to failure which may result in loss of information.

- **Stable storage**. Information residing in stable storage is *never* lost (*never* should be taken with a grain of salt, since theoretically *never* cannot be guaranteed—for example, it is possible, although extremely unlikely, that a black hole may envelop the earth and permanently destroy all data!). Although stable storage is theoretically impossible to obtain, it can be closely approximated by techniques that make data loss extremely unlikely. To implement stable storage, we replicate the information in several nonvolatile storage media (usually disk) with independent failure modes. Updates must be done with care to ensure that a failure during an update to stable storage does not cause a loss of information. Section 16.2.1 discusses stable-storage implementation.

The distinctions among the various storage types can be less clear in practice than in our presentation. For example, certain systems, for example some RAID controllers, provide battery backup, so that some main memory can survive system crashes and power failures.

For a transaction to be durable, its changes need to be written to stable storage. Similarly, for a transaction to be atomic, log records need to be written to stable storage before any changes are made to the database on disk. Clearly, the degree to which a system ensures durability and atomicity depends on how stable its implementation of stable storage really is. In some cases, a single copy on disk is considered sufficient, but applications whose data are highly valuable and whose transactions are highly important require multiple copies, or, in other words, a closer approximation of the idealized concept of stable storage.

14.4   Transaction Atomicity and Durability

As we noted earlier, a transaction may not always complete its execution successfully. Such a transaction is termed **aborted**. If we are to ensure the atomicity property, an aborted transaction must have no effect on the state of the database. Thus, any changes that the aborted transaction made to the database must be undone. Once the changes caused by an aborted transaction have been undone, we say that the transaction has been **rolled back**. It is part of the responsibility of the recovery scheme to manage transaction aborts. This is done typically by maintaining a **log**. Each database modification made by a transaction is first recorded in the log. We record the identifier of the transaction performing the modification, the identifier of the data item being modified, and both the old value (prior to modification) and the new value (after modification) of the data item. Only then is the database itself modified. Maintaining a log provides the possibility of redoing a modification to ensure atomicity and durability as well as the possibility of undoing a modification to ensure atomicity in case of a failure during transaction execution. Details of log-based recovery are discussed in Chapter 16.

A transaction that completes its execution successfully is said to be **committed**. A committed transaction that has performed updates transforms the database into a new consistent state, which must persist even if there is a system failure.

Once a transaction has committed, we cannot undo its effects by aborting it. The only way to undo the effects of a committed transaction is to execute a **compensating transaction**. For instance, if a transaction added $20 to an account, the compensating transaction would subtract $20 from the account. However, it is not always possible to create such a compensating transaction. Therefore, the responsibility of writing and executing a compensating transaction is left to the user, and is not handled by the database system. Chapter 26 includes a discussion of compensating transactions.

We need to be more precise about what we mean by *successful completion* of a transaction. We therefore establish a simple abstract transaction model. A transaction must be in one of the following states:

- **Active**, the initial state; the transaction stays in this state while it is executing.

- **Partially committed**, after the final statement has been executed.

- **Failed**, after the discovery that normal execution can no longer proceed.

- **Aborted**, after the transaction has been rolled back and the database has been restored to its state prior to the start of the transaction.

- **Committed**, after successful completion.

The state diagram corresponding to a transaction appears in Figure 14.1. We say that a transaction has committed only if it has entered the committed state.

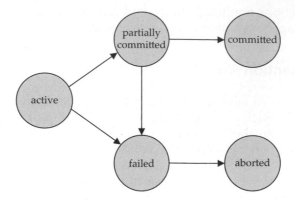

Figure 14.1   State diagram of a transaction.

Similarly, we say that a transaction has aborted only if it has entered the aborted state. A transaction is said to have **terminated** if it has either committed or aborted.

A transaction starts in the active state. When it finishes its final statement, it enters the partially committed state. At this point, the transaction has completed its execution, but it is still possible that it may have to be aborted, since the actual output may still be temporarily residing in main memory, and thus a hardware failure may preclude its successful completion.

The database system then writes out enough information to disk that, even in the event of a failure, the updates performed by the transaction can be re-created when the system restarts after the failure. When the last of this information is written out, the transaction enters the committed state.

As mentioned earlier, we assume for now that failures do not result in loss of data on disk. Chapter 16 discusses techniques to deal with loss of data on disk.

A transaction enters the failed state after the system determines that the transaction can no longer proceed with its normal execution (for example, because of hardware or logical errors). Such a transaction must be rolled back. Then, it enters the aborted state. At this point, the system has two options:

- It can **restart** the transaction, but only if the transaction was aborted as a result of some hardware or software error that was not created through the internal logic of the transaction. A restarted transaction is considered to be a new transaction.

- It can **kill** the transaction. It usually does so because of some internal logical error that can be corrected only by rewriting the application program, or because the input was bad, or because the desired data were not found in the database.

We must be cautious when dealing with **observable external writes**, such as writes to a user's screen, or sending email. Once such a write has occurred, it cannot be erased, since it may have been seen external to the database system.

Most systems allow such writes to take place only after the transaction has entered the committed state. One way to implement such a scheme is for the database system to store any value associated with such external writes temporarily in a special relation in the database, and to perform the actual writes only after the transaction enters the committed state. If the system should fail after the transaction has entered the committed state, but before it could complete the external writes, the database system will carry out the external writes (using the data in nonvolatile storage) when the system is restarted.

Handling external writes can be more complicated in some situations. For example, suppose the external action is that of dispensing cash at an automated teller machine, and the system fails just before the cash is actually dispensed (we assume that cash can be dispensed atomically). It makes no sense to dispense cash when the system is restarted, since the user may have left the machine. In such a case a compensating transaction, such as depositing the cash back in the user's account, needs to be executed when the system is restarted.

As another example, consider a user making a booking over the Web. It is possible that the database system or the application server crashes just after the booking transaction commits. It is also possible that the network connection to the user is lost just after the booking transaction commits. In either case, even though the transaction has committed, the external write has not taken place. To handle such situations, the application must be designed such that when the user connects to the Web application again, she will be able to see whether her transaction had succeeded or not.

For certain applications, it may be desirable to allow active transactions to display data to users, particularly for long-duration transactions that run for minutes or hours. Unfortunately, we cannot allow such output of observable data unless we are willing to compromise transaction atomicity. In Chapter 26, we discuss alternative transaction models that support long-duration, interactive transactions.

14.5   Transaction Isolation

Transaction-processing systems usually allow multiple transactions to run concurrently. Allowing multiple transactions to update data concurrently causes several complications with consistency of the data, as we saw earlier. Ensuring consistency in spite of concurrent execution of transactions requires extra work; it is far easier to insist that transactions run **serially**—that is, one at a time, each starting only after the previous one has completed. However, there are two good reasons for allowing concurrency:

- **Improved throughput and resource utilization**. A transaction consists of many steps. Some involve I/O activity; others involve CPU activity. The CPU and the disks in a computer system can operate in parallel. Therefore, I/O activity can be done in parallel with processing at the CPU. The parallelism of the CPU and the I/O system can therefore be exploited to run multiple transactions in parallel. While a read or write on behalf of one transaction is in progress on one disk, another transaction can be running in the CPU, while another disk may be executing a read or write on behalf of a third transaction. All of this increases the **throughput** of the system—that is, the number of transactions executed in a given amount of time. Correspondingly, the processor and disk **utilization** also increase; in other words, the processor and disk spend less time idle, or not performing any useful work.

- **Reduced waiting time**. There may be a mix of transactions running on a system, some short and some long. If transactions run serially, a short transaction may have to wait for a preceding long transaction to complete, which can lead to unpredictable delays in running a transaction. If the transactions are operating on different parts of the database, it is better to let them run concurrently, sharing the CPU cycles and disk accesses among them. Concurrent execution reduces the unpredictable delays in running transactions. Moreover, it also reduces the **average response time**: the average time for a transaction to be completed after it has been submitted.

The motivation for using concurrent execution in a database is essentially the same as the motivation for using **multiprogramming** in an operating system.

When several transactions run concurrently, the isolation property may be violated, resulting in database consistency being destroyed despite the correctness of each individual transaction. In this section, we present the concept of schedules to help identify those executions that are guaranteed to ensure the isolation property and thus database consistency.

The database system must control the interaction among the concurrent transactions to prevent them from destroying the consistency of the database. It does so through a variety of mechanisms called **concurrency-control schemes**. We study concurrency-control schemes in Chapter 15; for now, we focus on the concept of correct concurrent execution.

Consider again the simplified banking system of Section 14.1, which has several accounts, and a set of transactions that access and update those accounts. Let T_1 and T_2 be two transactions that transfer funds from one account to another. Transaction T_1 transfers \$50 from account A to account B. It is defined as:

$$T_1: \text{read}(A);$$
$$A := A - 50;$$
$$\text{write}(A);$$
$$\text{read}(B);$$
$$B := B + 50;$$
$$\text{write}(B).$$

Transaction T_2 transfers 10 percent of the balance from account A to account B. It is defined as:

TRENDS IN CONCURRENCY

Several current trends in the field of computing are giving rise to an increase in the amount of concurrency possible. As database systems exploit this concurrency to increase overall system performance, there will necessarily be an increasing number of transactions run concurrently.

Early computers had only one processor. Therefore, there was never any real concurrency in the computer. The only concurrency was apparent concurrency created by the operating system as it shared the processor among several distinct tasks or processes. Modern computers are likely to have many processors. These may be truly distinct processors all part of the one computer. However even a single processor may be able to run more than one process at a time by having multiple *cores*. The Intel Core Duo processor is a well-known example of such a multicore processor.

For database systems to take advantage of multiple processors and multiple cores, two approaches are being taken. One is to find parallelism within a single transaction or query. Another is to support a very large number of concurrent transactions.

Many service providers now use large collections of computers rather than large mainframe computers to provide their services. They are making this choice based on the lower cost of this approach. A result of this is yet a further increase in the degree of concurrency that can be supported.

The bibliographic notes refer to texts that describe these advances in computer architecture and parallel computing. Chapter 18 describes algorithms for building parallel database systems, which exploit multiple processors and multiple cores.

T_2: read(A);
  $temp := A * 0.1$;
  $A := A - temp$;
  write(A);
  read(B);
  $B := B + temp$;
  write(B).

Suppose the current values of accounts A and B are \$1000 and \$2000, respectively. Suppose also that the two transactions are executed one at a time in the order T_1 followed by T_2. This execution sequence appears in Figure 14.2. In the figure, the sequence of instruction steps is in chronological order from top to bottom, with instructions of T_1 appearing in the left column and instructions of T_2 appearing in the right column. The final values of accounts A and B, after the execution in Figure 14.2 takes place, are \$855 and \$2145, respectively. Thus, the total amount of money in accounts A and B—that is, the sum $A + B$—is preserved after the execution of both transactions.

T_1	T_2
read(A)	
$A := A - 50$	
write(A)	
read(B)	
$B := B + 50$	
write(B)	
commit	
	read(A)
	$temp := A * 0.1$
	$A := A - temp$
	write(A)
	read(B)
	$B := B + temp$
	write(B)
	commit

Figure 14.2   Schedule 1 — a serial schedule in which T_1 is followed by T_2.

Similarly, if the transactions are executed one at a time in the order T_2 followed by T_1, then the corresponding execution sequence is that of Figure 14.3. Again, as expected, the sum $A + B$ is preserved, and the final values of accounts A and B are $850 and $2150, respectively.

T_1	T_2
	read(A)
	$temp := A * 0.1$
	$A := A - temp$
	write(A)
	read(B)
	$B := B + temp$
	write(B)
	commit
read(A)	
$A := A - 50$	
write(A)	
read(B)	
$B := B + 50$	
write(B)	
commit	

Figure 14.3   Schedule 2 — a serial schedule in which T_2 is followed by T_1.

The execution sequences just described are called **schedules**. They represent the chronological order in which instructions are executed in the system. Clearly, a schedule for a set of transactions must consist of all instructions of those transactions, and must preserve the order in which the instructions appear in each individual transaction. For example, in transaction T_1, the instruction write(A) must appear before the instruction read(B), in any valid schedule. Note that we include in our schedules the **commit** operation to indicate that the transaction has entered the committed state. In the following discussion, we shall refer to the first execution sequence (T_1 followed by T_2) as schedule 1, and to the second execution sequence (T_2 followed by T_1) as schedule 2.

These schedules are **serial**: Each serial schedule consists of a sequence of instructions from various transactions, where the instructions belonging to one single transaction appear together in that schedule. Recalling a well-known formula from combinatorics, we note that, for a set of n transactions, there exist n factorial ($n!$) different valid serial schedules.

When the database system executes several transactions concurrently, the corresponding schedule no longer needs to be serial. If two transactions are running concurrently, the operating system may execute one transaction for a little while, then perform a context switch, execute the second transaction for some time, and then switch back to the first transaction for some time, and so on. With multiple transactions, the CPU time is shared among all the transactions.

Several execution sequences are possible, since the various instructions from both transactions may now be interleaved. In general, it is not possible to predict exactly how many instructions of a transaction will be executed before the CPU switches to another transaction.[1]

Returning to our previous example, suppose that the two transactions are executed concurrently. One possible schedule appears in Figure 14.4. After this execution takes place, we arrive at the same state as the one in which the transactions are executed serially in the order T_1 followed by T_2. The sum $A + B$ is indeed preserved.

Not all concurrent executions result in a correct state. To illustrate, consider the schedule of Figure 14.5. After the execution of this schedule, we arrive at a state where the final values of accounts A and B are \$950 and \$2100, respectively. This final state is an *inconsistent state*, since we have gained \$50 in the process of the concurrent execution. Indeed, the sum $A + B$ is not preserved by the execution of the two transactions.

If control of concurrent execution is left entirely to the operating system, many possible schedules, including ones that leave the database in an inconsistent state, such as the one just described, are possible. It is the job of the database system to ensure that any schedule that is executed will leave the database in a consistent state. The **concurrency-control** component of the database system carries out this task.

---

[1] The number of possible schedules for a set of n transactions is very large. There are $n!$ different serial schedules. Considering all the possible ways that steps of transactions might be interleaved, the total number of possible schedules is much larger than $n!$.

T_1	T_2
read(A)	
$A := A - 50$	
write(A)	
	read(A)
	$temp := A * 0.1$
	$A := A - temp$
	write(A)
read(B)	
$B := B + 50$	
write(B)	
commit	
	read(B)
	$B := B + temp$
	write(B)
	commit

Figure 14.4   Schedule 3 — a concurrent schedule equivalent to schedule 1.

We can ensure consistency of the database under concurrent execution by making sure that any schedule that is executed has the same effect as a schedule that could have occurred without any concurrent execution. That is, the schedule should, in some sense, be equivalent to a serial schedule. Such schedules are called **serializable** schedules.

T_1	T_2
read(A)	
$A := A - 50$	
	read(A)
	$temp := A * 0.1$
	$A := A - temp$
	write(A)
	read(B)
write(A)	
read(B)	
$B := B + 50$	
write(B)	
commit	
	$B := B + temp$
	write(B)
	commit

Figure 14.5   Schedule 4 — a concurrent schedule resulting in an inconsistent state.

14.6   Serializability

Before we can consider how the concurrency-control component of the database system can ensure serializability, we consider how to determine when a schedule is serializable. Certainly, serial schedules are serializable, but if steps of multiple transactions are interleaved, it is harder to determine whether a schedule is serializable. Since transactions are programs, it is difficult to determine exactly what operations a transaction performs and how operations of various transactions interact. For this reason, we shall not consider the various types of operations that a transaction can perform on a data item, but instead consider only two operations: read and write. We assume that, between a read(Q) instruction and a write(Q) instruction on a data item Q, a transaction may perform an arbitrary sequence of operations on the copy of Q that is residing in the local buffer of the transaction. In this model, the only significant operations of a transaction, from a scheduling point of view, are its read and write instructions. Commit operations, though relevant, are not considered until Section 14.7. We therefore may show only read and write instructions in schedules, as we do for schedule 3 in Figure 14.6.

In this section, we discuss different forms of schedule equivalence, but focus on a particular form called **conflict serializability**.

Let us consider a schedule S in which there are two consecutive instructions, I and J, of transactions T_i and T_j, respectively ($i \neq j$). If I and J refer to different data items, then we can swap I and J without affecting the results of any instruction in the schedule. However, if I and J refer to the same data item Q, then the order of the two steps may matter. Since we are dealing with only read and write instructions, there are four cases that we need to consider:

1. $I = \text{read}(Q)$, $J = \text{read}(Q)$. The order of I and J does not matter, since the same value of Q is read by T_i and T_j, regardless of the order.

2. $I = \text{read}(Q)$, $J = \text{write}(Q)$. If I comes before J, then T_i does not read the value of Q that is written by T_j in instruction J. If J comes before I, then T_i reads the value of Q that is written by T_j. Thus, the order of I and J matters.

T_1	T_2
read(A)	
write(A)	
	read(A)
	write(A)
read(B)	
write(B)	
	read(B)
	write(B)

Figure 14.6   Schedule 3 — showing only the read and write instructions.

T_1	T_2
read(A)	
write(A)	
	read(A)
read(B)	
	write(A)
write(B)	
	read(B)
	write(B)

Figure 14.7 Schedule 5 — schedule 3 after swapping of a pair of instructions.

3. I = write(Q), J = read(Q). The order of I and J matters for reasons similar to those of the previous case.

4. I = write(Q), J = write(Q). Since both instructions are write operations, the order of these instructions does not affect either T_i or T_j. However, the value obtained by the next read(Q) instruction of S is affected, since the result of only the latter of the two write instructions is preserved in the database. If there is no other write(Q) instruction after I and J in S, then the order of I and J directly affects the final value of Q in the database state that results from schedule S.

Thus, only in the case where both I and J are read instructions does the relative order of their execution not matter.

We say that I and J **conflict** if they are operations by different transactions on the same data item, and at least one of these instructions is a write operation.

To illustrate the concept of conflicting instructions, we consider schedule 3in Figure 14.6. The write(A) instruction of T_1 conflicts with the read(A) instruction of T_2. However, the write(A) instruction of T_2 does not conflict with the read(B) instruction of T_1, because the two instructions access different data items.

T_1	T_2
read(A)	
write(A)	
read(B)	
write(B)	
	read(A)
	write(A)
	read(B)
	write(B)

Figure 14.8 Schedule 6 — a serial schedule that is equivalent to schedule 3.

T_3	T_4
read(Q)	
	write(Q)
write(Q)	

Figure 14.9   Schedule 7.

Let I and J be consecutive instructions of a schedule S. If I and J are instructions of different transactions and I and J do not conflict, then we can swap the order of I and J to produce a new schedule S'. S is equivalent to S', since all instructions appear in the same order in both schedules except for I and J, whose order does not matter.

Since the write(A) instruction of T_2 in schedule 3 of Figure 14.6 does not conflict with the read(B) instruction of T_1, we can swap these instructions to generate an equivalent schedule, schedule 5, in Figure 14.7. Regardless of the initial system state, schedules 3 and 5 both produce the same final system state.

We continue to swap nonconflicting instructions:

- Swap the read(B) instruction of T_1 with the read(A) instruction of T_2.

- Swap the write(B) instruction of T_1 with the write(A) instruction of T_2.

- Swap the write(B) instruction of T_1 with the read(A) instruction of T_2.

The final result of these swaps, schedule 6 of Figure 14.8, is a serial schedule. Note that schedule 6 is exactly the same as schedule 1, but it shows only the read and write instructions. Thus, we have shown that schedule 3 is equivalent to a serial schedule. This equivalence implies that, regardless of the initial system state, schedule 3 will produce the same final state as will some serial schedule.

If a schedule S can be transformed into a schedule S' by a series of swaps of nonconflicting instructions, we say that S and S' are **conflict equivalent**.[2]

Not all serial schedules are conflict equivalent to each other. For example, schedules 1 and 2 are not conflict equivalent.

The concept of conflict equivalence leads to the concept of conflict serializability. We say that a schedule S is **conflict serializable** if it is conflict equivalent to a serial schedule. Thus, schedule 3 is conflict serializable, since it is conflict equivalent to the serial schedule 1.

Finally, consider schedule 7 of Figure 14.9; it consists of only the significant operations (that is, the read and write) of transactions T_3 and T_4. This schedule is not conflict serializable, since it is not equivalent to either the serial schedule $<T_3,T_4>$ or the serial schedule $<T_4,T_3>$.

---

[2]We use the term *conflict equivalent* to distinguish the way we have just defined equivalence from other definitions that we shall discuss later on in this section.

Figure 14.10   Precedence graph for (a) schedule 1 and (b) schedule 2.

We now present a simple and efficient method for determining conflict serializability of a schedule. Consider a schedule S. We construct a directed graph, called a **precedence graph**, from S. This graph consists of a pair $G = (V, E)$, where V is a set of vertices and E is a set of edges. The set of vertices consists of all the transactions participating in the schedule. The set of edges consists of all edges $T_i \rightarrow T_j$ for which one of three conditions holds:

1. T_i executes write(Q) before T_j executes read(Q).

2. T_i executes read(Q) before T_j executes write(Q).

3. T_i executes write(Q) before T_j executes write(Q).

If an edge $T_i \rightarrow T_j$ exists in the precedence graph, then, in any serial schedule S' equivalent to S, T_i must appear before T_j.

For example, the precedence graph for schedule 1 in Figure 14.10a contains the single edge $T_1 \rightarrow T_2$, since all the instructions of T_1 are executed before the first instruction of T_2 is executed. Similarly, Figure 14.10b shows the precedence graph for schedule 2 with the single edge $T_2 \rightarrow T_1$, since all the instructions of T_2 are executed before the first instruction of T_1 is executed.

The precedence graph for schedule 4 appears in Figure 14.11. It contains the edge $T_1 \rightarrow T_2$, because T_1 executes read(A) before T_2 executes write(A). It also contains the edge $T_2 \rightarrow T_1$, because T_2 executes read(B) before T_1 executes write(B).

If the precedence graph for S has a cycle, then schedule S is not conflict serializable. If the graph contains no cycles, then the schedule S is conflict serializable.

A **serializability order** of the transactions can be obtained by finding a linear order consistent with the partial order of the precedence graph. This process is called **topological sorting**. There are, in general, several possible linear orders that

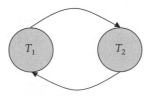

Figure 14.11   Precedence graph for schedule 4.

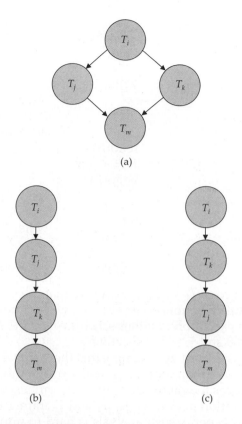

Figure 14.12 Illustration of topological sorting.

can be obtained through a topological sort. For example, the graph of Figure 14.12a has the two acceptable linear orderings shown in Figures 14.12b and 14.12c.

Thus, to test for conflict serializability, we need to construct the precedence graph and to invoke a cycle-detection algorithm. Cycle-detection algorithms can be found in standard textbooks on algorithms. Cycle-detection algorithms, such as those based on depth-first search, require on the order of n^2 operations, where n is the number of vertices in the graph (that is, the number of transactions).

Returning to our previous examples, note that the precedence graphs for schedules 1 and 2 (Figure 14.10) indeed do not contain cycles. The precedence graph for schedule 4 (Figure 14.11), on the other hand, contains a cycle, indicating that this schedule is not conflict serializable.

It is possible to have two schedules that produce the same outcome, but that are not conflict equivalent. For example, consider transaction T_5, which transfers $10 from account B to account A. Let schedule 8 be as defined in Figure 14.13. We claim that schedule 8 is not conflict equivalent to the serial schedule $<T_1, T_5>$, since, in schedule 8, the write(B) instruction of T_5 conflicts with the read(B) instruction of T_1. This creates an edge $T_5 \rightarrow T_1$ in the precedence graph. Similarly, we see that the write(A) instruction of T_1 conflicts with the read instruction of T_5

T_1	T_5
read(A) $A := A - 50$ write(A)	
	read(B) $B := B - 10$ write(B)
read(B) $B := B + 50$ write(B)	
	read(A) $A := A + 10$ write(A)

Figure 14.13   Schedule 8.

creating an edge $T_1 \to T_5$. This shows that the precedence graph has a cycle and that schedule 8 is not serializable. However, the final values of accounts A and B after the execution of either schedule 8 or the serial schedule $<T_1,T_5>$ are the same—$960 and $2040, respectively.

We can see from this example that there are less-stringent definitions of schedule equivalence than conflict equivalence. For the system to determine that schedule 8 produces the same outcome as the serial schedule $<T_1,T_5>$, it must analyze the computation performed by T_1 and T_5, rather than just the read and write operations. In general, such analysis is hard to implement and is computationally expensive. In our example, the final result is the same as that of a serial schedule because of the mathematical fact that addition and subtraction are commutative. While this may be easy to see in our simple example, the general case is not so easy since a transaction may be expressed as a complex SQL statement, a Java program with JDBC calls, etc.

However, there are other definitions of schedule equivalence based purely on the read and write operations. One such definition is *view equivalence*, a definition that leads to the concept of *view serializability*. View serializability is not used in practice due to its high degree of computational complexity.[3] We therefore defer discussion of view serializability to Chapter 15, but, for completeness, note here that the example of schedule 8 is not view serializable.

14.7   Transaction Isolation and Atomicity

So far, we have studied schedules while assuming implicitly that there are no transaction failures. We now address the effect of transaction failures during concurrent execution.

---

[3]Testing for view serializability has been proven to be NP-complete, which means that it is virtually certain that no efficient test for view serializability exists.

T_6	T_7
read(A)	
write(A)	
	read(A)
	commit
read(B)	

Figure 14.14 Schedule 9, a nonrecoverable schedule.

If a transaction T_i fails, for whatever reason, we need to undo the effect of this transaction to ensure the atomicity property of the transaction. In a system that allows concurrent execution, the atomicity property requires that any transaction T_j that is dependent on T_i (that is, T_j has read data written by T_i) is also aborted. To achieve this, we need to place restrictions on the type of schedules permitted in the system.

In the following two subsections, we address the issue of what schedules are acceptable from the viewpoint of recovery from transaction failure. We describe in Chapter 15 how to ensure that only such acceptable schedules are generated.

14.7.1 Recoverable Schedules

Consider the partial schedule 9 in Figure 14.14, in which T_7 is a transaction that performs only one instruction: read(A). We call this a **partial schedule** because we have not included a **commit** or **abort** operation for T_6. Notice that T_7 commits immediately after executing the read(A) instruction. Thus, T_7 commits while T_6 is still in the active state. Now suppose that T_6 fails before it commits. T_7 has read the value of data item A written by T_6. Therefore, we say that T_7 is **dependent** on T_6. Because of this, we must abort T_7 to ensure atomicity. However, T_7 has already committed and cannot be aborted. Thus, we have a situation where it is impossible to recover correctly from the failure of T_6.

Schedule 9 is an example of a *nonrecoverable* schedule. A **recoverable schedule** is one where, for each pair of transactions T_i and T_j such that T_j reads a data item previously written by T_i, the commit operation of T_i appears before the commit operation of T_j. For the example of schedule 9 to be recoverable, T_7 would have to delay committing until after T_6 commits.

14.7.2 Cascadeless Schedules

Even if a schedule is recoverable, to recover correctly from the failure of a transaction T_i, we may have to roll back several transactions. Such situations occur if transactions have read data written by T_i. As an illustration, consider the partial schedule of Figure 14.15. Transaction T_8 writes a value of A that is read by transaction T_9. Transaction T_9 writes a value of A that is read by transaction T_{10}. Suppose that, at this point, T_8 fails. T_8 must be rolled back. Since T_9 is dependent on T_8, T_9 must be rolled back. Since T_{10} is dependent on T_9, T_{10} must be rolled back. This

T_8	T_9	T_{10}
read(A)		
read(B)		
write(A)		
	read(A)	
	write(A)	
		read(A)
abort		

Figure 14.15 Schedule 10.

phenomenon, in which a single transaction failure leads to a series of transaction rollbacks, is called **cascading rollback**.

Cascading rollback is undesirable, since it leads to the undoing of a significant amount of work. It is desirable to restrict the schedules to those where cascading rollbacks cannot occur. Such schedules are called *cascadeless* schedules. Formally, a **cascadeless schedule** is one where, for each pair of transactions T_i and T_j such that T_j reads a data item previously written by T_i, the commit operation of T_i appears before the read operation of T_j. It is easy to verify that every cascadeless schedule is also recoverable.

14.8   Transaction Isolation Levels

Serializability is a useful concept because it allows programmers to ignore issues related to concurrency when they code transactions. If every transaction has the property that it maintains database consistency if executed alone, then serializability ensures that concurrent executions maintain consistency. However, the protocols required to ensure serializability may allow too little concurrency for certain applications. In these cases, weaker levels of consistency are used. The use of weaker levels of consistency places additional burdens on programmers for ensuring database correctness.

The SQL standard also allows a transaction to specify that it may be executed in such a way that it becomes nonserializable with respect to other transactions. For instance, a transaction may operate at the isolation level of **read uncommitted**, which permits the transaction to read a data item even if it was written by a transaction that has not been committed. SQL provides such features for the benefit of long transactions whose results do not need to be precise. If these transactions were to execute in a serializable fashion, they could interfere with other transactions, causing the others' execution to be delayed.

The isolation levels specified by the SQL standard are as follows:

- **Serializable** usually ensures serializable execution. However, as we shall explain shortly, some database systems implement this isolation level in a manner that may, in certain cases, allow nonserializable executions.

- **Repeatable read** allows only committed data to be read and further requires that, between two reads of a data item by a transaction, no other transaction is allowed to update it. However, the transaction may not be serializable with respect to other transactions. For instance, when it is searching for data satisfying some conditions, a transaction may find some of the data inserted by a committed transaction, but may not find other data inserted by the same transaction.

- **Read committed** allows only committed data to be read, but does not require repeatable reads. For instance, between two reads of a data item by the transaction, another transaction may have updated the data item and committed.

- **Read uncommitted** allows uncommitted data to be read. It is the lowest isolation level allowed by SQL.

All the isolation levels above additionally disallow **dirty writes**, that is, they disallow writes to a data item that has already been written by another transaction that has not yet committed or aborted.

Many database systems run, by default, at the read-committed isolation level. In SQL, it is possible to set the isolation level explicitly, rather than accepting the system's default setting. For example, the statement "**set transaction isolation level serializable;**" sets the isolation level to serializable; any of the other isolation levels may be specified instead. The above syntax is supported by Oracle, PostgreSQL and SQL Server; DB2 uses the syntax "**change isolation level**," with its own abbreviations for isolation levels.

Changing of the isolation level must be done as the first statement of a transaction. Further, automatic commit of individual statements must be turned off, if it is on by default; API functions, such as the JDBC method Connection.setAutoCommit(false) which we saw in Section 5.1.1.7, can be used to do so. Further, in JDBC the method Connection.setTransactionIsolation(int level) can be used to set the isolation level; see the JDBC manuals for details.

An application designer may decide to accept a weaker isolation level in order to improve system performance. As we shall see in Section 14.9 and Chapter 15, ensuring serializability may force a transaction to wait for other transactions or, in some cases, to abort because the transaction can no longer be executed as part of a serializable execution. While it may seem shortsighted to risk database consistency for performance, this trade-off makes sense if we can be sure that the inconsistency that may occur is not relevant to the application.

There are many means of implementing isolation levels. As long as the implementation ensures serializability, the designer of a database application or a user of an application does not need to know the details of such implementations, except perhaps for dealing with performance issues. Unfortunately, even if the isolation level is set to **serializable**, some database systems actually implement a weaker level of isolation, which does not rule out every possible nonserializable execution; we revisit this issue in Section 14.9. If weaker levels of isolation are used, either explicitly or implicitly, the application designer has to be aware of some details of the implementation, to avoid or minimize the chance of inconsistency due to lack of serializability.

SERIALIZABILITY IN THE REAL WORLD

Serializable schedules are the ideal way to ensure consistency, but in our day-to-day lives, we don't impose such stringent requirements. A Web site offering goods for sale may list an item as being in stock, yet by the time a user selects the item and goes through the checkout process, that item might no longer be available. Viewed from a database perspective, this would be a nonrepeatable read.

As another example, consider seat selection for air travel. Assume that a traveler has already booked an itinerary and now is selecting seats for each flight. Many airline Web sites allow the user to step through the various flights and choose a seat, after which the user is asked to confirm the selection. It could be that other travelers are selecting seats or changing their seat selections for the same flights at the same time. The seat availability that the traveler was shown is thus actually changing, but the traveler is shown a snapshot of the seat availability as of when the traveler started the seat selection process.

Even if two travelers are selecting seats at the same time, most likely they will select different seats, and if so there would be no real conflict. However, the transactions are not serializable, since each traveler has read data that was subsequently updated by the other traveler, leading to a cycle in the precedence graph. If two travelers performing seat selection concurrently actually selected the same seat, one of them would not be able to get the seat they selected; however, the situation could be easily resolved by asking the traveler to perform the selection again, with updated seat availability information.

It is possible to enforce serializability by allowing only one traveler to do seat selection for a particular flight at a time. However, doing so could cause significant delays as travelers would have to wait for their flight to become available for seat selection; in particular a traveler who takes a long time to make a choice could cause serious problems for other travelers. Instead, any such transaction is typically broken up into a part that requires user interaction, and a part that runs exclusively on the database. In the example above, the database transaction would check if the seats chosen by the user are still available, and if so update the seat selection in the database. Serializability is ensured only for the transactions that run on the database, without user interaction.

14.9   Implementation of Isolation Levels

So far, we have seen what properties a schedule must have if it is to leave the database in a consistent state and allow transaction failures to be handled in a safe manner.

There are various **concurrency-control** policies that we can use to ensure that, even when multiple transactions are executed concurrently, only acceptable schedules are generated, regardless of how the operating system time-shares resources (such as CPU time) among the transactions.

As a trivial example of a concurrency-control policy, consider this: A transaction acquires a **lock** on the entire database before it starts and releases the lock after it has committed. While a transaction holds a lock, no other transaction is allowed to acquire the lock, and all must therefore wait for the lock to be released. As a result of the locking policy, only one transaction can execute at a time. Therefore, only serial schedules are generated. These are trivially serializable, and it is easy to verify that they are recoverable and cascadeless as well.

A concurrency-control policy such as this one leads to poor performance, since it forces transactions to wait for preceding transactions to finish before they can start. In other words, it provides a poor degree of concurrency (indeed, no concurrency at all). As we saw in Section 14.5, concurrent execution has substantial performance benefits.

The goal of concurrency-control policies is to provide a high degree of concurrency, while ensuring that all schedules that can be generated are conflict or view serializable, recoverable, and cascadeless.

Here we provide an overview of how some of most important concurrency-control mechanisms work, and we defer the details to Chapter 15.

14.9.1 Locking

Instead of locking the entire database, a transaction could, instead, lock only those data items that it accesses. Under such a policy, the transaction must hold locks long enough to ensure serializability, but for a period short enough not to harm performance excessively. Complicating matters are SQL statements like those we saw in Section 14.10, where the data items accessed depend on a **where** clause. In Chapter 15, we present the two-phase locking protocol, a simple, widely used technique that ensures serializability. Stated simply, two-phase locking requires a transaction to have two phases, one where it acquires locks but does not release any, and a second phase where the transaction releases locks but does not acquire any. (In practice, locks are usually released only when the transaction completes its execution and has been either committed or aborted.)

Further improvements to locking result if we have two kinds of locks: shared and exclusive. Shared locks are used for data that the transaction reads and exclusive locks are used for those it writes. Many transactions can hold shared locks on the same data item at the same time, but a transaction is allowed an exclusive lock on a data item only if no other transaction holds any lock (regardless of whether shared or exclusive) on the data item. This use of two modes of locks along with two-phase locking allows concurrent reading of data while still ensuring serializability.

14.9.2 Timestamps

Another category of techniques for the implementation of isolation assigns each transaction a **timestamp**, typically when it begins. For each data item, the system keeps two timestamps. The read timestamp of a data item holds the largest (that is, the most recent) timestamp of those transactions that read the data item. The write timestamp of a data item holds the timestamp of the transaction that wrote the current value of the data item. Timestamps are used to ensure that transactions access each data item in order of the transactions' timestamps if their accesses conflict. When this is not possible, offending transactions are aborted and restarted with a new timestamp.

14.9.3 Multiple Versions and Snapshot Isolation

By maintaining more than one version of a data item, it is possible to allow a transaction to read an old version of a data item rather than a newer version written by an uncommitted transaction or by a transaction that should come later in the serialization order. There are a variety of multiversion concurrency-control techniques. One in particular, called **snapshot isolation**, is widely used in practice.

In snapshot isolation, we can imagine that each transaction is given its own version, or snapshot, of the database when it begins.[4] It reads data from this private version and is thus isolated from the updates made by other transactions. If the transaction updates the database, that update appears only in its own version, not in the actual database itself. Information about these updates is saved so that the updates can be applied to the "real" database if the transaction commits.

When a transaction T enters the partially committed state, it then proceeds to the committed state only if no other concurrent transaction has modified data that T intends to update. Transactions that, as a result, cannot commit abort instead.

Snapshot isolation ensures that attempts to read data never need to wait (unlike locking). Read-only transactions cannot be aborted; only those that modify data run a slight risk of aborting. Since each transaction reads its own version or snapshot of the database, reading data does not cause subsequent update attempts by other transactions to wait (unlike locking). Since most transactions are read-only (and most others read more data than they update), this is often a major source of performance improvement as compared to locking.

The problem with snapshot isolation is that, paradoxically, it provides *too much* isolation. Consider two transactions T and T'. In a serializable execution, either T sees all the updates made by T' or T' sees all the updates made by T, because one must follow the other in the serialization order. Under snapshot isolation, there are cases where neither transaction sees the updates of the other. This is a situation that cannot occur in a serializable execution. In many (indeed, most) cases, the data accesses by the two transactions do not conflict and there is no problem. However, if T reads some data item that T' updates and T' reads some data item that T updates, it is possible that both transactions fail to read the update made by the other. The result, as we shall see in Chapter 15, may be an inconsistent database state that, of course, could not be obtained in any serializable execution.

---

[4]Of course, in reality, the entire database is not copied. Multiple versions are kept only of those data items that are changed.

Oracle, PostgreSQL, and SQL Server offer the option of snapshot isolation. Oracle and PostgreSQL implement the **serializable** isolation level using snapshot isolation. As a result, their implementation of serializability can, in exceptional circumstances, result in a nonserializable execution being allowed. SQL Server instead includes an additional isolation level beyond the standard ones, called **snapshot**, to offer the option of snapshot isolation.

14.10 Transactions as SQL Statements

In Section 4.3, we presented the SQL syntax for specifying the beginning and end of transactions. Now that we have seen some of the issues in ensuring the ACID properties for transactions, we are ready to consider how those properties are ensured when transactions are specified as a sequence of SQL statements rather than the restricted model of simple reads and writes that we considered up to this point.

In our simple model, we assumed a set of data items exists. While our simple model allowed data-item values to be changed, it did not allow data items to be created or deleted. In SQL, however, **insert** statements create new data and **delete** statements delete data. These two statements are, in effect, **write** operations, since they change the database, but their interactions with the actions of other transactions are different from what we saw in our simple model. As an example, consider the following SQL query on our university database that finds all instructors who earn more than $90,000.

> **select** *ID*, *name*
> **from** *instructor*
> **where** *salary* > 90000;

Using our sample *instructor* relation (Appendix A.3), we find that only Einstein and Brandt satisfy the condition. Now assume that around the same time we are running our query, another user inserts a new instructor named "James" whose salary is $100,000.

> **insert into** *instructor* **values** ('11111', 'James', 'Marketing', 100000);

The result of our query will be different depending on whether this insert comes before or after our query is run. In a concurrent execution of these transactions, it is intuitively clear that they conflict, but this is a conflict not captured by our simple model. This situation is referred to as the **phantom phenomenon**, because a conflict may exist on "phantom" data.

Our simple model of transactions required that operations operate on a specific data item given as an argument to the operation. In our simple model, we can look at the **read** and **write** steps to see which data items are referenced. But in an SQL statement, the specific data items (tuples) referenced may be determined by a **where** clause predicate. So the same transaction, if run more than once, might reference different data items each time it is run if the values in the database change between runs.

One way of dealing with the above problem is to recognize that it is not sufficient for concurrency control to consider only the tuples that are accessed by a transaction; the information used to find the tuples that are accessed by the transaction must also be considered for the purpose of concurrency control. The information used to find tuples could be updated by an insertion or deletion, or in the case of an index, even by an update to a search-key attribute. For example, if locking is used for concurrency control, the data structures that track the tuples in a relation, as well as index structures, must be appropriately locked. However, such locking can lead to poor concurrency in some situations; index-locking protocols which maximize concurrency, while ensuring serializability in spite of inserts, deletes, and predicates in queries, are discussed in Section 15.8.3.

Let us consider again the query:

> **select** *ID*, *name*
> **from** *instructor*
> **where** *salary* > 90000;

and the following SQL update:

> **update** *instructor*
> **set** *salary* = *salary* * 0.9
> **where** *name* = 'Wu';

We now face an interesting situation in determining whether our query conflicts with the update statement. If our query reads the entire *instructor* relation, then it reads the tuple with Wu's data and conflicts with the update. However, if an index were available that allowed our query direct access to those tuples with *salary* > 90000, then our query would not have accessed Wu's data at all because Wu's salary is initially $90,000 in our example instructor relation, and reduces to $81,000 after the update.

However, using the above approach, it would appear that the existence of a conflict depends on a low-level query processing decision by the system that is unrelated to a user-level view of the meaning of the two SQL statements! An alternative approach to concurrency control treats an insert, delete or update as conflicting with a predicate on a relation, if it could affect the set of tuples selected by a predicate. In our example query above, the predicate is "*salary* > 90000", and an update of Wu's salary from $90,000 to a value greater than $90,000, or an update of Einstein's salary from a value greater that $90,000 to a value less than or equal to $90,000, would conflict with this predicate. Locking based on this idea is called **predicate locking**; however predicate locking is expensive, and not used in practice.

14.11   Summary

- A *transaction* is a *unit* of program execution that accesses and possibly updates various data items. Understanding the concept of a transaction is critical for understanding and implementing updates of data in a database in such a way that concurrent executions and failures of various forms do not result in the database becoming inconsistent.

- Transactions are required to have the ACID properties: atomicity, consistency, isolation, and durability.

    - Atomicity ensures that either all the effects of a transaction are reflected in the database, or none are; a failure cannot leave the database in a state where a transaction is partially executed.

    - Consistency ensures that, if the database is initially consistent, the execution of the transaction (by itself) leaves the database in a consistent state.

    - Isolation ensures that concurrently executing transactions are isolated from one another, so that each has the impression that no other transaction is executing concurrently with it.

    - Durability ensures that, once a transaction has been committed, that transaction's updates do not get lost, even if there is a system failure.

- Concurrent execution of transactions improves throughput of transactions and system utilization, and also reduces waiting time of transactions.

- The various types of storage in a computer are volatile storage, nonvolatile storage, and stable storage. Data in volatile storage, such as in RAM, are lost when the computer crashes. Data in nonvolatile storage, such as disk, are not lost when the computer crashes, but may occasionally be lost because of failures such as disk crashes. Data in stable storage are never lost.

- Stable storage that must be accessible online is approximated with mirrored disks, or other forms of RAID, which provide redundant data storage. Offline, or archival, stable storage may consist of multiple tape copies of data stored in physically secure locations.

- When several transactions execute concurrently on the database, the consistency of data may no longer be preserved. It is therefore necessary for the system to control the interaction among the concurrent transactions.

    - Since a transaction is a unit that preserves consistency, a serial execution of transactions guarantees that consistency is preserved.

    - A *schedule* captures the key actions of transactions that affect concurrent execution, such as read and write operations, while abstracting away internal details of the execution of the transaction.

○ We require that any schedule produced by concurrent processing of a set of transactions will have an effect equivalent to a schedule produced when these transactions are run serially in some order.

○ A system that guarantees this property is said to ensure *serializability*.

○ There are several different notions of equivalence leading to the concepts of *conflict serializability* and *view serializability*.

- Serializability of schedules generated by concurrently executing transactions can be ensured through one of a variety of mechanisms called *concurrency-control* policies.

- We can test a given schedule for conflict serializability by constructing a *precedence graph* for the schedule, and by searching for absence of cycles in the graph. However, there are more efficient concurrency-control policies for ensuring serializability.

- Schedules must be recoverable, to make sure that if transaction *a* sees the effects of transaction *b*, and *b* then aborts, then *a* also gets aborted.

- Schedules should preferably be cascadeless, so that the abort of a transaction does not result in cascading aborts of other transactions. Cascadelessness is ensured by allowing transactions to only read committed data.

- The concurrency-control–management component of the database is responsible for handling the concurrency-control policies. Chapter 15 describes concurrency-control policies.

Review Terms

- Transaction
- ACID properties
  - Atomicity
  - Consistency
  - Isolation
  - Durability
- Inconsistent state
- Storage types
  - Volatile storage
  - Nonvolatile storage
  - Stable storage
- Concurrency control system

- Recovery system
- Transaction state
  - Active
  - Partially committed
  - Failed
  - Aborted
  - Committed
  - Terminated
- Transaction
  - Restart
  - Kill

- Observable external writes
- Concurrent executions
- Serial execution
- Schedules
- Conflict of operations
- Conflict equivalence
- Conflict serializability
- Serializability testing
- Precedence graph

- Serializability order
- Recoverable schedules
- Cascading rollback
- Cascadeless schedules
- Concurrency-control
- Locking
- Multiple versions
- Snapshot isolation

Practice Exercises

14.1 Suppose that there is a database system that never fails. Is a recovery manager required for this system?

14.2 Consider a file system such as the one on your favorite operating system.

   a. What are the steps involved in creation and deletion of files, and in writing data to a file?

   b. Explain how the issues of atomicity and durability are relevant to the creation and deletion of files and to writing data to files.

14.3 Database-system implementers have paid much more attention to the ACID properties than have file-system implementers. Why might this be the case?

14.4 Justify the following statement: Concurrent execution of transactions is more important when data must be fetched from (slow) disk or when transactions are long, and is less important when data are in memory and transactions are very short.

14.5 Since every conflict-serializable schedule is view serializable, why do we emphasize conflict serializability rather than view serializability?

14.6 Consider the precedence graph of Figure 14.16. Is the corresponding schedule conflict serializable? Explain your answer.

14.7 What is a cascadeless schedule? Why is cascadelessness of schedules desirable? Are there any circumstances under which it would be desirable to allow noncascadeless schedules? Explain your answer.

14.8 The **lost update** anomaly is said to occur if a transaction T_j reads a data item, then another transaction T_k writes the data item (possibly based on a previous read), after which T_j writes the data item. The update performed by T_k has been lost, since the update done by T_j ignored the value written by T_k.

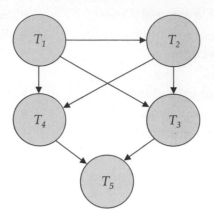

Figure 14.16 Precedence graph for Practice Exercise 14.6.

    a.   Give an example of a schedule showing the lost update anomaly.

    b.   Give an example schedule to show that the lost update anomaly is possible with the **read committed** isolation level.

    c.   Explain why the lost update anomaly is not possible with the **repeatable read** isolation level.

14.9   Consider a database for a bank where the database system uses snapshot isolation. Describe a particular scenario in which a nonserializable execution occurs that would present a problem for the bank.

14.10   Consider a database for an airline where the database system uses snapshot isolation. Describe a particular scenario in which a nonserializable execution occurs, but the airline may be willing to accept it in order to gain better overall performance.

14.11   The definition of a schedule assumes that operations can be totally ordered by time. Consider a database system that runs on a system with multiple processors, where it is not always possible to establish an exact ordering between operations that executed on different processors. However, operations on a data item can be totally ordered.

     Does the above situation cause any problem for the definition of conflict serializability? Explain your answer.

Exercises

14.12   List the ACID properties. Explain the usefulness of each.

14.13   During its execution, a transaction passes through several states, until it finally commits or aborts. List all possible sequences of states through which a transaction may pass. Explain why each state transition may occur.

14.14 Explain the distinction between the terms *serial schedule* and *serializable schedule*.

14.15 Consider the following two transactions:

$$T_{13}: \text{read}(A);$$
$$\text{read}(B);$$
$$\textbf{if } A = 0 \textbf{ then } B := B + 1;$$
$$\text{write}(B).$$
$$T_{14}: \text{read}(B);$$
$$\text{read}(A);$$
$$\textbf{if } B = 0 \textbf{ then } A := A + 1;$$
$$\text{write}(A).$$

Let the consistency requirement be $A = 0 \lor B = 0$, with $A = B = 0$ the initial values.

  a. Show that every serial execution involving these two transactions preserves the consistency of the database.

  b. Show a concurrent execution of T_{13} and T_{14} that produces a nonserializable schedule.

  c. Is there a concurrent execution of T_{13} and T_{14} that produces a serializable schedule?

14.16 Give an example of a serializable schedule with two transactions such that the order in which the transactions commit is different from the serialization order.

14.17 What is a recoverable schedule? Why is recoverability of schedules desirable? Are there any circumstances under which it would be desirable to allow nonrecoverable schedules? Explain your answer.

14.18 Why do database systems support concurrent execution of transactions, in spite of the extra programming effort needed to ensure that concurrent execution does not cause any problems?

14.19 Explain why the read-committed isolation level ensures that schedules are cascade-free.

14.20 For each of the following isolation levels, give an example of a schedule that respects the specified level of isolation, but is not serializable:

  a. Read uncommitted

  b. Read committed

  c. Repeatable read

14.21 Suppose that in addition to the operations read and write, we allow an operation pred_read(r, P), which reads all tuples in relation r that satisfy predicate P.

  a. Give an example of a schedule using the pred_read operation that exhibits the phantom phenomenon, and is nonserializable as a result.

  b. Give an example of a schedule where one transaction uses the pred_read operation on relation r and another concurrent transactions deletes a tuple from r, but the schedule does not exhibit a phantom conflict. (To do so, you have to give the schema of relation r, and show the attribute values of the deleted tuple.)

Bibliographical Notes

Gray and Reuter [1993] provides detailed textbook coverage of transaction-processing concepts, techniques and implementation details, including concurrency control and recovery issues. Bernstein and Newcomer [1997] provides textbook coverage of various aspects of transaction processing.

The concept of serializability was formalized by Eswaran et al. [1976] in connection to work on concurrency control for System R.

References covering specific aspects of transaction processing, such as concurrency control and recovery, are cited in Chapters 15, 16, and 26.

CHAPTER 15

Concurrency Control

We saw in Chapter 14 that one of the fundamental properties of a transaction is isolation. When several transactions execute concurrently in the database, however, the isolation property may no longer be preserved. To ensure that it is, the system must control the interaction among the concurrent transactions; this control is achieved through one of a variety of mechanisms called *concurrency-control* schemes. In Chapter 26, we discuss concurrency-control schemes that admit nonserializable schedules. In this chapter, we consider the management of concurrently executing transactions, and we ignore failures. In Chapter 16, we shall see how the system can recover from failures.

As we shall see, there are a variety of concurrency-control schemes. No one scheme is clearly the best; each one has advantages. In practice, the most frequently used schemes are *two-phase locking* and *snapshot isolation*.

15.1 Lock-Based Protocols

One way to ensure isolation is to require that data items be accessed in a mutually exclusive manner; that is, while one transaction is accessing a data item, no other transaction can modify that data item. The most common method used to implement this requirement is to allow a transaction to access a data item only if it is currently holding a **lock** on that item. We introduced the concept of locking in Section 14.9.

15.1.1 Locks

There are various modes in which a data item may be locked. In this section, we restrict our attention to two modes:

1. **Shared**. If a transaction T_i has obtained a **shared-mode lock** (denoted by S) on item Q, then T_i can read, but cannot write, Q.

2. **Exclusive**. If a transaction T_i has obtained an **exclusive-mode lock** (denoted by X) on item Q, then T_i can both read and write Q.

	S	X
S	true	false
X	false	false

Figure 15.1   Lock-compatibility matrix comp.

We require that every transaction **request** a lock in an appropriate mode on data item Q, depending on the types of operations that it will perform on Q. The transaction makes the request to the concurrency-control manager. The transaction can proceed with the operation only after the concurrency-control manager **grants** the lock to the transaction. The use of these two lock modes allows multiple transactions to read a data item but limits write access to just one transaction at a time.

To state this more generally, given a set of lock modes, we can define a **compatibility function** on them as follows: Let A and B represent arbitrary lock modes. Suppose that a transaction T_i requests a lock of mode A on item Q on which transaction T_j $(T_i \neq T_j)$ currently holds a lock of mode B. If transaction T_i can be granted a lock on Q immediately, in spite of the presence of the mode B lock, then we say mode A is **compatible** with mode B. Such a function can be represented conveniently by a matrix. The compatibility relation between the two modes of locking discussed in this section appears in the matrix comp of Figure 15.1. An element comp(A, B) of the matrix has the value *true* if and only if mode A is compatible with mode B.

Note that shared mode is compatible with shared mode, but not with exclusive mode. At any time, several shared-mode locks can be held simultaneously (by different transactions) on a particular data item. A subsequent exclusive-mode lock request has to wait until the currently held shared-mode locks are released.

A transaction requests a shared lock on data item Q by executing the lock-S(Q) instruction. Similarly, a transaction requests an exclusive lock through the lock-X(Q) instruction. A transaction can unlock a data item Q by the unlock(Q) instruction.

To access a data item, transaction T_i must first lock that item. If the data item is already locked by another transaction in an incompatible mode, the concurrency-control manager will not grant the lock until all incompatible locks held by other transactions have been released. Thus, T_i is made to **wait** until all incompatible locks held by other transactions have been released.

Transaction T_i may unlock a data item that it had locked at some earlier point. Note that a transaction must hold a lock on a data item as long as it accesses that item. Moreover, it is not necessarily desirable for a transaction to unlock a data item immediately after its final access of that data item, since serializability may not be ensured.

As an illustration, consider again the banking example that we introduced in Chapter 14. Let A and B be two accounts that are accessed by transactions T_1

$$T_1: \; \text{lock-X}(B);$$
$$\text{read}(B);$$
$$B := B - 50;$$
$$\text{write}(B);$$
$$\text{unlock}(B);$$
$$\text{lock-X}(A);$$
$$\text{read}(A);$$
$$A := A + 50;$$
$$\text{write}(A);$$
$$\text{unlock}(A).$$

Figure 15.2 Transaction T_1.

and T_2. Transaction T_1 transfers $50 from account B to account A (Figure 15.2). Transaction T_2 displays the total amount of money in accounts A and B—that is, the sum $A + B$ (Figure 15.3).

Suppose that the values of accounts A and B are $100 and $200, respectively. If these two transactions are executed serially, either in the order T_1, T_2 or the order T_2, T_1, then transaction T_2 will display the value $300. If, however, these transactions are executed concurrently, then schedule 1, in Figure 15.4, is possible. In this case, transaction T_2 displays $250, which is incorrect. The reason for this mistake is that the transaction T_1 unlocked data item B too early, as a result of which T_2 saw an inconsistent state.

The schedule shows the actions executed by the transactions, as well as the points at which the concurrency-control manager grants the locks. The transaction making a lock request cannot execute its next action until the concurrency-control manager grants the lock. Hence, the lock must be granted in the interval of time between the lock-request operation and the following action of the transaction. Exactly when within this interval the lock is granted is not important; we can safely assume that the lock is granted just before the following action of the transaction. We shall therefore drop the column depicting the actions of the concurrency-control manager from all schedules depicted in the rest of the chapter. We let you infer when locks are granted.

$$T_2: \; \text{lock-S}(A);$$
$$\text{read}(A);$$
$$\text{unlock}(A);$$
$$\text{lock-S}(B);$$
$$\text{read}(B);$$
$$\text{unlock}(B);$$
$$\text{display}(A + B).$$

Figure 15.3 Transaction T_2.

T_1	T_2	concurreny-control manager
lock-X(B)		
		grant-X(B, T_1)
read(B)		
$B := B - 50$		
write(B)		
unlock(B)		
	lock-S(A)	
		grant-S(A, T_2)
	read(A)	
	unlock(A)	
	lock-S(B)	
		grant-S(B, T_2)
	read(B)	
	unlock(B)	
	display($A + B$)	
lock-X(A)		
		grant-X(A, T_1)
read(A)		
$A := A - 50$		
write(A)		
unlock(A)		

Figure 15.4 Schedule 1.

Suppose now that unlocking is delayed to the end of the transaction. Transaction T_3 corresponds to T_1 with unlocking delayed (Figure 15.5). Transaction T_4 corresponds to T_2 with unlocking delayed (Figure 15.6).

You should verify that the sequence of reads and writes in schedule 1, which lead to an incorrect total of \$250 being displayed, is no longer possible with T_3

T_3: lock-X(B);
    read(B);
    $B := B - 50$;
    write(B);
    lock-X(A);
    read(A);
    $A := A + 50$;
    write(A);
    unlock(B);
    unlock(A).

Figure 15.5 Transaction T_3 (transaction T_1 with unlocking delayed).

T_4: lock-S(A);
  read(A);
  lock-S(B);
  read(B);
  display($A + B$);
  unlock(A);
  unlock(B).

Figure 15.6 Transaction T_4 (transaction T_2 with unlocking delayed).

and T_4. Other schedules are possible. T_4 will not print out an inconsistent result in any of them; we shall see why later.

Unfortunately, locking can lead to an undesirable situation. Consider the partial schedule of Figure 15.7 for T_3 and T_4. Since T_3 is holding an exclusive-mode lock on B and T_4 is requesting a shared-mode lock on B, T_4 is waiting for T_3 to unlock B. Similarly, since T_4 is holding a shared-mode lock on A and T_3 is requesting an exclusive-mode lock on A, T_3 is waiting for T_4 to unlock A. Thus, we have arrived at a state where neither of these transactions can ever proceed with its normal execution. This situation is called **deadlock**. When deadlock occurs, the system must roll back one of the two transactions. Once a transaction has been rolled back, the data items that were locked by that transaction are unlocked. These data items are then available to the other transaction, which can continue with its execution. We shall return to the issue of deadlock handling in Section 15.2.

If we do not use locking, or if we unlock data items too soon after reading or writing them, we may get inconsistent states. On the other hand, if we do not unlock a data item before requesting a lock on another data item, deadlocks may occur. There are ways to avoid deadlock in some situations, as we shall see in Section 15.1.5. However, in general, deadlocks are a necessary evil associated with locking, if we want to avoid inconsistent states. Deadlocks are definitely

T_3	T_4
lock-x(B)	
read(B)	
$B := B - 50$	
write(B)	
	lock-S(A)
	read(A)
	lock-S(B)
lock-x(A)	

Figure 15.7 Schedule 2.

preferable to inconsistent states, since they can be handled by rolling back transactions, whereas inconsistent states may lead to real-world problems that cannot
be handled by the database system.

We shall require that each transaction in the system follow a set of rules, called
a **locking protocol**, indicating when a transaction may lock and unlock each of the
data items. Locking protocols restrict the number of possible schedules. The set of
all such schedules is a proper subset of all possible serializable schedules. We shall
present several locking protocols that allow only conflict-serializable schedules,
and thereby ensure isolation. Before doing so, we introduce some terminology.

Let $\{T_0, T_1, \ldots, T_n\}$ be a set of transactions participating in a schedule S. We
say that T_i **precedes** T_j in S, written $T_i \rightarrow T_j$, if there exists a data item Q such
that T_i has held lock mode A on Q, and T_j has held lock mode B on Q later, and
comp(A,B) = false. If $T_i \rightarrow T_j$, then that precedence implies that in any equivalent
serial schedule, T_i must appear before T_j. Observe that this graph is similar to the
precedence graph that we used in Section 14.6 to test for conflict serializability.
Conflicts between instructions correspond to noncompatibility of lock modes.

We say that a schedule S is **legal** under a given locking protocol if S is a
possible schedule for a set of transactions that follows the rules of the locking
protocol. We say that a locking protocol **ensures** conflict serializability if and only
if all legal schedules are conflict serializable; in other words, for all legal schedules
the associated $\rightarrow$ relation is acyclic.

15.1.2   Granting of Locks

When a transaction requests a lock on a data item in a particular mode, and no
other transaction has a lock on the same data item in a conflicting mode, the lock
can be granted. However, care must be taken to avoid the following scenario.
Suppose a transaction T_2 has a shared-mode lock on a data item, and another
transaction T_1 requests an exclusive-mode lock on the data item. Clearly, T_1 has
to wait for T_2 to release the shared-mode lock. Meanwhile, a transaction T_3 may
request a shared-mode lock on the same data item. The lock request is compatible
with the lock granted to T_2, so T_3 may be granted the shared-mode lock. At this
point T_2 may release the lock, but still T_1 has to wait for T_3 to finish. But again,
there may be a new transaction T_4 that requests a shared-mode lock on the same
data item, and is granted the lock before T_3 releases it. In fact, it is possible that
there is a sequence of transactions that each requests a shared-mode lock on the
data item, and each transaction releases the lock a short while after it is granted,
but T_1 never gets the exclusive-mode lock on the data item. The transaction T_1
may never make progress, and is said to be **starved**.

We can avoid starvation of transactions by granting locks in the following
manner: When a transaction T_i requests a lock on a data item Q in a particular
mode M, the concurrency-control manager grants the lock provided that:

1. There is no other transaction holding a lock on Q in a mode that conflicts
    with M.

2. There is no other transaction that is waiting for a lock on Q and that made its lock request before T_i.

Thus, a lock request will never get blocked by a lock request that is made later.

15.1.3 The Two-Phase Locking Protocol

One protocol that ensures serializability is the **two-phase locking protocol**. This protocol requires that each transaction issue lock and unlock requests in two phases:

1. **Growing phase**. A transaction may obtain locks, but may not release any lock.

2. **Shrinking phase**. A transaction may release locks, but may not obtain any new locks.

Initially, a transaction is in the growing phase. The transaction acquires locks as needed. Once the transaction releases a lock, it enters the shrinking phase, and it can issue no more lock requests.

For example, transactions T_3 and T_4 are two phase. On the other hand, transactions T_1 and T_2 are not two phase. Note that the unlock instructions do not need to appear at the end of the transaction. For example, in the case of transaction T_3, we could move the unlock(B) instruction to just after the lock-X(A) instruction, and still retain the two-phase locking property.

We can show that the two-phase locking protocol ensures conflict serializability. Consider any transaction. The point in the schedule where the transaction has obtained its final lock (the end of its growing phase) is called the **lock point** of the transaction. Now, transactions can be ordered according to their lock points—this ordering is, in fact, a serializability ordering for the transactions. We leave the proof as an exercise for you to do (see Practice Exercise 15.1).

Two-phase locking does *not* ensure freedom from deadlock. Observe that transactions T_3 and T_4 are two phase, but, in schedule 2 (Figure 15.7), they are deadlocked.

Recall from Section 14.7.2 that, in addition to being serializable, schedules should be cascadeless. Cascading rollback may occur under two-phase locking. As an illustration, consider the partial schedule of Figure 15.8. Each transaction observes the two-phase locking protocol, but the failure of T_5 after the read(A) step of T_7 leads to cascading rollback of T_6 and T_7.

Cascading rollbacks can be avoided by a modification of two-phase locking called the **strict two-phase locking protocol**. This protocol requires not only that locking be two phase, but also that all exclusive-mode locks taken by a transaction be held until that transaction commits. This requirement ensures that any data written by an uncommitted transaction are locked in exclusive mode until the transaction commits, preventing any other transaction from reading the data.

Another variant of two-phase locking is the **rigorous two-phase locking protocol**, which requires that all locks be held until the transaction commits.

T_5	T_6	T_7
lock-x(A) read(A) lock-s(B) read(B) write(A) unlock(A)		
	lock-x(A) read(A) write(A) unlock(A)	
		lock-s(A) read(A)

Figure 15.8 Partial schedule under two-phase locking.

We can easily verify that, with rigorous two-phase locking, transactions can be serialized in the order in which they commit.

Consider the following two transactions, for which we have shown only some of the significant **read** and **write** operations:

$$T_8: \text{read}(a_1);$$
$$\text{read}(a_2);$$
$$\dots$$
$$\text{read}(a_n);$$
$$\text{write}(a_1).$$

$$T_9: \text{read}(a_1);$$
$$\text{read}(a_2);$$
$$\text{display}(a_1 + a_2).$$

If we employ the two-phase locking protocol, then T_8 must lock a_1 in exclusive mode. Therefore, any concurrent execution of both transactions amounts to a serial execution. Notice, however, that T_8 needs an exclusive lock on a_1 only at the end of its execution, when it writes a_1. Thus, if T_8 could initially lock a_1 in shared mode, and then could later change the lock to exclusive mode, we could get more concurrency, since T_8 and T_9 could access a_1 and a_2 simultaneously.

This observation leads us to a refinement of the basic two-phase locking protocol, in which **lock conversions** are allowed. We shall provide a mechanism for upgrading a shared lock to an exclusive lock, and downgrading an exclusive lock to a shared lock. We denote conversion from shared to exclusive modes by **upgrade**, and from exclusive to shared by **downgrade**. Lock conversion cannot be allowed arbitrarily. Rather, upgrading can take place in only the growing phase, whereas downgrading can take place in only the shrinking phase.

T_8	T_9
lock-S(a_1)	
	lock-S(a_1)
lock-S(a_2)	
	lock-S(a_2)
lock-S(a_3)	
lock-S(a_4)	
	unlock(a_1)
	unlock(a_2)
lock-S(a_n)	
upgrade(a_1)	

Figure 15.9 Incomplete schedule with a lock conversion.

Returning to our example, transactions T_8 and T_9 can run concurrently under the refined two-phase locking protocol, as shown in the incomplete schedule of Figure 15.9, where only some of the locking instructions are shown.

Note that a transaction attempting to upgrade a lock on an item Q may be forced to wait. This enforced wait occurs if Q is currently locked by *another* transaction in shared mode.

Just like the basic two-phase locking protocol, two-phase locking with lock conversion generates only conflict-serializable schedules, and transactions can be serialized by their lock points. Further, if exclusive locks are held until the end of the transaction, the schedules are cascadeless.

For a set of transactions, there may be conflict-serializable schedules that cannot be obtained through the two-phase locking protocol. However, to obtain conflict-serializable schedules through non-two-phase locking protocols, we need either to have additional information about the transactions or to impose some structure or ordering on the set of data items in the database. We shall see examples when we consider other locking protocols later in this chapter.

Strict two-phase locking and rigorous two-phase locking (with lock conversions) are used extensively in commercial database systems.

A simple but widely used scheme automatically generates the appropriate lock and unlock instructions for a transaction, on the basis of read and write requests from the transaction:

- When a transaction T_i issues a read(Q) operation, the system issues a lock-S(Q) instruction followed by the read(Q) instruction.

- When T_i issues a write(Q) operation, the system checks to see whether T_i already holds a shared lock on Q. If it does, then the system issues an upgrade(Q) instruction, followed by the write(Q) instruction. Otherwise, the system issues a lock-X(Q) instruction, followed by the write(Q) instruction.

- All locks obtained by a transaction are unlocked after that transaction commits or aborts.

15.1.4   Implementation of Locking

A **lock manager** can be implemented as a process that receives messages from transactions and sends messages in reply. The lock-manager process replies to lock-request messages with lock-grant messages, or with messages requesting rollback of the transaction (in case of deadlocks). Unlock messages require only an acknowledgment in response, but may result in a grant message to another waiting transaction.

The lock manager uses this data structure: For each data item that is currently locked, it maintains a linked list of records, one for each request, in the order in which the requests arrived. It uses a hash table, indexed on the name of a data item, to find the linked list (if any) for a data item; this table is called the **lock table**. Each record of the linked list for a data item notes which transaction made the request, and what lock mode it requested. The record also notes if the request has currently been granted.

Figure 15.10 shows an example of a lock table. The table contains locks for five different data items, I4, I7, I23, I44, and I912. The lock table uses overflow chaining, so there is a linked list of data items for each entry in the lock table. There is also a list of transactions that have been granted locks, or are waiting for locks, for each of the data items. Granted locks are the rectangles filled in a darker shade, while waiting requests are the rectangles filled in a lighter shade. We have omitted the lock mode to keep the figure simple. It can be seen, for example, that T23 has been granted locks on I912 and I7, and is waiting for a lock on I4.

Although the figure does not show it, the lock table should also maintain an index on transaction identifiers, so that it is possible to determine efficiently the set of locks held by a given transaction.

The lock manager processes requests this way:

- When a lock request message arrives, it adds a record to the end of the linked list for the data item, if the linked list is present. Otherwise it creates a new linked list, containing only the record for the request.

    It always grants a lock request on a data item that is not currently locked. But if the transaction requests a lock on an item on which a lock is currently held, the lock manager grants the request only if it is compatible with the locks that are currently held, and all earlier requests have been granted already. Otherwise the request has to wait.

- When the lock manager receives an unlock message from a transaction, it deletes the record for that data item in the linked list corresponding to that transaction. It tests the record that follows, if any, as described in the previous paragraph, to see if that request can now be granted. If it can, the lock manager grants that request, and processes the record following it, if any, similarly, and so on.

- If a transaction aborts, the lock manager deletes any waiting request made by the transaction. Once the database system has taken appropriate actions to undo the transaction (see Section 16.3), it releases all locks held by the aborted transaction.

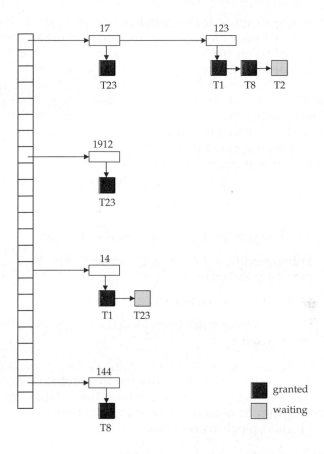

Figure 15.10   Lock table.

This algorithm guarantees freedom from starvation for lock requests, since a request can never be granted while a request received earlier is waiting to be granted. We study how to detect and handle deadlocks later, in Section 15.2.2. Section 17.2.1 describes an alternative implementation—one that uses shared memory instead of message passing for lock request/grant.

15.1.5   Graph-Based Protocols

As noted in Section 15.1.3, if we wish to develop protocols that are not two phase, we need additional information on how each transaction will access the database. There are various models that can give us the additional information, each differing in the amount of information provided. The simplest model requires that we have prior knowledge about the order in which the database items will be accessed. Given such information, it is possible to construct locking protocols that are not two phase, but that, nevertheless, ensure conflict serializability.

To acquire such prior knowledge, we impose a partial ordering $\rightarrow$ on the set $\mathbf{D} = \{d_1, d_2, \ldots, d_h\}$ of all data items. If $d_i \rightarrow d_j$, then any transaction accessing both d_i and d_j must access d_i before accessing d_j. This partial ordering may be the result of either the logical or the physical organization of the data, or it may be imposed solely for the purpose of concurrency control.

The partial ordering implies that the set **D** may now be viewed as a directed acyclic graph, called a **database graph**. In this section, for the sake of simplicity, we will restrict our attention to only those graphs that are rooted trees. We shall present a simple protocol, called the *tree protocol*, which is restricted to employ only *exclusive* locks. References to other, more complex, graph-based locking protocols are in the bibliographical notes.

In the **tree protocol**, the only lock instruction allowed is lock-X. Each transaction T_i can lock a data item at most once, and must observe the following rules:

1. The first lock by T_i may be on any data item.

2. Subsequently, a data item Q can be locked by T_i only if the parent of Q is currently locked by T_i.

3. Data items may be unlocked at any time.

4. A data item that has been locked and unlocked by T_i cannot subsequently be relocked by T_i.

All schedules that are legal under the tree protocol are conflict serializable.

To illustrate this protocol, consider the database graph of Figure 15.11. The following four transactions follow the tree protocol on this graph. We show only the lock and unlock instructions:

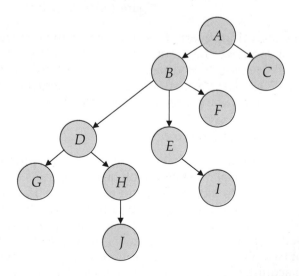

Figure 15.11   Tree-structured database graph.

T_{10}: lock-x(B); lock-x(E); lock-x(D); unlock(B); unlock(E); lock-x(G); unlock(D); unlock(G).

T_{11}: lock-x(D); lock-x(H); unlock(D); unlock(H).

T_{12}: lock-x(B); lock-x(E); unlock(E); unlock(B).

T_{13}: lock-x(D); lock-x(H); unlock(D); unlock(H).

One possible schedule in which these four transactions participated appears in Figure 15.12. Note that, during its execution, transaction T_{10} holds locks on two *disjoint* subtrees.

Observe that the schedule of Figure 15.12 is conflict serializable. It can be shown not only that the tree protocol ensures conflict serializability, but also that this protocol ensures freedom from deadlock.

The tree protocol in Figure 15.12 does not ensure recoverability and cascadelessness. To ensure recoverability and cascadelessness, the protocol can be modified to not permit release of exclusive locks until the end of the transaction. Holding exclusive locks until the end of the transaction reduces concurrency. Here is an alternative that improves concurrency, but ensures only recoverability: For each data item with an uncommitted write, we record which transaction performed the last write to the data item. Whenever a transaction T_i performs a read of an uncommitted data item, we record a **commit dependency** of T_i on the

T_{10}	T_{11}	T_{12}	T_{13}
lock-x(B)			
	lock-x(D)		
	lock-x(H)		
	unlock(D)		
lock-x(E)			
lock-x(D)			
unlock(B)			
unlock(E)			
		lock-x(B)	
		lock-x(E)	
	unlock(H)		
lock-x(G)			
unlock(D)			
			lock-x(D)
			lock-x(H)
			unlock(D)
			unlock(H)
		unlock(E)	
		unlock(B)	
unlock(G)			

Figure 15.12 Serializable schedule under the tree protocol.

transaction that performed the last write to the data item. Transaction T_i is then not permitted to commit until the commit of all transactions on which it has a commit dependency. If any of these transactions aborts, T_i must also be aborted.

The tree-locking protocol has an advantage over the two-phase locking protocol in that, unlike two-phase locking, it is deadlock-free, so no rollbacks are required. The tree-locking protocol has another advantage over the two-phase locking protocol in that unlocking may occur earlier. Earlier unlocking may lead to shorter waiting times, and to an increase in concurrency.

However, the protocol has the disadvantage that, in some cases, a transaction may have to lock data items that it does not access. For example, a transaction that needs to access data items A and J in the database graph of Figure 15.11 must lock not only A and J, but also data items B, D, and H. This additional locking results in increased locking overhead, the possibility of additional waiting time, and a potential decrease in concurrency. Further, without prior knowledge of what data items will need to be locked, transactions will have to lock the root of the tree, and that can reduce concurrency greatly.

For a set of transactions, there may be conflict-serializable schedules that cannot be obtained through the tree protocol. Indeed, there are schedules possible under the two-phase locking protocol that are not possible under the tree protocol, and vice versa. Examples of such schedules are explored in the exercises.

15.2   Deadlock Handling

A system is in a deadlock state if there exists a set of transactions such that every transaction in the set is waiting for another transaction in the set. More precisely, there exists a set of waiting transactions $\{T_0, T_1, \ldots, T_n\}$ such that T_0 is waiting for a data item that T_1 holds, and T_1 is waiting for a data item that T_2 holds, and $\ldots$, and T_{n-1} is waiting for a data item that T_n holds, and T_n is waiting for a data item that T_0 holds. None of the transactions can make progress in such a situation.

The only remedy to this undesirable situation is for the system to invoke some drastic action, such as rolling back some of the transactions involved in the deadlock. Rollback of a transaction may be partial: That is, a transaction may be rolled back to the point where it obtained a lock whose release resolves the deadlock.

There are two principal methods for dealing with the deadlock problem. We can use a **deadlock prevention** protocol to ensure that the system will *never* enter a deadlock state. Alternatively, we can allow the system to enter a deadlock state, and then try to recover by using a **deadlock detection** and **deadlock recovery** scheme. As we shall see, both methods may result in transaction rollback. Prevention is commonly used if the probability that the system would enter a deadlock state is relatively high; otherwise, detection and recovery are more efficient.

Note that a detection and recovery scheme requires overhead that includes not only the run-time cost of maintaining the necessary information and of executing the detection algorithm, but also the potential losses inherent in recovery from a deadlock.

15.2.1   Deadlock Prevention

There are two approaches to deadlock prevention. One approach ensures that no cyclic waits can occur by ordering the requests for locks, or requiring all locks to be acquired together. The other approach is closer to deadlock recovery, and performs transaction rollback instead of waiting for a lock, whenever the wait could potentially result in a deadlock.

The simplest scheme under the first approach requires that each transaction locks all its data items before it begins execution. Moreover, either all are locked in one step or none are locked. There are two main disadvantages to this protocol: (1) it is often hard to predict, before the transaction begins, what data items need to be locked; (2) data-item utilization may be very low, since many of the data items may be locked but unused for a long time.

Another approach for preventing deadlocks is to impose an ordering of all data items, and to require that a transaction lock data items only in a sequence consistent with the ordering. We have seen one such scheme in the tree protocol, which uses a partial ordering of data items.

A variation of this approach is to use a total order of data items, in conjunction with two-phase locking. Once a transaction has locked a particular item, it cannot request locks on items that precede that item in the ordering. This scheme is easy to implement, as long as the set of data items accessed by a transaction is known when the transaction starts execution. There is no need to change the underlying concurrency-control system if two-phase locking is used: All that is needed is to ensure that locks are requested in the right order.

The second approach for preventing deadlocks is to use preemption and transaction rollbacks. In preemption, when a transaction T_j requests a lock that transaction T_i holds, the lock granted to T_i may be **preempted** by rolling back of T_i, and granting of the lock to T_j. To control the preemption, we assign a unique timestamp, based on a counter or on the system clock, to each transaction when it begins. The system uses these timestamps only to decide whether a transaction should wait or roll back. Locking is still used for concurrency control. If a transaction is rolled back, it retains its *old* timestamp when restarted. Two different deadlock-prevention schemes using timestamps have been proposed:

1. The **wait–die** scheme is a nonpreemptive technique. When transaction T_i requests a data item currently held by T_j, T_i is allowed to wait only if it has a timestamp smaller than that of T_j (that is, T_i is older than T_j). Otherwise, T_i is rolled back (dies).

   For example, suppose that transactions T_{14}, T_{15}, and T_{16} have timestamps 5, 10, and 15, respectively. If T_{14} requests a data item held by T_{15}, then T_{14} will wait. If T_{24} requests a data item held by T_{15}, then T_{16} will be rolled back.

2. The **wound–wait** scheme is a preemptive technique. It is a counterpart to the wait–die scheme. When transaction T_i requests a data item currently held by T_j, T_i is allowed to wait only if it has a timestamp larger than that of T_j (that is, T_i is younger than T_j). Otherwise, T_j is rolled back (T_j is *wounded* by T_i).

Returning to our example, with transactions T_{14}, T_{15}, and T_{16}, if T_{14} requests a data item held by T_{15}, then the data item will be preempted from T_{15}, and T_{15} will be rolled back. If T_{16} requests a data item held by T_{15}, then T_{16} will wait.

The major problem with both of these schemes is that unnecessary rollbacks may occur.

Another simple approach to deadlock prevention is based on **lock timeouts**. In this approach, a transaction that has requested a lock waits for at most a specified amount of time. If the lock has not been granted within that time, the transaction is said to time out, and it rolls itself back and restarts. If there was in fact a deadlock, one or more transactions involved in the deadlock will time out and roll back, allowing the others to proceed. This scheme falls somewhere between deadlock prevention, where a deadlock will never occur, and deadlock detection and recovery, which Section 15.2.2 discusses.

The timeout scheme is particularly easy to implement, and works well if transactions are short and if long waits are likely to be due to deadlocks. However, in general it is hard to decide how long a transaction must wait before timing out. Too long a wait results in unnecessary delays once a deadlock has occurred. Too short a wait results in transaction rollback even when there is no deadlock, leading to wasted resources. Starvation is also a possibility with this scheme. Hence, the timeout-based scheme has limited applicability.

15.2.2   Deadlock Detection and Recovery

If a system does not employ some protocol that ensures deadlock freedom, then a detection and recovery scheme must be used. An algorithm that examines the state of the system is invoked periodically to determine whether a deadlock has occurred. If one has, then the system must attempt to recover from the deadlock. To do so, the system must:

- Maintain information about the current allocation of data items to transactions, as well as any outstanding data item requests.

- Provide an algorithm that uses this information to determine whether the system has entered a deadlock state.

- Recover from the deadlock when the detection algorithm determines that a deadlock exists.

In this section, we elaborate on these issues.

15.2.2.1   Deadlock Detection

Deadlocks can be described precisely in terms of a directed graph called a **wait-for graph**. This graph consists of a pair $G = (V, E)$, where V is a set of vertices and E is a set of edges. The set of vertices consists of all the transactions in the system. Each element in the set E of edges is an ordered pair $T_i \rightarrow T_j$. If $T_i \rightarrow T_j$ is in E,

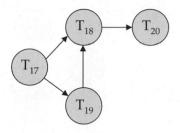

Figure 15.13   Wait-for graph with no cycle.

then there is a directed edge from transaction T_i to T_j, implying that transaction T_i is waiting for transaction T_j to release a data item that it needs.

When transaction T_i requests a data item currently being held by transaction T_j, then the edge $T_i \rightarrow T_j$ is inserted in the wait-for graph. This edge is removed only when transaction T_j is no longer holding a data item needed by transaction T_i.

A deadlock exists in the system if and only if the wait-for graph contains a cycle. Each transaction involved in the cycle is said to be deadlocked. To detect deadlocks, the system needs to maintain the wait-for graph, and periodically to invoke an algorithm that searches for a cycle in the graph.

To illustrate these concepts, consider the wait-for graph in Figure 15.13, which depicts the following situation:

- Transaction T_{17} is waiting for transactions T_{18} and T_{19}.

- Transaction T_{19} is waiting for transaction T_{18}.

- Transaction T_{18} is waiting for transaction T_{20}.

Since the graph has no cycle, the system is not in a deadlock state.

Suppose now that transaction T_{20} is requesting an item held by T_{19}. The edge $T_{20} \rightarrow T_{19}$ is added to the wait-for graph, resulting in the new system state in Figure 15.14. This time, the graph contains the cycle:

$$T_{18} \rightarrow T_{20} \rightarrow T_{19} \rightarrow T_{18}$$

implying that transactions T_{18}, T_{19}, and T_{20} are all deadlocked.

Consequently, the question arises: When should we invoke the detection algorithm? The answer depends on two factors:

1. How often does a deadlock occur?

2. How many transactions will be affected by the deadlock?

If deadlocks occur frequently, then the detection algorithm should be invoked more frequently. Data items allocated to deadlocked transactions will be

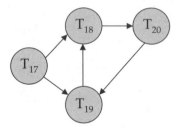

Figure 15.14 Wait-for graph with a cycle.

unavailable to other transactions until the deadlock can be broken. In addition, the number of cycles in the graph may also grow. In the worst case, we would invoke the detection algorithm every time a request for allocation could not be granted immediately.

15.2.2.2 Recovery from Deadlock

When a detection algorithm determines that a deadlock exists, the system must **recover** from the deadlock. The most common solution is to roll back one or more transactions to break the deadlock. Three actions need to be taken:

1. **Selection of a victim**. Given a set of deadlocked transactions, we must determine which transaction (or transactions) to roll back to break the deadlock. We should roll back those transactions that will incur the minimum cost. Unfortunately, the term *minimum cost* is not a precise one. Many factors may determine the cost of a rollback, including:

    a. How long the transaction has computed, and how much longer the transaction will compute before it completes its designated task.

    b. How many data items the transaction has used.

    c. How many more data items the transaction needs for it to complete.

    d. How many transactions will be involved in the rollback.

2. **Rollback**. Once we have decided that a particular transaction must be rolled back, we must determine how far this transaction should be rolled back.

    The simplest solution is a **total rollback**: Abort the transaction and then restart it. However, it is more effective to roll back the transaction only as far as necessary to break the deadlock. Such **partial rollback** requires the system to maintain additional information about the state of all the running transactions. Specifically, the sequence of lock requests/grants and updates performed by the transaction needs to be recorded. The deadlock detection mechanism should decide which locks the selected transaction needs to release in order to break the deadlock. The selected transaction must be rolled back to the point where it obtained the first of these locks, undoing all actions it took after that point. The recovery mechanism must be capable of performing such partial rollbacks. Furthermore, the transactions must be capable of resuming execution after a partial rollback. See the bibliographical notes for relevant references.

3. **Starvation**. In a system where the selection of victims is based primarily on cost factors, it may happen that the same transaction is always picked as a victim. As a result, this transaction never completes its designated task, thus there is **starvation**. We must ensure that a transaction can be picked as a victim only a (small) finite number of times. The most common solution is to include the number of rollbacks in the cost factor.

15.3 Multiple Granularity

In the concurrency-control schemes described thus far, we have used each individual data item as the unit on which synchronization is performed.

There are circumstances, however, where it would be advantageous to group several data items, and to treat them as one individual synchronization unit. For example, if a transaction T_i needs to access the entire database, and a locking protocol is used, then T_i must lock each item in the database. Clearly, executing these locks is time-consuming. It would be better if T_i could issue a *single* lock request to lock the entire database. On the other hand, if transaction T_j needs to access only a few data items, it should not be required to lock the entire database, since otherwise concurrency is lost.

What is needed is a mechanism to allow the system to define multiple levels of **granularity**. This is done by allowing data items to be of various sizes and defining a hierarchy of data granularities, where the small granularities are nested within larger ones. Such a hierarchy can be represented graphically as a tree. Note that the tree that we describe here is significantly different from that used by the tree protocol (Section 15.1.5). A nonleaf node of the multiple-granularity tree represents the data associated with its descendants. In the tree protocol, each node is an independent data item.

As an illustration, consider the tree of Figure 15.15, which consists of four levels of nodes. The highest level represents the entire database. Below it are nodes of type *area*; the database consists of exactly these areas. Each area in turn has nodes of type *file* as its children. Each area contains exactly those files that are its child nodes. No file is in more than one area. Finally, each file has nodes of type *record*. As before, the file consists of exactly those records that are its child nodes, and no record can be present in more than one file.

Each node in the tree can be locked individually. As we did in the two-phase locking protocol, we shall use **shared** and **exclusive** lock modes. When a transaction locks a node, in either shared or exclusive mode, the transaction also has implicitly locked all the descendants of that node in the same lock mode. For example, if transaction T_i gets an **explicit lock** on file F_c of Figure 15.15, in exclusive mode, then it has an **implicit lock** in exclusive mode on all the records belonging to that file. It does not need to lock the individual records of F_c explicitly.

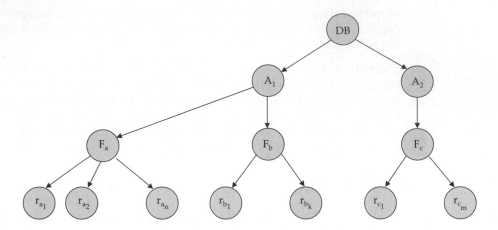

Figure 15.15 Granularity hierarchy.

Suppose that transaction T_j wishes to lock record r_{b_6} of file F_b. Since T_i has locked F_b explicitly, it follows that r_{b_6} is also locked (implicitly). But, when T_j issues a lock request for r_{b_6}, r_{b_6} is not explicitly locked! How does the system determine whether T_j can lock r_{b_6}? T_j must traverse the tree from the root to record r_{b_6}. If any node in that path is locked in an incompatible mode, then T_j must be delayed.

Suppose now that transaction T_k wishes to lock the entire database. To do so, it simply must lock the root of the hierarchy. Note, however, that T_k should not succeed in locking the root node, since T_i is currently holding a lock on part of the tree (specifically, on file F_b). But how does the system determine if the root node can be locked? One possibility is for it to search the entire tree. This solution, however, defeats the whole purpose of the multiple-granularity locking scheme. A more efficient way to gain this knowledge is to introduce a new class of lock modes, called **intention lock modes**. If a node is locked in an intention mode, explicit locking is done at a lower level of the tree (that is, at a finer granularity). Intention locks are put on all the ancestors of a node before that node is locked explicitly. Thus, a transaction does not need to search the entire tree to determine whether it can lock a node successfully. A transaction wishing to lock a node—say, Q—must traverse a path in the tree from the root to Q. While traversing the tree, the transaction locks the various nodes in an intention mode.

There is an intention mode associated with shared mode, and there is one with exclusive mode. If a node is locked in **intention-shared (IS) mode**, explicit locking is being done at a lower level of the tree, but with only shared-mode locks. Similarly, if a node is locked in **intention-exclusive (IX) mode**, then explicit locking is being done at a lower level, with exclusive-mode or shared-mode locks. Finally, if a node is locked in **shared and intention-exclusive (SIX) mode**, the subtree rooted by that node is locked explicitly in shared mode, and that explicit locking is being done at a lower level with exclusive-mode locks. The compatibility function for these lock modes is in Figure 15.16.

	IS	IX	S	SIX	X
IS	true	true	true	true	false
IX	true	true	false	false	false
S	true	false	true	false	false
SIX	true	false	false	false	false
X	false	false	false	false	false

Figure 15.16 Compatibility matrix.

The **multiple-granularity locking protocol** uses these lock modes to ensure serializability. It requires that a transaction T_i that attempts to lock a node Q must follow these rules:

1. Transaction T_i must observe the lock-compatibility function of Figure 15.16.

2. Transaction T_i must lock the root of the tree first, and can lock it in any mode.

3. Transaction T_i can lock a node Q in S or IS mode only if T_i currently has the parent of Q locked in either IX or IS mode.

4. Transaction T_i can lock a node Q in X, SIX, or IX mode only if T_i currently has the parent of Q locked in either IX or SIX mode.

5. Transaction T_i can lock a node only if T_i has not previously unlocked any node (that is, T_i is two phase).

6. Transaction T_i can unlock a node Q only if T_i currently has none of the children of Q locked.

Observe that the multiple-granularity protocol requires that locks be acquired in *top-down* (root-to-leaf) order, whereas locks must be released in *bottom-up* (leaf-to-root) order.

As an illustration of the protocol, consider the tree of Figure 15.15 and these transactions:

*   Suppose that transaction T_{21} reads record r_{a_2} in file F_a. Then, T_{21} needs to lock the database, area A_1, and F_a in IS mode (and in that order), and finally to lock r_{a_2} in S mode.

*   Suppose that transaction T_{22} modifies record r_{a_9} in file F_a. Then, T_{22} needs to lock the database, area A_1, and file F_a (and in that order) in IX mode, and finally to lock r_{a_9} in X mode.

*   Suppose that transaction T_{23} reads all the records in file F_a. Then, T_{23} needs to lock the database and area A_1 (and in that order) in IS mode, and finally to lock F_a in S mode.

- Suppose that transaction T_{24} reads the entire database. It can do so after locking the database in S mode.

We note that transactions T_{21}, T_{23}, and T_{24} can access the database concurrently. Transaction T_{22} can execute concurrently with T_{21}, but not with either T_{23} or T_{24}.

This protocol enhances concurrency and reduces lock overhead. It is particularly useful in applications that include a mix of:

- Short transactions that access only a few data items.

- Long transactions that produce reports from an entire file or set of files.

There is a similar locking protocol that is applicable to database systems in which data granularities are organized in the form of a directed acyclic graph. See the bibliographical notes for additional references. Deadlock is possible in the multiple-granularity protocol, as it is in the two-phase locking protocol. There are techniques to reduce deadlock frequency in the multiple-granularity protocol, and also to eliminate deadlock entirely. These techniques are referenced in the bibliographical notes.

15.4   Timestamp-Based Protocols

The locking protocols that we have described thus far determine the order between every pair of conflicting transactions at execution time by the first lock that both members of the pair request that involves incompatible modes. Another method for determining the serializability order is to select an ordering among transactions in advance. The most common method for doing so is to use a *timestamp-ordering* scheme.

15.4.1   Timestamps

With each transaction T_i in the system, we associate a unique fixed timestamp, denoted by $TS(T_i)$. This timestamp is assigned by the database system before the transaction T_i starts execution. If a transaction T_i has been assigned timestamp $TS(T_i)$, and a new transaction T_j enters the system, then $TS(T_i) < TS(T_j)$. There are two simple methods for implementing this scheme:

1. Use the value of the **system clock** as the timestamp; that is, a transaction's timestamp is equal to the value of the clock when the transaction enters the system.

2. Use a **logical counter** that is incremented after a new timestamp has been assigned; that is, a transaction's timestamp is equal to the value of the counter when the transaction enters the system.

The timestamps of the transactions determine the serializability order. Thus, if $TS(T_i) < TS(T_j)$, then the system must ensure that the produced schedule is equivalent to a serial schedule in which transaction T_i appears before transaction T_j.

To implement this scheme, we associate with each data item Q two timestamp values:

- **W-timestamp**(Q) denotes the largest timestamp of any transaction that executed write(Q) successfully.

- **R-timestamp**(Q) denotes the largest timestamp of any transaction that executed read(Q) successfully.

These timestamps are updated whenever a new read(Q) or write(Q) instruction is executed.

15.4.2   The Timestamp-Ordering Protocol

The **timestamp-ordering protocol** ensures that any conflicting read and write operations are executed in timestamp order. This protocol operates as follows:

1. Suppose that transaction T_i issues read(Q).

   a. If $TS(T_i) <$ W-timestamp(Q), then T_i needs to read a value of Q that was already overwritten. Hence, the read operation is rejected, and T_i is rolled back.

   b. If $TS(T_i) \geq$ W-timestamp(Q), then the read operation is executed, and R-timestamp(Q) is set to the maximum of R-timestamp(Q) and $TS(T_i)$.

2. Suppose that transaction T_i issues write(Q).

   a. If $TS(T_i) <$ R-timestamp(Q), then the value of Q that T_i is producing was needed previously, and the system assumed that that value would never be produced. Hence, the system rejects the write operation and rolls T_i back.

   b. If $TS(T_i) <$ W-timestamp(Q), then T_i is attempting to write an obsolete value of Q. Hence, the system rejects this write operation and rolls T_i back.

   c. Otherwise, the system executes the write operation and sets W-timestamp(Q) to $TS(T_i)$.

If a transaction T_i is rolled back by the concurrency-control scheme as result of issuance of either a read or write operation, the system assigns it a new timestamp and restarts it.

To illustrate this protocol, we consider transactions T_{25} and T_{26}. Transaction T_{25} displays the contents of accounts A and B:

$$T_{25}: \text{read}(B);$$
$$\text{read}(A);$$
$$\text{display}(A + B).$$

Transaction T_{26} transfers \$50 from account B to account A, and then displays the contents of both:

$$T_{26}: \text{read}(B);$$
$$B := B - 50;$$
$$\text{write}(B);$$
$$\text{read}(A);$$
$$A := A + 50;$$
$$\text{write}(A);$$
$$\text{display}(A + B).$$

In presenting schedules under the timestamp protocol, we shall assume that a transaction is assigned a timestamp immediately before its first instruction. Thus, in schedule 3 of Figure 15.17, $\text{TS}(T_{25}) < \text{TS}(T_{26})$, and the schedule is possible under the timestamp protocol.

We note that the preceding execution can also be produced by the two-phase locking protocol. There are, however, schedules that are possible under the two-phase locking protocol, but are not possible under the timestamp protocol, and vice versa (see Exercise 15.29).

The timestamp-ordering protocol ensures conflict serializability. This is because conflicting operations are processed in timestamp order.

The protocol ensures freedom from deadlock, since no transaction ever waits. However, there is a possibility of starvation of long transactions if a sequence of conflicting short transactions causes repeated restarting of the long transaction. If a transaction is suffering from repeated restarts, conflicting transactions need to be temporarily blocked to enable the transaction to finish.

T_{25}	T_{26}
read(B)	
	read(B)
	$B := B - 50$
	write(B)
read(A)	
	read(A)
display($A + B$)	
	$A := A + 50$
	write(A)
	display($A + B$)

Figure 15.17 Schedule 3.

The protocol can generate schedules that are not recoverable. However, it can be extended to make the schedules recoverable, in one of several ways:

- Recoverability and cascadelessness can be ensured by performing all writes together at the end of the transaction. The writes must be atomic in the following sense: While the writes are in progress, no transaction is permitted to access any of the data items that have been written.

- Recoverability and cascadelessness can also be guaranteed by using a limited form of locking, whereby reads of uncommitted items are postponed until the transaction that updated the item commits (see Exercise 15.30).

- Recoverability alone can be ensured by tracking uncommitted writes, and allowing a transaction T_i to commit only after the commit of any transaction that wrote a value that T_i read. Commit dependencies, outlined in Section 15.1.5, can be used for this purpose.

15.4.3 Thomas' Write Rule

We now present a modification to the timestamp-ordering protocol that allows greater potential concurrency than does the protocol of Section 15.4.2. Let us consider schedule 4 of Figure 15.18, and apply the timestamp-ordering protocol. Since T_{27} starts before T_{28}, we shall assume that $TS(T_{27}) < TS(T_{28})$. The read(Q) operation of T_{27} succeeds, as does the write(Q) operation of T_{28}. When T_{27} attempts its write(Q) operation, we find that $TS(T_{27}) < $ W-timestamp(Q), since W-timestamp(Q) = $TS(T_{28})$. Thus, the write(Q) by T_{27} is rejected and transaction T_{27} must be rolled back.

Although the rollback of T_{27} is required by the timestamp-ordering protocol, it is unnecessary. Since T_{28} has already written Q, the value that T_{27} is attempting to write is one that will never need to be read. Any transaction T_i with $TS(T_i) < TS(T_{28})$ that attempts a read(Q) will be rolled back, since $TS(T_i) < $ W-timestamp(Q). Any transaction T_j with $TS(T_j) > TS(T_{28})$ must read the value of Q written by T_{28}, rather than the value that T_{27} is attempting to write.

This observation leads to a modified version of the timestamp-ordering protocol in which obsolete write operations can be ignored under certain circumstances. The protocol rules for read operations remain unchanged. The protocol rules for write operations, however, are slightly different from the timestamp-ordering protocol of Section 15.4.2.

T_{27}	T_{28}
read(Q)	
	write(Q)
write(Q)	

Figure 15.18 Schedule 4.

The modification to the timestamp-ordering protocol, called **Thomas' write rule**, is this: Suppose that transaction T_i issues write(Q).

1. If $TS(T_i) <$ R-timestamp(Q), then the value of Q that T_i is producing was previously needed, and it had been assumed that the value would never be produced. Hence, the system rejects the write operation and rolls T_i back.

2. If $TS(T_i) <$ W-timestamp(Q), then T_i is attempting to write an obsolete value of Q. Hence, this write operation can be ignored.

3. Otherwise, the system executes the write operation and sets W-timestamp(Q) to $TS(T_i)$.

The difference between these rules and those of Section 15.4.2 lies in the second rule. The timestamp-ordering protocol requires that T_i be rolled back if T_i issues write(Q) and $TS(T_i) <$ W-timestamp(Q). However, here, in those cases where $TS(T_i) \geq$ R-timestamp(Q), we ignore the obsolete write.

By ignoring the write, Thomas' write rule allows schedules that are not conflict serializable but are nevertheless correct. Those non-conflict-serializable schedules allowed satisfy the definition of *view serializable* schedules (see example box). Thomas' write rule makes use of view serializability by, in effect, deleting obsolete write operations from the transactions that issue them. This modification of transactions makes it possible to generate serializable schedules that would not be possible under the other protocols presented in this chapter. For example, schedule 4 of Figure 15.18 is not conflict serializable and, thus, is not possible under the two-phase locking protocol, the tree protocol, or the timestamp-ordering protocol. Under Thomas' write rule, the write(Q) operation of T_{27} would be ignored. The result is a schedule that is *view equivalent* to the serial schedule $<T_{27}, T_{28}>$.

15.5   Validation-Based Protocols

In cases where a majority of transactions are read-only transactions, the rate of conflicts among transactions may be low. Thus, many of these transactions, if executed without the supervision of a concurrency-control scheme, would nevertheless leave the system in a consistent state. A concurrency-control scheme imposes overhead of code execution and possible delay of transactions. It may be better to use an alternative scheme that imposes less overhead. A difficulty in reducing the overhead is that we do not know in advance which transactions will be involved in a conflict. To gain that knowledge, we need a scheme for *monitoring* the system.

The **validation protocol** requires that each transaction T_i executes in two or three different phases in its lifetime, depending on whether it is a read-only or an update transaction. The phases are, in order:

VIEW SERIALIZABILITY

There is another form of equivalence that is less stringent than conflict equivalence, but that, like conflict equivalence, is based on only the read and write operations of transactions.

Consider two schedules S and S', where the same set of transactions participates in both schedules. The schedules S and S' are said to be **view equivalent** if three conditions are met:

1. For each data item Q, if transaction T_i reads the initial value of Q in schedule S, then transaction T_i must, in schedule S', also read the initial value of Q.

2. For each data item Q, if transaction T_i executes read(Q) in schedule S, and if that value was produced by a write(Q) operation executed by transaction T_j, then the read(Q) operation of transaction T_i must, in schedule S', also read the value of Q that was produced by the same write(Q) operation of transaction T_j.

3. For each data item Q, the transaction (if any) that performs the final write(Q) operation in schedule S must perform the final write(Q) operation in schedule S'.

Conditions 1 and 2 ensure that each transaction reads the same values in both schedules and, therefore, performs the same computation. Condition 3, coupled with conditions 1 and 2, ensures that both schedules result in the same final system state.

The concept of view equivalence leads to the concept of view serializability. We say that a schedule S is **view serializable** if it is view equivalent to a serial schedule.

As an illustration, suppose that we augment schedule 4 with transaction T_{29}, and obtain the following view serializable (schedule 5):

T_{27}	T_{28}	T_{29}
read (Q)		
	write (Q)	
write (Q)		
		write (Q)

Indeed, schedule 5 is view equivalent to the serial schedule $<T_{27}, T_{28}, T_{29}>$, since the one read(Q) instruction reads the initial value of Q in both schedules and T_{29} performs the final write of Q in both schedules.

Every conflict-serializable schedule is also view serializable, but there are view-serializable schedules that are not conflict serializable. Indeed, schedule 5 is not conflict serializable, since every pair of consecutive instructions conflicts, and, thus, no swapping of instructions is possible.

Observe that, in schedule 5, transactions T_{28} and T_{29} perform write(Q) operations without having performed a read(Q) operation. Writes of this sort are called **blind writes**. Blind writes appear in any view-serializable schedule that is not conflict serializable.

1. **Read phase**. During this phase, the system executes transaction T_i. It reads the values of the various data items and stores them in variables local to T_i. It performs all write operations on temporary local variables, without updates of the actual database.

2. **Validation phase**. The validation test (described below) is applied to transaction T_i. This determines whether T_i is allowed to proceed to the write phase without causing a violation of serializability. If a transaction fails the validation test, the system aborts the transaction.

3. **Write phase**. If the validation test succeeds for transaction T_i, the temporary local variables that hold the results of any write operations performed by T_i are copied to the database. Read-only transactions omit this phase.

Each transaction must go through the phases in the order shown. However, phases of concurrently executing transactions can be interleaved.

To perform the validation test, we need to know when the various phases of transactions took place. We shall, therefore, associate three different timestamps with each transaction T_i:

1. **Start**(T_i), the time when T_i started its execution.

2. **Validation**(T_i), the time when T_i finished its read phase and started its validation phase.

3. **Finish**(T_i), the time when T_i finished its write phase.

We determine the serializability order by the timestamp-ordering technique, using the value of the timestamp Validation(T_i). Thus, the value TS(T_i) = Validation(T_i) and, if TS(T_j) < TS(T_k), then any produced schedule must be equivalent to a serial schedule in which transaction T_j appears before transaction T_k. The reason we have chosen Validation(T_i), rather than Start(T_i), as the timestamp of transaction T_i is that we can expect faster response time provided that conflict rates among transactions are indeed low.

The **validation test** for transaction T_i requires that, for all transactions T_k with TS(T_k) < TS(T_i), one of the following two conditions must hold:

1. Finish(T_k) < Start(T_i). Since T_k completes its execution before T_i started, the serializability order is indeed maintained.

2. The set of data items written by T_k does not intersect with the set of data items read by T_i, and T_k completes its write phase before T_i starts its validation phase (Start(T_i) < Finish(T_k) < Validation(T_i)). This condition ensures that the writes of T_k and T_i do not overlap. Since the writes of T_k do not affect the read of T_i, and since T_i cannot affect the read of T_k, the serializability order is indeed maintained.

T_{25}	T_{26}
read(B)	
	read(B)
	$B := B - 50$
	read(A)
	$A := A + 50$
read(A)	
< validate>	
display($A + B$)	
	< validate>
	write(B)
	write(A)

Figure 15.19 Schedule 6, a schedule produced by using validation.

As an illustration, consider again transactions T_{25} and T_{26}. Suppose that $TS(T_{25})$ < $TS(T_{26})$. Then, the validation phase succeeds in the schedule 6 in Figure 15.19. Note that the writes to the actual variables are performed only after the validation phase of T_{26}. Thus, T_{25} reads the old values of B and A, and this schedule is serializable.

The validation scheme automatically guards against cascading rollbacks, since the actual writes take place only after the transaction issuing the write has committed. However, there is a possibility of starvation of long transactions, due to a sequence of conflicting short transactions that cause repeated restarts of the long transaction. To avoid starvation, conflicting transactions must be temporarily blocked, to enable the long transaction to finish.

This validation scheme is called the **optimistic concurrency-control** scheme since transactions execute optimistically, assuming they will be able to finish execution and validate at the end. In contrast, locking and timestamp ordering are pessimistic in that they force a wait or a rollback whenever a conflict is detected, even though there is a chance that the schedule may be conflict serializable.

15.6 Multiversion Schemes

The concurrency-control schemes discussed thus far ensure serializability by either delaying an operation or aborting the transaction that issued the operation. For example, a read operation may be delayed because the appropriate value has not been written yet; or it may be rejected (that is, the issuing transaction must be aborted) because the value that it was supposed to read has already been overwritten. These difficulties could be avoided if old copies of each data item were kept in a system.

In **multiversion concurrency-control** schemes, each write(Q) operation creates a new **version** of Q. When a transaction issues a read(Q) operation, the concurrency-control manager selects one of the versions of Q to be read. The concurrency-control scheme must ensure that the version to be read is selected in a manner that ensures serializability. It is also crucial, for performance reasons, that a transaction be able to determine easily and quickly which version of the data item should be read.

15.6.1 Multiversion Timestamp Ordering

The timestamp-ordering protocol can be extended to a multiversion protocol. With each transaction T_i in the system, we associate a unique static timestamp, denoted by $TS(T_i)$. The database system assigns this timestamp before the transaction starts execution, as described in Section 15.4.

With each data item Q, a sequence of versions $<Q_1, Q_2, \ldots, Q_m>$ is associated. Each version Q_k contains three data fields:

- **Content** is the value of version Q_k.

- **W-timestamp**(Q_k) is the timestamp of the transaction that created version Q_k.

- **R-timestamp**(Q_k) is the largest timestamp of any transaction that successfully read version Q_k.

A transaction—say, T_i—creates a new version Q_k of data item Q by issuing a write(Q) operation. The content field of the version holds the value written by T_i. The system initializes the W-timestamp and R-timestamp to $TS(T_i)$. It updates the R-timestamp value of Q_k whenever a transaction T_j reads the content of Q_k, and R-timestamp(Q_k) < $TS(T_j)$.

The **multiversion timestamp-ordering scheme** presented next ensures serializability. The scheme operates as follows: Suppose that transaction T_i issues a read(Q) or write(Q) operation. Let Q_k denote the version of Q whose write timestamp is the largest write timestamp less than or equal to $TS(T_i)$.

1. If transaction T_i issues a read(Q), then the value returned is the content of version Q_k.

2. If transaction T_i issues write(Q), and if $TS(T_i)$ < R-timestamp(Q_k), then the system rolls back transaction T_i. On the other hand, if $TS(T_i)$ = W-timestamp(Q_k), the system overwrites the contents of Q_k; otherwise (if $TS(T_i)$ > R-timestamp(Q_k)), it creates a new version of Q.

The justification for rule 1 is clear. A transaction reads the most recent version that comes before it in time. The second rule forces a transaction to abort if it is "too late" in doing a write. More precisely, if T_i attempts to write a version that some other transaction would have read, then we cannot allow that write to succeed.

Versions that are no longer needed are removed according to the following rule: Suppose that there are two versions, Q_k and Q_j, of a data item, and that both versions have a W-timestamp less than the timestamp of the oldest transaction in the system. Then, the older of the two versions Q_k and Q_j will not be used again, and can be deleted.

The multiversion timestamp-ordering scheme has the desirable property that a read request never fails and is never made to wait. In typical database systems, where reading is a more frequent operation than is writing, this advantage may be of major practical significance.

The scheme, however, suffers from two undesirable properties. First, the reading of a data item also requires the updating of the R-timestamp field, resulting in two potential disk accesses, rather than one. Second, the conflicts between transactions are resolved through rollbacks, rather than through waits. This alternative may be expensive. Section 15.6.2 describes an algorithm to alleviate this problem.

This multiversion timestamp-ordering scheme does not ensure recoverability and cascadelessness. It can be extended in the same manner as the basic timestamp-ordering scheme, to make it recoverable and cascadeless.

15.6.2 Multiversion Two-Phase Locking

The **multiversion two-phase locking protocol** attempts to combine the advantages of multiversion concurrency control with the advantages of two-phase locking. This protocol differentiates between **read-only transactions** and **update transactions**.

Update transactions perform rigorous two-phase locking; that is, they hold all locks up to the end of the transaction. Thus, they can be serialized according to their commit order. Each version of a data item has a single timestamp. The timestamp in this case is not a real clock-based timestamp, but rather is a counter, which we will call the ts-counter, that is incremented during commit processing.

The database system assigns read-only transactions a timestamp by reading the current value of ts-counter before they start execution; they follow the multiversion timestamp-ordering protocol for performing reads. Thus, when a read-only transaction T_i issues a read(Q), the value returned is the contents of the version whose timestamp is the largest timestamp less than or equal to TS(T_i).

When an update transaction reads an item, it gets a shared lock on the item, and reads the latest version of that item. When an update transaction wants to write an item, it first gets an exclusive lock on the item, and then creates a new version of the data item. The write is performed on the new version, and the timestamp of the new version is initially set to a value ∞, a value greater than that of any possible timestamp.

When the update transaction T_i completes its actions, it carries out commit processing: First, T_i sets the timestamp on every version it has created to 1 more than the value of ts-counter; then, T_i increments ts-counter by 1. Only one update transaction is allowed to perform commit processing at a time.

As a result, read-only transactions that start after T_i increments ts-counter will see the values updated by T_i, whereas those that start before T_i increments ts-counter will see the value before the updates by T_i. In either case, read-only transactions never need to wait for locks. Multiversion two-phase locking also ensures that schedules are recoverable and cascadeless.

Versions are deleted in a manner like that of multiversion timestamp ordering. Suppose there are two versions, Q_k and Q_j, of a data item, and that both versions have a timestamp less than or equal to the timestamp of the oldest read-only transaction in the system. Then, the older of the two versions Q_k and Q_j will not be used again and can be deleted.

15.7   Snapshot Isolation

Snapshot isolation is a particular type of concurrency-control scheme that has gained wide acceptance in commercial and open-source systems, including Oracle, PostgreSQL, and SQL Server. We introduced snapshot isolation in Section 14.9.3. Here, we take a more detailed look into how it works.

Conceptually, snapshot isolation involves giving a transaction a "snapshot" of the database at the time when it begins its execution. It then operates on that snapshot in complete isolation from concurrent transactions. The data values in the snapshot consist only of values written by committed transactions. This isolation is ideal for read-only transactions since they never wait and are never aborted by the concurrency manager. Transactions that update the database must, of course, interact with potentially conflicting concurrent update transactions before updates are actually placed in the database. Updates are kept in the transaction's private workspace until the transaction successfully commits, at which point the updates are written to the database. When a transaction T is allowed to commit, the transition of T to the committed state and the writing of all of the updates made by T to the database must be done as an atomic action so that any snapshot created for another transaction either includes all updates by transaction T or none of them.

15.7.1   Validation Steps for Update Transactions

Deciding whether or not to allow an update transaction to commit requires some care. Potentially, two transactions running concurrently might both update the same data item. Since these two transactions operate in isolation using their own private snapshots, neither transaction sees the update made by the other. If both transactions are allowed to write to the database, the first update written will be overwritten by the second. The result is a **lost update**. Clearly, this must be prevented. There are two variants of snapshot isolation, both of which prevent lost updates. They are called *first committer wins* and *first updater wins*. Both approaches are based on testing the transaction against concurrent transactions. A transaction is said to be **concurrent with** T if it was active or partially committed at any point from the start of T up to and including the time when this test is being performed.

Under **first committer wins**, when a transaction T enters the partially committed state, the following actions are taken in an atomic action:

- A test is made to see if any transaction that was concurrent with T has already written an update to the database for some data item that T intends to write.

- If some such transaction is found, then T aborts.

- If no such transaction is found, then T commits and its updates are written to the database.

This approach is called "first committer wins" because if transactions conflict, the first one to be tested using the above rule succeeds in writing its updates, while the subsequent ones are forced to abort. Details of how to implement the above tests are addressed in Exercise 15.19.

Under **first updater wins** the system uses a locking mechanism that applies only to updates (reads are unaffected by this, since they do not obtain locks). When a transaction T_i attempts to update a data item, it requests a *write lock* on that data item. If the lock is not held by a concurrent transaction, the following steps are taken after the lock is acquired:

- If the item has been updated by any concurrent transaction, then T_i aborts.

- Otherwise T_i may proceed with its execution including possibly committing.

If, however, some other concurrent transaction T_j already holds a write lock on that data item, then T_i cannot proceed and the following rules are followed:

- T_i waits until T_j aborts or commits.
  - If T_j aborts, then the lock is released and T_i can obtain the lock. After the lock is acquired, the check for an update by a concurrent transaction is performed as described earlier: T_i aborts if a concurrent transaction had updated the data item, and proceeds with its execution otherwise.
  - If T_j commits, then T_i must abort.

Locks are released when the transaction commits or aborts.

This approach is called "first updater wins" because if transactions conflict, the first one to obtain the lock is the one that is permitted to commit and perform its update. Those that attempt the update later abort unless the first updater subsequently aborts for some other reason. (As an alternative to waiting to see if the first updater T_j aborts, a subsequent updater T_i can be aborted as soon as it finds that the write lock it wishes to obtain is held by T_j.)

15.7.2   Serializability Issues

Snapshot isolation is attractive in practice because the overhead is low and no aborts occur unless two concurrent transactions update the same data item.

There is, however, one serious problem with the snapshot isolation scheme as we have presented it, and as it is implemented in practice: *snapshot isolation does* **not** *ensure serializability*. This is true even in Oracle, which uses snapshot isolation as the implementation for the serializable isolation level! Next, we give examples of possible nonserializable executions under snapshot isolation and show how to deal with them.

1. Suppose that we have two concurrent transactions T_i and T_j and two data items A and B. Suppose that T_i reads A and B, then updates B, while T_j reads A and B, then updates A. For simplicity, we assume there are no other concurrent transactions. Since T_i and T_j are concurrent, neither transaction sees the update by the other in its snapshot. But, since they update different data items, both are allowed to commit regardless of whether the system uses the first-update-wins policy or the first-committer-wins policy.

    However, the precedence graph has a cycle. There is an edge in the precedence graph from T_i to T_j because T_i reads the value of A that existed before T_j writes A. There is also an edge in the precedence graph from T_j to T_i because T_j reads the value of B that existed before T_i writes B. Since there is a cycle in the precedence graph, the result is a nonserializable schedule.

    This situation, where each of a pair of transactions has read data that is written by the other, but there is no data written by both transactions, is referred to as **write skew**. As a concrete example of write skew, consider a banking scenario. Suppose that the bank enforces the integrity constraint that the sum of the balances in the checking and the savings account of a customer must not be negative. Suppose the checking and savings balances for a customer are $100 and $200, respectively. Suppose that transaction T_{36} withdraws $200 from the checking account, after verifying the integrity constraint by reading both balances. Suppose that concurrently transaction T_{37} withdraws $200 from the savings account, again after verifying the integrity constraint. Since each of the transactions checks the integrity constraint on its own snapshot, if they run concurrently each will believe that the sum of the balances after the withdrawal is $100, and therefore its withdrawal does not violate the constraint. Since the two transactions update different data items, they do not have any update conflict, and under snapshot isolation both of them can commit.

    Unfortunately, in the final state after both T_{36} and T_{37} have committed, the sum of the balances is $-100, violating the integrity constraint. Such a violation could never have occurred in any serial execution of T_{36} and T_{37}.

    It is worth noting that integrity constraints that are enforced by the database, such as primary-key and foreign-key constraints, cannot be checked on a snapshot; otherwise it would be possible for two concurrent transactions to insert two tuples with the same primary key value, or for a transaction to insert a foreign key value that is concurrently deleted from the referenced table. Instead, the database system must check these constraints on the current state of the database, as part of validation at the time of commit.

2. For the next example, we shall consider two concurrent update transactions that do not themselves present any problem as regards serializability unless

a read-only transaction happens to show up at just the right time to cause a problem.

Suppose that we have two concurrent transactions T_i and T_j and two data items A and B. Suppose that T_i reads B and then updates B, while T_j reads A and B, then updates A. Running these two transactions concurrently causes no problem. Since T_i accesses only data item B, there are no conflicts on data item A and therefore there is no cycle in the precedence graph. The only edge in the precedence graph is the edge from T_j to T_i because T_j reads the value of B that existed before T_i writes B.

However, let us suppose that T_i commits while T_j is still active. Suppose that, after T_i commits but before T_j commits, a new read-only transaction T_k enters the system and T_k reads both A and B. Its snapshot includes the update by T_i because T_i has already committed. However, since T_j has not committed, its update has not yet been written to the database and is not included in the snapshot seen by T_k.

Consider the edges that are added to the precedence graph on account of T_k. There is an edge in the precedence graph from T_i to T_k because T_i writes the value of B that existed before T_k reads B. There is an edge in the precedence graph from T_k to T_j because T_k reads the value of A that existed before T_j writes A. That leads to a cycle in the precedence graph, showing that the resulting schedule is nonserializable.

The above anomalies may not be as troublesome as they first appear. Recall that the reason for serializability is to ensure that, despite concurrent execution of transactions, database consistency is preserved. Since consistency is the goal, we can accept the potential for nonserializable executions if we are sure that those nonserializable executions that might occur will not lead to inconsistency. The second example above is a problem only if the application that submits the read-only transaction (T_k) cares about seeing updates to A and B out of order. In that example, we did not specify the database consistency constraints that each transaction expects to hold. If we are dealing with a financial database, it might be a very serious matter for T_k to read updates out of proper serial order. On the other hand, if A and B are enrollments in two sections of the same course, then T_k may not demand perfect serialization and we may know from our applications that update rates are low enough that any inaccuracy in what T_k reads is not significant.

The fact that the database must check integrity constraints at the time of commit, and not on a snapshot, also helps avoid inconsistencies in some situations. Some financial applications create consecutive sequence numbers, for example to number bills, by taking the maximum current bill number and adding 1 to the value to get a new bill number. If two such transactions run concurrently, each would see the same set of bills in its snapshot, and each would create a new bill with the same number. Both transactions pass the validation tests for snapshot isolation, since they do not update any tuple in common. However, the execution is not serializable; the resultant database state cannot be obtained by any serial execution of the two transactions. Creating two bills with the same number could have serious legal implications.

The above problem is an example of the phantom phenomenon, since the insert performed by each transaction conflicts with the read performed by the other transaction to find the maximum bill number, but the conflict is not detected by snapshot isolation.[1]

Luckily, in most such applications the bill number would have been declared as a primary key, and the database system would detect the primary key violation outside the snapshot, and roll back one of the two transactions.[2]

An application developer can guard against certain snapshot anomalies by appending a **for update** clause to the SQL select query as illustrated below:

> **select** *
> **from** *instructor*
> **where** ID = 22222
> **for update**;

Adding the **for update** clause causes the system to treat data that are read as if they had been updated for purposes of concurrency control. In our first example of write skew, if the **for update** clause is appended to the select queries that read the account balances, only one of the two concurrent transactions would be allowed to commit since it appears that both transactions have updated both the checking and savings balances.

In our second example of nonserializable execution, if the author of transaction T_k wished to avoid this anomaly, the **for update** clause could be appended to the **select** query, even though there is in fact no update. In our example, if T_k used **select for update**, it would be treated as if it had updated A and B when it read them. The result would be that either T_k or T_j would be aborted, and retried later as a new transaction. This would lead to a serializable execution. In this example, the queries in the other two transactions do not need the **for update** clause to be added; unnecessary use of the **for update** clause can cause significant reduction in concurrency.

Formal methods exist (see the bibliographical notes) to determine whether a given mix of transactions runs the risk of nonserializable execution under snapshot isolation, and to decide on what conflicts to introduce (using the **for update** clause, for example), to ensure serializability. Of course, such methods can work only if we know in advance what transactions are being executed. In some applications, all transactions are from a predetermined set of transactions making this analysis possible. However, if the application allows unrestricted, ad-hoc transactions, then no such analysis is possible.

---

[1] The SQL standard uses the term phantom problem to refer to non-repeatable predicate reads, leading some to claim that snapshot isolation avoids the phantom problem; however, such a claim is not valid under our definition of phantom conflict.

[2] The problem of duplicate bill numbers actually occurred several times in a financial application in I.I.T. Bombay, where (for reasons too complex to discuss here) the bill number was not a primary key, and was detected by financial auditors.

Of the three widely used systems that support snapshot isolation, SQL Server offers the option of a *serializable* isolation level that truly ensures serializability along with a *snapshot* isolation level that provides the performance advantages of snapshot isolation (along with the potential for the anomalies discussed above). In Oracle and PostgreSQL, the *serializable* isolation level offers only snapshot isolation.

15.8   Insert Operations, Delete Operations, and Predicate Reads

Until now, we have restricted our attention to read and write operations. This restriction limits transactions to data items already in the database. Some transactions require not only access to existing data items, but also the ability to create new data items. Others require the ability to delete data items. To examine how such transactions affect concurrency control, we introduce these additional operations:

- **delete**(Q) deletes data item Q from the database.

- **insert**(Q) inserts a new data item Q into the database and assigns Q an initial value.

An attempt by a transaction T_i to perform a read(Q) operation after Q has been deleted results in a logical error in T_i. Likewise, an attempt by a transaction T_i to perform a read(Q) operation before Q has been inserted results in a logical error in T_i. It is also a logical error to attempt to delete a nonexistent data item.

15.8.1   Deletion

To understand how the presence of **delete** instructions affects concurrency control, we must decide when a **delete** instruction conflicts with another instruction. Let I_i and I_j be instructions of T_i and T_j, respectively, that appear in schedule S in consecutive order. Let $I_i = $ **delete**(Q). We consider several instructions I_j.

- $I_j = $ read(Q). I_i and I_j conflict. If I_i comes before I_j, T_j will have a logical error. If I_j comes before I_i, T_j can execute the read operation successfully.

- $I_j = $ write(Q). I_i and I_j conflict. If I_i comes before I_j, T_j will have a logical error. If I_j comes before I_i, T_j can execute the write operation successfully.

- $I_j = $ **delete**(Q). I_i and I_j conflict. If I_i comes before I_j, T_i will have a logical error. If I_j comes before I_i, T_i will have a logical error.

- $I_j = $ **insert**(Q). I_i and I_j conflict. Suppose that data item Q did not exist prior to the execution of I_i and I_j. Then, if I_i comes before I_j, a logical error results for T_i. If I_j comes before I_i, then no logical error results. Likewise, if Q existed prior to the execution of I_i and I_j, then a logical error results if I_j comes before I_i, but not otherwise.

We can conclude the following:

- Under the two-phase locking protocol, an exclusive lock is required on a data item before that item can be deleted.

- Under the timestamp-ordering protocol, a test similar to that for a write must be performed. Suppose that transaction T_i issues **delete**(Q).
  - If $TS(T_i) <$ R-timestamp(Q), then the value of Q that T_i was to delete has already been read by a transaction T_j with $TS(T_j) > TS(T_i)$. Hence, the **delete** operation is rejected, and T_i is rolled back.
  - If $TS(T_i) <$ W-timestamp(Q), then a transaction T_j with $TS(T_j) > TS(T_i)$ has written Q. Hence, this **delete** operation is rejected, and T_i is rolled back.
  - Otherwise, the **delete** is executed.

15.8.2 Insertion

We have already seen that an **insert**(Q) operation conflicts with a **delete**(Q) operation. Similarly, **insert**(Q) conflicts with a read(Q) operation or a write(Q) operation; no read or write can be performed on a data item before it exists.

Since an **insert**(Q) assigns a value to data item Q, an **insert** is treated similarly to a write for concurrency-control purposes:

- Under the two-phase locking protocol, if T_i performs an **insert**(Q) operation, T_i is given an exclusive lock on the newly created data item Q.

- Under the timestamp-ordering protocol, if T_i performs an **insert**(Q) operation, the values R-timestamp(Q) and W-timestamp(Q) are set to $TS(T_i)$.

15.8.3 Predicate Reads and The Phantom Phenomenon

Consider transaction T_{30} that executes the following SQL query on the university database:

> **select count**(*)
> **from** *instructor*
> **where** *dept_name* = 'Physics' ;

Transaction T_{30} requires access to all tuples of the *instructor* relation pertaining to the Physics department.

Let T_{31} be a transaction that executes the following SQL insertion:

> **insert into** *instructor*
>   **values** (11111,'Feynman', 'Physics', 94000);

Let S be a schedule involving T_{30} and T_{31}. We expect there to be potential for a conflict for the following reasons:

- If T_{30} uses the tuple newly inserted by T_{31} in computing **count**(*), then T_{30} reads a value written by T_{31}. Thus, in a serial schedule equivalent to S, T_{31} must come before T_{30}.

- If T_{30} does not use the tuple newly inserted by T_{31} in computing **count**(*), then in a serial schedule equivalent to S, T_{30} must come before T_{31}.

The second of these two cases is curious. T_{30} and T_{31} do not access any tuple in common, yet they conflict with each other! In effect, T_{30} and T_{31} conflict on a phantom tuple. If concurrency control is performed at the tuple granularity, this conflict would go undetected. As a result, the system could fail to prevent a nonserializable schedule. This problem is called the **phantom phenomenon**.

In addition to the phantom problem, we also need to deal with the situation we saw in Section 14.10, where a transaction used an index to find only tuples with *dept_name* = "Physics", and as a result did not read any tuples with other department names. If another transaction updates one of these tuples, changing its department name to Physics, a problem equivalent to the phantom problem occurs. Both problems are rooted in predicate reads, and have a common solution.

To prevent the above problems, we allow transaction T_{30} to prevent other transactions from creating new tuples in the *instructor* relation with *dept_name* = "Physics", and from updating the department name of an existing *instructor* tuple to Physics.

To find all *instructor* tuples with *dept_name* = "Physics", T_{30} must search either the whole *instructor* relation, or at least an index on the relation. Up to now, we have assumed implicitly that the only data items accessed by a transaction are tuples. However, T_{30} is an example of a transaction that reads information about what tuples are in a relation, and T_{31} is an example of a transaction that updates that information.

Clearly, it is not sufficient merely to lock the tuples that are accessed; the information used to find the tuples that are accessed by the transaction must also be locked.

Locking of information used to find tuples can be implemented by associating a data item with the relation; the data item represents the information used to find the tuples in the relation. Transactions, such as T_{30}, that read the information about what tuples are in a relation would then have to lock the data item corresponding to the relation in shared mode. Transactions, such as T_{31}, that update the information about what tuples are in a relation would have to lock the data item in exclusive mode. Thus, T_{30} and T_{31} would conflict on a real data item, rather than on a phantom. Similarly, transactions that use an index to retrieve tuples must lock the index itself.

Do not confuse the locking of an entire relation, as in multiple-granularity locking, with the locking of the data item corresponding to the relation. By locking the data item, a transaction only prevents other transactions from updating information about what tuples are in the relation. Locking is still required on tuples. A transaction that directly accesses a tuple can be granted a lock on the tuples even when another transaction has an exclusive lock on the data item corresponding to the relation itself.

The major disadvantage of locking a data item corresponding to the relation, or locking an entire index, is the low degree of concurrency—two transactions that insert different tuples into a relation are prevented from executing concurrently.

A better solution is an **index-locking** technique that avoids locking the whole index. Any transaction that inserts a tuple into a relation must insert information into every index maintained on the relation. We eliminate the phantom phenomenon by imposing a locking protocol for indices. For simplicity we shall consider only B$^+$-tree indices.

As we saw in Chapter 11, every search-key value is associated with an index leaf node. A query will usually use one or more indices to access a relation. An insert must insert the new tuple in all indices on the relation. In our example, we assume that there is an index on *instructor* for *dept_name*. Then, T_{31} must modify the leaf containing the key "Physics". If T_{30} reads the same leaf node to locate all tuples pertaining to the Physics department, then T_{30} and T_{31} conflict on that leaf node.

The **index-locking protocol** takes advantage of the availability of indices on a relation, by turning instances of the phantom phenomenon into conflicts on locks on index leaf nodes. The protocol operates as follows:

- Every relation must have at least one index.

- A transaction T_i can access tuples of a relation only after first finding them through one or more of the indices on the relation. For the purpose of the index-locking protocol, a relation scan is treated as a scan through all the leaves of one of the indices.

- A transaction T_i that performs a lookup (whether a range lookup or a point lookup) must acquire a shared lock on all the index leaf nodes that it accesses.

- A transaction T_i may not insert, delete, or update a tuple t_i in a relation r without updating all indices on r. The transaction must obtain exclusive locks on all index leaf nodes that are affected by the insertion, deletion, or update. For insertion and deletion, the leaf nodes affected are those that contain (after insertion) or contained (before deletion) the search-key value of the tuple. For updates, the leaf nodes affected are those that (before the modification) contained the old value of the search key, and nodes that (after the modification) contain the new value of the search key.

- Locks are obtained on tuples as usual.

- The rules of the two-phase locking protocol must be observed.

Note that the index-locking protocol does not address concurrency control on internal nodes of an index; techniques for concurrency control on indices, which minimize lock conflicts, are presented in Section 15.10.

Locking an index leaf node prevents any update to the node, even if the update did not actually conflict with the predicate. A variant called key-value locking, which minimizes such false lock conflicts, is presented in Section 15.10 as part of index concurrency control.

As noted in Section 14.10, it would appear that the existence of a conflict between transactions depends on a low-level query-processing decision by the system that is unrelated to a user-level view of the meaning of the two transactions. An alternative approach to concurrency control acquires shared locks on predicates in a query, such as the predicate *"salary > 90000"* on the *instructor* relation. Inserts and deletes of the relation must then be checked to see if they satisfy the predicate; if they do, there is a lock conflict, forcing the insert or delete to wait till the predicate lock is released. For updates, both the initial value and the final value of the tuple must be checked against the predicate. Such conflicting inserts, deletes and updates affect the set of tuples selected by the predicate, and cannot be allowed to execute concurrently with the query that acquired the (shared) predicate lock. We call the above protocol **predicate locking;**[3] predicate locking is not used in practice since it is more expensive to implement than the index-locking protocol, and does not give significant additional benefits.

Variants of the predicate-locking technique can be used for eliminating the phantom phenomenon under the other concurrency-control protocols presented in this chapter. However, many database systems, such as PostgreSQL (as of version 8.1) and (to the best of our knowledge) Oracle (as of version 10g) do not implement index locking or predicate locking, and are vulnerable to nonserializability due to phantom problems even if the isolation level is set to **serializable**.

15.9   Weak Levels of Consistency in Practice

In Section 14.5, we discussed the isolation levels specified by the SQL standard: serializable, repeatable read, read committed, and read uncommitted. In this section, we first briefly outline some older terminology relating to consistency levels weaker than serializability and relate it to the SQL standard levels. We then discuss the issue of concurrency control for transactions that involve user interaction, an issue that we briefly discussed earlier in Section 14.8.

15.9.1   Degree-Two Consistency

The purpose of **degree-two consistency** is to avoid cascading aborts without necessarily ensuring serializability. The locking protocol for degree-two consistency uses the same two lock modes that we used for the two-phase locking protocol: shared (S) and exclusive (X). A transaction must hold the appropriate lock mode when it accesses a data item, but two-phase behavior is not required.

In contrast to the situation in two-phase locking, S-locks may be released at any time, and locks may be acquired at any time. Exclusive locks, however,

---

[3]The term *predicate locking* was used for a version of the protocol that used shared and exclusive locks on predicates, and was thus more complicated. The version we present here, with only shared locks on predicates, is also referred to as **precision locking**.

T_{32}	T_{33}
lock-S(Q)	
read(Q)	
unlock(Q)	
	lock-X(Q)
	read(Q)
	write(Q)
	unlock(Q)
lock-S(Q)	
read(Q)	
unlock(Q)	

Figure 15.20 Nonserializable schedule with degree-two consistency.

cannot be released until the transaction either commits or aborts. Serializability is not ensured by this protocol. Indeed, a transaction may read the same data item twice and obtain different results. In Figure 15.20, T_{32} reads the value of Q before and after that value is written by T_{33}.

Clearly, reads are not repeatable, but since exclusive locks are held until transaction commit, no transaction can read an uncommitted value. Thus, degree-two consistency is one particular implementation of the read-committed isolation level.

15.9.2 Cursor Stability

Cursor stability is a form of degree-two consistency designed for programs that iterate over tuples of a relation by using cursors. Instead of locking the entire relation, cursor stability ensures that:

- The tuple that is currently being processed by the iteration is locked in shared mode.

- Any modified tuples are locked in exclusive mode until the transaction commits.

These rules ensure that degree-two consistency is obtained. Two-phase locking is not required. Serializability is not guaranteed. Cursor stability is used in practice on heavily accessed relations as a means of increasing concurrency and improving system performance. Applications that use cursor stability must be coded in a way that ensures database consistency despite the possibility of nonserializable schedules. Thus, the use of cursor stability is limited to specialized situations with simple consistency constraints.

15.9.3 Concurrency Control Across User Interactions

Concurrency-control protocols usually consider transactions that do not involve user interaction. Consider the airline seat selection example from Section 14.8, which involved user interaction. Suppose we treat all the steps from when the seat availability is initially shown to the user, till the seat selection is confirmed, as a single transaction.

If two-phase locking is used, the entire set of seats on a flight would be locked in shared mode till the user has completed the seat selection, and no other transaction would be able to update the seat allocation information in this period. Clearly such locking would be a very bad idea since a user may take a long time to make a selection, or even just abandon the transaction without explicitly cancelling it. Timestamp protocols or validation could be used instead, which avoid the problem of locking, but both these protocols would abort the transaction for a user A if any other user B has updated the seat allocation information, even if the seat selected by B does not conflict with the seat selected by user A. Snapshot isolation is a good option in this situation, since it would not abort the transaction of user A as long as B did not select the same seat as A.

However, snapshot isolation requires the database to remember information about updates performed by a transaction even after it has committed, as long as any other concurrent transaction is still active, which can be problematic for long duration transactions.

Another option is to split a transaction that involves user interaction into two or more transactions, such that no transaction spans a user interaction. If our seat selection transaction is split thus, the first transaction would read the seat availability, while the second transaction would complete the allocation of the selected seat. If the second transaction is written carelessly, it could assign the selected seat to the user, without checking if the seat was meanwhile assigned to some other user, resulting in a lost-update problem. To avoid the problem, as we outlined in Section 14.8, the second transaction should perform the seat allocation only if the seat was not meanwhile assigned to some other user.

The above idea has been generalized in an alternative concurrency control scheme, which uses version numbers stored in tuples to avoid lost updates. The schema of each relation is altered by adding an extra *version_number* attribute, which is initialized to 0 when the tuple is created. When a transaction reads (for the first time) a tuple that it intends to update, it remembers the version number of that tuple. The read is performed as a stand-alone transaction on the database, and hence any locks that may be obtained are released immediately. Updates are done locally, and copied to the database as part of commit processing, using the following steps which are executed atomically (that is, as part of a single database transaction):

- For each updated tuple, the transaction checks if the current version number is the same as the version number of the tuple when it was first read by the transaction.

    1. If the version numbers match, the update is performed on the tuple in the database, and its version number is incremented by 1.

    2. If the version numbers do not match, the transaction is aborted, rolling back all the updates it performed.

If the version number check succeeds for all updated tuples, the transaction commits. It is worth noting that a timestamp could be used instead of the version number, without impacting the scheme in any way.

Observe the close similarity between the above scheme and snapshot isolation. The version number check implements the first-committer-wins rule used in snapshot isolation, and can be used even if the transaction was active for a very long time. However, unlike snapshot isolation, the reads performed by transaction may not correspond to a snapshot of the database; and unlike the validation-based protocol, reads performed by the transaction are not validated.

We refer to the above scheme as **optimistic concurrency control without read validation**. Optimistic concurrency control without read validation provides a weak level of serializability, and does not ensure serializability. A variant of this scheme uses version numbers to validate reads at the time of commit, in addition to validating writes, to ensure that the tuples read by the transaction were not updated subsequent to the initial read; this scheme is equivalent to the optimistic concurrency-control scheme which we saw earlier.

The above scheme has been widely used by application developers to handle transactions that involve user interaction. An attractive feature of the scheme is that it can be implemented easily on top of a database system. The validation and update steps performed as part of commit processing are then executed as a single transaction in the database, using the concurrency-control scheme of the database to ensure atomicity for commit processing. The above scheme is also used by the Hibernate object-relational mapping system (Section 9.4.2), and other object-relational mapping systems, where it is referred to as optimistic concurrency control (even though reads are not validated by default). Transactions that involve user interaction are called **conversations** in Hibernate to differentiate them from regular transactions validation using version numbers is very useful for such transactions. Object-relational mapping systems also cache database tuples in the form of objects in memory, and execute transactions on the cached objects; updates on the objects are converted into updates on the database when the transaction commits. Data may remain in cache for a long time, and if transactions update such cached data, there is a risk of lost updates. Hibernate and other object-relational mapping systems therefore perform the version number checks transparently as part of commit processing. (Hibernate allows programmers to bypass the cache and execute transactions directly on the database, if serializability is desired.)

15.10   Concurrency in Index Structures**

It is possible to treat access to index structures like any other database structure, and to apply the concurrency-control techniques discussed earlier. However, since indices are accessed frequently, they would become a point of great lock contention, leading to a low degree of concurrency. Luckily, indices do not have to be treated like other database structures. It is perfectly acceptable for a transaction to perform a lookup on an index twice, and to find that the structure of the index has changed in between, as long as the index lookup returns the correct set of tuples. Thus, it is acceptable to have nonserializable concurrent access to an index, as long as the accuracy of the index is maintained.

We outline two techniques for managing concurrent access to B^+-trees. The bibliographical notes reference other techniques for B^+-trees, as well as techniques for other index structures.

The techniques that we present for concurrency control on B^+-trees are based on locking, but neither two-phase locking nor the tree protocol is employed. The algorithms for lookup, insertion, and deletion are those used in Chapter 11, with only minor modifications.

The first technique is called the **crabbing protocol**:

- When searching for a key value, the crabbing protocol first locks the root node in shared mode. When traversing down the tree, it acquires a shared lock on the child node to be traversed further. After acquiring the lock on the child node, it releases the lock on the parent node. It repeats this process until it reaches a leaf node.

- When inserting or deleting a key value, the crabbing protocol takes these actions:

  ○ It follows the same protocol as for searching until it reaches the desired leaf node. Up to this point, it obtains (and releases) only shared locks.

  ○ It locks the leaf node in exclusive mode and inserts or deletes the key value.

  ○ If it needs to split a node or coalesce it with its siblings, or redistribute key values between siblings, the crabbing protocol locks the parent of the node in exclusive mode. After performing these actions, it releases the locks on the node and siblings.

     If the parent requires splitting, coalescing, or redistribution of key values, the protocol retains the lock on the parent, and splitting, coalescing, or redistribution propagates further in the same manner. Otherwise, it releases the lock on the parent.

The protocol gets its name from the way in which crabs advance by moving sideways, moving the legs on one side, then the legs on the other, and so on alternately. The progress of locking while the protocol both goes down the tree and goes back up (in case of splits, coalescing, or redistribution) proceeds in a similar crab-like manner.

Once a particular operation releases a lock on a node, other operations can access that node. There is a possibility of deadlocks between search operations coming down the tree, and splits, coalescing, or redistribution propagating up the tree. The system can easily handle such deadlocks by restarting the search operation from the root, after releasing the locks held by the operation.

The second technique achieves even more concurrency, avoiding even holding the lock on one node while acquiring the lock on another node, by using a modified version of B^+-trees called **B-link trees**; B-link trees require that every node (including internal nodes, not just the leaves) maintain a pointer to its right sibling. This pointer is required because a lookup that occurs while a node is being split may have to search not only that node but also that node's right sibling (if one exists). We shall illustrate this technique with an example later, but we first present the modified procedures of the **B-link-tree locking protocol**.

- **Lookup**. Each node of the B^+-tree must be locked in shared mode before it is accessed. A lock on a nonleaf node is released before any lock on any other node in the B^+-tree is requested. If a split occurs concurrently with a lookup, the desired search-key value may no longer appear within the range of values represented by a node accessed during lookup. In such a case, the search-key value is in the range represented by a sibling node, which the system locates by following the pointer to the right sibling. However, the system locks leaf nodes following the two-phase locking protocol, as Section 15.8.3 describes, to avoid the phantom phenomenon.

- **Insertion and deletion**. The system follows the rules for lookup to locate the leaf node into which it will make the insertion or deletion. It upgrades the shared-mode lock on this node to exclusive mode, and performs the insertion or deletion. It locks leaf nodes affected by insertion or deletion following the two-phase locking protocol, as Section 15.8.3 describes, to avoid the phantom phenomenon.

- **Split**. If the transaction splits a node, it creates a new node according to the algorithm of Section 11.3 and makes it the right sibling of the original node. The right-sibling pointers of both the original node and the new node are set. Following this, the transaction releases the exclusive lock on the original node (provided it is an internal node; leaf nodes are locked in two-phase manner), and then requests an exclusive lock on the parent, so that it can insert a pointer to the new node. (There is no need to lock or unlock the new node.)

- **Coalescence**. If a node has too few search-key values after a deletion, the node with which it will be coalesced must be locked in exclusive mode. Once the transaction has coalesced these two nodes, it requests an exclusive lock on the parent so that the deleted node can be removed. At this point, the transaction releases the locks on the coalesced nodes. Unless the parent node must be coalesced also, its lock is released.

Observe this important fact: An insertion or deletion may lock a node, unlock it, and subsequently relock it. Furthermore, a lookup that runs concurrently with a split or coalescence operation may find that the desired search key has been moved to the right-sibling node by the split or coalescence operation.

As an illustration, consider the B-link tree in Figure 15.21. Assume that there are two concurrent operations on this B-link tree:

1. Insert "Chemistry".
2. Look up "Comp. Sci."

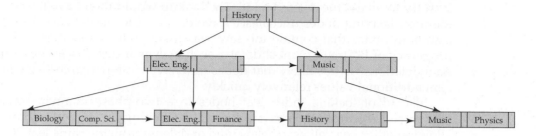

Figure 15.21   B-link tree for *department* file with $n = 3$.

Let us assume that the insertion operation begins first. It does a lookup on "Chemistry", and finds that the node into which "Chemistry" should be inserted is full. It therefore converts its shared lock on the node to exclusive mode, and creates a new node. The original node now contains the search-key values "Biology" and "Chemistry". The new node contains the search-key value "Comp. Sci."

Now assume that a context switch occurs that results in control passing to the lookup operation. This lookup operation accesses the root, and follows the pointer to the left child of the root. It then accesses that node, and obtains a pointer to the left child. This left-child node originally contained the search-key values "Biology" and "Comp. Sci.". Since this node is currently locked by the insertion operation in exclusive mode, the lookup operation must wait. Note that, at this point, the lookup operation holds no locks at all!

The insertion operation now unlocks the leaf node and relocks its parent, this time in exclusive mode. It completes the insertion, leaving the B-link tree as in Figure 15.22. The lookup operation proceeds. However, it is holding a pointer to an incorrect leaf node. It therefore follows the right-sibling pointer to locate the next node. If this node, too, turns out to be incorrect, the lookup follows that node's right-sibling pointer. It can be shown that, if a lookup holds a pointer to an incorrect node, then, by following right-sibling pointers, the lookup must eventually reach the correct node.

Lookup and insertion operations cannot lead to deadlock. Coalescing of nodes during deletion can cause inconsistencies, since a lookup may have read a pointer to a deleted node from its parent, before the parent node was updated, and may

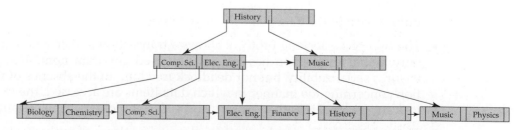

Figure 15.22   Insertion of "Chemistry" into the B-link tree of Figure 15.21.

then try to access the deleted node. The lookup would then have to restart from the root. Leaving nodes uncoalesced avoids such inconsistencies. This solution results in nodes that contain too few search-key values and that violate some properties of B^+-trees. In most databases, however, insertions are more frequent than deletions, so it is likely that nodes that have too few search-key values will gain additional values relatively quickly.

Instead of locking index leaf nodes in a two-phase manner, some index concurrency-control schemes use **key-value locking** on individual key values, allowing other key values to be inserted or deleted from the same leaf. Key-value locking thus provides increased concurrency. Using key-value locking naïvely, however, would allow the phantom phenomenon to occur; to prevent the phantom phenomenon, the **next-key locking** technique is used. In this technique, every index lookup must lock not only the keys found within the range (or the single key, in case of a point lookup) but also the next-key value—that is, the key value just greater than the last key value that was within the range. Also, every insert must lock not only the value that is inserted, but also the next-key value. Thus, if a transaction attempts to insert a value that was within the range of the index lookup of another transaction, the two transactions would conflict on the key value next to the inserted key value. Similarly, deletes must also lock the next-key value to the value being deleted, to ensure that conflicts with subsequent range lookups of other queries are detected.

15.11   Summary

- When several transactions execute concurrently in the database, the consistency of data may no longer be preserved. It is necessary for the system to control the interaction among the concurrent transactions, and this control is achieved through one of a variety of mechanisms called *concurrency-control* schemes.

- To ensure serializability, we can use various concurrency-control schemes. All these schemes either delay an operation or abort the transaction that issued the operation. The most common ones are locking protocols, timestamp-ordering schemes, validation techniques, and multiversion schemes.

- A locking protocol is a set of rules that state when a transaction may lock and unlock each of the data items in the database.

- The two-phase locking protocol allows a transaction to lock a new data item only if that transaction has not yet unlocked any data item. The protocol ensures serializability, but not deadlock freedom. In the absence of information concerning the manner in which data items are accessed, the two-phase locking protocol is both necessary and sufficient for ensuring serializability.

- The strict two-phase locking protocol permits release of exclusive locks only at the end of transaction, in order to ensure recoverability and cascadelessness of the resulting schedules. The rigorous two-phase locking protocol releases all locks only at the end of the transaction.

- Graph-based locking protocols impose restrictions on the order in which items are accessed, and can thereby ensure serializability without requiring the use of two-phase locking, and can additionally ensure deadlock freedom.

- Various locking protocols do not guard against deadlocks. One way to prevent deadlock is to use an ordering of data items, and to request locks in a sequence consistent with the ordering.

- Another way to prevent deadlock is to use preemption and transaction rollbacks. To control the preemption, we assign a unique timestamp to each transaction. The system uses these timestamps to decide whether a transaction should wait or roll back. If a transaction is rolled back, it retains its old timestamp when restarted. The wound–wait scheme is a preemptive scheme.

- If deadlocks are not prevented, the system must deal with them by using a deadlock detection and recovery scheme. To do so, the system constructs a wait-for graph. A system is in a deadlock state if and only if the wait-for graph contains a cycle. When the deadlock detection algorithm determines that a deadlock exists, the system must recover from the deadlock. It does so by rolling back one or more transactions to break the deadlock.

- There are circumstances where it would be advantageous to group several data items, and to treat them as one aggregate data item for purposes of working, resulting in multiple levels of granularity. We allow data items of various sizes, and define a hierarchy of data items, where the small items are nested within larger ones. Such a hierarchy can be represented graphically as a tree. Locks are acquired in root-to-leaf order; they are released in leaf-to-root order. The protocol ensures serializability, but not freedom from deadlock.

- A timestamp-ordering scheme ensures serializability by selecting an ordering in advance between every pair of transactions. A unique fixed timestamp is associated with each transaction in the system. The timestamps of the transactions determine the serializability order. Thus, if the timestamp of transaction T_i is smaller than the timestamp of transaction T_j, then the scheme ensures that the produced schedule is equivalent to a serial schedule in which transaction T_i appears before transaction T_j. It does so by rolling back a transaction whenever such an order is violated.

- A validation scheme is an appropriate concurrency-control method in cases where a majority of transactions are read-only transactions, and thus the rate of conflicts among these transactions is low. A unique fixed timestamp is associated with each transaction in the system. The serializability order is determined by the timestamp of the transaction. A transaction in this scheme is never delayed. It must, however, pass a validation test to complete. If it does not pass the validation test, the system rolls it back to its initial state.

- A multiversion concurrency-control scheme is based on the creation of a new version of a data item for each transaction that writes that item. When a read operation is issued, the system selects one of the versions to be read. The concurrency-control scheme ensures that the version to be read is selected in a manner that ensures serializability, by using timestamps. A read operation always succeeds.

  ○ In multiversion timestamp ordering, a write operation may result in the rollback of the transaction.

  ○ In multiversion two-phase locking, write operations may result in a lock wait or, possibly, in deadlock.

- Snapshot isolation is a multiversion concurrency-control protocol based on validation, which, unlike multiversion two-phase locking, does not require transactions to be declared as read-only or update. Snapshot isolation does not guarantee serializability, but is nevertheless supported by many database systems.

- A **delete** operation may be performed only if the transaction deleting the tuple has an exclusive lock on the tuple to be deleted. A transaction that inserts a new tuple into the database is given an exclusive lock on the tuple.

- Insertions can lead to the phantom phenomenon, in which an insertion logically conflicts with a query even though the two transactions may access no tuple in common. Such conflict cannot be detected if locking is done only on tuples accessed by the transactions. Locking is required on the data used to find the tuples in the relation. The index-locking technique solves this problem by requiring locks on certain index nodes. These locks ensure that all conflicting transactions conflict on a real data item, rather than on a phantom.

- Weak levels of consistency are used in some applications where consistency of query results is not critical, and using serializability would result in queries adversely affecting transaction processing. Degree-two consistency is one such weaker level of consistency; cursor stability is a special case of degree-two consistency, and is widely used.

- Concurrency control is a challenging task for transactions that span user interactions. Applications often implement a scheme based on validation of writes using version numbers stored in tuples; this scheme provides a weak level of serializability, and can be implemented at the application level without modifications to the database.

- Special concurrency-control techniques can be developed for special data structures. Often, special techniques are applied in B^+-trees to allow greater concurrency. These techniques allow nonserializable access to the B^+-tree, but they ensure that the B^+-tree structure is correct, and ensure that accesses to the database itself are serializable.

Review Terms

- Concurrency control
- Lock types
  - Shared-mode (S) lock
  - Exclusive-mode (X) lock
- Lock
  - Compatibility
  - Request
  - Wait
  - Grant
- Deadlock
- Starvation
- Locking protocol
- Legal schedule
- Two-phase locking protocol
  - Growing phase
  - Shrinking phase
  - Lock point
  - Strict two-phase locking
  - Rigorous two-phase locking
- Lock conversion
  - Upgrade
  - Downgrade
- Graph-based protocols
  - Tree protocol
  - Commit dependency
- Deadlock handling
  - Prevention
  - Detection
  - Recovery
- Deadlock prevention

- Ordered locking
- Preemption of locks
- Wait–die scheme
- Wound–wait scheme
- Timeout-based schemes
- Deadlock detection
  - Wait-for graph
- Deadlock recovery
  - Total rollback
  - Partial rollback
- Multiple granularity
  - Explicit locks
  - Implicit locks
  - Intention locks
- Intention lock modes
  - Intention-shared (IS)
  - Intention-exclusive (IX)
  - Shared and intention-exclusive (SIX)
- Multiple-granularity locking protocol
- Timestamp
  - System clock
  - Logical counter
  - W-timestamp(Q)
  - R-timestamp(Q)
- Timestamp-ordering protocol
  - Thomas' write rule
- Validation-based protocols
  - Read phase

- Validation phase
- Write phase
- Validation test
- Multiversion timestamp ordering
- Multiversion two-phase locking
  - Read-only transactions
  - Update transactions
- Snapshot isolation
  - Lost update
  - First committer wins
  - First updater wins
  - Write skew
  - Select for update

- Insert and delete operations
- Phantom phenomenon
- Index-locking protocol
- Predicate locking
- Weak levels of consistency
  - Degree-two consistency
  - Cursor stability
- Optimistic concurrency control without read validation
- Conversations
- Concurrency in indices
  - Crabbing
  - B-link trees
  - B-link-tree locking protocol
  - Next-key locking

Practice Exercises

15.1   Show that the two-phase locking protocol ensures conflict serializability, and that transactions can be serialized according to their lock points.

15.2   Consider the following two transactions:

$$T_{34}: \text{read}(A);$$
$$\text{read}(B);$$
$$\textbf{if } A \; = \; 0 \textbf{ then } B := B + 1;$$
$$\text{write}(B).$$

$$T_{35}: \text{read}(B);$$
$$\text{read}(A);$$
$$\textbf{if } B \; = \; 0 \textbf{ then } A := A + 1;$$
$$\text{write}(A).$$

Add lock and unlock instructions to transactions T_{31} and T_{32}, so that they observe the two-phase locking protocol. Can the execution of these transactions result in a deadlock?

15.3   What benefit does rigorous two-phase locking provide? How does it compare with other forms of two-phase locking?

15.4 Consider a database organized in the form of a rooted tree. Suppose that we insert a dummy vertex between each pair of vertices. Show that, if we follow the tree protocol on the new tree, we get better concurrency than if we follow the tree protocol on the original tree.

15.5 Show by example that there are schedules possible under the tree protocol that are not possible under the two-phase locking protocol, and vice versa.

15.6 Consider the following extension to the tree-locking protocol, which allows both shared and exclusive locks:

- A transaction can be either a read-only transaction, in which case it can request only shared locks, or an update transaction, in which case it can request only exclusive locks.

- Each transaction must follow the rules of the tree protocol. Read-only transactions may lock any data item first, whereas update transactions must lock the root first.

Show that the protocol ensures serializability and deadlock freedom.

15.7 Consider the following graph-based locking protocol, which allows only exclusive lock modes, and which operates on data graphs that are in the form of a rooted directed acyclic graph.

- A transaction can lock any vertex first.

- To lock any other vertex, the transaction must be holding a lock on the majority of the parents of that vertex.

Show that the protocol ensures serializability and deadlock freedom.

15.8 Consider the following graph-based locking protocol, which allows only exclusive lock modes and which operates on data graphs that are in the form of a rooted directed acyclic graph.

- A transaction can lock any vertex first.

- To lock any other vertex, the transaction must have visited all the parents of that vertex and must be holding a lock on one of the parents of the vertex.

Show that the protocol ensures serializability and deadlock freedom.

15.9 Locking is not done explicitly in persistent programming languages. Rather, objects (or the corresponding pages) must be locked when the objects are accessed. Most modern operating systems allow the user to set access protections (no access, read, write) on pages, and memory access that violate the access protections result in a protection violation (see the Unix `mprotect` command, for example). Describe how the access-protection mechanism can be used for page-level locking in a persistent programming language.

	S	X	I
S	true	false	false
X	false	false	false
I	false	false	true

Figure 15.23 Lock-compatibility matrix.

15.10 Consider a database system that includes an atomic **increment** operation, in addition to the read and write operations. Let V be the value of data item X. The operation

$$\text{increment}(X) \text{ by } C$$

sets the value of X to $V + C$ in an atomic step. The value of X is not available to the transaction unless the latter executes a read(X). Figure 15.23 shows a lock-compatibility matrix for three lock modes: share mode, exclusive mode, and incrementation mode.

a. Show that, if all transactions lock the data that they access in the corresponding mode, then two-phase locking ensures serializability.

b. Show that the inclusion of **increment** mode locks allows for increased concurrency. (Hint: Consider check-clearing transactions in our bank example.)

15.11 In timestamp ordering, **W-timestamp**(Q) denotes the largest timestamp of any transaction that executed write(Q) successfully. Suppose that, instead, we defined it to be the timestamp of the most recent transaction to execute write(Q) successfully. Would this change in wording make any difference? Explain your answer.

15.12 Use of multiple-granularity locking may require more or fewer locks than an equivalent system with a single lock granularity. Provide examples of both situations, and compare the relative amount of concurrency allowed.

15.13 Consider the validation-based concurrency-control scheme of Section 15.5. Show that by choosing Validation(T_i), rather than Start(T_i), as the timestamp of transaction T_i, we can expect better response time, provided that conflict rates among transactions are indeed low.

15.14 For each of the following protocols, describe aspects of practical applications that would lead you to suggest using the protocol, and aspects that would suggest not using the protocol:

- Two-phase locking.
- Two-phase locking with multiple-granularity locking.

- The tree protocol.

- Timestamp ordering.

- Validation.

- Multiversion timestamp ordering.

- Multiversion two-phase locking.

15.15 Explain why the following technique for transaction execution may provide better performance than just using strict two-phase locking: First execute the transaction without acquiring any locks and without performing any writes to the database as in the validation-based techniques, but unlike the validation techniques do not perform either validation or writes on the database. Instead, rerun the transaction using strict two-phase locking. (Hint: Consider waits for disk I/O.)

15.16 Consider the timestamp-ordering protocol, and two transactions, one that writes two data items p and q, and another that reads the same two data items. Give a schedule whereby the timestamp test for a write operation fails and causes the first transaction to be restarted, in turn causing a cascading abort of the other transaction. Show how this could result in starvation of both transactions. (Such a situation, where two or more processes carry out actions, but are unable to complete their task because of interaction with the other processes, is called a **livelock**.)

15.17 Devise a timestamp-based protocol that avoids the phantom phenomenon.

15.18 Suppose that we use the tree protocol of Section 15.1.5 to manage concurrent access to a B$^+$-tree. Since a split may occur on an insert that affects the root, it appears that an insert operation cannot release any locks until it has completed the entire operation. Under what circumstances is it possible to release a lock earlier?

15.19 The snapshot isolation protocol uses a validation step which, before performing a write of a data item by transaction T, checks if a transaction concurrent with T has already written the data item.

   a. A straightforward implementation uses a start timestamp and a commit timestamp for each transaction, in addition to an *update set*, that is the set of data items updated by the transaction. Explain how to perform validation for the first-committer-wins scheme by using the transaction timestamps along with the update sets. You may assume that validation and other commit processing steps are executed serially, that is for one transaction at a time,

   b. Explain how the validation step can be implemented as part of commit processing for the first-committer-wins scheme, using a modification of the above scheme, where instead of using update sets, each data item has a write timestamp associated with it. Again, you may assume that validation and other commit processing steps are executed serially.

c. The first-updater-wins scheme can be implemented using timestamps as described above, except that validation is done immediately after acquiring an exclusive lock, instead of being done at commit time.

i. Explain how to assign write timestamps to data items to implement the first-updater-wins scheme.

ii. Show that as a result of locking, if the validation is repeated at commit time the result would not change.

iii. Explain why there is no need to perform validation and other commit processing steps serially in this case.

Exercises

15.20 What benefit does strict two-phase locking provide? What disadvantages result?

15.21 Most implementations of database systems use strict two-phase locking. Suggest three reasons for the popularity of this protocol.

15.22 Consider a variant of the tree protocol called the *forest* protocol. The database is organized as a forest of rooted trees. Each transaction T_i must follow the following rules:

- The first lock in each tree may be on any data item.
- The second, and all subsequent, locks in a tree may be requested only if the parent of the requested node is currently locked.
- Data items may be unlocked at any time.
- A data item may not be relocked by T_i after it has been unlocked by T_i.

Show that the forest protocol does *not* ensure serializability.

15.23 Under what conditions is it less expensive to avoid deadlock than to allow deadlocks to occur and then to detect them?

15.24 If deadlock is avoided by deadlock-avoidance schemes, is starvation still possible? Explain your answer.

15.25 In multiple-granularity locking, what is the difference between implicit and explicit locking?

15.26 Although SIX mode is useful in multiple-granularity locking, an exclusive and intention-shared (XIS) mode is of no use. Why is it useless?

15.27 The multiple-granularity protocol rules specify that a transaction T_i can lock a node Q in S or IS mode only if T_i currently has the parent of Q locked in either IX or IS mode. Given that SIX and S locks are stronger than IX or IS locks, why does the protocol not allow locking a node in S or IS mode if the parent is locked in either SIX or S mode?

15.28 When a transaction is rolled back under timestamp ordering, it is assigned a new timestamp. Why can it not simply keep its old timestamp?

15.29 Show that there are schedules that are possible under the two-phase locking protocol, but are not possible under the timestamp protocol, and vice versa.

15.30 Under a modified version of the timestamp protocol, we require that a commit bit be tested to see whether a read request must wait. Explain how the commit bit can prevent cascading abort. Why is this test not necessary for write requests?

15.31 As discussed in Exercise 15.19, snapshot isolation can be implemented using a form of timestamp validation. However, unlike the multiversion timestamp-ordering scheme, which guarantees serializability, snapshot isolation does not guarantee serializability. Explain what is the key difference between the protocols that results in this difference.

15.32 Outline the key similarities and differences between the timestamp based implementation of the first-committer-wins version of snapshot isolation, described in Exercise 15.19, and the optimistic-concurrency-control-without-read-validation scheme, described in Section 15.9.3.

15.33 Explain the phantom phenomenon. Why may this phenomenon lead to an incorrect concurrent execution despite the use of the two-phase locking protocol?

15.34 Explain the reason for the use of degree-two consistency. What disadvantages does this approach have?

15.35 Give example schedules to show that with key-value locking, if any of lookup, insert, or delete do not lock the next-key value, the phantom phenomenon could go undetected.

15.36 Many transactions update a common item (e.g., the cash balance at a branch), and private items (e.g., individual account balances). Explain how you can increase concurrency (and throughput) by ordering the operations of the transaction.

15.37 Consider the following locking protocol: All items are numbered, and once an item is unlocked, only higher-numbered items may be locked. Locks may be released at any time. Only X-locks are used. Show by an example that this protocol does not guarantee serializability.

Bibliographical Notes

Gray and Reuter [1993] provides detailed textbook coverage of transaction-processing concepts, including concurrency-control concepts and implementation details. Bernstein and Newcomer [1997] provides textbook coverage of various aspects of transaction processing including concurrency control.

The two-phase locking protocol was introduced by Eswaran et al. [1976]. The tree-locking protocol is from Silberschatz and Kedem [1980]. Other non-two-phase locking protocols that operate on more general graphs are described in Yannakakis et al. [1979], Kedem and Silberschatz [1983], and Buckley and Silberschatz [1985]. Korth [1983] explores various lock modes that can be obtained from the basic shared and exclusive lock modes.

Practice Exercise 15.4 is from Buckley and Silberschatz [1984]. Practice Exercise 15.6 is from Kedem and Silberschatz [1983]. Practice Exercise 15.7 is from Kedem and Silberschatz [1979]. Practice Exercise 15.8 is from Yannakakis et al. [1979]. Practice Exercise 15.10 is from Korth [1983].

The locking protocol for multiple-granularity data items is from Gray et al. [1975]. A detailed description is presented by Gray et al. [1976]. Kedem and Silberschatz [1983] formalizes multiple-granularity locking for an arbitrary collection of lock modes (allowing for more semantics than simply read and write). This approach includes a class of lock modes called *update* modes to deal with lock conversion. Carey [1983] extends the multiple-granularity idea to timestamp-based concurrency control. An extension of the protocol to ensure deadlock freedom is presented by Korth [1982].

The timestamp-based concurrency-control scheme is from Reed [1983]. A timestamp algorithm that does not require any rollback to ensure serializability is presented by Buckley and Silberschatz [1983]. The validation concurrency-control scheme is from Kung and Robinson [1981].

Multiversion timestamp order was introduced in Reed [1983]. A multiversion tree-locking algorithm appears in Silberschatz [1982].

Degree-two consistency was introduced in Gray et al. [1975]. The levels of consistency—or isolation—offered in SQL are explained and critiqued in Berenson et al. [1995]. Many commercial database systems use version-based approaches in combination with locking. PostgreSQL, Oracle, and SQL Server all support forms of the snapshot isolation protocol mentioned in Section 15.6.2. Details can be found in Chapters 27, 28, and 30, respectively.

It should be noted that on PostgreSQL (as of version 8.1.4) and Oracle (as of version 10g), setting the isolation level to serializable results in the use of snapshot isolation, which does not guarantee serializability. Fekete et al. [2005] describes how to ensure serializable executions under snapshot isolation, by rewriting certain transactions to introduce conflicts; these conflicts ensure that the transactions cannot run concurrently under snapshot isolation; Jorwekar et al. [2007] describes an approach, that given a set of (parametrized) transactions running under snapshot isolation, can check if the transactions are vulnerability to nonserializability,

Concurrency in B$^+$-trees was studied by Bayer and Schkolnick [1977] and Johnson and Shasha [1993]. The techniques presented in Section 15.10 are based on Kung and Lehman [1980] and Lehman and Yao [1981]. The technique of key-value locking used in ARIES provides for very high concurrency on B$^+$-tree access and is described in Mohan [1990a] and Mohan and Narang [1992]. Ellis [1987] presents a concurrency-control technique for linear hashing.

CHAPTER 16

Recovery System

A computer system, like any other device, is subject to failure from a variety of causes: disk crash, power outage, software error, a fire in the machine room, even sabotage. In any failure, information may be lost. Therefore, the database system must take actions in advance to ensure that the atomicity and durability properties of transactions, introduced in Chapter 14, are preserved. An integral part of a database system is a **recovery scheme** that can restore the database to the consistent state that existed before the failure. The recovery scheme must also provide **high availability**; that is, it must minimize the time for which the database is not usable after a failure.

16.1 Failure Classification

There are various types of failure that may occur in a system, each of which needs to be dealt with in a different manner. In this chapter, we shall consider only the following types of failure:

- **Transaction failure**. There are two types of errors that may cause a transaction to fail:

  ○ **Logical error**. The transaction can no longer continue with its normal execution because of some internal condition, such as bad input, data not found, overflow, or resource limit exceeded.

  ○ **System error**. The system has entered an undesirable state (for example, deadlock), as a result of which a transaction cannot continue with its normal execution. The transaction, however, can be reexecuted at a later time.

- **System crash**. There is a hardware malfunction, or a bug in the database software or the operating system, that causes the loss of the content of volatile storage, and brings transaction processing to a halt. The content of nonvolatile storage remains intact, and is not corrupted.

721

The assumption that hardware errors and bugs in the software bring the system to a halt, but do not corrupt the nonvolatile storage contents, is known as the **fail-stop assumption**. Well-designed systems have numerous internal checks, at the hardware and the software level, that bring the system to a halt when there is an error. Hence, the fail-stop assumption is a reasonable one.

- **Disk failure**. A disk block loses its content as a result of either a head crash or failure during a data-transfer operation. Copies of the data on other disks, or archival backups on tertiary media, such as DVD or tapes, are used to recover from the failure.

To determine how the system should recover from failures, we need to identify the failure modes of those devices used for storing data. Next, we must consider how these failure modes affect the contents of the database. We can then propose algorithms to ensure database consistency and transaction atomicity despite failures. These algorithms, known as recovery algorithms, have two parts:

1. Actions taken during normal transaction processing to ensure that enough information exists to allow recovery from failures.

2. Actions taken after a failure to recover the database contents to a state that ensures database consistency, transaction atomicity, and durability.

16.2   Storage

As we saw in Chapter 10, the various data items in the database may be stored and accessed in a number of different storage media. In Section 14.3, we saw that storage media can be distinguished by their relative speed, capacity, and resilience to failure. We identified three categories of storage:

- **Volatile storage**
- **Nonvolatile storage**
- **Stable storage**

Stable storage or, more accurately, an approximation thereof, plays a critical role in recovery algorithms.

16.2.1   Stable-Storage Implementation

To implement stable storage, we need to replicate the needed information in several nonvolatile storage media (usually disk) with independent failure modes, and to update the information in a controlled manner to ensure that failure during data transfer does not damage the needed information.

Recall (from Chapter 10) that RAID systems guarantee that the failure of a single disk (even during data transfer) will not result in loss of data. The simplest and fastest form of RAID is the mirrored disk, which keeps two copies of each block, on separate disks. Other forms of RAID offer lower costs, but at the expense of lower performance.

RAID systems, however, cannot guard against data loss due to disasters such as fires or flooding. Many systems store archival backups of tapes off site to guard against such disasters. However, since tapes cannot be carried off site continually, updates since the most recent time that tapes were carried off site could be lost in such a disaster. More secure systems keep a copy of each block of stable storage at a remote site, writing it out over a computer network, in addition to storing the block on a local disk system. Since the blocks are output to a remote system as and when they are output to local storage, once an output operation is complete, the output is not lost, even in the event of a disaster such as a fire or flood. We study such *remote backup* systems in Section 16.9.

In the remainder of this section, we discuss how storage media can be protected from failure during data transfer. Block transfer between memory and disk storage can result in:

- **Successful completion**. The transferred information arrived safely at its destination.

- **Partial failure**. A failure occurred in the midst of transfer, and the destination block has incorrect information.

- **Total failure**. The failure occurred sufficiently early during the transfer that the destination block remains intact.

We require that, if a **data-transfer failure** occurs, the system detects it and invokes a recovery procedure to restore the block to a consistent state. To do so, the system must maintain two physical blocks for each logical database block; in the case of mirrored disks, both blocks are at the same location; in the case of remote backup, one of the blocks is local, whereas the other is at a remote site. An output operation is executed as follows:

1. Write the information onto the first physical block.

2. When the first write completes successfully, write the same information onto the second physical block.

3. The output is completed only after the second write completes successfully.

If the system fails while blocks are being written, it is possible that the two copies of a block are inconsistent with each other. During recovery, for each block, the system would need to examine two copies of the blocks. If both are the same and no detectable error exists, then no further actions are necessary. (Recall that errors in a disk block, such as a partial write to the block, are detected by storing a checksum with each block.) If the system detects an error in one block, then it replaces its content with the content of the other block. If both blocks contain no detectable error, but they differ in content, then the system replaces the content of the first block with the value of the second. This recovery procedure ensures that a write to stable storage either succeeds completely (that is, updates all copies) or results in no change.

The requirement of comparing every corresponding pair of blocks during recovery is expensive to meet. We can reduce the cost greatly by keeping track of block writes that are in progress, using a small amount of nonvolatile RAM. On recovery, only blocks for which writes were in progress need to be compared.

The protocols for writing out a block to a remote site are similar to the protocols for writing blocks to a mirrored disk system, which we examined in Chapter 10, and particularly in Practice Exercise 10.3.

We can extend this procedure easily to allow the use of an arbitrarily large number of copies of each block of stable storage. Although a large number of copies reduces the probability of a failure to even lower than two copies do, it is usually reasonable to simulate stable storage with only two copies.

16.2.2   Data Access

As we saw in Chapter 10, the database system resides permanently on nonvolatile storage (usually disks) and only parts of the database are in memory at any time.[1] The database is partitioned into fixed-length storage units called **blocks**. Blocks are the units of data transfer to and from disk, and may contain several data items. We shall assume that no data item spans two or more blocks. This assumption is realistic for most data-processing applications, such as a bank or a university.

Transactions input information from the disk to main memory, and then output the information back onto the disk. The input and output operations are done in block units. The blocks residing on the disk are referred to as **physical blocks**; the blocks residing temporarily in main memory are referred to as **buffer blocks**. The area of memory where blocks reside temporarily is called the **disk buffer**.

Block movements between disk and main memory are initiated through the following two operations:

1. input(B) transfers the physical block B to main memory.

2. output(B) transfers the buffer block B to the disk, and replaces the appropriate physical block there.

Figure 16.1 illustrates this scheme.

Conceptually, each transaction T_i has a private work area in which copies of data items accessed and updated by T_i are kept. The system creates this work area when the transaction is initiated; the system removes it when the transaction

---

[1]There is a special category of database system, called *main-memory database systems*, where the entire database can be loaded into memory at once. We consider such systems in Section 26.4.

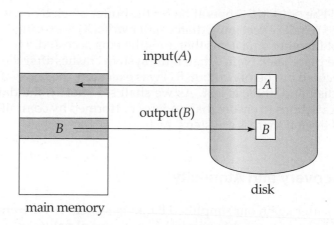

input(A)

output(B)

main memory

disk

Figure 16.1 Block storage operations.

either commits or aborts. Each data item X kept in the work area of transaction T_i is denoted by x_i. Transaction T_i interacts with the database system by transferring data to and from its work area to the system buffer. We transfer data by these two operations:

1. read(X) assigns the value of data item X to the local variable x_i. It executes this operation as follows:

    a. If block B_X on which X resides is not in main memory, it issues input(B_X).

    b. It assigns to x_i the value of X from the buffer block.

2. write(X) assigns the value of local variable x_i to data item X in the buffer block. It executes this operation as follows:

    a. If block B_X on which X resides is not in main memory, it issues input(B_X).

    b. It assigns the value of x_i to X in buffer B_X.

Note that both operations may require the transfer of a block from disk to main memory. They do not, however, specifically require the transfer of a block from main memory to disk.

A buffer block is eventually written out to the disk either because the buffer manager needs the memory space for other purposes or because the database system wishes to reflect the change to B on the disk. We shall say that the database system performs a **force-output** of buffer B if it issues an output(B).

When a transaction needs to access a data item X for the first time, it must execute read(X). The system then performs all updates to X on x_i. At any point during its execution a transaction may execute write(X) to reflect the change to X in the database itself; write(X) must certainly be done after the final write to X.

The output(B_X) operation for the buffer block B_X on which X resides does not need to take effect immediately after write(X) is executed, since the block B_X may contain other data items that are still being accessed. Thus, the actual output may take place later. Notice that, if the system crashes after the write(X) operation was executed but before output(B_X) was executed, the new value of X is never written to disk and, thus, is lost. As we shall see shortly, the database system executes extra actions to ensure that updates performed by committed transactions are not lost even if there is a system crash.

16.3   Recovery and Atomicity

Consider again our simplified banking system and a transaction T_i that transfers $50 from account A to account B, with initial values of A and B being $1000 and $2000, respectively. Suppose that a system crash has occurred during the execution of T_i, after output(B_A) has taken place, but before output(B_B) was executed, where B_A and B_B denote the buffer blocks on which A and B reside. Since the memory contents were lost, we do not know the fate of the transaction.

When the system restarts, the value of A would be $950, while that of B would be $2000, which is clearly inconsistent with the atomicity requirement for transaction T_i. Unfortunately, there is no way to find out by examining the database state what blocks had been output, and what had not, before the crash. It is possible that the transaction completed, updating the database on stable storage from an initial state with the values of A and B being $1000 and $1950; it is also possible that the transaction did not affect the stable storage at all, and the values of A and B were $950 and $2000 initially; or that the updated B was output but not the updated A; or that the updated A was output but the updated B was not.

Our goal is to perform either all or no database modifications made by T_i. However, if T_i performed multiple database modifications, several output operations may be required, and a failure may occur after some of these modifications have been made, but before all of them are made.

To achieve our goal of atomicity, we must first output to stable storage information describing the modifications, without modifying the database itself. As we shall see, this information can help us ensure that all modifications performed by committed transactions are reflected in the database (perhaps during the course of recovery actions after a crash). This information can also help us ensure that no modifications made by an aborted transaction persist in the database.

16.3.1   Log Records

The most widely used structure for recording database modifications is the **log**. The log is a sequence of **log records**, recording all the update activities in the database.

There are several types of log records. An **update log record** describes a single database write. It has these fields:

SHADOW COPIES AND SHADOW PAGING

In the **shadow-copy** scheme, a transaction that wants to update the database first creates a complete copy of the database. All updates are done on the new database copy, leaving the original copy, the **shadow copy**, untouched. If at any point the transaction has to be aborted, the system merely deletes the new copy. The old copy of the database has not been affected. The current copy of the database is identified by a pointer, called db-pointer, which is stored on disk.

If the transaction partially commits (that is, executes its final statement) it is committed as follows: First, the operating system is asked to make sure that all pages of the new copy of the database have been written out to disk. (Unix systems use the fsync command for this purpose.) After the operating system has written all the pages to disk, the database system updates the pointer db-pointer to point to the new copy of the database; the new copy then becomes the current copy of the database. The old copy of the database is then deleted. The transaction is said to have been *committed* at the point where the updated db-pointer is written to disk.

The implementation actually depends on the write to db-pointer being atomic; that is, either all its bytes are written or none of its bytes are written. Disk systems provide atomic updates to entire blocks, or at least to a disk sector. In other words, the disk system guarantees that it will update db-pointer atomically, as long as we make sure that db-pointer lies entirely in a single sector, which we can ensure by storing db-pointer at the beginning of a block.

Shadow copy schemes are commonly used by text editors (saving the file is equivalent to transaction commit, while quitting without saving the file is equivalent to transaction abort). Shadow copying can be used for small databases, but copying a large database would be extremely expensive. A variant of shadow-copying, called **shadow-paging**, reduces copying as follows: the scheme uses a page table containing pointers to all pages; the page table itself and all updated pages are copied to a new location. Any page which is not updated by a transaction is not copied, but instead the new page table just stores a pointer to the original page. When a transaction commits, it atomically updates the pointer to the page table, which acts as db-pointer, to point to the new copy.

Shadow paging unfortunately does not work well with concurrent transactions and is not widely used in databases.

- **Transaction identifier**, which is the unique identifier of the transaction that performed the write operation.

- **Data-item identifier**, which is the unique identifier of the data item written. Typically, it is the location on disk of the data item, consisting of the block identifier of the block on which the data item resides, and an offset within the block.

- **Old value**, which is the value of the data item prior to the write.

- **New value**, which is the value that the data item will have after the write.

We represent an update log record as $<T_i, X_j, V_1, V_2>$, indicating that transaction T_i has performed a write on data item X_j. X_j had value V_1 before the write, and has value V_2 after the write. Other special log records exist to record significant events during transaction processing, such as the start of a transaction and the commit or abort of a transaction. Among the types of log records are:

- $<T_i$ start$>$. Transaction T_i has started.

- $<T_i$ commit$>$. Transaction T_i has committed.

- $<T_i$ abort$>$. Transaction T_i has aborted.

We shall introduce several other types of log records later.

Whenever a transaction performs a write, it is essential that the log record for that write be created and added to the log, before the database is modified. Once a log record exists, we can output the modification to the database if that is desirable. Also, we have the ability to *undo* a modification that has already been output to the database. We undo it by using the old-value field in log records.

For log records to be useful for recovery from system and disk failures, the log must reside in stable storage. For now, we assume that every log record is written to the end of the log on stable storage as soon as it is created. In Section 16.5, we shall see when it is safe to relax this requirement so as to reduce the overhead imposed by logging. Observe that the log contains a complete record of all database activity. As a result, the volume of data stored in the log may become unreasonably large. In Section 16.3.6, we shall show when it is safe to erase log information.

16.3.2   Database Modification

As we noted earlier, a transaction creates a log record prior to modifying the database. The log records allow the system to undo changes made by a transaction in the event that the transaction must be aborted; they allow the system also to redo changes made by a transaction if the transaction has committed but the system crashed before those changes could be stored in the database on disk. In order for us to understand the role of these log records in recovery, we need to consider the steps a transaction takes in modifying a data item:

1. The transaction performs some computations in its own private part of main memory.

2. The transaction modifies the data block in the disk buffer in main memory holding the data item.

3. The database system executes the output operation that writes the data block to disk.

We say a transaction *modifies the database* if it performs an update on a disk buffer, or on the disk itself; updates to the private part of main memory do not count as database modifications. If a transaction does not modify the database until it has committed, it is said to use the **deferred-modification** technique. If database modifications occur while the transaction is still active, the transaction is said to use the **immediate-modification** technique. Deferred modification has the overhead that transactions need to make local copies of all updated data items; further, if a transaction reads a data item that it has updated, it must read the value from its local copy.

The recovery algorithms we describe in this chapter support immediate modification. As described, they work correctly even with deferred modification, but can be optimized to reduce overhead when used with deferred modification; we leave details as an exercise.

A recovery algorithm must take into account a variety of factors, including:

- The possibility that a transaction may have committed although some of its database modifications exist only in the disk buffer in main memory and not in the database on disk.

- The possibility that a transaction may have modified the database while in the active state and, as a result of a subsequent failure, may need to abort.

Because all database modifications must be preceded by the creation of a log record, the system has available both the old value prior to the modification of the data item and the new value that is to be written for the data item. This allows the system to perform *undo* and *redo* operations as appropriate.

- **Undo** using a log record sets the data item specified in the log record to the old value.

- **Redo** using a log record sets the data item specified in the log record to the new value.

16.3.3 Concurrency Control and Recovery

If the concurrency control scheme allows a data item X that has been modified by a transaction T_1 to be further modified by another transaction T_2 before T_1 commits, then undoing the effects of T_1 by restoring the old value of X (before T_1 updated X) would also undo the effects of T_2. To avoid such situations, recovery algorithms usually require that if a data item has been modified by a transaction, no other transaction can modify the data item until the first transaction commits or aborts.

This requirement can be ensured by acquiring an exclusive lock on any updated data item and holding the lock until the transaction commits; in other words, by using strict two-phase locking. Snapshot-isolation and validation-based concurrency-control techniques also acquire exclusive locks on data items at the time of validation, before modifying the data items, and hold the locks until the transaction is committed; as a result the above requirement is satisfied even by these concurrency control protocols.

We discuss later, in Section 16.7, how the above requirement can be relaxed in certain cases.

When either snapshot-isolation or validation is used for concurrency control, database updates of a transaction are (conceptually) deferred until the transaction is partially committed; the deferred-modification technique is a natural fit with these concurrency control schemes. However, it is worth noting that some implementations of snapshot isolation use immediate modification, but provide a logical snapshot on demand: when a transaction needs to read an item that a concurrent transaction has updated, a copy of the (already updated) item is made, and updates made by concurrent transactions are rolled back on the copy of the item. Similarly, immediate modification of the database is a natural fit with two-phase locking, but deferred modification can also be used with two-phase locking.

16.3.4   Transaction Commit

We say that a transaction has **committed** when its commit log record, which is the last log record of the transaction, has been output to stable storage; at that point all earlier log records have already been output to stable storage. Thus, there is enough information in the log to ensure that even if there is a system crash, the updates of the transaction can be redone. If a system crash occurs before a log record $< T_i$ commit$>$ is output to stable storage, transaction T_i will be rolled back. Thus, the output of the block containing the commit log record is the single atomic action that results in a transaction getting committed.[2]

With most log-based recovery techniques, including the ones we describe in this chapter, blocks containing the data items modified by a transaction do not have to be output to stable storage when the transaction commits, but can be output some time later. We discuss this issue further in Section 16.5.2.

16.3.5   Using the Log to Redo and Undo Transactions

We now provide an overview of how the log can be used to recover from a system crash, and to roll back transactions during normal operation. However, we postpone details of the procedures for failure recovery and rollback to Section 16.4.

Consider our simplified banking system. Let T_0 be a transaction that transfers $50 from account A to account B:

---

[2]The output of a block can be made atomic by techniques for dealing with data-transfer failure, as described earlier in Section 16.2.1.

$$\langle T_0 \text{ start}\rangle$$
$$\langle T_0, A, 1000, 950\rangle$$
$$\langle T_0, B, 2000, 2050\rangle$$
$$\langle T_0 \text{ commit}\rangle$$
$$\langle T_1 \text{ start}\rangle$$
$$\langle T_1, C, 700, 600\rangle$$
$$\langle T_1 \text{ commit}\rangle$$

Figure 16.2   Portion of the system log corresponding to T_0 and T_1.

$$T_0: \text{read}(A);$$
$$A := A - 50;$$
$$\text{write}(A);$$
$$\text{read}(B);$$
$$B := B + 50;$$
$$\text{write}(B).$$

Let T_1 be a transaction that withdraws \$100 from account C:

$$T_1: \text{read}(C);$$
$$C := C - 100;$$
$$\text{write}(C).$$

The portion of the log containing the relevant information concerning these two transactions appears in Figure 16.2.

Figure 16.3 shows one possible order in which the actual outputs took place in both the database system and the log as a result of the execution of T_0 and T_1.[3]

Using the log, the system can handle any failure that does not result in the loss of information in nonvolatile storage. The recovery scheme uses two recovery procedures. Both these procedures make use of the log to find the set of data items updated by each transaction T_i, and their respective old and new values.

- redo(T_i) sets the value of all data items updated by transaction T_i to the new values.

  The order in which updates are carried out by redo is important; when recovering from a system crash, if updates to a particular data item are applied in an order different from the order in which they were applied originally, the final state of that data item will have a wrong value. Most recovery algorithms, including the one we describe in Section 16.4, do not perform redo of each transaction separately; instead they perform a single scan of the log, during which redo actions are performed for each log record as it is encountered. This approach ensures the order of updates is preserved,

---

[3]Notice that this order could not be obtained using the deferred-modification technique, because the database is modified by T_0 before it commits, and likewise for T_1.

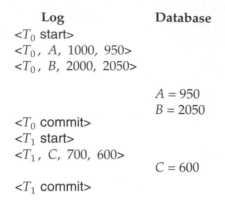

Log   Database

$<T_0$ start$>$

$<T_0,\ A,\ 1000,\ 950>$

$<T_0,\ B,\ 2000,\ 2050>$

                                 $A = 950$
                                 $B = 2050$

$<T_0$ commit$>$

$<T_1$ start$>$

$<T_1,\ C,\ 700,\ 600>$

                                 $C = 600$

$<T_1$ commit$>$

Figure 16.3   State of system log and database corresponding to T_0 and T_1.

and is more efficient since the log needs to be read only once overall, instead of once per transaction.

- undo(T_i) restores the value of all data items updated by transaction T_i to the old values.

  In the recovery scheme that we describe in Section 16.4:

  ○ The undo operation not only restores the data items to their old value, but also writes log records to record the updates performed as part of the undo process. These log records are special **redo-only** log records, since they do not need to contain the old-value of the updated data item.

    As with the redo procedure, the order in which undo operations are performed is important; again we postpone details to Section 16.4.

  ○ When the undo operation for transaction T_i completes, it writes a $<T_i$ abort$>$ log record, indicating that the undo has completed.

    As we shall see in Section 16.4, the undo(T_i) procedure is executed only once for a transaction, if the transaction is rolled back during normal processing or if on recovering from a system crash, neither a commit nor an abort record is found for transaction T_i. As a result, every transaction will eventually have either a commit or an abort record in the log.

After a system crash has occurred, the system consults the log to determine which transactions need to be redone, and which need to be undone so as to ensure atomicity.

- Transaction T_i needs to be undone if the log contains the record $<T_i$ start$>$, but does not contain either the record $<T_i$ commit$>$ or the record $<T_i$ abort$>$.

- Transaction T_i needs to be redone if the log contains the record $<T_i$ start$>$ and either the record $<T_i$ commit$>$ or the record $<T_i$ abort$>$. It may seem strange to redo T_i if the record $<T_i$ abort$>$ is in the log. To see why this works, note

(a)	(b)	(c)
$<T_0$ start$>$	$<T_0$ start$>$	$<T_0$ start$>$
$<T_0, A, 1000, 950>$	$<T_0, A, 1000, 950>$	$<T_0, A, 1000, 950>$
$<T_0, B, 2000, 2050>$	$<T_0, B, 2000, 2050>$	$<T_0, B, 2000, 2050>$
	$<T_0$ commit$>$	$<T_0$ commit$>$
	$<T_1$ start$>$	$<T_1$ start$>$
	$<T_1, C, 700, 600>$	$<T_1, C, 700, 600>$
		$<T_1$ commit$>$

Figure 16.4 The same log, shown at three different times.

that if $<T_i$ abort$>$ is in the log, so are the redo-only records written by the undo operation. Thus, the end result will be to undo T_i's modifications in this case. This slight redundancy simplifies the recovery algorithm and enables faster overall recovery time.

As an illustration, return to our banking example, with transaction T_0 and T_1 executed one after the other in the order T_0 followed by T_1. Suppose that the system crashes before the completion of the transactions. We shall consider three cases. The state of the logs for each of these cases appears in Figure 16.4.

First, let us assume that the crash occurs just after the log record for the step:

$$\text{write}(B)$$

of transaction T_0 has been written to stable storage (Figure 16.4a). When the system comes back up, it finds the record $<T_0$ start$>$ in the log, but no corresponding $<T_0$ commit$>$ or $<T_0$ abort$>$ record. Thus, transaction T_0 must be undone, so an undo(T_0) is performed. As a result, the values in accounts A and B (on the disk) are restored to $1000 and $2000, respectively.

Next, let us assume that the crash comes just after the log record for the step:

$$\text{write}(C)$$

of transaction T_1 has been written to stable storage (Figure 16.4b). When the system comes back up, two recovery actions need to be taken. The operation undo(T_1) must be performed, since the record $<T_1$ start$>$ appears in the log, but there is no record $<T_1$ commit$>$ or $<T_1$ abort$>$. The operation redo(T_0) must be performed, since the log contains both the record $<T_0$ start$>$ and the record $<T_0$ commit$>$. At the end of the entire recovery procedure, the values of accounts A, B, and C are $950, $2050, and $700, respectively.

Finally, let us assume that the crash occurs just after the log record:

$$<T_1 \text{ commit}>$$

has been written to stable storage (Figure 16.4c). When the system comes back up, both T_0 and T_1 need to be redone, since the records $<T_0$ start$>$ and $<T_0$ commit$>$ appear in the log, as do the records $<T_1$ start$>$ and $<T_1$ commit$>$. After the system performs the recovery procedures redo(T_0) and redo(T_1), the values in accounts A, B, and C are \$950, \$2050, and \$600, respectively.

16.3.6 Checkpoints

When a system crash occurs, we must consult the log to determine those transactions that need to be redone and those that need to be undone. In principle, we need to search the entire log to determine this information. There are two major difficulties with this approach:

1. The search process is time-consuming.

2. Most of the transactions that, according to our algorithm, need to be redone have already written their updates into the database. Although redoing them will cause no harm, it will nevertheless cause recovery to take longer.

To reduce these types of overhead, we introduce checkpoints.

We describe below a simple checkpoint scheme that (a) does not permit any updates to be performed while the checkpoint operation is in progress, and (b) outputs all modified buffer blocks to disk when the checkpoint is performed. We discuss later how to modify the checkpointing and recovery procedures to provide more flexibility by relaxing both these requirements.

A checkpoint is performed as follows:

1. Output onto stable storage all log records currently residing in main memory.

2. Output to the disk all modified buffer blocks.

3. Output onto stable storage a log record of the form $<$checkpoint $L>$, where L is a list of transactions active at the time of the checkpoint.

Transactions are not allowed to perform any update actions, such as writing to a buffer block or writing a log record, while a checkpoint is in progress. We discuss how this requirement can be enforced, later, in Section 16.5.2.

The presence of a $<$checkpoint $L>$ record in the log allows the system to streamline its recovery procedure. Consider a transaction T_i that completed prior to the checkpoint. For such a transaction, the $<T_i$ commit$>$ record (or $< T_i$ abort$>$ record) appears in the log before the $<$checkpoint$>$ record. Any database modifications made by T_i must have been written to the database either prior to the checkpoint or as part of the checkpoint itself. Thus, at recovery time, there is no need to perform a redo operation on T_i.

After a system crash has occurred, the system examines the log to find the last $<$checkpoint $L>$ record (this can be done by searching the log backward, from the end of the log, until the first $<$checkpoint $L>$ record is found).

The redo or undo operations need to be applied only to transactions in L, and to all transactions that started execution after the <checkpoint L> record was written to the log. Let us denote this set of transactions as T.

- For all transactions T_k in T that have no <T_k commit> record or <T_k abort> record in the log, execute undo(T_k).

- For all transactions T_k in T such that either the record <T_k commit> or the record <T_k abort> appears in the log, execute redo(T_k).

Note that we need only examine the part of the log starting with the last checkpoint log record to find the set of transactions T, and to find out whether a commit or abort record occurs in the log for each transaction in T.

As an illustration, consider the set of transactions $\{T_0, T_1, \ldots, T_{100}\}$. Suppose that the most recent checkpoint took place during the execution of transaction T_{67} and T_{69}, while T_{68} and all transactions with subscripts lower than 67 completed before the checkpoint. Thus, only transactions $T_{67}, T_{69}, \ldots, T_{100}$ need to be considered during the recovery scheme. Each of them needs to be redone if it has completed (that is, either committed or aborted); otherwise, it was incomplete, and needs to be undone.

Consider the set of transactions L in a checkpoint log record. For each transaction T_i in L, log records of the transaction that occur prior to the checkpoint log record may be needed to undo the transaction, in case it does not commit. However, all log records prior to the earliest of the $< T_i$ start> log records, among transactions T_i in L, are not needed once the checkpoint has completed. These log records can be erased whenever the database system needs to reclaim the space occupied by these records.

The requirement that transactions must not perform any updates to buffer blocks or to the log during checkpointing can be bothersome, since transaction processing has to halt while a checkpoint is in progress. A **fuzzy checkpoint** is a checkpoint where transactions are allowed to perform updates even while buffer blocks are being written out. Section 16.5.4 describes fuzzy-checkpointing schemes. Later in Section 16.8 we describe a checkpoint scheme that is not only fuzzy, but does not even require all modified buffer blocks to be output to disk at the time of the checkpoint.

16.4 Recovery Algorithm

Until now, in discussing recovery, we have identified transactions that need to be redone and those that need to be undone, but we have not given a precise algorithm for performing these actions. We are now ready to present the full recovery algorithm using log records for recovery from transaction failure and a combination of the most recent checkpoint and log records to recover from a system crash.

The recovery algorithm described in this section requires that a data item that has been updated by an uncommitted transaction cannot be modified by any other transaction, until the first transaction has either committed or aborted. Recall that this restriction was discussed earlier, in Section 16.3.3.

16.4.1 Transaction Rollback

First consider transaction rollback during normal operation (that is, not during recovery from a system crash). Rollback of a transaction T_i is performed as follows:

1. The log is scanned backward, and for each log record of T_i of the form $<T_i, X_j, V_1, V_2>$ that is found:

    a. The value V_1 is written to data item X_j, and

    b. A special redo-only log record $<T_i, X_j, V_1>$ is written to the log, where V_1 is the value being restored to data item X_j during the rollback. These log records are sometimes called **compensation log records**. Such records do not need undo information, since we never need to undo such an undo operation. We shall explain later how they are used.

2. Once the log record $<T_i \text{ start}>$ is found the backward scan is stopped, and a log record $<T_i \text{ abort}>$ is written to the log.

Observe that every update action performed by the transaction or on behalf of the transaction, including actions taken to restore data items to their old value, have now been recorded in the log. In Section 16.4.2 we shall see why this is a good idea.

16.4.2 Recovery After a System Crash

Recovery actions, when the database system is restarted after a crash, take place in two phases:

1. In the **redo phase**, the system replays updates of *all* transactions by scanning the log forward from the last checkpoint. The log records that are replayed include log records for transactions that were rolled back before system crash, and those that had not committed when the system crash occurred. This phase also determines all transactions that were incomplete at the time of the crash, and must therefore be rolled back. Such incomplete transactions would either have been active at the time of the checkpoint, and thus would appear in the transaction list in the checkpoint record, or would have started later; further, such incomplete transactions would have neither a $<T_i \text{ abort}>$ nor a $<T_i \text{ commit}>$ record in the log.
    The specific steps taken while scanning the log are as follows:

    a. The list of transactions to be rolled back, undo-list, is initially set to the list L in the $<\text{checkpoint } L>$ log record.

b. Whenever a normal log record of the form $<T_i, X_j, V_1, V_2>$, or a redo-only log record of the form $<T_i, X_j, V_2>$ is encountered, the operation is redone; that is, the value V_2 is written to data item X_j.

c. Whenever a log record of the form $<T_i$ start$>$ is found, T_i is added to undo-list.

d. Whenever a log record of the form $<T_i$ abort$>$ or $<T_i$ commit$>$ is found, T_i is removed from undo-list.

At the end of the redo phase, undo-list contains the list of all transactions that are incomplete, that is, they neither committed nor completed rollback before the crash.

2. In the **undo phase**, the system rolls back all transactions in the undo-list. It performs rollback by scanning the log backward from the end.

a. Whenever it finds a log record belonging to a transaction in the undo-list, it performs undo actions just as if the log record had been found during the rollback of a failed transaction.

b. When the system finds a $<T_i$ start$>$ log record for a transaction T_i in undo-list, it writes a $<T_i$ abort$>$ log record to the log, and removes T_i from undo-list.

c. The undo phase terminates once undo-list becomes empty, that is, the system has found $<T_i$ start$>$ log records for all transactions that were initially in undo-list.

After the undo phase of recovery terminates, normal transaction processing can resume.

Observe that the redo phase replays every log record since the most recent checkpoint record. In other words, this phase of restart recovery repeats all the update actions that were executed after the checkpoint, and whose log records reached the stable log. The actions include actions of incomplete transactions and the actions carried out to rollback failed transactions. The actions are repeated in the same order in which they were originally carried out; hence, this process is called **repeating history**. Although it may appear wasteful, repeating history even for failed transactions simplifies recovery schemes.

Figure 16.5 shows an example of actions logged during normal operation, and actions performed during failure recovery. In the log shown in the figure, transaction T_1 had committed, and transaction T_0 had been completely rolled back, before the system crashed. Observe how the value of data item B is restored during the rollback of T_0. Observe also the checkpoint record, with the list of active transactions containing T_0 and T_1.

When recovering from a crash, in the redo phase, the system performs a redo of all operations after the last checkpoint record. In this phase, the list undo-list initially contains T_0 and T_1; T_1 is removed first when its commit log record is found, while T_2 is added when its start log record is found. Transaction T_0 is

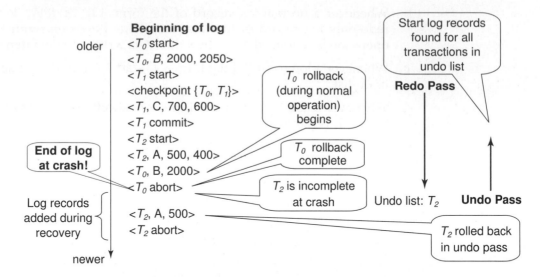

Figure 16.5 Example of logged actions, and actions during recovery.

removed from undo-list when its abort log record is found, leaving only T_2 in undo-list. The undo phase scans the log backwards from the end, and when it finds a log record of T_2 updating A, the old value of A is restored, and a redo-only log record written to the log. When the start record for T_2 is found, an **abort** record is added for T_2. Since undo-list contains no more transactions, the undo phase terminates, completing recovery.

16.5   Buffer Management

In this section, we consider several subtle details that are essential to the implementation of a crash-recovery scheme that ensures data consistency and imposes a minimal amount of overhead on interactions with the database.

16.5.1   Log-Record Buffering

So far, we have assumed that every log record is output to stable storage at the time it is created. This assumption imposes a high overhead on system execution for several reasons: Typically, output to stable storage is in units of blocks. In most cases, a log record is much smaller than a block. Thus, the output of each log record translates to a much larger output at the physical level. Furthermore, as we saw in Section 16.2.1, the output of a block to stable storage may involve several output operations at the physical level.

The cost of outputting a block to stable storage is sufficiently high that it is desirable to output multiple log records at once. To do so, we write log records to a log buffer in main memory, where they stay temporarily until they are output to stable storage. Multiple log records can be gathered in the log buffer and output to stable storage in a single output operation. The order of log records in the stable storage must be exactly the same as the order in which they were written to the log buffer.

As a result of log buffering, a log record may reside in only main memory (volatile storage) for a considerable time before it is output to stable storage. Since such log records are lost if the system crashes, we must impose additional requirements on the recovery techniques to ensure transaction atomicity:

- Transaction T_i enters the commit state after the $<T_i$ commit$>$ log record has been output to stable storage.

- Before the $<T_i$ commit$>$ log record can be output to stable storage, all log records pertaining to transaction T_i must have been output to stable storage.

- Before a block of data in main memory can be output to the database (in nonvolatile storage), all log records pertaining to data in that block must have been output to stable storage.

  This rule is called the **write-ahead logging (WAL)** rule. (Strictly speaking, the WAL rule requires only that the undo information in the log has been output to stable storage, and it permits the redo information to be written later. The difference is relevant in systems where undo information and redo information are stored in separate log records.)

The three rules state situations in which certain log records *must* have been output to stable storage. There is no problem resulting from the output of log records *earlier* than necessary. Thus, when the system finds it necessary to output a log record to stable storage, it outputs an entire block of log records, if there are enough log records in main memory to fill a block. If there are insufficient log records to fill the block, all log records in main memory are combined into a partially full block and are output to stable storage.

Writing the buffered log to disk is sometimes referred to as a **log force**.

16.5.2   Database Buffering

In Section 16.2.2, we described the use of a two-level storage hierarchy. The system stores the database in nonvolatile storage (disk), and brings blocks of data into main memory as needed. Since main memory is typically much smaller than the entire database, it may be necessary to overwrite a block B_1 in main memory when another block B_2 needs to be brought into memory. If B_1 has been modified, B_1 must be output prior to the input of B_2. As discussed in Section 10.8.1 in Chapter 10, this storage hierarchy is similar to the standard operating-system concept of *virtual memory*.

One might expect that transactions would force-output all modified blocks to disk when they commit. Such a policy is called the **force** policy. The alternative, the **no-force** policy, allows a transaction to commit even if it has modified some blocks that have not yet been written back to disk. All the recovery algorithms described in this chapter work correctly even with the no-force policy. The no-force policy allows faster commit of transactions; moreover it allows multiple updates to accumulate on a block before it is output to stable storage, which can reduce the number of output operations greatly for frequently updated blocks. As a result, the standard approach taken by most systems is the no-force policy.

Similarly, one might expect that blocks modified by a transaction that is still active should not be written to disk. This policy is called the **no-steal** policy. The alternative, the **steal** policy, allows the system to write modified blocks to disk even if the transactions that made those modifications have not all committed. As long as the write-ahead logging rule is followed, all the recovery algorithms we study in the chapter work correctly even with the steal policy. Further, the no-steal policy does not work with transactions that perform a large number of updates, since the buffer may get filled with updated pages that cannot be evicted to disk, and the transaction cannot then proceed. As a result, the standard approach taken by most systems is the steal policy.

To illustrate the need for the write-ahead logging requirement, consider our banking example with transactions T_0 and T_1. Suppose that the state of the log is:

$$<T_0 \text{ start}>$$
$$<T_0, \ A, \ 1000, \ 950>$$

and that transaction T_0 issues a read(B). Assume that the block on which B resides is not in main memory, and that main memory is full. Suppose that the block on which A resides is chosen to be output to disk. If the system outputs this block to disk and then a crash occurs, the values in the database for accounts A, B, and C are \$950, \$2000, and \$700, respectively. This database state is inconsistent. However, because of the WAL requirements, the log record:

$$<T_0, \ A, \ 1000, \ 950>$$

must be output to stable storage prior to output of the block on which A resides. The system can use the log record during recovery to bring the database back to a consistent state.

When a block B_1 is to be output to disk, all log records pertaining to data in B_1 must be output to stable storage before B_1 is output. It is important that no writes to the block B_1 be in progress while the block is being output, since such a write could violate the write-ahead logging rule. We can ensure that there are no writes in progress by using a special means of locking:

- Before a transaction performs a write on a data item, it acquires an exclusive lock on the block in which the data item resides. The lock is released immediately after the update has been performed.

- The following sequence of actions is taken when a block is to be output:

  ○ Obtain an exclusive lock on the block, to ensure that no transaction is performing a write on the block.

- ○ Output log records to stable storage until all log records pertaining to block B_1 have been output.

- ○ Output block B_1 to disk.

- ○ Release the lock once the block output has completed.

Locks on buffer blocks are unrelated to locks used for concurrency-control of transactions, and releasing them in a non-two-phase manner does not have any implications on transaction serializability. These locks, and other similar locks that are held for a short duration, are often referred to as **latches**.

Locks on buffer blocks can also be used to ensure that buffer blocks are not updated, and log records are not generated, while a checkpoint is in progress. This restriction may be enforced by acquiring exclusive locks on all buffer blocks, as well as an exclusive lock on the log, before the checkpoint operation is performed. These locks can be released as soon as the checkpoint operation has completed.

Database systems usually have a process that continually cycles through the buffer blocks, outputting modified buffer blocks back to disk. The above locking protocol must of course be followed when the blocks are output. As a result of continuous output of modified blocks, the number of **dirty blocks** in the buffer, that is, blocks that have been modified in the buffer but have not been subsequently output, is minimized. Thus, the number of blocks that have to be output during a checkpoint is minimized; further, when a block needs to be evicted from the buffer it is likely that there will be a non-dirty block available for eviction, allowing the input to proceed immediately instead of waiting for an output to complete.

16.5.3 Operating System Role in Buffer Management

We can manage the database buffer by using one of two approaches:

1. The database system reserves part of main memory to serve as a buffer that it, rather than the operating system, manages. The database system manages data-block transfer in accordance with the requirements in Section 16.5.2.

   This approach has the drawback of limiting flexibility in the use of main memory. The buffer must be kept small enough that other applications have sufficient main memory available for their needs. However, even when the other applications are not running, the database will not be able to make use of all the available memory. Likewise, non-database applications may not use that part of main memory reserved for the database buffer, even if some of the pages in the database buffer are not being used.

2. The database system implements its buffer within the virtual memory provided by the operating system. Since the operating system knows about the memory requirements of all processes in the system, ideally it should be in charge of deciding what buffer blocks must be force-output to disk, and when. But, to ensure the write-ahead logging requirements in Section 16.5.1, the operating system should not write out the database buffer pages itself,

but instead should request the database system to force-output the buffer blocks. The database system in turn would force-output the buffer blocks to the database, after writing relevant log records to stable storage.

Unfortunately, almost all current-generation operating systems retain complete control of virtual memory. The operating system reserves space on disk for storing virtual-memory pages that are not currently in main memory; this space is called **swap space**. If the operating system decides to output a block B_x, that block is output to the swap space on disk, and there is no way for the database system to get control of the output of buffer blocks.

Therefore, if the database buffer is in virtual memory, transfers between database files and the buffer in virtual memory must be managed by the database system, which enforces the write-ahead logging requirements that we discussed.

This approach may result in extra output of data to disk. If a block B_x is output by the operating system, that block is not output to the database. Instead, it is output to the swap space for the operating system's virtual memory. When the database system needs to output B_x, the operating system may need first to input B_x from its swap space. Thus, instead of a single output of B_x, there may be two outputs of B_x (one by the operating system, and one by the database system) and one extra input of B_x.

Although both approaches suffer from some drawbacks, one or the other must be chosen unless the operating system is designed to support the requirements of database logging.

16.5.4   Fuzzy Checkpointing

The checkpointing technique described in Section 16.3.6 requires that all updates to the database be temporarily suspended while the checkpoint is in progress. If the number of pages in the buffer is large, a checkpoint may take a long time to finish, which can result in an unacceptable interruption in processing of transactions.

To avoid such interruptions, the checkpointing technique can be modified to permit updates to start once the checkpoint record has been written, but before the modified buffer blocks are written to disk. The checkpoint thus generated is a **fuzzy checkpoint**.

Since pages are output to disk only after the checkpoint record has been written, it is possible that the system could crash before all pages are written. Thus, a checkpoint on disk may be incomplete. One way to deal with incomplete checkpoints is this: The location in the log of the checkpoint record of the last completed checkpoint is stored in a fixed position, last-checkpoint, on disk. The system does not update this information when it writes the checkpoint record. Instead, before it writes the checkpoint record, it creates a list of all modified buffer blocks. The last-checkpoint information is updated only after all buffer blocks in the list of modified buffer blocks have been output to disk.

Even with fuzzy checkpointing, a buffer block must not be updated while it is being output to disk, although other buffer blocks may be updated concurrently. The write-ahead log protocol must be followed so that (undo) log records pertaining to a block are on stable storage before the block is output.

16.6   Failure with Loss of Nonvolatile Storage

Until now, we have considered only the case where a failure results in the loss of information residing in volatile storage while the content of the nonvolatile storage remains intact. Although failures in which the content of nonvolatile storage is lost are rare, we nevertheless need to be prepared to deal with this type of failure. In this section, we discuss only disk storage. Our discussions apply as well to other nonvolatile storage types.

The basic scheme is to **dump** the entire contents of the database to stable storage periodically—say, once per day. For example, we may dump the database to one or more magnetic tapes. If a failure occurs that results in the loss of physical database blocks, the system uses the most recent dump in restoring the database to a previous consistent state. Once this restoration has been accomplished, the system uses the log to bring the database system to the most recent consistent state.

One approach to database dumping requires that no transaction may be active during the dump procedure, and uses a procedure similar to checkpointing:

1. Output all log records currently residing in main memory onto stable storage.

2. Output all buffer blocks onto the disk.

3. Copy the contents of the database to stable storage.

4. Output a log record <dump> onto the stable storage.

Steps 1, 2, and 4 correspond to the three steps used for checkpoints in Section 16.3.6.

To recover from the loss of nonvolatile storage, the system restores the database to disk by using the most recent dump. Then, it consults the log and redoes all the actions since the most recent dump occurred. Notice that no undo operations need to be executed.

In case of a partial failure of nonvolatile storage, such as the failure of a single block or a few blocks, only those blocks need to be restored, and redo actions performed only for those blocks.

A dump of the database contents is also referred to as an **archival dump**, since we can archive the dumps and use them later to examine old states of the database. Dumps of a database and checkpointing of buffers are similar.

Most database systems also support an **SQL dump**, which writes out SQL DDL statements and SQL insert statements to a file, which can then be reexecuted to re-create the database. Such dumps are useful when migrating data to a different instance of the database, or to a different version of the database software, since the physical locations and layout may be different in the other database instance or database software version.

The simple dump procedure described here is costly for the following two reasons. First, the entire database must be copied to stable storage, resulting in considerable data transfer. Second, since transaction processing is halted during the dump procedure, CPU cycles are wasted. **Fuzzy dump** schemes have been developed that allow transactions to be active while the dump is in progress. They are similar to fuzzy-checkpointing schemes; see the bibliographical notes for more details.

16.7 Early Lock Release and Logical Undo Operations

Any index used in processing a transaction, such as a B^+-tree, can be treated as normal data, but to increase concurrency, we can use the B^+-tree concurrency-control algorithm described in Section 15.10 to allow locks to be released early, in a non-two-phase manner. As a result of early lock release, it is possible that a value in a B^+-tree node is updated by one transaction T_1, which inserts an entry $(V1, R1)$, and subsequently by another transaction T_2, which inserts an entry $(V2, R2)$ in the same node, moving the entry $(V1, R1)$ even before T_1 completes execution.[4] At this point, we cannot undo transaction T_1 by replacing the contents of the node with the old value prior to T_1 performing its insert, since that would also undo the insert performed by T_2; transaction T_2 may still commit (or may have already committed). In this example, the only way to undo the effect of insertion of $(V1, R1)$ is to execute a corresponding delete operation.

In the rest of this section, we see how to extend the recovery algorithm of Section 16.4 to support early lock release.

16.7.1 Logical Operations

The insertion and deletion operations are examples of a class of operations that require logical undo operations since they release locks early; we call such operations **logical operations**. Such early lock release is important not only for indices, but also for operations on other system data structures that are accessed and updated very frequently; examples include data structures that track the blocks containing records of a relation, the free space in a block, and the free blocks in a database. If locks were not released early after performing operations on such data structures, transactions would tend to run serially, affecting system performance.

The theory of conflict serializability has been extended to operations, based on what operations conflict with what other operations. For example, two insert

---

[4]Recall that an entry consists of a key value and a record identifier, or a key value and a record in the case of the leaf level of a B^+-tree file organization.

operations on a B^+-tree do not conflict if they insert different key values, even if they both update overlapping areas of the same index page. However, insert and delete operations conflict with other insert and delete operations, as well as with read operations, if they use the same key value. See the bibliographical notes for references to more information on this topic.

Operations acquire *lower-level locks* while they execute, but release them when they complete; the corresponding transaction must however retain a *higher-level lock* in a two-phase manner to prevent concurrent transactions from executing conflicting actions. For example, while an insert operation is being performed on a B^+-tree page, a short-term lock is obtained on the page, allowing entries in the page to be shifted during the insert; the short-term lock is released as soon as the page has been updated. Such early lock release allows a second insert to execute on the same page. However, each transaction must obtain a lock on the key values being inserted or deleted, and retain it in a two-phase manner, to prevent a concurrent transaction from executing a conflicting read, insert or delete operation on the same key value.

Once the lower-level lock is released, the operation cannot be undone by using the old values of updated data items, and must instead be undone by executing a compensating operation; such an operation is called a **logical undo operation**. It is important that the lower-level locks acquired during an operation are sufficient to perform a subsequent logical undo of the operation, for reasons explained later in Section 16.7.4.

16.7.2 Logical Undo Log Records

To allow logical undo of operations, before an operation is performed to modify an index, the transaction creates a log record $<T_i, O_j,$ operation-begin$>$, where O_j is a unique identifier for the operation instance.[5] While the system is executing the operation, it creates update log records in the normal fashion for all updates performed by the operation. Thus, the usual old-value and new-value information is written out as usual for each update performed by the operation; the old-value information is required in case the transaction needs to be rolled back before the operation completes. When the operation finishes, it writes an **operation-end** log record of the form $<T_i, O_j,$ **operation-end**, $U>$, where the U denotes undo information.

For example, if the operation inserted an entry in a B^+-tree, the undo information U would indicate that a deletion operation is to be performed, and would identify the B^+-tree and what entry to delete from the tree. Such logging of information about operations is called **logical logging**. In contrast, logging of old-value and new-value information is called **physical logging**, and the corresponding log records are called **physical log records**.

Note that in the above scheme, logical logging is used only for undo, not for redo; redo operations are performed exclusively using physical log record. This is because the state of the database after a system failure may reflect some updates

---

[5]The position in the log of the **operation-begin** log record can be used as the unique identifier.

of an operation and not other operations, depending on what buffer blocks had been written to disk before the failure. Data structures such as B^+-trees would not be in a consistent state, and neither logical redo nor logical undo operations can be performed on an inconsistent data structure. To perform logical redo or undo, the database state on disk must be **operation consistent**, that is, it should not have partial effects of any operation. However, as we shall see, the physical redo processing in the redo phase of the recovery scheme, along with undo processing using physical log records ensures that the parts of the database accessed by a logical undo operation are in an operation consistent state, before the logical undo operation is performed.

An operation is said to be **idempotent** if executing it several times in a row gives the same result as executing it once. Operations such as inserting an entry into a B^+-tree may not be idempotent, and the recovery algorithm must therefore make sure that an operation that has already been performed is not performed again. On the other hand, a physical log record is idempotent, since the corresponding data item would have the same value regardless of whether the logged update is executed one or multiple times.

16.7.3   Transaction Rollback With Logical Undo

When rolling back a transaction T_i, the log is scanned backwards, and log records corresponding to T_i are processed as follows:

1. Physical log records encountered during the scan are handled as described earlier, except those that are skipped as described shortly. Incomplete logical operations are undone using the physical log records generated by the operation.

2. Completed logical operations, identified by operation-end records, are rolled back differently. Whenever the system finds a log record $<T_i, O_j,$ operation-end, $U>$, it takes special actions:

    a. It rolls back the operation by using the undo information U in the log record. It logs the updates performed during the rollback of the operation just like updates performed when the operation was first executed.

        At the end of the operation rollback, instead of generating a log record $<T_i, O_j,$ operation-end, $U>$, the database system generates a log record $<T_i, O_j,$ operation-abort$>$.

    b. As the backward scan of the log continues, the system skips all log records of transaction T_i until it finds the log record $<T_i, O_j,$ operation-begin$>$. After it finds the operation-begin log record, it processes log records of transaction T_i in the normal manner again.

Observe that the system logs physical undo information for the updates performed during rollback, instead of using a redo-only compensation log records. This is because a crash may occur while a logical undo is in progress, and on recovery the system has to complete the logical undo; to do so, restart recovery will undo the partial effects of the earlier undo, using the physical undo information, and then perform the logical undo again.

Observe also that skipping over physical log records when the operation-end log record is found during rollback ensures that the old values in the physical log record are not used for rollback, once the operation completes.

3. If the system finds a record $<T_i, O_j, \text{operation-abort}>$, it skips all preceding records (including the operation-end record for O_j) until it finds the record $<T_i, O_j, \text{operation-begin}>$.

   An operation-abort log record would be found only if a transaction that is being rolled back had been partially rolled back earlier. Recall that logical operations may not be idempotent, and hence a logical undo operation must not be performed multiple times. These preceding log records must be skipped to prevent multiple rollback of the same operation, in case there had been a crash during an earlier rollback, and the transaction had already been partly rolled back.

4. As before, when the $<T_i \text{ start}>$ log record has been found, the transaction rollback is complete, and the system adds a record $<T_i \text{ abort}>$ to the log.

If a failure occurs while a logical operation is in progress, the operation-end log record for the operation will not be found when the transaction is rolled back. However, for every update performed by the operation, undo information—in the form of the old value in the physical log records—is available in the log. The physical log records will be used to roll back the incomplete operation.

Now suppose an operation undo was in progress when the system crash occurred, which could happen if a transaction was being rolled back when the crash occurred. Then the physical log records written during operation undo would be found, and the partial operation undo would itself be undone using these physical log records. Continuing in the backward scan of the log, the original operation's operation-end record would then be found, and the operation undo would be executed again. Rolling back the partial effects of the earlier undo operation using the physical log records brings the database to a consistent state, allowing the logical undo operation to be executed again.

Figure 16.6 shows an example of a log generated by two transactions, which add or subtract a value from a data item. Early lock release on the data item C by transaction T_0 after operation O_1 completes allows transaction T_1 to update the data item using O_2, even before T_0 completes, but necessitates logical undo. The logical undo operation needs to add or subtract a value from the data item, instead of restoring an old value to the data item.

The annotations on the figure indicate that before an operation completes, rollback can perform physical undo; after the operation completes and releases lower-level locks, the undo must be performed by subtracting or adding a value, instead of restoring the old value. In the example in the figure, T_0 rolls back operation O_1 by adding 100 to C; on the other hand, for data item B, which was not subject to early lock release, undo is performed physically. Observe that T_1,

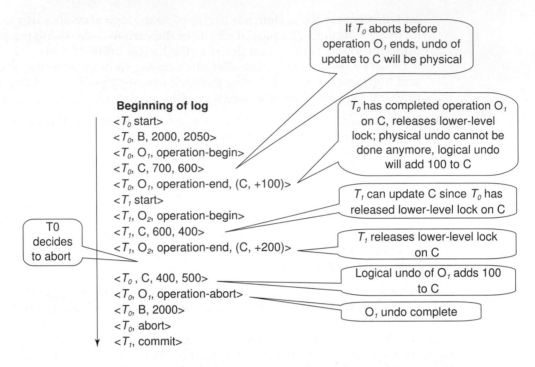

Figure 16.6 Transaction rollback with logical undo operations.

which had performed an update on C commits, and its update O_2, which added 200 to C and was performed before the undo of O_1, has persisted even though O_1 has been undone.

Figure 16.7 shows an example of recovery from a crash, with logical undo logging. In this example, operation T_1 was active and executing operation O_4 at the time of checkpoint. In the redo pass, the actions of O_4 that are after the checkpoint log record are redone. At the time of crash, operation O_5 was being executed by T_2, but the operation was not complete. The undo-list contains T_1 and T_2 at the end of the redo pass. During the undo pass, the undo of operation O_5 is carried out using the old value in the physical log record, setting C to 400; this operation is logged using a redo-only log record. The **start** record of T_2 is encountered next, resulting in the addition of $< T_2$ **abort**$>$ to the log, and removal of T_2 from undo-list.

The next log record encountered is the **operation-end** record of O_4; logical undo is performed for this operation by adding 300 to C, which is logged physically, and an **operation-abort** log record is added for O_4. The physical log records that were part of O_4 are skipped until the **operation-begin** log record for O_4 is encountered. In this example, there are no other intervening log records, but in general log records from other transactions may be found before we reach the **operation-begin** log record; such log records should of course not be skipped (unless they are part of a completed operation for the corresponding transaction and the algorithm skips those records). After the **operation-begin** log record is

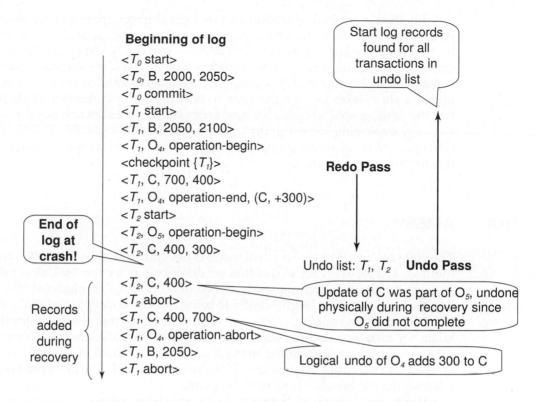

Figure 16.7 Failure recovery actions with logical undo operations

found for O_4, a physical log record is found for T_1, which is rolled back physically. Finally the start log record for T_1 is found; this results in $< T_1$ abort$>$ being added to the log, and T_1 being deleted from undo-list. At this point undo-list is empty, and the undo phase is complete.

16.7.4 Concurrency Issues in Logical Undo

As mentioned earlier, it is important that the lower-level locks acquired during an operation are sufficient to perform a subsequent logical undo of the operation; otherwise concurrent operations that execute during normal processing may cause problems in the undo-phase. For example, suppose the logical undo of operation O_1 of transaction T_1 can conflict at the data item level with a concurrent operation O_2 of transaction T_2, and O_1 completes while O_2 does not. Assume also that neither transaction had committed when the system crashed. The physical update log records of O_2 may appear before and after the operation-end record for O_1, and during recovery updates done during the logical undo of O_1 may get fully or partially overwritten by old values during the physical undo of O_2. This problem cannot occur if O_1 had obtained all the lower-level locks required for the logical undo of O_1, since then there cannot be such a concurrent O_2.

If both the original operation and its logical undo operation access a single page (such operations are called physiological operations, and are discussed in Section 16.8), the locking requirement above is met easily. Otherwise the details of the specific operation need to be considered when deciding on what lower-level locks need to be obtained. For example, update operations on a B$^+$-tree could obtain a short-term lock on the root, to ensure that operations execute serially. See the bibliographical notes for references on B$^+$-tree concurrency control and recovery exploiting logical undo logging. See the bibliographical notes also for references to an alternative approach, called multi-level recovery, which relaxes this locking requirement.

16.8   ARIES**

The state of the art in recovery methods is best illustrated by the ARIES recovery method. The recovery technique that we described in Section 16.4, along with the logical undo logging techniques described in Section 16.7, is modeled after ARIES, but has been simplified significantly to bring out key concepts and make it easier to understand. In contrast, ARIES uses a number of techniques to reduce the time taken for recovery, and to reduce the overhead of checkpointing. In particular, ARIES is able to avoid redoing many logged operations that have already been applied and to reduce the amount of information logged. The price paid is greater complexity; the benefits are worth the price.

The major differences between ARIES and the recovery algorithm presented earlier are that ARIES:

1. Uses a **log sequence number** (LSN) to identify log records, and stores LSNs in database pages to identify which operations have been applied to a database page.

2. Supports **physiological redo** operations, which are physical in that the affected page is physically identified, but can be logical within the page.

    For instance, the deletion of a record from a page may result in many other records in the page being shifted, if a slotted page structure (Section 10.5.2) is used. With physical redo logging, all bytes of the page affected by the shifting of records must be logged. With physiological logging, the deletion operation can be logged, resulting in a much smaller log record. Redo of the deletion operation would delete the record and shift other records as required.

3. Uses a **dirty page table** to minimize unnecessary redos during recovery. As mentioned earlier, dirty pages are those that have been updated in memory, and the disk version is not up-to-date.

4. Uses a fuzzy-checkpointing scheme that records only information about dirty pages and associated information and does not even require writing

of dirty pages to disk. It flushes dirty pages in the background, continuously, instead of writing them during checkpoints.

In the rest of this section, we provide an overview of ARIES. The bibliographical notes list references that provide a complete description of ARIES.

16.8.1 Data Structures

Each log record in ARIES has a log sequence number (LSN) that uniquely identifies the record. The number is conceptually just a logical identifier whose value is greater for log records that occur later in the log. In practice, the LSN is generated in such a way that it can also be used to locate the log record on disk. Typically, ARIES splits a log into multiple log files, each of which has a file number. When a log file grows to some limit, ARIES appends further log records to a new log file; the new log file has a file number that is higher by 1 than the previous log file. The LSN then consists of a file number and an offset within the file.

Each page also maintains an identifier called the **PageLSN**. Whenever an update operation (whether physical or physiological) occurs on a page, the operation stores the LSN of its log record in the PageLSN field of the page. During the redo phase of recovery, any log records with LSN less than or equal to the PageLSN of a page should not be executed on the page, since their actions are already reflected on the page. In combination with a scheme for recording PageLSNs as part of checkpointing, which we present later, ARIES can avoid even reading many pages for which logged operations are already reflected on disk. Thereby, recovery time is reduced significantly.

The PageLSN is essential for ensuring idempotence in the presence of physiological redo operations, since reapplying a physiological redo that has already been applied to a page could cause incorrect changes to a page.

Pages should not be flushed to disk while an update is in progress, since physiological operations cannot be redone on the partially updated state of the page on disk. Therefore, ARIES uses latches on buffer pages to prevent them from being written to disk while they are being updated. It releases the buffer page latch only after the update is completed, and the log record for the update has been written to the log.

Each log record also contains the LSN of the previous log record of the same transaction. This value, stored in the PrevLSN field, permits log records of a transaction to be fetched backward, without reading the whole log. There are special redo-only log records generated during transaction rollback, called **compensation log records** (CLRs) in ARIES. These serve the same purpose as the redo-only log records in our earlier recovery scheme. In addition CLRs serve the role of the operation-abort log records in our scheme. The CLRs have an extra field, called the UndoNextLSN, that records the LSN of the log that needs to be undone next, when the transaction is being rolled back. This field serves the same purpose as the operation identifier in the operation-abort log record in our earlier recovery scheme, which helps to skip over log records that have already been rolled back.

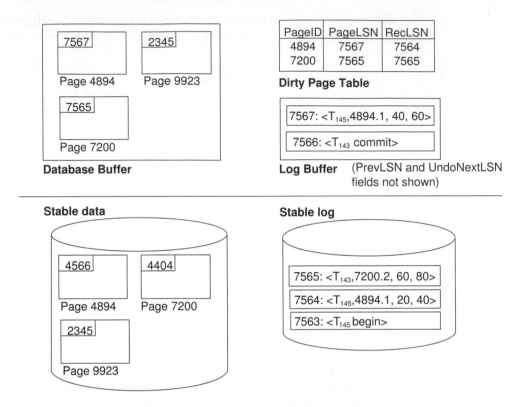

Figure 16.8   Data structures used in ARIES.

The **DirtyPageTable** contains a list of pages that have been updated in the database buffer. For each page, it stores the PageLSN and a field called the RecLSN, which helps identify log records that have been applied already to the version of the page on disk. When a page is inserted into the DirtyPageTable (when it is first modified in the buffer pool), the value of RecLSN is set to the current end of log. Whenever the page is flushed to disk, the page is removed from the DirtyPageTable.

A **checkpoint log record** contains the DirtyPageTable and a list of active transactions. For each transaction, the checkpoint log record also notes LastLSN, the LSN of the last log record written by the transaction. A fixed position on disk also notes the LSN of the last (complete) checkpoint log record.

Figure 16.8 illustrates some of the data structures used in ARIES. The log records shown in the figure are prefixed by their LSN; these may not be explicitly stored, but inferred from the position in the log, in an actual implementation. The data item identifier in a log record is shown in two parts, for example 4894.1; the first identifies the page, and the second part identifies a record within the page (we assume a slotted page record organization within a page). Note that the log is shown with newest records on top, since older log records, which are on disk, are shown lower in the figure.

Each page (whether in the buffer or on disk) has an associated PageLSN field. You can verify that the LSN for the last log record that updated page 4894 is 7567. By comparing PageLSNs for the pages in the buffer with the PageLSNs for the corresponding pages in stable storage, you can observe that the DirtyPageTable contains entries for all pages in the buffer that have been modified since they were fetched from stable storage. The RecLSN entry in the DirtyPageTable reflects the LSN at the end of the log when the page was added to DirtyPageTable, and would be greater than or equal to the PageLSN for that page on stable storage.

16.8.2 Recovery Algorithm

ARIES recovers from a system crash in three passes.

- **Analysis pass**: This pass determines which transactions to undo, which pages were dirty at the time of the crash, and the LSN from which the redo pass should start.

- **Redo pass**: This pass starts from a position determined during analysis, and performs a redo, repeating history, to bring the database to a state it was in before the crash.

- **Undo pass**: This pass rolls back all transactions that were incomplete at the time of crash.

16.8.2.1 Analysis Pass

The analysis pass finds the last complete checkpoint log record, and reads in the DirtyPageTable from this record. It then sets RedoLSN to the minimum of the RecLSNs of the pages in the DirtyPageTable. If there are no dirty pages, it sets RedoLSN to the LSN of the checkpoint log record. The redo pass starts its scan of the log from RedoLSN. All the log records earlier than this point have already been applied to the database pages on disk. The analysis pass initially sets the list of transactions to be undone, undo-list, to the list of transactions in the checkpoint log record. The analysis pass also reads from the checkpoint log record the LSNs of the last log record for each transaction in undo-list.

The analysis pass continues scanning forward from the checkpoint. Whenever it finds a log record for a transaction not in the undo-list, it adds the transaction to undo-list. Whenever it finds a transaction end log record, it deletes the transaction from undo-list. All transactions left in undo-list at the end of analysis have to be rolled back later, in the undo pass. The analysis pass also keeps track of the last record of each transaction in undo-list, which is used in the undo pass.

The analysis pass also updates DirtyPageTable whenever it finds a log record for an update on a page. If the page is not in DirtyPageTable, the analysis pass adds it to DirtyPageTable, and sets the RecLSN of the page to the LSN of the log record.

16.8.2.2   Redo Pass

The redo pass repeats history by replaying every action that is not already reflected in the page on disk. The redo pass scans the log forward from RedoLSN. Whenever it finds an update log record, it takes this action:

1. If the page is not in DirtyPageTable or the LSN of the update log record is less than the RecLSN of the page in DirtyPageTable, then the redo pass skips the log record.

2. Otherwise the redo pass fetches the page from disk, and if the PageLSN is less than the LSN of the log record, it redoes the log record.

Note that if either of the tests is negative, then the effects of the log record have already appeared on the page; otherwise the effects of the log record are not reflected on the page. Since ARIES allows non-idempotent physiological log records, a log record should not be redone if its effect is already reflected on the page. If the first test is negative, it is not even necessary to fetch the page from disk to check its PageLSN.

16.8.2.3   Undo Pass and Transaction Rollback

The undo pass is relatively straightforward. It performs a single backward scan of the log, undoing all transactions in undo-list. The undo pass examines only log records of transactions in undo-list; the last LSN recorded during the analysis pass is used to find the last log record for each transaction in undo-list.

Whenever an update log record is found, it is used to perform an undo (whether for transaction rollback during normal processing, or during the restart undo pass). The undo pass generates a CLR containing the undo action performed (which must be physiological). It sets the UndoNextLSN of the CLR to the PrevLSN value of the update log record.

If a CLR is found, its UndoNextLSN value indicates the LSN of the next log record to be undone for that transaction; later log records for that transaction have already been rolled back. For log records other than CLRs, the PrevLSN field of the log record indicates the LSN of the next log record to be undone for that transaction. The next log record to be processed at each stop in the undo pass is the maximum, across all transactions in undo-list, of next log record LSN.

Figure 16.9 illustrates the recovery actions performed by ARIES, on an example log. We assume that the last completed checkpoint pointer on disk points to the checkpoint log record with LSN 7568. The PrevLSN values in the log records are shown using arrows in the figure, while the UndoNextLSN value is shown using a dashed arrow for the one compensation log record, with LSN 7565, in the figure. The analysis pass would start from LSN 7568, and when it is complete, RedoLSN would be 7564. Thus, the redo pass must start at the log record with LSN 7564. Note that this LSN is less than the LSN of the checkpoint log record, since the ARIES checkpointing algorithm does not flush modified pages to stable storage. The DirtyPageTable at the end of analysis would include pages 4894, 7200 from

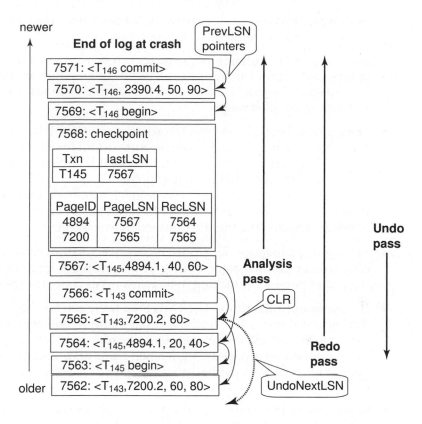

Figure 16.9 Recovery actions in ARIES.

the checkpoint log record, and 2390 which is updated by the log record with LSN 7570. At the end of the analysis pass, the list of transactions to be undone consists of only T_{145} in this example.

The redo pass for the above example starts from LSN 7564 and performs redo of log records whose pages appear in DirtyPageTable. The undo pass needs to undo only transaction T_{145}, and hence starts from its LastLSN value 7567, and continues backwards until the record $< T_{145}$ start$>$ is found at LSN 7563.

16.8.3 Other Features

Among other key features that ARIES provides are:

- **Nested top actions**: ARIES allows the logging of operations that should not be undone even if a transaction gets rolled back; for example, if a transaction allocates a page to a relation, even if the transaction is rolled back the page allocation should not be undone since other transactions may have stored records in the page. Such operations that should not be undone are called nested top actions. Such operations can be modeled as operations whose undo action does nothing. In ARIES, such operations are implemented by creating a dummy CLR whose UndoNextLSN is set such that transaction rollback skips the log records generated by the operation.

- **Recovery independence**: Some pages can be recovered independently from others, so that they can be used even while other pages are being recovered. If some pages of a disk fail, they can be recovered without stopping transaction processing on other pages.

- **Savepoints**: Transactions can record savepoints, and can be rolled back partially, up to a savepoint. This can be quite useful for deadlock handling, since transactions can be rolled back up to a point that permits release of required locks, and then restarted from that point.

   Programmers can also use savepoints to undo a transaction partially, and then continue execution; this approach can be useful to handle certain kinds of errors detected during the transaction execution.

- **Fine-grained locking**: The ARIES recovery algorithm can be used with index concurrency-control algorithms that permit tuple-level locking on indices, instead of page-level locking, which improves concurrency significantly.

- **Recovery optimizations**: The DirtyPageTable can be used to prefetch pages during redo, instead of fetching a page only when the system finds a log record to be applied to the page. Out-of-order redo is also possible: Redo can be postponed on a page being fetched from disk, and performed when the page is fetched. Meanwhile, other log records can continue to be processed.

In summary, the ARIES algorithm is a state-of-the-art recovery algorithm, incorporating a variety of optimizations designed to improve concurrency, reduce logging overhead, and reduce recovery time.

16.9   Remote Backup Systems

Traditional transaction-processing systems are centralized or client–server systems. Such systems are vulnerable to environmental disasters such as fire, flooding, or earthquakes. Increasingly, there is a need for transaction-processing systems that can function in spite of system failures or environmental disasters. Such systems must provide **high availability**; that is, the time for which the system is unusable must be extremely small.

We can achieve high availability by performing transaction processing at one site, called the **primary site**, and having a **remote backup** site where all the data from the primary site are replicated. The remote backup site is sometimes also called the **secondary site**. The remote site must be kept synchronized with the primary site, as updates are performed at the primary. We achieve synchronization by sending all log records from primary site to the remote backup site. The remote backup site must be physically separated from the primary—for example, we can locate it in a different state—so that a disaster at the primary does not damage

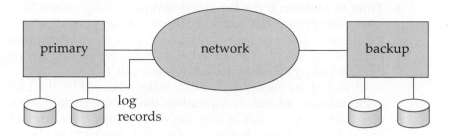

Figure 16.10   Architecture of remote backup system.

the remote backup site. Figure 16.10 shows the architecture of a remote backup system.

When the primary site fails, the remote backup site takes over processing. First, however, it performs recovery, using its (perhaps outdated) copy of the data from the primary, and the log records received from the primary. In effect, the remote backup site is performing recovery actions that would have been performed at the primary site when the latter recovered. Standard recovery algorithms, with minor modifications, can be used for recovery at the remote backup site. Once recovery has been performed, the remote backup site starts processing transactions.

Availability is greatly increased over a single-site system, since the system can recover even if all data at the primary site are lost.

Several issues must be addressed in designing a remote backup system:

- **Detection of failure**. It is important for the remote backup system to detect when the primary has failed. Failure of communication lines can fool the remote backup into believing that the primary has failed. To avoid this problem, we maintain several communication links with independent modes of failure between the primary and the remote backup. For example, several independent network connections, including perhaps a modem connection over a telephone line, may be used. These connections may be backed up via manual intervention by operators, who can communicate over the telephone system.

- **Transfer of control**. When the primary fails, the backup site takes over processing and becomes the new primary. When the original primary site recovers, it can either play the role of remote backup, or take over the role of primary site again. In either case, the old primary must receive a log of updates carried out by the backup site while the old primary was down.

  The simplest way of transferring control is for the old primary to receive redo logs from the old backup site, and to catch up with the updates by applying them locally. The old primary can then act as a remote backup site. If control must be transferred back, the old backup site can pretend to have failed, resulting in the old primary taking over.

- **Time to recover**. If the log at the remote backup grows large, recovery will take a long time. The remote backup site can periodically process the redo log records that it has received and can perform a checkpoint, so that earlier parts of the log can be deleted. The delay before the remote backup takes over can be significantly reduced as a result.

  A **hot-spare** configuration can make takeover by the backup site almost instantaneous. In this configuration, the remote backup site continually processes redo log records as they arrive, applying the updates locally. As soon as the failure of the primary is detected, the backup site completes recovery by rolling back incomplete transactions; it is then ready to process new transactions.

- **Time to commit**. To ensure that the updates of a committed transaction are durable, a transaction must not be declared committed until its log records have reached the backup site. This delay can result in a longer wait to commit a transaction, and some systems therefore permit lower degrees of durability. The degrees of durability can be classified as follows:

  ○ **One-safe**. A transaction commits as soon as its commit log record is written to stable storage at the primary site.

     The problem with this scheme is that the updates of a committed transaction may not have made it to the backup site, when the backup site takes over processing. Thus, the updates may appear to be lost. When the primary site recovers, the lost updates cannot be merged in directly, since the updates may conflict with later updates performed at the backup site. Thus, human intervention may be required to bring the database to a consistent state.

  ○ **Two-very-safe**. A transaction commits as soon as its commit log record is written to stable storage at the primary and the backup site.

     The problem with this scheme is that transaction processing cannot proceed if either the primary or the backup site is down. Thus, availability is actually less than in the single-site case, although the probability of data loss is much less.

  ○ **Two-safe**. This scheme is the same as two-very-safe if both primary and backup sites are active. If only the primary is active, the transaction is allowed to commit as soon as its commit log record is written to stable storage at the primary site.

     This scheme provides better availability than does two-very-safe, while avoiding the problem of lost transactions faced by the one-safe scheme. It results in a slower commit than the one-safe scheme, but the benefits generally outweigh the cost.

Several commercial shared-disk systems provide a level of fault tolerance that is intermediate between centralized and remote backup systems. In these commercial systems, the failure of a CPU does not result in system failure. Instead, other CPUs take over, and they carry out recovery. Recovery actions include rollback of transactions running on the failed CPU, and recovery of locks held by those transactions. Since data are on a shared disk, there is no need for transfer of log records. However, we should safeguard the data from disk failure by using, for example, a RAID disk organization.

An alternative way of achieving high availability is to use a distributed database, with data replicated at more than one site. Transactions are then required to update all replicas of any data item that they update. We study distributed databases, including replication, in Chapter 19.

16.10 Summary

- A computer system, like any other mechanical or electrical device, is subject to failure. There are a variety of causes of such failure, including disk crash, power failure, and software errors. In each of these cases, information concerning the database system is lost.

- In addition to system failures, transactions may also fail for various reasons, such as violation of integrity constraints or deadlocks.

- An integral part of a database system is a recovery scheme that is responsible for the detection of failures and for the restoration of the database to a state that existed before the occurrence of the failure.

- The various types of storage in a computer are volatile storage, nonvolatile storage, and stable storage. Data in volatile storage, such as in RAM, are lost when the computer crashes. Data in nonvolatile storage, such as disk, are not lost when the computer crashes, but may occasionally be lost because of failures such as disk crashes. Data in stable storage are never lost.

- Stable storage that must be accessible online is approximated with mirrored disks, or other forms of RAID, which provide redundant data storage. Offline, or archival, stable storage may consist of multiple tape copies of data stored in a physically secure location.

- In case of failure, the state of the database system may no longer be consistent; that is, it may not reflect a state of the world that the database is supposed to capture. To preserve consistency, we require that each transaction be atomic. It is the responsibility of the recovery scheme to ensure the atomicity and durability property.

- In log-based schemes, all updates are recorded on a log, which must be kept in stable storage. A transaction is considered to have committed when its last log record, which is the commit log record for the transaction, has been output to stable storage.

- Log records contain old values and new values for all updated data items. The new values are used in case the updates need to be redone after a system crash. The old values are used to roll back the updates of the transaction if the transaction aborts during normal operation, as well as to roll back the updates of the transaction in case the system crashed before the transaction committed.

- In the deferred-modifications scheme, during the execution of a transaction, all the write operations are deferred until the transaction has been committed, at which time the system uses the information on the log associated with the transaction in executing the deferred writes. With deferred modification, log records do not need to contain old values of updated data items.

- To reduce the overhead of searching the log and redoing transactions, we can use checkpointing techniques.

- Modern recovery algorithms are based on the concept of repeating history, whereby all actions taken during normal operation (since the last completed checkpoint) are replayed during the redo pass of recovery. Repeating history restores the system state to what it was at the time the last log record was output to stable storage before the system crashed. Undo is then performed from this state, by executing an undo pass that processes log records of incomplete transactions in reverse order.

- Undo of an incomplete transaction writes out special redo-only log records, and an abort log record. After that, the transaction can be considered to have completed, and it will not be undone again.

- Transaction processing is based on a storage model in which main memory holds a log buffer, a database buffer, and a system buffer. The system buffer holds pages of system object code and local work areas of transactions.

- Efficient implementation of a recovery scheme requires that the number of writes to the database and to stable storage be minimized. Log records may be kept in volatile log buffer initially, but must be written to stable storage when one of the following conditions occurs:

  - Before the $<T_i$ commit$>$ log record may be output to stable storage, all log records pertaining to transaction T_i must have been output to stable storage.

  - Before a block of data in main memory is output to the database (in nonvolatile storage), all log records pertaining to data in that block must have been output to stable storage.

- Modern recovery techniques support high-concurrency locking techniques, such as those used for B^+-tree concurrency control. These techniques allow early release of lower-level locks obtained by operations such as inserts or deletes, which allows other such operations to be performed by other transactions. After lower-level locks are released, physical undo is not possible, and instead logical undo, such as a deletion to undo an insertion, is required. Transactions retain higher-level locks that ensure that concurrent transactions cannot perform actions that could make logical undo of an operation impossible.

- To recover from failures that result in the loss of nonvolatile storage, we must dump the entire contents of the database onto stable storage periodically—say, once per day. If a failure occurs that results in the loss of physical database blocks, we use the most recent dump in restoring the database to a previous consistent state. Once this restoration has been accomplished, we use the log to bring the database system to the most recent consistent state.

- The ARIES recovery scheme is a state-of-the-art scheme that supports a number of features to provide greater concurrency, reduce logging overheads, and minimize recovery time. It is also based on repeating history, and allows logical undo operations. The scheme flushes pages on a continuous basis and does not need to flush all pages at the time of a checkpoint. It uses log sequence numbers (LSNs) to implement a variety of optimizations that reduce the time taken for recovery.

- Remote backup systems provide a high degree of availability, allowing transaction processing to continue even if the primary site is destroyed by a fire, flood, or earthquake. Data and log records from a primary site are continually backed up to a remote backup site. If the primary site fails, the remote backup site takes over transaction processing, after executing certain recovery actions.

Review Terms

- Recovery scheme
- Failure classification
  - Transaction failure
  - Logical error
  - System error
  - System crash
  - Data-transfer failure
- Fail-stop assumption
- Disk failure
- Storage types
  - Volatile storage
  - Nonvolatile storage
  - Stable storage
- Blocks
  - Physical blocks
  - Buffer blocks
- Disk buffer
- Force-output
- Log-based recovery
- Log
- Log records
- Update log record
- Deferred modification
- Immediate modification
- Uncommitted modifications
- Checkpoints
- Recovery algorithm

- Restart recovery
- Transaction rollback
- Physical undo
- Physical logging
- Transaction rollback
- Checkpoints
- Restart recovery
- Redo phase
- Undo phase
- Repeating history
- Buffer management
- Log-record buffering
- Write-ahead logging (WAL)
- Log force
- Database buffering
- Latches
- Operating system and buffer management
- Fuzzy checkpointing
- Early lock release
- Logical operations
- Logical logging
- Logical undo
- Loss of nonvolatile storage
- Archival dump
- Fuzzy dump
- ARIES

  - Log sequence number (LSN)
  - PageLSN
  - Physiological redo
  - Compensation log record (CLR)
  - DirtyPageTable
  - Checkpoint log record
  - Analysis phase
  - Redo phase
  - Undo phase

- High availability
- Remote backup systems

  - Primary site
  - Remote backup site
  - Secondary site

- Detection of failure
- Transfer of control
- Time to recover
- Hot-spare configuration
- Time to commit

  - One-safe
  - Two-very-safe
  - Two-safe

Practice Exercises

16.1 Explain why log records for transactions on the undo-list must be pro-cessed in reverse order, whereas redo is performed in a forward direction.

16.2 Explain the purpose of the checkpoint mechanism. How often should checkpoints be performed? How does the frequency of checkpoints affect:

- System performance when no failure occurs?
- The time it takes to recover from a system crash?
- The time it takes to recover from a media (disk) failure?

16.3 Some database systems allow the administrator to choose between two forms of logging: *normal logging,* used to recover from system crashes, and *archival logging,* used to recover from media (disk) failure. When can a log record be deleted, in each of these cases, using the recovery algorithm of Section 16.4?

16.4 Describe how to modify the recovery algorithm of Section 16.4 to implement savepoints, and to perform rollback to a savepoint. (Savepoints are described in Section 16.8.3.)

16.5 Suppose the deferred modification technique is used in a database.

    a. Is the old-value part of an update log record required any more? Why or why not?

    b. If old values are not stored in update log records, transaction undo is clearly not feasible. How would the redo-phase of recovery have to be modified as a result?

    c. Deferred modification can be implemented by keeping updated data items in local memory of transactions, and reading data items that have not been updated directly from the database buffer. Suggest how to efficiently implement a data item read, ensuring that a transaction sees its own updates.

    d. What problem would arise with the above technique, if transactions perform a large number of updates?

16.6 The shadow-paging scheme requires the page table to be copied. Suppose the page table is represented as a B^+-tree.

    a. Suggest how to share as many nodes as possible between the new copy and the shadow-copy of the B^+-tree, assuming that updates are made only to leaf entries, with no insertions and deletions.

    b. Even with the above optimization, logging is much cheaper than a shadow-copy scheme, for transactions that perform small updates. Explain why.

16.7 Suppose we (incorrectly) modify the recovery algorithm of Section 16.4 to not log actions taken during transaction rollback. When recovering from a system crash, transactions that were rolled back earlier would then be included in undo-list, and rolled back again. Give an example to show how actions taken during the undo phase of recovery could result in an incorrect database state. (Hint: Consider a data item updated by an aborted transaction, and then updated by a transaction that commits.)

16.8 Disk space allocated to a file as a result of a transaction should not be released even if the transaction is rolled back. Explain why, and explain how ARIES ensures that such actions are not rolled back.

16.9 Suppose a transaction deletes a record, and the free space generated thus is allocated to a record inserted by another transaction, even before the first transaction commits.

    a. What problem can occur if the first transaction needs to be rolled back?

    b. Would this problem be an issue if page-level locking is used instead of tuple-level locking?

    c. Suggest how to solve this problem while supporting tuple-level locking, by logging post-commit actions in special log records, and executing them after commit. Make sure your scheme ensures that such actions are performed exactly once.

16.10 Explain the reasons why recovery of interactive transactions is more difficult to deal with than is recovery of batch transactions. Is there a simple way to deal with this difficulty? (Hint: Consider an automatic teller machine transaction in which cash is withdrawn.)

16.11 Sometimes a transaction has to be undone after it has committed because it was erroneously executed, for example because of erroneous input by a bank teller.

    a. Give an example to show that using the normal transaction undo mechanism to undo such a transaction could lead to an inconsistent state.

    b. One way to handle this situation is to bring the whole database to a state prior to the commit of the erroneous transaction (called *point-in-time* recovery). Transactions that committed later have their effects rolled back with this scheme.

        Suggest a modification to the recovery algorithm of Section 16.4 to implement point-in-time recovery using database dumps.

    c. Later nonerroneous transactions can be re-executed logically, if the updates are available in the form of SQL but cannot be re-executed using their log records. Why?

Exercises

16.12 Explain the difference between the three storage types—volatile, nonvolatile, and stable—in terms of I/O cost.

16.13 Stable storage cannot be implemented.

    a. Explain why it cannot be.

    b. Explain how database systems deal with this problem.

16.14 Explain how the database may become inconsistent if some log records pertaining to a block are not output to stable storage before the block is output to disk.

16.15 Outline the drawbacks of the no-steal and force buffer management policies.

16.16 Physiological redo logging can reduce logging overheads significantly, especially with a slotted page record organization. Explain why.

16.17 Explain why logical undo logging is used widely, whereas logical redo logging (other than physiological redo logging) is rarely used.

16.18 Consider the log in Figure 16.5. Suppose there is a crash just before the $< T_0 \text{ abort}>$ log record is written out. Explain what would happen during recovery.

16.19 Suppose there is a transaction that has been running for a very long time, but has performed very few updates.

  a. What effect would the transaction have on recovery time with the recovery algorithm of Section 16.4, and with the ARIES recovery algorithm.

  b. What effect would the transaction have on deletion of old log records?

16.20 Consider the log in Figure 16.6. Suppose there is a crash during recovery, just after before the operation abort log record is written for operation O_1. Explain what would happen when the system recovers again.

16.21 Compare log-based recovery with the shadow-copy scheme in terms of their overheads, for the case when data is being added to newly allocated disk pages (in other words, there is no old value to be restored in case the transaction aborts).

16.22 In the ARIES recovery algorithm:

  a. If at the beginning of the analysis pass, a page is not in the checkpoint dirty page table, will we need to apply any redo records to it? Why?

  b. What is RecLSN, and how is it used to minimize unnecessary redos?

16.23 Explain the difference between a system crash and a "disaster."

16.24 For each of the following requirements, identify the best choice of degree of durability in a remote backup system:

  a. Data loss must be avoided but some loss of availability may be tolerated.

  b. Transaction commit must be accomplished quickly, even at the cost of loss of some committed transactions in a disaster.

  c. A high degree of availability and durability is required, but a longer running time for the transaction commit protocol is acceptable.

16.25   The Oracle database system uses undo log records to provide a snapshot view of the database, under snapshot-isolation. The snapshot view seen by transaction T_i reflects updates of all transactions that had committed when T_i started, and the updates of T_i; updates of all other transactions are not visible to T_i.

Describe a scheme for buffer handling whereby transactions are given a snapshot view of pages in the buffer. Include details of how to use the log to generate the snapshot view. You can assume that operations as well as their undo actions affect only one page.

Bibliographical Notes

Gray and Reuter [1993] is an excellent textbook source of information about recovery, including interesting implementation and historical details. Bernstein and Goodman [1981] is an early textbook source of information on concurrency control and recovery.

An overview of the recovery scheme of System R is presented by Gray et al. [1981]. Tutorial and survey papers on various recovery techniques for database systems include Gray [1978], Lindsay et al. [1980], and Verhofstad [1978]. The concepts of fuzzy checkpointing and fuzzy dumps are described in Lindsay et al. [1980]. A comprehensive presentation of the principles of recovery is offered by Haerder and Reuter [1983].

The state-of-the-art in recovery methods is best illustrated by the ARIES recovery method, described in Mohan et al. [1992] and Mohan [1990b]. Mohan and Levine [1992] presents ARIES IM, an extension of ARIES to optimize B^+-tree concurrency control and recovery using logical undo logging. ARIES and its variants are used in several database products, including IBM DB2 and Microsoft SQL Server. Recovery in Oracle is described in Lahiri et al. [2001].

Specialized recovery techniques for index structures are described in Mohan and Levine [1992] and Mohan [1993]; Mohan and Narang [1994] describes recovery techniques for client–server architectures, while Mohan and Narang [1992] describes recovery techniques for parallel-database architectures.

A generalized version of the theory of serializability, with short duration lower-level locks during operations, combined with longer duration higher-level locks, is described by Weikum [1991]. In Section 16.7.3, we saw the requirement that an operation should acquire all lower-level locks that may be needed for the logical undo of the operation. This requirement can be relaxed by performing all physical undo operations first, before perfoming any logical undo operations. A generalized version of this idea, called multi-level recovery, presented in Weikum et al. [1990], allows multiple levels of logical operations, with level-by-level undo passes during recovery.

Remote backup algorithms for disaster recovery are presented in King et al. [1991] and Polyzois and Garcia-Molina [1994].

PART 5

SYSTEM ARCHITECTURE

The architecture of a database system is greatly influenced by the underlying computer system on which the database system runs. Database systems can be centralized, where one server machine executes operations on the database. Database systems can also be designed to exploit parallel computer architectures. Distributed databases span multiple geographically separated machines.

Chapter 17 first outlines the architectures of database systems running on server systems, which are used in centralized and client–server architectures. The various processes that together implement the functionality of a database are outlined here. The chapter then outlines parallel computer architectures, and parallel database architectures designed for different types of parallel computers. Finally, the chapter outlines architectural issues in building a distributed database system.

Chapter 18 describes how various actions of a database, in particular query processing, can be implemented to exploit parallel processing.

Chapter 19 presents a number of issues that arise in a distributed database, and describes how to deal with each issue. The issues include how to store data, how to ensure atomicity of transactions that execute at multiple sites, how to perform concurrency control, and how to provide high availability in the presence of failures.a Cloud-based data storage systems, distributed query processing and directory systems are also described in this chapter.

CHAPTER 17

Database-System Architectures

The architecture of a database system is greatly influenced by the underlying computer system on which it runs, in particular by such aspects of computer architecture as networking, parallelism, and distribution:

- Networking of computers allows some tasks to be executed on a server system and some tasks to be executed on client systems. This division of work has led to *client–server database systems*.

- Parallel processing within a computer system allows database-system activities to be speeded up, allowing faster response to transactions, as well as more transactions per second. Queries can be processed in a way that exploits the parallelism offered by the underlying computer system. The need for parallel query processing has led to *parallel database systems*.

- Distributing data across sites in an organization allows those data to reside where they are generated or most needed, but still to be accessible from other sites and from other departments. Keeping multiple copies of the database across different sites also allows large organizations to continue their database operations even when one site is affected by a natural disaster, such as flood, fire, or earthquake. *Distributed database systems* handle geographically or administratively distributed data spread across multiple database systems.

We study the architecture of database systems in this chapter, starting with the traditional centralized systems, and covering client–server, parallel, and distributed database systems.

17.1 Centralized and Client–Server Architectures

Centralized database systems are those that run on a single computer system and do not interact with other computer systems. Such database systems span a range from single-user database systems running on personal computers to high-performance database systems running on high-end server systems. Client

769

–server systems, on the other hand, have functionality split between a server system and multiple client systems.

17.1.1 Centralized Systems

A modern, general-purpose computer system consists of one to a few processors and a number of device controllers that are connected through a common bus that provides access to shared memory (Figure 17.1). The processors have local cache memories that store local copies of parts of the memory, to speed up access to data. Each processor may have several independent **cores**, each of which can execute a separate instruction stream. Each device controller is in charge of a specific type of device (for example, a disk drive, an audio device, or a video display). The processors and the device controllers can execute concurrently, competing for memory access. Cache memory reduces the contention for memory access, since it reduces the number of times that the processor needs to access the shared memory.

We distinguish two ways in which computers are used: as single-user systems and as multiuser systems. Personal computers and workstations fall into the first category. A typical **single-user system** is a desktop unit used by a single person, usually with only one processor and one or two hard disks, and usually only one person using the machine at a time. A typical **multiuser system**, on the other hand, has more disks and more memory and may have multiple processors. It serves a large number of users who are connected to the system remotely.

Database systems designed for use by single users usually do not provide many of the facilities that a multiuser database provides. In particular, they may not support concurrency control, which is not required when only a single user can generate updates. Provisions for crash recovery in such systems are either absent or primitive—for example, they may consist of simply making a backup of the database before any update. Some such systems do not support SQL, and they provide a simpler query language, such as a variant of QBE. In contrast,

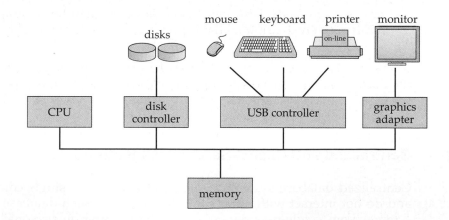

Figure 17.1 A centralized computer system.

database systems designed for multiuser systems support the full transactional features that we have studied earlier.

Although most general-purpose computer systems in use today have multiple processors, they have **coarse-granularity parallelism**, with only a few processors (about two to four, typically), all sharing the main memory. Databases running on such machines usually do not attempt to partition a single query among the processors; instead, they run each query on a single processor, allowing multiple queries to run concurrently. Thus, such systems support a higher throughput; that is, they allow a greater number of transactions to run per second, although individual transactions do not run any faster.

Databases designed for single-processor machines already provide multitasking, allowing multiple processes to run on the same processor in a time-shared manner, giving a view to the user of multiple processes running in parallel. Thus, coarse-granularity parallel machines logically appear to be identical to single-processor machines, and database systems designed for time-shared machines can be easily adapted to run on them.

In contrast, machines with **fine-granularity parallelism** have a large number of processors, and database systems running on such machines attempt to parallelize single tasks (queries, for example) submitted by users. We study the architecture of parallel database systems in Section 17.3.

Parallelism is emerging as a critical issue in the future design of database systems. Whereas today those computer systems with multicore processors have only a few cores, future processors will have large numbers of cores.[1] As a result, parallel database systems, which once were specialized systems running on specially designed hardware, will become the norm.

17.1.2 Client–Server Systems

As personal computers became faster, more powerful, and cheaper, there was a shift away from the centralized system architecture. Personal computers supplanted terminals connected to centralized systems. Correspondingly, personal computers assumed the user-interface functionality that used to be handled directly by the centralized systems. As a result, centralized systems today act as **server systems** that satisfy requests generated by *client systems*. Figure 17.2 shows the general structure of a client–server system.

Functionality provided by database systems can be broadly divided into two parts—the front end and the back end. The back end manages access structures, query evaluation and optimization, concurrency control, and recovery. The front end of a database system consists of tools such as the SQL user interface, forms interfaces, report generation tools, and data mining and analysis tools (see Figure 17.3). The interface between the front end and the back end is through SQL, or through an application program.

---

[1] The reasons for this pertain to issues in computer architecture related to heat generation and power consumption. Rather than make processors significantly faster, computer architects are using advances in chip design to put more cores on a single chip, a trend likely to continue for some time.

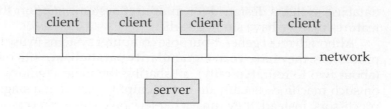

Figure 17.2   General structure of a client–server system.

Standards such as *ODBC* and *JDBC*, which we saw in Chapter 3, were developed to interface clients with servers. Any client that uses the ODBC or JDBC interface can connect to any server that provides the interface.

Certain application programs, such as spreadsheets and statistical-analysis packages, use the client–server interface directly to access data from a back-end server. In effect, they provide front ends specialized for particular tasks.

Systems that deal with large numbers of users adopt a three-tier architecture, which we saw earlier in Figure 1.6 (Chapter 1), where the front end is a Web browser that talks to an application server. The application server, in effect, acts as a client to the database server.

Some transaction-processing systems provide a **transactional remote procedure call** interface to connect clients with a server. These calls appear like ordinary procedure calls to the programmer, but all the remote procedure calls from a client are enclosed in a single transaction at the server end. Thus, if the transaction aborts, the server can undo the effects of the individual remote procedure calls.

17.2   Server System Architectures

Server systems can be broadly categorized as transaction servers and data servers.

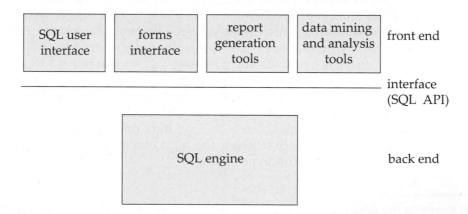

Figure 17.3   Front-end and back-end functionality.

- **Transaction-server** systems, also called **query-server** systems, provide an interface to which clients can send requests to perform an action, in response to which they execute the action and send back results to the client. Usually, client machines ship transactions to the server systems, where those transactions are executed, and results are shipped back to clients that are in charge of displaying the data. Requests may be specified by using SQL, or through a specialized application program interface.

- **Data-server systems** allow clients to interact with the servers by making requests to read or update data, in units such as files or pages. For example, file servers provide a file-system interface where clients can create, update, read, and delete files. Data servers for database systems offer much more functionality; they support units of data—such as pages, tuples, or objects —that are smaller than a file. They provide indexing facilities for data, and provide transaction facilities so that the data are never left in an inconsistent state if a client machine or process fails.

Of these, the transaction-server architecture is by far the more widely used architecture. We shall elaborate on the transaction-server and data-server architectures in Sections 17.2.1 and 17.2.2.

17.2.1   Transaction Servers

A typical transaction-server system today consists of multiple processes accessing data in shared memory, as in Figure 17.4. The processes that form part of the database system include:

- **Server processes**: These are processes that receive user queries (transactions), execute them, and send the results back. The queries may be submitted to the server processes from a user interface, or from a user process running embedded SQL, or via JDBC, ODBC, or similar protocols. Some database systems use a separate process for each user session, and a few use a single database process for all user sessions, but with multiple threads so that multiple queries can execute concurrently. (A **thread** is like a process, but multiple threads execute as part of the same process, and all threads within a process run in the same virtual-memory space. Multiple threads within a process can execute concurrently.) Many database systems use a hybrid architecture, with multiple processes, each one running multiple threads.

- **Lock manager process**: This process implements lock manager functionality, which includes lock grant, lock release, and deadlock detection.

- **Database writer process**: There are one or more processes that output modified buffer blocks back to disk on a continuous basis.

- **Log writer process**: This process outputs log records from the log record buffer to stable storage. Server processes simply add log records to the log

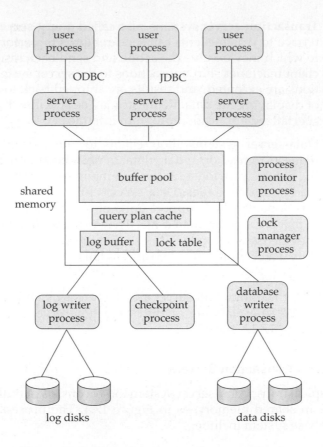

Figure 17.4 Shared memory and process structure.

record buffer in shared memory, and if a log force is required, they request the log writer process to output log records.

- **Checkpoint process**: This process performs periodic checkpoints.

- **Process monitor process**: This process monitors other processes, and if any of them fails, it takes recovery actions for the process, such as aborting any transaction being executed by the failed process, and then restarting the process.

The shared memory contains all shared data, such as:

- Buffer pool.

- Lock table.

- Log buffer, containing log records waiting to be output to the log on stable storage.

- Cached query plans, which can be reused if the same query is submitted again.

All database processes can access the data in shared memory. Since multiple processes may read or perform updates on data structures in shared memory, there must be a mechanism to ensure that a data structure is modified by at most one process at a time, and no process is reading a data structure while it is being written by others. Such **mutual exclusion** can be implemented by means of operating system functions called semaphores. Alternative implementations, with less overhead, use special **atomic instructions** supported by the computer hardware; one type of atomic instruction tests a memory location and sets it to 1 atomically. Further implementation details of mutual exclusion can be found in any standard operating system textbook. The mutual exclusion mechanisms are also used to implement latches.

To avoid the overhead of message passing, in many database systems, server processes implement locking by directly updating the lock table (which is in shared memory), instead of sending lock request messages to a lock manager process. The lock request procedure executes the actions that the lock manager process would take on getting a lock request. The actions on lock request and release are like those in Section 15.1.4, but with two significant differences:

- Since multiple server processes may access shared memory, mutual exclusion must be ensured on the lock table.

- If a lock cannot be obtained immediately because of a lock conflict, the lock request code may monitor the lock table to check when the lock has been granted. The lock release code updates the lock table to note which process has been granted the lock.

  To avoid repeated checks on the lock table, operating system semaphores can be used by the lock request code to wait for a lock grant notification. The lock release code must then use the semaphore mechanism to notify waiting transactions that their locks have been granted.

Even if the system handles lock requests through shared memory, it still uses the lock manager process for deadlock detection.

17.2.2   Data Servers

Data-server systems are used in local-area networks, where there is a high-speed connection between the clients and the server, the client machines are comparable in processing power to the server machine, and the tasks to be executed are computation intensive. In such an environment, it makes sense to ship data to client machines, to perform all processing at the client machine (which may take a while), and then to ship the data back to the server machine. Note that this architecture requires full back-end functionality at the clients. Data-server architectures have been particularly popular in object-oriented database systems (Chapter 22).

Interesting issues arise in such an architecture, since the time cost of communication between the client and the server is high compared to that of a local memory reference (milliseconds, versus less than 100 nanoseconds):

- **Page shipping** versus **item shipping**. The unit of communication for data can be of coarse granularity, such as a page, or fine granularity, such as a tuple (or an object, in the context of object-oriented database systems). We use the term **item** to refer to both tuples and objects.

  If the unit of communication is a single item, the overhead of message passing is high compared to the amount of data transmitted. Instead, when an item is requested, it makes sense also to send back other items that are likely to be used in the near future. Fetching items even before they are requested is called **prefetching**. Page shipping can be considered a form of prefetching if multiple items reside on a page, since all the items in the page are shipped when a process desires to access a single item in the page.

- **Adaptive lock granularity**. Locks are usually granted by the server for the data items that it ships to the client machines. A disadvantage of page shipping is that client machines may be granted locks of too coarse a granularity —a lock on a page implicitly locks all items contained in the page. Even if the client is not accessing some items in the page, it has implicitly acquired locks on all prefetched items. Other client machines that require locks on those items may be blocked unnecessarily. Techniques for lock **de-escalation** have been proposed where the server can request its clients to transfer back locks on prefetched items. If the client machine does not need a prefetched item, it can transfer locks on the item back to the server, and the locks can then be allocated to other clients.

- **Data caching**. Data that are shipped to a client on behalf of a transaction can be **cached** at the client, even after the transaction completes, if sufficient storage space is available. Successive transactions at the same client may be able to make use of the cached data. However, **cache coherency** is an issue: Even if a transaction finds cached data, it must make sure that those data are up to date, since they may have been updated by a different client after they were cached. Thus, a message must still be exchanged with the server to check validity of the data, and to acquire a lock on the data.

- **Lock caching**. If the use of data is mostly partitioned among the clients, with clients rarely requesting data that are also requested by other clients, locks can also be cached at the client machine. Suppose that a client finds a data item in the cache, and that it also finds the lock required for an access to the data item in the cache. Then, the access can proceed without any communication with the server. However, the server must keep track of cached locks; if a client requests a lock from the server, the server must **call back** all conflicting locks on the data item from any other client machines that have cached the locks. The task becomes more complicated when machine failures are taken into account. This technique differs from lock de-escalation in that lock caching takes place across transactions; otherwise, the two techniques are similar.

The bibliographical references provide more information about client–server database systems.

17.2.3 Cloud-Based Servers

Servers are usually owned by the enterprise providing the service, but there is an increasing trend for service providers to rely at least in part upon servers that are owned by a "third party" that is neither the client nor the service provider.

One model for using third-party servers is to outsource the entire service to another company that hosts the service on its own computers using its own software. This allows the service provider to ignore most details of technology and focus on the marketing of the service.

Another model for using third-party servers is **cloud computing**, in which the service provider runs its own software, but runs it on computers provided by another company. Under this model, the third party does not provide any of the application software; it provides only a collection of machines. These machines are not "real" machines, but rather simulated by software that allows a single real computer to simulate several independent computers. Such simulated machines are called **virtual machines**. The service provider runs its software (possibly including a database system) on these virtual machines. A major advantage of cloud computing is that the service provider can add machines as needed to meet demand and release them at times of light load. This can prove to be highly cost-effective in terms of both money and energy.

A third model uses a cloud computing service as a data server; such *cloud-based data storage* systems are covered in detail in Section 19.9. Database applications using cloud-based storage may run on the same cloud (that is, the same set of machines), or on another cloud. The bibliographical references provide more information about cloud-computing systems.

17.3   Parallel Systems

Parallel systems improve processing and I/O speeds by using multiple processors and disks in parallel. Parallel machines are becoming increasingly common, making the study of parallel database systems correspondingly more important. The driving force behind parallel database systems is the demands of applications that have to query extremely large databases (of the order of terabytes—that is, 10^{12} bytes) or that have to process an extremely large number of transactions per second (of the order of thousands of transactions per second). Centralized and client–server database systems are not powerful enough to handle such applications.

In parallel processing, many operations are performed simultaneously, as opposed to serial processing, in which the computational steps are performed sequentially. A **coarse-grain** parallel machine consists of a small number of powerful processors; a **massively parallel** or **fine-grain parallel** machine uses thousands of smaller processors. Virtually all high-end machines today offer some degree of coarse-grain parallelism: at least two or four processors. Massively parallel computers can be distinguished from the coarse-grain parallel machines by the much larger degree of parallelism that they support. Parallel computers with hundreds of processors and disks are available commercially.

There are two main measures of performance of a database system: (1) **throughput**, the number of tasks that can be completed in a given time interval, and (2) **response time**, the amount of time it takes to complete a single task from the time it is submitted. A system that processes a large number of small transactions can improve throughput by processing many transactions in parallel. A system that processes large transactions can improve response time as well as throughput by performing subtasks of each transaction in parallel.

17.3.1   Speedup and Scaleup

Two important issues in studying parallelism are speedup and scaleup. Running a given task in less time by increasing the degree of parallelism is called **speedup**. Handling larger tasks by increasing the degree of parallelism is called **scaleup**.

Consider a database application running on a parallel system with a certain number of processors and disks. Now suppose that we increase the size of the system by increasing the number of processors, disks, and other components of the system. The goal is to process the task in time inversely proportional to the number of processors and disks allocated. Suppose that the execution time of a task on the larger machine is T_L, and that the execution time of the same task on the smaller machine is T_S. The speedup due to parallelism is defined as T_S/T_L. The parallel system is said to demonstrate **linear speedup** if the speedup is N when the larger system has N times the resources (processors, disk, and so on) of the smaller system. If the speedup is less than N, the system is said to demonstrate **sublinear speedup**. Figure 17.5 illustrates linear and sublinear speedup.

Scaleup relates to the ability to process larger tasks in the same amount of time by providing more resources. Let Q be a task, and let Q_N be a task that is N times bigger than Q. Suppose that the execution time of task Q on a given machine

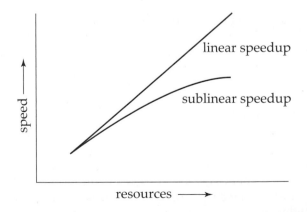

Figure 17.5   Speedup with increasing resources.

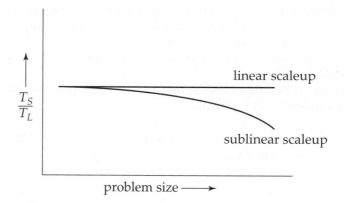

Figure 17.6 Scaleup with increasing problem size and resources.

M_S is T_S, and the execution time of task Q_N on a parallel machine M_L, which is N times larger than M_S, is T_L. The scaleup is then defined as T_S/T_L. The parallel system M_L is said to demonstrate **linear scaleup** on task Q if $T_L = T_S$. If $T_L > T_S$, the system is said to demonstrate **sublinear scaleup**. Figure 17.6 illustrates linear and sublinear scaleups (where the resources increase in proportion to problem size). There are two kinds of scaleup that are relevant in parallel database systems, depending on how the size of the task is measured:

- In **batch scaleup**, the size of the database increases, and the tasks are large jobs whose runtime depends on the size of the database. An example of such a task is a scan of a relation whose size is proportional to the size of the database. Thus, the size of the database is the measure of the size of the problem. Batch scaleup also applies in scientific applications, such as executing a query at an N-times finer resolution or performing an N-times longer simulation.

- In **transaction scaleup**, the rate at which transactions are submitted to the database increases and the size of the database increases proportionally to the transaction rate. This kind of scaleup is what is relevant in transaction-processing systems where the transactions are small updates—for example, a deposit or withdrawal from an account—and transaction rates grow as more accounts are created. Such transaction processing is especially well adapted for parallel execution, since transactions can run concurrently and independently on separate processors, and each transaction takes roughly the same amount of time, even if the database grows.

Scaleup is usually the more important metric for measuring efficiency of parallel database systems. The goal of parallelism in database systems is usually to make sure that the database system can continue to perform at an acceptable speed, even as the size of the database and the number of transactions increases. Increasing the capacity of the system by increasing the parallelism provides a smoother path for growth for an enterprise than does replacing a centralized system with a faster machine (even assuming that such a machine exists). However, we must also look at absolute performance numbers when using scaleup measures; a machine that scales up linearly may perform worse than a machine that scales less than linearly, simply because the latter machine is much faster to start off with.

A number of factors work against efficient parallel operation and can diminish both speedup and scaleup.

- **Start-up costs**. There is a start-up cost associated with initiating a single process. In a parallel operation consisting of thousands of processes, the *start-up time* may overshadow the actual processing time, affecting speedup adversely.

- **Interference**. Since processes executing in a parallel system often access shared resources, a slowdown may result from the *interference* of each new process as it competes with existing processes for commonly held resources, such as a system bus, or shared disks, or even locks. Both speedup and scaleup are affected by this phenomenon.

- **Skew**. By breaking down a single task into a number of parallel steps, we reduce the size of the average step. Nonetheless, the service time for the single slowest step will determine the service time for the task as a whole. It is often difficult to divide a task into exactly equal-sized parts, and the way that the sizes are distributed is therefore *skewed*. For example, if a task of size 100 is divided into 10 parts, and the division is skewed, there may be some tasks of size less than 10 and some tasks of size more than 10; if even one task happens to be of size 20, the speedup obtained by running the tasks in parallel is only five, instead of ten as we would have hoped.

17.3.2 Interconnection Networks

Parallel systems consist of a set of components (processors, memory, and disks) that can communicate with each other via an **interconnection network**. Figure 17.7 shows three commonly used types of interconnection networks:

- **Bus**. All the system components can send data on and receive data from a single communication bus. This type of interconnection is shown in Figure 17.7a. The bus could be an Ethernet or a parallel interconnect. Bus architectures work well for small numbers of processors. However, they do not scale well with increasing parallelism, since the bus can handle communication from only one component at a time.

- **Mesh**. The components are nodes in a grid, and each component connects to all its adjacent components in the grid. In a two-dimensional mesh each node connects to four adjacent nodes, while in a three-dimensional mesh each node connects to six adjacent nodes. Figure 17.7b shows a two-dimensional mesh.

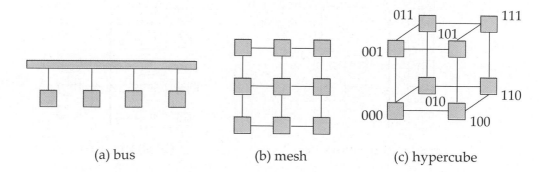

(a) bus   (b) mesh   (c) hypercube

Figure 17.7 Interconnection networks.

Nodes that are not directly connected can communicate with one another by routing messages via a sequence of intermediate nodes that are directly connected to one another. The number of communication links grows as the number of components grows, and the communication capacity of a mesh therefore scales better with increasing parallelism.

- **Hypercube**. The components are numbered in binary, and a component is connected to another if the binary representations of their numbers differ in exactly one bit. Thus, each of the n components is connected to $\log(n)$ other components. Figure 17.7c shows a hypercube with eight nodes. In a hypercube interconnection, a message from a component can reach any other component by going through at most $\log(n)$ links. In contrast, in a mesh architecture a component may be $2(\sqrt{n} - 1)$ links away from some of the other components (or $\sqrt{n}$ links away, if the mesh interconnection wraps around at the edges of the grid). Thus communication delays in a hypercube are significantly lower than in a mesh.

17.3.3 Parallel Database Architectures

There are several architectural models for parallel machines. Among the most prominent ones are those in Figure 17.8 (in the figure, M denotes memory, P denotes a processor, and disks are shown as cylinders):

- **Shared memory**. All the processors share a common memory (Figure 17.8a).
- **Shared disk**. All the processors share a common set of disks (Figure 17.8b). Shared-disk systems are sometimes called **clusters**.
- **Shared nothing**. The processors share neither a common memory nor common disk (Figure 17.8c).
- **Hierarchical**. This model is a hybrid of the preceding three architectures (Figure 17.8d).

In Sections 17.3.3.1 through 17.3.3.4, we elaborate on each of these models.

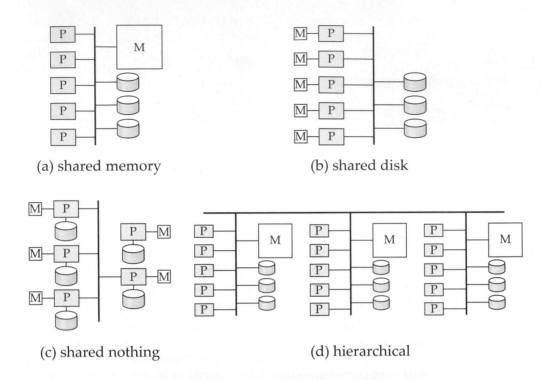

Figure 17.8 Parallel database architectures.

Techniques used to speed up transaction processing on data-server systems, such as data and lock caching and lock de-escalation, outlined in Section 17.2.2, can also be used in shared-disk parallel databases as well as in shared-nothing parallel databases. In fact, they are very important for efficient transaction processing in such systems.

17.3.3.1   Shared Memory

In a **shared-memory** architecture, the processors and disks have access to a common memory, typically via a bus or through an interconnection network. The benefit of shared memory is extremely efficient communication between processors—data in shared memory can be accessed by any processor without being moved with software. A processor can send messages to other processors much faster by using memory writes (which usually take less than a microsecond) than by sending a message through a communication mechanism. The downside of shared-memory machines is that the architecture is not scalable beyond 32 or 64 processors because the bus or the interconnection network becomes a bottleneck (since it is shared by all processors). Adding more processors does not help after a point, since the processors will spend most of their time waiting for their turn on the bus to access memory.

Shared-memory architectures usually have large memory caches at each processor, so that referencing of the shared memory is avoided whenever possible.

However, at least some of the data will not be in the cache, and accesses will have to go to the shared memory. Moreover, the caches need to be kept coherent; that is, if a processor performs a write to a memory location, the data in that memory location should be either updated at or removed from any processor where the data are cached. Maintaining cache coherency becomes an increasing overhead with increasing numbers of processors. Consequently, shared-memory machines are not capable of scaling up beyond a point; current shared-memory machines cannot support more than 64 processors.

17.3.3.2 Shared Disk

In the **shared-disk** model, all processors can access all disks directly via an interconnection network, but the processors have private memories. There are two advantages of this architecture over a shared-memory architecture. First, since each processor has its own memory, the memory bus is not a bottleneck. Second, it offers a cheap way to provide a degree of **fault tolerance**: If a processor (or its memory) fails, the other processors can take over its tasks, since the database is resident on disks that are accessible from all processors. We can make the disk subsystem itself fault tolerant by using a RAID architecture, as described in Chapter 10. The shared-disk architecture has found acceptance in many applications.

The main problem with a shared-disk system is again scalability. Although the memory bus is no longer a bottleneck, the interconnection to the disk subsystem is now a bottleneck; it is particularly so in a situation where the database makes a large number of accesses to disks. Compared to shared-memory systems, shared-disk systems can scale to a somewhat larger number of processors, but communication across processors is slower (up to a few milliseconds in the absence of special-purpose hardware for communication), since it has to go through a communication network.

17.3.3.3 Shared Nothing

In a **shared-nothing** system, each node of the machine consists of a processor, memory, and one or more disks. The processors at one node may communicate with another processor at another node by a high-speed interconnection network. A node functions as the server for the data on the disk or disks that the node owns. Since local disk references are serviced by local disks at each processor, the shared-nothing model overcomes the disadvantage of requiring all I/O to go through a single interconnection network; only queries, accesses to nonlocal disks, and result relations pass through the network. Moreover, the interconnection networks for shared-nothing systems are usually designed to be scalable, so that their transmission capacity increases as more nodes are added. Consequently, shared-nothing architectures are more scalable and can easily support a large number of processors. The main drawbacks of shared-nothing systems are the costs of communication and of nonlocal disk access, which are higher than in a shared-memory or shared-disk architecture since sending data involves software interaction at both ends.

17.3.3.4   Hierarchical

The **hierarchical architecture** combines the characteristics of shared-memory, shared-disk, and shared-nothing architectures. At the top level, the system consists of nodes that are connected by an interconnection network and do not share disks or memory with one another. Thus, the top level is a shared-nothing architecture. Each node of the system could actually be a shared-memory system with a few processors. Alternatively, each node could be a shared-disk system, and each of the systems sharing a set of disks could be a shared-memory system. Thus, a system could be built as a hierarchy, with shared-memory architecture with a few processors at the base, and a shared-nothing architecture at the top, with possibly a shared-disk architecture in the middle. Figure 17.8d illustrates a hierarchical architecture with shared-memory nodes connected together in a shared-nothing architecture. Commercial parallel database systems today run on several of these architectures.

Attempts to reduce the complexity of programming such systems have yielded **distributed virtual-memory** architectures, where logically there is a single shared memory, but physically there are multiple disjoint memory systems; the virtual-memory-mapping hardware, coupled with system software, allows each processor to view the disjoint memories as a single virtual memory. Since access speeds differ, depending on whether the page is available locally or not, such an architecture is also referred to as a **nonuniform memory architecture** (NUMA).

17.4   Distributed Systems

In a **distributed database system**, the database is stored on several computers. The computers in a distributed system communicate with one another through various communication media, such as high-speed private networks or the Internet. They do not share main memory or disks. The computers in a distributed system may vary in size and function, ranging from workstations up to mainframe systems.

The computers in a distributed system are referred to by a number of different names, such as **sites** or **nodes**, depending on the context in which they are mentioned. We mainly use the term **site**, to emphasize the physical distribution of these systems. The general structure of a distributed system appears in Figure 17.9.

The main differences between shared-nothing parallel databases and distributed databases are that distributed databases are typically geographically separated, are separately administered, and have a slower interconnection. Another major difference is that, in a distributed database system, we differentiate between local and global transactions. A **local transaction** is one that accesses data only from sites where the transaction was initiated. A **global transaction**, on the other hand, is one that either accesses data in a site different from the one at which the transaction was initiated, or accesses data in several different sites.

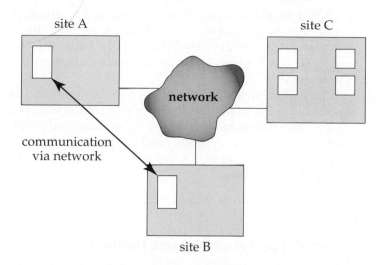

Figure 17.9   A distributed system.

There are several reasons for building distributed database systems, including sharing of data, autonomy, and availability.

- **Sharing data.** The major advantage in building a distributed database system is the provision of an environment where users at one site may be able to access the data residing at other sites. For instance, in a distributed university system, where each campus stores data related to that campus, it is possible for a user in one campus to access data in another campus. Without this capability, the transfer of student records from one campus to another campus would have to resort to some external mechanism that would couple existing systems.

- **Autonomy.** The primary advantage of sharing data by means of data distribution is that each site is able to retain a degree of control over data that are stored locally. In a centralized system, the database administrator of the central site controls the database. In a distributed system, there is a global database administrator responsible for the entire system. A part of these responsibilities is delegated to the local database administrator for each site. Depending on the design of the distributed database system, each administrator may have a different degree of **local autonomy**. The possibility of local autonomy is often a major advantage of distributed databases.

- **Availability.** If one site fails in a distributed system, the remaining sites may be able to continue operating. In particular, if data items are **replicated** in several sites, a transaction needing a particular data item may find that item in any of several sites. Thus, the failure of a site does not necessarily imply the shutdown of the system.

The failure of one site must be detected by the system, and appropriate action may be needed to recover from the failure. The system must no longer use the services of the failed site. Finally, when the failed site recovers or is repaired, mechanisms must be available to integrate it smoothly back into the system.

Although recovery from failure is more complex in distributed systems than in centralized systems, the ability of most of the system to continue to operate despite the failure of one site results in increased availability. Availability is crucial for database systems used for real-time applications. Loss of access to data by, for example, an airline may result in the loss of potential ticket buyers to competitors.

17.4.1   An Example of a Distributed Database

Consider a banking system consisting of four branches in four different cities. Each branch has its own computer, with a database of all the accounts maintained at that branch. Each such installation is thus a site. There also exists one single site that maintains information about all the branches of the bank.

To illustrate the difference between the two types of transactions—local and global—at the sites, consider a transaction to add $50 to account number A-177 located at the Valleyview branch. If the transaction was initiated at the Valleyview branch, then it is considered local; otherwise, it is considered global. A transaction to transfer $50 from account A-177 to account A-305, which is located at the Hillside branch, is a global transaction, since accounts in two different sites are accessed as a result of its execution.

In an ideal distributed database system, the sites would share a common global schema (although some relations may be stored only at some sites), all sites would run the same distributed database-management software, and the sites would be aware of each other's existence. If a distributed database is built from scratch, it would indeed be possible to achieve the above goals. However, in reality a distributed database has to be constructed by linking together multiple already-existing database systems, each with its own schema and possibly running different database-management software. Such systems are sometimes called **multidatabase systems** or **heterogeneous distributed database systems**. We discuss these systems in Section 19.8, where we show how to achieve a degree of global control despite the heterogeneity of the component systems.

17.4.2   Implementation Issues

Atomicity of transactions is an important issue in building a distributed database system. If a transaction runs across two sites, unless the system designers are careful, it may commit at one site and abort at another, leading to an inconsistent state. Transaction commit protocols ensure such a situation cannot arise. The *two-phase commit protocol* (2PC) is the most widely used of these protocols.

The basic idea behind 2PC is for each site to execute the transaction until it enters the partially committed state, and then leave the commit decision to a single coordinator site; the transaction is said to be in the *ready* state at a site at this point. The coordinator decides to commit the transaction only if the transaction reaches the ready state at every site where it executed; otherwise (for example, if the transaction aborts at any site), the coordinator decides to abort the transaction. Every site where the transaction executed must follow the decision of the coordinator. If a site fails when a transaction is in ready state, when the site recovers from failure it should be in a position to either commit or abort the transaction, depending on the decision of the coordinator. The 2PC protocol is described in detail in Section 19.4.1.

Concurrency control is another issue in a distributed database. Since a transaction may access data items at several sites, transaction managers at several sites may need to coordinate to implement concurrency control. If locking is used, locking can be performed locally at the sites containing accessed data items, but there is also a possibility of deadlock involving transactions originating at multiple sites. Therefore deadlock detection needs to be carried out across multiple sites. Failures are more common in distributed systems since not only may computers fail, but communication links may also fail. Replication of data items, which is the key to the continued functioning of distributed databases when failures occur, further complicates concurrency control. Section 19.5 provides detailed coverage of concurrency control in distributed databases.

The standard transaction models, based on multiple actions carried out by a single program unit, are often inappropriate for carrying out tasks that cross the boundaries of databases that cannot or will not cooperate to implement protocols such as 2PC. Alternative approaches, based on *persistent messaging* for communication, are generally used for such tasks; persistent messaging is discussed in Section 19.4.3.

When the tasks to be carried out are complex, involving multiple databases and/or multiple interactions with humans, coordination of the tasks and ensuring transaction properties for the tasks become more complicated. *Workflow management systems* are systems designed to help with carrying out such tasks, and are described in Section 26.2.

In case an organization has to choose between a distributed architecture and a centralized architecture for implementing an application, the system architect must balance the advantages against the disadvantages of distribution of data. We have already seen the advantages of using distributed databases. The primary disadvantage of distributed database systems is the added complexity required to ensure proper coordination among the sites. This increased complexity takes various forms:

- **Software-development cost**. It is more difficult to implement a distributed database system; thus, it is more costly.

- **Greater potential for bugs**. Since the sites that constitute the distributed system operate in parallel, it is harder to ensure the correctness of algorithms, especially operation during failures of part of the system, and recovery from failures. The potential exists for extremely subtle bugs.

- **Increased processing overhead**. The exchange of messages and the additional computation required to achieve intersite coordination are a form of overhead that does not arise in centralized systems.

There are several approaches to distributed database design, ranging from fully distributed designs to ones that include a large degree of centralization. We study them in Chapter 19.

17.5   Network Types

Distributed databases and client–server systems are built around communication networks. There are basically two types of networks: **local-area networks** and **wide-area networks**. The main difference between the two is the way in which they are distributed geographically. In local-area networks, processors are distributed over small geographical areas, such as a single building or a number of adjacent buildings. In wide-area networks, on the other hand, a number of autonomous processors are distributed over a large geographical area (such as the United States or the entire world). These differences imply major variations in the speed and reliability of the communication network, and are reflected in the distributed operating-system design.

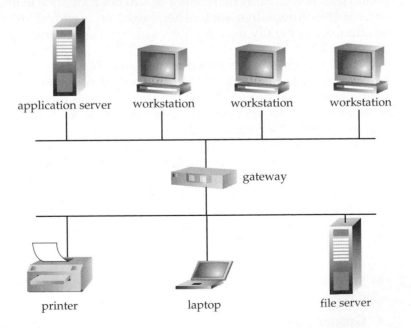

Figure 17.10   Local-area network.

17.5.1 Local-Area Networks

Local-area networks (LANs) (Figure 17.10) emerged in the early 1970s as a way for computers to communicate and to share data with one another. People recognized that, for many enterprises, numerous small computers, each with its own self-contained applications, are more economical than a single large system. Because each small computer is likely to need access to a full complement of peripheral devices (such as disks and printers), and because some form of data sharing is likely to occur in a single enterprise, it was a natural step to connect these small systems into a network.

LANs are generally used in an office environment. All the sites in such systems are close to one another, so the communication links tend to have a higher speed and lower error rate than do their counterparts in wide-area networks. The most common links in a local-area network are twisted pair, coaxial cable, fiber optics, and wireless connections. Communication speeds range from tens of megabits per second (for wireless local-area networks), to 1 gigabit per second for Gigabit Ethernet. The most recent Ethernet standard is 10-gigabit Ethernet.

A **storage-area network** (**SAN**) is a special type of high-speed local-area network designed to connect large banks of storage devices (disks) to computers that use the data (see Figure 17.11).

Thus storage-area networks help build large-scale *shared-disk systems*. The motivation for using storage-area networks to connect multiple computers to large banks of storage devices is essentially the same as that for shared-disk databases, namely:

- Scalability by adding more computers.

- High availability, since data are still accessible even if a computer fails.

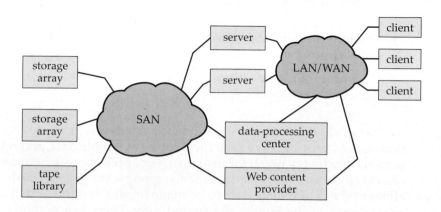

Figure 17.11 Storage-area network.

RAID organizations are used in the storage devices to ensure high availability of the data, permitting processing to continue even if individual disks fail. Storage-area networks are usually built with redundancy, such as multiple paths between nodes, so if a component such as a link or a connection to the network fails, the network continues to function.

17.5.2   Wide-Area Networks

Wide-area networks (WANs) emerged in the late 1960s, mainly as an academic research project to provide efficient communication among sites, allowing hardware and software to be shared conveniently and economically by a wide community of users. Systems that allowed remote terminals to be connected to a central computer via telephone lines were developed in the early 1960s, but they were not true WANs. The first WAN to be designed and developed was the *Arpanet*. Work on the Arpanet began in 1968. The Arpanet has grown from a four-site experimental network to a worldwide network of networks, the **Internet**, comprising hundreds of millions of computer systems. Typical links on the Internet are fiber-optic lines and, sometimes, satellite channels. Data rates for wide-area links typically range from a few megabits per second to hundreds of gigabits per second. The last link, to end user sites, has traditionally been the slowest link, using such technologies as *digital subscriber line* (DSL) technology (supporting a few megabits per second) or dial-up modem connections over land-based telephone lines (supporting up to 56 kilobits per second). Today, the last link is typically a cable modem or fiber optic connection (each supporting tens of megabits per second), or a wireless connection supporting several megabits per second.

In addition to limits on data rates, communication in a WAN must also contend with significant **latency**: a message may take up to a few hundred milliseconds to be delivered across the world, both due to speed of light delays, and due to queuing delays at a number of routers in the path of the message. Applications whose data and computing resources are distributed geographically have to be carefully designed to ensure latency does not affect system performance excessively.

WANs can be classified into two types:

- In **discontinuous connection** WANs, such as those based on mobile wireless connections, hosts are connected to the network only part of the time.

- In **continuous connection** WANs, such as the wired Internet, hosts are connected to the network at all times.

Networks that are not continuously connected typically do not allow transactions across sites, but may keep local copies of remote data, and refresh the copies periodically (every night, for instance). For applications where consistency is not critical, such as sharing of documents, groupware systems such as Lotus Notes allow updates of remote data to be made locally, and the updates are then propagated back to the remote site periodically. There is a potential for conflicting updates at different sites, conflicts that have to be detected and resolved. A mechanism for detecting conflicting updates is described later, in Section 25.5.4; the resolution mechanism for conflicting updates is, however, application dependent.

17.6   Summary

- Centralized database systems run entirely on a single computer. With the growth of personal computers and local-area networking, the database front-end functionality has moved increasingly to clients, with server systems providing the back-end functionality. Client–server interface protocols have helped the growth of client–server database systems.

- Servers can be either transaction servers or data servers, although the use of transaction servers greatly exceeds the use of data servers for providing database services.

   ○ Transaction servers have multiple processes, possibly running on multiple processors. So that these processes have access to common data, such as the database buffer, systems store such data in shared memory. In addition to processes that handle queries, there are system processes that carry out tasks such as lock and log management and checkpointing.

   ○ Data-server systems supply raw data to clients. Such systems strive to minimize communication between clients and servers by caching data and locks at the clients. Parallel database systems use similar optimizations.

- Parallel database systems consist of multiple processors and multiple disks connected by a fast interconnection network. Speedup measures how much we can increase processing speed by increasing parallelism for a single transaction. Scaleup measures how well we can handle an increased number of transactions by increasing parallelism. Interference, skew, and start-up costs act as barriers to getting ideal speedup and scaleup.

- Parallel database architectures include the shared-memory, shared-disk, shared-nothing, and hierarchical architectures. These architectures have different trade-offs of scalability versus communication speed.

- A distributed database system is a collection of partially independent database systems that (ideally) share a common schema, and coordinate processing of transactions that access nonlocal data. The systems communicate with one another through a communication network.

- Local-area networks connect nodes that are distributed over small geographical areas, such as a single building or a few adjacent buildings. Wide-area networks connect nodes spread over a large geographical area. The Internet is the most extensively used wide-area network today.

- Storage-area networks are a special type of local-area network designed to provide fast interconnection between large banks of storage devices and multiple computers.

Review Terms

- Centralized systems
- Server systems
- Coarse-granularity parallelism
- Fine-granularity parallelism
- Database process structure
- Mutual exclusion
- Thread
- Server processes
    - Lock manager process
    - Database writer process
    - Log writer process
    - Checkpoint process
    - Process monitor process
- Client–server systems
- Transaction server
- Query server
- Data server
    - Prefetching
    - De-escalation
    - Data caching
    - Cache coherency
    - Lock caching
    - Call back
- Parallel systems
- Throughput
- Response time
- Speedup
    - Linear speedup
    - Sublinear speedup
- Scaleup
    - Linear scaleup

- Sublinear scaleup
- Batch scaleup
- Transaction scaleup
- Start-up costs
- Interference
- Skew
- Interconnection networks
    - Bus
    - Mesh
    - Hypercube
- Parallel database architectures
    - Shared memory
    - Shared disk (clusters)
    - Shared nothing
    - Hierarchical
- Fault tolerance
- Distributed virtual memory
- Nonuniform memory architecture (NUMA)
- Distributed systems
- Distributed database
    - Sites (nodes)
    - Local transaction
    - Global transaction
    - Local autonomy
- Multidatabase systems
- Network types
    - Local-area networks (LAN)
    - Wide-area networks (WAN)
    - Storage-area network (SAN)

Practice Exercises

17.1 Instead of storing shared structures in shared memory, an alternative architecture would be to store them in the local memory of a special process, and access the shared data by interprocess communication with the process. What would be the drawback of such an architecture?

17.2 In typical client–server systems the server machine is much more powerful than the clients; that is, its processor is faster, it may have multiple processors, and it has more memory and disk capacity. Consider instead a scenario where client and server machines have exactly the same power. Would it make sense to build a client–server system in such a scenario? Why? Which scenario would be better suited to a data-server architecture?

17.3 Consider a database system based on a client–server architecture, with the server acting as a data server.

    a.   What is the effect of the speed of the interconnection between the client and the server on the choice between tuple and page shipping?

    b.   If page shipping is used, the cache of data at the client can be organized either as a tuple cache or a page cache. The page cache stores data in units of a page, while the tuple cache stores data in units of tuples. Assume tuples are smaller than pages. Describe one benefit of a tuple cache over a page cache.

17.4 Suppose a transaction is written in C with embedded SQL, and about 80 percent of the time is spent in the SQL code, with the remaining 20 percent spent in C code. How much speedup can one hope to attain if parallelism is used only for the SQL code? Explain.

17.5 Some database operations such as joins can see a significant difference in speed when data (for example, one of the relations involved in a join) fits in memory as compared to the situation where the data does not fit in memory. Show how this fact can explain the phenomenon of **superlinear speedup**, where an application sees a speedup greater than the amount of resources allocated to it.

17.6 Parallel systems often have a network structure where sets of n processors connect to a single Ethernet switch, and the Ethernet switches themselves connect to another Ethernet switch. Does this architecture correspond to a bus, mesh or hypercube architecture? If not, how would you describe this interconnection architecture?

Exercises

17.7 Why is it relatively easy to port a database from a single processor machine to a multiprocessor machine if individual queries need not be parallelized?

17.8   Transaction-server architectures are popular for client–server relational databases, where transactions are short. On the other hand, data-server architectures are popular for client–server object-oriented database systems, where transactions are expected to be relatively long. Give two reasons why data servers may be popular for object-oriented databases but not for relational databases.

17.9   What is lock de-escalation, and under what conditions is it required? Why is it not required if the unit of data shipping is an item?

17.10   Suppose you were in charge of the database operations of a company whose main job is to process transactions. Suppose the company is growing rapidly each year, and has outgrown its current computer system. When you are choosing a new parallel computer, what measure is most relevant—speedup, batch scaleup, or transaction scaleup? Why?

17.11   Database systems are typically implemented as a set of processes (or threads) sharing a shared memory area.

    a.   How is access to the shared memory area controlled?

    b.   Is two-phase locking appropriate for serializing access to the data structures in shared memory? Explain your answer.

17.12   Is it wise to allow a user process to access the shared memory area of a database system? Explain your answer.

17.13   What are the factors that can work against linear scaleup in a transaction processing system? Which of the factors are likely to be the most important in each of the following architectures: shared memory, shared disk, and shared nothing?

17.14   Memory systems can be divided into multiple modules, each of which can be serving a separate request at a given time. What impact would such a memory architecture have on the number of processors that can be supported in a shared-memory system?

17.15   Consider a bank that has a collection of sites, each running a database system. Suppose the only way the databases interact is by electronic transfer of money between themselves, using persistent messaging. Would such a system qualify as a distributed database? Why?

Bibliographical Notes

Hennessy et al. [2006] provides an excellent introduction to the area of computer architecture. Abadi [2009] provides an excellent introduction to cloud computing and the challenges of running database transactions in such an environment.

    Gray and Reuter [1993] provides a textbook description of transaction processing, including the architecture of client–server and distributed systems. The bibliographical notes of Chapter 5 provide references to more information on ODBC, JDBC, and other database access APIs.

DeWitt and Gray [1992] surveys parallel database systems, including their architecture and performance measures. A survey of parallel computer architectures is presented by Duncan [1990]. Dubois and Thakkar [1992] is a collection of papers on scalable shared-memory architectures. DEC clusters running Rdb were among the early commercial users of the shared-disk database architecture. Rdb is now owned by Oracle, and is called Oracle Rdb. The Teradata database machine was among the earliest commercial systems to use the shared-nothing database architecture. The Grace and the Gamma research prototypes also used shared-nothing architectures.

Ozsu and Valduriez [1999] provides textbook coverage of distributed database systems. Further references pertaining to parallel and distributed database systems appear in the bibliographical notes of Chapters 18 and 19, respectively.

Comer [2009], Halsall [2006], and Thomas [1996] describe computer networking and the Internet. Tanenbaum [2002], Kurose and Ross [2005], and Peterson and Davie [2007] provide general overviews of computer networks.

Parallel Databases

In this chapter, we discuss fundamental algorithms for parallel database systems that are based on the relational data model. In particular, we focus on the placement of data on multiple disks and the parallel evaluation of relational operations, both of which have been instrumental in the success of parallel databases.

18.1 Introduction

At one point over two decades ago, parallel database systems had been nearly written off, even by some of their staunchest advocates. Today, they are successfully marketed by practically every database-system vendor. Several trends fueled this transition:

- The transaction requirements of organizations have grown with increasing use of computers. Moreover, the growth of the World Wide Web has created many sites with millions of viewers, and the increasing amounts of data collected from these viewers has produced extremely large databases at many companies.

- Organizations are using these increasingly large volumes of data—such as data about what items people buy, what Web links users click on, and when people make telephone calls—to plan their activities and pricing. Queries used for such purposes are called **decision-support queries**, and the data requirements for such queries may run into terabytes. Single-processor systems are not capable of handling such large volumes of data at the required rates.

- The set-oriented nature of database queries naturally lends itself to parallelization. A number of commercial and research systems have demonstrated the power and scalability of parallel query processing.

- As microprocessors have become cheap, parallel machines have become common and relatively inexpensive.

- Individual processors have themselves become parallel machines using multicore architectures.

As we discussed in Chapter 17, parallelism is used to provide speedup, where queries are executed faster because more resources, such as processors and disks, are provided. Parallelism is also used to provide scaleup, where increasing workloads are handled without increased response time, via an increase in the degree of parallelism.

We outlined in Chapter 17 the different architectures for parallel database systems: shared-memory, shared-disk, shared-nothing, and hierarchical architectures. Briefly, in shared-memory architectures, all processors share a common memory and disks; in shared-disk architectures, processors have independent memories, but share disks; in shared-nothing architectures, processors share neither memory nor disks; and hierarchical architectures have nodes that share neither memory nor disks with each other, but internally each node has a shared-memory or a shared-disk architecture.

18.2   I/O Parallelism

In its simplest form, **I/O parallelism** refers to reducing the time required to retrieve relations from disk by partitioning the relations over multiple disks. The most common form of data partitioning in a parallel database environment is *horizontal partitioning*. In **horizontal partitioning**, the tuples of a relation are divided (or declustered) among many disks, so that each tuple resides on one disk. Several partitioning strategies have been proposed.

18.2.1   Partitioning Techniques

We present three basic data-partitioning strategies. Assume that there are n disks, $D_0, D_1, \ldots, D_{n-1}$, across which the data are to be partitioned.

- **Round-robin**. This strategy scans the relation in any order and sends the ith tuple to disk number $D_{i \bmod n}$. The round-robin scheme ensures an even distribution of tuples across disks; that is, each disk has approximately the same number of tuples as the others.

- **Hash partitioning**. This declustering strategy designates one or more attributes from the given relation's schema as the partitioning attributes. A hash function is chosen whose range is $\{0, 1, \ldots, n-1\}$. Each tuple of the original relation is hashed on the partitioning attributes. If the hash function returns i, then the tuple is placed on disk D_i.[1]

- **Range partitioning**. This strategy distributes tuples by assigning contiguous attribute-value ranges to each disk. It chooses a partitioning attribute, A, and a **partitioning vector** $[v_0, v_1, \ldots, v_{n-2}]$, such that, if $i < j$, then $v_i < v_j$. The relation is partitioned as follows: Consider a tuple t such that $t[A] = x$. If

---

[1]Hash-function design is discussed in Section 11.6.1.

$x < v_0$, then t goes on disk D_0. If $x \geq v_{n-2}$, then t goes on disk D_{n-1}. If $v_i \leq x < v_{i+1}$, then t goes on disk D_{i+1}.

For example, range partitioning with three disks numbered 0, 1, and 2 may assign tuples with values less than 5 to disk 0, values between 5 and 40 to disk 1, and values greater than 40 to disk 2.

18.2.2   Comparison of Partitioning Techniques

Once a relation has been partitioned among several disks, we can retrieve it in parallel, using all the disks. Similarly, when a relation is being partitioned, it can be written to multiple disks in parallel. Thus, the transfer rates for reading or writing an entire relation are much faster with I/O parallelism than without it. However, reading an entire relation, or *scanning a relation*, is only one kind of access to data. Access to data can be classified as follows:

1. Scanning the entire relation.

2. Locating a tuple associatively (for example, *employee_name* = "Campbell"); these queries, called **point queries**, seek tuples that have a specified value for a specific attribute.

3. Locating all tuples for which the value of a given attribute lies within a specified range (for example, $10000 < salary < 20000$); these queries are called **range queries**.

The different partitioning techniques support these types of access at different levels of efficiency:

- **Round-robin.** The scheme is ideally suited for applications that wish to read the entire relation sequentially for each query. With this scheme, both point queries and range queries are complicated to process, since each of the n disks must be used for the search.

- **Hash partitioning.** This scheme is best suited for point queries based on the partitioning attribute. For example, if a relation is partitioned on the *telephone_number* attribute, then we can answer the query "Find the record of the employee with *telephone_number* = 555-3333" by applying the partitioning hash function to 555-3333 and then searching that disk. Directing a query to a single disk saves the start-up cost of initiating a query on multiple disks, and leaves the other disks free to process other queries.

  Hash partitioning is also useful for sequential scans of the entire relation. If the hash function is a good randomizing function, and the partitioning attributes form a key of the relation, then the number of tuples in each of the disks is approximately the same, without much variance. Hence, the time taken to scan the relation is approximately $1/n$ of the time required to scan the relation in a single disk system.

  The scheme, however, is not well suited for point queries on nonpartitioning attributes. Hash-based partitioning is also not well suited for answering range queries, since, typically, hash functions do not preserve proximity within a range. Therefore, all the disks need to be scanned for range queries to be answered.

- **Range partitioning.** This scheme is well suited for point and range queries on the partitioning attribute. For point queries, we can consult the partitioning vector to locate the disk where the tuple resides. For range queries, we consult the partitioning vector to find the range of disks on which the tuples may reside. In both cases, the search narrows to exactly those disks that might have any tuples of interest.

  An advantage of this feature is that, if there are only a few tuples in the queried range, then the query is typically sent to one disk, as opposed to all the disks. Since other disks can be used to answer other queries, range partitioning results in higher throughput while maintaining good response time. On the other hand, if there are many tuples in the queried range (as there are when the queried range is a larger fraction of the domain of the relation), many tuples have to be retrieved from a few disks, resulting in an I/O bottleneck (hot spot) at those disks. In this example of **execution skew**, all processing occurs in one—or only a few—partitions. In contrast, hash partitioning and round-robin partitioning would engage all the disks for such queries, giving a faster response time for approximately the same throughput.

The type of partitioning also affects other relational operations, such as joins, as we shall see in Section 18.5. Thus, the choice of partitioning technique also depends on the operations that need to be executed. In general, hash partitioning or range partitioning are preferred to round-robin partitioning.

In a system with many disks, the number of disks across which to partition a relation can be chosen in this way: If a relation contains only a few tuples that will fit into a single disk block, then it is better to assign the relation to a single disk. Large relations are preferably partitioned across all the available disks. If a relation consists of m disk blocks and there are n disks available in the system, then the relation should be allocated $\mathbf{min}(m, n)$ disks.

18.2.3 Handling of Skew

When a relation is partitioned (by a technique other than round-robin), there may be a **skew** in the distribution of tuples, with a high percentage of tuples placed in some partitions and fewer tuples in other partitions. The ways that skew may appear are classified as:

- Attribute-value skew.
- Partition skew.

Attribute-value skew refers to the fact that some values appear in the partitioning attributes of many tuples. All the tuples with the same value for the partitioning attribute end up in the same partition, resulting in skew. **Partition skew** refers to the fact that there may be load imbalance in the partitioning, even when there is no attribute skew.

Attribute-value skew can result in skewed partitioning regardless of whether range partitioning or hash partitioning is used. If the partition vector is not chosen carefully, range partitioning may result in partition skew. Partition skew is less likely with hash partitioning, if a good hash function is chosen.

As Section 17.3.1 noted, even a small skew can result in a significant decrease in performance. Skew becomes an increasing problem with a higher degree of parallelism. For example, if a relation of 1000 tuples is divided into 10 parts, and the division is skewed, then there may be some partitions of size less than 100 and some partitions of size more than 100; if even one partition happens to be of size 200, the speedup that we would obtain by accessing the partitions in parallel is only 5, instead of the 10 for which we would have hoped. If the same relation has to be partitioned into 100 parts, a partition will have 10 tuples on an average. If even one partition has 40 tuples (which is possible, given the large number of partitions) the speedup that we would obtain by accessing them in parallel would be 25, rather than 100. Thus, we see that the loss of speedup due to skew increases with parallelism.

A **balanced range-partitioning vector** can be constructed by sorting: The relation is first sorted on the partitioning attributes. The relation is then scanned in sorted order. After every $1/n$ of the relation has been read, the value of the partitioning attribute of the next tuple is added to the partition vector. Here, n denotes the number of partitions to be constructed. In case there are many tuples with the same value for the partitioning attribute, the technique can still result in some skew. The main disadvantage of this method is the extra I/O overhead incurred in doing the initial sort.

The I/O overhead for constructing balanced range-partition vectors can be reduced by constructing and storing a frequency table, or **histogram**, of the attribute values for each attribute of each relation. Figure 18.1 shows an example of a histogram for an integer-valued attribute that takes values in the range 1 to 25. A histogram takes up only a little space, so histograms on several different attributes can be stored in the system catalog. It is straightforward to construct a balanced range-partitioning function given a histogram on the partitioning attributes. If the histogram is not stored, it can be computed approximately by sampling the relation, using only tuples from a randomly chosen subset of the disk blocks of the relation.

Another approach to minimizing the effect of skew, particularly with range partitioning, is to use *virtual processors*. In the **virtual processor** approach, we pretend there are several times as many *virtual processors* as the number of real processors. Any of the partitioning techniques and query-evaluation techniques that we study later in this chapter can be used, but they map tuples and work to virtual processors instead of to real processors. Virtual processors, in turn, are mapped to real processors, usually by round-robin partitioning.

The idea is that even if one range had many more tuples than the others because of skew, these tuples would get split across multiple virtual processor

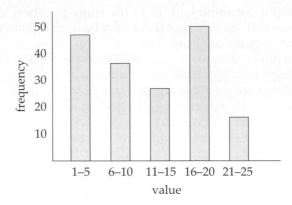

Figure 18.1 Example of histogram.

ranges. Round-robin allocation of virtual processors to real processors would distribute the extra work among multiple real processors, so that one processor does not have to bear all the burden.

18.3   Interquery Parallelism

In **interquery parallelism**, different queries or transactions execute in parallel with one another. Transaction throughput can be increased by this form of parallelism. However, the response times of individual transactions are no faster than they would be if the transactions were run in isolation. Thus, the primary use of interquery parallelism is to scale up a transaction-processing system to support a larger number of transactions per second.

Interquery parallelism is the easiest form of parallelism to support in a database system—particularly in a shared-memory parallel system. Database systems designed for single-processor systems can be used with few or no changes on a shared-memory parallel architecture, since even sequential database systems support concurrent processing. Transactions that would have operated in a time-shared concurrent manner on a sequential machine operate in parallel in the shared-memory parallel architecture.

Supporting interquery parallelism is more complicated in a shared-disk or shared-nothing architecture. Processors have to perform some tasks, such as locking and logging, in a coordinated fashion, and that requires that they pass messages to each other. A parallel database system must also ensure that two processors do not update the same data independently at the same time. Further, when a processor accesses or updates data, the database system must ensure that the processor has the latest version of the data in its buffer pool. The problem of ensuring that the version is the latest is known as the **cache-coherency** problem.

Various protocols are available to guarantee cache coherency; often, cache-coherency protocols are integrated with concurrency-control protocols so that their overhead is reduced. One such protocol for a shared-disk system is this:

1. Before any read or write access to a page, a transaction locks the page in shared or exclusive mode, as appropriate. Immediately after the transaction obtains either a shared or exclusive lock on a page, it also reads the most recent copy of the page from the shared disk.

2. Before a transaction releases an exclusive lock on a page, it flushes the page to the shared disk; then, it releases the lock.

This protocol ensures that, when a transaction sets a shared or exclusive lock on a page, it gets the correct copy of the page.

More complex protocols avoid the repeated reading and writing to disk required by the preceding protocol. Such protocols do not write pages to disk when exclusive locks are released. When a shared or exclusive lock is obtained, if the most recent version of a page is in the buffer pool of some processor, the page is obtained from there. The protocols have to be designed to handle concurrent requests. The shared-disk protocols can be extended to shared-nothing architectures by this scheme: Each page has a **home processor** P_i, and is stored on disk D_i. When other processors want to read or write the page, they send requests to the home processor P_i of the page, since they cannot directly communicate with the disk. The other actions are the same as in the shared-disk protocols.

The Oracle and Oracle Rdb systems are examples of shared-disk parallel database systems that support interquery parallelism.

18.4 Intraquery Parallelism

Intraquery parallelism refers to the execution of a single query in parallel on multiple processors and disks. Using intraquery parallelism is important for speeding up long-running queries. Interquery parallelism does not help in this task, since each query is run sequentially.

To illustrate the parallel evaluation of a query, consider a query that requires a relation to be sorted. Suppose that the relation has been partitioned across multiple disks by range partitioning on some attribute, and the sort is requested on the partitioning attribute. The sort operation can be implemented by sorting each partition in parallel, then concatenating the sorted partitions to get the final sorted relation.

Thus, we can parallelize a query by parallelizing individual operations. There is another source of parallelism in evaluating a query: The *operator tree* for a query can contain multiple operations. We can parallelize the evaluation of the operator tree by evaluating in parallel some of the operations that do not depend on one another. Further, as Chapter 12 mentions, we may be able to pipeline the output of one operation to another operation. The two operations can be executed in parallel on separate processors, one generating output that is consumed by the other, even as it is generated.

In summary, the execution of a single query can be parallelized in two different ways:

- **Intraoperation parallelism**. We can speed up processing of a query by parallelizing the execution of each individual operation, such as sort, select, project, and join. We consider intraoperation parallelism in Section 18.5.

- **Interoperation parallelism**. We can speed up processing of a query by executing in parallel the different operations in a query expression. We consider this form of parallelism in Section 18.6.

The two forms of parallelism are complementary, and can be used simultaneously on a query. Since the number of operations in a typical query is small, compared to the number of tuples processed by each operation, the first form of parallelism can scale better with increasing parallelism. However, with the relatively small number of processors in typical parallel systems today, both forms of parallelism are important.

In the following discussion of parallelization of queries, we assume that the queries are **read only**. The choice of algorithms for parallelizing query evaluation depends on the machine architecture. Rather than present algorithms for each architecture separately, we use a shared-nothing architecture model in our description. Thus, we explicitly describe when data have to be transferred from one processor to another. We can simulate this model easily by using the other architectures, since transfer of data can be done via shared memory in a shared-memory architecture, and via shared disks in a shared-disk architecture. Hence, algorithms for shared-nothing architectures can be used on the other architectures, too. We mention occasionally how the algorithms can be further optimized for shared-memory or shared-disk systems.

To simplify the presentation of the algorithms, assume that there are n processors, $P_0, P_1, \ldots, P_{n-1}$, and n disks $D_0, D_1, \ldots, D_{n-1}$, where disk D_i is associated with processor P_i. A real system may have multiple disks per processor. It is not hard to extend the algorithms to allow multiple disks per processor: We simply allow D_i to be a set of disks. However, for simplicity, we assume here that D_i is a single disk.

18.5   Intraoperation Parallelism

Since relational operations work on relations containing large sets of tuples, we can parallelize the operations by executing them in parallel on different subsets of the relations. Since the number of tuples in a relation can be large, the degree of parallelism is potentially enormous. Thus, intraoperation parallelism is natural in a database system. We shall study parallel versions of some common relational operations in Sections 18.5.1 through 18.5.3.

18.5.1   Parallel Sort

Suppose that we wish to sort a relation that resides on n disks $D_0, D_1, \ldots, D_{n-1}$. If the relation has been range-partitioned on the attributes on which it is to be sorted, then, as noted in Section 18.2.2, we can sort each partition separately, and can concatenate the results to get the full sorted relation. Since the tuples are partitioned on n disks, the time required for reading the entire relation is reduced by the parallel access.

If the relation has been partitioned in any other way, we can sort it in one of two ways:

1. We can range-partition it on the sort attributes, and then sort each partition separately.

2. We can use a parallel version of the external sort–merge algorithm.

18.5.1.1   Range-Partitioning Sort

Range-partitioning sort works in two steps: first range partitioning the relation, then sorting each partition separately. When we sort by range partitioning the relation, it is not necessary to range-partition the relation on the same set of processors or disks as those on which that relation is stored. Suppose that we choose processors $P_0, P_1, \ldots, P_m$, where $m < n$, to sort the relation. There are two steps involved in this operation:

1. Redistribute the tuples in the relation, using a range-partition strategy, so that all tuples that lie within the ith range are sent to processor P_i, which stores the relation temporarily on disk D_i.

    To implement range partitioning, in parallel every processor reads the tuples from its disk and sends the tuples to their destination processors. Each processor $P_0, P_1, \ldots, P_m$ also receives tuples belonging to its partition, and stores them locally. This step requires disk I/O and communication overhead.

2. Each of the processors sorts its partition of the relation locally, without interaction with the other processors. Each processor executes the same operation—namely, sorting—on a different data set. (Execution of the same operation in parallel on different sets of data is called **data parallelism**.)

    The final merge operation is trivial, because the range partitioning in the first phase ensures that, for $1 \leq i < j \leq m$, the key values in processor P_i are all less than the key values in P_j.

We must do range partitioning with a good range-partition vector, so that each partition will have approximately the same number of tuples. Virtual processor partitioning can also be used to reduce skew.

18.5.1.2   Parallel External Sort–Merge

Parallel external sort–merge is an alternative to range partitioning. Suppose that a relation has already been partitioned among disks $D_0, D_1, \ldots, D_{n-1}$ (it does not matter how the relation has been partitioned). Parallel external sort–merge then works this way:

1. Each processor P_i locally sorts the data on disk D_i.

2. The system then merges the sorted runs on each processor to get the final sorted output.

The merging of the sorted runs in step 2 can be parallelized by this sequence of actions:

1. The system range-partitions the sorted partitions at each processor P_i (all by the same partition vector) across the processors $P_0, P_1, \ldots, P_{m-1}$. It sends the tuples in sorted order, so that each processor receives the tuples in sorted streams.

2. Each processor P_i performs a merge on the streams as they are received, to get a single sorted run.

3. The system concatenates the sorted runs on processors $P_0, P_1, \ldots, P_{m-1}$ to get the final result.

As described, this sequence of actions results in an interesting form of **execution skew**, since at first every processor sends all blocks of partition 0 to P_0, then every processor sends all blocks of partition 1 to P_1, and so on. Thus, while sending happens in parallel, receiving tuples becomes sequential: First only P_0 receives tuples, then only P_1 receives tuples, and so on. To avoid this problem, each processor repeatedly sends a block of data to each partition. In other words, each processor sends the first block of every partition, then sends the second block of every partition, and so on. As a result, all processors receive data in parallel.

Some machines, such as the Teradata Purpose-Built Platform Family machines, use specialized hardware to perform merging. The BYNET interconnection network in the Teradata machines can merge output from multiple processors to give a single sorted output.

18.5.2   Parallel Join

The join operation requires that the system test pairs of tuples to see whether they satisfy the join condition; if they do, the system adds the pair to the join output. Parallel join algorithms attempt to split the pairs to be tested over several processors. Each processor then computes part of the join locally. Then, the system collects the results from each processor to produce the final result.

18.5.2.1 Partitioned Join

For certain kinds of joins, such as equi-joins and natural joins, it is possible to *partition* the two input relations across the processors and to compute the join locally at each processor. Suppose that we are using n processors and that the relations to be joined are r and s. **Partitioned join** then works this way: The system partitions the relations r and s each into n partitions, denoted $r_0, r_1, \ldots, r_{n-1}$ and $s_0, s_1, \ldots, s_{n-1}$. The system sends partitions r_i and s_i to processor P_i, where their join is computed locally.

The partitioned join technique works correctly only if the join is an equi-join (for example, $r \bowtie_{r.A=s.B} s$) and if we partition r and s by the same partitioning function on their join attributes. The idea of partitioning is exactly the same as that behind the partitioning step of hash join. In a partitioned join, however, there are two different ways of partitioning r and s:

- Range partitioning on the join attributes.

- Hash partitioning on the join attributes.

In either case, the same partitioning function must be used for both relations. For range partitioning, the same partition vector must be used for both relations. For hash partitioning, the same hash function must be used on both relations. Figure 18.2 depicts the partitioning in a partitioned parallel join.

Once the relations are partitioned, we can use any join technique locally at each processor P_i to compute the join of r_i and s_i. For example, hash join, merge join, or nested-loop join could be used. Thus, we can use partitioning to parallelize any join technique.

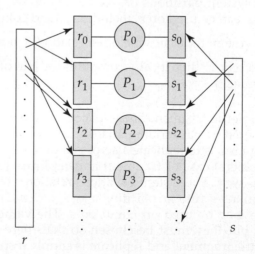

Figure 18.2 Partitioned parallel join.

If one or both of the relations r and s are already partitioned on the join attributes (by either hash partitioning or range partitioning), the work needed for partitioning is reduced greatly. If the relations are not partitioned, or are partitioned on attributes other than the join attributes, then the tuples need to be repartitioned. Each processor P_i reads in the tuples on disk D_i, computes for each tuple t the partition j to which t belongs, and sends tuple t to processor P_j. Processor P_j stores the tuples on disk D_j.

We can optimize the join algorithm used locally at each processor to reduce I/O by buffering some of the tuples to memory, instead of writing them to disk. We describe such optimizations in Section 18.5.2.3.

Skew presents a special problem when range partitioning is used, since a partition vector that splits one relation of the join into equal-sized partitions may split the other relations into partitions of widely varying size. The partition vector should be such that $|r_i| + |s_i|$ (that is, the sum of the sizes of r_i and s_i) is roughly equal over all the $i = 0, 1, \ldots, n-1$. With a good hash function, hash partitioning is likely to have a smaller skew, except when there are many tuples with the same values for the join attributes.

18.5.2.2   Fragment-and-Replicate Join

Partitioning is not applicable to all types of joins. For instance, if the join condition is an inequality, such as $r \bowtie_{r.a < s.b} s$, it is possible that all tuples in r join with some tuple in s (and vice versa). Thus, there may be no easy way of partitioning r and s so that tuples in partition r_i join with only tuples in partition s_i.

We can parallelize such joins by using a technique called *fragment and replicate*. We first consider a special case of fragment and replicate—**asymmetric fragment-and-replicate join**—which works as follows:

1. The system partitions one of the relations—say, r. Any partitioning technique can be used on r, including round-robin partitioning.

2. The system replicates the other relation, s, across all the processors.

3. Processor P_i then locally computes the join of r_i with all of s, using any join technique.

The asymmetric fragment-and-replicate scheme appears in Figure 18.3a. If r is already stored by partitioning, there is no need to partition it further in step 1. All that is required is to replicate s across all processors.

The general case of **fragment-and-replicate join** appears in Figure 18.3b; it works this way: The system partitions relation r into n partitions, $r_0, r_1, \ldots, r_{n-1}$, and partitions s into m partitions, $s_0, s_1, \ldots, s_{m-1}$. As before, any partitioning technique may be used on r and on s. The values of m and n do not need to be equal, but they must be chosen so that there are at least $m * n$ processors. Asymmetric fragment and replicate is simply a special case of general fragment and replicate, where $m = 1$. Fragment and replicate reduces the sizes of the relations at each processor, compared to asymmetric fragment and replicate.

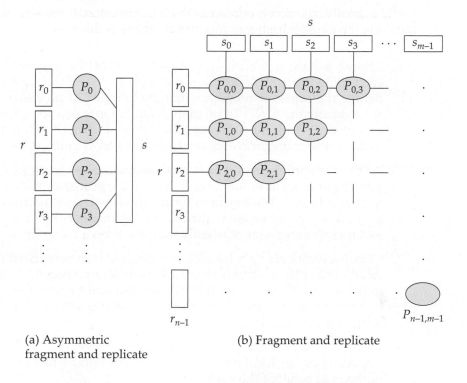

(a) Asymmetric
fragment and replicate

(b) Fragment and replicate

Figure 18.3 Fragment-and-replicate schemes.

Let the processors be $P_{0,0}, P_{0,1}, \ldots, P_{0,m-1}, P_{1,0}, \ldots, P_{n-1,m-1}$. Processor $P_{i,j}$ computes the join of r_i with s_j. Each processor must get those tuples in the partitions on which it works. To accomplish this, the system replicates r_i to processors $P_{i,0}, P_{i,1}, \ldots, P_{i,m-1}$ (which form a row in Figure 18.3b), and replicates s_i to processors $P_{0,i}, P_{1,i}, \ldots, P_{n-1,i}$ (which form a column in Figure 18.3b). Any join technique can be used at each processor $P_{i,j}$.

Fragment and replicate works with any join condition, since every tuple in r can be tested with every tuple in s. Thus, it can be used where partitioning cannot be.

Fragment and replicate usually has a higher cost than partitioning when both relations are of roughly the same size, since at least one of the relations has to be replicated. However, if one of the relations—say, s—is small, it may be cheaper to replicate s across all processors, rather than to repartition r and s on the join attributes. In such a case, asymmetric fragment and replicate is preferable, even though partitioning could be used.

18.5.2.3 Partitioned Parallel Hash Join

The partitioned hash join of Section 12.5.5 can be parallelized. Suppose that we have n processors, $P_0, P_1, \ldots, P_{n-1}$, and two relations r and s, such that the relations r and s are partitioned across multiple disks. Recall from Section 12.5.5

that the smaller relation is chosen as the build relation. If the size of s is less than that of r, the parallel hash-join algorithm proceeds this way:

1. Choose a hash function—say, h_1—that takes the join attribute value of each tuple in r and s and maps the tuple to one of the n processors. Let r_i denote the tuples of relation r that are mapped to processor P_i; similarly, let s_i denote the tuples of relation s that are mapped to processor P_i. Each processor P_i reads the tuples of s that are on its disk D_i and sends each tuple to the appropriate processor on the basis of hash function h_1.

2. As the destination processor P_i receives the tuples of s_i, it further partitions them by another hash function, h_2, which the processor uses to compute the hash join locally. The partitioning at this stage is exactly the same as in the partitioning phase of the sequential hash-join algorithm. Each processor P_i executes this step independently from the other processors.

3. Once the tuples of s have been distributed, the system redistributes the larger relation r across the n processors by the hash function h_1, in the same way as before. As it receives each tuple, the destination processor repartitions it by the function h_2, just as the probe relation is partitioned in the sequential hash-join algorithm.

4. Each processor P_i executes the build and probe phases of the hash-join algorithm on the local partitions r_i and s_i of r and s to produce a partition of the final result of the hash join.

The hash join at each processor is independent of that at other processors, and receiving the tuples of r_i and s_i is similar to reading them from disk. Therefore, any of the optimizations of the hash join described in Chapter 12 can be applied as well to the parallel case. In particular, we can use the hybrid hash-join algorithm to cache some of the incoming tuples in memory, and thus avoid the costs of writing them and of reading them back in.

18.5.2.4   Parallel Nested-Loop Join

To illustrate the use of fragment-and-replicate–based parallelization, consider the case where the relation s is much smaller than relation r. Suppose that relation r is stored by partitioning; the attribute on which it is partitioned does not matter. Suppose too that there is an index on a join attribute of relation r at each of the partitions of relation r.

We use asymmetric fragment and replicate, with relation s being replicated and with the existing partitioning of relation r. Each processor P_j where a partition of relation s is stored reads the tuples of relation s stored in D_j, and replicates the tuples to every other processor P_i. At the end of this phase, relation s is replicated at all sites that store tuples of relation r.

Now, each processor P_i performs an indexed nested-loop join of relation s with the ith partition of relation r. We can overlap the indexed nested-loop join with the distribution of tuples of relation s, to reduce the costs of writing the tuples of relation s to disk, and of reading them back. However, the replication of relation s must be synchronized with the join so that there is enough space in the in-memory buffers at each processor P_i to hold the tuples of relation s that have been received but that have not yet been used in the join.

18.5.3 Other Relational Operations

The evaluation of other relational operations also can be parallelized:

- **Selection.** Let the selection be $\sigma_\theta(r)$. Consider first the case where θ is of the form $a_i = v$, where a_i is an attribute and v is a value. If the relation r is partitioned on a_i, the selection proceeds at a single processor. If θ is of the form $l \le a_i \le u$—that is, θ is a range selection—and the relation has been range-partitioned on a_i, then the selection proceeds at each processor whose partition overlaps with the specified range of values. In all other cases, the selection proceeds in parallel at all the processors.

- **Duplicate elimination.** Duplicates can be eliminated by sorting; either of the parallel sort techniques can be used, optimized to eliminate duplicates as soon as they appear during sorting. We can also parallelize duplicate elimination by partitioning the tuples (by either range or hash partitioning) and eliminating duplicates locally at each processor.

- **Projection.** Projection without duplicate elimination can be performed as tuples are read in from disk in parallel. If duplicates are to be eliminated, either of the techniques just described can be used.

- **Aggregation.** Consider an aggregation operation. We can parallelize the operation by partitioning the relation on the grouping attributes, and then computing the aggregate values locally at each processor. Either hash partitioning or range partitioning can be used. If the relation is already partitioned on the grouping attributes, the first step can be skipped.

  We can reduce the cost of transferring tuples during partitioning by partly computing aggregate values before partitioning, at least for the commonly used aggregate functions. Consider an aggregation operation on a relation r, using the **sum** aggregate function on attribute B, with grouping on attribute A. The system can perform the operation at each processor P_i on those r tuples stored on disk D_i. This computation results in tuples with partial sums at each processor; there is one tuple at P_i for each value for attribute A present in r tuples stored on D_i. The system partitions the result of the local aggregation on the grouping attribute A, and performs the aggregation again (on tuples with the partial sums) at each processor P_i to get the final result.

  As a result of this optimization, fewer tuples need to be sent to other processors during partitioning. This idea can be extended easily to the **min** and **max** aggregate functions. Extensions to the **count** and **avg** aggregate functions are left for you to do in Exercise 18.12.

The parallelization of other operations is covered in several of the exercises.

18.5.4 Cost of Parallel Evaluation of Operations

We achieve parallelism by partitioning the I/O among multiple disks, and partitioning the CPU work among multiple processors. If such a split is achieved without any overhead, and if there is no skew in the splitting of work, a parallel operation using n processors will take $1/n$ times as long as the same operation on a single processor. We already know how to estimate the cost of an operation such as a join or a selection. The time cost of parallel processing would then be $1/n$ of the time cost of sequential processing of the operation.

We must also account for the following costs:

- **Start-up costs** for initiating the operation at multiple processors.

- **Skew** in the distribution of work among the processors, with some processors getting a larger number of tuples than others.

- **Contention for resources**—such as memory, disk, and the communication network—resulting in delays.

- **Cost of assembling** the final result by transmitting partial results from each processor.

The time taken by a parallel operation can be estimated as:

$$T_{\text{part}} + T_{\text{asm}} + \max(T_0, T_1, \ldots, T_{n-1})$$

where T_{part} is the time for partitioning the relations, T_{asm} is the time for assembling the results, and T_i is the time taken for the operation at processor P_i. Assuming that the tuples are distributed without any skew, the number of tuples sent to each processor can be estimated as $1/n$ of the total number of tuples. Ignoring contention, the cost T_i of the operations at each processor P_i can then be estimated by the techniques in Chapter 12.

The preceding estimate will be an optimistic estimate, since skew is common. Even though breaking down a single query into a number of parallel steps reduces the size of the average step, it is the time for processing the single slowest step that determines the time taken for processing the query as a whole. A partitioned parallel evaluation, for instance, is only as fast as the slowest of the parallel executions. Thus, any skew in the distribution of the work across processors greatly affects performance.

The problem of skew in partitioning is closely related to the problem of partition overflow in sequential hash joins (Chapter 12). We can use overflow resolution and avoidance techniques developed for hash joins to handle skew when hash partitioning is used. We can use balanced range partitioning and virtual processor partitioning to minimize skew due to range partitioning, as in Section 18.2.3.

18.6   Interoperation Parallelism

There are two forms of interoperation parallelism: pipelined parallelism and independent parallelism.

18.6.1   Pipelined Parallelism

As discussed in Chapter 12, pipelining forms an important source of economy of computation for database query processing. Recall that, in pipelining, the output tuples of one operation, A, are consumed by a second operation, B, even before the first operation has produced the entire set of tuples in its output. The major advantage of pipelined execution in a sequential evaluation is that we can carry out a sequence of such operations without writing any of the intermediate results to disk.

Parallel systems use pipelining primarily for the same reason that sequential systems do. However, pipelines are a source of parallelism as well, in the same way that instruction pipelines are a source of parallelism in hardware design. It is possible to run operations A and B simultaneously on different processors, so that B consumes tuples in parallel with A producing them. This form of parallelism is called **pipelined parallelism**.

Consider a join of four relations:

$$r_1 \bowtie r_2 \bowtie r_3 \bowtie r_4$$

We can set up a pipeline that allows the three joins to be computed in parallel. Suppose processor P_1 is assigned the computation of $temp_1 \leftarrow r_1 \bowtie r_2$, and P_2 is assigned the computation of $r_3 \bowtie temp_1$. As P_1 computes tuples in $r_1 \bowtie r_2$, it makes these tuples available to processor P_2. Thus, P_2 has available to it some of the tuples in $r_1 \bowtie r_2$ before P_1 has finished its computation. P_2 can use those tuples that are available to begin computation of $temp_1 \bowtie r_3$, even before $r_1 \bowtie r_2$ is fully computed by P_1. Likewise, as P_2 computes tuples in $(r_1 \bowtie r_2) \bowtie r_3$, it makes these tuples available to P_3, which computes the join of these tuples with r_4.

Pipelined parallelism is useful with a small number of processors, but does not scale up well. First, pipeline chains generally do not attain sufficient length to provide a high degree of parallelism. Second, it is not possible to pipeline relational operators that do not produce output until all inputs have been accessed, such as the set-difference operation. Third, only marginal speedup is obtained for the frequent cases in which one operator's execution cost is much higher than are those of the others.

All things considered, when the degree of parallelism is high, pipelining is a less important source of parallelism than partitioning. The real reason for using pipelining is that pipelined executions can avoid writing intermediate results to disk.

18.6.2   Independent Parallelism

Operations in a query expression that do not depend on one another can be executed in parallel. This form of parallelism is called **independent parallelism**.

Consider the join $r_1 \bowtie r_2 \bowtie r_3 \bowtie r_4$. Clearly, we can compute $temp_1 \leftarrow r_1 \bowtie r_2$ in parallel with $temp_2 \leftarrow r_3 \bowtie r_4$. When these two computations complete, we compute:

$$temp_1 \bowtie temp_2$$

To obtain further parallelism, we can pipeline the tuples in $temp_1$ and $temp_2$ into the computation of $temp_1 \bowtie temp_2$, which is itself carried out by a pipelined join (Section 12.7.2.2).

Like pipelined parallelism, independent parallelism does not provide a high degree of parallelism and is less useful in a highly parallel system, although it is useful with a lower degree of parallelism.

18.7   Query Optimization

Query optimizers account in large measure for the success of relational technology. Recall that a query optimizer takes a query and finds the cheapest execution plan among the many possible execution plans that give the same answer.

Query optimizers for parallel query evaluation are more complicated than query optimizers for sequential query evaluation. First, the cost models are more complicated, since partitioning costs have to be accounted for, and issues such as skew and resource contention must be taken into account. More important is the issue of how to parallelize a query. Suppose that we have somehow chosen an expression (from among those equivalent to the query) to be used for evaluating the query. The expression can be represented by an operator tree, as in Section 12.1.

To evaluate an operator tree in a parallel system, we must make the following decisions:

- How to parallelize each operation, and how many processors to use for it.

- What operations to pipeline across different processors, what operations to execute independently in parallel, and what operations to execute sequentially, one after the other.

These decisions constitute the task of **scheduling** the execution tree.

Determining the resources of each kind—such as processors, disks, and memory—that should be allocated to each operation in the tree is another aspect of the optimization problem. For instance, it may appear wise to use the maximum amount of parallelism available, but it is a good idea not to execute certain operations in parallel. Operations whose computational requirements are significantly smaller than the communication overhead should be clustered with one of their neighbors. Otherwise, the advantage of parallelism is negated by the overhead of communication.

One concern is that long pipelines do not lend themselves to good resource utilization. Unless the operations are coarse grained, the final operation of the pipeline may wait for a long time to get inputs, while holding precious resources, such as memory. Hence, long pipelines should be avoided.

The number of parallel evaluation plans from which to choose is much larger than the number of sequential evaluation plans. Optimizing parallel queries by considering all alternatives is therefore much more expensive than optimizing sequential queries. Hence, we usually adopt heuristic approaches to reduce the number of parallel execution plans that we have to consider. We describe two popular heuristics here.

The first heuristic is to consider only evaluation plans that parallelize every operation across all processors, and that do not use any pipelining. This approach is used in the Teradata systems. Finding the best such execution plan is like doing query optimization in a sequential system. The main differences lie in how the partitioning is performed and what cost-estimation formula is used.

The second heuristic is to choose the most efficient sequential evaluation plan, and then to parallelize the operations in that evaluation plan. The Volcano parallel database popularized a model of parallelization called the **exchange-operator** model. This model uses existing implementations of operations, operating on local copies of data, coupled with an exchange operation that moves data around between different processors. Exchange operators can be introduced into an evaluation plan to transform it into a parallel evaluation plan.

Yet another dimension of optimization is the design of physical-storage organization to speed up queries. The optimal physical organization differs for different queries. The database administrator must choose a physical organization that appears to be good for the expected mix of database queries. Thus, the area of parallel query optimization is complex, and it is still an area of active research.

18.8   Design of Parallel Systems

So far this chapter has concentrated on parallelization of data storage and of query processing. Since large-scale parallel database systems are used primarily for storing large volumes of data, and for processing decision-support queries on those data, these topics are the most important in a parallel database system. Parallel loading of data from external sources is an important requirement, if we are to handle large volumes of incoming data.

A large parallel database system must also address these availability issues:

- Resilience to failure of some processors or disks.

- Online reorganization of data and schema changes.

We consider these issues here.

With a large number of processors and disks, the probability that at least one processor or disk will malfunction is significantly greater than in a single-processor system with one disk. A poorly designed parallel system will stop functioning if any component (processor or disk) fails. Assuming that the probability of failure of a single processor or disk is small, the probability of failure of the system goes up linearly with the number of processors and disks. If a single processor or disk would fail once every 5 years, a system with 100 processors would have a failure every 18 days.

Therefore, large-scale parallel database systems, such as Teradata, and IBM Informix XPS, are designed to operate even if a processor or disk fails. Data are replicated across at least two processors. If a processor fails, the data that it stored can still be accessed from the other processors. The system keeps track of failed processors and distributes the work among functioning processors. Requests for data stored at the failed site are automatically routed to the backup sites that store a replica of the data. If all the data of a processor A are replicated at a single processor B, B will have to handle all the requests to A as well as those to itself, and that will result in B becoming a bottleneck. Therefore, the replicas of the data of a processor are partitioned across multiple other processors.

When we are dealing with large volumes of data (ranging in the terabytes), simple operations, such as creating indices, and changes to schema, such as adding a column to a relation, can take a long time—perhaps hours or even days. Therefore, it is unacceptable for the database system to be unavailable while such operations are in progress. Most database systems allow such operations to be performed **online,** that is, while the system is executing other transactions.

Consider, for instance, **online index construction.** A system that supports this feature allows insertions, deletions, and updates on a relation even as an index is being built on the relation. The index-building operation therefore cannot lock the entire relation in shared mode, as it would have done otherwise. Instead, the process keeps track of updates that occur while it is active and incorporates the changes into the index being constructed. (Most database systems today support online index construction, since this feature is very important even for non-parallel database systems.)

In recent years, a number of companies have developed new parallel database products, including Netezza, DATAllegro (which was acquired by Microsoft), Greenplum, and Aster Data. Each of these products runs on systems containing tens to thousands of nodes, with each node running an instance of an underlying database; Each product manages the partitioning of data, as well as parallel processing of queries, across the database instances.

Netezza, Greenplum and Aster Data use PostgreSQL as the underlying database; DATAllegro originally used Ingres as the underlying database system, but moved to SQL Server subsequent to its acquisition by Microsoft. By building on top of an existing database system, these systems are able to leverage the data storage, query processing, and transaction management features of the underlying database, leaving them free to focus on data partitioning (including replication for fault tolerance), fast interprocessor communication, parallel query processing, and parallel-query optimization. Another benefit of using a public domain database such as PostgreSQL is that the software cost per node is very low; in contrast commercial databases have a significant per-processor cost.

It is also worth mentioning that Netezza and DATAllegro actually sell data warehouse "appliances", which include hardware and software, allowing customers to build parallel databases with minimal effort.

18.9   Parallelism on Multicore Processors

Parallelism has become commonplace on most computers today, even some of the smallest, due to current trends in computer architecture. As a result, virtually all database systems today run on a parallel platform. In this section, we shall explore briefly the reasons for this architectural trend and the effects this has on database system design and implementation.

18.9.1   Parallelism versus Raw Speed

Since the dawn of computers, processor speed has increased at an exponential rate, doubling every 18 to 24 months. This increase results from an exponential growth in the number of transistors that could be fit within a unit area of a silicon chip, and is known popularly as **Moore's law**, named after Intel co-founder Gordon Moore. Technically, Moore's law is not a *law*, but rather an observation and a prediction regarding technology trends. Until recently, the increase in the number of transistors and the decrease in their size led to ever-faster processors. Although technological progress continues to behave as predicted by Moore's law, another factor has emerged to slow the growth in processor speed. Fast processors are power inefficient. This is problematic in terms of energy consumption and cost, battery life for mobile computers, and heat dissipation (all the power used eventually turns into heat). As a result, modern processors typically are not one single processor but rather consist of several processors on one chip. To maintain a distinction between on-chip multiprocessors and traditional processors, the term **core** is used for an on-chip processor. Thus we say that a machine has a multicore processor.[2]

18.9.2   Cache Memory and Multithreading

Each core is capable of processing an independent stream of machine instructions. However, because processors are able to process data faster than it can be accessed from main memory, main memory can become a bottleneck that limits overall performance. For this reason, computer designers include one or more levels of **cache** memory in a computer system. Cache memory is more costly than main memory on a per-byte basis, but offers a faster access time. In multilevel cache designs, the levels are called L1, L2, and so on, with L1 being the fastest cache (and thus the most costly per byte and therefore the smallest), L2 the next fastest,

---

[2]The use of the term *core* here is different from the use of that term in the early days of computing to refer to a main-memory technology based on magnetic cores.

and so on. The result is an extension of the storage hierarchy that we discussed in Chapter 10 to include the various levels of cache below main memory.

Although the database system can control the transfer of data between disk and main memory, the computer hardware maintains control over the transfer of data among the various levels of cache and between cache and main memory. Despite this lack of direct control, the database system's performance can be affected by how cache is utilized. If a core needs to access a data item that is not in cache, it must be fetched from main memory. Because main memory is so much slower than processors, a significant amount of potential processing speed may be lost while a core waits for data from main memory. These waits are referred to as **cache misses**.

One way in which computer designers attempt to limit the impact of cache misses is via *multithreading*. A **thread** is an execution stream that shares memory[3] with other threads running on the same core. If the thread currently executing on a core suffers a cache miss (or other type of wait), the core proceeds to execute another thread, thereby not wasting computing speed while waiting.

Threads introduce yet another source of parallelism beyond the multiplicity of cores. Each new generation of processors supports more cores and more threads. The Sun UltraSPARC T2 processor has 8 cores, each of which supports 8 threads, for a total of 64 threads on one processor chip.

The architecture trend of slower increase in raw speed accompanied by the growth in the number of cores has significant implications for database system design, as we shall see shortly.

18.9.3   Adapting Database System Design for Modern Architectures

It would appear that database systems are an ideal application to take advantage of large numbers of cores and threads, since database systems support large numbers of concurrent transactions. However, there are a variety of factors that make optimal use of modern processors challenging.

As we allow a higher degree of concurrency to take advantage of the parallelism of modern processors, we increase the amount of data that needs to be in cache. This can result in more cache misses, perhaps so many that even a multithreaded core has to wait for data from memory.

Concurrent transactions need some sort of concurrency control to ensure the ACID properties that we discussed in Chapter 14. When concurrent transactions access data in common, some sort of restrictions must be imposed on that concurrent access. Those restrictions, whether based on locks, timestamps, or validation, result in waiting or the loss of work due to transaction aborts. To avoid excessive amounts of waiting or lost work, it is ideal that concurrent transactions conflict rarely, but attempting to ensure that can increase the amount of data needed in cache, resulting in more cache misses.

Finally, there are components of a database system shared by all transactions. In a system using locking, the lock table is shared by all transactions and access to

---

[3]Technically, in operating-system terminology, its address space.

it can become a bottleneck. Similar problems exist for other forms of concurrency control. Similarly, the buffer manager, the log manager, and the recovery manager serve all transactions and are potential bottlenecks.

Because having a large number of concurrent transactions may not take optimal advantage of modern processors, it is desirable to find ways to allow multiple cores to work on a single transaction. This requires the database query processor to find effective ways to parallelize queries without creating excessive demands on cache. This can be done by creating pipelines of database operations from queries and by finding ways to parallelize individual database operations.

The adaptation of database system design and database query processing to multicore and multithreaded systems remains an area of active research. See the bibliographical notes for further details.

18.10 Summary

- Parallel databases have gained significant commercial acceptance in the past 20 years.

- In I/O parallelism, relations are partitioned among available disks so that they can be retrieved faster. Three commonly used partitioning techniques are round-robin partitioning, hash partitioning, and range partitioning.

- Skew is a major problem, especially with increasing degrees of parallelism. Balanced partitioning vectors, using histograms, and virtual processor partitioning are among the techniques used to reduce skew.

- In interquery parallelism, we run different queries concurrently to increase throughput.

- Intraquery parallelism attempts to reduce the cost of running a query. There are two types of intraquery parallelism: intraoperation parallelism and interoperation parallelism.

- We use intraoperation parallelism to execute relational operations, such as sorts and joins, in parallel. Intraoperation parallelism is natural for relational operations, since they are set oriented.

- There are two basic approaches to parallelizing a binary operation such as a join.

  ○ In partitioned parallelism, the relations are split into several parts, and tuples in r_i are joined only with tuples from s_i. Partitioned parallelism can be used only for natural and equi-joins.

  ○ In fragment and replicate, both relations are partitioned and each partition is replicated. In asymmetric fragment and replicate, one of the relations is replicated while the other is partitioned. Unlike partitioned parallelism, fragment and replicate and asymmetric fragment and replicate can be used with any join condition.

Both parallelization techniques can work in conjunction with any join technique.

- In independent parallelism, different operations that do not depend on one another are executed in parallel.

- In pipelined parallelism, processors send the results of one operation to another operation as those results are computed, without waiting for the entire operation to finish.

- Query optimization in parallel databases is significantly more complex than query optimization in sequential databases.

- Modern multicore processors are introducing new research problems in parallel databases.

Review Terms

- Decision-support queries
- I/O parallelism
- Horizontal partitioning
- Partitioning techniques
  - Round-robin
  - Hash partitioning
  - Range partitioning
- Partitioning attribute
- Partitioning vector
- Point query
- Range query
- Skew
  - Execution skew
  - Attribute-value skew
  - Partition skew
- Handling of skew
  - Balanced range-partitioning vector
  - Histogram
  - Virtual processors
- Interquery parallelism

- Cache coherency
- Intraquery parallelism
  - Intraoperation parallelism
  - Interoperation parallelism
- Parallel sort
  - Range-partitioning sort
  - Parallel external sort–merge
- Data parallelism
- Parallel join
  - Partitioned join
  - Fragment-and-replicate join
  - Asymmetric fragment-and-replicate join
  - Partitioned parallel hash join
  - Parallel nested-loop join
- Parallel selection
- Parallel duplicate elimination
- Parallel projection
- Parallel aggregation
- Cost of parallel evaluation

- Interoperation parallelism
  - Pipelined parallelism
  - Independent parallelism
- Query optimization

- Scheduling
- Exchange-operator model
- Design of parallel systems
- Online index construction
- Multicore processors

Practice Exercises

18.1 In a range selection on a range-partitioned attribute, it is possible that only one disk may need to be accessed. Describe the benefits and drawbacks of this property.

18.2 What form of parallelism (interquery, interoperation, or intraoperation) is likely to be the most important for each of the following tasks?

    a. Increasing the throughput of a system with many small queries

    b. Increasing the throughput of a system with a few large queries, when the number of disks and processors is large

18.3 With pipelined parallelism, it is often a good idea to perform several operations in a pipeline on a single processor, even when many processors are available.

    a. Explain why.

    b. Would the arguments you advanced in part *a* hold if the machine has a shared-memory architecture? Explain why or why not.

    c. Would the arguments in part *a* hold with independent parallelism? (That is, are there cases where, even if the operations are not pipelined and there are many processors available, it is still a good idea to perform several operations on the same processor?)

18.4 Consider join processing using symmetric fragment and replicate with range partitioning. How can you optimize the evaluation if the join condition is of the form $| r.A - s.B | \leq k$, where k is a small constant? Here, $| x |$ denotes the absolute value of x. A join with such a join condition is called a **band join**.

18.5 Recall that histograms are used for constructing load-balanced range partitions.

    a. Suppose you have a histogram where values are between 1 and 100, and are partitioned into 10 ranges, 1–10, 11–20, ..., 91–100, with frequencies 15, 5, 20, 10, 10, 5, 5, 20, 5, and 5, respectively. Give a load-balanced range partitioning function to divide the values into 5 partitions.

b.   Write an algorithm for computing a balanced range partition with p partitions, given a histogram of frequency distributions containing n ranges.

18.6   Large-scale parallel database systems store an extra copy of each data item on disks attached to a different processor, to avoid loss of data if one of the processors fails.

a.   Instead of keeping the extra copy of data items from a processor at a single backup processor, it is a good idea to partition the copies of the data items of a processor across multiple processors. Explain why.

b.   Explain how virtual-processor partitioning can be used to efficiently implement the partitioning of the copies as described above.

c.   What are the benefits and drawbacks of using RAID storage instead of storing an extra copy of each data item?

18.7   Suppose we wish to index a large relation that is partitioned. Can the idea of partitioning (including virtual processor partitioning) be applied to indices? Explain your answer, considering the following two cases (assuming for simplicity that partitioning as well as indexing are on single attributes):

a.   Where the index is on the partitioning attribute of the relation.

b.   Where the index is on an attribute other than the partitioning attribute of the relation.

18.8   Suppose a well-balanced range-partitioning vector had been chosen for a relation, but the relation is subsequently updated, making the partitioning unbalanced. Even if virtual-processor partitioning is used, a particular virtual processor may end up with a very large number of tuples after the update, and repartitioning would then be required.

a.   Suppose a virtual processor has a significant excess of tuples (say, twice the average). Explain how repartitioning can be done by splitting the partition, thereby increasing the number of virtual processors.

b.   If, instead of round-robin allocation of virtual processors, virtual partitions can be allocated to processors in an arbitrary fashion, with a mapping table tracking the allocation. If a particular node has excess load (compared to the others), explain how load can be balanced.

c.   Assuming there are no updates, does query processing have to be stopped while repartitioning, or reallocation of virtual processors, is carried out? Explain your answer.

Exercises

18.9   For each of the three partitioning techniques, namely round-robin, hash partitioning, and range partitioning, give an example of a query for which that partitioning technique would provide the fastest response.

18.10   What factors could result in skew when a relation is partitioned on one of its attributes by:

    a.   Hash partitioning?

    b.   Range partitioning?

    In each case, what can be done to reduce the skew?

18.11   Give an example of a join that is not a simple equi-join for which partitioned parallelism can be used. What attributes should be used for partitioning?

18.12   Describe a good way to parallelize each of the following:

    a.   The difference operation

    b.   Aggregation by the **count** operation

    c.   Aggregation by the **count distinct** operation

    d.   Aggregation by the **avg** operation

    e.   Left outer join, if the join condition involves only equality

    f.   Left outer join, if the join condition involves comparisons other than equality

    g.   Full outer join, if the join condition involves comparisons other than equality

18.13   Describe the benefits and drawbacks of pipelined parallelism.

18.14   Suppose you wish to handle a workload consisting of a large number of small transactions by using shared-nothing parallelism.

    a.   Is intraquery parallelism required in such a situation? If not, why, and what form of parallelism is appropriate?

    b.   What form of skew would be of significance with such a workload?

    c.   Suppose most transactions accessed one *account* record, which includes an *account_type* attribute, and an associated *account_type_master* record, which provides information about the account type. How would you partition and/or replicate data to speed up transactions? You may assume that the *account_type_master* relation is rarely updated.

18.15   The attribute on which a relation is partitioned can have a significant impact on the cost of a query.

    a.   Given a workload of SQL queries on a single relation, what attributes would be candidates for partitioning?

    b.   How would you choose between the alternative partitioning techniques, based on the workload?

    c.   Is it possible to partition a relation on more than one attribute? Explain your answer.

Bibliographical Notes

In the late 1970s and early 1980s, as the relational model gained reasonably sound footing, people recognized that relational operators are highly parallelizable and have good dataflow properties. Several research projects including GAMMA (DeWitt [1990]), XPRS (Stonebraker et al. [1989]) and Volcano (Graefe [1990]) were launched to investigate the practicality of parallel execution of relational operators.

Teradata was one of the first commercial parallel database systems, and continues to have a large market share. The Red Brick Warehouse was another early parallel database system; Red Brick was was acquired by Informix, which was itself acquired by IBM. More recent parallel database systems include Netezza, DATAllegro (now part of Microsoft), Greenplum, and Aster Data.

Locking in parallel databases is discussed in Joshi [1991] and Mohan and Narang [1992]. Cache-coherency protocols for parallel database systems are discussed by Dias et al. [1989], Mohan and Narang [1992], and Rahm [1993]. Carey et al. [1991] discusses caching issues in a client–server system.

Graefe and McKenna [1993b] presents an excellent survey of query processing, including parallel processing of queries. The exchange-operator model was advocated by Graefe [1990] and Graefe and McKenna [1993b].

Parallel sorting is discussed in DeWitt et al. [1992]. Parallel sorting on multicore and multithreaded processors is discussed in Garcia and Korth [2005] and Chen et al. [2007]. Parallel join algorithms are described by Nakayama et al. [1984], Richardson et al. [1987], Kitsuregawa and Ogawa [1990], and Wilschut et al. [1995], among other works.

Skew handling in parallel joins is described by Walton et al. [1991], Wolf [1991], and DeWitt et al. [1992].

Parallel query-optimization techniques are described by Lu et al. [1991] and Ganguly et al. [1992].

The adaptation of database-system design and query-processing algorithms to multicore and multithreaded architectures is discussed in the proceedings of the International Workshop on Data Management on Modern Hardware (DaMoN), held annually since 2005.

CHAPTER 19

Distributed Databases

Unlike parallel systems, in which the processors are tightly coupled and constitute a single database system, a distributed database system consists of loosely coupled sites that share no physical components. Furthermore, the database systems that run on each site may have a substantial degree of mutual independence. We discussed the basic structure of distributed systems in Chapter 17.

Each site may participate in the execution of transactions that access data at one site, or several sites. The main difference between centralized and distributed database systems is that, in the former, the data reside in one single location, whereas in the latter, the data reside in several locations. This distribution of data is the cause of many difficulties in transaction processing and query processing. In this chapter, we address these difficulties.

We start by classifying distributed databases as homogeneous or heterogeneous, in Section 19.1. We then address the question of how to store data in a distributed database in Section 19.2. In Section 19.3, we outline a model for transaction processing in a distributed database. In Section 19.4, we describe how to implement atomic transactions in a distributed database by using special commit protocols. In Section 19.5, we describe concurrency control in distributed databases. In Section 19.6, we outline how to provide high availability in a distributed database by exploiting replication, so the system can continue processing transactions even when there is a failure. We address query processing in distributed databases in Section 19.7. In Section 19.8, we outline issues in handling heterogeneous databases. In Section 19.10, we describe directory systems, which can be viewed as a specialized form of distributed databases.

In this chapter, we illustrate all our examples using the bank database of Figure 19.1.

19.1 Homogeneous and Heterogeneous Databases

In a **homogeneous distributed database** system, all sites have identical database-management system software, are aware of one another, and agree to cooperate in processing users' requests. In such a system, local sites surrender a portion of their autonomy in terms of their right to change schemas or database-management

825

$$branch(branch\_name, branch\_city, assets)$$
$$account \ (account\_number, branch\_name, balance)$$
$$depositor \ (customer\_name, account\_number)$$

Figure 19.1 Banking database.

system software. That software must also cooperate with other sites in exchanging information about transactions, to make transaction processing possible across multiple sites.

In contrast, in a **heterogeneous distributed database**, different sites may use different schemas, and different database-management system software. The sites may not be aware of one another, and they may provide only limited facilities for cooperation in transaction processing. The differences in schemas are often a major problem for query processing, while the divergence in software becomes a hindrance for processing transactions that access multiple sites.

In this chapter, we concentrate on homogeneous distributed databases. However, in Section 19.8 we briefly discuss issues in heterogeneous distributed database systems.

19.2   Distributed Data Storage

Consider a relation r that is to be stored in the database. There are two approaches to storing this relation in the distributed database:

- **Replication**. The system maintains several identical replicas (copies) of the relation, and stores each replica at a different site. The alternative to replication is to store only one copy of relation r.

- **Fragmentation**. The system partitions the relation into several fragments, and stores each fragment at a different site.

Fragmentation and replication can be combined: A relation can be partitioned into several fragments and there may be several replicas of each fragment. In the following subsections, we elaborate on each of these techniques.

19.2.1   Data Replication

If relation r is replicated, a copy of relation r is stored in two or more sites. In the most extreme case, we have **full replication**, in which a copy is stored in every site in the system.

There are a number of advantages and disadvantages to replication.

- **Availability**. If one of the sites containing relation r fails, then the relation r can be found in another site. Thus, the system can continue to process queries involving r, despite the failure of one site.

- **Increased parallelism**. In the case where the majority of accesses to the relation r result in only the reading of the relation, then several sites can process queries involving r in parallel. The more replicas of r there are, the greater the chance that the needed data will be found in the site where the transaction is executing. Hence, data replication minimizes movement of data between sites.

- **Increased overhead on update**. The system must ensure that all replicas of a relation r are consistent; otherwise, erroneous computations may result. Thus, whenever r is updated, the update must be propagated to all sites containing replicas. The result is increased overhead. For example, in a banking system, where account information is replicated in various sites, it is necessary to ensure that the balance in a particular account agrees in all sites.

In general, replication enhances the performance of read operations and increases the availability of data to read-only transactions. However, update transactions incur greater overhead. Controlling concurrent updates by several transactions to replicated data is more complex than in centralized systems, which we studied in Chapter 15. We can simplify the management of replicas of relation r by choosing one of them as the **primary copy** of r. For example, in a banking system, an account can be associated with the site in which the account has been opened. Similarly, in an airline-reservation system, a flight can be associated with the site at which the flight originates. We shall examine the primary copy scheme and other options for distributed concurrency control in Section 19.5.

19.2.2 Data Fragmentation

If relation r is fragmented, r is divided into a number of *fragments* $r_1, r_2, \ldots, r_n$. These fragments contain sufficient information to allow reconstruction of the original relation r. There are two different schemes for fragmenting a relation: *horizontal* fragmentation and *vertical* fragmentation. Horizontal fragmentation splits the relation by assigning each tuple of r to one or more fragments. Vertical fragmentation splits the relation by decomposing the scheme R of relation r.

In **horizontal fragmentation**, a relation r is partitioned into a number of subsets, $r_1, r_2, \ldots, r_n$. Each tuple of relation r must belong to at least one of the fragments, so that the original relation can be reconstructed, if needed.

As an illustration, the *account* relation can be divided into several different fragments, each of which consists of tuples of accounts belonging to a particular branch. If the banking system has only two branches—Hillside and Valleyview—then there are two different fragments:

$$account_1 = \sigma_{branch\_name = \text{"Hillside"}} (account)$$
$$account_2 = \sigma_{branch\_name = \text{"Valleyview"}} (account)$$

Horizontal fragmentation is usually used to keep tuples at the sites where they are used the most, to minimize data transfer.

In general, a horizontal fragment can be defined as a *selection* on the global relation r. That is, we use a predicate P_i to construct fragment r_i:

$$r_i = \sigma_{P_i}(r)$$

We reconstruct the relation r by taking the union of all fragments; that is:

$$r = r_1 \cup r_2 \cup \cdots \cup r_n$$

In our example, the fragments are disjoint. By changing the selection predicates used to construct the fragments, we can have a particular tuple of r appear in more than one of the r_i.

In its simplest form, vertical fragmentation is the same as decomposition (see Chapter 8). **Vertical fragmentation** of $r(R)$ involves the definition of several subsets of attributes $R_1, R_2, \ldots, R_n$ of the schema R so that:

$$R = R_1 \cup R_2 \cup \cdots \cup R_n$$

Each fragment r_i of r is defined by:

$$r_i = \Pi_{R_i}(r)$$

The fragmentation should be done in such a way that we can reconstruct relation r from the fragments by taking the natural join:

$$r = r_1 \bowtie r_2 \bowtie r_3 \bowtie \cdots \bowtie r_n$$

One way of ensuring that the relation r can be reconstructed is to include the primary-key attributes of R in each R_i. More generally, any superkey can be used. It is often convenient to add a special attribute, called a *tuple-id*, to the schema R. The tuple-id value of a tuple is a unique value that distinguishes the tuple from all other tuples. The tuple-id attribute thus serves as a candidate key for the augmented schema, and is included in each R_i. The physical or logical address for a tuple can be used as a tuple-id, since each tuple has a unique address.

To illustrate vertical fragmentation, consider a university database with a relation *employee_info* that stores, for each employee, *employee_id*, *name*, *designation*, and *salary*. For privacy reasons, this relation may be fragmented into a relation *employee_private_info* containing *employee_id* and *salary*, and another relation *employee_public_info* containing attributes *employee_id*, *name*, and *designation*. These may be stored at different sites, again, possibly for security reasons.

The two types of fragmentation can be applied to a single schema; for instance, the fragments obtained by horizontally fragmenting a relation can be further partitioned vertically. Fragments can also be replicated. In general, a fragment can be replicated, replicas of fragments can be fragmented further, and so on.

19.2.3 Transparency

The user of a distributed database system should not be required to know where the data are physically located nor how the data can be accessed at the specific local site. This characteristic, called **data transparency**, can take several forms:

- **Fragmentation transparency.** Users are not required to know how a relation has been fragmented.

- **Replication transparency.** Users view each data object as logically unique. The distributed system may replicate an object to increase either system performance or data availability. Users do not have to be concerned with what data objects have been replicated, or where replicas have been placed.

- **Location transparency.** Users are not required to know the physical location of the data. The distributed database system should be able to find any data as long as the data identifier is supplied by the user transaction.

Data items—such as relations, fragments, and replicas—must have unique names. This property is easy to ensure in a centralized database. In a distributed database, however, we must take care to ensure that two sites do not use the same name for distinct data items.

One solution to this problem is to require all names to be registered in a central **name server**. The name server helps to ensure that the same name does not get used for different data items. We can also use the name server to locate a data item, given the name of the item. This approach, however, suffers from two major disadvantages. First, the name server may become a performance bottle-neck when data items are located by their names, resulting in poor performance. Second, if the name server crashes, it may not be possible for any site in the distributed system to continue to run.

A more widely used alternative approach requires that each site prefix its own site identifier to any name that it generates. This approach ensures that no two sites generate the same name (since each site has a unique identifier). Furthermore, no central control is required. This solution, however, fails to achieve location transparency, since site identifiers are attached to names. Thus, the *account* relation might be referred to as *site17. account*, or *account@site17*, rather than as simply *account*. Many database systems use the Internet address (IP address) of a site to identify it.

To overcome this problem, the database system can create a set of alternative names, or **aliases**, for data items. A user may thus refer to data items by simple names that are translated by the system to complete names. The mapping of aliases to the real names can be stored at each site. With aliases, the user can be unaware of the physical location of a data item. Furthermore, the user will be unaffected if the database administrator decides to move a data item from one site to another.

Users should not have to refer to a specific replica of a data item. Instead, the system should determine which replica to reference on a read request, and should update all replicas on a write request. We can ensure that it does so by maintaining a catalog table, which the system uses to determine all replicas for the data item.

19.3   Distributed Transactions

Access to the various data items in a distributed system is usually accomplished through transactions, which must preserve the ACID properties (Section 14.1). There are two types of transaction that we need to consider. The **local transactions** are those that access and update data in only one local database; the **global transactions** are those that access and update data in several local databases. Ensuring the ACID properties of the local transactions can be done as described in Chapters 14, 15, and 16. However, for global transactions, this task is much more complicated, since several sites may be participating in execution. The failure of one of these sites, or the failure of a communication link connecting these sites, may result in erroneous computations.

In this section, we study the system structure of a distributed database and its possible failure modes. In Section 19.4, we study protocols for ensuring atomic commit of global transactions, and in Section 19.5 we study protocols for concurrency control in distributed databases. In Section 19.6, we study how a distributed database can continue functioning even in the presence of various types of failure.

19.3.1   System Structure

Each site has its own *local* transaction manager, whose function is to ensure the ACID properties of those transactions that execute at that site. The various transaction managers cooperate to execute global transactions. To understand how such a manager can be implemented, consider an abstract model of a transaction system, in which each site contains two subsystems:

- The **transaction manager** manages the execution of those transactions (or subtransactions) that access data stored in a local site. Note that each such transaction may be either a local transaction (that is, a transaction that executes at only that site) or part of a global transaction (that is, a transaction that executes at several sites).

- The **transaction coordinator** coordinates the execution of the various transactions (both local and global) initiated at that site.

The overall system architecture appears in Figure 19.2.

The structure of a transaction manager is similar in many respects to the structure of a centralized system. Each transaction manager is responsible for:

- Maintaining a log for recovery purposes.

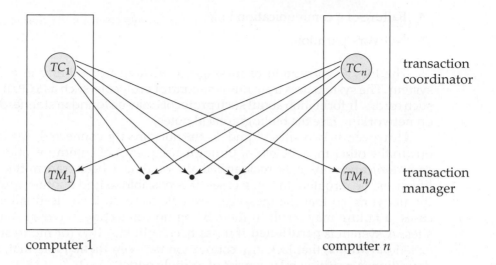

Figure 19.2 System architecture.

- Participating in an appropriate concurrency-control scheme to coordinate the concurrent execution of the transactions executing at that site.

As we shall see, we need to modify both the recovery and concurrency schemes to accommodate the distribution of transactions.

The transaction coordinator subsystem is not needed in the centralized environment, since a transaction accesses data at only a single site. A transaction coordinator, as its name implies, is responsible for coordinating the execution of all the transactions initiated at that site. For each such transaction, the coordinator is responsible for:

- Starting the execution of the transaction.

- Breaking the transaction into a number of subtransactions and distributing these subtransactions to the appropriate sites for execution.

- Coordinating the termination of the transaction, which may result in the transaction being committed at all sites or aborted at all sites.

19.3.2 System Failure Modes

A distributed system may suffer from the same types of failure that a centralized system does (for example, software errors, hardware errors, or disk crashes). There are, however, additional types of failure with which we need to deal in a distributed environment. The basic failure types are:

- Failure of a site.

- Loss of messages.

- Failure of a communication link.

- Network partition.

The loss or corruption of messages is always a possibility in a distributed system. The system uses transmission-control protocols, such as TCP/IP, to handle such errors. Information about such protocols may be found in standard textbooks on networking (see the bibliographical notes).

However, if two sites A and B are not directly connected, messages from one to the other must be *routed* through a sequence of communication links. If a communication link fails, messages that would have been transmitted across the link must be rerouted. In some cases, it is possible to find another route through the network, so that the messages are able to reach their destination. In other cases, a failure may result in there being no connection between some pairs of sites. A system is **partitioned** if it has been split into two (or more) subsystems, called **partitions**, that lack any connection between them. Note that, under this definition, a partition may consist of a single node.

19.4   Commit Protocols

If we are to ensure atomicity, all the sites in which a transaction T executed must agree on the final outcome of the execution. T must either commit at all sites, or it must abort at all sites. To ensure this property, the transaction coordinator of T must execute a *commit protocol*.

Among the simplest and most widely used commit protocols is the **two-phase commit protocol** (2PC), which is described in Section 19.4.1. An alternative is the **three-phase commit protocol** (3PC), which avoids certain disadvantages of the 2PC protocol but adds to complexity and overhead. Section 19.4.2 briefly outlines the 3PC protocol.

19.4.1   Two-Phase Commit

We first describe how the two-phase commit protocol (2PC) operates during normal operation, then describe how it handles failures and finally how it carries out recovery and concurrency control.

Consider a transaction T initiated at site S_i, where the transaction coordinator is C_i.

19.4.1.1   The Commit Protocol

When T completes its execution—that is, when all the sites at which T has executed inform C_i that T has completed—C_i starts the 2PC protocol.

- **Phase 1.** C_i adds the record <prepare T> to the log, and forces the log onto stable storage. It then sends a prepare T message to all sites at which T executed. On receiving such a message, the transaction manager at that site determines whether it is willing to commit its portion of T. If the answer is no, it adds a record <no T> to the log, and then responds by sending an **abort** T message to C_i. If the answer is yes, it adds a record <ready T> to the log, and forces the log (with all the log records corresponding to T) onto stable storage. The transaction manager then replies with a **ready** T message to C_i.

- **Phase 2**. When C_i receives responses to the **prepare** T message from all the sites, or when a prespecified interval of time has elapsed since the **prepare** T message was sent out, C_i can determine whether the transaction T can be committed or aborted. Transaction T can be committed if C_i received a **ready** T message from all the participating sites. Otherwise, transaction T must be aborted. Depending on the verdict, either a record <commit T> or a record <abort T> is added to the log and the log is forced onto stable storage. At this point, the fate of the transaction has been sealed. Following this point, the coordinator sends either a **commit** T or an **abort** T message to all participating sites. When a site receives that message, it records the message in the log.

A site at which T executed can unconditionally abort T at any time before it sends the message **ready** T to the coordinator. Once the message is sent, the transaction is said to be in the **ready state** at the site. The **ready** T message is, in effect, a promise by a site to follow the coordinator's order to commit T or to abort T. To make such a promise, the needed information must first be stored in stable storage. Otherwise, if the site crashes after sending **ready** T, it may be unable to make good on its promise. Further, locks acquired by the transaction must continue to be held until the transaction completes.

Since unanimity is required to commit a transaction, the fate of T is sealed as soon as at least one site responds **abort** T. Since the coordinator site S_i is one of the sites at which T executed, the coordinator can decide unilaterally to abort T. The final verdict regarding T is determined at the time that the coordinator writes that verdict (commit or abort) to the log and forces that verdict to stable storage. In some implementations of the 2PC protocol, a site sends an **acknowledge** T message to the coordinator at the end of the second phase of the protocol. When the coordinator receives the **acknowledge** T message from all the sites, it adds the record <complete T> to the log.

19.4.1.2 Handling of Failures

The 2PC protocol responds in different ways to various types of failures:

- **Failure of a participating site**. If the coordinator C_i detects that a site has failed, it takes these actions: If the site fails before responding with a **ready** T message to C_i, the coordinator assumes that it responded with an **abort** T message. If the site fails after the coordinator has received the **ready** T message from the site, the coordinator executes the rest of the commit protocol in the normal fashion, ignoring the failure of the site.

  When a participating site S_k recovers from a failure, it must examine its log to determine the fate of those transactions that were in the midst of execution when the failure occurred. Let T be one such transaction. We consider each of the possible cases:

○ The log contains a <commit T> record. In this case, the site executes redo(T).

○ The log contains an <abort T> record. In this case, the site executes undo(T).

○ The log contains a <ready T> record. In this case, the site must consult C_i to determine the fate of T. If C_i is up, it notifies S_k regarding whether T committed or aborted. In the former case, it executes redo(T); in the latter case, it executes undo(T). If C_i is down, S_k must try to find the fate of T from other sites. It does so by sending a querystatus T message to all the sites in the system. On receiving such a message, a site must consult its log to determine whether T has executed there, and if T has, whether T committed or aborted. It then notifies S_k about this outcome. If no site has the appropriate information (that is, whether T committed or aborted), then S_k can neither abort nor commit T. The decision concerning T is postponed until S_k can obtain the needed information. Thus, S_k must periodically resend the querystatus message to the other sites. It continues to do so until a site that contains the needed information recovers. Note that the site at which C_i resides always has the needed information.

○ The log contains no control records (abort, commit, ready) concerning T. Thus, we know that S_k failed before responding to the prepare T message from C_i. Since the failure of S_k precludes the sending of such a response, by our algorithm C_i must abort T. Hence, S_k must execute undo(T).

• **Failure of the coordinator**. If the coordinator fails in the midst of the execution of the commit protocol for transaction T, then the participating sites must decide the fate of T. We shall see that, in certain cases, the participating sites cannot decide whether to commit or abort T, and therefore these sites must wait for the recovery of the failed coordinator.

○ If an active site contains a <commit T> record in its log, then T must be committed.

○ If an active site contains an <abort T> record in its log, then T must be aborted.

○ If some active site does *not* contain a <ready T> record in its log, then the failed coordinator C_i cannot have decided to commit T, because a site that does not have a <ready T> record in its log cannot have sent a ready T message to C_i. However, the coordinator may have decided to abort T, but not to commit T. Rather than wait for C_i to recover, it is preferable to abort T.

○ If none of the preceding cases holds, then all active sites must have a <ready T> record in their logs, but no additional control records (such as <abort T> or <commit T>). Since the coordinator has failed, it is impossible to determine whether a decision has been made, and if one has, what that decision is, until the coordinator recovers. Thus, the active sites must wait for C_i to recover. Since the fate of T remains in doubt, T may continue to hold system resources. For example, if locking is used, T may hold locks on data at active sites. Such a situation is undesirable, because it may be hours or days before C_i is again active. During this time, other transactions may be forced to wait for T. As a result, data items may be unavailable not only on the failed site (C_i), but on active sites as well. This situation is called the **blocking** problem, because T is blocked pending the recovery of site C_i.

- **Network partition**. When a network partitions, two possibilities exist:

  1. The coordinator and all its participants remain in one partition. In this case, the failure has no effect on the commit protocol.

  2. The coordinator and its participants belong to several partitions. From the viewpoint of the sites in one of the partitions, it appears that the sites in other partitions have failed. Sites that are not in the partition containing the coordinator simply execute the protocol to deal with failure of the coordinator. The coordinator and the sites that are in the same partition as the coordinator follow the usual commit protocol, assuming that the sites in the other partitions have failed.

Thus, the major disadvantage of the 2PC protocol is that coordinator failure may result in blocking, where a decision either to commit or to abort T may have to be postponed until C_i recovers.

19.4.1.3 Recovery and Concurrency Control

When a failed site restarts, we can perform recovery by using, for example, the recovery algorithm described in Section 16.4. To deal with distributed commit protocols, the recovery procedure must treat **in-doubt transactions** specially; in-doubt transactions are transactions for which a <ready T> log record is found, but neither a <commit T> log record nor an <abort T> log record is found. The recovering site must determine the commit–abort status of such transactions by contacting other sites, as described in Section 19.4.1.2.

If recovery is done as just described, however, normal transaction processing at the site cannot begin until all in-doubt transactions have been committed or rolled back. Finding the status of in-doubt transactions can be slow, since multiple sites may have to be contacted. Further, if the coordinator has failed, and no other site has information about the commit–abort status of an incomplete transaction, recovery potentially could become blocked if 2PC is used. As a result, the site performing restart recovery may remain unusable for a long period.

To circumvent this problem, recovery algorithms typically provide support for noting lock information in the log. (We are assuming here that locking is used for concurrency control.) Instead of writing a <ready T> log record, the algorithm writes a <ready T, L> log record, where L is a list of all write locks held by the transaction T when the log record is written. At recovery time, after performing local recovery actions, for every in-doubt transaction T, all the write locks noted in the <ready T, L> log record (read from the log) are reacquired.

After lock reacquisition is complete for all in-doubt transactions, transaction processing can start at the site, even before the commit–abort status of the in-doubt transactions is determined. The commit or rollback of in-doubt transactions proceeds concurrently with the execution of new transactions. Thus, site recovery is faster, and never gets blocked. Note that new transactions that have a lock conflict with any write locks held by in-doubt transactions will be unable to make progress until the conflicting in-doubt transactions have been committed or rolled back.

19.4.2   Three-Phase Commit

The three-phase commit (3PC) protocol is an extension of the two-phase commit protocol that avoids the blocking problem under certain assumptions. In particular, it is assumed that no network partition occurs, and not more than k sites fail, where k is some predetermined number. Under these assumptions, the protocol avoids blocking by introducing an extra third phase where multiple sites are involved in the decision to commit. Instead of directly noting the commit decision in its persistent storage, the coordinator first ensures that at least k other sites know that it intended to commit the transaction. If the coordinator fails, the remaining sites first select a new coordinator. This new coordinator checks the status of the protocol from the remaining sites; if the coordinator had decided to commit, at least one of the other k sites that it informed will be up and will ensure that the commit decision is respected. The new coordinator restarts the third phase of the protocol if some site knew that the old coordinator intended to commit the transaction. Otherwise the new coordinator aborts the transaction.

While the 3PC protocol has the desirable property of not blocking unless k sites fail, it has the drawback that a partitioning of the network may appear to be the same as more than k sites failing, which would lead to blocking. The protocol also has to be implemented carefully to ensure that network partitioning (or more than k sites failing) does not result in inconsistencies, where a transaction is committed in one partition and aborted in another. Because of its overhead, the 3PC protocol is not widely used. See the bibliographical notes for references giving more details of the 3PC protocol.

19.4.3   Alternative Models of Transaction Processing

For many applications, the blocking problem of two-phase commit is not acceptable. The problem here is the notion of a single transaction that works across multiple sites. In this section, we describe how to use *persistent messaging* to avoid the problem of distributed commit, and then briefly outline the larger issue of *workflows*; workflows are considered in more detail in Section 26.2.

To understand persistent messaging, consider how one might transfer funds between two different banks, each with its own computer. One approach is to have a transaction span the two sites and use two-phase commit to ensure atomicity. However, the transaction may have to update the total bank balance, and blocking could have a serious impact on all other transactions at each bank, since almost all transactions at the bank would update the total bank balance.

In contrast, consider how funds transfer by a bank check occurs. The bank first deducts the amount of the check from the available balance and prints out a check. The check is then physically transferred to the other bank where it is deposited. After verifying the check, the bank increases the local balance by the amount of the check. The check constitutes a message sent between the two banks. So that funds are not lost or incorrectly increased, the check must not be lost, and must not be duplicated and deposited more than once. When the bank computers are connected by a network, persistent messages provide the same service as the check (but much faster, of course).

Persistent messages are messages that are guaranteed to be delivered to the recipient exactly once (neither less nor more), regardless of failures, if the transaction sending the message commits, and are guaranteed to not be delivered if the transaction aborts. Database recovery techniques are used to implement persistent messaging on top of the normal network channels, as we shall see shortly. In contrast, regular messages may be lost or may even be delivered multiple times in some situations.

Error handling is more complicated with persistent messaging than with two-phase commit. For instance, if the account where the check is to be deposited has been closed, the check must be sent back to the originating account and credited back there. Both sites must therefore be provided with error-handling code, along with code to handle the persistent messages. In contrast, with two-phase commit, the error would be detected by the transaction, which would then never deduct the amount in the first place.

The types of exception conditions that may arise depend on the application, so it is not possible for the database system to handle exceptions automatically. The application programs that send and receive persistent messages must include code to handle exception conditions and bring the system back to a consistent state. For instance, it is not acceptable to just lose the money being transferred if the receiving account has been closed; the money must be credited back to the originating account, and if that is not possible for some reason, humans must be alerted to resolve the situation manually.

There are many applications where the benefit of eliminating blocking is well worth the extra effort to implement systems that use persistent messages. In fact, few organizations would agree to support two-phase commit for transactions originating outside the organization, since failures could result in blocking of access to local data. Persistent messaging therefore plays an important role in carrying out transactions that cross organizational boundaries.

Workflows provide a general model of transaction processing involving multiple sites and possibly human processing of certain steps. For instance, when a bank receives a loan application, there are many steps it must take, including contacting external credit-checking agencies, before approving or rejecting a loan application. The steps, together, form a workflow. We study workflows in more detail in Section 26.2. We also note that persistent messaging forms the underlying basis for workflows in a distributed environment.

We now consider the **implementation** of persistent messaging. Persistent messaging can be implemented on top of an unreliable messaging infrastructure, which may lose messages or deliver them multiple times, by these protocols:

- **Sending site protocol**. When a transaction wishes to send a persistent message, it writes a record containing the message in a special relation *messages_to _send*, instead of directly sending out the message. The message is also given a unique message identifier.

  A *message delivery process* monitors the relation, and when a new message is found, it sends the message to its destination. The usual database concurrency-control mechanisms ensure that the system process reads the message only after the transaction that wrote the message commits; if the transaction aborts, the usual recovery mechanism would delete the message from the relation.

  The message delivery process deletes a message from the relation only after it receives an acknowledgment from the destination site. If it receives no acknowledgement from the destination site, after some time it sends the message again. It repeats this until an acknowledgment is received. In case of permanent failures, the system will decide, after some period of time, that the message is undeliverable. Exception handling code provided by the application is then invoked to deal with the failure.

  Writing the message to a relation and processing it only after the transaction commits ensures that the message will be delivered if and only if the transaction commits. Repeatedly sending it guarantees it will be delivered even if there are (temporary) system or network failures.

- **Receiving site protocol**. When a site receives a persistent message, it runs a transaction that adds the message to a special *received_messages* relation, provided it is not already present in the relation (the unique message identifier allows duplicates to be detected). After the transaction commits, or if the message was already present in the relation, the receiving site sends an acknowledgment back to the sending site.

  Note that sending the acknowledgment before the transaction commits is not safe, since a system failure may then result in loss of the message. Checking whether the message has been received earlier is essential to avoid multiple deliveries of the message.

  In many messaging systems, it is possible for messages to get delayed arbitrarily, although such delays are very unlikely. Therefore, to be safe, the message must never be deleted from the *received_messages* relation. Deleting it could result in a duplicate delivery not being detected. But as a result, the *received_messages* relation may grow indefinitely. To deal with this problem, each message is given a timestamp, and if the timestamp of a received message is older than some cutoff, the message is discarded. All messages recorded in the *received_messages* relation that are older than the cutoff can be deleted.

19.5   Concurrency Control in Distributed Databases

We show here how some of the concurrency-control schemes discussed in Chapter 15 can be modified so that they can be used in a distributed environment. We assume that each site participates in the execution of a commit protocol to ensure global transaction atomicity.

The protocols we describe in this section require updates to be done on all replicas of a data item. If any site containing a replica of a data item has failed, updates to the data item cannot be processed. In Section 19.6, we describe protocols that can continue transaction processing even if some sites or links have failed, thereby providing high availability.

19.5.1   Locking Protocols

The various locking protocols described in Chapter 15 can be used in a distributed environment. The only change that needs to be incorporated is in the way the lock manager deals with replicated data. We present several possible schemes that are applicable to an environment where data can be replicated in several sites. As in Chapter 15, we shall assume the existence of the *shared* and *exclusive* lock modes.

19.5.1.1   Single Lock-Manager Approach

In the **single lock-manager** approach, the system maintains a *single* lock manager that resides in a *single* chosen site—say S_i. All lock and unlock requests are made at site S_i. When a transaction needs to lock a data item, it sends a lock request to S_i. The lock manager determines whether the lock can be granted immediately. If the lock can be granted, the lock manager sends a message to that effect to the site at which the lock request was initiated. Otherwise, the request is delayed until it can be granted, at which time a message is sent to the site at which the lock request was initiated. The transaction can read the data item from *any* one of the sites at which a replica of the data item resides. In the case of a write, all the sites where a replica of the data item resides must be involved in the writing.

The scheme has these advantages:

- **Simple implementation**. This scheme requires two messages for handling lock requests and one message for handling unlock requests.

- **Simple deadlock handling**. Since all lock and unlock requests are made at one site, the deadlock-handling algorithms discussed in Chapter 15 can be applied directly.

The disadvantages of the scheme are:

- **Bottleneck**. The site S_i becomes a bottleneck, since all requests must be processed there.

- **Vulnerability**. If the site S_i fails, the concurrency controller is lost. Either processing must stop, or a recovery scheme must be used so that a backup site can take over lock management from S_i, as described in Section 19.6.5.

19.5.1.2   Distributed Lock Manager

A compromise between the advantages and disadvantages can be achieved through the **distributed-lock-manager** approach, in which the lock-manager function is distributed over several sites.

Each site maintains a local lock manager whose function is to administer the lock and unlock requests for those data items that are stored in that site. When a transaction wishes to lock a data item Q that is not replicated and resides at site S_i, a message is sent to the lock manager at site S_i requesting a lock (in a particular lock mode). If data item Q is locked in an incompatible mode, then the request is delayed until it can be granted. Once it has determined that the lock request can be granted, the lock manager sends a message back to the initiator indicating that it has granted the lock request.

We discuss several alternative ways of dealing with replication of data items in Sections 19.5.1.3 to 19.5.1.6.

The distributed-lock-manager scheme has the advantage of simple implementation, and reduces the degree to which the coordinator is a bottleneck. It has a reasonably low overhead, requiring two message transfers for handling lock requests, and one message transfer for handling unlock requests. However, deadlock handling is more complex, since the lock and unlock requests are no longer made at a single site: There may be intersite deadlocks even when there is no deadlock within a single site. The deadlock-handling algorithms discussed in Chapter 15 must be modified, as we shall discuss in Section 19.5.4, to detect global deadlocks.

19.5.1.3   Primary Copy

When a system uses data replication, we can choose one of the replicas as the **primary copy**. For each data item Q, the primary copy of Q must reside in precisely one site, which we call the **primary site** of Q.

When a transaction needs to lock a data item Q, it requests a lock at the primary site of Q. As before, the response to the request is delayed until it can be granted. The primary copy enables concurrency control for replicated data to be handled like that for unreplicated data. This similarity allows for a simple implementation. However, if the primary site of Q fails, Q is inaccessible, even though other sites containing a replica may be accessible.

19.5.1.4   Majority Protocol

The **majority protocol** works this way: If data item Q is replicated in n different sites, then a lock-request message must be sent to more than one-half of the n sites in which Q is stored. Each lock manager determines whether the lock can be granted immediately (as far as it is concerned). As before, the response is delayed until the request can be granted. The transaction does not operate on Q until it has successfully obtained a lock on a majority of the replicas of Q.

We assume for now that writes are performed on all replicas, requiring all sites containing replicas to be available. However, the major benefit of the majority protocol is that it can be extended to deal with site failures, as we shall see in Section 19.6.1. The protocol also deals with replicated data in a decentralized manner, thus avoiding the drawbacks of central control. However, it suffers from these disadvantages:

- **Implementation**. The majority protocol is more complicated to implement than are the previous schemes. It requires at least $2(n/2 + 1)$ messages for handling lock requests and at least $(n/2 + 1)$ messages for handling unlock requests.

- **Deadlock handling**. In addition to the problem of global deadlocks due to the use of a distributed-lock-manager approach, it is possible for a deadlock to occur even if only one data item is being locked. As an illustration, consider a system with four sites and full replication. Suppose that transactions T_1 and T_2 wish to lock data item Q in exclusive mode. Transaction T_1 may succeed in locking Q at sites S_1 and S_3, while transaction T_2 may succeed in locking Q at sites S_2 and S_4. Each then must wait to acquire the third lock; hence, a deadlock has occurred. Luckily, we can avoid such deadlocks with relative ease, by requiring all sites to request locks on the replicas of a data item in the same predetermined order.

19.5.1.5   Biased Protocol

The **biased protocol** is another approach to handling replication. The difference from the majority protocol is that requests for shared locks are given more favorable treatment than requests for exclusive locks.

- **Shared locks**. When a transaction needs to lock data item Q, it simply requests a lock on Q from the lock manager at one site that contains a replica of Q.

- **Exclusive locks**. When a transaction needs to lock data item Q, it requests a lock on Q from the lock manager at all sites that contain a replica of Q.

As before, the response to the request is delayed until it can be granted.

The biased scheme has the advantage of imposing less overhead on read operations than does the majority protocol. This savings is especially significant in common cases in which the frequency of read is much greater than the frequency of write. However, the additional overhead on writes is a disadvantage. Furthermore, the biased protocol shares the majority protocol's disadvantage of complexity in handling deadlock.

19.5.1.6   Quorum Consensus Protocol

The **quorum consensus** protocol is a generalization of the majority protocol. The quorum consensus protocol assigns each site a nonnegative weight. It assigns read and write operations on an item x two integers, called **read quorum** Q_r and **write quorum** Q_w, that must satisfy the following condition, where S is the total weight of all sites at which x resides:

$$Q_r + Q_w > S \text{ and } 2 * Q_w > S$$

To execute a read operation, enough replicas must be locked that their total weight is at least r. To execute a write operation, enough replicas must be locked so that their total weight is at least w.

A benefit of the quorum consensus approach is that it can permit the cost of either read or write locking to be selectively reduced by appropriately defining the read and write quorums. For instance, with a small read quorum, reads need to obtain fewer locks, but the write quorum will be higher, hence writes need to obtain more locks. Also, if higher weights are given to some sites (for example, those less likely to fail), fewer sites need to be accessed for acquiring locks. In fact, by setting weights and quorums appropriately, the quorum consensus protocol can simulate the majority protocol and the biased protocols.

Like the majority protocol, quorum consensus can be extended to work even in the presence of site failures, as we shall see in Section 19.6.1.

19.5.2   Timestamping

The principal idea behind the timestamping scheme in Section 15.4 is that each transaction is given a *unique* timestamp that the system uses in deciding the serialization order. Our first task, then, in generalizing the centralized scheme to a distributed scheme is to develop a scheme for generating unique timestamps. Then, the various protocols can operate directly to the nonreplicated environment.

There are two primary methods for generating unique timestamps, one centralized and one distributed. In the centralized scheme, a single site distributes the timestamps. The site can use a logical counter or its own local clock for this purpose.

In the distributed scheme, each site generates a unique local timestamp by using either a logical counter or the local clock. We obtain the unique global timestamp by concatenating the unique local timestamp with the site identifier, which also must be unique (Figure 19.3). The order of concatenation is important! We use the site identifier in the least significant position to ensure that the global timestamps generated in one site are not always greater than those generated in another site. Compare this technique for generating unique timestamps with the one that we presented in Section 19.2.3 for generating unique names.

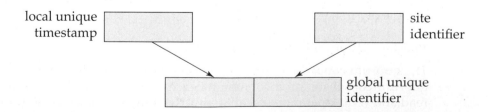

Figure 19.3   Generation of unique timestamps.

We may still have a problem if one site generates local timestamps at a rate faster than that of the other sites. In such a case, the fast site's logical counter will be larger than that of other sites. Therefore, all timestamps generated by the fast site will be larger than those generated by other sites. What we need is a mechanism to ensure that local timestamps are generated fairly across the system. We define within each site S_i a **logical clock** (LC_i), which generates the unique local timestamp. The logical clock can be implemented as a counter that is incremented after a new local timestamp is generated. To ensure that the various logical clocks are synchronized, we require that a site S_i advance its logical clock whenever a transaction T_i with timestamp $<x,y>$ visits that site and x is greater than the current value of LC_i. In this case, site S_i advances its logical clock to the value $x + 1$.

If the system clock is used to generate timestamps, then timestamps will be assigned fairly, provided that no site has a system clock that runs fast or slow. Since clocks may not be perfectly accurate, a technique similar to that for logical clocks must be used to ensure that no clock gets far ahead of or behind another clock.

19.5.3   Replication with Weak Degrees of Consistency

Many commercial databases today support replication, which can take one of several forms. With **master–slave replication**, the database allows updates at a primary site, and automatically propagates updates to replicas at other sites. Transactions may read the replicas at other sites, but are not permitted to update them.

An important feature of such replication is that transactions do not obtain locks at remote sites. To ensure that transactions running at the replica sites see a consistent (but perhaps outdated) view of the database, the replica should reflect a **transaction-consistent snapshot** of the data at the primary; that is, the replica should reflect all updates of transactions up to some transaction in the serialization order, and should not reflect any updates of later transactions in the serialization order.

The database may be configured to propagate updates immediately after they occur at the primary, or to propagate updates only periodically.

Master–slave replication is particularly useful for distributing information, for instance from a central office to branch offices of an organization. Another use for this form of replication is in creating a copy of the database to run large queries, so that queries do not interfere with transactions. Updates should be propagated periodically—every night, for example—so that update propagation does not interfere with query processing.

The Oracle database system supports a **create snapshot** statement, which can create a transaction-consistent snapshot copy of a relation, or set of relations, at a remote site. It also supports snapshot refresh, which can be done either by recomputing the snapshot or by incrementally updating it. Oracle supports automatic refresh, either continuously or at periodic intervals.

With **multimaster replication** (also called **update-anywhere replication**) updates are permitted at any replica of a data item, and are automatically propagated to all replicas. This model is the basic model used to manage replicas in distributed databases. Transactions update the local copy and the system updates other replicas transparently.

One way of updating replicas is to apply immediate update with two-phase commit, using one of the distributed concurrency-control techniques we have seen. Many database systems use the biased protocol, where writes have to lock and update all replicas and reads lock and read any one replica, as their currency-control technique.

Many database systems provide an alternative form of updating: They update at one site, with **lazy propagation** of updates to other sites, instead of immediately applying updates to all replicas as part of the transaction performing the update. Schemes based on lazy propagation allow transaction processing (including updates) to proceed even if a site is disconnected from the network, thus improving availability, but, unfortunately, do so at the cost of consistency. One of two approaches is usually followed when lazy propagation is used:

- Updates at replicas are translated into updates at a primary site, which are then propagated lazily to all replicas. This approach ensures that updates to an item are ordered serially, although serializability problems can occur, since transactions may read an old value of some other data item and use it to perform an update.

- Updates are performed at any replica and propagated to all other replicas. This approach can cause even more problems, since the same data item may be updated concurrently at multiple sites.

Some conflicts due to the lack of distributed concurrency control can be detected when updates are propagated to other sites (we shall see how in Section 25.5.4), but resolving the conflict involves rolling back committed transactions, and durability of committed transactions is therefore not guaranteed. Further, human intervention may be required to deal with conflicts. The above schemes should therefore be avoided or used with care.

19.5.4   Deadlock Handling

The deadlock-prevention and deadlock-detection algorithms in Chapter 15 can be used in a distributed system, provided that modifications are made. For example, we can use the tree protocol by defining a *global* tree among the system data items. Similarly, the timestamp-ordering approach could be directly applied to a distributed environment, as we saw in Section 19.5.2.

Deadlock prevention may result in unnecessary waiting and rollback. Furthermore, certain deadlock-prevention techniques may require more sites to be involved in the execution of a transaction than would otherwise be the case.

If we allow deadlocks to occur and rely on deadlock detection, the main problem in a distributed system is deciding how to maintain the wait-for graph.

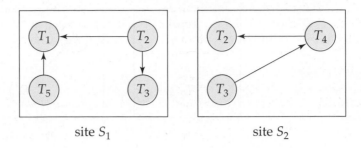

site S_1 site S_2

Figure 19.4 Local wait-for graphs.

Common techniques for dealing with this issue require that each site keep a **local wait-for graph**. The nodes of the graph correspond to all the transactions (local as well as nonlocal) that are currently either holding or requesting any of the items local to that site. For example, Figure 19.4 depicts a system consisting of two sites, each maintaining its local wait-for graph. Note that transactions T_2 and T_3 appear in both graphs, indicating that the transactions have requested items at both sites.

These local wait-for graphs are constructed in the usual manner for local transactions and data items. When a transaction T_i on site S_1 needs a resource in site S_2, it sends a request message to site S_2. If the resource is held by transaction T_j, the system inserts an edge $T_i \rightarrow T_j$ in the local wait-for graph of site S_2.

Clearly, if any local wait-for graph has a cycle, deadlock has occurred. On the other hand, the fact that there are no cycles in any of the local wait-for graphs does not mean that there are no deadlocks. To illustrate this problem, we consider the local wait-for graphs of Figure 19.4. Each wait-for graph is acyclic; nevertheless, a deadlock exists in the system because the *union* of the local wait-for graphs contains a cycle. This graph appears in Figure 19.5.

In the **centralized deadlock detection** approach, the system constructs and maintains a **global wait-for graph** (the union of all the local graphs) in a *single* site: the deadlock-detection coordinator. Since there is communication delay in the system, we must distinguish between two types of wait-for graphs. The *real* graph describes the real but unknown state of the system at any instance in time, as would be seen by an omniscient observer. The *constructed* graph is an

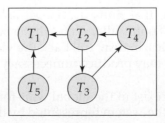

Figure 19.5 Global wait-for graph for Figure 19.4.

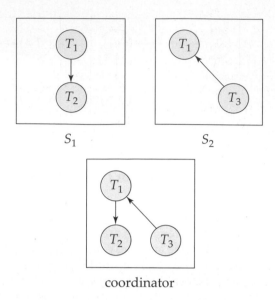

Figure 19.6   False cycles in the global wait-for graph.

approximation generated by the controller during the execution of the controller's algorithm. Obviously, the controller must generate the constructed graph in such a way that, whenever the detection algorithm is invoked, the reported results are correct. *Correct* means in this case that, if a deadlock exists, it is reported promptly, and if the system reports a deadlock, it is indeed in a deadlock state.

The global wait-for graph can be reconstructed or updated under these conditions:

- Whenever a new edge is inserted in or removed from one of the local wait-for graphs.

- Periodically, when a number of changes have occurred in a local wait-for graph.

- Whenever the coordinator needs to invoke the cycle-detection algorithm.

When the coordinator invokes the deadlock-detection algorithm, it searches its global graph. If it finds a cycle, it selects a victim to be rolled back. The coordinator must notify all the sites that a particular transaction has been selected as victim. The sites, in turn, roll back the victim transaction.

This scheme may produce unnecessary rollbacks if:

- **False cycles** exist in the global wait-for graph. As an illustration, consider a snapshot of the system represented by the local wait-for graphs of Figure 19.6. Suppose that T_2 releases the resource that it is holding in site S_1, resulting in the deletion of the edge $T_1 \rightarrow T_2$ in S_1. Transaction T_2 then requests a resource held by T_3 at site S_2, resulting in the addition of the edge $T_2 \rightarrow T_3$ in S_2. If the insert $T_2 \rightarrow T_3$ message from S_2 arrives before the remove $T_1 \rightarrow T_2$ message from S_1, the coordinator may discover the false cycle $T_1 \rightarrow T_2 \rightarrow T_3$ after the insert (but before the remove). Deadlock recovery may be initiated, although no deadlock has occurred.

Note that the false-cycle situation could not occur under two-phase locking. The likelihood of false cycles is usually sufficiently low that they do not cause a serious performance problem.

- A *deadlock* has indeed occurred and a victim has been picked, while one of the transactions was aborted for reasons unrelated to the deadlock. For example, suppose that site S_1 in Figure 19.4 decides to abort T_2. At the same time, the coordinator has discovered a cycle, and has picked T_3 as a victim. Both T_2 and T_3 are now rolled back, although only T_2 needed to be rolled back.

Deadlock detection can be done in a distributed manner, with several sites taking on parts of the task, instead of it being done at a single site. However, such algorithms are more complicated and more expensive. See the bibliographical notes for references to such algorithms.

19.6 Availability

One of the goals in using distributed databases is **high availability**; that is, the database must function almost all the time. In particular, since failures are more likely in large distributed systems, a distributed database must continue functioning even when there are various types of failures. The ability to continue functioning even during failures is referred to as **robustness**.

For a distributed system to be robust, it must *detect* failures, *reconfigure* the system so that computation may continue, and *recover* when a processor or a link is repaired.

The different types of failures are handled in different ways. For example, message loss is handled by retransmission. Repeated retransmission of a message across a link, without receipt of an acknowledgment, is usually a symptom of a link failure. The network usually attempts to find an alternative route for the message. Failure to find such a route is usually a symptom of network partition.

It is generally not possible, however, to differentiate clearly between site failure and network partition. The system can usually detect that a failure has occurred, but it may not be able to identify the type of failure. For example, suppose that site S_1 is not able to communicate with S_2. It could be that S_2 has failed. However, another possibility is that the link between S_1 and S_2 has failed, resulting in network partition. The problem is partly addressed by using multiple links between sites, so that even if one link fails the sites will remain connected. However, multiple link failure can still occur, so there are situations where we cannot be sure whether a site failure or network partition has occurred.

Suppose that site S_1 has discovered that a failure has occurred. It must then initiate a procedure that will allow the system to reconfigure, and to continue with the normal mode of operation.

- If transactions were active at a failed/inaccessible site at the time of the failure, these transactions should be aborted. It is desirable to abort such transactions promptly, since they may hold locks on data at sites that are still active; waiting for the failed/inaccessible site to become accessible again may impede other transactions at sites that are operational. However, in some cases, when data objects are replicated it may be possible to proceed with reads and updates even though some replicas are inaccessible. In this case, when a failed site recovers, if it had replicas of any data object, it must obtain the current values of these data objects, and must ensure that it receives all future updates. We address this issue in Section 19.6.1.

- If replicated data are stored at a failed/inaccessible site, the catalog should be updated so that queries do not reference the copy at the failed site. When a site rejoins, care must be taken to ensure that data at the site are consistent, as we shall see in Section 19.6.3.

- If a failed site is a central server for some subsystem, an *election* must be held to determine the new server (see Section 19.6.5). Examples of central servers include a name server, a concurrency coordinator, or a global deadlock detector.

Since it is, in general, not possible to distinguish between network link failures and site failures, any reconfiguration scheme must be designed to work correctly in case of a partitioning of the network. In particular, these situations must be avoided to ensure consistency:

- Two or more central servers are elected in distinct partitions.

- More than one partition updates a replicated data item.

Although traditional database systems place a premium on consistency, there are many applications today that value availability more than consistency. The design of replication protocols is different for such systems, and is discussed in Section 19.6.6.

19.6.1 Majority-Based Approach

The majority-based approach to distributed concurrency control in Section 19.5.1.4 can be modified to work in spite of failures. In this approach, each data object stores with it a version number to detect when it was last written. Whenever a transaction writes an object it also updates the version number in this way:

- If data object a is replicated in n different sites, then a lock-request message must be sent to more than one-half of the n sites at which a is stored. The transaction does not operate on a until it has successfully obtained a lock on a majority of the replicas of a.

- Read operations look at all replicas on which a lock has been obtained, and read the value from the replica that has the highest version number. (Optionally, they may also write this value back to replicas with lower version numbers.) Writes read all the replicas just like reads to find the highest version number (this step would normally have been performed earlier in the transaction by a read, and the result can be reused). The new version number is one more than the highest version number. The write operation writes all the replicas on which it has obtained locks, and sets the version number at all the replicas to the new version number.

Failures during a transaction (whether network partitions or site failures) can be tolerated as long as (1) the sites available at commit contain a majority of replicas of all the objects written to and (2) during reads, a majority of replicas are read to find the version numbers. If these requirements are violated, the transaction must be aborted. As long as the requirements are satisfied, the two-phase commit protocol can be used, as usual, on the sites that are available.

In this scheme, reintegration is trivial; nothing needs to be done. This is because writes would have updated a majority of the replicas, while reads will read a majority of the replicas and find at least one replica that has the latest version.

The version numbering technique used with the majority protocol can also be used to make the quorum consensus protocol work in the presence of failures. We leave the (straightforward) details to the reader. However, the danger of failures preventing the system from processing transactions increases if some sites are given higher weights.

19.6.2 Read One, Write All Available Approach

As a special case of quorum consensus, we can employ the biased protocol by giving unit weights to all sites, setting the read quorum to 1, and setting the write quorum to n (all sites). In this special case, there is no need to use version numbers; however, if even a single site containing a data item fails, no write to the item can proceed, since the write quorum will not be available. This protocol is called the **read one, write all** protocol since all replicas must be written.

To allow work to proceed in the event of failures, we would like to be able to use a **read one, write all available** protocol. In this approach, a read operation proceeds as in the **read one, write all** scheme; any available replica can be read, and a read lock is obtained at that replica. A write operation is shipped to all replicas; and write locks are acquired on all the replicas. If a site is down, the transaction manager proceeds without waiting for the site to recover.

While this approach appears very attractive, there are several complications. In particular, temporary communication failure may cause a site to appear to be unavailable, resulting in a write not being performed, but when the link is restored, the site is not aware that it has to perform some reintegration actions to catch up on writes it has lost. Further, if the network partitions, each partition may proceed to update the same data item, believing that sites in the other partitions are all dead.

The read one, write all available scheme can be used if there is never any network partitioning, but it can result in inconsistencies in the event of network partitions.

19.6.3   Site Reintegration

Reintegration of a repaired site or link into the system requires care. When a failed site recovers, it must initiate a procedure to update its system tables to reflect changes made while it was down. If the site had replicas of any data items, it must obtain the current values of these data items and ensure that it receives all future updates. Reintegration of a site is more complicated than it may seem to be at first glance, since there may be updates to the data items processed during the time that the site is recovering.

An easy solution is to halt the entire system temporarily while the failed site rejoins it. In most applications, however, such a temporary halt is unacceptably disruptive. Techniques have been developed to allow failed sites to reintegrate while concurrent updates to data items proceed concurrently. Before a read or write lock is granted on any data item, the site must ensure that it has caught up on all updates to the data item. If a failed link recovers, two or more partitions can be rejoined. Since a partitioning of the network limits the allowable operations by some or all sites, all sites should be informed promptly of the recovery of the link. See the bibliographical notes for more information on recovery in distributed systems.

19.6.4   Comparison with Remote Backup

Remote backup systems, which we studied in Section 16.9, and replication in distributed databases are two alternative approaches to providing high availability. The main difference between the two schemes is that with remote backup systems, actions such as concurrency control and recovery are performed at a single site, and only data and log records are replicated at the other site. In particular, remote backup systems help avoid two-phase commit, and its resultant overheads. Also, transactions need to contact only one site (the primary site), and thus avoid the overhead of running transaction code at multiple sites. Thus remote backup systems offer a lower-cost approach to high availability than replication.

On the other hand, replication can provide greater availability by having multiple replicas available and using the majority protocol.

19.6.5   Coordinator Selection

Several of the algorithms that we have presented require the use of a coordinator. If the coordinator fails because of a failure of the site at which it resides, the system can continue execution only by restarting a new coordinator on another site. One way to continue execution is by maintaining a backup to the coordinator, which is ready to assume responsibility if the coordinator fails.

A **backup coordinator** is a site that, in addition to other tasks, maintains enough information locally to allow it to assume the role of coordinator with minimal disruption to the distributed system. All messages directed to the coordinator are received by both the coordinator and its backup. The backup coordinator executes the same algorithms and maintains the same internal state information (such as, for a concurrency coordinator, the lock table) as does the actual coordinator. The only difference in function between the coordinator and its backup is that the backup does not take any action that affects other sites. Such actions are left to the actual coordinator.

In the event that the backup coordinator detects the failure of the actual coordinator, it assumes the role of coordinator. Since the backup has all the information available to it that the failed coordinator had, processing can continue without interruption.

The prime advantage to the backup approach is the ability to continue processing immediately. If a backup were not ready to assume the coordinator's responsibility, a newly appointed coordinator would have to seek information from all sites in the system so that it could execute the coordination tasks. Frequently, the only source of some of the requisite information is the failed coordinator. In this case, it may be necessary to abort several (or all) active transactions, and to restart them under the control of the new coordinator.

Thus, the backup-coordinator approach avoids a substantial amount of delay while the distributed system recovers from a coordinator failure. The disadvantage is the overhead of duplicate execution of the coordinator's tasks. Furthermore, a coordinator and its backup need to communicate regularly to ensure that their activities are synchronized.

In short, the backup-coordinator approach incurs overhead during normal processing to allow fast recovery from a coordinator failure.

In the absence of a designated backup coordinator, or in order to handle multiple failures, a new coordinator may be chosen dynamically by sites that are live. **Election algorithms** enable the sites to choose the site for the new coordinator in a decentralized manner. Election algorithms require that a unique identification number be associated with each active site in the system.

The **bully algorithm** for election works as follows: To keep the notation and the discussion simple, assume that the identification number of site S_i is i and that the chosen coordinator will always be the active site with the largest identification number. Hence, when a coordinator fails, the algorithm must elect the active site that has the largest identification number. The algorithm must send this number to each active site in the system. In addition, the algorithm must provide a mechanism by which a site recovering from a crash can identify the current coordinator. Suppose that site S_i sends a request that is not answered by the coordinator within a prespecified time interval T. In this situation, it is assumed that the coordinator has failed, and S_i tries to elect itself as the site for the new coordinator.

Site S_i sends an election message to every site that has a higher identification number. Site S_i then waits, for a time interval T, for an answer from any one of these sites. If it receives no response within time T, it assumes that all sites with numbers greater than i have failed, and it elects itself as the site for the new coordinator and sends a message to inform all active sites with identification numbers lower than i that it is the site at which the new coordinator resides.

If S_i does receive an answer, it begins a time interval T', to receive a message informing it that a site with a higher identification number has been elected. (Some other site is electing itself coordinator, and should report the results within time T'.) If S_i receives no message within T', then it assumes the site with a higher number has failed, and site S_i restarts the algorithm.

After a failed site recovers, it immediately begins execution of the same algorithm. If there are no active sites with higher numbers, the recovered site forces all sites with lower numbers to let it become the coordinator site, even if there is a currently active coordinator with a lower number. It is for this reason that the algorithm is termed the *bully* algorithm. If the network partitions, the bully algorithm elects a separate coordinator in each partition; to ensure that at most one coordinator is elected, winning sites should additionally verify that a majority of the sites are in their partition.

19.6.6   Trading Off Consistency for Availability

The protocols we have seen so far require a (weighted) majority of sites be in a partition for updates to proceed. Sites that are in a minority partition cannot process updates; if a network failure results in more than two partitions, no partition may have a majority of sites. Under such a situation, the system would be completely unavailable for updates, and depending on the read-quorum, may even become unavailable for reads. The write-all-available protocol which we saw earlier provides availability, but not consistency.

Ideally, we would like to have consistency and availability, even in the face of partitions. Unfortunately, this is not possible, a fact that is crystallized in the so-called **CAP theorem**, which states that any distributed database can have at most two of the following three properties:

- Consistency.
- Availability.
- Partition-tolerance.

The proof of the CAP theorem uses the following definition of consistency, with replicated data: an execution of a set of operations (reads and writes) on replicated data is said to be **consistent** if its result is the same as if the operations were executed on a single site, in some sequential order, and the sequential order is consistent with the ordering of operations issued by each process (transaction).

The notion of consistency is similar to atomicity of transactions, but with each operation treated as a transaction, and is weaker than the atomicity property of transactions.

In any large-scale distributed system, partitions cannot be prevented, and as a result either of availability or consistency has to be sacrificed. The schemes we have seen earlier sacrifice availability for consistency in the face of partitions.

Consider a Web-based social-networking system that replicates its data on three servers, and a network partition occurs that prevents the servers from communicating with each other. Since none of the partitions has a majority, it would not be possible to execute updates on any of the partitions. If one of these servers is in the same partition as a user, the user actually has access to data, but would be unable to update the data, since another user may be concurrently updating the same object in another partition, which could potentially lead to inconsistency. Inconsistency is not as great a risk in a social-networking system as in a banking database. A designer of such a system may decide that a user who can access the system should be allowed to perform updates on whatever replicas are accessible, even at the risk of inconsistency.

In contrast to systems such as banking databases that require the ACID properties, systems such as the social-networking system mentioned above are said to require the **BASE** properties:

- Basically available.

- Soft state.

- Eventually consistent.

The primary requirement is availability, even at the cost of consistency. Updates should be allowed, even in the event of partitioning, following for example the write-all-available protocol (which is similar to multimaster replication described in Section 19.5.3). Soft state refers to the property that the state of the database may not be precisely defined, with each replica possibly having a somewhat different state due to partitioning of the network. Eventually consistent is the requirement that once a partitioning is resolved, eventually all replicas will become consistent with each other.

This last step requires that inconsistent copies of data items be identified; if one is an earlier version of the other, the earlier version can be replaced by the later version. It is possible, however, that the two copies were the result of independent updates to a common base copy. A scheme for detecting such inconsistent updates, called the version-vector scheme, is described in Section 25.5.4.

Restoring consistency in the face of inconsistent updates requires that the updates be merged in some way that is meaningful to the application. This step cannot be handled by the database; instead the database detects and informs the application about the inconsistency, and the application then decides how to resolve the inconsistency.

19.7   Distributed Query Processing

In Chapter 13, we saw that there are a variety of methods for computing the answer to a query. We examined several techniques for choosing a strategy for processing a query that minimize the amount of time that it takes to compute the answer. For centralized systems, the primary criterion for measuring the cost of a particular strategy is the number of disk accesses. In a distributed system, we must take into account several other matters, including:

- The cost of data transmission over the network.

- The potential gain in performance from having several sites process parts of the query in parallel.

The relative cost of data transfer over the network and data transfer to and from disk varies widely depending on the type of network and on the speed of the disks. Thus, in general, we cannot focus solely on disk costs or on network costs. Rather, we must find a good trade-off between the two.

19.7.1   Query Transformation

Consider an extremely simple query: "Find all the tuples in the *account* relation." Although the query is simple—indeed, trivial—processing it is not trivial, since the *account* relation may be fragmented, replicated, or both, as we saw in Section 19.2. If the *account* relation is replicated, we have a choice of replica to make. If no replicas are fragmented, we choose the replica for which the transmission cost is lowest. However, if a replica is fragmented, the choice is not so easy to make, since we need to compute several joins or unions to reconstruct the *account* relation. In this case, the number of strategies for our simple example may be large. Query optimization by exhaustive enumeration of all alternative strategies may not be practical in such situations.

Fragmentation transparency implies that a user may write a query such as:

$$\sigma_{branch\_name\,=\,\text{"Hillside"}}\,(account)$$

Since *account* is defined as:

$$account_1\ \cup\ account_2$$

the expression that results from the name translation scheme is:

$$\sigma_{branch\_name\,=\,\text{"Hillside"}}\,(account_1\ \cup\ account_2)$$

Using the query-optimization techniques of Chapter 13, we can simplify the preceding expression automatically. The result is the expression:

$$\sigma_{branch\_name = \text{"Hillside"}} (account_1) \ \cup \ \sigma_{branch\_name = \text{"Hillside"}} (account_2)$$

which includes two subexpressions. The first involves only $account_1$, and thus can be evaluated at the Hillside site. The second involves only $account_2$, and thus can be evaluated at the Valleyview site.

There is a further optimization that can be made in evaluating:

$$\sigma_{branch\_name = \text{"Hillside"}} (account_1)$$

Since $account_1$ has only tuples pertaining to the Hillside branch, we can eliminate the selection operation. In evaluating:

$$\sigma_{branch\_name = \text{"Hillside"}} (account_2)$$

we can apply the definition of the $account_2$ fragment to obtain:

$$\sigma_{branch\_name = \text{"Hillside"}} (\sigma_{branch\_name = \text{"Valleyview"}} (account))$$

This expression is the empty set, regardless of the contents of the *account* relation.

Thus, our final strategy is for the Hillside site to return $account_1$ as the result of the query.

19.7.2 Simple Join Processing

As we saw in Chapter 13, a major decision in the selection of a query-processing strategy is choosing a join strategy. Consider the following relational-algebra expression:

$$account \bowtie depositor \bowtie branch$$

Assume that the three relations are neither replicated nor fragmented, and that *account* is stored at site S_1, *depositor* at S_2, and *branch* at S_3. Let S_I denote the site at which the query was issued. The system needs to produce the result at site S_I. Among the possible strategies for processing this query are these:

- Ship copies of all three relations to site S_I. Using the techniques of Chapter 13, choose a strategy for processing the entire query locally at site S_I.

- Ship a copy of the *account* relation to site S_2, and compute $temp_1 = account \bowtie depositor$ at S_2. Ship $temp_1$ from S_2 to S_3, and compute $temp_2 = temp_1 \bowtie branch$ at S_3. Ship the result $temp_2$ to S_I.

- Devise strategies similar to the previous one, with the roles of S_1, S_2, S_3 exchanged.

No one strategy is always the best one. Among the factors that must be considered are the volume of data being shipped, the cost of transmitting a block of data between a pair of sites, and the relative speed of processing at each site. Consider the first two strategies listed. Suppose indices present at S_2 and S_3 are useful for computing the join. If we ship all three relations to S_I, we would need to either re-create these indices at S_I, or use a different, possibly more expensive, join strategy. Re-creation of indices entails extra processing overhead and extra disk accesses. With the second strategy a potentially large relation (*account* $\bowtie$ *depositor*) must be shipped from S_2 to S_3. This relation repeats the name of a customer once for each account that the customer has. Thus, the second strategy may result in extra network transmission compared to the first strategy.

19.7.3   Semijoin Strategy

Suppose that we wish to evaluate the expression $r_1 \bowtie r_2$, where r_1 and r_2 are stored at sites S_1 and S_2, respectively. Let the schemas of r_1 and r_2 be R_1 and R_2. Suppose that we wish to obtain the result at S_1. If there are many tuples of r_2 that do not join with any tuple of r_1, then shipping r_2 to S_1 entails shipping tuples that fail to contribute to the result. We want to remove such tuples before shipping data to S_1, particularly if network costs are high.

A possible strategy to accomplish all this is:

1. Compute $temp_1 \leftarrow \Pi_{R_1 \cap R_2}(r_1)$ at S_1.
2. Ship $temp_1$ from S_1 to S_2.
3. Compute $temp_2 \leftarrow r_2 \bowtie temp_1$ at S_2.
4. Ship $temp_2$ from S_2 to S_1.
5. Compute $r_1 \bowtie temp_2$ at S_1. The resulting relation is the same as $r_1 \bowtie r_2$.

Before considering the efficiency of this strategy, let us verify that the strategy computes the correct answer. In step 3, $temp_2$ has the result of $r_2 \bowtie \Pi_{R_1 \cap R_2}(r_1)$. In step 5, we compute:

$$r_1 \bowtie r_2 \bowtie \Pi_{R_1 \cap R_2}(r_1)$$

Since join is associative and commutative, we can rewrite this expression as:

$$(r_1 \bowtie \Pi_{R_1 \cap R_2}(r_1)) \bowtie r_2$$

Since $r_1 \bowtie \Pi_{(R_1 \cap R_2)}(r_1) = r_1$, the expression is, indeed, equal to $r_1 \bowtie r_2$, the expression we are trying to evaluate.

This strategy is particularly advantageous when relatively few tuples of r_2 contribute to the join. This situation is likely to occur if r_1 is the result of a relational-algebra expression involving selection. In such a case, $temp_2$ may have significantly fewer tuples than r_2. The cost savings of the strategy result from having to ship only $temp_2$, rather than all of r_2, to S_1. Additional cost is incurred in shipping $temp_1$ to S_2. If a sufficiently small fraction of tuples in r_2 contribute to the join, the overhead of shipping $temp_1$ will be dominated by the savings of shipping only a fraction of the tuples in r_2.

This strategy is called a **semijoin strategy**, after the semijoin operator of the relational algebra, denoted $\ltimes$. The semijoin of r_1 with r_2, denoted $r_1 \ltimes r_2$, is:

$$\Pi_{R_1}(r_1 \bowtie r_2)$$

Thus, $r_1 \ltimes r_2$ selects those tuples of relation r_1 that contributed to $r_1 \bowtie r_2$. In step 3, $temp_2 = r_2 \ltimes r_1$.

For joins of several relations, this strategy can be extended to a series of semijoin steps. A substantial body of theory has been developed regarding the use of semijoins for query optimization. Some of this theory is referenced in the bibliographical notes.

19.7.4   Join Strategies that Exploit Parallelism

Consider a join of four relations:

$$r_1 \bowtie r_2 \bowtie r_3 \bowtie r_4$$

where relation r_i is stored at site S_i. Assume that the result must be presented at site S_1. There are many possible strategies for parallel evaluation. (We studied the issue of parallel processing of queries in detail in Chapter 18.) In one such strategy, r_1 is shipped to S_2, and $r_1 \bowtie r_2$ computed at S_2. At the same time, r_3 is shipped to S_4, and $r_3 \bowtie r_4$ computed at S_4. Site S_2 can ship tuples of $(r_1 \bowtie r_2)$ to S_1 as they are produced, rather than wait for the entire join to be computed. Similarly, S_4 can ship tuples of $(r_3 \bowtie r_4)$ to S_1. Once tuples of $(r_1 \bowtie r_2)$ and $(r_3 \bowtie r_4)$ arrive at S_1, the computation of $(r_1 \bowtie r_2) \bowtie (r_3 \bowtie r_4)$ can begin, with the pipelined join technique of Section 12.7.2.2. Thus, computation of the final join result at S_1 can be done in parallel with the computation of $(r_1 \bowtie r_2)$ at S_2, and with the computation of $(r_3 \bowtie r_4)$ at S_4.

19.8   Heterogeneous Distributed Databases

Many new database applications require data from a variety of preexisting databases located in a heterogeneous collection of hardware and software environments. Manipulation of information located in a heterogeneous distributed database requires an additional software layer on top of existing database systems. This software layer is called a **multidatabase system**. The local database systems may employ different logical models and data-definition and data-manipulation languages, and may differ in their concurrency-control and transaction-management mechanisms. A multidatabase system creates the illusion of logical database integration without requiring physical database integration.

Full integration of heterogeneous systems into a homogeneous distributed database is often difficult or impossible:

- **Technical difficulties.** The investment in application programs based on existing database systems may be huge, and the cost of converting these applications may be prohibitive.

- **Organizational difficulties.** Even if integration is *technically* possible, it may not be *politically* possible, because the existing database systems belong to different corporations or organizations. In such cases, it is important for a multidatabase system to allow the local database systems to retain a high degree of **autonomy** over the local database and transactions running against that data.

For these reasons, multidatabase systems offer significant advantages that outweigh their overhead. In this section, we provide an overview of the challenges faced in constructing a multidatabase environment from the standpoint of data definition and query processing.

19.8.1   Unified View of Data

Each local database management system may use a different data model. For instance, some may employ the relational model, whereas others may employ older data models, such as the network model (see Appendix D) or the hierarchical model (see Appendix E).

Since the multidatabase system is supposed to provide the illusion of a single, integrated database system, a common data model must be used. A commonly used choice is the relational model, with SQL as the common query language. Indeed, there are several systems available today that allow SQL queries to a nonrelational database-management system.

Another difficulty is the provision of a common conceptual schema. Each local system provides its own conceptual schema. The multidatabase system must integrate these separate schemas into one common schema. Schema integration is a complicated task, mainly because of the semantic heterogeneity.

Schema integration is not simply straightforward translation between data-definition languages. The same attribute names may appear in different local databases but with different meanings. The data types used in one system may not be supported by other systems, and translation between types may not be simple. Even for identical data types, problems may arise from the physical representation of data: One system may use 8-bit ASCII, another 16-bit Unicode, and yet another EBCDIC; floating-point representations may differ; integers may be represented in *big-endian* or *little-endian* form. At the semantic level, an integer value for length may be inches in one system and millimeters in another, thus creating an awkward situation in which equality of integers is only an approximate notion (as is always the case for floating-point numbers). The same name may appear in different languages in different systems. For example, a system based in the United States may refer to the city "Cologne," whereas one in Germany refers to it as "Köln."

All these seemingly minor distinctions must be properly recorded in the common global conceptual schema. Translation functions must be provided. Indices must be annotated for system-dependent behavior (for example, the sort order of nonalphanumeric characters is not the same in ASCII as in EBCDIC). As we noted earlier, the alternative of converting each database to a common format may not be feasible without obsoleting existing application programs.

19.8.2 Query Processing

Query processing in a heterogeneous database can be complicated. Some of the issues are:

- Given a query on a global schema, the query may have to be translated into queries on local schemas at each of the sites where the query has to be executed. The query results have to be translated back into the global schema.

  The task is simplified by writing **wrappers** for each data source, which provide a view of the local data in the global schema. Wrappers also translate queries on the global schema into queries on the local schema, and translate results back into the global schema. Wrappers may be provided by individual sites, or may be written separately as part of the multidatabase system.

  Wrappers can even be used to provide a relational view of nonrelational data sources, such as Web pages (possibly with forms interfaces), flat files, hierarchical and network databases, and directory systems.

- Some data sources may provide only limited query capabilities; for instance, they may support selections, but not joins. They may even restrict the form of selections, allowing selections only on certain fields; Web data sources with form interfaces are an example of such data sources. Queries may therefore have to be broken up, to be partly performed at the data source and partly at the site issuing the query.

- In general, more than one site may need to be accessed to answer a given query. Answers retrieved from the sites may have to be processed to remove duplicates. Suppose one site contains *account* tuples satisfying the selection $balance < 100$, while another contains *account* tuples satisfying $balance > 50$. A query on the entire account relation would require access to both sites and removal of duplicate answers resulting from tuples with balance between 50 and 100, which are replicated at both sites.

- Global query optimization in a heterogeneous database is difficult, since the query execution system may not know what the costs are of alternative query plans at different sites. The usual solution is to rely on only local-level optimization, and just use heuristics at the global level.

Mediator systems are systems that integrate multiple heterogeneous data sources, providing an integrated global view of the data and providing query facilities on the global view. Unlike full-fledged multidatabase systems, mediator systems do not bother about transaction processing. (The terms mediator and multidatabase are often used in an interchangeable fashion, and systems that are called mediators may support limited forms of transactions.) The term **virtual**

database is used to refer to multidatabase/mediator systems, since they provide the appearance of a single database with a global schema, although data exist on multiple sites in local schemas.

19.8.3 Transaction Management in Multidatabases

A multidatabase system supports two types of transactions:

1. **Local transactions**. These transactions are executed by each local database system outside of the multidatabase system's control.

2. **Global transactions**. These transactions are executed under the multidatabase system's control.

The multidatabase system is aware of the fact that local transactions may run at the local sites, but it is not aware of what specific transactions are being executed, or of what data they may access.

Ensuring the local autonomy of each database system requires that no changes be made to its software. A database system at one site thus is not able to communicate directly with one at any other site to synchronize the execution of a global transaction active at several sites.

Since the multidatabase system has no control over the execution of local transactions, each local system must use a concurrency-control scheme (for example, two-phase locking or timestamping) to ensure that its schedule is serializable. In addition, in case of locking, the local system must be able to guard against the possibility of local deadlocks.

The guarantee of local serializability is not sufficient to ensure global serializability. As an illustration, consider two global transactions T_1 and T_2, each of which accesses and updates two data items, A and B, located at sites S_1 and S_2, respectively. Suppose that the local schedules are serializable. It is still possible to have a situation where, at site S_1, T_2 follows T_1, whereas, at S_2, T_1 follows T_2, resulting in a nonserializable global schedule. Indeed, even if there is no concurrency among global transactions (that is, a global transaction is submitted only after the previous one commits or aborts), local serializability is not sufficient to ensure global serializability (see Practice Exercise 19.14).

Depending on the implementation of the local database systems, a global transaction may not be able to control the precise locking behavior of its local subtransactions. Thus, even if all local database systems follow two-phase locking, it may be possible only to ensure that each local transaction follows the rules of the protocol. For example, one local database system may commit its subtransaction and release locks, while the subtransaction at another local system is still executing. If the local systems permit control of locking behavior and all systems follow two-phase locking, then the multidatabase system can ensure that global transactions lock in a two-phase manner and the lock points of conflicting transactions would then define their global serialization order. If different local systems follow different concurrency-control mechanisms, however, this straightforward sort of global control does not work.

There are many protocols for ensuring consistency despite concurrent execution of global and local transactions in multidatabase systems. Some are based on imposing sufficient conditions to ensure global serializability. Others ensure only a form of consistency weaker than serializability, but achieve this consistency by less restrictive means. Section 26.6 describes approaches to consistency without serializability; other approaches are cited in the bibliographical notes.

Early multidatabase systems restricted global transactions to be read only. They thus avoided the possibility of global transactions introducing inconsistency to the data, but were not sufficiently restrictive to ensure global serializability. It is indeed possible to get such global schedules and to develop a scheme to ensure global serializability, and we ask you to do both in Practice Exercise 19.15.

There are a number of general schemes to ensure global serializability in an environment where update as well as read-only transactions can execute. Several of these schemes are based on the idea of a **ticket**. A special data item called a ticket is created in each local database system. Every global transaction that accesses data at a site must write the ticket at that site. This requirement ensures that global transactions conflict directly at every site they visit. Furthermore, the global transaction manager can control the order in which global transactions are serialized, by controlling the order in which the tickets are accessed. References to such schemes appear in the bibliographical notes.

If we want to ensure global serializability in an environment where no direct local conflicts are generated in each site, some assumptions must be made about the schedules allowed by the local database system. For example, if the local schedules are such that the commit order and serialization order are always identical, we can ensure serializability by controlling only the order in which transactions commit.

A related problem in multidatabase systems is that of global atomic commit. If all local systems follow the two-phase commit protocol, that protocol can be used to achieve global atomicity. However, local systems not designed to be part of a distributed system may not be able to participate in such a protocol. Even if a local system is capable of supporting two-phase commit, the organization owning the system may be unwilling to permit waiting in cases where blocking occurs. In such cases, compromises may be made that allow for lack of atomicity in certain failure modes. Further discussion of these matters appears in the literature (see the bibliographical notes).

19.9 Cloud-Based Databases

Cloud computing is a relatively new concept in computing that emerged in the late 1990s and the 2000s, first under the name *software as a service*. Initial vendors of software services provided specific customizable applications that they hosted on their own machines. The concept of cloud computing developed as vendors began to offer generic computers as a service on which clients could run software applications of their choosing. A client can make arrangements with a cloud-computing vendor to obtain a certain number of machines of a certain capacity as well as a certain amount of data storage. Both the number of machines and the amount of storage can grow and shrink as needed. In addition to providing computing services, many vendors also provide other services such as data storage services, map services, and other services that can be accessed using a Web-service application programming interface.

Many enterprises are finding the model of cloud computing and services beneficial. It saves client enterprises the need to maintain a large system-support staff and allows new enterprises to begin operation without having to make a large, up-front capital investment in computing systems. Further, as the needs of the enterprise grow, more resources (computing and storage) can be added as required; the cloud-computing vendor generally has very large clusters of computers, making it easy for the vendor to allocate resources on demand.

A variety of vendors offer cloud services. They include traditional computing vendors as well as companies, such as Amazon and Google, that are seeking to leverage the large infrastructure they have in place for their core businesses.

Web applications that need to store and retrieve data for very large numbers of users (ranging from millions to hundreds of millions) have been a major driver of cloud-based databases. The needs of these applications differ from those of traditional database applications, since they value availability and scalability over consistency. Several cloud-based data-storage systems have been developed in recent years to serve the needs of such applications. We discuss issues in building such data-storage systems on the cloud in Section 19.9.1.

In Section 19.9.2, we consider issues in running traditional database systems on a cloud. Cloud-based databases have features of both homogeneous and heterogeneous systems. Although the data are owned by one organization (the client) and are part of one unified distributed database, the underlying computers are owned and operated by another organization (the service vendor). The computers are remote from the client's location(s) and are accessed over the Internet. As a result, some of the challenges of heterogeneous distributed systems remain, particularly as regards transaction processing. However, many of the organizational and political challenges of heterogeneous systems are avoided.

Finally, in Section 19.9.3, we discuss several technical as well as nontechnical challenges that cloud databases face today.

19.9.1   Data Storage Systems on the Cloud

Applications on the Web have extremely high scalability requirements. Popular applications have hundreds of millions of users, and many applications have seen their load increase manyfold within a single year, or even within a few months. To handle the data management needs of such applications, data must be partitioned across thousands of processors.

A number of systems for data storage on the cloud have been developed and deployed over the past few years to address data management requirements of such applications; these include *Bigtable* from Google, *Simple Storage Service* (*S3*) from Amazon, which provides a Web interface to *Dynamo*, which is a key-value storage system, *Cassandra*, from FaceBook, which is similar to Bigtable, and

Sherpa/*PNUTS* from Yahoo!, the data storage component of the *Azure* environment from Microsoft, and several other systems.

In this section, we provide an overview of the architecture of such data-storage systems. Although some people refer to these systems as distributed database systems, they do not provide many of the features which are viewed as standard on database systems today, such as support for SQL, or for transactions with the ACID properties.

19.9.1.1 Data Representation

As an example of data management needs of Web applications, consider the profile of a user, which needs to be accessible to a number of different applications that are run by an organization. The profile contains a variety of attributes, and there are frequent additions to the attributes stored in the profile. Some attributes may contain complex data. A simple relational representation is often not sufficient for such complex data.

Some cloud-based data-storage systems support XML (described in Chapter 23) for representing such complex data. Others support the **JavaScript Object Notation** (**JSON**) representation, which has found increasing acceptance for representing complex data. The XML and JSON representations provide flexibility in the set of attributes that a record contains, as well as the types of these attributes. Yet others, such as Bigtable, define their own data model for complex data including support for records with a very large number of optional columns. We revisit the Bigtable data model later in this section.

Further, many such Web applications either do not need extensive query language support, or at least, can manage without such support. The primary mode of data access is to store data with an associated key, and to retrieve data with that key. In the above user profile example, the key for user-profile data would be the user's identifier. There are applications that conceptually require joins, but implement the joins by a form of view materialization. For example, in a social-networking application, each user should be shown new posts from all her friends. Unfortunately, finding the set of friends and then querying each one to find their posts may lead to a significant amount of delay when the data are distributed across a large number of machines. An alternative is as follows: whenever a user makes a post, a message is sent to all friends of that user, and the data associated with each of the friends is updated with a summary of the new post. When that user checks for updates, all required data are available in one place and can be retrieved quickly.

Thus, cloud data-storage systems are, at their core, based on two primitive functions, put(key, value), used to store values with an associated key, and get(key), which retrieves the stored value associated with the specified key. Some systems such as Bigtable additionally provide range queries on key values.

In Bigtable, a record is not stored as a single value, but is instead split into component attributes that are stored separately. Thus, the key for an attribute value conceptually consists of (record-identifier, attribute-name). Each attribute value is just a string as far as Bigtable is concerned. To fetch all attributes of a

JSON

JavaScript Object Notation, or JSON, is a textual representation of complex data types which is widely used for transmitting data between applications, as well as to store complex data. JSON supports the primitive data types integer, real and string, as well as arrays, and "objects", which are a collection of (attribute-name, value) pairs. An example of a JSON object is:

```
{
    "ID": "22222",
    "name": {
        "firstname: "Albert",
        "lastname: "Einstein"
    },
    "deptname": "Physics",
    "children": [
        { "firstname": "Hans", "lastname": "Einstein" },
        { "firstname": "Eduard", "lastname": "Einstein" }
    ]
}
```

The above example illustrates objects, which contain (attribute-name, value) pairs, as well as arrays, delimited by square brackets. JSON can be viewed as a simplified form of XML; XML is covered in Chapter 23.

Libraries have been developed to transform data between the JSON representation and the object representation used in the JavaScript and PHP scripting languages, as well as other programming languages.

record, a range query, or more precisely a prefix-match query consisting of just the record identifier, is used. The get() function returns the attribute names along with the values. For efficient retrieval of all attributes of a record, the storage system stores entries sorted by the key, so all attribute values of a particular record are clustered together.

In fact, the record identifier can itself be structured hierarchically, although to Bigtable itself the record identifier is just a string. For example, an application that stores pages retrieved from a web crawl could map a URL of the form:

www.cs.yale.edu/people/silberschatz.html

to the record identifier:

edu.yale.cs.www/people/silberschatz.html

so that pages are clustered in a useful order. As another example, the record shown in the JSON example (see example box on JSON) can be represented by a record with identifier "22222", with multiple attribute names such as "name.firstname", "deptname", "children[1].firstname" or "children[2].lastname".

Further, a single instance of Bigtable can store data for multiple applications, with multiple tables per application, by simply prefixing the application name and table name to the record identifier.

Data-storage systems typically allow multiple versions of data items to be stored. Versions are often identified by timestamp, but may be alternatively identified by an integer value that is incremented whenever a new version of a data item is created. Lookups can specify the required version of a data item, or can pick the version with the highest version number. In Bigtable, for example, a key actually consists of three parts: (record-identifier, attribute-name, timestamp).

19.9.1.2 Partitioning and Retrieving Data

Partitioning of data is, of course, the key to handling extremely large scale in data-storage systems. Unlike regular parallel databases, it is usually not possible to decide on a partitioning function ahead of time. Further, if load increases, more servers need to be added and each server should be able to take on parts of the load incrementally.

To solve both these problems, data-storage systems typically partition data into relatively small units (small on such systems may mean of the order of hundreds of megabytes). These partitions are often called **tablets**, reflecting the fact that each tablet is a fragment of a table. The partitioning of data should be done on the search key, so that a request for a specific key value is directed to a single tablet; otherwise each request would require processing at multiple sites, increasing the load on the system greatly. Two approaches are used: either range partitioning is used directly on the key, or a hash function is applied on the key, and range partitioning is applied on the result of the hash function.

The site to which a tablet is assigned acts as the master site for that tablet. All updates are routed through this site, and updates are then propagated to replicas of the tablet. Lookups are also sent to the same site, so that reads are consistent with writes.

The partitioning of data into tablets is not fixed up front, but happens dynamically. As data are inserted, if a tablet grows too big, it is broken into smaller parts. Further, even if a tablet is not large enough to merit being broken up, if the load (get/put operations) on that tablet are excessive, the tablet may be broken into smaller tablets, which can be distributed across two or more sites to share the load. Usually the number of tablets is much larger than the number of sites, for the same reason that virtual partitioning is used in parallel databases.

It is important to know which site in the overall system is responsible for a particular tablet. This can be done by having a tablet controller site which tracks the partitioning function, to map a get() request to one or more tablets, and a mapping function from tablets to sites, to find which site were responsible for which tablet. Each request coming into the system must be routed to the correct site; if a single tablet controller site is responsible for this task, it would soon

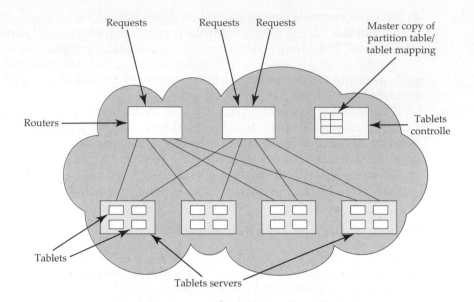

Figure 19.7   Architecture of a cloud data storage system.

get overloaded. Instead, the mapping information can be replicated on a set of router sites, which route requests to the site with the appropriate tablet. Protocols to update mapping information when a tablet is split or moved are designed in such a way that no locking is used; a request may as a result end up at a wrong site. The problem is handled by detecting that the site is no longer responsible for the key specified by the request, and rerouting the request based on up-to-date mapping information.

Figure 19.7 depicts the architecture of a cloud data-storage system, based loosely on the PNUTS architecture. Other systems provide similar functionality, although their architecture may vary. For example, Bigtable does not have separate routers; the partitioning and tablet-server mapping information is stored in the Google file system, and clients read the information from the file system, and decide where to send their requests.

19.9.1.3   Transactions and Replication

Data-storage systems on the cloud typically do not fully support ACID transactions. The cost of two-phase commit is too high, and two-phase commit can lead to blocking in the event of failures, which is not acceptable to typical Web applications. This means that such systems typically do not even support a transactionally consistent secondary index: the secondary index would be partitioned on a different attribute from the key used for storing the data, and an insert or update would then need to update two sites, which would require two-phase commit. At best, such systems support transactions on data within a single tablet, which is controlled by a a single master site. Sherpa/PNUTS also provides a test-

and-set function, which allows an update to a data item to be conditional on the current version of the data item being the same as a specified version number. If the current version number of the data item is more recent than the specified version number, the update is not performed. The test-and-set function can be used by applications to implement a limited form of validation-based concurrency control, with validation restricted to data items in a single tablet.

In a system with thousands of sites, at any time it is almost guaranteed that several of the sites will be down. A data-storage system on the cloud must be able to continue normal processing even with many sites down. Such systems replicate data (such as tablets) to multiple machines in a cluster, so that a copy of the data is likely to be available even if some machines of a cluster are down. (A **cluster** is a collection of machines in a data center.) For example, the *Google File System* (GFS), which is a distributed fault-tolerant file system, replicates all file system blocks at three or more nodes in a cluster. Normal operation can continue as long as at least one copy of the data is available (key system data, such as the mapping of files to nodes, is replicated at more nodes, a majority of which need to be available). In addition, replication is also used across geographically distributed clusters, for reasons that we shall see shortly.

Since each tablet is controlled by a single master site, if the site fails the tablet should be reassigned to a different site that has a copy of the tablet, which becomes the new master site for the tablet. Updates to a tablet are logged, and the log is itself replicated. When a site fails, the tablets at the site are assigned to other sites; the new master site of each tablet is responsible for performing recovery actions using the log to bring its copy of the tablet to an up-to-date consistent state, after which updates and lookups can be performed on the tablet.

In Bigtable, as an example, mapping information is stored in an index structure, and the index as well as the actual tablet data are stored in the file system. Tablet data updates are not flushed immediately, but log data are. The file system ensures that the file system data are replicated and will be available even in the face of failure of a few nodes in the cluster. Thus, when a tablet is reassigned, the new master site for the tablet has access to up-to-date log data. Yahoo!'s Sherpa/PNUTS system, on the other hand, explicitly replicates tablets to multiple nodes in a cluster, instead of using a distributed file system, and uses a reliable distributed-messaging system to implement a highly available log.

Unfortunately, it is not uncommon for an entire data center to become unavailable-for example, due to natural disasters or fires. Replication at a remote site is therefore essential for high availability. For many Web applications, round-trip delays across a long-distance network can affect performance significantly, a problem that is increasing with the use of Ajax applications that require multiple rounds of communication between the browser and the application. To deal with this problem, users are connected with application servers that are closest to them geographically, and data are replicated at multiple data centers so that one of the replicas is likely to be close to the application server.

However, the danger of partitioning of the network is increased as a result. Given that most Web applications place a greater premium on availability than on consistency, data-storage systems on the cloud usually allow updates to proceed even in the event of a partitioning, and provide support for restoring consistency later, as discussed earlier in Section 19.6.6. Multimaster replication with lazy propagation of updates, which we saw in Section 19.5.3, is typically used for processing updates. Lazy propagation implies that updates are not propagated to replicas as part of the updating transaction, although they are typically propagated as soon as possible, typically using a messaging infrastructure.

In addition to propagating updates to replicas of a data item, updates to secondary indices, or to certain kinds of materialized views (such as the updates from friends, in a social-networking application we saw earlier in Section 19.9.1.1), can be sent using the messaging infrastructure. Secondary indices are basically tables, partitioned just like regular tables, based on the index search key; an update of a record in a table can be mapped to updates of one or more tablets in a secondary index on the table. There is no transactional guarantee on the updates of such secondary indices or materialized views, and only a best-effort guarantee in terms of when the updates reach their destination.

19.9.2 Traditional Databases on the Cloud

We now consider the issue of implementing a traditional distributed database system, supporting ACID properties and queries, on a cloud.

The concept of computing utilities is an old one, envisioned back in the 1960s. The first manifestation of the concept was in timesharing systems in which several users shared access to a single mainframe computer. Later, in the late 1960s, the concept of **virtual machines** was developed, in which a user was given the illusion of having a private computer, while in reality a single computer simulated several virtual machines.

Cloud computing makes extensive use of the virtual-machine concept to provide computing services. Virtual machines provide great flexibility since clients may choose their own software environment including not only the application software but also the operating system. Virtual machines of several clients can run on a single physical computer, if the computing needs of the clients are low. On the other hand, an entire computer can be allocated to each virtual machine of a client whose virtual machines have a high load. A client may request several virtual machines over which to run an application. This makes it easy to add or subtract computing power as workloads grow and shrink simply by adding or releasing virtual machines.

Having a set of virtual machines works well for applications that are easily parallelized. Database systems, as we have seen, fall into this category. Each virtual machine can run database system code locally and behave in a manner similar to a site in a homogeneous distributed database system.

19.9.3 Challenges with Cloud-Based Databases

Cloud-based databases certainly have several important advantages compared to building a computing infrastructure from scratch, and are in fact essential for certain applications.

However, cloud-based database systems also have several disadvantages that we shall now explore. Unlike purely computational applications in which parallel computations run largely independently, distributed database systems require frequent communication and coordination among sites for:

- access to data on another physical machine, either because the data are owned by another virtual machine or because the data are stored on a storage server separate from the computer hosting the virtual machine.

- obtaining locks on remote data.

- ensuring atomic transaction commit via two-phase commit.

In our earlier study of distributed databases, we assumed (implicitly) that the database administrator had control over the physical location of data. In a cloud system, the physical location of data is under the control of the vendor, not the client. As a result, the physical placement of data may be suboptimal in terms of communication cost, and this may result in a large number of remote lock requests and large transfers of data across virtual machines. Effective query optimization requires that the optimizer have accurate cost measures for operations. Lacking knowledge of the physical placement of data, the optimizer has to rely on estimates that may be highly inaccurate, resulting in poor execution strategies. Because remote accesses are relatively slow compared to local access, these issues can have a significant impact on performance.

The above issues are a particular challenge for implementing traditional database applications on the cloud, although less challenging for simple data-storage systems. The next few challenges we discuss apply equally to both application scenarios.

The matter of replication further complicates cloud-based data management. Cloud systems replicate client data for availability. Indeed many contracts have clauses imposing penalties on the vendor if a certain level of availability is not maintained. This replication is done by the vendor without specific knowledge of the application. Since replication is under control of the cloud and not under the control of the database system, care must be used when the database system accesses data so as to ensure that the latest versions of the data are read. Failure to take these issues properly into account can result in a loss of the atomicity or isolation properties. In many current cloud database applications, the application itself may need to take some responsibility for consistency.

Users of cloud computing must be willing to accept that their data are held by another organization. This may present a variety of risks in terms of security and legal liability. If the cloud vendor suffers a security breach, client data may be divulged, causing the client to face legal challenges from its customers. Yet the client has no direct control over cloud-vendor security. These issues become more complex if the cloud vendor chooses to store data (or replicas of data) in a foreign country. Various legal jurisdictions differ in their privacy laws. So, for example, if a German company's data are replicated on a server in New York, then the privacy laws of the United States rather than those of Germany or the

European Union apply. The cloud vendor might be required to release client data to the U.S. government even though the client never knew that its data would wind up under U.S. jurisdiction.

Specific cloud vendors offer their clients varying degrees of control over how their data are distributed and replicated. Some vendors offer database services directly to their clients rather than require clients to contract for raw storage and virtual machines over which to run their own database systems.

The market for cloud services continues to evolve rapidly, but it is clear that a database administrator who is contracting for cloud services has to consider a wide variety of technical, economic, and legal issues in order to ensure the privacy and security of data, guarantees of the ACID properties (or an acceptable approximation thereof), and adequate performance despite the likelihood of data being distributed over a wide geographic area. The bibliographical notes provide some of the current thinking on these topics. Much new literature is likely to appear in the next few years, and many of the current issues in cloud databases are being addressed by the research community.

19.10   Directory Systems

Consider an organization that wishes to make data about its employees available to a variety of people in the organization; examples of the kinds of data include name, designation, employee-id, address, email address, phone number, fax number, and so on. In the precomputerization days, organizations would create physical directories of employees and distribute them across the organization. Even today, telephone companies create physical directories of customers.

In general, a directory is a listing of information about some class of objects such as persons. Directories can be used to find information about a specific object, or in the reverse direction to find objects that meet a certain requirement. In the world of physical telephone directories, directories that satisfy lookups in the forward direction are called **white pages**, while directories that satisfy lookups in the reverse direction are called **yellow pages**.

In today's networked world, the need for directories is still present and, if anything, even more important. However, directories today need to be available over a computer network, rather than in a physical (paper) form.

19.10.1   Directory Access Protocols

Directory information can be made available through Web interfaces, as many organizations, and phone companies in particular, do. Such interfaces are good for humans. However, programs too need to access directory information. Directories can be used for storing other types of information, much like file system directories. For instance, Web browsers can store personal bookmarks and other browser settings in a directory system. A user can thus access the same settings from multiple locations, such as at home and at work, without having to share a file system.

Several **directory access protocols** have been developed to provide a standardized way of accessing data in a directory. The most widely used among them today is the **Lightweight Directory Access Protocol (LDAP)**.

Obviously all the types of data in our examples can be stored without much trouble in a database system, and accessed through protocols such as JDBC or ODBC. The question then is, why come up with a specialized protocol for accessing directory information? There are at least two answers to the question.

- First, directory access protocols are simplified protocols that cater to a limited type of access to data. They evolved in parallel with the database access protocols.

- Second, and more important, directory systems provide a simple mechanism to name objects in a hierarchical fashion, similar to file system directory names, which can be used in a distributed directory system to specify what information is stored in each of the directory servers. For example, a particular directory server may store information for Bell Laboratories employees in Murray Hill, while another may store information for Bell Laboratories employees in Bangalore, giving both sites autonomy in controlling their local data. The directory access protocol can be used to obtain data from both directories across a network. More important, the directory system can be set up to automatically forward queries made at one site to the other site, without user intervention.

For these reasons, several organizations have directory systems to make organizational information available online through a directory access protocol. Information in an organizational directory can be used for a variety of purposes, such as to find addresses, phone numbers, or email addresses of people, to find which departments people are in, and to track department hierarchies. Directories are also used to authenticate users: applications can collect authentication information such as passwords from users and authenticate them using the directory.

As may be expected, several directory implementations find it beneficial to use relational databases to store data, instead of creating special-purpose storage systems.

19.10.2 LDAP: Lightweight Directory Access Protocol

In general a directory system is implemented as one or more servers, which service multiple clients. Clients use the application programmer interface defined by the directory system to communicate with the directory servers. Directory access protocols also define a data model and access control.

The **X.500 directory access protocol**, defined by the International Organization for Standardization (ISO), is a standard for accessing directory information. However, the protocol is rather complex, and is not widely used. The **Lightweight Directory Access Protocol (LDAP)** provides many of the X.500 features, but with less complexity, and is widely used. In the rest of this section, we shall outline the data model and access protocol details of LDAP.

19.10.2.1   LDAP Data Model

In LDAP, directories store **entries**, which are similar to objects. Each entry must have a **distinguished name (DN)**, which uniquely identifies the entry. A DN is in turn made up of a sequence of **relative distinguished names (RDNs)**. For example, an entry may have the following distinguished name:

cn=Silberschatz, ou=Computer Science, o=Yale University, c=USA

As you can see, the distinguished name in this example is a combination of a name and (organizational) address, starting with a person's name, then giving the organizational unit (ou), the organization (o), and country (c). The order of the components of a distinguished name reflects the normal postal address order, rather than the reverse order used in specifying path names for files. The set of RDNs for a DN is defined by the schema of the directory system.

Entries can also have attributes. LDAP provides binary, string, and time types, and additionally the types tel for telephone numbers, and PostalAddress for addresses (lines separated by a "$" character). Unlike those in the relational model, attributes are multivalued by default, so it is possible to store multiple telephone numbers or addresses for an entry.

LDAP allows the definition of **object classes** with attribute names and types. Inheritance can be used in defining object classes. Moreover, entries can be specified to be of one or more object classes. It is not necessary that there be a single most-specific object class to which an entry belongs.

Entries are organized into a **directory information tree (DIT)**, according to their distinguished names. Entries at the leaf level of the tree usually represent specific objects. Entries that are internal nodes represent objects such as organizational units, organizations, or countries. The children of a node have a DN containing all the RDNs of the parent, and one or more additional RDNs. For instance, an internal node may have a DN c=USA, and all entries below it have the value USA for the RDN c.

The entire distinguished name need not be stored in an entry. The system can generate the distinguished name of an entry by traversing up the DIT from the entry, collecting the RDN=value components to create the full distinguished name.

Entries may have more than one distinguished name—for example, an entry for a person in more than one organization. To deal with such cases, the leaf level of a DIT can be an **alias**, which points to an entry in another branch of the tree.

19.10.2.2   Data Manipulation

Unlike SQL, LDAP does not define either a data-definition language or a data-manipulation language. However, LDAP defines a network protocol for carrying out data definition and manipulation. Users of LDAP can either use an application programming interface or use tools provided by various vendors to perform data definition and manipulation. LDAP also defines a file format called **LDAP Data Interchange Format (LDIF)** that can be used for storing and exchanging information.

The querying mechanism in LDAP is very simple, consisting of just selections and projections, without any join. A query must specify the following:

- A base—that is, a node within a DIT—by giving its distinguished name (the path from the root to the node).

- A search condition, which can be a Boolean combination of conditions on individual attributes. Equality, matching by wild-card characters, and approximate equality (the exact definition of approximate equality is system dependent) are supported.

- A scope, which can be just the base, the base and its children, or the entire subtree beneath the base.

- Attributes to return.

- Limits on number of results and resource consumption.

The query can also specify whether to automatically dereference aliases; if alias dereferences are turned off, alias entries can be returned as answers.

One way of querying an LDAP data source is by using LDAP URLs. Examples of LDAP URLs are:

```
ldap://codex.cs.yale.edu/o=Yale University,c=USA
ldap://codex.cs.yale.edu/o=Yale University,c=USA??sub?cn=Silberschatz
```

The first URL returns all attributes of all entries at the server with organization being Yale University, and country being USA. The second URL executes a search query (selection) cn=Silberschatz on the subtree of the node with distinguished name o=Yale University, c=USA. The question marks in the URL separate different fields. The first field is the distinguished name, here o=Yale University,c=USA. The second field, the list of attributes to return, is left empty, meaning return all attributes. The third attribute, sub, indicates that the entire subtree is to be searched. The last parameter is the search condition.

A second way of querying an LDAP directory is by using an application programming interface. Figure 19.8 shows a piece of C code used to connect to an LDAP server and run a query against the server. The code first opens a connection to an LDAP server by ldap_open and ldap_bind. It then executes a query by ldap_search_s. The arguments to ldap_search_s are the LDAP connection handle, the DN of the base from which the search should be done, the scope of the search, the search condition, the list of attributes to be returned, and an attribute called attrsonly, which, if set to 1, would result in only the schema of the result being returned, without any actual tuples. The last argument is an output argument that returns the result of the search as an LDAPMessage structure.

The first **for** loop iterates over and prints each entry in the result. Note that an entry may have multiple attributes, and the second **for** loop prints each attribute. Since attributes in LDAP may be multivalued, the third **for** loop prints each value of an attribute. The calls ldap_msgfree and ldap_value_free free memory that is

```
#include <stdio.h>
#include <ldap.h>
main() {
    LDAP *ld;
    LDAPMessage *res, *entry;
    char *dn, *attr, *attrList[] = {"telephoneNumber", NULL};
    BerElement *ptr;
    int vals, i;
    ld = ldap_open("codex.cs.yale.edu", LDAP_PORT);
    ldap_simple_bind(ld, "avi", "avi-passwd") ;
    ldap_search_s(ld, "o=Yale University, c=USA", LDAP_SCOPE_SUBTREE,
                    "cn=Silberschatz", attrList, /*attrsonly*/ 0, &res);
    printf("found %d entries", ldap_count_entries(ld, res));
    for (entry=ldap_first_entry(ld, res); entry != NULL;
                            entry = ldap_next_entry(ld, entry))
    {
        dn = ldap_get_dn(ld, entry);
        printf("dn: %s", dn);
        ldap_memfree(dn);
        for (attr = ldap_first_attribute(ld, entry, &ptr);
                    attr ! NULL;
                    attr = ldap_next_attribute(ld, entry, ptr))
        {
            printf("%s: ", attr);
            vals = ldap_get_values(ld, entry, attr);
            for (i=0; vals[i] != NULL; i++)
                printf("%s, ", vals[i]);
            ldap_value_free(vals);
        }
    }
    ldap_msgfree(res);
    ldap_unbind(ld);
}
```

Figure 19.8   Example of LDAP code in C.

allocated by the LDAP libraries. Figure 19.8 does not show code for handling error conditions.

The LDAP API also contains functions to create, update, and delete entries, as well as other operations on the DIT. Each function call behaves like a separate transaction; LDAP does not support atomicity of multiple updates.

19.10.2.3   Distributed Directory Trees

Information about an organization may be split into multiple DITs, each of which stores information about some entries. The **suffix** of a DIT is a sequence of

RDN=value pairs that identify what information the DIT stores; the pairs are concatenated to the rest of the distinguished name generated by traversing from the entry to the root. For instance, the suffix of a DIT may be o=Lucent, c=USA, while another may have the suffix o=Lucent, c=India. The DITs may be organizationally and geographically separated.

A node in a DIT may contain a **referral** to another node in another DIT; for instance, the organizational unit Bell Labs under o=Lucent, c=USA may have its own DIT, in which case the DIT for o=Lucent, c=USA would have a node ou=Bell Labs representing a referral to the DIT for Bell Labs.

Referrals are the key component that help organize a distributed collection of directories into an integrated system. When a server gets a query on a DIT, it may return a referral to the client, which then issues a query on the referenced DIT. Access to the referenced DIT is transparent, proceeding without the user's knowledge. Alternatively, the server itself may issue the query to the referred DIT and return the results along with locally computed results.

The hierarchical naming mechanism used by LDAP helps break up control of information across parts of an organization. The referral facility then helps integrate all the directories in an organization into a single virtual directory.

Although it is not an LDAP requirement, organizations often choose to break up information either by geography (for instance, an organization may maintain a directory for each site where the organization has a large presence) or by organizational structure (for instance, each organizational unit, such as department, maintains its own directory).

Many LDAP implementations support master–slave and multimaster replication of DITs, although replication is not part of the current LDAP version 3 standard. Work on standardizing replication in LDAP is in progress.

19.11 Summary

- A distributed database system consists of a collection of sites, each of which maintains a local database system. Each site is able to process local transactions: those transactions that access data in only that single site. In addition, a site may participate in the execution of global transactions: those transactions that access data in several sites. The execution of global transactions requires communication among the sites.

- Distributed databases may be homogeneous, where all sites have a common schema and database system code, or heterogeneous, where the schemas and system codes may differ.

- There are several issues involved in storing a relation in the distributed database, including replication and fragmentation. It is essential that the system minimize the degree to which a user needs to be aware of how a relation is stored.

- A distributed system may suffer from the same types of failure that can afflict a centralized system. There are, however, additional failures with which we need to deal in a distributed environment, including the failure of a site, the failure of a link, loss of a message, and network partition. Each of these problems needs to be considered in the design of a distributed recovery scheme.

- To ensure atomicity, all the sites in which a transaction T executed must agree on the final outcome of the execution. T either commits at all sites or aborts at all sites. To ensure this property, the transaction coordinator of T must execute a commit protocol. The most widely used commit protocol is the two-phase commit protocol.

- The two-phase commit protocol may lead to blocking, the situation in which the fate of a transaction cannot be determined until a failed site (the coordinator) recovers. We can use the three-phase commit protocol to reduce the probability of blocking.

- Persistent messaging provides an alternative model for handling distributed transactions. The model breaks a single transaction into parts that are executed at different databases. Persistent messages (which are guaranteed to be delivered exactly once, regardless of failures), are sent to remote sites to request actions to be taken there. While persistent messaging avoids the blocking problem, application developers have to write code to handle various types of failures.

- The various concurrency-control schemes used in a centralized system can be modified for use in a distributed environment.

  - In the case of locking protocols, the only change that needs to be incorporated is in the way that the lock manager is implemented. There are a variety of different approaches here. One or more central coordinators may be used. If, instead, a distributed-lock-manager approach is taken, replicated data must be treated specially.

  - Protocols for handling replicated data include the primary copy, majority, biased, and quorum consensus protocols. These have different trade-offs in terms of cost and ability to work in the presence of failures.

  - In the case of timestamping and validation schemes, the only needed change is to develop a mechanism for generating unique global timestamps.

  - Many database systems support lazy replication, where updates are propagated to replicas outside the scope of the transaction that performed the update. Such facilities must be used with great care, since they may result in nonserializable executions.

- Deadlock detection in a distributed-lock-manager environment requires cooperation between multiple sites, since there may be global deadlocks even when there are no local deadlocks.

- To provide high availability, a distributed database must detect failures, reconfigure itself so that computation may continue, and recover when a processor or a link is repaired. The task is greatly complicated by the fact that it is hard to distinguish between network partitions and site failures.

  The majority protocol can be extended by using version numbers to permit transaction processing to proceed even in the presence of failures. While the protocol has a significant overhead, it works regardless of the type of failure. Less-expensive protocols are available to deal with site failures, but they assume network partitioning does not occur.

- Some of the distributed algorithms require the use of a coordinator. To provide high availability, the system must maintain a backup copy that is ready to assume responsibility if the coordinator fails. Another approach is to choose the new coordinator after the coordinator has failed. The algorithms that determine which site should act as a coordinator are called **election algorithms**.

- Queries on a distributed database may need to access multiple sites. Several optimization techniques are available to identify the best set of sites to access. Queries can be rewritten automatically in terms of fragments of relations and then choices can be made among the replicas of each fragment. Semijoin techniques may be employed to reduce data transfer involved in joining relations (or fragments or relicas thereof) across distinct sites.

- Heterogeneous distributed databases allow sites to have their own schemas and database system code. A multidatabase system provides an environment in which new database applications can access data from a variety of pre-existing databases located in various heterogeneous hardware and software environments. The local database systems may employ different logical models and data-definition and data-manipulation languages, and may differ in their concurrency-control and transaction-management mechanisms. A multidatabase system creates the illusion of logical database integration, without requiring physical database integration.

- A large number of data-storage systems on the cloud have been built in recent years, in response to data storage needs of extremely large-scale Web applications. These data-storage systems allow scalability to thousands of nodes, with geographic distribution, and high availability. However, they do not support the usual ACID properties, and they achieve availability during partitions at the cost of consistency of replicas. Current data-storage systems also do not support SQL, and provide only a simple put()/get() interface. While cloud computing is attractive even for traditional databases, there are several challenges due to lack of control on data placement and geographic replication.

- Directory systems can be viewed as a specialized form of database, where information is organized in a hierarchical fashion similar to the way files are organized in a file system. Directories are accessed by standardized directory access protocols such as LDAP. Directories can be distributed across multiple sites to provide autonomy to individual sites. Directories can contain referrals to other directories, which help build an integrated view whereby a query is sent to a single directory, and it is transparently executed at all relevant directories.

Review Terms

- Homogeneous distributed database
- Heterogeneous distributed database
- Data replication
- Primary copy
- Data fragmentation
  - Horizontal fragmentation
  - Vertical fragmentation
- Data transparency
  - Fragmentation transparency
  - Replication transparency
  - Location transparency
- Name server
- Aliases
- Distributed transactions
  - Local transactions
  - Global transactions
- Transaction manager
- Transaction coordinator
- System failure modes
- Network partition
- Commit protocols
- Two-phase commit protocol (2PC)
  - Ready state
  - In-doubt transactions
  - Blocking problem

- Three-phase commit protocol (3PC)
- Persistent messaging
- Concurrency control
- Single lock manager
- Distributed lock manager
- Protocols for replicas
  - Primary copy
  - Majority protocol
  - Biased protocol
  - Quorum consensus protocol
- Timestamping
- Master–slave replication
- Multimaster (update-anywhere) replication
- Transaction-consistent snapshot
- Lazy propagation
- Deadlock handling
  - Local wait-for graph
  - Global wait-for graph
  - False cycles
- Availability
- Robustness
  - Majority-based approach
  - Read one, write all
  - Read one, write all available
  - Site reintegration
- Coordinator selection

- Backup coordinator
- Election algorithms
- Bully algorithm
- Distributed query processing
- Semijoin strategy
- Multidatabase system
  - Autonomy
  - Mediators
  - Local transactions
  - Global transactions
  - Ensuring global serializability
  - Ticket
- Cloud computing

- Cloud data storage
- Tablet
- Directory systems
- LDAP: Lightweight Directory Access Protocol
  - Distinguished name (DN)
  - Relative distinguished names (RDNs)
  - Directory information tree (DIT)
- Distributed directory trees
  - DIT suffix
  - Referral

Practice Exercises

19.1 How might a distributed database designed for a local-area network differ from one designed for a wide-area network?

19.2 To build a highly available distributed system, you must know what kinds of failures can occur.

    a.   List possible types of failure in a distributed system.

    b.   Which items in your list from part a are also applicable to a centralized system?

19.3 Consider a failure that occurs during 2PC for a transaction. For each possible failure that you listed in Practice Exercise 19.2a, explain how 2PC ensures transaction atomicity despite the failure.

19.4 Consider a distributed system with two sites, A and B. Can site A distinguish among the following?

- B goes down.
- The link between A and B goes down.
- B is extremely overloaded and response time is 100 times longer than normal.

What implications does your answer have for recovery in distributed systems?

19.5 The persistent messaging scheme described in this chapter depends on timestamps combined with discarding of received messages if they are too old. Suggest an alternative scheme based on sequence numbers instead of timestamps.

19.6 Give an example where the read one, write all available approach leads to an erroneous state.

19.7 Explain the difference between data replication in a distributed system and the maintenance of a remote backup site.

19.8 Give an example where lazy replication can lead to an inconsistent database state even when updates get an exclusive lock on the primary (master) copy.

19.9 Consider the following deadlock-detection algorithm. When transaction T_i, at site S_1, requests a resource from T_j, at site S_3, a request message with timestamp n is sent. The edge (T_i, T_j, n) is inserted in the local wait-for graph of S_1. The edge (T_i, T_j, n) is inserted in the local wait-for graph of S_3 only if T_j has received the request message and cannot immediately grant the requested resource. A request from T_i to T_j in the same site is handled in the usual manner; no timestamps are associated with the edge (T_i, T_j). A central coordinator invokes the detection algorithm by sending an initiating message to each site in the system.

On receiving this message, a site sends its local wait-for graph to the coordinator. Note that such a graph contains all the local information that the site has about the state of the real graph. The wait-for graph reflects an instantaneous state of the site, but it is not synchronized with respect to any other site.

When the controller has received a reply from each site, it constructs a graph as follows:

- The graph contains a vertex for every transaction in the system.

- The graph has an edge (T_i, T_j) if and only if:

    ○ There is an edge (T_i, T_j) in one of the wait-for graphs.

    ○ An edge (T_i, T_j, n) (for some n) appears in more than one wait-for graph.

Show that, if there is a cycle in the constructed graph, then the system is in a deadlock state, and that, if there is no cycle in the constructed graph, then the system was not in a deadlock state when the execution of the algorithm began.

19.10 Consider a relation that is fragmented horizontally by *plant_number*:

employee (name, address, salary, plant_number)

Assume that each fragment has two replicas: one stored at the New York site and one stored locally at the plant site. Describe a good processing strategy for the following queries entered at the San Jose site.

a. Find all employees at the Boca plant.

b. Find the average salary of all employees.

c. Find the highest-paid employee at each of the following sites: Toronto, Edmonton, Vancouver, Montreal.

d. Find the lowest-paid employee in the company.

19.11 Compute $r \bowtie s$ for the relations of Figure 19.9.

19.12 Give an example of an application ideally suited for the cloud and another that would be hard to implement successfully in the cloud. Explain your answer.

19.13 Given that the LDAP functionality can be implemented on top of a database system, what is the need for the LDAP standard?

19.14 Consider a multidatabase system in which it is guaranteed that at most one global transaction is active at any time, and every local site ensures local serializability.

a. Suggest ways in which the multidatabase system can ensure that there is at most one active global transaction at any time.

b. Show by example that it is possible for a nonserializable global schedule to result despite the assumptions.

19.15 Consider a multidatabase system in which every local site ensures local serializability, and all global transactions are read only.

a. Show by example that nonserializable executions may result in such a system.

b. Show how you could use a ticket scheme to ensure global serializability.

A	B	C
1	2	3
4	5	6
1	2	4
5	3	2
8	9	7

r

C	D	E
3	4	5
3	6	8
2	3	2
1	4	1
1	2	3

s

Figure 19.9 Relations for Practice Exercise 19.11.

Exercises

19.16   Discuss the relative advantages of centralized and distributed databases.

19.17   Explain how the following differ: fragmentation transparency, replication transparency, and location transparency.

19.18   When is it useful to have replication or fragmentation of data? Explain your answer.

19.19   Explain the notions of transparency and autonomy. Why are these notions desirable from a human-factors standpoint?

19.20   If we apply a distributed version of the multiple-granularity protocol of Chapter 15 to a distributed database, the site responsible for the root of the DAG may become a bottleneck. Suppose we modify that protocol as follows:

- Only intention-mode locks are allowed on the root.

- All transactions are given all possible intention-mode locks on the root automatically.

Show that these modifications alleviate this problem without allowing any nonserializable schedules.

19.21   Study and summarize the facilities that the database system you are using provides for dealing with inconsistent states that can be reached with lazy propagation of updates.

19.22   Discuss the advantages and disadvantages of the two methods that we presented in Section 19.5.2 for generating globally unique timestamps.

19.23   Consider the relations:

$$employee\ (name,\ address,\ salary,\ plant\_number)$$
$$machine\ (machine\_number,\ type,\ plant\_number)$$

Assume that the *employee* relation is fragmented horizontally by *plant _number*, and that each fragment is stored locally at its corresponding plant site. Assume that the *machine* relation is stored in its entirety at the Armonk site. Describe a good strategy for processing each of the following queries.

   a.   Find all employees at the plant that contains machine number 1130.

   b.   Find all employees at plants that contain machines whose type is "milling machine."

   c.   Find all machines at the Almaden plant.

   d.   Find employee ⋈ machine.

19.24 For each of the strategies of Exercise 19.23, state how your choice of a strategy depends on:

  a. The site at which the query was entered.

  b. The site at which the result is desired.

19.25 Is the expression $r_i \bowtie r_j$ necessarily equal to $r_j \bowtie r_i$? Under what conditions does $r_i \bowtie r_j = r_j \bowtie r_i$ hold?

19.26 If a cloud data-storage service is used to store two relations r and s and we need to join r and s, why might it be useful to maintain the join as a materialized view? In your answer, be sure to distinguish among various meanings of "useful": overall throughput, efficient use of space, and response time to user queries.

19.27 Why do cloud-computing services support traditional database systems best by using a virtual machine instead of running directly on the service provider's actual machine?

19.28 Describe how LDAP can be used to provide multiple hierarchical views of data, without replicating the base-level data.

Bibliographical Notes

Textbook discussions of distributed databases are offered by Ozsu and Valduriez [1999]. Breitbart et al. [1999b] presents an overview of distributed databases.

The implementation of the transaction concept in a distributed database is presented by Gray [1981] and Traiger et al. [1982]. The 2PC protocol was developed by Lampson and Sturgis [1976]. The three-phase commit protocol is from Skeen [1981]. Mohan and Lindsay [1983] discusses two modified versions of 2PC, called *presume commit* and *presume abort,* that reduce the overhead of 2PC by defining default assumptions regarding the fate of transactions.

The bully algorithm in Section 19.6.5 is from Garcia-Molina [1982]. Distributed clock synchronization is discussed in Lamport [1978]. Distributed concurrency control is covered by Bernstein and Goodman [1981].

The transaction manager of R* is described in Mohan et al. [1986]. Validation techniques for distributed concurrency-control schemes are described by Schlageter [1981] and Bassiouni [1988].

The problem of concurrent updates to replicated data was revisited in the context of data warehouses by Gray et al. [1996]. Anderson et al. [1998] discusses issues concerning lazy replication and consistency. Breitbart et al. [1999a] describes lazy update protocols for handling replication.

The user manuals of various database systems provide details of how they handle replication and consistency. Huang and Garcia-Molina [2001] addresses exactly-once semantics in a replicated messaging system.

Knapp [1987] surveys the distributed deadlock-detection literature. Practice Exercise 19.9 is from Stuart et al. [1984].

Distributed query processing is discussed in Epstein et al. [1978] and Hevner and Yao [1979]. Daniels et al. [1982] discusses the approach to distributed query processing taken by R*.

Dynamic query optimization in multidatabases is addressed by Ozcan et al. [1997]. Adali et al. [1996] and Papakonstantinou et al. [1996] describe query-optimization issues in mediator systems.

Transaction processing in multidatabase systems is discussed in Mehrotra et al. [2001]. The ticket scheme is presented in Georgakopoulos et al. [1994]. 2LSR is introduced in Mehrotra et al. [1991].

A collection of papers on data management on cloud systems is in Ooi and S. Parthasarathy [2009]. The implementation of Google's Bigtable is described in Chang et al. [2008], while Cooper et al. [2008] describe Yahoo!'s PNUTS system. Experience in building a database using Amazon's S3 cloud-based storage is described in Brantner et al. [2008]. An approach to making transactions work correctly in cloud systems is discussed in Lomet et al. [2009]. The CAP theorem was conjectured by Brewer [2000], and was formalized and proved by Gilbert and Lynch [2002].

Howes et al. [1999] provides textbook coverage of LDAP.

PART 6

DATA WAREHOUSING, DATA MINING, AND INFORMATION RETRIEVAL

Database queries are often designed to extract specific information, such as the balance of an account or the sum of a customer's account balances. However, queries designed to help formulate a corporate strategy usually requires access to large amounts of data originating at multiple sources.

A data warehouse is a repository of data gathered from multiple sources and stored under a common, unified database schema. Data stored in warehouse are analyzed by a variety of complex aggregations and statistical analyses, often exploiting SQL constructs for data analysis which we saw in Chapter 5. Furthermore, knowledge-discovery techniques may be used to attempt to discover rules and patterns from the data. For example, a retailer may discover that certain products tend to be purchased together, and may use that information to develop marketing strategies. This process of knowledge discovery from data is called *data mining*. Chapter 20 addresses the issues of data warehousing and data mining.

In our discussions so far, we have focused on relatively simple, well-structured data. However, there is an enormous amount of unstructured textual data on the Internet, on intranets within organizations, and on the computers of individual users. Users wish to find relevant information from this vast body of mostly textual information, using simple query mechanisms such as keyword queries. The field of information retrieval deals with querying of such unstructured data, and pays particular attention to the ranking of query results. Although this area of research is several decades old, it has undergone tremendous growth with the development of the World Wide Web. Chapter 21 provides an introduction to the field of information retrieval.

CHAPTER 20

Data Warehousing and Mining

Businesses have begun to exploit the burgeoning data online to make better decisions about their activities, such as what items to stock and how best to target customers to increase sales. There are two aspects to exploiting such data. The first aspect is to gather data from multiple sources into a central repository, called a data warehouse. Issues involved in warehousing include techniques for dealing with dirty data, that is, data with some errors, and with techniques for efficient storage and indexing of large volumes of data.

The second aspect is to analyze the gathered data to find information or knowledge that can be the basis for business decisions. Some kinds of data analysis can be done by using SQL constructs for online analytical processing (OLAP), which we saw in Section 5.6 (Chapter 5), and by using tools and graphical interfaces for OLAP. Another approach to getting knowledge from data is to use *data mining*, which aims at detecting various types of patterns in large volumes of data. Data mining supplements various types of statistical techniques with similar goals.

20.1   Decision-Support Systems

Database applications can be broadly classified into transaction-processing and decision-support systems. Transaction-processing systems are systems that record information about transactions, such as product sales information for companies, or course registration and grade information for universities. Transaction-processing systems are widely used today, and organizations have accumulated a vast amount of information generated by these systems. Decision-support systems aim to get high-level information out of the detailed information stored in transaction-processing systems, and to use the high-level information to make a variety of decisions. Decision-support systems help managers to decide what products to stock in a shop, what products to manufacture in a factory, or which of the applicants should be admitted to a university.

For example, company databases often contain enormous quantities of information about customers and transactions. The size of the information storage required may range up to hundreds of gigabytes, or even terabytes, for large retail chains. Transaction information for a retailer may include the name or identifier (such as credit-card number) of the customer, the items purchased, the price paid, and the dates on which the purchases were made. Information about the items purchased may include the name of the item, the manufacturer, the model number, the color, and the size. Customer information may include credit history, annual income, residence, age, and even educational background.

Such large databases can be treasure troves of information for making business decisions, such as what items to stock and what discounts to offer. For instance, a retail company may notice a sudden spurt in purchases of flannel shirts in the Pacific Northwest, may realize that there is a trend, and may start stocking a larger number of such shirts in shops in that area. As another example, a car company may find, on querying its database, that most of its small sports cars are bought by young women whose annual incomes are above $50,000. The company may then target its marketing to attract more such women to buy its small sports cars, and may avoid wasting money trying to attract other categories of people to buy those cars. In both cases, the company has identified patterns in customer behavior and has used the patterns to make business decisions.

The storage and retrieval of data for decision support raises several issues:

- Although many decision-support queries can be written in SQL, others either cannot be expressed in SQL or cannot be expressed easily in SQL. Several SQL extensions have therefore been proposed to make data analysis easier. In Section 5.6, we covered SQL extensions for data analysis and techniques for online analytical processing (OLAP).

- Database query languages are not suited to the performance of detailed **statistical analyses** of data. There are several packages, such as SAS and S++, that help in statistical analysis. Such packages have been interfaced with databases, to allow large volumes of data to be stored in the database and retrieved efficiently for analysis. The field of statistical analysis is a large discipline on its own; see the references in the bibliographical notes for more information.

- Large companies have diverse sources of data that they need to use for making business decisions. The sources may store the data under different schemas. For performance reasons (as well as for reasons of organization control), the data sources usually will not permit other parts of the company to retrieve data on demand.

  To execute queries efficiently on such diverse data, companies have built *data warehouses*. Data warehouses gather data from multiple sources under a unified schema, at a single site. Thus, they provide the user a single uniform interface to data. We study issues in building and maintaining a data warehouse in Section 20.2.

- Knowledge-discovery techniques attempt to discover automatically statistical rules and patterns from data. The field of *data mining* combines knowledge-discovery techniques invented by artificial intelligence researchers and statistical analysts, with efficient implementation techniques that enable them to be used on extremely large databases. Section 20.3 discusses data mining.

The area of **decision support** can be broadly viewed as covering all the above areas, although some people use the term in a narrower sense that excludes statistical analysis and data mining.

20.2   Data Warehousing

Large companies have presences in many places, each of which may generate a large volume of data. For instance, large retail chains have hundreds or thousands of stores, whereas insurance companies may have data from thousands of local branches. Further, large organizations have a complex internal organization structure, and therefore different data may be present in different locations, or on different operational systems, or under different schemas. For instance, manufacturing-problem data and customer-complaint data may be stored on different database systems. Organizations often purchase data from external sources, such as mailing lists that are used for product promotions, or credit scores of customers that are provided by credit bureaus, to decide on credit-worthiness of customers.[1]

Corporate decision makers require access to information from multiple such sources. Setting up queries on individual sources is both cumbersome and inefficient. Moreover, the sources of data may store only current data, whereas decision makers may need access to past data as well; for instance, information about how purchase patterns have changed in the past year could be of great importance. Data warehouses provide a solution to these problems.

A **data warehouse** is a repository (or archive) of information gathered from multiple sources, stored under a unified schema, at a single site. Once gathered, the data are stored for a long time, permitting access to historical data. Thus, data warehouses provide the user a single consolidated interface to data, making decision-support queries easier to write. Moreover, by accessing information for decision support from a data warehouse, the decision maker ensures that online transaction-processing systems are not affected by the decision-support workload.

20.2.1   Components of a Data Warehouse

Figure 20.1 shows the architecture of a typical data warehouse, and illustrates the gathering of data, the storage of data, and the querying and data analysis support. Among the issues to be addressed in building a warehouse are the following:

---

[1]Credit bureaus are companies that gather information about consumers from multiple sources and compute a credit-worthiness score for each consumer.

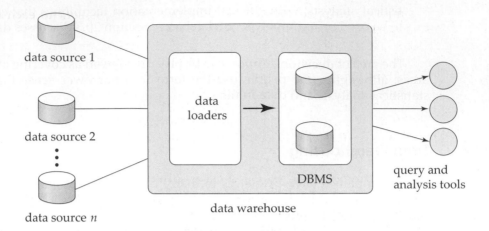

Figure 20.1   Data-warehouse architecture.

- **When and how to gather data.** In a **source-driven architecture** for gathering data, the data sources transmit new information, either continually (as transaction processing takes place), or periodically (nightly, for example). In a **destination-driven architecture**, the data warehouse periodically sends requests for new data to the sources.

    Unless updates at the sources are replicated at the warehouse via two-phase commit, the warehouse will never be quite up-to-date with the sources. Two-phase commit is usually far too expensive to be an option, so data warehouses typically have slightly out-of-date data. That, however, is usually not a problem for decision-support systems.

- **What schema to use.** Data sources that have been constructed independently are likely to have different schemas. In fact, they may even use different data models. Part of the task of a warehouse is to perform schema integration, and to convert data to the integrated schema before they are stored. As a result, the data stored in the warehouse are not just a copy of the data at the sources. Instead, they can be thought of as a materialized view of the data at the sources.

- **Data transformation and cleansing.** The task of correcting and preprocessing data is called **data cleansing**. Data sources often deliver data with numerous minor inconsistencies, which can be corrected. For example, names are often misspelled, and addresses may have street, area, or city names misspelled, or postal codes entered incorrectly. These can be corrected to a reasonable extent by consulting a database of street names and postal codes in each city. The approximate matching of data required for this task is referred to as **fuzzy lookup**.

    Address lists collected from multiple sources may have duplicates that need to be eliminated in a **merge–purge operation** (this operation is also referred to as **deduplication**). Records for multiple individuals in a house may be grouped together so only one mailing is sent to each house; this operation is called **householding**.

Data may be **transformed** in ways other than cleansing, such as changing the units of measure, or converting the data to a different schema by joining data from multiple source relations. Data warehouses typically have graphical tools to support data transformation. Such tools allow transformation to be specified as boxes, and edges can be created between boxes to indicate the flow of data. Conditional boxes can route data to an appropriate next step in transformation. See Figure 30.7 for an example of a transformation specified using the graphical tool provided by Microsoft SQL Server.

- **How to propagate updates**. Updates on relations at the data sources must be propagated to the data warehouse. If the relations at the data warehouse are exactly the same as those at the data source, the propagation is straightforward. If they are not, the problem of propagating updates is basically the *view-maintenance* problem, which was discussed in Section 13.5.

- **What data to summarize.** The raw data generated by a transaction-processing system may be too large to store online. However, we can answer many queries by maintaining just summary data obtained by aggregation on a relation, rather than maintaining the entire relation. For example, instead of storing data about every sale of clothing, we can store total sales of clothing by item_name and category.

    Suppose that a relation r has been replaced by a summary relation s. Users may still be permitted to pose queries as though the relation r were available online. If the query requires only summary data, it may be possible to transform it into an equivalent one using s instead; see Section 13.5.

The different steps involved in getting data into a data warehouse are called **extract, transform, and load** or ETL tasks; extraction refers to getting data from the sources, while load refers to loading the data into the data warehouse.

20.2.2 Warehouse Schemas

Data warehouses typically have schemas that are designed for data analysis, using tools such as OLAP tools. Thus, the data are usually multidimensional data, with dimension attributes and measure attributes. Tables containing multidimensional data are called **fact tables** and are usually very large. A table recording sales information for a retail store, with one tuple for each item that is sold, is a typical example of a fact table. The dimensions of the *sales* table would include what the item is (usually an item identifier such as that used in bar codes), the date when the item is sold, which location (store) the item was sold from, which customer bought the item, and so on. The measure attributes may include the number of items sold and the price of the items.

To minimize storage requirements, dimension attributes are usually short identifiers that are foreign keys into other tables called **dimension tables**. For instance, a fact table *sales* would have attributes *item_id*, *store_id*, *customer_id*, and

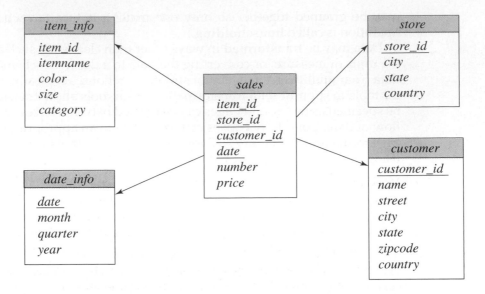

Figure 20.2   Star schema for a data warehouse.

date, and measure attributes *number* and *price*. The attribute *store_id* is a foreign key into a dimension table *store*, which has other attributes such as store location (city, state, country). The *item_id* attribute of the *sales* table would be a foreign key into a dimension table *item_info*, which would contain information such as the name of the item, the category to which the item belongs, and other item details such as color and size. The *customer_id* attribute would be a foreign key into a *customer* table containing attributes such as name and address of the customer. We can also view the *date* attribute as a foreign key into a *date_info* table giving the month, quarter, and year of each date.

The resultant schema appears in Figure 20.2. Such a schema, with a fact table, multiple dimension tables, and foreign keys from the fact table to the dimension tables, is called a **star schema**. More complex data-warehouse designs may have multiple levels of dimension tables; for instance, the *item_info* table may have an attribute *manufacturer_id* that is a foreign key into another table giving details of the manufacturer. Such schemas are called **snowflake schemas**. Complex data-warehouse designs may also have more than one fact table.

20.2.3   Column-Oriented Storage

Databases traditionally store all attributes of a tuple together, and tuples are stored sequentially in a file. Such a storage layout is referred to as *row-oriented storage*. In contrast, in **column-oriented storage**, each attribute of a relation is stored in a separate file, with values from successive tuples stored at successive positions in the file. Assuming fixed-size data types, the value of attribute A of the ith tuple of a relation can be found by accessing the file corresponding to attribute A, and reading the value at offset $(i - 1)$ times the size (in bytes) of values in attribute A.

Column-oriented storage has at least two major benefits over row-oriented storage:

1. When a query needs to access only a few attributes of a relation with a large number of attributes, the remaining attributes need not be fetched from disk into memory. In contrast, in row-oriented storage, not only are irrelevant attributes fetched into memory, but they may also get prefetched into processor cache, wasting cache space and memory bandwidth, if they are stored adjacent to attributes used in the query.

2. Storing values of the same type together increases the effectiveness of compression; compression can greatly reduce both the disk storage cost and the time to retrieve data from disk.

On the other hand, column-oriented storage has the drawback that storing or fetching a single tuple requires multiple I/O operations.

As a result of the above trade-offs, column-oriented storage is not widely used for transaction-processing applications. However, column-oriented storage is gaining increasing acceptance for data-warehousing applications, where accesses are rarely to individual tuples, but rather require scanning and aggregating multiple tuples.

Sybase IQ was one of the early products to use column-oriented storage, but there are now several research projects and companies that have developed databases based on column-oriented storage systems. These systems have been able to demonstrate significant performance gains for many data-warehousing applications. See the bibliographical notes for references on how column-oriented stores are implemented, and queries optimized and processed on such stores.

20.3   Data Mining

The term **data mining** refers loosely to the process of semiautomatically analyzing large databases to find useful patterns. Like knowledge discovery in artificial intelligence (also called machine learning) or statistical analysis, data mining attempts to discover rules and patterns from data. However, data mining differs from machine learning and statistics in that it deals with large volumes of data, stored primarily on disk. That is, data mining deals with "knowledge discovery in databases."

Some types of knowledge discovered from a database can be represented by a set of **rules**. The following is an example of a rule, stated informally: "Young women with annual incomes greater than $50,000 are the most likely people to buy small sports cars." Of course such rules are not universally true, and have degrees of "support" and "confidence," as we shall see. Other types of knowledge are represented by equations relating different variables to each other, or by other mechanisms for predicting outcomes when the values of some variables are known.

There are a variety of possible types of patterns that may be useful, and different techniques are used to find different types of patterns. We shall study a few examples of patterns and see how they may be automatically derived from a database.

Usually there is a manual component to data mining, consisting of preprocessing data to a form acceptable to the algorithms and postprocessing of discovered patterns to find novel ones that could be useful. There may also be more than one type of pattern that can be discovered from a given database, and manual interaction may be needed to pick useful types of patterns. For this reason, data mining is really a semiautomatic process in real life. However, in our description we concentrate on the automatic aspect of mining.

The discovered knowledge has numerous applications. The most widely used applications are those that require some sort of **prediction**. For instance, when a person applies for a credit card, the credit-card company wants to predict if the person is a good credit risk. The prediction is to be based on known attributes of the person, such as age, income, debts, and past debt-repayment history. Rules for making the prediction are derived from the same attributes of past and current credit-card holders, along with their observed behavior, such as whether they defaulted on their credit-card dues. Other types of prediction include predicting which customers may switch over to a competitor (these customers may be offered special discounts to tempt them not to switch), predicting which people are likely to respond to promotional mail ("junk mail"), or predicting what types of phone calling card usage are likely to be fraudulent.

Another class of applications looks for **associations**, for instance, books that tend to be bought together. If a customer buys a book, an online bookstore may suggest other associated books. If a person buys a camera, the system may suggest accessories that tend to be bought along with cameras. A good salesperson is aware of such patterns and exploits them to make additional sales. The challenge is to automate the process. Other types of associations may lead to discovery of causation. For instance, discovery of unexpected associations between a newly introduced medicine and cardiac problems led to the finding that the medicine may cause cardiac problems in some people. The medicine was then withdrawn from the market.

Associations are an example of **descriptive patterns**. **Clusters** are another example of such patterns. For example, over a century ago a cluster of typhoid cases was found around a well, which led to the discovery that the water in the well was contaminated and was spreading typhoid. Detection of clusters of disease remains important even today.

20.4   Classification

As mentioned in Section 20.3, prediction is one of the most important types of data mining. We describe classification, study techniques for building one type of classifiers, called decision-tree classifiers, and then study other prediction techniques.

Abstractly, the **classification** problem is this: Given that items belong to one of several classes, and given past instances (called **training instances**) of items along with the classes to which they belong, the problem is to predict the class to which a new item belongs. The class of the new instance is not known, so other attributes of the instance must be used to predict the class.

Classification can be done by finding rules that partition the given data into disjoint groups. For instance, suppose that a credit-card company wants to decide whether or not to give a credit card to an applicant. The company has a variety of information about the person, such as her age, educational background, annual income, and current debts, that it can use for making a decision.

Some of this information could be relevant to the credit-worthiness of the applicant, whereas some may not be. To make the decision, the company assigns a credit-worthiness level of excellent, good, average, or bad to each of a sample set of *current* customers according to each customer's payment history. Then, the company attempts to find rules that classify its current customers into excellent, good, average, or bad, on the basis of the information about the person, other than the actual payment history (which is unavailable for new customers). Let us consider just two attributes: education level (highest degree earned) and income. The rules may be of the following form:

$$\forall person \ P, \ P.degree = masters \text{ and } P.income > 75,000$$
$$\Rightarrow P.credit = excellent$$

$$\forall person \ P, \ P.degree = bachelors \text{ or}$$
$$(P.income \geq 25,000 \text{ and } P.income \leq 75,000) \Rightarrow P.credit = good$$

Similar rules would also be present for the other credit-worthiness levels (average and bad).

The process of building a classifier starts from a sample of data, called a **training set**. For each tuple in the training set, the class to which the tuple belongs is already known. For instance, the training set for a credit-card application may be the existing customers, with their credit-worthiness determined from their payment history. The actual data, or population, may consist of all people, including those who are not existing customers. There are several ways of building a classifier, as we shall see.

20.4.1 Decision-Tree Classifiers

The decision-tree classifier is a widely used technique for classification. As the name suggests, **decision-tree classifiers** use a tree; each leaf node has an associated class, and each internal node has a predicate (or more generally, a function) associated with it. Figure 20.3 shows an example of a decision tree.

To classify a new instance, we start at the root and traverse the tree to reach a leaf; at an internal node we evaluate the predicate (or function) on the data instance, to find which child to go to. The process continues until we reach a leaf node. For example, if the degree level of a person is masters, and the person's

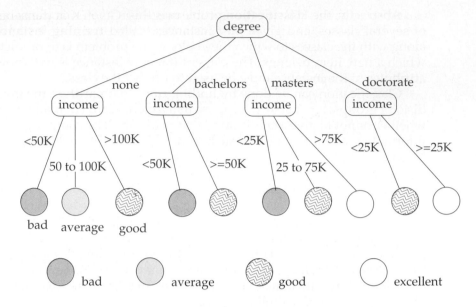

Figure 20.3 Classification tree.

income is 40K, starting from the root we follow the edge labeled "masters," and from there the edge labeled "25K to 75K," to reach a leaf. The class at the leaf is "good," so we predict that the credit risk of that person is good.

20.4.1.1 Building Decision-Tree Classifiers

The question then is how to build a decision-tree classifier, given a set of training instances. The most common way of doing so is to use a **greedy** algorithm, which works recursively, starting at the root and building the tree downward. Initially there is only one node, the root, and all training instances are associated with that node.

At each node, if all, or "almost all" training instances associated with the node belong to the same class, then the node becomes a leaf node associated with that class. Otherwise, a **partitioning attribute** and **partitioning conditions** must be selected to create child nodes. The data associated with each child node is the set of training instances that satisfy the partitioning condition for that child node. In our example, the attribute *degree* is chosen, and four children, one for each value of degree, are created. The conditions for the four children nodes are *degree* = none, *degree* = bachelors, *degree* = masters, and *degree* = doctorate, respectively. The data associated with each child consist of training instances satisfying the condition associated with that child. At the node corresponding to masters, the attribute *income* is chosen, with the range of values partitioned into intervals 0 to 25K, 25K to 50K, 50K to 75K, and over 75K. The data associated with each node consist of training instances with the *degree* attribute being masters and the *income* attribute being in each of these ranges, respectively. As an optimization, since the class for the range 25K to 50K and the range 50K to 75K is the same under the node *degree* = masters, the two ranges have been merged into a single range 25K to 75K.

20.4.1.2 Best Splits

Intuitively, by choosing a sequence of partitioning attributes, we start with the set of all training instances, which is "impure" in the sense that it contains instances from many classes, and ends up with leaves which are "pure" in the sense that at each leaf all training instances belong to only one class. We shall see shortly how to measure purity quantitatively. To judge the benefit of picking a particular attribute and condition for partitioning of the data at a node, we measure the purity of the data at the children resulting from partitioning by that attribute. The attribute and condition that result in the maximum purity are chosen.

The purity of a set S of training instances can be measured quantitatively in several ways. Suppose there are k classes, and of the instances in S the fraction of instances in class i is p_i. One measure of purity, the **Gini measure**, is defined as:

$$\text{Gini}(S) = 1 - \sum_{i-1}^{k} p_i^2$$

When all instances are in a single class, the Gini value is 0, while it reaches its maximum (of $1 - 1/k$) if each class has the same number of instances. Another measure of purity is the **entropy measure**, which is defined as:

$$\text{Entropy}(S) = - \sum_{i-1}^{k} p_i \log_2 p_i$$

The entropy value is 0 if all instances are in a single class, and reaches its maximum when each class has the same number of instances. The entropy measure derives from information theory.

When a set S is split into multiple sets $S_i, i = 1, 2, \ldots, r$, we can measure the purity of the resultant set of sets as:

$$\text{Purity}(S_1, S_2, \ldots, S_r) = \sum_{i=1}^{r} \frac{|S_i|}{|S|} \text{purity}(S_i)$$

That is, the purity is the weighted average of the purity of the sets S_i. The above formula can be used with both the Gini measure and the entropy measure of purity.

The **information gain** due to a particular split of S into $S_i, i = 1, 2, \ldots, r$ is then:

$$\text{Information\_gain}(S, \{S_1, S_2, \ldots, S_r\}) = \text{purity}(S) - \text{purity}(S_1, S_2, \ldots, S_r)$$

Splits into fewer sets are preferable to splits into many sets, since they lead to simpler and more meaningful decision trees. The number of elements in each of the sets S_i may also be taken into account; otherwise, whether a set S_i has 0 elements or 1 element would make a big difference in the number of sets, although the split is the same for almost all the elements. The **information content** of a particular split can be defined in terms of entropy as:

$$\text{Information\_content}(S, \{S_1, S_2, \ldots, S_r\}) = -\sum_{i-1}^{r} \frac{|S_i|}{|S|} \log_2 \frac{|S_i|}{|S|}$$

All of this leads to a definition: The **best split** for an attribute is the one that gives the maximum **information gain ratio**, defined as:

$$\frac{\text{Information\_gain}(S, \{S_1, S_2, \ldots, S_r\})}{\text{Information\_content}(S, \{S_1, S_2, \ldots, S_r\})}$$

20.4.1.3   Finding Best Splits

How do we find the best split for an attribute? How to split an attribute depends on the type of the attribute. Attributes can be either **continuous valued**, that is, the values can be ordered in a fashion meaningful to classification, such as age or income, or they can be **categorical**; that is, they have no meaningful order, such as department names or country names. We do not expect the sort order of department names or country names to have any significance to classification.

Usually attributes that are numbers (integers/reals) are treated as continuous valued while character string attributes are treated as categorical, but this may be controlled by the user of the system. In our example, we have treated the attribute *degree* as categorical, and the attribute *income* as continuous valued.

We first consider how to find best splits for continuous-valued attributes. For simplicity, we shall consider only **binary splits** of continuous-valued attributes, that is, splits that result in two children. The case of **multiway splits** is more complicated; see the bibliographical notes for references on the subject.

To find the best binary split of a continuous-valued attribute, we first sort the attribute values in the training instances. We then compute the information gain obtained by splitting at each value. For example, if the training instances have values 1, 10, 15, and 25 for an attribute, the split points considered are 1, 10, and 15; in each case values less than or equal to the split point form one partition and the rest of the values form the other partition. The best binary split for the attribute is the split that gives the maximum information gain.

For a categorical attribute, we can have a multiway split, with a child for each value of the attribute. This works fine for categorical attributes with only a few distinct values, such as degree or gender. However, if the attribute has many distinct values, such as department names in a large company, creating a child for each value is not a good idea. In such cases, we would try to combine multiple values into each child, to create a smaller number of children. See the bibliographical notes for references on how to do so.

procedure GrowTree(*S*)
    Partition(*S*);

procedure Partition (*S*)
    if ($purity(S) > \delta_p$ **or** $|S| < \delta_s$) **then**
        return;
    for each attribute *A*
        evaluate splits on attribute *A*;
    Use best split found (across all attributes) to partition
          S into $S_1, S_2, \ldots, S_r$;
    for $i = 1, 2, \ldots, r$
        Partition(S_i);

Figure 20.4 Recursive construction of a decision tree.

20.4.1.4 Decision-Tree Construction Algorithm

The main idea of decision-tree construction is to evaluate different attributes and different partitioning conditions, and pick the attribute and partitioning condition that results in the maximum information-gain ratio. The same procedure works recursively on each of the sets resulting from the split, thereby recursively constructing a decision tree. If the data can be perfectly classified, the recursion stops when the purity of a set is 0. However, often data are noisy, or a set may be so small that partitioning it further may not be justified statistically. In this case, the recursion stops when the purity of a set is "sufficiently high," and the class of the resulting leaf is defined as the class of the majority of the elements of the set. In general, different branches of the tree could grow to different levels.

Figure 20.4 shows pseudocode for a recursive tree-construction procedure, which takes a set of training instances *S* as parameter. The recursion stops when the set is sufficiently pure or the set *S* is too small for further partitioning to be statistically significant. The parameters δ_p and δ_s define cutoffs for purity and size; the system may give them default values, which may be overridden by users.

There are a wide variety of decision-tree construction algorithms, and we outline the distinguishing features of a few of them. See the bibliographical notes for details. With very large data sets, partitioning may be expensive, since it involves repeated copying. Several algorithms have therefore been developed to minimize the I/O and computation cost when the training data are larger than available memory.

Several of the algorithms also prune subtrees of the generated decision tree to reduce **overfitting**: A subtree is overfitted if it has been so highly tuned to the specifics of the training data that it makes many classification errors on other data. A subtree is pruned by replacing it with a leaf node. There are different pruning heuristics; one heuristic uses part of the training data to build the tree and another part of the training data to test it. The heuristic prunes a subtree if it finds that misclassification on the test instances would be reduced if the subtree were replaced by a leaf node.

We can generate classification rules from a decision tree, if we so desire. For each leaf we generate a rule as follows: The left-hand side is the conjunction of all the split conditions on the path to the leaf, and the class is the class of the majority of the training instances at the leaf. An example of such a classification rule is:

$$degree = masters \text{ and } income > 75000 \Rightarrow excellent$$

20.4.2 Other Types of Classifiers

There are several types of classifiers other than decision-tree classifiers. Two types that have been quite useful are *neural-net classifiers*, *Bayesian classifiers*, and *Support Vector Machine* classifiers. Neural-net classifiers use the training data to train artificial neural nets. There is a large body of literature on neural nets, and we do not consider them further here.

Bayesian classifiers find the distribution of attribute values for each class in the training data; when given a new instance d, they use the distribution information to estimate, for each class c_j, the probability that instance d belongs to class c_j, denoted by $p(c_j|d)$, in a manner outlined here. The class with maximum probability becomes the predicted class for instance d.

To find the probability $p(c_j|d)$ of instance d being in class c_j, Bayesian classifiers use **Bayes' theorem**, which says:

$$p(c_j|d) = \frac{p(d|c_j)p(c_j)}{p(d)}$$

where $p(d|c_j)$ is the probability of generating instance d given class c_j, $p(c_j)$ is the probability of occurrence of class c_j, and $p(d)$ is the probability of instance d occurring. Of these, $p(d)$ can be ignored since it is the same for all classes. $p(c_j)$ is simply the fraction of training instances that belong to class c_j.

For example, let us consider a special case where only one attribute, *income*, is used for classification, and suppose we need to classify a person whose income is 76000. We assume that income values are broken up into buckets, and assume that the bucket containing 76000 contains values in the range (75000, 80000). Suppose among instances of class *excellent*, the probability of income being in (75000, 80000) is 0.1, while among instances of class *good*, the probability of income being in (75000, 80000) is 0.05. Suppose also that overall 0.1 fraction of people are classified as *excellent*, and 0.3 are classified as *good*. Then, $p(d|c_j)p(c_j)$ for class *excellent* is .01, while for class *good*, it is 0.015. The person would therefore be classified in class *good*.

In general, multiple attributes need to be considered for classification. Then, finding $p(d|c_j)$ exactly is difficult, since it requires the distribution of instances of c_j, across all combinations of values for the attributes used for classification. The number of such combinations (for example of income buckets, with degree values and other attributes) can be very large. With a limited training set used to find the distribution, most combinations would not have even a single training set matching them, leading to incorrect classification decisions. To avoid this problem, as well as to simplify the task of classification, **naive Bayesian classifiers** assume attributes have independent distributions, and thereby estimate:

$$p(d|c_j) = p(d_1|c_j) * p(d_2|c_j) * \cdots * p(d_n|c_j)$$

That is, the probability of the instance d occurring is the product of the probability of occurrence of each of the attribute values d_i of d, given the class is c_j.

The probabilities $p(d_i|c_j)$ derive from the distribution of values for each attribute i, for each class c_j. This distribution is computed from the training instances that belong to each class c_j; the distribution is usually approximated by a histogram. For instance, we may divide the range of values of attribute i into equal intervals, and store the fraction of instances of class c_j that fall in each interval. Given a value d_i for attribute i, the value of $p(d_i|c_j)$ is simply the fraction of instances belonging to class c_j that fall in the interval to which d_i belongs.

A significant benefit of Bayesian classifiers is that they can classify instances with unknown and null attribute values—unknown or null attributes are just omitted from the probability computation. In contrast, decision-tree classifiers cannot meaningfully handle situations where an instance to be classified has a null value for a partitioning attribute used to traverse further down the decision tree.

The **Support Vector Machine** (SVM) is a type of classifier that has been found to give very accurate classification across a range of applications. We provide some basic intuition about Support Vector Machine classifiers here; see the references in the bibliographical notes for further information.

Support Vector Machine classifiers can best be understood geometrically. In the simplest case, consider a set of points in a two-dimensional plane, some belonging to class A, and some belonging to class B. We are given a training set of points whose class (A or B) is known, and we need to build a classifier of points, using these training points. This situation is illustrated in Figure 20.5, where the points in class A are denoted by X marks, while those in class B are denoted by O marks.

Suppose we can draw a line on the plane, such that all points in class A lie to one side and all points in line B lie to the other. Then, the line can be used to classify new points, whose class we don't already know. But there may be many possible such lines that can separate points in class A from points in class B. A few such lines are shown in Figure 20.5. The Support Vector Machine classifier chooses the line whose distance from the nearest point in either class (from the points in the training data set) is maximum. This line (called the *maximum margin line*) is then used to classify other points into class A or B, depending on which side of the line they lie on. In Figure 20.5, the maximum margin line is shown in bold, while the other lines are shown as dashed lines.

The above intuition can be generalized to more than two dimensions, allowing multiple attributes to be used for classification; in this case, the classifier finds a dividing plane, not a line. Further, by first transforming the input points using certain functions, called *kernel functions*, Support Vector Machine classifiers can find nonlinear curves separating the sets of points. This is important for cases

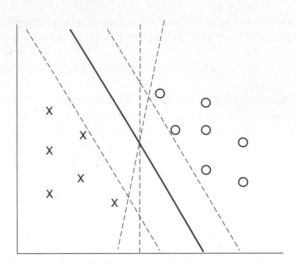

Figure 20.5   Example of a support vector machine classifier.

where the points are not separable by a line or plane. In the presence of noise, some points of one class may lie in the midst of points of the other class. In such cases, there may not be any line or meaningful curve that separates the points in the two classes; then, the line or curve that most accurately divides the points into the two classes is chosen.

Although the basic formulation of Support Vector Machines is for binary classifiers, i.e., those with only two classes, they can be used for classification into multiple classes as follows: If there are N classes, we build N classifiers, with classifier i performing a binary classification, classifying a point either as in class i or not in class i. Given a point, each classifier i also outputs a value indicating how related a given point is to class i. We then apply all N classifiers on a given point, and choose the class for which the relatedness value is the highest.

20.4.3 Regression

Regression deals with the prediction of a value, rather than a class. Given values for a set of variables, $X_1, X_2, \ldots, X_n$, we wish to predict the value of a variable Y. For instance, we could treat the level of education as a number and income as another number, and, on the basis of these two variables, we wish to predict the likelihood of default, which could be a percentage chance of defaulting, or the amount involved in the default.

One way is to infer coefficients $a_0, a_1, a_2, \ldots, a_n$ such that:

$$Y = a_0 + a_1 * X_1 + a_2 * X_2 + \cdots + a_n * X_n$$

Finding such a linear polynomial is called **linear regression**. In general, we wish to find a curve (defined by a polynomial or other formula) that fits the data; the process is also called **curve fitting**.

The fit may be only approximate, because of noise in the data or because the relationship is not exactly a polynomial, so regression aims to find coefficients that give the best possible fit. There are standard techniques in statistics for finding regression coefficients. We do not discuss these techniques here, but the bibliographical notes provide references.

20.4.4 Validating a Classifier

It is important to validate a classifier, that is, to measure its classification error rate, before deciding to use it for an application. Consider an example of a classification problem where a classifier has to predict, based on some inputs (the exact inputs are not relevant here), whether a person is suffering from a particular disease X or not. A positive prediction says that the person has the disease, and a negative prediction says the person does not have the disease. (The terminology of positive/negative prediction can be used for any binary classification problem, not just disease classification.)

A set of test cases where the outcome is already known (in our example, cases where it is already known whether or not the person actually has the disease) is used to measure the quality (that is, the error rate) of the classifier. A **true positive** is a case where the prediction was positive, and the person actually had the disease, while a **false positive** is a case where the prediction was positive, but the person did not have the disease. **True negative** and **false negative** are defined similarly for the case where the prediction was negative.

Given a set of test cases, let t_pos, f_pos, t_neg and f_neg denote the number of true positives, false positives, true negatives and false negatives generated. Let pos and neg denote the actual number of positives and negatives (it is easy to see that $pos = t\_pos + f\_neg$, and $neg = f\_pos + t\_neg$).

The quality of classification can be measured in several different ways:

1. **Accuracy**, defined as $(t\_pos + t\_neg)/(pos+neg)$, that is, the fraction of the time when the classifier gives the correct classification.

2. **Recall** (also known as **sensitivity**) defined as t_pos/pos, that is, how many of the actual positive cases are classified as positive.

3. **Precision**, defined as $t\_pos/(t\_pos+f\_pos)$, that is, how often the positive prediction is correct.

4. **Specificity**, defined as t_neg/neg.

Which of these measures should be used for a specific application depends on the needs of that application. For example, a high recall is important for a screening test, which is to be followed up by a more precise test, so that patients with the disease are not missed out. In contrast a researcher who wants to find a few actual patients of the disease for further follow up, but is not interested in finding all patients, may value high precision over recall. Different classifiers may be appropriate for each of these applications. This issue is explored further in Exercise 20.5.

A set of test cases where the outcome is already known can be used either to train or to measure the quality the classifier. It is a bad idea to use exactly the same set of test cases to train as well as to measure the quality of the classifier, since the classifier has already seen the correct classification of the test cases during training; this can lead to artificially high measures of quality. The quality of a classifier must therefore be measured on test cases that have not been seen during training.

Therefore, a subset of the available test cases is used for training and a disjoint subset is used for validation. In **cross validation**, the available test cases are divided into k parts numbered 1 to k, from which k different test sets are created as follows: test set i uses the ith part for validation, after training the classifier using the other $k-1$ parts. The results (t_pos, f_pos, etc.) from all k test sets are added up before computing the quality measures. Cross validation provides much more accurate measures than merely partitioning the data into a single training and a single test set.

20.5   Association Rules

Retail shops are often interested in **associations** between different items that people buy. Examples of such associations are:

- Someone who buys bread is quite likely also to buy milk.

- A person who bought the book *Database System Concepts* is quite likely also to buy the book *Operating System Concepts*.

Association information can be used in several ways. When a customer buys a particular book, an online shop may suggest associated books. A grocery shop may decide to place bread close to milk, since they are often bought together, to help shoppers finish their task faster. Or, the shop may place them at opposite ends of a row, and place other associated items in between to tempt people to buy those items as well, as the shoppers walk from one end of the row to the other. A shop that offers discounts on one associated item may not offer a discount on the other, since the customer will probably buy the other anyway.

An example of an association rule is:

$$bread \Rightarrow milk$$

In the context of grocery-store purchases, the rule says that customers who buy bread also tend to buy milk with a high probability. An association rule must have an associated **population**: The population consists of a set of **instances**. In the grocery-store example, the population may consist of all grocery-store purchases; each purchase is an instance. In the case of a bookstore, the population may consist of all people who made purchases, regardless of when they made a purchase. Each customer is an instance. In the bookstore example, the analyst has decided that when a purchase is made is not significant, whereas for the grocery-store example, the analyst may have decided to concentrate on single purchases, ignoring multiple visits by the same customer.

Rules have an associated *support*, as well as an associated *confidence*. These are defined in the context of the population:

- **Support** is a measure of what fraction of the population satisfies both the antecedent and the consequent of the rule.

  For instance, suppose only 0.001 percent of all purchases include milk and screwdrivers. The support for the rule:

  $$milk \Rightarrow screwdrivers$$

  is low. The rule may not even be statistically significant—perhaps there was only a single purchase that included both milk and screwdrivers. Businesses are usually not interested in rules that have low support, since they involve few customers, and are not worth bothering about.

  On the other hand, if 50 percent of all purchases involve milk and bread, then support for rules involving bread and milk (and no other item) is relatively high, and such rules may be worth attention. Exactly what minimum degree of support is considered desirable depends on the application.

- **Confidence** is a measure of how often the consequent is true when the antecedent is true. For instance, the rule:

  $$bread \Rightarrow milk$$

  has a confidence of 80 percent if 80 percent of the purchases that include bread also include milk. A rule with a low confidence is not meaningful. In business applications, rules usually have confidences significantly less than 100 percent, whereas in other domains, such as in physics, rules may have high confidences.

  Note that the confidence of $bread \Rightarrow milk$ may be very different from the confidence of $milk \Rightarrow bread$, although both have the same support.

To discover association rules of the form:

$$i_1, i_2, \ldots, i_n \Rightarrow i_0$$

we first find sets of items with sufficient support, called **large itemsets**. In our example, we find sets of items that are included in a sufficiently large number of instances. We shall see shortly how to compute large itemsets.

For each large itemset, we then output all rules with sufficient confidence that involve all and only the elements of the set. For each large itemset S, we output a rule $S - s \Rightarrow s$ for every subset $s \subset S$, provided $S - s \Rightarrow s$ has sufficient confidence; the confidence of the rule is given by support of s divided by support of S.

We now consider how to generate all large itemsets. If the number of possible sets of items is small, a single pass over the data suffices to detect the level of support for all the sets. A count, initialized to 0, is maintained for each set of items. When a purchase record is fetched, the count is incremented for each set of items such that all items in the set are contained in the purchase. For instance, if a purchase included items a, b, and c, counts would be incremented for $\{a\}$, $\{b\}$, $\{c\}$, $\{a, b\}$, $\{b, c\}$, $\{a, c\}$, and $\{a, b, c\}$. Those sets with a sufficiently high count at the end of the pass correspond to items that have a high degree of association.

The number of sets grows exponentially, making the procedure just described infeasible if the number of items is large. Luckily, almost all the sets would normally have very low support; optimizations have been developed to eliminate most such sets from consideration. These techniques use multiple passes on the database, considering only some sets in each pass.

In the **a priori** technique for generating large itemsets, only sets with single items are considered in the first pass. In the second pass, sets with two items are considered, and so on.

At the end of a pass, all sets with sufficient support are output as large itemsets. Sets found to have too little support at the end of a pass are eliminated. Once a set is eliminated, none of its supersets needs to be considered. In other words, in pass i we need to count only supports for sets of size i such that all subsets of the set have been found to have sufficiently high support; it suffices to test all subsets of size $i - 1$ to ensure this property. At the end of some pass i, we would find that no set of size i has sufficient support, so we do not need to consider any set of size $i + 1$. Computation then terminates.

20.6   Other Types of Associations

Using plain association rules has several shortcomings. One of the major shortcomings is that many associations are not very interesting, since they can be predicted. For instance, if many people buy cereal and many people buy bread, we can predict that a fairly large number of people would buy both, even if there is no connection between the two purchases. In fact, even if buying cereal has a mild negative influence on buying bread (that is, customers who buy cereal tend to purchase bread less often than the average customer), the association between cereal and bread may still have a high support.

What would be more interesting is if there is a **deviation** from the expected co-occurrence of the two. In statistical terms, we look for **correlations** between items; correlations can be positive, in that the co-occurrence is higher than would have been expected, or negative, in that the items co-occur less frequently than predicted. Thus, if purchase of bread is not correlated with cereal, it would not be reported, even if there was a strong association between the two. There are standard measures of correlation, widely used in the area of statistics. See a standard textbook on statistics for more information about correlations.

Another important class of data-mining applications is sequence associations (or sequence correlations). Time-series data, such as stock prices on a sequence of days, form an example of sequence data. Stock-market analysts want to find associations among stock-market price sequences. An example of such an association is the following rule: "Whenever bond rates go up, the stock prices go down within 2 days." Discovering such associations between sequences can help us to make intelligent investment decisions. See the bibliographical notes for references to research on this topic.

Deviations from temporal patterns are often interesting. For instance, if a company has been growing at a steady rate each year, a deviation from the usual growth rate is surprising. If sales of winter clothes go down in summer, it is not surprising, since we can predict it from past years; a deviation that we could not have predicted from past experience would be considered interesting. Mining techniques can find deviations from what one would have expected on the basis of past temporal or sequential patterns. See the bibliographical notes for references to research on this topic.

20.7 Clustering

Intuitively, clustering refers to the problem of finding clusters of points in the given data. The problem of **clustering** can be formalized from distance metrics in several ways. One way is to phrase it as the problem of grouping points into k sets (for a given k) so that the average distance of points from the *centroid* of their assigned cluster is minimized.[2] Another way is to group points so that the average distance between every pair of points in each cluster is minimized. There are other definitions too; see the bibliographical notes for details. But the intuition behind all these definitions is to group similar points together in a single set.

Another type of clustering appears in classification systems in biology. (Such classification systems do not attempt to *predict* classes; rather they attempt to cluster related items together.) For instance, leopards and humans are clustered under the class mammalia, while crocodiles and snakes are clustered under reptilia. Both mammalia and reptilia come under the common class chordata. The clustering of mammalia has further subclusters, such as carnivora and primates. We thus have **hierarchical clustering**. Given characteristics of different species, biologists have created a complex hierarchical clustering scheme grouping related species together at different levels of the hierarchy.

Hierarchical clustering is also useful in other domains—for clustering documents, for example. Internet directory systems (such as the Yahoo! directory) cluster related documents in a hierarchical fashion (see Section 21.9). Hierarchical clustering algorithms can be classified as **agglomerative clustering** algorithms, which start by building small clusters and then create higher levels, or **divisive**

---

[2]The centroid of a set of points is defined as a point whose coordinate on each dimension is the average of the coordinates of all the points of that set on that dimension. For example in two dimensions, the centroid of a set of points { (x_1, y_1), $(x_2, y_2), \ldots, (x_n, y_n)$ } is given by $\left(\frac{\sum_{i=1}^{n} x_i}{n}, \frac{\sum_{i=1}^{n} y_i}{n} \right)$.

clustering algorithms, which first create higher levels of the hierarchical clustering, then refine each resulting cluster into lower-level clusters.

The statistics community has studied clustering extensively. Database research has provided scalable clustering algorithms that can cluster very large data sets (that may not fit in memory). The Birch clustering algorithm is one such algorithm. Intuitively, data points are inserted into a multidimensional tree structure (based on R-trees, described in Section 25.3.5.3), and guided to appropriate leaf nodes on the basis of nearness to representative points in the internal nodes of the tree. Nearby points are thus clustered together in leaf nodes, and summarized if there are more points than fit in memory. The result of this first phase of clustering is to create a partially clustered data set that fits in memory. Standard clustering techniques can then be executed on the in-memory data to get the final clustering. See the bibliographical notes for references to the Birch algorithm, and other techniques for clustering, including algorithms for hierarchical clustering.

An interesting application of clustering is to predict what new movies (or books or music) a person is likely to be interested in, on the basis of:

1. The person's past preferences in movies.

2. Other people with similar past preferences.

3. The preferences of such people for new movies.

One approach to this problem is as follows: To find people with similar past preferences we create clusters of people based on their preferences for movies. The accuracy of clustering can be improved by previously clustering movies by their similarity, so even if people have not seen the same movies, if they have seen similar movies they would be clustered together. We can repeat the clustering, alternately clustering people, then movies, then people, and so on until we reach an equilibrium. Given a new user, we find a cluster of users most similar to that user, on the basis of the user's preferences for movies already seen. We then predict movies in movie clusters that are popular with that user's cluster as likely to be interesting to the new user. In fact, this problem is an instance of *collaborative filtering*, where users collaborate in the task of filtering information to find information of interest.

20.8   Other Forms of Data Mining

Text mining applies data-mining techniques to textual documents. For instance, there are tools that form clusters on pages that a user has visited; this helps users when they browse the history of their browsing to find pages they have visited earlier. The distance between pages can be based, for instance, on common words in the pages (see Section 21.2.2). Another application is to classify pages into a Web directory automatically, according to their similarity with other pages (see Section 21.9).

Data-visualization systems help users to examine large volumes of data, and to detect patterns visually. Visual displays of data—such as maps, charts, and other graphical representations—allow data to be presented compactly to users. A single graphical screen can encode as much information as a far larger number of text screens. For example, if the user wants to find out whether production problems at plants are correlated to the locations of the plants, the problem locations can be encoded in a special color—say, red—on a map. The user can then quickly discover locations where problems are occurring. The user may then form hypotheses about why problems are occurring in those locations, and may verify the hypotheses quantitatively against the database.

As another example, information about values can be encoded as a color, and can be displayed with as little as one pixel of screen area. To detect associations between pairs of items, we can use a two-dimensional pixel matrix, with each row and each column representing an item. The percentage of transactions that buy both items can be encoded by the color intensity of the pixel. Items with high association will show up as bright pixels in the screen—easy to detect against the darker background.

Data-visualization systems do not automatically detect patterns, but they provide system support for users to detect patterns. Since humans are very good at detecting visual patterns, data visualization is an important component of data mining.

20.9 Summary

- Decision-support systems analyze online data collected by transaction-processing systems, to help people make business decisions. Since most organizations are extensively computerized today, a very large body of information is available for decision support. Decision-support systems come in various forms, including OLAP systems and data-mining systems.

- Data warehouses help gather and archive important operational data. Warehouses are used for decision support and analysis on historical data, for instance, to predict trends. Data cleansing from input data sources is often a major task in data warehousing. Warehouse schemas tend to be multidimensional, involving one or a few very large fact tables and several much smaller dimension tables.

- Column-oriented storage systems provide good performance for many data warehousing applications.

- Data mining is the process of semiautomatically analyzing large databases to find useful patterns. There are a number of applications of data mining, such as prediction of values based on past examples, finding of associations between purchases, and automatic clustering of people and movies.

- Classification deals with predicting the class of test instances by using attributes of the test instances, based on attributes of training instances, and the actual class of training instances. There are several types of classifiers, such as:

- Decision-tree classifiers, which perform classification by constructing a tree based on training instances with leaves having class labels. The tree is traversed for each test instance to find a leaf, and the class of the leaf is the predicted class. Several techniques are available to construct decision trees, most of them based on greedy heuristics.

- Bayesian classifiers are simpler to construct than decision-tree classifiers, and they work better in the case of missing/null attribute values.

- The Support Vector Machine is another widely used classification technique.

- Association rules identify items that co-occur frequently, for instance, items that tend to be bought by the same customer. Correlations look for deviations from expected levels of association.

- Other types of data mining include clustering, text mining, and data visualization.

Review Terms

- Decision-support systems
- Statistical analysis
- Data warehousing
  - Gathering data
  - Source-driven architecture
  - Destination-driven architecture
  - Data cleansing
    - Merge–purge
    - Householding
  - Extract, transform, load (ETL)
- Warehouse schemas
  - Fact table
  - Dimension tables
  - Star schema
- Column-oriented storage

- Data mining
- Prediction
- Associations
- Classification
  - Training data
  - Test data
- Decision-tree classifiers
  - Partitioning attribute
  - Partitioning condition
  - Purity
    - Gini measure
    - Entropy measure
  - Information gain
  - Information content
  - Information gain ratio
  - Continuous-valued attribute

- ○ Categorical attribute
- ○ Binary split
- ○ Multiway split
- ○ Overfitting
- • Bayesian classifiers
    - ○ Bayes' theorem
    - ○ Naive Bayesian classifiers
- • Support Vector Machine (SVM)
- • Regression
    - ○ Linear regression
    - ○ Curve fitting
- • Validation
    - ○ Accuracy
    - ○ Recall

- ○ Precision
- ○ Specificity
- ○ Cross validation
- • Association rules
    - ○ Population
    - ○ Support
    - ○ Confidence
    - ○ Large itemsets
- • Other types of associations
- • Clustering
    - ○ Hierarchical clustering
    - ○ Agglomerative clustering
    - ○ Divisive clustering
- • Text mining
- • Data visualization

Practice Exercises

20.1 Describe benefits and drawbacks of a source-driven architecture for gathering of data at a data warehouse, as compared to a destination-driven architecture.

20.2 Why is column-oriented storage potentially advantageous in a database system that supports a data warehouse?

20.3 Suppose that there are two classification rules, one that says that people with salaries between $10,000 and $20,000 have a credit rating of *good*, and another that says that people with salaries between $20,000 and $30,000 have a credit rating of *good*. Under what conditions can the rules be replaced, without any loss of information, by a single rule that says people with salaries between $10,000 and $30,000 have a credit rating of *good*?

20.4 Consider the schema depicted in Figure 20.2. Give an SQL query to summarize sales numbers and price by store and date, along with the hierarchies on store and date.

20.5 Consider a classification problem where the classifier predicts whether a person has a particular disease. Suppose that 95% of the people tested do not suffer from the disease. (That is, *pos* corresponds to 5% and *neg* to 95% of the test cases.) Consider the following classifiers:

- Classifier C_1 which always predicts negative (a rather useless classifier of course).

- Classifier C_2 which predicts positive in 80% of the cases where the person actually has the disease, but also predicts positive in 5% of the cases where the person does not have the disease.

- Classifier C_3 which predicts positive in 95% of the cases where the person actually has the disease, but also predicts positive in 20% of the cases where the person does not have the disease.

Given the above classifiers, answer the following questions.

a. For each of the above classifiers, compute the accuracy, precision, recall and specificity.

b. If you intend to use the results of classification to perform further screening for the disease, how would you choose between the classifiers.

c. On the other hand, if you intend to use the result of classification to start medication, where the medication could have harmful effects if given to someone who does not have the disease, how would you choose between the classifiers?

Exercises

20.6 Draw a diagram that shows how the *classroom* relation of our university example as shown in Appendix A would be stored under a column-oriented storage structure.

20.7 Explain why the nested-loops join algorithm (see Section 12.5.1) would work poorly on database stored in a column-oriented manner. Describe an alternative algorithm that would work better and explain why your solution is better.

20.8 Construct a decision-tree classifier with binary splits at each node, using tuples in relation $r(A, B, C)$ shown below as training data; attribute C denotes the class. Show the final tree, and with each node show the best split for each attribute along with its information gain value.

$$(1, 2, a), (2, 1, a), (2, 5, b), (3, 3, b), (3, 6, b),$$
$$(4, 5, b), (5, 5, c), (6, 3, b), (6, 7, c)$$

20.9 Suppose half of all the transactions in a clothes shop purchase jeans, and one third of all transactions in the shop purchase T-shirts. Suppose also that half of the transactions that purchase jeans also purchase T-shirts. Write down all the (nontrivial) association rules you can deduce from the above information, giving support and confidence of each rule.

20.10 Consider the problem of finding large itemsets.

    a. Describe how to find the support for a given collection of itemsets by using a single scan of the data. Assume that the itemsets and associated information, such as counts, will fit in memory.

    b. Suppose an itemset has support less than j. Show that no superset of this itemset can have support greater than or equal to j.

20.11 Create a small example of a set of transactions showing that although many transactions contain two items, that is, the itemset containing the two items has a high support, purchase of one of the items may have a negative correlation with purchase of the other.

20.12 The organization of parts, chapters, sections, and subsections in a book is related to clustering. Explain why, and to what form of clustering.

20.13 Suggest how predictive mining techniques can be used by a sports team, using your favorite sport as an example.

Tools

A variety of tools are available for each of the applications we have studied in this chapter. Most database vendors provide OLAP tools as part of their database systems, or as add-on applications. These include OLAP tools from Microsoft Corp., SAP, IBM and Oracle. The Mondrian OLAP server is a public-domain OLAP server. Many companies also provide analysis tools for specific applications, such as customer relationship management.

Major database vendors also offer data warehousing products coupled with their database systems. These provide support functionality for data modeling, cleansing, loading, and querying. The Web site www.dwinfocenter.org provides information on data-warehousing products.

There is also a wide variety of general-purpose data-mining tools, including data-mining suites from the SAS Institute, IBM Intelligent Miner, and Oracle. There are also several open-source data-mining tools, such as the widely used Weka, and RapidMiner. The open-source business intelligence suite Pentaho has several components including an ETL tool, the Mondrian OLAP server, and data-mining tools based on Weka.

A good deal of expertise is required to apply general-purpose mining tools for specific applications. As a result, a large number of mining tools have been developed to address specialized applications. The Web site www.kdnuggets.com provides an extensive directory of mining software, solutions, publications, and so on.

Bibliographical Notes

Definitions of statistical functions can be found in standard statistics textbooks such as Bulmer [1979] and Ross [1999].

Poe [1995] and Mattison [1996] provide textbook coverage of data warehousing. Zhuge et al. [1995] describes view maintenance in a data-warehousing environment. Chaudhuri et al. [2003] describes techniques for fuzzy matching for data cleaning, while Sarawagi et al. [2002] describes a system for deduplication using active learning techniques.

Abadi et al. [2008] presents a comparison of column-oriented and row-oriented storage, including issues related to query processing and optimization.

Witten and Frank [1999] and Han and Kamber [2000] provide textbook coverage of data mining. Mitchell [1997] is a classic textbook on machine learning, and covers classification techniques in detail. Fayyad et al. [1995] presents an extensive collection of articles on knowledge discovery and data mining. Kohavi and Provost [2001] presents a collection of articles on applications of data mining to electronic commerce.

Agrawal et al. [1993b] provides an early overview of data mining in databases. Algorithms for computing classifiers with large training sets are described by Agrawal et al. [1992] and Shafer et al. [1996]; the decision-tree construction algorithm described in this chapter is based on the SPRINT algorithm of Shafer et al. [1996]. Cortes and Vapnik [1995] introduced several key results on Support Vector Machines, while Cristianini and Shawe-Taylor [2000] provides textbook coverage of Support Vector Machines.

Agrawal et al. [1993a] introduced the notion of association rules, and an efficient algorithm for association rule mining was presented by Agrawal and Srikant [1994]. Algorithms for mining of different forms of association rules are described by Srikant and Agrawal [1996a] and Srikant and Agrawal [1996b]. Chakrabarti et al. [1998] describes techniques for mining surprising temporal patterns. Techniques for integrating data cubes with data mining are described by Sarawagi [2000].

Clustering has long been studied in the area of statistics, and Jain and Dubes [1988] provides textbook coverage of clustering. Ng and Han [1994] describes spatial clustering techniques. Clustering techniques for large datasets are described by Zhang et al. [1996]. Breese et al. [1998] provides an empirical analysis of different algorithms for collaborative filtering. Techniques for collaborative filtering of news articles are described by Konstan et al. [1997].

Chakrabarti [2002] and Manning et al. [2008] provide textbook description of information retrieval, including extensive coverage of data-mining tasks related to textual and hypertext data, such as classification and clustering. Chakrabarti [2000] provides a survey of hypertext mining techniques such as hypertext classification and clustering.

CHAPTER **21**

Information Retrieval

Textual data is unstructured, unlike the rigidly structured data in relational databases. The term **information retrieval** generally refers to the querying of unstructured textual data. Information-retrieval systems have much in common with database systems, in particular, the storage and retrieval of data on secondary storage. However, the emphasis in the field of information systems is different from that in database systems, concentrating on issues such as querying based on keywords; the relevance of documents to the query; and the analysis, classification, and indexing of documents. Web search engines today go beyond the paradigm of retrieving documents, and address broader issues such as what information to display in response to a keyword query, to satisfy the information needs of a user.

21.1 Overview

The field of **information retrieval** has developed in parallel with the field of databases. In the traditional model used in the field of information retrieval, information is organized into documents, and it is assumed that there is a large number of documents. Data contained in documents are unstructured, without any associated schema. The process of information retrieval consists of locating relevant documents, on the basis of user input, such as keywords or example documents.

The Web provides a convenient way to get to, and to interact with, information sources across the Internet. However, a persistent problem facing the Web is the explosion of stored information, with little guidance to help the user to locate what is interesting. Information retrieval has played a critical role in making the Web a productive and useful tool, especially for researchers.

Traditional examples of information-retrieval systems are online library catalogs and online document-management systems such as those that store newspaper articles. The data in such systems are organized as a collection of *documents*; a newspaper article and a catalog entry (in a library catalog) are examples of documents. In the context of the Web, usually each HTML page is considered to be a document.

A user of such a system may want to retrieve a particular document or a particular class of documents. The intended documents are typically described by a set of **keywords**—for example, the keywords "database system" may be used to locate books on database systems, and the keywords "stock" and "scandal" may be used to locate articles about stock-market scandals. Documents have associated with them a set of keywords, and documents whose keywords contain those supplied by the user are retrieved.

Keyword-based information retrieval can be used not only for retrieving textual data, but also for retrieving other types of data, such as video and audio data, that have descriptive keywords associated with them. For instance, a video movie may have associated with it keywords such as its title, director, actors, and genre, while an image or video clip may have tags, which are keywords describing the image or video clip, associated with it.

There are several differences between this model and the models used in traditional database systems.

- Database systems deal with several operations that are not addressed in information-retrieval systems. For instance, database systems deal with updates and with the associated transactional requirements of concurrency control and durability. These matters are viewed as less important in information systems. Similarly, database systems deal with structured information organized with relatively complex data models (such as the relational model or object-oriented data models), whereas information-retrieval systems traditionally have used a much simpler model, where the information in the database is organized simply as a collection of unstructured documents.

- Information-retrieval systems deal with several issues that have not been addressed adequately in database systems. For instance, the field of information retrieval has dealt with the issue of querying collections of unstructured documents, focusing on issues such as keyword queries, and of ranking of documents on estimated degree of relevance of the documents to the query.

In addition to simple keyword queries that are just sets of words, information-retrieval systems typically allow query expressions formed using keywords and the logical connectives *and, or*, and *not*. For example, a user could ask for all documents that contain the keywords "motorcycle *and* maintenance," or documents that contain the keywords "computer *or* microprocessor," or even documents that contain the keyword "computer *but not* database." A query containing keywords without any of the above connectives is assumed to have *and*s implicitly connecting the keywords.

In **full text** retrieval, all the words in each document are considered to be keywords. For unstructured documents, full text retrieval is essential since there may be no information about what words in the document are keywords. We shall use the word **term** to refer to the words in a document, since all words are keywords.

In its simplest form, an information-retrieval system locates and returns all documents that contain all the keywords in the query, if the query has no connectives; connectives are handled as you would expect. More-sophisticated systems estimate relevance of documents to a query so that the documents can be shown in order of estimated relevance. They use information about term occurrences, as well as hyperlink information, to estimate relevance.

Information-retrieval systems, as exemplified by Web search engines, have today evolved beyond just retrieving documents based on a ranking scheme. Today, search engines aim to satisfy a user's information needs, by judging what topic a query is about, and displaying not only Web pages judged as relevant, but also displaying other kinds of information about the topic. For example, given a query term "cricket", a search engine may display scores from ongoing or recent cricket matches, rather than just display top-ranked documents related to cricket. As another example, in response to a query "New York", a search engine may show a map of New York, and images of New York, in addition to Web pages related to New York.

21.2   Relevance Ranking Using Terms

The set of all documents that satisfy a query expression may be very large; in particular, there are billions of documents on the Web, and most keyword queries on a Web search engine find hundreds of thousands of documents containing the keywords. Full text retrieval makes this problem worse: each document may contain many terms, and even terms that are mentioned only in passing are treated equivalently with documents where the term is indeed relevant. Irrelevant documents may be retrieved as a result.

Information-retrieval systems therefore estimate relevance of documents to a query, and return only highly ranked documents as answers. Relevance ranking is not an exact science, but there are some well-accepted approaches.

21.2.1   Ranking Using TF-IDF

The first question to address is, given a particular term t, how relevant is a particular document d to the term. One approach is to use the the number of occurrences of the term in the document as a measure of its relevance, on the assumption that relevant terms are likely to be mentioned many times in a document. Just counting the number of occurrences of a term is usually not a good indicator: first, the number of occurrences depends on the length of the document, and second, a document containing 10 occurrences of a term may not be 10 times as relevant as a document containing one occurrence.

One way of measuring $TF(d, t)$, the relevance of a document d to a term t, is:

$$TF(d, t) = \log \left(1 + \frac{n(d, t)}{n(d)} \right)$$

where $n(d)$ denotes the number of terms in the document and $n(d, t)$ denotes the number of occurrences of term t in the document d. Observe that this metric takes the length of the document into account. The relevance grows with more occurrences of a term in the document, although it is not directly proportional to the number of occurrences.

Many systems refine the above metric by using other information. For instance, if the term occurs in the title, or the author list, or the abstract, the document would be considered more relevant to the term. Similarly, if the first occurrence of a term is late in the document, the document may be considered less relevant than if the first occurrence is early in the document. The above notions can be formalized by extensions of the formula we have shown for $TF(d, t)$. In the information retrieval community, the relevance of a document to a term is referred to as **term frequency** (TF), regardless of the exact formula used.

A query Q may contain multiple keywords. The relevance of a document to a query with two or more keywords is estimated by combining the relevance measures of the document to each keyword. A simple way of combining the measures is to add them up. However, not all terms used as keywords are equal. Suppose a query uses two terms, one of which occurs frequently, such as "database", and another that is less frequent, such as "Silberschatz". A document containing "Silberschatz" but not "database" should be ranked higher than a document containing the term "database" but not "Silberschatz".

To fix the above problem, weights are assigned to terms using the **inverse document frequency** (IDF), defined as:

$$IDF(t) = \frac{1}{n(t)}$$

where $n(t)$ denotes the number of documents (among those indexed by the system) that contain the term t. The **relevance** of a document d to a set of terms Q is then defined as:

$$r(d, Q) = \sum_{t \in Q} TF(d, t) * IDF(t)$$

This measure can be further refined if the user is permitted to specify weights $w(t)$ for terms in the query, in which case the user-specified weights are also taken into account by multiplying $TF(t)$ by $w(t)$ in the above formula.

The above approach of using term frequency and inverse document frequency as a measure of the relevance of a document is called the **TF–IDF** approach.

Almost all text documents (in English) contain words such as "and," "or," "a," and so on, and hence these words are useless for querying purposes since their inverse document frequency is extremely low. Information-retrieval systems define a set of words, called **stop words**, containing 100 or so of the most common words, and ignore these words when indexing a document. Such words are not used as keywords, and are discarded if present in the keywords supplied by the user.

Another factor taken into account when a query contains multiple terms is the **proximity** of the terms in the document. If the terms occur close to each other in the document, the document would be ranked higher than if they occur far apart. The formula for $r(d, Q)$ can be modified to take proximity of the terms into account.

Given a query Q, the job of an information-retrieval system is to return documents in descending order of their relevance to Q. Since there may be a very large number of documents that are relevant, information-retrieval systems typically return only the first few documents with the highest degree of estimated relevance, and permit users to interactively request further documents.

21.2.2 Similarity-Based Retrieval

Certain information-retrieval systems permit **similarity-based retrieval**. Here, the user can give the system document A, and ask the system to retrieve documents that are "similar" to A. The similarity of a document to another may be defined, for example, on the basis of common terms. One approach is to find k terms in A with highest values of $TF(A, t) * IDF(t)$, and to use these k terms as a query to find relevance of other documents. The terms in the query are themselves weighted by $TF(A, t) * IDF(t)$.

More generally, the similarity of documents is defined by the **cosine similarity** metric. Let the terms occurring in either of the two documents be $t_1, t_2, \ldots, t_n$. Let $r(d, t) = TF(d, t) * IDF(t)$. Then the cosine similarity metric between documents d and e is defined as:

$$\frac{\sum_{i=1}^{n} r(d, t_i) r(e, t_i)}{\sqrt{\sum_{i=1}^{n} r(d, t_i)^2} \sqrt{\sum_{i=1}^{n} r(e, t_i)^2}}$$

You can easily verify that the cosine similarity metric of a document with itself is 1, while that between two documents that do not share any terms is 0.

The name "cosine similarity" comes from the fact that the above formula computes the cosine of the angle between two vectors, one representing each document, defined as follows: Let there be n words overall across all the documents being considered. An n-dimensional space is defined, with each word as one of the dimensions. A document d is represented by a point in this space, with the value of the ith coordinate of the point being $r(d, t_i)$. The vector for document d connects the origin (all coordinates = 0) to the point representing the document. The model of documents as points and vectors in an n-dimensional space is called the **vector space model**.

If the set of documents similar to a query document A is large, the system may present the user a few of the similar documents, allow the user to choose the most relevant few, and start a new search based on similarity to A *and* to the chosen documents. The resultant set of documents is likely to be what the user intended to find. This idea is called **relevance feedback**.

Relevance feedback can also be used to help users find relevant documents from a large set of documents matching the given query keywords. In such a situation, users may be allowed to identify one or a few of the returned documents as relevant; the system then uses the identified documents to find other similar ones. The resultant set of documents is likely to be what the user intended to find. An alternative to the relevance feedback approach is to require users to modify the query by adding more keywords; relevance feedback can be easier to use, in addition to giving a better final set of documents as the answer.

In order to show the user a representative set of documents when the number of documents is very large, a search system may cluster the documents, based on their cosine similarity. Then, a few documents from each cluster may be shown, so that more than one cluster is represented in the set of answers. Clustering was described earlier in Section 20.7, and several techniques have been developed to cluster sets of documents. See the bibliographical notes for references to more information on clustering.

As a special case of similarity, there are often multiple copies of a document on the Web; this could happen, for example, if a Web site mirrors the contents of another Web site. In this case, it makes no sense to return multiple copies of a highly ranked document as separate answers; duplicates should be detected, and only one copy should be returned as an answer.

21.3   Relevance Using Hyperlinks

Early Web-search engines ranked documents by using only TF–IDF based relevance measures like those described in Section 21.2. However, these techniques had some limitations when used on very large collections of documents, such as the set of all Web pages. In particular, many Web pages have all the keywords specified in a typical search engine query; further, some of the pages that users want as answers often have just a few occurrences of the query terms, and would not get a very high TF–IDF score.

However, researchers soon realized that Web pages have very important information that plain text documents do not have, namely hyperlinks. These can be exploited to get better relevance ranking; in particular, the relevance ranking of a page is influenced greatly by hyperlinks that point *to* the page. In this section, we study how hyperlinks are used for ranking of Web pages.

21.3.1   Popularity Ranking

The basic idea of **popularity ranking** (also called **prestige ranking**) is to find pages that are popular, and to rank them higher than other pages that contain the specified keywords. Since most searches are intended to find information from popular pages, ranking such pages higher is generally a good idea. For instance, the term "google" may occur in vast numbers of pages, but the page google.com is the most popular among the pages that contain the term "google." The page google.com should therefore be ranked as the most relevant answer to a query consisting of the term "google".

Traditional measures of relevance of a page such as the TF–IDF based measures that we saw in Section 21.2, can be combined with the popularity of the page to get an overall measure of the relevance of the page to the query. Pages with the highest overall relevance value are returned as the top answers to a query.

This raises the question of how to define and how to find the popularity of a page. One way would be to find how many times a page is accessed and use the number as a measure of the site's popularity. However, getting such information is impossible without the cooperation of the site, and while a few sites may be persuaded to reveal this information, it is difficult to get it for all sites. Further, sites may lie about their access frequency, in order to get ranked higher.

A very effective alternative is to use hyperlinks to a page as a measure of its popularity. Many people have bookmark files that contain links to sites that they use frequently. Sites that appear in a large number of bookmark files can be inferred to be very popular sites. Bookmark files are usually stored privately and not accessible on the Web. However, many users do maintain Web pages with links to their favorite Web pages. Many Web sites also have links to other related sites, which can also be used to infer the popularity of the linked sites. A Web search engine can fetch Web pages (by a process called crawling, which we describe in Section 21.7), and analyze them to find links between the pages.

A first solution to estimating the popularity of a page is to use the number of pages that link to the page as a measure of its popularity. However, this by itself has the drawback that many sites have a number of useful pages, yet external links often point only to the root page of the site. The root page in turn has links to other pages in the site. These other pages would then be wrongly inferred to be not very popular, and would have a low ranking in answering queries.

One alternative is to associate popularity with sites, rather than with pages. All pages at a site then get the popularity of the site, and pages other than the root page of a popular site would also benefit from the site's popularity. However, the question of what constitutes a site then arises. In general the Internet address prefix of a page URL would constitute the site corresponding to the page. However, there are many sites that host a large number of mostly unrelated pages, such as home page servers in universities and Web portals such as groups.yahoo.com or groups.google.com. For such sites, the popularity of one part of the site does not imply popularity of another part of the site.

A simpler alternative is to allow **transfer of prestige** from popular pages to pages to which they link. Under this scheme, in contrast to the one-person one-vote principles of democracy, a link from a popular page x to a page y is treated as conferring more prestige to page y than a link from a not-so-popular page z.[1]

This notion of popularity is in fact circular, since the popularity of a page is defined by the popularity of other pages, and there may be cycles of links between pages. However, the popularity of pages can be defined by a system of simultaneous linear equations, which can be solved by matrix manipulation

---

[1]This is similar in some sense to giving extra weight to endorsements of products by celebrities (such as film stars), so its significance is open to question, although it is effective and widely used in practice.

techniques. The linear equations can be defined in such a way that they have a unique and well-defined solution.

It is interesting to note that the basic idea underlying popularity ranking is actually quite old, and first appeared in a theory of social networking developed by sociologists in the 1950s. In the social-networking context, the goal was to define the prestige of people. For example, the president of the United States has high prestige since a large number of people know him. If someone is known by multiple prestigious people, then she also has high prestige, even if she is not known by as large a number of people. The use of a set of linear equations to define the popularity measure also dates back to this work.

21.3.2   PageRank

The Web search engine Google introduced **PageRank**, which is a measure of popularity of a page based on the popularity of pages that link to the page. Using the PageRank popularity measure to rank answers to a query gave results so much better than previously used ranking techniques that Google became the most widely used search engine, in a rather short period of time.

PageRank can be understood intuitively using a **random walk model**. Suppose a person browsing the Web performs a random walk (traversal) on Web pages as follows: the first step starts at a random Web page, and in each step, the random walker does one of the following. With a probability δ the walker jumps to a randomly chosen Web page, and with a probability of $1 - \delta$ the walker randomly chooses one of the outlinks from the current Web page and follows the link. The PageRank of a page is then the probability that the random walker is visiting the page at any given point in time.

Note that pages that are pointed to from many Web pages are more likely to be visited, and thus will have a higher PageRank. Similarly, pages pointed to by Web pages with a high PageRank will also have a higher probability of being visited, and thus will have a higher PageRank.

PageRank can be defined by a set of linear equations, as follows: First, Web pages are given integer identifiers. The jump probability matrix T is defined with $T[i, j]$ set to the probability that a random walker who is following a link out of page i follows the link to page j. Assuming that each link from i has an equal probability of being followed $T[i, j] = 1/N_i$, where N_i is the number of links out of page i. Most entries of T are 0 and it is best represented as an adjacency list. Then the PageRank $P[j]$ for each page j can be defined as:

$$P[j] = \delta/N + (1 - \delta) * \sum_{i=1}^{N}(T[i, j] * P[i])$$

where δ is a constant between 0 and 1, and N the number of pages; δ represents the probability of a step in the random walk being a jump.

The set of equations generated as above are usually solved by an an iterative technique, starting with each $P[i]$ set to $1/N$. Each step of the iteration computes new values for each $P[i]$ using the P values from the previous iteration. Iteration stops when the maximum change in any $P[i]$ value in an iteration goes below some cutoff value.

21.3.3 Other Measures of Popularity

Basic measures of popularity such as PageRank play an important role in ranking of query answers, but are by no means the only factor. The TF–IDF scores of a page are used to judge its relevance to the query keywords, and must be combined with the popularity ranking. Other factors must also be taken into account, to handle limitations of PageRank and related popularity measures.

Information about how often a site is visited would be a useful measure of popularity, but as mentioned earlier it is hard to obtain in general. However, search engines do track what fraction of times users click on a page, when it is returned as an answer. This fraction can be used as a measure of the site's popularity. To measure the click fraction, instead of providing a direct link to the page, the search engine provides an indirect link through the search engine's site, which records the page click, and transparently redirects the browser to the original link.[2]

One drawback of the PageRank algorithm is that it assigns a measure of popularity that does not take query keywords into account. For example, the page google.com is likely to have a very high PageRank because many sites contain a link to it. Suppose it contains a word mentioned in passing, such as "Stanford" (the advanced search page at Google did in fact contain this word at one point several years ago). A search on the keyword Stanford would then return google.com as the highest-ranked answer, ahead of a more relevant answer such as the Stanford University Web page.

One widely used solution to this problem is to use keywords in the anchor text of links to a page to judge what topics the page is highly relevant to. The anchor text of a link consists of the text that appears within the HTML a href tag. For example, the anchor text of the link:

<a href="http://stanford.edu"> Stanford University</a>

is "Stanford University". If many links to the page stanford.edu have the word Stanford in their anchor text, the page can be judged to be very relevant to the keyword Stanford. Text near the anchor text may also be taken into account; for example, a Web site may contain the text "Stanford's home page is here", but may have used only the word "here" as anchor text in the link to the Stanford Web site.

Popularity based on anchor text is combined with other measures of popularity, and with TF–IDF measures, to get an overall ranking for query answers, as discussed in Section 21.3.5. As an implementation trick, the words in the anchor

---

[2]Sometimes this indirection is hidden from the user. For example when you point the mouse at a link (such as db-book.com) in a Google query result, the link appears to point directly to the site. However, at least as of mid 2009, when you actually click on the link, Javascript code associated with the page actually rewrites the link to go indirectly through Google's site. If you use the back button of the browser to go back to the query result page, and point to the link again, the change in the linked URL becomes visible.

text are often treated as part of the page, with a term frequency based on the the popularity of the pages where the anchor text appears. Then, TF–IDF ranking automatically takes anchor text into account.

An alternative approach to taking keywords into account when defining popularity is to compute a measure of popularity using *only* pages that contain the query keywords, instead of computing popularity using all available Web pages. This approach is more expensive, since the computation of popularity ranking has to be done dynamically when a query is received, whereas PageRank is computed statically once, and reused for all queries. Web search engines handling billions of queries per day cannot afford to spend so much time answering a query. As a result, although this approach can give better answers, it is not very widely used.

The HITS algorithm was based on the above idea of first finding pages that contain the query keywords, and then computing a popularity measure using just this set of related pages. In addition it introduced a notion of *hubs* and *authorities*. A **hub** is a page that stores links to many related pages; it may not in itself contain actual information on a topic, but points to pages that contain actual information. In contrast, an **authority** is a page that contains actual information on a topic, although it may not store links to many related pages. Each page then gets a prestige value as a hub (*hub-prestige*), and another prestige value as an authority (*authority-prestige*). The definitions of prestige, as before, are cyclic and are defined by a set of simultaneous linear equations. A page gets higher hub-prestige if it points to many pages with high authority-prestige, while a page gets higher authority-prestige if it is pointed to by many pages with high hub-prestige. Given a query, pages with highest authority-prestige are ranked higher than other pages. See the bibliographical notes for references giving further details.

21.3.4   Search Engine Spamming

Search engine spamming refers to the practice of creating Web pages, or sets of Web pages, designed to get a high relevance rank for some queries, even though the sites are not actually popular sites. For example, a travel site may want to be ranked high for queries with the keyword "travel". It can get high TF–IDF scores by repeating the word "travel" many times in its page.[3] Even a site unrelated to travel, such as a pornographic site, could do the same thing, and would get highly ranked for a query on the word travel. In fact, this sort of spamming of TF–IDF was common in the early days of Web search, and there was a constant battle between such sites and search engines that tried to detect spamming and deny them a high ranking.

Popularity ranking schemes such as PageRank make the job of search engine spamming more difficult, since just repeating words to get a high TF–IDF score was no longer sufficient. However, even these techniques can be spammed, by creating a collection of Web pages that point to each other, increasing their popularity

---

[3]Repeated words in a Web page may confuse users; spammers can tackle this problem by delivering different pages to search engines than to other users, for the same URL, or by making the repeated words invisible, for example, by formatting the words in small white font on a white background.

rank. Techniques such as using sites instead of pages as the unit of ranking (with appropriately normalized jump probabilities) have been proposed to avoid some spamming techniques, but are not fully effective against other spamming techniques. The war between search engine spammers and the search engines continues even today.

The hubs and authorities approach of the HITS algorithm is more susceptible to spamming. A spammer can create a Web page containing links to good authorities on a topic, and gains a high hub score as a result. In addition the spammer's Web page includes links to pages that they wish to popularize, which may not have any relevance to the topic. Because these linked pages are pointed to by a page with high hub score, they get a high but undeserved authority score.

21.3.5 Combining TF-IDF and Popularity Ranking Measures

We have seen two broad kinds of features used in ranking, namely TF–IDF and popularity scores such as PageRank. TF–IDF itself reflects a combination of several factors including raw term frequency and inverse document frequency, occurrence of a term in anchor text linking to the page, and a variety of other factors such as occurrence of the term in the title, occurrence of the term early in the document, and larger font size for the term, among other factors.

How to combine the scores of a page on each these factors, to generate an overall page score, is a major problem that must be addressed by any information retrieval system. In the early days of search engines, humans created functions to combine scores into an overall score. But today, search engines use machine-learning techniques to decide how to combine scores. Typically, a score combining formula is fixed, but the formula takes as parameters weights for different scoring factors. By using a training set of query results ranked by humans, a machine-learning algorithm can come up with an assignment of weights for each scoring factor that results in the best ranking performance across multiple queries.

We note that most search engines do not reveal how they compute relevance rankings; they believe that revealing their ranking techniques would allow competitors to catch up, and would make the job of search engine spamming easier, resulting in poorer quality of results.

21.4 Synonyms, Homonyms, and Ontologies

Consider the problem of locating documents about motorcycle maintenance, using the query "motorcycle maintenance". Suppose that the keywords for each document are the words in the title and the names of the authors. The document titled *Motorcycle Repair* would not be retrieved, since the word "maintenance" does not occur in its title.

We can solve that problem by making use of **synonyms**. Each word can have a set of synonyms defined, and the occurrence of a word can be replaced by the *or* of all its synonyms (including the word itself). Thus, the query "motorcycle *and* repair" can be replaced by "motorcycle *and* (repair *or* maintenance)." This query would find the desired document.

Keyword-based queries also suffer from the opposite problem, of **homonyms**, that is single words with multiple meanings. For instance, the word "object" has different meanings as a noun and as a verb. The word "table" may refer to a dinner table, or to a table in a relational database.

In fact, a danger even with using synonyms to extend queries is that the synonyms may themselves have different meanings. For example, "allowance" is a synonym for one meaning of the word "maintenance", but has a different meaning than what the user intended in the query "motorcycle maintenance". Documents that use the synonyms with an alternative intended meaning would be retrieved. The user is then left wondering why the system thought that a particular retrieved document (for example, using the word "allowance") is relevant, if it contains neither the keywords the user specified, nor words whose intended meaning in the document is synonymous with specified keywords! It is therefore a bad idea to use synonyms to extend a query without first verifying the synonyms with the user.

A better approach to the above problem is for the system to understand what **concept** each word in a document represents, and similarly to understand what concepts a user is looking for, and to return documents that address the concepts that the user is interested in. A system that supports **concept-based querying** has to analyze each document to disambiguate each word in the document, and replace it with the concept that it represents; disambiguation is usually done by looking at other surrounding words in the document. For example, if a document contains words such as database or query, the word table probably should be replaced by the concept "table: data" whereas if the document contains words such as furniture, chair, or wood near the word table, the word table should be replaced by the concept "table: furniture." Disambiguation based on nearby words is usually harder for user queries, since queries contain very few words, so concept-based query systems would offer several alternative concepts to the user, who picks one or more before the search continues.

Concept-based querying has several advantages; for example, a query in one language can retrieve documents in other languages, so long as they relate to the same concept. Automated translation mechanisms can be used subsequently if the user does not understand the language in which the document is written. However, the overhead of processing documents to disambiguate words is very high when billions of documents are being handled. Internet search engines therefore generally did not support concept-based querying initially, but interest in concept-based approaches is growing rapidly. However, concept-based querying systems have been built and used for other large collections of documents.

Querying based on concepts can be extended further by exploiting concept hierarchies. For example, suppose a person issues a query "flying animals"; a document containing information about "flying mammals" is certainly relevant, since a mammal is an animal. However, the two concepts are not the same, and just matching concepts would not allow the document to be returned as an answer. Concept-based querying systems can support retrieval of documents based on concept hierarchies.

Ontologies are hierarchical structures that reflect relationships between concepts. The most common relationship is the **is-a** relationship; for example, a leopard *is-a* mammal, and a mammal *is-a* animal. Other relationships, such as *part-of* are also possible; for example, an airplane wing is *part-of* an airplane.

The WordNet system defines a large variety of concepts with associated words (called a *synset* in WordNet terminology). The words associated with a synset are synonyms for the concept; a word may of course be a synonym for several different concepts. In addition to synonyms, WordNet defines homonyms and other relationships. In particular, the *is-a* and *part-of* relationships that it defines connect concepts, and in effect define an ontology. The Cyc project is another effort to create an ontology.

In addition to language-wide ontologies, ontologies have been defined for specific areas to deal with terminology relevant to those areas. For example, ontologies have been created to standardize terms used in businesses; this is an important step in building a standard infrastructure for handling order processing and other interorganization flow of data. As another example, consider a medical insurance company that needs to get reports from hospitals containing diagnosis and treatment information. An ontology that standardizes the terms helps hospital staff to understand the reports unambiguously. This can greatly help in analysis of the reports, for example to track how many cases of a particular disease occurred in a particular time frame.

It is also possible to build ontologies that link multiple languages. For example, WordNets have been built for different languages, and common concepts between languages can be linked to each other. Such a system can be used for translation of text. In the context of information retrieval, a multilingual ontology can be used to implement a concept-based search across documents in multiple languages.

The largest effort in using ontologies for concept-based queries is the **Semantic Web**. The Semantic Web is led by the World Wide Web Consortium and consists of a collection of tools, standards, and languages that permit data on the Web to be connected based on their semantics, or meaning. Instead of being a centralized repository, the Semantic Web is designed to permit the same kind of decentralized, distributed growth that has made the World Wide Web so successful. Key to this is the capability to integrate multiple, distributed ontologies. As a result, anyone with access to the Internet can add to the Semantic Web.

21.5   Indexing of Documents

An effective index structure is important for efficient processing of queries in an information-retrieval system. Documents that contain a specified keyword can be located efficiently by using an **inverted index** that maps each keyword K_i to a list S_i of (identifiers of) the documents that contain K_i. For example, if documents d_1, d_9 and d_{21} contain the term "Silberschatz", the inverted list for the keyword Silberschatz would be "$d_1; d_9; d_{21}$". To support relevance ranking based on proximity of keywords, such an index may provide not just identifiers of documents, but also a list of locations within the document where the keyword appears. For example, if "Silberschatz" appeared at position 21 in d_1, positions 1 and 19 in d_2, and positions 4, 29 and 46 in d_3, the inverted list with positions would be "$d_1/21; d_9/1, 19; d_{21}/4, 29, 46$". The inverted lists may also include with each document the term frequency of the term.

Such indices must be stored on disk, and each list S_i can span multiple disk pages. To minimize the number of I/O operations to retrieve each list S_i, the system would attempt to keep each list S_i in a set of consecutive disk pages, so the entire list can be retrieved with just one disk seek. A B^+-tree index can be used to map each keyword K_i to its associated inverted list S_i.

The *and* operation finds documents that contain all of a specified set of keywords $K_1, K_2, \ldots, K_n$. We implement the *and* operation by first retrieving the sets of document identifiers $S_1, S_2, \ldots, S_n$ of all documents that contain the respective keywords. The intersection, $S_1 \cap S_2 \cap \cdots \cap S_n$, of the sets gives the document identifiers of the desired set of documents. The *or* operation gives the set of all documents that contain at least one of the keywords $K_1, K_2, \ldots, K_n$. We implement the *or* operation by computing the union, $S_1 \cup S_2 \cup \cdots \cup S_n$, of the sets. The *not* operation finds documents that do not contain a specified keyword K_i. Given a set of document identifiers S, we can eliminate documents that contain the specified keyword K_i by taking the difference $S - S_i$, where S_i is the set of identifiers of documents that contain the keyword K_i.

Given a set of keywords in a query, many information-retrieval systems do not insist that the retrieved documents contain all the keywords (unless an *and* operation is used explicitly). In this case, all documents containing at least one of the words are retrieved (as in the *or* operation), but are ranked by their relevance measure.

To use term frequency for ranking, the index structure should additionally maintain the number of times terms occur in each document. To reduce this effort, they may use a compressed representation with only a few bits that approximates the term frequency. The index should also store the document frequency of each term (that is, the number of documents in which the term appears).

If the popularity ranking is independent of the index term (as is the case for Page Rank), the list S_i can be sorted on the popularity ranking (and secondarily, for documents with the same popularity ranking, on document-id). Then, a simple merge can be used to compute *and* and *or* operations. For the case of the *and* operation, if we ignore the TF–IDF contribution to the relevance score, and merely require that the document should contain the given keywords, merging can stop once K answers have been obtained, if the user requires only the top K answers. In general, the results with highest final score (after including TF–IDF scores) are likely to have high popularity scores, and would appear near the front of the lists. Techniques have been developed to estimate the best possible scores of remaining results, and these can be used to recognize that answers not yet seen cannot be part of the top K answers. Processing of the lists can then terminate early.

However, sorting on popularity score is not fully effective in avoiding long inverted list scans, since it ignores the contribution of the TF–IDF scores. An alternative in such cases is to break up the inverted list for each term into two parts. The first part contains documents that have a high TF–IDF score for that term (for example, documents where the term occurs in the document title, or in anchor text referencing the document). The second part contains all documents. Each part of the list can be sorted in order of (popularity, document-id). Given a query, merging the first parts of the list for each term is likely to give several answers with an overall high score. If sufficient high-scoring answers are not found using the first parts of the lists, the second parts of the lists are used to find all remaining answers. If a document scores high on TF–IDF, it is likely to be found when merging the first parts of the lists. See the bibliographical notes for related references.

21.6 Measuring Retrieval Effectiveness

Each keyword may be contained in a large number of documents; hence, a compact representation is critical to keep space usage of the index low. Thus, the sets of documents for a keyword are maintained in a compressed form. So that storage space is saved, the index is sometimes stored such that the retrieval is approximate; a few relevant documents may not be retrieved (called a **false drop** or **false negative**), or a few irrelevant documents may be retrieved (called a **false positive**). A good index structure will not have *any* false drops, but may permit a few false positives; the system can filter them away later by looking at the keywords that they actually contain. In Web indexing, false positives are not desirable either, since the actual document may not be quickly accessible for filtering.

Two metrics are used to measure how well an information-retrieval system is able to answer queries. The first, **precision**, measures what percentage of the retrieved documents are actually relevant to the query. The second, **recall**, measures what percentage of the documents relevant to the query were retrieved. Ideally both should be 100 percent.

Precision and recall are also important measures for understanding how well a particular document-ranking strategy performs. Ranking strategies can result in false negatives and false positives, but in a more subtle sense.

- False negatives may occur when documents are ranked, as a result of relevant documents receiving a low ranking. If the system fetched all documents down to those with very low ranking there would be very few false negatives. However, humans would rarely look beyond the first few tens of returned documents, and may thus miss relevant documents because they are not ranked high. Exactly what is a false negative depends on how many documents are examined. Therefore instead of having a single number as the measure of recall, we can measure the recall as a function of the number of documents fetched.

- False positives may occur because irrelevant documents get higher rankings than relevant documents. This too depends on how many documents are examined. One option is to measure precision as a function of number of documents fetched.

A better and more intuitive alternative for measuring precision is to measure it as a function of recall. With this combined measure, both precision and recall can be computed as a function of number of documents, if required.

For instance, we can say that with a recall of 50 percent the precision was 75 percent, whereas at a recall of 75 percent the precision dropped to 60 percent. In general, we can draw a graph relating precision to recall. These measures can be computed for individual queries, then averaged out across a suite of queries in a query benchmark.

Yet another problem with measuring precision and recall lies in how to define which documents are really relevant and which are not. In fact, it requires understanding of natural language, and understanding of the intent of the query, to decide if a document is relevant or not. Researchers therefore have created collections of documents and queries, and have manually tagged documents as relevant or irrelevant to the queries. Different ranking systems can be run on these collections to measure their average precision and recall across multiple queries.

21.7   Crawling and Indexing the Web

Web crawlers are programs that locate and gather information on the Web. They recursively follow hyperlinks present in known documents to find other documents. Crawlers start from an initial set of URLs, which may be created manually. Each of the pages identified by these URLs are fetched from the Web. The Web crawler then locates all URL links in these pages, and adds them to the set of URLs to be crawled, if they have not already been fetched, or added to the to-be-crawled set. This process is again repeated by fetching all pages in the to-be-crawled set, and processing the links in these pages in the same fashion. By repeating the process, all pages that are reachable by any sequence of links from the initial set of URLs would be eventually fetched.

Since the number of documents on the Web is very large, it is not possible to crawl the whole Web in a short period of time; and in fact, all search engines cover only some portions of the Web, not all of it, and their crawlers may take weeks or months to perform a single crawl of all the pages they cover. There are usually many processes, running on multiple machines, involved in crawling. A database stores a set of links (or sites) to be crawled; it assigns links from this set to each crawler process. New links found during a crawl are added to the database, and may be crawled later if they are not crawled immediately. Pages have to be refetched (that is, links recrawled) periodically to obtain updated information, and to discard sites that no longer exist, so that the information in the search index is kept reasonably up-to-date.

See the references in the bibliography for a number of practical details in performing a Web crawl, such as infinite sequences of links created by dynamically generated pages (called a **spider trap**), prioritization of page fetches, and ensuring that Web sites are not flooded by a burst of requests from a crawler.

Pages fetched during a crawl are handed over to a prestige computation and indexing system, which may be running on a different machine. The prestige computation and indexing systems themselves run on multiple machines in parallel. Pages can be discarded after they are used for prestige computation and added to the index; however, they are usually cached by the search engine, to give search engine users fast access to a cached copy of a page, even if the original Web site containing the page is not accessible.

It is not a good idea to add pages to the same index that is being used for queries, since doing so would require concurrency control on the index, and would affect query and update performance. Instead, one copy of the index is used to answer queries while another copy is updated with newly crawled pages. At periodic intervals the copies switch over, with the old one being updated while the new copy is being used for queries.

To support very high query rates, the indices may be kept in main memory, and there are multiple machines; the system selectively routes queries to the machines to balance the load among them. Popular search engines often have tens of thousands of machines carrying out the various tasks of crawling, indexing, and answering user queries.

Web crawlers depend on all relevant pages being reachable through hyperlinks. However, many sites containing large collections of data may not make all the data available as hyperlinked pages. Instead, they provide search interfaces, where users can enter terms, or select menu options, and get results. As an example, a database of flight information is usually made available using such a search interface, without any hyperlinks to the pages containing flight information. As a result, the information inside such sites is not accessible to a normal Web crawler. The information in such sites is often referred to as **deep Web** information.

Deep Web crawlers extract some such information by guessing what terms would make sense to enter, or what menu options to choose, in such search interfaces. By entering each possible term/option and executing the search interface, they are able to extract pages with data that they would not have been able to find otherwise. The pages extracted by a deep Web crawl may be indexed just like regular Web pages. The Google search engine, for example, includes results from deep Web crawls.

21.8   Information Retrieval: Beyond Ranking of Pages

Information-retrieval systems were originally designed to find textual documents related to a query, and later extended to finding pages on the Web that are related to a query. People use search engines for many different tasks, from simple tasks such as locating a Web site that they want to use, to a broader goal of finding information on a topic of interest. Web search engines have become extremely good at the task of locating Web sites that a user wants to visit. The task of providing information on a topic of interest is much harder, and we study some approaches in this section.

There is also an increasing need for systems that try to understand documents (to a limited extent), and answer questions based on the (limited) understanding. One approach is to create structured information from unstructured documents and to answer questions based on the structured information. Another approach applies natural language techniques to find documents related to a question (phrased in natural language) and return relevant segments of the documents as an answer to the question.

21.8.1 Diversity of Query Results

Today, search engines do not just return a ranked list of Web pages relevant to a query. They also return image and video results relevant to a query. Further, there are a variety of sites providing dynamically changing content such as sports scores, or stock market tickers. To get current information from such sites, users would have to first click on the query result. Instead, search engines have created "gadgets," which take data from a particular domain, such as sports updates, stock prices, or weather conditions, and format them in a nice graphical manner, to be displayed as results for a query. Search engines have to rank the set of gadgets available in terms of relevance to a query, and display the most relevant gadgets, along with Web pages, images, videos, and other types of results. Thus a query result has a diverse set of result types.

Search terms are often ambiguous. For example, a query "eclipse" may be referring to a solar or lunar eclipse, or to the integrated development environment (IDE) called Eclipse. If all the highly ranked pages for the term "eclipse" are about the IDE, a user looking for information about solar or lunar eclipses may be very dissatisfied. Search engines therefore attempt to provide a set of results that are *diverse* in terms of their topics, to minimize the chance that a user would be dissatisfied. To do so, at indexing time the search engine must disambiguate the sense in which a word is used in a page; for example, it must decide whether the use of the word "eclipse" in a page refers to the IDE or the astronomical phenomenon. Then, given a query, the search engine attempts to provide results that are relevant to the most common senses in which the query words are used.

The results obtained from a Web page need to be summarized as a **snippet** in a query result. Traditionally, search engines provided a few words surrounding the query keywords as a snippet that helps indicate what the page contains. However, there are many domains where the snippet can be generated in a much more meaningful manner. For example, if a user queries about a restaurant, a search engine can generate a snippet containing the restaurant's rating, a phone number, and a link to a map, in addition to providing a link to the restaurant's home page. Such specialized snippets are often generated for results retrieved from a database, for example, a database of restaurants.

21.8.2 Information Extraction

Information-extraction systems convert information from textual form to a more structured form. For example, a real-estate advertisement may describe attributes of a home in textual form, such as "two-bedroom three-bath house in Queens, $1 million", from which an information extraction system may extract attributes such as number of bedrooms, number of bathrooms, cost and neighborhood. The original advertisement could have used various terms such as 2BR, or two BR, or two bed, to denote two bedrooms. The extracted information can be used to structure the data in a standard way. Thus, a user could specify that he is interested in two-bedroom houses, and a search system would be able to return all relevant houses based on the structured data, regardless of the terms used in the advertisement.

An organization that maintains a database of company information may use an information-extraction system to extract information automatically from newspaper articles; the information extracted would relate to changes in attributes of interest, such as resignations, dismissals, or appointments of company officers.

As another example, search engines designed for finding scholarly research articles, such as Citeseer and Google Scholar, crawl the Web to retrieve documents that are likely to be research articles. They examine some features of each retrieved document, such as the presence of words such as "bibliography", "references", and "abstract", to judge if a document is in fact a scholarly research article. They then extract the title, list of authors, and the citations at the end of the article, by using information extraction techniques. The extracted citation information can be used to link each article to articles that it cites, or to articles that cite it; such citation links between articles can be very useful for a researcher.

Several systems have been built for information extraction for specialized applications. They use linguistic techniques, page structure, and user-defined rules for specific domains such as real estate advertisements or scholarly publications. For limited domains, such as a specific Web site, it is possible for a human to specify patterns that can be used to extract information. For example, on a particular Web site, a pattern such as "Price: <number> $", where <number> indicates any number, may match locations where the price is specified. Such patterns can be created manually for a limited number of Web sites.

However, on the Web scale with millions of Web sites, manual creation of such patterns is not feasible. Machine-learning techniques, which can learn such patterns given a set of training examples, are widely used to automate the process of information extraction.

Information extraction usually has errors in some fraction of the extracted information; typically this is because some page had information in a format that syntactically matched a pattern, but did not actually specify a value (such as the price). Information extraction using simple patterns, which separately match parts of a page, is relatively error prone. Machine-learning techniques can perform much more sophisticated analysis, based on interactions between patterns, to minimize errors in the information extracted, while maximizing the amount of information extracted. See the references in the bibliographical notes for more information.

21.8.3   Question Answering

Information retrieval systems focus on finding documents relevant to a given query. However, the answer to a query may lie in just one part of a document, or in small parts of several documents. **Question answering** systems attempt to provide direct answers to questions posed by users. For example, a question of the form "Who killed Lincoln?" may best be answered by a line that says "Abraham Lincoln was shot by John Wilkes Booth in 1865." Note that the answer does not actually contain the words "killed" or "who", but the system infers that "who" can be answered by a name, and "killed" is related to "shot".

Question answering systems targeted at information on the Web typically generate one or more keyword queries from a submitted question, execute the keyword queries against Web search engines, and parse returned documents to find segments of the documents that answer the question. A number of linguistic techniques and heuristics are used to generate keyword queries, and to find relevant segments from the document.

An issue in answering questions is that different documents may indicate different answers to a question. For example, if the question is "How tall is a giraffe?" different documents may give different numbers as an answer. These answers form a distribution of values, and a question answering system may choose the average, or median value of the distribution as the answer to be returned; to reflect the fact that the answer is not expected to be precise, the system may return the average along with the standard deviation (for example, average of 16 feet, with a standard deviation of 2 feet), or a range based on the average and the standard deviation (for example, between 14 and 18 feet).

Current-generation question answering systems are limited in power, since they do not really understand either the question or the documents used to answer the question. However, they are useful for a number of simple question answering tasks.

21.8.4 Querying Structured Data

Structured data are primarily represented in either relational or XML form. Several systems have been built to support keyword querying on relational and XML data (see Chapter 23). A common theme between these systems lies in finding nodes (tuples or XML elements) containing the specified keywords, and finding connecting paths (or common ancestors, in the case of XML data) between them.

For example, a query "Zhang Katz" on a university database may find the *name* "Zhang" occurring in a *student* tuple, and the *name* "Katz" in an *instructor* tuple, and a path through the *advisor* relation connecting the two tuples. Other paths, such as student "Zhang" taking a course taught by "Katz" may also be found in response to this query. Such queries may be used for ad hoc browsing and querying of data, when the user does not know the exact schema and does not wish to take the effort to write an SQL query defining what she is searching for. Indeed it is unreasonable to expect lay users to write queries in a structured query language, whereas keyword querying is quite natural.

Since queries are not fully defined, they may have many different types of answers, which must be ranked. A number of techniques have been proposed to rank answers in such a setting, based on the lengths of connecting paths, and on techniques for assigning directions and weights to edges. Techniques have also been proposed for assigning popularity ranks to tuples and XML elements, based on links such as foreign key and IDREF links. See the bibliographical notes for more information on keyword searching of relational and XML data.

21.9   Directories and Categories

A typical library user may use a catalog to locate a book for which she is looking. When she retrieves the book from the shelf, however, she is likely to *browse* through other books that are located nearby. Libraries organize books in such a way that related books are kept close together. Hence, a book that is physically near the desired book may be of interest as well, making it worthwhile for users to browse through such books.

To keep related books close together, libraries use a **classification hierarchy**. Books on science are classified together. Within this set of books, there is a finer classification, with computer-science books organized together, mathematics books organized together, and so on. Since there is a relation between mathematics and computer science, relevant sets of books are stored close to each other physically. At yet another level in the classification hierarchy, computer-science books are broken down into subareas, such as operating systems, languages, and algorithms. Figure 21.1 illustrates a classification hierarchy that may be used by a library. Because books can be kept at only one place, each book in a library is classified into exactly one spot in the classification hierarchy.

In an information-retrieval system, there is no need to store related documents close together. However, such systems need to *organize documents logically* so as to permit browsing. Thus, such a system could use a classification hierarchy similar

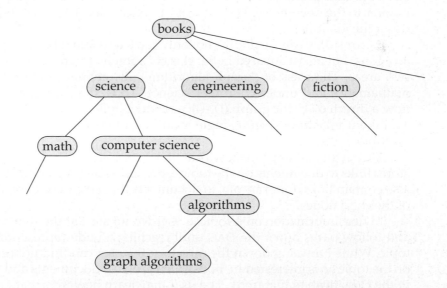

Figure 21.1 A classification hierarchy for a library system.

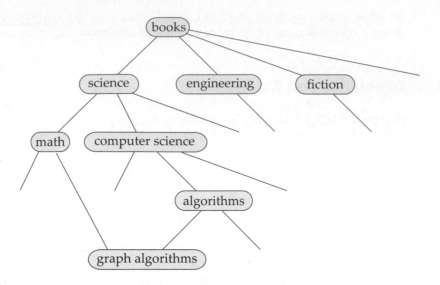

Figure 21.2   A classification DAG for a library information-retrieval system.

to one that libraries use, and, when it displays a particular document, it can also display a brief description of documents that are close in the hierarchy.

In an information-retrieval system, there is no need to keep a document in a single spot in the hierarchy. A document that talks of mathematics for computer scientists could be classified under mathematics as well as under computer science. All that is stored at each spot is an identifier of the document (that is, a pointer to the document), and it is easy to fetch the contents of the document by using the identifier.

As a result of this flexibility, not only can a document be classified under two locations, but also a subarea in the classification hierarchy can itself occur under two areas. The class of "graph algorithm" documents can appear both under mathematics and under computer science. Thus, the classification hierarchy is now a directed acyclic graph (DAG), as shown in Figure 21.2. A graph-algorithm document may appear in a single location in the DAG, but can be reached via multiple paths.

A **directory** is simply a classification DAG structure. Each leaf of the directory stores links to documents on the topic represented by the leaf. Internal nodes may also contain links, for example, to documents that cannot be classified under any of the child nodes.

To find information on a topic, a user would start at the root of the directory and follow paths down the DAG until reaching a node representing the desired topic. While browsing down the directory, the user can find not only documents on the topic he is interested in, but also find related documents and related classes in the classification hierarchy. The user may learn new information by browsing through documents (or subclasses) within the related classes.

Organizing the enormous amount of information available on the Web into a directory structure is a daunting task.

- The first problem is determining what exactly the directory hierarchy should be.

- The second problem is, given a document, deciding which nodes of the directory are categories relevant to the document.

To tackle the first problem, portals such as Yahoo! have teams of "Internet librarians" who come up with the classification hierarchy and continually refine it.

The second problem can also be tackled manually by librarians, or Web site maintainers may be responsible for deciding where their sites should lie in the hierarchy. There are also techniques for deciding automatically the location of documents based on computing their similarity to documents that have already been classified.

Wikipedia, the online encyclopedia, addresses the classification problem in the reverse direction. Each page in Wikipedia has a list of **categories** to which it belongs. For example, as of 2009, the Wikipedia page on giraffes had several categories including "Mammals of Africa". In turn, the "Mammals of Africa" category itself belongs to the category "Mammals by geography", which in turn belongs to the category "Mammals", which in turn has a category "Vertebrates", and so on. The category structure is useful to browse other instances of the same category, for example, to find other mammals of Africa, or other mammals. Conversely, a query that looks for mammals can use the category information to infer that a giraffe is a mammal. The Wikipedia category structure is not a tree, but is almost a DAG; it is not actually a DAG since it has a few instances of loops, which probably reflect categorization errors.

21.10 Summary

- Information-retrieval systems are used to store and query textual data such as documents. They use a simpler data model than do database systems, but provide more powerful querying capabilities within the restricted model.

- Queries attempt to locate documents that are of interest by specifying, for example, sets of keywords. The query that a user has in mind usually cannot be stated precisely; hence, information-retrieval systems order answers on the basis of potential relevance.

- Relevance ranking makes use of several types of information, such as:

    ○ Term frequency: how important each term is to each document.

    ○ Inverse document frequency.

    ○ Popularity ranking.

- Similarity of documents is used to retrieve documents similar to an example document. The cosine metric is used to define similarity, and is based on the vector space model.

- PageRank and hub/authority rank are two ways to assign prestige to pages on the basis of links to the page. The PageRank measure can be understood intuitively using a random-walk model. Anchor text information is also used to compute a per-keyword notion of popularity. Information-retrieval systems need to combine scores on multiple factors such as TF–IDF and PageRank, to get an overall score for a page.

- Search engine spamming attempts to get (an undeserved) high ranking for a page.

- Synonyms and homonyms complicate the task of information retrieval. Concept-based querying aims at finding documents containing specified concepts, regardless of the exact words (or language) in which the concept is specified. Ontologies are used to relate concepts using relationships such as is-a or part-of.

- Inverted indices are used to answer keyword queries.

- Precision and recall are two measures of the effectiveness of an information retrieval system.

- Web search engines crawl the Web to find pages, analyze them to compute prestige measures, and index them.

- Techniques have been developed to extract structured information from textual data, to perform keyword querying on structured data, and to give direct answers to simple questions posed in natural language.

- Directory structures and categories are used to classify documents with other similar documents.

Review Terms

- Information-retrieval systems
- Keyword search
- Full text retrieval
- Term
- Relevance ranking

  - Term frequency
  - Inverse document frequency
  - Relevance

- Proximity
- Similarity-based retrieval
  - Vector space model
  - Cosine similarity metric
  - Relevance feedback
- Stop words
- Relevance using hyperlinks
  - Popularity/prestige

- Transfer of prestige
- PageRank
  - Random walk model
- Anchor-text–based relevance
- Hub/authority ranking
- Search engine spamming
- Synonyms
- Homonyms
- Concepts
- Concept-based querying
- Ontologies
- Semantic Web
- Inverted index

- False drop
- False negative
- False positive
- Precision
- Recall
- Web crawlers
- Deep Web
- Query result diversity
- Information extraction
- Question answering
- Querying structured data
- Directories
- Classification hierarchy
- Categories

Practice Exercises

21.1 Compute the relevance (using appropriate definitions of term frequency and inverse document frequency) of each of the Practice Exercises in this chapter to the query "SQL relation".

21.2 Suppose you want to find documents that contain at least k of a given set of n keywords. Suppose also you have a keyword index that gives you a (sorted) list of identifiers of documents that contain a specified keyword. Give an efficient algorithm to find the desired set of documents.

21.3 Suggest how to implement the iterative technique for computing Page-Rank given that the T matrix (even in adjacency list representation) does not fit in memory.

21.4 Suggest how a document containing a word (such as "leopard") can be indexed such that it is efficiently retrieved by queries using a more general concept (such as "carnivore" or "mammal"). You can assume that the concept hierarchy is not very deep, so each concept has only a few generalizations (a concept can, however, have a large number of specializations). You can also assume that you are provided with a function that returns the concept for each word in a document. Also suggest how a query using a specialized concept can retrieve documents using a more general concept.

21.5 Suppose inverted lists are maintained in blocks, with each block noting the largest popularity rank and TF–IDF scores of documents in the remaining blocks in the list. Suggest how merging of inverted lists can stop early if the user wants only the top K answers.

Exercises

21.6   Using a simple definition of term frequency as the number of occurrences of the term in a document, give the TF–IDF scores of each term in the set of documents consisting of this and the next exercise.

21.7   Create a small example of four small documents, each with a PageRank, and create inverted lists for the documents sorted by the PageRank. You do not need to compute PageRank, just assume some values for each page.

21.8   Suppose you wish to perform keyword querying on a set of tuples in a database, where each tuple has only a few attributes, each containing only a few words. Does the concept of term frequency make sense in this context? And that of inverse document frequency? Explain your answer. Also suggest how you can define the similarity of two tuples using TF–IDF concepts.

21.9   Web sites that want to get some publicity can join a Web ring, where they create links to other sites in the ring, in exchange for other sites in the ring creating links to their site. What is the effect of such rings on popularity ranking techniques such as PageRank?

21.10   The Google search engine provides a feature whereby Web sites can display advertisements supplied by Google. The advertisements supplied are based on the contents of the page. Suggest how Google might choose which advertisements to supply for a page, given the page contents.

21.11   One way to create a keyword-specific version of PageRank is to modify the random jump such that a jump is only possible to pages containing the keyword. Thus pages that do not contain the keyword but are close (in terms of links) to pages that contain the keyword also get a nonzero rank for that keyword.

    a.   Give equations defining such a keyword-specific version of Page-Rank.

    b.   Give a formula for computing the relevance of a page to a query containing multiple keywords.

21.12   The idea of popularity ranking using hyperlinks can be extended to relational and XML data, using foreign key and IDREF edges in place of hyperlinks. Suggest how such a ranking scheme may be of value in the following applications:

    a.   A bibliographic database that has links from articles to authors of the articles and links from each article to every article that it references.

    b. A sales database that has links from each sales record to the items that were sold.

Also suggest why prestige ranking can give less than meaningful results in a movie database that records which actor has acted in which movies.

21.13 What is the difference between a false positive and a false drop? If it is essential that no relevant information be missed by an information retrieval query, is it acceptable to have either false positives or false drops? Why?

Tools

Google (www.google.com) is currently the most popular search engine, but there are a number of other search engines, such as Microsoft Bing (www.bing.com) and Yahoo! search (search.yahoo.com). The site searchenginewatch.com provides a variety of information about search engines. Yahoo! (dir.yahoo.com) and the Open Directory Project (dmoz.org) provide classification hierarchies for Web sites.

Bibliographical Notes

Manning et al. [2008], Chakrabarti [2002], Grossman and Frieder [2004], Witten et al. [1999], and Baeza-Yates and Ribeiro-Neto [1999] provide textbook descriptions of information retrieval. In particular, Chakrabarti [2002] and Manning et al. [2008] provide detailed coverage of Web crawling, ranking techniques, and mining techniques related to information retrieval such as text classification and clustering.

Brin and Page [1998] describes the anatomy of the Google search engine, including the PageRank technique, while a hubs- and authorities-based ranking technique called HITS is described by Kleinberg [1999]. Bharat and Henzinger [1998] presents a refinement of the HITS ranking technique. These techniques, as well as other popularity-based ranking techniques (and techniques to avoid search engine spamming) are described in detail in Chakrabarti [2002]. Chakrabarti et al. [1999] addresses focused crawling of the Web to find pages related to a specific topic. Chakrabarti [1999] provides a survey of Web resource discovery.

Indexing of documents is covered in detail by Witten et al. [1999]. Jones and Willet [1997] is a collection of articles on information retrieval. Salton [1989] is an early textbook on information-retrieval systems. A number of practical issues in ranking and indexing of Web pages, as done in an early version of the Google search engine, are discussed in Brin and Page [1998]. Unfortunately, there are no publicly available details of how exactly ranking is done currently by any of the leading search engines.

The Citeseer system (citeseer.ist.psu.edu) maintains a very large database of research articles, with citation links between the publications, and uses citations to rank publications. It includes a technique for adjusting the citation ranking based on the age of a publication, to compensate for the fact that citations to a publication increase as time passes; without the adjustment, older documents tend to get a higher ranking than they truly deserve. Google Scholar (scholar.google.com) provides a similar searchable database of research articles incorporating citations between articles. It is worth noting that these systems use information extraction techniques to infer the title and list of authors of an article, as well as the citations at the end of the article. They then create citation links between articles based on (approximate) matching of the article title and author list with the citation text.

Information extraction and question answering have had a fairly long history in the artificial intelligence community. Jackson and Moulinier [2002] provides textbook coverage of natural language processing techniques with an emphasis on information extraction. Soderland [1999] describes information extraction using the WHISK system, while Appelt and Israel [1999] provides a tutorial on information extraction.

The annual Text Retrieval Conference (TREC) has a number of tracks, each of which defines a problem and infrastructure to test the quality of solutions to the problem. Details on TREC may be found at trec.nist.gov. More information about WordNet can be found at wordnet.princeton.edu and globalwordnet.org. The goal of the Cyc system is to provide a formal representation of large amounts of human knowledge. Its knowledge base contains a large number of terms, and assertions about each term. Cyc also includes a support for natural language understanding and disambiguation. Information about the Cyc system may be found at cyc.com and opencyc.org.

The evolution of Web search toward concepts and semantics rather than keywords is discussed in Dalvi et al. [2009]. The annual International Semantic Web Conference (ISWC) is one of the major conferences where new developments in the Semantic Web are presented. Details may be found at semanticweb.org.

Agrawal et al. [2002], Bhalotia et al. [2002] and Hristidis and Papakonstantinou [2002] cover keyword querying of relational data. Keyword querying of XML data is addressed by Florescu et al. [2000] and Guo et al. [2003], among others.

PART 7

SPECIALTY DATABASES

Several application areas for database systems are limited by the restrictions of the relational data model. As a result, researchers have developed several data models based on an object-oriented approach, to deal with these application domains.

The object-relational model, described in Chapter 22, combines features of the relational and object-oriented models. This model provides the rich type system of object-oriented languages, combined with relations as the basis for storage of data. It applies inheritance to relations, not just to types. The object-relational data model provides a smooth migration path from relational databases, which is attractive to relational database vendors. As a result, starting with SQL:1999, the SQL standard includes a number of object-oriented features in its type system, while continuing to use the relational model as the underlying model.

The term object-oriented database is used to describe a database system that supports direct access to data from object-oriented programming languages, without requiring a relational query language as the database interface. Chapter 22 also provides a brief overview of object-oriented databases.

The XML language was initially designed as a way of adding markup information to text documents, but has become important because of its applications in data exchange. XML provides a way to represent data that have nested structure, and furthermore allows a great deal of flexibility in structuring of data, which is important for certain kinds of nontraditional data. Chapter 23 describes the XML language, and then presents different ways of expressing queries on data represented in XML, including the XQuery XML query language, and SQL/XML, an extension of SQL which allows the creation of nested XML output.

CHAPTER **22**

Object-Based Databases

Traditional database applications consist of data-processing tasks, such as banking and payroll management, with relatively simple data types that are well suited to the relational data model. As database systems were applied to a wider range of applications, such as computer-aided design and geographical information systems, limitations imposed by the relational model emerged as an obstacle. The solution was the introduction of object-based databases, which allow one to deal with complex data types.

22.1 Overview

The first obstacle faced by programmers using the relational data model was the limited type system supported by the relational model. Complex application domains require correspondingly complex data types, such as nested record structures, multivalued attributes, and inheritance, which are supported by traditional programming languages. Such features are in fact supported in the E-R and extended E-R notations, but had to be translated to simpler SQL data types. The **object-relational data model** extends the relational data model by providing a richer type system including complex data types and object orientation. Relational query languages, in particular SQL, need to be correspondingly extended to deal with the richer type system. Such extensions attempt to preserve the relational foundations—in particular, the declarative access to data—while extending the modeling power. **Object-relational database systems**, that is, database systems based on the object-relation model, provide a convenient migration path for users of relational databases who wish to use object-oriented features.

The second obstacle was the difficulty in accessing database data from programs written in programming languages such as C++ or Java. Merely extending the type system supported by the database was not enough to solve this problem completely. Differences between the type system of the database and the type system of the programming language make data storage and retrieval more complicated, and need to be minimized. Having to express database access using a language (SQL) that is different from the programming language again makes the job of the programmer harder. It is desirable, for many applications, to have programming language constructs or extensions that permit direct access to data in the database, without having to go through an intermediate language such as SQL.

In this chapter, we first explain the motivation for the development of complex data types. We then study object-relational database systems, specifically using features that were introduced in SQL:1999 and SQL:2003. Note that most database products support only a subset of the SQL features described here and for supported features, the syntax often differs slightly from the standard. This is the result of commercial systems introducing object-relational features to the market before the standards were finalized. Refer to the user manual of the database system you use to find out what features it supports.

We then address the issue of supporting persistence for data that is in the native type system of an object-oriented programming language. Two approaches are used in practice:

1. Build an **object-oriented database system**, that is, a database system that natively supports an object-oriented type system, and allows direct access to data from an object-oriented programming language using the native type system of the language.

2. Automatically convert data from the native type system of the programming language to a relational representation, and vice versa. Data conversion is specified using an **object-relational mapping**.

We provide a brief introduction to both these approaches.

Finally, we outline situations in which the object-relational approach is better than the object-oriented approach, and vice versa, and mention criteria for choosing between them.

22.2   Complex Data Types

Traditional database applications have conceptually simple data types. The basic data items are records that are fairly small and whose fields are atomic—that is, they are not further structured, and first normal form holds (see Chapter 8). Further, there are only a few record types.

In recent years, demand has grown for ways to deal with more complex data types. Consider, for example, addresses. While an entire address could be viewed as an atomic data item of type string, this view would hide details such as the street address, city, state, and postal code, which could be of interest to queries. On the other hand, if an address were represented by breaking it into the components (street address, city, state, and postal code), writing queries would be more complicated since they would have to mention each field. A better alternative is to allow structured data types that allow a type *address* with subparts *street_address*, *city*, *state*, and *postal_code*.

As another example, consider multivalued attributes from the E-R model. Such attributes are natural, for example, for representing phone numbers, since people

title	author_array	publisher	keyword_set
		(name, branch)	
Compilers	[Smith, Jones]	(McGraw-Hill, NewYork)	{parsing, analysis}
Networks	[Jones, Frick]	(Oxford, London)	{Internet, Web}

Figure 22.1 Non-1NF books relation, *books*.

may have more than one phone. The alternative of normalization by creating a new relation is expensive and artificial for this example.

With complex type systems we can represent E-R model concepts, such as composite attributes, multivalued attributes, generalization, and specialization directly, without a complex translation to the relational model.

In Chapter 8, we defined *first normal form* (1NF), which requires that all attributes have *atomic domains*. Recall that a domain is *atomic* if elements of the domain are considered to be indivisible units.

The assumption of 1NF is a natural one in the database application examples we have considered. However, not all applications are best modeled by 1NF relations. For example, rather than view a database as a set of records, users of certain applications view it as a set of objects (or entities). These objects may require several records for their representation. A simple, easy-to-use interface requires a one-to-one correspondence between the user's intuitive notion of an object and the database system's notion of a data item.

Consider, for example, a library application, and suppose we wish to store the following information for each book:

- Book title.

- List of authors.

- Publisher.

- Set of keywords.

We can see that, if we define a relation for the preceding information, several domains will be nonatomic.

- **Authors**. A book may have a list of authors, which we can represent as an array. Nevertheless, we may want to find all books of which Jones was one of the authors. Thus, we are interested in a subpart of the domain element "authors."

- **Keywords**. If we store a set of keywords for a book, we expect to be able to retrieve all books whose keywords include one or more specified keywords. Thus, we view the domain of the set of keywords as nonatomic.

- **Publisher**. Unlike *keywords* and *authors*, *publisher* does not have a set-valued domain. However, we may view *publisher* as consisting of the subfields *name* and *branch*. This view makes the domain of *publisher* nonatomic.

Figure 22.1 shows an example relation, *books*.

title	author	position
Compilers	Smith	1
Compilers	Jones	2
Networks	Jones	1
Networks	Frick	2

authors

title	keyword
Compilers	parsing
Compilers	analysis
Networks	Internet
Networks	Web

keywords

title	pub_name	pub_branch
Compilers	McGraw-Hill	New York
Networks	Oxford	London

books4

Figure 22.2   4NF version of the relation *books*.

For simplicity, we assume that the title of a book uniquely identifies the book.[1] We can then represent the same information using the following schema, where the primary key attributes are underlined:

- *authors*(<u>title</u>, *author*, *position*)

- *keywords*(*title*, *keyword*)

- *books4*(<u>title</u>, *pub_name*, *pub_branch*)

The above schema satisfies 4NF. Figure 22.2 shows the normalized representation of the data from Figure 22.1.

Although our example book database can be adequately expressed without using nested relations, the use of nested relations leads to an easier-to-understand model. The typical user or programmer of an information-retrieval system thinks of the database in terms of books having sets of authors, as the non-1NF design models. The 4NF design requires queries to join multiple relations, whereas the non-1NF design makes many types of queries easier.

On the other hand, it may be better to use a first normal form representation in other situations. For instance, consider the *takes* relationship in our university example. The relationship is many-to-many between *student* and *section*. We could

---

[1]This assumption does not hold in the real world. Books are usually identified by a 10-digit ISBN number that uniquely identifies each published book.

conceivably store a set of sections with each student, or a set of students with each section, or both. If we store both, we would have data redundancy (the relationship of a particular student to a particular section would be stored twice).

The ability to use complex data types such as sets and arrays can be useful in many applications but should be used with care.

22.3   Structured Types and Inheritance in SQL

Before SQL:1999, the SQL type system consisted of a fairly simple set of predefined types. SQL:1999 added an extensive type system to SQL, allowing structured types and type inheritance.

22.3.1   Structured Types

Structured types allow composite attributes of E-R designs to be represented directly. For instance, we can define the following structured type to represent a composite attribute *name* with component attribute *firstname* and *lastname*:

> **create type** *Name* **as**
>   (*firstname* **varchar**(20),
>   *lastname* **varchar**(20))
>   **final**;

Similarly, the following structured type can be used to represent a composite attribute *address*:

> **create type** *Address* **as**
>   (*street* **varchar**(20),
>   *city* **varchar**(20),
>   *zipcode* **varchar**(9))
>   **not final**;

Such types are called **user-defined** types in SQL[2]. The above definition corresponds to the E-R diagram in Figure 7.4. The **final** and **not final** specifications are related to subtyping, which we describe later, in Section 22.3.2.[3]

We can now use these types to create composite attributes in a relation, by simply declaring an attribute to be of one of these types. For example, we could create a table *person* as follows:

---

[2]To illustrate our earlier note about commercial implementations defining their syntax before the standards were developed, we point out that Oracle requires the keyword **object** following **as**.

[3]The **final** specification for *Name* indicates that we cannot create subtypes for *name*, whereas the **not final** specification for *Address* indicates that we can create subtypes of *address*.

> **create table** *person* (
> *name Name,*
> *address Address,*
> *dateOfBirth* **date**);

The components of a composite attribute can be accessed using a "dot" notation; for instance *name.firstname* returns the firstname component of the name attribute. An access to attribute *name* would return a value of the structured type *Name*.

We can also create a table whose rows are of a user-defined type. For example, we could define a type *PersonType* and create the table *person* as follows:[4]

> **create type** *PersonType* **as** (
> *name Name,*
> *address Address,*
> *dateOfBirth* **date**)
> **not final**
> **create table** *person* **of** *PersonType*;

An alternative way of defining composite attributes in SQL is to use unnamed **row types**. For instance, the relation representing person information could have been created using row types as follows:

> **create table** *person_r* (
> *name* **row** (*firstname* **varchar**(20),
> *lastname* **varchar**(20)),
> *address* **row** (*street* **varchar**(20),
> *city* **varchar**(20),
> *zipcode* **varchar**(9)),
> *dateOfBirth* **date**);

This definition is equivalent to the preceding table definition, except that the attributes *name* and *address* have unnamed types, and the rows of the table also have an unnamed type.

The following query illustrates how to access component attributes of a composite attribute. The query finds the last name and city of each person.

> **select** *name.lastname, address.city*
> **from** *person*;

A structured type can have **methods** defined on it. We declare methods as part of the type definition of a structured type:

---

[4]Most actual systems, being case insensitive, would not permit *name* to be used both as an attribute name and a data type.

> **create type** *PersonType* **as** (
>   *name Name,*
>   *address Address,*
>   *dateOfBirth* **date**)
>   **not final**
> **method** *ageOnDate(onDate* **date**)
>   **returns interval year**;

We create the method body separately:

> **create instance method** *ageOnDate* (*onDate* **date**)
>   **returns interval year**
>   **for** *PersonType*
> **begin**
>   **return** *onDate* − **self**.*dateOfBirth*;
> **end**

Note that the **for** clause indicates which type this method is for, while the keyword **instance** indicates that this method executes on an instance of the *Person* type. The variable **self** refers to the *Person* instance on which the method is invoked. The body of the method can contain procedural statements, which we saw earlier in Section 5.2. Methods can update the attributes of the instance on which they are executed.

Methods can be invoked on instances of a type. If we had created a table *person* of type *PersonType*, we could invoke the method *ageOnDate()* as illustrated below, to find the age of each person.

> **select** *name.lastname, ageOnDate*(**current_date**)
> **from** *person*;

In SQL:1999, **constructor functions** are used to create values of structured types. A function with the same name as a structured type is a constructor function for the structured type. For instance, we could declare a constructor for the type *Name* like this:

> **create function** *Name* (*firstname* **varchar**(20), *lastname* **varchar**(20))
> **returns** *Name*
> **begin**
>   **set self**.*firstname* = *firstname*;
>   **set self**.*lastname* = *lastname*;
> **end**

We can then use **new** *Name*('John', 'Smith') to create a value of the type *Name*. We can construct a row value by listing its attributes within parentheses. For instance, if we declare an attribute *name* as a row type with components *firstname* and *lastname* we can construct this value for it: ('Ted', 'Codd') without using a constructor.

By default every structured type has a constructor with no arguments, which sets the attributes to their default values. Any other constructors have to be created explicitly. There can be more than one constructor for the same structured type; although they have the same name, they must be distinguishable by the number of arguments and types of their arguments.

The following statement illustrates how we can create a new tuple in the *Person* relation. We assume that a constructor has been defined for *Address*, just like the constructor we defined for *Name*.

> **insert into** *Person*
> > **values**
> > > (**new** *Name*('John', 'Smith'),
> > > **new** *Address*('20 Main St', 'New York', '11001'),
> > > **date** '1960-8-22');

22.3.2   Type Inheritance

Suppose that we have the following type definition for people:

> **create type** *Person*
> > (*name* **varchar**(20),
> > *address* **varchar**(20));

We may want to store extra information in the database about people who are students, and about people who are teachers. Since students and teachers are also people, we can use inheritance to define the student and teacher types in SQL:

> **create type** *Student*
> > **under** *Person*
> > (*degree* **varchar**(20),
> > *department* **varchar**(20));

> **create type** *Teacher*
> > **under** *Person*
> > (*salary* **integer**,
> > *department* **varchar**(20));

Both *Student* and *Teacher* inherit the attributes of *Person*—namely, *name* and *address*. *Student* and *Teacher* are said to be subtypes of *Person*, and *Person* is a supertype of *Student*, as well as of *Teacher*.

Methods of a structured type are inherited by its subtypes, just as attributes are. However, a subtype can redefine the effect of a method by declaring the method again, using **overriding method** in place of **method** in the method declaration.

The SQL standard requires an extra field at the end of the type definition, whose value is either **final** or **not final**. The keyword **final** says that subtypes may not be created from the given type, while **not final** says that subtypes may be created.

Now suppose that we want to store information about teaching assistants, who are simultaneously students and teachers, perhaps even in different departments. We can do this if the type system supports **multiple inheritance**, where a type is declared as a subtype of multiple types. Note that the SQL standard does not support multiple inheritance, although future versions of the SQL standard may support it, so we discuss the concept here.

For instance, if our type system supports multiple inheritance, we can define a type for teaching assistant as follows:

> **create type** *TeachingAssistant*
> **under** *Student, Teacher*;

TeachingAssistant inherits all the attributes of *Student* and *Teacher*. There is a problem, however, since the attributes *name, address*, and *department* are present in *Student*, as well as in *Teacher*.

The attributes *name* and *address* are actually inherited from a common source, *Person*. So there is no conflict caused by inheriting them from *Student* as well as *Teacher*. However, the attribute *department* is defined separately in *Student* and *Teacher*. In fact, a teaching assistant may be a student of one department and a teacher in another department. To avoid a conflict between the two occurrences of *department*, we can rename them by using an **as** clause, as in this definition of the type *TeachingAssistant*:

> **create type** *TeachingAssistant*
> **under** *Student* **with** (*department* **as** *student_dept*),
> *Teacher* **with** (*department* **as** *teacher_dept*);

In SQL, as in most other languages, a value of a structured type must have exactly one *most-specific type*. That is, each value must be associated with one specific type, called its **most-specific type**, when it is created. By means of inheritance, it is also associated with each of the supertypes of its most-specific type. For example, suppose that an entity has the type *Person*, as well as the type *Student*. Then, the most-specific type of the entity is *Student*, since *Student* is a subtype of *Person*. However, an entity cannot have the type *Student* as well as the type *Teacher* unless it has a type, such as *TeachingAssistant*, that is a subtype of *Teacher*, as well as of *Student* (which is not possible in SQL since multiple inheritance is not supported by SQL).

22.4   Table Inheritance

Subtables in SQL correspond to the E-R notion of specialization/generalization. For instance, suppose we define the *people* table as follows:

create table *people* **of** *Person*;

We can then define tables *students* and *teachers* as **subtables** of *people*, as follows:

create table *students* **of** *Student*
        under *people*;

create table *teachers* **of** *Teacher*
        under *people*;

The types of the subtables (*Student* and *Teacher* in the above example) are subtypes of the type of the parent table (*Person* in the above example). As a result, every attribute present in the table *people* is also present in the subtables *students* and *teachers*.

Further, when we declare *students* and *teachers* as subtables of *people*, every tuple present in *students* or *teachers* becomes implicitly present in *people*. Thus, if a query uses the table *people*, it will find not only tuples directly inserted into that table, but also tuples inserted into its subtables, namely *students* and *teachers*. However, only those attributes that are present in *people* can be accessed by that query.

SQL permits us to find tuples that are in *people* but not in its subtables by using "**only** *people*" in place of *people* in a query. The **only** keyword can also be used in delete and update statements. Without the **only** keyword, a delete statement on a supertable, such as *people*, also deletes tuples that were originally inserted in subtables (such as *students*); for example, a statement:

delete from *people* **where** *P*;

would delete all tuples from the table *people*, as well as its subtables *students* and *teachers*, that satisfy *P*. If the **only** keyword is added to the above statement, tuples that were inserted in subtables are not affected, even if they satisfy the **where** clause conditions. Subsequent queries on the supertable would continue to find these tuples.

Conceptually, multiple inheritance is possible with tables, just as it is possible with types. For example, we can create a table of type *TeachingAssistant*:

create table *teaching_assistants*
of *TeachingAssistant*
        under *students, teachers*;

As a result of the declaration, every tuple present in the *teaching_assistants* table is also implicitly present in the *teachers* and in the *students* table, and in turn in the *people* table. We note, however, that multiple inheritance of tables is not supported by SQL.

There are some consistency requirements for subtables. Before we state the constraints, we need a definition: we say that tuples in a subtable and parent table **correspond** if they have the same values for all inherited attributes. Thus, corresponding tuples represent the same entity.

The consistency requirements for subtables are:

1. Each tuple of the supertable can correspond to at most one tuple in each of its immediate subtables.

2. SQL has an additional constraint that all the tuples corresponding to each other must be derived from one tuple (inserted into one table).

For example, without the first condition, we could have two tuples in *students* (or *teachers*) that correspond to the same person.

The second condition rules out a tuple in *people* corresponding to both a tuple in *students* and a tuple in *teachers*, unless all these tuples are implicitly present because a tuple was inserted in a table *teaching_assistants*, which is a subtable of both *teachers* and *students*.

Since SQL does not support multiple inheritance, the second condition actually prevents a person from being both a teacher and a student. Even if multiple inheritance were supported, the same problem would arise if the subtable *teaching_assistants* were absent. Obviously it would be useful to model a situation where a person can be a teacher and a student, even if a common subtable *teaching_assistants* is not present. Thus, it can be useful to remove the second consistency constraint. Doing so would allow an object to have multiple types, without requiring it to have a most-specific type.

For example, suppose we again have the type *Person*, with subtypes *Student* and *Teacher*, and the corresponding table *people*, with subtables *teachers* and *students*. We can then have a tuple in *teachers* and a tuple in *students* corresponding to the same tuple in *people*. There is no need to have a type *TeachingAssistant* that is a subtype of both *Student* and *Teacher*. We need not create a type *TeachingAssistant* unless we wish to store extra attributes or redefine methods in a manner specific to people who are both students and teachers.

We note, however, that SQL unfortunately prohibits such a situation, because of consistency requirement 2. Since SQL also does not support multiple inheritance, we cannot use inheritance to model a situation where a person can be both a student and a teacher. As a result, SQL subtables cannot be used to represent overlapping specializations from the E-R model.

We can of course create separate tables to represent the overlapping specializations/generalizations without using inheritance. The process was described earlier, in Section 7.8.6.1. In the above example, we would create tables *people*, *students*, and *teachers*, with the *students* and *teachers* tables containing the primary-key attribute of *Person* and other attributes specific to *Student* and *Teacher*, respectively. The *people* table would contain information about all persons, including students and teachers. We would then have to add appropriate referential-integrity constraints to ensure that students and teachers are also represented in the *people* table.

In other words, we can create our own improved implementation of the subtable mechanism using existing features of SQL, with some extra effort in defining the table, as well as some extra effort at query time to specify joins to access required attributes.

We note that SQL defines a privilege called **under**, which is required in order to create a subtype or subtable under another type or table. The motivation for this privilege is similar to that for the **references** privilege.

22.5   Array and Multiset Types in SQL

SQL supports two collection types: arrays and multisets; array types were added in SQL:1999, while multiset types were added in SQL:2003. Recall that a *multiset* is an unordered collection, where an element may occur multiple times. Multisets are like sets, except that a set allows each element to occur at most once.

Suppose we wish to record information about books, including a set of keywords for each book. Suppose also that we wished to store the names of authors of a book as an array; unlike elements in a multiset, the elements of an array are ordered, so we can distinguish the first author from the second author, and so on. The following example illustrates how these array and multiset-valued attributes can be defined in SQL:

> **create type** *Publisher* **as**
>   (*name* **varchar**(20),
>   *branch* **varchar**(20));
>
> **create type** *Book* **as**
>   (*title* **varchar**(20),
>   *author_array* **varchar**(20) **array** [10],
>   *pub_date* **date**,
>   *publisher Publisher*,
>   *keyword_set* **varchar**(20) **multiset**);
>
> **create table** *books* **of** *Book*;

The first statement defines a type called *Publisher* with two components: a name and a branch. The second statement defines a structured type *Book* that contains a *title*, an *author_array*, which is an array of up to 10 author names, a publication date, a publisher (of type *Publisher*), and a multiset of keywords. Finally, a table *books* containing tuples of type *Book* is created.

Note that we used an array, instead of a multiset, to store the names of authors, since the ordering of authors generally has some significance, whereas we believe that the ordering of keywords associated with a book is not significant.

In general, multivalued attributes from an E-R schema can be mapped to multiset-valued attributes in SQL; if ordering is important, SQL arrays can be used instead of multisets.

22.5.1   Creating and Accessing Collection Values

An array of values can be created in SQL:1999 in this way:

$$\textbf{array}['Silberschatz', 'Korth', 'Sudarshan']$$

Similarly, a multiset of keywords can be constructed as follows:

$$\textbf{multiset}['computer', 'database', 'SQL']$$

Thus, we can create a tuple of the type defined by the *books* relation as:

('Compilers', **array**['Smith', 'Jones'], **new** *Publisher*('McGraw-Hill', 'New York'), **multiset**['parsing', 'analysis'])

Here we have created a value for the attribute *Publisher* by invoking a *constructor* function for *Publisher* with appropriate arguments. Note that this constructor for *Publisher* must be created explicitly, and is not present by default; it can be declared just like the constructor for *Name*, which we saw earlier in Section 22.3.

If we want to insert the preceding tuple into the relation *books*, we could execute the statement:

> **insert into** *books*
> **values** ('Compilers', **array**['Smith', 'Jones'],
>   **new** *Publisher*('McGraw-Hill', 'New York'),
>   **multiset**['parsing', 'analysis']);

We can access or update elements of an array by specifying the array index, for example *author_array*[1].

22.5.2   Querying Collection-Valued Attributes

We now consider how to handle collection-valued attributes in queries. An expression evaluating to a collection can appear anywhere that a relation name may appear, such as in a **from** clause, as the following paragraphs illustrate. We use the table *books* that we defined earlier.

If we want to find all books that have the word "database" as one of their keywords, we can use this query:

> **select** *title*
> **from** *books*
> **where** 'database' **in** (**unnest**(*keyword_set*));

Note that we have used **unnest**(*keyword_set*) in a position where SQL without nested relations would have required a **select-from-where** subexpression.

If we know that a particular book has three authors, we could write:

> **select** *author_array*[1], *author_array*[2], *author_array*[3]
> **from** *books*
> **where** *title* = 'Database System Concepts';

Now, suppose that we want a relation containing pairs of the form "title, author_name" for each book and each author of the book. We can use this query:

> **select** *B.title, A.author*
> **from** *books* **as** *B*, **unnest**(*B.author_array*) **as** *A*(*author*);

Since the *author_array* attribute of *books* is a collection-valued field, **unnest**(*B.author_array*) can be used in a **from** clause, where a relation is expected. Note that the tuple variable *B* is visible to this expression since it is defined *earlier* in the **from** clause.

When unnesting an array, the previous query loses information about the ordering of elements in the array. The **unnest with ordinality** clause can be used to get this information, as illustrated by the following query. This query can be used to generate the *authors* relation, which we saw earlier, from the *books* relation.

> **select** *title, A.author, A.position*
> **from** *books* **as** *B*,
>   **unnest**(*B.author_array*) **with ordinality as** *A*(*author, position*);

The **with ordinality** clause generates an extra attribute which records the position of the element in the array. A similar query, but without the **with ordinality** clause, can be used to generate the *keyword* relation.

22.5.3   Nesting and Unnesting

The transformation of a nested relation into a form with fewer (or no) relation-valued attributes is called **unnesting**. The *books* relation has two attributes, *author_array* and *keyword_set*, that are collections, and two attributes, *title* and *publisher*, that are not. Suppose that we want to convert the relation into a single flat relation, with no nested relations or structured types as attributes. We can use the following query to carry out the task:

title	author	pub_name	pub_branch	keyword
Compilers	Smith	McGraw-Hill	New York	parsing
Compilers	Jones	McGraw-Hill	New York	parsing
Compilers	Smith	McGraw-Hill	New York	analysis
Compilers	Jones	McGraw-Hill	New York	analysis
Networks	Jones	Oxford	London	Internet
Networks	Frick	Oxford	London	Internet
Networks	Jones	Oxford	London	Web
Networks	Frick	Oxford	London	Web

Figure 22.3 *flat_books*: result of unnesting attributes *author_array* and *keyword_set* of relation *books*.

> **select** *title, A.author, publisher.name* **as** *pub_name, publisher.branch*
> **as** *pub_branch, K.keyword*
> **from** *books* **as** *B,* **unnest**(*B.author_array*) **as** *A(author),*
> **unnest** (*B.keyword_set*) **as** *K(keyword)*;

The variable *B* in the **from** clause is declared to range over *books*. The variable *A* is declared to range over the authors in *author_array* for the book *B*, and *K* is declared to range over the keywords in the *keyword_set* of the book *B*. Figure 22.1 shows an instance *books* relation, and Figure 22.3 shows the relation, which we call *flat_books*, that is the result of the preceding query. Note that the relation *flat_books* is in 1NF, since all its attributes are atomic valued.

The reverse process of transforming a 1NF relation into a nested relation is called **nesting**. Nesting can be carried out by an extension of grouping in SQL. In the normal use of grouping in SQL, a temporary multiset relation is (logically) created for each group, and an aggregate function is applied on the temporary relation to get a single (atomic) value. The **collect** function returns the multiset of values, so instead of creating a single value, we can create a nested relation. Suppose that we are given the 1NF relation *flat_books*, as in Figure 22.3. The following query nests the relation on the attribute *keyword*:

> **select** *title, author, Publisher(pub_name, pub_branch)* **as** *publisher,*
> **collect**(*keyword*) **as** *keyword_set*
> **from** *flat_books*
> **group by** *title, author, publisher*;

The result of the query on the *flat_books* relation from Figure 22.3 appears in Figure 22.4.

If we want to nest the author attribute also into a multiset, we can use the query:

title	author	publisher	keyword_set
		(pub_name, pub_branch)	
Compilers	Smith	(McGraw-Hill, New York)	{parsing, analysis}
Compilers	Jones	(McGraw-Hill, New York)	{parsing, analysis}
Networks	Jones	(Oxford, London)	{Internet, Web}
Networks	Frick	(Oxford, London)	{Internet, Web}

Figure 22.4 A partially nested version of the *flat_books* relation.

> **select** *title*, **collect**(*author*) **as** *author_set*,
>   *Publisher*(*pub_name, pub_branch*) **as** *publisher*,
>   **collect**(*keyword*) **as** *keyword_set*
> **from** *flat_books*
> **group by** *title, publisher*;

Another approach to creating nested relations is to use subqueries in the **select** clause. An advantage of the subquery approach is that an **order by** clause can be used in the subquery to generate results in the order desired for the creation of an array. The following query illustrates this approach; the keywords **array** and **multiset** specify that an array and multiset (respectively) are to be created from the results of the subqueries.

> **select** *title*,
>   **array**(**select** *author*
>   **from** *authors* **as** *A*
>   **where** *A.title* = *B.title*
>   **order by** *A.position*) **as** *author_array*,
>   *Publisher*(*pub_name, pub_branch*) **as** *publisher*,
>   **multiset**(**select** *keyword*
>   **from** *keywords* **as** *K*
>   **where** *K.title* = *B.title*) **as** *keyword_set*,
> **from** *books4* **as** *B*;

The system executes the nested subqueries in the **select** clause for each tuple generated by the **from** and **where** clauses of the outer query. Observe that the attribute *B.title* from the outer query is used in the nested queries, to ensure that only the correct sets of authors and keywords are generated for each title.

SQL:2003 provides a variety of operators on multisets, including a function **set**(*M*) that returns a duplicate-free version of a multiset *M*, an **intersection** aggregate operation, which returns the intersection of all the multisets in a group, a **fusion** aggregate operation, which returns the union of all multisets in a group, and a **submultiset** predicate, which checks if a multiset is contained in another multiset.

The SQL standard does not provide any way to update multiset attributes except by assigning a new value. For example, to delete a value v from a multiset attribute A, we would have to set it to (A **except all multiset**[v]).

22.6   Object-Identity and Reference Types in SQL

Object-oriented languages provide the ability to refer to objects. An attribute of a type can be a reference to an object of a specified type. For example, in SQL we can define a type *Department* with a field *name* and a field *head* that is a reference to the type *Person*, and a table *departments* of type *Department*, as follows:

> **create type** *Department* (
>   *name* **varchar(20)**,
>   *head* **ref**(*Person*) **scope** *people*);
>
> **create table** *departments* **of** *Department*;

Here, the reference is restricted to tuples of the table *people*. The restriction of the **scope** of a reference to tuples of a table is mandatory in SQL, and it makes references behave like foreign keys.

We can omit the declaration **scope** *people* from the type declaration and instead make an addition to the **create table** statement:

> **create table** *departments* **of** *Department*
>   (*head* **with options scope** *people*);

The referenced table must have an attribute that stores the identifier of the tuple. We declare this attribute, called the **self-referential attribute**, by adding a **ref is** clause to the **create table** statement:

> **create table** *people* **of** *Person*
>   **ref is** *person_id* **system generated**;

Here, *person_id* is an attribute name, not a keyword, and the **create table** statement specifies that the identifier is generated automatically by the database.

In order to initialize a reference attribute, we need to get the identifier of the tuple that is to be referenced. We can get the identifier value of a tuple by means of a query. Thus, to create a tuple with the reference value, we may first create the tuple with a null reference and then set the reference separately:

> **insert into** *departments*
> **values** ('CS', null);
>
> **update** *departments*
>   **set** *head* = (**select** *p.person_id*
>   **from** *people* **as** *p*
>   **where** *name* = 'John')
>   **where** *name* = 'CS';

An alternative to system-generated identifiers is to allow users to generate identifiers. The type of the self-referential attribute must be specified as part of the type definition of the referenced table, and the table definition must specify that the reference is **user generated**:

> **create type** *Person*
>   (*name* **varchar**(20),
>   *address* **varchar**(20))
>   **ref using varchar**(20);
>
> **create table** *people* **of** *Person*
>   **ref is** *person_id* **user generated**;

When inserting a tuple in *people*, we must then provide a value for the identifier:

> **insert into** *people* (*person_id, name, address*) **values**
>   ('01284567', 'John', '23 Coyote Run');

No other tuple for *people* or its supertables or subtables can have the same identifier. We can then use the identifier value when inserting a tuple into *departments*, without the need for a separate query to retrieve the identifier:

> **insert into** *departments*
>   **values** ('CS', '01284567');

It is even possible to use an existing primary-key value as the identifier, by including the **ref from** clause in the type definition:

> **create type** *Person*
>   (*name* **varchar**(20) **primary key**,
>   *address* **varchar**(20))
>   **ref from**(*name*);
>
> **create table** *people* **of** *Person*
>   **ref is** *person_id* **derived**;

Note that the table definition must specify that the reference is derived, and must still specify a self-referential attribute name. When inserting a tuple for *departments*, we can then use:

> **insert into** *departments*
> **values** ('CS', 'John');

References are dereferenced in SQL:1999 by the $->$ symbol. Consider the *departments* table defined earlier. We can use this query to find the names and addresses of the heads of all departments:

> **select** *head$->$name, head$->$address*
> **from** *departments*;

An expression such as "*head$->$name*" is called a **path expression**.

Since *head* is a reference to a tuple in the *people* table, the attribute *name* in the preceding query is the *name* attribute of the tuple from the *people* table. References can be used to hide join operations; in the preceding example, without the references, the *head* field of *department* would be declared a foreign key of the table *people*. To find the name and address of the head of a department, we would require an explicit join of the relations *departments* and *people*. The use of references simplifies the query considerably.

We can use the operation **deref** to return the tuple pointed to by a reference, and then access its attributes, as shown below:

> **select deref**(*head*).*name*
> **from** *departments*;

22.7 Implementing O-R Features

Object-relational database systems are basically extensions of existing relational database systems. Changes are clearly required at many levels of the database system. However, to minimize changes to the storage-system code (relation storage, indices, etc.), the complex data types supported by object-relational systems can be translated to the simpler type system of relational databases.

To understand how to do this translation, we need look only at how some features of the E-R model are translated into relations. For instance, multivalued attributes in the E-R model correspond to multiset-valued attributes in the object-relational model. Composite attributes roughly correspond to structured types. ISA hierarchies in the E-R model correspond to table inheritance in the object-relational model.

The techniques for converting E-R model features to tables, which we saw in Section 7.6, can be used, with some extensions, to translate object-relational data to relational data at the storage level.

Subtables can be stored in an efficient manner, without replication of all inherited fields, in one of two ways:

- Each table stores the primary key (which may be inherited from a parent table) and the attributes that are defined locally. Inherited attributes (other than the primary key) do not need to be stored, and can be derived by means of a join with the supertable, based on the primary key.

- Each table stores all inherited and locally defined attributes. When a tuple is inserted, it is stored only in the table in which it is inserted, and its presence is inferred in each of the supertables. Access to all attributes of a tuple is faster, since a join is not required.

  However, in case the type system allows an entity to be represented in two subtables without being present in a common subtable of both, this representation can result in replication of information. Further, it is hard to translate foreign keys referring to a supertable into constraints on the subtables; to implement such foreign keys efficiently, the supertable has to be defined as a view, and the database system would have to support foreign keys on views.

Implementations may choose to represent array and multiset types directly, or may choose to use a normalized representation internally. Normalized representations tend to take up more space and require an extra join/grouping cost to collect data in an array or multiset. However, normalized representations may be easier to implement.

The ODBC and JDBC application program interfaces have been extended to retrieve and store structured types. JDBC provides a method `getObject()` that is similar to `getString()` but returns a Java `Struct` object, from which the components of the structured type can be extracted. It is also possible to associate a Java class with an SQL structured type, and JDBC will then convert between the types. See the ODBC or JDBC reference manuals for details.

22.8   Persistent Programming Languages

Database languages differ from traditional programming languages in that they directly manipulate data that are persistent—that is, data that continue to exist even after the program that created it has terminated. A relation in a database and tuples in a relation are examples of persistent data. In contrast, the only persistent data that traditional programming languages directly manipulate are files.

Access to a database is only one component of any real-world application. While a data-manipulation language like SQL is quite effective for accessing data, a programming language is required for implementing other components of the application such as user interfaces or communication with other computers. The traditional way of interfacing database languages to programming languages is by embedding SQL within the programming language.

A **persistent programming language** is a programming language extended with constructs to handle persistent data. Persistent programming languages can be distinguished from languages with embedded SQL in at least two ways:

1. With an embedded language, the type system of the host language usually differs from the type system of the data-manipulation language. The programmer is responsible for any type conversions between the host language and SQL. Having the programmer carry out this task has several drawbacks:

   - The code to convert between objects and tuples operates outside the object-oriented type system, and hence has a higher chance of having undetected errors.

   - Conversion between the object-oriented format and the relational format of tuples in the database takes a substantial amount of code. The format translation code, along with the code for loading and unloading data from a database, can form a significant percentage of the total code required for an application.

   In contrast, in a persistent programming language, the query language is fully integrated with the host language, and both share the same type system. Objects can be created and stored in the database without any explicit type or format changes; any format changes required are carried out transparently.

2. The programmer using an embedded query language is responsible for writing explicit code to fetch data from the database into memory. If any updates are performed, the programmer must write code explicitly to store the updated data back in the database.

   In contrast, in a persistent programming language, the programmer can manipulate persistent data without writing code explicitly to fetch it into memory or store it back to disk.

In this section, we describe how object-oriented programming languages, such as C++ and Java, can be extended to make them persistent programming languages. These language features allow programmers to manipulate data directly from the programming language, without having to go through a data-manipulation language such as SQL. They thereby provide tighter integration of the programming languages with the database than, for example, embedded SQL.

There are certain drawbacks to persistent programming languages, however, that we must keep in mind when deciding whether to use them. Since the programming language is usually a powerful one, it is relatively easy to make programming errors that damage the database. The complexity of the language makes automatic high-level optimization, such as to reduce disk I/O, harder. Support for declarative querying is important for many applications, but persistent programming languages currently do not support declarative querying well.

In this section, we describe a number of conceptual issues that must be addressed when adding persistence to an existing programming language. We first address language-independent issues, and in subsequent sections we discuss issues that are specific to the C++ language and to the Java language. However, we do not cover details of language extensions; although several standards have been proposed, none has met universal acceptance. See the references in the bibliographical notes to learn more about specific language extensions and further details of implementations.

22.8.1 Persistence of Objects

Object-oriented programming languages already have a concept of objects, a type system to define object types, and constructs to create objects. However, these objects are *transient*—they vanish when the program terminates, just as variables in a Java or C program vanish when the program terminates. If we wish to turn such a language into a database programming language, the first step is to provide a way to make objects persistent. Several approaches have been proposed.

- **Persistence by class**. The simplest, but least convenient, way is to declare that a class is persistent. All objects of the class are then persistent objects by default. Objects of nonpersistent classes are all transient.

  This approach is not flexible, since it is often useful to have both transient and persistent objects in a single class. Many object-oriented database systems interpret declaring a class to be persistent as saying that objects in the class potentially can be made persistent, rather than that all objects in the class are persistent. Such classes might more appropriately be called "persistable" classes.

- **Persistence by creation**. In this approach, new syntax is introduced to create persistent objects, by extending the syntax for creating transient objects. Thus, an object is either persistent or transient, depending on how it was created. Several object-oriented database systems follow this approach.

- **Persistence by marking**. A variant of the preceding approach is to mark objects as persistent after they are created. All objects are created as transient objects, but, if an object is to persist beyond the execution of the program, it must be marked explicitly as persistent before the program terminates. This approach, unlike the previous one, postpones the decision on persistence or transience until after the object is created.

- **Persistence by reachability**. One or more objects are explicitly declared as (root) persistent objects. All other objects are persistent if (and only if) they are reachable from the root object through a sequence of one or more references.

  Thus, all objects referenced by (that is, whose object identifiers are stored in) the root persistent objects are persistent. But also, all objects referenced from these objects are persistent, and objects to which they refer are in turn persistent, and so on.

  A benefit of this scheme is that it is easy to make entire data structures persistent by merely declaring the root of such structures as persistent. However, the database system has the burden of following chains of references to detect which objects are persistent, and that can be expensive.

22.8.2 Object Identity and Pointers

In an object-oriented programming language that has not been extended to handle persistence, when an object is created, the system returns a transient object identifier. Transient object identifiers are valid only when the program that created them is executing; after that program terminates, the objects are deleted, and the identifier is meaningless. When a persistent object is created, it is assigned a persistent object identifier.

The notion of object identity has an interesting relationship to pointers in programming languages. A simple way to achieve built-in identity is through pointers to physical locations in storage. In particular, in many object-oriented languages such as C++, a transient object identifier is actually an in-memory pointer.

However, the association of an object with a physical location in storage may change over time. There are several degrees of permanence of identity:

- **Intraprocedure**. Identity persists only during the execution of a single procedure. Examples of intraprogram identity are local variables within procedures.

- **Intraprogram**. Identity persists only during the execution of a single program or query. Examples of intraprogram identity are global variables in programming languages. Main-memory or virtual-memory pointers offer only intraprogram identity.

- **Interprogram**. Identity persists from one program execution to another. Pointers to file-system data on disk offer interprogram identity, but they may change if the way data is stored in the file system is changed.

- **Persistent**. Identity persists not only among program executions, but also among structural reorganizations of the data. It is the persistent form of identity that is required for object-oriented systems.

In persistent extensions of languages such as C++, object identifiers for persistent objects are implemented as "persistent pointers." A *persistent pointer* is a type of pointer that, unlike in-memory pointers, remains valid even after the end of a program execution, and across some forms of data reorganization. A programmer may use a persistent pointer in the same ways that she may use an in-memory pointer in a programming language. Conceptually, we may think of a persistent pointer as a pointer to an object in the database.

22.8.3 Storage and Access of Persistent Objects

What does it mean to store an object in a database? Clearly, the data part of an object has to be stored individually for each object. Logically, the code that implements methods of a class should be stored in the database as part of the database schema, along with the type definitions of the classes. However, many implementations simply store the code in files outside the database, to avoid having to integrate system software such as compilers with the database system.

There are several ways to find objects in the database. One way is to give names to objects, just as we give names to files. This approach works for a relatively small number of objects, but does not scale to millions of objects. A second way is to expose object identifiers or persistent pointers to the objects, which can be stored externally. Unlike names, these pointers do not have to be mnemonic, and they can even be physical pointers into a database.

A third way is to store collections of objects, and to allow programs to iterate over the collections to find required objects. Collections of objects can themselves be modeled as objects of a *collection type*. Collection types include sets, multisets (that is, sets with possibly many occurrences of a value), lists, and so on. A special case of a collection is a **class extent**, which is the collection of all objects belonging to the class. If a class extent is present for a class, then, whenever an object of the class is created, that object is inserted in the class extent automatically, and, whenever an object is deleted, that object is removed from the class extent. Class extents allow classes to be treated like relations in that we can examine all objects in the class, just as we can examine all tuples in a relation.

Most object-oriented database systems support all three ways of accessing persistent objects. They give identifiers to all objects. They usually give names only to class extents and other collection objects, and perhaps to other selected objects, but not to most objects. They usually maintain class extents for all classes that can have persistent objects, but, in many of the implementations, the class extents contain only persistent objects of the class.

22.8.4 Persistent C++ Systems

There are several object-oriented databases based on persistent extensions to C++ (see the bibliographical notes). There are differences among them in terms of the system architecture, yet they have many common features in terms of the programming language.

Several of the object-oriented features of the C++ language provide support for persistence without changing the language itself. For example, we can declare a class called Persistent_Object with attributes and methods to support persistence; any other class that should be persistent can be made a subclass of this class, and thereby inherit the support for persistence. The C++ language (like some other modern programming languages) also lets us redefine standard function names and operators—such as $+$, $-$, the pointer dereference operator $->$, and so on—according to the types of the operands on which they are applied. This ability is called *overloading*; it is used to redefine operators to behave in the required manner when they are operating on persistent objects.

Providing persistence support via class libraries has the benefit of making only minimal changes to C++ necessary; moreover, it is relatively easy to implement. However, it has the drawback that the programmer has to spend much more time to write a program that handles persistent objects, and it is not easy for the programmer to specify integrity constraints on the schema or to provide support for declarative querying. Some persistent C++ implementations support extensions to the C++ syntax to make these tasks easier.

The following aspects need to be addressed when adding persistence support to C++ (and other languages):

- **Persistent pointers**: A new data type has to be defined to represent persistent pointers. For example, the ODMG C++ standard defines a template class d_Ref< T > to represent persistent pointers to a class T. The dereference operator on this class is redefined to fetch the object from disk (if not already present in memory), and it returns an in-memory pointer to the buffer where the object has been fetched. Thus if p is a persistent pointer to a class T, one can use standard syntax such as p->A or p->f(v) to access attribute A of class T or invoke method f of class T.

  The ObjectStore database system uses a different approach to persistent pointers. It uses normal pointer types to store persistent pointers. This poses two problems: (1) in-memory pointer sizes may be only 4 bytes, which is too small to use with databases larger than 4 gigabytes, and (2) when an object is moved on disk, in-memory pointers to its old physical location are meaningless. ObjectStore uses a technique called "hardware swizzling" to address both problems; it prefetches objects from the database into memory, and replaces persistent pointers with in-memory pointers, and when data are stored back on disk, in-memory pointers are replaced by persistent pointers. When on disk, the value stored in the in-memory pointer field is not the actual persistent pointer; instead, the value is looked up in a table that contains the full persistent pointer value.

- **Creation of persistent objects**: The C++ new operator is used to create persistent objects by defining an "overloaded" version of the operator that takes extra arguments specifying that it should be created in the database. Thus instead of new T(), one would call new (db) T() to create a persistent object, where db identifies the database.

- **Class extents**: Class extents are created and maintained automatically for each class. The ODMG C++ standard requires the name of the class to be passed as an additional parameter to the new operation. This also allows multiple extents to be maintained for a class, by passing different names.

- **Relationships**: Relationships between classes are often represented by storing pointers from each object to the objects to which it is related. Objects related to multiple objects of a given class store a set of pointers. Thus if a pair of objects is in a relationship, each should store a pointer to the other. Persistent C++ systems provide a way to specify such integrity constraints and to enforce them by automatically creating and deleting pointers: For example, if a pointer is created from an object a to an object b, a pointer to a is added automatically to object b.

- **Iterator interface**: Since programs need to iterate over class members, an interface is required to iterate over members of a class extent. The iterator interface also allows selections to be specified, so that only objects satisfying the selection predicate need to be fetched.

- **Transactions**: Persistent C++ systems provide support for starting a transaction, and for committing it or rolling it back.

- **Updates**: One of the goals of providing persistence support in a programming language is to allow transparent persistence. That is, a function that operates on an object should not need to know that the object is persistent; the same functions can thus be used on objects regardless of whether they are persistent or not.

  However, one resultant problem is that it is difficult to detect when an object has been updated. Some persistent extensions to C++ require the programmer to specify explicitly that an object has been modified by calling a function mark_modified(). In addition to increasing programmer effort, this approach increases the chance that programming errors can result in a corrupt database. If a programmer omits a call to mark_modified(), it is possible that one update made by a transaction may never be propagated to the database, while another update made by the same transaction is propagated, violating atomicity of transactions.

  Other systems, such as ObjectStore, use memory-protection support provided by the operating system/hardware to detect writes to a block of memory and mark the block as a dirty block that should be written later to disk.

- **Query language**: Iterators provide support for simple selection queries. To support more complex queries, persistent C++ systems define a query language.

A large number of object-oriented database systems based on C++ were developed in the late 1980s and early 1990s. However, the market for such databases turned out to be much smaller than anticipated, since most application requirements are more than met by using SQL through interfaces such as ODBC or JDBC. As a result, most of the object-oriented database systems developed in that period do not exist any longer. In the 1990s, the Object Data Management Group (ODMG) defined standards for adding persistence to C++ and Java. However, the group wound up its activities around 2002. ObjectStore and Versant are among the original object-oriented database systems that are still in existence.

Although object-oriented database systems did not find the commercial success that they had hoped for, the motivation for adding persistence to programming language remains. There are several applications with high performance requirements that run on object-oriented database systems; using SQL would impose too high a performance overhead for many such systems. With object-relational database systems now providing support for complex data types, including references, it is easier to store programming language objects in an SQL database. A new generation of object-oriented database systems using object-relational databases as a backend may yet emerge.

22.8.5 Persistent Java Systems

The Java language has seen an enormous growth in usage in recent years. Demand for support for persistence of data in Java programs has grown correspondingly. Initial attempts at creating a standard for persistence in Java were led by the ODMG consortium; the consortium wound up its efforts later, but transferred its design to the **Java Database Objects (JDO)** effort, which is coordinated by Sun Microsystems.

The JDO model for object persistence in Java programs differs from the model for persistence support in C++ programs. Among its features are:

- **Persistence by reachability**: Objects are not explicitly created in a database. Explicitly registering an object as persistent (using the `makePersistent()` method of the `PersistenceManager` class) makes the object persistent. In addition, any object reachable from a persistent object becomes persistent.

- **Byte code enhancement**: Instead of declaring a class to be persistent in the Java code, classes whose objects may be made persistent are specified in a configuration file (with suffix `.jdo`). An implementation-specific *enhancer* program is executed that reads the configuration file and carries out two tasks. First, it may create structures in a database to store objects of the class. Second, it modifies the byte code (generated by compiling the Java program) to handle tasks related to persistence. Below are some examples of such modifications:

  - Any code that accesses an object could be changed to check first if the object is in memory, and if not, take steps to bring it into memory.

  - Any code that modifies an object is modified to record additionally that the object has been modified, and perhaps to save a pre-updated value used in case the update needs to be undone (that is, if the transaction is rolled back).

  Other modifications to the byte code may also be carried out. Such byte code modification is possible since the byte code is standard across all platforms, and includes much more information than compiled object code.

- **Database mapping**: JDO does not define how data are stored in the back-end database. For example, a common scenario is to store objects in a relational database. The enhancer program may create an appropriate schema in the database to store class objects. How exactly it does this is implementation dependent and not defined by JDO. Some attributes could be mapped to relational attributes, while others may be stored in a serialized form, treated as a binary object by the database. JDO implementations may allow existing relational data to be viewed as objects by defining an appropriate mapping.

- **Class extents**: Class extents are created and maintained automatically for each class declared to be persistent. All objects made persistent are added automatically to the class extent corresponding to their class. JDO programs may access a class extent, and iterate over selected members. The `Iterator` interface provided by Java can be used to create iterators on class extents, and to step through the members of the class extent. JDO also allows selections to be specified when an iterator is created on a class extent, and only objects satisfying the selection are fetched.

- **Single reference type**: There is no difference in type between a reference to a transient object and a reference to a persistent object.

  One approach to achieving such a unification of pointer types would be to load the entire database into memory, replacing all persistent pointers with in-memory pointers. After updates were done, the process would be reversed, storing updated objects back on disk. Such an approach would be very inefficient for large databases.

  We now describe an alternative approach that allows persistent objects to be fetched automatically into memory when required, while allowing all references contained in in-memory objects to be in-memory references. When an object A is fetched, a **hollow object** is created for each object B_i that it references, and the in-memory copy of A has references to the corresponding hollow object for each B_i. Of course the system has to ensure that if an object B_i was fetched already, the reference points to the already fetched object instead of creating a new hollow object. Similarly, if an object B_i has not been fetched, but is referenced by another object fetched earlier, it would already have a hollow object created for it; the reference to the existing hollow object is reused, instead of creating a new hollow object.

  Thus, for every object O_i that has been fetched, every reference from O_i is either to an already fetched object or to a hollow object. The hollow objects form a *fringe* surrounding fetched objects.

  Whenever the program actually accesses a hollow object O, the enhanced byte code detects this and fetches the object from the database. When this object is fetched, the same process of creating hollow objects is carried out for all objects referenced by O. After this the access to the object is allowed to proceed.[5]

  An in-memory index structure mapping persistent pointers to in-memory references is required to implement this scheme. In writing objects back to disk, this index would be used to replace in-memory references with persistent pointers in the copy written to disk.

---

[5]The technique using hollow objects described above is closely related to the hardware swizzling technique (mentioned earlier in Section 22.8.4). Hardware swizzling is used by some persistent C++ implementations to provide a single pointer type for persistent and in-memory pointers. Hardware swizzling uses virtual-memory protection techniques provided by the operating system to detect accesses to pages, and fetches the pages from the database when required. In contrast, the Java version modifies byte code to check for hollow objects, instead of using memory protection, and fetches objects when required, instead of fetching whole pages from the database.

22.9   Object-Relational Mapping

So far we have seen two approaches to integrating object-oriented data models and programming languages with database systems. **Object-relational mapping** systems provide a third approach to integration of object-oriented programming languages and databases.

Object-relational mapping systems are built on top of a traditional relational database, and allow a programmer to define a mapping between tuples in database relations and objects in the programming language. Unlike in persistent programming languages, objects are transient, and there is no permanent object identity.

An object, or a set of objects, can be retrieved based on a selection condition on its attributes; relevant data are retrieved from the underlying database based on the selection conditions, and one or more objects are created from the retrieved data, based on the prespecified mapping between objects and relations. The program can optionally update such objects, create new objects, or specify that an object is to be deleted, and then issue a save command; the mapping from objects to relations is then used to correspondingly update, insert or delete tuples in the database.

Object-relational mapping systems in general, and in particular the widely used Hibernate system which provides an object-relational mapping to Java, are described in more detail in Section 9.4.2.

The primary goal of object-relational mapping systems is to ease the job of programmers who build applications, by providing them an object-model, while retaining the benefits of using a robust relational database underneath. As an added benefit, when operating on objects cached in memory, object-relational systems can provide significant performance gains over direct access to the underlying database.

Object-relational mapping systems also provide query languages that allow programmers to write queries directly on the object model; such queries are translated into SQL queries on the underlying relational database, and result objects created from the SQL query results.

On the negative side, object-relational mapping systems can suffer from significant overheads for bulk database updates, and may provide only limited querying capabilities. However, it is possible to directly update the database, bypassing the object-relational mapping system, and to write complex queries directly in SQL. The benefits or object-relational models exceed the drawbacks for many applications, and object-relational mapping systems have seen widespread adoption in recent years.

22.10   Object-Oriented versus Object-Relational

We have now studied object-relational databases, which are object-oriented databases built on top of the relation model, as well as object-oriented databases, which are built around persistent programming languages, and object-relational mapping systems, which build an object layer on top of a traditional relational database.

Each of these approaches targets a different market. The declarative nature and limited power (compared to a programming language) of the SQL language provides good protection of data from programming errors, and makes high-level optimizations, such as reducing I/O, relatively easy. (We covered optimization of relational expressions in Chapter 13.) Object-relational systems aim at making data modeling and querying easier by using complex data types. Typical applications include storage and querying of complex data, including multimedia data.

A declarative language such as SQL, however, imposes a significant performance penalty for certain kinds of applications that run primarily in main memory, and that perform a large number of accesses to the database. Persistent programming languages target such applications that have high performance requirements. They provide low-overhead access to persistent data and eliminate the need for data translation if the data are to be manipulated by a programming language. However, they are more susceptible to data corruption by programming errors, and they usually do not have a powerful querying capability. Typical applications include CAD databases.

Object-relational mapping systems allow programmers to build applications using an object model, while using a traditional database system to store the data. Thus, they combine the robustness of widely used relational database systems, with the power of object models for writing applications. However, they suffer from overheads of data conversion between the object model and the relational model used to store data.

We can summarize the strengths of the various kinds of database systems in this way:

- **Relational systems**: Simple data types, powerful query languages, high protection.

- **Persistent programming language–based OODBs**: Complex data types, integration with programming language, high performance.

- **Object-relational systems**: Complex data types, powerful query languages, high protection.

- **Object-relational mapping systems**: Complex data types integrated with programming languages, designed as a layer on top of a relational database system.

These descriptions hold in general, but keep in mind that some database systems blur the boundaries. For example, object-oriented database systems built around a persistent programming language can be implemented on top of a relational or object-relational database system. Such systems may provide lower performance than object-oriented database systems built directly on a storage system, but provide some of the stronger protection guarantees of relational systems.

22.11 Summary

- The object-relational data model extends the relational data model by providing a richer type system including collection types and object orientation.

- Collection types include nested relations, sets, multisets, and arrays, and the object-relational model permits attributes of a table to be collections.

- Object orientation provides inheritance with subtypes and subtables, as well as object (tuple) references.

- The SQL standard includes extensions of the SQL data-definition and query language to deal with new data types and with object orientation. These include support for collection-valued attributes, inheritance, and tuple references. Such extensions attempt to preserve the relational foundations—in particular, the declarative access to data—while extending the modeling power.

- Object-relational database systems (that is, database systems based on the object-relation model) provide a convenient migration path for users of relational databases who wish to use object-oriented features.

- Persistent extensions to C++ and Java integrate persistence seamlessly and orthogonally with existing programming language constructs and so are easy to use.

- The ODMG standard defines classes and other constructs for creating and accessing persistent objects from C++, while the JDO standard provides equivalent functionality for Java.

- Object-relational mapping systems provide an object view of data that is stored in a relational database. Objects are transient, and there is no notion of persistent object identity. Objects are created on-demand from relational data, and updates to objects are implemented by updating the relational data. Object-relational mapping systems have been widely adopted, unlike the more limited adoption of persistent programming languages.

- We discussed differences between persistent programming languages and object-relational systems, and we mention criteria for choosing between them.

Review Terms

- Nested relations
- Nested relational model
- Complex types
- Collection types
- Large object types
- Sets
- Arrays
- Multisets
- Structured types
- Methods

- Row types
- Constructors
- Inheritance
    - Single inheritance
    - Multiple inheritance
- Type inheritance
- Most-specific type
- Table inheritance
- Subtable
- Overlapping subtables
- Reference types
- Scope of a reference
- Self-referential attribute
- Path expressions
- Nesting and unnesting
- SQL functions and procedures

- Persistent programming languages
- Persistence by
    - Class
    - Creation
    - Marking
    - Reachability
- ODMG C++ binding
- ObjectStore
- JDO
    - Persistence by reachability
    - Roots
    - Hollow objects
- Object-relational mapping

Practice Exercises

22.1 A car-rental company maintains a database for all vehicles in its current fleet. For all vehicles, it includes the vehicle identification number, license number, manufacturer, model, date of purchase, and color. Special data are included for certain types of vehicles:

- Trucks: cargo capacity.
- Sports cars: horsepower, renter age requirement.
- Vans: number of passengers.
- Off-road vehicles: ground clearance, drivetrain (four- or two-wheel drive).

Construct an SQL schema definition for this database. Use inheritance where appropriate.

22.2 Consider a database schema with a relation *Emp* whose attributes are as shown below, with types specified for multivalued attributes.

Emp = (ename, ChildrenSet **multiset***(Children), SkillSet* **multiset***(Skills))*
Children = (name, birthday)
Skills = (type, ExamSet **setof***(Exams))*
Exams = (year, city)

    a. Define the above schema in SQL, with appropriate types for each attribute.

    b. Using the above schema, write the following queries in SQL.

       i. Find the names of all employees who have a child born on or after January 1, 2000.

      ii. Find those employees who took an examination for the skill type "typing" in the city "Dayton".

     iii. List all skill types in the relation *Emp*.

22.3 Consider the E-R diagram in Figure 22.5, which contains composite, multivalued, and derived attributes.

    a. Give an SQL schema definition corresponding to the E-R diagram.

    b. Give constructors for each of the structured types defined above.

22.4 Consider the relational schema shown in Figure 22.6.

    a. Give a schema definition in SQL corresponding to the relational schema, but using references to express foreign-key relationships.

    b. Write each of the queries given in Exercise 6.13 on the above schema, using SQL.

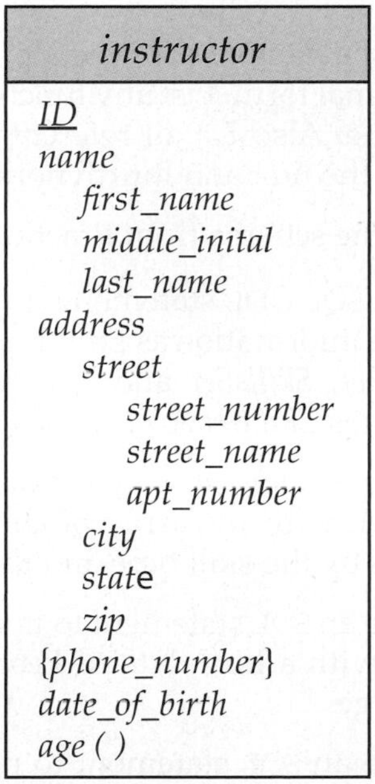

instructor

ID
name
  first_name
  middle_inital
  last_name
address
  street
    street_number
    street_name
    apt_number
  city
  state
  zip
{phone_number}
date_of_birth
age ( )

Figure 22.5 E-R diagram with composite, multivalued, and derived attributes.

employee (*person_name*, street, city)
works (*person_name*, company_name, salary)
company (*company_name*, city)
manages (*person_name*, manager_name)

Figure 22.6 Relational database for Practice Exercise 22.4.

22.5 Suppose that you have been hired as a consultant to choose a database system for your client's application. For each of the following applications, state what type of database system (relational, persistent programming language–based OODB, object relational; do not specify a commercial product) you would recommend. Justify your recommendation.

a. A computer-aided design system for a manufacturer of airplanes.

b. A system to track contributions made to candidates for public office.

c. An information system to support the making of movies.

22.6 How does the concept of an object in the object-oriented model differ from the concept of an entity in the entity-relationship model?

Exercises

22.7 Redesign the database of Practice Exercise 22.2 into first normal form and fourth normal form. List any functional or multivalued dependencies that you assume. Also list all referential-integrity constraints that should be present in the first and fourth normal form schemas.

22.8 Consider the schema from Practice Exercise 22.2.

a. Give SQL DDL statements to create a relation *EmpA* which has the same information as *Emp*, but where multiset-valued attributes *ChildrenSet*, *SkillsSet* and *ExamsSet* are replaced by array-valued attributes *ChildrenArray*, *SkillsArray* and *ExamsArray*.

b. Write a query to convert data from the schema of *Emp* to that of *EmpA*, with the array of children sorted by birthday, the array of skills by the skill type and the array of exams by the year.

c. Write an SQL statement to update the *Emp* relation by adding a child Jeb, with a birthdate of February 5, 2001, to the employee named George.

d. Write an SQL statement to perform the same update as above but on the *EmpA* relation. Make sure that the array of children remains sorted by year.

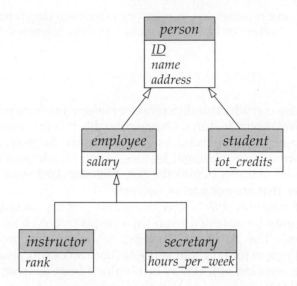

Figure 22.7 Specialization and generalization.

22.9 Consider the schemas for the table *people*, and the tables *students* and *teachers*, which were created under *people*, in Section 22.4. Give a relational schema in third normal form that represents the same information. Recall the constraints on subtables, and give all constraints that must be imposed on the relational schema so that every database instance of the relational schema can also be represented by an instance of the schema with inheritance.

22.10 Explain the distinction between a type x and a reference type **ref**(x). Under what circumstances would you choose to use a reference type?

22.11 Consider the E-R diagram in Figure 22.7, which contains specializations, using subtypes and subtables.

    a.   Give an SQL schema definition of the E-R diagram.

    b.   Give an SQL query to find the names of all people who are not secretaries.

    c.   Give an SQL query to print the names of people who are neither employees nor students.

    d.   Can you create a person who is an employee and a student with the schema you created? Explain how, or explain why it is not possible.

22.12 Suppose a JDO database had an object A, which references object B, which in turn references object C. Assume all objects are on disk initially. Suppose a program first dereferences A, then dereferences B by following the reference from A, and then finally dereferences C. Show the objects that are represented in memory after each dereference, along with their state (hollow or filled, and values in their reference fields).

Tools

There are considerable differences between database products in their support for object-relational features. Oracle probably has the most extensive support among the major database vendors. The Informix database system provides support for many object-relational features. Both Oracle and Informix provided object-relational features before the SQL:1999 standard was finalized, and have some features that are not part of SQL:1999.

Information about ObjectStore and Versant, including download of trial versions, may be obtained from their respective Web sites (objectstore.com and versant.com). The Apache DB project (db.apache.org) provides an object-relational mapping tool for Java that supports both an ODMG Java and JDO APIs. A reference implementation of JDO may be obtained from sun.com; use a search engine to get the full URL.

Bibliographical Notes

Several object-oriented extensions to SQL have been proposed. POSTGRES (Stonebraker and Rowe [1986] and Stonebraker [1986]) was an early implementation of an object-relational system. Other early object-relational systems include the SQL extensions of O_2 (Bancilhon et al. [1989]) and UniSQL (UniSQL [1991]). SQL:1999 was the product of an extensive (and long-delayed) standardization effort, which originally started off as adding object-oriented features to SQL and ended up adding many more features, such as procedural constructs, which we saw earlier. Support for multiset types was added as part of SQL:2003.

Melton [2002] concentrates on the object-relational features of SQL:1999. Eisenberg et al. [2004] provides an overview of SQL:2003, including its support for multisets.

A number of object-oriented database systems were developed in the late 1980s and early 1990s. Among the notable commercial ones were ObjectStore (Lamb et al. [1991]), O_2 (Lecluse et al. [1988]), and Versant. The object database standard ODMG is described in detail in Cattell [2000]. JDO is described by Roos [2002], Tyagi et al. [2003], and Jordan and Russell [2003].

CHAPTER **23**

XML

The **Extensible Markup Language** (**XML**) was not designed for database applications. In fact, like the *Hyper-Text Markup Language* (HTML) on which the World Wide Web is based, XML has its roots in document management, and is derived from a language for structuring large documents known as the *Standard Generalized Markup Language* (SGML). However, unlike SGML and HTML, XML is designed to represent data. It is particularly useful as a data format when an application must communicate with another application, or integrate information from several other applications. When XML is used in these contexts, many database issues arise, including how to organize, manipulate, and query the XML data. In this chapter, we introduce XML and discuss both the management of XML data with database techniques and the exchange of data formatted as XML documents.

23.1   Motivation

To understand XML, it is important to understand its roots as a document markup language. The term **markup** refers to anything in a document that is not intended to be part of the printed output. For example, a writer creating text that will eventually be typeset in a magazine may want to make notes about how the typesetting should be done. It would be important to type these notes in a way so that they could be distinguished from the actual content, so that a note like "set this word in large size, bold font" or "insert a line break here" does not end up printed in the magazine. Such notes convey extra information about the text. In electronic document processing, a **markup language** is a formal description of what part of the document is content, what part is markup, and what the markup means.

Just as database systems evolved from physical file processing to provide a separate logical view, markup languages evolved from specifying instructions for how to print parts of the document to specifying the *function* of the content. For instance, with functional markup, text representing section headings (for this section, the word "Motivation") would be marked up as being a section heading, instead of being marked up as text to be printed in large size, bold font. From the viewpoint of typesetting, such functional markup allows the document to be

981

formatted differently in different situations. It also helps different parts of a large document, or different pages in a large Web site, to be formatted in a uniform manner. More importantly, functional markup also helps record what each part of the text represents semantically, and correspondingly helps automate extraction of key parts of documents.

For the family of markup languages that includes HTML, SGML, and XML, the markup takes the form of **tags** enclosed in angle brackets, <>. Tags are used in pairs, with <tag> and </tag> delimiting the beginning and the end of the portion of the document to which the tag refers. For example, the title of a document might be marked up as follows:

<title>Database System Concepts</title>

Unlike HTML, XML does not prescribe the set of tags allowed, and the set may be chosen as needed by each application. This feature is the key to XML's major role in data representation and exchange, whereas HTML is used primarily for document formatting.

```
<university>
    <department>
        <dept_name> Comp. Sci. </dept_name>
        <building> Taylor </building>
        <budget> 100000 </budget>
    </department>
    <department>
        <dept_name> Biology </dept_name>
        <building> Watson </building>
        <budget> 90000 </budget>
    </department>
    <course>
        <course_id> CS-101 </course_id>
        <title> Intro. to Computer Science </title>
        <dept_name> Comp. Sci </dept_name>
        <credits> 4 </credits>
    </course>
    <course>
        <course_id> BIO-301 </course_id>
        <title> Genetics </title>
        <dept_name> Biology </dept_name>
        <credits> 4 </credits>
    </course>
```

continued in Figure 23.2

Figure 23.1   XML representation of (part of) university information.

```
<instructor>
        <IID> 10101 </IID>
        <name> Srinivasan </name>
        <dept_name> Comp. Sci. </dept_name>
        <salary> 65000 </salary>
</instructor>
<instructor>
        <IID> 83821 </IID>
        <name> Brandt </name>
        <dept_name> Comp. Sci. </dept_name>
        <salary> 92000 </salary>
</instructor>
<instructor>
        <IID> 76766 </IID>
        <name> Crick </name>
        <dept_name> Biology </dept_name>
        <salary> 72000 </salary>
</instructor>
<teaches>
        <IID> 10101 </IID>
        <course_id> CS-101 </course_id>
</teaches>
<teaches>
        <IID> 83821 </IID>
        <course_id> CS-101 </course_id>
</teaches>
<teaches>
        <IID> 76766 </IID>
        <course_id> BIO-301 </course_id>
</teaches>
</university>
```

Figure 23.2 Continuation of Figure 23.1.

For example, in our running university application, department, course and instructor information can be represented as part of an XML document as in Figures 23.1 and 23.2. Observe the use of tags such as department, course, instructor, and teaches. To keep the example short, we use a simplified version of the university schema that ignores section information for courses. We have also used the tag IID to denote the identifier of the instructor, for reasons we shall see later.

These tags provide context for each value and allow the semantics of the value to be identified. For this example, the XML data representation does not provide any significant benefit over the traditional relational data representation; however, we use this example as our running example because of its simplicity.

```
<purchase_order>
    <identifier> P-101 </identifier>
    <purchaser>
            <name> Cray Z. Coyote </name>
            <address> Mesa Flats, Route 66, Arizona 12345, USA  </address>
    </purchaser>
    <supplier>
            <name> Acme Supplies  </name>
            <address> 1 Broadway, New York, NY, USA  </address>
    </supplier>
    <itemlist>
        <item>
            <identifier>  RS1  </identifier>
            <description> Atom powered rocket sled  </description>
            <quantity> 2 </quantity>
            <price> 199.95 </price>
        </item>
        <item>
            <identifier>  SG2  </identifier>
            <description> Superb glue  </description>
            <quantity> 1 </quantity>
            <unit-of-measure> liter </unit-of-measure>
            <price> 29.95 </price>
        </item>
    </itemlist>
    <total_cost> 429.85 </total_cost>
    <payment_terms> Cash-on-delivery </payment_terms>
    <shipping_mode> 1-second-delivery </shipping_mode>
</purchaseorder>
```

Figure 23.3   XML representation of a purchase order.

Figure 23.3, which shows how information about a purchase order can be represented in XML, illustrates a more realistic use of XML. Purchase orders are typically generated by one organization and sent to another. Traditionally they were printed on paper by the purchaser and sent to the supplier; the data would be manually re-entered into a computer system by the supplier. This slow process can be greatly sped up by sending the information electronically between the purchaser and supplier. The nested representation allows all information in a purchase order to be represented naturally in a single document. (Real purchase orders have considerably more information than that depicted in this simplified example.) XML provides a standard way of tagging the data; the two organizations must of course agree on what tags appear in the purchase order, and what they mean.

Compared to storage of data in a relational database, the XML representation may be inefficient, since tag names are repeated throughout the document. However, in spite of this disadvantage, an XML representation has significant advantages when it is used to exchange data between organizations, and for storing complex structured information in files:

- First, the presence of the tags makes the message **self-documenting**; that is, a schema need not be consulted to understand the meaning of the text. We can readily read the fragment above, for example.

- Second, the format of the document is not rigid. For example, if some sender adds additional information, such as a tag last_accessed noting the last date on which an account was accessed, the recipient of the XML data may simply ignore the tag. As another example, in Figure 23.3, the item with identifier SG2 has a tag called unit-of-measure specified, which the first item does not. The tag is required for items that are ordered by weight or volume, and may be omitted for items that are simply ordered by number.

  The ability to recognize and ignore unexpected tags allows the format of the data to evolve over time, without invalidating existing applications. Similarly, the ability to have multiple occurrences of the same tag makes it easy to represent multivalued attributes.

- Third, XML allows nested structures. The purchase order shown in Figure 23.3 illustrates the benefits of having a nested structure. Each purchase order has a purchaser and a list of items as two of its nested structures. Each item in turn has an item identifier, description and a price nested within it, while the purchaser has a name and address nested within it.

  Such information would have been split into multiple relations in a relational schema. Item information would have been stored in one relation, purchaser information in a second relation, purchase orders in a third, and the relationship between purchase orders, purchasers, and items would have been stored in a fourth relation.

  The relational representation helps to avoid redundancy; for example, item descriptions would be stored only once for each item identifier in a normalized relational schema. In the XML purchase order, however, the descriptions may be repeated in multiple purchase orders that order the same item. However, gathering all information related to a purchase order into a single nested structure, even at the cost of redundancy, is attractive when information has to be exchanged with external parties.

- Finally, since the XML format is widely accepted, a wide variety of tools are available to assist in its processing, including programming language APIs to create and to read XML data, browser software, and database tools.

We describe several applications for XML data later, in Section 23.7. Just as SQL is the dominant *language* for querying relational data, XML has become the dominant *format* for data exchange.

23.2   Structure of XML Data

The fundamental construct in an XML document is the **element**. An element is simply a pair of matching start- and end-tags and all the text that appears between them.

XML documents must have a single **root** element that encompasses all other elements in the document. In the example in Figure 23.1, the <university> element forms the root element. Further, elements in an XML document must **nest** properly. For instance:

<course> ... <title> ... </title> ... </course>

is properly nested, whereas:

<course> ... <title> ... </course> ... </title>

is not properly nested.

While proper nesting is an intuitive property, we may define it more formally. Text is said to appear **in the context of** an element if it appears between the start-tag and end-tag of that element. Tags are properly nested if every start-tag has a unique matching end-tag that is in the context of the same parent element.

Note that text may be mixed with the subelements of an element, as in Figure 23.4. As with several other features of XML, this freedom makes more sense in a document-processing context than in a data-processing context, and is not particularly useful for representing more-structured data such as database content in XML.

The ability to nest elements within other elements provides an alternative way to represent information. Figure 23.5 shows a representation of part of the university information from Figure 23.1, but with course elements nested within department elements. The nested representation makes it easy to find all courses offered by a department. Similarly, identifiers of courses taught by an instructor are nested within the instructor elements. If an instructor teaches more than one course, there would be multiple course_id elements within the correspond-

```
    . . .
        <course>
            This course is being offered for the first time in 2009.
            <course_id> BIO-399 </course_id>
            <title> Computational Biology </title>
            <dept_name> Biology </dept_name>
            <credits> 3 </credits>
        </course>
    . . .
```

Figure 23.4   Mixture of text with subelements.

```
<university-1>
    <department>
        <dept_name> Comp. Sci. </dept_name>
        <building> Taylor </building>
        <budget> 100000 </budget>
        <course>
            <course_id> CS-101 </course_id>
            <title> Intro. to Computer Science </title>
            <credits> 4 </credits>
        </course>
        <course>
            <course_id> CS-347 </course_id>
            <title> Database System Concepts </title>
            <credits> 3 </credits>
        </course>
    </department>
    <department>
        <dept_name> Biology </dept_name>
        <building> Watson </building>
        <budget> 90000 </budget>
        <course>
            <course_id> BIO-301 </course_id>
            <title> Genetics </title>
            <credits> 4 </credits>
        </course>
    </department>
    <instructor>
        <IID> 10101 </IID>
        <name> Srinivasan </name>
        <dept_name> Comp. Sci. </dept_name>
        <salary> 65000. </salary>
        <course_id> CS-101 </coursr_id>
    </instructor>
</university-1>
```

Figure 23.5   Nested XML representation of university information.

ing instructor element. Details of instructors Brandt and Crick are omitted from Figure 23.5 for lack of space, but are similar in structure to that for Srinivasan.

Although nested representations are natural in XML, they may lead to redundant storage of data. For example, suppose details of courses taught by an instructor are stored nested within the instructor element as shown in Figure 23.6. If a course is taught by more than one instructor, course information such as title, department, and credits would be stored redundantly with every instructor associated with the course.

```
<university-2>
    <instructor>
        <ID> 10101 </ID>
        <name> Srinivasan </name>
        <dept_name> Comp. Sci.</dept_name>
        <salary> 65000 </salary>
        <teaches>
            <course>
                <course_id> CS-101 </course_id>
                <title> Intro. to Computer Science </title>
                <dept_name> Comp. Sci. </dept_name>
                <credits> 4 </credits>
            </course>
        </teaches>
    </instructor>

    <instructor>
        <ID> 83821 </ID>
        <name> Brandt </name>
        <dept_name> Comp. Sci.</dept_name>
        <salary> 92000 </salary>
        <teaches>
            <course>
                <course_id> CS-101 </course_id>
                <title> Intro. to Computer Science </title>
                <dept_name> Comp. Sci. </dept_name>
                <credits> 4 </credits>
            </course>
        </teaches>
    </instructor>
</university-2>
```

Figure 23.6 Redundancy in nested XML representation.

Nested representations are widely used in XML data interchange applications to avoid joins. For instance, a purchase order would store the full address of sender and receiver redundantly on multiple purchase orders, whereas a normalized representation may require a join of purchase order records with a *company_address* relation to get address information.

In addition to elements, XML specifies the notion of an **attribute**. For instance, the course identifier of a course can be represented as an attribute, as shown in Figure 23.7. The attributes of an element appear as *name=value* pairs before the closing ">" of a tag. Attributes are strings and do not contain markup. Furthermore, attributes can appear only once in a given tag, unlike subelements, which may be repeated.

. . .

```
<course course_id= "CS-101">
    <title> Intro. to Computer Science</title>
    <dept_name> Comp. Sci. </dept_name>
    <credits> 4 </credits>
</course>
```

. . .

Figure 23.7 Use of attributes.

Note that in a document construction context, the distinction between subelement and attribute is important—an attribute is implicitly text that does not appear in the printed or displayed document. However, in database and data exchange applications of XML, this distinction is less relevant, and the choice of representing data as an attribute or a subelement is frequently arbitrary. In general, it is advisable to use attributes only to represent identifiers, and to store all other data as subelements.

One final syntactic note is that an element of the form <element></element> that contains no subelements or text can be abbreviated as <element/>; abbreviated elements may, however, contain attributes.

Since XML documents are designed to be exchanged between applications, a **namespace** mechanism has been introduced to allow organizations to specify globally unique names to be used as element tags in documents. The idea of a namespace is to prepend each tag or attribute with a universal resource identifier (for example, a Web address). Thus, for example, if Yale University wanted to ensure that XML documents it created would not duplicate tags used by any business partner's XML documents, it could prepend a unique identifier with a colon to each tag name. The university may use a Web URL such as:

http://www.yale.edu

as a unique identifier. Using long unique identifiers in every tag would be rather inconvenient, so the namespace standard provides a way to define an abbreviation for identifiers.

In Figure 23.8, the root element (university) has an attribute xmlns:yale, which declares that yale is defined as an abbreviation for the URL given above. The abbreviation can then be used in various element tags, as illustrated in the figure.

A document can have more than one namespace, declared as part of the root element. Different elements can then be associated with different namespaces. A *default namespace* can be defined by using the attribute xmlns instead of xmlns:yale in the root element. Elements without an explicit namespace prefix would then belong to the default namespace.

Sometimes we need to store values containing tags without having the tags interpreted as XML tags. So that we can do so, XML allows this construct:

<![CDATA[<course> · · ·</course>]]>

```
<university xmlns:yale="http://www.yale.edu">
    . . .
    <yale:course>
        <yale:course_id> CS-101 </yale:course_id>
        <yale:title> Intro. to Computer Science</yale:title>
        <yale:dept_name> Comp. Sci. </yale:dept_name>
        <yale:credits> 4 </yale:credits>
    </yale:course>
    . . .
</university>
```

Figure 23.8 Unique tag names can be assigned by using namespaces.

Because it is enclosed within CDATA, the text <course> is treated as normal text data, not as a tag. The term CDATA stands for character data.

23.3   XML Document Schema

Databases have schemas, which are used to constrain what information can be stored in the database and to constrain the data types of the stored information. In contrast, by default, XML documents can be created without any associated schema: an element may then have any subelement or attribute. While such freedom may occasionally be acceptable given the self-describing nature of the data format, it is not generally useful when XML documents must be processed automatically as part of an application, or even when large amounts of related data are to be formatted in XML.

Here, we describe the first schema-definition language included as part of the XML standard, the *Document Type Definition*, as well as its more recently defined replacement, *XML Schema*. Another XML schema-definition language called Relax NG is also in use, but we do not cover it here; for more information on Relax NG see the references in the bibliographical notes section.

23.3.1   Document Type Definition

The **document type definition** (DTD) is an optional part of an XML document. The main purpose of a DTD is much like that of a schema: to constrain and type the information present in the document. However, the DTD does not in fact constrain types in the sense of basic types like integer or string. Instead, it constrains only the appearance of subelements and attributes within an element. The DTD is primarily a list of rules for what pattern of subelements may appear within an element. Figure 23.9 shows a part of an example DTD for a university information document; the XML document in Figure 23.1 conforms to this DTD.

Each declaration is in the form of a regular expression for the subelements of an element. Thus, in the DTD in Figure 23.9, a university element consists of one or more course, department, or instructor elements; the | operator specifies "or"

```
<!DOCTYPE university [
    <!ELEMENT university ( (department|course|instructor|teaches)+)>
    <!ELEMENT department ( dept_name, building, budget)>
    <!ELEMENT course ( course_id, title, dept_name, credits)>
    <!ELEMENT instructor (IID, name, dept_name, salary)>
    <!ELEMENT teaches (IID, course_id)>
    <!ELEMENT dept_name( #PCDATA )>
    <!ELEMENT building( #PCDATA )>
    <!ELEMENT budget( #PCDATA )>
    <!ELEMENT course_id ( #PCDATA )>
    <!ELEMENT title ( #PCDATA )>
    <!ELEMENT credits( #PCDATA )>
    <!ELEMENT IID( #PCDATA )>
    <!ELEMENT name( #PCDATA )>
    <!ELEMENT salary( #PCDATA )>
] >
```

Figure 23.9 Example of a DTD.

while the + operator specifies "one or more." Although not shown here, the ∗ operator is used to specify "zero or more," while the ? operator is used to specify an optional element (that is, "zero or one").

The course element contains subelements course_id, title, dept_name, and credits (in that order). Similarly, department and instructor have the attributes of their relational schema defined as subelements in the DTD.

Finally, the elements course_id, title, dept_name, credits, building, budget, IID, name, and salary are all declared to be of type #PCDATA. The keyword #PCDATA indicates text data; it derives its name, historically, from "parsed character data." Two other special type declarations are empty, which says that the element has no contents, and any, which says that there is no constraint on the subelements of the element; that is, any elements, even those not mentioned in the DTD, can occur as subelements of the element. The absence of a declaration for an element is equivalent to explicitly declaring the type as any.

The allowable attributes for each element are also declared in the DTD. Unlike subelements, no order is imposed on attributes. Attributes may be specified to be of type CDATA, ID, IDREF, or IDREFS; the type CDATA simply says that the attribute contains character data, while the other three are not so simple; they are explained in more detail shortly. For instance, the following line from a DTD specifies that element course has an attribute of type course_id, and a value must be present for this attribute:

<!ATTLIST course course_id CDATA #REQUIRED>

Attributes must have a type declaration and a default declaration. The default declaration can consist of a default value for the attribute or #REQUIRED, meaning

```
<!DOCTYPE university-3 [
    <!ELEMENT university ( (department|course|instructor)+)>
    <!ELEMENT department ( building, budget )>
    <!ATTLIST department
        dept_name ID #REQUIRED >
    <!ELEMENT course (title, credits )>
    <!ATTLIST course
        course_id ID #REQUIRED
        dept_name IDREF #REQUIRED
        instructors IDREFS #IMPLIED >
    <!ELEMENT instructor ( name, salary )>
    <!ATTLIST instructor
        IID ID #REQUIRED >
        dept_name IDREF #REQUIRED >
    ⋯ declarations for title, credits, building,
        budget, name and salary ⋯
] >
```

Figure 23.10   DTD with ID and IDREFS attribute types.

that a value must be specified for the attribute in each element, or #IMPLIED, meaning that no default value has been provided, and the document may omit this attribute. If an attribute has a default value, for every element that does not specify a value for the attribute, the default value is filled in automatically when the XML document is read.

An attribute of type ID provides a unique identifier for the element; a value that occurs in an ID attribute of an element must not occur in any other element in the same document. At most one attribute of an element is permitted to be of type ID. (We renamed the attribute *ID* of the *instructor* relation to IID in the XML representation, in order to avoid confusion with the type ID.)

An attribute of type IDREF is a reference to an element; the attribute must contain a value that appears in the ID attribute of some element in the document. The type IDREFS allows a list of references, separated by spaces.

Figure 23.10 shows an example DTD in which identifiers of course, department and instructor are represented by ID attributes, and relationships between them are represented by IDREF and IDREFS attributes. The course elements use course_id as their identifier attribute; to do so, course_id has been made an attribute of course instead of a subelement. Additionally, each course element also contains an IDREF of the department corresponding to the course, and an IDREFS attribute instructors identifying the instructors who teach the course. The department elements have an identifier attribute called dept_name. The instructor elements have an identifier attribute called IID, and an IDREF attribute dept_name identifying the department to which the instructor belongs.

Figure 23.11 shows an example XML document based on the DTD in Figure 23.10.

```
<university-3>
    <department dept_name="Comp. Sci.">
        <building> Taylor </building>
        <budget> 100000 </budget>
    </department>
    <department dept_name="Biology">
        <building> Watson </building>
        <budget> 90000 </budget>
    </department>
    <course course_id="CS-101" dept_name="Comp. Sci"
                            instructors="10101 83821">
        <title> Intro. to Computer Science </title>
        <credits> 4 </credits>
    </course>
    <course course_id="BIO-301" dept_name="Biology"
                            instructors="76766">
        <title> Genetics </title>
        <credits> 4 </credits>
    </course>
    <instructor IID="10101" dept_name="Comp. Sci.">
        <name> Srinivasan </name>
        <salary> 65000 </salary>
    </instructor>
    <instructor IID="83821" dept_name="Comp. Sci.">
        <name> Brandt </name>
        <salary> 72000 </salary>
    </instructor>
    <instructor IID="76766" dept_name="Biology">
        <name> Crick </name>
        <salary> 72000 </salary>
    </instructor>
</university-3>
```

Figure 23.11 XML data with ID and IDREF attributes.

The ID and IDREF attributes serve the same role as reference mechanisms in object-oriented and object-relational databases, permitting the construction of complex data relationships.

Document type definitions are strongly connected to the document formatting heritage of XML. Because of this, they are unsuitable in many ways for serving as the type structure of XML for data-processing applications. Nevertheless, a number of data exchange formats have been defined in terms of DTDs, since they were part of the original standard. Here are some of the limitations of DTDs as a schema mechanism:

- Individual text elements and attributes cannot be typed further. For instance, the element balance cannot be constrained to be a positive number. The lack of such constraints is problematic for data processing and exchange applications, which must then contain code to verify the types of elements and attributes.

- It is difficult to use the DTD mechanism to specify unordered sets of subelements. Order is seldom important for data exchange (unlike document layout, where it is crucial). While the combination of alternation (the | operation) and the * or the + operation as in Figure 23.9 permits the specification of unordered collections of tags, it is much more difficult to specify that each tag may only appear once.

- There is a lack of typing in IDs and IDREFSs. Thus, there is no way to specify the type of element to which an IDREF or IDREFS attribute should refer. As a result, the DTD in Figure 23.10 does not prevent the "dept_name" attribute of a course element from referring to other courses, even though this makes no sense.

23.3.2   XML Schema

An effort to redress the deficiencies of the DTD mechanism resulted in the development of a more sophisticated schema language, **XML Schema**. We provide a brief overview of XML Schema, and then we list some areas in which it improves DTDs.

XML Schema defines a number of built-in types such as string, integer, decimal date, and boolean. In addition, it allows user-defined types; these may be simple types with added restrictions, or complex types constructed using constructors such as complexType and sequence.

Figures 23.12 and 23.13 show how the DTD in Figure 23.9 can be represented by XML Schema; we describe below XML Schema features illustrated by the figures.

The first thing to note is that schema definitions in XML Schema are themselves specified in XML syntax, using a variety of tags defined by XML Schema. To avoid conflicts with user-defined tags, we prefix the XML Schema tag with the namespace prefix "xs:"; this prefix is associated with the XML Schema namespace by the xmlns:xs specification in the root element:

<xs:schema xmlns:xs="http://www.w3.org/2001/XMLSchema">

Note that any namespace prefix could be used in place of xs; thus we could replace all occurrences of "xs:" in the schema definition with "xsd:" without changing the meaning of the schema definition. All types defined by XML Schema must be prefixed by this namespace prefix.

The first element is the root element university, whose type is specified to be UniversityType, which is declared later. The example then defines the types of elements department, course, instructor, and teaches. Note that each of these

```
<xs:schema xmlns:xs="http://www.w3.org/2001/XMLSchema">
<xs:element name="university" type="universityType" />
<xs:element name="department">
    <xs:complexType>
        <xs:sequence>
            <xs:element name="dept_name" type="xs:string"/>
            <xs:element name="building" type="xs:string"/>
            <xs:element name="budget" type="xs:decimal"/>
        </xs:sequence>
    </xs:complexType>
</xs:element>
<xs:element name="course">
            <xs:element name="course_id" type="xs:string"/>
            <xs:element name="title" type="xs:string"/>
            <xs:element name="dept_name" type="xs:string"/>
            <xs:element name="credits" type="xs:decimal"/>
</xs:element>
<xs:element name="instructor">
    <xs:complexType>
        <xs:sequence>
            <xs:element name="IID" type="xs:string"/>
            <xs:element name="name" type="xs:string"/>
            <xs:element name="dept_name" type="xs:string"/>
            <xs:element name="salary" type="xs:decimal"/>
        </xs:sequence>
    </xs:complexType>
</xs:element>
```

continued in Figure 23.13.

Figure 23.12 XML Schema version of DTD from Figure 23.9.

is specified by an element with tag xs:element, whose body contains the type definition.

The type of department is defined to be a complex type, which is further specified to consist of a sequence of elements dept_name, building, and budget. Any type that has either attributes or nested subelements must be specified to be a complex type.

Alternatively, the type of an element can be specified to be a predefined type by the attribute type; observe how the XML Schema types xs:string and xs:decimal are used to constrain the types of data elements such as dept_name and credits.

Finally the example defines the type UniversityType as containing zero or more occurrences of each of department, course, instructor, and teaches. Note the use of ref to specify the occurrence of an element defined earlier. XML Schema can define the minimum and maximum number of occurrences of subelements by

```
<xs:element name="teaches">
    <xs:complexType>
        <xs:sequence>
            <xs:element name="IID" type="xs:string"/>
            <xs:element name="course_id" type="xs:string"/>
        </xs:sequence>
    </xs:complexType>
</xs:element>
<xs:complexType name="UniversityType">
    <xs:sequence>
        <xs:element ref="department" minOccurs="0"
                maxOccurs="unbounded"/>
        <xs:element ref="course" minOccurs="0"
                maxOccurs="unbounded"/>
        <xs:element ref="instructor" minOccurs="0"
                maxOccurs="unbounded"/>
        <xs:element ref="teaches" minOccurs="0"
                maxOccurs="unbounded"/>
    </xs:sequence>
</xs:complexType>
</xs:schema>
```

Figure 23.13 Continuation of Figure 23.12.

using minOccurs and maxOccurs. The default for both minimum and maximum occurrences is 1, so these have to be specified explicitly to allow zero or more department, course, instructor, and teaches elements.

Attributes are specified using the xs:attribute tag. For example, we could have defined dept_name as an attribute by adding:

<xs:attribute name = "dept_name"/>

within the declaration of the department element. Adding the attribute use = "required" to the above attribute specification declares that the attribute must be specified, whereas the default value of use is optional. Attribute specifications would appear directly under the enclosing complexType specification, even if elements are nested within a sequence specification.

We can use the xs:complexType element to create named complex types; the syntax is the same as that used for the xs:complexType element in Figure 23.12, except that we add an attribute name = typeName to the xs:complexType element, where typeName is the name we wish to give to the type. We can then use the named type to specify the type of an element using the type attribute, just as we used xs:decimal and xs:string in our example.

In addition to defining types, a relational schema also allows the specification of constraints. XML Schema allows the specification of keys and key references, corresponding to the primary-key and foreign-key definition in SQL. In SQL, a primary-key constraint or unique constraint ensures that the attribute values do not recur within the relation. In the context of XML, we need to specify a scope within which values are unique and form a key. The **selector** is a path expression that defines the scope for the constraint, and **field** declarations specify the elements or attributes that form the key.[1] To specify that **dept_name** forms a key for **department** elements under the root **university** element, we add the following constraint specification to the schema definition:

```
<xs:key name = "deptKey">
    <xs:selector xpath = "/university/department"/>
    <xs:field xpath = "dept_name"/>
</xs:key>
```

Correspondingly a foreign-key constraint from **course** to **department** may be defined as follows:

```
<xs: name = "courseDeptFKey" refer="deptKey">
    <xs:selector xpath = "/university/course"/>
    <xs:field xpath = "dept_name"/>
</xs:keyref>
```

Note that the **refer** attribute specifies the name of the key declaration that is being referenced, while the **field** specification identifies the referring attributes.

XML Schema offers several benefits over DTDs, and is widely used today. Among the benefits that we have seen in the examples above are these:

- It allows the text that appears in elements to be constrained to specific types, such as numeric types in specific formats or complex types such as sequences of elements of other types.

- It allows user-defined types to be created.

- It allows uniqueness and foreign-key constraints.

- It is integrated with namespaces to allow different parts of a document to conform to different schemas.

In addition to the features we have seen, XML Schema supports several other features that DTDs do not, such as these:

- It allows types to be restricted to create specialized types, for instance by specifying minimum and maximum values.

- It allows complex types to be extended by using a form of inheritance.

---

[1] We use simple path expressions here that are in a familiar syntax. XML has a rich syntax for path expressions, called XPath, which we explore in Section 23.4.2.

Our description of XML Schema is just an overview; to learn more about XML Schema, see the references in the bibliographical notes.

23.4   Querying and Transformation

Given the increasing number of applications that use XML to exchange, mediate, and store data, tools for effective management of XML data are becoming increasingly important. In particular, tools for querying and transformation of XML data are essential to extract information from large bodies of XML data, and to convert data between different representations (schemas) in XML. Just as the output of a relational query is a relation, the output of an XML query can be an XML document. As a result, querying and transformation can be combined into a single tool.

In this section, we describe the XPath and XQuery languages:

- XPath is a language for path expressions and is actually a building block for XQuery.

- XQuery is the standard language for querying XML data. It is modeled after SQL but is significantly different, since it has to deal with nested XML data. XQuery also incorporates XPath expressions.

The XSLT language is another language designed for transforming XML. However, it is used primarily in document-formatting applications, rather in data-management applications, so we do not discuss it in this book.

The tools section at the end of this chapter provides references to software that can be used to execute queries written in XPath and XQuery.

23.4.1   Tree Model of XML

A **tree model** of XML data is used in all these languages. An XML document is modeled as a **tree**, with **nodes** corresponding to elements and attributes. Element nodes can have child nodes, which can be subelements or attributes of the element. Correspondingly, each node (whether attribute or element), other than the root element, has a parent node, which is an element. The order of elements and attributes in the XML document is modeled by the ordering of children of nodes of the tree. The terms parent, child, ancestor, descendant, and siblings are used in the tree model of XML data.

The text content of an element can be modeled as a text-node child of the element. Elements containing text broken up by intervening subelements can have multiple text-node children. For instance, an element containing "this is a <bold> wonderful </bold> book" would have a subelement child corresponding to the element bold and two text node children corresponding to "this is a" and "book." Since such structures are not commonly used in data representation, we shall assume that elements do not contain both text and subelements.

23.4.2   XPath

XPath addresses parts of an XML document by means of path expressions. The language can be viewed as an extension of the simple path expressions in object-oriented and object-relational databases (see Section 22.6). The current version of the XPath standard is XPath 2.0, and our description is based on this version.

A **path expression** in XPath is a sequence of location steps separated by "/" (instead of the "." operator that separates location steps in SQL). The result of a path expression is a set of nodes. For instance, on the document in Figure 23.11, the XPath expression:

/university-3/instructor/name

returns these elements:

<name>Srinivasan</name>
<name>Brandt</name>

The expression:

/university-3/instructor/name/text()

returns the same names, but without the enclosing tags.

Path expressions are evaluated from left to right. Like a directory hierarchy, the initial '/' indicates the root of the document. Note that this is an abstract root "above" <university-3> that is the document tag.

As a path expression is evaluated, the result of the path at any point consists of an ordered set of nodes from the document. Initially, the "current" set of elements contains only one node, the abstract root. When the next step in a path expression is an element name, such as instructor, the result of the step consists of the nodes corresponding to elements of the specified name that are children of elements in the current element set. These nodes then become the current element set for the next step of the path expression evaluation. Thus, the expression:

/university-3

returns a single node corresponding to the:

<university-3>

tag, while:

/university-3/instructor

returns the two nodes corresponding to the:

instructor

elements that are children of the:

university-3

node.

The result of a path expression is then the set of nodes after the last step of path expression evaluation. The nodes returned by each step appear in the same order as their appearance in the document.

Since multiple children can have the same name, the number of nodes in the node set can increase or decrease with each step. Attribute values may also be accessed, using the "@" symbol. For instance, /university-3/course/@course_id returns a set of all values of course_id attributes of course elements. By default, IDREF links are not followed; we shall see how to deal with IDREFs later.

XPath supports a number of other features:

- Selection predicates may follow any step in a path, and are contained in square brackets. For example,

    /university-3/course[credits >= 4]

    returns course elements with a credits value greater than or equal to 4, while:

    /university-3/course[credits >= 4]/@course_id

    returns the course identifiers of those courses.

    We can test the existence of a subelement by listing it without any comparison operation; for instance, if we removed just ">= 4" from the above, the expression would return course identifiers of all courses that have a credits subelement, regardless of its value.

- XPath provides several functions that can be used as part of predicates, including testing the position of the current node in the sibling order and the aggregate function count(), which counts the number of nodes matched by the expression to which it is applied. For example, on the XML representation in Figure 23.6, the path expression:

    /university-2/instructor[count(./teaches/course)> 2]

    returns instructors who teach more than two courses. Boolean connectives and and or can be used in predicates, while the function not(. . .) can be used for negation.

- The function id("foo") returns the node (if any) with an attribute of type ID and value "foo". The function id can even be applied on sets of references, or even strings containing multiple references separated by blanks, such as IDREFS. For instance, the path:

/university-3/course/id(@dept_name)

returns all department elements referred to from the dept_name attribute of course elements, while:

/university-3/course/id(@instructors)

returns the instructor elements referred to in the instuctors attribute of course elements.

- The | operator allows expression results to be unioned. For example, given data using the schema from Figure 23.11, we could find the union of Computer Science and Biology courses using the expression:

/university-3/course[@dept_name="Comp. Sci"] |
/university-3/course[@dept_name="Biology"]

However, the | operator cannot be nested inside other operators. It is also worth noting that the nodes in the union are returned in the order in which they appear in the document.

- An XPath expression can skip multiple levels of nodes by using "//". For instance, the expression /university-3//name finds all name elements *anywhere* under the /university-3 element, regardless of the elements in which they are contained, and regardless of how many levels of enclosing elements are present between the university-3 and name elements. This example illustrates the ability to find required data without full knowledge of the schema.

- A step in the path need not just select from the children of the nodes in the current node set. In fact, this is just one of several directions along which a step in the path may proceed, such as parents, siblings, ancestors, and descendants. We omit details, but note that "//", described above, is a short form for specifying "all descendants," while ".." specifies the parent.

- The built-in function doc(name) returns the root of a named document; the name could be a file name or a URL. The root returned by the function can then be used in a path expression to access the contents of the document. Thus, a path expression can be applied on a specified document, instead of being applied on the current default document.

  For example, if the university data in our university example is contained in a file "university.xml", the following path expression would return all departments at the university:

doc("university.xml")/university/department

The function collection(name) is similar to doc, but returns a collection of documents identified by name. The function collection can be used, for example, to open an XML database, which can be viewed as a collection of documents; the following element in the XPath expression would select the appropriate document(s) from the collection.

In most of our examples, we assume that the expressions are evaluated in the context of a database, which implicitly provides a collection of "documents" on which XPath expressions are evaluated. In such cases, we do not need to use the functions doc and collection.

23.4.3   XQuery

The World Wide Web Consortium (W3C) has developed XQuery as the standard query language for XML. Our discussion is based on XQuery 1.0, which was released as a W3C recommendation on 23 January 2007.

23.4.3.1   FLWOR Expressions

XQuery queries are modeled after SQL queries, but differ significantly from SQL. They are organized into five sections: **for**, **let**, **where**, **order by**, and **return**. They are referred to as "FLWOR" (pronounced "flower") expressions, with the letters in FLWOR denoting the five sections.

A simple FLWOR expression that returns course identifiers of courses with greater than 3 credits, shown below, is based on the XML document of Figure 23.11, which uses ID and IDREFS:

> **for** \$x **in** /university-3/course
> **let** \$courseId := \$x/@course_id
> **where** \$x/credits > 3
> **return** <course_id> { \$courseId } </course_id>

The **for** clause is like the **from** clause of SQL, and specifies variables that range over the results of XPath expressions. When more than one variable is specified, the results include the Cartesian product of the possible values the variables can take, just as the SQL **from** clause does.

The **let** clause simply allows the results of XPath expressions to be assigned to variable names for simplicity of representation. The **where** clause, like the SQL **where** clause, performs additional tests on the joined tuples from the **for** clause. The **order by** clause, like the SQL **order by** clause, allows sorting of the output. Finally, the **return** clause allows the construction of results in XML.

A FLWOR query need not contain all the clauses; for example a query may contain just the **for** and **return** clauses, and omit the **let**, **where**, and **order by** clauses. The preceding XQuery query did not contain an **order by** clause. In fact, since this query is simple, we can easily do away with the **let** clause, and the variable \$courseId in the **return** clause could be replaced with \$x/@course_id. Note further that, since the **for** clause uses XPath expressions, selections may occur within the XPath expression. Thus, an equivalent query may have only **for** and **return** clauses:

> **for** $x **in** /university-3/course[credits > 3]
> **return** <course_id> { $x/@course_id } </course_id>

However, the **let** clause helps simplify complex queries. Note also that variables assigned by **let** clauses may contain sequences with multiple elements or values, if the path expression on the right-hand side returns a sequence of multiple elements or values.

Observe the use of curly brackets ("{}") in the **return** clause. When XQuery finds an element such as <course_id> starting an expression, it treats its contents as regular XML text, except for portions enclosed within curly brackets, which are evaluated as expressions. Thus, if we omitted the curly brackets in the above **return** clause, the result would contain several copies of the string "$x/@course_id" each enclosed in a course_id tag. The contents within the curly brackets are, however, treated as expressions to be evaluated. Note that this convention applies even if the curly brackets appear within quotes. Thus, we could modify the above query to return an element with tag course, with the course identifier as an attribute, by replacing the **return** clause with the following:

> **return** <course course_id="{$x/@course_id}" />

XQuery provides another way of constructing elements using the **element** and **attribute** constructors. For example, if the **return** clause in the previous query is replaced by the following **return** clause, the query would return course elements with course_id and dept_name as attributes and title and credits as subelements.

> **return element** course {
>   **attribute** course_id {$x/@course_id},
>   **attribute** dept_name {$x/dept_name},
>   **element** title {$x/title},
>   **element** credits {$x/credits}
> }

Note that, as before, the curly brackets are required to treat a string as an expression to be evaluated.

23.4.3.2 Joins

Joins are specified in XQuery much as they are in SQL. The join of course, instructor, and teaches elements in Figure 23.1 can be written in XQuery this way:

```
      for $c in /university/course,
          $i in /university/instructor,
          $t in /university/teaches
      where $c/course_id= $t/course_id
          and $t/IID = $i/IID
      return <course_instructor> { $c $i } </course_instructor>
```

The same query can be expressed with the selections specified as XPath selections:

```
      for $c in /university/course,
          $i in /university/instructor,
          $t in /university/teaches[ $c/course_id= $t/course_id
              and $t/IID = $i/IID]
      return <course_instructor> { $c $i } </course_instructor>
```

Path expressions in XQuery are the same as path expressions in XPath2.0. Path expressions may return a single value or element, or a sequence of values or elements. In the absence of schema information, it may not be possible to infer whether a path expression returns a single value or a sequence of values. Such path expressions may participate in comparison operations such as $=$, $<$, and $>=$.

XQuery has an interesting definition of comparison operations on sequences. For example, the expression $x/credits > 3 would have the usual interpretation if the result of $x/credits is a single value, but if the result is a sequence containing multiple values, the expression evaluates to true if at least one of the values is greater than 3. Similarly, the expression $x/credits = $y/credits evaluates to true if any one of the values returned by the first expression is equal to any one of the values returned by the second expression. If this behavior is not appropriate, the operators eq, ne, lt, gt, le, ge can be used instead. These raise an error if either of their inputs is a sequence with multiple values.

23.4.3.3 Nested Queries

XQuery FLWOR expressions can be nested in the **return** clause, in order to generate element nestings that do not appear in the source document. For instance, the XML structure shown in Figure 23.5, with course elements nested within department elements, can be generated from the structure in Figure 23.1 by the query shown in Figure 23.14.

The query also introduces the syntax $d/*, which refers to all the children of the node (or sequence of nodes) bound to the variable $d. Similarly, $d/text() gives the text content of an element, without the tags.

XQuery provides a variety of aggregate functions such as sum() and count() that can be applied on sequences of elements or values. The function distinct-values() applied on a sequence returns a sequence without duplication. The sequence (collection) of values returned by a path expression may have some values repeated because they are repeated in the document, although an XPath expres-

```
<university-1>
{
    for $d in /university/department
    return
        <department>
            { $d/* }
            { for $c in /university/course[dept_name = $d/dept_name]
                return $c }
        </department>
}
{
    for $i in /university/instructor
    return
        <instructor>
            { $i/* }
            { for $c in /university/teaches[IID = $i/IID]
                return $c/course_id }
        </instructor>
}
</university-1>
```

Figure 23.14 Creating nested structures in XQuery

sion result can contain at most one occurrence of each node in the document. XQuery supports many other functions; see the references in the bibliographical notes for more information. These functions are actually common to XPath 2.0 and XQuery, and can be used in any XPath path expression.

To avoid namespace conflicts, functions are associated with a namespace:

http://www.w3.org/2005/xpath-functions

which has a default namespace prefix of fn. Thus, these functions can be referred to unambiguously as fn:sum or fn:count.

While XQuery does not provide a **group by** construct, aggregate queries can be written by using the aggregate functions on path or FLWOR expressions nested within the **return** clause. For example, the following query on the university XML schema finds the total salary of all instructors in each department:

```
for $d in /university/department
return
    <department-total-salary>
        <dept_name> { $d/dept_name } </dept_name>
        <total_salary> { fn:sum(
            for $i in /university/instructor[dept_name = $d/dept_name]
            return $i/salary
        ) } </total_salary>
    </department-total-salary>
```

23.4.3.4   Sorting of Results

Results can be sorted in XQuery by using the **order by** clause. For instance, this query outputs all instructor elements sorted by the name subelement:

```
for $i in /university/instructor
order by $i/name
return <instructor> { $i/* } </instructor>
```

To sort in descending order, we can use **order by** $i/name **descending**.

Sorting can be done at multiple levels of nesting. For instance, we can get a nested representation of university information with departments sorted in department name order, with courses sorted by course identifiers, as follows:

```
<university-1> {
    for $d in /university/department
    order by $d/dept_name
    return
        <department>
            { $d/* }
            { for $c in /university/course[dept_name = $d/dept_name]
            order by $c/course_id
            return <course> { $c/* } </course> }
        </department>
} </university-1>
```

23.4.3.5   Functions and Types

XQuery provides a variety of built-in functions, such as numeric functions and string matching and manipulation functions. In addition, XQuery supports user-defined functions. The following user-defined function takes as input an instructor identifier, and returns a list of all courses offered by the department to which the instructor belongs:

```
declare function local:dept_courses($iid as xs:string) as element(course)* {
    for $i in /university/instructor[IID = $iid],
        $c in /university/courses[dept_name = $i/dept_name]
    return $c
}
```

The namespace prefix xs: used in the above example is predefined by XQuery to be associated with the XML Schema namespace, while the namespace local: is predefined to be associated with XQuery local functions.

The type specifications for function arguments and return values are optional, and may be omitted. XQuery uses the type system of XML Schema. The type element allows elements with any tag, while element(course) allows elements with the tag course. Types can be suffixed with a * to indicate a sequence of values of that type; for example, the definition of function dept_courses specifies the return value as a sequence of course elements.

The following query, which illustrates function invocation, prints out the department courses for the instructor(s) named Srinivasan:

> for $i in /university/instructor[name = "Srinivasan"],
> returnlocal:inst_dept_courses($i/IID)

XQuery performs type conversion automatically whenever required. For example, if a numeric value represented by a string is compared to a numeric type, type conversion from string to the numeric type is done automatically. When an element is passed to a function that expects a string value, type conversion to a string is done by concatenating all the text values contained (nested) within the element. Thus, the function contains(a,b), which checks if string a contains string b, can be used with its first argument set to an element, in which case it checks if the element a contains the string b nested anywhere inside it. XQuery also provides functions to convert between types. For instance, number(x) converts a string to a number.

23.4.3.6 Other Features

XQuery offers a variety of other features, such as if-then-else constructs that can be used within **return** clauses, and existential and universal quantification that can be used in predicates in **where** clauses. For example, existential quantification can be expressed in the **where** clause by using:

> some $e in path satisfies P

where path is a path expression and P is a predicate that can use $e. Universal quantification can be expressed by using **every** in place of **some**.

For example, to find departments where every instructor has a salary greater than $50,000, we can use the following query:

> for $d in /university/department
> where every $i in /university/instructor[dept_name=$d/dept_name]
>   satisfies $i/salary > 50000
> return $d

Note, however, that if a department has no instructor, it will trivially satisfy the above condition. An extra clause:

> and fn:exists(/university/instructor[dept_name=$d/dept_name])

can be used to ensure that there is at least one instructor in the department. The built-in function exists() used in the clause returns true if its input argument is nonempty.

The **XQJ** standard provides an API to submit XQuery queries to an XML database system and to retrieve the XML results. Its functionality is similar to the JDBC API.

23.5 Application Program Interfaces to XML

With the wide acceptance of XML as a data representation and exchange format, software tools are widely available for manipulation of XML data. There are two standard models for programmatic manipulation of XML, each available for use with a number of popular programming languages. Both these APIs can be used to parse an XML document and create an in-memory representation of the document. They are used for applications that deal with individual XML documents. Note, however, that they are not suitable for querying large collections of XML data; declarative querying mechanisms such as XPath and XQuery are better suited to this task.

One of the standard APIs for manipulating XML is based on the *document object model* (DOM), which treats XML content as a tree, with each element represented by a node, called a DOMNode. Programs may access parts of the document in a navigational fashion, beginning with the root.

DOM libraries are available for most common programming languages and are even present in Web browsers, where they may be used to manipulate the document displayed to the user. We outline here some of the interfaces and methods in the Java API for DOM, to give a flavor of DOM.

- The Java DOM API provides an interface called Node, and interfaces Element and Attribute, which inherit from the Node interface.

- The Node interface provides methods such as getParentNode(), getFirstChild(), and getNextSibling(), to navigate the DOM tree, starting with the root node.

- Subelements of an element can be accessed by name, using getElementsBy-TagName(name), which returns a list of all child elements with a specified tag name; individual members of the list can be accessed by the method item(i), which returns the *i*th element in the list.

- Attribute values of an element can be accessed by name, using the method getAttribute(name).

- The text value of an element is modeled as a Text node, which is a child of the element node; an element node with no subelements has only one such child node. The method getData() on the Text node returns the text contents.

DOM also provides a variety of functions for updating the document by adding and deleting attribute and element children of a node, setting node values, and so on.

Many more details are required for writing an actual DOM program; see the bibliographical notes for references to further information.

DOM can be used to access XML data stored in databases, and an XML database can be built with DOM as its primary interface for accessing and modifying data. However, the DOM interface does not support any form of declarative querying.

The second commonly used programming interface, the *Simple API for XML* (SAX) is an *event* model, designed to provide a common interface between parsers and applications. This API is built on the notion of *event handlers*, which consist of user-specified functions associated with parsing events. Parsing events correspond to the recognition of parts of a document; for example, an event is generated when the start-tag is found for an element, and another event is generated when the end-tag is found. The pieces of a document are always encountered in order from start to finish.

The SAX application developer creates handler functions for each event, and registers them. When a document is read in by the SAX parser, as each event occurs, the handler function is called with parameters describing the event (such as element tag or text contents). The handler functions then carry out their task. For example, to construct a tree representing the XML data, the handler functions for an attribute or element start event could add a node (or nodes) to a partially constructed tree. The start- and end-tag event handlers would also have to keep track of the current node in the tree to which new nodes must be attached; the element start event would set the new element as the node that is the point where further child nodes must be attached. The corresponding element end event would set the parent of the node as the current node where further child nodes must be attached.

SAX generally requires more programming effort than DOM, but it helps avoid the overhead of creating a DOM tree in situations where the application needs to create its own data representation. If DOM were used for such applications, there would be unnecessary space and time overhead for constructing the DOM tree.

23.6 Storage of XML Data

Many applications require storage of XML data. One way to store XML data is to store it as documents in a file system, while a second is to build a special-purpose database to store XML data. Another approach is to convert the XML data to a relational representation and store it in a relational database. Several alternatives for storing XML data are briefly outlined in this section.

23.6.1 Nonrelational Data Stores

There are several alternatives for storing XML data in nonrelational data-storage systems:

- **Store in flat files.** Since XML is primarily a file format, a natural storage mechanism is simply a flat file. This approach has many of the drawbacks, outlined in Chapter 1, of using file systems as the basis for database applications. In particular, it lacks data isolation, atomicity, concurrent access, and security. However, the wide availability of XML tools that work on file data makes it relatively easy to access and query XML data stored in files. Thus, this storage format may be sufficient for some applications.

- **Create an XML database.** XML databases are databases that use XML as their basic data model. Early XML databases implemented the Document Object Model on a C++-based object-oriented database. This allows much of the object-oriented database infrastructure to be reused, while providing a standard XML interface. The addition of XQuery or other XML query languages provides declarative querying. Other implementations have built the entire XML storage and querying infrastructure on top of a storage manager that provides transactional support.

Although several databases designed specifically to store XML data have been built, building a full-featured database system from ground up is a very complex task. Such a database must support not only XML data storage and querying but also other database features such as transactions, security, support for data access from clients, and a variety of administration facilities. It makes sense to instead use an existing database system to provide these facilities and implement XML data storage and querying either on top of the relational abstraction, or as a layer parallel to the relational abstraction. We study these approaches in Section 23.6.2.

23.6.2 Relational Databases

Since relational databases are widely used in existing applications, there is a great benefit to be had in storing XML data in relational databases, so that the data can be accessed from existing applications.

Converting XML data to relational form is usually straightforward if the data were generated from a relational schema in the first place and XML is used merely as a data exchange format for relational data. However, there are many applications where the XML data are not generated from a relational schema, and translating the data to relational form for storage may not be straightforward. In particular, nested elements and elements that recur (corresponding to set-valued attributes) complicate storage of XML data in relational format. Several alternative approaches are available, which we describe below.

23.6.2.1 Store as String

Small XML documents can be stored as string (**clob**) values in tuples in a relational database. Large XML documents with the top-level element having many children can be handled by storing each child element as a string in a separate tuple. For instance, the XML data in Figure 23.1 could be stored as a set of tuples in a relation *elements*(*data*), with the attribute *data* of each tuple storing one XML element (department, course, instructor, or teaches) in string form.

While the above representation is easy to use, the database system does not know the schema of the stored elements. As a result, it is not possible to query the data directly. In fact, it is not even possible to implement simple selections such as finding all department elements, or finding the department element with department name "Comp. Sci.", without scanning all tuples of the relation and examining the string contents.

A partial solution to this problem is to store different types of elements in different relations, and also store the values of some critical elements as attributes of the relation to enable indexing. For instance, in our example, the relations would be *department_elements*, *course_elements*, *instructor_elements*, and *teaches_elements*, each with an attribute *data*. Each relation may have extra attributes to store the values of some subelements, such as *dept_name*, *course_id*, or *name*. Thus, a query that requires department elements with a specified department name can be answered efficiently with this representation. Such an approach depends on type information about XML data, such as the DTD of the data.

Some database systems, such as Oracle, support **function indices**, which can help avoid replication of attributes between the XML string and relation attributes. Unlike normal indices, which are on attribute values, function indices can be built on the result of applying user-defined functions on tuples. For instance, a function index can be built on a user-defined function that returns the value of the dept_name subelement of the XML string in a tuple. The index can then be used in the same way as an index on a *dept_name* attribute.

The above approaches have the drawback that a large part of the XML information is stored within strings. It is possible to store all the information in relations in one of several ways that we examine next.

23.6.2.2 Tree Representation

Arbitrary XML data can be modeled as a tree and stored using a relation:

$$nodes(id, parent\_id, type, label, value)$$

Each element and attribute in the XML data is given a unique identifier. A tuple inserted in the *nodes* relation for each element and attribute with its identifier (*id*), the identifier of its parent node (*parent_id*), the type of the node (attribute or element), the name of the element or attribute (*label*), and the text value of the element or attribute (*value*).

If order information of elements and attributes must be preserved, an extra attribute *position* can be added to the *nodes* relation to indicate the relative position of the child among the children of the parent. As an exercise, you can represent the XML data of Figure 23.1 by using this technique.

This representation has the advantage that all XML information can be represented directly in relational form, and many XML queries can be translated into relational queries and executed inside the database system. However, it has the drawback that each element gets broken up into many pieces, and a large number of joins are required to reassemble subelements into an element.

23.6.2.3   Map to Relations

In this approach, XML elements whose schema is known are mapped to relations and attributes. Elements whose schema is unknown are stored as strings or as a tree.

A relation is created for each element type (including subelements) whose schema is known and whose type is a complex type (that is, contains attributes or subelements). The root element of the document can be ignored in this step if it does not have any attributes. The attributes of the relation are defined as follows:

- All attributes of these elements are stored as string-valued attributes of the relation.

- If a subelement of the element is a simple type (that is, cannot have attributes or subelements), an attribute is added to the relation to represent the subelement. The type of the relation attribute defaults to a string value, but if the subelement had an XML Schema type, a corresponding SQL type may be used.

    For example, when applied to the element *department* in the schema (DTD or XML Schema) of the data in Figure 23.1, the subelements *dept_name*, *building* and *budget* of the element *department* all become attributes of a relation *department*. Applying this procedure to the remaining elements, we get back the original relational schema that we have used in earlier chapters.

- Otherwise, a relation is created corresponding to the subelement (using the same rules recursively on its subelements). Further:

    ○ An identifier attribute is added to the relations representing the element. (The identifier attribute is added only once even if an element has several subelements.)

    ○ An attribute *parent_id* is added to the relation representing the subelement, storing the identifier of its parent element.

    ○ If ordering is to be preserved, an attribute *position* is added to the relation representing the subelement.

For example, if we apply the above procedure to the schema corresponding to the data in Figure 23.5, we get the following relations:

$$department(id, dept\_name, building, budget)$$
$$course(parent\_id, course\_id, dept\_name, title, credits)$$

Variants of this approach are possible. For example, the relations corresponding to subelements that can occur at most once can be "flattened" into the parent relation by moving all their attributes into the parent relation. The bibliographical notes provide references to different approaches to represent XML data as relations.

23.6.2.4 Publishing and Shredding XML Data

When XML is used to exchange data between business applications, the data most often originates in relational databases. Data in relational databases must be *published*, that is, converted to XML form, for export to other applications. Incoming data must be *shredded*, that is, converted back from XML to normalized relation form and stored in a relational database. While application code can perform the publishing and shredding operations, the operations are so common that the conversions should be done automatically, without writing application code, where possible. Database vendors have spent a lot of effort to *XML-enable* their database products.

An XML-enabled database supports an automatic mechanism for publishing relational data as XML. The mapping used for publishing data may be simple or complex. A simple relation to XML mapping might create an XML element for every row of a table, and make each column in that row a subelement of the XML element. The XML schema in Figure 23.1 can be created from a relational representation of university information, using such a mapping. Such a mapping is straightforward to generate automatically. Such an XML view of relational data can be treated as a *virtual* XML document, and XML queries can be executed against the virtual XML document.

A more complicated mapping would allow nested structures to be created. Extensions of SQL with nested queries in the **select** clause have been developed to allow easy creation of nested XML output. We outline these extensions in Section 23.6.3.

Mappings also have to be defined to shred XML data into a relational representation. For XML data created from a relational representation, the mapping required to shred the data is a straightforward inverse of the mapping used to publish the data. For the general case, a mapping can be generated as outlined in Section 23.6.2.3.

23.6.2.5 Native Storage within a Relational Database

Some relational databases support **native storage** of XML. Such systems store XML data as strings or in more efficient binary representations, without converting the data to relational form. A new data type **xml** is introduced to represent XML data, although the CLOB and BLOB data types may provide the underlying storage mechanism. XML query languages such as XPath and XQuery are supported to query XML data.

A relation with an attribute of type **xml** can be used to store a collection of XML documents; each document is stored as a value of type **xml** in a separate tuple. Special-purpose indices are created to index the XML data.

Several database systems provide native support for XML data. They provide an **xml** data type and allow XQuery queries to be embedded within SQL queries. An XQuery query can be executed on a single XML document and can be embedded within an SQL query to allow it to execute on each of a collection of documents, with each document stored in a separate tuple. For example, see Section 30.11 for more details on native XML support in Microsoft SQL Server 2005.

```
<university>
    <department>
        <row>
            <dept_name> Comp. Sci. </dept_name>
            <building> Taylor </building>
            <budget> 100000 </budget>
        </row>
        <row>
            <dept_name> Biology </dept_name>
            <building> Watson </building>
            <budget> 90000 </budget>
        </row>
    </department>
    <course>
        <row>
            <course_id> CS-101 </course_id>
            <title> Intro. to Computer Science </title>
            <dept_name> Comp. Sci </dept_name>
            <credits> 4 </credits>
        </row>
        <row>
            <course_id> BIO-301 </course_id>
            <title> Genetics </title>
            <dept_name> Biology </dept_name>
            <credits> 4 </credits>
        </row>
    <course>
</university>
```

Figure 23.15   SQL/XML representation of (part of) university information.

23.6.3 SQL/XML

While XML is used widely for data interchange, structured data is still widely stored in relational databases. There is often a need to convert relational data to XML representation. The SQL/XML standard, developed to meet this need, defines a standard extension of SQL, allowing the creation of nested XML output. The standard has several parts, including a standard way of mapping SQL types to XML Schema types, and a standard way to map relational schemas to XML schemas, as well as SQL query language extensions.

For example, the SQL/XML representation of the *department* relation would have an XML schema with outermost element *department*, with each tuple mapped to an XML element *row*, and each relation attribute mapped to an XML element of the same name (with some conventions to resolve incompatibilities with special characters in names). An entire SQL schema, with multiple relations, can also be mapped to XML in a similar fashion. Figure 23.15 shows the SQL/XML representation of (part of) the *university* data from 23.1, containing the relations *department* and *course*.

SQL/XML adds several operators and aggregate operations to SQL to allow the construction of XML output directly from the extended SQL. The **xmlelement** function can be used to create XML elements, while **xmlattributes** can be used to create attributes, as illustrated by the following query.

> **select xmlelement** (**name** "course",
>   **xmlattributes** (*course_id* **as** *course_id*, *dept_name* **as** *dept_name*),
>   **xmlelement** (**name** "title", *title*),
>   **xmlelement** (**name** "credits", *credits*))
>   **from** *course*

The above query creates an XML element for each course, with the course identifier and department name represented as attributes, and title and credits as subelements. The result would look like the course elements shown in Figure 23.11, but without the instructor attribute. The **xmlattributes** operator creates the XML attribute name using the SQL attribute name, which can be changed using an **as** clause as shown.

The **xmlforest** operator simplifies the construction of XML structures. Its syntax and behavior are similar to those of **xmlattributes**, except that it creates a forest (collection) of subelements, instead of a list of attributes. It takes multiple arguments, creating an element for each argument, with the attribute's SQL name used as the XML element name. The **xmlconcat** operator can be used to concatenate elements created by subexpressions into a forest.

When the SQL value used to construct an attribute is null, the attribute is omitted. Null values are omitted when the body of an element is constructed.

SQL/XML also provides an aggregate function **xmlagg** that creates a forest (collection) of XML elements from the collection of values on which it is applied. The following query creates an element for each department with a course, containing as subelements all the courses in that department. Since the query has a clause **group by** *dept_name*, the aggregate function is applied on all courses in each department, creating a sequence of *course_id* elements.

> **select xmlelement** (**name** "department",
>   *dept_name*,
>   **xmlagg** (**xmlforest**(*course_id*)
>   **order by** *course_id*))
>   **from** *course*
>   **group by** *dept_name*

SQL/XML allows the sequence created by **xmlagg** to be ordered, as illustrated in the preceding query. See the bibliographical notes for references to more information on SQL/XML.

23.7   XML Applications

We now outline several applications of XML for storing and communicating (exchanging) data and for accessing Web services (information resources).

23.7.1   Storing Data with Complex Structure

Many applications need to store data that are structured, but are not easily modeled as relations. Consider, for example, user preferences that must be stored by an application such as a browser. There are usually a large number of fields, such as home page, security settings, language settings, and display settings, that must be recorded. Some of the fields are multivalued, for example, a list of trusted sites, or maybe ordered lists, for example, a list of bookmarks. Applications traditionally used some type of textual representation to store such data. Today, a majority of such applications prefer to store such configuration information in XML format. The ad hoc textual representations used earlier require effort to design and effort to create parsers that can read the file and convert the data into a form that a program can use. The XML representation avoids both these steps.

XML-based representations are now widely used for storing documents, spreadsheet data and other data that are part of office application packages. The *Open Document Format (ODF)*, supported by the Open Office software suite as well as other office suites, and the *Office Open XML (OOXML)* format, supported by the Microsoft Office suite, are document representation standards based on XML. They are the two most widely used formats for editable document representation.

XML is also used to represent data with complex structure that must be exchanged between different parts of an application. For example, a database system may represent a query execution plan (a relational-algebra expression with extra information on how to execute operations) by using XML. This allows one part of the system to generate the query execution plan and another part to display it, without using a shared data structure. For example, the data may be generated at a server system and sent to a client system where the data are displayed.

23.7.2   Standardized Data Exchange Formats

XML-based standards for representation of data have been developed for a variety of specialized applications, ranging from business applications such as banking and shipping to scientific applications such as chemistry and molecular biology. Some examples:

- The chemical industry needs information about chemicals, such as their molecular structure, and a variety of important properties, such as boiling and melting points, calorific values, and solubility in various solvents. *ChemML* is a standard for representing such information.

- In shipping, carriers of goods and customs and tax officials need shipment records containing detailed information about the goods being shipped, from whom and to where they were sent, to whom and to where they are being shipped, the monetary value of the goods, and so on.

- An online marketplace in which business can buy and sell goods [a so-called business-to-business (B2B) market] requires information such as product catalogs, including detailed product descriptions and price information, product inventories, quotes for a proposed sale, and purchase orders. For example, the *RosettaNet* standards for e-business applications define XML schemas and semantics for representing data as well as standards for message exchange.

Using normalized relational schemas to model such complex data requirements would result in a large number of relations that do not correspond directly to the objects that are being modeled. The relations would often have large numbers of attributes; explicit representation of attribute/element names along with values in XML helps avoid confusion between attributes. Nested element representations help reduce the number of relations that must be represented, as well as the number of joins required to get required information, at the possible cost of redundancy. For instance, in our university example, listing departments with course elements nested within department elements, as in Figure 23.5, results in a format that is more natural for some applications—in particular, for humans to read—than is the normalized representation in Figure 23.1.

23.7.3 Web Services

Applications often require data from outside of the organization, or from another department in the same organization that uses a different database. In many such situations, the outside organization or department is not willing to allow direct access to its database using SQL, but is willing to provide limited forms of information through predefined interfaces.

When the information is to be used directly by a human, organizations provide Web-based forms, where users can input values and get back desired information in HTML form. However, there are many applications where such information needs to be accessed by software programs, rather than by end users. Providing the results of a query in XML form is a clear requirement. In addition, it makes sense to specify the input values to the query also in XML format.

In effect, the provider of the information defines procedures whose input and output are both in XML format. The HTTP protocol is used to communicate the input and output information, since it is widely used and can go through firewalls that institutions use to keep out unwanted traffic from the Internet.

The **Simple Object Access Protocol** (**SOAP**) defines a standard for invoking procedures, using XML for representing the procedure input and output. SOAP defines a standard XML schema for representing the name of the procedure, and result status indicators such as failure/error indicators. The procedure parameters and results are application-dependent XML data embedded within the SOAP XML headers.

Typically, HTTP is used as the transport protocol for SOAP, but a message-based protocol (such as email over the SMTP protocol) may also be used. The

SOAP standard is widely used today. For example, Amazon and Google provide SOAP-based procedures to carry out search and other activities. These procedures can be invoked by other applications that provide higher-level services to users. The SOAP standard is independent of the underlying programming language, and it is possible for a site running one language, such as C#, to invoke a service that runs on a different language, such as Java.

A site providing such a collection of SOAP procedures is called a **Web service**. Several standards have been defined to support Web services. The **Web Services Description Language** (**WSDL**) is a language used to describe a Web service's capabilities. WSDL provides facilities that interface definitions (or function definitions) provide in a traditional programming language, specifying what functions are available and their input and output types. In addition WSDL allows specification of the URL and network port number to be used to invoke the Web service. There is also a standard called **Universal Description, Discovery, and Integration** (**UDDI**) that defines how a directory of available Web services may be created and how a program may search in the directory to find a Web service satisfying its requirements.

The following example illustrates the value of Web services. An airline may define a Web service providing a set of procedures that can be invoked by a travel Web site; these may include procedures to find flight schedules and pricing information, as well as to make flight bookings. The travel Web site may interact with multiple Web services, provided by different airlines, hotels, and other companies, to provide travel information to a customer and to make travel bookings. By supporting Web services, the individual companies allow a useful service to be constructed on top, integrating the individual services. Users can interact with a single Web site to make their travel bookings, without having to contact multiple separate Web sites.

To invoke a Web service, a client must prepare an appropriate SOAP XML message and send it to the service; when it gets the result encoded in XML, the client must then extract information from the XML result. There are standard APIs in languages such as Java and C# to create and extract information from SOAP messages.

See the bibliographical notes for references to more information on Web services.

23.7.4   Data Mediation

Comparison shopping is an example of a mediation application, in which data about items, inventory, pricing, and shipping costs are extracted from a variety of Web sites offering a particular item for sale. The resulting aggregated information is significantly more valuable than the individual information offered by a single site.

A personal financial manager is a similar application in the context of banking. Consider a consumer with a variety of accounts to manage, such as bank accounts, credit-card accounts, and retirement accounts. Suppose that these accounts may be held at different institutions. Providing centralized management for all accounts of a customer is a major challenge. XML-based mediation addresses the problem by extracting an XML representation of account information from the respective Web sites of the financial institutions where the individual holds accounts. This information may be extracted easily if the institution exports it in a standard XML format, for example, as a Web service. For those that do not, *wrapper* software is used to generate XML data from HTML Web pages returned by the Web site. Wrapper applications need constant maintenance, since they depend on formatting details of Web pages, which change often. Nevertheless, the value provided by mediation often justifies the effort required to develop and maintain wrappers.

Once the basic tools are available to extract information from each source, a *mediator* application is used to combine the extracted information under a single schema. This may require further transformation of the XML data from each site, since different sites may structure the same information differently. They may also use different names for the same information (for instance, acct_number and account_id), or may even use the same name for different information. The mediator must decide on a single schema that represents all required information, and must provide code to transform data between different representations. Such issues are discussed in more detail in Section 19.8, in the context of distributed databases. XML query languages such as XSLT and XQuery play an important role in the task of transformation between different XML representations.

23.8 Summary

- Like the Hyper-Text Markup Language (HTML) on which the Web is based, the Extensible Markup Language (XML) is derived from the Standard Generalized Markup Language (SGML). XML was originally intended for providing functional markup for Web documents, but has now become the de facto standard data format for data exchange between applications.

- XML documents contain elements with matching starting and ending tags indicating the beginning and end of an element. Elements may have subelements nested within them, to any level of nesting. Elements may also have attributes. The choice between representing information as attributes and subelements is often arbitrary in the context of data representation.

- Elements may have an attribute of type ID that stores a unique identifier for the element. Elements may also store references to other elements by using attributes of type IDREF. Attributes of type IDREFS can store a list of references.

- Documents optionally may have their schema specified by a Document Type Declaration (DTD). The DTD of a document specifies what elements may occur, how they may be nested, and what attributes each element may have. Although DTDs are widely used, they have several limitations. For instance, they do not provide a type system.

- XML Schema is now the standard mechanism for specifying the schema of an XML document. It provides a large set of basic types, as well as constructs for creating complex types and specifying integrity constraints, including key constraints and foreign-key (**keyref**) constraints.

- XML data can be represented as tree structures, with nodes corresponding to elements and attributes. Nesting of elements is reflected by the parent-child structure of the tree representation.

- Path expressions can be used to traverse the XML tree structure and locate data. XPath is a standard language for path expressions, and allows required elements to be specified by a file-system-like path, and additionally allows selections and other features. XPath also forms part of other XML query languages.

- The XQuery language is the standard language for querying XML data. It has a structure not unlike SQL, with **for**, **let**, **where**, **order by**, and **return** clauses. However, it supports many extensions to deal with the tree nature of XML and to allow for the transformation of XML documents into other documents with a significantly different structure. XPath path expressions form a part of XQuery. XQuery supports nested queries and user-defined functions.

- The DOM and SAX APIs are widely used for programmatic access to XML data. These APIs are available from a variety of programming languages.

- XML data can be stored in any of several different ways. XML data may also be stored in file systems, or in XML databases, which use XML as their internal representation.

- XML data can be stored as strings in a relational database. Alternatively, relations can represent XML data as trees. As another alternative, XML data can be mapped to relations in the same way that E-R schemas are mapped to relational schemas. Native storage of XML in relational databases is facilitated by adding an **xml** data type to SQL.

- XML is used in a variety of applications, such as storing complex data, exchange of data between organizations in a standardized form, data mediation, and Web services. Web services provide a remote-procedure call interface, with XML as the mechanism for encoding parameters as well as results.

Review Terms

- Extensible Markup Language (XML)
- Hyper-Text Markup Language (HTML)
- Standard Generalized Markup Language
- Markup language

- Tags
- Self-documenting
- Element
- Root element
- Nested elements
- Attribute

- Namespace
- Default namespace
- Schema definition
- Document Type Definition (DTD)
  - ID
  - IDREF and IDREFS
- XML Schema
  - Simple and complex types
  - Sequence type
  - Key and keyref
  - Occurrence constraints
- Tree model of XML data
- Nodes
- Querying and transformation
- Path expressions
- XPath
- XQuery
  - FLWOR expressions
    - **for**
    - **let**
    - **where**
    - **order by**
    - **return**
  - Joins
  - Nested FLWOR expression
  - Sorting
- XML API
- Document Object Model (DOM)
- Simple API for XML (SAX)
- Storage of XML data
  - In nonrelational data stores
  - In relational databases
    - Store as string
    - Tree representation
    - Map to relations
    - Publish and shred
    - XML-enabled database
    - Native storage
    - SQL/XML
- XML applications
  - Storing complex data
  - Exchange of data
  - Data mediation
  - SOAP
  - Web services

Practice Exercises

23.1 Give an alternative representation of university information containing the same data as in Figure 23.1, but using attributes instead of subelements. Also give the DTD or XML Schema for this representation.

23.2 Give the DTD or XML Schema for an XML representation of the following nested-relational schema:

> *Emp = (ename, ChildrenSet* **setof***(Children), SkillsSet* **setof***(Skills))*
> *Children = (name, Birthday)*
> *Birthday = (day, month, year)*
> *Skills = (type, ExamsSet* **setof***(Exams))*
> *Exams = (year, city)*

```
<!DOCTYPE bibliography [
    <!ELEMENT book (title, author+, year, publisher, place?)>
    <!ELEMENT article (title, author+, journal, year, number, volume, pages?)>
    <!ELEMENT author ( last_name, first_name) >
    <!ELEMENT title ( #PCDATA )>
    · · · similar PCDATA declarations for year, publisher, place, journal, year,
        number, volume, pages, last_name and first_name
] >
```

Figure 23.16 DTD for bibliographical data.

23.3 Write a query in XPath on the schema of Practice Exercise 23.2 to list all skill types in *Emp*.

23.4 Write a query in XQuery on the XML representation in Figure 23.11 to find the total salary of all instructors in each department.

23.5 Write a query in XQuery on the XML representation in Figure 23.1 to compute the left outer join of **department** elements with **course** elements. (Hint: Use universal quantification.)

23.6 Write queries in XQuery to output department elements with associated course elements nested within the department elements, given the university information representation using ID and IDREFS in Figure 23.11.

23.7 Give a relational schema to represent bibliographical information specified according to the DTD fragment in Figure 23.16. The relational schema must keep track of the order of **author** elements. You can assume that only books and articles appear as top-level elements in XML documents.

23.8 Show the tree representation of the XML data in Figure 23.1, and the representation of the tree using *nodes* and *child* relations described in Section 23.6.2.

23.9 Consider the following recursive DTD:

```
<!DOCTYPE parts [
    <!ELEMENT part (name, subpartinfo*)>
    <!ELEMENT subpartinfo (part, quantity)>
    <!ELEMENT name ( #PCDATA )>
    <!ELEMENT quantity ( #PCDATA )>
] >
```

a. Give a small example of data corresponding to this DTD.

b. Show how to map this DTD to a relational schema. You can assume that part names are unique; that is, wherever a part appears, its subpart structure will be the same.

c. Create a schema in XML Schema corresponding to this DTD.

Exercises

23.10 Show, by giving a DTD, how to represent the non-1NF *books* relation from Section 22.2, using XML.

23.11 Write the following queries in XQuery, assuming the schema from Practice Exercise 23.2.

    a. Find the names of all employees who have a child who has a birthday in March.

    b. Find those employees who took an examination for the skill type "typing" in the city "Dayton".

    c. List all skill types in *Emp*.

23.12 Consider the XML data shown in Figure 23.3. Suppose we wish to find purchase orders that ordered two or more copies of the part with identifier 123. Consider the following attempt to solve this problem:

```
for $p in purchaseorder
where $p/part/id = 123 and $p/part/quantity >= 2
return $p
```

Explain why the query may return some purchase orders that order less than two copies of part 123. Give a correct version of the above query.

23.13 Give a query in XQuery to flip the nesting of data from Exercise 23.10. That is, at the outermost level of nesting the output must have elements corresponding to authors, and each such element must have nested within it items corresponding to all the books written by the author.

23.14 Give the DTD for an XML representation of the information in Figure 7.29. Create a separate element type to represent each relationship, but use ID and IDREF to implement primary and foreign keys.

23.15 Give an XML Schema representation of the DTD from Exercise 23.14.

23.16 Write queries in XQuery on the bibliography DTD fragment in Figure 23.16, to do the following:

    a. Find all authors who have authored a book and an article in the same year.

    b. Display books and articles sorted by year.

    c. Display books with more than one author.

    d. Find all books that contain the word "database" in their title and the word "Hank" in an author's name (whether first or last).

23.17   Give a relational mapping of the XML purchase order schema illustrated in Figure 23.3, using the approach described in Section 23.6.2.3. Suggest how to remove redundancy in the relational schema, if item identifiers functionally determine the description and purchase and supplier names functionally determine the purchase and supplier address, respectively.

23.18   Write queries in SQL/XML to convert university data from the relational schema we have used in earlier chapters to the *university-1* and *university-2* XML schemas.

23.19   As in Exercise 23.18, write queries to convert university data to the *university-1* and *university-2* XML schemas, but this time by writing XQuery queries on the default SQL/XML database to XML mapping.

23.20   One way to shred an XML document is to use XQuery to convert the schema to an SQL/XML mapping of the corresponding relational schema, and then use the SQL/XML mapping in the backward direction to populate the relation.

   As an illustration, give an XQuery query to convert data from the *university-1* XML schema to the SQL/XML schema shown in Figure 23.15.

23.21   Consider the example XML schema from Section 23.3.2, and write XQuery queries to carry out the following tasks:

   a.   Check if the key constraint shown in Section 23.3.2 holds.

   b.   Check if the keyref constraint shown in Section 23.3.2 holds.

23.22   Consider Practice Exercise 23.7, and suppose that authors could also appear as top-level elements. What change would have to be done to the relational schema?

Tools

A number of tools to deal with XML are available in the public domain. The W3C Web site www.w3.org has pages describing the various XML-related standards, as well as pointers to software tools such as language implementations. An extensive list of XQuery implementations is available at www.w3.org/XML/Query. Saxon D (saxon.sourceforge.net) and Galax (http://www.galaxquery.org/) are useful as learning tools, although not designed to handle large databases. Exist (exist-db.org) is an open source XML database, supporting a variety of features. Several commercial databases, including IBM DB2, Oracle, and Microsoft SQL Server support XML storage, publishing using various SQL extensions, and querying using XPath and XQuery.

Bibliographical Notes

The World Wide Web Consortium (W3C) acts as the standards body for Web-related standards, including basic XML and all the XML-related languages such as

XPath, XSLT, and XQuery. A large number of technical reports defining the XML-related standards are available at www.w3.org. This site also contains tutorials and pointers to software implementing the various standards.

The XQuery language derives from an XML query language called Quilt; Quilt itself included features from earlier languages such as XPath, discussed in Section 23.4.2, and two other XML query languages, XQL and XML-QL. Quilt is described in Chamberlin et al. [2000]. Deutsch et al. [1999] describes the XML-QL language. The W3C issued a *candidate recommendation* for an extension of XQuery in mid-2009 that includes updates.

Katz et al. [2004] provides detailed textbook coverage of XQuery. The XQuery specification may be found at www.w3.org/TR/xquery. Specifications of XQuery extensions, including the XQuery Update facility and the XQuery Scripting Extension are also available at this site. Integration of keyword querying into XML is outlined by Florescu et al. [2000] and Amer-Yahia et al. [2004].

Funderburk et al. [2002a], Florescu and Kossmann [1999], Kanne and Moerkotte [2000], and Shanmugasundaram et al. [1999] describe storage of XML data. Eisenberg and Melton [2004a] provides an overview of SQL/XML, while Funderburk et al. [2002b] provides overviews of SQL/XML and XQuery. See Chapters 28 through 30 for more information on XML support in commercial databases. Eisenberg and Melton [2004b] provides an overview of the XQJ API for XQuery, while the standard definition may be found online at http://www.w3.org/TR/xquery.

XML Indexing, Query Processing and Optimization: Indexing of XML data, and query processing and optimization of XML queries, has been an area of great interest in the past few years. A large number of papers have been published in this area. One of the challenges in indexing is that queries may specify a selection on a path, such as */a/b//c[d=*"CSE"]; the index must support efficient retrieval of nodes that satisfy the path specification and the value selection. Work on indexing of XML data includes Pal et al. [2004] and Kaushik et al. [2004]. If data is shredded and stored in relations, evaluating a path expression maps to computation of a join. Several techniques have been proposed for efficiently computing such joins, in particular when the path expression specifies any descendant (//). Several techniques for numbering of nodes in XML data have been proposed that can be used to efficiently check if a node is a descendant of another; see, for example, O'Neil et al. [2004]. Work on optimization of XML queries includes McHugh and Widom [1999], Wu et al. [2003] and Krishnaprasad et al. [2004].

PART 8

ADVANCED TOPICS

Chapter 24 covers a number of advanced topics in application development, starting with performance tuning to improve application speed. It then discusses standard benchmarks that are used as measures of commercial database-system performance. Issues in application development, such as application testing and application migration are discussed next. The chapter concludes with an overview of the standardization process and existing database-language standards.

Chapter 25 describes spatial and temporal data types, and multimedia data, and the issues in storing such data in databases. Database issues related to mobile computing systems are also described in this chapter.

Finally, Chapter 26 describes several advanced transaction-processing techniques, including transaction-processing monitors, transactional workflows, and transaction processing issues in electronic commerce. The chapter then discusses main-memory database systems and real-time transaction systems, and concludes with a discussion of long-duration transactions.

CHAPTER 24

Advanced Application Development

There are a number of tasks in application development. We saw earlier in Chapters 7 to 9 how to design and build an application. One of the aspects of application design is the performance one expects out of the application. In fact, it is common to find that once an application has been built, it runs slower than the designers wanted, or handles fewer transactions per second than they required. An application that takes an excessive amount of time to perform requested actions can cause user dissatisfaction at best and be completely unusable at worst.

Applications can be made to run significantly faster by performance tuning, which consists of finding and eliminating bottlenecks and adding appropriate hardware such as memory or disks. There are many things an application developer can do to tune the application, and there are things that a database-system administrator can do to speed up processing for an application.

Benchmarks are standardized sets of tasks that help to characterize the performance of database systems. They are useful to get a rough idea of the hardware and software requirements of an application, even before the application is built.

Applications must be tested as they are being developed. Testing requires generation of database states and test inputs, and verifying that the outputs match the expected outputs. We discuss issues in application testing. Legacy systems are application systems that are outdated and usually based on older-generation technology. However, they are often at the core of organizations, and run mission-critical applications. We outline issues in interfacing with and issues in migrating away from legacy systems, replacing them with more modern systems.

Standards are very important for application development, especially in the age of the Internet, since applications need to communicate with each other to perform useful tasks. A variety of standards have been proposed that affect database-application development.

24.1 Performance Tuning

Tuning the performance of a system involves adjusting various parameters and design choices to improve its performance for a specific application. Various aspects of a database-system design—ranging from high-level aspects such as the schema and transaction design to database parameters such as buffer sizes, down to hardware issues such as number of disks—affect the performance of an application. Each of these aspects can be adjusted so that performance is improved.

24.1.1   Improving Set Orientation

When SQL queries are executed from an application program, it is often the case that a query is executed frequently, but with different values for a parameter. Each call has an overhead of communication with the server, in addition to processing overheads at the server.

For example, consider a program that steps through each department, invoking an embedded SQL query to find the total salary of all instructors in the department:

$$\textbf{select sum}(\textit{salary})$$
$$\textbf{from } \textit{instructor}$$
$$\textbf{where } \textit{dept\_name} = ?$$

If the *instructor* relation does not have a clustered index on *dept_name*, each such query will result in a scan of the relation. Even if there is such an index, a random I/O operation will be required for each *dept_name* value.

Instead, we can use a single SQL query to find total salary expenses of each department:

$$\textbf{select } \textit{dept\_name}, \textbf{sum}(\textit{salary})$$
$$\textbf{from } \textit{instructor}$$
$$\textbf{group by } \textit{dept\_name};$$

This query can be evaluated with a single scan of the *instructor* relation, avoiding random I/O for each department. The results can be fetched to the client side using a single round of communication, and the client program can then step through the results to find the aggregate for each department. Combining multiple SQL queries into a single SQL query as above can reduce execution costs greatly in many cases–for example, if the *instructor* relation is very large and has a large number of departments.

The JDBC API also provides a feature called **batch update** that allows a number of inserts to be performed using a single communication with the database. Figure 24.1 illustrates the use of this feature. The code shown in the figure requires only one round of communication with the database, when the executeBatch() method is executed, in contrast to similar code without the batch update feature that we saw earlier in Figure 5.2. In the absence of batch update, as many rounds of communication with the database are required as there are instructors to be inserted. The batch update feature also enables the database to process a batch of

```
PreparedStatement pStmt = conn.prepareStatement(
                "insert into instructor values(?,?,?,?)");
pStmt.setString(1, "88877");
pStmt.setString(2, "Perry");
pStmt.setInt(3, "Finance");
pStmt.setInt(4, 125000);
pStmt.addBatch( );
pStmt.setString(1, "88878");
pStmt.setString(2, "Thierry");
pStmt.setInt(3, "Physics");
pStmt.setInt(4, 100000);
pStmt.addBatch( ); pStmt.executeBatch( );
```

Figure 24.1 Batch update in JDBC.

inserts at once, which can potentially be done much more efficiently than a series of single record inserts.

Another technique used widely in client–server systems to reduce the cost of communication and SQL compilation is to use stored procedures, where queries are stored at the server in the form of procedures, which may be precompiled. Clients can invoke these stored procedures, rather than communicate a series of queries.

Another aspect of improving set orientation lies in rewriting queries with **nested subqueries**. In the past, optimizers on many database systems were not particularly good, so how a query was written would have a big influence on how it was executed, and therefore on the performance. Today's advanced optimizers can transform even badly written queries and execute them efficiently, so the need for tuning individual queries is less important than it used to be. However, complex queries containing nested subqueries are not optimized very well by many optimizers.

We saw techniques for nested subquery decorrelation in Section 13.4.4. If a subquery is not decorrelated, it gets executed repeatedly, potentially resulting in a great deal of random I/O. In contrast, decorrelation allows efficient set-oriented operations such as joins to be used, minimizing random I/O. Most database query optimizers incorporate some forms of decorrelation, but some can handle only very simple nested subqueries. The execution plan chosen by the optimizer can be found as described earlier in Chapter 13. If the optimizer has not succeeded in decorrelating a nested subquery, the query can be decorrelated by rewriting it manually.

24.1.2 Tuning of Bulk Loads and Updates

When loading a large volume of data into a database (called a **bulk load** operation), performance is usually very poor if the inserts are carried out a separate SQL insert statements. One reason is the overhead of parsing each SQL query; a more important reason is that performing integrity constraint checks and index updates separately for each inserted tuple results in a large number of random I/O operations. If the inserts were done as a large batch, integrity-constraint checking and index update can be done in a much more set-oriented fashion, reducing overheads greatly; performance improvements of an order-of-magnitude or more are not uncommon.

To support bulk load operations, most database systems provide a **bulk import** utility, and a corresponding **bulk export** utility. The bulk-import utility reads data from a file, and performs integrity constraint checking as well as index maintenance in a very efficient manner. Common input and output file format supported by such bulk import/export utilities include text files with characters such as commas or tabs separating attribute values, with each record in a line of its own (such file formats are referred to as *comma-separated values* or *tab-separated values* formats). Database specific binary formats, as well as XML formats are also supported by bulk import/export utilities. The names of the bulk import/export utilities differ by database. In PostgreSQL, the utilities are called pg_dump and pg _restore (PostgreSQL also provides an SQL command **copy** which provides similar functionality). The bulk import/export utility in Oracle is called **SQL*Loader**, the utility in DB2 is called load, and the utility in SQL Server is called bcp (SQL Server also provides an SQL command called **bulk insert**).

We now consider the case of tuning of bulk updates. Suppose we have a relation *funds_received*(*dept_name*, *amount*) that stores funds received (say, by electronic funds transfer) for each of a set of departments. Suppose now that we want to add the amounts to the balances of the corresponding department budgets. In order to use the SQL update statement to carry out this task, we have to perform a look up on the *funds_received* relation for each tuple in the *department* relation. We can use subqueries in the update clause to carry out this task, as follows: We assume for simplicity that the relation *funds_received* contains at most one tuple for each department.

> **update** *department* **set** *budget* = *budget* +
>   (**select** *amount*
>   **from** *funds_received*
>   **where** *funds_received.dept_name* = *department.dept_name*)
>   **where exists**(
>   **select** *
>   **from** *funds_received*
>   **where** *funds_received.dept_name* = *department.dept_name*);

Note that the condition in the **where** clause of the update ensures that only accounts with corresponding tuples in *funds_received* are updated, while the subquery within the **set** clause computes the amount to be added to each such department.

There are many applications that require updates such as that illustrated above. Typically, there is a table, which we shall call the **master table**, and updates to the master table are received as a batch. Now the master table has to be correspondingly updated. SQL:2003 provides a special construct, called the **merge** construct, to simplify the task of performing such merging of information. For example, the above update can be expressed using **merge** as follows:

> **merge into** *department* **as** *A*
> **using**   (**select** *
>   **from** *funds_received*) **as** *F*
>   **on** (*A.dept_name* = *F.dept_name*)
> **when matched then**
>   **update set** *budget* = *budget* + *F.amount*;

When a record from the subquery in the **using** clause matches a record in the *department* relation, the **when matched** clause is executed, which can execute an update on the relation; in this case, the matching record in the *department* relation is updated as shown.

The **merge** statement can also have a **when not matched then** clause, which permits insertion of new records into the relation. In the above example, when there is no matching department for a *funds_received* tuple, the insertion action could create a new department record (with a null *building*) using the following clause:

> **when not matched then**
>   **insert values** (*F.dept_name*, null, *F.budget*)

Although not very meaningful in this example,[1] the **when not matched then** clause can be quite useful in other cases. For example, suppose the local relation is a copy of a master relation, and we receive updated as well as newly inserted records from the master relation. The **merge** statement can update matched records (these would be updated old records) and insert records that are not matched (these would be new records).

Not all SQL implementations support the **merge** statement currently; see the respective system manuals for further details.

24.1.3 Location of Bottlenecks

The performance of most systems (at least before they are tuned) is usually limited primarily by the performance of one or a few components, called **bottlenecks**. For instance, a program may spend 80 percent of its time in a small loop deep in the code, and the remaining 20 percent of the time on the rest of the code; the small loop then is a bottleneck. Improving the performance of a component that is not a bottleneck does little to improve the overall speed of the system; in the example, improving the speed of the rest of the code cannot lead to more than a

---

[1] A better action here would have been to insert these records into an error relation, but that cannot be done with the **merge** statement.

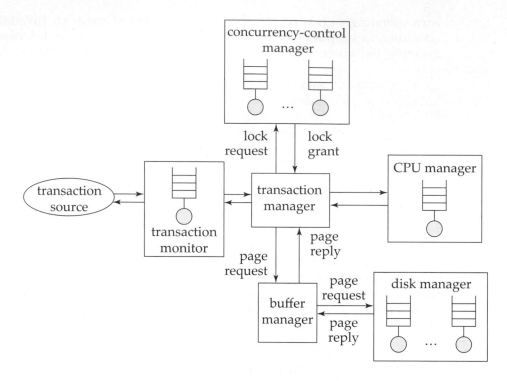

Figure 24.2   Queues in a database system.

20 percent improvement overall, whereas improving the speed of the bottleneck loop could result in an improvement of nearly 80 percent overall, in the best case.

Hence, when tuning a system, we must first try to discover what the bottlenecks are and then eliminate them by improving the performance of system components causing the bottlenecks. When one bottleneck is removed, it may turn out that another component becomes the bottleneck. In a well-balanced system, no single component is the bottleneck. If the system contains bottlenecks, components that are not part of the bottleneck are underutilized, and could perhaps have been replaced by cheaper components with lower performance.

For simple programs, the time spent in each region of the code determines the overall execution time. However, database systems are much more complex, and can be modeled as **queueing systems**. A transaction requests various services from the database system, starting from entry into a server process, disk reads during execution, CPU cycles, and locks for concurrency control. Each of these services has a queue associated with it, and small transactions may spend most of their time waiting in queues—especially in disk I/O queues—instead of executing code. Figure 24.2 illustrates some of the queues in a database system.

As a result of the numerous queues in the database, bottlenecks in a database system typically show up in the form of long queues for a particular service, or, equivalently, in high utilizations for a particular service. If requests are spaced exactly uniformly, and the time to service a request is less than or equal to the time before the next request arrives, then each request will find the resource idle and can therefore start execution immediately without waiting. Unfortunately, the arrival of requests in a database system is never so uniform and is instead random.

If a resource, such as a disk, has a low utilization, then, when a request is made, the resource is likely to be idle, in which case the waiting time for the request will be 0. Assuming uniformly randomly distributed arrivals, the length of the queue (and correspondingly the waiting time) go up exponentially with utilization; as utilization approaches 100 percent, the queue length increases sharply, resulting in excessively long waiting times. The utilization of a resource should be kept low enough that queue length is short. As a rule of the thumb, utilizations of around 70 percent are considered to be good, and utilizations above 90 percent are considered excessive, since they will result in significant delays. To learn more about the theory of queueing systems, generally referred to as **queueing theory**, you can consult the references cited in the bibliographical notes.

24.1.4 Tunable Parameters

Database administrators can tune a database system at three levels. The lowest level is at the hardware level. Options for tuning systems at this level include adding disks or using a RAID system if disk I/O is a bottleneck, adding more memory if the disk buffer size is a bottleneck, or moving to a faster processor if CPU use is a bottleneck.

The second level consists of the database-system parameters, such as buffer size and checkpointing intervals. The exact set of database-system parameters that can be tuned depends on the specific database system. Most database-system manuals provide information on what database-system parameters can be adjusted, and how you should choose values for the parameters. Well-designed database systems perform as much tuning as possible automatically, freeing the user or database administrator from the burden. For instance, in many database systems the buffer size is fixed but tunable. If the system automatically adjusts the buffer size by observing indicators such as page-fault rates, then the database administrator will not have to worry about tuning the buffer size.

The third level is the highest level. It includes the schema and transactions. The administrator can tune the design of the schema, the indices that are created, and the transactions that are executed, to improve performance. Tuning at this level is comparatively system independent.

The three levels of tuning interact with one another; we must consider them together when tuning a system. For example, tuning at a higher level may result in the hardware bottleneck changing from the disk system to the CPU, or vice versa.

24.1.5 Tuning of Hardware

Even in a well-designed transaction processing system, each transaction usually has to do at least a few I/O operations, if the data required by the transaction are on disk. An important factor in tuning a transaction processing system is to make sure that the disk subsystem can handle the rate at which I/O operations are required. For instance, consider a disk that supports an access time of about 10 milliseconds, and average transfer rate of 25 to 100 megabytes per second (a fairly typical disk today). Such a disk would support a little under 100 random-access I/O operations of 4 kilobytes each per second. If each transaction requires just 2 I/O operations, a single disk would support at most 50 transactions per second. The only way to support more transactions per second is to increase the number of disks. If the system needs to support n transactions per second, each performing 2 I/O operations, data must be striped (or otherwise partitioned) across at least $n/50$ disks (ignoring skew).

Notice here that the limiting factor is not the capacity of the disk, but the speed at which random data can be accessed (limited in turn by the speed at which the disk arm can move). The number of I/O operations per transaction can be reduced by storing more data in memory. If all data are in memory, there will be no disk I/O except for writes. Keeping frequently used data in memory reduces the number of disk I/Os, and is worth the extra cost of memory. Keeping very infrequently used data in memory would be a waste, since memory is much more expensive than disk.

The question is, for a given amount of money available for spending on disks or memory, what is the best way to spend the money to achieve the maximum number of transactions per second. A reduction of 1 I/O per second saves:

$$(price\ per\ disk\ drive)/(access\ per\ second\ per\ disk)$$

Thus, if a particular page is accessed n times per second, the saving due to keeping it in memory is n times the above value. Storing a page in memory costs:

$$(price\ per\ megabyte\ of\ memory)/(pages\ per\ megabyte\ of\ memory)$$

Thus, the break-even point is:

$$n * \frac{price\ per\ disk\ drive}{access\ per\ second\ per\ disk} = \frac{price\ per\ megabyte\ of\ memory}{pages\ per\ megabyte\ of\ memory}$$

We can rearrange the equation and substitute current values for each of the above parameters to get a value for n; if a page is accessed more frequently than this, it is worth buying enough memory to store it. Current disk technology and memory and disk prices (which we assume to be about $50 per disk, and $0.020 per megabyte) give a value of n around 1/6400 times per second (or equivalently, once in nearly 2 hours) for pages that are randomly accessed; with disk and memory cost and speeds as of some years ago, the corresponding value was in 5 minutes.

This reasoning is captured by the rule of thumb that was originally called the **5-minute rule**: if a page is used more frequently than once in 5 minutes, it should be cached in memory. In other words, some years ago, the rule suggested buying enough memory to cache all pages that are accessed at least once in 5 minutes on average. Today, it is worth buying enough memory to cache all pages that are accessed at least once in 2 hours on average. For data that are accessed less frequently, buy enough disks to support the rate of I/O required for the data.

For data that are sequentially accessed, significantly more pages can be read per second. Assuming 1 megabyte of data is read at a time, some years ago we had the **1-minute rule**, which said that sequentially accessed data should be cached in memory if they are used at least once in 1 minute. The corresponding number, with current memory and disk costs from our earlier example, is around 30 seconds. Surprisingly, this figure has not changed all that much over the years, since disk transfer rates have increased greatly, even though the price of a megabyte of memory has reduced greatly compared to the price of a disk.

Clearly the amount of data read per I/O operation greatly affects the time above; in fact the 5-minute rule still holds if about 100 kilobytes of data are read or written per I/O operation.

The 5-minute rule of thumb and its variants take only the number of I/O operations into account, and do not consider factors such as response time. Some applications need to keep even infrequently used data in memory, to support response times that are less than or comparable to disk-access time.

With the wide availability of flash memory, and "solid-state disks" based on flash memory, system designers can now choose to store frequently used data in flash storage, instead of storing it on disk. Alternatively, in the **flash-as-buffer** approach, flash storage is used as a persistent buffer, with each block having a permanent location on disk, but stored in flash instead of being written to disk as long as it is frequently used. When flash storage is full, a block that is not frequently used is evicted, and flushed back to disk if it was updated after being read from disk.

The flash-as-buffer approach requires changes in the database system itself. Even if a database system does not support flash as a buffer, a database administrator can control the mapping of relations or indices to disks, and allocate frequently used relations/indices to flash storage. The tablespace feature, supported by most database systems, can be used to control the mapping, by creating a tablespace on flash storage and assigning desired relations and indices to that tablespace. Controlling the mapping at a finer level of granularity than a relation, however, requires changes to the database-system code.

The "5-minute" rule has been extended to the case where data can be stored on flash, in addition to main memory and disk. See the bibliographical notes for references to more information.

Another aspect of tuning is whether to use RAID 1 or RAID 5. The answer depends on how frequently the data are updated, since RAID 5 is much slower than RAID 1 on random writes: RAID 5 requires 2 reads and 2 writes to execute a single random write request. If an application performs r random reads and w random writes per second to support a particular throughput rate, a RAID 5 implementation would require $r + 4w$ I/O operations per second whereas a RAID 1 implementation would require $r + 2w$ I/O operations per second. We can then calculate the number of disks required to support the required I/O operations per second by dividing the result of the calculation by 100 I/O operations per second (for current-generation disks). For many applications, r and w are large enough that the $(r + w)/100$ disks can easily hold two copies of all the data. For such applications, if RAID 1 is used, the required number of disks is actually less than the required number of disks if RAID 5 is used! Thus RAID 5 is useful only when the data storage requirements are very large, but the update rates, and particularly random update rates, are small, that is, for very large and very "cold" data.

24.1.6 Tuning of the Schema

Within the constraints of the chosen normal form, it is possible to partition relations vertically. For example, consider the *course* relation, with the schema:

$$course\ (\underline{course\_id},\ title,\ dept\_name,\ credits)$$

for which *course_id* is a key. Within the constraints of the normal forms (BCNF and third normal forms), we can partition the *course* relation into two relations:

$$course\_credit\ (\underline{course\_id},\ credits)$$
$$course\_title\_dept\ (\underline{course\_id},\ title,\ dept\_name)$$

The two representations are logically equivalent, since *course_id* is a key, but they have different performance characteristics.

If most accesses to course information look at only the *course_id* and *credits*, then they can be run against the *course_credit* relation, and access is likely to be somewhat faster, since the *title* and *dept_name* attributes are not fetched. For the same reason, more tuples of *course_credit* will fit in the buffer than corresponding tuples of *course*, again leading to faster performance. This effect would be particularly marked if the *title* and *dept_name* attributes were large. Hence, a schema consisting of *course_credit* and *course_title_dept* would be preferable to a schema consisting of the *course* relation in this case.

On the other hand, if most accesses to course information require both *dept _name* and *credits*, using the *course* relation would be preferable, since the cost of the join of *course_credit* and *course_title_dept* would be avoided. Also, the storage overhead would be lower, since there would be only one relation, and the attribute *course_id* would not be replicated.

The **column store** approach to storing data is based on vertical partitioning, but takes it to the limit by storing each attribute (column) of the relation in a separate file. Column stores have been shown to perform well for several data-warehouse applications.

Another trick to improve performance is to store a *denormalized relation*, such as a join of *instructor* and *department*, where the information about *dept_name*, *building*, and *budget* is repeated for every instructor. More effort has to be expended to make sure the relation is consistent whenever an update is carried out. However, a query that fetches the names of the instructors and the associated buildings will be speeded up, since the join of *instructor* and *department* will have been precomputed. If such a query is executed frequently, and has to be performed as efficiently as possible, the denormalized relation could be beneficial.

Materialized views can provide the benefits that denormalized relations provide, at the cost of some extra storage; we describe performance tuning of materialized views in Section 24.1.8. A major advantage to materialized views over denormalized relations is that maintaining consistency of redundant data becomes the job of the database system, not the programmer. Thus, materialized views are preferable, whenever they are supported by the database system.

Another approach to speed up the computation of the join without materializing it, is to cluster records that would match in the join on the same disk page. We saw such clustered file organizations in Section 10.6.2.

24.1.7 Tuning of Indices

We can tune the indices in a database system to improve performance. If queries are the bottleneck, we can often speed them up by creating appropriate indices on relations. If updates are the bottleneck, there may be too many indices, which have to be updated when the relations are updated. Removing indices may speed up certain updates.

The choice of the type of index also is important. Some database systems support different kinds of indices, such as hash indices and B-tree indices. If range queries are common, B-tree indices are preferable to hash indices. Whether to make an index a clustered index is another tunable parameter. Only one index on a relation can be made clustered, by storing the relation sorted on the index attributes. Generally, the index that benefits the greatest number of queries and updates should be made clustered.

To help identify what indices to create, and which index (if any) on each relation should be clustered, most commercial database systems provide *tuning wizards*; these are described in more detail in Section 24.1.9. These tools use the past history of queries and updates (called the *workload*) to estimate the effects of various indices on the execution time of the queries and updates in the workload. Recommendations on what indices to create are based on these estimates.

24.1.8 Using Materialized Views

Maintaining materialized views can greatly speed up certain types of queries, in particular aggregate queries. Recall the example from Section 13.5 where the total salary for each department (obtained by summing the salary of each instructor in the department) is required frequently. As we saw in that section, creating a materialized view storing the total salary for each department can greatly speed up such queries.

Materialized views should be used with care, however, since there is not only space overhead for storing them but, more important, there is also time overhead for maintaining materialized views. In the case of **immediate view maintenance**, if the updates of a transaction affect the materialized view, the materialized view must be updated as part of the same transaction. The transaction may therefore run slower. In the case of **deferred view maintenance**, the materialized view is updated later; until it is updated, the materialized view may be inconsistent with the database relations. For instance, the materialized view may be brought up-to-date when a query uses the view, or periodically. Using deferred maintenance reduces the burden on update transactions.

The database administrator is responsible for the selection of materialized views and for view-maintenance policies. The database administrator can make the selection manually by examining the types of queries in the workload, and finding out which queries need to run faster and which updates/queries may be executed more slowly. From the examination, the database administrator may choose an appropriate set of materialized views. For instance, the administrator may find that a certain aggregate is used frequently, and choose to materialize it, or may find that a particular join is computed frequently, and choose to materialize it.

However, manual choice is tedious for even moderately large sets of query types, and making a good choice may be difficult, since it requires understanding the costs of different alternatives; only the query optimizer can estimate the costs with reasonable accuracy, without actually executing the query. Thus a good set of views may be found only by trial and error—that is, by materializing one or more views, running the workload, and measuring the time taken to run the queries in the workload. The administrator repeats the process until a set of views is found that gives acceptable performance.

A better alternative is to provide support for selecting materialized views within the database system itself, integrated with the query optimizer. This approach is described in more detail in Section 24.1.9.

24.1.9 Automated Tuning of Physical Design

Most commercial database systems today provide tools to help the database administrator with index and materialized view selection, and other tasks related to physical database design such as how to partition data in a parallel database system.

These tools examine the **workload** (the history of queries and updates) and suggest indices and views to be materialized. The database administrator may specify the importance of speeding up different queries, which the tool takes into account when selecting views to materialize. Often tuning must be done before the application is fully developed, and the actual database contents may be small on the development database, but expected to be much larger on a production database. Thus, some tuning tools also allow the database administrator to specify information about the expected size of the database and related statistics.

Microsoft's Database Tuning Assistant, for example, allows the user to ask "what if" questions, whereby the user can pick a view, and the optimizer then estimates the effect of materializing the view on the total cost of the workload and on the individual costs of different types of queries and updates in the workload.

The automatic selection of indices and materialized views is usually implemented by enumerating different alternatives and using the query optimizer to estimate the costs and benefits of selecting each alternative by using the workload. Since the number of design alternatives may be extremely large, as also the workload, the selection techniques must be designed carefully.

The first step is to generate a workload. This is usually done by recording all the queries and updates that are executed during some time period. Next, the selection tools perform **workload compression**, that is, create a representation of the workload using a small number of updates and queries. For example, updates of the same form can be represented by a single update with a weight corresponding to how many times the update occurred. Queries of the same form can be similarly replaced by a representative with appropriate weight. After this, queries that are very infrequent and do not have a high cost may be discarded from consideration. The most expensive queries may be chosen to be addressed first. Such workload compression is essential for large workloads.

With the help of the optimizer, the tool would come up with a set of indices and materialized views that could help the queries and updates in the compressed workload. Different combinations of these indices and materialized views can be tried out to find the best combination. However, an exhaustive approach would be totally impractical, since the number of potential indices and materialized views is already large, and each subset of these is a potential design alternative, leading to an exponential number of alternatives. Heuristics are used to reduce the space of alternatives, that is, to reduce the number of combinations considered.

Greedy heuristics for index and materialized view selection operate as follows: They estimate the benefits of materializing different indices or views (using the optimizer's cost estimation functionality as a subroutine). They then choose the index or view that gives either the maximum benefit or the maximum benefit per unit space (that is, benefit divided by the space required to store the index or view). The cost of maintaining the index or view must be taken into account when computing the benefit. Once the heuristic has selected an index or view, the benefits of other indices or views may have changed, so the heuristic recomputes these, and chooses the next best index or view for materialization. The process continues until either the available disk space for storing indices or materialized views is exhausted, or the cost of maintaining the remaining candidates is more than the benefit to queries that could use the indices or views.

Real-world index and materialized-view selection tools usually incorporate some elements of greedy selection, but use other techniques to get better results. They also support other aspects of physical database design, such as deciding how to partition a relation in a parallel database, or what physical storage mechanism to use for a relation.

24.1.10 Tuning of Concurrent Transactions

Concurrent execution of different types of transactions can sometimes lead to poor performance because of contention on locks. We first consider the case of read-write contention, which is more common, and then consider the case of write-write contention.

As an example of **read-write contention**, consider the following situation on a banking database. During the day, numerous small update transactions are executed almost continuously. Suppose that a large query that computes statistics on branches is run at the same time. If the query performs a scan on a relation, it may block out all updates on the relation while it runs, and that can have a disastrous effect on the performance of the system.

Several database systems—Oracle, PostgreSQL, and Microsoft SQL Server, for example— support snapshot isolation, whereby queries are executed on a snapshot of the data, and updates can go on concurrently. (Snapshot isolation is described in detail in Section 15.7.) Snapshot isolation should be used, if available, for large queries, to avoid lock contention in the above situation. In SQL Server, executing the statement

set transaction isolation level snapshot

at the beginning of a transaction results in snapshot isolation being used for that transaction. In Oracle and PostgreSQL, using the keyword **serializable** in place of the keyword **snapshot** in the above command has the same effect, since both these systems actually use snapshot isolation when the isolation level is set to serializable.

If snapshot isolation is not available, an alternative option is to execute large queries at times when updates are few or nonexistent. However, for databases supporting Web sites, there may be no such quiet period for updates.

Another alternative is to use weaker levels of consistency, such as the **read committed** isolation level, whereby evaluation of the query has a minimal impact on concurrent updates, but the query results are not guaranteed to be consistent. The application semantics determine whether approximate (inconsistent) answers are acceptable.

We now consider the case of **write-write contention**. Data items that are updated very frequently can result in poor performance with locking, with many transactions waiting for locks on those data items. Such data items are called **update hot spots**. Update hot spots can cause problems even with snapshot isolation, causing frequent transaction aborts due to write validation failures. A commonly occurring situation that results in an update hot spot is as follows: transactions need to assign unique identifiers to data items being inserted into the database, and to do so they read and increment a sequence counter stored in a tuple in the database. If inserts are frequent, and the sequence counter is locked in a two-phase manner, the tuple containing the sequence counter becomes a hot spot.

One way to improve concurrency is to release the lock on the sequence counter immediately after it is read and incremented; however, after doing so, even if the transaction aborts, the update to the sequence counter should not be rolled back. To understand why, suppose T_1 increments the sequence counter, and then T_2 increments the sequence counter before T_1 commits; if T_1 then aborts, rolling back its update, either by restoring the counter to the original value, or by decrementing the counter, will result in the sequence value used by T_2 getting reused by a subsequent transaction.

Most databases provide a special construct for creating **sequence counters** that implement early, non-two-phase, lock release, coupled with special case treatment of undo logging so that updates to the counter are not rolled back if the transaction aborts. The SQL standard allows a sequence counter to be created using the command:

create sequence *counter1*;

In the above command, *counter1* is the name of the sequence; multiple sequences can be created with different names. The syntax to get a value from the sequence is not standardized; in Oracle, *counter1.nextval* would return the next value of the sequence, after incrementing it, while the function call *nextval('counter1')* would have the same effect in PostgreSQL, and DB2 uses the syntax **nextval for** *counter1*.

The SQL standard provides an alternative to using an explicit sequence counter, which is useful when the goal is to give unique identifiers to tuples inserted into a relation. To do so, the keyword **identity** can be added to the declaration of an integer attribute of a relation (usually this attribute would also be declared as the primary key). If the value for that attribute is left unspecified in an insert statement for that relation, a unique new value is created automatically for each newly inserted tuple. A non-two-phase locked sequence counter is used internally to implement the **identity** declaration, with the counter incremented each time a tuple is inserted. Several databases including DB2 and SQL Server support the **identity** declaration, although the syntax varies. PostgreSQL supports a data type called **serial**, which provides the same effect; the PostgreSQL type **serial** is implemented by transparently creating a non-two-phase locked sequence.

It is worth noting that since the acquisition of a sequence number by a transaction cannot be rolled back if the transaction aborts (for reasons discussed earlier), transaction aborts may result in *gaps in the sequence numbers* in tuple inserted in the database. For example, there may be tuples with identifier value 1001 and 1003, but no tuple with value 1002, if the transaction that acquired the sequence number 1002 did not commit. Such gaps are not acceptable in some applications; for example, some financial applications require that there be no gaps in bill or receipt numbers. Database provided sequences and automatically incremented attributes should not be used for such applications, since they can result in gaps. A sequence counter stored in normal tuple, which is locked in a two-phase manner, would not be susceptible to such gaps since a transaction abort would restore the sequence counter value, and the next transaction would get the same sequence number, avoiding a gap.

Long update transactions can cause performance problems with system logs, and can increase the time taken to recover from system crashes. If a transaction performs many updates, the system log may become full even before the transaction completes, in which case the transaction will have to be rolled back. If an update transaction runs for a long time (even with few updates), it may block deletion of old parts of the log, if the logging system is not well designed. Again, this blocking could lead to the log getting filled up.

To avoid such problems, many database systems impose strict limits on the number of updates that a single transaction can carry out. Even if the system does not impose such limits, it is often helpful to break up a large update transaction into a set of smaller update transactions where possible. For example, a transaction that gives a raise to every employee in a large corporation could be split up into a series of small transactions, each of which updates a small range of employee-ids. Such transactions are called **minibatch transactions**. However, minibatch transactions must be used with care. First, if there are concurrent updates on the set of employees, the result of the set of smaller transactions may not be equivalent to that of the single large transaction. Second, if there is a failure, the salaries of some of the employees would have been increased by committed transactions, but salaries of other employees would not. To avoid this problem, as soon as the system recovers from failure, we must execute the transactions remaining in the batch.

Long transactions, whether read-only or update, can also result in the lock table becoming full. If a single query scans a large relation, the query optimizer would ensure that a relation lock is obtained instead of acquiring a large number of tuple locks. However, if a transaction executes a large number of small queries or updates, it may acquire a large number of locks, resulting in the lock table becoming full.

To avoid this problem, some databases provide for automatic **lock escalation**; with this technique, if a transaction has acquired a large number of tuple locks, tuple locks are upgraded to page locks, or even full relation locks. Recall that with multiple-granularity locking (Section 15.3), once a coarser level lock is obtained, there is no need to record finer-level locks, so tuple lock entries can be removed from the lock table, freeing up space. On databases that do not support lock escalation, it is possible for the transaction to explicitly acquire a relation lock, thereby avoiding the acquisition of tuple locks.

24.1.11   Performance Simulation

To test the performance of a database system even before it is installed, we can create a performance-simulation model of the database system. Each service shown in Figure 24.2, such as the CPU, each disk, the buffer, and the concurrency control, is modeled in the simulation. Instead of modeling details of a service, the simulation model may capture only some aspects of each service, such as the **service time**—that is, the time taken to finish processing a request once processing has begun. Thus, the simulation can model a disk access from just the average disk-access time.

Since requests for a service generally have to wait their turn, each service has an associated queue in the simulation model. A transaction consists of a series of requests. The requests are queued up as they arrive, and are serviced according to the policy for that service, such as first come, first served. The models for services such as CPU and the disks conceptually operate in parallel, to account for the fact that these subsystems operate in parallel in a real system.

Once the simulation model for transaction processing is built, the system administrator can run a number of experiments on it. The administrator can use experiments with simulated transactions arriving at different rates to find how the system would behave under various load conditions. The administrator could run other experiments that vary the service times for each service to find out how sensitive the performance is to each of them. System parameters, too, can be varied, so that performance tuning can be done on the simulation model.

24.2 Performance Benchmarks

As database servers become more standardized, the differentiating factor among the products of different vendors is those products' performance. **Performance benchmarks** are suites of tasks that are used to quantify the performance of software systems.

24.2.1 Suites of Tasks

Since most software systems, such as databases, are complex, there is a good deal of variation in their implementation by different vendors. As a result, there is a significant amount of variation in their performance on different tasks. One system may be the most efficient on a particular task; another may be the most efficient on a different task. Hence, a single task is usually insufficient to quantify the performance of the system. Instead, the performance of a system is measured by suites of standardized tasks, called *performance benchmarks*.

Combining the performance numbers from multiple tasks must be done with care. Suppose that we have two tasks, T_1 and T_2, and that we measure the throughput of a system as the number of transactions of each type that run in a given amount of time—say, 1 second. Suppose that system A runs T_1 at 99 transactions per second and T_2 at 1 transaction per second. Similarly, let system B run both T_1 and T_2 at 50 transactions per second. Suppose also that a workload has an equal mixture of the two types of transactions.

If we took the average of the two pairs of numbers (that is, 99 and 1, versus 50 and 50), it might appear that the two systems have equal performance. However, it is *wrong* to take the averages in this fashion—if we ran 50 transactions of each type, system A would take about 50.5 seconds to finish, whereas system B would finish in just 2 seconds!

The example shows that a simple measure of performance is misleading if there is more than one type of transaction. The right way to average out the numbers is to take the **time to completion** for the workload, rather than the average *throughput* for each transaction type. We can then compute system performance accurately in transactions per second for a specified workload. Thus, system A takes 50.5/100, which is 0.505 seconds per transaction, whereas system B takes 0.02 seconds per transaction, on average. In terms of throughput, system A runs at an average of 1.98 transactions per second, whereas system B runs at 50 transactions per second. Assuming that transactions of all the types are equally likely, the correct way to average out the throughputs on different transaction types is to take the **harmonic mean** of the throughputs. The harmonic mean of n throughputs $t_1, \ldots, t_n$ is defined as:

$$\frac{n}{\frac{1}{t_1} + \frac{1}{t_2} + \cdots + \frac{1}{t_n}}$$

For our example, the harmonic mean for the throughputs in system A is 1.98. For system B, it is 50. Thus, system B is approximately 25 times faster than system A on a workload consisting of an equal mixture of the two example types of transactions.

24.2.2   Database-Application Classes

Online transaction processing (OLTP) and **decision support**, including **online analytical processing** (OLAP), are two broad classes of applications handled by database systems. These two classes of tasks have different requirements. High concurrency and clever techniques to speed up commit processing are required for supporting a high rate of update transactions. On the other hand, good query-evaluation algorithms and query optimization are required for decision support. The architecture of some database systems has been tuned to transaction processing; that of others, such as the Teradata series of parallel database systems, has been tuned to decision support. Other vendors try to strike a balance between the two tasks.

Applications usually have a mixture of transaction-processing and decision-support requirements. Hence, which database system is best for an application depends on what mix of the two requirements the application has.

Suppose that we have throughput numbers for the two classes of applications separately, and the application at hand has a mix of transactions in the two classes. We must be careful even about taking the harmonic mean of the throughput numbers, because of **interference** between the transactions. For example, a long-running decision-support transaction may acquire a number of locks, which may prevent all progress of update transactions. The harmonic mean of throughputs should be used only if the transactions do not interfere with one another.

24.2.3   The TPC Benchmarks

The **Transaction Processing Performance Council** (TPC) has defined a series of benchmark standards for database systems.

The TPC benchmarks are defined in great detail. They define the set of relations and the sizes of the tuples. They define the number of tuples in the relations not as a fixed number, but rather as a multiple of the number of claimed transactions per second, to reflect that a larger rate of transaction execution is likely to be correlated with a larger number of accounts. The performance metric is throughput, expressed as **transactions per second** (TPS). When its performance is measured, the system must provide a response time within certain bounds, so that a high throughput cannot be obtained at the cost of very long response times.

Further, for business applications, cost is of great importance. Hence, the TPC benchmark also measures performance in terms of **price per TPS**. A large system may have a high number of transactions per second, but may be expensive (that is, have a high price per TPS). Moreover, a company cannot claim TPC benchmark numbers for its systems *without* an external audit that ensures that the system faithfully follows the definition of the benchmark, including full support for the ACID properties of transactions.

The first in the series was the **TPC-A benchmark**, which was defined in 1989. This benchmark simulates a typical bank application by a single type of transaction that models cash withdrawal and deposit at a bank teller. The transaction updates several relations—such as the bank balance, the teller's balance, and the customer's balance—and adds a record to an audit trail relation. The benchmark also incorporates communication with terminals, to model the end-to-end performance of the system realistically. The **TPC-B benchmark** was designed to test the core performance of the database system, along with the operating system on which the system runs. It removes the parts of the TPC-A benchmark that deal with users, communication, and terminals, to focus on the back-end database server. Neither TPC-A nor TPC-B is in use today.

The **TPC-C benchmark** was designed to model a more complex system than the TPC-A benchmark. The TPC-C benchmark concentrates on the main activities in an order-entry environment, such as entering and delivering orders, recording payments, checking status of orders, and monitoring levels of stock. The TPC-C benchmark is still widely used for benchmarking online transaction processing (OLTP) systems. The more recent TPC-E benchmark is also aimed at OLTP systems, but is based on a model of a brokerage firm, with customers who interact with the firm and generate transactions. The firm in turn interacts with financial markets to execute transactions.

The **TPC-D benchmark** was designed to test the performance of database systems on decision-support queries. Decision-support systems are becoming increasingly important today. The TPC-A, TPC-B, and TPC-C benchmarks measure performance on transaction-processing workloads, and should not be used as a measure of performance on decision-support queries. The D in TPC-D stands for **decision support**. The TPC-D benchmark schema models a sales/distribution application, with parts, suppliers, customers, and orders, along with some auxiliary information. The sizes of the relations are defined as a ratio, and database size is the total size of all the relations, expressed in gigabytes. TPC-D at scale factor 1 represents the TPC-D benchmark on a 1-gigabyte database, while scale factor 10 represents a 10-gigabyte database. The benchmark workload consists of a set of 17 SQL queries modeling common tasks executed on decision-support systems. Some of the queries make use of complex SQL features, such as aggregation and nested queries.

The benchmark's users soon realized that the various TPC-D queries could be significantly speeded up by using materialized views and other redundant information. There are applications, such as periodic reporting tasks, where the queries are known in advance and materialized view can be carefully selected to speed up the queries. It is necessary, however, to account for the overhead of maintaining materialized views.

The **TPC-H benchmark** (where H represents **ad hoc**) is a refinement of the TPC-D benchmark. The schema is the same, but there are 22 queries, of which 16 are from TPC-D. In addition, there are two updates, a set of inserts, and a set of deletes. TPC-H prohibits materialized views and other redundant information, and permits indices only on primary and foreign keys. This benchmark models ad hoc querying where the queries are not known beforehand, so it is not possible to create appropriate materialized views ahead of time. A variant, TPC-R (where R stands for "reporting"), which is no longer in use, allowed the use of materialized views and other redundant information.

TPC-H measures performance in this way: The **power test** runs the queries and updates one at a time sequentially, and 3600 seconds divided by the geometric mean of the execution times of the queries (in seconds) gives a measure of queries per hour. The **throughput test** runs multiple streams in parallel, with each stream executing all 22 queries. There is also a parallel update stream. Here the total time for the entire run is used to compute the number of queries per hour.

The **composite query per hour metric**, which is the overall metric, is then obtained as the square root of the product of the power and throughput metrics. A **composite price/performance metric** is defined by dividing the system price by the composite metric.

The **TPC-W Web commerce benchmark** is an end-to-end benchmark that models Web sites having static content (primarily images) and dynamic content generated from a database. Caching of dynamic content is specifically permitted, since it is very useful for speeding up Web sites. The benchmark models an electronic bookstore, and like other TPC benchmarks, provides for different scale factors. The primary performance metrics are **Web interactions per second (WIPS)** and price per WIPS. However, the TPC-W benchmark is no longer in use.

24.3 Other Issues in Application Development

In this section, we discuss two issues in application development: testing of applications, and migration of applications.

24.3.1 Testing Applications

Testing of programs involves designing a **test suite**, that is, a collection of test cases. Testing is not a one-time process, since programs evolve continuously, and bugs may appear as an unintended consequence of a change in the program; such a bug is referred to as program **regression**. Thus, after every change to a program, the program must be tested again. It is usually infeasible to have a human perform tests after every change to a program. Instead, expected test outputs are stored with each test case in a test suite. **Regression testing** involves running the program on each test case in a test suite, and checking that the program generates the expected test output.

In the context of database applications, a test case consists of two parts: a database state, and an input to a specific interface of the application.

SQL queries can have subtle bugs that can be difficult to catch. For example, a query may execute $r \bowtie s$, when it should have actually performed $r \rightinnerjoin s$. The difference between these two queries would be found only if the test database had an r tuple with no matching s tuple. Thus, it is important to create test databases that can catch commonly occurring errors. Such errors are referred to as **mutations**, since they are usually small changes to a query (or program). A test case that produces different outputs on an intended query and a mutant of the query is said to **kill the mutant**. A test suite should have test cases that kill (most) commonly occurring mutants.

If a test case performs an update on the database, to check that it executed properly one must verify that the contents of the database match the expected contents. Thus, the expected output consists not only of data displayed on the user's screen, but also (updates to) the database state.

Since the database state can be rather large, multiple test cases would share a common database state. Testing is complicated by the fact that if a test case performs an update on the database, the results of other test cases run subsequently on the same database may not match the expected results. The other test cases would then be erroneously reported as having failed. To avoid this problem, whenever a test case performs an update, the database state must be restored to its original state after running the test.

Testing can also be used to ensure that an application meets performance requirements. To carry out such **performance testing**, the test database must be of the same size as the real database would be. In some cases, there is already existing data on which performance testing can be carried out. In other cases, a test database of the required size must be generated; there are several tools available for generating such test databases. These tools ensure that the generated data satisfies constraints such as primary and foreign key constraints. They may additionally generate data that looks meaningful, for example, by populating a name attribute using meaningful names instead of random strings. Some tools also allow data distributions to be specified; for example, a university database may require a distribution with most students in the range of 18 to 25 years, and most faculty in the range of 25 to 65 years.

Even if there is an existing database, organizations usually do not want to reveal sensitive data to an external organization that may be carrying out the performance tests. In such a situation, a copy of the real database may be made, and the values in the copy may be modified in such a way that any sensitive data, such as credit-card numbers, social-security numbers, or dates of birth, are **obfuscated**. Obfuscation is done in most cases by replacing a real value with a randomly generated value (taking care to also update all references to that value, in case the value is a primary key). On the other hand, if the application execution depends on the value, such as the date of birth in an application that performs different actions based on the date of birth, obfuscation may make small random changes in the value instead of replacing it completely.

24.3.2   Application Migration

Legacy systems are older-generation application systems that are in use by an organization, but that the organization wishes to replace with a different application. For example, many organizations developed applications in house, but may decide to replace them with a commercial product. In some cases, a legacy system may use old technology that is incompatible with current-generation standards and systems. Some legacy systems in operation today are several decades old and are based on technologies such as databases that use the network or hierarchical data models, or use Cobol and file systems without a database. Such systems may still contain valuable data, and may support critical applications.

Replacing legacy applications with new applications is often costly in terms of both time and money, since they are often very large, consisting of millions of lines of code developed by teams of programmers, often over several decades. They contain large amounts of data that must be ported to the new application, which may use a completely different schema. Switchover from an old to a new application involves retraining large numbers of staff. Switchover must usually be done without any disruption, with data entered in the old system available through the new system as well.

Many organizations attempt to avoid replacing legacy systems, and instead try to interoperate them with newer systems. One approach used to interoperate between relational databases and legacy databases is to build a layer, called a **wrapper**, on top of the legacy systems that can make the legacy system appear to be a relational database. The wrapper may provide support for ODBC or other interconnection standards such as OLE-DB, which can be used to query and update the legacy system. The wrapper is responsible for converting relational queries and updates into queries and updates on the legacy system.

When an organization decides to replace a legacy system with a new system, it may follow a process called **reverse engineering**, which consists of going over the code of the legacy system to come up with schema designs in the required data model (such as an E-R model or an object-oriented data model). Reverse engineering also examines the code to find out what procedures and processes were implemented, in order to get a high-level model of the system. Reverse engineering is needed because legacy systems usually do not have high-level documentation of their schema and overall system design. When coming up with the design of a new system, developers review the design, so that it can be improved rather than just reimplemented as is. Extensive coding is required to support all the functionality (such as user interface and reporting systems) that was provided by the legacy system. The overall process is called **re-engineering**.

When a new system has been built and tested, the system must be populated with data from the legacy system, and all further activities must be carried out on the new system. However, abruptly transitioning to a new system, which is called the **big-bang approach**, carries several risks. First, users may not be familiar with the interfaces of the new system. Second, there may be bugs or performance problems in the new system that were not discovered when it was tested. Such problems may lead to great losses for companies, since their ability to carry out critical transactions such as sales and purchases may be severely affected. In some extreme cases the new system has even been abandoned, and the legacy system reused, after an attempted switchover failed.

An alternative approach, called the **chicken-little approach**, incrementally replaces the functionality of the legacy system. For example, the new user interfaces may be used with the old system in the back end, or vice versa. Another option is to use the new system only for some functionality that can be decoupled from the legacy system. In either case, the legacy and new systems coexist for some time. There is therefore a need for developing and using wrappers on the legacy system to provide required functionality to interoperate with the new system. This approach therefore has a higher development cost associated with it.

24.4 Standardization

Standards define the interface of a software system; for example, standards define the syntax and semantics of a programming language, or the functions in an application-program interface, or even a data model (such as the object-oriented database standards). Today, database systems are complex, and are often made up of multiple independently created parts that need to interact. For example, client programs may be created independently of back-end systems, but the two must be able to interact with each other. A company that has multiple heterogeneous database systems may need to exchange data between the databases. Given such a scenario, standards play an important role.

Formal standards are those developed by a standards organization or by industry groups, through a public process. Dominant products sometimes become **de facto standards**, in that they become generally accepted as standards without any formal process of recognition. Some formal standards, like many aspects of the SQL-92 and SQL:1999 standards, are **anticipatory standards** that lead the marketplace; they define features that vendors then implement in products. In other cases, the standards, or parts of the standards, are **reactionary standards**, in that they attempt to standardize features that some vendors have already implemented, and that may even have become de facto standards. SQL-89 was in many ways reactionary, since it standardized features, such as integrity checking, that were already present in the IBM SAA SQL standard and in other databases.

Formal standards committees are typically composed of representatives of the vendors and of members from user groups and standards organizations such as the International Organization for Standardization (ISO) or the American National Standards Institute (ANSI), or professional bodies, such as the Institute of Electrical and Electronics Engineers (IEEE). Formal standards committees meet periodically, and members present proposals for features to be added to or modified in the standard. After a (usually extended) period of discussion, modifications to the proposal, and public review, members vote on whether to accept or reject a feature. Some time after a standard has been defined and implemented, its shortcomings become clear and new requirements become apparent. The process of updating the standard then begins, and a new version of the standard is usually released after a few years. This cycle usually repeats every few years, until eventually (perhaps many years later) the standard becomes technologically irrelevant, or loses its user base.

The DBTG CODASYL standard for network databases, formulated by the Database Task Group, was one of the early formal standards for databases. IBM database products formerly established de facto standards, since IBM commanded much of the database market. With the growth of relational databases came a number of new entrants in the database business; hence, the need for formal standards arose. In recent years, Microsoft has created a number of specifications that also have become de facto standards. A notable example is ODBC, which is now used in non-Microsoft environments. JDBC, whose specification was created by Sun Microsystems, is another widely used de facto standard.

This section gives a very high-level overview of different standards, concentrating on the goals of the standard. The bibliographical notes at the end of the chapter provide references to detailed descriptions of the standards mentioned in this section.

24.4.1   SQL Standards

Since SQL is the most widely used query language, much work has been done on standardizing it. ANSI and ISO, with the various database vendors, have played a leading role in this work. The SQL-86 standard was the initial version. The IBM Systems Application Architecture (SAA) standard for SQL was released in 1987. As people identified the need for more features, updated versions of the formal SQL standard were developed, called SQL-89 and SQL-92.

The SQL:1999 version of the SQL standard added a variety of features to SQL. We have seen many of these features in earlier chapters. The SQL:2003 version of the SQL standard is a minor extension of the SQL:1999 standard. Some features such as the SQL:1999 OLAP features (Section 5.6.3) were specified as an amendment to the earlier version of the SQL:1999 standard, instead of waiting for the release of SQL:2003.

The SQL:2003 standard was broken into several parts:

- Part 1: SQL/Framework provides an overview of the standard.

- Part 2: SQL/Foundation defines the basics of the standard: types, schemas, tables, views, query and update statements, expressions, security model, predicates, assignment rules, transaction management, and so on.

- Part 3: SQL/CLI (Call Level Interface) defines application program interfaces to SQL.

- Part 4: SQL/PSM (Persistent Stored Modules) defines extensions to SQL to make it procedural.

- Part 9: SQL/MED (Management of External Data) defines standards or interfacing an SQL system to external sources. By writing wrappers, system designers can treat external data sources, such as files or data in nonrelational databases, as if they were "foreign" tables.

- Part 10: SQL/OLB (Object Language Bindings) defines standards for embedding SQL in Java.

- Part 11: SQL/Schemata (Information and Definition Schema) defines a standard catalog interface.

- Part 13: SQL/JRT (Java Routines and Types) defines standards for accessing routines and types in Java.

- Part 14: SQL/XML defines XML-Related Specifications.

The missing numbers cover features such as temporal data, distributed transaction processing, and multimedia data, for which there is as yet no agreement on the standards.

The latest versions of the SQL standard are SQL:2006, which added several features related to XML, and SQL:2008, which introduces a number of extensions to the SQL language.

24.4.2 Database Connectivity Standards

The **ODBC** standard is a widely used standard for communication between client applications and database systems. ODBC is based on the SQL **Call Level Interface (CLI)** standards developed by the **X/Open** industry consortium and the SQL Access Group, but it has several extensions. The ODBC API defines a CLI, an SQL syntax definition, and rules about permissible sequences of CLI calls. The standard also defines conformance levels for the CLI and the SQL syntax. For example, the core level of the CLI has commands to connect to a database, to prepare and execute SQL statements, to get back results or status values, and to manage transactions. The next level of conformance (level 1) requires support for catalog information retrieval and some other features over and above the core-level CLI; level 2 requires further features, such as ability to send and retrieve arrays of parameter values and to retrieve more detailed catalog information.

ODBC allows a client to connect simultaneously to multiple data sources and to switch among them, but transactions on each are independent; ODBC does not support two-phase commit.

A distributed system provides a more general environment than a client–server system. The X/Open consortium has also developed the **X/Open XA standards** for interoperation of databases. These standards define transaction-management primitives (such as transaction begin, commit, abort, and prepare-to-commit) that compliant databases should provide; a transaction manager can invoke these primitives to implement distributed transactions by two-phase commit. The XA standards are independent of the data model and of the specific interfaces between clients and databases to exchange data. Thus, we can use the XA protocols to implement a distributed transaction system in which a single transaction can access relational as well as object-oriented databases, yet the transaction manager ensures global consistency via two-phase commit.

There are many data sources that are not relational databases, and in fact may not be databases at all. Examples are flat files and email stores. Microsoft's **OLE-DB** is a C++ API with goals similar to ODBC, but for nondatabase data sources that may provide only limited querying and update facilities. Just like ODBC, OLE-DB provides constructs for connecting to a data source, starting a session, executing commands, and getting back results in the form of a rowset, which is a set of result rows.

However, OLE-DB differs from ODBC in several ways. To support data sources with limited feature support, features in OLE-DB are divided into a number of interfaces, and a data source may implement only a subset of the interfaces. An OLE-DB program can negotiate with a data source to find what interfaces are supported. In ODBC commands are always in SQL. In OLE-DB, commands may be in any language supported by the data source; while some sources may support SQL, or a limited subset of SQL, other sources may provide only simple capabilities such as accessing data in a flat file, without any query capability. Another major difference of OLE-DB from ODBC is that a rowset is an object that can be shared by multiple applications through shared memory. A rowset object can be updated by one application, and other applications sharing that object will get notified about the change.

The **Active Data Objects (ADO)** API, also created by Microsoft, provides an easy-to-use interface to the OLE-DB functionality, which can be called from scripting languages, such as VBScript and JScript. The newer **ADO.NET** API is designed for applications written in the .NET languages such as C# and Visual Basic.NET. In addition to providing simplified interfaces, it provides an abstraction called the *DataSet* that permits disconnected data access.

24.4.3   Object Database Standards

Standards in the area of object-oriented databases have so far been driven primarily by OODB vendors. The **Object Database Management Group** (ODMG) was a group formed by OODB vendors to standardize the data model and language interfaces to OODBs. The C++ language interface specified by ODMG was briefly outlined in Chapter 22. ODMG is no longer active. JDO is a standard for adding persistence to Java.

The **Object Management Group** (OMG) is a consortium of companies, formed with the objective of developing a standard architecture for distributed software applications based on the object-oriented model. OMG brought out the *Object Management Architecture* (OMA) reference model. The *Object Request Broker* (ORB) is a component of the OMA architecture that provides message dispatch to distributed objects transparently, so the physical location of the object is not important. The **Common Object Request Broker Architecture** (CORBA) provides a detailed specification of the ORB, and includes an **Interface Description Language** (IDL), which is used to define the data types used for data interchange. The IDL helps to support data conversion when data are shipped between systems with different data representations.

Microsoft introduced the **Entity data model**, which incorporates ideas from the entity-relationship and object-oriented data models, and an approach to integrating querying with the programming language, called **Language Integrated Querying** or **LINQ**. These are likely to become de facto standards.

24.4.4 XML-Based Standards

A wide variety of standards based on XML (see Chapter 23) have been defined for a wide variety of applications. Many of these standards are related to e-commerce. They include standards promulgated by nonprofit consortia and corporate-backed efforts to create de facto standards.

RosettaNet, which falls into the former category, is an industry consortium that uses XML-based standards to facilitate supply-chain management in the computer and information technology industries. Supply-chain management refers to the purchases of material and services that an organization needs to function. In contrast, customer-relationship management refers to the front end of a company's interaction, dealing with customers. Supply-chain management requires standardization of a variety of things such as:

- **Global company identifier:** RosettaNet specifies a system for uniquely identifying companies, using a 9-digit identifier called *Data Universal Numbering System* (DUNS).

- **Global product identifier:** RosettaNet specifies a 14-digit *Global Trade Item Number* (GTIN) for identifying products and services.

- **Global class identifier:** This is a 10-digit hierarchical code for classifying products and services called the *United Nations/Standard Product and Services Code* (UN/SPSC).

- **Interfaces between trading partners:** RosettaNet *Partner Interface Processes* (PIPs) define business processes between partners. PIPs are system-to-system XML-based dialogs: They define the formats and semantics of business documents involved in a process and the steps involved in completing a transaction. Examples of steps could include getting product and service information, purchase orders, order invoicing, payment, order status requests, inventory management, post-sales support including service warranty, and so on. Exchange of design, configuration, process, and quality information is also possible to coordinate manufacturing activities across organizations.

Participants in electronic marketplaces may store data in a variety of database systems. These systems may use different data models, data formats, and data types. Furthermore, there may be semantic differences (metric versus English measure, distinct monetary currencies, and so forth) in the data. Standards for electronic marketplaces include methods for *wrapping* each of these heterogeneous systems with an XML schema. These XML *wrappers* form the basis of a unified view of data across all of the participants in the marketplace.

Simple Object Access Protocol (SOAP) is a remote procedure call standard that uses XML to encode data (both parameters and results), and uses HTTP as the transport protocol; that is, a procedure call becomes an HTTP request. SOAP is backed by the World Wide Web Consortium (W3C) and has gained wide acceptance in industry. SOAP can be used in a variety of applications. For instance, in business-to-business e-commerce, applications running at one site can access data from and execute actions at other sites through SOAP.

SOAP and Web services were described in more detail in Section 23.7.3.

24.5   Summary

- Tuning of the database-system parameters, as well as the higher-level database design—such as the schema, indices, and transactions—is important for good performance. Queries can be tuned to improve set-orientation, while bulk-loading utilities can greatly speed up data import into a database.

  Tuning is best done by identifying bottlenecks and eliminating them. Database systems usually have a variety of tunable parameters, such as buffer sizes, memory size, and number of disks. The set of indices and materialized views can be appropriately chosen to minimize overall cost. Transactions can be tuned to minimize lock contention; snapshot isolation, and sequence numbering facilities supporting early lock release are useful tools for reducing read-write and write-write contention.

- Performance benchmarks play an important role in comparisons of database systems, especially as systems become more standards compliant. The TPC benchmark suites are widely used, and the different TPC benchmarks are useful for comparing the performance of databases under different workloads.

- Applications need to be tested extensively as they are developed, and before they are deployed. Testing is used to catch errors, as well as to ensure that performance goals are met.

- Legacy systems are systems based on older-generation technologies such as nonrelational databases or even directly on file systems. Interfacing legacy systems with new-generation systems is often important when they run mission-critical systems. Migrating from legacy systems to new-generation systems must be done carefully to avoid disruptions, which can be very expensive.

- Standards are important because of the complexity of database systems and their need for interoperation. Formal standards exist for SQL. De facto standards, such as ODBC and JDBC, and standards adopted by industry groups, such as CORBA, have played an important role in the growth of client–server database systems.

Review Terms

- Performance tuning
- Set-orientation
- Batch update (JDBC)
- Bulk load
- Bulk update
- Merge statement
- Bottlenecks
- Queueing systems
- Tunable parameters
- Tuning of hardware
- Five-minute rule
- One-minute rule
- Tuning of the schema
- Tuning of indices
- Materialized views
- Immediate view maintenance
- Deferred view maintenance
- Tuning of transactions
- Lock contention
- Sequences
- Minibatch transactions
- Performance simulation
- Performance benchmarks
- Service time
- Time to completion
- Database-application classes
- The TPC benchmarks
  - TPC-A
  - TPC-B
  - TPC-C
  - TPC-D
  - TPC-E
  - TPC-H
- Web interactions per second
- Regression testing
- Killing mutants
- Legacy systems
- Reverse engineering
- Re-engineering
- Standardization
  - Formal standards
  - De facto standards
  - Anticipatory standards
  - Reactionary standards
- Database connectivity standards
  - ODBC
  - OLE-DB
  - X/Open XA standards
- Object database standards
  - ODMG
  - CORBA
- XML-based standards

Practice Exercises

24.1 Many applications need to generate sequence numbers for each transaction.

  a. If a sequence counter is locked in two-phase manner, it can become a concurrency bottleneck. Explain why this may be the case.

       b.   Many database systems support built-in sequence counters that are not locked in two-phase manner; when a transaction requests a sequence number, the counter is locked, incremented and unlocked.

          i.   Explain how such counters can improve concurrency.

         ii.   Explain why there may be gaps in the sequence numbers belonging to the final set of committed transactions.

24.2   Suppose you are given a relation $r(a, b, c)$.

     a.   Give an example of a situation under which the performance of equality selection queries on attribute a can be greatly affected by how r is clustered.

     b.   Suppose you also had range selection queries on attribute b. Can you cluster r in such a way that the equality selection queries on $r.a$ and the range selection queries on $r.b$ can both be answered efficiently? Explain your answer.

     c.   If clustering as above is not possible, suggest how both types of queries can be executed efficiently by choosing appropriate indices, assuming your database supports index-only plans (that is, if all information required for a query is available in an index, the database can generate a plan that uses the index but does not access the relation).

24.3   Suppose that a database application does not appear to have a single bottleneck; that is, CPU and disk utilization are both high, and all database queues are roughly balanced. Does that mean the application cannot be tuned further? Explain your answer.

24.4   Suppose a system runs three types of transactions. Transactions of type A run at the rate of 50 per second, transactions of type B run at 100 per second, and transactions of type C run at 200 per second. Suppose the mix of transactions has 25 percent of type A, 25 percent of type B, and 50 percent of type C.

     a.   What is the average transaction throughput of the system, assuming there is no interference between the transactions?

     b.   What factors may result in interference between the transactions of different types, leading to the calculated throughput being incorrect?

24.5   List some benefits and drawbacks of an anticipatory standard compared to a reactionary standard.

Exercises

24.6   Find out all performance information your favorite database system provides. Look for at least the following: what queries are currently executing or executed recently, what resources each of them consumed (CPU and I/O), what fraction of page requests resulted in buffer misses (for each query, if available), and what locks have a high degree of contention. You may also be able to get information about CPU and I/O utilization from the operating system.

24.7   a.   What are the three broad levels at which a database system can be tuned to improve performance?

   b.   Give two examples of how tuning can be done for each of the levels.

24.8   When carrying out performance tuning, should you try to tune your hardware (by adding disks or memory) first, or should you try to tune your transactions (by adding indices or materialized views) first? Explain your answer.

24.9   Suppose that your application has transactions that each access and update a single tuple in a very large relation stored in a B^+-tree file organization. Assume that all internal nodes of the B^+-tree are in memory, but only a very small fraction of the leaf pages can fit in memory. Explain how to calculate the minimum number of disks required to support a workload of 1000 transactions per second. Also calculate the required number of disks, using values for disk parameters given in Section 10.2.

24.10   What is the motivation for splitting a long transaction into a series of small ones? What problems could arise as a result, and how can these problems be averted?

24.11   Suppose the price of memory falls by half, and the speed of disk access (number of accesses per second) doubles, while all other factors remain the same. What would be the effect of this change on the 5-minute and 1-minute rules?

24.12   List at least four features of the TPC benchmarks that help make them realistic and dependable measures.

24.13   Why was the TPC-D benchmark replaced by the TPC-H and TPC-R benchmarks?

24.14   Explain what application characteristics would help you decide which of TPC-C, TPC-H, or TPC-R best models the application.

Bibliographical Notes

The classic text on queueing theory is Kleinrock [1975].

An early proposal for a database-system benchmark (the Wisconsin benchmark) was made by Bitton et al. [1983]. The TPC-A, -B, and -C benchmarks are described in Gray [1991]. An online version of all the TPC benchmark descriptions, as well as benchmark results, is available on the World Wide Web at the URL www.tpc.org; the site also contains up-to-date information about new benchmark proposals. The OO1 benchmark for OODBs is described in Cattell and Skeen [1992]; the OO7 benchmark is described in Carey et al. [1993].

Shasha and Bonnet [2002] provides detailed coverage of database tuning. O'Neil and O'Neil [2000] provides a very good textbook coverage of performance measurement and tuning. The 5-minute and 1-minute rules are described in Gray and Graefe [1997], and more recently extended to consider combinations of main memory, flash, and disk, in Graefe [2008].

Index selection and materialized view selection are addressed by Ross et al. [1996], Chaudhuri and Narasayya [1997], Agrawal et al. [2000], and Mistry et al. [2001]. Zilio et al. [2004], Dageville et al. [2004], and Agrawal et al. [2004] describe tuning support in IBM DB2, Oracle and Microsoft SQL Server.

Information about ODBC, OLE-DB, ADO, and ADO.NET can be found on the Web site www.microsoft.com/data and in a number of books on the subject that can be found through www.amazon.com. *ACM Sigmod Record*, which is published quarterly, has a regular section on standards in databases.

A wealth of information on XML-based standards and tools is available online on the Web site www.w3c.org. Information about RosettaNet can be found on the Web at www.rosettanet.org.

Business process re-engineering is covered by Cook [1996]. Umar [1997] covers re-engineering and issues in dealing with legacy systems.

CHAPTER 25

Spatial and Temporal Data and Mobility

For most of the history of databases, the types of data stored in databases were relatively simple, and this was reflected in the rather limited support for data types in earlier versions of SQL. Over time, however, there developed increasing need for handling more complex data types in databases, such as temporal data, spatial data, and multimedia data.

Another major trend has created its own set of issues: the growth of mobile computers, starting with laptop computers and pocket organizers and extending in more recent years to mobile phones with built-in computers and a variety of wearable computers that are increasingly used in commercial applications.

In this chapter, we study several data types and other database issues dealing with these applications.

25.1 Motivation

Before we address each of the topics in detail, we summarize the motivation for, and some important issues in dealing with, each of these types of data.

- **Temporal data**. Most database systems model the current state of the world, for instance, current customers, current students, and courses currently being offered. In many applications, it is very important to store and retrieve information about past states. Historical information can be incorporated manually into a schema design. However, the task is greatly simplified by database support for temporal data, which we study in Section 25.2.

- **Spatial data**. Spatial data include **geographic data**, such as maps and associated information, and **computer-aided-design data**, such as integrated-circuit designs or building designs. Applications of spatial data initially stored data as files in a file system, as did early-generation business applications. But as the complexity and volume of the data, and the number of users, have grown, ad hoc approaches to storing and retrieving data in a file system have proved insufficient for the needs of many applications that use spatial data.

Spatial-data applications require facilities offered by a database system—in particular, the ability to store and query large amounts of data efficiently. Some applications may also require other database features, such as atomic updates to parts of the stored data, durability, and concurrency control. In Section 25.3, we study the extensions needed in traditional database systems to support spatial data.

- **Multimedia data**. In Section 25.4, we study the features required in database systems that store multimedia data such as image, video, and audio data. The main distinguishing feature of video and audio data is that the display of the data requires retrieval at a steady, predetermined rate; hence, such data are called **continuous-media data**.

- **Mobile databases**. In Section 25.5, we study the database requirements of mobile computing systems, such as laptop and netbook computers and high-end cell phones that are connected to base stations via wireless digital communication networks. Such computers may need to be able to operate while disconnected from the network, unlike the distributed database systems discussed in Chapter 19. They also have limited storage capacity, and thus require special techniques for memory management.

25.2   Time in Databases

A database models the state of some aspect of the real world outside itself. Typically, databases model only one state—the current state—of the real world, and do not store information about past states, except perhaps as audit trails. When the state of the real world changes, the database gets updated, and information about the old state gets lost. However, in many applications, it is important to store and retrieve information about past states. For example, a patient database must store information about the medical history of a patient. A factory monitoring system may store information about current and past readings of sensors in the factory, for analysis. Databases that store information about states of the real world across time are called **temporal databases**.

When considering the issue of time in database systems, we must distinguish between time as measured by the system and time as observed in the real world. The **valid time** for a fact is the set of time intervals during which the fact is true in the real world. The **transaction time** for a fact is the time interval during which the fact is current within the database system. This latter time is based on the transaction serialization order and is generated automatically by the system. Note that valid-time intervals, being a real-world concept, cannot be generated automatically and must be provided to the system.

A **temporal relation** is one where each tuple has an associated time when it is true; the time may be either valid time or transaction time. Of course, both valid time and transaction time can be stored, in which case the relation is said

ID	name	dept_name	salary	from	to
10101	Srinivasan	Comp. Sci.	61000	2007/1/1	2007/12/31
10101	Srinivasan	Comp. Sci.	65000	2008/1/1	2008/12/31
12121	Wu	Finance	82000	2005/1/1	2006/12/31
12121	Wu	Finance	87000	2007/1/1	2007/12/31
12121	Wu	Finance	90000	2008/1/1	2008/12/31
98345	Kim	Elec. Eng.	80000	2005/1/1	2008/12/31

Figure 25.1 A temporal *instructor* relation.

to be a **bitemporal relation**. Figure 25.1 shows an example of a temporal relation. To simplify the representation, each tuple has only one time interval associated with it; thus, a tuple is represented once for every disjoint time interval in which it is true. Intervals are shown here as a pair of attributes *from* and *to*; an actual implementation would have a structured type, perhaps called *Interval*, that contains both fields. Note that some of the tuples have a "*" in the *to* time column; these asterisks indicate that the tuple is true until the value in the *to* time column is changed; thus, the tuple is true at the current time. Although times are shown in textual form, they are stored internally in a more compact form, such as the number of seconds since some fixed time on a fixed date (such as 12:00 A.M., January 1, 1900) that can be translated back to the normal textual form.

25.2.1 Time Specification in SQL

The SQL standard defines the types **date**, **time**, and **timestamp** as we saw in Chapter 4. The type **date** contains four digits for the year (1–9999), two digits for the month (1–12), and two digits for the date (1–31). The type **time** contains two digits for the hour, two digits for the minute, and two digits for the second, plus optional fractional digits. The seconds field can go beyond 60, to allow for leap seconds that are added during some years to correct for small variations in the speed of rotation of Earth. The type **timestamp** contains the fields of **date** and **time**, with six fractional digits for the seconds field.

Since different places in the world have different local times, there is often a need for specifying the time zone along with the time. The **Universal Coordinated Time** (UTC) is a standard reference point for specifying time, with local times defined as offsets from UTC. (The standard abbreviation is UTC, rather than UCT, since it is an abbreviation of "Universal Coordinated Time" written in French as *universel temps coordonné*.) SQL also supports two types, **time with time zone**, and **timestamp with time zone**, which specify the time as a local time plus the offset of the local time from UTC. For instance, the time could be expressed in terms of U.S. Eastern Standard Time, with an offset of −6:00, since U.S. Eastern Standard time is 6 hours behind UTC.

SQL supports a type called **interval**, which allows us to refer to a period of time such as "1 day" or "2 days and 5 hours," without specifying a particular time when this period starts. This notion differs from the notion of interval we used previously, which refers to an interval of time with specific starting and ending times.[1]

25.2.2 Temporal Query Languages

A database relation without temporal information is sometimes called a **snapshot relation**, since it reflects the state in a snapshot of the real world. Thus, a snapshot of a temporal relation at a point in time t is the set of tuples in the relation that are true at time t, with the time-interval attributes projected out. The snapshot operation on a temporal relation gives the snapshot of the relation at a specified time (or the current time, if the time is not specified).

A **temporal selection** is a selection that involves the time attributes; a **temporal projection** is a projection where the tuples in the projection inherit their times from the tuples in the original relation. A **temporal join** is a join, with the time of a tuple in the result being the intersection of the times of the tuples from which it is derived. If the times do not intersect, the tuple is removed from the result.

The predicates *precedes*, *overlaps*, and *contains* can be applied on intervals; their meanings should be clear. The *intersect* operation can be applied on two intervals, to give a single (possibly empty) interval. However, the union of two intervals may or may not be a single interval.

Functional dependencies must be used with care in a temporal relation, as we saw in Section 8.9. Although the instructor *ID* may functionally determine the salary at any given point in time, obviously the salary can change over time. A **temporal functional dependency** $X \xrightarrow{\text{T}} Y$ holds on a relation schema R if, for all legal instances r of R, all snapshots of r satisfy the functional dependency $X \rightarrow Y$.

Several proposals have been made for extending SQL to improve its support of temporal data, but at least until SQL:2008, SQL has not provided any special support for temporal data beyond the time-related data types and operations.

25.3   Spatial and Geographic Data

Spatial data support in databases is important for efficiently storing, indexing, and querying of data on the basis of spatial locations. For example, suppose that we want to store a set of polygons in a database and to query the database to find all polygons that intersect a given polygon. We cannot use standard index structures, such as B-trees or hash indices, to answer such a query efficiently. Efficient processing of the above query would require special-purpose index structures, such as R-trees (which we study later) for the task.

Two types of spatial data are particularly important:

- **Computer-aided-design (CAD) data**, which includes spatial information about how objects—such as buildings, cars, or aircraft—are constructed. Other im-

---

[1]Many temporal database researchers feel this type should have been called **span** since it does not specify an exact start or end time, only the time span between the two.

portant examples of computer-aided-design databases are integrated-circuit and electronic-device layouts.

- **Geographic data** such as road maps, land-usage maps, topographic elevation maps, political maps showing boundaries, land-ownership maps, and so on. **Geographic information systems** are special-purpose databases tailored for storing geographic data.

Support for geographic data has been added to many database systems, such as the IBM DB2 Spatial Extender, the Informix Spatial Datablade, and Oracle Spatial.

25.3.1 Representation of Geometric Information

Figure 25.2 illustrates how various geometric constructs can be represented in a database, in a normalized fashion. We stress here that geometric information can be represented in several different ways, only some of which we describe.

A *line segment* can be represented by the coordinates of its endpoints. For example, in a map database, the two coordinates of a point would be its latitude and longitude. A **polyline** (also called a **linestring**) consists of a connected sequence of line segments and can be represented by a list containing the coordinates of the endpoints of the segments, in sequence. We can approximately represent an arbitrary curve by polylines, by partitioning the curve into a sequence of segments. This representation is useful for two-dimensional features such as roads; here, the width of the road is small enough relative to the size of the full map that it can be considered to be a line. Some systems also support *circular arcs* as primitives, allowing curves to be represented as sequences of arcs.

We can represent a *polygon* by listing its vertices in order, as in Figure 25.2.[2] The list of vertices specifies the boundary of a polygonal region. In an alternative representation, a polygon can be divided into a set of triangles, as shown in Figure 25.2. This process is called **triangulation**, and any polygon can be triangulated. The complex polygon can be given an identifier, and each of the triangles into which it is divided carries the identifier of the polygon. Circles and ellipses can be represented by corresponding types, or can be approximated by polygons.

List-based representations of polylines or polygons are often convenient for query processing. Such non-first-normal-form representations are used when supported by the underlying database. So that we can use fixed-size tuples (in first normal form) for representing polylines, we can give the polyline or curve an identifier, and can represent each segment as a separate tuple that also carries with it the identifier of the polyline or curve. Similarly, the triangulated representation of polygons allows a first normal form relational representation of polygons.

The representation of points and line segments in three-dimensional space is similar to their representation in two-dimensional space, the only difference being that points have an extra z component. Similarly, the representation of planar figures—such as triangles, rectangles, and other polygons—does not change

---

[2]Some references use the term *closed polygon* to refer to what we call polygons, and refer to polylines as open polygons.

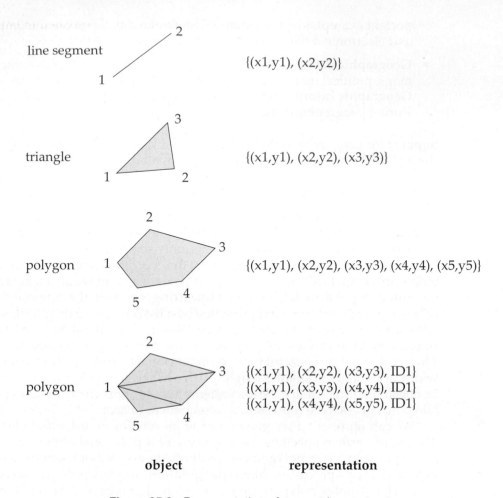

line segment   {(x1,y1), (x2,y2)}

triangle   {(x1,y1), (x2,y2), (x3,y3)}

polygon   {(x1,y1), (x2,y2), (x3,y3), (x4,y4), (x5,y5)}

polygon   {(x1,y1), (x2,y2), (x3,y3), ID1}
                                                {(x1,y1), (x3,y3), (x4,y4), ID1}
                                                {(x1,y1), (x4,y4), (x5,y5), ID1}

object   **representation**

Figure 25.2 Representation of geometric constructs.

much when we move to three dimensions. Tetrahedrons and cuboids can be represented in the same way as triangles and rectangles. We can represent arbitrary polyhedra by dividing them into tetrahedrons, just as we triangulate polygons. We can also represent them by listing their faces, each of which is itself a polygon, along with an indication of which side of the face is inside the polyhedron.

25.3.2 Design Databases

Computer-aided-design (**CAD**) systems traditionally stored data in memory during editing or other processing, and wrote the data back to a file at the end of a session of editing. The drawbacks of such a scheme include the cost (programming complexity, as well as time cost) of transforming data from one form to another, and the need to read in an entire file even if only parts of it are required. For large designs, such as the design of a large-scale integrated circuit or the design of an entire airplane, it may be impossible to hold the complete design in memory. Designers of object-oriented databases were motivated in large part by the database requirements of CAD systems. Object-oriented databases represent components of the design as objects, and the connections between the objects indicate how the design is structured.

The objects stored in a design database are generally geometric objects. Simple two-dimensional geometric objects include points, lines, triangles, rectangles, and, in general, polygons. Complex two-dimensional objects can be formed from simple objects by means of union, intersection, and difference operations. Similarly, complex three-dimensional objects may be formed from simpler objects such as spheres, cylinders, and cuboids, by union, intersection, and difference operations, as in Figure 25.3. Three-dimensional surfaces may also be represented by **wireframe models**, which essentially model the surface as a set of simpler objects, such as line segments, triangles, and rectangles.

Design databases also store nonspatial information about objects, such as the material from which the objects are constructed. We can usually model such information by standard data-modeling techniques. We concern ourselves here with only the spatial aspects.

Various spatial operations must be performed on a design. For instance, the designer may want to retrieve that part of the design that corresponds to a particular region of interest. Spatial-index structures, discussed in Section 25.3.5, are useful for such tasks. Spatial-index structures are multidimensional, dealing with two- and three-dimensional data, rather than dealing with just the simple one-dimensional ordering provided by the B$^+$-trees.

Spatial-integrity constraints, such as "two pipes should not be in the same location," are important in design databases to prevent interference errors. Such errors often occur if the design is performed manually, and are detected only when a prototype is being constructed. As a result, these errors can be expensive to fix. Database support for spatial-integrity constraints helps people to avoid design

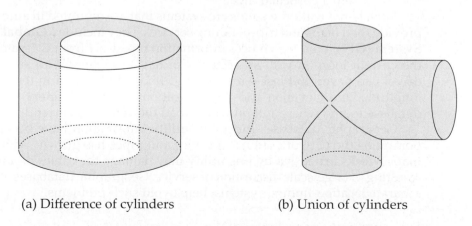

(a) Difference of cylinders (b) Union of cylinders

Figure 25.3 Complex three-dimensional objects.

errors, thereby keeping the design consistent. Implementing such integrity checks again depends on the availability of efficient multidimensional index structures.

25.3.3 Geographic Data

Geographic data are spatial in nature, but differ from design data in certain ways. Maps and satellite images are typical examples of geographic data. Maps may provide not only location information—about boundaries, rivers, and roads, for example—but also much more detailed information associated with locations, such as elevation, soil type, land usage, and annual rainfall.

25.3.3.1 Applications of Geographic Data

Geographic databases have a variety of uses, including online map services; vehicle-navigation systems; distribution-network information for public-service utilities such as telephone, electric-power, and water-supply systems; and land-usage information for ecologists and planners.

Web-based road map services form a very widely used application of map data. At the simplest level, these systems can be used to generate online road maps of a desired region. An important benefit of online maps is that it is easy to scale the maps to the desired size—that is, to zoom in and out to locate relevant features. Road map services also store information about roads and services, such as the layout of roads, speed limits on roads, road conditions, connections between roads, and one-way restrictions. With this additional information about roads, the maps can be used for getting directions to go from one place to another and for automatic trip planning. Users can query online information about services to locate, for example, hotels, gas stations, or restaurants with desired offerings and price ranges. In recent years, several Web-based map services have defined APIs that allow programmers to create customized maps that include data from the map service along with data from other sources. Such customized maps can be used to display, for example, houses available for sale or rent, or shops and restaurants, in a particular area.

Vehicle-navigation systems are systems that are mounted in automobiles and provide road maps and trip-planning services. They include a **Global Positioning System (GPS)** unit, which uses information broadcast from GPS satellites to find the current location with an accuracy of tens of meters. With such a system, a driver can never[3] get lost—the GPS unit finds the location in terms of latitude, longitude, and elevation and the navigation system can query the geographic database to find where and on which road the vehicle is currently located.

Geographic databases for public-utility information have become very important as the network of buried cables and pipes has grown. Without detailed maps, work carried out by one utility may damage the cables of another utility, resulting in large-scale disruption of service. Geographic databases, coupled with accurate location-finding systems, help avoid such problems.

---

[3]Well, hardly ever!

25.3.3.2 Representation of Geographic Data

Geographic data can be categorized into two types:

- **Raster data**. Such data consist of bit maps or pixel maps, in two or more dimensions. A typical example of a two-dimensional raster image is a satellite image of an area. In addition to the actual image, the data includes the location of the image, specified for example by the latitude and longitude of its corners, and the resolution, specified either by the total number of pixels, or, more commonly in the context of geographic data, by the area covered by each pixel.

  Raster data is often represented as **tiles**, each covering a fixed sized area. A larger area can be displayed by displaying all the tiles that overlap with the area. To allow the display of data at different zoom levels, a separate set of tiles is created for each zoom level. Once the zoom level is set by the user interface (for example a Web browser), tiles at that zoom level, which overlap the area being displayed, are retrieved and displayed.

  Raster data can be three-dimensional—for example, the temperature at different altitudes at different regions, again measured with the help of a satellite. Time could form another dimension—for example, the surface temperature measurements at different points in time.

- **Vector data**. Vector data are constructed from basic geometric objects, such as points, line segments, polylines, triangles, and other polygons in two dimensions, and cylinders, spheres, cuboids, and other polyhedrons in three dimensions. In the context of geographic data, points are usually represented by latitude and longitude, and where the height is relevant, additionally by elevation.

  Map data are often represented in vector format. Roads are often represented as polylines. Geographic features, such as large lakes, or even political features such as states and countries, are represented as complex polygons. Some features, such as rivers, may be represented either as complex curves or as complex polygons, depending on whether their width is relevant.

Geographic information related to regions, such as annual rainfall, can be represented as an array—that is, in raster form. For space efficiency, the array can be stored in a compressed form. In Section 25.3.5.2, we study an alternative representation of such arrays by a data structure called a *quadtree*.

As another alternative, we can represent region information in vector form, using polygons, where each polygon is a region within which the array value is the same. The vector representation is more compact than the raster representation in some applications. It is also more accurate for some tasks, such as depicting roads, where dividing the region into pixels (which may be fairly large) leads to a loss of precision in location information. However, the vector representation is unsuitable for applications where the data are intrinsically raster based, such as satellite images.

Topographical information, that is information about the elevation (height) of each point on a surface, can be represented in raster form. Alternatively it can be represented in vector form by dividing the surface into polygons covering regions of (approximately) equal elevation, with a single elevation value associated with each polygon. As another alternative, the surface can be **triangulated** (that is, divided into triangles), with each triangle represented by the latitude, longitude, and elevation of each of its corners. The latter representation, called the **triangulated irregular network** (TIN) representation, is a compact representation which is particularly useful for generating three-dimensional views of an area.

Geographic information systems usually contain both raster and vector data, and can merge the two kinds of data when displaying results to users. For example, maps applications usually contain both satellite images and vector data about roads, building and other landmarks. A map display usually **overlays** different kinds of information; for example, road information can be overlaid on a background satellite image, to create a hybrid display. In fact, a map typically consists of multiple layers, which are displayed in bottom-to-top order; data from higher layers appears on top of data from lower layers.

It is also interesting to note that even information that is actually stored in vector form may be converted to raster form before it is sent to a user interface such as a Web browser. One reason is that even Web browsers that do not support scripting languages (required to interpret and display vector data) can then display map data; a second reason may be to prevent end users from extracting and using the vector data.

Map services such as Google Maps and Yahoo! Maps provide APIs that allow users to create specialized map displays, containing application specific data overlaid on top of standard map data. For example, a Web site may show a map of an area with information about restaurants overlaid on the map. The overlays can be constructed dynamically, displaying only restaurants with a specific cuisine, for example, or allowing users to change the zoom level, or pan the display. The maps APIs for a specific language (typically JavaScript or Flash) are built on top of a Web service that provides the underlying map data.

25.3.4 Spatial Queries

There are a number of types of queries that involve spatial locations.

- **Nearness queries** request objects that lie near a specified location. A query to find all restaurants that lie within a given distance of a given point is an example of a nearness query. The **nearest-neighbor query** requests the object that is nearest to a specified point. For example, we may want to find the nearest gasoline station. Note that this query does not have to specify a limit on the distance, and hence we can ask it even if we have no idea how far the nearest gasoline station lies.

- **Region queries** deal with spatial regions. Such a query can ask for objects that lie partially or fully inside a specified region. A query to find all retail shops within the geographic boundaries of a given town is an example.

- Queries may also request **intersections** and **unions** of regions. For example, given region information, such as annual rainfall and population density, a query may request all regions with a low annual rainfall as well as a high population density.

Queries that compute intersections of regions can be thought of as computing the **spatial join** of two spatial relations—for example, one representing rainfall and the other representing population density—with the location playing the role of join attribute. In general, given two relations, each containing spatial objects, the spatial join of the two relations generates either pairs of objects that intersect, or the intersection regions of such pairs.

Several join algorithms efficiently compute spatial joins on vector data. Although nested-loop join and indexed nested-loop join (with spatial indices) can be used, hash joins and sort–merge joins cannot be used on spatial data. Researchers have proposed join techniques based on coordinated traversal of spatial index structures on the two relations. See the bibliographical notes for more information.

In general, queries on spatial data may have a combination of spatial and nonspatial requirements. For instance, we may want to find the nearest restaurant that has vegetarian selections and that charges less than $10 for a meal.

Since spatial data are inherently graphical, we usually query them by using a graphical query language. Results of such queries are also displayed graphically, rather than in tables. The user can invoke various operations on the interface, such as choosing an area to be viewed (for example, by pointing and clicking on suburbs west of Manhattan), zooming in and out, choosing what to display on the basis of selection conditions (for example, houses with more than three bedrooms), overlay of multiple maps (for example, houses with more than three bedrooms overlaid on a map showing areas with low crime rates), and so on. The graphical interface constitutes the front end. Extensions of SQL have been proposed to permit relational databases to store and retrieve spatial information efficiently, and also to allow queries to mix spatial and nonspatial conditions. Extensions include allowing abstract data types, such as lines, polygons, and bit maps, and allowing spatial conditions, such as *contains* or *overlaps*.

25.3.5   Indexing of Spatial Data

Indices are required for efficient access to spatial data. Traditional index structures, such as hash indices and B-trees, are not suitable, since they deal only with one-dimensional data, whereas spatial data are typically of two or more dimensions.

25.3.5.1   k-d Trees

To understand how to index spatial data consisting of two or more dimensions, we consider first the indexing of points in one-dimensional data. Tree structures, such as binary trees and B-trees, operate by successively dividing space into smaller parts. For instance, each internal node of a binary tree partitions a one-

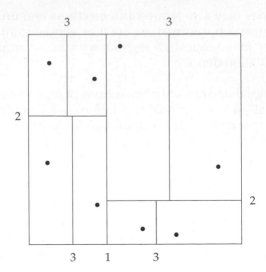

Figure 25.4   Division of space by a k-d tree.

dimensional interval in two. Points that lie in the left partition go into the left subtree; points that lie in the right partition go into the right subtree. In a balanced binary tree, the partition is chosen so that approximately one-half of the points stored in the subtree fall in each partition. Similarly, each level of a B-tree splits a one-dimensional interval into multiple parts.

We can use that intuition to create tree structures for two-dimensional space, as well as in higher-dimensional spaces. A tree structure called a **k-d tree** was one of the early structures used for indexing in multiple dimensions. Each level of a k-d tree partitions the space into two. The partitioning is done along one dimension at the node at the top level of the tree, along another dimension in nodes at the next level, and so on, cycling through the dimensions. The partitioning proceeds in such a way that, at each node, approximately one-half of the points stored in the subtree fall on one side and one-half fall on the other. Partitioning stops when a node has less than a given maximum number of points. Figure 25.4 shows a set of points in two-dimensional space, and a k-d tree representation of the set of points. Each line corresponds to a node in the tree, and the maximum number of points in a leaf node has been set at 1. Each line in the figure (other than the outside box) corresponds to a node in the k-d tree. The numbering of the lines in the figure indicates the level of the tree at which the corresponding node appears.

The **k-d-B tree** extends the k-d tree to allow multiple child nodes for each internal node, just as a B-tree extends a binary tree, to reduce the height of the tree. k-d-B trees are better suited for secondary storage than k-d trees.

25.3.5.2   Quadtrees

An alternative representation for two-dimensional data is a **quadtree**. An example of the division of space by a quadtree appears in Figure 25.5. The set of points

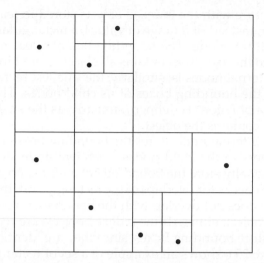

Figure 25.5 Division of space by a quadtree.

is the same as that in Figure 25.4. Each node of a quadtree is associated with a rectangular region of space. The top node is associated with the entire target space. Each nonleaf node in a quadtree divides its region into four equal-sized quadrants, and correspondingly each such node has four child nodes corresponding to the four quadrants. Leaf nodes have between zero and some fixed maximum number of points. Correspondingly, if the region corresponding to a node has more than the maximum number of points, child nodes are created for that node. In the example in Figure 25.5, the maximum number of points in a leaf node is set to 1.

This type of quadtree is called a **PR quadtree**, to indicate it stores points, and that the division of space is divided based on regions, rather than on the actual set of points stored. We can use **region quadtrees** to store array (raster) information. A node in a region quadtree is a leaf node if all the array values in the region that it covers are the same. Otherwise, it is subdivided further into four children of equal area, and is therefore an internal node. Each node in the region quadtree corresponds to a subarray of values. The subarrays corresponding to leaves either contain just a single array element or have multiple array elements, all of which have the same value.

Indexing of line segments and polygons presents new problems. There are extensions of k-d trees and quadtrees for this task. However, a line segment or polygon may cross a partitioning line. If it does, it has to be split and represented in each of the subtrees in which its pieces occur. Multiple occurrences of a line segment or polygon can result in inefficiencies in storage, as well as inefficiencies in querying.

25.3.5.3 R-Trees

A storage structure called an **R-tree** is useful for indexing of objects such as points, line segments, rectangles, and other polygons. An R-tree is a balanced tree structure with the indexed objects stored in leaf nodes, much like a B$^+$-tree. However, instead of a range of values, a rectangular **bounding box** is associated with each tree node. The bounding box of a leaf node is the smallest rectangle parallel to the axes that contains all objects stored in the leaf node. The bounding box of internal nodes is, similarly, the smallest rectangle parallel to the axes that contains the bounding boxes of its child nodes. The bounding box of an object (such as a polygon) is defined, similarly, as the smallest rectangle parallel to the axes that contains the object.

Each internal node stores the bounding boxes of the child nodes along with the pointers to the child nodes. Each leaf node stores the indexed objects, and may optionally store the bounding boxes of the objects; the bounding boxes help speed up checks for overlaps of the rectangle with the indexed objects—if a query rectangle does not overlap with the bounding box of an object, it cannot overlap with the object, either. (If the indexed objects are rectangles, there is of course no need to store bounding boxes, since they are identical to the rectangles.)

Figure 25.6 shows an example of a set of rectangles (drawn with a solid line) and the bounding boxes (drawn with a dashed line) of the nodes of an R-tree for the set of rectangles. Note that the bounding boxes are shown with extra space inside them, to make them stand out pictorially. In reality, the boxes would be smaller and fit tightly on the objects that they contain; that is, each side of a bounding box B would touch at least one of the objects or bounding boxes that are contained in B.

The R-tree itself is at the right side of Figure 25.6. The figure refers to the coordinates of bounding box i as BB_i in the figure.

We shall now see how to implement search, insert, and delete operations on an R-tree.

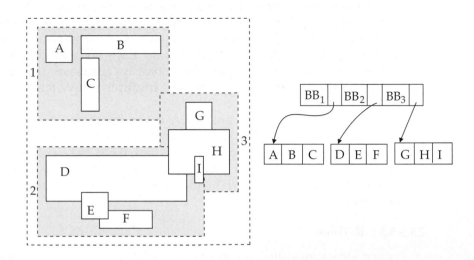

Figure 25.6 An R-tree.

- **Search**. As the figure shows, the bounding boxes associated with sibling nodes may overlap; in B$^+$-trees, k-d trees, and quadtrees, in contrast, the ranges do not overlap. A search for objects containing a point therefore has to follow *all* child nodes whose associated bounding boxes contain the point; as a result, multiple paths may have to be searched. Similarly, a query to find all objects that intersect a given object has to go down every node where the associated rectangle intersects the given object.

- **Insert**. When we insert an object into an R-tree, we select a leaf node to hold the object. Ideally we should pick a leaf node that has space to hold a new entry, and whose bounding box contains the bounding box of the object. However, such a node may not exist; even if it did, finding the node may be very expensive, since it is not possible to find it by a single traversal down from the root. At each internal node we may find multiple children whose bounding boxes contain the bounding box of the object, and each of these children needs to be explored. Therefore, as a heuristic, in a traversal from the root, if any of the child nodes has a bounding box containing the bounding box of the object, the R-tree algorithm chooses one of them arbitrarily. If none of the children satisfy this condition, the algorithm chooses a child node whose bounding box has the maximum overlap with the bounding box of the object for continuing the traversal.

  Once the leaf node has been reached, if the node is already full, the algorithm performs node splitting (and propagates splitting upward if required) in a manner very similar to B$^+$-tree insertion. Just as with B$^+$-tree insertion, the R-tree insertion algorithm ensures that the tree remains balanced. Additionally, it ensures that the bounding boxes of leaf nodes, as well as internal nodes, remain consistent; that is, bounding boxes of leaves contain all the bounding boxes of the objects stored at the leaf, while the bounding boxes for internal nodes contain all the bounding boxes of the children nodes.

  The main difference of the insertion procedure from the B$^+$-tree insertion procedure lies in how the node is split. In a B$^+$-tree, it is possible to find a value such that half the entries are less than the midpoint and half are greater than the value. This property does not generalize beyond one dimension; that is, for more than one dimension, it is not always possible to split the entries into two sets so that their bounding boxes do not overlap. Instead, as a heuristic, the set of entries S can be split into two disjoint sets S_1 and S_2 so that the bounding boxes of S_1 and S_2 have the minimum total area; another heuristic would be to split the entries into two sets S_1 and S_2 in such a way that S_1 and S_2 have minimum overlap. The two nodes resulting from the split would contain the entries in S_1 and S_2, respectively. The cost of finding splits with minimum total area or overlap can itself be large, so cheaper heuristics, such as the *quadratic split* heuristic, are used. (The heuristic gets is name from the fact that it takes time quadratic in the number of entries.)

  The **quadratic split** heuristic works this way: First, it picks a pair of entries a and b from S such that putting them in the same node would result in a bounding box with the maximum wasted space; that is, the area of the minimum bounding box of a and b minus the sum of the areas of a and b is the largest. The heuristic places the entries a and b in sets S_1 and S_2, respectively.

It then iteratively adds the remaining entries, one entry per iteration, to one of the two sets S_1 or S_2. At each iteration, for each remaining entry e, let $i_{e,1}$ denote the increase in the size of the bounding box of S_1 if e is added to S_1 and let $i_{e,2}$ denote the corresponding increase for S_2. In each iteration, the heuristic chooses one of the entries with the maximum difference of $i_{e,1}$ and $i_{e,2}$ and adds it to S_1 if $i_{e,1}$ is less than $i_{e,2}$, and to S_2 otherwise. That is, an entry with "maximum preference" for one of S_1 or S_2 is chosen at each iteration. The iteration stops when all entries have been assigned, or when one of the sets S_1 or S_2 has enough entries that all remaining entries have to be added to the other set so the nodes constructed from S_1 and S_2 both have the required minimum occupancy. The heuristic then adds all unassigned entries to the set with fewer entries.

- **Deletion**. Deletion can be performed like a B$^+$-tree deletion, borrowing entries from sibling nodes, or merging sibling nodes if a node becomes underfull. An alternative approach redistributes all the entries of underfull nodes to sibling nodes, with the aim of improving the clustering of entries in the R-tree.

See the bibliographical references for more details on insertion and deletion operations on R-trees, as well as on variants of R-trees, called R*-trees or R$^+$-trees.

The storage efficiency of R-trees is better than that of k-d trees or quadtrees, since an object is stored only once, and we can ensure easily that each node is at least half full. However, querying may be slower, since multiple paths have to be searched. Spatial joins are simpler with quadtrees than with R-trees, since all quadtrees on a region are partitioned in the same manner. However, because of their better storage efficiency, and their similarity to B-trees, R-trees and their variants have proved popular in database systems that support spatial data.

25.4   Multimedia Databases

Multimedia data, such as images, audio, and video—an increasingly popular form of data—are today almost always stored outside the database, in file systems. This kind of storage is not a problem when the number of multimedia objects is relatively small, since features provided by databases are usually not important.

However, database features become important when the number of multimedia objects stored is large. Issues such as transactional updates, querying facilities, and indexing then become important. Multimedia objects often have descriptive attributes, such as those indicating when they were created, who created them, and to what category they belong. One approach to building a database for such multimedia objects is to use databases for storing the descriptive attributes and for keeping track of the files in which the multimedia objects are stored.

However, storing multimedia outside the database makes it harder to provide database functionality, such as indexing on the basis of actual multimedia data content. It can also lead to inconsistencies, such as a file that is noted in the database, but whose contents are missing, or vice versa. It is therefore desirable to store the data themselves in the database.

Several issues must be addressed if multimedia data are to be stored in a database.

- The database must support large objects, since multimedia data such as videos can occupy up to a few gigabytes of storage. Many database systems do not support objects larger than a few gigabytes. Larger objects could be split into smaller pieces and stored in the database. Alternatively, the multimedia object may be stored in a file system, but the database may contain a pointer to the object; the pointer would typically be a file name. The SQL/MED standard (MED stands for Management of External Data) allows external data, such as files, to be treated as if they are part of the database. With SQL/MED, the object would appear to be part of the database, but can be stored externally. We discuss multimedia data formats in Section 25.4.1.

- The retrieval of some types of data, such as audio and video, has the requirement that data delivery must proceed at a guaranteed steady rate. Such data are sometimes called **isochronous data**, or **continuous-media data**. For example, if audio data are not supplied in time, there will be gaps in the sound. If the data are supplied too fast, system buffers may overflow, resulting in loss of data. We discuss continuous-media data in Section 25.4.2.

- Similarity-based retrieval is needed in many multimedia database applications. For example, in a database that stores fingerprint images, a query fingerprint image is provided, and fingerprints in the database that are similar to the query fingerprint must be retrieved. Index structures such as B^+-trees and R-trees cannot be used for this purpose; special index structures need to be created. We discuss similarity-based retrieval in Section 25.4.3.

25.4.1 Multimedia Data Formats

Because of the large number of bytes required to represent multimedia data, it is essential that multimedia data be stored and transmitted in compressed form. For image data, the most widely used format is *JPEG*, named after the standards body that created it, the *Joint Picture Experts Group*. We can store video data by encoding each frame of video in JPEG format, but such an encoding is wasteful, since successive frames of a video are often nearly the same. The *Moving Picture Experts Group* has developed the MPEG series of standards for encoding video and audio data; these encodings exploit commonalities among a sequence of frames to achieve a greater degree of compression. The *MPEG-1* standard stores a minute of 30-frame-per-second video and audio in approximately 12.5 megabytes (compared to approximately 75 megabytes for video in only JPEG). However, MPEG-1 encoding introduces some loss of video quality, to a level roughly comparable to that of VHS videotape. The *MPEG-2* standard is designed for digital broadcast systems and digital video disks (DVDs); it introduces only a negligible loss of video quality. MPEG-2 compresses 1 minute of video and audio to approximately 17 megabytes. MPEG-4 provides techniques for further compression of video, with variable bandwidth to support delivery of video data over networks with a wide range of bandwidths. Several competing standards are used for audio encoding, including *MP3*, which stands for MPEG-1 Layer 3, RealAudio, Windows Media Audio, and other formats. High-definition video with audio is encoded in several variants of MPEG-4 that include MPEG-4 AVC and AVCHD.

25.4.2 Continuous-Media Data

The most important types of continuous-media data are video and audio data (for example, a database of movies). Continuous-media systems are characterized by their real-time information-delivery requirements:

- Data must be delivered sufficiently fast that no gaps in the audio or video result.

- Data must be delivered at a rate that does not cause overflow of system buffers.

- Synchronization among distinct data streams must be maintained. This need arises, for example, when the video of a person speaking must show lips moving synchronously with the audio of the person speaking.

To supply data predictably at the right time to a large number of consumers of the data, the fetching of data from disk must be coordinated carefully. Usually, data are fetched in periodic cycles. In each cycle, say of n seconds, n seconds' worth of data is fetched for each consumer and stored in memory buffers, while the data fetched in the previous cycle is being sent to the consumers from the memory buffers. The cycle period is a compromise: A short period uses less memory but requires more disk-arm movement, which is a waste of resources, while a long period reduces disk-arm movement but increases memory requirements and may delay initial delivery of data. When a new request arrives, **admission control** comes into play: That is, the system checks if the request can be satisfied with available resources (in each period); if so, it is admitted; otherwise it is rejected.

Extensive research on delivery of continuous-media data has dealt with such issues as handling arrays of disks and dealing with disk failure. See the bibliographical references for details.

Several vendors offer video-on-demand servers. Current systems are based on file systems, because existing database systems do not provide the real-time response that these applications need. The basic architecture of a video-on-demand system comprises:

- **Video server**. Multimedia data are stored on several disks (usually in a RAID configuration). Systems containing a large volume of data may use tertiary storage for less frequently accessed data.

- **Terminals.** People view multimedia data through various devices, collectively referred to as *terminals*. Examples are personal computers and televisions attached to a small, inexpensive computer called a **set-top box**.

- **Network.** Transmission of multimedia data from a server to multiple terminals requires a high-capacity network.

Video-on-demand service over cable networks is widely available.

25.4.3 Similarity-Based Retrieval

In many multimedia applications, data are described only approximately in the database. An example is the fingerprint data in Section 25.4. Other examples are:

- **Pictorial data.** Two pictures or images that are slightly different as represented in the database may be considered the same by a user. For instance, a database may store trademark designs. When a new trademark is to be registered, the system may need first to identify all similar trademarks that were registered previously.

- **Audio data.** Speech-based user interfaces are being developed that allow the user to give a command or identify a data item by speaking. The input from the user must then be tested for similarity to those commands or data items stored in the system.

- **Handwritten data.** Handwritten input can be used to identify a handwritten data item or command stored in the database. Here again, similarity testing is required.

The notion of similarity is often subjective and user specific. However, similarity testing is often more successful than speech or handwriting recognition, because the input can be compared to data already in the system and, thus, the set of choices available to the system is limited.

Several algorithms exist for finding the best matches to a given input by similarity testing. Many voice-activated systems have been deployed commercially, particularly for phone applications and in-vehicle controls. See the bibliographical notes for references.

25.5 Mobility and Personal Databases

Large-scale, commercial databases have traditionally been stored in central computing facilities. In distributed database applications, there has usually been strong central database and network administration. Several technology trends have combined to create applications in which this assumption of central control and administration is not entirely correct:

- The widespread use of laptop, notebook, or netbook computers.

- The widespread use of cell phones with the capabilities of a computer.

- The development of a relatively low-cost wireless digital communication infrastructure, based on wireless local-area networks, cellular digital packet networks, and other technologies.

Mobile computing has proved useful in many applications. Many business travelers use laptop computers so that they can work and access data en route. Delivery services use mobile computers to assist in package tracking. Emergency-response services use mobile computers at the scene of disasters, medical emergencies, and the like to access information and to enter data pertaining to the situation. Cell phones are increasingly becoming devices that provide not only phone services, but are also mobile computers allowing email and Web access. New applications of mobile computers continue to emerge.

Wireless computing creates a situation where machines no longer have fixed locations and network addresses. **Location-dependent queries** are an interesting class of queries that are motivated by mobile computers; in such queries, the location of the user (computer) is a parameter of the query. The value of the location parameter is provided by a global positioning system (GPS). An example is a traveler's information system that provides data on hotels, roadside services, and the like to motorists. Processing of queries about services that are ahead on the current route must be based on knowledge of the user's location, direction of motion, and speed. Increasingly, navigational aids are being offered as a built-in feature in automobiles.

Energy (battery power) is a scarce resource for most mobile computers. This limitation influences many aspects of system design. Among the more interesting consequences of the need for energy efficiency is that small mobile devices spend most of their time sleeping, waking up for a fraction of a second every second or so to check for incoming data and to send outgoing data. This behavior has a significant impact on protocols used to communicate with mobile devices. The use of scheduled data broadcasts to reduce the need for mobile systems to transmit queries is another way to reduce energy requirements.

Increasing amounts of data may reside on machines administered by users, rather than by database administrators. Furthermore, these machines may, at times, be disconnected from the network. In many cases, there is a conflict between the user's need to continue to work while disconnected and the need for global data consistency.

A user is likely to use more than one mobile device. Such users need to be able to view their data in its most up-to-date version regardless of which device is being used at a given time. Often, this capability is supported by some variant of cloud computing, which we discussed in Section 19.9.

In Sections 25.5.1 through 25.5.4, we discuss techniques in use and under development to deal with the problems of mobility and personal computing.

25.5.1   A Model of Mobile Computing

The mobile-computing environment consists of mobile computers, referred to as **mobile hosts**, and a wired network of computers. Mobile hosts communicate with the wired network via computers referred to as **mobile support stations**. Each mobile support station manages those mobile hosts within its **cell**—that is, the geographical area that it covers. Mobile hosts may move between cells, thus necessitating a **handoff** of control from one mobile support station to another. Since mobile hosts may, at times, be powered down, a host may leave one cell and rematerialize later at some distant cell. Therefore, moves between cells are not necessarily between adjacent cells. Within a small area, such as a building, mobile hosts may be connected by a wireless local-area network (LAN) that provides lower-cost connectivity than would a wide-area cellular network, and that reduces the overhead of handoffs.

It is possible for mobile hosts to communicate directly without the intervention of a mobile support station. However, such communication can occur only between nearby hosts. Such direct forms of communication often use **Bluetooth**, a short-range digital radio standard that allows wireless connectivity within a 10-meter range at high speed (up to 721 kilobits per second). Initially conceived as a replacement for cables, Bluetooth's greatest benefit is in easy ad hoc connection of mobile computers, PDAs, mobile phones, and so-called intelligent appliances.

Wireless local-area network systems based on the 801.11 (a/b/g/n) standards are very widely used today, and systems based on the 802.16 (Wi-Max) standard are being deployed.

The network infrastructure for mobile computing consists in large part of two technologies: wireless local-area networks and packet-based cellular telephony networks. Early cellular systems used analog technology and were designed for voice communication. Second-generation digital systems retained the focus on voice applications. Third-generation (3G) and so-called 2.5G systems use packet-based networking and are more suited to data applications. In these networks, voice is just one of many applications (albeit an economically important one). Fourth-generation (4G) technologies include Wi-Max as well as several competitors.

Bluetooth, wireless LANs, and 2.5G and 3G cellular networks make it possible for a wide variety of devices to communicate at low cost. While such communication itself does not fit the domain of a usual database application, the accounting, monitoring, and management data pertaining to this communication generate huge databases. The immediacy of wireless communication generates a need for real-time access to many of these databases. This need for timeliness adds another dimension to the constraints on the system—a matter we shall discuss further in Section 26.4.

The size and power limitations of many mobile computers have led to alternative memory hierarchies. Instead of, or in addition to, disk storage, flash memory, which we discussed in Section 10.1, may be included. If the mobile host includes a hard disk, the disk may be allowed to spin down when it is not in use, to save energy. The same considerations of size and energy limit the type and size of the display used in a mobile device. Designers of mobile devices often create special-purpose user interfaces to work within these constraints. However, the need to present Web-based data has necessitated the creation of presentation standards. **Wireless application protocol** (WAP) is a standard for wireless Internet access. WAP-based browsers access special Web pages that use **wireless markup language** (WML), an XML-based language designed for the constraints of mobile and wireless Web browsing.

25.5.2 Routing and Query Processing

The route between a pair of hosts may change over time if one of the two hosts is mobile. This simple fact has a dramatic effect at the network level, since location-based network addresses are no longer constants within the system.

Mobility also directly affects database query processing. As we saw in Chapter 19, we must consider the communication costs when we choose a distributed query-processing strategy. Mobility results in dynamically changing communication costs, thus complicating the optimization process. Furthermore, there are competing notions of cost to consider:

- **User time** is a highly valuable commodity in many business applications.

- **Connection time** is the unit by which monetary charges are assigned in some cellular systems.

- **Number of bytes, or packets, transferred** is the unit by which charges are computed in some digital cellular systems.

- **Time-of-day-based charges** vary, depending on whether communication occurs during peak or off-peak periods.

- **Energy** is limited. Often, battery power is a scarce resource whose use must be optimized. A basic principle of radio communication is that it requires less energy to receive than to transmit radio signals. Thus, transmission and reception of data impose different power demands on the mobile host.

25.5.3 Broadcast Data

It is often desirable for frequently requested data to be broadcast in a continuous cycle by mobile support stations, rather than transmitted to mobile hosts on demand. A typical application of such **broadcast data** is stock-market price information. There are two reasons for using broadcast data. First, the mobile host avoids the energy cost for transmitting data requests. Second, the broadcast data can be received by a large number of mobile hosts at once, at no extra cost. Thus, the available transmission bandwidth is utilized more effectively.

A mobile host can then receive data as they are transmitted, rather than consuming energy by transmitting a request. The mobile host may have local nonvolatile storage available to cache the broadcast data for possible later use. Given a query, the mobile host may optimize energy costs by determining whether it can process that query with only cached data. If the cached data are insufficient, there are two options: wait for the data to be broadcast, or transmit a request for data. To make this decision, the mobile host must know when the relevant data will be broadcast.

Broadcast data may be transmitted according to a fixed schedule or a changeable schedule. In the former case, the mobile host uses the known fixed schedule to determine when the relevant data will be transmitted. In the latter case, the broadcast schedule must itself be broadcast at a well-known radio frequency and at well-known time intervals.

In effect, the broadcast medium can be modeled as a disk with a high latency. Requests for data can be thought of as being serviced when the requested data are broadcast. The transmission schedules behave like indices on the disk. The bibliographical notes list recent research papers in the area of broadcast data management.

25.5.4 Disconnectivity and Consistency

Since wireless communication may be paid for on the basis of connection time, there is an incentive for certain mobile hosts to be disconnected for substantial periods. Mobile computers without wireless connectivity are disconnected most of the time when they are being used, except periodically when they are connected to their host computers, either physically or through a computer network.

During these periods of disconnection, the mobile host may remain in operation. The user of the mobile host may issue queries and updates on data that reside or are cached locally. This situation creates several problems, in particular:

- **Recoverability**: Updates entered on a disconnected machine may be lost if the mobile host experiences a catastrophic failure. Since the mobile host represents a single point of failure, stable storage cannot be simulated well.

- **Consistency**: Locally cached data may become out-of-date, but the mobile host cannot discover this situation until it is reconnected. Likewise, updates occurring in the mobile host cannot be propagated until reconnection occurs.

We explored the consistency problem in Chapter 19, where we discussed network partitioning, and we elaborate on it here. In wired distributed systems, partitioning is considered to be a failure mode; in mobile computing, partitioning via disconnection is part of the normal mode of operation. It is therefore necessary to allow data access to proceed despite partitioning, even at the risk of some loss of consistency.

For data updated by only the mobile host, it is a simple matter to propagate the updates when the mobile host reconnects. However, if the mobile host caches read-only copies of data that may be updated by other computers, the cached data may become inconsistent. When the mobile host is connected, it can be sent **invalidation reports** that inform it of out-of-date cache entries. However, when the mobile host is disconnected, it may miss an invalidation report. A simple solution to this problem is to invalidate the entire cache on reconnection, but such an extreme solution is highly costly. Several caching schemes are cited in the bibliographical notes.

If updates can occur at both the mobile host and elsewhere, detecting conflicting updates is more difficult. **Version-numbering**-based schemes allow updates of shared files from disconnected hosts. These schemes do not guarantee that the updates will be consistent. Rather, they guarantee that, if two hosts independently update the same version of a document, the clash will be detected eventually, when the hosts exchange information either directly or through a common host.

The **version-vector scheme** detects inconsistencies when copies of a document are independently updated. This scheme allows copies of a *document* to be stored at multiple hosts. Although we use the term *document*, the scheme can be applied to any other data items, such as tuples of a relation.

The basic idea is for each host i to store, with its copy of each document d, a **version vector**—that is, a set of version numbers $\{V_{d,i}[j]\}$, with one entry for each other host j on which the document could potentially be updated. When a host i updates a document d, it increments the version number $V_{d,i}[i]$ by one.

Whenever two hosts i and j connect with each other, they exchange updated documents, so that both obtain new versions of the documents. However, before exchanging documents, the hosts have to discover whether the copies are consistent:

1. If the version vectors are the same on both hosts—that is, for each k, $V_{d,i}[k] = V_{d,j}[k]$—then the copies of document d are identical.

2. If, for each k, $V_{d,i}[k] \leq V_{d,j}[k]$ and the version vectors are not identical, then the copy of document d at host i is older than the one at host j. That is, the copy of document d at host j was obtained by one or more modifications of the copy of the document at host i. Host i replaces its copy of d, as well as its copy of the version vector for d, with the copies from host j.

3. If there are a pair of hosts k and m such that $V_{d,i}[k] < V_{d,j}[k]$ and $V_{d,i}[m] > V_{d,j}[m]$, then the copies are *inconsistent*; that is, the copy of d at i contains updates performed by host k that have not been propagated to host j, and, similarly, the copy of d at j contains updates performed by host m that have not been propagated to host i. Then, the copies of d are inconsistent, since two or more updates have been performed on d independently. Manual intervention may be required to merge the updates.

The version-vector scheme was initially designed to deal with failures in distributed file systems. The scheme gained importance because mobile computers often store copies of files that are also present on server systems, in effect constituting a distributed file system that is often disconnected. Another application of the scheme is in groupware systems, where hosts are connected periodically, rather than continuously, and must exchange updated documents.

The version-vector scheme also has applications in replicated databases, where it can be applied to individual tuples. For example, if a calendar or address book is maintained on a mobile device as well as on a host, inserts, deletes and updates can happen either on the mobile device or on the host. By applying the version-vector scheme to individual calendar entries or contacts, it is easy to handle situations where a particular entry has been updated on the mobile device while a different one has been updated on the host; such a situation would not be considered a conflict. However, if the same entry is updated independently at both places, a conflict would be detected by the version-vector scheme.

The version-vector scheme, however, fails to address the most difficult and most important issue arising from updates to shared data—the reconciliation of inconsistent copies of data. Many applications can perform reconciliation automatically by executing in each computer those operations that had performed updates on remote computers during the period of disconnection. This solution works if update operations commute—that is, they generate the same result, regardless of the order in which they are executed. Alternative techniques may be available in certain applications; in the worst case, however, it must be left to the users to resolve the inconsistencies. Dealing with such inconsistency automatically, and assisting users in resolving inconsistencies that cannot be handled automatically, remains an area of research.

Another weakness is that the version-vector scheme requires substantial communication between a reconnecting mobile host and that host's mobile support station. Consistency checks can be delayed until the data are needed, although this delay may increase the overall inconsistency of the database.

The potential for disconnection and the cost of wireless communication limit the practicality of transaction-processing techniques discussed in Chapter 19 for distributed systems. Often, it is preferable to let users prepare transactions on mobile hosts, but to require that, instead of executing the transactions locally, they submit transactions to a server for execution. Transactions that span more than one computer and that include a mobile host face long-term blocking during transaction commit, unless disconnectivity is rare or predictable.

25.6 Summary

- Time plays an important role in database systems. Databases are models of the real world. Whereas most databases model the state of the real world at a point in time (at the current time), temporal databases model the states of the real world across time.

- Facts in temporal relations have associated times when they are valid, which can be represented as a union of intervals. Temporal query languages simplify modeling of time, as well as time-related queries.

- Spatial databases are finding increasing use today to store computer-aided-design data as well as geographic data.

- Design data are stored primarily as vector data; geographic data consist of a combination of vector and raster data. Spatial-integrity constraints are important for design data.

- Vector data can be encoded as first-normal-form data, or they can be stored using non-first-normal-form structures, such as lists. Special-purpose index structures are particularly important for accessing spatial data, and for processing spatial queries.

- R-trees are a multidimensional extension of B-trees; with variants such as R+-trees and R*-trees, they have proved popular in spatial databases. Index structures that partition space in a regular fashion, such as quadtrees, help in processing spatial join queries.

- Multimedia databases are growing in importance. Issues such as similarity-based retrieval and delivery of data at guaranteed rates are topics of current research.

- Mobile computing systems have become common, leading to interest in database systems that can run on such systems. Query processing in such systems may involve lookups on server databases. The query cost model must include the cost of communication, including monetary cost and battery-power cost, which is relatively high for mobile systems.

- Broadcast is much cheaper per recipient than is point-to-point communication, and broadcast of data such as stock-market data helps mobile systems to pick up data inexpensively.

- Disconnected operation, use of broadcast data, and caching of data are three important issues being addressed in mobile computing.

Review Terms

- Temporal data
- Valid time
- Transaction time
- Temporal relation
- Bitemporal relation
- Universal coordinated time (UTC)
- Snapshot relation
- Temporal query languages
- Temporal selection
- Temporal projection
- Temporal join
- Spatial and geographic data
- Computer-aided-design (CAD) data
- Geographic data
- Geographic information systems
- Triangulation
- Design databases

- Geographic data
- Raster data
- Vector data
- Global positioning system (GPS)
- Spatial queries
- Nearness queries
- Nearest-neighbor queries
- Region queries
- Spatial join
- Indexing of spatial data
- k-d trees
- k-d-B trees
- Quadtrees
  - PR quadtree
  - Region quadtree
- R-trees
  - Bounding box

- ○ Quadratic split
- Multimedia databases
- Isochronous data
- Continuous-media data
- Similarity-based retrieval
- Multimedia data formats
- Video servers
- Mobile computing
  - ○ Mobile hosts

- ○ Mobile support stations
- ○ Cell
- ○ Handoff
- Location-dependent queries
- Broadcast data
- Consistency
  - ○ Invalidation reports
  - ○ Version-vector scheme

Practice Exercises

25.1 What are the two types of time, and how are they different? Why does it make sense to have both types of time associated with a tuple?

25.2 Suppose you have a relation containing the x, y coordinates and names of restaurants. Suppose also that the only queries that will be asked are of the following form: The query specifies a point, and asks if there is a restaurant exactly at that point. Which type of index would be preferable, R-tree or B-tree? Why?

25.3 Suppose you have a spatial database that supports region queries (with circular regions) but not nearest-neighbor queries. Describe an algorithm to find the nearest neighbor by making use of multiple region queries.

25.4 Suppose you want to store line segments in an R-tree. If a line segment is not parallel to the axes, the bounding box for it can be large, containing a large empty area.

- Describe the effect on performance of having large bounding boxes on queries that ask for line segments intersecting a given region.

- Briefly describe a technique to improve performance for such queries and give an example of its benefit. Hint: You can divide segments into smaller pieces.

25.5 Give a recursive procedure to efficiently compute the spatial join of two relations with R-tree indices. (Hint: Use bounding boxes to check if leaf entries under a pair of internal nodes may intersect.)

25.6 Describe how the ideas behind the RAID organization (Section 10.3) can be used in a broadcast-data environment, where there may occasionally be noise that prevents reception of part of the data being transmitted.

25.7 Define a model of repeatedly broadcast data in which the broadcast medium is modeled as a virtual disk. Describe how access time and data-transfer rate for this virtual disk differ from the corresponding values for a typical hard disk.

25.8 Consider a database of documents in which all documents are kept in a central database. Copies of some documents are kept on mobile computers. Suppose that mobile computer A updates a copy of document 1 while it is disconnected, and, at the same time, mobile computer B updates a copy of document 2 while it is disconnected. Show how the version-vector scheme can ensure proper updating of the central database and mobile computers when a mobile computer reconnects.

Exercises

25.9 Will functional dependencies be preserved if a relation is converted to a temporal relation by adding a time attribute? How is the problem handled in a temporal database?

25.10 Consider two-dimensional vector data where the data items do not overlap. Is it possible to convert such vector data to raster data? If so, what are the drawbacks of storing raster data obtained by such conversion, instead of the original vector data?

25.11 Study the support for spatial data offered by the database system that you use, and implement the following:

    a. A schema to represent the geographic location of restaurants along with features such as the cuisine served at the restaurant and the level of expensiveness.

    b. A query to find moderately priced restaurants that serve Indian food and are within 5 miles of your house (assume any location for your house).

    c. A query to find for each restaurant the distance from the nearest restaurant serving the same cuisine and with the same level of expensiveness.

25.12 What problems can occur in a continuous-media system if data are delivered either too slowly or too fast?

25.13 List three main features of mobile computing over wireless networks that are distinct from traditional distributed systems.

25.14 List three factors that need to be considered in query optimization for mobile computing that are not considered in traditional query optimizers.

25.15 Give an example to show that the version-vector scheme does not ensure serializability. (Hint: Use the example from Practice Exercise 25.8, with the assumption that documents 1 and 2 are available on both mobile computers A and B, and take into account the possibility that a document may be read without being updated.)

Bibliographical Notes

Stam and Snodgrass [1988] and Soo [1991] provide surveys on temporal data management. Jensen et al. [1994] presents a glossary of temporal-database concepts, aimed at unifying the terminology. Tansel et al. [1993] is a collection of articles on different aspects of temporal databases. Chomicki [1995] presents techniques for managing temporal integrity constraints.

Heywood et al. [2002] provides textbook coverage of geographical information systems. Samet [1995b] provides an overview of the large amount of work on spatial index structures. Samet [1990] and Samet [2006] provides a textbook coverage of spatial data structures. An early description of the quad tree is provided by Finkel and Bentley [1974]. Samet [1990] and Samet [1995b] describe numerous variants of quad trees. Bentley [1975] describes the k-d tree, and Robinson [1981] describes the k-d-B tree. The R-tree was originally presented in Guttman [1984]. Extensions of the R-tree are presented by Sellis et al. [1987], which describes the R^+ tree, and Beckmann et al. [1990], which describes the R^* tree.

Brinkhoff et al. [1993] discusses an implementation of spatial joins using R-trees. Lo and Ravishankar [1996] and Patel and DeWitt [1996] present partitioning-based methods for computation of spatial joins. Samet and Aref [1995] provides an overview of spatial data models, spatial operations, and the integration of spatial and nonspatial data.

Revesz [2002] provides textbook coverage of the area of constraint databases; temporal intervals and spatial regions can be thought of as special cases of constraints.

Samet [1995a] describes research issues in multimedia databases. Indexing of multimedia data is discussed in Faloutsos and Lin [1995].

Dashti et al. [2003] provides a textbook description of streaming media server design, including extensive coverage of data organization on disk subsystems. Video servers are discussed in Anderson et al. [1992], Rangan et al. [1992], Ozden et al. [1994], Freedman and DeWitt [1995], and Ozden et al. [1996b]. Fault tolerance is discussed in Berson et al. [1995] and Ozden et al. [1996a].

Information management in systems that include mobile computers is studied in Alonso and Korth [1993] and Imielinski and Badrinath [1994]. Imielinski and Korth [1996] presents an introduction to mobile computing and a collection of research papers on the subject.

The version-vector scheme for detecting inconsistency in distributed file systems is described by Popek et al. [1981] and Parker et al. [1983].

CHAPTER **26**

Advanced Transaction Processing

In Chapters 14, 15, and 16, we introduced the concept of a transaction, a program unit that accesses—and possibly updates—various data items, and whose execution ensures the preservation of the ACID properties. We discussed in those chapters a variety of techniques for ensuring the ACID properties in an environment where failure can occur, and where the transactions may run concurrently.

In this chapter, we go beyond the basic schemes discussed previously, and cover advanced transaction-processing concepts, including transaction-processing monitors, transactional workflows, and transaction processing in the context of electronic commerce. We also cover main-memory databases, real-time databases, long-duration transactions, and nested transactions.

26.1 Transaction-Processing Monitors

Transaction-processing monitors (**TP monitors**) are systems that were developed in the 1970s and 1980s, initially in response to a need to support a large number of remote terminals (such as airline-reservation terminals) from a single computer. The term *TP monitor* initially stood for *teleprocessing monitor*.

TP monitors have since evolved to provide the core support for distributed transaction processing, and the term TP monitor has acquired its current meaning. The CICS TP monitor from IBM was one of the earliest TP monitors, and has been very widely used. Other TP monitors include Oracle Tuxedo and Microsoft Transaction Server.

Web application server architectures, including servlets, which we studied earlier in Section 9.3, support many of the features of TP monitors and are sometimes referred to as "TP lite." Web application servers are in widespread use, and have supplanted traditional TP monitors for many applications. However, the concepts underlying them, which we study in this section, are essentially the same.

26.1.1   TP-Monitor Architectures

Large-scale transaction-processing systems are built around a client–server architecture. One way of building such systems is to have a server process for each client; the server performs authentication, and then executes actions requested by the client. This **process-per-client model** is illustrated in Figure 26.1a. This model presents several problems with respect to memory utilization and processing speed:

- Per-process memory requirements are high. Even if memory for program code is shared by all processes, each process consumes memory for local data and open file descriptors, as well as for operating-system overhead, such as page tables to support virtual memory.

- The operating system divides up available CPU time among processes by switching among them; this technique is called **multitasking**. Each **context switch** between one process and the next has considerable CPU overhead; even on today's fast systems, a context switch can take hundreds of microseconds.

The above problems can be avoided by having a single-server process to which all remote clients connect; this model is called the **single-server model**,

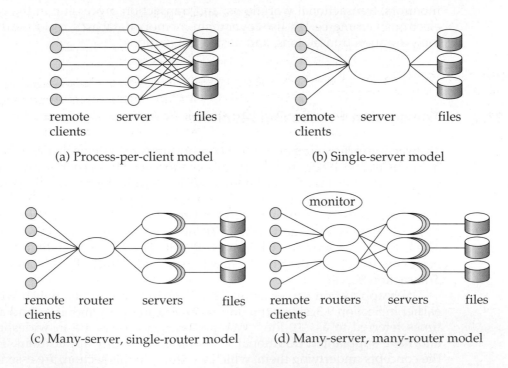

(a) Process-per-client model   (b) Single-server model

(c) Many-server, single-router model   (d) Many-server, many-router model

Figure 26.1 TP-monitor architectures.

illustrated in Figure 26.1b. Remote clients send requests to the server process, which then executes those requests. This model is also used in client–server environments, where clients send requests to a single-server process. The server process handles tasks, such as user authentication, that would normally be handled by the operating system. To avoid blocking other clients when processing a long request for one client, the server process is **multithreaded**: The server process has a thread of control for each client, and, in effect, implements its own low-overhead multitasking. It executes code on behalf of one client for a while, then saves the internal context and switches to the code for another client. Unlike the overhead of full multitasking, the cost of switching between threads is low (typically only a few microseconds).

Systems based on the single-server model, such as the original version of the IBM CICS TP monitor and file servers such as Novel's NetWare, successfully provided high transaction rates with limited resources. However, they had problems, especially when multiple applications accessed the same database:

- Since all the applications run as a single process, there is no protection among them. A bug in one application can affect all the other applications as well. It would be best to run each application as a separate process.

- Such systems are not suited for parallel or distributed databases, since a server process cannot execute on multiple computers at once. (However, concurrent threads within a process can be supported in a shared-memory multiprocessor system.) This is a serious drawback in large organizations, where parallel processing is critical for handling large workloads, and distributed data are becoming increasingly common.

One way to solve these problems is to run multiple application-server processes that access a common database, and to let the clients communicate with the application through a single communication process that routes requests. This model is called the **many-server, single-router model**, illustrated in Figure 26.1c. This model supports independent server processes for multiple applications; further, each application can have a pool of server processes, any one of which can handle a client session. The request can, for example, be routed to the most lightly loaded server in a pool. As before, each server process can itself be multithreaded, so that it can handle multiple clients concurrently. As a further generalization, the application servers can run on different sites of a parallel or distributed database, and the communication process can handle the coordination among the processes.

The above architecture is also widely used in Web servers. A Web server has a main process that receives HTTP requests, and then assigns the task of handling each request to a separate process (chosen from among a pool of processes). Each of the processes is itself multithreaded, so that it can handle multiple requests. The use of safe programming languages, such as Java, C#, or Visual Basic, allows Web application servers to protect threads from errors in other threads. In contrast, with a language like C or C++, errors such as memory allocation errors in one thread can cause other threads to fail.

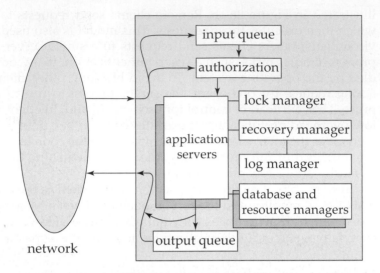

Figure 26.2   TP-monitor components.

A more general architecture has multiple processes, rather than just one, to communicate with clients. The client communication processes interact with one or more router processes, which route their requests to the appropriate server. Later-generation TP monitors therefore have a different architecture, called the **many-server, many-router model**, illustrated in Figure 26.1d. A controller process starts up the other processes and supervises their functioning. Very high performance Web-server systems also adopt such an architecture. The router processes are often network routers that direct traffic addressed to the same Internet address to different server computers, depending on where the traffic comes from. What looks like a single server with a single address to the outside world may be a collection of servers.

The detailed structure of a TP monitor appears in Figure 26.2. A TP monitor does more than simply pass messages to application servers. When messages arrive, they may have to be queued; thus, there is a **queue manager** for incoming messages. The queue may be a **durable queue**, whose entries survive system failures. Using a durable queue helps ensure that once received and stored in the queue, the messages will be processed eventually, regardless of system failures. Authorization and application-server management (for example, server start-up and routing of messages to servers) are further functions of a TP monitor. TP monitors often provide logging, recovery, and concurrency-control facilities, allowing application servers to implement the ACID transaction properties directly if required.

Finally, TP monitors also provide support for persistent messaging. Recall that persistent messaging (Section 19.4.3) provides a guarantee that the message will be delivered if (and only if) the transaction commits.

In addition to these facilities, many TP monitors also provided *presentation facilities* to create menus/forms interfaces for dumb clients such as terminals;

these facilities are no longer important since dumb clients are no longer widely used.

26.1.2 Application Coordination Using TP monitors

Applications today often have to interact with multiple databases. They may also have to interact with legacy systems, such as special-purpose data-storage systems built directly on file systems. Finally, they may have to communicate with users or other applications at remote sites. Hence, they also have to interact with communication subsystems. It is important to be able to coordinate data accesses, and to implement ACID properties for transactions across such systems.

Modern TP monitors provide support for the construction and administration of such large applications, built up from multiple subsystems such as databases, legacy systems, and communication systems. A TP monitor treats each subsystem as a **resource manager** that provides transactional access to some set of resources. The interface between the TP monitor and the resource manager is defined by a set of transaction primitives, such as *begin_transaction*, *commit_transaction*, *abort_transaction*, and *prepare_to_commit_transaction* (for two-phase commit). Of course, the resource manager must also provide other services, such as supplying data, to the application.

The resource-manager interface is defined by the X/Open Distributed Transaction Processing standard. Many database systems support the X/Open standards, and can act as resource managers. TP monitors—as well as other products, such as SQL systems, that support the X/Open standards—can connect to the resource managers.

In addition, services provided by a TP monitor, such as persistent messaging and durable queues, act as resource managers supporting transactions. The TP monitor can act as coordinator of two-phase commit for transactions that access these services as well as database systems. For example, when a queued update transaction is executed, an output message is delivered, and the request transaction is removed from the request queue. Two-phase commit between the database and the resource managers for the durable queue and persistent messaging helps ensure that, regardless of failures, either all these actions occur or none occurs.

We can also use TP monitors to administer complex client–server systems consisting of multiple servers and a large number of clients. The TP monitor coordinates activities such as system checkpoints and shutdowns. It provides security and authentication of clients. It administers server pools by adding servers or removing servers without interruption of the the database system. Finally, it controls the scope of failures. If a server fails, the TP monitor can detect this failure, abort the transactions in progress, and restart the transactions. If a node fails, the TP monitor can migrate transactions to servers at other nodes, again backing out incomplete transactions. When failed nodes restart, the TP monitor can govern the recovery of the node's resource managers.

TP monitors can be used to hide database failures in replicated systems; remote backup systems (Section 16.9) are an example of replicated systems. Transaction requests are sent to the TP monitor, which relays the messages to one of the database replicas (the primary site, in case of remote backup systems). If one site fails, the TP monitor can transparently route messages to a backup site, masking the failure of the first site.

In client–server systems, clients often interact with servers via a **remote-procedure-call** (RPC) mechanism, where a client invokes a procedure call, which is actually executed at the server, with the results sent back to the client. As far as the client code that invokes the RPC is concerned, the call looks like a local procedure-call invocation. TP monitor systems provide a **transactional RPC** interface to their services. In such an interface, the RPC mechanism provides calls that can be used to enclose a series of RPC calls within a transaction. Thus, updates performed by an RPC are carried out within the scope of the transaction, and can be rolled back if there is any failure.

26.2   Transactional Workflows

A **workflow** is an activity in which multiple tasks are executed in a coordinated way by different processing entities. A **task** defines some work to be done and can be specified in a number of ways, including a textual description in a file or electronic-mail message, a form, a message, or a computer program. The **processing entity** that performs the tasks may be a person or a software system (for example, a mailer, an application program, or a database-management system).

Figure 26.3 shows a few examples of workflows. A simple example is that of an electronic-mail system. The delivery of a single mail message may involve several mail systems that receive and forward the mail message, until the message reaches its destination, where it is stored. Other terms used in the database and related literature to refer to workflows include **task flow** and **multisystem applications**. Workflow tasks are also sometimes called **steps**.

In general, workflows may involve one or more humans. For instance, consider the processing of a loan. The relevant workflow appears in Figure 26.4. The person who wants a loan fills out a form, which is then checked by a loan officer. An employee who processes loan applications verifies the data in the form, using sources such as credit-reference bureaus. When all the required information has been collected, the loan officer may decide to approve the loan; that decision may

Workflow application	Typical task	Typical processing entity
electronic-mail routing	electronic-mail message	mailers
loan processing	form processing	humans, application software
purchase-order processing	form processing	humans, application software, DBMSs

Figure 26.3 Examples of workflows.

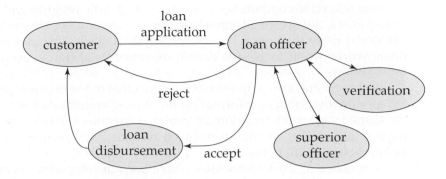

Figure 26.4 Workflow in loan processing.

then have to be approved by one or more superior officers, after which the loan can be made. Each human here performs a task; in a bank that has not automated the task of loan processing, the coordination of the tasks is typically carried out by passing of the loan application, with attached notes and other information, from one employee to the next. Other examples of workflows include processing of expense vouchers, of purchase orders, and of credit-card transactions.

Today, all the information related to a workflow is more than likely to be stored in a digital form on one or more computers, and, with the growth of networking, information can be easily transferred from one computer to another. Hence, it is feasible for organizations to automate their workflows. For example, to automate the tasks involved in loan processing, we can store the loan application and associated information in a database. The workflow itself then involves handing of responsibility from one human to the next, and possibly even to programs that can automatically fetch the required information. Humans can coordinate their activities by means such as electronic mail.

Workflows are becoming increasingly important for multiple reasons within as well as between organizations. Many organizations today have multiple software systems that need to work together. For example, when an employee joins an organization, information about the employee may have to be provided to the payroll system, to the library system, to authentication systems that allow the user to log on to computers, to a system that manages cafeteria accounts, an so on. Updates, such as when the employee changes status or leaves the organization, also have to be propagated to all the systems.

Organizations are increasingly automating their services; for example, a supplier may provide an automated system for customers to place orders. Several tasks may need to be carried out when an order is placed, including reserving production time to create the ordered product and delivery services to deliver the product.

We have to address two activities, in general, to automate a workflow. The first is **workflow specification**: detailing the tasks that must be carried out and defining the execution requirements. The second problem is **workflow execution**, which we must do while providing the safeguards of traditional database systems related to computation correctness and data integrity and durability. For example, it is not acceptable for a loan application or a voucher to be lost, or to be processed more than once, because of a system crash. The idea behind transactional workflows is to use and extend the concepts of transactions to the context of workflows.

Both activities are complicated by the fact that many organizations use several independently managed information-processing systems that, in most cases, were developed separately to automate different functions. Workflow activities may require interactions among several such systems, each performing a task, as well as interactions with humans.

A number of workflow systems have been developed in recent years. Here, we study properties of workflow systems at a relatively abstract level, without going into the details of any particular system.

26.2.1   Workflow Specification

Internal aspects of a task do not need to be modeled for the purpose of specification and management of a workflow. In an abstract view of a task, a task may use parameters stored in its input variables, may retrieve and update data in the local system, may store its results in its output variables, and may be queried about its execution state. At any time during the execution, the **workflow state** consists of the collection of states of the workflow's constituent tasks, and the states (values) of all variables in the workflow specification.

The coordination of tasks can be specified either statically or dynamically. A static specification defines the tasks—and dependencies among them—before the execution of the workflow begins. For instance, the tasks in an expense-voucher workflow may consist of the approvals of the voucher by a secretary, a manager, and an accountant, in that order, and finally the delivery of a check. The dependencies among the tasks may be simple—each task has to be completed before the next begins.

A generalization of this strategy is to have a precondition for execution of each task in the workflow, so that all possible tasks in a workflow and their dependencies are known in advance, but only those tasks whose preconditions are satisfied are executed. The preconditions can be defined through dependencies such as the following:

- **Execution states** of other tasks—for example, "task t_i cannot start until task t_j has ended," or "task t_i must abort if task t_j has committed."

- **Output values** of other tasks—for example, "task t_i can start if task t_j returns a value greater than 25," or "the manager-approval task can start if the secretary-approval task returns a value of OK."

- **External variables** modified by external events—for example, "task t_i cannot be started before 9 A.M.," or "task t_i must be started within 24 hours of the completion of task t_j."

We can combine the dependencies by the regular logical connectors (**or**, **and**, **not**) to form complex scheduling preconditions.

An example of dynamic scheduling of tasks is an electronic-mail routing system. The next task to be scheduled for a given mail message depends on what the destination address of the message is, and on which intermediate routers are functioning.

26.2.2 Failure-Atomicity Requirements of a Workflow

The workflow designer may specify the **failure-atomicity** requirements of a workflow according to the semantics of the workflow. The traditional notion of failure atomicity would require that a failure of any task result in the failure of the workflow. However, a workflow can, in many cases, survive the failure of one of its tasks—for example, by executing a functionally equivalent task at another site. Therefore, we should allow the designer to define failure-atomicity requirements of a workflow. The system must guarantee that every execution of a workflow will terminate in a state that satisfies the failure-atomicity requirements defined by the designer. We call those states **acceptable termination states** of a workflow. All other execution states of a workflow constitute a set of **nonacceptable termination states**, in which the failure-atomicity requirements may be violated.

An acceptable termination state can be designated as committed or aborted. A **committed acceptable termination state** is an execution state in which the objectives of a workflow have been achieved. In contrast, an **aborted acceptable termination state** is a valid termination state in which a workflow has failed to achieve its objectives. If an aborted acceptable termination state has been reached, all undesirable effects of the partial execution of the workflow must be undone in accordance with that workflow's failure-atomicity requirements.

A workflow must reach an acceptable termination state *even in the presence of system failures*. Thus, if a workflow is in a nonacceptable termination state at the time of failure, during system recovery it must be brought to an acceptable termination state (whether aborted or committed).

For example, in the loan-processing workflow, in the final state, either the loan applicant is told that a loan cannot be made or the loan is disbursed. In case of failures such as a long failure of the verification system, the loan application could be returned to the loan applicant with a suitable explanation; this outcome would constitute an aborted acceptable termination. A committed acceptable termination would be either the acceptance or the rejection of the loan.

In general, a task can commit and release its resources before the workflow reaches a termination state. However, if the multitask transaction later aborts, its failure atomicity may require that we undo the effects of already completed tasks (for example, committed subtransactions) by executing compensating tasks (as subtransactions). The semantics of compensation requires that a compensating transaction eventually complete its execution successfully, possibly after a number of resubmissions.

In an expense-voucher-processing workflow, for example, a department-budget balance may be reduced on the basis of an initial approval of a voucher by the manager. If the voucher is later rejected, whether because of failure or for other reasons, the budget may have to be restored by a compensating transaction.

26.2.3   Execution of Workflows

The execution of the tasks may be controlled by a human coordinator or by a software system called a **workflow-management system**. A workflow-management system consists of a scheduler, task agents, and a mechanism to query the state of the workflow system. A task agent controls the execution of a task by a processing entity. A scheduler is a program that processes workflows by submitting various tasks for execution, monitoring various events, and evaluating conditions related to intertask dependencies. A scheduler may submit a task for execution (to a task agent), or may request that a previously submitted task be aborted. In the case of multidatabase transactions, the tasks are subtransactions, and the processing entities are local database-management systems. In accordance with the workflow specifications, the scheduler enforces the scheduling dependencies and is responsible for ensuring that tasks reach acceptable termination states.

There are three architectural approaches to the development of a workflow-management system. A **centralized architecture** has a single scheduler that schedules the tasks for all concurrently executing workflows. The **partially distributed architecture** has one scheduler instantiated for each workflow. When the issues of concurrent execution can be separated from the scheduling function, the latter option is a natural choice. A **fully distributed architecture** has no scheduler, but the task agents coordinate their execution by communicating with one another to satisfy task dependencies and other workflow execution requirements.

The simplest workflow-execution systems follow the fully distributed approach just described and are based on messaging. Messaging may be implemented by persistent messaging mechanisms, to provide guaranteed delivery. Some implementations use email for messaging; such implementations provide many of the features of persistent messaging, but generally do not guarantee atomicity of message delivery and transaction commit. Each site has a task agent that executes tasks received through messages. Execution may also involve presenting messages to humans, who have then to carry out some action. When a task is completed at a site, and needs to be processed at another site, the task agent dispatches a message to the next site. The message contains all relevant information about the task to be performed. Such message-based workflow systems are particularly useful in networks that may be disconnected for part of the time.

The centralized approach is used in workflow systems where the data are stored in a central database. The scheduler notifies various agents, such as humans or computer programs, that a task has to be carried out, and keeps track of task completion. It is easier to keep track of the state of a workflow with a centralized approach than it is with a fully distributed approach.

The scheduler must guarantee that a workflow will terminate in one of the specified acceptable termination states. Ideally, before attempting to execute a workflow, the scheduler should examine that workflow to check whether the workflow may terminate in a nonacceptable state. If the scheduler cannot guarantee that a workflow will terminate in an acceptable state, it should reject such specifications without attempting to execute the workflow. As an example, let us consider a workflow consisting of two tasks represented by subtransactions S_1 and S_2, with the failure-atomicity requirements indicating that either both or neither of the subtransactions should be committed. If S_1 and S_2 do not provide prepared-to-commit states (for a two-phase commit), and further do not have compensating transactions, then it is possible to reach a state where one subtransaction is committed and the other aborted, and there is no way to bring both to the same state. Therefore, such a workflow specification is **unsafe**, and should be rejected.

Safety checks such as the one just described may be impossible or impractical to implement in the scheduler; it then becomes the responsibility of the person designing the workflow specification to ensure that the workflows are safe.

26.2.4 Recovery of a Workflow

The objective of **workflow recovery** is to enforce the failure atomicity of the workflows. The recovery procedures must make sure that, if a failure occurs in any of the workflow-processing components (including the scheduler), the workflow will eventually reach an acceptable termination state (whether aborted or committed). For example, the scheduler could continue processing after failure and recovery, as though nothing happened, thus providing forward recoverability. Otherwise, the scheduler could abort the whole workflow (that is, reach one of the global abort states). In either case, some subtransactions may need to be committed or even submitted for execution (for example, compensating subtransactions).

We assume that the processing entities involved in the workflow have their own recovery systems and handle their local failures. To recover the execution-environment context, the failure-recovery routines need to restore the state information of the scheduler at the time of failure, including the information about the execution states of each task. Therefore, the appropriate status information must be logged on stable storage.

We also need to consider the contents of the message queues. When one agent hands off a task to another, the handoff should be carried out exactly once: If the handoff happens twice a task may get executed twice; if the handoff does not occur, the task may get lost. Persistent messaging (Section 19.4.3) provides exactly the features to ensure positive, single handoff.

26.2.5 Workflow-Management Systems

Workflows are often hand coded as part of application systems. For instance, enterprise resource planning (ERP) systems, which help coordinate activities across an entire enterprise, have numerous workflows built into them.

The goal of workflow-management systems is to simplify the construction of workflows and make them more reliable, by permitting them to be specified in a high-level manner and executed in accordance with the specification. There are a large number of commercial workflow-management systems; some are general-purpose workflow-management systems, while others are specific to particular workflows, such as order processing or bug/failure reporting systems.

In today's world of interconnected organizations, it is not sufficient to manage workflows only within an organization. Workflows that cross organizational boundaries are becoming increasingly common. For instance, consider an order placed by an organization and communicated to another organization that fulfills the order. In each organization there may be a workflow associated with the order, and it is important that the workflows be able to interoperate, in order to minimize human intervention.

The term **business process management** is used to refer to the management of workflows related to business processes. Today, applications are increasingly making their functionality available as services that can be invoked by other applications, often using a Web service architecture. A system architecture based on invoking services provided by multiple applications is referred to as a **service oriented architecture** SOA. Such services are the base layer on top of which workflow management is implemented today. The process logic that controls the workflow by invoking the services is referred to as **orchestration**.

Business process management systems based on the SOA architecture include Microsoft's BizTalk Server, IBMs WebSphere Business Integration Server Foundation, and BEAs WebLogic Process Edition, among others.

The **Web Services Business Process Execution Language** (WS-BPEL) is an XML based standard for specifying Web services and business processes (workflows) based on the Web services, which can be executed by a business process management system. The **Business Process Modeling Notation** (BPMN), is a standard for graphical modeling of business processes in a workflow, and **XML Process Definition Language** (XPDL) is an XML based representation of business process definitions, based on BPMN diagrams.

26.3 E-Commerce

E-commerce refers to the process of carrying out various activities related to commerce, through electronic means, primarily through the Internet. The types of activities include:

- Presale activities, needed to inform the potential buyer about the product or service being sold.

- The sale process, which includes negotiations on price and quality of service, and other contractual matters.

- The marketplace: When there are multiple sellers and buyers for a product, a marketplace, such as a stock exchange, helps in negotiating the price to be paid for the product. Auctions are used when there is a single seller and multiple buyers, and reverse auctions are used when there is a single buyer and multiple sellers.

- Payment for the sale.

- Activities related to delivery of the product or service. Some products and services can be delivered over the Internet; for others the Internet is used only for providing shipping information and for tracking shipments of products.

- Customer support and postsale service.

Databases are used extensively to support these activities. For some of the activities, the use of databases is straightforward, but there are interesting application development issues for the other activities.

26.3.1 E-Catalogs

Any e-commerce site provides users with a catalog of the products and services that the site supplies. The services provided by an e-catalog may vary considerably.

At the minimum, an e-catalog must provide browsing and search facilities to help customers find the product for which they are looking. To help with browsing, products should be organized into an intuitive hierarchy, so a few clicks on hyperlinks can lead customers to the products in which they are interested. Keywords provided by the customer (for example, "digital camera" or "computer") should speed up the process of finding required products. E-catalogs should also provide a means for customers to easily compare alternatives from which to choose among competing products.

E-catalogs can be customized for the customer. For instance, a retailer may have an agreement with a large company to supply some products at a discount. An employee of the company, viewing the catalog to purchase products for the company, should see prices with the negotiated discount, instead of the regular prices. Because of legal restrictions on sales of some types of items, customers who are underage, or from certain states or countries, should not be shown items that cannot legally be sold to them. Catalogs can also be personalized to individual users, on the basis of past buying history. For instance, frequent customers may be offered special discounts on some items.

Supporting such customization requires customer information as well as special pricing/discount information and sales restriction information to be stored in a database. There are also challenges in supporting very high transaction rates, which are often tackled by caching of query results or generated Web pages.

26.3.2 Marketplaces

When there are multiple sellers or multiple buyers (or both) for a product, a marketplace helps in negotiating the price to be paid for the product. There are several different types of marketplaces:

- In a **reverse auction** system a buyer states requirements, and sellers bid for supplying the item. The supplier quoting the lowest price wins. In a closed bidding system, the bids are not made public, whereas in an open bidding system the bids are made public.

- In an **auction** there are multiple buyers and a single seller. For simplicity, assume that there is only one instance of each item being sold. Buyers bid for the items being sold, and the highest bidder for an item gets to buy the item at the bid price.

  When there are multiple copies of an item, things become more complicated: Suppose there are four items, and one bidder may want three copies for $10 each, while another wants two copies for $13 each. It is not possible to satisfy both bids. If the items will be of no value if they are not sold (for instance, airline seats, which must be sold before the plane leaves), the seller simply picks a set of bids that maximizes the income. Otherwise the decision is more complicated.

- In an **exchange**, such as a stock exchange, there are multiple sellers and multiple buyers. Buyers can specify the maximum price they are willing to pay, while sellers specify the minimum price they want. There is usually a *market maker* who matches buy and sell bids, deciding on the price for each trade (for instance, at the price of the sell bid).

There are other more complex types of marketplaces.

Among the database issues in handling marketplaces are these:

- Bidders need to be authenticated before they are allowed to bid.

- Bids (buy or sell) need to be recorded securely in a database. Bids need to be communicated quickly to other people involved in the marketplace (such as all the buyers or all the sellers), who may be numerous.

- Delays in broadcasting bids can lead to financial losses to some participants.

- The volumes of trades may be extremely large at times of stock market volatility, or toward the end of auctions. Thus, very high performance databases with large degrees of parallelism are used for such systems.

26.3.3   Order Settlement

After items have been selected (perhaps through an electronic catalog) and the price determined (perhaps by an electronic marketplace), the order has to be settled. Settlement involves payment for goods and the delivery of the goods.

A simple but unsecure way of paying electronically is to send a credit-card number. There are two major problems. First, credit-card fraud is possible. When a buyer pays for physical goods, companies can ensure that the address for delivery matches the cardholder's address, so no one else can receive the goods, but for goods delivered electronically no such check is possible. Second, the seller has to be trusted to bill only for the agreed-on item and to not pass on the card number to unauthorized people who may misuse it.

Several protocols are available for secure payments that avoid both the problems listed above. In addition, they provide for better privacy, whereby the seller may not be given any unnecessary details about the buyer, and the credit-card company is not provided any unnecessary information about the items purchased. All information transmitted must be encrypted so that anyone intercepting the data on the network cannot find out the contents. Public-/private-key encryption is widely used for this task.

The protocols must also prevent **person-in-the-middle attacks**, where someone can impersonate the bank or credit-card company, or even the seller, or buyer, and steal secret information. Impersonation can be perpetrated by passing off a fake key as someone else's public key (the bank's or credit-card company's, or the merchant's or the buyer's). Impersonation is prevented by a system of **digital certificates**, whereby public keys are signed by a certification agency, whose public key is well known (or which in turn has its public key certified by another certification agency and so on up to a key that is well known). From the well-known public key, the system can authenticate the other keys by checking the certificates in reverse sequence. Digital certificates were described earlier, in Section 9.8.3.2.

Several novel payment systems were developed in the early days of the Web. One of these was a secure payment protocol called the *Secure Electronic Transaction* (*SET*) protocol. The protocol requires several rounds of communication between the buyer, seller, and the bank, in order to guarantee safety of the transaction. There were also systems that provide for greater anonymity, similar to that provided by physical cash. The *DigiCash* payment system was one such system. When a payment is made in such a system, it is not possible to identify the purchaser. In contrast, identifying purchasers is very easy with credit cards, and even in the case of SET, it is possible to identify the purchaser with the cooperation of the credit-card company or bank. However, none of these systems was successful commercially, for both technical and non-technical reasons.

Today, many banks provide **secure payment gateways** which allow a purchaser to pay online at the banks Web site, without exposing credit card or bank account information to the online merchant. When making a purchase at an online merchant, the purchaser's Web browser is redirected to the gateway to complete the payment by providing credit card or bank account information, after which the purchaser is again redirected back to the merchant's site to complete the purchase. Unlike the SET or DigiCash protocols, there is no software running on the purchasers machine, except a Web browser; as a result this approach has found wide success where the earlier approaches failed.

An alternative approach which is used by the PayPal system is for both the purchaser and the merchant to have an account on a common platform, and the money transfer happens entirely within the common platform. The purchaser first loads her account with money using a credit card, and can then transfer money to the merchants account. This approach has been very successful with small merchants, since it does not require either the purchaser or the merchant to run any software.

26.4   Main-Memory Databases

To allow a high rate of transaction processing (hundreds or thousands of transactions per second), we must use high-performance hardware, and must exploit parallelism. These techniques alone, however, are insufficient to obtain very low response times, since disk I/O remains a bottleneck—about 10 milliseconds are required for each I/O, and this number has not decreased at a rate comparable to the increase in processor speeds. Disk I/O is often the bottleneck for reads, as well as for transaction commits. The long disk latency increases not only the time to access a data item, but also limits the number of accesses per second.[1]

We can make a database system less disk bound by increasing the size of the database buffer. Advances in main-memory technology let us construct large main memories at relatively low cost. Today, commercial 64-bit systems can support main memories of tens of gigabytes. Oracle TimesTen is a currently available main-memory database. Additional information on main-memory databases is given in the references in the bibliographical notes.

For some applications, such as real-time control, it is necessary to store data in main memory to meet performance requirements. The memory size required for most such systems is not exceptionally large, although there are at least a few applications that require multiple gigabytes of data to be memory resident. Since memory sizes have been growing at a very fast rate, an increasing number of applications can be expected to have data that fit into main memory.

Large main memories allow faster processing of transactions, since data are memory resident. However, there are still disk-related limitations:

- Log records must be written to stable storage before a transaction is committed. The improved performance made possible by a large main memory may result in the logging process becoming a bottleneck. We can reduce commit time by creating a stable log buffer in main memory, using nonvolatile RAM (implemented, for example, by battery-backed-up memory). The overhead imposed by logging can also be reduced by the *group-commit* technique discussed later in this section. Throughput (number of transactions per second) is still limited by the data-transfer rate of the log disk.

- Buffer blocks marked as modified by committed transactions still have to be written so that the amount of log that has to be replayed at recovery time is reduced. If the update rate is extremely high, the disk data-transfer rate may become a bottleneck.

- If the system crashes, all of main memory is lost. On recovery, the system has an empty database buffer, and data items must be input from disk when they are accessed. Therefore, even after recovery is complete, it takes some time before the database is fully loaded in main memory and high-speed processing of transactions can resume.

On the other hand, a main-memory database provides opportunities for optimizations:

---

[1]Write latency for flash depends on whether an erase operation must be done first.

- Since memory is costlier than disk space, internal data structures in main-memory databases have to be designed to reduce space requirements. However, data structures can have pointers crossing multiple pages, unlike those in disk databases, where the cost of the I/Os to traverse multiple pages would be excessively high. For example, tree structures in main-memory databases can be relatively deep, unlike B^+-trees, but should minimize space requirements.

  However, the speed difference between cache memory and main-memory, and the fact that data is transferred between main-memory and cache in units of a *cache-line* (typically about 64 bytes), results in a situation where the relationship between cache and main-memory is not dissimilar to the relationship between main-memory and disk (although with smaller speed differences). As a result, B^+-trees with small nodes that fit in a cache line have been found quite useful even in main-memory databases.

- There is no need to pin buffer pages in memory before data are accessed, since buffer pages will never be replaced.

- Query-processing techniques should be designed to minimize space overhead, so that main-memory limits are not exceeded while a query is being evaluated; that situation would result in paging to swap area, and would slow down query processing.

- Once the disk I/O bottleneck is removed, operations such as locking and latching may become bottlenecks. Such bottlenecks must be eliminated by improvements in the implementation of these operations.

- Recovery algorithms can be optimized, since pages rarely need to be written out to make space for other pages.

The process of committing a transaction T requires these records to be written to stable storage:

- All log records associated with T that have not been output to stable storage.

- The <T **commit**> log record.

These output operations frequently require the output of blocks that are only partially filled. To ensure that nearly full blocks are output, we use the **group-commit** technique. Instead of attempting to commit T when T completes, the system waits until several transactions have completed, or a certain period of time has passed since a transaction completed execution. It then commits the group of transactions that are waiting, together. Blocks written to the log on stable storage would contain records of several transactions. By careful choice of group size and maximum waiting time, the system can ensure that blocks are full when they are written to stable storage without making transactions wait excessively. This technique results, on average, in fewer output operations per committed transaction.

Although group commit reduces the overhead imposed by logging, it results in a slight delay in commit of transactions that perform updates. The delay can be made quite small (say, 10 milliseconds), which is acceptable for many applications. These delays can be eliminated if disks or disk controllers support nonvolatile RAM buffers for write operations. Transactions can commit as soon as the write is performed on the nonvolatile RAM buffer. In this case, there is no need for group commit.

Note that group commit is useful even in databases with disk-resident data, not just for main-memory databases. If flash storage is used instead of magnetic disk for storing log records, the commit delay is significantly reduced. However, group commit can still be useful since it minimizes the number of pages written; this translates to performance benefits in flash storage, since pages cannot be overwritten, and the erase operation is expensive. (Flash storage systems remap logical pages to a pre-erased physical page, avoiding delay at the time a page is written, but the erase operation must be performed eventually as part of garbage collection of old versions of pages.)

26.5   Real-Time Transaction Systems

The integrity constraints that we have considered thus far pertain to the values stored in the database. In certain applications, the constraints include **deadlines** by which a task must be completed. Examples of such applications include plant management, traffic control, and scheduling. When deadlines are included, correctness of an execution is no longer solely an issue of database consistency. Rather, we are concerned with how many deadlines are missed, and by how much time they are missed. Deadlines are characterized as follows:

- **Hard deadline**. Serious problems, such as system crash, may occur if a task is not completed by its deadline.

- **Firm deadline**. The task has zero value if it is completed after the deadline.

- **Soft deadlines**. The task has diminishing value if it is completed after the deadline, with the value approaching zero as the degree of lateness increases.

Systems with deadlines are called **real-time systems**.

Transaction management in real-time systems must take deadlines into account. If the concurrency-control protocol determines that a transaction T_i must wait, it may cause T_i to miss the deadline. In such cases, it may be preferable to pre-empt the transaction holding the lock, and to allow T_i to proceed. Pre-emption must be used with care, however, because the time lost by the pre-empted transaction (due to rollback and restart) may cause the pre-empted transaction to miss its deadline. Unfortunately, it is difficult to determine whether rollback or waiting is preferable in a given situation.

A major difficulty in supporting real-time constraints arises from the variance in transaction execution time. In the best case, all data accesses reference data in the database buffer. In the worst case, each access causes a buffer page to be written to disk (preceded by the requisite log records), followed by the reading from disk of the page containing the data to be accessed. Because the two or more disk accesses required in the worst case take several orders of magnitude more time than the main-memory references required in the best case, transaction execution time can be estimated only very poorly if data are resident on disk. Hence, main-memory databases are often used if real-time constraints have to be met.

However, even if data are resident in main memory, variances in execution time arise from lock waits, transaction aborts, and so on. Researchers have devoted considerable effort to concurrency control for real-time databases. They have extended locking protocols to provide higher priority for transactions with early deadlines. They have found that optimistic concurrency protocols perform well in real-time databases; that is, these protocols result in fewer missed deadlines than even the extended locking protocols. The bibliographical notes provide references to research in the area of real-time databases.

In real-time systems, deadlines, rather than absolute speed, are the most important issue. Designing a real-time system involves ensuring that there is enough processing power to meet deadlines without requiring excessive hardware resources. Achieving this objective, despite the variance in execution time resulting from transaction management, remains a challenging problem.

26.6 Long-Duration Transactions

The transaction concept developed initially in the context of data-processing applications, in which most transactions are noninteractive and of short duration. Although the techniques presented here and earlier in Chapters 14, 15, and 16 work well in those applications, serious problems arise when this concept is applied to database systems that involve human interaction. Such transactions have these key properties:

- **Long duration**. Once a human interacts with an active transaction, that transaction becomes a **long-duration transaction** from the perspective of the computer, since human response time is slow relative to computer speed. Furthermore, in design applications, the human activity may involve hours, days, or an even longer period. Thus, transactions may be of long duration in human terms, as well as in machine terms.

- **Exposure of uncommitted data**. Data generated and displayed to a user by a long-duration transaction are uncommitted, since the transaction may abort. Thus, users—and, as a result, other transactions—may be forced to read uncommitted data. If several users are cooperating on a project, user transactions may need to exchange data prior to transaction commit.

- **Subtasks**. An interactive transaction may consist of a set of subtasks initiated by the user. The user may wish to abort a subtask without necessarily causing the entire transaction to abort.

- **Recoverability**. It is unacceptable to abort a long-duration interactive transaction because of a system crash. The active transaction must be recovered to a state that existed shortly before the crash so that relatively little human work is lost.

- **Performance**. Good performance in an interactive transaction system is defined as fast response time. This definition is in contrast to that in a noninteractive system, in which high throughput (number of transactions per second) is the goal. Systems with high throughput make efficient use of system resources. However, in the case of interactive transactions, the most costly resource is the user. If the efficiency and satisfaction of the user is to be optimized, response time should be fast (from a human perspective). In those cases where a task takes a long time, response time should be predictable (that is, the variance in response times should be low), so that users can manage their time well.

In Sections 26.6.1 through 26.6.5, we shall see why these five properties are incompatible with the techniques presented thus far and shall discuss how those techniques can be modified to accommodate long-duration interactive transactions.

26.6.1   Nonserializable Executions

The properties that we discussed make it impractical to enforce the requirement used in earlier chapters that only serializable schedules be permitted. Each of the concurrency-control protocols of Chapter 15 has adverse effects on long-duration transactions:

- **Two-phase locking**. When a lock cannot be granted, the transaction requesting the lock is forced to wait for the data item in question to be unlocked. The duration of this wait is proportional to the duration of the transaction holding the lock. If the data item is locked by a short-duration transaction, we expect that the waiting time will be short (except in case of deadlock or extraordinary system load). However, if the data item is locked by a long-duration transaction, the wait will be of long duration. Long waiting times lead to both longer response time and an increased chance of deadlock.

- **Graph-based protocols**. Graph-based protocols allow for locks to be released earlier than under the two-phase locking protocols, and they prevent deadlock. However, they impose an ordering on the data items. Transactions must lock data items in a manner consistent with this ordering. As a result, a transaction may have to lock more data than it needs. Furthermore, a transaction must hold a lock until there is no chance that the lock will be needed again. Thus, long-duration lock waits are likely to occur.

- **Timestamp-based protocols**. Timestamp protocols never require a transaction to wait. However, they do require transactions to abort under certain circumstances. If a long-duration transaction is aborted, a substantial amount of work is lost. For noninteractive transactions, this lost work is a performance issue. For interactive transactions, the issue is also one of user satisfaction. It is highly undesirable for a user to find that several hours' worth of work have been undone.

- **Validation protocols**. Like timestamp-based protocols, validation protocols enforce serializability by means of transaction abort.

Thus, it appears that the enforcement of serializability results in long-duration waits, in abort of long-duration transactions, or in both. There are theoretical results, cited in the bibliographical notes, that substantiate this conclusion.

Further difficulties with the enforcement of serializability arise when we consider recovery issues. We previously discussed the problem of cascading rollback, in which the abort of a transaction may lead to the abort of other transactions. This phenomenon is undesirable, particularly for long-duration transactions. If locking is used, exclusive locks must be held until the end of the transaction, if cascading rollback is to be avoided. This holding of exclusive locks, however, increases the length of transaction waiting time.

Thus, it appears that the enforcement of transaction atomicity must either lead to an increased probability of long-duration waits or create a possibility of cascading rollback.

Snapshot isolation, described in Section 15.7, can provide a partial solution to these issues, as can the *optimistic concurrency control without read validation* protocol described in Section 15.9.3. The latter protocol was in fact designed specifically to deal with long duration transactions that involve user interaction. Although it does not guarantee serializability, optimistic concurrency control without read validation is quite widely used.

However, when transactions are of long duration, conflicting updates are more likely, resulting in additional waits or aborts. These considerations are the basis for the alternative concepts of correctness of concurrent executions and transaction recovery that we consider in the remainder of this section.

26.6.2 Concurrency Control

The fundamental goal of database concurrency control is to ensure that concurrent execution of transactions does not result in a loss of database consistency. The concept of serializability can be used to achieve this goal, since all serializable schedules preserve consistency of the database. However, not all schedules that preserve consistency of the database are serializable. For an example, consider again a bank database consisting of two accounts A and B, with the consistency requirement that the sum $A + B$ be preserved. Although the schedule of Figure 26.5 is not conflict serializable, it nevertheless preserves the sum of $A + B$. It also illustrates two important points about the concept of correctness without serializability.

- Correctness depends on the specific consistency constraints for the database.

- Correctness depends on the properties of operations performed by each transaction.

T_1	T_2
read(A)	
$A := A - 50$	
write(A)	
	read(B)
	$B := B - 10$
	write(B)
read(B)	
$B := B + 50$	
write(B)	
	read(A)
	$A := A + 10$
	write(A)

Figure 26.5   A non-conflict-serializable schedule.

In general it is not possible to perform an automatic analysis of low-level operations by transactions and check their effect on database consistency constraints. However, there are simpler techniques. One is to use the database consistency constraints as the basis for a split of the database into subdatabases on which concurrency can be managed separately. Another is to treat some operations besides **read** and **write** as fundamental low-level operations and to extend concurrency control to deal with them.

The bibliographical notes reference other techniques for ensuring consistency without requiring serializability. Many of these techniques exploit variants of multiversion concurrency control (see Section 15.6). For older data-processing applications that need only one version, multiversion protocols impose a high space overhead to store the extra versions. Since many of the new database applications require the maintenance of versions of data, concurrency-control techniques that exploit multiple versions are practical.

26.6.3 Nested and Multilevel Transactions

A long-duration transaction can be viewed as a collection of related subtasks or subtransactions. By structuring a transaction as a set of subtransactions, we are able to enhance parallelism, since it may be possible to run several subtransactions in parallel. Furthermore, it is possible to deal with failure of a subtransaction (due to abort, system crash, and so on) without having to roll back the entire long-duration transaction.

A nested or multilevel transaction T consists of a set $T = \{t_1, t_2, \ldots, t_n\}$ of subtransactions and a partial order P on T. A subtransaction t_i in T may abort without forcing T to abort. Instead, T may either restart t_i or simply choose not to run t_i. If t_i commits, this action does not make t_i permanent (unlike the situation in Chapter 16). Instead, t_i *commits to* T, and may still abort (or require compensation —see Section 26.6.4) if T aborts. An execution of T must not violate the partial order P. That is, if an edge $t_i \rightarrow t_j$ appears in the precedence graph, then $t_j \rightarrow t_i$ must not be in the transitive closure of P.

Nesting may be several levels deep, representing a subdivision of a transaction into subtasks, subsubtasks, and so on. At the lowest level of nesting, we have the standard database operations **read** and **write** that we have used previously.

If a subtransaction of T is permitted to release locks on completion, T is called a **multilevel transaction**. When a multilevel transaction represents a long-duration activity, the transaction is sometimes referred to as a **saga**. Alternatively, if locks held by a subtransaction t_i of T are automatically assigned to T on completion of t_i, T is called a **nested transaction**.

Although the main practical value of multilevel transactions arises in complex, long-duration transactions, we shall use the simple example of Figure 26.5 to show how nesting can create higher-level operations that may enhance concurrency. We rewrite transaction T_1, using subtransactions $T_{1,1}$ and $T_{1,2}$, which perform increment or decrement operations:

- T_1 consists of:

    - $T_{1,1}$, which subtracts 50 from A.

    - $T_{1,2}$, which adds 50 to B.

Similarly, we rewrite transaction T_2, using subtransactions $T_{2,1}$ and $T_{2,2}$, which also perform increment or decrement operations:

- T_2 consists of:

    - $T_{2,1}$, which subtracts 10 from B.

    - $T_{2,2}$, which adds 10 to A.

No ordering is specified on $T_{1,1}$, $T_{1,2}$, $T_{2,1}$, and $T_{2,2}$. Any execution of these subtransactions will generate a correct result. The schedule of Figure 26.5 corresponds to the schedule $< T_{1,1}, T_{2,1}, T_{1,2}, T_{2,2} >$.

26.6.4 Compensating Transactions

To reduce the frequency of long-duration waiting, we arrange for uncommitted updates to be exposed to other concurrently executing transactions. Indeed, multilevel transactions may allow this exposure. However, the exposure of uncommitted data creates the potential for cascading rollbacks. The concept of **compensating transactions** helps us to deal with this problem.

Let transaction T be divided into several subtransactions $t_1, t_2, \ldots, t_n$. After a subtransaction t_i commits, it releases its locks. Now, if the outer-level transaction T has to be aborted, the effect of its subtransactions must be undone. Suppose that subtransactions $t_1, \ldots, t_k$ have committed, and that t_{k+1} was executing when the decision to abort is made. We can undo the effects of t_{k+1} by aborting that subtransaction. However, it is not possible to abort subtransactions $t_1, \ldots, t_k$, since they have committed already.

Instead, we execute a new subtransaction ct_i, called a *compensating transaction*, to undo the effect of a subtransaction t_i. Each subtransaction t_i is required to have a compensating transaction ct_i. The compensating transactions must be executed in the inverse order $ct_k, \ldots, ct_1$. Here are several examples of compensation:

- Consider the schedule of Figure 26.5, which we have shown to be correct, although not conflict serializable. Each subtransaction releases its locks once it completes. Suppose that T_2 fails just prior to termination, after $T_{2,2}$ has released its locks. We then run a compensating transaction for $T_{2,2}$ that subtracts 10 from A and a compensating transaction for $T_{2,1}$ that adds 10 to B.

- Consider a database insert by transaction T_i that, as a side effect, causes a B^+-tree index to be updated. The insert operation may have modified several nodes of the B^+-tree index. Other transactions may have read these nodes in accessing data other than the record inserted by T_i. As mentioned in Section 16.7, we can undo the insertion by deleting the record inserted by T_i. The result is a correct, consistent B^+-tree, but is not necessarily one with exactly the same structure as the one we had before T_i started. Thus, deletion is a compensating action for insertion.

- Consider a long-duration transaction T_i representing a travel reservation. Transaction T has three subtransactions: $T_{i,1}$, which makes airline reservations; $T_{i,2}$, which reserves rental cars; and $T_{i,3}$, which reserves a hotel room. Suppose that the hotel cancels the reservation. Instead of undoing all of T_i, we compensate for the failure of $T_{i,3}$ by deleting the old hotel reservation and making a new one.

If the system crashes in the middle of executing an outer-level transaction, its subtransactions must be rolled back when it recovers. The techniques described in Section 16.7 can be used for this purpose.

Compensation for the failure of a transaction requires that the semantics of the failed transaction be used. For certain operations, such as incrementation or insertion into a B^+-tree, the corresponding compensation is easily defined. For more complex transactions, the application programmers may have to define the correct form of compensation at the time that the transaction is coded. For complex interactive transactions, it may be necessary for the system to interact with the user to determine the proper form of compensation.

26.6.5   Implementation Issues

The transaction concepts discussed in this section create serious difficulties for implementation. We present a few of them here, and discuss how we can address these problems.

Long-duration transactions must survive system crashes. We can ensure that they will by performing a **redo** on committed subtransactions, and by performing either an **undo** or compensation for any short-duration subtransactions that were active at the time of the crash. However, these actions solve only part of the problem. In typical database systems, such internal system data as lock tables and transaction timestamps are kept in volatile storage. For a long-duration transaction to be resumed after a crash, these data must be restored. Therefore, it is necessary to log not only changes to the database, but also changes to internal system data pertaining to long-duration transactions.

Logging of updates is made more complex when certain types of data items exist in the database. A data item may be a CAD design, text of a document, or another form of composite design. Such data items are physically large. Thus, storing both the old and new values of the data item in a log record is undesirable.

There are two approaches to reducing the overhead of ensuring the recoverability of large data items:

- **Operation logging**. Only the operation performed on the data item and the data-item name are stored in the log. Operation logging is also called **logical logging**. For each operation, an inverse operation must exist. We perform **undo** using the inverse operation and **redo** using the operation itself. Recovery through operation logging is more difficult, since **redo** and **undo** are not idempotent. Further, using logical logging for an operation that updates multiple pages is greatly complicated by the fact that some, but not all, of the updated pages may have been written to the disk, so it is hard to apply either the **redo** or the **undo** of the operation on the disk image during recovery. Using physical redo logging and logical undo logging, as described in Section 16.7, provides the concurrency benefits of logical logging while avoiding the above pitfalls.

- **Logging and shadow paging**. Logging is used for modifications to small data items, but large data items are often made recoverable via a shadowing, or copy-on-write, technique. When we use shadowing, it is possible to reduce the overhead by keeping copies of only those pages that are actually modified.

Regardless of the technique used, the complexities introduced by long-duration transactions and large data items complicate the recovery process. Thus, it is desirable to allow certain noncritical data to be exempt from logging, and to rely instead on offline backups and human intervention.

26.7 Summary

- Workflows are activities that involve the coordinated execution of multiple tasks performed by different processing entities. They exist not just in computer applications, but also in almost all organizational activities. With the growth of networks, and the existence of multiple autonomous database systems, workflows provide a convenient way of carrying out tasks that involve multiple systems.

- Although the usual ACID transactional requirements are too strong or are unimplementable for such workflow applications, workflows must satisfy a limited set of transactional properties that guarantee that a process is not left in an inconsistent state.

- Transaction-processing monitors were initially developed as multithreaded servers that could service large numbers of terminals from a single process. They have since evolved, and today they provide the infrastructure for building and administering complex transaction-processing systems that have a large number of clients and multiple servers. They provide services such as durable queueing of client requests and server responses, routing of client messages to servers, persistent messaging, load balancing, and coordination of two-phase commit when transactions access multiple servers.

- E-commerce systems have become a core part of commerce. There are several database issues in e-commerce systems. Catalog management, especially personalization of the catalog, is done with databases. Electronic marketplaces help in pricing of products through auctions, reverse auctions, or exchanges. High-performance database systems are needed to handle such trading. Orders are settled by electronic payment systems, which also need high-performance database systems to handle very high transaction rates.

- Large main memories are exploited in certain systems to achieve high system throughput. In such systems, logging is a bottleneck. Under the group-commit concept, the number of outputs to stable storage can be reduced, thus releasing this bottleneck.

- The efficient management of long-duration interactive transactions is more complex, because of the long-duration waits and because of the possibility of aborts. Since the concurrency-control techniques used in Chapter 15 use waits, aborts, or both, alternative techniques must be considered. These techniques must ensure correctness without requiring serializability.

- A long-duration transaction is represented as a nested transaction with atomic database operations at the lowest level. If a transaction fails, only active short-duration transactions abort. Active long-duration transactions resume once any short-duration transactions have recovered. A compensating transaction is needed to undo updates of nested transactions that have committed, if the outer-level transaction fails.

- In systems with real-time constraints, correctness of execution involves not only database consistency but also deadline satisfaction. The wide variance of execution times for read and write operations complicates the transaction-management problem for time-constrained systems.

Review Terms

- TP monitor
- TP-monitor architectures
  - ○ Process per client
  - ○ Single server

- Many server, single router
- Many server, many router
- Multitasking
- Context switch
- Multithreaded server
- Queue manager
- Application coordination
  - Resource manager
  - Remote procedure call (RPC)
- Transactional workflows
  - Task
  - Processing entity
  - Workflow specification
  - Workflow execution
- Workflow state
  - Execution states
  - Output values
  - External variables
- Workflow failure atomicity
- Workflow termination states
  - Acceptable
  - Nonacceptable
  - Committed
  - Aborted
- Workflow recovery
- Workflow-management system
- Workflow-management system architectures

- Centralized
- Partially distributed
- Fully distributed
- Business process management
- Orchestration
- E-commerce
- E-catalogs
- Marketplaces
  - Auctions
  - Reverse auctions
  - Exchange
- Order settlement
- Digital certificates
- Main-memory databases
- Group commit
- Real-time systems
- Deadlines
  - Hard deadline
  - Firm deadline
  - Soft deadline
- Real-time databases
- Long-duration transactions
- Exposure of uncommitted data
- Nonserializable executions
- Nested transactions
- Multilevel transactions
- Saga
- Compensating transactions
- Logical logging

Practice Exercises

26.1 Like database systems, workflow systems also require concurrency and recovery management. List three reasons why we cannot simply apply a relational database system using 2PL, physical undo logging, and 2PC.

26.2   Consider a main-memory database system recovering from a system crash. Explain the relative merits of:

- Loading the entire database back into main memory before resuming transaction processing.

- Loading data as it is requested by transactions.

26.3   Is a high-performance transaction system necessarily a real-time system? Why or why not?

26.4   Explain why it may be impractical to require serializability for long-duration transactions.

26.5   Consider a multithreaded process that delivers messages from a durable queue of persistent messages. Different threads may run concurrently, attempting to deliver different messages. In case of a delivery failure, the message must be restored in the queue. Model the actions that each thread carries out as a multilevel transaction, so that locks on the queue need not be held until a message is delivered.

26.6   Discuss the modifications that need to be made in each of the recovery schemes covered in Chapter 16 if we allow nested transactions. Also, explain any differences that result if we allow multilevel transactions.

Exercises

26.7   Explain how a TP monitor manages memory and processor resources more effectively than a typical operating system.

26.8   Compare TP-monitor features with those provided by Web servers supporting servlets (such servers have been nicknamed *TP-lite*).

26.9   Consider the process of admitting new students at your university (or new employees at your organization).

a.   Give a high-level picture of the workflow starting from the student application procedure.

b.   Indicate acceptable termination states and which steps involve human intervention.

c.   Indicate possible errors (including deadline expiry) and how they are dealt with.

d.   Study how much of the workflow has been automated at your university.

26.10   Answer the following questions regarding electronic payment systems:

    a. Explain why electronic transactions carried out using credit-card numbers may be insecure.

    b. An alternative is to have an electronic payment gateway maintained by the credit-card company, and the site receiving payment redirects customers to the gateway site to make the payment.

       i. Explain what benefits such a system offers if the gateway does not authenticate the user.

      ii. Explain what further benefits are offered if the gateway has a mechanism to authenticate the user.

    c. Some credit-card companies offer a one-time-use credit-card number as a more secure method of electronic payment. Customers connect to the credit-card company's Web site to get the one-time-use number. Explain what benefit such a system offers, as compared to using regular credit-card numbers. Also explain its benefits and drawbacks as compared to electronic payment gateways with authentication.

    d. Does either of the above systems guarantee the same privacy that is available when payments are made in cash? Explain your answer.

26.11 If the entire database fits in main memory, do we still need a database system to manage the data? Explain your answer.

26.12 In the group-commit technique, how many transactions should be part of a group? Explain your answer.

26.13 In a database system using write-ahead logging, what is the worst-case number of disk accesses required to read a data item from a specified disk page. Explain why this presents a problem to designers of real-time database systems. Hint: consider the case when the disk buffer is full.

26.14 What is the purpose of compensating transactions? Present two examples of their use.

26.15 Explain the connections between a workflow and a long-duration transaction.

Bibliographical Notes

Gray and Reuter [1993] provides a detailed (and excellent) textbook description of transaction-processing systems, including chapters on TP monitors. X/Open [1991] defines the X/Open XA interface.

Fischer [2006] is a handbook on workflow systems, which is published in association with the Workflow Management Coalition. The Web site of the coalition is www.wfmc.org. Our description of workflows follows the model of Rusinkiewicz and Sheth [1995].

Loeb [1998] provides a detailed description of secure electronic transactions.

Garcia-Molina and Salem [1992] provides an overview of main-memory databases. Jagadish et al. [1993] describes a recovery algorithm designed for main-memory databases. A storage manager for main-memory databases is described in Jagadish et al. [1994].

Real-time databases are discussed by Lam and Kuo [2001]. Concurrency control and scheduling in real-time databases are discussed by Haritsa et al. [1990], Hong et al. [1993], and Pang et al. [1995]. Ozsoyoglu and Snodgrass [1995] is a survey of research in real-time and temporal databases.

Nested and multilevel transactions are presented by Moss [1985], Lynch and Merritt [1986], Moss [1987], Haerder and Rothermel [1987], Rothermel and Mohan [1989], Weikum et al. [1990], Korth and Speegle [1990], Weikum [1991], and Korth and Speegle [1994], Theoretical aspects of multilevel transactions are presented in Lynch et al. [1988]. The concept of Saga was introduced in Garcia-Molina and Salem [1987].

PART 9

CASE STUDIES

This part describes how different database systems integrate the various concepts described earlier in the book. We begin by covering a widely used open-source database system, PostgreSQL, in Chapter 27. Three widely used commercial database systems—IBM DB2, Oracle, and Microsoft SQL Server—are covered in Chapters 28, 29, and 30. These three represent three of the most widely used commercial database systems.

Each of these chapters highlights unique features of each database system: tools, SQL variations and extensions, and system architecture, including storage organization, query processing, concurrency control and recovery, and replication.

The chapters cover only key aspects of the database products they describe, and therefore should not be regarded as a comprehensive coverage of the product. Furthermore, since products are enhanced regularly, details of the product may change. When using a particular product version, be sure to consult the user manuals for specific details.

Keep in mind that the chapters in this part often use industrial rather than academic terminology. For instance, they use table instead of relation, row instead of tuple, and column instead of attribute.

CHAPTER 27

PostgreSQL

Anastasia Ailamaki, Sailesh Krishnamurthy, Spiros Papadimitriou, Bianca Schroeder, Karl Schnaitter, and Gavin Sherry

PostgreSQL is an open-source object-relational database management system. It is a descendant of one of the earliest such systems, the POSTGRES system developed under Professor Michael Stonebraker at the University of California, Berkeley. The name "postgres" is derived from the name of a pioneering relational database system, Ingres, also developed under Stonebraker at Berkeley. Currently, PostgreSQL supports many aspects of SQL:2003 and offers features such as complex queries, foreign keys, triggers, views, transactional integrity, full-text searching, and limited data replication. In addition, users can extend PostgreSQL with new data types, functions, operators, or index methods. PostgreSQL supports a variety of programming languages (including C, C++, Java, Perl, Tcl, and Python) as well as the database interfaces JDBC and ODBC. Another notable point of PostgreSQL is that it, along with MySQL, is one of the two most widely used open-source relational database systems. PostgreSQL is released under the BSD license, which grants permission to anyone for the use, modification, and distribution of the PostgreSQL code and documentation for any purpose without fee.

27.1 Introduction

In the course of two decades, PostgreSQL has undergone several major releases. The first prototype system, under the name POSTGRES, was demonstrated at the 1988 ACM SIGMOD conference. The first version, distributed to users in 1989, provided features such as extensible data types, a preliminary rule system, and a query language named POSTQUEL. After the subsequent versions added a new rule system, support for multiple storage managers, and an improved query executor, the system developers focused on portability and performance until 1994, when an SQL language interpreter was added. Under a new name, Postgres95, the system was released to the Web and later commercialized by Illustra Information Technologies (later merged into Informix, which is now owned by IBM). By 1996, the name Postgres95 was replaced by PostgreSQL, to reflect the relationship between the original POSTGRES and the more recent versions with SQL capability.

PostgreSQL runs under virtually all Unix-like operating systems, including Linux and Apple Macintosh OS X. Early versions of the PostgreSQL server can be run under Microsoft Windows in the Cygwin environment, which provides Linux emulation under Windows. Version 8.0, released in January 2005, introduced native support for Microsoft Windows.

Today, PostgreSQL is used to implement several different research and production applications (such as the PostGIS system for geographic information) and an educational tool at several universities. The system continues to evolve through the contributions of a community of about 1000 developers. In this chapter, we explain how PostgreSQL works, starting from user interfaces and languages and continuing into the heart of the system (the data structures and the concurrency-control mechanism).

27.2   User Interfaces

The standard distribution of PostgreSQL comes with command-line tools for administering the database. However, there is a wide range of commercial and open-source graphical administration and design tools that support PostgreSQL. Software developers may also access PostgreSQL through a comprehensive set of programming interfaces.

27.2.1   Interactive Terminal Interfaces

Like most database systems, PostgreSQL offers command-line tools for database administration. The main interactive terminal client is psql, which is modeled after the Unix shell and allows execution of SQL commands on the server, as well as several other operations (such as client-side copying). Some of its features are:

- **Variables.** psql provides variable substitution features, similar to common Unix command shells.

- **SQL interpolation.** The user can substitute ("interpolate") psql variables into regular SQL statements by placing a colon in front of the variable name.

- **Command-line editing.** psql uses the GNU readline library for convenient line editing, with tab-completion support.

PostgreSQL may also be accessed from a Tcl/Tk shell, which provides a flexible scripting language commonly used for rapid prototyping. This functionality is enabled in Tcl/Tk by loading the pgtcl library, which is distributed as an optional extension to PostgreSQL.

27.2.2   Graphical Interfaces

The standard distribution of PostgreSQL does not contain any graphical tools. However, several graphical user interface tools exist, and users can choose among

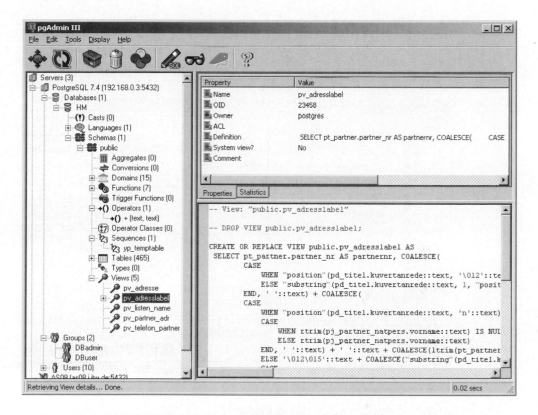

Figure 27.1 pgAdmin III: An open-source database administration GUI.

commercial and open-source alternatives. Many of these go through rapid release cycles; the following list reflects the state of affairs at the time of this writing.

There are graphical tools for administration, including pgAccess and pgAdmin, the latter of which is shown in Figure 27.1. Tools for database design include TORA and Data Architect, the latter of which is shown in Figure 27.2. PostgreSQL works with several commercial forms-design and report-generation tools. Open-source alternatives include Rekall (shown in Figures 27.3 and 27.4), GNU Report Generator, and a more comprehensive tool suite, GNU Enterprise.

27.2.3 Programming Language Interfaces

PostgreSQL provides native interfaces for ODBC and JDBC, as well as bindings for most programming languages, including C, C++, PHP, Perl, Tcl/Tk, ECPG, Python, and Ruby.

The libpq library provides the C API for PostgreSQL; libpq is also the underlying engine for most programming-language bindings. The libpq library supports both synchronous and asynchronous execution of SQL commands and prepared statements, through a reentrant and thread-safe interface. The connection parameters of libpq may be configured in several flexible ways, such as

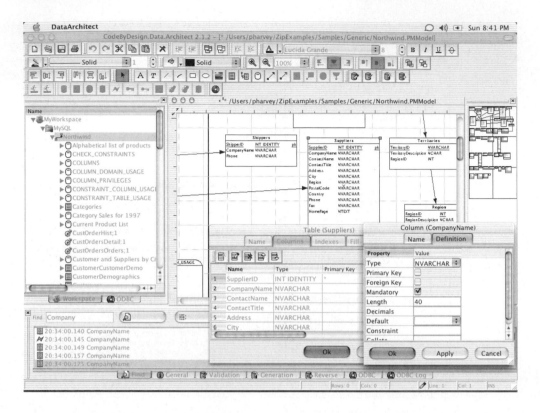

Figure 27.2   Data Architect: A multiplatform database design GUI.

setting environment variables, placing settings in a local file, or creating entries on an LDAP server.

27.3   SQL Variations and Extensions

The current version of PostgreSQL supports almost all entry-level SQL-92 features, as well as many of the intermediate- and full-level features. It also supports many SQL:1999 and SQL:2003 features, including most object-relational features described in Chapter 22 and the SQL/XML features for parsed XML data described in Chapter 23. In fact, some features of the current SQL standard (such as arrays, functions, and inheritance) were pioneered by PostgreSQL or its ancestors. It lacks OLAP features (most notably, **cube** and **rollup**), but data from PostgreSQL can be easily loaded into open-source external OLAP servers (such as Mondrian) as well as commercial products.

27.3.1   PostgreSQL Types

PostgreSQL has support for several nonstandard types, useful for specific application domains. Furthermore, users can define new types with the **create type**

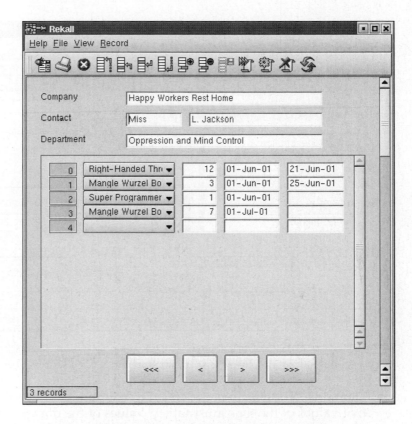

Figure 27.3 Rekall: Form-design GUI.

command. This includes new low-level base types, typically written in C (see Section 27.3.3.1).

27.3.1.1 The PostgreSQL Type System

PostgreSQL types fall into the following categories:

- **Base types.** Base types are also known as **abstract data types**; that is, modules that encapsulate both state and a set of operations. These are implemented below the SQL level, typically in a language such as C (see Section 27.3.3.1). Examples are **int4** (already included in PostgreSQL) or **complex** (included as an optional extension type). A base type may represent either an individual scalar value or a variable-length array of values. For each scalar type that exists in a database, PostgreSQL automatically creates an array type that holds values of the same scalar type.

- **Composite types.** These correspond to table rows; that is, they are a list of field names and their respective types. A composite type is created implicitly whenever a table is created, but users may also construct them explicitly.

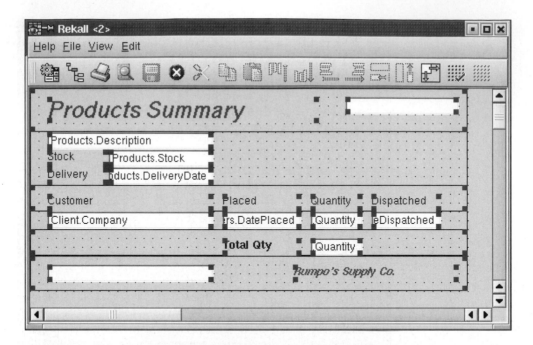

Figure 27.4 Rekall: Report-design GUI.

- **Domains.** A domain type is defined by coupling a base type with a constraint that values of the type must satisfy. Values of the domain type and the associated base type may be used interchangeably, provided that the constraint is satisfied. A domain may also have an optional default value, whose meaning is similar to the default value of a table column.

- **Enumerated types.** These are similar to enum types used in programming languages such as C and Java. An enumerated type is essentially a fixed list of named values. In PostgreSQL, enumerated types may be converted to the textual representation of their name, but this conversion must be specified explicitly in some cases to ensure type safety. For instance, values of different enumerated types may not be compared without explicit conversion to compatible types.

- **Pseudotypes.** Currently, PostgreSQL supports the following pseudotypes: *any, anyarray, anyelement, anyenum, anynonarray cstring, internal, opaque, language_handler, record, trigger,* and *void.* These cannot be used in composite types (and thus cannot be used for table columns), but can be used as argument and return types of user-defined functions.

- **Polymorphic types.** Four of the pseudotypes *anyelement, anyarray, anynonarray,* and *anyenum* are collectively known as **polymorphic**. Functions with arguments of these types (correspondingly called **polymorphic functions**) may operate on any actual type. PostgreSQL has a simple type-resolution scheme that requires that: (1) in any particular invocation of a polymorphic function, all occurrences of a polymorphic type must be bound to the same actual type (that is, a function defined as *f(anyelement, anyelement)* may operate only on pairs of the same actual type), and (2) if the return type is polymorphic, then at least one of the arguments must be of the same polymorphic type.

27.3.1.2 Nonstandard Types

The types described in this section are included in the standard distribution. Furthermore, thanks to the open nature of PostgreSQL, there are several contributed extension types, such as complex numbers, and ISBN/ISSNs (see Section 27.3.3).

Geometric data types (*point, line, lseg, box, polygon, path, circle*) are used in geographic information systems to represent two-dimensional spatial objects such as points, line segments, polygons, paths, and circles. Numerous functions and operators are available in PostgreSQL to perform various geometric operations such as scaling, translation, rotation, and determining intersections. Furthermore, PostgreSQL supports indexing of these types using R-trees (Sections 25.3.5.3 and 27.5.2.1).

Full-text searching is performed in PostgreSQL using the *tsvector* type that represents a document and the *tsquery* type that represents a full-text query. A *tsvector* stores the distinct words in a document, after converting variants of each word to a common normal form (for example, removing word stems). PostgreSQL provides functions to convert raw text to a *tsvector* and concatenate documents. A *tsquery* specifies words to search for in candidate documents, with multiple words connected by Boolean operators. For example, the query 'index & !(tree | hash)' finds documents that contain "index" without using the words "tree" or "hash." PostgreSQL natively supports operations on full-text types, including language features and indexed search.

PostgreSQL offers data types to store network addresses. These data types allow network-management applications to use a PostgreSQL database as their data store. For those familiar with computer networking, we provide a brief summary of this feature here. Separate types exist for IPv4, IPv6, and Media Access Control (MAC) addresses (*cidr, inet* and *macaddr*, respectively). Both *inet* and *cidr* types can store IPv4 and IPv6 addresses, with optional subnet masks. Their main difference is in input/output formatting, as well as the restriction that classless Internet domain routing (CIDR) addresses do not accept values with nonzero bits to the right of the netmask. The *macaddr* type is used to store MAC addresses (typically, Ethernet card hardware addresses). PostgreSQL supports indexing and sorting on these types, as well as a set of operations (including subnet testing, and mapping MAC addresses to hardware manufacturer names). Furthermore, these types offer input-error checking. Thus, they are preferable over plain text fields.

The PostgreSQL *bit* type can store both fixed- and variable-length strings of 1s and 0s. PostgreSQL supports bit-logical operators and string-manipulation functions for these values.

27.3.2   Rules and Other Active-Database Features

PostgreSQL supports SQL constraints and triggers (and stored procedures; see Section 27.3.3). Furthermore, it features query-rewriting rules that can be declared on the server.

PostgreSQL allows **check** constraints, **not null** constraints, and primary-key and foreign-key constraints (with restricting and cascading deletes).

Like many other relational database systems, PostgreSQL supports triggers, which are useful for nontrivial constraints and consistency checking or enforcement. Trigger functions can be written in a procedural language such as PL/pgSQL (see Section 27.3.3.4) or in C, but not in plain SQL. Triggers can execute before or after **insert**, **update**, or **delete** operations and either once per modified row, or once per SQL statement.

The PostgreSQL rules system allows users to define query-rewrite rules on the database server. Unlike stored procedures and triggers, the rule system intervenes between the query parser and the planner and modifies queries on the basis of the set of rules. After the original query tree has been transformed into one or more trees, they are passed to the query planner. Thus, the planner has all the necessary information (tables to be scanned, relationships between them, qualifications, join information, and so forth) and can come up with an efficient execution plan, even when complex rules are involved.

The general syntax for declaring rules is:

> **create rule** *rule_name* **as**
>   **on** { **select** | **insert** | **update** | **delete** }
>   **to** *table* [**where** *rule_qualification*]
>   **do** [**instead**] { **nothing** | *command* | (*command* ; *command* ...) }

The rest of this section provides examples that illustrate the rule system's capabilities. More details on how rules are matched to query trees and how the latter are subsequently transformed can be found in the PostgreSQL documentation (see the bibliographical notes). The rule system is implemented in the rewrite phase of query processing and explained in Section 27.6.1.

First, PostgreSQL uses rules to implement views. A view definition such as:

> **create view** *myview* **as select** * **from** *mytab*;

is converted into the following rule definition:

> **create table** *myview* (*same column list as mytab*);
> **create rule** *_return* **as on select to** *myview* **do instead**
>   **select** * **from** *mytab*;

Queries on *myview* are transformed before execution to queries on the underlying table *mytab*. The **create view** syntax is considered better programming form in this case, since it is more concise and it also prevents creation of views that reference each other (which is possible if rules are carelessly declared, resulting in potentially confusing runtime errors). However, rules can be used to define update actions on views explicitly (**create view** statements do not allow this).

As another example, consider the case where the user wants to log all increases of instructor salaries. This could be achieved by a rule such as:

> **create rule** *salary_audit* **as on update to** *instructor*
> **where new**.*salary* <> **old**.*salary*
> **do insert into** *salary_audit*
> **values** (current_timestamp, current_user,
>   **new**.*name*, **old**.*salary*, **new**.*salary*);

Finally, we give a slightly more complicated insert/update rule. Assume that pending salary increases are stored in a table *salary_increases(name, increase)*. We can declare a "dummy" table *approved_increases* with the same fields and then define the following rule:

> **create rule** *approved_increases_insert*
>   **as on insert to** *approved_increases*
>   **do instead**
>   **update** *instructor*
>   **set** *salary* = *salary* + **new**.*increase*
>   **where** *name* = **new**.*name*;

Then the following query:

> **insert into** *approved_increases* **select** * **from** *salary_increases*;

will update all salaries in the *instructor* table at once. Since the **instead** keyword was specified in the rule, the *approved_increases* table is unchanged.

There is some overlap between the functionality provided by rules and per-row triggers. The PostgreSQL rule system can be used to implement most triggers, but some kinds of constraints (in particular, foreign keys) cannot be implemented by rules. Also, triggers have the added ability to generate error messages to signal constraint violations, whereas a rule may only enforce data integrity by silently suppressing invalid values. On the other hand, triggers cannot be used for the **update** or **delete** actions that rules enable on views. Since there is no real data in a view relation, the trigger would never be called.

An important difference between triggers and views is that a trigger is executed iteratively for every affected row. A rule, on the other hand, manipulates the query tree before query planning. So if a statement affects many rows, a rule is far more efficient than a trigger.

The implementation of triggers and constraints in PostgreSQL is outlined briefly in Section 27.6.4.

27.3.3 Extensibility

Like most relational database systems, PostgreSQL stores information about data-bases, tables, columns, and so forth, in what are commonly known as **system catalogs**, which appear to the user as normal tables. Other relational database systems are typically extended by changing hard-coded procedures in the source code or by loading special extension modules written by the vendor.

Unlike most relational database systems, PostgreSQL goes one step further and stores much more information in its catalogs: not only information about tables and columns, but also information about data types, functions, access methods, and so on. Therefore, PostgreSQL is easy for users to extend and facilitates rapid prototyping of new applications and storage structures. PostgreSQL can also in-corporate user-written code into the server, through dynamic loading of shared objects. This provides an alternative approach to writing extensions that can be used when catalog-based extensions are not sufficient.

Furthermore, the `contrib` module of the PostgreSQL distribution includes nu-merous user functions (for example, array iterators, fuzzy string matching, cryp-tographic functions), base types (for example, encrypted passwords, ISBN/ISSNs, n-dimensional cubes) and index extensions (for example, RD-trees, indexing for hierarchical labels). Thanks to the open nature of PostgreSQL, there is a large community of PostgreSQL professionals and enthusiasts who also actively extend PostgreSQL on an almost daily basis. Extension types are identical in functionality to the built-in types (see also Section 27.3.1.2); the latter are simply already linked into the server and preregistered in the system catalog. Similarly, this is the only difference between built-in and extension functions.

27.3.3.1 Types

PostgreSQL allows users to define composite types, enumeration types, and even new base types.

A composite-type definition is similar to a table definition (in fact, the latter implicitly does the former). Stand-alone composite types are typically useful for function arguments. For example, the definition:

create type *city_t* **as** (*name* **varchar**(80), *state* **char**(2));

allows functions to accept and return *city_t* tuples, even if there is no table that explicitly contains rows of this type.

Enumeration types are easy to define, by simply listing the names of the values. The following example creates an enumerated type to represent the status of a software product.

create type *status_t* **as enum** ('alpha', 'beta', 'release');

The order of listed names is significant in comparing values of an enumerated type. This can be useful for a statement such as:

> **select** *name* **from** *products*
> **where** *status* > 'alpha';

which retrieves the names of products that have moved past the alpha stage.

Adding base types to PostgreSQL is straightforward; an example can be found in `complex.sql` and `complex.c` in the tutorials of the PostgreSQL distribution. The base type can be declared in C, for example:

```
typedef struct Complex {
    double x;
    double y;
} Complex;
```

The next step is to define functions to read and write values of the new type in text format (see Section 27.3.3.2). Subsequently, the new type can be registered using the statement:

> **create type** *complex* {
>   *internallength* = 16,
>   *input* = *complex_in*,
>   *output* = *complex_out*,
>   *alignment* = **double**
> };

assuming the text I/O functions have been registered as *complex_in* and *complex_out*.

The user has the option of defining binary I/O functions as well (for more efficient data dumping). Extension types can be used like the existing base types of PostgreSQL. In fact, their only difference is that the extension types are dynamically loaded and linked into the server. Furthermore, indices may be extended easily to handle new base types; see Section 27.3.3.3.

27.3.3.2 Functions

PostgreSQL allows users to define functions that are stored and executed on the server. PostgreSQL also supports function overloading (that is, functions may be declared by using the same name but with arguments of different types). Functions can be written as plain SQL statements, or in several procedural languages (covered in Section 27.3.3.4). Finally, PostgreSQL has an application programmer interface for adding functions written in C (explained in this section).

User-defined functions can be written in C (or a language with compatible calling conventions, such as C++). The actual coding conventions are essentially the same for dynamically loaded, user-defined functions, as well as for internal functions (which are statically linked into the server). Hence, the standard internal function library is a rich source of coding examples for user-defined C functions.

Once the shared library containing the function has been created, a declaration such as the following registers it on the server:

> **create function** *complex_out*(*complex*)
> **returns cstring**
> **as** 'shared_object_filename'
> **language C immutable strict**;

The entry point to the shared object file is assumed to be the same as the SQL function name (here, *complex_out*), unless otherwise specified.

The example here continues the one from Section 27.3.3.1. The application program interface hides most of PostgreSQL's internal details. Hence, the actual C code for the above text output function of *complex* values is quite simple:

```
PG_FUNCTION_INFO_V1(complex_out);
Datum complex_out(pg_function_args) {
    Complex *complex = (Complex *) pg_getarg_pointer(0);
    char *result;
    result = (char *) palloc(100);
    snprintf(result, 100, "(%g,%g)", complex->x, complex->y);
    pg_return_cstring(result);
}
```

The first line declares the function **complex_out**, and the following lines implement the output function. The code uses several PostgreSQL-specific constructs, such as the **palloc** function, which dynamically allocates memory controlled by PostgreSQL's memory manager. More details may be found in the PostgreSQL documentation (see the bibliographical notes).

Aggregate functions in PostgreSQL operate by updating a **state value** via a **state transition** function that is called for each tuple value in the aggregation group. For example, the state for the **avg** operator consists of the running sum and the count of values. As each tuple arrives, the transition function should simply add its value to the running sum and increment the count by one. Optionally, a *final* function may be called to compute the return value based on the state information. For example, the final function for **avg** would simply divide the running sum by the count and return it.

Thus, defining a new aggregate is as simple as defining these two functions. For the *complex* type example, if *complex_add* is a user-defined function that takes two complex arguments and returns their sum, then the **sum** aggregate operator can be extended to complex numbers using the simple declaration:

```
create aggregate sum (
    sfunc = complex_add,
    basetype = complex,
    stype = complex,
    initcond = '(0,0)'
);
```

Note the use of function overloading: PostgreSQL will call the appropriate *sum* aggregate function, on the basis of the actual type of its argument during invocation. The *basetype* is the argument type and *stype* is the state value type. In this case, a final function is unnecessary, since the return value is the state value itself (that is, the running sum in both cases).

User-defined functions can also be invoked by using operator syntax. Beyond simple "syntactic sugar" for function invocation, operator declarations can also provide hints to the query optimizer in order to improve performance. These hints may include information about commutativity, restriction and join selectivity estimation, and various other properties related to join algorithms.

27.3.3.3 Index Extensions

PostgreSQL currently supports the usual B-tree and hash indices, as well as two index methods that are unique to PostgreSQL: the Generalized Search Tree (GiST) and the Generalized Inverted Index (GIN), which is useful for full-text indexing (these index structures are explained in Section 27.5.2.1). Finally, PostgreSQL provides indexing of two-dimensional spatial objects with an R-tree index, which is implemented using a GiST index behind the scenes. All of these can be easily extended to accommodate new base types.

Adding index extensions for a type requires definition of an **operator class**, which encapsulates the following:

- **Index-method strategies.** These are a set of operators that can be used as qualifiers in **where** clauses. The particular set depends on the index type. For example, B-tree indices can retrieve ranges of objects, so the set consists of five operators ($<$, $<=$, $=$, $>=$, and $>$), all of which can appear in a **where** clause involving a B-tree index. A hash index allows only equality testing and an R-tree index allows a number of spatial relationships (for example contained, to-the-left, and so forth).

- **Index-method support routines.** The above set of operators is typically not sufficient for the operation of the index. For example, a hash index requires a function to compute the hash value for each object. An R-tree index needs to be able to compute intersections and unions and to estimate the size of indexed objects.

For example, if the following functions and operators are defined to compare the magnitude of *complex* numbers (see Section 27.3.3.1), then we can make such objects indexable by the following declaration:

> **create operator class** *complex_abs_ops*
> **default for type** *complex* **using btree as**
> **operator** 1 < (*complex*, *complex*),
> **operator** 2 <= (*complex*, *complex*),
> **operator** 3 = (*complex*, *complex*),
> **operator** 4 >= (*complex*, *complex*),
> **operator** 5 > (*complex*, *complex*),
> **function** 1 *complex_abs_cmp*(*complex*, *complex*);

The **operator** statements define the strategy methods and the **function** statements define the support methods.

27.3.3.4 Procedural Languages

Stored functions and procedures can be written in a number of procedural languages. Furthermore, PostgreSQL defines an application programmer interface for hooking up any programming language for this purpose. Programming languages can be registered on demand and are either **trusted** or **untrusted**. The latter allow unlimited access to the DBMS and the file system, and writing stored functions in them requires superuser privileges.

- **PL/pgSQL**. This is a trusted language that adds procedural programming capabilities (for example, variables and control flow) to SQL. It is very similar to Oracle's PL/SQL. Although code cannot be transferred verbatim from one to the other, porting is usually simple.

- **PL/Tcl**, **PL/Perl**, and **PL/Python**. These leverage the power of Tcl, Perl, and Python to write stored functions and procedures on the server. The first two come in both trusted and untrusted versions (PL/Tcl, PL/Perl and PL/TclU, PL/PerlU, respectively), while PL/Python is untrusted at the time of this writing. Each of these has bindings that allow access to the database system via a language-specific interface.

27.3.3.5 Server Programming Interface

The server programming interface (SPI) is an application programmer interface that allows user-defined C functions (see Section 27.3.3.2) to run arbitrary SQL commands inside their functions. This gives writers of user-defined functions the ability to implement only essential parts in C and easily leverage the full power of the relational database system engine to do most of the work.

27.4   Transaction Management in PostgreSQL

Transaction management in PostgreSQL uses both both snapshot isolation and two-phase locking. Which one of the two protocols is used depends on the type of statement being executed. For DML statements[1] the snapshot isolation technique presented in Section 15.7 is used; the snapshot isolation scheme is referred to as the multiversion concurrency control (MVCC) scheme in PostgreSQL. Concurrency control for DDL statements, on the other hand, is based on standard two-phase locking.

27.4.1   PostgreSQL Concurrency Control

Since the concurrency control protocol used by PostgreSQL depends on the *isolation level* requested by the application, we begin with an overview of the isolation levels offered by PostgreSQL. We then describe the key ideas behind the MVCC scheme, followed by a discussion of their implementation in PostgreSQL and some of the implications of MVCC. We conclude this section with an overview of locking for DDL statements and a discussion of concurrency control for indices.

27.4.1.1   PostgreSQL Isolation Levels

The SQL standard defines three weak levels of consistency, in addition to the serializable level of consistency, on which most of the discussion in this book is based. The purpose of providing the weak consistency levels is to allow a higher degree of concurrency for applications that don't require the strong guarantees that serializability provides. Examples of such applications include long-running transactions that collect statistics over the database and whose results do not need to be precise.

The SQL standard defines the different isolation levels in terms of three phenomena that violate serializability. The three phenomena are called *dirty read*, *nonrepeatable read*, and *phantom read*, and are defined as follows:

- **Dirty read.** The transaction reads values written by another transaction that hasn't committed yet.

- **Nonrepeatable read.** A transaction reads the same object twice during execution and finds a different value the second time, although the transaction has not changed the value in the meantime.

- **Phantom read.** A transaction re-executes a query returning a set of rows that satisfy a search condition and finds that the set of rows satisfying the condition has changed as a result of another recently committed transaction. (A more detailed explanation of the phantom phenomenon, including the

---

[1]A DML statement is any statement that updates or reads data within a table, that is, **select**, **insert**, **update**, **fetch**, and **copy**. DDL statements affect entire tables; they can remove a table or change the schema of a table, for example. DDL statements and some other PostgreSQL-specific statements will be discussed later in this section.

Isolated level	Dirty Read	Non repeatable Read	Phantom Read
Read Uncommitted	Maybe	Maybe	Maybe
Read Committed	No	Maybe	Maybe
Repeated Read	No	No	Maybe
Serializable	No	No	No

Figure 27.5 Definition of the four standard SQL isolation levels.

concept of a phantom conflict, can be found in Section 15.8.3; eliminating phantom reads does not eliminate all phantom conflicts.)

It should be obvious that each of the above phenomena violates transaction isolation, and hence violates serializability. Figure 27.5 shows the definition of the four SQL isolation levels specified in the SQL standard—read uncommitted, read committed, repeatable read, and serializable—in terms of these phenomena. PostgreSQL supports two of the four different isolation levels, read committed (which is the default isolation level in PostgreSQL) and serializable. However, the PostgreSQL implementation of the serializable isolation level uses snapshot isolation, which does not truly ensure serializability as we have seen earlier in Section 15.7.

27.4.1.2 Concurrency Control for DML Commands

The MVCC scheme used in PostgreSQL is an implementation of the snapshot isolation protocol which we saw in Section 15.7. The key idea behind MVCC is to maintain different versions of each row that correspond to instances of the row at different points in time. This allows a transaction to see a consistent **snapshot** of the data, by selecting the most recent version of each row that was committed before taking the snapshot. The MVCC protocol uses snapshots to ensure that every transaction sees a consistent view of the database: before executing a command, the transaction chooses a snapshot of the data and processes the row versions that are either in the snapshot or created by earlier commands of the same transaction. This view of the data is "consistent" since it only takes full transactions into account, but the snapshot is not necessarily equal to the current state of the data.

The motivation for using MVCC is that readers never block writers and vice versa. Readers access the most recent version of a row that is part of the transaction's snapshot. Writers create their own separate copy of the row to be updated. Section 27.4.1.3 shows that the only conflict that causes a transaction to be blocked arises if two writers try to update the same row. In contrast, under the standard two-phase locking approach, both readers and writers might be blocked, since there is only one version of each data object and both read and write operations are required to obtain a lock before accessing any data.

The MVCC scheme in PostgreSQL implements the first-updater-wins version of the snapshot isolation protocol, by acquiring exclusive locks on rows that are written, but using a snapshot (without any locking) when reading rows;

additional validation is done when exclusive locks are obtained, as outlined earlier in Section 15.7.

27.4.1.3   PostgreSQL Implementation of MVCC

At the core of PostgreSQL MVCC is the notion of *tuple visibility*. A PostgreSQL tuple refers to a version of a row. Tuple visibility defines which of the potentially many versions of a row in a table is valid within the context of a given statement or transaction. A transaction determines tuple visibility based on a database snapshot that is chosen before executing a command.

A tuple is visible for a transaction T if the following two conditions hold:

1. The tuple was created by a transaction that committed before transaction T took its snapshot.

2. Updates to the tuple (if any) were executed by a transaction that is either

    *   aborted, *or*

    *   started running after T took its snapshot, *or*

    *   was active when T took its snapshot.

To be precise, a tuple is also visible to T if it was created by T and not subsequently updated by T. We omit the details of this special case for simplicity.

The goal of the above conditions is to ensure that each transaction sees a consistent view of the data. PostgreSQL maintains the following state information to check these conditions efficiently:

*   A *transaction ID*, which at the same time serves as a timestamp, is assigned to every transaction at transaction start time. PostgreSQL uses a logical counter (as described in Section 15.4.1) for assigning transaction IDs.

*   A log file called *pg_clog* contains the current status of each transaction. The status can be either in progress, committed, or aborted.

*   Each tuple in a table has a header with three fields: *xmin*, which contains the transaction ID of the transaction that created the tuple and which is therefore also called the *creation-transaction ID*; *xmax*, which contains the transaction ID of the replacing/deleting transaction (or *null* if not deleted/replaced) and which is also referred to as the *expire-transaction ID*; and a forward link to new versions of the same logical row, if there are any.

*   A *SnapshotData* data structure is created either at transaction start time or at query start time, depending on the isolation level (described in more detail below). Its main purpose is to decide whether a tuple is visible to the current command. The *SnapshotData* stores information about the state of transactions at the time it is created, which includes a list of active transactions and *xmax*, a value equal to 1 + the highest ID of any transaction that has started so far.

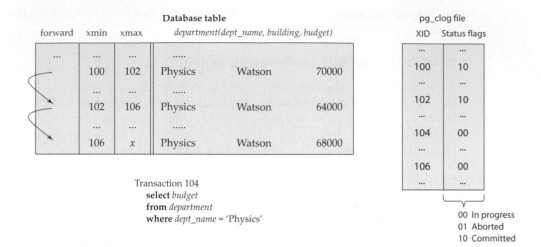

Figure 27.6 The PostgreSQL data structures used for MVCC.

The value *xmax* serves as a "cutoff" for transactions that may be considered visible.

Figure 27.6 illustrates some of this state information through a simple example involving a database with only one table, the *department* table from Figure 27.7. The *department* table has three columns, the name of the department, the building where the department is located, and the budget of the department. Figure 27.6 shows a fragment of the *department* table containing only the (versions of) the row corresponding to the Physics department. The tuple headers indicate that the row was originally created by transaction 100, and later updated by transaction 102 and transaction 106. Figure 27.6 also shows a fragment of the corresponding *pg _clog* file. On the basis of the *pg_clog* file, transactions 100 and 102 are committed, while transactions 104 and 106 are in progress.

Given the above state information, the two conditions that need to be satisfied for a tuple to be visible can be rewritten as follows:

dept_name	building	budget
Biology	Watson	90000
Comp. Sci.	Taylor	100000
Elec. Eng.	Taylor	85000
Finance	Painter	120000
History	Painter	50000
Music	Packard	80000
Physics	Watson	70000

Figure 27.7 The *department* relation.

1. The creation-transaction ID in the tuple header

   a. is a committed transaction according to the *pg_clog* file, *and*

   b. is less than the cutoff transaction ID *xmax* recorded by *SnapshotData*, *and*

   c. is not one of the active transactions stored in *SnapshotData*.

2. The expire-transaction ID, if it exists,

   a. is an aborted transaction according to the *pg_clog* file, *or*

   b. is greater than or equal to the cutoff transaction ID *xmax* recorded by *SnapshotData*, *or*

   c. is one of the active transactions stored in *SnapshotData*.

Consider the example database in Figure 27.6 and assume that the *Snapshot-Data* used by transaction 104 simply uses 103 as the cutoff transaction ID *xmax* and does not show any earlier transactions to be active. In this case, the only version of the row corresponding to the Physics department that is visible to transaction 104 is the second version in the table, created by transaction 102. The first version, created by transaction 100, is not visible, since it violates condition 2: The expire-transaction ID of this tuple is 102, which corresponds to a transaction that is not aborted and that has a transaction ID less than or equal to 103. The third version of the Physics tuple is not visible, since it was created by transaction 106, which has a transaction ID larger than transaction 103, implying that this version had not been committed at the time *SnapshotData* was created. Moreover, transaction 106 is still in progress, which violates another one of the conditions. The second version of the row meets all the conditions for tuple visibility.

The details of how PostgreSQL MVCC interacts with the execution of SQL statements depends on whether the statement is an **insert**, **select**, **update**, or **delete** statement. The simplest case is an **insert** statement, which may simply create a new tuple based on the data in the statement, initialize the tuple header (the creation ID), and insert the new tuple into the table. Unlike two-phase locking, this does not require any interaction with the concurrency-control protocol unless the insertion needs to be checked for integrity conditions, such as uniqueness or foreign key constraints.

When the system executes a **select**, **update**, or **delete** statement the interaction with the MVCC protocol depends on the isolation level specified by the application. If the isolation level is read committed, the processing of a new statement begins with creating a new *SnapshotData* data structure (independent of whether the statement starts a new transaction or is part of an existing transaction). Next, the system identifies *target tuples*, that is, the tuples that are visible with respect to the *SnapshotData* and that match the search criteria of the statement. In the case of a **select** statement, the set of target tuples make up the result of the query.

In the case of an **update** or **delete** statement in read committed mode, an extra step is necessary after identifying the target tuples, before the actual update or delete operation can take place. The reason is that visibility of a tuple ensures only that the tuple has been created by a transaction that committed before the **update**/**delete** statement in question started. However, it is possible that, since query start, this tuple has been updated or deleted by another concurrently executing transaction. This can be detected by looking at the expire-transaction ID of the tuple. If the expire-transaction ID corresponds to a transaction that is still in progress, it is necessary to wait for the completion of this transaction first. If the transaction aborts, the **update** or **delete** statement can proceed and perform the actual modification. If the transaction commits, the search criteria of the statement need to be evaluated again, and only if the tuple still meets these criteria can the row be modified. If the row is to be deleted, the main step is to update the expire-transaction ID of the old tuple. A row update also performs this step, and additionally creates a new version of the row, sets its creation-transaction ID, and sets the forward link of the old tuple to reference the new tuple.

Going back to the example from Figure 27.6, transaction 104, which consists of a **select** statement only, identifies the second version of the Physics row as a target tuple and returns it immediately. If transaction 104 were an update statement instead, for example, trying to increment the budget of the Physics department by some amount, it would have to wait for transaction 106 to complete. It would then re-evaluate the search condition and, only if it is still met, proceed with its update.

Using the protocol described above for **update** and **delete** statements provides only the read-committed isolation level. Serializability can be violated in several ways. First, nonrepeatable reads are possible. Since each query within a transaction may see a different snapshot of the database, a query in a transaction might see the effects of an **update** command completed in the meantime that weren't visible to earlier queries within the same transaction. Following the same line of thought, phantom reads are possible when a relation is modified between queries.

In order to provide the PostgreSQL serializable isolation level, PostgreSQL MVCC eliminates violations of serializability in two ways: First, when it is determining tuple visibility, all queries within a transaction use a snapshot as of the start of the transaction, rather than the start of the individual query. This way successive queries within a transaction always see the same data.

Second, the way updates and deletes are processed is different in serializable mode compared to read-committed mode. As in read-committed mode, transactions wait after identifying a visible target row that meets the search condition and is currently updated or deleted by another concurrent transaction. If the concurrent transaction that executes the update or delete aborts, the waiting transaction can proceed with its own update. However, if the concurrent transaction commits, there is no way for PostgreSQL to ensure serializability for the waiting transaction. Therefore, the waiting transaction is rolled back and returns with the error message "could not serialize access due to concurrent update."

It is up to the application to handle an error message like the above appropriately, by aborting the current transaction and restarting the entire transaction from the beginning. Observe that rollbacks due to serializability issues are possible only for **update** and **delete** statements. It is still the case that **select** statements never conflict with any other transactions.

27.4.1.4 Implications of Using MVCC

Using the PostgreSQL MVCC scheme has implications in three different areas: (1) extra burden is placed on the storage system, since it needs to maintain different versions of tuples; (2) developing concurrent applications takes some extra care, since PostgreSQL MVCC can lead to subtle, but important, differences in how concurrent transactions behave, compared to systems where standard two-phase locking is used; (3) PostgreSQL performance depends on the characteristics of the workload running on it. The implications of PostgreSQL MVCC are described in more detail below.

Creating and storing multiple versions of every row can lead to excessive storage consumption. To alleviate this problem, PostgreSQL frees up space when possible by identifying and deleting versions of tuples that cannot be visible to any active or future transactions, and are therefore no longer needed. The task of freeing space is nontrivial, because indices may refer to the location of an unneeded tuple, so these references need to be deleted before reusing the space. To lessen this issue, PostgreSQL avoids indexing multiple versions of a tuple that have identical index attributes. This allows the space taken by nonindexed tuples to be freed efficiently by any transaction that finds such a tuple.

For more aggressive space reuse, PostgreSQL provides the **vacuum** command, which correctly updates indices for each freed tuple. PostgreSQL employs a background process to **vacuum** tables automatically, but the command can also be executed by the user directly. The **vacuum** command offers two modes of operation: Plain **vacuum** simply identifies tuples that are not needed, and makes their space available for reuse. This form of the command can operate in parallel with normal reading and writing of the table. **Vacuum full** does more extensive processing, including moving of tuples across blocks to try to compact the table to the minimum number of disk blocks. This form is much slower and requires an exclusive lock on each table while it is being processed.

Because of the use of multiversion concurrency control in PostgreSQL, porting applications from other environments to PostgreSQL might require some extra care to ensure data consistency. As an example, consider a transaction T_A executing a **select** statement. Since readers in PostgreSQL don't lock data, data read and selected by T_A can be overwritten by another concurrent transaction T_B, while T_A is still running. As a result some of the data that T_A returns might not be current anymore at the time of completion of T_A. T_A might return rows that in the meantime have been changed or deleted by other transactions. To ensure the current validity of a row and protect it against concurrent updates, an application must either use **select for share** or explicitly acquire a lock with the appropriate **lock table** command.

PostgreSQL's approach to concurrency control performs best for workloads containing many more reads than updates, since in this case there is a very low chance that two updates will conflict and force a transaction to roll back. Two-phase locking may be more efficient for some update-intensive workloads, but this depends on many factors, such as the length of transactions and the frequency of deadlocks.

27.4.1.5 DDL Concurrency Control

The MVCC mechanisms described in the previous section do not protect transactions against operations that affect entire tables, for example, transactions that drop a table or change the schema of a table. Toward this end, PostgreSQL provides explicit locks that DDL commands are forced to acquire before starting their execution. These locks are always table based (rather than row based) and are acquired and released in accordance with the strict two-phase locking protocol.

Figure 27.8 lists all types of locks offered by PostgreSQL, which locks they conflict with, and some commands that use them (the **create index concurrently**

Lock name	Conflicts with	Acquired by
ACCESS SHARE	ACCESS EXCLUSIVE	**select** query
ROW SHARE	EXCLUSIVE ACCESS EXCLUSIVE	**select for update** query **select for share** query
ROW EXCLUSIVE	SHARE SHARE ROW EXCLUSIVE EXCLUSIVE ACCESS EXCLUSIVE	**update** **delete** **insert** queries
SHARE UPDATE EXCLUSIVE	SHARE UPDATE EXCLUSIVE SHARE SHARE ROW EXCLUSIVE EXCLUSIVE ACCESS EXCLUSIVE	**vacuum** **analyze** **create index concurrently**
SHARE	ROW EXCLUSIVE SHARE UPDATE EXCLUSIVE SHARE ROW EXCLUSIVE EXCLUSIVE ACCESS EXCLUSIVE	**create index**
SHARE ROW EXCLUSIVE	ROW EXCLUSIVE SHARE UPDATE EXCLUSIVE SHARE SHARE ROW EXCLUSIVE EXCLUSIVE ACCESS EXCLUSIVE	---
EXCLUSIVE	All except ACCESS SHARE	---
ACCESS EXCLUSIVE	All modes	**drop table** **alter table** **vaccum full**

Figure 27.8 Table-level lock modes.

command is covered in Section 27.5.2.3). The names of the lock types are often historical and don't necessarily reflect the use of the lock. For example, all the locks are table-level locks, although some contain the word "row" in the name. DML commands acquire only locks of the first three types. These three lock types are compatible with each other, since MVCC takes care of protecting these operations against each other. DML commands acquire these locks only for protection against DDL commands.

While their main purpose is providing PostgreSQL internal concurrency control for DDL commands, all locks in Figure 27.8 can also be acquired explicitly by PostgreSQL applications through the **lock table** command.

Locks are recorded in a lock table that is implemented as a shared-memory hash table keyed by a signature that identifies the object being locked. If a transaction wants to acquire a lock on an object that is held by another transaction in a conflicting mode, it needs to wait until the lock is released. Lock waits are implemented through semaphores, each of which is associated with a unique transaction. When waiting for a lock, a transaction actually waits on the semaphore associated with the transaction holding the lock. Once the lock holder releases the lock, it will signal the waiting transaction(s) through the semaphore. By implementing lock waits on a per-lock-holder basis, rather than on a per-object basis, PostgreSQL requires at most one semaphore per concurrent transaction, rather than one semaphore per lockable object.

Deadlock detection in PostgreSQL is based on time-outs. By default, deadlock detection is triggered if a transaction has been waiting for a lock for more than 1 second. The deadlock-detection algorithm constructs a wait-for graph based on the information in the lock table and searches this graph for circular dependencies. If it finds any, meaning a deadlock was detected, the transaction that triggered the deadlock detection aborts and returns an error to the user. If no cycle is detected, the transaction continues waiting on the lock. Unlike some commercial systems, PostgreSQL does not tune the lock time-out parameter dynamically, but it allows the administrator to tune it manually. Ideally, this parameter should be chosen on the order of a transaction lifetime, in order to optimize the trade-off between the time it takes to detect a deadlock and the work wasted for running the deadlock detection algorithm when there is no deadlock.

27.4.1.6 Locking and Indices

All current types of indices in PostgreSQL allow for concurrent access by multiple transactions. This is typically enabled by page-level locks, so that different transactions may access the index in parallel if they do not request conflicting locks on a page. These locks are usually held for a short time to avoid deadlock, with the exception of hash indices, which lock pages for longer periods and may participate in deadlock.

27.4.2 Recovery

Historically, PostgreSQL did not use write-ahead logging (WAL) for recovery, and therefore was not able to guarantee consistency in the case of crash. A crash could potentially result in inconsistent index structures or, worse, totally corrupted table contents, because of partially written data pages. As a result, starting with version 7.1, PostgreSQL employs WAL-based recovery. The approach is similar to standard recovery techniques such as ARIES (Section 16.8), but recovery in PostgreSQL is simplified in some ways because of the MVCC protocol.

First, under PostgreSQL, recovery doesn't have to undo the effects of aborted transactions: an aborting transaction makes an entry in the *pg_clog* file, recording the fact that it is aborting. Consequently, all versions of rows it leaves behind will never be visible to any other transactions. The only case where this approach could potentially lead to problems is when a transaction aborts because of a crash of the corresponding PostgreSQL process and the PostgreSQL process doesn't have a chance to create the *pg_clog* entry before the crash. PostgreSQL handles this as follows: Before checking the status of another transaction in the *pg_clog* file, it checks whether the transaction is running on any of the PostgreSQL processes. If no PostgreSQL process is currently running the transaction and the *pg_clog* file shows the transaction as still running, it is safe to assume that the transaction crashed and the transaction's *pg_clog* entry is updated to "aborted".

Second, recovery is simplified by the fact that PostgreSQL MVCC already keeps track of some of the information required by WAL logging. More precisely, there is no need for logging the start, commit, and abort of transactions, since MVCC logs the status of every transaction in the *pg_clog*.

27.5   Storage and Indexing

PostgreSQL's approach to data layout and storage is aimed at the goals of (1) a simple and clean implementation and (2) ease of administration. As a step toward these goals, PostgreSQL relies on "cooked" file systems, instead of handling the physical layout of data on raw disk partitions by itself. PostgreSQL maintains a list of directories in the file hierarchy to use for storage, which are conventionally referred to as **tablespaces**. Each PostgreSQL installation is initialized with a default tablespace, and additional tablespaces may be added at any time. When creating a table, index, or entire database, the user may specify any existing tablespace in which to store the related files. It is particularly useful to create multiple tablespaces if they reside on different physical devices, so that the faster devices may be dedicated to data that are in higher demand. Moreover, data that are stored on separate disks may be accessed in parallel more efficiently.

The design of the PostgreSQL storage system potentially leads to some performance limitations, due to clashes between PostgreSQL and the file system. The use of cooked file systems results in double buffering, where blocks are first fetched from disk into the file system's cache (in kernel space) before being copied to PostgreSQL's buffer pool. Performance can also be limited by the fact that PostgreSQL stores data in 8-KB blocks, which may not match the block size used by the kernel. It is possible to change the PostgreSQL block size when the server is installed, but this may have undesired consequences: small blocks limit

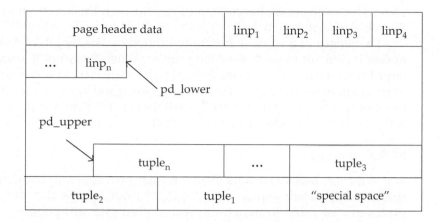

Figure 27.9 Slotted-page format for PostgreSQL tables.

the ability of PostgreSQL to store large tuples efficiently, while large blocks are wasteful when a small region of a file is accessed.

On the other hand, modern enterprises increasingly use external storage systems, such as network-attached storage and storage-area networks, instead of disks attached to servers. The philosophy here is that storage is a service that is easily administered and tuned for performance separately. One approach used by these systems is RAID, which offers both parallelism and redundant storage as explained in Section 10.3. PostgreSQL may directly leverage these technologies because of its reliance on cooked file systems. Thus, the feeling of many PostgreSQL developers is that, for a vast majority of applications, and indeed PostgreSQL's audience, the performance limitations are minimal and justified by the ease of administration and management, as well as simplicity of implementation.

27.5.1 Tables

The primary unit of storage in PostgreSQL is a table. In PostgreSQL, tables are stored in *heap files*. These files use a form of the standard *slotted-page* format described in Section 10.5. The PostgreSQL format is shown in Figure 27.9. In each page, a header is followed by an array of "line pointers." A line pointer holds the offset (relative to the start of the page) and length of a specific tuple in the page. The actual tuples are stored in reverse order of line pointers from the end of the page.

A record in a heap file is identified by its **tuple ID** (TID). The TID consists of a 4-byte block ID that specifies the page in the file containing the tuple and a 2-byte slot ID. The slot ID is an index into the line pointer array that in turn is used to access the tuple.

Although this infrastructure permits tuples in a page to be deleted or updated, under PostgreSQL's MVCC approach, neither operation actually deletes or replaces old versions of rows immediately. As explained in Section 27.4.1.4, expired tuples may be physically deleted by later commands, causing holes to be formed in a page. The indirection of accessing tuples through the line pointer array permits the reuse of such holes.

The length of a tuple is normally limited by the length of a data page. This makes it difficult to store very long tuples. When PostgreSQL encounters such a large tuple, it tries to "*toast*" individual large attributes. In some cases, toasting an attribute may be accomplished by compressing the value. If this does not shrink the tuple enough to fit in the page (often the case), the data in the toasted attribute is replaced with a reference to a copy that is stored outside the page.

27.5.2 Indices

A PostgreSQL index is a data structure that provides a dynamic mapping from search predicates to sequences of tuple IDs from a particular table. The returned tuples are intended to match the search predicate, although in some cases the predicate must be rechecked in the heap file. PostgreSQL supports several different index types, including those that are based on user-extensible access methods. Although an access method may use a different page format, all the indices available in PostgreSQL use the same slotted-page format described above in Section 27.5.1.

27.5.2.1 Index Types

PostgreSQL supports the following types of indices:

- **B-tree.** The default index type is a B^+-tree index based on Lehman and Yao's B-link trees (B-link trees, described in Section 15.10, support high concurrency of operations). These indices are useful for equality and range queries on sortable data and also for certain pattern-matching operations such as the **like** expression.

- **Hash.** PostgreSQL's hash indices are an implementation of linear hashing (for more information on hash indices, see Section 11.6.3). Such indices are useful only for simple equality operations. The hash indices used by PostgreSQL have been shown to have lookup performance no better than that of B-trees, but have considerably larger size and maintenance costs. Moreover, hash indices are the only indices in PostgreSQL that do not support crash recovery. Thus it is almost always preferable to use B-tree indices instead of hash indices.

- **GiST.** PostgreSQL supports a highly extensible index called GiST, or Generalized Search Tree. GiST is a balanced, tree-structured access method that makes it easy for a domain expert who is well versed in a particular data type (such as image data) to develop performance-enhancing indices without having to deal with the internal details of the database system. Examples of some indices built using GiST include B-trees and R-trees, as well as less conventional indices for multidimensional cubes and full-text search. New GiST access methods can be implemented by creating an operator class as explained in Section 27.3.3.3. Operator classes for GiST are different from B-trees, as each GiST operator class may have a different set of strategies that indicate the search predicates implemented by the index. GiST also relies on seven support functions for operations such as testing set membership and splitting sets of entries for page overflows.

It is interesting to note that the original PostgreSQL implementation of R-trees (Section 25.3.5.3) was replaced by GiST operator classes in version 8.2. This allowed R-trees to take advantage of the WAL logging and concurrency capabilities that were added to GiST in version 8.1. Since the original R-tree implementation did not have these features, this change illustrates the benefits of an extensible indexing method. See the bibliographical notes for references to more information on the GiST index.

- **GIN.** The newest type of index in PostgreSQL is the Generalized Inverted Index (GIN). A GIN index interprets both index keys and search keys as sets, making the index type appropriate for set-oriented operators. One of the intended uses of GIN is to index documents for full-text search, which is implemented by reducing documents and queries to sets of search terms. Like GiST, a GIN index may be extended to handle any comparison operator by creating an operator class with appropriate support functions.

  To evaluate a search, GIN efficiently identifies index keys that overlap the search key, and computes a bitmap indicating which searched-for elements are members of the index key. This is accomplished using support functions that extract members from a set and compare individual members. Another support function decides if the search predicate is satisfied based on the bitmap and the original predicate. If the search predicate cannot be resolved without the full indexed attribute, the decision function must report a match and recheck the predicate in the heap file.

27.5.2.2 Other Index Variations

For some of the index types described above, PostgreSQL supports more complex variations such as:

- **Multicolumn indices.** These are useful for conjuncts of predicates over multiple columns of a table. Multicolumn indices are only supported for B-tree and GiST indices.

- **Unique indices.** Unique and primary-key constraints can be enforced by using unique indices in PostgreSQL. Only B-tree indices may be defined as being unique.

- **Indices on expressions.** In PostgreSQL, it is possible to create indices on arbitrary scalar expressions of columns, and not just specific columns, of a table. This is especially useful when the expressions in question are "expensive" —say, involving complicated user-defined computation. An example is to support case-insensitive comparisons by defining an index on the expression *lower(column)* and using the predicate *lower(column)* = 'value' in queries. One disadvantage is that the maintenance costs of indices on expressions is high.

- **Operator classes.** The specific comparison functions used to build, maintain, and use an index on a column are tied to the data type of that column. Each data type has associated with it a default "operator class" (described in Section 27.3.3.3) that identifies the actual operators that would normally be used for it. While this default operator class is normally sufficient for most uses, some data types might possess multiple "meaningful" classes. For instance, in dealing with complex numbers, it might be desirable to index either the real or imaginary component. PostgreSQL provides some built-in operator classes for pattern-matching operations (such as **like**) on text data that do not use the standard locale-specific collation rules (in other words, language specific sort orders).

- **Partial indices.** These are indices built over a subset of a table defined by a predicate. The index contains only entries for tuples that satisfy the predicate. Partial indices are suited for cases where a column might contain a large number of occurrences of a very small number of values. In such cases, the common values are not worth indexing, since index scans are not beneficial for queries that require a large subset of the base table. A partial index that excludes the common values is small and incurs less I/O. The partial indices are less expensive to maintain, as a large fraction of inserts do not participate in the index.

27.5.2.3   Index Construction

An index may be added to the database using the **create index** command. For example, the following DDL statement creates a B-tree index on instructor salaries.

$$\textbf{create index } \textit{inst\_sal\_idx} \textbf{ on } \textit{instructor } (\textit{salary});$$

This statement is executed by scanning the *instructor* relation to find row versions that might be visible to a future transaction, then sorting their index attributes and building the index structure. During this process, the building transaction holds a lock on the *instructor* relation that prevents concurrent **insert**, **delete**, and **update** statements. Once the process is finished, the index is ready to use and the table lock is released.

The lock acquired by the **create index** command may present a major inconvenience for some applications where it is difficult to suspend updates while the index is built. For these cases, PostgreSQL provides the **create index concurrently** variant, which allows concurrent updates during index construction. This is achieved by a more complex construction algorithm that scans the base table twice. The first table scan builds an initial version of the index, in a way similar to normal index construction described above. This index may be missing tuples if the table was concurrently updated; however, the index is well formed, so it is flagged as being ready for insertions. Finally, the algorithm scans the table a second time and inserts all tuples it finds that still need to be indexed. This scan may also miss concurrently updated tuples, but the algorithm synchronizes with other transactions to guarantee that tuples that are updated during the second scan will be added to the index by the updating transaction. Hence, the index is ready to use after the second table scan. Since this two-pass approach can be expensive, the plain **create index** command is preferred if it is easy to suspend table updates temporarily.

27.6 Query Processing and Optimization

When PostgreSQL receives a query, it is first parsed into an internal representation, which goes through a series of transformations, resulting in a query plan that is used by the **executor** to process the query.

27.6.1 Query Rewrite

The first stage of a query's transformation is **rewrite** and it is this stage that is responsible for the PostgreSQL **rules** system. As explained in Section 27.3, in PostgreSQL, users can create **rules** that are fired on different events such as **update**, **delete**, **insert**, and **select** statements. A view is implemented by the system by converting a view definition into a **select** rule. When a query involving a **select** statement on the view is received, the **select** rule for the view is fired, and the query is rewritten using the definition of the view.

A rule is registered in the system using the **create rule** command, at which point information on the rule is stored in the catalog. This catalog is then used during query rewrite to uncover all candidate rules for a given query.

The rewrite phase first deals with all **update**, **delete**, and **insert** statements by firing all appropriate rules. Such statements might be complicated and contain **select** clauses. Subsequently, all the remaining rules involving only **select** statements are fired. Since the firing of a rule may cause the query to be rewritten to a form that may require another rule to be fired, the rules are repeatedly checked on each form of the rewritten query until a fixed point is reached and no more rules need to be fired.

There exist no default rules in PostgreSQL—only those defined explicitly by users and implicitly by the definition of views.

27.6.2 Query Planning and Optimization

Once the query has been rewritten, it is subject to the planning and optimization phase. Here, each query block is treated in isolation and a plan is generated for it. This planning begins bottom-up from the rewritten query's innermost subquery, proceeding to its outermost query block.

The optimizer in PostgreSQL is, for the most part, cost based. The idea is to generate an access plan whose estimated cost is minimal. The cost model includes as parameters the I/O cost of sequential and random page fetches, as well as the CPU costs of processing heap tuples, index tuples, and simple predicates.

The actual process of optimization is based on one of the following two forms:

- **Standard planner.** The standard planner uses the the bottom-up dynamic programming algorithm for join order optimization, originally used in System R, the pioneering relational system developed by IBM research in the 1970s. The System R dynamic programming algorithm is described in detail in Section 13.4.1. The algorithm is used on a single query block at a time.

- **Genetic query optimizer.** When the number of tables in a query block is very large, System R's dynamic programming algorithm becomes very expensive. Unlike other commercial systems that default to greedy or rule-based techniques, PostgreSQL uses a more radical approach: a genetic algorithm that was developed initially to solve traveling-salesman problems. There exists anecdotal evidence of the successful use of genetic query optimization in production systems for queries with around 45 tables.

Since the planner operates in a bottom-up fashion on query blocks, it is able to perform certain transformations on the query plan as it is being built. One example is the common subquery-to-join transformation that is present in many commercial systems (usually implemented in the rewrite phase). When PostgreSQL encounters a noncorrelated subquery (such as one caused by a query on a view), it is generally possible to "pull up" the planned subquery and merge it into the upper-level query block. However, transformations that push duplicate elimination into lower-level query blocks are generally not possible in PostgreSQL.

The query-optimization phase results in a query plan that is a tree of relational operators. Each operator represents a specific operation on one or more sets of tuples. The operators can be unary (for example, sort, aggregation), binary (for example, nested-loop join), or n-ary (for example, set union).

Crucial to the cost model is an accurate estimate of the total number of tuples that will be processed at each operator in the plan. This is inferred by the optimizer on the basis of statistics that are maintained on each relation in the system. These indicate the total number of tuples for each relation and specific information on each column of a relation, such as the column cardinality, a list of most common values in the table and the number of occurrences, and a histogram that divides the column's values into groups of equal population (that is, an equi-depth histogram, described in Section 13.3.1). In addition, PostgreSQL also maintains a statistical correlation between the physical and logical row orderings of a column's values —this indicates the cost of an index scan to retrieve tuples that pass predicates on the column. The DBA must ensure that these statistics are current by running the **analyze** command periodically.

27.6.3 Query Executor

The executor module is responsible for processing a query plan produced by the optimizer. The executor follows the **iterator** model with a set of four functions implemented for each operator (open, next, rescan, and close). Iterators are also discussed as part of demand-driven pipelining in Section 12.7.2.1. PostgreSQL iterators have an extra function, rescan, which is used to reset a subplan (say for an inner loop of a join) with parameters such as index key ranges.

Some of the important operators of the executor can be categorized as follows:

1. **Access methods.** The actual access methods that are used to retrieve data from on-disk objects in PostgreSQL are sequential scans of heap files, index scans, and bitmap index scans.

   - **Sequential scans.** The tuples of a relation are scanned sequentially from the first to last blocks of the file. Each tuple is returned to the caller only if it is "visible" according to the transaction isolation rules in Section 27.4.1.3.

   - **Index scans.** Given a search condition such as a range or equality predicate, this access method returns a set of matching tuples from the associated heap file. The operator processes one tuple at a time, starting by reading an entry from the index and then fetching the corresponding tuple from the heap file. This can result in a random page fetch for each tuple in the worst case.

   - **Bitmap index scans.** A bitmap index scan reduces the danger of excessive random page fetches in index scans. This is achieved by processing tuples in two phases. The first phase reads all index entries and stores the heap tuple IDs in a bitmap, and the second phase fetches the matching heap tuples in sequential order. This guarantees that each heap page is accessed only once, and increases the chance of sequential page fetches. Moreover, bitmaps from multiple indexes can be merged and intersected to evaluate complex Boolean predicates before accessing the heap.

2. **Join methods.** PostgreSQL supports three join methods: sorted merge joins, nested-loop joins (including index-nested loop variants for the inner), and a hybrid hash join (Section 12.5).

3. **Sort.** External sorting is implemented in PostgreSQL by algorithms explained in Section 12.4. The input is divided into sorted runs that are then merged in a polyphase merge. The initial runs are formed using replacement selection, using a priority tree instead of a data structure that fixes the number of in-memory records. This is because PostgreSQL may deal with tuples that vary considerably in size and tries to ensure full utilization of the configured sort memory space.

4. **Aggregation.** Grouped aggregation in PostgreSQL can be either sort-based or hash-based. When the estimated number of distinct groups is very large the former is used and otherwise the hash-based approach is preferred.

27.6.4 Triggers and Constraints

In PostgreSQL (unlike some commercial systems) active-database features such as triggers and constraints are not implemented in the rewrite phase. Instead they are implemented as part of the query executor. When the triggers and constraints are registered by the user, the details are associated with the catalog information for each appropriate relation and index. The executor processes an **update**, **delete**, and **insert** statement by repeatedly generating tuple changes for a relation. For each row modification, the executor explicitly identifies, fires, and enforces candidate triggers and constraints, before or after the change as required.

27.7   System Architecture

The PostgreSQL system architecture follows the process-per-transaction model. A running PostgreSQL site is managed by a central coordinating process, called the **postmaster.** The postmaster process is responsible for initializing and shutting down the server and also for handling connection requests from new clients. The postmaster assigns each new connecting client to a back-end server process that is responsible for executing the queries on behalf of the client and for returning the results to the client. This architecture is depicted in Figure 27.10.

Client applications can connect to the PostgreSQL server and submit queries through one of the many database application programmer interfaces supported by PostgreSQL (libpq, JDBC, ODBC, Perl DBD) that are provided as client-side libraries. An example client application is the command-line psql program, included in the standard PostgreSQL distribution. The postmaster is responsible for handling the initial client connections. For this, it constantly listens for new connections on a known port. After performing initialization steps such as user authentication, the postmaster will spawn a new back-end server process to handle the new client. After this initial connection, the client interacts only with the back-end server process, submitting queries and receiving query results. This is the essence of the process-per-connection model adopted by PostgreSQL.

The back-end server process is responsible for executing the queries submitted by the client by performing the necessary query-execution steps, including parsing, optimization, and execution. Each back-end server process can handle

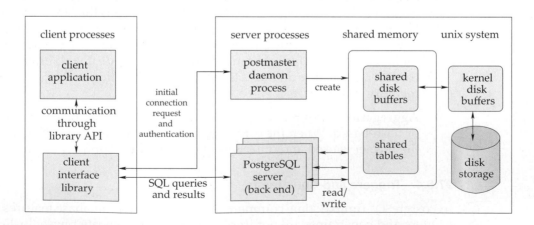

Figure 27.10   The PostgreSQL system architecture.

only a single query at a time. In order to execute more than one query in parallel, an application must maintain multiple connections to the server.

At any given time, there may be multiple clients connected to the system and thus multiple back-end server processes may be executing concurrently. The back-end server processes access database data through the main-memory buffer pool, which is placed in shared memory, so that all the processes have the same view of the data. Shared memory is also used to implement other forms of synchronization between the server processes, for example, the locking of data items.

The use of shared memory as a communication medium suggests that a PostgreSQL server should run on a single machine; a single-server site cannot be spread across multiple machines without the assistance of third-party packages, such as the Slony replication tool. However, it is possible to build a shared-nothing parallel database system with an instance of PostgreSQL running on each node; in fact, several commercial parallel database systems have been built with exactly this architecture, as described in Section 18.8.

Bibliographical Notes

There is extensive online documentation of PostgreSQL at www.postgresql.org. This Web site is the authoritative source for information on new releases of PostgreSQL, which occur on a frequent basis. Until PostgreSQL version 8, the only way to run PostgreSQL under Microsoft Windows was by using Cygwin. Cygwin is a Linux-like environment that allows rebuilding of Linux applications from source to run under Windows. Details are at www.cygwin.com. Books on PostgreSQL include Douglas and Douglas [2003] and Stinson [2002]. Rules as used in PostgreSQL are presented in Stonebraker et al. [1990]. The GiST structure is described in Hellerstein et al. [1995].

Many tools and extensions for PostgreSQL are documented by the pgFoundry at www.pgfoundry.org. These include the `pgtcl` library and the pgAccess administration tool mentioned in this chapter. The pgAdmin tool is described on the Web at www.pgadmin.org. The database-design tools, TORA and Data Architect, are described at tora.sourceforge.net and www.thekompany.com/products/dataarchitect, respectively. The report-generation tools, GNU Report Generator and GNU Enterprise, are described at www.gnu.org/software/grg and www.gnuenterprise.org, respectively. The open-source Mondrian OLAP server is described at mondrian.pentaho.org.

An open-source alternative to PostgreSQL is MySQL, which is available for noncommercial use under the GNU General Public License. MySQL may be embedded in commercial software that does not have freely distributed source code, but this requires a special license to be purchased. Comparisons between the most recent versions of the two systems are readily available on the Web.

CHAPTER 28

Oracle

Hakan Jakobsson

When Oracle was founded in 1977 as Software Development Laboratories by Larry Ellison, Bob Miner, and Ed Oates, there were no commercial relational database products. The company, which was later renamed Oracle, set out to build a relational database management system as a commercial product, and became a pioneer of the RDBMS market and has held a leading position in this market ever since. Over the years, its product and service offerings have grown beyond the relational database server to include middleware and applications.

In addition to products developed inside the company, Oracle's offerings include software that was originally developed in companies that Oracle acquired. Oracle's acquisitions have ranged from small companies to large, publicly traded ones, including Peoplesoft, Siebel, Hyperion, and BEA. As a result of these acquisitions, Oracle has a very broad portfolio of enterprise software products.

This chapter is focused on Oracle's main relational database server and closely related products. New versions of the products are being developed continually, so all product descriptions are subject to change. The feature set described here is based on the first release of Oracle11g, which is Oracle's flagship database product.

28.1   Database Design and Querying Tools

Oracle provides a variety of tools for database design, querying, report generation and data analysis, including OLAP. These tools, along with various other application development tools, are part of a portfolio of software products called Oracle Fusion Middleware. Products include both traditional tools using Oracle's PL/SQL programming language and newer ones based on Java/J2EE technologies. The software supports open standards such as SOAP, XML, BPEL, and UML.

28.1.1   Database and Application Design Tools

The Oracle Application Development Framework (ADF) is an end-to-end J2EE-based development framework for a Model-View-Control design pattern. In this framework, an application consists of multiple layers. The Model and Business Services layers handle the interaction with the data sources and contains the business logic. The View layer handles the user interface, and the Controller layer handles the flow of the application and the interaction between the other layers.

The primary development tool for Oracle ADF is Oracle JDeveloper, which provides an integrated development environment with support for Java, XML, PHP, HTML, Javascript, BPEL, SQL, and PL/SQL development. It has built-in support for UML modeling.

Oracle Designer is a database design tool, which translates business logic and data flows into schema definitions and procedural scripts for application logic. It supports such modeling techniques as E-R diagrams, information engineering, and object analysis and design.

Oracle also has an application development tool for data warehousing, Oracle Warehouse Builder. Warehouse Builder is a tool for design and deployment of all aspects of a data warehouse, including schema design, data mapping and transformations, data load processing, and metadata management. Oracle Warehouse Builder supports both 3NF and star schemas and can also import designs from Oracle Designer. This tool, in conjunction with database features, such as external tables and table functions, typically eliminates the need for third-party extraction, transformation, and loading (ETL) tools.

28.1.2 Querying Tools

Oracle provides tools for ad hoc querying, report generation, and data analysis, including OLAP.

Oracle Business Intelligence Suite (OBI) is a comprehensive suite of tools sharing a common service-oriented architecture. Components include a Business Intelligence server and tools for ad hoc querying, dashboard generation, reporting, and alerting. The components share infrastructure and services for data access and metadata management and have a common security model and administration tool.

The component for ad hoc querying, Oracle BI Answers, is an interactive tool that presents the user with a logical view of the data hiding the details of the physical implementation. Objects available to the user are displayed graphically and the user can build a query with a point-and-click interface. This logical query is sent to the Oracle BI Server component, which then generates the physical query or queries. Multiple physical data sources are supported, and a query could combine data stored in relational databases, OLAP sources, and Excel spreadsheets. Results can be presented as charts, reports, pivot tables, or dashboards that are drillable and can be saved and later modified.

28.2   SQL Variations and Extensions

Oracle supports all core SQL:2003 features fully or partially, with the exception of features-and-conformance views. In addition, Oracle supports a large number of other language constructs, some of which conform with Optional Features of SQL Foundation:2003, while others are Oracle-specific in syntax or functionality.

28.2.1 Object-Relational Features

Oracle has extensive support for object-relational constructs, including:

- **Object types**. A single-inheritance model is supported for type hierarchies.

- **Collection types**. Oracle supports **varrays**, which are variable length arrays, and nested tables.

- **Object tables**. These are used to store objects while providing a relational view of the attributes of the objects.

- **Table functions**. These are functions that produce sets of rows as output, and can be used in the **from** clause of a query. Table functions in Oracle can be nested. If a table function is used to express some form of data transformation, nesting multiple functions allows multiple transformations to be expressed in a single statement.

- **Object views**. These provide a virtual object table view of data stored in a regular relational table. They allow data to be accessed or viewed in an object-oriented style even if the data are really stored in a traditional relational format.

- **Methods**. These can be written in PL/SQL, Java, or C.

- **User-defined aggregate functions**. These can be used in SQL statements in the same way as built-in functions such as **sum** and **count**.

28.2.2 Oracle XML DB

Oracle XML DB provides in-database storage for XML data and support for a broad set of XML functionality including XML Schema and XQuery. It is built on the **XMLType** abstract data type, which is treated as a native Oracle data type. XML DB provides several options for how data of this data type are stored in the database, including:

- Structured in object-relational format. This format is usually space efficient and allows the use of a variety of standard relational features, such as B-tree indices, but incurs some overhead when mapping XML documents to the storage format and back. It is mainly suitable for XML data that are highly structured and the mapping includes a manageable number of relational tables and joins.

- Unstructured as a text string. This representation does not require any mapping and provides high throughput when inserting or retrieving an entire XML document. However, it is usually not very space efficient and provides for less intelligent processing when operating on parts of an XML document.

- Binary XML storage. This representation is a post-parse, XML Schema-aware, binary format. It is more space efficient than unstructured storage and can handle operations against parts of an XML document. It is also better than the structured format at handling data that are highly unstructured, but may not always be as space efficient. This format may make the processing of XQuery statements less efficient than when the structured format is used.

Both the binary and unstructured representation can be indexed with a special type of index called **XMLIndex**. This type of index allows document fragments to be indexed based on their corresponding XPath expression.

Storing XML data inside the database means that they get the benefit of Oracle's functionality in areas such as backup, recovery, security, and query processing. It allows for accessing relational data as part of doing XML processing as well as accessing XML data as part of doing SQL processing. Some very high-level features of XML DB include:

- Support for the XQuery language (W3C XQuery 1.0 Recommendation).

- An XSLT process that lets XSL transformations be performed inside the database.

- An XPath rewrite optimization that can speed up queries against data stored in object-relational representation. By translating an expression used in an XQuery into conditions directly on the object-relational columns, regular indices on these columns can be used to speed up query processing.

28.2.3 Procedural Languages

Oracle has two main procedural languages, PL/SQL and Java. PL/SQL was Oracle's original language for stored procedures and it has syntax similar to that used in the Ada language. Java is supported through a Java virtual machine inside the database engine. Oracle provides a package to encapsulate related procedures, functions, and variables into single units. Oracle supports SQLJ (SQL embedded in Java) and JDBC, and provides a tool to generate Java class definitions corresponding to user-defined database types.

28.2.4 Dimensions

Dimensional modeling is a commonly used design technique for relational star schemas as well as multidimensional databases. Oracle supports the creation of **dimensions** as metadata objects in order to support query processing against databases designed based on this technique. The metadata objects can be used to store information about various kinds of attributes of a dimension, but perhaps more importantly, about hierarchical relationships. See Section 28.3.10 for examples.

28.2.5 OLAP

Oracle provides support for analytical database processing in several different ways. In addition to support for a rich set of analytical SQL constructs (cube, rollup, grouping sets, window functions, etc.), Oracle provides native multidimensional storage inside the relational database server. The multidimensional data structures allow for array-based access to the data, and, in the right circumstances, this type of access can be vastly more efficient than traditional relational access methods. Using these data structures as an integrated part of a relational database provides a choice of storing data in a relational or multidimensional format while still taking advantage of Oracle features in areas such as backup and recovery, security, and administration tools.

Oracle provides storage containers for multidimensional data known as **analytic workspaces**. An analytic workspace contains both the dimensional data and measures (or facts) of an OLAP cube and is stored inside an Oracle table. From a traditional relational perspective, a cube stored inside a table would be an opaque object where the data could not normally be interpreted directly in terms of the table's rows and columns. However, Oracle's OLAP server inside the database has the knowledge to interpret and access the data and makes it possible to give SQL access to it as if it had been stored in a regular table format. Hence, it is possible to store data in either a multidimensional format or a traditional relational format, depending on what is optimal, and still be able to join data stored in both types of representations in a single SQLquery. A materialized view can use either representation.

In addition to Oracle's OLAP support inside its relational database, Oracle's product suite includes Essbase. Essbase is a widely used multidimensional database that came to be part of Oracle with the acquisition of Hyperion.

28.2.6 Triggers

Oracle provides several types of triggers and several options for when and how they are invoked. (See Section 5.3 for an introduction to triggers in SQL.) Triggers can be written in PL/SQL or Java or as C callouts.

For triggers that execute on DML statements such as insert, update, and delete, Oracle supports **row triggers** and **statement triggers**. Row triggers execute once for every row that is affected (updated or deleted, for example) by the DML operation. A statement trigger is executed just once per statement. In each case, the trigger can be defined as either a *before* or *after* trigger, depending on whether it is to be invoked before or after the DML operation is carried out.

Oracle allows the creation of **instead of** triggers for views that cannot be subject to DML operations. Depending on the view definition, it may not be possible for Oracle to translate a DML statement on a view to modifications of the underlying base tables unambiguously. Hence, DML operations on views are subject to numerous restrictions. A user can create an **instead of** trigger on a view to specify manually what operations on the base tables are to be carried out in response to a DML operation on the view. Oracle executes the trigger instead of the

DML operation and therefore provides a mechanism to circumvent the restrictions on DML operations against views.

Oracle also has triggers that execute on a variety of other events, such as database start-up or shutdown, server error messages, user logon or logoff, and DDL statements such as **create**, **alter** and **drop** statements.

28.3   Storage and Indexing

In Oracle parlance, a **database** consists of information stored in files and is accessed through an **instance**, which is a shared memory area and a set of processes that interact with the data in the files. The **control file** is a small file that contains some very high-level metadata required to start or operate an instance. The storage structure of the regular data and metadata is described in the next section.

28.3.1   Table Spaces

A database consists of one or more logical storage units called **table spaces**. Each table space, in turn, consists of one or more physical structures called *data files*. These may be either part of a file system or raw devices.

Usually, an Oracle database has the following table spaces:

- The **system** and the auxiliary **sysaux** table spaces, which are always created. They contain the data dictionary tables and storage for triggers and stored procedures.

- Table spaces created to store user data. While user data can be stored in the **system** table space, it is often desirable to separate the user data from the system data. Usually, the decision about what other table spaces should be created is based on performance, availability, maintainability, and ease of administration. For example, having multiple table spaces can be useful for partial backup and recovery operations.

- The **undo** table space, which is used solely for storing undo information for transaction management and recovery.

- **Temporary** table spaces. Many database operations require sorting the data, and the sort routine may have to store data temporarily on disk if the sort cannot be done in memory. Temporary table spaces are allocated for sorting and hashing to make the space management operations involved in spilling to disk more efficient.

Table spaces can also be used as a means of moving data between databases. For example, it is common to move data from a transactional system to a data warehouse at regular intervals. Oracle allows moving all the data in a table space from one system to the other by simply copying the data files and exporting and importing a small amount of data-dictionary metadata. These operations can be much faster than unloading the data from one database and then using a loader to insert it into the other. This Oracle feature is known as **transportable table spaces**.

28.3.2 Segments

The space in a table space is divided into units, called **segments**, each of which contains data for a specific data structure. There are four types of segments:

- **Data segments**. Each table in a table space has its own data segment where the table data are stored unless the table is partitioned; if so, there is one data segment per partition. (Partitioning in Oracle is described in Section 28.3.9.)

- **Index segments**. Each index in a table space has its own index segment, except for partitioned indices, which have one index segment per partition.

- **Temporary segments**. These are segments used when a sort operation needs to write data to disk or when data are inserted into a temporary table.

- **Undo segments**. These segments contain undo information so that an uncommitted transaction can be rolled back. These segments are automatically allocated in a special undo table space. They also play an important role in Oracle's concurrency control model and for database recovery, described in Sections 28.5.1 and 28.5.2. In older implementations of Oracle's undo management, the term "rollback segment" was used.

Below the level of segment, space is allocated at a level of granularity called an **extent**. Each extent consists of a set of contiguous database *blocks*. A database block is the lowest level of granularity at which Oracle performs disk I/O. A database block does not have to be the same as an operating system block in size, but should be a multiple thereof.

Oracle provides storage parameters that allow for detailed control of how space is allocated and managed, parameters such as:

- The size of a new extent that is to be allocated to provide room for rows that are inserted into a table.

- The percentage of space utilization at which a database block is considered full and at which no more rows will be inserted into that block. (Leaving some free space in a block can allow the existing rows to grow in size through updates, without running out of space in the block.)

28.3.3 Tables

A standard table in Oracle is heap organized; that is, the storage location of a row in a table is not based on the values contained in the row, and is fixed when the row is inserted. However, if the table is partitioned, the content of the row affects the partition in which it is stored. There are several features and variations. Heap tables can optionally be compressed, as described in Section 28.3.3.2.

Oracle supports nested tables; that is, a table can have a column whose data type is another table. The nested table is not stored in line in the parent table, but is stored in a separate table.

Oracle supports temporary tables where the duration of the data is either the transaction in which the data are inserted, or the user session. The data are private to the session and are automatically removed at the end of its duration.

A **cluster** is another form of file organization for table data, described earlier in Section 10.6.2 where it is called *multitable clustering*. The use of the term "cluster" in this context, should not be confused with other meanings of the word cluster, such as those relating to hardware architecture. In a cluster file organization, rows from different tables are stored together in the same block on the basis of some common columns. For example, a department table and an employee table could be clustered so that each row in the department table is stored together with all the employee rows for those employees who work in that department. The primary key/foreign key values are used to determine the storage location.

The cluster organization implies that a row belongs in a specific place; for example, a new employee row must be inserted with the other rows for the same department. Therefore, an index on the clustering column is mandatory. An alternative organization is a **hash cluster**. Here, Oracle computes the location of a row by applying a hash function to the value for the cluster column. The hash function maps the row to a specific block in the hash cluster. Since no index traversal is needed to access a row according to its cluster column value, this organization can save significant amounts of disk I/O.

28.3.3.1   Index-Organized Tables

In an **index-organized table** (IOT), records are stored in an Oracle B-tree index instead of in a heap; this file organization is described earlier in Section 11.4.1, where it is called B^+-*tree file organization*. An IOT requires that a unique key be identified for use as the index key. While an entry in a regular index contains the key value and row-id of the indexed row, an IOT replaces the row-id with the column values for the remaining columns of the row. Compared to storing the data in a regular heap table and creating an index on the key columns, using an IOT can improve both performance and space utilization. Consider looking up all the column values of a row, given its primary key value. For a heap table, that would require an index probe followed by a table access by row-id. For an IOT, only the index probe is necessary.

Secondary indices on nonkey columns of an index-organized table are different from indices on a regular heap table. In a heap table, each row has a fixed row-id that does not change. However, a B-tree is reorganized as it grows or shrinks when entries are inserted or deleted, and there is no guarantee that a row will stay in a fixed place inside an IOT. Hence, a secondary index on an IOT contains not normal row-ids, but **logical row-ids** instead. A logical row-id consists of two parts: a physical row-id corresponding to where the row was when the index was created or last rebuilt and a value for the unique key. The physical row-id is referred to as a "guess" since it could be incorrect if the row has been moved. If so, the other part of a logical row-id, the key value for the row, is used to access the row; however, this access is slower than if the guess had been correct, since it involves a traversal of the B-tree for the IOT from the root all the way to the leaf nodes, potentially incurring several disk I/Os. However, if a table is highly volatile and a large percentage of the guesses are likely to be wrong, it can be better to create the secondary index with only key values (as described in Section 11.4.1), since using an incorrect guess may result in a wasted disk I/O.

28.3.3.2 Compression

Oracle's compression feature allows data to be stored in a compressed format, something that can drastically reduce the amount of space needed to store the data and the number of I/O operations needed to retrieve it. Oracle's compression method is a lossless dictionary-based algorithm that compresses each block individually. All the information needed to uncompress a block is contained in that block itself. The algorithm works by replacing repeated occurrences of a value in that block with pointers to an entry for that value in a symbol table (or dictionary) in the block. Entries can be based on repeated values for individual columns or a combination of columns.

Oracle's original table compression generated the compressed block format as the data were bulk-loaded into a table and was mainly intended for data warehousing environments. A newer OLTP compression feature supports compression in conjunction with regular DML operations as well. In the latter case, Oracle compresses blocks only after certain thresholds have been reached for how much data have been written into the block. As a result, only transactions that cause a threshold to be passed will occur any overhead for compressing a block.

28.3.3.3 Data Security

In addition to regular access control features such as passwords, user privileges, and user roles, Oracle supports several features to protect the data from unauthorized access, including:

- **Encryption.** Oracle can automatically store table data in an encrypted format and transparently encrypt and decrypt data using the AES or 3DES algorithms. Encryption can be enabled for an entire database or just for individual table columns. The main motivation for this feature is to protect sensitive data outside the normally protected environment, such as when backup media is sent to a remote location.

- **Database Vault.** This feature is aimed at providing a separation of duties for users with access to the database. A database administrator is a highly privileged user that typically can do almost anything with the database. However, it may be inappropriate or illegal to let that person access sensitive corporate financial data or personal information about other employees. Database vault includes a variety of mechanisms that can be used to restrict or monitor access to sensitive data by highly privileged database users.

- **Virtual Private Database.** This feature, described earlier in Section 9.7.5, allows additional predicates to be automatically added to the **where** clause of a query that accesses a given table or view. Typically, the feature would be used so that the additional predicate filters out all the rows that the user does not have the right to see. For example, two users could submit identical queries to find all the employee information in the entire employee table. However, if a policy exists that limits each user to seeing only the information for the employee number that matches the user ID, the automatically added predicates will ensure that each query only returns the employee information for the user who submitted the query. Hence, each user will be left with the impression of accessing a virtual database that contains only a subset of the data of the physical database.

28.3.4 Indices

Oracle supports several different types of indices. The most commonly used type is a B-tree index, created on one or multiple columns. Note that in the terminology of Oracle (as also in several other database systems) a B-tree index is what is referred to as a B^+-tree index in Chapter 11. Index entries have the following format: for an index on columns col_1, col_2, and col_3, each row in the table where at least one of the columns has a nonnull value would result in the index entry:

$$<col_1><col_2><col_3><row\text{-}id>$$

where $<col_i>$ denotes the value for column i and $<row\text{-}id>$ is the row-id for the row. Oracle can optionally compress the prefix of the entry to save space. For example, if there are many repeated combinations of $<col_1><col_2>$ values, the representation of each distinct $<col_1><col_2>$ prefix can be shared between the entries that have that combination of values, rather than stored explicitly for each such entry. Prefix compression can lead to substantial space savings.

28.3.5 Bitmap Indices

Bitmap indices (described in Section 11.9) use a bitmap representation for index entries, which can lead to substantial space saving (and therefore disk I/O savings), when the indexed column has a moderate number of distinct values. Bitmap indices in Oracle use the same kind of B-tree structure to store the entries as a regular index. However, where a regular index on a column would have entries of the form $<col_1><row\text{-}id>$, a bitmap index entry has the form:

$$<col_1><start\ row\text{-}id><end\ row\text{-}id><compressed\ bitmap>$$

The bitmap conceptually represents the space of all possible rows in the table between the start and end row-id. The number of such possible rows in a block depends on how many rows can fit into a block, which is a function of the number of columns in the table and their data types. Each bit in the bitmap represents one such possible row in a block. If the column value of that row is that of the index entry, the bit is set to 1. If the row has some other value, or the row does not actually exist in the table, the bit is set to 0. (It is possible that the row does not actually exist because a table block may well have a smaller number of rows than the number that was calculated as the maximum possible.) If the difference is large, the result may be long strings of consecutive zeros in the bitmap, but the compression algorithm deals with such strings of zeros, so the negative effect is limited.

The compression algorithm is a variation of a compression technique called Byte-Aligned Bitmap Compression (BBC). Essentially, a section of the bitmap where the distance between two consecutive 1s is small enough is stored as verbatim bitmaps. If the distance between two 1s is sufficiently large—that is, there is a sufficient number of adjacent 0s between them—a runlength of 0s, that is, the number of 0s, is stored.

Bitmap indices allow multiple indices on the same table to be combined in the same access path if there are multiple conditions on indexed columns in the **where** clause of a query. Bitmaps from the different indices are retrieved and combined using Boolean operations corresponding to the conditions in the **where** clause. All Boolean operations are performed directly on the compressed representation of the bitmaps—no decompression is necessary—and the resulting (compressed) bitmap represents those rows that match all the logical conditions.

The ability to use the Boolean operations to combine multiple indices is not limited to bitmap indices. Oracle can convert row-ids to the compressed bitmap representation, so it can use a regular B-tree index anywhere in a Boolean tree of bitmap operation simply by putting a row-id-to-bitmap operator on top of the index access in the execution plan.

As a rule of thumb, bitmap indices tend to be more space efficient than regular B-tree indices if the number of distinct key values is less than half the number of rows in the table. For example, in a table with 1 million rows, an index on a column with less than 500,000 distinct values would probably be smaller if it were created as a bitmap index. For columns with a very small number of distinct values—for example, columns referring to properties such as country, state, gender, marital status, and various status flags—a bitmap index might require only a small fraction of the space of a regular B-tree index. Any such space advantage can also give rise to corresponding performance advantages in the form of fewer disk I/Os when the index is scanned.

28.3.6 Function-Based Indices

In addition to creating indices on one or multiple columns of a table, Oracle allows indices to be created on expressions that involve one or more columns, such as $col_1 + col_2 * 5$. For example, by creating an index on the expression *upper(name)*, where *upper* is a function that returns the uppercase version of a string, and *name* is a column, it is possible to do case-insensitive searches on the *name* column. In order to find all rows with name "van Gogh" efficiently, the condition:

$$upper(name) = \text{'VAN GOGH'}$$

would be used in the **where** clause of the query. Oracle then matches the condition with the index definition and concludes that the index can be used to retrieve all the rows matching "van Gogh" regardless of how the name was capitalized when it was stored in the database. A function-based index can be created as either a bitmap or a B-tree index.

28.3.7   Join Indices

A join index is an index where the key columns are not in the table that is referenced by the row-ids in the index. Oracle supports bitmap join indices primarily for use with star schemas (see Section 20.2.2). For example, if there is a column for product names in a product dimension table, a bitmap join index on the fact table with this key column could be used to retrieve the fact table rows that correspond to a product with a specific name, although the name is not stored in the fact table. How the rows in the fact and dimension tables correspond is based on a join condition that is specified when the index is created, and becomes part of the index metadata. When a query is processed, the optimizer will look for the same join condition in the **where** clause of the query in order to determine if the join index is applicable.

Oracle can combine a bitmap join index on a fact table with other indices on the same table—whether join indices or not—by using the operators for Boolean bitmap operations.

28.3.8   Domain Indices

Oracle allows tables to be indexed by index structures that are not native to Oracle. This extensibility feature of the Oracle server allows software vendors to develop so-called **cartridges** with functionality for specific application domains, such as text, spatial data, and images, with indexing functionality beyond that provided by the standard Oracle index types. In implementing the logic for creating, maintaining, and searching the index, the index designer must ensure that it adheres to a specific protocol in its interaction with the Oracle server.

A domain index must be registered in the data dictionary, together with the operators it supports. Oracle's optimizer considers domain indices as one of the possible access paths for a table. Oracle allows cost functions to be registered with the operators so that the optimizer can compare the cost of using the domain index to those of other access paths.

For example, a domain index for advanced text searches may support an operator *contains*. Once this operator has been registered, the domain index will be considered as an access path for a query like:

```
select *
from employees
where contains(resume, 'LINUX');
```

where *resume* is a text column in the *employee* table. The domain index can be stored in either an external data file or inside an Oracle index-organized table.

A domain index can be combined with other (bitmap or B-tree) indices in the same access path by converting between the row-id and bitmap representation and using Boolean bitmap operations.

28.3.9 Partitioning

Oracle supports various kinds of horizontal partitioning of tables and indices, and this feature plays a major role in Oracle's ability to support very large databases. The ability to partition a table or index has advantages in many areas.

- Backup and recovery are easier and faster, since they can be done on individual partitions rather than on the table as a whole.

- Loading operations in a data warehousing environment are less intrusive: data can be added to a newly created partition, and then the partition added to a table, which is an instantaneous operation. Likewise, dropping a partition with obsolete data from a table is very easy in a data warehouse that maintains a rolling window of historical data.

- Query performance benefits substantially, since the optimizer can recognize that only a subset of the partitions of a table need to be accessed in order to resolve a query (partition pruning). Also, the optimizer can recognize that in a join, it is not necessary to try to match all rows in one table with all rows in the other, but that the joins need to be done only between matching pairs of partitions (partitionwise join).

An index on a partitioned table can be either a **global index** or a **local index**. Entries in a global index can refer to rows in any partition. A locally indexed table has one physical index for each partition that only contains entries for that partition. Unless partition pruning restricts a query to a single partition, a table accessed through a local index will require multiple individual physical index probes. However, a local index has advantages in data warehousing environments where new data can be loaded into a new partition and indexed without the need to maintain any existing index. (Loading followed by index creation is much more efficient than maintaining an existing index while the data are being loaded.) Similarly, dropping an old partition and the physical part of its local index can be done without causing any index maintenance.

Each row in a partitioned table is associated with a specific partition. This association is based on the partitioning column or columns that are part of the definition of a partitioned table. There are several ways to map column values to partitions, giving rise to several types of partitioning, each with different characteristics: range, hash, list, and composite partitioning.

28.3.9.1   Range Partitioning

In range partitioning, the partitioning criteria are ranges of values. This type of partitioning is especially well suited to date columns, in which case all rows in the same date range, say a day or a month, belong in the same partition. In a data warehouse where data are loaded from the transactional systems at regular intervals, range partitioning can be used to implement a rolling window of historical data efficiently. Each data load gets its own new partition, making the loading process faster and more efficient. The system actually loads the data into a separate table with the same column definition as the partitioned table. It can then check the data for consistency, cleanse them, and index them. After that, the system can make the separate table a new partition of the partitioned table, by a simple change to the metadata in the data dictionary—a nearly instantaneous operation.

Up until the metadata change, the loading process does not affect the existing data in the partitioned table in any way. There is no need to do any maintenance of existing indices as part of the loading. Old data can be removed from a table by simply dropping its partition; this operation does not affect the other partitions.

In addition, queries in a data warehousing environment often contain conditions that restrict them to a certain time period, such as a quarter or month. If date-range partitioning is used, the query optimizer can restrict the data access to those partitions that are relevant to the query, and avoid a scan of the entire table.

Partitions can either be created with explicitly set end points or be defined based on a fixed range, such as a day or a month. In the latter case, called **interval partitioning**, the creation of the partition happens automatically under the covers when trying to insert a row with a value in a previously nonexistent interval.

28.3.9.2   Hash Partitioning

In hash partitioning, a hash function maps rows to partitions according to the values in the partitioning columns. This type of partitioning is primarily useful when it is important to distribute the rows evenly among partitions or when partitionwise joins are important for query performance.

28.3.9.3   List Partitioning

In list partitioning, the values associated with a particular partition are stated in a list. This type of partitioning is useful if the data in the partitioning column have a relatively small set of discrete values. For instance, a table with a state column can be implicitly partitioned by geographical region if each partition list has the states that belong in the same region.

28.3.9.4   Composite Partitioning

In composite partitioning, tables that are range, interval, or list partitioned can be subpartitioned by range, list, or hash. For example, a table may be range partitioned on a date column and hash subpartitioned on a column that is frequently used as a join column. The subpartitioning allows partition-wise joins to be used when the table is joined.

28.3.9.5 Reference Partitioning

In reference partitioning, the partitioning key is resolved based on a foreign-key constraint with another table. The dependency between the tables allows maintenance operations to be automatically cascaded.

28.3.10 Materialized Views

The materialized-view feature (see Section 4.2.3) allows the result of an SQL query to be stored in a table and used for later query processing. In addition, Oracle maintains the materialized result, updating it when the tables that were referenced in the query are updated. Materialized views are used in data warehousing to speed up query processing, but the technology is also used for replication in distributed and mobile environments.

In data warehousing, a common usage for materialized views is to summarize data. For example, a common type of query asks for "the sum of sales for each quarter during the last 2 years." Precomputing the result, or some partial result, of such a query can speed up query processing dramatically compared to computing it from scratch by aggregating all detail-level sales records.

Oracle supports automatic query rewrites that take advantage of any useful materialized view when resolving a query. The rewrite consists of changing the query to use the materialized view instead of the original tables in the query. In addition, the rewrite may add additional joins or aggregate processing as may be required to get the correct result. For example, if a query needs sales by quarter, the rewrite can take advantage of a view that materializes sales by month, by adding additional aggregation to roll up the months to quarters. Oracle has a type of metadata object called dimension that allows hierarchical relationships in tables to be defined. For example, for a time-dimension table in a star schema, Oracle can define a dimension metadata object to specify how days roll up to months, months to quarters, quarters to years, and so forth. Likewise, hierarchical properties relating to geography can be specified—for example, how sales districts roll up to regions. The query rewrite logic looks at these relationships since they allow a materialized view to be used for wider classes of queries.

The container object for a materialized view is a table, which means that a materialized view can be indexed, partitioned, or subjected to other controls, to improve query performance.

When there are changes to the data in the tables referenced in the query that defines a materialized view, the materialized view must be refreshed to reflect those changes. Oracle supports both complete refresh of a materialized view and fast, incremental refresh. In a complete refresh, Oracle recomputes the materialized view from scratch, which may be the best option if the underlying tables have had significant changes, for example, changes due to a bulk load. In a fast refresh, Oracle updates the view using the records that were changed in the underlying tables. The refresh to the view can be executed *on commit* as part of the transaction that changed the underlying tables or at some later point in time *on demand*. Fast refresh may be better if the number of rows that were changed is low. There are some restrictions on the classes of queries for which a materialized view can be incrementally refreshed (and others for when a materialized view can be created at all).

A materialized view is similar to an index in the sense that, while it can improve query performance, it uses up space, and creating and maintaining it consumes resources. To help resolve this trade-off, Oracle provides an advisor that can help a user create the most cost-effective materialized views, given a particular query workload as input.

28.4   Query Processing and Optimization

Oracle supports a large variety of processing techniques in its query processing engine. Some of the more important ones are described here briefly.

28.4.1   Execution Methods

Data can be accessed through a variety of access methods:

- **Full table scan**. The query processor scans the entire table by getting information about the blocks that make up the table from the extent map, and scanning those blocks.

- **Index scan**. The processor creates a start and/or stop key from conditions in the query and uses it to scan to a relevant part of the index. If there are columns that need to be retrieved, that are not part of the index, the index scan would be followed by a table access by index row-id. If no start or stop key is available, the scan would be a full index scan.

- **Index fast full scan**. The processor scans the extents the same way as the table extent in a full table scan. If the index contains all the table columns that are needed for that table, and there are no good start/stop keys that would significantly reduce that portion of the index that would be scanned in a regular index scan, this method may be the fastest way to access the data. This is because the fast full scan can take full advantage of multiblock disk I/O. However, unlike a regular full scan, which traverses the index leaf blocks in order, a fast full scan does not guarantee that the output preserves the sort order of the index.

- **Index join**. If a query needs only a small subset of the columns of a wide table, but no single index contains all those columns, the processor can use an index join to generate the relevant information without accessing the table, by joining several indices that together contain the needed columns. It performs the joins as hash joins on the row-ids from the different indices.

- **Cluster** and **hash cluster access**. The processor accesses the data by using the cluster key.

Oracle has several ways to combine information from multiple indices in a single access path. This ability allows multiple **where**-clause conditions to be used together to compute the result set as efficiently as possible. The functionality includes the ability to perform Boolean operations **and**, **or**, and **minus** on bitmaps representing row-ids. There are also operators that map a list of row-ids into bitmaps and vice versa, which allows regular B-tree indices and bitmap indices to be used together in the same access path. In addition, for many queries involving **count**(*) on selections on a table, the result can be computed by just counting the bits that are set in the bitmap generated by applying the **where** clause conditions, without accessing the table.

Oracle supports several types of joins in the execution engine: inner joins, outer joins, semijoins, and antijoins. (An antijoin in Oracle returns rows from the left-hand side input that do not match any row in the right-hand side input; this operation is called anti-semijoin in other literature.) It evaluates each type of join by one of three methods: hash join, sort–merge join, or nested-loop join.

28.4.2   Optimization

Chapter 13 discusses the general topic of query optimization. Here, we discuss optimization in the context of Oracle.

28.4.2.1   Query Transformations

Oracle does query optimization in several steps. One such step is to perform various query transformations and rewrites that fundamentally change the structure of the query. Another step is to perform access path selection to determine access paths, join methods, and join order. Since some transformations are not always beneficial, Oracle uses cost-based query transformations where the transformations and access path selection are interleaved. For each transformation that is tried, access path selection is performed in order to generate a cost estimate, and the transformation is accepted or rejected based on the cost for the resulting execution plan.

Some of the major types of transformations and rewrites supported by Oracle are as follows:

- **View merging**. A view reference in a query is replaced by the view definition. This transformation is not applicable to all views.

- **Complex view merging**. Oracle offers this feature for certain classes of views that are not subject to regular view merging because they have a **group by** or **select distinct** in the view definition. If such a view is joined to other tables, Oracle can commute the joins and the sort or hash operation used for the **group by** or **distinct**.

- **Subquery flattening**. Oracle has a variety of transformations that convert various classes of subqueries into joins, semijoins, or antijoins. Such conversion is also called *decorrelation*, and is described briefly in Section 13.4.4.

- **Materialized view rewrite**. Oracle has the ability to rewrite a query automatically to take advantage of materialized views. If some part of the query can be matched up with an existing materialized view, Oracle can replace that part of the query with a reference to the table in which the view is materialized. If need be, Oracle adds join conditions or **group by** operations to preserve the semantics of the query. If multiple materialized views are applicable, Oracle picks the one that gives the greatest advantage in reducing the amount of data that have to be processed. In addition, Oracle subjects both the rewritten query and the original version to the full optimization process producing an execution plan and an associated cost estimate for each. Oracle then decides whether to execute the rewritten or the original version of the query on the basis of the cost estimates.

- **Star transformation**. Oracle supports a technique for evaluating queries against star schemas, known as the star transformation. When a query contains a join of a fact table with dimension tables, and selections on attributes from the dimension tables, the query is transformed by deleting the join condition between the fact table and the dimension tables, and replacing the selection condition on each dimension table by a subquery of the form:

  $fact\_table.fk_i$ **in**
      (**select** pk **from** $dimension\_table_i$
        where <conditions on $dimension\_table_i$ >)

  One such subquery is generated for each dimension that has some constraining predicate. If the dimension has a snowflake schema (see Section 20.2), the subquery will contain a join of the applicable tables that make up the dimension.

  Oracle uses the values that are returned from each subquery to probe an index on the corresponding fact table column, getting a bitmap as a result. The bitmaps generated from different subqueries are combined by a bitmap **and** operation. The resultant bitmap can be used to access matching fact table rows. Hence, only those rows in the fact table that simultaneously match the conditions on the constrained dimensions will be accessed. Both the decision on whether the use of a subquery for a particular dimension is cost-effective, and the decision on whether the rewritten query is better than the original, are based on the optimizer's cost estimates.

28.4.2.2   Access Path Selection

Oracle has a cost-based optimizer that determines join order, join methods, and access paths. Each operation that the optimizer considers has an associated cost function, and the optimizer tries to generate the combination of operations that has the lowest overall cost.

In estimating the cost of an operation, the optimizer relies on statistics that have been computed for schema objects such as tables and indices. The statistics contain information about the size of the object, the cardinality, the data distribution of table columns, and so forth. Oracle supports height-balanced and frequency histograms for data distributions. Height-balanced histograms are also referred to as *equi-depth histograms*, and are described in Section 13.3.1.

To facilitate the collection of optimizer statistics, Oracle can monitor modification activity on tables and keep track of those tables that have been subject to enough changes that recalculating the statistics may be appropriate. Oracle also tracks what columns are used in **where** clauses of queries, which makes them potential candidates for histogram creation. With a single command, a user can tell Oracle to refresh the statistics for those tables that were marked as sufficiently changed. Oracle uses sampling to speed up the process of gathering the new statistics and automatically chooses the smallest adequate sample percentage. It also determines whether the distribution of the marked columns merits the creation of histograms; if the distribution is close to uniform, Oracle uses a simpler representation of the column statistics.

In some cases, it may be impossible for the optimizer to accurately estimate the selectivity of a condition in the **where** clause of a query just based on simple column statistics. For example, the condition may be an expression involving a column, such as $f(col + 3) > 5$. Another class of problematic queries is those that have multiple predicates on columns that have some form of correlation. Assessing the combined selectivity of those predicates may be hard. Oracle therefore allows statistics to be created for expressions as well as for groups of columns. In addition, Oracle can address these issues through *dynamic sampling*. The optimizer can randomly sample a small portion of a table and apply all the relevant predicates to the sample to see the percentage of the rows that match. This feature can also handle temporary tables where the lifespan and visibility of the data may prevent regular statistics collection.

Oracle uses both CPU cost and disk I/Os in the optimizer cost model. To balance the two components, it stores measures about CPU speed and disk I/O performance as part of the optimizer statistics. Oracle's package for gathering optimizer statistics computes these measures.

For queries involving a nontrivial number of joins, the search space is an issue for a query optimizer. Oracle addresses this issue in several ways. The optimizer generates an initial join order and then decides on the best join methods and access paths for that join order. It then changes the order of the tables and determines the best join methods and access paths for the new join order and so forth, while keeping the best plan that has been found so far. Oracle cuts the optimization short if the number of different join orders that have been considered becomes so large that the time spent in the optimizer may be noticeable compared to the time it would take to execute the best plan found so far. Since this cutoff depends on the cost estimate for the best plan found so far, finding a good plan early is important so that the optimization can be stopped after a smaller number of join orders, resulting in better response time. Oracle uses several initial ordering heuristics to increase the likelihood that the first join order considered is a good one.

For each join order that is considered, the optimizer may make additional passes over the tables to decide join methods and access paths. Such additional passes would target specific global side effects of the access path selection. For instance, a specific combination of join methods and access paths may eliminate the need to perform an **order by** sort. Since such a global side effect may not be obvious when the costs of the different join methods and access paths are considered locally, a separate pass targeting a specific side effect is used to find a possible execution plan with a better overall cost.

28.4.2.3   Partition Pruning

For partitioned tables, the optimizer tries to match conditions in the **where** clause of a query with the partitioning criteria for the table, in order to avoid accessing partitions that are not needed for the result. For example, if a table is partitioned by date range and the query is constrained to data between two specific dates, the optimizer determines which partitions contain data between the specified dates and ensures that only those partitions are accessed. This scenario is very common, and the speedup can be dramatic if only a small subset of the partitions are needed.

28.4.2.4   SQL Tuning Advisor

In addition to the regular optimization process, Oracle's optimizer can be used in tuning mode as part of the SQL Tuning Advisor in order to generate more efficient execution plans than it normally would. This feature is especially useful for packaged applications that generate the same set of SQL statements repeatedly so that effort to tune these statements for performance can have future benefits.

Oracle monitors the database activity and automatically stores information about high-load SQL statements in a workload repository; see Section 28.8.2. High-load SQL statements are those that use up the most resources because they are executed a very large number of times or because each execution is very expensive. Such statements are logical candidates for tuning since their impact on the system is the greatest. The SQL Tuning Advisor can be used to improve the performance of these statements by making making various kinds of recommendations that fall into the following different categories:

- **Statistics Analysis**. Oracle checks whether statistics needed by the optimizer are missing or stale and makes recommendations for collecting them.

- **SQL Profiling**. A profile for an SQL statement is a set of information that is intended to help the optimizer make better decisions the next time the statement is optimized. An optimizer can sometimes generate inefficient execution plans if it is unable to accurately estimate cardinalities and selectivities, something that can happen because of data correlation or the use of certain types of constructs. When running the optimizer in tuning mode to create a profile, the optimizer tries to verify that its assumptions are correct using dynamic sampling and partial evaluation of the SQL statement. If it finds that there are steps in the optimization process where the optimizer's assumptions are wrong, it will generate a correction factor for that step that will become part of the profile. Optimizing in tuning mode can be very time-consuming, but it can be worthwhile if the use of the profile significantly improves the performance of the statement. If a profile is created, it will be stored persistently and used whenever the statement is optimized in the future. Profiles can be used to tune SQL statements without changing the text of the statement, something that is important since it is often impossible for the database administrator to modify statements generated by an application.

- **Access Path Analysis.** Based on analysis by the optimizer, Oracle suggests the creation of additional indices that could speed up the statement.

- **SQL Structure Analysis.** Oracle suggests changes in the structure of the SQLstatement that would allow for more efficient execution.

28.4.2.5 SQL Plan Management

Packaged applications often generate a large number of SQL statements that are executed repeatedly. If the application is performing adequately, it is common that database administrators are averse to changes in database behavior. If the change results in better performance, there is limited perceived upside since the performance was already good enough. On the other hand, if the change leads to a performance degradation, it may break an application if a critical query deteriorates to a response time that is unacceptable.

An example of a change of behavior is a change of an execution plan for a query. Such a change may be a perfectly legitimate reflection of changes to properties of the data, such as a table having grown much larger. But the change could also be an unintended consequence of a number of other actions, such as a change in the routines for collecting optimizer statistics or an upgrade to a new version of the RDBMS with new optimizer behavior.

Oracle's SQL Plan Management feature addresses the risk associated with execution plan changes by maintaining a set of trusted execution plans for a workload and phasing in plans changed by the query optimizer only after they have been verified not to cause any performance degradations. The feature has three major components:

1. **SQL plan baseline capture.** Oracle can capture execution plans for a workload and store a plan history for each SQL statement. The plan baseline is a set of plans for a workload with trusted performance characteristics and against which future plan changes can be compared. A statement could have more than one baseline plan.

2. **SQL plan baseline selection.** After the optimizer generates a plan for an SQL statement, it checks whether there exists a baseline plan for the statement.

If the statement exists in the baseline but the new plan is different from any existing one, the baseline plan that the optimizer considers to be the best will be used. The newly generated plan will be added to the plan history for the statement and could become part of a future baseline.

3. **SQL plan baseline evolution.** Periodically, it may make sense to try to make newly generated execution plans part of the trusted plans in the baseline. Oracle supports adding new plans to the baseline with or without *verification*. If verification is the chosen option, Oracle will execute a newly generated plan and compare its performance to the baseline in order to make sure it does not cause performance regressions.

28.4.3 Parallel Execution

Oracle allows the execution of a single SQL statement to be parallelized by dividing the work between multiple processes on a multiprocessor computer. This feature is especially useful for computationally intensive operations that would otherwise take an unacceptably long time to perform. Representative examples are decision support queries that need to process large amounts of data, data loads in a data warehouse, and index creation or rebuild.

In order to achieve good speedup through parallelism, it is important that the work involved in executing the statement be divided into granules that can be processed independently by the different parallel processors. Depending on the type of operation, Oracle has several ways to split up the work.

For operations that access base objects (tables and indices), Oracle can divide the work by horizontal slices of the data. For some operations, such as a full table scan, each such slice can be a range of blocks—each parallel query process scans the table from the block at the start of the range to the block at the end. For some operations on a partitioned table, such as an index range scan, the slice would be a partition. Parallelism based on block ranges is more flexible since these can be determined dynamically based on a variety of criteria and are not tied to the table definition.

Joins can be parallelized in several different ways. One way is to divide one of the inputs to the join between parallel processes and let each process join its slice with the other input to the join; this is the asymmetric fragment-and-replicate method of Section 18.5.2.2. For example, if a large table is joined to a small one by a hash join, Oracle divides the large table among the processes and broadcasts a copy of the small table to each process, which then joins its slice with the smaller table. If both tables are large, it would be prohibitively expensive to broadcast one of them to all processes. In that case, Oracle achieves parallelism by partitioning the data among processes by hashing on the values of the join columns (the partitioned hash-join method of Section 18.5.2.1). Each table is scanned in parallel by a set of processes and each row in the output is passed on to one of a set of processes that are to perform the join. Which one of these processes gets the row is determined by a hash function on the values of the join column. Hence, each join process gets only rows that could potentially match, and no rows that could match could end up in different processes.

Oracle parallelizes sort operations by value ranges of the column on which the sort is performed (that is, using the range-partitioning sort of Section 18.5.1). Each process participating in the sort is sent rows with values in its range, and it sorts the rows in its range. To maximize the benefits of parallelism, the rows need to be divided as evenly as possible among the parallel processes, and the problem of determining range boundaries that generates a good distribution then arises. Oracle solves the problem by dynamically sampling a subset of the rows in the input to the sort before deciding on the range boundaries.

28.4.3.1 Process Structure

The processes involved in the parallel execution of an SQL statement consist of a coordinator process and a number of parallel server processes. The coordinator is responsible for assigning work to the parallel servers and for collecting and returning data to the user process that issued the statement. The degree of parallelism is the number of parallel server processes that are assigned to execute a primitive operation as part of the statement. The degree of parallelism is determined by the optimizer, but can be throttled back dynamically if the load on the system increases.

The parallel servers operate on a producer/consumer model. When a sequence of operations is needed to process a statement, the producer set of servers performs the first operation and passes the resulting data to the consumer set. For example, if a full table scan is followed by a sort and the degree of parallelism is 32, there would be 32 producer servers performing the table scan and passing the result to 32 consumer servers that perform the sort. If a subsequent operation is needed, such as another sort, the roles of the two sets of servers switch. The servers that originally performed the table scan take on the role of consumers of the output produced by the first sort and use it to perform the second sort. Hence, a sequence of operations proceeds by passing data back and forth between two sets of servers that alternate in their roles as producers and consumers. The servers communicate with each other through memory buffers on shared-memory hardware and through high-speed network connections on MPP (shared nothing) configurations and clustered (shared disk) systems.

For shared-nothing systems, the cost of accessing data on disk is not uniform among processes. A process running on a node that has direct access to a device is able to process data on that device faster than a process that has to retrieve the data over a network. Oracle uses knowledge about device-to-node and device-to-process affinity—that is, the ability to access devices directly—when distributing work among parallel execution servers.

28.4.4 Result Caching

Oracle's result caching feature allows the result of a query or query block (e.g., a view referenced in a query) to be cached in memory and reused if the same query is executed again. Updates of the data in the underlying tables invalidate the cached results, so this feature works best for queries against tables that are relatively static and where the result sets are relatively small. Consider, as a usage example, some part of a Web page that is stored in the database and does not change very frequently compared to how often it accessed. For such an application, result caching would be a much more lightweight alternative to using materialized views, which would require explicitly creating and administering new persistent database objects.

28.5   Concurrency Control and Recovery

Oracle supports concurrency control and recovery techniques that provide a number of useful features.

28.5.1   Concurrency Control

Oracle's multiversion concurrency control mechanism is based on the snapshot isolation protocol described in Section 15.7. Read-only queries are given a read-consistent snapshot, which is a view of the database as it existed at a specific point in time, containing all updates that were committed by that point in time, and not containing any updates that were not committed at that point in time. Thus, read locks are not used and read-only queries do not interfere with other database activity in terms of locking.

Oracle supports both statement- and transaction-level read consistency: at the beginning of the execution of either a statement or a transaction (depending on what level of consistency is used), Oracle determines the current system change number (SCN). The SCN essentially acts as a timestamp, where the time is measured in terms of transaction commits instead of wall-clock time.

If in the course of a query a data block is found that has a higher SCN than the one being associated with the query, it is evident that the data block has been modified after the time of the original query's SCN by some other transaction that may or may not have committed. Hence, the data in the block cannot be included in a consistent view of the database as it existed at the time of the query's SCN. Instead, an older version of the data in the block must be used; specifically, the one that has the highest SCN that does not exceed the SCN of the query. Oracle retrieves that version of the data from the undo segment (undo segments are described in Section 28.5.2). Hence, provided that the undo space is sufficiently large, Oracle can return a consistent result of the query even if the data items have been modified several times since the query started execution. Should the block with the desired SCN no longer exist in the undo, the query will return an error. It would be an indication that the undo table space has not been properly sized, given the activity on the system.

In the Oracle concurrency model, read operations do not block write operations and write operations do not block read operations, a property that allows a high degree of concurrency. In particular, the scheme allows for long-running queries (for example, reporting queries) to run on a system with a large amount of transactional activity. This kind of scenario is often problematic for database systems where queries use read locks, since the query may either fail to acquire them or lock large amounts of data for a long time, thereby preventing transactional activity against that data and reducing concurrency. (An alternative that is used in some systems is to use a lower degree of consistency, such as degree-two consistency, but that could result in inconsistent query results.)

Oracle's concurrency model is used as a basis for the **flashback** feature. This feature allows a user to set a certain SCN number or wall-clock time in his session and perform operations on the data that existed at that point in time (provided that the data still exist in the undo). Normally in a database system, once a change has been committed, there is no way to get back to the previous state of the data other than performing point-in-time recovery from backups. However, recovery of a very large database can be very costly, especially if the goal is just to retrieve some data item that had been inadvertently deleted by a user. The flashback feature provides a much simpler mechanism to deal with user errors. The flashback feature includes the ability to restore a table or an entire database to an earlier point in time without recovering from backups, the ability to perform queries on the data as they existed at an earlier point in time, the ability to track how one or more rows have changed over time, and the ability to examine changes to the database at the transaction level.

It may be desirable to be able to track changes to a table beyond what would be possible through normal undo retention. (For instance, corporate governance regulations may require that such changes be trackable for a certain number of years.) For this purpose, a table can be tracked by the **flashback archive** feature, which creates an internal, history version of the table. A background process converts the undo information into entries in the history table, which can be used to provide flashback functionality for arbitrarily long periods of time.

Oracle supports two ANSI/ISO isolation levels, **read committed** and **serializable**. There is no support for dirty reads since it is not needed. Statement-level read consistency corresponds to the read committed isolation level, while transaction-level read consistency corresponds to the serializable isolation level. The isolation level can be set for a session or an individual transaction. Statement-level read consistency (that is, read committed) is the default.

Oracle uses row-level locking. Updates to different rows do not conflict. If two writers attempt to modify the same row, one waits until the other either commits or is rolled back, and then it can either return a write-conflict error or go ahead and modify the row; write-conflict errors are detected based on the first-updater-wins version of snapshot isolation, described in Section 15.7. (Section 15.7 also describes certain cases of non-serializable execution that can occur with snapshot isolation, and outlines techniques for preventing such problems.) Locks are held for the duration of a transaction.

In addition to row-level locks that prevent inconsistencies due to DML activity, Oracle uses table locks that prevent inconsistencies due to DDL activity. These locks prevent one user from, say, dropping a table while another user has an uncommitted transaction that is accessing that table. Oracle does not use lock escalation to convert row locks to table locks for the purpose of its regular concurrency control.

Oracle detects deadlocks automatically and resolves them by rolling back one of the transactions involved in the deadlock.

Oracle supports autonomous transactions, which are independent transactions generated within other transactions. When Oracle invokes an autonomous transaction, it generates a new transaction in a separate context. The new transaction can be either committed or rolled back before control returns to the calling transaction. Oracle supports multiple levels of nesting of autonomous transactions.

28.5.2   Basic Structures for Recovery

Oracle's Flashback technology, described in Section 28.5.1, can be used as a recovery mechanism, but Oracle also supports media recovery where files are backed up physically. We describe this more traditional form of backup and recovery here.

In order to understand how Oracle recovers from a failure, such as a disk crash, it is important to understand the basic structures that are involved. In addition to the data files that contain tables and indices, there are control files, redo logs, archived redo logs, and undo segments.

The control file contains various metadata that are needed to operate the database, including information about backups.

Oracle records any transactional modification of a database buffer in the redo log, which consists of two or more files. It logs the modification as part of the operation that causes it and regardless of whether the transaction eventually commits. It logs changes to indices and undo segments as well as changes to table data. As the redo logs fill up, they are archived by one or several background processes (if the database is running in **archivelog** mode).

The undo segment contains information about older versions of the data (that is, undo information). In addition to its role in Oracle's consistency model, the information is used to restore the old version of data items when a transaction that has modified the data items is rolled back.

To be able to recover from a storage failure, the data files and control files should be backed up regularly. The frequency of the backup determines the worst-case recovery time, since it takes longer to recover if the backup is old. Oracle supports hot backups—backups performed on an online database that is subject to transactional activity.

During recovery from a backup, Oracle performs two steps to reach a consistent state of the database as it existed just prior to the failure. First, Oracle rolls forward by applying the (archived) redo logs to the backup. This action takes the database to a state that existed at the time of the failure, but not necessarily a consistent state since the redo logs include uncommitted data. Second, Oracle rolls back uncommitted transactions by using the undo segment data. The database is now in a consistent state.

Recovery on a database that has been subject to heavy transactional activity since the last backup can be time-consuming. Oracle supports parallel recovery in which several processes are used to apply redo information simultaneously.

Oracle provides a GUI tool, Recovery Manager, which automates most tasks associated with backup and recovery.

28.5.3 Oracle Data Guard

To ensure high availability, Oracle provides a standby database feature, **data guard**. (This feature is the same as remote backups, described in Section 16.9.) A standby database is a copy of the regular database that is installed on a separate system. If a catastrophic failure occurs on the primary system, the standby system is activated and takes over, thereby minimizing the effect of the failure on availability. Oracle keeps the standby database up-to-date by constantly applying archived redo logs that are shipped from the primary database. The backup database can be brought online in read-only mode and used for reporting and decision support queries.

28.6   System Architecture

Whenever a database application executes an SQL statement, there is an operating system process that executes code in the database server. Oracle can be configured so that the operating system process is *dedicated* exclusively to the statement it is processing or so that the process can be *shared* among multiple statements. The latter configuration, known as the **shared server**, has somewhat different properties with regard to the process and memory architecture. We shall discuss the **dedicated server** architecture first and the multithreaded server architecture later.

28.6.1 Dedicated Server: Memory Structures

The memory used by Oracle falls mainly into three categories: software code areas, which are the parts of the memory where the Oracle server code resides, the system global area (SGA), and the program global area (PGA).

A PGA is allocated for each process to hold its local data and control information. This area contains stack space for various session data and the private memory for the SQL statement that it is executing. It also contains memory for sorting and hashing operations that may occur during the evaluation of the statement. The performance of such operations is sensitive to the amount of memory that is available. For example, a hash join that can be performed in memory will be faster than if it is necessary to spill to disk. Since there can be a large number of sorting and hashing operations active simultaneously (because of multiple queries as well as multiple operations within each query), deciding how much memory should be allocated to each operation is nontrivial, especially as the load on the system may fluctuate. Underallocation of memory can lead to extra disk I/Os if an operation needlessly spills to disk and overallocation of memory can lead to thrashing. Oracle lets the database administrator specify a *target* parameter for the total amount of memory that should be considered available for these operations. The size of this target would typically be based on the total amount of memory available on the system and some calculation as to how it should be divided between various Oracle and non-Oracle activities. Oracle will dynamically decide the best way to divide the memory available within the target between the active operations in order to maximize throughput. The memory allocation algorithm knows the relationship between memory and performance for the different operations and seeks to ensure that the available memory is used as efficiently as possible.

The SGA is a memory area for structures that are shared among users. It is made up of several major structures, including the following.

- **Buffer cache**. This cache keeps frequently accessed data blocks (from tables as well as indices) in memory to reduce the need to perform physical disk I/O. A least recently used replacement policy is used except for blocks accessed during a full table scan. However, Oracle allows multiple buffer pools to be created that have different criteria for aging out data. Some Oracle operations bypass the buffer cache and read data directly from disk.

- **Redo log buffer**. This buffer contains the part of the redo log that has not yet been written to disk.

- **Shared pool**. Oracle seeks to maximize the number of users that can use the database concurrently by minimizing the amount of memory that is needed for each user. One important concept in this context is the ability to share the internal representation of SQL statements and procedural code written in PL/SQL. When multiple users execute the same SQL statement, they can share most data structures that represent the execution plan for the statement. Only data that are local to each specific invocation of the statement need to be kept in private memory.

  The sharable parts of the data structures representing the SQL statement are stored in the shared pool, including the text of the statement. The caching of SQL statements in the shared pool also saves compilation time, since a new invocation of a statement that is already cached does not have to go through the complete compilation process. The determination of whether an SQL statement is the same as one existing in the shared pool is based on exact text matching and the setting of certain session parameters. Oracle can automatically replace constants in an SQL statement with bind variables; future queries that are the same except for the values of constants will then match the earlier query in the shared pool.

  The shared pool also contains caches for dictionary information and various control structures. Caching dictionary metadata is important for speeding up the compilation time for SQL statements. In addition, the shared pool is used for Oracle's result cache feature.

28.6.2 Dedicated Server: Process Structures

There are two types of processes that execute Oracle server code: server processes that process SQL statements and background processes that perform various administrative and performance-related tasks. Some of these processes are optional, and in some cases, multiple processes of the same type can be used for performance reasons. Oracle can generate about two dozen different types of background processes. Some of the most important ones are:

- **Database writer**. When a buffer is removed from the buffer cache, it must be written back to disk if it has been modified since it entered the cache. This task is performed by the database writer processes, which help the performance of the system by freeing up space in the buffer cache.

- **Log writer**. The log-writer process writes entries in the redo log buffer to the redo log file on disk. It also writes a commit record to disk whenever a transaction commits.

- **Checkpoint**. The checkpoint process updates the headers of the data file when a checkpoint occurs.

- **System monitor**. This process performs crash recovery if needed. It also performs some space management to reclaim unused space in temporary segments.

- **Process monitor**. This process performs process recovery for server processes that fail, releasing resources and performing various cleanup operations.

- **Recoverer**. The recoverer process resolves failures and conducts cleanup for distributed transactions.

- **Archiver**. The archiver copies the online redo log file to an archived redo log every time the online log file fills up.

28.6.3 Shared Server

The shared-server configuration increases the number of users that a given number of server processes can support by sharing server processes among statements. It differs from the dedicated server architecture in these major aspects:

- A background dispatch process routes user requests to the next available server process. In doing so, it uses a request queue and a response queue in the SGA. The dispatcher puts a new request in the request queue where it will be picked up by a server process. As a server process completes a request, it puts the result in the response queue to be picked up by the dispatcher and returned to the user.

- Since a server process is shared among multiple SQL statements, Oracle does not keep private data in the PGA. Instead, it stores the session-specific data in the SGA.

28.6.4 Oracle Real Application Clusters

Oracle Real Application Clusters (RAC) is a feature that allows multiple instances of Oracle to run against the same database. (Recall that, in Oracle terminology, an instance is the combination of background processes and memory areas.) This feature enables Oracle to run on clustered and MPP (shared disk and shared nothing) hardware architectures. The ability to cluster multiple nodes has important benefits for scalability and availability that are useful in both OLTP and data warehousing environments.

The scalability benefits of the feature are obvious, since more nodes mean more processing power. On shared-nothing architectures, adding nodes to a cluster typically requires redistributing the data between the nodes. Oracle uses a shared-disk architecture where all the nodes have access to all the data and as a result, more nodes can be added to a RAC cluster without worrying how the data should be divided between the nodes. Oracle further optimizes the use of the hardware through features such as affinity and partitionwise joins.

RAC can also be used to achieve high availability. If one node fails, the remaining ones are still available to the application accessing the database. The remaining instances will automatically roll back uncommitted transactions that were being processed on the failed node in order to prevent them from blocking activity on the remaining nodes. RAC also allows rolling patching so that software patches can be applied to one node at a time without database downtime.

Oracle's shared-disk architecture avoids many of the issues that shared-nothing architectures have with data on disk either being local to a node or not. Still, having multiple instances run against the same database gives rise to some technical issues that do not exist on a single instance. While it is sometimes possible to partition an application among nodes so that nodes rarely access the same data, there is always the possibility of overlaps, which affects cache management. In order to achieve efficient cache management over multiple nodes, Oracle's **cache fusion** feature allows data blocks to flow directly among caches on different instances using the interconnect, without being written to disk.

28.6.5 Automatic Storage Manager

The Automatic Storage Manager (ASM) is a volume manager and file system developed by Oracle. While Oracle can be used with other volume managers and file systems as well as raw devices, ASM is specifically designed to simplify storage management for the Oracle database while optimizing performance.

ASM manages collections of disks, known as **disk groups**, and exposes a file system interface to the database. (Recall that an Oracle table space is defined in terms of data files.) Examples of what could constitute ASM disks include disks or partitions of disk arrays, logical volumes, and network attached files. ASM automatically stripes the data over the disks in a disk group and provides several options for different levels of mirroring.

If the disk configuration changes, e.g., when more disks are added to increase storage capacity, a disk group may need to be rebalanced so that the data are spread evenly over all the disks. The rebalancing operation can be done in the background while the database remains fully operational and with minimal impact on database performance.

28.6.6 Oracle Exadata

Exadata is a set of Oracle libraries that can run on the storage array CPUs on certain types of storage hardware. While Oracle is fundamentally based on a shared-disk architecture, Exadata contains a shared-nothing flavor in that some operations that would normally be executed on the database server are moved to storage cells that can only access data that are local to each cell. (Each storage cell consists of a number of disks and several multicore CPUs.)

The are major advantages to offloading certain types of processing to storage CPUs:

- It allows a large, but relatively inexpensive, expansion of the amount of processing power that is available.

- The amount of data that needs to be transferred from a storage cell to the database server can be dramatically reduced, which can be very important since the bandwidth between the storage cell and database server is usually expensive and often a bottleneck.

When executing a query against Exadata storage, the reduction of the amount of data that needs to be retrieved comes from several techniques that can be pushed to the storage cells and executed there locally:

- **Projection.** A table may have hundreds of columns, but a given query may only need to access a very small subset of them. The storage cells can project out the unneeded columns and only send the relevant ones back to the database server.

- **Table filtering.** The database server can send a list of predicates that are local to a table to the storage cells and only rows matching these predicates get sent back to the server.

- **Join filtering.** The filtering mechanism allows for predicates that are *Bloom filters* allowing rows to be filtered out based on join conditions as well.

In combination, offloading these techniques to the storage cells can speed up query processing by orders of magnitude. It requires that the storage cells, in addition to sending back regular, unaltered database blocks to the server, can send back a compacted version where certain columns and rows have been removed. This ability in turn requires the storage software to understand Oracle's block format and data types, and to include Oracle's expression and predicate evaluation routines.

In addition to providing benefits for query processing, Exadata can also speed up incremental backups by performing block-level change tracking and only returning blocks that have changed. Also, the work of formatting extents when creating a new table space is offloaded to Exadata storage.

Exadata storage supports all regular Oracle features, and it is possible to have a database that includes both Exadata and non-Exadata storage.

28.7   Replication, Distribution, and External Data

Oracle provides support for replication and distributed transactions with two-phase commit.

28.7.1   Replication

Oracle supports several types of replication. (See Section 19.2.1 for an introduction to replication.) In one form, data in a master site are replicated to other sites in the form of *materialized views*. A materialized view does not have to contain all the master data—it can, for example, exclude certain columns from a table for security reasons. Oracle supports two types of materialized views for replication: *read-only* and *updatable*. An updatable materialized view can be modified and the modifications propagated to the master table. However, read-only materialized views allow for a wider range of view definitions. For instance, a read-only materialized view can be defined in terms of set operations on tables at the master site. Changes to the master data are propagated to the replicas through the materialized view refresh mechanism.

Oracle also supports multiple master sites for the same data, where all master sites act as peers. A replicated table can be updated at any of the master sites and the update is propagated to the other sites. The updates can be propagated either asynchronously or synchronously.

For asynchronous replication, the update information is sent in batches to the other master sites and applied. Since the same data could be subject to conflicting modifications at different sites, conflict resolution based on some business rules might be needed. Oracle provides a number of built-in conflict resolution methods and allows users to write their own if need be.

With synchronous replication, an update to one master site is propagated immediately to all other sites.

28.7.2   Distributed Databases

Oracle supports queries and transactions spanning multiple databases on different systems. With the use of gateways, the remote systems can include non-Oracle databases. Oracle has built-in capability to optimize a query that includes tables at different sites, retrieve the relevant data, and return the result as if it had been a normal, local query. Oracle also transparently supports transactions spanning multiple sites by a built-in two-phase-commit protocol.

28.7.3 External Data Sources

Oracle has several mechanisms for supporting external data sources. The most common usage is in data warehousing when large amounts of data are regularly loaded from a transactional system.

28.7.3.1 SQL*Loader

Oracle has a direct-load utility, SQL*Loader, that supports fast parallel loads of large amounts of data from external files. It supports a variety of data formats and it can perform various filtering operations on the data being loaded.

28.7.3.2 External Tables

Oracle allows external data sources, such as flat files, to be referenced in the **from** clause of a query as if they were regular tables. An external table is defined by metadata that describe the Oracle column types and the mapping of the external data into those columns. An access driver is also needed to access the external data. Oracle provides a default driver for flat files.

The external table feature is primarily intended for extraction, transformation, and loading (ETL) operations in a data warehousing environment. Data can be loaded into the data warehouse from a flat file using

> **create table** *table* **as**
> **select** ... **from** < external table >
> **where** ...

By adding operations on the data in either the **select** list or **where** clause, transformations and filtering can be done as part of the same SQL statement. Since these operations can be expressed either in native SQL or in functions written in PL/SQL or Java, the external table feature provides a very powerful mechanism for expressing all kinds of data transformation and filtering operations. For scalability, the access to the external table can be parallelized by Oracle's parallel execution feature.

28.7.3.3 Data Pump Export and Import

Oracle provides an export utility for unloading data and metadata into dump files. These files are regular files using a proprietary format that can be moved to another system and loaded into another Oracle database using the corresponding import utility.

28.8 Database Administration Tools

Oracle provides users a number of tools and features for system management and application development. In recent releases of Oracle, a lot of emphasis was put on the concept of *manageability*, that is, reducing the complexity of all aspects of creating and administering an Oracle database. This effort covered a wide variety of areas, including database creation, tuning, space management, storage management, backup and recovery, memory management, performance diagnostics, and workload management.

28.8.1   Oracle Enterprise Manager

Oracle Enterprise Manager (OEM) is Oracle's main tool for database systems management. It provides an easy-to-use graphical user interface for most tasks associated with administering an Oracle database including configuration, performance monitoring, resource management, security management, and access to the various advisors. In addition to database management, OEM provides integrated management of Oracle's applications and middleware software stack.

28.8.2   Automatic Workload Repository

The Automatic Workload Repository (AWR) is one of the central pieces of infrastructure for Oracle's manageability effort. Oracle monitors the activity on the database system and records a variety of information relating to workloads and resource consumption and records them in AWR at regular intervals. By tracking the characteristics of a workload over time, Oracle can detect and help diagnose deviations from normal behavior such as a significant performance degradation of a query, lock contention, and CPU bottlenecks.

The information recorded in AWR provides a basis for a variety of **advisors** that provide analysis of various aspects of the performance of the system and advice for how it can be improved. Oracle has advisors for SQL tuning, creating access structures, such as indices and materialized views, and memory sizing. Oracle also provides advisors for segment defragmentation and undo sizing.

28.8.3   Database Resource Management

A database administrator needs to be able to control how the processing power of the hardware is divided among users or groups of users. Some groups may execute interactive queries where response time is critical; others may execute long-running reports that can be run as batch jobs in the background when the system load is low. It is also important to be able to prevent a user from inadvertently submitting an extremely expensive ad hoc query that will unduly delay other users.

Oracle's Database Resource Management feature allows the database administrator to divide users into resource consumer groups with different priorities and properties. For example, a group of high-priority, interactive users may be guaranteed at least 60 percent of the CPU. The remainder, plus any part of the 60 percent not used up by the high-priority group, would be allocated among resource consumer groups with lower priority. A really low-priority group could get assigned 0 percent, which would mean that queries issued by this group would run only when there are spare CPU cycles available. Limits for the degree of parallelism for parallel execution can be set for each group. The database administrator can also set time limits for how long an SQL statement is allowed to run for each group. When a user submits a statement, the resource manager estimates how long it would take to execute it and returns an error if the statement violates the limit. The resource manager can also limit the number of user sessions that can be active concurrently for each resource consumer group. Other resources that can be controlled by the resource manager include undo space.

28.9 Data Mining

Oracle Data Mining provides a variety of algorithms that embed the data mining process inside the database both for building a model on a training set of data and for applying the model for scoring the actual production data. The fact the data never needs to leave the database is a significant advantage compared to using other data mining engines. Having to extract and insert potentially very large data sets into a separate engine is cumbersome, costly, and may prevent new data from being scored instantaneously as they are entered into the database. Oracle provides algorithms for both supervised and unsupervised learning including:

- Classification—Naive Bayes, generalized linear models, Support Vector Machines, and Decision Trees.

- Regression—Support vector machines and generalized linear models.

- Attribute importance—Minimum description length.

- Anomaly detection—One class support vector machines.

- Clustering—Enhanced k-means clustering and orthogonal Partitioning Clustering.

- Association rules—Apriori.

- Feature extraction—Nonnegative matrix factorization.

In addition, Oracle provides a wide range of statistical functions inside the database covering areas including linear regression, correlation, cross tabs, hypothesis testing, distribution fitting, and Pareto analysis.

Oracle provides two interfaces to the data mining functionality, one based on Java and one that is based on Oracle's procedural language PL/SQL. Once a model has been built on an Oracle database, it can be shipped to be deployed on other Oracle databases.

Bibliographical Notes

Up-to-date product information, including documentation, on Oracle products can be found at the Web sites http://www.oracle.com and http://technet.oracle.com.

Oracle's intelligent algorithms for allocating available memory for operations such as hashing and sorting are discussed in Dageville and Zaït [2002]. Murthy and Banerjee [2003] discussed XML schemas. Table compression in Oracle is described in Pöss and Potapov [2003]. Automatic SQL tuning is described in Dageville et al. [2004]. The optimizer's cost-based query transformation framework is described in Ahmed et al. [2006]. The SQL Plan-Management feature is discussed in Ziauddin et al. [2008]. Antoshenkov [1995] describes the byte-aligned bitmap compression technique used in Oracle; see also Johnson [1999].

CHAPTER 29

IBM DB2 Universal Database

Sriram Padmanabhan

IBM's DB2 Universal Database family of products consists of flagship database servers and suites of related products for business intelligence, information integration, and content management. The DB2 Universal Database Server is available on a variety of hardware and operating-system platforms. The list of server platforms supported includes high-end systems such as mainframes, massively parallel processors (MPP), and large symmetric multiprocessors (SMP) servers; medium-scale systems such as four-way and eight-way SMPs; workstations; and even small handheld devices. Operating systems that are supported include Unix variants such as Linux, IBM AIX, Solaris, and HP-UX, as well as Microsoft Windows, IBM MVS, IBM VM, IBM OS/400, and a number of others. The DB2 Everyplace edition supports operating systems such as PalmOS and Windows CE. There is even a no-charge (free) version of DB2 called DB2 Express-C. Applications can migrate seamlessly from the low-end platforms to high-end servers because of the portability of the DB2 interfaces and services. Besides the core database engine, the DB2 family consists of several other products that provide tooling, administration, replication, distributed data access, pervasive data access, OLAP, and many other features. Figure 29.1 describes the different products in the family.

29.1 Overview

The origin of DB2 can be traced back to the System R project at IBM's Almaden Research Center (then called the IBM San Jose Research Laboratory). The first DB2 product was released in 1984 on the IBM mainframe platform, and this was followed over time with versions for the other platforms. IBM research contributions have continually enhanced the DB2 product in areas such as transaction processing (write-ahead logging and ARIES recovery algorithms), query processing and optimization (Starburst), parallel processing (DB2 Parallel Edition), active-database support (constraints, triggers), advanced query and warehousing techniques such as materialized views, multidimensional clustering, "autonomic" features, and object-relational support (ADTs, UDFs).

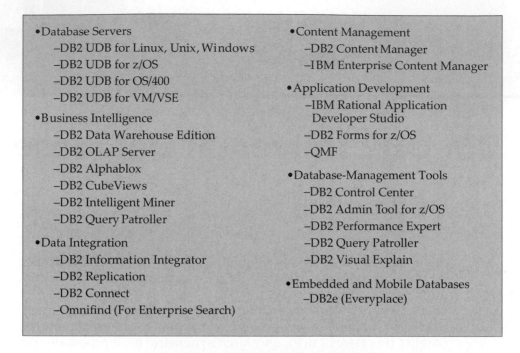

- Database Servers
  - DB2 UDB for Linux, Unix, Windows
  - DB2 UDB for z/OS
  - DB2 UDB for OS/400
  - DB2 UDB for VM/VSE
- Business Intelligence
  - DB2 Data Warehouse Edition
  - DB2 OLAP Server
  - DB2 Alphablox
  - DB2 CubeViews
  - DB2 Intelligent Miner
  - DB2 Query Patroller
- Data Integration
  - DB2 Information Integrator
  - DB2 Replication
  - DB2 Connect
  - Omnifind (For Enterprise Search)

- Content Management
  - DB2 Content Manager
  - IBM Enterprise Content Manager
- Application Development
  - IBM Rational Application Developer Studio
  - DB2 Forms for z/OS
  - QMF
- Database-Management Tools
  - DB2 Control Center
  - DB2 Admin Tool for z/OS
  - DB2 Performance Expert
  - DB2 Query Patroller
  - DB2 Visual Explain
- Embedded and Mobile Databases
  - DB2e (Everyplace)

Figure 29.1   The DB2 family of products.

Since IBM supports a number of server and operating-system platforms, the DB2 database engine consists of four code base types: (1) Linux, Unix, and Windows, (2) z/OS (3) VM, and (4) OS/400. All of these support a common subset of data-definition language, SQL, and administration interfaces. However, the engines have somewhat different features due to their platform origins. In this chapter, the focus is on the DB2 Universal Database (UDB) engine that supports Linux, Unix, and Windows. Specific features of interest in other DB2 systems are highlighted in appropriate sections.

The latest version of DB2 UDB for Linux, Unix, and Windows as of 2009 is version 9.7. DB2 version 9.7 includes several new feature such as extension of native support for XML to shared-nothing environments, native compression for tables and indexes, automatic storage management, and improved support for procedural languages such as SQL PL and Oracle's PL/SQL.

29.2   Database-Design Tools

Most industry database-design and CASE tools can be used to design a DB2 database. In particular, data modeling tools such as ERWin and Rational Rose allow the designer to generate DB2-specific DDL syntax. For instance, Rational Rose's UML Data Modeler tool can generate DB2-specific **create distinct type** DDL statements for user-defined types and use them subsequently in column definitions. Most design tools also support a reverse-engineering feature that reads the DB2 catalog tables and builds a logical design for additional manipulation. The tools support the generation of constraints and indices.

DB2 provides support for many logical and physical database features using SQL. The features include constraints, triggers, and recursion using SQL constructs. Likewise, certain physical database features such as tablespaces, bufferpools, and partitioning are also supported by using SQL statements. The Control Center GUI tool for DB2 allows a designer or an administrator to issue the appropriate DDL for these features. Another tool, *db2look*, allows the administrator to obtain a full set of DDL statements for a database including tablespaces, tables, indices, constraints, triggers, and functions that can be used to create an exact replica of the database schema for testing or replication.

The DB2 Control Center includes a variety of design- and administration-related tools. For design, the Control Center provides a tree view of a server, its databases, tables, views, and all other objects. It also allows users to define new objects, create ad hoc SQL queries, and view query results. Design tools for ETL, OLAP, replication, and federation also integrate into the Control Center. The entire DB2 family supports the Control Center for database definition as well as related tools. DB2 also provides plug-in modules for application development in the IBM Rational Application Developer product as well as in the Microsoft Visual Studio product.

29.3   SQL Variations and Extensions

DB2 provides support for a rich set of SQL features for various aspects of database processing. Many of the DB2 features and syntax have provided the basis for standards in SQL-92, or SQL:1999. In this section, we highlight the XML object-relational and application-integration features in DB2 UDB version 8, along with some new features from version 9.

29.3.1   XML Features

A rich set of XML functions have been included in DB2. The following is a list of several important XML functions that can be used in SQL, as part of the SQL/XML extension to SQL (described earlier in Section 23.6.3):

- **xmlelement.** Constructs an element tag with given name. For example the function call, **xmlelement**(*book*) creates the book element.

- **xmlattributes.** Constructs the set of attributes for an element.

- **xmlforest.** Constructs a sequence of XML elements from arguments.

- **xmlconcat.** Returns the concatenation of a variable number of XML arguments.

- **xmlserialize.** Provides a character-oriented serialized version of the argument.

```
select xmlemement(name 'PO',
            xmlattributes(poid, orderdate),
            (select xmlagg(xmlelement(name 'item',
                        xmlattributes(itemid, qty, shipdate),
                        (select xmlelement(name 'itemdesc',
                                    xmlattributes(name, price))
                        from product
                        where product.itemid = lineitem.itemid)))
            from lineitem
            where lineitem.poid = orders.poid))
    from orders
    where orders.poid= 349;
```

Figure 29.2   DB2 SQL XML query.

- **xmlagg.** Returns a concatenation of a set of XML values.
- **xml2clob.** Constructs a character large object (**clob**) representation of the XML. This **clob** can then be retrieved by SQL applications.

The XML functions can be incorporated into SQL effectively to provide extensive XML manipulation capabilities. For instance, suppose that one needs to construct a purchase-order XML document from relational tables *orders*, *lineitem*, and *product* for order number 349. In Figure 29.2, we show an SQL query with XML extensions that can be used to create such a purchase order. The resultant output is as shown in Figure 29.3.

Version 9 of DB2 supports native storage of XML data as an **xml** type. and native support for the XQuery language. Specialized storage, indexing, query processing and optimization techniques have been introduced for efficient processing of XML data and queries in the XQuery language, and APIs have been extended to deal with XML data and XQuery.

29.3.2   Support for Data Types

DB2 provides support for user-defined data types (UDTs). Users can define *distinct* or *structured* data types. Distinct data types are based on DB2 built-in data types.

```
<PO poid = "349" orderdate = "2004-10-01">
    <item itemid="1", qty="10", shipdate="2004-10-03">
    <itemdesc name = "IBM ThinkPad T41", Price = "1000.00 USD"/>
    </item>
</PO>
```

Figure 29.3   Purchase order in XML for id=349.

However, the user can define additional or alternative semantics for these new types. For example, the user can define a distinct data type called *us_dollar*, using:

create distinct type *us_dollar* **as decimal**(9,2);

Subsequently, the user can create a field (e.g., *price*) in a table with type *us_dollar*. Queries may now use the typed field in predicates such as the following:

select *product* **from** *us_sales*
where *price* > *us_dollar*(1000);

Structured data types are complex objects that usually consist of two or more attributes. For example, one can use the following DDL to create a structured type called *department_t*:

create type *department_t* **as**
(*deptname* **varchar**(32),
depthead **varchar**(32),
faculty_count **integer**)
mode db2/sql;

create type *point_t* **as**
(*x_coord* **float**,
y_coord **float**)
mode db2/sql;

Structured types can be used to define *typed tables*:

create table *dept* **of** *department_t*;

One can create a type hierarchy and tables in the hierarchy that can inherit specific methods and privileges. Structured types can also be used to define nested attributes inside a column of a table. Although such a definition would violate normalization rules, it may be suitable for object-oriented applications that rely on encapsulation and well-defined methods on objects.

29.3.3 User-Defined Functions and Methods

Another important feature is the ability for users to define their own functions and methods. These functions can subsequently be included in SQL statements and queries. Functions can generate scalars (single attribute) or tables (multiattribute row) as their result. Users can register functions (scalar or table) using the **create function** statement. The functions can be written in common programming languages such as C or Java or scripts such as REXX or PERL. User-defined functions (UDFs) can operate in fenced or unfenced modes. In fenced mode, the functions are executed by a separate thread in its own address space. In unfenced

```
create function db2gse.GsegeFilterDist (
        operation integer, g1XMin double, g1XMax double,
        g1YMin double, g1YMax double, dist double,
        g2XMin double, g2XMax double, g2YMin double,
        g2YMax double )
    returns integer
    specific db2gse.GsegeFilterDist
    external name 'db2gsefn!gsegeFilterDist'
    language C
    parameter style db2 sql
    deterministic
    not fenced
    threadsafe
    called on null input
    no sql
    no external action
    no scratchpad
    no final call
    allow parallel
    no dbinfo;
```

Figure 29.4   Definition of a UDF.

mode, the database-processing agent is allowed to execute the function in the server's address space. UDFs can define a scratch pad (work) area where they can maintain local and static variables across different invocations. Thus, UDFs can perform powerful manipulations of intermediate rows that are its inputs. In Figure 29.4, we show a definition of a UDF, *db2gse.GsegeFilterDist*, in DB2 pointing to a particular external method that performs the actual function.

Methods are another feature that define the behavior of objects. Unlike UDFs, they are tightly encapsulated with a particular structured data type. Methods are registered by using the **create method** statement.

DB2 also supports procedural extensions to SQL, using the DB2's SQL PL extension, including procedures, functions, and control flow. Procedural features of the SQL standard are described in Section 5.2). In addition, as of version 9.7, DB2 also supports much of Oracle's PL/SQL language, for compatibility with applications developed on Oracle.

29.3.4   Large Objects

New database applications require the ability to manipulate text, images, video, and other types of data that are typically quite large in size. DB2 supports these requirements by providing three different large object (LOB) types. Each LOB can be as large as two gigabytes in size. The large objects in DB2 are (1) binary large objects (**blob**s), (2) single byte character large objects (**clob**s), and (3) double byte character large objects (**dbclob**s). DB2 organizes these LOBs as separate objects with

create index extension *db2gse.spatial_index(*
  gS1 **double**, *gS2* **double**, *gS3* **double**)
from source key(*geometry db2gse.ST_Geometry*)
generate key using
  db2gse.GseGridIdxKeyGen(geometry..srid,
  geometry..xMin, geometry..xMax,
  geometry..yMin, geometry..yMax,
  gS1, gS2, gS3)

with target key(*srsId* **integer**,
  lvl **integer**, *gX* **integer**, *gY* **integer**, *xMin* **double**,
  xMax **double**, *yMin* **double**, *yMax* **double**)
search methods <conditions> <actions>

Figure 29.5 Spatial index extension in DB2.

each row in the table maintaining pointers to its corresponding LOBs. Users can register UDFs that manipulate these LOBs according to application requirements.

29.3.5 Indexing Extensions and Constraints

A recent feature of DB2 enables users to create index extensions to generate keys from structured data types by using the **create index extension** statement. For example, one can create an index on an attribute based on the *department_t* data type defined earlier by generating keys, using the department name. DB2's spatial extender uses the index extension method to create indices as shown in Figure 29.5.

Finally, users can take advantage of the rich set of constraint checking features available in DB2 for enforcing object semantics such as uniqueness, validity, and inheritance.

29.3.6 Web Services

DB2 can integrate Web services as producer or consumer. A Web service can be defined to invoke DB2, using SQL statements. The resultant Web-service call is processed by an embedded Web-service engine in DB2 and the appropriate SOAP response generated. For example, if there is a Web service called *GetRecentActivity(cust_id)* that invokes the following SQL, the result should be the last transaction for this customer.

```
select trn_id, amount, date
from transactions
where cust_id = <input>
order by date
fetch first 1 row only;
```

The following SQL shows DB2 acting as a consumer of a Web service. In this example, the *GetQuote()* user-defined function is a Web service. DB2 makes the Web-service call using an embedded Web-service engine. In this case, *GetQuote* returns a numeric quote value for each *ticker_id* in the portfolio table.

> **select** *ticker_id*, *GetQuote*(*ticker_id*)
> **from** *portfolio*;

29.3.7 Other Features

DB2 also supports IBM's Websphere MQ product by defining appropriate UDFs. UDFs are defined for both read and write interfaces. These UDFs can be incorporated in SQL for reading from or writing to message queues.

From version 9, DB2 supports fine-grained authorization through the label-based access control feature, which plays a role similar to Oracle's Virtual Private Database (described earlier in Section 9.7.5).

29.4   Storage and Indexing

The storage and indexing architecture in DB2 consists of the file-system or disk-management layer, the services to manage the buffer pools, data objects such as tables, LOBs, index objects, and concurrency and recovery managers. We overview the general storage architecture in this section. In addition, we describe a new feature in DB2 version 8 called multidimensional clustering in the following section.

29.4.1 Storage Architecture

DB2 provides storage abstractions for managing logical database tables usefully in a multinode and multidisk environment. *Nodegroups* can be defined to support table partitioning across a specific set of nodes in a multinode system. This allows complete flexibility in allocating table partitions to different nodes in a system. For example, large tables may be partitioned across all nodes in a system while small tables may reside on a single node.

Within a node, DB2 uses *tablespaces* to organize tables. A tablespace consists of one or more *containers*, which are references to directories, devices, or files. A tablespace may contain zero or more database objects such as tables, indices, or LOBs. Figure 29.6 illustrates these concepts. In this figure, two tablespaces have been defined for a nodegroup. The *humanres* tablespace is assigned four containers, while the *sched* tablespace has only one container. The *employee* and *department* tables are assigned to the *humanres* tablespace, while the *project* table is in the *sched* tablespace. Striping is used to allocate fragments (extents) of the *employee* and *department* table to the containers of the *humanres* tablespace. DB2 permits the administrator to create either *system*-managed or *DBMS*-managed tablespaces. System-managed spaces (SMS) are directories or file systems that are maintained by the underlying operating system. In SMS, DB2 creates file objects

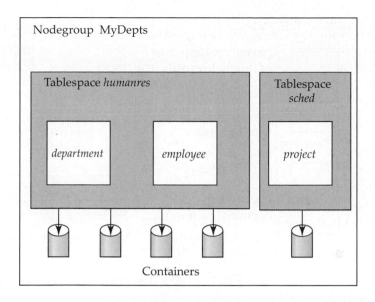

Figure 29.6 Tablespaces and containers in DB2.

in the directories and allocates data to each of the files. Data-managed spaces (DMS) are raw devices or preallocated files that are then controlled by DB2. The size of these containers can never grow or shrink. DB2 creates allocation maps and manages the DMS tablespace itself. In both cases, an extent of pages is the unit of space management. The administrator can choose the extent size for a tablespace.

DB2 supports striping across the different containers as a default behavior. For example, when data are inserted into a newly created table, the first extent is assigned to a container. Once the extent is full, the next data items are allocated to the next container in round-robin fashion. Striping provides two significant benefits: parallel I/O and load balancing.

29.4.2 Buffer Pools

One or more buffer pools may be associated with each tablespace for managing different objects such as data and indices. The buffer pool is a common shared data area that maintains memory copies of objects. These objects are typically organized as pages for management in the buffer pool. DB2 allows buffer pools to be defined by SQL statements. DB2 version 8 has the ability to grow or shrink buffer pools online and also automatically by choosing the **automatic** setting for the buffer pool configuration parameter. An administrator can add more pages to a buffer pool or decrease its size without quiescing the database activity.

```
create bufferpool <buffer-pool> ....
alter bufferpool <buffer-pool> size <n>
```

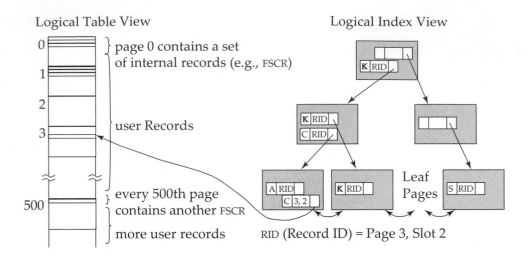

Figure 29.7 Logical view of tables and indices in DB2.

DB2 also supports prefetching and asynchronous writes using separate threads. The data manager component triggers prefetch of data and index pages based on the query access patterns. For instance, a table scan always triggers prefetch of data pages. Index scans can trigger prefetch of index pages as well as data pages if they are being accessed in a clustered fashion. The number of prefetchers and the prefetch size are configurable parameters that need to be initialized according to the number of disks or containers in the tablespace.

29.4.3 Tables, Records, and Indices

DB2 organizes the relational data as records in pages. Figure 29.7 shows the logical view of a table and an associated index. The table consists of a set of pages. Each page consists of a set of records that are either user data records or special system records. Page zero of the table contains special system records about the table and its status. DB2 uses a space-map record called free space control record (FSCR) to find free space in the table. The FSCR record usually contains a space map for 500 pages. The FSCR entry is a bit mask that provides a rough indication of the possibility of free space in a page. The insert or update algorithm must validate the FSCR entries by performing a physical check of the available space in a page.

Indices are also organized as pages containing index records and pointers to child and sibling pages. DB2 provides support for the B^+-tree index mechanisms internally. The B^+-tree index contains internal pages and leaf pages. The indices have bidirectional pointers at the leaf level to support forward and reverse scans. Leaf pages contain index entries that point to records in the table. Each record in the table can be uniquely identified by using its page and slot information, which are called the *record ID* or RID.

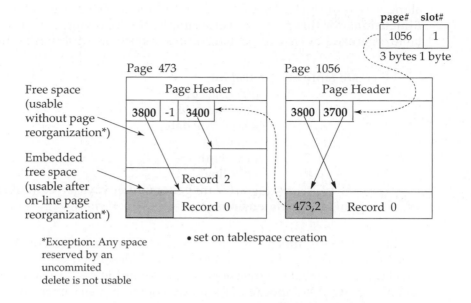

Figure 29.8 Data page and record layout in DB2.

DB2 supports "include columns" in the index definition, as:

create unique index I1 **on** T1 (C1) **include** (C2);

The included index columns enable DB2 to extend the use of "index-only" query-processing techniques whenever possible. Additional directives such as **minpctused** and **pctfree** can be used to control the merge and initial space allocation of index pages.

Figure 29.8 shows the typical data page format in DB2. Each data page contains a header and a slot directory. The slot directory is an array of 255 entries that points to record offsets in the page. The figure shows that page number 473 contains record zero at offset 3800 and record 2 at offset 3400. Page 1056 contains record 1 at offset 3700, which is a forward pointer to the record <473,2>. Hence, record <473,2> is an overflow record that was created as a result of an update operation of the original record <1056,1>. DB2 supports different page sizes such as 4, 8, 16, and 32 kilobytes. However, each page may contain only 255 user records in it. Larger page sizes are useful in applications such as data warehousing, where the table contains many columns. Smaller page sizes are useful for operational data with frequent updates.

29.5 Multidimensional Clustering

This section provides a brief overview of the main features of MDC. With this feature, a DB2 table may be created by specifying one or more keys as dimensions along which to cluster the table's data. DB2 includes a clause called **organize by dimensions** for this purpose. For example, the following DDL describes a sales table organized by *storeId*, *year(orderDate)*, and *itemId* attributes as dimensions.

> **create table** *sales(storeId* **int**,
>   *orderDate* **date**,
>   *shipDate* **date**,
>   *receiptDate* **date**,
>   *region* **int**,
>   *itemId* **int**,
>   *price* **float**
>   *yearOd* **int generated always as** *year(orderDate)*)
> **organized by dimensions** *(region, yearOd, itemId)*;

Each of these dimensions may consist of one or more columns, similar to index keys. In fact, a "dimension block index" (described below) is automatically created for each of the dimensions specified and is used to access data quickly and efficiently. A composite block index, containing all dimension key columns, is created automatically if necessary, and is used to maintain the clustering of data over insert and update activity.

Every unique combination of dimension values forms a logical "cell," that is physically organized as blocks of pages, where a block is a set of consecutive pages on disk. The set of blocks that contain pages with data having a certain key value of one of the dimension block indices is called a "slice." Every page of the table is part of exactly one block, and all blocks of the table consist of the same number of pages, namely, the block size. DB2 has associated the block size with the extent size of the tablespace so that block boundaries line up with extent boundaries.

Figure 29.9 illustrates these concepts. This MDC table is clustered along the dimensions *year(orderDate)*,[1] *region*, and *itemId*. The figure shows a simple logical cube with only two values for each dimension attribute. In reality, dimension attributes can easily extend to large numbers of values without requiring any administration. Logical cells are represented by the subcubes in the figure. Records in the table are stored in blocks, which contain an extent's worth of consecutive pages on disk. In the diagram, a block is represented by a shaded oval, and is numbered according to the logical order of allocated extents in the table. We show only a few blocks of data for the cell identified by the dimension values <1997,Canada,2>. A column or row in the grid represents a slice for a particular dimension. For example, all records containing the value "Canada" in the *region* dimension are found in the blocks contained in the slice defined by the "Canada" column in the cube. In fact, each block in this slice only contains records having "Canada" in the *region* field.

---

[1] Dimensions can be created by using a generated function.

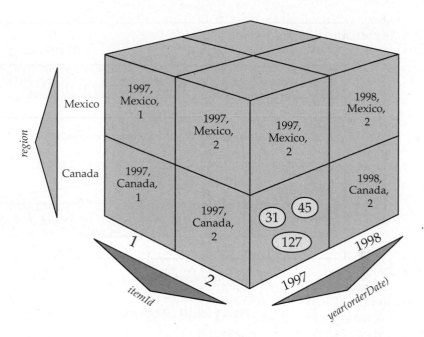

Figure 29.9   Logical view of physical layout of an MDC table.

29.5.1   Block Indices

In our example, a dimension block index is created on each of the *year(orderDate)*, *region*, and *itemId* attributes. Each dimension block index is structured in the same manner as a traditional B-tree index except that, at the leaf level, the keys point to a *block identifier* (BID) instead of a record identifier (RID). Since each block contains potentially many pages of records, these block indices are much smaller than RID indices and need be updated only when a new block is added to a cell or existing blocks are emptied and removed from a cell. A slice, or the set of blocks containing pages with all records having a particular key value in a dimension, are represented in the associated dimension block index by a BID list for that key value. Figure 29.10 illustrates slices of blocks for specific values of *region* and *itemId* dimensions, respectively.

In the example above, to find the slice containing all records with "Canada" for the *region* dimension, we would look up this key value in the *region* dimension block index and find a key as shown in Figure 29.10a. This key points to the exact set of BIDs for the particular value.

29.5.2   Block Map

A block map is also associated with the table. This map records the state of each block belonging to the table. A block may be in a number of states such as **in use**, **free**, **loaded**, **requiring constraint enforcement**. The states of the block are used

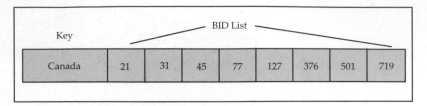

(a) Dimension block index entry for *region* 'Canada'

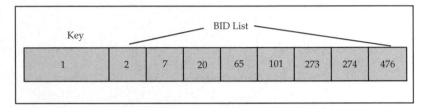

(b) Dimension block index entry for *itemId* = 1

Figure 29.10   Block index key entries.

by the data-management layer in order to determine various processing options. Figure 29.11 shows an example block map for a table.

Element 0 in the block map represents block 0 in the MDC table diagram. Its availability status is "U," indicating that it is in use. However, it is a special block and does not contain any user records. Blocks 2, 3, 9, 10, 13, 14, and 17 are not being used in the table and are considered "F," or free, in the block map. Blocks 7 and 18 have recently been loaded into the table. Block 12 was previously loaded and requires that a constraint check be performed on it.

29.5.3   Design Considerations

A crucial aspect of MDC is to choose the right set of dimensions for clustering a table and the right block size parameter to minimize the space utilization. If the dimensions and block sizes are chosen appropriately, then the clustering benefits translate into significant performance and maintenance advantages. On the other hand, if chosen incorrectly, the performance may degrade and the space utilization could be significantly worse. There are a number of tuning knobs that can be exploited to organize the table. These include varying the number of dimensions, and varying the granularity of one or more dimensions, varying the

Figure 29.11   Block map entries.

block size (extent size) and page size of the tablespace containing the table. One or more of these techniques can be used jointly to identify the best organization of the table.

29.5.4 Impact on Existing Techniques

It is natural to ask whether the new MDC feature has an adverse impact or disables some existing features of DB2 for normal tables. All existing features such as secondary RID indices, constraints, triggers, defining materialized views, and query processing options, are available for MDC tables. Hence, MDC tables behave just like normal tables except for their enhanced clustering and processing aspects.

29.6 Query Processing and Optimization

DB2 queries are transformed into a tree of operations by the query compiler. The query operator tree is used at execution time for processing. DB2 supports a rich set of query operators that enables it to consider the best processing strategies and provides the flexibility to execute complex query tasks.

Figures 29.12 and 29.13 show a query and its associated query plan in DB2. The query is a representative complex query (query 5) from the TPC-H benchmark and contains several joins and aggregations. The query plan chosen for this particular example is rather simple since many indices and other auxiliary structures such as materialized views were not defined for these tables. DB2 provides various "explain" facilities including a powerful visual explain feature in the Control Center that can help users understand the details of a query-execution plan. The query plan shown in the figure is based on the visual explain for the query. Visual

```
-- 'TPCD Local Supplier Volume Query (Q5)';
select n_name, sum(l_extendedprice*(1-l_discount)) as revenue
from tpcd.customer, tpcd.orders, tpcd.lineitem,
      tpcd.supplier, tpcd.nation, tpcd.region
where c_custkey = o_custkey and
      o_orderkey = l_orderkey and
      l_suppkey = s_suppkey and
      c_nationkey = s_nationkey and
      s_nationkey = n_nationkey and
      n_regionkey = r_regionkey and
      r_name = 'MIDDLE EAST' and
      o_orderdate >= date('1995-01-01') and
      o_orderdate < date('1995-01-01') + 1 year
group by n_name
order by revenue desc;
```

Figure 29.12 SQL query.

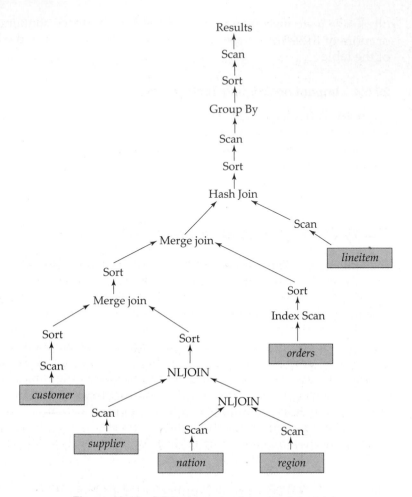

Figure 29.13   DB2 query plan (graphical explain).

explain allows the user to understand cost and other relevant properties of the different operations of the query plan.

All SQL queries and statements, however complex they may be, are transformed into a query tree. The base or leaf operators of the query tree manipulate records in database tables. These operations are also called as *access methods*. Intermediate operations of the tree include relational-algebra operations such as join, set operations, and aggregation. The root of the tree produces the results of the query or SQL statement.

29.6.1   Access Methods

DB2 supports a comprehensive set of access methods on relational tables. The list of access methods includes:

- **Table scan**. This is the most basic method and performs a page-by-page access of all records in the table.

- **Index scan**. An index is used to select the specific records that satisfy the query. The qualifying records are accessed using the RIDs in the index. DB2 detects opportunities to prefetch data pages when it observes a sequential-access pattern.

- **Block index scan**. This is a new access method for MDC tables. One of the block indices is used to scan a specific set of MDC data blocks. The qualifying blocks are accessed and processed in block table scan operations.

- **Index only**. In this case, the index contains all the attributes that are required by the query. Hence, a scan of the index entries is sufficient. The index-only technique is usually a good performance solution.

- **List prefetch**. This access method is chosen for an unclustered index scan with a significant number of RIDs. DB2 has a sort operation on the RIDs and performs a fetch of the records in sorted order from the data pages. Sorted access changes the I/O pattern from random to sequential and also enables prefetching opportunities. List prefetch has been extended to deal with block indices as well.

- **Block and record index ANDing**. This method is used when DB2 determines that more than one index can be used to constrain the number of satisfying records in a base table. The most selective index is processed to generate a list of BIDs or RIDs. The next selective index is then processed to return the BIDs or RIDs that it qualifies. A BID or RID qualifies for further processing only if it is present in the intersection (AND operation) of the index scan results. The result of an index AND operation is a small list of qualifying BIDs or RIDs which are used to fetch the corresponding records from the base table.

- **Block and record index ordering**. This strategy is used if two or more block or record indices can be used to satisfy query predicates that are combined by using the OR operator. DB2 eliminates duplicate BIDs or RIDs by performing a sort and then fetching the resulting set of records. Index ORing has been extended to consider block and RID index combinations.

All the selection and projection predicates of a query are usually pushed down to the access methods. In addition, DB2 performs certain operations such as sorting and aggregation in "pushed down" mode in order to reduce instruction paths.

This MDC feature takes advantage of the new set of access-method improvements for block index scans, block index prefetch, block index ANDing, and block index ORing to process blocks of data.

29.6.2 Join, Aggregation, and Set Operations

DB2 supports a number of techniques for these operations. For join, DB2 can choose between nested-loop, sort-merge, and hash-join techniques. In describing the join and set binary operations, we use the notation of "outer" and "inner" tables to distinguish the two input streams. The nested-loop technique is useful if the inner table is very small or can be accessed by using an index on a join predicate. Sort-merge-join and hash-join techniques are used for joins involving large outer and inner tables. Set operations are implemented by using sorting and merging techniques. The merging technique eliminates duplicates in the case of union while duplicates are forwarded in the case of intersection. DB2 also supports outer-join operations of all kinds.

DB2 processes aggregation operations in early or "push-down" mode whenever possible. For instance, a group by aggregation can be performed by incorporating the aggregation into the sort phase. The join and aggregation algorithms can take advantage of superscalar processing in modern CPUs using block-oriented and cache-conscious techniques.

29.6.3 Support for Complex SQL Processing

One of the most important aspects of DB2 is that it uses the query-processing infrastructure in an extensible fashion to support complex SQL operations. The complex SQL operations include support for deeply nested and correlated queries as well as constraints, referential integrity, and triggers. Because most of these actions are built into the query plan, DB2 is able to scale and provide support for a larger number of these constraints and actions. Constraints and integrity checks are built as query tree operations on insert, delete, or update SQL statements. DB2 also supports maintenance of materialized view by using built-in triggers.

29.6.4 Multiprocessor Query-Processing Features

DB2 extends the base set of query operations with control and data exchange primitives to support SMP (that is, shared memory), MPP (that is, shared nothing), and SMP cluster (that is, shared disk) modes of query processing. DB2 uses a "tablequeue" abstraction for data exchange between threads on different nodes or on the same node. The tablequeue is used as a buffer that redirects data to appropriate receivers using broadcast, one-to-one, or directed multicast methods. Control operations are used to create threads and coordinate the operation of different processes and threads.

In all these modes, DB2 employs a coordinator process to control the query operations and final result gathering. Coordinator processes can also perform some global database-processing actions if required. An example is the global aggregation operation to combine the local aggregation results. Subagents or slave threads perform the base database operations in one or more nodes. In SMP mode, the subagents use shared memory to synchronize between themselves when sharing data. In an MPP, the tablequeue mechanisms provide buffering and flow control to synchronize across different nodes during execution. DB2 employs extensive techniques to optimize and process queries efficiently in an MPP or SMP environment. Figure 29.14 shows a simple query executing in a four-node MPP system. In this example, the *sales* table is partitioned across the four nodes $P_1, \ldots, P_4$. The query is executed by spawning agents that execute at each

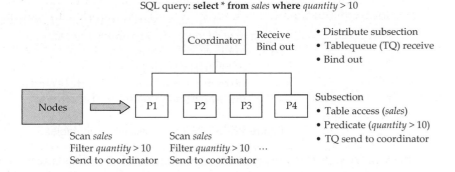

Figure 29.14 DB2 MPP query processing using function shipping.

of these nodes to scan and filter the rows of the sales table at that node (called function shipping), and the resulting rows are sent to the coordinator node.

29.6.5 Query Optimization

DB2's query compiler uses an internal representation of the query, called the query-graph model (QGM), in order to perform transformations and optimizations. After parsing the SQL statement, DB2 performs semantic transformations on the QGM to enforce constraints, referential integrity, and triggers. The result of these transformations is an enhanced QGM. Next, DB2 attempts to perform *query rewrite* transformations that are considered mostly beneficial. Rewrite rules are fired if applicable to perform the required transformations. Examples of rewrite transformations include (1) decorrelation of correlated subqueries, (2) transforming certain subqueries into joins using early-out processing, (3) pushing the **group by** operation below joins if applicable, and (4) using materialized views for portions of the original query.

The query optimizer component uses this enhanced and transformed QGM as its input for optimization. The optimizer is cost based and uses an extensible, rule-driven framework. The optimizer can be configured to operate at different levels of complexity. At the highest level, it uses a dynamic-programming algorithm to consider all query-plan options and chooses the optimal cost plan. At an intermediate level, the optimizer does not consider certain plans, access methods (e.g., index ORing), or rewrite rules. At the lowest level of complexity, the optimizer uses a simple greedy heuristic to choose a good but not necessarily optimal query plan. The optimizer uses detailed models of the query-processing operations, including memory sizes and prefetching, to obtain accurate estimates of the I/O and CPU costs. It relies on the statistics of the data to estimate the cardinality and selectivities of the operations. DB2 allows the user to obtain detailed histograms of column-level distributions and combinations of columns using the **runstats** utility. The detailed histograms contain information about the most frequent value occurrences as well as quantile-based frequency distributions of the attributes. The optimizer generates an internal query plan that is considered the

create table *emp_dept*(*dept_id* **integer**, *emp_id* **integer**,
                        emp_name **varchar**(100), *mgr_id* **integer**) **as**
        select *dept_id*, *emp_id*, *emp_name*, *mgr_id*
        from *employee*, *department*
                data initially deferred
                refresh immediate – – (or **deferred**)
                maintained by user – – (or **system**)

Figure 29.15   DB2 materialized query tables.

best query plan for the particular optimization level. This query plan is converted into threads of query operators and associated data structures for execution by the query-processing engine.

29.7   Materialized Query Tables

Materialized views are supported in DB2 in Linux, Unix, and Windows as well as on the z/OS platforms. A materialized view can be any general view definition on one or more tables or views. A materialized view is useful since it maintains a persistent copy of the view data to enable faster query processing. In DB2 a materialized view is called a **materialized query table** (**MQT**). MQTs are specified by using the **create table** statement as shown by the example in Figure 29.15.

In DB2, MQTs can reference other MQTs to create a tree or forest of dependent views. These MQTs are highly scalable as they can be partitioned in an MPP environment and can have MDC clustering keys. MQTs are most valuable if the database engine can route queries to them seamlessly and also if the database engine can maintain them efficiently whenever possible. DB2 provides both of these features.

29.7.1   Query Routing to MQTs

The query-compiler infrastructure in DB2 is ideally suited to leverage the full power of MQTs. The internal QGM model allows the compiler to match the input query against the available MQT definitions and choose appropriate MQTs for consideration. After matching, the compiler considers several options for optimization. They include the base query as well as suitable MQT reroute versions. The optimizer loops through these options before choosing the optimal version for execution. The entire flow of the reroute and optimization is shown in Figure 29.16.

29.7.2   Maintenance of MQTs

MQTs are useful only if the database engine provides efficient techniques for maintenance. There are two dimensions to maintenance: time and cost. In the time dimension, the two choices are *immediate* or *deferred*. DB2 supports both these choices. If one selects immediate, then internal triggers are created and compiled

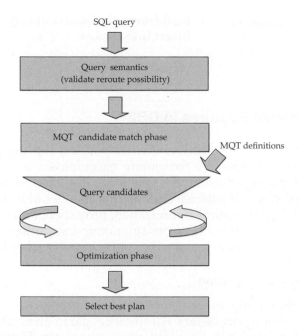

Figure 29.16 MQT matching and optimization in DB2.

into the **insert**, **update**, or **delete** statements of the source objects to process the updates to the dependent MQTs. In the case of deferred maintenance, the updated tables are moved into an integrity mode and an explicit **refresh** statement must be issued to perform the maintenance. In the size dimension, the choices are *incremental* or *full*. Incremental maintenance implies that only the recently updated rows should be used for maintenance. Full maintenance implies that the entire MQT be refreshed from its sources. The matrix in Figure 29.17 shows the two dimensions and the options that are most useful along these dimensions. For instance, immediate and full maintenance are not compatible unless the sources are extremely small. DB2 also allows for the MQTs to be maintained by **user**. In this case, the refresh of the MQTs is determined by users performing explicit processing using SQL or utilities.

The following commands provide one simple example of performing deferred maintenance for the *emp_dept* materialized view after a load operation to one of its sources.

Choices	Incremental	Full
Immediate	Yes, After insert/update/delete	Usually no
Deferred	Yes, After load	Yes

Figure 29.17 Options for MQT maintenance in DB2.

> **load from** newdata.txt **of type del**
> **insert into** *employee;*
>
> **refresh table** *emp_dept*

29.8   Autonomic Features in DB2

DB2 UDB provides features for simplifying the design and manageability of databases. Autonomic computing encompasses a set of techniques that allow the computing environment to manage itself and reduce the external dependencies in the face of external and internal changes in security, system load, or other factors. Configuration, optimization, protection, and monitoring are examples of subject areas that benefit from autonomic-computing enhancements. The following sections briefly describe the configuration and optimization areas.

29.8.1   Configuration

DB2 is providing support for automatic tuning of various memory and system configuration parameters. For instance, parameters such as buffer pool sizes and sort heap sizes can be specified as automatic. In this case, DB2 monitors the system and slowly grows or shrinks these heap memory sizes, depending on the workload characteristics.

29.8.2   Optimization

Auxiliary data structures (indices, MQTs) and data organization features (partitioning, clustering) are important aspects of improving the performance of database processing in DB2. In the past, the database administrator (DBA) had to use experience and known guidelines to choose meaningful indices, MQTs, partition keys, and clustering keys. Given the potential number of choices, even the best experts are not capable of finding the right mix of these features for a given workload in a short time. DB2 includes a *Design Advisor* that provides workload-based advice for all of these features. The Design Advisor tool automatically analyzes a workload, using optimization techniques to present a set of recommendations. The Design Advisor command syntax is:

> db2advis -d <DB name> -i <workloadfile> -m MICP

The "-m " parameter allows the user to specify the following options:

- **M**—Materialized query tables.
- **I**—Indices.
- **C**—Clustering, namely, MDC.
- **P**—Partitioning key selection.

The advisor uses the full power of the DB2 query-optimization framework in these recommendations. It uses an input workload and constraints on size and time of advise as its parameters. Given that it leverages the DB2 optimization framework, it has full knowledge of the schema and statistics of the underlying data. The advisor uses several combinatorial techniques to identify indices, MQTs, MDCs, and partitioning keys to improve the performance of the given workload.

Another aspect of optimization is balancing the processing load on the system. In particular, utilities tend to increase the load on a system and cause significant reduction in user workload performance. Given the trend toward online utilities, there is a need to balance the load consumption of utilities. DB2 includes a utility load-throttling mechanism. The throttling technique is based on feedback control theory. It continually adjusts and throttles the performance of the backup utility, using specific control parameters.

29.9   Tools and Utilities

DB2 provides a number of tools for ease of use and administration. This core set of tools is augmented and enhanced by a large number of tools from vendors.

The DB2 Control Center is the primary tool for use and administration of DB2 databases. The Control Center runs on many workstation platforms. It is organized from data objects such as servers, databases, tables, and indices. It contains task-oriented interfaces to perform commands and allows users to generate SQL scripts. Figure 29.18 shows a screen shot of the main panel of the Control Center. This screen shot shows a list of tables in the *Sample* database in the *DB2* instance on node *Crankarm*. The administrator can use the menu to invoke a suite of component tools. The main components of the Control Center include command center, script center, journal, license management, alert center, performance monitor, visual explain, remote database management, storage management, and support for replication. The command center allows users and administrators to issue database commands and SQL. The script center allows users to run SQL scripts constructed interactively or from a file. The performance monitor allows users to monitor various events in the database system and obtain snapshots of performance. "SmartGuides" provide help on configuring parameters and setting up the DB2 system. A stored-procedure builder helps the user to develop and install stored procedures. Visual explain allows the user to obtain graphical views of the query-execution plan. An index wizard helps the administrator by suggesting indices for performance.

While the Control Center is an integrated interface for many of the tasks, DB2 also provides direct access to most tools. For users, tools such as the explain facility, explain tables, and graphical explain provide a detailed breakdown of the query plans. Users are also allowed to modify statistics (if permitted) in order to generate the best query plans.

Administrators are supported by a number of tools. DB2 provides comprehensive support for load, import, export, reorg, redistribute, and other data-related utilities. Most of these support incremental and online processing capability. For

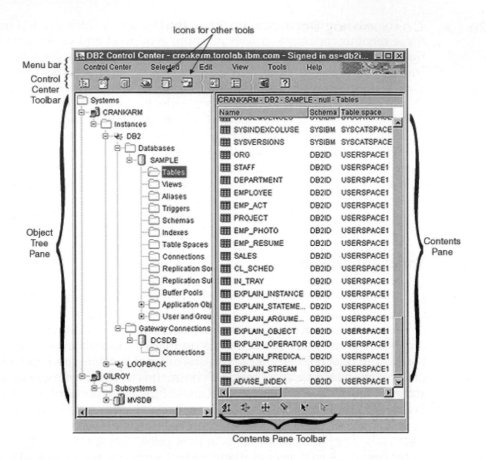

Figure 29.18   DB2 Control Center.

instance, one can issue a load command in online mode to allow applications to access the original contents of a table concurrently. DB2's utilities are all fully enabled to run in parallel mode.

Additionally, DB2 supports a number of tools such as:

- Audit facility for maintaining the audit trace of database actions.

- Governor facility for controlling the priority and execution times of different applications.

- Query patroller facility for managing the query jobs in the system.

- Trace and diagnostic facilities for debugging.

- Event monitoring facilities for tracking the resources and events during system execution.

DB2 for OS/390 has a very rich set of tools. QMF is a widely used tool for generating ad hoc queries and integrating it into applications.

29.10   Concurrency Control and Recovery

DB2 supports a comprehensive set of concurrency-control, isolation, and recovery techniques.

29.10.1   Concurrency and Isolation

For isolation, DB2 supports the *repeatable read* (RR), *read stability* (RS), *cursor stability* (CS), and *uncommitted read* (UR) modes. RR, CS, and UR modes need no further explanation. The RS isolation mode locks only the rows that an application retrieves in a unit of work. On a subsequent scan, the application is guaranteed to see all these rows (like RR) but might also see new rows that qualify. However, this might be an acceptable trade-off for some applications with respect to strict RR isolation. Typically, the default isolation level is CS. Applications can choose their level of isolation at the binding stage. Most commercially available applications are bound using most isolation levels, enabling users to choose the right version of the application for their requirement.

The various isolation modes are implemented by using locks. DB2 supports record-level and table-level locks. A separate lock-table data structure is maintained with the lock information. DB2 escalates from record-level to table-level locks if the space in the lock table becomes tight. DB2 implements strict two-phase locking for all update transactions. Write locks or update locks are held until commit or rollback time. Figure 29.19 shows the different lock modes and their descriptions. The set of lock modes supported includes intent locks at the table

Lock Mode	Objects	Interpretation
IN (intent none)	Tablespaces, tables	Read with no row locks
IS (intent share)	Tablespaces, tables	Read with row locks
NS (next key share)	Rows	Read locks for RS or CS isolation levels
S (share)	Rows, tables	Read lock
IX (intent exclusive)	Tablespaces, tables	Intend to update rows
SIX (share with intent exclusive)	Tables	No read locks on rows but X locks on updated rows
U (update)	Rows, tables	Update lock but allows others to read
NX (next-key exclusive)	Rows	Next key lock for inserts/deletes to prevent phantom reads during RR index scans
X (exclusive)	Rows, tables	Only uncommitted readers allowed
Z (superexclusive)	Tablespaces, tables	Complete exclusive access

Figure 29.19   DB2 lock modes.

level in order to maximize concurrency. Also, DB2 implements next-key locking and variant schemes for updates affecting index scans to eliminate the Halloween and phantom-read problems.

The transaction can set the lock granularity to table level by using the **lock table** statement. This is useful for applications that know their desired level of isolation is at the table level. Also, DB2 chooses the appropriate locking granularities for utilities such as reorg and load. The offline versions of these utilities usually lock the table in exclusive mode. The online versions of the utilities allow other transactions to proceed concurrently by acquiring row locks.

A deadlock detection agent is activated for each database and periodically checks for deadlocks between transactions. The interval for deadlock detection is a configurable parameter. In case of a deadlock, the agent chooses a victim and aborts it with a deadlock SQL error code.

29.10.2 Commit and Rollback

Applications can commit or roll back by using explicit **commit** or **rollback** statements. Applications can also issue **begin transaction** and **end transaction** statements to control the scope of transactions. Nested transactions are not supported. Normally, DB2 releases all locks that it holds on behalf of a transaction at **commit** or **rollback**. However, if a cursor statement has been declared by using the **with hold** clause, then some locks are maintained across commits.

29.10.3 Logging and Recovery

DB2 implements strict ARIES logging and recovery schemes. Write-ahead logging is employed to flush log records to the persistent log file before data pages are written or at **commit** time. DB2 supports two types of log modes: circular logging and archive logging. In circular logging, a predefined set of primary and secondary log files is used. Circular logging is useful for crash recovery or application failure recovery. In archival logging, DB2 creates new log files and the old log files must be archived in order to free up space in the file system. Archival logging is required to perform roll-forward recovery. In both cases, DB2 allows the user to configure the number of log files and the sizes of the log files.

In update-intensive environments, DB2 can be configured to look for group commits in order to bunch log writes.

DB2 supports transaction rollback and crash recovery as well as point-in-time or roll-forward recovery. In the case of crash recovery, DB2 performs the standard phases of *undo* processing and *redo* processing up to and from the last checkpoint in order to recover the proper committed state of the database. For point-in-time recovery, the database can be restored from a backup and can be rolled forward to a specific point in time, using the archived logs. The roll-forward recovery command supports both database and tablespace levels. It can also be issued on specific nodes on a multinode system. A parallel recovery scheme improves the performance in SMP systems by utilizing many CPUs. DB2 performs coordinated recovery across MPP nodes by implementing a global checkpointing scheme.

29.11 System Architecture

Figure 29.20 shows some of the different processes or threads in a DB2 server. Remote client applications connect to the database server by using communication agents such as *db2tcpcm*. Each application is assigned an agent (coordinator agent in MPP or SMP environments) called the *db2agent* thread. This agent and its subordinate agents perform the application-related tasks. Each database has a set of processes or threads that performs tasks such as prefetching, page cleaning from buffer pool, logging, and deadlock detection. Finally, there is a set of agents at the level of the server to perform tasks such as crash detection, license server, process creation, and control of system resources. DB2 provides configuration parameters to control the number of threads and processes in a server. Almost all the different types of agents can be controlled by using the configuration parameters.

Figure 29.21 shows the different types of memory segments in DB2. Private memory in agents or threads is mainly used for local variables and data structures that are relevant only for the current activity. For example, a private sort could allocate memory from the agent's private heap. Shared memory is partitioned into *server shared memory*, *database shared memory*, and *application shared memory*.

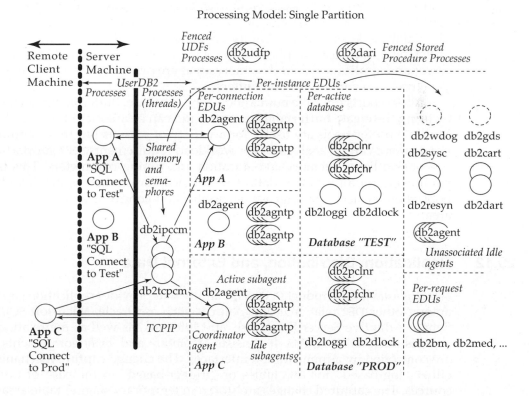

Figure 29.20 Process model in DB2.

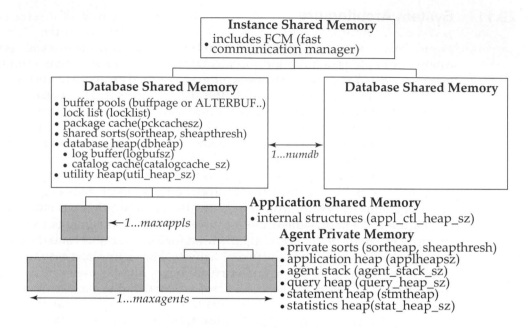

Figure 29.21   DB2 memory model.

The database-level shared memory contains useful data structures such as the buffer pool, lock lists, application package caches, and shared sort areas. The server and application shared memory areas are primarily used for common data structures and communication buffers.

DB2 supports multiple buffer pools for a database. Buffer pools can be created by using the **create bufferpool** statement and can be associated with tablespaces. Multiple buffer pools are useful for a variety of reasons but they should be defined after a careful analysis of the workload requirements. DB2 supports a comprehensive list of memory configuration and tuning parameters. This includes parameters for all the large data structure heap areas such as the default buffer pool, the sort heap, package cache, application-control heaps, and the lock-list area.

29.12   Replication, Distribution, and External Data

DB2 Replication is a product in the DB2 family that provides replication capabilities among other DB2 relational data sources such as Oracle, Microsoft SQL Server, Sybase Adaptive Server Enterprise, and Informix, as well as nonrelational data sources such as IBM's IMS. It consists of *capture* and *apply* components, which are controlled by administration interfaces. The change-capture mechanisms are either "log-based" for DB2 tables or "trigger-based" in the case of other data sources. The captured changes are stored in temporary staging table areas under the control of DB2 Replication. These staged intermediate tables with changes are then applied to destination tables using regular SQL statements: inserts, updates, and deletes. SQL-based transformations can be performed on the intermediate staging tables by using filtering conditions as well as aggregations. The resulting rows can be applied to one or more target tables. All of these actions are controlled by the administration facility.

DB2 supports a feature called *queue replication*. Queue (Q) replication creates a queue transport mechanism using IBM's message-queue product to ship captured log records as messages. These messages are extracted from the queues at the receiving end and applied against targets. The apply process can be parallelized and allows for user-specified conflict resolution rules.

Another member of the DB2 family is the DB2 information-integrator product, which provides federation, replication (using the replication engine described above), and search capabilities. The federated edition integrates tables in remote DB2 or other relational databases into a single distributed database. Users and developers can access various nonrelational data sources in tabular format, using wrapper technology. The federation engine provides a cost-based method for query optimization across the different data sites.

DB2 supports user-defined table functions that enable access to nonrelational and external data sources. User-defined table functions are created by using the **create function** statement with the clause **returns table**. Using these features, DB2 is able to participate in the OLE DB protocols.

Finally, DB2 provides full support for distributed transaction processing using the two-phase commit protocol. DB2 can act as the coordinator or agent for distributed XA support. As a coordinator, DB2 can perform all stages of the two-phase commit protocol. As a participant, DB2 can interact with any commercial distributed transaction manager.

29.13 Business Intelligence Features

DB2 Data Warehouse Edition is an offering in the DB2 family that incorporates business intelligence features. Data Warehouse Edition has at its foundation the DB2 engine, and enhances it with features for ETL, OLAP, mining, and online reporting. The DB2 engine provides scalability using its MPP features. In the MPP mode, DB2 can support configurations that can scale to several hundreds of nodes for large database sizes (terabytes). Additionally, features such as MDC and MQT provide support for the complex query-processing requirements of business intelligence.

Another aspect of business intelligence is online analytical processing or OLAP. The DB2 family includes a feature called *cube views* that provides a mechanism to construct appropriate data structures and MQTs inside DB2 that can be used for relational OLAP processing. Cube views provide modeling support for multidimensional cubes and provides a mapping mechanism to a relational star schema. This model is then used to recommend appropriate MQTs, indices, and MDC definitions to improve the performance of OLAP queries against the database. In addition, cube views can take advantage of DB2's native support for the **cube by** and **rollup** operations for generating aggregated cubes. Cube views is a tool that can be used to integrate DB2 tightly with OLAP vendors such as Business Objects, Microstrategy, and Cognos.

In addition, DB2 also provides multidimensional OLAP support using the DB2 OLAP server. The DB2 OLAP server can create a multidimensional data mart from an underlying DB2 database for analysis by OLAP techniques. The OLAP engine from the Essbase product is used in the DB2 OLAP server.

DB2 Alphablox is a new feature that provides online, interactive, reporting, and analysis capabilities. A very attractive feature of the Alphablox feature is the ability to construct new Web-based analysis forms rapidly, using a building block approach called *blox*.

For deep analytics, DB2 Intelligent Miner provides various components for modeling, scoring, and visualizing data. Mining enables users to perform classification, prediction, clustering, segmentation, and association against large data sets.

Bibliographical Notes

The origin of DB2 can be traced back to the System R project (Chamberlin et al. [1981]). IBM Research contributions include areas such as transaction processing (write-ahead logging and ARIES recovery algorithms) (Mohan et al. [1992]), query processing and optimization (Starburst) (Haas et al. [1990]), parallel processing (DB2 Parallel Edition) (Baru et al. [1995]), active database support (constraints, triggers) (Cochrane et al. [1996]), advanced query and warehousing techniques such as materialized views (Zaharioudakis et al. [2000], Lehner et al. [2000]), multidimensional clustering (Padmanabhan et al. [2003], Bhattacharjee et al. [2003]), autonomic features (Zilio et al. [2004]), and object-relational support (ADTs, UDFs) (Carey et al. [1999]). Multiprocessor query-processing details can be found in Baru et al. [1995]. Don Chamberlin's books provide a good review of the SQL and programming features of earlier versions of DB2 (Chamberlin [1996], Chamberlin [1998]). Earlier books by C. J. Date and others provide a good review of the features of DB2 Universal Database for OS/390 (Date [1989], Martin et al. [1989]).

The DB2 manuals provide the definitive view of each version of DB2. Most of these manuals are available online (http://www.software.ibm.com/db2). Books on DB2 for developers and administrators include Gunning [2008], Zikopoulos et al. [2004], Zikopoulos et al. [2007] and Zikopoulos et al. [2009].

CHAPTER 30

Microsoft SQL Server

Sameet Agarwal, José A. Blakeley, Thierry D'Hers,
Ketan Duvedi, César A. Galindo-Legaria, Gerald
Hinson, Dirk Myers, Vaqar Pirzada, Bill Ramos,
Balaji Rathakrishnan, Jack Richins, Michael Rys,
Florian Waas, Michael Zwilling

Microsoft SQL Server is a relational database-management system that scales from laptops and desktops to enterprise servers, with a compatible version, based on the Windows Mobile operating system, available for handheld devices such as Pocket PCs, SmartPhones, and Portable Media Centers. SQL Server was originally developed in the 1980s at Sybase for UNIX systems and later ported to Windows NT systems by Microsoft. Since 1994, Microsoft has shipped SQL Server releases developed independently of Sybase, which stopped using the SQL Server name in the late 1990s. The latest release, SQL Server 2008, is available in express, standard, and enterprise editions and localized for many languages around the world. In this chapter, the term SQL Server refers to all of these editions of SQL Server 2008.

SQL Server provides replication services among multiple copies of SQL Server and with other database systems. Its Analysis Services, an integral part of the system, includes online analytical processing (OLAP) and data-mining facilities. SQL Server provides a large collection of graphical tools and "wizards" that guide database administrators through tasks such as setting up regular backups, replicating data among servers, and tuning a database for performance. Many development environments support SQL Server, including Microsoft's Visual Studio and related products, in particular the .NET products and services.

30.1 Management, Design, and Querying Tools

SQL Server provides a suite of tools for managing all aspects of SQL Server development, querying, tuning, testing, and administration. Most of these tools center around the SQL Server Management Studio. SQL ServerManagement Studio provides a common shell for administering all services associated with SQL Server, which includes Database Engine, Analysis Services, Reporting Services, SQL ServerMobile, and Integration Services.

30.1.1   Database Development and Visual Database Tools

While designing a database, the database administrator creates database objects such as tables, columns, keys, indices, relationships, constraints, and views. To help create these objects, the SQL Server Management Studio provides access to visual database tools. These tools provide three mechanisms to aid in database design: the Database Designer, the Table Designer, and the View Designer.

The Database Designer is a visual tool that allows the database owner or the owner's delegates to create tables, columns, keys, indices, relationships, and constraints. Within this tool, a user can interact with database objects through database diagrams, which graphically show the structure of the database. The View Designer provides a visual query tool that allows the user to create or modify SQL views through the use of Windows drag-and-drop capabilities. Figure 30.1 shows a view opened from the Management Studio.

30.1.2   Database Query and Tuning Tools

SQL Server Management Studio provides several tools to aid the application development process. Queries and stored procedures can be developed and tested using the integrated Query Editor. The Query Editor supports creating and editing scripts for a variety of environments, including Transact-SQL, the SQL Server scripting language SQLCMD, the multidimensional expression language MDX which is used for data analysis, the SQL Server data-mining language DMX, the XML-analysis language XMLA, and SQL Server Mobile. Further analysis can be done using the SQL ServerProfiler. Database tuning recommendations are provided by the Database Tuning Advisor.

30.1.2.1   Query Editor

The integrated Query Editor provides a simple graphical user interface for running SQL queries and viewing the results. The Query Editor also provides a graphical representation of **showplan**, the steps chosen by the optimizer for query execution. The Query Editor is integrated with Management Studio's Object Explorer, which lets a user drag and drop object or table names into a query window and helps build **select, insert, update,** or **delete** statements for any table.

A database administrator or developer can use Query Editor to:

- **Analyze queries:** Query Editor can show a graphical or textual execution plan for any query, as well as displaying statistics regarding the time and resources required to execute any query.

- **Format SQL queries:** Including indenting and color syntax coding.

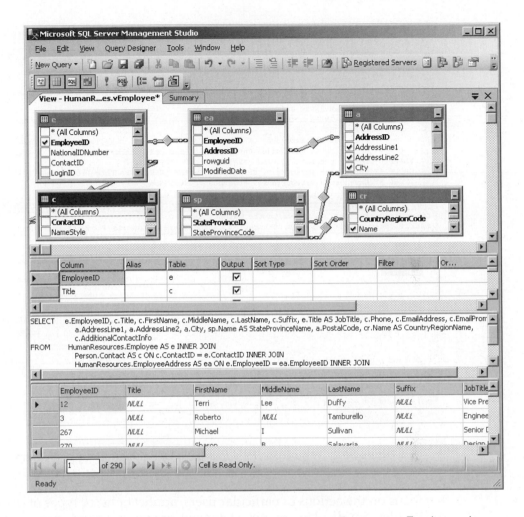

Figure 30.1 The View Designer opened for the HumanResources.vEmployee view.

- **Use templates for stored procedures, functions, and basic SQL statements:** The Management Studio comes with dozens of predefined templates for building DDL commands, or users can define their own.

Figure 30.2 shows the Management Studio with the Query Editor displaying the graphical execution plan for a query involving a four-table join and an aggregation.

30.1.2.2 SQL Profiler

SQL Profiler is a graphical utility that allows database administrators to monitor and record database activity of the SQL Server Database Engine and Analysis Services. SQL Profiler can display all server activity in real time, or it can create filters

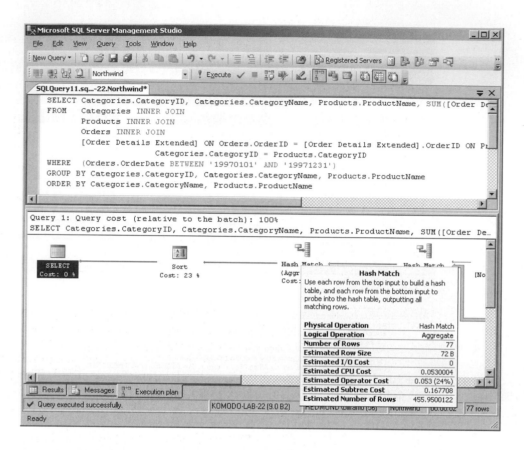

Figure 30.2 A showplan for a four-table join with **group by** aggregation.

that focus on the actions of particular users, applications, or types of commands. SQL Profiler can display any SQL statement or stored procedure sent to any instance of SQL Server (if the security privileges allow it) in addition to performance data indicating how long the query took to run, how much CPU and I/O was needed, and the execution plan that the query used.

SQL Profiler allows drilling down even deeper into SQL Server to monitor every statement executed as part of a stored procedure, every data modification operation, every lock acquired or released, or every occurrence of a database file growing automatically. Dozens of different events can be captured, and dozens of data items can be captured for each event. SQL Server actually divides the tracing functionality into two separate but connected components. The SQL Profiler is the client-side trace facility. Using SQL Profiler, a user can choose to save the captured data to a file or a table, in addition to displaying it in the Profiler User Interface (UI). The Profiler tool displays every event that meets the filter criteria as it occurs. Once trace data are saved, SQL Profiler can read the saved data for display or analysis purposes.

On the server side is the SQL trace facility, which manages queues of events generated by event producers. A consumer thread reads events from the queues and filters them before sending them to the process that requested them. Events are the main unit of activity as far as tracing is concerned, and an event can be anything that happens inside SQL Server, or between SQL Server and a client. For example, creating or dropping an object is an event, executing a stored procedure is an event, acquiring or releasing a lock is an event, and sending a Transact-SQL batch from a client to the SQL Server is an event. There is a set of stored system procedures to define which events should be traced, what data for each event are interesting, and where to save the information collected from the events. Filters applied to the events can reduce the amount of information collected and stored.

SQL Server guarantees that certain critical information will always be gathered, and it can be used as a useful auditing mechanism. SQL Server is certified for U.S. government C2-level security, and many of the traceable events are available solely to support C2-certification requirements.

30.1.2.3 The Database Tuning Advisor

Queries and updates can often execute much faster if an appropriate set of indices is available. Designing the best possible indices for the tables in a large database is a complex task; it not only requires a thorough knowledge of how SQL Server uses indices and how the query optimizer makes its decisions, but how the data will actually be used by applications and interactive queries. The SQL Server Database Tuning Advisor (DTA) is a powerful tool for designing the best possible indices and indexed (materialized) views based on observed query and update workloads.

DTA can tune across multiple databases and it bases its recommendations on a workload that can be a file of captured trace events, a file of SQL statements, or an XML input file. SQL Profiler can be used to capture all SQL statements submitted by all users over a period of time. DTA can then look at the data access patterns for all users, for all applications, for all tables, and make balanced recommendations.

30.1.3 SQL Server Management Studio

In addition to providing access to the database design and visual database tools, the easy-to-use SQL Server Management Studio supports centralized management of all aspects of multiple installations of the SQL Server Database Engine, Analysis Services, Reporting Services, Integration Services, and SQL Server Mobile, including security, events, alerts, scheduling, backup, server configuration, tuning, full-text search, and replication. SQL Server Management Studio allows a database administrator to create, modify, and copy SQL Server database schemas and objects such as tables, views, and triggers. Because multiple installations of SQL Server can be organized into groups and treated as a unit, SQL Server Management Studio can manage hundreds of servers simultaneously.

Although it can run on the same computer as the SQL Server engine, SQL Server Management Studio offers the same management capabilities while running on

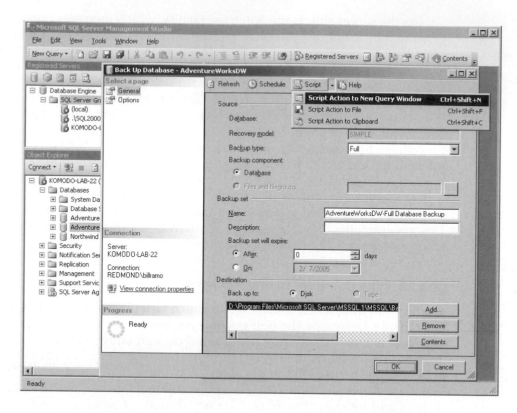

Figure 30.3   The SQL Server Management Studio interface.

any Windows 2000 (or later) machine. In addition, the efficient client–server architecture of SQL Server makes it practical to use the remote-access (dial-up networking) capabilities of Windows for administration and management.

SQL Server Management Studio relieves the database administrator from having to know the specific steps and syntax to complete a job. It provides wizards to guide the database administrator through the process of setting up and maintaining an installation of SQL Server. Management Studio's interface is shown in Figure 30.3 and illustrates how a script for database backup can be created directly from its dialogs.

30.2   SQL Variations and Extensions

SQL Server allows application developers to write server-side business logic using Transact-SQL or a .NET programming language such as C#, Visual Basic, COBOL, or J++. Transact-SQL is a complete database programming language that includes data-definition and data-manipulation statements, iterative and conditional statements, variables, procedures, and functions. Transact-SQL supports most of the **mandatory** DDL query and data modification statements and constructs in the

SQL:2003 standard. See Section 30.2.1 for the list of SQL:2003 data types supported. In addition to the mandatory features, Transact-SQL also supports many **optional** features in the SQL:2003 standard such as recursive queries, common table expressions, user-defined functions, and relational operators such as **intersect** and **except** among others.

30.2.1 Data Types

SQL Server 2008 supports all the mandatory scalar data types in the SQL:2003 standard. SQL Server also supports the ability to alias system types using user-supplied names; the aliasing is similar in functionality to the SQL:2003 distinct types, but not fully compliant with them.

Some primitive types unique to SQL Server include:

- Large character and binary string types of variable size up to $2^{31} - 1$ bytes, using the **varchar/nvarchar/varbinary(max)** data type, which has a programming model that is similar to the small-character and byte-string types. Additionally, they support a storage attribute called FILESTREAM to specify that data for each individual column value is stored as a separate file in the filesystem. FILESTREAM storage allows higher performance streaming access to applications using the native filesystem API.

- An XML type, described in Section 30.11, which is used to store XML data inside a table column. The XML type can optionally have an associated XML *schema collection* specifying a constraint that the instances of the type should adhere to one of the XML types defined in the schema collection.

- **sql_variant** is a scalar data type that can contain values of any SQL scalar type (except large character and binary types and **sql_variant**). This type is used by applications that need to store data whose type cannot be anticipated at data-definition time. **sql_variant** is also the type of a column formed from the execution of an **unpivot** relational operator (see Section 30.2.2). Internally, the system keeps track of the original type of the data. It is possible to filter, join, and sort on **sql_variant** columns. The system function **sql_variant_property** returns details on the actual data stored in a column of type **sql_variant**, including the base type and size information.

- The **hierarchyId** data type makes it easier to store and query hierarchical data. Hierarchical data are defined as a set of data items related to one another by hierarchical relationships where one item of data is the parent of another item. Common examples include: an organizational structure, a hierarchical file system, a set of tasks in a project, a taxonomy of language terms, a single-inheritance type hierarchy, part-subpart relationships, and a graph of links among Web pages.

- SQL Server supports storing and querying of geospatial data, that is, location data referenced to the earth. Common models of these data are the planar and geodetic coordinate systems. The main distinction between these two systems is that the latter takes into account the curvature of the earth. SQL

Server supports geometry and geography, which correspond to the planar and geodetic models.

In addition, SQL Server supports a table type and a cursor type that cannot be used as columns in a table, but can be used in the Transact-SQL language as variables:

- A **table** type enables a variable to hold a set of rows. An instance of this type is used primarily to hold temporary results in a stored procedure or as the return value of a table-valued function. A table variable behaves like a local variable. It has a well-defined scope, which is the function, stored procedure, or batch in which it is declared. Within its scope, a table variable may be used like a regular table. It may be applied anywhere a table or table expression is used in **select, insert, update,** and **delete** statements.

- A **cursor** type that enables references to a cursor object. The cursor type can be used to declare variables, or routine input/output arguments to reference cursors across routine calls.

30.2.2   Query Language Enhancements

In addition to the SQL relational operators such as **inner join** and **outer join**, SQL Server supports the relational operators **pivot**, **unpivot**, and **apply**.

- **pivot** is an operator that transforms the shape of its input result set from two columns that represent name-value pairs into multiple columns, one for each name from the input. The name column from the input is called the pivot column. The user needs to indicate which names to transpose from the input into individual columns in the output. Consider the table *MonthlySales(ProductID, Month, SalesQty)*. The following query, using the **pivot** operator, returns the *SalesQty* for each of the months Jan, Feb, and Mar as separate columns. Note that the **pivot** operator also performs an implicit aggregation on all the other columns in the table and an explicit aggregation on the pivot column.

  select *
  from *MonthlySales* **pivot(sum(***SalesQty***) for** *Month* **in** ('Jan', 'Feb', 'Mar')) *T*;

  The inverse operation of **pivot** is **unpivot**.

- The **apply** operator is similar to join, except its right input is an expression that may contain references to columns in the left input, for example a table-valued function invocation that takes as arguments one or more columns from the left input. The set of columns produced by the operator is the union of the columns from its two inputs. The **apply** operator can be used to evaluate its right input for each row of its left input and perform a **union all** of the rows across all these evaluations. There are two flavors of the **apply** operator similar to **join**, namely, **cross** and **outer**. The two flavors differ in terms of how they handle the case of the right input producing an empty result-set. In the case of **cross apply**, this causes the corresponding row from the left input to not appear in the result. In the case of **outer apply**, the row appears from the left input with NULL values for the columns in the right input. Consider a table-valued function called *FindReports* that takes as input the ID of a given employee and returns the set of employees reporting directly or indirectly to that employee in an organization. The following query calls this function for the manager of each department from the *Departments* table:

> **select** *
> **from** *Departments* D **cross apply** *FindReports(D.ManagerID)*

30.2.3 Routines

Users can write routines that run inside the server process as scalar or table functions, stored procedures, and triggers using Transact-SQL or a .NET language. All these routines are defined to the database by using the corresponding **create [function, procedure, trigger]** DDL statement. Scalar functions can be used in any scalar expression inside an SQL DML or DDL statement. Table-valued functions can be used anywhere a table is allowed in a **select** statement. Transact-SQL table-valued functions whose body contains a single SQL **select** statement are treated as a view (expanded inline) in the query that references the function. Since table-valued functions allow input arguments, inline table-valued functions can be considered parameterized views.

30.2.3.1 Indexed Views

In addition to traditional views as defined in ANSI SQL, SQL Server supports indexed (materialized) views. Indexed views can substantially enhance the performance of complex decision support queries that retrieve large numbers of base table rows and aggregate large amounts of information into concise sums, counts, and averages. SQL Server supports creating a clustered index on a view and subsequently any number of nonclustered indices. Once a view is indexed, the optimizer can use its indices in queries that reference the view or its base tables. There is no need for queries to refer to the view explicitly for the indexed view to be used in the query plan, as the matching is done automatically from the view definition. This way, existing queries can benefit from the improved efficiency of retrieving data directly from the indexed view without having to be rewritten. The indexed view is maintained consistent with the base tables by automatically propagating all updates.

30.2.4 Filtered Indexes

A filtered index is an optimized nonclustered index, especially suited to cover queries that select from a well-defined subset of data. It uses a filter predicate to index a portion of rows in the table. A well-designed filtered index can improve query performance, reduce index-maintenance costs, and reduce index-storage costs compared with full-table indices. Filtered indices can provide the following advantages over full-table indices:

- **Improved query performance and plan quality**. A well-designed filtered index improves query performance and execution plan quality because it is smaller than a full-table nonclustered index and has filtered statistics. The filtered statistics are more accurate than full-table statistics because they cover only the rows in the filtered index.

- **Reduced index maintenance costs**. An index is maintained only when data manipulation language (DML) statements affect the data in the index. A filtered index reduces index maintenance costs compared to a full-table nonclustered index because it is smaller and is only maintained when the data in the index are affected. It is possible to have a large number of filtered indices, especially when they contain data that are affected infrequently. Similarly, if a filtered index contains only the frequently affected data, the smaller size of the index reduces the cost of updating the statistics.

- **Reduced index storage costs**. Creating a filtered index can reduce disk storage for nonclustered indices when a full-table index is not necessary. You can replace a full-table nonclustered index with multiple filtered indices without significantly increasing the storage requirements.

Filtered statistics can also be created explicitly, independently from filtered indices.

30.2.4.1 Updatable Views and Triggers

Generally, views can be the target of **update, delete**, or **insert** statements if the data modification applies to only one of the view's base tables. Updates to partitioned views can be propagated to multiple base tables. For example, the following **update** will increase the prices for publisher "0736" by 10 percent:

> **update** *titleview*
> **set** *price = price* * 1.10
> **where** *pub_id* = '0736';

For data modifications that affect more than one base table, the view can be updated if there is an **instead** trigger defined for the operation; **instead** triggers for **insert, update**, or **delete** operations can be defined on a view, to specify the updates that must be performed on the base tables to reflect the corresponding modifications on the view.

Triggers are Transact-SQL or .NET procedures that are automatically executed when either a DML (**update, insert**, or **delete**) or DDL statement is issued against a base table or view. Triggers are mechanisms that enable enforcement of business logic automatically when data are modified or when DDL statements are executed. Triggers can extend the integrity checking logic of declarative constraints, defaults, and rules, although declarative constraints should be used preferably whenever they suffice, as they can be used by the query optimizer to reason about the data contents.

Triggers can be classified into DML and DDL triggers depending on the kind of event that fires the trigger. DML triggers are defined against a table or view that is being modified. DDL triggers are defined against an entire database for one or more DDL statements such as **create table**, **drop procedure**, etc.

Triggers can be classified into **after** and **instead** triggers according to when the trigger gets invoked relative to the action that fires the trigger. **After** triggers execute after the triggering statement and subsequent declarative constraints are enforced. **Instead** triggers execute instead of the triggering action. **Instead** triggers can be thought of as similar to **before** triggers, but they actually replace the triggering action. In SQL Server, DML **after** triggers can be defined only on base tables, while DML **instead** triggers can be defined on base tables or views. **Instead** triggers allow practically any view to be made updatable via user-provided logic. DDL **instead** triggers can be defined on any DDL statement.

30.3   Storage and Indexing

In SQL Server, a database refers to a collection of files that contain data and are supported by a single transaction log. The database is the primary unit of administration in SQL Server and also provides a container for physical structures such as tables and indices and for logical structures such as constraints and views.

30.3.1   Filegroups

In order to manage space effectively in a database, the set of data files in a database is divided into groups called filegroups. Each filegroup contains one or more operating-system files.

Every database has at least one filegroup known as the primary filegroup. This filegroup contains all the metadata for the database in system tables. The primary filegroup may also store user data.

If additional, user-defined filegroups have been created, a user can explicitly control the placement of individual tables, indices, or the large-object columns of a table by placing them in a particular filegroup. For example, the user may choose to store performance critical indices on a filegroup located on solid state disks. Likewise they may choose to place varbinary(max) columns containing video data on an I/O subsystem optimized for streaming.

30.3.2   Space Management within Filegroups

One of the main purposes for filegroups is to allow for effective space management. All data files are divided into fixed-size 8-kilobyte units called **pages**. The allocation system is responsible for allocating these pages to tables and indices.

The goal of the allocation system is to minimize the amount of space wasted while, at the same time, keeping the amount of fragmentation in the database to a minimum to ensure good scan performance. In order to achieve this goal, the allocation manager usually allocates and deallocates all the pages in units of eight contiguous pages called **extents**.

The allocation system manages these extents through various bitmaps. These bitmaps allow the allocation system to find a page or an extent for allocation quickly. These bitmaps are also used when a full table or index scan is executed. The advantage of using allocation-based bitmaps for scanning is that it allows disk-order traversals of all the extents belonging to a table or index-leaf level, which significantly improves the scan performance.

If there is more than one file in a filegroup, the allocation system allocates extents for any object on that filegroup by using a "proportional fill" algorithm. Each file is filled up in the proportion of the amount of free space in that file compared to other files. This fills all the files in a filegroup at roughly the same rate and allows the system to utilize all the files in the filegroup evenly. Files can also be configured to grow automatically if the filegroup is running out of space. SQL Server allows files to shrink. In order to shrink a data file, SQL Server moves all the data from the physical end of the file to a point closer to the beginning of the file and then actually shrinks the file, releasing space back to the operating system.

30.3.3 Tables

SQL Server supports heap and clustered organizations for tables. In a heap-organized table, the location of every row of the table is determined entirely by the system and is not specified in any way by the user. The rows of a heap have a fixed identifier known as the row (RID), and this value never changes unless the file is shrunk and the row is moved. If the row becomes large enough that it cannot fit in the page in which it was originally inserted, the record is moved to a different place but a forwarding stub is left in the original place so that the record can still be found by using its original RID.

In a clustered-index organization for a table, the rows of the table are stored in a B^+-tree sorted by the clustering key of the index. The clustered-index key also serves as the unique identifier for each row. The key for a clustered index can be defined to be nonunique, in which case SQL Server adds an additional hidden column to make the key unique. The clustered index also serves as a search structure to identify a row of the table with a particular key or scan a set of rows of the table with keys within a certain range. A clustered index is the most common type of table organization.

30.3.4 Indices

SQL Server also supports secondary (nonclustered) B^+-tree indices. Queries that refer only to columns that are available through secondary indices are processed by retrieving pages from the leaf level of the indices without having to retrieve data from the clustered index or heap. Nonclustered indices over a table with a clustered index contain the key columns of the clustered index. Thus, the clustered index rows can move to a different page (via splits, defragmentation, or even index rebuilds) without requiring changes to the nonclustered indices.

SQL Server supports the addition of computed columns to a table. A computed column is a column whose value is an expression, usually based on the value of other columns in that row. SQL Server allows the user to build secondary indices on computed columns.

30.3.5 Partitions

SQL Server supports range partitioning on tables and nonclustered indices. A partitioned index is made up of multiple B^+-trees, one per partition. A partitioned table without an index (a heap) is made up of multiple heaps, one per partition. For brevity, we refer only to partitioned indices (clustered or nonclustered) and ignore heaps for the rest of this discussion.

Partitioning a large index allows an administrator more flexibility in managing the storage for the index and can improve some query performance because the partitions act as a coarse-grained index.

The partitioning for an index is specified by providing both a partitioning function and a partitioning scheme. A partitioning function maps the domain of a partitioning column (any column in the index) to partitions numbered 1 to N. A partitioning scheme maps partition numbers produced by a partitioning function to specific filegroups where the partitions are stored.

30.3.6 Online Index Build

Building new indices and rebuilding existing indices on a table can be performed online, i.e., while **select**, **insert**, **delete**, and **update** operations are being performed on the table. The creation of a new index happens in three phases. The first phase is simply creating an empty B^+-tree for the new index with the catalog showing the new index is available for maintenance operations. That is, the new index must be maintained by all subsequent **insert**, **delete**, and **update** operations, but it is not available for queries. The second phase consists of scanning the table to retrieve the index columns for each row, sorting the rows and inserting them into the new B^+-tree. These inserts must be careful to interact with the other rows in the new B^+-tree placed there by index maintenance operations from updates on the base table. The scan is a snapshot scan that, without locking, ensures the scan sees the entire table with only the results of committed transactions as of the start of the scan. This is achieved by using the snapshot isolation technique described in Section 30.5.1. The final phase of the index build involves updating the catalog to indicate the index build is complete and the index is available for queries.

30.3.7 Scans and Read-ahead

Execution of queries in SQL Server can involve a variety of different scan modes on the underlying tables and indices. These include ordered versus unordered scans, serial versus parallel scans, unidirectional versus bidirectional scans, forward versus backward scans, and entire table or index scans versus range or filtered scans.

Each of the scan modes has a read-ahead mechanism that tries to keep the scan ahead of the needs of the query execution, in order to reduce seek and latency overheads and utilize disk idle time. The SQL Server read-ahead algorithm uses the knowledge from the query-execution plan in order to drive the read-ahead and make sure that only data that are actually needed by the query are read. Also, the amount of read-ahead is automatically scaled according to the size of the buffer pool, the amount of I/O the disk subsystem can sustain, and the rate at which the data are being consumed by query execution.

30.3.8 Compression

SQL Server supports both *row* and *page* compression for tables and indices. Row compression uses a variable-length format for data types such as integers that are traditionally considered fixed-length. Page compression removes common prefixes on columns and builds a per-page dictionary for common values.

30.4   Query Processing and Optimization

The query processor of SQL Server is based on an extensible framework that allows rapid incorporation of new execution and optimization techniques. Any SQL query can be expressed as a tree of operators in an extended relational algebra. Abstracting operators of this algebra into **iterators**, query execution encapsulates data-processing algorithms as logical units that communicate with each other by using a GetNextRow() interface. Starting out with an initial query tree, the query optimizer generates alternatives by using tree transformations and estimates their execution cost by taking into account iterator behavior and statistical models to estimate the number of rows to process.

30.4.1   Overview of Compilation Process

Complex queries present significant optimization opportunities that require re-ordering operators across query block boundaries and selecting plans solely on the basis of estimated costs. To go after these opportunities, the query optimizer deviates from traditional query-optimization approaches used in other commercial systems in favor of a more general, purely algebraic framework that is based on the Cascades optimizer prototype. Query optimization is part of the query-compilation process, which consists of four steps:

- **Parsing/binding**. After parsing, the binder resolves table and column names by using the catalogs. SQL Server utilizes a plan cache to avoid repeated optimization of identical or structurally similar queries. If no cached plan is available, an initial operator tree is generated. The operator tree is simply a combination of relational operators and is not constrained by concepts such as query blocks or derived tables, which typically obstruct optimization.

- **Simplification/normalization**. The optimizer applies simplification rules on the operator tree to obtain a normal, simplified form. During simplification, the optimizer determines and loads statistics required for cardinality estimation.

- **Cost-based optimization**. The optimizer applies exploration and implementation rules to generate alternatives, estimates execution cost, and chooses the plan with the cheapest anticipated cost. Exploration rules implement reordering for an extensive set of operators, including join and aggregation reordering. Implementation rules introduce execution alternatives such as merge join and hash join.

- **Plan preparation**. The optimizer creates query-execution structures for the selected plan.

To achieve best results, cost-based optimization is not divided into phases that optimize different aspects of the query independently; also, it is not restricted to a single dimension such as join enumeration. Instead, a collection of transformation rules defines the space of interest, and cost estimation is used uniformly to select an efficient plan.

30.4.2 Query Simplification

During simplification, only transformations that are guaranteed to generate less costly substitutes are applied. The optimizer pushes selects down the operator tree as far as possible; it checks predicates for contradictions, taking into account declared constraints. It uses contradictions to identify subexpressions that can be removed from the tree. A common scenario is the elimination of **union** branches that retrieve data from tables with different constraints.

A number of simplification rules are *context dependent*; that is, the substitution is valid only in the context of utilization of the subexpression. For example, an outer join can be simplified into an inner join if a later filter operation will discard nonmatching rows that were padded with **null**. Another example is the elimination of joins on foreign keys, when there are no later uses of columns from the referenced table. A third example is the context of duplicate insensitivity, which specifies that delivering one or multiple copies of a row does not affect the query result. Subexpressions under semijoins and under **distinct** are duplicate insensitive, which allows turning **union** into **union all**, for example.

For grouping and aggregation, the *GbAgg* operator is used, which creates groups and optionally applies an aggregate function on each group. Duplicate removal, expressed in SQL by the **distinct** keyword, is simply a *GbAgg* with no aggregate functions to compute. During simplification, information about keys and functional dependencies is used to reduce grouping columns.

Subqueries are normalized by removing correlated query specifications and using some join variant instead. Removing correlations is not a "subquery execution strategy," but simply a normalization step. A variety of execution strategies is then considered during cost-based optimization.

30.4.3   Reordering and Cost-Based Optimization

In SQL Server, transformations are fully integrated into the cost-based generation and selection of execution plans. The query optimizer includes about 350 logical and physical transformation rules. In addition to inner-join reordering, the query optimizer employs reordering transformations for the operators outer join, semijoin, and antisemijoin, from the standard relational algebra (with duplicates, for SQL). *GbAgg* is reordered as well, by moving it below or above joins when possible. Partial aggregation, that is, introducing a new *GbAgg* with grouping on a superset of the columns of a subsequent *GbAgg*, is considered below joins and **union all**, and also in parallel plans. See the references given in the bibliographical notes for details.

Correlated execution is considered during plan exploration, the simplest case being index-lookup join. SQL Server models correlated execution as a single algebraic operator, called **apply**, which operates on a table T and a parameterized relational expression $E(t)$. **Apply** executes E for each row of T, which provides parameter values. Correlated execution is considered as an execution alternative, regardless of the use of subqueries in the original SQL formulation. It is a very efficient strategy when table T is small and indices support efficient parameterized execution of $E(t)$. Furthermore, we consider reduction on the number of executions of $E(t)$ when there are duplicate parameter values, by means of two techniques: Sort T on parameter values so that a single result of $E(t)$ is reused while the parameter value remains the same, or else use a hash table that keeps track of the result of $E(t)$ for (some subset of) earlier parameter values.

Some applications select rows on the basis of some aggregate result for their group. For example, "Find customers whose balance is more than twice the average for their market segment." The SQL formulation requires a self-join. During exploration, this pattern is detected and per-segment execution over a single scan is considered as an alternative to self-join.

Materialized-view utilization is also considered during cost-based optimization. View matching interacts with operator reordering in that utilization may not be apparent until some other reordering has taken place. When a view is found to match some subexpression, the table that contains the view result is added as an alternative for the corresponding expression. Depending on data distribution and indices available, it may or may not be better than the original expression—selection will be based on cost estimation.

To estimate the execution cost of a plan, the model takes into account the number of times a subexpression is executed, as well as the **row goal**, which is the number of rows expected to be consumed by the parent operator. The row goal can be less than the cardinality estimate in the case of top-n queries, and for *Apply/semijoin*. For example, *Apply/semijoin* outputs row t from T as soon as a single row is produced by $E(t)$ (that is, it tests **exists** $E(t)$). Thus, the row goal of the output of $E(t)$ is 1, and the row goals of subtrees of $E(t)$ are computed for this row goal for $E(t)$ and used for cost estimation.

30.4.4 Update Plans

Update plans optimize maintenance of indices, verify constraints, apply cascading actions, and maintain materialized views. For index maintenance, instead of taking each row and maintaining all indices for it, update plans may apply modifications per index, sorting rows and applying the update operation in key order. This minimizes random I/O, especially when the number of rows to update is large. Constraints are handled by an **assert** operator, which executes a predicate and raises an error if the result is **false**. Referential constraints are defined by **exists** predicates, which in turn become semijoins and are optimized by considering all execution algorithms.

The Halloween problem (described earlier in Section 13.6) refers to the following anomaly: Suppose a salary index is read in ascending order, and salaries are being raised by 10 percent. As a result of the update, rows will move forward in the index and will be found and updated again, leading to an infinite loop. One way to address this problem is to separate processing into two phases: First read all rows that will be updated and make a copy of them in some temporary place, then read from this place and apply all updates. Another alternative is to read from a different index where rows will not move as a result of the update. Some execution plans provide phase separation automatically, if they sort or build a hash table on the rows to be updated. Halloween protection is modeled as a property of plans. Multiple plans that provide the required property are considered, and one is selected on the basis of estimated execution cost.

30.4.5 Data Analysis at Optimization Time

SQL pioneered techniques to perform gathering of statistics as part of an ongoing optimization. The computation of result size estimates is based on statistics for columns used in a given expression. These statistics consist of max-diff histograms on the column values and a number of counters that capture densities and row sizes, among others. Database administrators may create statistics explicitly by using extended SQL syntax.

If no statistics are available for a given column, however, SQL Server's optimizer puts the ongoing optimization on hold and gathers statistics as needed. As soon as the statistics are computed, the original optimization is resumed, leveraging the newly created statistics. Optimization of subsequent queries reuses previously generated statistics. Typically, after a short period of time, statistics for frequently used columns have been created and interruptions to gather new statistics become infrequent. By keeping track of the number of rows modified in a table, a measure of staleness is maintained for all affected statistics. Once the staleness exceeds a certain threshold the statistics are recomputed and cached plans are recompiled to take changed data distributions into account.

Statistics can be recomputed asynchronously, which avoids potentially long compile times caused by synchronous computation. The optimization that triggers the computation of statistics uses potentially stale statistics. However, subsequent queries are able to leverage the recomputed statistics. This allows striking an acceptable balance between time spent in optimization and the quality of the resulting query plan.

30.4.6   Partial Search and Heuristics

Cost-based query optimizers face the issue of search-space explosion because applications do issue queries involving dozens of tables. To address this, SQL Server uses multiple optimization stages, each of which uses query transformations to explore successively larger regions of the search space.

There are simple and complete transformations geared toward exhaustive optimization, as well as smart transformations that implement various heuristics. Smart transformations generate plans that are very far apart in the search space, while simple transformations explore neighborhoods. Optimization stages apply a mix of both kinds of transformations, first emphasizing smart transformations, and later transitioning to simple transformations. Optimum results on subtrees are preserved, so that later stages can take advantage of results generated earlier. Each stage needs to balance opposing plan generation techniques:

- **Exhaustive generation of alternatives**: To generate the complete space, the optimizer uses complete, local, nonredundant transformations—a transformation rule that is equivalent to a sequence of more primitive transformations would only introduce additional overhead.

- **Heuristic generation of candidates**: A handful of interesting candidates (selected on the basis of estimated cost) are likely to be far apart in terms of primitive transformation rules. Here, desirable transformations are incomplete, global, and redundant.

Optimization can be terminated at any point after a first plan has been generated. Such termination is based on the estimated cost of the best plan found and the time spent already in optimization. For example, if a query requires only looking up a few rows in some indices, a very cheap plan will likely be produced quickly in the early stages, terminating optimization. This approach enabled adding new heuristics easily over time, without compromising either cost-based selection of plans, or exhaustive exploration of the search space, when appropriate.

30.4.7   Query Execution

Execution algorithms support both sort-based and hash-based processing, and their data structures are designed to optimize use of processor cache. Hash operations support basic aggregation and join, with a number of optimizations, extensions, and dynamic tuning for data skew. The **flow-distinct** operation is a variant of hash-distinct, where rows are output early, as soon as a new distinct value is found, instead of waiting to process the complete input. This operator is effective for queries that use **distinct** and request only a few rows, say using the **top n** construct. Correlated plans specify executing $E(t)$, often including some index lookup based on the parameter, for each row t of a table T. **Asynchronous prefetching** allows issuing multiple index-lookup requests to the storage engine. It is implemented this way: A nonblocking index-lookup request is made for a row t of T, then t is placed in a prefetch queue. Rows are taken out of the queue and used by **apply** to execute $E(t)$. Execution of $E(t)$ does not require that data be already in the buffer pool, but having outstanding prefetch operations maximizes hardware utilization and increases performance. The size of the queue is determined dynamically as a function of cache hits. If no ordering is required on the output rows of **apply**, rows from the queue may be taken out of order, to minimize waiting on I/O.

Parallel execution is implemented by the **exchange** operator, which manages multiple threads, partitions or broadcasts data, and feeds the data to multiple processes. The query optimizer decides **exchange** placement on the basis of estimated cost. The degree of parallelism is determined dynamically at runtime, according to the current system utilization.

Index plans are made up of the pieces described earlier. For example, we consider the use of an index join to resolve predicate conjunctions (or index union, for disjunctions), in a cost-based way. Such a join can be done in parallel, using any of SQL Server's join algorithms. We also consider joining indices for the sole purpose of assembling a row with the set of columns needed on a query, which is sometimes faster than scanning a base table. Taking record IDs from a secondary index and locating the corresponding row in a base table is effectively equivalent to performing index-lookup join. For this, we use our generic correlated execution techniques such as asynchronous prefetch.

Communication with the storage engine is done through OLE-DB, which allows accessing other data providers that implement this interface. OLE-DB is the mechanism used for distributed and remote queries, which are driven directly by the query processor. Data providers are categorized according to the range of functionality they provide, ranging from simple rowset providers with no indexing capabilities to providers with full SQL support.

30.5 Concurrency and Recovery

SQL Server's transaction, logging, locking, and recovery subsystems realize the ACID properties expected of a database system.

30.5.1 Transactions

In SQL Server all statements are atomic and applications can specify various levels of isolation for each statement. A single transaction can include statements that not only select, insert, delete, or update records, but also create or drop tables, build indices, and bulk-import data. Transactions can span databases on remote servers. When transactions are spread across servers, SQL Server uses a

Windows operating-system service called the Microsoft Distributed Transaction Coordinator (MS DTC) to perform two-phase commit processing. MS DTC supports the XA transaction protocol and, along with OLE-DB, provides the foundation for ACID transactions among heterogeneous systems.

Concurrency control based on locking is the default for SQL Server. SQL Server also offers optimistic concurrency control for cursors. Optimistic concurrency control is based on the assumption that resource conflicts between multiple users are unlikely (but not impossible), and allows transactions to execute without locking any resources. Only when attempting to change data does SQL Server check resources to determine if any conflicts have occurred. If a conflict occurs, the application must read the data and attempt the change again. Applications can choose to detect changes either by comparing values or by checking a special row version column on a row.

SQL Server supports the SQL isolation levels of read uncommitted, read committed, repeatable read, and serializable. Read committed is the default level. In addition, SQL Server supports two snapshot-based isolation levels (snapshot isolation is described earlier in Section 15.7).

- **Snapshot**: Specifies that data read by any statement in a transaction will be the transactionally consistent version of the data that existed at the start of the transaction. The effect is as if the statements in a transaction see a snapshot of the committed data as it existed at the start of the transaction. Writes are validated using the validation steps described in Section 15.7, and permitted to complete only if the validation is successful.

- **Read committed snapshot**: Specifies that each statement executed within a transaction sees a transactionally consistent snapshot of the data as it existed at the start of the statement. This contrasts with read committed isolation where the statement may see committed updates of transactions that commit while the statement is executing.

30.5.2 Locking

Locking is the primary mechanism used to enforce the semantics of the isolation levels. All updates acquire sufficient exclusive locks held for the duration of the transaction to prevent conflicting updates from occurring. Shared locks are held for various durations to provide the different SQL isolation levels for queries.

SQL Server provides multigranularity locking that allows different types of resources to be locked by a transaction (see Figure 30.4, where the resources are listed in order of increasing granularity). To minimize the cost of locking, SQL Server locks resources automatically at a granularity appropriate to the task. Locking at a smaller granularity, such as rows, increases concurrency, but has a higher overhead because more locks must be held if many rows are locked.

The fundamental SQL Server lock modes are shared (S), update (U), and exclusive (X); intent locks are also supported for multigranularity locking. Update locks are used to prevent a common form of deadlock that occurs when multiple sessions are reading, locking, and potentially updating resources later. Additional

Resource	Description
RID	Row identifier; used to lock a single row within a table
Key	Row lock within an index; protects key ranges in serializable transactions
Page	8-kilobyte table or index page
Extent	Contiguous group of eight data pages or index pages
Table	Entire table, including all data and indices
DB	Database

Figure 30.4 Lockable resources.

lock modes—called key-range locks—are taken only in serializable isolation level for locking the range between two rows in an index.

30.5.2.1 Dynamic Locking

Fine-granularity locking can improve concurrency at the cost of extra CPU cycles and memory to acquire and hold many locks. For many queries, a coarser locking granularity provides better performance with no (or minimal) loss of concurrency. Database systems have traditionally required query hints and table options for applications to specify locking granularity. In addition, there are configuration parameters (often static) for how much memory to dedicate to the lock manager.

In SQL Server, locking granularity is optimized automatically for optimal performance and concurrency for each index used in a query. In addition, the memory dedicated to the lock manager is adjusted dynamically on the basis of feedback from other parts of the system, including other applications on the machine.

Lock granularity is optimized before query execution for each table and index used in the query. The lock optimization process takes into account isolation level (that is, how long locks are held), scan type (range, probe, or entire table), estimated number of rows to be scanned, selectivity (percentage of visited rows that qualify for the query), row density (number of rows per page), operation type (scan, update), user limits on the granularity, and available system memory.

Once a query is executing, the lock granularity is **escalated** automatically to table level if the system acquires significantly more locks than the optimizer expected or if the amount of available memory drops and cannot support the number of locks required.

30.5.2.2 Deadlock Detection

SQL Server automatically detects deadlocks involving both locks and other resources. For example, if transaction *A* is holding a lock on Table1 and is waiting for memory to become available and transaction *B* has some memory it can't release until it acquires a lock on Table1, the transactions will deadlock. Threads and communication buffers can also be involved in deadlocks. When SQL Server detects a deadlock, it chooses as the deadlock victim the transaction that would be the least expensive to roll back, considering the amount of work the transaction has already done.

Frequent deadlock detection can hurt system performance. SQL Server automatically adjusts the frequency of deadlock detection to how often deadlocks are occurring. If deadlocks are infrequent, the detection algorithm runs every 5 seconds. If they are frequent it will begin checking every time a transaction waits for a lock.

30.5.2.3   Row Versioning for Snapshot Isolation

The two snapshot-based isolation levels use row versioning to achieve isolation for queries while not blocking the queries behind updates and vice versa. Under snapshot isolation, update and delete operations generate versions of the affected rows and store them in a temporary database. The versions are garbage-collected when there are no active transactions that could require them. Therefore, a query run under snapshot isolation does not need to acquire locks and instead can read the older versions of any record that gets updated/deleted by another transaction. Row versioning is also used to provide a snapshot of a table for online index build operations.

30.5.3   Recovery and Availability

SQL Server is designed to recover from system and media failures, and the recovery system can scale to machines with very large buffer pools (100 gigabytes) and thousands of disk drives.

30.5.3.1   Crash Recovery

Logically, the log is a potentially infinite stream of log records identified by log sequence numbers (LSNs). Physically, a portion of the stream is stored in log files. Log records are saved in the log files until they have been backed up and are no longer needed by the system for rollback or replication. Log files grow and shrink in size to accommodate the records that need to be stored. Additional log files can be added to a database (on new disks, for example) while the system is running and without blocking any current operations, and all logs are treated as if they were one continuous file.

SQL Server's recovery system has many aspects in common with the ARIES recovery algorithm (see Section 16.8), and some of the key differences are highlighted in this section.

SQL Server has a configuration option called **recovery interval**, which allows an administrator to limit the length of time SQL Server should take to recover after a crash. The server dynamically adjusts the checkpoint frequency to reduce recovery time to within the recovery interval. Checkpoints flush all dirty pages from the buffer pool and adjust to the capabilities of the I/O system and its current workload to effectively eliminate any impact on running transactions.

Upon start-up after a crash, the system starts multiple threads (automatically scaled to the number of CPUs) to start recovering multiple databases in parallel.

The first phase of recovery is an analysis pass on the log, which builds a dirty page table and active transaction list. The next phase is a redo pass starting from the last checkpoint and redoing all operations. During the redo phase, the dirty page table is used to drive read-ahead of data pages. The final phase is an undo phase where incomplete transactions are rolled back. The undo phase is actually divided into two parts as SQL Server uses a two-level recovery scheme. Transactions at the first level (those involving internal operations such as space allocation and page splits) are rolled back first, followed by user transactions. Once the transactions at the first level are rolled back, the database is brought online and is available for new user transactions to start while the final rollback operations are performed. This is achieved by having the redo pass reacquire locks for all incomplete user transactions that will be rolled back in the undo phase.

30.5.3.2   Media Recovery

SQL Server's backup and restore capabilities allow recovery from many failures, including loss or corruption of disk media, user errors, and permanent loss of a server. Additionally, backing up and restoring databases is useful for other purposes, such as copying a database from one server to another and maintaining standby systems.

SQL Server has three different recovery models that users can choose from for each database. By specifying a recovery model, an administrator declares the type of recovery capabilities required (such as point-in-time restore and log shipping) and the required backups to achieve them. Backups can be taken on databases, files, file-groups, and the transaction log. All backups are fuzzy and completely online; that is, they do not block any DML or DDL operations while they execute. Restores can also be done online such that only the portion of the database being restored (e.g., a corrupt disk block) is taken offline. Backup and restore operations are highly optimized and limited only by the speed of the media onto which the backup is targeted. SQL Server can back up to both disk and tape devices (up to 64 in parallel) and has high-performance backup APIs for use by third-party backup products.

30.5.3.3   Database Mirroring

Database mirroring involves immediately reproducing every update to a database (the principal database) onto a separate, complete copy of the database (the mirror database) generally located on another machine. In the event of a disaster on the primary server or even just maintenance, the system can automatically failover to the mirror in a matter of seconds. The communication library used by applications is aware of the mirroring and will automatically reconnect to the mirror machine in the event of a failover. A tight coupling between the primary database and the mirror is achieved by sending blocks of transaction log to the mirror as it is generated on the primary and redoing the log records on the mirror. In full-safety mode, a transaction cannot commit until the log records for the transaction have made it to disk on the mirror. Besides supporting failover, a mirror can also be used to automatically restore a page by copying it from the mirror in the event that the page is found to be corrupt during an attempt to read it.

30.6   System Architecture

An SQL Server instance is a single operating-system process that is also a named endpoint for requests for SQL execution. Applications interact with SQL Server via various client-side libraries (like ODBC, OLE-DB, and ADO.NET) in order to execute SQL.

30.6.1   Thread Pooling on the Server

In order to minimize the context switching on the server and to control the degree of multiprogramming, the SQL Server process maintains a pool of threads that execute client requests. As requests arrive from the client, they are assigned a thread on which to execute. The thread executes the SQL statements issued by the client and sends the results back to it. Once the user request completes, the thread is returned back to the thread pool. In addition to user requests, the thread pool is used to assign threads for internal background tasks such as:

- **Lazywriter:** This thread is dedicated to making sure a certain amount of the buffer pool is free and available at all times for allocation by the system. The thread also interacts with the operating system to determine the optimal amount of memory that should be consumed by the SQL Server process.

- **Checkpoint:** This thread periodically checkpoints all databases in order to maintain a fast recovery interval for the databases on server restart.

- **Deadlock monitor:** This thread monitors the other threads, looking for a deadlock in the system. It is responsible for the detection of deadlocks and also picking a victim in order to allow the system to make progress.

When the query processor chooses a parallel plan to execute a particular query, it can allocate multiple threads that work on behalf of the main thread to execute the query. Since the Windows NT family of operating systems provides native thread support, SQL Server uses NT threads for its execution. However, SQL Server can be configured to run with user-mode threads in addition to kernel threads in very high-end systems to avoid the cost of a kernel context switch on a thread switch.

30.6.2   Memory Management

There are many different uses of memory within the SQL Server process:

- **Buffer pool.** The biggest consumer of memory in the system is the buffer pool. The buffer pool maintains a cache of the most recently used database pages. It uses a clock replacement algorithm with a steal, no-force policy; that is, buffer pages with uncommitted updates may be replaced ("stolen"), and buffer pages are not forced to disk on transaction commit. The buffers also obey the write-ahead logging protocol to ensure correctness of crash and media recovery.

- **Dynamic memory allocation.** This is the memory that is allocated dynamically to execute requests submitted by the user.

- **Plan and execution cache.** This cache stores the compiled plans for various queries that have been previously executed by users in the system. This allows various users to share the same plan (saving memory) and also saves on query compilation time for similar queries.

- **Large memory grants.** These are for query operators that consume large amounts of memory, such as hash join and sort.

SQL Server uses an elaborate scheme of memory management to divide its memory among the various uses described above. A single memory manager centrally manages all the memory used by SQL Server. The memory manager is responsible for dynamically partitioning and redistributing the memory between the various consumers of memory in the system. It distributes this memory in accordance with an analysis of the relative cost benefit of memory for any particular use. A generalized LRU infrastructure mechanism is available to all components. This caching infrastructure tracks not only the lifetime of cached data but also the relative CPU and I/O costs incurred to create and cache it. This information is used to determine the relative costs of various cached data. The memory manager focuses on throwing out the cached data that have not been touched recently and were cheap to cache. As an example, complex query plans that require seconds of CPU time to compile are more likely to stay in memory than trivial plans, given equivalent access frequencies.

The memory manager interacts with the operating system to decide dynamically how much memory it should consume out of the total amount of memory in the system. This allows SQL Server to be quite aggressive in using the memory on the system but still return memory back to the system when other programs need it without causing excessive page faults.

In addition the memory manager is aware of the CPU and memory topology of the system. Specifically, it leverages the NUMA (nonuniform memory access) that many machines employ and attempts to maintain locality between the processor that a thread is executing on and the memory it accesses.

30.6.3 Security

SQL Server provides comprehensive security mechanisms and policies for authentication, authorization, audit, and encryption. Authentication can be either through a username–password pair managed by SQL Server, or through a Windows OS account. Authorization is managed by permission grants to schema objects or covering permissions on container objects such as the database or server instance. At authorization-check time, permissions are rolled up and calculated, accounting for covering permissions and role memberships of the principal. Audits are defined in the same way as permissions — they are defined on schema objects for a given principal or containing objects and at the time of the operation they are dynamically calculated based on audit definitions on the object and accounting for any covering audits or role memberships of the principal. Multiple audits may be defined so that audits for different purposes, such as for Sarbanes-Oxley and HIPAA,[1] may be managed independently without risk of breaking each other. Audits records are written either in a file or to the Windows Security Log.

SQL Server provides both manual encryption of data and Transparent Data Encryption. Transparent Data Encryption encrypts all data pages and log pages when written to disk and decrypts when read from the disk so that the data are encrypted at rest on the disk but is plaintext to SQL Server users without application modification. Transparent Data Encryption can be more CPU efficient than manual encryption as data is only encrypted when written to disk and it is done in larger units, pages, rather than individual cells of data.

Two things are even more critical to users' security: (1) the quality of the entire code base itself and (2) the ability for users to determine if they have secured the system properly. The quality of the code base is enhanced by using the Security Development Lifecycle. All developers and testers of the product go through security training. All features are threat modeled to assure assets are appropriately protected. Wherever possible, SQL Server utilizes the underlying security features of the operating system rather than implementing its own, such as Windows OS Authorization and the Windows Security Log for an audit record. Furthermore, numerous internal tools are utilized to analyze the code base looking for potential security flaws. Security is verified using fuzz testing[2] and testing of the threat model. Before release, there is a final security review of the product and a response plan is in place for dealing with security issues found after release — which is then executed as issues are discovered.

A number of features are provided to help users secure the system properly. One such feature is a fundamental policy called off-by-default, where many less commonly used components or those requiring extra care for security, are completely disabled by default. Another feature is a best-practices analyzer that warns users about configurations of system settings that could lead to a security vulnerability. Policy-based management further allows users to define what the settings should be and either warns of or prevents changes that would conflict with the approved settings.

30.7   Data Access

SQL Server supports the following application programming interfaces (APIs) for building data-intensive applications:

---

[1]The Sarbanes-Oxley Act is a U.S. government financial regulation law. HIPAA is a U.S. government health-care law that includes regulation of health-care-related information.
[2]Fuzz testing A randomization-based technique for testing for unexpected, possibly invalid, input.

- **ODBC.** This is Microsoft's implementation of the standard SQL:1999 call-level interface (CLI). It includes object models—Remote Data Objects (RDOs) and Data Access Objects (DAOs)—that make it easier to program multitier database applications from programming languages like Visual Basic.

- **OLE-DB.** This is a low-level, systems-oriented API designed for programmers building database components. The interface is architected according to the Microsoft Component Object Model (COM), and it enables the encapsulation of low-level database services such as rowset providers, ISAM providers, and query engines. OLE-DB is used inside SQL Server to integrate the relational query processor and the storage engine and to enable replication and distributed access to SQL and other external data sources. Like ODBC, OLE-DB includes a higher-level object model called ActiveX Data Objects (ADO) to make it easier to program database applications from Visual Basic.

- **ADO.NET.** This is an API designed for applications written in .NET languages such as C# and Visual Basic.NET. This interface simplifies some common data access patterns supported by ODBC and OLE-DB. In addition, it provides a new *data set* model to enable stateless, disconnected data access applications. ADO.NET includes the ADO.NET **Entity Framework**, which is a platform for programming against data that raises the level of abstraction from the logical (relational) level to the conceptual (entity) level, and thereby significantly reduces the impedance mismatch for applications and data services such as reporting, analysis, and replication. The conceptual data model is implemented using an extended relational model, the **Entity Data Model** (EDM) that embraces entities and relationships as first-class concepts. It includes a query language for the EDM called **Entity SQL**, a comprehensive mapping engine that translates from the conceptual to the logical (relational) level, and a set of model-driven tools that help developers define mappings between objects and entities to tables.

- **LINQ. Language-integrated query**, or **LINQ** for short, allows declarative, set-oriented constructs to be used directly in programming languages such as C# and Visual Basic. The query expressions are not processed by an external tool or language preprocessor but instead are first-class expressions of the languages themselves. LINQ allows query expressions to benefit from the rich metadata, compile-time syntax checking, static typing and auto-completion that was previously available only to imperative code. LINQ defines a set of general-purpose standard query operators that allow traversal, filter, join, projection, sorting, and grouping operations to be expressed in a direct yet declarative way in any .NET-based programming language. C# and Visual Basic also support query comprehensions, i.e., language syntax extensions that leverage the standard query operators.

- **DB-Lib**. The DB-Library for C API that was developed specifically to be used with earlier versions of SQL Server that predate the SQL-92 standard.

- **HTTP/SOAP.** Applications can use HTTP/SOAP requests to invoke SQL Server queries and procedures. Applications can use URLs that specify Internet Information Server (IIS) virtual roots that reference an instance of SQL Server. The URL can contain an XPath query, a Transact-SQL statement, or an XML template.

30.8   Distributed Heterogeneous Query Processing

SQL Server distributed heterogeneous query capability allows transactional queries and updates against a variety of relational and nonrelational sources via OLE-DB data providers running in one or more computers. SQL Server supports two methods for referencing heterogeneous OLE-DB data sources in Transact-SQL statements. The linked-server-names method uses system-stored procedures to associate a server name with an OLE-DB data source. Objects in these linked servers can be referenced in Transact-SQL statements using the four-part name convention described below. For example, if a linked server name of *DeptSQLSrvr* is defined against another copy of SQL Server, the following statement references a table on that server:

> **select** *
> **from** *DeptSQLSrvr.Northwind.dbo.Employees;*

An OLE-DB data source is registered in SQL Server as a linked server. Once a linked server is defined, its data can be accessed using the four-part name:

> <linked- server>.<catalog>.<schema>.<object>

The following example establishes a linked server to an Oracle server via an OLE-DB provider for Oracle:

> **exec** sp_addlinkedserver OraSvr, 'Oracle 7.3', 'MSDAORA', 'OracleServer'

A query against this linked server is expressed as:

> **select** *
> **from** *OraSvr.CORP.ADMIN.SALES;*

In addition, SQL Server supports built-in, parameterized table-valued functions called **openrowset** and **openquery**, which allow sending uninterpreted queries to a provider or linked server, respectively, in the dialect supported by the provider. The following query combines information stored in an Oracle server and a Microsoft Index Server. It lists all documents and their author containing the words Data and Access ordered by the author's department and name.

select *e.dept, f.DocAuthor, f.FileName*
from *OraSvr.Corp.Admin.Employee e,*
openquery(EmpFiles,
      'select DocAuthor, FileName
      from scope("c:\EmpDocs")
      where contains(' ' "Data" near() "Access" ' ')>0') **as** *f*
where *e.name = f.DocAuthor*
order by *e.dept, f.DocAuthor;*

The relational engine uses the OLE-DB interfaces to open the rowsets on linked servers, to fetch the rows, and to manage transactions. For each OLE-DB data source accessed as a linked server, an OLE-DB provider must be present on the server running SQL Server. The set of Transact-SQL operations that can be used against a specific OLE-DB data source depends on the capabilities of the OLE-DB provider. Whenever it is cost-effective, SQL Server pushes relational operations such as joins, restrictions, projections, sorts, and group by operations to the OLE-DB data source. SQL Server uses Microsoft Distributed Transaction Coordinator and the OLE-DB transaction interfaces of the provider to ensure atomicity of transactions spanning multiple data sources.

30.9   Replication

SQL Server replication is a set of technologies for copying and distributing data and database objects from one database to another, tracking changes, and synchronizing between databases to maintain consistency. SQL Server replication also provides inline replication of most database schema changes without requiring any interruptions or reconfiguration.

Data are typically replicated to increase availability of data. Replication can roll up corporate data from geographically dispersed sites for reporting purposes and disseminate data to remote users on a local-area network or mobile users on dial-up connections or the Internet. Microsoft SQL Server replication also enhances application performance by scaling out for improved total read performance among replicas, as is common in providing midtier data-caching services for Web sites.

30.9.1   Replication Model

SQL Server introduced the **Publish–Subscribe** metaphor to database replication and extends this publishing-industry metaphor throughout its replication administration and monitoring tools.

The **publisher** is a server that makes data available for replication to other servers. The publisher can have one or more publications, each representing a logically related set of data and database objects. The discrete objects within a publication, including tables, stored procedures, user-defined functions, views, materialized views, and more, are called **articles**. The addition of an article to a publication allows for extensive customizing of the way the object is replicated, e.g., restrictions on which users can subscribe to receive its data and how the data set should be filtered on the basis of a projection or selection of a table, by a "horizontal" or a "vertical" filter, respectively.

Subscribers are servers that receive replicated data from a publisher. Subscribers can conveniently subscribe to only the publications they require from one or more publishers regardless of the number or type of replication options each implements. Depending on the type of replication options selected, the subscriber either can be used as a read-only replica or can make data changes that are automatically propagated back to the publisher and subsequently to all other replicas. Subscribers can also republish the data they subscribe to, supporting as flexible a replication topology as the enterprise requires.

The **distributor** is a server that plays different roles, depending on the replication options chosen. At a minimum it is used as a repository for history and error state information. In other cases, it is used additionally as an intermediate store-and-forward queue to scale up the delivery of the replicated payload to all the subscribers.

30.9.2 Replication Options

Microsoft SQL Server replication offers a wide spectrum of replication options. To decide on the appropriate replication options to use, a database designer must determine the application's needs with respect to autonomous operation of the sites involved and the degree of transactional consistency required.

Snapshot replication copies and distributes data and database objects exactly as they appear at a moment in time. Snapshot replication does not require continuous change tracking because changes are not propagated incrementally to subscribers. Subscribers are updated with a complete refresh of the data set defined by the publication on a periodic basis. Options available with snapshot replication can filter published data and can enable subscribers to modify replicated data and propagate those changes back to the publisher. This type of replication is best suited for smaller sizes of data and when updates typically affect enough of the data that replicating a complete refresh of the data is efficient.

With **transactional replication**, the publisher propagates an initial snapshot of data to subscribers, then forwards incremental data modifications to subscribers as discrete transactions and commands. Incremental change tracking occurs inside the core engine of SQL Server, which marks transactions affecting replicated objects in the publishing database's transaction log. A replication process called the **log reader agent** reads these transactions from the database transaction log, applies an optional filter, and stores them in the distribution database, which acts as the reliable queue supporting the store-and-forward mechanism of transactional replication. (Reliable queues are the same as durable queues, described in Section 26.1.1.) Another replication process, called the **distribution agent**, then forwards the changes to each subscriber. Like snapshot replication, transactional replication offers subscribers the option to make updates that either use two-phase commit to reflect those changes consistently at the publisher and subscriber or queue the changes at the subscriber for asynchronous retrieval by a replication process that later propagates the change to the publisher. This type of replication is suitable when intermediate states between multiple updates need to be preserved.

Merge replication allows each replica in the enterprise to work with total autonomy whether online or offline. The system tracks metadata on the changes to published objects at publishers and subscribers in each replicated database, and the replication agent merges those data modifications together during synchronization between replicated pairs and ensures data convergence through automatic conflict detection and resolution. Numerous conflict resolution policy options are built into the replication agent used in the synchronization process, and custom conflict resolution can be written by using stored procedures or by using an extensible **component object model** (COM) interface. This type of replication does not replicate all intermediate states but only the current state of the data at the time of synchronization. It is suitable when replicas require the ability to make autonomous updates while not connected to any network.

30.10 Server Programming in .NET

SQL Server supports the hosting of the .NET Common Language Runtime (CLR) inside the SQL Server process to enable database programmers to write business logic as functions, stored procedures, triggers, data types, and aggregates. The ability to run application code inside the database adds flexibility to the design of application architectures that require business logic to execute close to the data and cannot afford the cost of shipping data to a middle-tier process to perform computation outside the database.

The .NET Common Language Runtime (CLR) is a runtime environment with a strongly typed intermediate language that executes multiple modern programming languages such as C#, Visual Basic, C++, COBOL, and J++, among others, and has garbage-collected memory, preemptive threading, metadata services (type reflection), code verifiability, and code access security. The runtime uses metadata to locate and load classes, lay out instances in memory, resolve method invocations, generate native code, enforce security, and set runtime context boundaries.

Application code is deployed inside the database by using **assemblies**, which are the units of packaging, deployment, and versioning of application code in .NET. Deployment of application code inside the database provides a uniform way to administer, back up, and restore complete database applications (code and data). Once an assembly is registered inside the database, users can expose entry points within the assembly via SQL DDL statements, which can act as scalar or table functions, procedures, triggers, types, and aggregates, by using well-defined extensibility contracts enforced during the execution of these DDL statements. Stored procedures, triggers, and functions usually need to execute SQL queries and updates. This is achieved through a component that implements the ADO.NET data-access API for use inside the database process.

30.10.1 Basic .NET Concepts

In the .NET framework, a programmer writes program code in a high-level programming language that implements a class defining its structure (e.g., the fields or properties of the class) and methods. Some of these methods can be static functions. The compilation of the program produces a file, called an *assembly*, containing the compiled code in the **Microsoft Intermediate Language** (MSIL), and a *manifest* containing all references to dependent assemblies. The manifest is an integral part of every assembly that renders the assembly self-describing. The assembly manifest contains the assembly's metadata, which describes all structures, fields, properties, classes, inheritance relationships, functions, and methods defined in the program. The manifest establishes the assembly identity, specifies the files that make up the assembly implementation, specifies the types and resources that make up the assembly, itemizes the compile-time dependencies on other assemblies, and specifies the set of permissions required for the assembly to run properly. This information is used at runtime to resolve references, enforce version-binding policy, and validate the integrity of loaded assemblies. The .NET framework supports an out-of-band mechanism called *custom attributes* for annotating classes, properties, functions and methods with additional information or facets the application may want to capture in metadata. All .NET compilers consume these annotations without interpretation and store them in the assembly's metadata. All these annotations can be examined in the same way as any other metadata by using a common set of reflection APIs. **Managed code** refers to MSIL executed in the CLR rather than directly by the operating system. Managed-code applications gain common-language runtime services such as automatic garbage collection, runtime type checking, and security support. These services help provide uniform platform- and language-independent behavior of managed-code applications. At execution time, a **just-in-time** (JIT) compiler translates the MSIL into native code (e.g., Intel X86 code). During this translation, code must pass a verification process that examines the MSIL and metadata to find out whether the code can be determined to be type safe.

30.10.2 SQL CLR Hosting

SQL Server and the CLR are two different runtimes with different internal models for threading, scheduling and memory management. SQL Server supports a cooperative non-preemptive threading model in which the DBMS threads voluntarily yield execution periodically or when they are waiting on locks or I/O, whereas the CLR supports a preemptive threading model. If user code running inside the DBMS can directly call the operating-system (OS) threading primitives, then it does not integrate well with the SQL Server task scheduler and can degrade the scalability of the system. CLR does not distinguish between virtual and physical memory, while SQL Server directly manages physical memory and is required to use physical memory within a configurable limit.

The different models for threading, scheduling, and memory management present an integration challenge for a DBMS that scales to support thousands of concurrent user sessions. SQL Server solves this challenge by becoming the

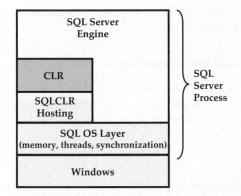

Figure 30.5 Integration of CLR with SQL Server operating-system services.

operating system for the CLR when it is hosted inside the SQL Server process. The CLR calls low-level primitives implemented by SQL Server for threading, scheduling, synchronization, and memory management (see Figure 30.5). This approach provides the following scalability and reliability benefits:

Common threading, scheduling, and synchronization. CLR calls SQL Server APIs for creating threads both for running user code and for its own internal use such as the garbage collector and the class finalizer thread. In order to synchronize between multiple threads, the CLR calls SQL Server synchronization objects. This allows SQL Server scheduler to schedule other tasks when a thread is waiting on a synchronization object. For instance, when the CLR initiates garbage collection, all of its threads wait for garbage collection to finish. Since the CLR threads and the synchronization objects they are waiting on are known to the SQL Server scheduler, it can schedule threads that are running other database tasks not involving the CLR. Further, this enables SQL Server to detect deadlocks that involve locks taken by CLR synchronization objects and employ traditional techniques for deadlock removal. The SQL Server scheduler has the ability to detect and stop threads that have not yielded for a significant amount of time. The ability to hook CLR threads to SQL Server threads implies that the SQL Server scheduler can identify runaway threads running in the CLR and manage their priority, so that they do not consume significant CPU resources, thereby affecting the throughput of the system. Such runaway threads are suspended and put back in the queue. Repeat offenders are not allowed timeslices that are unfair to other executing workers. If an offender took 50 times the allowed quantum, it is punished for 50 "rounds" before being allowed to run again because the scheduler cannot tell when a computation is long and runaway versus long and legitimate.

Common memory management. The CLR calls SQL Server primitives for allocating and deallocating its memory. Since the memory used by the CLR is accounted for in the total memory usage of the system, SQL Server can stay within its configured memory limits and ensure the CLR and SQL Server are not competing with each other for memory. Also, SQL Server can reject CLR memory requests when the system is constrained and ask CLR to reduce its memory use when other tasks need memory.

30.10.3 Extensibility Contracts

All user-managed code running within the SQL Server process interacts with DBMS components as an extension. Current extensions include scalar functions, table functions, procedures, triggers, scalar types, and scalar aggregates. For each extension there is a mutual contract defining the properties or services user code must implement to act as one of these extensions as well as the services the extension can expect from the DBMS when the managed code is called. SQL CLR leverages the class and custom attributes information stored in assembly metadata to enforce that user code implements these extensibility contracts. All user assemblies are stored inside the database. All relational and assembly metadata are processed inside the SQL engine through a uniform set of interfaces and data structures. When data-definition language (DDL) statements registering a particular extension function, type, or aggregate are processed, the system ensures the user code implements the appropriate contract by analyzing its assembly metadata. If the contract is implemented, then the DDL statement succeeds, otherwise it fails. The next subsections describe key aspects of the specific contracts currently enforced by SQL Server.

30.10.3.1   Routines

We classify scalar functions, procedures, and triggers generically as routines. Routines, implemented as static class methods, can specify the following properties through custom attributes.

- **IsPrecise.** If this Boolean property is **false**, then it indicates the routine body involves imprecise computations such as floating-point operations. Expressions involving imprecise functions cannot be indexed.

- **UserDataAccess.** If the value of this property is **read**, then the routine reads user-data tables. Otherwise, the value of the property is *None* indicating the routine does not access data. Queries that do not access any user tables (directly or indirectly through views and functions) are not considered to have user-data access.

- **SystemDataAccess.** If the value of this property is **read**, then the routine reads system catalogs or virtual system tables.

- **IsDeterministic.** If this property is **true**, then the routine is assumed to produce the same output value given the same input values, state of the local database, and execution context.

- **IsSystemVerified.** This indicates whether the determinism and precision properties can be ascertained or enforced by SQL Server (e.g., built-ins, Transact-SQL functions) or it is as specified by the user (e.g., CLR functions).

- **HasExternalAccess.** If the value of this property is true, then the routine accesses resources outside SQL Server such as files, network, Web access, and registry.

30.10.3.2 Table Functions

A class implementing a table-valued function must implement an interface IEnumerable to enable iteration over the rows returned by the function, a method to describe the schema of the table returned (i.e., columns, types), a method to describe what columns can be unique keys, and a method to insert rows into the table.

30.10.3.3 Types

Classes implementing user-defined types are annotated with an SqlUserDefinedType() attribute that specifies the following properties:

- **Format.** SQL Server supports three storage formats: native, user-defined, and .NET serialization.

- **MaxByteSize.** This is the maximum size of the serialized binary representation of type instances in bytes. UDTs can be up to 2 GB in length.

- **IsFixedLength.** This is a Boolean property specifying whether the instances of the type have fixed or variable length.

- **IsByteOrdered.** This is a Boolean property indicating whether the serialized binary representation of the type instances is binary ordered. When this property is true, the system can perform comparisons directly against this representation without the need to instantiate type instances as objects.

- **Nullability.** All UDTs in our system must be capable of holding the *null* value by supporting the INullable interface containing the Boolean IsNull method.

- **Type conversions.** All UDTs must implement conversions to and from character strings via the ToString and Parse methods.

30.10.3.4 Aggregates

In addition to supporting the contract for types, user-defined aggregates must implement four methods required by the query-execution engine to initialize the computation of an aggregate instance, to accumulate input values into the function provided by the aggregate, to merge partial computations of the aggregate, and to retrieve the final aggregate result. Aggregates can declare additional properties, via custom attributes, in their class definition; these properties are used by the query optimizer to derive alternative plans for the aggregate computation.

- **IsInvariantToDuplicates.** If this property is true, then the computation delivering the data to the aggregate can be modified by either discarding or introducing new duplication-removal operations.

- **IsInvariantToNulls.** If this property is true, then null rows can be discarded from the input. However, care must be taken in the context of **group by** operations not to discard entire groups.

- **IsInvariantToOrder.** If this property is true, then the query processor can ignore **order by** clauses and explore plans that avoid having to sort the data.

30.11   XML Support

Relational database systems have embraced XML in many different ways in recent years. First-generation XML support in relational database systems was mainly concerned with exporting relational data as XML ("publish XML"), and to import relational data in XML markup form back into a relational representation ("shred XML"). The main usage scenario supported by these systems is information exchange in contexts where XML is used as the "wire format" and where the relational and XML schemas are often predefined independently of each other. In order to cover this scenario, Microsoft SQL Server provides extensive functionality such as the **for xml** publishing rowset aggregator, the OpenXML rowset provider, and the XML view technology based on annotated schemas.

Shredding of XML data into a relational schema can be quite difficult or inefficient for storing semistructured data whose structure may vary over time, and for storing documents. To support such applications SQL Server implements native XML based on the SQL:2003 **xml** data type. Figure 30.6 provides a high-

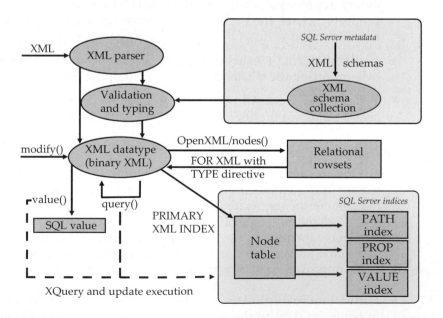

Figure 30.6 Architectural overview of the native XML support in SQL Server.

level architectural diagram of SQL Server's native XML support in the database. It consists of the ability to store XML natively, to constrain and type the stored XML data with collections of XML schemas, and to query and update the XML data. In order to provide efficient query executions, several types of XML-specific indices are provided. Finally, the native XML support also integrates with the "shredding" and "publishing" to and from relational data.

30.11.1 Natively Storing and Organizing XML

The **xml** data type can store XML documents and content fragments (multiple text or element nodes at the top) and is defined on the basis of the XQuery 1.0/XPath 2.0 data model. The data type can be used for parameters of stored procedures, for variables, and as a column type.

SQL Server stores data of type **xml** in an internal binary format as a **blob** and provides indexing mechanisms for executing queries. The internal binary format provides efficient retrieval and reconstruction of the original XML document, in addition to some space savings (on average, 20 percent). The indices support an efficient query mechanism that can utilize the relational query engine and optimizer; more details are provided later, in Section 30.11.3.

SQL Server provides a database-metadata concept called an **XML schema collection** that associates an SQL identifier with a collection of schema components of one or multiple target namespaces.

30.11.2 Querying and Updating the XML Data Type

SQL Server provides several XQuery-based query and modification capabilities on the XML data type. These query and modification capabilities are supported by using methods defined on the **xml** data type. Some of these methods are described in the rest of this section.

Each method takes a string literal as the query string and potentially other arguments. The XML data type (on which the method is applied) provides the context item for the path expressions and populates the in-scope schema definitions with all the type information provided by the associated XML schema collection (if no collection is provided, the XML data is assumed to be untyped). The SQL Server XQuery implementation is statically typed, thereby supporting early detection of path expression typing mistakes, type errors, and cardinality mismatch, as well as some additional optimizations.

The *query* method takes an XQuery expression and returns an untyped XML data type instance (that can then be cast to a target schema collection if the data need to be typed). In XQuery specification terminology, we have set the construction mode to "strip." The following example shows a simple XQuery expression that summarizes a complex Customer element in a trip report document that contains among other information a name, anIDattribute, and sales-lead information that are contained in the marked-up actual trip report notes. The summary shows the name and sales leads for Customer elements that have sales leads.

```
            select Report.query('
                    declare namespace c = "urn:example/customer";
                        for $cust in /c:doc/c:customer
                        where $cust/c:notes//c:saleslead
                        return
                            <customer_id="$cust/@id"> {
                                $cust/c:name,
                                $cust/c:notes//c:saleslead
                            }</customer>')
            from TripReports;
```

The above XQuery query gets executed on the XML value stored in the *doc* attribute of each row of the table *TripReports*. Each row in the result of the SQL query contains the result of executing the XQuery query on the data in one input row.

The *value* method takes an XQuery expression and an SQL type name, extracts a single atomic value from the result of the XQuery expression, and casts its lexical form into the specified SQL type. If the XQuery expression results in a node, the typed value of the node will implicitly be extracted as the atomic value to be cast into the SQL type (in XQuery terminology the node will be "atomized"; the result is cast to SQL). Note that the *value* method performs a static type check that at most one value is being returned.

The *exist* method takes an XQuery expression and returns 1 if the expression produces a nonempty result and 0 otherwise.

Finally, the *modify* method provides a mechanism to change an XML value at the subtree level, inserting new subtrees at specific locations inside a tree, changing the value of an element or attribute, and deleting subtrees. The following example deletes all customer `saleslead` elements of years previous to the year given by an SQL variable or parameter with the name `@year`:

```
    update TripReports
    set Report.modify(
        'declare namespace c = "urn:example/customer";
        delete /c:doc/c:customer//c:saleslead[@year < sql:variable("@year")]');
```

30.11.3 Execution of XQuery Expressions

As mentioned earlier, the XML data are stored in an internal binary representation. However, in order to execute the XQuery expressions, the XML data type is internally transformed into a so-called node table. The internal node table basically uses a row to represent a node. Each node receives an OrdPath identifier as its nodeID (an OrdPath identifier is a modified Dewey decimal numbering scheme; see the bibliographical notes for references to more information on OrdPath). Each node also contains key information to point back to the original SQL row to which the node belongs, information about the name and type (in a tokenized form), values, and more. Since the OrdPath encodes both the document order and the hierarchy information, the node table then is clustered on the basis of the key information and OrdPath, so that a path expression or recomposition of a subtree can be achieved with a simple table scan.

All XQuery and update expressions are then translated into an algebraic operator tree against this internal node table; the tree uses the common relational operators and some operators specifically designed for the XQuery algebraization. The resulting tree is then grafted into the algebra tree of the relational expression so that in the end, the query-execution engine receives a single execution tree that it can optimize and execute. In order to avoid costly runtime transformations, a user can prematerialize the node table by using the primary XML index. SQL Server in addition provides three secondary XML indices so that the query execution can take further advantage of index structures:

- The *path* index provides support for simple types of path expressions.

- The *properties* index provides support for the common scenario of property-value comparisons.

- The *value* index is well suited if the query uses wild-cards in comparisons.

See the bibliographical notes for references to more information on XML indexing and query processing in SQL Server.

30.12 SQL Server Service Broker

Service Broker helps developers create loosely coupled distributed applications by providing support for queued, reliable messaging in SQL Server. Many database applications use asynchronous processing to improve scalability and response times for interactive sessions. One common approach to asynchronous processing is to use work tables. Instead of performing all of the work for a business process in a single database transaction, an application makes a change indicating that outstanding work is present and then inserts a record of the work to be performed into a work table. As resources permit, the application processes the work table and completes the business process. Service Broker is a part of the database server that directly supports this approach for application development. The Transact-SQL language includes DDL and DML statements for Service Broker. In addition, SQL Server Management Objects (SMO) for Service Broker are provided in SQL Server. These allow programmatic access to Service Broker objects from managed code.

Previous message-queuing technologies concentrated on individual messages. With Service Broker, the basic unit of communication is the **conversation** — a persistent, reliable, full-duplex stream of messages. SQL Server guarantees that the messages within a conversation are delivered to an application exactly once, in order. It is also possible to assign a priority from 1 to 10 to a conversation. Messages from conversations with higher priority are sent and received faster than messages from conversations with a lower priority. Conversations occur between two services. A *service* is a named endpoint for a conversation. Each conversation is part of a *conversation group*. Related conversations can be associated with the same conversation group.

Messages are strongly typed, i.e., each message has a specific type. SQL Server can optionally validate that messages are well-formed XML, that messages are empty, or that messages conform to an XML schema. A *contract* defines the message types that are allowable for a conversation, and which participant in the conversation may send messages of that type. SQL Server provides a default contract and message type for applications that only need a reliable stream.

SQL Server stores messages in internal tables. These tables are not directly accessible; instead, SQL Server exposes *queues* as views of those internal tables. Applications receive messages from a queue. A receive operation returns one or more messages from the same conversation group. By controlling access to the underlying table, SQL Server can efficiently enforce message ordering, correlation of related messages, and locking. Because queues are internal tables, queues require no special treatment for backup, restore, failover, or database mirroring. Both application tables and the associated, queued messages are backed up, restored, and failed-over with the database. Broker conversations that exist in mirrored databases continue where they left off when the mirrored failover is complete — even if the conversation was between two services that live in separate databases.

The locking granularity for Service Broker operations is the conversation group rather than a specific conversation or individual messages. By enforcing locking on the conversation group, Service Broker automatically helps applications avoid concurrency issues while processing messages. When a queue contains multiple conversations, SQL Server guarantees that only one queue reader at a time can process messages that belong to a given conversation group. This eliminates the need for the application itself to include deadlock-avoidance logic — a common source of errors in many messaging applications. Another nice side effect of this locking semantic is that applications may choose to use the conversation group as a key for storing and retrieving application state. These programming-model benefits are just two examples of the advantages that derive from the decision to formalize the conversation as the communication primitive versus the atomic message primitive found in traditional message-queuing systems.

SQL Server can automatically activate stored procedures when a queue contains messages to be processed. To scale the number of running stored procedures to the incoming traffic, the activation logic monitors the queue to see if there is useful work for another queue reader. SQL Server considers both the rate at which existing readers receive messages and the number of conversation groups available to decide when to start another queue reader. The stored procedure to be activated, the security context of the stored procedure, and the maximum number of instances to be started are configured for an individual queue. SQL Server also provides an External Activator. This feature allows an application outside of SQL Server to be activated when new messages are inserted into a queue. The application can then receive and process the messages. By doing this, CPU-intensive work can be offloaded out of SQL Server to an application, possibly in a different computer. Also, long-duration tasks, e.g., invoking a Web service, can be executed without tying up database resources. The External Activator follows the same logic as internal activation, and can be configured to activate multiple instances of an application when messages accumulate in a queue.

As a logical extension to asynchronous messaging within the instance, Service Broker also provides reliable messaging between SQL Server instances to allow developers to easily build distributed applications. Conversations can occur within a single instance of SQL Server or between two instances of SQL Server. Local and remote conversations use the same programming model.

Security and routing are configured declaratively, without requiring changes to the queue readers. SQL Server uses *routes* to map a service name to the network address of the other participant in the conversation. SQL Server can also perform message forwarding and simple load balancing for conversations. SQL Server provides reliable, exactly once in-order delivery regardless of the number of instances that a message travels through. A conversation that spans instances of SQL Server can be secured both at the networking level (point to point) and at the conversation level (end to end). When end-to-end security is used, the contents of the message remain encrypted until the message reaches the final destination, while the headers are available to each SQL Server instance that the message travels through. Standard SQL Server permissions apply within an instance. Encryption occurs when messages leave an instance.

SQL Server uses a binary protocol for sending messages between instances. The protocol fragments large messages and permits interleaved fragments from multiple messages. Fragmentation allows SQL Server to quickly transmit smaller messages even in cases where a large message is in the process of being transmitted. The binary protocol does not use distributed transactions or two-phase commit. Instead, the protocol requires that a recipient acknowledge message fragments. SQL Server simply retries message fragments periodically until the fragment is acknowledged by the recipient. Acknowledgments are most often included as part of the headers of a return message, although dedicated return messages are used if no return message is available.

SQL Server includes a command line diagnostics tool (*ssbdiagnose*) to help analyze a Service Broker deployment and investigate problems. The tool can run in either *configuration* or *runtime* mode. In configuration mode, the tool checks whether a pair of services can exchange messages and returns any configuration errors. Examples of these errors are disabled queues and missing return routes. In the second mode, the tool connects to two or more SQL Server instances and monitors SQL Profiler events to discover Service Broker problems at runtime. The tool output can be sent into a file for automated processing.

30.13 Business Intelligence

The business intelligence component of SQL Server contains three subcomponents:

- SQL Server Integration Services (SSIS), which provides the means to integrate data from multiple sources, performs transformations related to cleaning the data and bringing it to a common form, and loading the data into a database system.

- SQL Server Analysis Services (SSAS), which provides OLAP and data-mining capabilities.

- SQL Server Reporting Services (SSRS).

Integration Services, Analysis Services, and Reporting Services are each implemented in separate servers and can be installed independently from one another on the same or different machines. They can connect to a variety of data sources, such as flat files, spreadsheets, or a variety of relational database systems, through native connectors, OLE-DB, or ODBC drivers.

Together they provide an end-to-end solution for extracting, transforming, and loading data, then modeling and adding analytical capability to the data, and finally building and distributing reports on the data. The different Business Intelligence components of SQL Server can integrate and leverage each others' capability. Here are a few common scenarios that will leverage a combination of components:

- Build an SSIS package that cleanses data, using patterns generated by SSAS data mining.

- Use SSIS to load data to an SSAS cube, process it, and execute reports against the SSAS cube.

- Build an SSRS report to publish the findings of a mining model or the data contained in an SSAS OLAP component.

The following sections give an overview of the capabilities and architecture of each of these server components.

30.13.1 SQL Server Integration Services

Microsoft SQL Server Integration Services (SSIS) is an enterprise data transformation and data integration solution that you can use to extract, transform, aggregate, and consolidate data from disparate sources and move it to single or multiple destinations. You can use SSIS to perform the following tasks:

- Merge data from heterogeneous data stores.

- Refresh data in data warehouses and data marts.

- Cleanse data before loading it into destinations.

- Bulk-load data into online transaction processing (OLTP) and online analytical processing (OLAP) databases.

- Send notifications.

- Build business intelligence into a data transformation process.

- Automate administrative functions.

SSIS provides a complete set of services, graphical tools, programmable objects, and APIs for the above tasks. These provide the ability to build large, robust, and complex data transformation solutions without any custom programming. However, an API and programmable objects are available when they are needed to create custom elements or integrate data transformation capabilities into custom applications.

The SSIS data-flow engine provides the in-memory buffers that move data from source to destination and calls the source adapters that extract data from files and relational databases. The engine also provides the transformations that modify data and the destination adapters that load data into data stores. Duplicate elimination based on fuzzy (approximate) match is an example of a transformation provided by SSIS. Users can program their own transformations if required. Figure 30.7 shows an example of how various transformations can be combined to cleanse and load book sales information; the book titles from the sales data

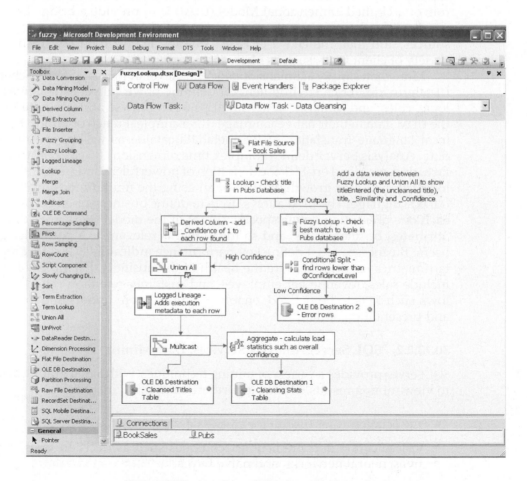

Figure 30.7 Loading of data by using fuzzy lookup.

are matched against a publications database, and in case there is no match, fuzzy lookup is performed to handle titles with minor errors (such as spelling errors). Information about confidence and data lineage is stored with the cleansed data.

30.13.2 SQL Server Analysis Services

The Analysis Services component delivers online analytical processing (OLAP) and data-mining functionality for business intelligence applications. Analysis Services supports a thin client architecture. The calculation engine is on the server, so queries are resolved on the server, avoiding the need to transfer large amounts of data between the client and the server.

30.13.2.1 SQL Server Analysis Services: OLAP

Analysis Services utilizes a Unified Dimensional Model (UDM), which bridges the gap between traditional relational reporting and OLAP ad hoc analysis. The role of a Unified Dimensional Model (UDM) is to provide a bridge between the user and the data sources. A UDM is constructed over one or more physical data sources, and then the end user issues queries against the UDM, using one of a variety of client tools, such as Microsoft Excel.

More than simply a dimension modeling layer of the DataSource schemas, the UDM provides a rich environment for defining powerful yet exhaustive business logic, rules, and semantic definition. Users can browse and generate reports on the UDM data in their native language (for example, French or Hindi) by defining local language translation of the metadata catalog as well as the dimensional data. Analysis Server defines complex time dimensions (fiscal, reporting, manufacturing, etc.), and enables the definition of powerful multidimensional business logic (year-to-year growth, year-to-date) using the multidimensional expression (MDX) language. The UDM allows users to define business-oriented perspectives, each one presenting only a specific subset of the model (measures, dimensions, attributes, business rules, and so forth) that is relevant to a particular group of users. Businesses often define key performance indicators (KPIs) that are important metrics used to measure the health of the business. Examples of such KPIs include sales, revenue per employee, and customer retention rate. The UDM allows such KPIs to be defined, enabling a much more understandable grouping and presentation of data.

30.13.2.2 SQL Server Analysis Services: Data Mining

SQL Server provides a variety of mining techniques, with a rich graphical interface to view mining results. Mining algorithms supported include:

- Association rules (useful for cross-sales applications).
- Classification and prediction techniques such as decision trees, regression trees, neural networks, and naive Bayes.
- Time series forecasting techniques including ARIMA and ARTXP.

- Clustering techniques such as expectation maximization and K-means (coupled with techniques for sequence clustering).

In addition, SQL Server provides an extensible architecture for plugging in third-party data mining algorithms and visualizers.

SQL Server also supports the *Data-Mining Extensions* (DMX) extensions for SQL. DMX is the language used to interact with data-mining models just as SQL is used to interact with tables and views. With DMX, models can be created and trained and then stored in an Analysis Services database. The model can then be browsed to look at patterns or, by using a special **prediction join** syntax, applied against new data to perform predictions. The DMX language supports functions and constructs to easily determine a predicted class along with its confidence, predict a list of associated items as in a recommendation engine, or even return information and supporting facts about a prediction. Data mining in SQL Server can be used against data stored in relational or multidimensional data sources. Other data sources are supported as well through specialized tasks and transforms, allowing data mining directly in the operational data pipeline of Integration Services. Data-mining results can be exposed in graphical controls, special data-mining dimensions for OLAP cubes, or simply in Reporting Services reports.

30.13.3 SQL Server Reporting Services

Reporting Services is a server-based reporting platform that can be used to create and manage tabular, matrix, graphical, and free-form reports that contain data from relational and multidimensional data sources. The reports that you create can be viewed and managed over a Web-based connection. Matrix reports can summarize data for high-level reviews, while providing supporting detail in drilldown reports. Parameterized reports can be used to filter data on the basis of values that are provided at runtime. Users can choose from a variety of viewing formats to render reports on the fly in preferred formats for data manipulation or printing. An API is also available to extend or integrate report capabilities into custom solutions. Server-based reporting provides a way to centralize report storage and management, set policies and secure access to reports and folders, control how reports are processed and distributed, and standardize how reports are used in your business.

Bibliographical Notes

Detailed information about using a C2 certified system with SQL Server is available at www.microsoft.com/Downloads/Release.asp?ReleaseID=25503.

SQL Server's optimization framework is based on the Cascades optimizer prototype, which Graefe [1995] proposed. Simmen et al. [1996] discusses the scheme for reducing grouping columns. Galindo-Legaria and Joshi [2001] and Elhemali et al. [2007] present the variety of execution strategies that SQL Server considers for cost-based optimization of subqueries. Additional information on the self-tuning aspects of SQL Server are discussed by Chaudhuri et al. [1999]. Chaudhuri and Shim [1994] and Yan and Larson [1995] discuss reordering of aggregation operations.

Chatziantoniou and Ross [1997] and Galindo-Legaria and Joshi [2001] proposed the alternative used by SQL Server for SQL queries requiring a self-join. Under this scheme, the optimizer detects the pattern and considers per-segment execution. Pellenkoft et al. [1997] discusses the optimization scheme for generating the complete search space using a set of transformations that are complete, local and nonredundant. Graefe et al. [1998] offers discussion concerning hash operations that support basic aggregation and join, with a number of optimizations, extensions, and dynamic tuning for data skew. Graefe et al. [1998] presents the idea of joining indices for the sole purpose of assembling a row with the set of columns needed on a query. It argues that this sometimes is faster than scanning a base table.

Blakeley [1996] and Blakeley and Pizzo [2001] offer discussions concerning communication with the storage engine through OLE-DB. Blakeley et al. [2005] details the implementation of the distributed and heterogeneous query capabilities of SQL Server. Acheson et al. [2004] provides details on the integration of the .NET CLR inside the SQL Server process.

Blakeley et al. [2008] describes the contracts for UDTs, UDAggs, and UDFs in more detail. Blakeley et al. [2006] describes the ADO.NET Entity Framework. Melnik et al. [2007] describes the mapping technology behind the ADO.NET Entity Framework. Adya et al. [2007] provides an overview of the ADO.NET Entity Framework architecture. The SQL:2003 standard is defined in SQL/XML [2004]. Rys [2001] provides more details on the SQL Server 2000 XML functionality. Rys [2004] provides an overview of the extensions to the **for xml** aggregation. For information on XML capabilities that can be used on the client side or inside CLR, refer to the collection of white papers at http://msdn.microsoft.com/XML/Building-XML/XMLandDatabase/default.aspx. The XQuery 1.0/XPath 2.0 data model is defined in Walsh et al. [2007]. Rys [2003] provides an overview of implementation techniques for XQuery in the context of relational databases. The OrdPath numbering scheme is described in O'Neil et al. [2004]; Pal et al. [2004] and Baras et al. [2005] provide more information on XML indexing and XQuery algebraization and optimization in SQL Server 2005.

PART 10

APPENDICES

Appendix A presents the full details of the university database that we have used as our running example, including an E-R diagram, SQL DDL, and sample data that we have used throughout the book. (The DDL and sample data are also available on the Web site of the book, db-book.com, for use in laboratory exercises.)

The remaining appendices are not part of the printed book, but are available online on the Web site of the book, db-book.com. These include:

- Appendix B (Advanced Relational Database Design), first covers the theory of multivalued dependencies; recall that multivalued dependencies were introduced in Chapter 8. The project-join normal form, which is based on a type of constraint called join dependency is presented next; join dependencies are a generalization of multivalued dependencies. The chapter concludes with another normal form called the domain-key normal form.

- Appendix C (Other Relational Query Languages) first presents the relational query language Query-by-Example (QBE), which was designed to be used by non-programmers. In QBE, queries look like a collection of tables containing an example of data to be retrieved. The graphical query language of Microsoft Access, which is based on QBE, is presented next, followed by the Datalog language, which has a syntax modeled after the logic-programming language Prolog.

- Appendix D (Network Model), and Appendix E (Hierarchical Model), cover the network and hierarchical data models. Both these data models predate the relational model, and provide a level of abstraction that is lower than the relational model. They abstract away some, but not all, details of the actual data structures used to store data on disks. These models are only used in a few legacy applications.

For appendices B through E, we illsutrate our concepts using a bank enterprise with the schema shown in Figure 2.15.

Detailed University Schema

In this appendix, we present the full details of our running-example university database. In Section A.1 we present the full schema as used in the text and the E-R diagram that corresponds to that schema. In Section A.2 we present a relatively complete SQL data definition for our running university example. Besides listing a datatype for each attribute, we include a substantial number of constraints. Finally, in Section A.3 we present sample data that correspond to our schema. SQL scripts to create all the relations in the schema, and to populate them with sample data, are available on the Web site of the book, db-book.com.

A.1 Full Schema

The full schema of the University database as used in the text is shown in Figure A.1. The E-R diagram that corresponds to that schema, and used throughout the text, is shown in Figure A.2.

> *classroom*(*building*, *room_number*, *capacity*)
> *department*(*dept_name*, *building*, *budget*)
> *course*(*course_id*, *title*, *dept_name*, *credits*)
> *instructor*(*ID*, *name*, *dept_name*, *salary*)
> *section*(*course_id*, *sec_id*, *semester*, *year*, *building*, *room_number*, *time_slot_id*)
> *teaches*(*ID*, *course_id*, *sec_id*, *semester*, *year*)
> *student*(*ID*, *name*, *dept_name*, *tot_cred*)
> *takes*(*ID*, *course_id*, *sec_id*, *semester*, *year*, *grade*)
> *advisor*(*s_ID*, *i_ID*)
> *time_slot*(*time_slot_id*, *day*, *start_time*, *end_time*)
> *prereq*(*course_id*, *prereq_id*)

Figure A.1 Schema of the University database.

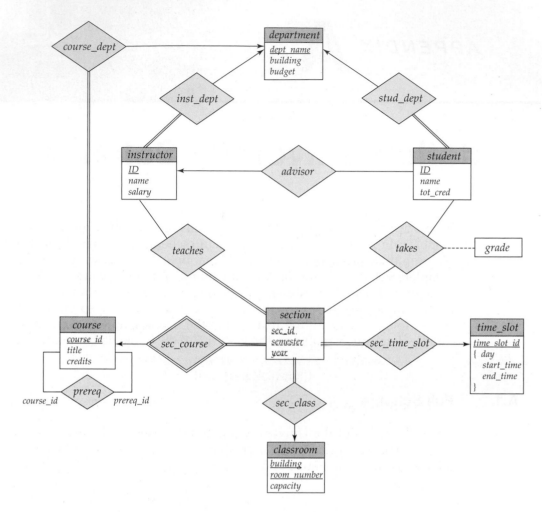

Figure A.2   E-R diagram for a university enterprise.

A.2   DDL

In this section, we present a relatively complete SQL data definition for our example. Besides listing a datatype for each attribute, we include a substantial number of constraints.

```
create table classroom
    (building        varchar (15),
     room_number     varchar (7),
     capacity        numeric (4,0),
     primary key (building, room_number));
```

create table *department*
    (*dept_name*   **varchar** (20),
    building   **varchar** (15),
    budget   **numeric** (12,2) **check** (*budget* > 0),
    primary key (*dept_name*));

create table *course*
    (*course_id*   **varchar** (8),
    title   **varchar** (50),
    dept_name   **varchar** (20),
    credits   **numeric** (2,0) **check** (*credits* > 0),
    primary key (*course_id*),
    foreign key (*dept_name*) **references** *department*
           on delete set null);

create table *instructor*
    (*ID*   **varchar** (5),
    name   **varchar** (20) **not null**,
    dept_name   **varchar** (20),
    salary   **numeric** (8,2) **check** (*salary* > 29000),
    primary key (*ID*),
    foreign key (*dept_name*) **references** *department*
           on delete set null);

create table *section*
    (*course_id*   **varchar** (8),
    sec_id   **varchar** (8),
    semester   **varchar** (6) **check** (*semester* **in**
                          ('Fall', 'Winter', 'Spring', 'Summer')),
    year   **numeric** (4,0) **check** (*year* > 1701 and *year* < 2100),
    building   **varchar** (15),
    room_number **varchar** (7),
    time_slot_id **varchar** (4),
    primary key (*course_id*, *sec_id*, *semester*, *year*),
    foreign key (*course_id*) **references** *course*
           on delete cascade,
    foreign key (*building*, *room_number*) **references** *classroom*
           on delete set null);

In the above DDL we add the **on delete cascade** specification to a foreign key constraint if the existence of the tuple depends on the referenced tuple. For example we add the **on delete cascade** specification to the foreign key constraint from *section* (which was generated from weak entity *section*), to *course* (which was its identifying relationship). In other foreign key constraints we either specify **on delete set null**, which allows deletion of a referenced tuple by setting the referencing value to null, or do not add any specification, which prevents the deletion of any referenced tuple. For example, if a department is deleted, we would not wish to delete associated instructors; the foreign key constraint from *instructor* to *department* instead sets the *dept_name* attribute to null. On the other hand, the foreign key constraint for the *prereq* relation, shown later, prevents the deletion of a course that is required as a prerequisite for another course. For the *advisor* relation, shown later, we allow *i_ID* to be set to null if an instructor is deleted, but delete an *advisor* tuple if the referenced student is deleted.

```
create table teaches
    (ID              varchar (5),
    course_id        varchar (8),
    sec_id           varchar (8),
    semester         varchar (6),
    year             numeric (4,0),
    primary key (ID, course_id, sec_id, semester, year),
    foreign key (course_id, sec_id, semester, year) references section
                on delete cascade,
    foreign key (ID) references instructor
                on delete cascade);

create table student
    (ID              varchar (5),
    name             varchar (20) not null,
    dept_name        varchar (20),
    tot_cred         numeric (3,0) check (tot_cred >= 0),
    primary key (ID),
    foreign key (dept_name) references department
                on delete set null);

create table takes
    (ID              varchar (5),
    course_id        varchar (8),
    sec_id           varchar (8),
    semester         varchar (6),
    year             numeric (4,0),
    grade            varchar (2),
    primary key (ID, course_id, sec_id, semester, year),
    foreign key (course_id, sec_id, semester, year) references section
                on delete cascade,
    foreign key (ID) references student
                on delete cascade);
```

```
create table advisor
    (s_ID           varchar (5),
    i_ID            varchar (5),
    primary key (s_ID),
    foreign key (i_ID) references instructor (ID)
                    on delete set null,
    foreign key (s_ID) references student (ID)
                    on delete cascade);
```

```
create table prereq
    (course_id      varchar(8),
    prereq_id       varchar(8),
    primary key (course_id, prereq_id),
    foreign key (course_id) references course
                    on delete cascade,
    foreign key (prereq_id) references course);
```

The following **create table** statement for the table *time_slot* can be run on most database systems, but does not work on Oracle (at least as of Oracle version 11), since Oracle does not support the SQL standard type **time**.

```
create table timeslot
    (time_slot_id   varchar (4),
    day             varchar (1) check (day in ('M', 'T', 'W', 'R', 'F', 'S', 'U')),
    start_time      time,
    end_time        time,
    primary key (time_slot_id, day, start_time));
```

The syntax for specifying time in SQL is illustrated by these examples: '08:30', '13:55', and '5:30 PM'. Since Oracle does not support the **time** type, for Oracle we use the following schema instead:

```
create table timeslot
    (time_slot_id   varchar (4),
    day             varchar (1),
    start_hr        numeric (2) check (start_hr >= 0 and end_hr < 24),
    start_min       numeric (2) check (start_min >= 0 and start_min < 60),
    end_hr          numeric (2) check (end_hr >= 0 and end_hr < 24),
    end_min         numeric (2) check (end_min >= 0 and end_min < 60),
    primary key (time_slot_id, day, start_hr, start_min));
```

The difference is that *start_time* has been replaced by two attributes *start_hr* and *start_min*, and similarly *end_time* has been replaced by attributes *end_hr* and *end_min*. These attributes also have constraints that ensure that only numbers representing valid time values appear in those attributes. This version of the schema for *time_slot* works on all databases, including Oracle. Note that although Oracle supports the **datetime** datatype, **datetime** includes a specific day, month, and year as well as a time, and is not appropriate here since we want only a time. There are two alternatives to splitting the time attributes into an hour and a minute component, but neither is desirable. The first alternative is to use a **varchar** type, but that makes it hard to enforce validity constraints on the string as well as to perform comparison on time. The second alternative is to encode time as an integer representing a number of minutes (or seconds) from midnight, but this alternative requires extra code with each query to covert values between the standard time representation and the integer encoding. We therefore chose the two-part solution.

A.3   Sample Data

In this section we provide sample data for each of the relations defined in the previous section.

building	room_number	capacity
Packard	101	500
Painter	514	10
Taylor	3128	70
Watson	100	30
Watson	120	50

Figure A.3 The *classroom* relation.

dept_name	building	budget
Biology	Watson	90000
Comp. Sci.	Taylor	100000
Elec. Eng.	Taylor	85000
Finance	Painter	120000
History	Painter	50000
Music	Packard	80000
Physics	Watson	70000

Figure A.4 The *department* relation.

course_id	title	dept_name	credits
BIO-101	Intro. to Biology	Biology	4
BIO-301	Genetics	Biology	4
BIO-399	Computational Biology	Biology	3
CS-101	Intro. to Computer Science	Comp. Sci.	4
CS-190	Game Design	Comp. Sci.	4
CS-315	Robotics	Comp. Sci.	3
CS-319	Image Processing	Comp. Sci.	3
CS-347	Database System Concepts	Comp. Sci.	3
EE-181	Intro. to Digital Systems	Elec. Eng.	3
FIN-201	Investment Banking	Finance	3
HIS-351	World History	History	3
MU-199	Music Video Production	Music	3
PHY-101	Physical Principles	Physics	4

Figure A.5 The *course* relation.

ID	name	dept_name	salary
10101	Srinivasan	Comp. Sci.	65000
12121	Wu	Finance	90000
15151	Mozart	Music	40000
22222	Einstein	Physics	95000
32343	El Said	History	60000
33456	Gold	Physics	87000
45565	Katz	Comp. Sci.	75000
58583	Califieri	History	62000
76543	Singh	Finance	80000
76766	Crick	Biology	72000
83821	Brandt	Comp. Sci.	92000
98345	Kim	Elec. Eng.	80000

Figure A.6 The *instructor* relation.

course_id	sec_id	semester	year	building	room_number	time_slot_id
BIO-101	1	Summer	2009	Painter	514	B
BIO-301	1	Summer	2010	Painter	514	A
CS-101	1	Fall	2009	Packard	101	H
CS-101	1	Spring	2010	Packard	101	F
CS-190	1	Spring	2009	Taylor	3128	E
CS-190	2	Spring	2009	Taylor	3128	A
CS-315	1	Spring	2010	Watson	120	D
CS-319	1	Spring	2010	Watson	100	B
CS-319	2	Spring	2010	Taylor	3128	C
CS-347	1	Fall	2009	Taylor	3128	A
EE-181	1	Spring	2009	Taylor	3128	C
FIN-201	1	Spring	2010	Packard	101	B
HIS-351	1	Spring	2010	Painter	514	C
MU-199	1	Spring	2010	Packard	101	D
PHY-101	1	Fall	2009	Watson	100	A

Figure A.7 The *section* relation.

ID	course_id	sec_id	semester	year
10101	CS-101	1	Fall	2009
10101	CS-315	1	Spring	2010
10101	CS-347	1	Fall	2009
12121	FIN-201	1	Spring	2010
15151	MU-199	1	Spring	2010
22222	PHY-101	1	Fall	2009
32343	HIS-351	1	Spring	2010
45565	CS-101	1	Spring	2010
45565	CS-319	1	Spring	2010
76766	BIO-101	1	Summer	2009
76766	BIO-301	1	Summer	2010
83821	CS-190	1	Spring	2009
83821	CS-190	2	Spring	2009
83821	CS-319	2	Spring	2010
98345	EE-181	1	Spring	2009

Figure A.8 The *teaches* relation.

ID	name	dept_name	tot_cred
00128	Zhang	Comp. Sci.	102
12345	Shankar	Comp. Sci.	32
19991	Brandt	History	80
23121	Chavez	Finance	110
44553	Peltier	Physics	56
45678	Levy	Physics	46
54321	Williams	Comp. Sci.	54
55739	Sanchez	Music	38
70557	Snow	Physics	0
76543	Brown	Comp. Sci.	58
76653	Aoi	Elec. Eng.	60
98765	Bourikas	Elec. Eng.	98
98988	Tanaka	Biology	120

Figure A.9 The *student* relation.

ID	course_id	sec_id	semester	year	grade
00128	CS-101	1	Fall	2009	A
00128	CS-347	1	Fall	2009	A-
12345	CS-101	1	Fall	2009	C
12345	CS-190	2	Spring	2009	A
12345	CS-315	1	Spring	2010	A
12345	CS-347	1	Fall	2009	A
19991	HIS-351	1	Spring	2010	B
23121	FIN-201	1	Spring	2010	C+
44553	PHY-101	1	Fall	2009	B-
45678	CS-101	1	Fall	2009	F
45678	CS-101	1	Spring	2010	B+
45678	CS-319	1	Spring	2010	B
54321	CS-101	1	Fall	2009	A-
54321	CS-190	2	Spring	2009	B+
55739	MU-199	1	Spring	2010	A-
76543	CS-101	1	Fall	2009	A
76543	CS-319	2	Spring	2010	A
76653	EE-181	1	Spring	2009	C
98765	CS-101	1	Fall	2009	C-
98765	CS-315	1	Spring	2010	B
98988	BIO-101	1	Summer	2009	A
98988	BIO-301	1	Summer	2010	*null*

Figure A.10 The *takes* relation.

s_id	i_id
00128	45565
12345	10101
23121	76543
44553	22222
45678	22222
76543	45565
76653	98345
98765	98345
98988	76766

Figure A.11   The *advisor* relation.

time_slot_id	day	start_time	end_time
A	M	8:00	8:50
A	W	8:00	8:50
A	F	8:00	8:50
B	M	9:00	9:50
B	W	9:00	9:50
B	F	9:00	9:50
C	M	11:00	11:50
C	W	11:00	11:50
C	F	11:00	11:50
D	M	13:00	13:50
D	W	13:00	13:50
D	F	13:00	13:50
E	T	10:30	11:45
E	R	10:30	11:45
F	T	14:30	15:45
F	R	14:30	15:45
G	M	16:00	16:50
G	W	16:00	16:50
G	F	16:00	16:50
H	W	10:00	12:30

Figure A.12   The *time_slot* relation.

course_id	prereq_id
BIO-301	BIO-101
BIO-399	BIO-101
CS-190	CS-101
CS-315	CS-101
CS-319	CS-101
CS-347	CS-101
EE-181	PHY-101

Figure A.13 The *prereq* relation.

time_slot_id	day	start_hr	start_min	end_hr	end_min
A	M	8	0	8	50
A	W	8	0	8	50
A	F	8	0	8	50
B	M	9	0	9	50
B	W	9	0	9	50
B	F	9	0	9	50
C	M	11	0	11	50
C	W	11	0	11	50
C	F	11	0	11	50
D	M	13	0	13	50
D	W	13	0	13	50
D	F	13	0	13	50
E	T	10	30	11	45
E	R	10	30	11	45
F	T	14	30	15	45
F	R	14	30	15	45
G	M	16	0	16	50
G	W	16	0	16	50
G	F	16	0	16	50
H	W	10	0	12	30

Figure A.14 The *time_slot* relation with start and end time separated into hour and minute.

Bibliography

[Abadi 2009] D. Abadi, "Data Management in the Cloud: Limitations and Opportunities", *Data Engineering Bulletin*, Volume 32, Number 1 (2009), pages 3–12.

[Abadi et al. 2008] D. J. Abadi, S. Madden, and N. Hachem, "Column-stores vs. row-stores: how different are they really?", In *Proc. of the ACM SIGMOD Conf. on Management of Data* (2008), pages 967–980.

[Abiteboul et al. 1995] S. Abiteboul, R. Hull, and V. Vianu, *Foundations of Databases*, Addison Wesley (1995).

[Abiteboul et al. 2003] S. Abiteboul, R. Agrawal, P. A. Bernstein, M. J. Carey, et al. "The Lowell Database Research Self Assessment" (2003).

[Acheson et al. 2004] A. Acheson, M. Bendixen, J. A. Blakeley, I. P. Carlin, E. Ersan, J. Fang, X. Jiang, C. Kleinerman, B. Rathakrishnan, G. Schaller, B. Sezgin, R. Venkatesh, and H. Zhang, "Hosting the .NET Runtime in Microsoft SQL Server", In *Proc. of the ACM SIGMOD Conf. on Management of Data* (2004), pages 860–865.

[Adali et al. 1996] S. Adali, K. S. Candan, Y. Papakonstantinou, and V. S. Subrahmanian, "Query Caching and Optimization in Distributed Mediator Systems", In *Proc. of the ACM SIGMOD Conf. on Management of Data* (1996), pages 137–148.

[Adya et al. 2007] A. Adya, J. A. Blakeley, S. Melnik, and S. Muralidhar, "Anatomy of the ADO.NET entity framework", In *Proc. of the ACM SIGMOD Conf. on Management of Data* (2007), pages 877–888.

[Agarwal et al. 1996] S. Agarwal, R. Agrawal, P. M. Deshpande, A. Gupta, J. F. Naughton, R. Ramakrishnan, and S. Sarawagi, "On the Computation of Multidimensional Attributes", In *Proc. of the International Conf. on Very Large Databases* (1996), pages 506–521.

[Agrawal and Srikant 1994] R. Agrawal and R. Srikant, "Fast Algorithms for Mining Association Rules in Large Databases", In *Proc. of the International Conf. on Very Large Databases* (1994), pages 487–499.

[Agrawal et al. 1992]   R. Agrawal, S. P. Ghosh, T. Imielinski, B. R. Iyer, and A. N. Swami, "An Interval Classifier for Database Mining Applications", In *Proc. of the International Conf. on Very Large Databases* (1992), pages 560–573.

[Agrawal et al. 1993a]   R. Agrawal, T. Imielinski, and A. Swami, "Mining Association Rules between Sets of Items in Large Databases", In *Proc. of the ACM SIGMOD Conf. on Management of Data* (1993).

[Agrawal et al. 1993b]   R. Agrawal, T. Imielinski, and A. N. Swami, "Database Mining: A Performance Perspective", *IEEE Transactions on Knowledge and Data Engineering*, Volume 5, Number 6 (1993), pages 914–925.

[Agrawal et al. 2000]   S. Agrawal, S. Chaudhuri, and V. R. Narasayya, "Automated Selection of Materialized Views and Indexes in SQL Databases", In *Proc. of the International Conf. on Very Large Databases* (2000), pages 496–505.

[Agrawal et al. 2002]   S. Agrawal, S. Chaudhuri, and G. Das, "DBXplorer: A System for Keyword-Based Search over Relational Databases", In *Proc. of the International Conf. on Data Engineering* (2002).

[Agrawal et al. 2004]   S. Agrawal, S. Chaudhuri, L. Kollar, A. Marathe, V. Narasayya, and M. Syamala, "Database Tuning Advisor for Microsoft SQL Server 2005", In *Proc. of the International Conf. on Very Large Databases* (2004).

[Agrawal et al. 2009]   R. Agrawal, A. Ailamaki, P. A. Bernstein, E. A. Brewer, M. J. Carey, S. Chaudhuri, A. Doan, D. Florescu, M. J. Franklin, H. Garcia-Molina, J. Gehrke, L. Gruenwald, L. M. Haas, A. Y. Halevy, J. M. Hellerstein, Y. E. Ioannidis, H. F. Korth, D. Kossmann, S. Madden, R. Magoulas, B. C. Ooi, T. O^Reilly, R. Ramakrishnan, S. Sarawagi, and G. W. Michael Stonebraker, Alexander S. Szalay, "The Claremont Report on Database Research", *Communications of the ACM*, Volume 52, Number 6 (2009), pages 56–65.

[Ahmed et al. 2006]   R. Ahmed, A. Lee, A. Witkowski, D. Das, H. Su, M. Zaït, and T. Cruanes, "Cost-Based Query Transformation in Oracle", In *Proc. of the International Conf. on Very Large Databases* (2006), pages 1026–1036.

[Aho et al. 1979a]   A. V. Aho, C. Beeri, and J. D. Ullman, "The Theory of Joins in Relational Databases", *ACM Transactions on Database Systems*, Volume 4, Number 3 (1979), pages 297–314.

[Aho et al. 1979b]   A. V. Aho, Y. Sagiv, and J. D. Ullman, "Equivalences among Relational Expressions", *SIAM Journal of Computing*, Volume 8, Number 2 (1979), pages 218–246.

[Ailamaki et al. 2001]   A. Ailamaki, D. J. DeWitt, M. D. Hill, and M. Skounakis, "Weaving Relations for Cache Performance", In *Proc. of the International Conf. on Very Large Databases* (2001), pages 169–180.

[Alonso and Korth 1993]   R. Alonso and H. F. Korth, "Database System Issues in Nomadic Computing", In *Proc. of the ACM SIGMOD Conf. on Management of Data* (1993), pages 388–392.

[Amer-Yahia et al. 2004]   S. Amer-Yahia, C. Botev, and J. Shanmugasundaram, "TeXQuery: A Full-Text Search Extension to XQuery", In *Proc. of the International World Wide Web Conf.* (2004).

[Anderson et al. 1992]   D. P. Anderson, Y. Osawa, and R. Govindan, "A File System for Continuous Media", *ACM Transactions on Database Systems*, Volume 10, Number 4 (1992), pages 311–337.

[Anderson et al. 1998]   T. Anderson, Y. Breitbart, H. F. Korth, and A. Wool, "Replication, Consistency and Practicality: Are These Mutually Exclusive?", In *Proc. of the ACM SIGMOD Conf. on Management of Data* (1998).

[ANSI 1986]   *American National Standard for Information Systems: Database Language SQL.* American National Standards Institute (1986).

[ANSI 1989]   *Database Language SQL with Integrity Enhancement, ANSI X3, 135–1989.* American National Standards Institute, New York (1989).

[ANSI 1992]   *Database Language SQL, ANSI X3,135–1992.* American National Standards Institute, New York (1992).

[Antoshenkov 1995]   G. Antoshenkov, "Byte-aligned Bitmap Compression (poster abstract)", In *IEEE Data Compression Conf.* (1995).

[Appelt and Israel 1999]   D. E. Appelt and D. J. Israel, "Introduction to Information Extraction Technology", In *Proc. of the International Joint Conferences on Artificial Intelligence* (1999).

[Apt and Pugin 1987]   K. R. Apt and J. M. Pugin, "Maintenance of Stratified Database Viewed as a Belief Revision System", In *Proc. of the ACM Symposium on Principles of Database Systems* (1987), pages 136–145.

[Armstrong 1974]   W. W. Armstrong, "Dependency Structures of Data Base Relationships", In *Proc. of the 1974 IFIP Congress* (1974), pages 580–583.

[Astrahan et al. 1976]   M. M. Astrahan, M. W. Blasgen, D. D. Chamberlin, K. P. Eswaran, J. N. Gray, P. P. Griffiths, W. F. King, R. A. Lorie, P. R. McJones, J. W. Mehl, G. R. Putzolu, I. L. Traiger, B. W. Wade, and V. Watson, "System R, A Relational Approach to Data Base Management", *ACM Transactions on Database Systems*, Volume 1, Number 2 (1976), pages 97–137.

[Atreya et al. 2002]   M. Atreya, B. Hammond, S. Paine, P. Starrett, and S. Wu, *Digital Signatures*, RSA Press (2002).

[Atzeni and Antonellis 1993]   P. Atzeni and V. D. Antonellis, *Relational Database Theory*, Benjamin Cummings (1993).

[Baeza-Yates and Ribeiro-Neto 1999]   R. Baeza-Yates and B. Ribeiro-Neto, *Modern Information Retrieval*, Addison Wesley (1999).

[Bancilhon et al. 1989]   F. Bancilhon, S. Cluet, and C. Delobel, "A Query Language for the O_2 Object-Oriented Database", In *Proc. of the Second Workshop on Database Programming Languages* (1989).

[Baras et al. 2005] A. Baras, D. Churin, I. Cseri, T. Grabs, E. Kogan, S. Pal, M. Rys, and O. Seeliger. "Implementing XQuery in a Relational Database System" (2005).

[Baru et al. 1995] C. Baru et al., "DB2 Parallel Edition", *IBM Systems Journal*, Volume 34, Number 2 (1995), pages 292–322.

[Bassiouni 1988] M. Bassiouni, "Single-site and Distributed Optimistic Protocols for Concurrency Control", *IEEE Transactions on Software Engineering*, Volume SE-14, Number 8 (1988), pages 1071–1080.

[Batini et al. 1992] C. Batini, S. Ceri, and S. Navathe, *Database Design: An Entity-Relationship Approach*, Benjamin Cummings (1992).

[Bayer 1972] R. Bayer, "Symmetric Binary B-trees: Data Structure and Maintenance Algorithms", *Acta Informatica*, Volume 1, Number 4 (1972), pages 290–306.

[Bayer and McCreight 1972] R. Bayer and E. M. McCreight, "Organization and Maintenance of Large Ordered Indices", *Acta Informatica*, Volume 1, Number 3 (1972), pages 173–189.

[Bayer and Schkolnick 1977] R. Bayer and M. Schkolnick, "Concurrency of Operating on B-trees", *Acta Informatica*, Volume 9, Number 1 (1977), pages 1–21.

[Bayer and Unterauer 1977] R. Bayer and K. Unterauer, "Prefix B-trees", *ACM Transactions on Database Systems*, Volume 2, Number 1 (1977), pages 11–26.

[Bayer et al. 1978] R. Bayer, R. M. Graham, and G. Seegmuller, editors, *Operating Systems: An Advanced Course*, Springer Verlag (1978).

[Beckmann et al. 1990] N. Beckmann, H. P. Kriegel, R. Schneider, and B. Seeger, "The R*-tree: An Efficient and Robust Access Method for Points and Rectangles", In *Proc. of the ACM SIGMOD Conf. on Management of Data* (1990), pages 322–331.

[Beeri et al. 1977] C. Beeri, R. Fagin, and J. H. Howard, "A Complete Axiomatization for Functional and Multivalued Dependencies", In *Proc. of the ACM SIGMOD Conf. on Management of Data* (1977), pages 47–61.

[Bentley 1975] J. L. Bentley, "Multidimensional Binary Search Trees Used for Associative Searching", *Communications of the ACM*, Volume 18, Number 9 (1975), pages 509–517.

[Berenson et al. 1995] H. Berenson, P. Bernstein, J. Gray, J. Melton, E. O'Neil, and P. O'Neil, "A Critique of ANSI SQL Isolation Levels", In *Proc. of the ACM SIGMOD Conf. on Management of Data* (1995), pages 1–10.

[Bernstein and Goodman 1981] P. A. Bernstein and N. Goodman, "Concurrency Control in Distributed Database Systems", *ACM Computing Survey*, Volume 13, Number 2 (1981), pages 185–221.

[Bernstein and Newcomer 1997] P. A. Bernstein and E. Newcomer, *Principles of Transaction Processing*, Morgan Kaufmann (1997).

[Bernstein et al. 1998]   P. Bernstein, M. Brodie, S. Ceri, D. DeWitt, M. Franklin, H. Garcia-Molina, J. Gray, J. Held, J. Hellerstein, H. V. Jagadish, M. Lesk, D. Maier, J. Naughton, H. Pirahesh, M. Stonebraker, and J. Ullman, "The Asilomar Report on Database Research", *ACM SIGMOD Record*, Volume 27, Number 4 (1998).

[Berson et al. 1995]   S. Berson, L. Golubchik, and R. R. Muntz, "Fault Tolerant Design of Multimedia Servers", In *Proc. of the ACM SIGMOD Conf. on Management of Data* (1995), pages 364–375.

[Bhalotia et al. 2002]   G. Bhalotia, A. Hulgeri, C. Nakhe, S. Chakrabarti, and S. Sudarshan, "Keyword Searching and Browsing in Databases using BANKS", In *Proc. of the International Conf. on Data Engineering* (2002).

[Bharat and Henzinger 1998]   K. Bharat and M. R. Henzinger, "Improved Algorithms for Topic Distillation in a Hyperlinked Environment", In *Proc. of the ACM SIGIR Conf. on Research and Development in Information Retrieval* (1998), pages 104–111.

[Bhattacharjee et al. 2003]   B. Bhattacharjee, S. Padmanabhan, T. Malkemus, T. Lai, L. Cranston, and M. Huras, "Efficient Query Processing for Multi-Dimensionally Clustered Tables in DB2", In *Proc. of the International Conf. on Very Large Databases* (2003), pages 963–974.

[Biskup et al. 1979]   J. Biskup, U. Dayal, and P. A. Bernstein, "Synthesizing Independent Database Schemas", In *Proc. of the ACM SIGMOD Conf. on Management of Data* (1979), pages 143–152.

[Bitton et al. 1983]   D. Bitton, D. J. DeWitt, and C. Turbyfill, "Benchmarking Database Systems: A Systematic Approach", In *Proc. of the International Conf. on Very Large Databases* (1983).

[Blakeley 1996]   J. A. Blakeley, "Data Access for the Masses through OLE DB", In *Proc. of the ACM SIGMOD Conf. on Management of Data* (1996), pages 161–172.

[Blakeley and Pizzo 2001]   J. A. Blakeley and M. Pizzo, "Enabling Component Databases with OLE DB", In K. R. Dittrich and A. Geppert, editors, *Component Database Systems*, Morgan Kaufmann Publishers (2001), pages 139–173.

[Blakeley et al. 1986]   J. A. Blakeley, P. Larson, and F. W. Tompa, "Efficiently Updating Materialized Views", In *Proc. of the ACM SIGMOD Conf. on Management of Data* (1986), pages 61–71.

[Blakeley et al. 2005]   J. A. Blakeley, C. Cunningham, N. Ellis, B. Rathakrishnan, and M.-C. Wu, "Distributed/Heterogeneous Query Processing in Microsoft SQL Server", In *Proc. of the International Conf. on Data Engineering* (2005).

[Blakeley et al. 2006]   J. A. Blakeley, D. Campbell, S. Muralidhar, and A. Nori, "The ADO.NET entity framework: making the conceptual level real", *SIGMOD Record*, Volume 35, Number 4 (2006), pages 32–39.

[Blakeley et al. 2008]   J. A. Blakeley, V. Rao, I. Kunen, A. Prout, M. Henaire, and C. Kleinerman, ".NET database programmability and extensibility in Microsoft

SQL server", In *Proc. of the ACM SIGMOD Conf. on Management of Data* (2008), pages 1087–1098.

[Blasgen and Eswaran 1976]   M. W. Blasgen and K. P. Eswaran, "On the Evaluation of Queries in a Relational Database System", *IBM Systems Journal*, Volume 16, (1976), pages 363–377.

[Boyce et al. 1975]   R. Boyce, D. D. Chamberlin, W. F. King, and M. Hammer, "Specifying Queries as Relational Expressions", *Communications of the ACM*, Volume 18, Number 11 (1975), pages 621–628.

[Brantner et al. 2008]   M. Brantner, D. Florescu, D. Graf, D. Kossmann, and T. Kraska, "Building a Database on S3", In *Proc. of the ACM SIGMOD Conf. on Management of Data* (2008), pages 251–263.

[Breese et al. 1998]   J. Breese, D. Heckerman, and C. Kadie, "Empirical Analysis of Predictive Algorithms for Collaborative Filtering", In *Procs. Conf. on Uncertainty in Artificial Intelligence*, Morgan Kaufmann (1998).

[Breitbart et al. 1999a]   Y. Breitbart, R. Komondoor, R. Rastogi, S. Seshadri, and A. Silberschatz, "Update Propagation Protocols For Replicated Databases", In *Proc. of the ACM SIGMOD Conf. on Management of Data* (1999), pages 97–108.

[Breitbart et al. 1999b]   Y. Breitbart, H. Korth, A. Silberschatz, and S. Sudarshan, "Distributed Databases", In *Encyclopedia of Electrical and Electronics Engineering*, John Wiley and Sons (1999).

[Brewer 2000]   E. A. Brewer, "Towards robust distributed systems (abstract)", In *Proc. of the ACM Symposium on Principles of Distributed Computing* (2000), page 7.

[Brin and Page 1998]   S. Brin and L. Page, "The Anatomy of a Large-Scale Hypertextual Web Search Engine", In *Proc. of the International World Wide Web Conf.* (1998).

[Brinkhoff et al. 1993]   T. Brinkhoff, H.-P. Kriegel, and B. Seeger, "Efficient Processing of Spatial Joins Using R-trees", In *Proc. of the ACM SIGMOD Conf. on Management of Data* (1993), pages 237–246.

[Bruno et al. 2002]   N. Bruno, S. Chaudhuri, and L. Gravano, "Top-k Selection Queries Over Relational Databases: Mapping Strategies and Performance Evaluation", *ACM Transactions on Database Systems*, Volume 27, Number 2 (2002), pages 153–187.

[Buckley and Silberschatz 1983]   G. Buckley and A. Silberschatz, "Obtaining Progressive Protocols for a Simple Multiversion Database Model", In *Proc. of the International Conf. on Very Large Databases* (1983), pages 74–81.

[Buckley and Silberschatz 1984]   G. Buckley and A. Silberschatz, "Concurrency Control in Graph Protocols by Using Edge Locks", In *Proc. of the ACM SIGMOD Conf. on Management of Data* (1984), pages 45–50.

[Buckley and Silberschatz 1985]   G. Buckley and A. Silberschatz, "Beyond Two-Phase Locking", *Journal of the ACM*, Volume 32, Number 2 (1985), pages 314–326.

[Bulmer 1979] M. G. Bulmer, *Principles of Statistics*, Dover Publications (1979).

[Burkhard 1976] W. A. Burkhard, "Hashing and Trie Algorithms for Partial Match Retrieval", *ACM Transactions on Database Systems*, Volume 1, Number 2 (1976), pages 175–187.

[Burkhard 1979] W. A. Burkhard, "Partial-match Hash Coding: Benefits of Redundancy", *ACM Transactions on Database Systems*, Volume 4, Number 2 (1979), pages 228–239.

[Cannan and Otten 1993] S. Cannan and G. Otten, *SQL—The Standard Handbook*, McGraw Hill (1993).

[Carey 1983] M. J. Carey, "Granularity Hierarchies in Concurrency Control", In *Proc. of the ACM SIGMOD Conf. on Management of Data* (1983), pages 156–165.

[Carey and Kossmann 1998] M. J. Carey and D. Kossmann, "Reducing the Braking Distance of an SQL Query Engine", In *Proc. of the International Conf. on Very Large Databases* (1998), pages 158–169.

[Carey et al. 1991] M. Carey, M. Franklin, M. Livny, and E. Shekita, "Data Caching Tradeoffs in Client-Server DBMS Architectures", In *Proc. of the ACM SIGMOD Conf. on Management of Data* (1991).

[Carey et al. 1993] M. J. Carey, D. DeWitt, and J. Naughton, "The OO7 Benchmark", In *Proc. of the ACM SIGMOD Conf. on Management of Data* (1993).

[Carey et al. 1999] M. J. Carey, D. D. Chamberlin, S. Narayanan, B. Vance, D. Doole, S. Rielau, R. Swagerman, and N. Mattos, "O-O, What Have They Done to DB2?", In *Proc. of the International Conf. on Very Large Databases* (1999), pages 542–553.

[Cattell 2000] R. Cattell, editor, *The Object Database Standard: ODMG 3.0*, Morgan Kaufmann (2000).

[Cattell and Skeen 1992] R. Cattell and J. Skeen, "Object Operations Benchmark", *ACM Transactions on Database Systems*, Volume 17, Number 1 (1992).

[Chakrabarti 1999] S. Chakrabarti, "Recent Results in Automatic Web Resource Discovery", *ACM Computing Surveys*, Volume 31, Number 4 (1999).

[Chakrabarti 2000] S. Chakrabarti, "Data Mining for Hypertext: A Tutorial Survey", *SIGKDD Explorations*, Volume 1, Number 2 (2000), pages 1–11.

[Chakrabarti 2002] S. Chakrabarti, *Mining the Web: Discovering Knowledge from HyperText Data*, Morgan Kaufmann (2002).

[Chakrabarti et al. 1998] S. Chakrabarti, S. Sarawagi, and B. Dom, "Mining Surprising Patterns Using Temporal Description Length", In *Proc. of the International Conf. on Very Large Databases* (1998), pages 606–617.

[Chakrabarti et al. 1999] S. Chakrabarti, M. van den Berg, and B. Dom, "Focused Crawling: A New Approach to Topic Specific Web Resource Discovery", In *Proc. of the International World Wide Web Conf.* (1999).

[Chamberlin 1996]   D. Chamberlin, *Using the New DB2: IBM's Object-Relational Database System*, Morgan Kaufmann (1996).

[Chamberlin 1998]   D. D. Chamberlin, *A Complete Guide to DB2 Universal Database*, Morgan Kaufmann (1998).

[Chamberlin and Boyce 1974]   D. D. Chamberlin and R. F. Boyce, "SEQUEL: A Structured English Query Language", In *ACM SIGMOD Workshop on Data Description, Access, and Control* (1974), pages 249–264.

[Chamberlin et al. 1976]   D. D. Chamberlin, M. M. Astrahan, K. P. Eswaran, P. P. Griffiths, R. A. Lorie, J. W. Mehl, P. Reisner, and B. W. Wade, "SEQUEL 2: A Unified Approach to Data Definition, Manipulation, and Control", *IBM Journal of Research and Development*, Volume 20, Number 6 (1976), pages 560–575.

[Chamberlin et al. 1981]   D. D. Chamberlin, M. M. Astrahan, M. W. Blasgen, J. N. Gray, W. F. King, B. G. Lindsay, R. A. Lorie, J. W. Mehl, T. G. Price, P. G. Selinger, M. Schkolnick, D. R. Slutz, I. L. Traiger, B. W. Wade, and R. A. Yost, "A History and Evaluation of System R", *Communications of the ACM*, Volume 24, Number 10 (1981), pages 632–646.

[Chamberlin et al. 2000]   D. D. Chamberlin, J. Robie, and D. Florescu, "Quilt: An XML Query Language for Heterogeneous Data Sources", In *Proc. of the International Workshop on the Web and Databases (WebDB)* (2000), pages 53–62.

[Chan and Ioannidis 1998]   C.-Y. Chan and Y. E. Ioannidis, "Bitmap Index Design and Evaluation", In *Proc. of the ACM SIGMOD Conf. on Management of Data* (1998).

[Chan and Ioannidis 1999]   C.-Y. Chan and Y. E. Ioannidis, "An Efficient Bitmap Encoding Scheme for Selection Queries", In *Proc. of the ACM SIGMOD Conf. on Management of Data* (1999).

[Chandra and Harel 1982]   A. K. Chandra and D. Harel, "Structure and Complexity of Relational Queries", *Journal of Computer and System Sciences*, Volume 15, Number 10 (1982), pages 99–128.

[Chandrasekaran et al. 2003]   S. Chandrasekaran, O. Cooper, A. Deshpande, M. J. Franklin, J. M. Hellerstein, W. Hong, S. Krishnamurthy, S. Madden, V. Raman, F. Reiss, and M. Shah, "TelegraphCQ: Continuous Dataflow Processing for an Uncertain World", In *First Biennial Conference on Innovative Data Systems Research* (2003).

[Chang et al. 2008]   F. Chang, J. Dean, S. Ghemawat, W. C. Hsieh, D. A. Wallach, M. Burrows, T. Chandra, A. Fikes, and R. E. Gruber, "Bigtable: A Distributed Storage System for Structured Data", *ACM Trans. Comput. Syst.*, Volume 26, Number 2 (2008).

[Chatziantoniou and Ross 1997]   D. Chatziantoniou and K. A. Ross, "Groupwise Processing of Relational Queries", In *Proc. of the International Conf. on Very Large Databases* (1997), pages 476–485.

[Chaudhuri and Narasayya 1997]   S. Chaudhuri and V. Narasayya, "An Efficient Cost-Driven Index Selection Tool for Microsoft SQL Server", In *Proc. of the International Conf. on Very Large Databases* (1997).

[Chaudhuri and Shim 1994]   S. Chaudhuri and K. Shim, "Including Group-By in Query Optimization", In *Proc. of the International Conf. on Very Large Databases* (1994).

[Chaudhuri et al. 1995]   S. Chaudhuri, R. Krishnamurthy, S. Potamianos, and K. Shim, "Optimizing Queries with Materialized Views", In *Proc. of the International Conf. on Data Engineering* (1995).

[Chaudhuri et al. 1998]   S. Chaudhuri, R. Motwani, and V. Narasayya, "Random sampling for histogram construction: how much is enough?", In *Proc. of the ACM SIGMOD Conf. on Management of Data* (1998), pages 436–447.

[Chaudhuri et al. 1999]   S. Chaudhuri, E. Christensen, G. Graefe, V. Narasayya, and M. Zwilling, "Self Tuning Technology in Microsoft SQL Server", *IEEE Data Engineering Bulletin*, Volume 22, Number 2 (1999).

[Chaudhuri et al. 2003]   S. Chaudhuri, K. Ganjam, V. Ganti, and R. Motwani, "Robust and Efficient Fuzzy Match for Online Data Cleaning", In *Proc. of the ACM SIGMOD Conf. on Management of Data* (2003).

[Chen 1976]   P. P. Chen, "The Entity-Relationship Model: Toward a Unified View of Data", *ACM Transactions on Database Systems*, Volume 1, Number 1 (1976), pages 9–36.

[Chen et al. 1994]   P. M. Chen, E. K. Lee, G. A. Gibson, R. H. Katz, and D. A. Patterson, "RAID: High-Performance, Reliable Secondary Storage", *ACM Computing Survey*, Volume 26, Number 2 (1994).

[Chen et al. 2007]   S. Chen, A. Ailamaki, P. B. Gibbons, and T. C. Mowry, "Improving hash join performance through prefetching", *ACM Transactions on Database Systems*, Volume 32, Number 3 (2007).

[Chomicki 1995]   J. Chomicki, "Efficient Checking of Temporal Integrity Constraints Using Bounded History Encoding", *ACM Transactions on Database Systems*, Volume 20, Number 2 (1995), pages 149–186.

[Chou and Dewitt 1985]   H. T. Chou and D. J. Dewitt, "An Evaluation of Buffer Management Strategies for Relational Database Systems", In *Proc. of the International Conf. on Very Large Databases* (1985), pages 127–141.

[Cieslewicz et al. 2009]   J. Cieslewicz, W. Mee, and K. A. Ross, "Cache-Conscious Buffering for Database Operators with State", In *Proc. Fifth International Workshop on Data Management on New Hardware (DaMoN 2009)* (2009).

[Cochrane et al. 1996]   R. Cochrane, H. Pirahesh, and N. M. Mattos, "Integrating Triggers and Declarative Constraints in SQL Database Sytems", In *Proc. of the International Conf. on Very Large Databases* (1996), pages 567–578.

[Codd 1970]   E. F. Codd, "A Relational Model for Large Shared Data Banks", *Communications of the ACM*, Volume 13, Number 6 (1970), pages 377–387.

[Codd 1972]   E. F. Codd. "Further Normalization of the Data Base Relational Model", In *Rustin [1972]*, pages 33–64 (1972).

[Codd 1979]   E. F. Codd, "Extending the Database Relational Model to Capture More Meaning", *ACM Transactions on Database Systems*, Volume 4, Number 4 (1979), pages 397–434.

[Codd 1982]   E. F. Codd, "The 1981 ACM Turing Award Lecture: Relational Database: A Practical Foundation for Productivity", *Communications of the ACM*, Volume 25, Number 2 (1982), pages 109–117.

[Codd 1990]   E. F. Codd, *The Relational Model for Database Management: Version 2*, Addison Wesley (1990).

[Comer 1979]   D. Comer, "The Ubiquitous B-tree", *ACM Computing Survey*, Volume 11, Number 2 (1979), pages 121–137.

[Comer 2009]   D. E. Comer, *Computer Networks and Internets*, 5th edition, Prentice Hall (2009).

[Cook 1996]   M. A. Cook, *Building Enterprise Information Architecture: Reengineering Information Systems*, Prentice Hall (1996).

[Cooper et al. 2008]   B. F. Cooper, R. Ramakrishnan, U. Srivastava, A. Silberstein, P. Bohannon, H.-A. Jacobsen, N. Puz, D. Weaver, and R. Yerneni, "PNUTS: Yahoo!'s hosted data serving platform", *Proceedings of the VLDB Endowment*, Volume 1, Number 2 (2008), pages 1277–1288.

[Cormen et al. 1990]   T. Cormen, C. Leiserson, and R. Rivest, *Introduction to Algorithms*, MIT Press (1990).

[Cortes and Vapnik 1995]   C. Cortes and V. Vapnik, *Machine Learning*, Volume 20, Number 3 (1995), pages 273–297.

[Cristianini and Shawe-Taylor 2000]   N. Cristianini and J. Shawe-Taylor, *An Introduction to Support Vector Machines and other Kernel-Based Learning Methods*, Cambridge University Press (2000).

[Dageville and Zaït 2002]   B. Dageville and M. Zaït, "SQL Memory Management in Oracle9i", In *Proc. of the International Conf. on Very Large Databases* (2002), pages 962–973.

[Dageville et al. 2004]   B. Dageville, D. Das, K. Dias, K. Yagoub, M. Zaït, and M. Ziauddin, "Automatic SQL Tuning in Oracle 10g", In *Proc. of the International Conf. on Very Large Databases* (2004), pages 1098–1109.

[Dalvi et al. 2009]   N. Dalvi, R. Kumar, B. Pang, R. Ramakrishnan, A. Tomkins, P. Bohannon, S. Keerthi, and S. Merugu, "A Web of Concepts", In *Proc. of the ACM Symposium on Principles of Database Systems* (2009).

[Daniels et al. 1982] D. Daniels, P. G. Selinger, L. M. Haas, B. G. Lindsay, C. Mohan, A. Walker, and P. F. Wilms. "An Introduction to Distributed Query Compilation in R*", In *Schneider [1982]* (1982).

[Dashti et al. 2003] A. Dashti, S. H. Kim, C. Shahabi, and R. Zimmermann, *Streaming Media Server Design*, Prentice Hall (2003).

[Date 1983] C. J. Date, "The Outer Join", In *Proc. of the International Conference on Databases*, John Wiley and Sons (1983), pages 76–106.

[Date 1989] C. Date, *A Guide to DB2*, Addison Wesley (1989).

[Date 1993] C. J. Date, "How SQL Missed the Boat", *Database Programming and Design*, Volume 6, Number 9 (1993).

[Date 2003] C. J. Date, *An Introduction to Database Systems*, 8th edition, Addison Wesley (2003).

[Date and Darwen 1997] C. J. Date and G. Darwen, *A Guide to the SQL Standard*, 4th edition, Addison Wesley (1997).

[Davis et al. 1983] C. Davis, S. Jajodia, P. A. Ng, and R. Yeh, editors, *Entity-Relationship Approach to Software Engineering*, North Holland (1983).

[Davison and Graefe 1994] D. L. Davison and G. Graefe, "Memory-Contention Responsive Hash Joins", In *Proc. of the International Conf. on Very Large Databases* (1994).

[Dayal 1987] U. Dayal, "Of Nests and Trees: A Unified Approach to Processing Queries that Contain Nested Subqueries, Aggregates and Quantifiers", In *Proc. of the International Conf. on Very Large Databases* (1987), pages 197–208.

[Deutsch et al. 1999] A. Deutsch, M. Fernandez, D. Florescu, A. Levy, and D. Suciu, "A Query Language for XML", In *Proc. of the International World Wide Web Conf.* (1999).

[DeWitt 1990] D. DeWitt, "The Gamma Database Machine Project", *IEEE Transactions on Knowledge and Data Engineering*, Volume 2, Number 1 (1990).

[DeWitt and Gray 1992] D. DeWitt and J. Gray, "Parallel Database Systems: The Future of High Performance Database Systems", *Communications of the ACM*, Volume 35, Number 6 (1992), pages 85–98.

[DeWitt et al. 1992] D. DeWitt, J. Naughton, D. Schneider, and S. Seshadri, "Practical Skew Handling in Parallel Joins", In *Proc. of the International Conf. on Very Large Databases* (1992).

[Dias et al. 1989] D. Dias, B. Iyer, J. Robinson, and P. Yu, "Integrated Concurrency-Coherency Controls for Multisystem Data Sharing", *Software Engineering*, Volume 15, Number 4 (1989), pages 437–448.

[Donahoo and Speegle 2005] M. J. Donahoo and G. D. Speegle, *SQL: Practical Guide for Developers*, Morgan Kaufmann (2005).

[Douglas and Douglas 2003]   K. Douglas and S. Douglas, *PostgreSQL*, Sam's Publishing (2003).

[Dubois and Thakkar 1992]   M. Dubois and S. Thakkar, editors, *Scalable Shared Memory Multiprocessors*, Kluwer Academic Publishers (1992).

[Duncan 1990]   R. Duncan, "A Survey of Parallel Computer Architectures", *IEEE Computer*, Volume 23, Number 2 (1990), pages 5–16.

[Eisenberg and Melton 1999]   A. Eisenberg and J. Melton, "SQL:1999, formerly known as SQL3", *ACM SIGMOD Record*, Volume 28, Number 1 (1999).

[Eisenberg and Melton 2004a]   A. Eisenberg and J. Melton, "Advancements in SQL/XML", *ACM SIGMOD Record*, Volume 33, Number 3 (2004), pages 79–86.

[Eisenberg and Melton 2004b]   A. Eisenberg and J. Melton, "An Early Look at XQuery API for Java (XQJ)", *ACM SIGMOD Record*, Volume 33, Number 2 (2004), pages 105–111.

[Eisenberg et al. 2004]   A. Eisenberg, J. Melton, K. G. Kulkarni, J.-E. Michels, and F. Zemke, "SQL:2003 Has Been Published", *ACM SIGMOD Record*, Volume 33, Number 1 (2004), pages 119–126.

[Elhemali et al. 2007]   M. Elhemali, C. A. Galindo-Legaria, T. Grabs, and M. Joshi, "Execution strategies for SQL subqueries", In *Proc. of the ACM SIGMOD Conf. on Management of Data* (2007), pages 993–1004.

[Ellis 1987]   C. S. Ellis, "Concurrency in Linear Hashing", *ACM Transactions on Database Systems*, Volume 12, Number 2 (1987), pages 195–217.

[Elmasri and Navathe 2006]   R. Elmasri and S. B. Navathe, *Fundamentals of Database Systems*, 5th edition, Addison Wesley (2006).

[Epstein et al. 1978]   R. Epstein, M. R. Stonebraker, and E. Wong, "Distributed Query Processing in a Relational Database System", In *Proc. of the ACM SIGMOD Conf. on Management of Data* (1978), pages 169–180.

[Escobar-Molano et al. 1993]   M. Escobar-Molano, R. Hull, and D. Jacobs, "Safety and Translation of Calculus Queries with Scalar Functions", In *Proc. of the ACM SIGMOD Conf. on Management of Data* (1993), pages 253–264.

[Eswaran et al. 1976]   K. P. Eswaran, J. N. Gray, R. A. Lorie, and I. L. Traiger, "The Notions of Consistency and Predicate Locks in a Database System", *Communications of the ACM*, Volume 19, Number 11 (1976), pages 624–633.

[Fagin 1977]   R. Fagin, "Multivalued Dependencies and a New Normal Form for Relational Databases", *ACM Transactions on Database Systems*, Volume 2, Number 3 (1977), pages 262–278.

[Fagin 1979]   R. Fagin, "Normal Forms and Relational Database Operators", In *Proc. of the ACM SIGMOD Conf. on Management of Data* (1979), pages 153–160.

[Fagin 1981]   R. Fagin, "A Normal Form for Relational Databases That Is Based on Domains and Keys", *ACM Transactions on Database Systems*, Volume 6, Number 3 (1981), pages 387–415.

[Fagin et al. 1979]   R. Fagin, J. Nievergelt, N. Pippenger, and H. R. Strong, "Extendible Hashing — A Fast Access Method for Dynamic Files", *ACM Transactions on Database Systems*, Volume 4, Number 3 (1979), pages 315–344.

[Faloutsos and Lin 1995]   C. Faloutsos and K.-I. Lin, "Fast Map: A Fast Algorithm for Indexing, Data-Mining and Visualization of Traditional and Multimedia Datasets", In *Proc. of the ACM SIGMOD Conf. on Management of Data* (1995), pages 163–174.

[Fayyad et al. 1995]   U. Fayyad, G. Piatetsky-Shapiro, P. Smyth, and R. Uthurusamy, *Advances in Knowledge Discovery and Data Mining*, MIT Press (1995).

[Fekete et al. 2005]   A. Fekete, D. Liarokapis, E. O'Neil, P. O'Neil, and D. Shasha, "Making Snapshot Isolation Serializable", *ACM Transactions on Database Systems*, Volume 30, Number 2 (2005).

[Finkel and Bentley 1974]   R. A. Finkel and J. L. Bentley, "Quad Trees: A Data Structure for Retrieval on Composite Keys", *Acta Informatica*, Volume 4, (1974), pages 1–9.

[Fischer 2006]   L. Fischer, editor, *Workflow Handbook 2001*, Future Strategies (2006).

[Florescu and Kossmann 1999]   D. Florescu and D. Kossmann, "Storing and Querying XML Data Using an RDBMS", *IEEE Data Engineering Bulletin (Special Issue on XML)* (1999), pages 27–35.

[Florescu et al. 2000]   D. Florescu, D. Kossmann, and I. Monalescu, "Integrating Keyword Search into XML Query Processing", In *Proc. of the International World Wide Web Conf.* (2000), pages 119–135. Also appears in *Computer Networks*, Vol. 33, pages 119-135.

[Fredkin 1960]   E. Fredkin, "Trie Memory", *Communications of the ACM*, Volume 4, Number 2 (1960), pages 490–499.

[Freedman and DeWitt 1995]   C. S. Freedman and D. J. DeWitt, "The SPIFFI Scalable Video-on-Demand Server", In *Proc. of the ACM SIGMOD Conf. on Management of Data* (1995), pages 352–363.

[Funderburk et al. 2002a]   J. E. Funderburk, G. Kiernan, J. Shanmugasundaram, E. Shekita, and C. Wei, "XTABLES: Bridging Relational Technology and XML", *IBM Systems Journal*, Volume 41, Number 4 (2002), pages 616–641.

[Funderburk et al. 2002b]   J. E. Funderburk, S. Malaika, and B. Reinwald, "XML Programming with SQL/XML and XQuery", *IBM Systems Journal*, Volume 41, Number 4 (2002), pages 642–665.

[Galindo-Legaria 1994]   C. Galindo-Legaria, "Outerjoins as Disjunctions", In *Proc. of the ACM SIGMOD Conf. on Management of Data* (1994).

[Galindo-Legaria and Joshi 2001]   C. A. Galindo-Legaria and M. M. Joshi, "Orthogonal Optimization of Subqueries and Aggregation", In *Proc. of the ACM SIGMOD Conf. on Management of Data* (2001).

[Galindo-Legaria and Rosenthal 1992]   C. Galindo-Legaria and A. Rosenthal, "How to Extend a Conventional Optimizer to Handle One- and Two-Sided Outerjoin", In *Proc. of the International Conf. on Data Engineering* (1992), pages 402–409.

[Galindo-Legaria et al. 2004]   C. Galindo-Legaria, S. Stefani, and F. Waas, "Query Processing for SQL Updates", In *Proc. of the ACM SIGMOD Conf. on Management of Data* (2004), pages 844–849.

[Ganguly 1998]   S. Ganguly, "Design and Analysis of Parametric Query Optimization Algorithms", In *Proc. of the International Conf. on Very Large Databases* (1998).

[Ganguly et al. 1992]   S. Ganguly, W. Hasan, and R. Krishnamurthy, "Query Optimization for Parallel Execution", In *Proc. of the ACM SIGMOD Conf. on Management of Data* (1992).

[Ganguly et al. 1996]   S. Ganguly, P. Gibbons, Y. Matias, and A. Silberschatz, "A Sampling Algorithm for Estimating Join Size", In *Proc. of the ACM SIGMOD Conf. on Management of Data* (1996).

[Ganski and Wong 1987]   R. A. Ganski and H. K. T. Wong, "Optimization of Nested SQL Queries Revisited", In *Proc. of the ACM SIGMOD Conf. on Management of Data* (1987).

[Garcia and Korth 2005]   P. Garcia and H. F. Korth, "Multithreaded Architectures and the Sort Benchmark", In *Proc. of the First International Workshop on Data Management on Modern Hardward (DaMoN)* (2005).

[Garcia-Molina 1982]   H. Garcia-Molina, "Elections in Distributed Computing Systems", *IEEE Transactions on Computers*, Volume C-31, Number 1 (1982), pages 48–59.

[Garcia-Molina and Salem 1987]   H. Garcia-Molina and K. Salem, "Sagas", In *Proc. of the ACM SIGMOD Conf. on Management of Data* (1987), pages 249–259.

[Garcia-Molina and Salem 1992]   H. Garcia-Molina and K. Salem, "Main Memory Database Systems: An Overview", *IEEE Transactions on Knowledge and Data Engineering*, Volume 4, Number 6 (1992), pages 509–516.

[Garcia-Molina et al. 2008]   H. Garcia-Molina, J. D. Ullman, and J. D. Widom, *Database Systems: The Complete Book*, 2nd edition, Prentice Hall (2008).

[Georgakopoulos et al. 1994]   D. Georgakopoulos, M. Rusinkiewicz, and A. Seth, "Using Tickets to Enforce the Serializability of Multidatabase Transactions", *IEEE Transactions on Knowledge and Data Engineering*, Volume 6, Number 1 (1994), pages 166–180.

[Gilbert and Lynch 2002]   S. Gilbert and N. Lynch, "Brewer's conjecture and the feasibility of consistent, available, partition-tolerant web services", *SIGACT News*, Volume 33, Number 2 (2002), pages 51–59.

[Graefe 1990] G. Graefe, "Encapsulation of Parallelism in the Volcano Query Processing System", In *Proc. of the ACM SIGMOD Conf. on Management of Data* (1990), pages 102–111.

[Graefe 1995] G. Graefe, "The Cascades Framework for Query Optimization", *Data Engineering Bulletin*, Volume 18, Number 3 (1995), pages 19–29.

[Graefe 2008] G. Graefe, "The Five-Minute Rule 20 Years Later: and How Flash Memory Changes the Rules", *ACM Queue*, Volume 6, Number 4 (2008), pages 40–52.

[Graefe and McKenna 1993a] G. Graefe and W. McKenna, "The Volcano Optimizer Generator", In *Proc. of the International Conf. on Data Engineering* (1993), pages 209–218.

[Graefe and McKenna 1993b] G. Graefe and W. J. McKenna, "Extensibility and Search Efficiency in the Volcano Optimizer Generator", In *Proc. of the International Conf. on Data Engineering* (1993).

[Graefe et al. 1998] G. Graefe, R. Bunker, and S. Cooper, "Hash Joins and Hash Teams in Microsoft SQL Server", In *Proc. of the International Conf. on Very Large Databases* (1998), pages 86–97.

[Gray 1978] J. Gray. "Notes on Data Base Operating System", In *Bayer et al. [1978]*, pages 393–481 (1978).

[Gray 1981] J. Gray, "The Transaction Concept: Virtues and Limitations", In *Proc. of the International Conf. on Very Large Databases* (1981), pages 144–154.

[Gray 1991] J. Gray, *The Benchmark Handbook for Database and Transaction Processing Systems*, 2nd edition, Morgan Kaufmann (1991).

[Gray and Graefe 1997] J. Gray and G. Graefe, "The Five-Minute Rule Ten Years Later, and Other Computer Storage Rules of Thumb", *SIGMOD Record*, Volume 26, Number 4 (1997), pages 63–68.

[Gray and Reuter 1993] J. Gray and A. Reuter, *Transaction Processing: Concepts and Techniques*, Morgan Kaufmann (1993).

[Gray et al. 1975] J. Gray, R. A. Lorie, and G. R. Putzolu, "Granularity of Locks and Degrees of Consistency in a Shared Data Base", In *Proc. of the International Conf. on Very Large Databases* (1975), pages 428–451.

[Gray et al. 1976] J. Gray, R. A. Lorie, G. R. Putzolu, and I. L. Traiger, *Granularity of Locks and Degrees of Consistency in a Shared Data Base*, Nijssen (1976).

[Gray et al. 1981] J. Gray, P. R. McJones, and M. Blasgen, "The Recovery Manager of the System R Database Manager", *ACM Computing Survey*, Volume 13, Number 2 (1981), pages 223–242.

[Gray et al. 1995] J. Gray, A. Bosworth, A. Layman, and H. Pirahesh, "Data Cube: A Relational Aggregation Operator Generalizing Group-By, Cross-Tab and Sub-Totals", Technical report, Microsoft Research (1995).

[Gray et al. 1996]   J. Gray, P. Helland, and P. O'Neil, "The Dangers of Replication and a Solution", In *Proc. of the ACM SIGMOD Conf. on Management of Data* (1996), pages 173–182.

[Gray et al. 1997]   J. Gray, S. Chaudhuri, A. Bosworth, A. Layman, D. Reichart, M. Venkatrao, F. Pellow, and H. Pirahesh, "Data Cube: A Relational Aggregation Operator Generalizing Group-by, Cross-Tab, and Sub Totals", *Data Mining and Knowledge Discovery*, Volume 1, Number 1 (1997), pages 29–53.

[Gregersen and Jensen 1999]   H. Gregersen and C. S. Jensen, "Temporal Entity-Relationship Models-A Survey", *IEEE Transactions on Knowledge and Data Engineering*, Volume 11, Number 3 (1999), pages 464–497.

[Grossman and Frieder 2004]   D. A. Grossman and O. Frieder, *Information Retrieval: Algorithms and Heuristics*, 2nd edition, Springer Verlag (2004).

[Gunning 2008]   P. K. Gunning, *DB2 9 for Developers*, MC Press (2008).

[Guo et al. 2003]   L. Guo, F. Shao, C. Botev, and J. Shanmugasundaram, "XRANK: Ranked Keyword Search over XML Documents", In *Proc. of the ACM SIGMOD Conf. on Management of Data* (2003).

[Guttman 1984]   A. Guttman, "R-Trees: A Dynamic Index Structure for Spatial Searching", In *Proc. of the ACM SIGMOD Conf. on Management of Data* (1984), pages 47–57.

[Haas et al. 1989]   L. M. Haas, J. C. Freytag, G. M. Lohman, and H. Pirahesh, "Extensible Query Processing in Starburst", In *Proc. of the ACM SIGMOD Conf. on Management of Data* (1989), pages 377–388.

[Haas et al. 1990]   L. M. Haas, W. Chang, G. M. Lohman, J. McPherson, P. F. Wilms, G. Lapis, B. G. Lindsay, H. Pirahesh, M. J. Carey, and E. J. Shekita, "Starburst Mid-Flight: As the Dust Clears", *IEEE Transactions on Knowledge and Data Engineering*, Volume 2, Number 1 (1990), pages 143–160.

[Haerder and Reuter 1983]   T. Haerder and A. Reuter, "Principles of Transaction-Oriented Database Recovery", *ACM Computing Survey*, Volume 15, Number 4 (1983), pages 287–318.

[Haerder and Rothermel 1987]   T. Haerder and K. Rothermel, "Concepts for Transaction Recovery in Nested Transactions", In *Proc. of the ACM SIGMOD Conf. on Management of Data* (1987), pages 239–248.

[Halsall 2006]   F. Halsall, *Computer Networking and the Internet : With Internet and Multiamedia Applications*, Addison Wesley (2006).

[Han and Kamber 2000]   J. Han and M. Kamber, *Data Mining: Concepts and Techniques*, Morgan Kaufmann (2000).

[Harinarayan et al. 1996]   V. Harinarayan, J. D. Ullman, and A. Rajaraman, "Implementing Data Cubes Efficiently", In *Proc. of the ACM SIGMOD Conf. on Management of Data* (1996).

[Haritsa et al. 1990]   J. Haritsa, M. Carey, and M. Livny, "On Being Optimistic about Real-Time Constraints", In *Proc. of the ACM SIGMOD Conf. on Management of Data* (1990).

[Harizopoulos and Ailamaki 2004]   S. Harizopoulos and A. Ailamaki, "STEPS towards Cache-resident Transaction Processing", In *Proc. of the International Conf. on Very Large Databases* (2004), pages 660–671.

[Hellerstein and Stonebraker 2005]   J. M. Hellerstein and M. Stonebraker, editors, *Readings in Database Systems*, 4th edition, Morgan Kaufmann (2005).

[Hellerstein et al. 1995]   J. M. Hellerstein, J. F. Naughton, and A. Pfeffer, "Generalized Search Trees for Database Systems", In *Proc. of the International Conf. on Very Large Databases* (1995), pages 562–573.

[Hennessy et al. 2006]   J. L. Hennessy, D. A. Patterson, and D. Goldberg, *Computer Architecture: A Quantitative Approach*, 4th edition, Morgan Kaufmann (2006).

[Hevner and Yao 1979]   A. R. Hevner and S. B. Yao, "Query Processing in Distributed Database Systems", *IEEE Transactions on Software Engineering*, Volume SE-5, Number 3 (1979), pages 177–187.

[Heywood et al. 2002]   I. Heywood, S. Cornelius, and S. Carver, *An Introduction to Geographical Information Systems*, 2nd edition, Prentice Hall (2002).

[Hong et al. 1993]   D. Hong, T. Johnson, and S. Chakravarthy, "Real-Time Transaction Scheduling: A Cost Conscious Approach", In *Proc. of the ACM SIGMOD Conf. on Management of Data* (1993).

[Howes et al. 1999]   T. A. Howes, M. C. Smith, and G. S. Good, *Understanding and Deploying LDAP Directory Services*, Macmillan Publishing (1999).

[Hristidis and Papakonstantinou 2002]   V. Hristidis and Y. Papakonstantinou, "DISCOVER: Keyword Search in Relational Databases", In *Proc. of the International Conf. on Very Large Databases* (2002).

[Huang and Garcia-Molina 2001]   Y. Huang and H. Garcia-Molina, "Exactly-once Semantics in a Replicated Messaging System", In *Proc. of the International Conf. on Data Engineering* (2001), pages 3–12.

[Hulgeri and Sudarshan 2003]   A. Hulgeri and S. Sudarshan, "AniPQO: Almost Non-Intrusive Parametric Query Optimization for Non-Linear Cost Functions", In *Proc. of the International Conf. on Very Large Databases* (2003).

[IBM 1987]   IBM, "Systems Application Architecture: Common Programming Interface, Database Reference", Technical report, IBM Corporation, IBM Form Number SC26–4348–0 (1987).

[Ilyas et al. 2008]   I. Ilyas, G. Beskales, and M. A. Soliman, "A Survey of top-k query processing techniques in relational database systems", *ACM Computing Surveys*, Volume 40, Number 4 (2008).

[Imielinski and Badrinath 1994]   T. Imielinski and B. R. Badrinath, "Mobile Computing — Solutions and Challenges", *Communications of the ACM*, Volume 37, Number 10 (1994).

[Imielinski and Korth 1996]   T. Imielinski and H. F. Korth, editors, *Mobile Computing*, Kluwer Academic Publishers (1996).

[Ioannidis and Christodoulakis 1993]   Y. Ioannidis and S. Christodoulakis, "Optimal Histograms for Limiting Worst-Case Error Propagation in the Size of Join Results", *ACM Transactions on Database Systems*, Volume 18, Number 4 (1993), pages 709–748.

[Ioannidis and Poosala 1995]   Y. E. Ioannidis and V. Poosala, "Balancing Histogram Optimality and Practicality for Query Result Size Estimation", In *Proc. of the ACM SIGMOD Conf. on Management of Data* (1995), pages 233–244.

[Ioannidis et al. 1992]   Y. E. Ioannidis, R. T. Ng, K. Shim, and T. K. Sellis, "Parametric Query Optimization", In *Proc. of the International Conf. on Very Large Databases* (1992), pages 103–114.

[Jackson and Moulinier 2002]   P. Jackson and I. Moulinier, *Natural Language Processing for Online Applications: Text Retrieval, Extraction, and Categorization*, John Benjamin (2002).

[Jagadish et al. 1993]   H. V. Jagadish, A. Silberschatz, and S. Sudarshan, "Recovering from Main-Memory Lapses", In *Proc. of the International Conf. on Very Large Databases* (1993).

[Jagadish et al. 1994]   H. Jagadish, D. Lieuwen, R. Rastogi, A. Silberschatz, and S. Sudarshan, "Dali: A High Performance Main Memory Storage Manager", In *Proc. of the International Conf. on Very Large Databases* (1994).

[Jain and Dubes 1988]   A. K. Jain and R. C. Dubes, *Algorithms for Clustering Data*, Prentice Hall (1988).

[Jensen et al. 1994]   C. S. Jensen et al., "A Consensus Glossary of Temporal Database Concepts", *ACM SIGMOD Record*, Volume 23, Number 1 (1994), pages 52–64.

[Jensen et al. 1996]   C. S. Jensen, R. T. Snodgrass, and M. Soo, "Extending Existing Dependency Theory to Temporal Databases", *IEEE Transactions on Knowledge and Data Engineering*, Volume 8, Number 4 (1996), pages 563–582.

[Johnson 1999]   T. Johnson, "Performance Measurements of Compressed Bitmap Indices", In *Proc. of the International Conf. on Very Large Databases* (1999).

[Johnson and Shasha 1993]   T. Johnson and D. Shasha, "The Performance of Concurrent B-Tree Algorithms", *ACM Transactions on Database Systems*, Volume 18, Number 1 (1993).

[Jones and Willet 1997]   K. S. Jones and P. Willet, editors, *Readings in Information Retrieval*, Morgan Kaufmann (1997).

[Jordan and Russell 2003]   D. Jordan and C. Russell, *Java Data Objects*, O'Reilly (2003).

[Jorwekar et al. 2007]   S. Jorwekar, A. Fekete, K. Ramamritham, and S. Sudarshan, "Automating the Detection of Snapshot Isolation Anomalies", In *Proc. of the International Conf. on Very Large Databases* (2007), pages 1263–1274.

[Joshi 1991]   A. Joshi, "Adaptive Locking Strategies in a Multi-Node Shared Data Model Environment", In *Proc. of the International Conf. on Very Large Databases* (1991).

[Kanne and Moerkotte 2000]   C.-C. Kanne and G. Moerkotte, "Efficient Storage of XML Data", In *Proc. of the International Conf. on Data Engineering* (2000), page 198.

[Katz et al. 2004]   H. Katz, D. Chamberlin, D. Draper, M. Fernandez, M. Kay, J. Robie, M. Rys, J. Simeon, J. Tivy, and P. Wadler, *XQuery from the Experts: A Guide to the W3C XML Query Language*, Addison Wesley (2004).

[Kaushik et al. 2004]   R. Kaushik, R. Krishnamurthy, J. F. Naughton, and R. Ramakrishnan, "On the Integration of Structure Indexes and Inverted Lists", In *Proc. of the ACM SIGMOD Conf. on Management of Data* (2004).

[Kedem and Silberschatz 1979]   Z. M. Kedem and A. Silberschatz, "Controlling Concurrency Using Locking Protocols", In *Proc. of the Annual IEEE Symposium on Foundations of Computer Science* (1979), pages 275–285.

[Kedem and Silberschatz 1983]   Z. M. Kedem and A. Silberschatz, "Locking Protocols: From Exclusive to Shared Locks", *Journal of the ACM*, Volume 30, Number 4 (1983), pages 787–804.

[Kifer et al. 2005]   M. Kifer, A. Bernstein, and P. Lewis, *Database Systems: An Application Oriented Approach, Complete Version*, 2nd edition, Addison Wesley (2005).

[Kim 1982]   W. Kim, "On Optimizing an SQL-like Nested Query", *ACM Transactions on Database Systems*, Volume 3, Number 3 (1982), pages 443–469.

[Kim 1995]   W. Kim, editor, *Modern Database Systems*, ACM Press (1995).

[King et al. 1991]   R. P. King, N. Halim, H. Garcia-Molina, and C. Polyzois, "Management of a Remote Backup Copy for Disaster Recovery", *ACM Transactions on Database Systems*, Volume 16, Number 2 (1991), pages 338–368.

[Kitsuregawa and Ogawa 1990]   M. Kitsuregawa and Y. Ogawa, "Bucket Spreading Parallel Hash: A New, Robust, Parallel Hash Join Method for Skew in the Super Database Computer", In *Proc. of the International Conf. on Very Large Databases* (1990), pages 210–221.

[Kleinberg 1999]   J. M. Kleinberg, "Authoritative Sources in a Hyperlinked Environment", *Journal of the ACM*, Volume 46, Number 5 (1999), pages 604–632.

[Kleinrock 1975]   L. Kleinrock, *Queueing Systems*, Wiley-Interscience (1975).

[Klug 1982]   A. Klug, "Equivalence of Relational Algebra and Relational Calculus Query Languages Having Aggregate Functions", *Journal of the ACM*, Volume 29, Number 3 (1982), pages 699–717.

[Knapp 1987]   E. Knapp, "Deadlock Detection in Distributed Databases", *ACM Computing Survey*, Volume 19, Number 4 (1987).

[Knuth 1973]   D. E. Knuth, *The Art of Computer Programming, Volume 3*, Addison Wesley, Sorting and Searching (1973).

[Kohavi and Provost 2001]   R. Kohavi and F. Provost, editors, *Applications of Data Mining to Electronic Commerce*, Kluwer Academic Publishers (2001).

[Konstan et al. 1997]   J. A. Konstan, B. N. Miller, D. Maltz, J. L. Herlocker, L. R. Gordon, and J. Riedl, "GroupLens: Applying Collaborative Filtering to Usenet News", *Communications of the ACM*, Volume 40, Number 3 (1997), pages 77–87.

[Korth 1982]   H. F. Korth, "Deadlock Freedom Using Edge Locks", *ACM Transactions on Database Systems*, Volume 7, Number 4 (1982), pages 632–652.

[Korth 1983]   H. F. Korth, "Locking Primitives in a Database System", *Journal of the ACM*, Volume 30, Number 1 (1983), pages 55–79.

[Korth and Speegle 1990]   H. F. Korth and G. Speegle, "Long Duration Transactions in Software Design Projects", In *Proc. of the International Conf. on Data Engineering* (1990), pages 568–575.

[Korth and Speegle 1994]   H. F. Korth and G. Speegle, "Formal Aspects of Concurrency Control in Long Duration Transaction Systems Using the NT/PV Model", *ACM Transactions on Database Systems*, Volume 19, Number 3 (1994), pages 492–535.

[Krishnaprasad et al. 2004]   M. Krishnaprasad, Z. Liu, A. Manikutty, J. W. Warner, V. Arora, and S. Kotsovolos, "Query Rewrite for XML in Oracle XML DB", In *Proc. of the International Conf. on Very Large Databases* (2004), pages 1122–1133.

[Kung and Lehman 1980]   H. T. Kung and P. L. Lehman, "Concurrent Manipulation of Binary Search Trees", *ACM Transactions on Database Systems*, Volume 5, Number 3 (1980), pages 339–353.

[Kung and Robinson 1981]   H. T. Kung and J. T. Robinson, "Optimistic Concurrency Control", *ACM Transactions on Database Systems*, Volume 6, Number 2 (1981), pages 312–326.

[Kurose and Ross 2005]   J. Kurose and K. Ross, *Computer Networking—A Top-Down Approach Featuring the Internet*, 3rd edition, Addison Wesley (2005).

[Lahiri et al. 2001]   T. Lahiri, A. Ganesh, R. Weiss, and A. Joshi, "Fast-Start: Quick Fault Recovery in Oracle", In *Proc. of the ACM SIGMOD Conf. on Management of Data* (2001).

[Lam and Kuo 2001]   K.-Y. Lam and T.-W. Kuo, editors, *Real-Time Database Systems*, Kluwer Academic Publishers (2001).

[Lamb et al. 1991]   C. Lamb, G. Landis, J. Orenstein, and D. Weinreb, "The Object-Store Database System", *Communications of the ACM*, Volume 34, Number 10 (1991), pages 51–63.

[Lamport 1978]   L. Lamport, "Time, Clocks, and the Ordering of Events in a Distributed System", *Communications of the ACM*, Volume 21, Number 7 (1978), pages 558–565.

[Lampson and Sturgis 1976]   B. Lampson and H. Sturgis, "Crash Recovery in a Distributed Data Storage System", Technical report, Computer Science Laboratory, Xerox Palo Alto Research Center,Palo Alto (1976).

[Lecluse et al. 1988]   C. Lecluse, P. Richard, and F. Velez, "O2: An Object-Oriented Data Model", In *Proc. of the International Conf. on Very Large Databases* (1988), pages 424–433.

[Lehman and Yao 1981]   P. L. Lehman and S. B. Yao, "Efficient Locking for Concurrent Operations on B-trees", *ACM Transactions on Database Systems*, Volume 6, Number 4 (1981), pages 650–670.

[Lehner et al. 2000]   W. Lehner, R. Sidle, H. Pirahesh, and R. Cochrane, "Maintenance of Automatic Summary Tables", In *Proc. of the ACM SIGMOD Conf. on Management of Data* (2000), pages 512–513.

[Lindsay et al. 1980]   B. G. Lindsay, P. G. Selinger, C. Galtieri, J. N. Gray, R. A. Lorie, T. G. Price, G. R. Putzolu, I. L. Traiger, and B. W. Wade. "Notes on Distributed Databases", In Draffen and Poole, editors, *Distributed Data Bases*, pages 247–284. Cambridge University Press (1980).

[Litwin 1978]   W. Litwin, "Virtual Hashing: A Dynamically Changing Hashing", In *Proc. of the International Conf. on Very Large Databases* (1978), pages 517–523.

[Litwin 1980]   W. Litwin, "Linear Hashing: A New Tool for File and Table Addressing", In *Proc. of the International Conf. on Very Large Databases* (1980), pages 212–223.

[Litwin 1981]   W. Litwin, "Trie Hashing", In *Proc. of the ACM SIGMOD Conf. on Management of Data* (1981), pages 19–29.

[Lo and Ravishankar 1996]   M.-L. Lo and C. V. Ravishankar, "Spatial Hash-Joins", In *Proc. of the ACM SIGMOD Conf. on Management of Data* (1996).

[Loeb 1998]   L. Loeb, *Secure Electronic Transactions: Introduction and Technical Reference*, Artech House (1998).

[Lomet 1981]   D. G. Lomet, "Digital B-trees", In *Proc. of the International Conf. on Very Large Databases* (1981), pages 333–344.

[Lomet et al. 2009]   D. Lomet, A. Fekete, G. Weikum, and M. Zwilling, "Unbundling Transaction Services in the Cloud", In *Proc. 4th Biennial Conference on Innovative Data Systems Research* (2009).

[Lu et al. 1991]   H. Lu, M. Shan, and K. Tan, "Optimization of Multi-Way Join Queries for Parallel Execution", In *Proc. of the International Conf. on Very Large Databases* (1991), pages 549–560.

[Lynch and Merritt 1986]   N. A. Lynch and M. Merritt, "Introduction to the Theory of Nested Transactions", In *Proc. of the International Conf. on Database Theory* (1986).

[Lynch et al. 1988]   N. A. Lynch, M. Merritt, W. Weihl, and A. Fekete, "A Theory of Atomic Transactions", In *Proc. of the International Conf. on Database Theory* (1988), pages 41–71.

[Maier 1983]   D. Maier, *The Theory of Relational Databases*, Computer Science Press (1983).

[Manning et al. 2008]   C. D. Manning, P. Raghavan, and H. Schütze, *Introduction to Information Retrieval*, Cambridge University Press (2008).

[Martin et al. 1989]   J. Martin, K. K. Chapman, and J. Leben, *DB2, Concepts, Design, and Programming*, Prentice Hall (1989).

[Mattison 1996]   R. Mattison, *Data Warehousing: Strategies, Technologies, and Techniques*, McGraw Hill (1996).

[McHugh and Widom 1999]   J. McHugh and J. Widom, "Query Optimization for XML", In *Proc. of the International Conf. on Very Large Databases* (1999), pages 315–326.

[Mehrotra et al. 1991]   S. Mehrotra, R. Rastogi, H. F. Korth, and A. Silberschatz, "Non-Serializable Executions in Heterogeneous Distributed Database Systems", In *Proc. of the International Conf. on Parallel and Distributed Information Systems* (1991).

[Mehrotra et al. 2001]   S. Mehrotra, R. Rastogi, Y. Breitbart, H. F. Korth, and A. Silberschatz, "Overcoming Heterogeneity and Autonomy in Multidatabase Systems.", *Inf. Comput.*, Volume 167, Number 2 (2001), pages 137–172.

[Melnik et al. 2007]   S. Melnik, A. Adya, and P. A. Bernstein, "Compiling mappings to bridge applications and databases", In *Proc. of the ACM SIGMOD Conf. on Management of Data* (2007), pages 461–472.

[Melton 2002]   J. Melton, *Advanced SQL:1999 – Understanding Object-Relational and Other Advanced Features*, Morgan Kaufmann (2002).

[Melton and Eisenberg 2000]   J. Melton and A. Eisenberg, *Understanding SQL and Java Together : A Guide to SQLJ, JDBC, and Related Technologies*, Morgan Kaufmann (2000).

[Melton and Simon 1993]   J. Melton and A. R. Simon, *Understanding The New SQL: A Complete Guide*, Morgan Kaufmann (1993).

[Melton and Simon 2001]   J. Melton and A. R. Simon, *SQL:1999, Understanding Relational Language Components*, Morgan Kaufmann (2001).

[Microsoft 1997]   Microsoft, *Microsoft ODBC 3.0 Software Development Kit and Programmer's Reference*, Microsoft Press (1997).

[Mistry et al. 2001]   H. Mistry, P. Roy, S. Sudarshan, and K. Ramamritham, "Materialized View Selection and Maintenance Using Multi-Query Optimization", In *Proc. of the ACM SIGMOD Conf. on Management of Data* (2001).

[Mitchell 1997]   T. M. Mitchell, *Machine Learning*, McGraw Hill (1997).

[Mohan 1990a] C. Mohan, "ARIES/KVL: A Key-Value Locking Method for Concurrency Control of Multiaction Transactions Operations on B-Tree indexes", In *Proc. of the International Conf. on Very Large Databases* (1990), pages 392–405.

[Mohan 1990b] C. Mohan, "Commit-LSN: A Novel and Simple Method for Reducing Locking and Latching in Transaction Processing Systems", In *Proc. of the International Conf. on Very Large Databases* (1990), pages 406–418.

[Mohan 1993] C. Mohan, "IBM's Relational Database Products:Features and Technologies", In *Proc. of the ACM SIGMOD Conf. on Management of Data* (1993).

[Mohan and Levine 1992] C. Mohan and F. Levine, "ARIES/IM:An Efficient and High-Concurrency Index Management Method Using Write-Ahead Logging", In *Proc. of the ACM SIGMOD Conf. on Management of Data* (1992).

[Mohan and Lindsay 1983] C. Mohan and B. Lindsay, "Efficient Commit Protocols for the Tree of Processes Model of Distributed Transactions", In *Proc. of the ACM Symposium on Principles of Distributed Computing* (1983).

[Mohan and Narang 1992] C. Mohan and I. Narang, "Efficient Locking and Caching of Data in the Multisystem Shared Disks Transaction Environment", In *Proc. of the International Conf. on Extending Database Technology* (1992).

[Mohan and Narang 1994] C. Mohan and I. Narang, "ARIES/CSA: A Method for Database Recovery in Client-Server Architectures", In *Proc. of the ACM SIGMOD Conf. on Management of Data* (1994), pages 55–66.

[Mohan et al. 1986] C. Mohan, B. Lindsay, and R. Obermarck, "Transaction Management in the R* Distributed Database Management System", *ACM Transactions on Database Systems*, Volume 11, Number 4 (1986), pages 378–396.

[Mohan et al. 1992] C. Mohan, D. Haderle, B. Lindsay, H. Pirahesh, and P. Schwarz, "ARIES: A Transaction Recovery Method Supporting Fine-Granularity Locking and Partial Rollbacks Using Write-Ahead Logging", *ACM Transactions on Database Systems*, Volume 17, Number 1 (1992).

[Moss 1985] J. E. B. Moss, *Nested Transactions: An Approach to Reliable Distributed Computing*, MIT Press (1985).

[Moss 1987] J. E. B. Moss, "Log-Based Recovery for Nested Transactions", In *Proc. of the International Conf. on Very Large Databases* (1987), pages 427–432.

[Murthy and Banerjee 2003] R. Murthy and S. Banerjee, "XML Schemas in Oracle XML DB", In *Proc. of the International Conf. on Very Large Databases* (2003), pages 1009–1018.

[Nakayama et al. 1984] T. Nakayama, M. Hirakawa, and T. Ichikawa, "Architecture and Algorithm for Parallel Execution of a Join Operation", In *Proc. of the International Conf. on Data Engineering* (1984).

[Ng and Han 1994] R. T. Ng and J. Han, "Efficient and Effective Clustering Methods for Spatial Data Mining", In *Proc. of the International Conf. on Very Large Databases* (1994).

[NIST 1993]   NIST, "Integration Definition for Information Modeling (IDEF1X)", Technical Report Federal Information Processing Standards Publication 184, National Institute of Standards and Technology (NIST), Available at www.idef.com/Downloads/pdf/Idef1x.pdf (1993).

[Nyberg et al. 1995]   C. Nyberg, T. Barclay, Z. Cvetanovic, J. Gray, and D. B. Lomet, "AlphaSort: A Cache-Sensitive Parallel External Sort", *VLDB Journal*, Volume 4, Number 4 (1995), pages 603–627.

[O'Neil and O'Neil 2000]   P. O'Neil and E. O'Neil, *Database: Principles, Programming, Performance*, 2nd edition, Morgan Kaufmann (2000).

[O'Neil and Quass 1997]   P. O'Neil and D. Quass, "Improved Query Performance with Variant Indexes", In *Proc. of the ACM SIGMOD Conf. on Management of Data* (1997).

[O'Neil et al. 2004]   P. E. O'Neil, E. J. O'Neil, S. Pal, I. Cseri, G. Schaller, and N. Westbury, "ORDPATHs: Insert-Friendly XML Node Labels", In *Proc. of the ACM SIGMOD Conf. on Management of Data* (2004), pages 903–908.

[Ooi and S. Parthasarathy 2009]   B. C. Ooi and e. S. Parthasarathy, "Special Issue on Data Management on Cloud Computing Platforms", *Data Engineering Bulletin*, Volume 32, Number 1 (2009).

[Orenstein 1982]   J. A. Orenstein, "Multidimensional Tries Used for Associative Searching", *Information Processing Letters*, Volume 14, Number 4 (1982), pages 150–157.

[Ozcan et al. 1997]   F. Ozcan, S. Nural, P. Koksal, C. Evrendilek, and A. Dogac, "Dynamic Query Optimization in Multidatabases", *Data Engineering Bulletin*, Volume 20, Number 3 (1997), pages 38–45.

[Ozden et al. 1994]   B. Ozden, A. Biliris, R. Rastogi, and A. Silberschatz, "A Low-cost Storage Server for a Movie on Demand Database", In *Proc. of the International Conf. on Very Large Databases* (1994).

[Ozden et al. 1996a]   B. Ozden, R. Rastogi, P. Shenoy, and A. Silberschatz, "Fault-Tolerant Architectures for Continuous Media Servers", In *Proc. of the ACM SIGMOD Conf. on Management of Data* (1996).

[Ozden et al. 1996b]   B. Ozden, R. Rastogi, and A. Silberschatz, "On the Design of a Low-Cost Video-on-Demand Storage System", *Multimedia Systems Journal*, Volume 4, Number 1 (1996), pages 40–54.

[Ozsoyoglu and Snodgrass 1995]   G. Ozsoyoglu and R. Snodgrass, "Temporal and Real-Time Databases: A Survey", *IEEE Transactions on Knowledge and Data Engineering*, Volume 7, Number 4 (1995), pages 513–532.

[Ozsu and Valduriez 1999]   T. Ozsu and P. Valduriez, *Principles of Distributed Database Systems*, 2nd edition, Prentice Hall (1999).

[Padmanabhan et al. 2003]   S. Padmanabhan, B. Bhattacharjee, T. Malkemus, L. Cranston, and M. Huras, "Multi-Dimensional Clustering: A New Data Layout Scheme in DB2", In *Proc. of the ACM SIGMOD Conf. on Management of Data* (2003), pages 637–641.

[Pal et al. 2004]   S. Pal, I. Cseri, G. Schaller, O. Seeliger, L. Giakoumakis, and V. Zolotov, "Indexing XML Data Stored in a Relational Database", In *Proc. of the International Conf. on Very Large Databases* (2004), pages 1134–1145.

[Pang et al. 1995]   H.-H. Pang, M. J. Carey, and M. Livny, "Multiclass Scheduling in Real-Time Database Systems", *IEEE Transactions on Knowledge and Data Engineering*, Volume 2, Number 4 (1995), pages 533–551.

[Papakonstantinou et al. 1996]   Y. Papakonstantinou, A. Gupta, and L. Haas, "Capabilities-Based Query Rewriting in Mediator Systems", In *Proc. of the International Conf. on Parallel and Distributed Information Systems* (1996).

[Parker et al. 1983]   D. S. Parker, G. J. Popek, G. Rudisin, A. Stoughton, B. J. Walker, E. Walton, J. M. Chow, D. Edwards, S. Kiser, and C. Kline, "Detection of Mutual Inconsistency in Distributed Systems", *IEEE Transactions on Software Engineering*, Volume 9, Number 3 (1983), pages 240–246.

[Patel and DeWitt 1996]   J. Patel and D. J. DeWitt, "Partition Based Spatial-Merge Join", In *Proc. of the ACM SIGMOD Conf. on Management of Data* (1996).

[Patterson 2004]   D. P. Patterson, "Latency Lags Bandwidth", *Communications of the ACM*, Volume 47, Number 10 (2004), pages 71–75.

[Patterson et al. 1988]   D. A. Patterson, G. Gibson, and R. H. Katz, "A Case for Redundant Arrays of Inexpensive Disks (RAID)", In *Proc. of the ACM SIGMOD Conf. on Management of Data* (1988), pages 109–116.

[Pellenkoft et al. 1997]   A. Pellenkoft, C. A. Galindo-Legaria, and M. Kersten, "The Complexity of Transformation-Based Join Enumeration", In *Proc. of the International Conf. on Very Large Databases* (1997), pages 306–315.

[Peterson and Davie 2007]   L. L. Peterson and B. S. Davie, *Computer Networks: a Systems Approach*, Morgan Kaufmann Publishers Inc. (2007).

[Pless 1998]   V. Pless, *Introduction to the Theory of Error-Correcting Codes*, 3rd edition, John Wiley and Sons (1998).

[Poe 1995]   V. Poe, *Building a Data Warehouse for Decision Support*, Prentice Hall (1995).

[Polyzois and Garcia-Molina 1994]   C. Polyzois and H. Garcia-Molina, "Evaluation of Remote Backup Algorithms for Transaction-Processing Systems", *ACM Transactions on Database Systems*, Volume 19, Number 3 (1994), pages 423–449.

[Poosala et al. 1996]   V. Poosala, Y. E. Ioannidis, P. J. Haas, and E. J. Shekita, "Improved Histograms for Selectivity Estimation of Range Predicates", In *Proc. of the ACM SIGMOD Conf. on Management of Data* (1996), pages 294–305.

[Popek et al. 1981]   G. J. Popek, B. J. Walker, J. M. Chow, D. Edwards, C. Kline, G. Rudisin, and G. Thiel, "LOCUS: A Network Transparent, High Reliability Distributed System", In *Proc. of the Eighth Symposium on Operating System Principles* (1981), pages 169–177.

[Pöss and Potapov 2003]   M. Pöss and D. Potapov, "Data Compression in Oracle", In *Proc. of the International Conf. on Very Large Databases* (2003), pages 937–947.

[Rahm 1993]   E. Rahm, "Empirical Performance Evaluation of Concurrency and Coherency Control Protocols for Database Sharing Systems", *ACM Transactions on Database Systems*, Volume 8, Number 2 (1993).

[Ramakrishna and Larson 1989]   M. V. Ramakrishna and P. Larson, "File Organization Using Composite Perfect Hashing", *ACM Transactions on Database Systems*, Volume 14, Number 2 (1989), pages 231–263.

[Ramakrishnan and Gehrke 2002]   R. Ramakrishnan and J. Gehrke, *Database Management Systems*, 3rd edition, McGraw Hill (2002).

[Ramakrishnan and Ullman 1995]   R. Ramakrishnan and J. D. Ullman, "A Survey of Deductive Database Systems", *Journal of Logic Programming*, Volume 23, Number 2 (1995), pages 125–149.

[Ramakrishnan et al. 1992]   R. Ramakrishnan, D. Srivastava, and S. Sudarshan, *Controlling the Search in Bottom-up Evaluation* (1992).

[Ramesh et al. 1989]   R. Ramesh, A. J. G. Babu, and J. P. Kincaid, "Index Optimization: Theory and Experimental Results", *ACM Transactions on Database Systems*, Volume 14, Number 1 (1989), pages 41–74.

[Rangan et al. 1992]   P. V. Rangan, H. M. Vin, and S. Ramanathan, "Designing an On-Demand Multimedia Service", *Communications Magazine*, Volume 1, Number 1 (1992), pages 56–64.

[Rao and Ross 2000]   J. Rao and K. A. Ross, "Making B+-Trees Cache Conscious in Main Memory", In *Proc. of the ACM SIGMOD Conf. on Management of Data* (2000), pages 475–486.

[Rathi et al. 1990]   A. Rathi, H. Lu, and G. E. Hedrick, "Performance Comparison of Extendable Hashing and Linear Hashing Techniques", In *Proc. ACM SIGSmall/PC Symposium on Small Systems* (1990), pages 178–185.

[Reed 1983]   D. Reed, "Implementing Atomic Actions on Decentralized Data", *Transactions on Computer Systems*, Volume 1, Number 1 (1983), pages 3–23.

[Revesz 2002]   P. Revesz, *Introduction to Constraint Databases*, Springer Verlag (2002).

[Richardson et al. 1987]   J. Richardson, H. Lu, and K. Mikkilineni, "Design and Evaluation of Parallel Pipelined Join Algorithms", In *Proc. of the ACM SIGMOD Conf. on Management of Data* (1987).

[Rivest 1976]   R. L. Rivest, "Partial Match Retrieval Via the Method of Superimposed Codes", *SIAM Journal of Computing*, Volume 5, Number 1 (1976), pages 19–50.

[Robinson 1981]   J. Robinson, "The k-d-B Tree: A Search Structure for Large Multidimensional Indexes", In *Proc. of the ACM SIGMOD Conf. on Management of Data* (1981), pages 10–18.

[Roos 2002]   R. M. Roos, *Java Data Objects*, Pearson Education (2002).

[Rosch 2003]   W. L. Rosch, *The Winn L. Rosch Hardware Bible*, 6th edition, Que (2003).

[Rosenthal and Reiner 1984]   A. Rosenthal and D. Reiner, "Extending the Algebraic Framework of Query Processing to Handle Outerjoins", In *Proc. of the International Conf. on Very Large Databases* (1984), pages 334–343.

[Ross 1990]   K. A. Ross, "Modular Stratification and Magic Sets for DATALOG Programs with Negation", In *Proc. of the ACM SIGMOD Conf. on Management of Data* (1990).

[Ross 1999]   S. M. Ross, *Introduction to Probability and Statistics for Engineers and Scientists*, Harcourt/Academic Press (1999).

[Ross and Srivastava 1997]   K. A. Ross and D. Srivastava, "Fast Computation of Sparse Datacubes", In *Proc. of the International Conf. on Very Large Databases* (1997), pages 116–125.

[Ross et al. 1996]   K. Ross, D. Srivastava, and S. Sudarshan, "Materialized View Maintenance and Integrity Constraint Checking: Trading Space for Time", In *Proc. of the ACM SIGMOD Conf. on Management of Data* (1996).

[Rothermel and Mohan 1989]   K. Rothermel and C. Mohan, "ARIES/NT: A Recovery Method Based on Write-Ahead Logging for Nested Transactions", In *Proc. of the International Conf. on Very Large Databases* (1989), pages 337–346.

[Roy et al. 2000]   P. Roy, S. Seshadri, S. Sudarshan, and S. Bhobhe, "Efficient and Extensible Algorithms for Multi-Query Optimization", In *Proc. of the ACM SIGMOD Conf. on Management of Data* (2000).

[Rusinkiewicz and Sheth 1995]   M. Rusinkiewicz and A. Sheth. "Specification and Execution of Transactional Workflows", In *Kim [1995]*, pages 592–620 (1995).

[Rustin 1972]   R. Rustin, *Data Base Systems*, Prentice Hall (1972).

[Rys 2001]   M. Rys, "Bringing the Internet to Your Database: Using SQL Server 2000 and XML to Build Loosely-Coupled Systems", In *Proc. of the International Conf. on Data Engineering* (2001), pages 465–472.

[Rys 2003]   M. Rys. "XQuery and Relational Database Systems", In H. Katz, editor, *XQuery From the Experts*, pages 353–391. Addison Wesley (2003).

[Rys 2004]   M. Rys. "What's New in FOR XML in Microsoft SQL Server 2005". http://msdn.microsoft.com/en-us/library/ms345137(SQL.90).aspx (2004).

[Sagiv and Yannakakis 1981]   Y. Sagiv and M. Yannakakis, "Equivalence among Relational Expressions with the Union and Difference Operators", *Proc. of the ACM SIGMOD Conf. on Management of Data* (1981).

[Salton 1989]   G. Salton, *Automatic Text Processing*, Addison Wesley (1989).

[Samet 1990]   H. Samet, *The Design and Analysis of Spatial Data Structures*, Addison Wesley (1990).

[Samet 1995a]   H. Samet, "General Research Issues in Multimedia Database Systems", *ACM Computing Survey*, Volume 27, Number 4 (1995), pages 630–632.

[Samet 1995b]   H. Samet. "Spatial Data Structures", In *Kim [1995]*, pages 361–385 (1995).

[Samet 2006]   H. Samet, *Foundations of Multidimenional and Metric Data Structures*, Morgan Kaufmann (2006).

[Samet and Aref 1995]   H. Samet and W. Aref. "Spatial Data Models and Query Processing", In *Kim [1995]*, pages 338–360 (1995).

[Sanders 1998]   R. E. Sanders, *ODBC 3.5 Developer's Guide*, McGraw Hill (1998).

[Sarawagi 2000]   S. Sarawagi, "User-Adaptive Exploration of Multidimensional Data", In *Proc. of the International Conf. on Very Large Databases* (2000), pages 307–316.

[Sarawagi et al. 2002]   S. Sarawagi, A. Bhamidipaty, A. Kirpal, and C. Mouli, "ALIAS: An Active Learning Led Interactive Deduplication System", In *Proc. of the International Conf. on Very Large Databases* (2002), pages 1103–1106.

[Schlageter 1981]   G. Schlageter, "Optimistic Methods for Concurrency Control in Distributed Database Systems", In *Proc. of the International Conf. on Very Large Databases* (1981), pages 125–130.

[Schneider 1982]   H. J. Schneider, "Distributed Data Bases", In *Proc. of the International Symposium on Distributed Databases* (1982).

[Selinger et al. 1979]   P. G. Selinger, M. M. Astrahan, D. D. Chamberlin, R. A. Lorie, and T. G. Price, "Access Path Selection in a Relational Database System", In *Proc. of the ACM SIGMOD Conf. on Management of Data* (1979), pages 23–34.

[Sellis 1988]   T. K. Sellis, "Multiple Query Optimization", *ACM Transactions on Database Systems*, Volume 13, Number 1 (1988), pages 23–52.

[Sellis et al. 1987]   T. K. Sellis, N. Roussopoulos, and C. Faloutsos, "TheR$^+$-Tree: A Dynamic Index for Multi-Dimensional Objects", In *Proc. of the International Conf. on Very Large Databases* (1987), pages 507–518.

[Seshadri et al. 1996]   P. Seshadri, H. Pirahesh, and T. Y. C. Leung, "Complex Query Decorrelation", In *Proc. of the International Conf. on Data Engineering* (1996), pages 450–458.

[Shafer et al. 1996]   J. C. Shafer, R. Agrawal, and M. Mehta, "SPRINT: A Scalable Parallel Classifier for Data Mining", In *Proc. of the International Conf. on Very Large Databases* (1996), pages 544–555.

[Shanmugasundaram et al. 1999]   J. Shanmugasundaram, G. He, K. Tufte, C. Zhang, D. DeWitt, and J. Naughton, "Relational Databases for Querying XML

Documents: Limitations and Opportunities", In *Proc. of the International Conf. on Very Large Databases* (1999).

[Shapiro 1986] L. D. Shapiro, "Join Processing in Database Systems with Large Main Memories", *ACM Transactions on Database Systems*, Volume 11, Number 3 (1986), pages 239–264.

[Shasha and Bonnet 2002] D. Shasha and P. Bonnet, *Database Tuning: Principles, Experiments, and Troubleshooting Techniques*, Morgan Kaufmann (2002).

[Silberschatz 1982] A. Silberschatz, "A Multi-Version Concurrency Control Scheme With No Rollbacks", In *Proc. of the ACM Symposium on Principles of Distributed Computing* (1982), pages 216–223.

[Silberschatz and Kedem 1980] A. Silberschatz and Z. Kedem, "Consistency in Hierarchical Database Systems", *Journal of the ACM*, Volume 27, Number 1 (1980), pages 72–80.

[Silberschatz et al. 1990] A. Silberschatz, M. R. Stonebraker, and J. D. Ullman, "Database Systems: Achievements and Opportunities", *ACM SIGMOD Record*, Volume 19, Number 4 (1990).

[Silberschatz et al. 1996] A. Silberschatz, M. Stonebraker, and J. Ullman, "Database Research: Achievements and Opportunities into the 21st Century", Technical Report CS-TR-96-1563, Department of Computer Science, Stanford University, Stanford (1996).

[Silberschatz et al. 2008] A. Silberschatz, P. B. Galvin, and G. Gagne, *Operating System Concepts*, 8th edition, John Wiley and Sons (2008).

[Simmen et al. 1996] D. Simmen, E. Shekita, and T. Malkemus, "Fundamental Techniques for Order Optimization", In *Proc. of the ACM SIGMOD Conf. on Management of Data* (1996), pages 57–67.

[Skeen 1981] D. Skeen, "Non-blocking Commit Protocols", In *Proc. of the ACM SIGMOD Conf. on Management of Data* (1981), pages 133–142.

[Soderland 1999] S. Soderland, "Learning Information Extraction Rules for Semi-structured and Free Text", *Machine Learning*, Volume 34, Number 1–3 (1999), pages 233–272.

[Soo 1991] M. Soo, "Bibliography on Temporal Databases", *ACM SIGMOD Record*, Volume 20, Number 1 (1991), pages 14–23.

[SQL/XML 2004] SQL/XML. "ISO/IEC 9075-14:2003, Information Technology: Database languages: SQL.Part 14: XML-Related Specifications (SQL/XML)" (2004).

[Srikant and Agrawal 1996a] R. Srikant and R. Agrawal, "Mining Quantitative Association Rules in Large Relational Tables", In *Proc. of the ACM SIGMOD Conf. on Management of Data* (1996).

[Srikant and Agrawal 1996b]   R. Srikant and R. Agrawal, "Mining Sequential Patterns: Generalizations and Performance Improvements", In *Proc. of the International Conf. on Extending Database Technology* (1996), pages 3–17.

[Stam and Snodgrass 1988]   R. Stam and R. Snodgrass, "A Bibliography on Temporal Databases", *IEEE Transactions on Knowledge and Data Engineering*, Volume 7, Number 4 (1988), pages 231–239.

[Stinson 2002]   B. Stinson, *PostgreSQL Essential Reference*, New Riders (2002).

[Stonebraker 1986]   M. Stonebraker, "Inclusion of New Types in Relational Database Systems", In *Proc. of the International Conf. on Data Engineering* (1986), pages 262–269.

[Stonebraker and Rowe 1986]   M. Stonebraker and L. Rowe, "The Design of POSTGRES", In *Proc. of the ACM SIGMOD Conf. on Management of Data* (1986).

[Stonebraker et al. 1989]   M. Stonebraker, P. Aoki, and M. Seltzer, "Parallelism in XPRS", In *Proc. of the ACM SIGMOD Conf. on Management of Data* (1989).

[Stonebraker et al. 1990]   M. Stonebraker, A. Jhingran, J. Goh, and S. Potamianos, "On Rules, Procedure, Caching and Views in Database Systems", In *Proc. of the ACM SIGMOD Conf. on Management of Data* (1990), pages 281–290.

[Stuart et al. 1984]   D. G. Stuart, G. Buckley, and A. Silberschatz, "A Centralized Deadlock Detection Algorithm", Technical report, Department of Computer Sciences, University of Texas, Austin (1984).

[Tanenbaum 2002]   A. S. Tanenbaum, *Computer Networks*, 4th edition, Prentice Hall (2002).

[Tansel et al. 1993]   A. Tansel, J. Clifford, S. Gadia, S. Jajodia, A. Segev, and R. Snodgrass, *Temporal Databases: Theory, Design and Implementation*, Benjamin Cummings (1993).

[Teorey et al. 1986]   T. J. Teorey, D. Yang, and J. P. Fry, "A Logical Design Methodology for Relational Databases Using the Extended Entity-Relationship Model", *ACM Computing Survey*, Volume 18, Number 2 (1986), pages 197–222.

[Thalheim 2000]   B. Thalheim, *Entity-Relationship Modeling: Foundations of Database Technology*, Springer Verlag (2000).

[Thomas 1996]   S. A. Thomas, *IPng and the TCP/IP Protocols: Implementing the Next Generation Internet*, John Wiley and Sons (1996).

[Traiger et al. 1982]   I. L. Traiger, J. N. Gray, C. A. Galtieri, and B. G. Lindsay, "Transactions and Consistency in Distributed Database Management Systems", *ACM Transactions on Database Systems*, Volume 7, Number 3 (1982), pages 323–342.

[Tyagi et al. 2003]   S. Tyagi, M. Vorburger, K. McCammon, and H. Bobzin, *Core Java Data Objects*, prenticehall (2003).

[Umar 1997]   A. Umar, *Application (Re)Engineering : Building Web-Based Applications and Dealing With Legacies*, Prentice Hall (1997).

[UniSQL 1991]   *UniSQL/X Database Management System User's Manual: Release 1.2.* UniSQL, Inc. (1991).

[Verhofstad 1978]   J. S. M. Verhofstad, "Recovery Techniques for Database Systems", *ACM Computing Survey*, Volume 10, Number 2 (1978), pages 167–195.

[Vista 1998]   D. Vista, "Integration of Incremental View Maintenance into Query Optimizers", In *Proc. of the International Conf. on Extending Database Technology* (1998).

[Vitter 2001]   J. S. Vitter, "External Memory Algorithms and Data Structures: Dealing with Massive Data", *ACM Computing Surveys*, Volume 33, (2001), pages 209–271.

[Walsh et al. 2007]   N. Walsh et al. "XQuery 1.0 and XPath 2.0 Data Model". http://www.w3.org/TR/xpath-datamodel. currently a W3C Recommendation (2007).

[Walton et al. 1991]   C. Walton, A. Dale, and R. Jenevein, "A Taxonomy and Performance Model of Data Skew Effects in Parallel Joins", In *Proc. of the International Conf. on Very Large Databases* (1991).

[Weikum 1991]   G. Weikum, "Principles and Realization Strategies of Multilevel Transaction Management", *ACM Transactions on Database Systems*, Volume 16, Number 1 (1991).

[Weikum et al. 1990]   G. Weikum, C. Hasse, P. Broessler, and P. Muth, "Multi-Level Recovery", In *Proc. of the ACM SIGMOD Conf. on Management of Data* (1990), pages 109–123.

[Wilschut et al. 1995]   A. N. Wilschut, J. Flokstra, and P. M. Apers, "Parallel Evaluation of Multi-Join Queues", In *Proc. of the ACM SIGMOD Conf. on Management of Data* (1995), pages 115–126.

[Witten and Frank 1999]   I. H. Witten and E. Frank, *Data Mining: Practical Machine Learning Tools and Techniques with Java Implementations*, Morgan Kaufmann (1999).

[Witten et al. 1999]   I. H. Witten, A. Moffat, and T. C. Bell, *Managing Gigabytes: Compressing and Indexing Documents and images*, 2nd edition, Morgan Kaufmann (1999).

[Wolf 1991]   J. Wolf, "An Effective Algorithm for Parallelizing Hash Joins in the Presence of Data Skew", In *Proc. of the International Conf. on Data Engineering* (1991).

[Wu and Buchmann 1998]   M. Wu and A. Buchmann, "Encoded Bitmap Indexing for Data Warehouses", In *Proc. of the International Conf. on Data Engineering* (1998).

[Wu et al. 2003]   Y. Wu, J. M. Patel, and H. V. Jagadish, "Structural Join Order Selection for XML Query Optimization", In *Proc. of the International Conf. on Data Engineering* (2003).

[X/Open 1991]   *X/Open Snapshot: X/Open DTP: XA Interface.* X/Open Company, Ltd. (1991).

[Yan and Larson 1995]   W. P. Yan and P. A. Larson, "Eager Aggregation and Lazy Aggregation", In *Proc. of the International Conf. on Very Large Databases* (1995).

[Yannakakis et al. 1979]   M. Yannakakis, C. H. Papadimitriou, and H. T. Kung, "Locking Protocols: Safety and Freedom from Deadlock", In *Proc. of the IEEE Symposium on the Foundations of Computer Science* (1979), pages 286–297.

[Zaharioudakis et al. 2000]   M. Zaharioudakis, R. Cochrane, G. Lapis, H. Pirahesh, and M. Urata, "Answering Complex SQL Queries using Automatic Summary Tables", In *Proc. of the ACM SIGMOD Conf. on Management of Data* (2000), pages 105–116.

[Zeller and Gray 1990]   H. Zeller and J. Gray, "An Adaptive Hash Join Algorithm for Multiuser Environments", In *Proc. of the International Conf. on Very Large Databases* (1990), pages 186–197.

[Zhang et al. 1996]   T. Zhang, R. Ramakrishnan, and M. Livny, "BIRCH: An Efficient Data Clustering Method for Very Large Databases", In *Proc. of the ACM SIGMOD Conf. on Management of Data* (1996), pages 103–114.

[Zhou and Ross 2004]   J. Zhou and K. A. Ross, "Buffering Database Operations for Enhanced Instruction Cache Performance", In *Proc. of the ACM SIGMOD Conf. on Management of Data* (2004), pages 191–202.

[Zhuge et al. 1995]   Y. Zhuge, H. Garcia-Molina, J. Hammer, and J. Widom, "View maintenance in a warehousing environment", In *Proc. of the ACM SIGMOD Conf. on Management of Data* (1995), pages 316–327.

[Ziauddin et al. 2008]   M. Ziauddin, D. Das, H. Su, Y. Zhu, and K. Yagoub, "Optimizer plan change management: improved stability and performance in Oracle 11g", *Proceedings of the VLDB Endowment*, Volume 1, Number 2 (2008), pages 1346–1355.

[Zikopoulos et al. 2004]   P. Zikopoulos, G. Baklarz, D. deRoos, and R. B. Melnyk, *DB2 Version 8: The Official Guide*, IBM Press (2004).

[Zikopoulos et al. 2007]   P. Zikopoulos, G. Baklarz, L. Katsnelson, and C. Eaton, *IBM DB2 9 New Features*, McGraw Hill (2007).

[Zikopoulos et al. 2009]   P. Zikopoulos, B. Tassi, G. Baklarz, and C. Eaton, *Break Free with DB2 9.7*, McGraw Hill (2009).

[Zilio et al. 2004]   D. C. Zilio, J. Rao, S. Lightstone, G. M. Lohman, A. Storm, C. Garcia-Arellano, and S. Fadden, "DB2 Design Advisor: Integrated Automatic Physical Database Design", In *Proc. of the International Conf. on Very Large Databases* (2004), pages 1087–1097.

[Zloof 1977]   M. M. Zloof, "Query-by-Example: A Data Base Language", *IBM Systems Journal*, Volume 16, Number 4 (1977), pages 324–343.

Index